24th EDITION

GUNS ILLUSTRATED®

1992

Edited by Harold A. Murtz
and the Editors of Gun Digest

DBI BOOKS, INC.

About Our Covers

Apple pie, baseball and the Ruger P85 pistol!? They don't rhyme but they all go together because they're genuinely American. Designed and made entirely in the United States, the Ruger P85 pistol evolved into a whole series of centerfire autoloaders, four of which you see on our covers.

At the top on the front cover is the latest and long-awaited Ruger, the KP90DC in 45 ACP. The "K" prefix means the slide is of stainless steel, while the "DC" suffix indicates a decocking lever instead of a safety lever on the slide. With a seven-shot, single-column magazine, this big-bore auto meets the needs of the many serious shooters who've been asking for the 45-caliber chambering.

Below is the KP89DC, the 9mm Parabellum brother that also has the decocker feature. This gun is available in either traditional blued steel or Ruger's exclusive "Terhune Anticorro" stainless steel, specially formulated to resist the corrosive action caused by saltwater, sweat and powder residue in humid climates.

On our back cover, two Mark II P85s are shown, the stainless steel version at left, blued steel on the right. These are the second generation P85 pistols, which offer several new features and field-tested refinements of the original design. Like the KP89DC on the front cover, the Mark II has a 4½-inch barrel, overall length of 7⅞ inches, and an empty weight of about 32 ounces. The magazine holds 15 rounds of 9mm Parabellum ammunition. The P85MKII has a manual safety that both decocks the gun and locks the firing pin in place, a feature which positively stops the gun from firing unless the safety lever is moved to the "fire" position.

All of Ruger's P-series pistols are optionally available with a moulded, high-impact, lockable case and extra magazine, as well as a thumb-saving magazine loader.

For the history and development of these excellent pistols, see "The P85 Pistol" by Nick Steadman beginning on page 9 of this edition.

Photos by John Hanusin.

GUNS ILLUSTRATED STAFF

EDITOR
Harold A. Murtz

ASSOCIATE EDITOR
Robert S.L. Anderson

PRODUCTION MANAGER
John L. Duoba

EDITORIAL/PRODUCTION ASSOCIATE
Jamie L. Puffpaff

ASSISTANT TO THE EDITOR
Lilo Anderson

ELECTRONIC PUBLISHING MANAGER
Nancy J. Mellem

GRAPHIC DESIGN
Jim Billy

MANAGING EDITOR
Pamela J. Johnson

PUBLISHER
Sheldon L. Factor

DBI BOOKS, INC.

PRESIDENT
Charles T. Hartigan

VICE PRESIDENT & PUBLISHER
Sheldon L. Factor

VICE PRESIDENT—SALES
John G. Strauss

TREASURER
Frank R. Serpone

Manuscripts, contributions and inquiries, including first class return postage, should be sent to the GUNS ILLUSTRATED Editorial Offices, 4092 Commercial Ave., Northbrook, IL 60062. All materials received will receive reasonable care, but we will not be responsible for its safe return. Material accepted is subject to our requirements for editing and revisions. Author payment covers all rights and title to the accepted material, including photos, drawings and other illustrations. Payment is at our current rates.

CAUTION: Technical data presented here, particularly technical data on handloading and on firearms adjustment and alteration, inevitably reflects individual experience with particular equipment and components under specific circumstances the reader cannot duplicate exactly. Such data presentations therefore should be used for guidance only and with caution. DBI Books, Inc. accepts no responsibility for results obtained using this data.

Arms and Armour Press, London, G.B. exclusive licensees and distributor in Britain and Europe; New Zealand; Nigeria, South Africa and Zimbabwe; India and Pakistan. Lothian Books, Port Melbourne, Aust., exclusive distributors in Australia.

ISBN 0-87349-118-1 Library of Congress Catalog #69-11342

CONTENTS

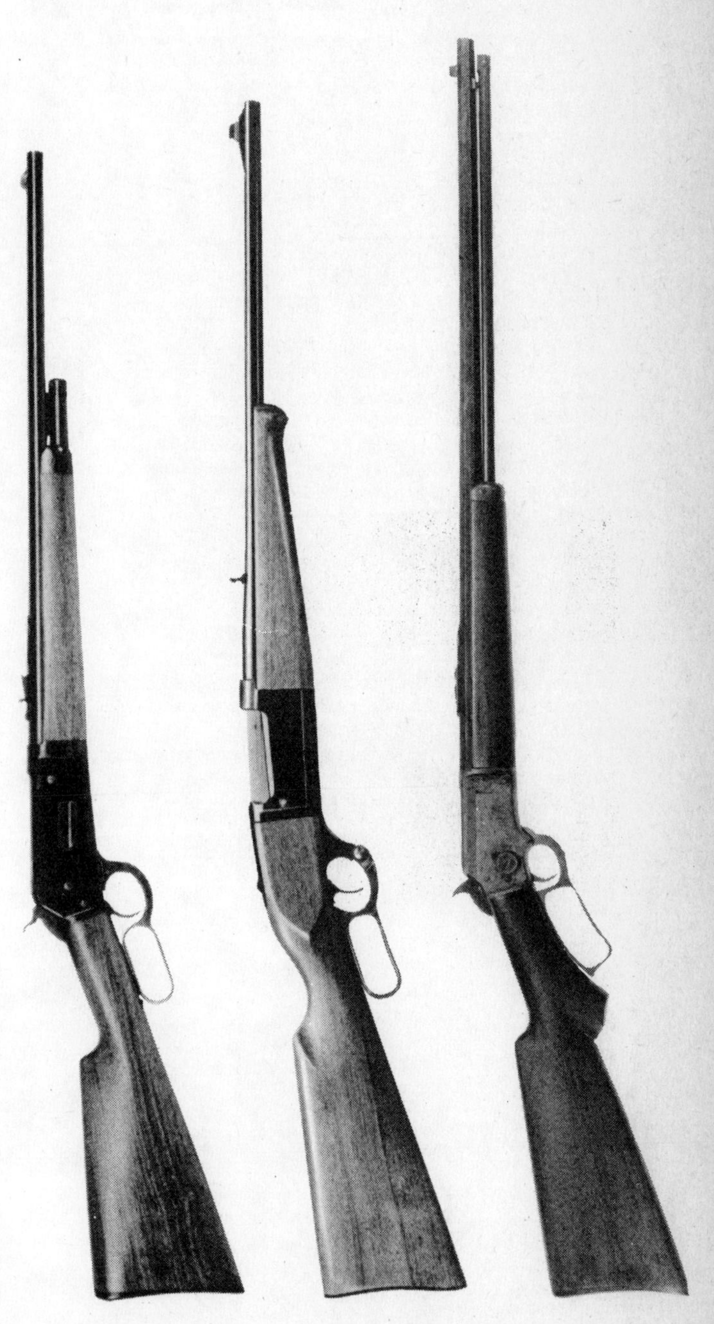

FEATURES

DEPARTMENTS

My Dream 22 Rifle

For years the author lusted after a modern 22 rimfire rifle that was different, and finally ordered what he wanted.

by STAN TRZONIEC

A beautiful blend of old and new is reflected here with the author's new Remington 40XR custom rimfire and his childhood favorite, the Winchester Model 67A.

WHEN I WAS a young lad popping off woodchucks in upper New York state some 35 years ago, I used an old Winchester Model 67A rifle. Still in my possession, that rifle, along with "penny-a-shot" 22 rimfire ammunition accounted for many a chuck in those relaxing summer afternoons looking over 300 acres of farmland. For a young hunter, certainly there was no better way to spend a school vacation.

Single shot in design, that basic Model 67 was introduced to the public in early 1934 with continued production until 1963. According to factory records, over 383,500 units were made. For use as a young man's rifle it was great, although at times I questioned the maker's decision to equip the gun with a 27-inch round barrel. Unknown to me at the time however, Winchester did produce a gun known as a "boys rifle" with a 20-inch tube. But on a 50-cent-a-week allowance it would have made little difference; the probability of buying one of them at the time was about as remote as seeing the sun shine every single day of the year. As I graduated up through the years into centerfire armament for such long (read longer) range sniping duties, nevertheless on calm, warm, lazy summer afternoons, I still longed for a modern 22 rimfire single shot rifle.

Over the years, the temptation was almost filled with such premium entries like the Kimber and Anschutz rifles but for some reason there was still something missing. Now don't get me wrong—there's absolutely nothing amiss about these rifles as they are top quality, very accurate rimfire rifles. However, like most everything else in this world that has to be very special, you sometimes don't know what you want until you actually see it. So was the case until a press release came along noting the reintroduction of the Remington Model 40XR rimfire sporter. Things were starting to look up.

First and foremost, this was a full-race custom rifle made only on special order at Remington's famed Custom Shop in Ilion, New York. This would add yet another dimension to the project as my "chuckin' haunts" just happened to be a stone's throw from the factory. Boy was I getting hyped! Not only could I sink my teeth into this rifle by getting involved in the final outcome, I also had the neat luxury of dressing her out in my choice of wood, metal finish and yes, even to the type of buttpad. But more on that in a minute.

Company lineage on this series of target rifles runs as long as your arm. The year 1937 witnessed the introduc-

Tim McCormack (right), Custom Shop supervisor, is discussing a Grade IV stock with John Remington. The Custom Shop does everything possible to match the wood to the customer's desires.

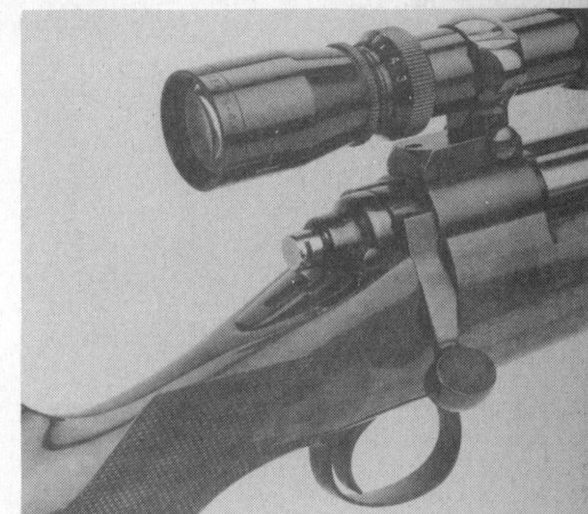

Details abound here. The bolt knob is checkered and the safety lever is just under the thumb. Note that the bolt head protrudes from the shroud to signal the cocked (and maybe loaded!) condition. Scope is a Leupold 3x-9x Compact in Redfield rings and bases. Point-pattern checkering is standard on Grade I rifles.

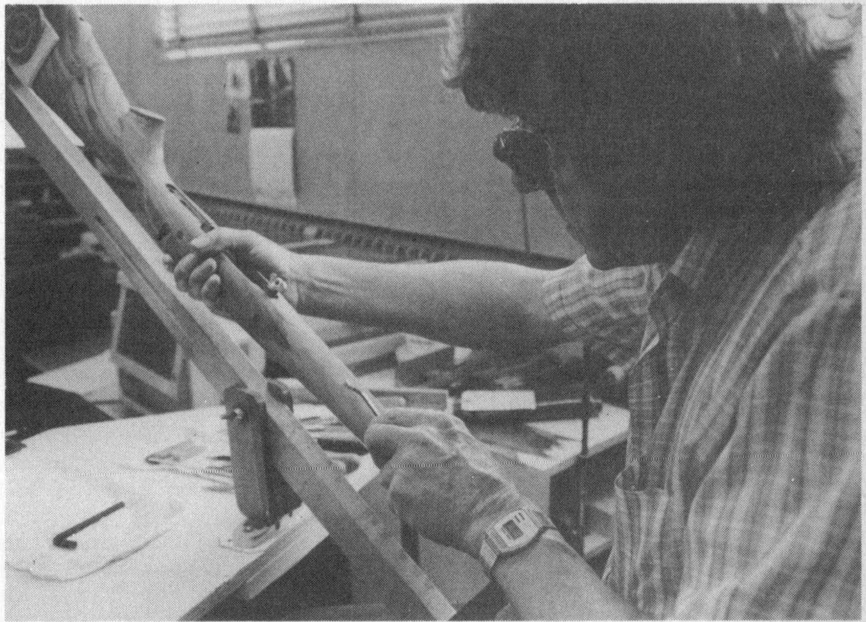

Leo Bala is completing the checkering pattern on a Grade I stock. The figure in the Claro walnut is outstanding.

For small game, the 22 rimfire is a natural. Trzoniec feels his custom rifle is not just a pretty wall-hanger—it's a using gun that just happens to be extremely handsome.

This 22 cartridge is ready to be driven home. Note the heavy-duty extractor at 3 o'clock on the bolt, and the bolt locking notch just forward of the rear receiver bridge. Redfield mount system looks great!

tion of the Model 37, a premium rifle slated for hole-punching duties. Remington made about 25,000 of these from 1937 to 1955. Depending upon options, you could spend upward of $75.80 for one, complete with very spiffy Redfield sights. In 1940 you could add a "selected, figured American walnut stock" for a mere $4.80. I guess there was nothing like the good old days.

Within the same time frame, several target 22s appeared in an overlapping pattern. The Model 37 was replaced by the Model 513 MatchMaster, which ran from 1940 to 1968. Following that we also saw the Model 521TL with production from 1948 to 1968. And in between all this the 40X had a start in 1956 and continued until 1963. First supplied in 22 LR, a super deluxe model could be had for around $187.50 with a heavy barrel sans sights, or with a standard barrel topped off with Redfield Olympic iron sights.

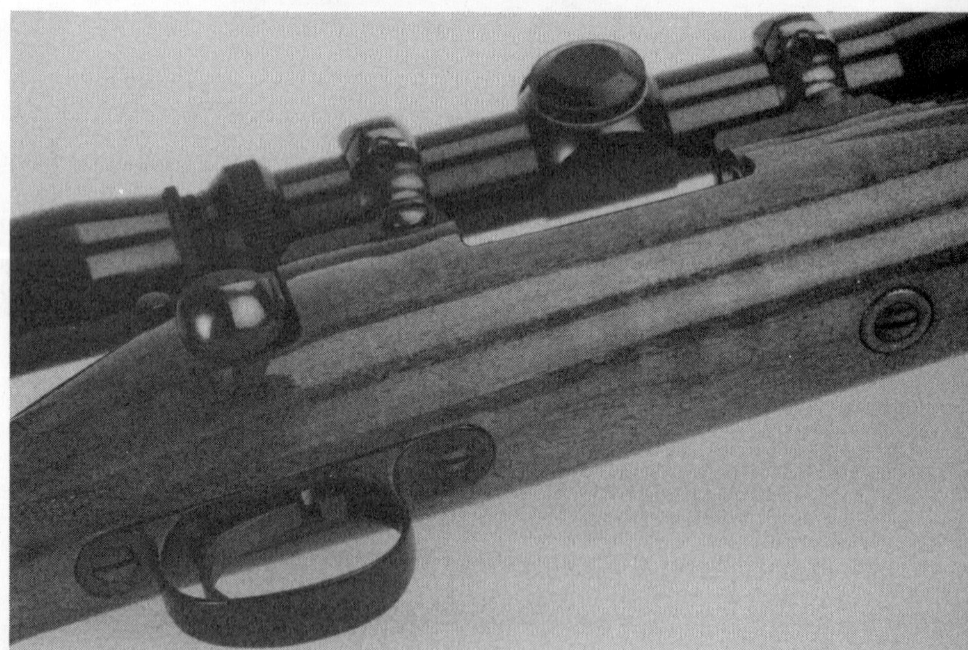

The lack of a magazine sticking out the bottom of the stock adds elegance to the rifle, as well as stability. Note that the guard and action screw slots are all lined up—another mark of a custom rifle.

While all this was well and good for benchrest shooters whose whole crusade in life is to put all those bullets into one tiny hole, the hunting and sporting fraternity had, for the most part, been denied a super accurate rimfire rifle until 1969 when Remington stuck her corporate neck out with the Model 40XR Rimfire Sporter. I'm sure you remember the gun; I've seen them now and then commanding high prices in selected gun shops. Made only by the Remington Custom Shop, what we had here was a barreled action from a 40XR mated to a Model 700 custom-made stock. They sold every last one of them. Dropped from the line for 8 years, it emerged again in 1986 to become a full-time line item in four ascending grades for discriminating rimfire shooters. If you've ever considered a fully custom rifle from a premium builder and wondered just how much effort goes into such an order, let me say that everything you heard or read about such an operation is true. Take my word for it; I've been to the shop many times on both photographic and journalistic assignments. The work is slow, intense, time consuming and letter perfect. Tim McCormack, the shop supervisor, wouldn't want it any other way. I know.

Options are more than plentiful, so many in fact you may become overwhelmed by the choices. To begin, de-

Trzoniec specified a .600-inch rubber buttpad for his "dream gun," as well as an ebony grip cap. The striking wood figure is enhanced by the high gloss finish. Sling swivel studs are standard.

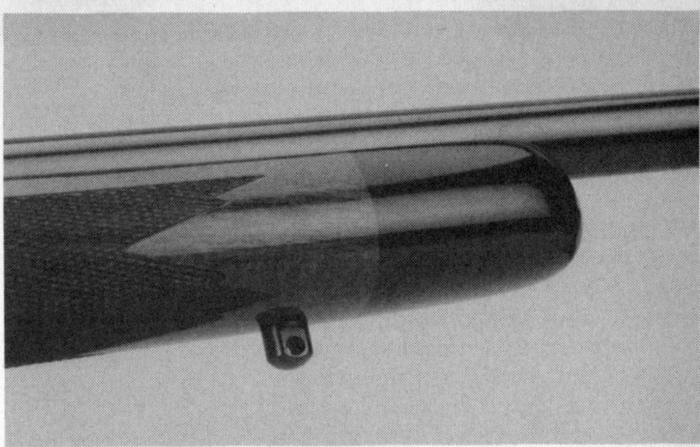

Also of ebony, the forend tip compliments the classic lines of the rifle. The checkering has a bobble or two, just enough to remind you that it was hand cut, not done by machine.

pending upon your wallet volume, the 40XR, like her Model 700 cousins, is available in four grades as Grade I, II, III and IV. In price, you're talking between $1300 to over $5000, depending on wood, final finish, engraving and inlays. Although I've never personally seen a Grade IV 40XR, if it approaches other examples of Ilion craftsmanship, it would be a knockout.

Rate of barrel twist is 1:16; chambering is 22 Long Rifle only. You can have your choice of any length from 18½ to 24 inches in light, medium or heavy contour. Adjustable sights are optionally available; otherwise count on receiving a clean barrel. As a final metal finish, a polished surface is available on all grades; matte finish is optional except on the Grade IV.

To further customize your 40XR, stock modifications are available on all grades. Length of pull, a most important dimension, is standard at 13⅜ inches with other measurements optional except on the higher Grade IV. For wood you have a choice of California claro, American walnut or English walnut on most grades. If you have something specific in mind (grain, pattern or color) let the shop know when you place the order. They will do their very best to come as close to your request as humanly possible. Additionally, styles can be had with a Monte Carlo, classic straight comb with or without a cheekpiece and/or white line spacers. Accents include a forend tip and cross-bolt plugs (if desired) in traditional rosewood or polished ebony. Grip caps can be had in the same wood with a skeleton or solid steel cap as an option. Recoil pads are available in all grades from .600-inch to 1-inch in Old English design. And to compliment the affair in total, a high gloss (for that extra fancy wood), satin or hand-rubbed oil finish can be specified.

Cut after the final finish is applied, hand checkering is the icing on the cake. In Grade I you receive a straight-line point pattern, 20 lines to the inch. In Grade II or III, a ribbon pattern is offered at 22 lpi. Finally, in Grade IV, a stunning fleur-de-lis pattern is standard. If you're like me, the obvious question always comes up: Can I order a Grade I with Grade III wood and checkering? While the Custom Shop bends over backward to handle most requests, to keep costs from going out of line you must be satisfied with what is available in each ascending grade. If you want extra fancy wood or different checkering you are bumped up to that model rifle with the appropriate increase in price. In other words, no Fords with Lincoln trim level. Delivery time is about 10 to 12 months from the time the order is placed at your dealer.

In the course of my work I was very privileged to be at the Custom Shop when my particular 40XR was in progress. The wood had been picked and roughed out, and when I arrived, Pat Bielanski was detailing it before the final finish. I had made a note to Tim McCormack to make the stock a bit oversize in width to allow for a more "man-sized" rifle. The request was honored and upon picking it up I found the stock exactly the way I had envisioned it. The wood was dark in color (another request) and included just a bit of crotch coloring denoting the Grade I price as specified. Some 6 weeks later, my 40XR arrived at the office. Opening the box, I noted that for extra protection Remington ships all custom guns in a hard case to protect your investment. Snapping open the locks revealed a 22 rimfire that was perfect in every way. I was thrilled to death.

Physically, this modern 40XR still has traits of her ancestors introduced some 40 years prior. Minor differences aside, our recent 40XR has a bolting system that sets her apart from serious 22 rimfire competition. The bolt can be considered a two-piece affair as the front part remains stationary within the receiver as the rear half turns and locks. Locking recesses for the bolt are stationed at a point just forward of the rear receiver bridge. The size of the 22 rimfire round lends itself to this design handily as traditional forward bolt locking lugs within the receiver walls would make loading difficult, if not impossible. Cocking, loading and extraction is effortless with this rifle; the attention to detail within the shop shows up in moving parts like this.

As it came from Ilion, the trigger pull was set for a click over 3 pounds. After cleaning the gun and getting it ready for range testing, a bit of tuning by myself brought it down to 2½ pounds without a hint of slack. Typical of Remington products, the safety is just under the thumb on the right-hand side of the bolt shroud. Untypical and rating an A+ in safety items is the way the rear of the bolt protrudes from the shroud by a good ⅜-inch. Polished bright, this is a sure indicator the gun is cocked and/or loaded. Per my request, the barrel was cut to 22 inches, a length I find just about perfect for 22 rimfire rifles. Contrary to what you may hear, the 22 rimfire gains little or no advantage in longer barrels.

Though I had gotten excited over this stock in the rough, the finished product was even better. The high gloss finish added depth to the wood and the combination of black ebony tip and grip cap made the rifle really stand out among the pack. I had chosen the classic-style stock with a cheekpiece and, now complete, it reinforced my convictions that I had indeed made the right choice. The point checkering was almost faultless—I say almost as there is a bobble or two along the border. No big deal really; as a matter of fact it adds a bit of "humanness" to it all, unlike modern machine checkering which is really too perfect on today's production guns.

With the gun all cleaned up I proceeded with the outfitting, which included a pair of Redfield bases and special high polish rings from the same company. Because I didn't order iron sights on this 40XR, a scope was in order. For this duty I picked a Leupold 3x-9x in their Compact line. As you can well see by the photographs, this scope compliments the whole assembly in just right proportions. All adjusted and bore-sighted, I headed for the range with none other than my trusty Model 67A sans optical goods.

At 50 yards both guns showed this shooter a thing or two. My Winchester single shot gave groups that somewhat satisfied me and, considering no scope was used, I really can't complain. Best shot of the day was with Federal Spitfires with a 1¾-inch group. From iron sights it even surprised me! After I got done patting myself on the back, my attention turned to that brand new 40XR. You'll notice on the chart nearby there are two entries. The first one for the 40XR (center) was shot in "competition" with the 67A just for ole times' sake. Not too shabby, and again those Spitfires blasted their way to victory with groups measuring ¾-inch.

The second time out was a blend of some previously tested ammo as well as newer, untried types. I could not have been more pleased. Remington led the way with some pretty impressive groups of ½-inch or slightly better with Winchester right on her heels with group sizes a mere ¼-inch more. At 50 yards I'll take either product any day.

To say I was pleased with my new possession would be an understatement. The quality of the piece in total reflects the ongoing commitment by Remington to supply first-rate, first-class rifles for those of us who want to go the distance. Furthermore, and this is important, the project rekindled fond memories of my younger days afield.

Yes, I found my 22 dream rifle at Remington's Custom Shop. Expensive? You bet, but worth every penny. In this day of heavy ballistic coefficients, compact discs and state of the art technology, it sure is nice to settle down with my regal rimfire. Single shot, you say? Ho hum. Well, sir, you just keep that attitude. Me, I'll take it with pleasure while I romance the days when I had to make due with my 67A. Now if I miss, I just reload, lean back and enjoy yesterday—*today*. ●

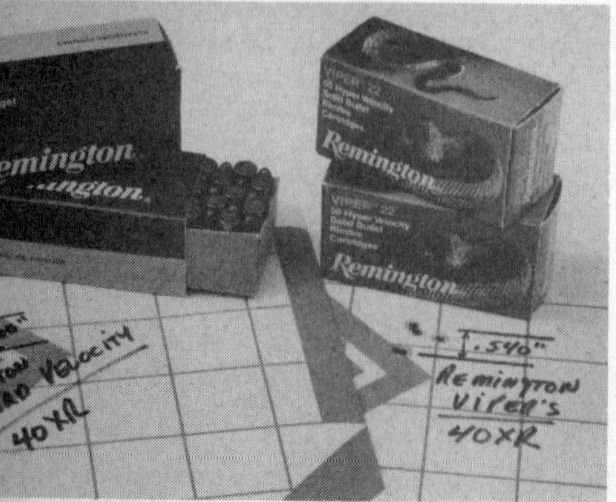

She shoots as good as she looks. Here are two groups shot at 50 yards with the custom 40XR and Remington ammunition. Fine performance, we'd say.

Accuracy Tests
22 Rimfire
Remington Model 40XR
50 Yards, 5-shot groups

Ammunition	Win. 67A	Rem. 40XR	Rem. 40XR
Winchester Super-X—Short	2½	1½	—
Remington Standard Velocity—Long	3½	1½	—
Winchester Standard Velocity—LR	—	—	¾
Federal Standard Velocity—LR	—	—	1
Remington Standard Velocity—Target, LR	2	1	⅝
Federal High Velocity—LR	—	—	1⅛
Winchester Super-X High Velocity—LR	2¼	⅞	¾
Remington Viper Hyper Velocity—LR	—	—	½
Federal Spitfire Hyper Velocity—LR	1¾	¾	—
CCI Stinger Hyper Velocity—LR	3	1½	—

Groups shown in inches

Specifications
Remington Model 40XR
Custom Rimfire Rifle

Options	Grades I	II	III	IV
Barrel length 18½″ to 24″	A	A	A	A
Light, medium or heavy contour	A	A	A	A
Adjustable open sights	A	A	A	A
Polished blue finish	A	A	A	A
Matte blue finish	O	O	O	A
Solid steel trigger guard	—	A	A	A
13⅜″ standard length of pull	A	A	A	A
Non-standard length of pull	O	O	O	A
Claro or American walnut stock	A	A	A	A
English walnut stock	—	A	A	A
Monte Carlo or classic-style butt	A	A	A	A
Cheekpiece	A	A	A	A
White line spacers	A	A	A	A
Forend tip and grip cap	A	A	A	A
Steel skeleton grip cap	—	O	O	A
Solid steel grip cap	O	O	O	A
Satin or high gloss wood finish	A	A	A	A
Hand-rubbed oil finish	O	O	O	A
Rubber butt pad (brown or black)	A	A	A	A
Checkered or skeleton buttplate	—	O	O	A
Point-pattern checkering (20 lpi)	A	—	—	—
Ribbon-pattern checkering (22 lpi)	—	A	A	—
Fleur-de-lis checkering (24 lpi)	—	—	—	A

A = Available at no additional charge
O = Extra cost option
A dash in any column indicates that feature not available; standard Remington part or style is supplied

by NICK STEADMAN

The P85 PISTOL A Shining Star in the Ruger Cast

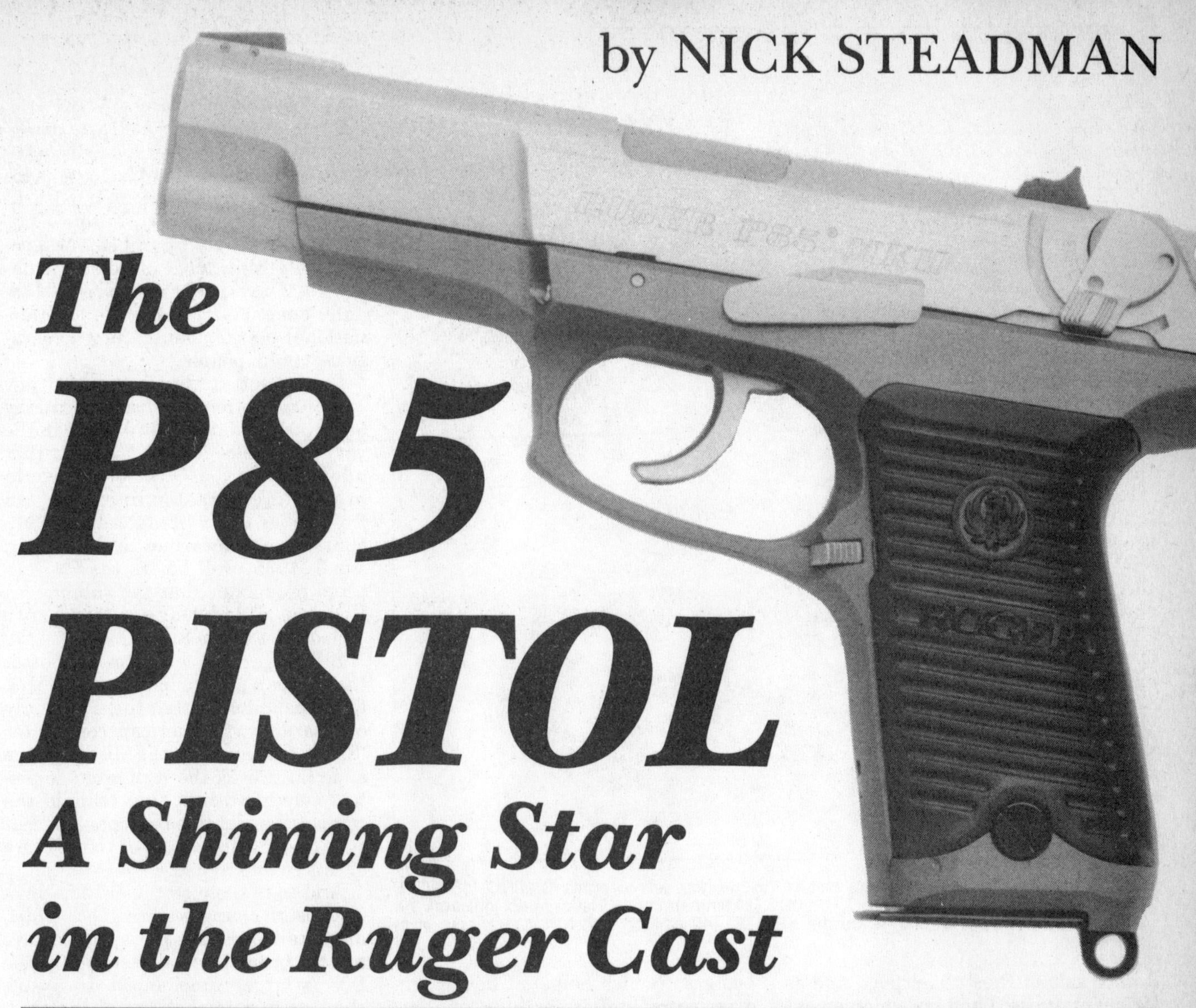

It's the best-value 9mm on the market, and here's the story of how it got there.

THOUGH MOST would say it was worth the wait, not even Bill Ruger himself would deny that his P85 pistol, which is Sturm, Ruger & Co.'s first venture into the 9mm semi-auto market, got off to a slightly shaky start. It was, however, something of a victim of premature publicity, a pitfall often hard to avoid. With the benefit of hindsight, Ruger probably wishes he'd called it the P88!

Early press photos issued in 1985 were subsequently withdrawn due to design changes, and a hiatus followed until mid-1986, when new illustrations and data were released. The pistol itself was not seen until the January, 1987 SHOT Show, and later the same year at the IWA exhibition in Nuremberg, Germany.

Shortly afterward, the first 100 P85s, newly assembled at the pilot Ruger plant in Prescott, Arizona, went out to the U.S. gun press and police agencies. But while field tests were under way, Ruger headquarters notified recipients that this initial batch of pistols was deemed unsatisfactory; further internal modifications were to be made. The first raft of magazine reviews, however, went ahead regardless, appearing in issues for the second half of 1987. Some were able to include comment on the modifications made to the initial design.

By May of 1988, Prescott was reporting P85 orders "in six figures" from the civil, police and military markets, but at the 1989 SHOT Show dealers were still complaining they could not obtain supplies of the new pistol. Ruger, however, confirmed that in the same month over a thousand pistols were being shipped each week—demand had simply outstripped supply. April, 1989, saw Ruger complete the transfer of P85 production to its new 200,000-square-foot plant on the

Current-production Ruger centerfire pistols include, top, left to right: KP90DC (45 ACP), P85MKII, KP85MKII; bottom: P89DC, KP89DC (all 9mms). The "K" letter prefix indicates the stainless steel slide. Not shown are the KP91DC (40 caliber) and KP89DAO, not yet in production.

other side of Prescott airport, and as 1989 progressed and law enforcement orders were satisfied, P85s became available in increasing quantities on the civil market, spawning yet another flurry of reviews.

Though the P85 has many novel qualities, not the least its very low price (still only $390.00), for some reason it so far has not attracted the same frenetic interest from the shooting press as some other inherently less innovative designs which have since been launched by rival gunmakers. Over 200,000 P85s have, in fact, already been shipped, of which more than 25 percent have gone to U.S. and foreign law enforcement and military agencies, but the high-profile publicity for Smith & Wesson's "model of the week," the plastic-framed Glocks and the Beretta saga (not to mention the 10mm/40 S&W story) have edged the Ruger 9mm to one side.

Despite all this, by any standards the P85 has to be the best-value 9mm on the market anywhere today, and apart from its "apple-pie" American pedigree (which helps), it has an impressive reputation for functional reliability, confirmed by repeated evaluations. Our aim in these pages is to document (warts and all) what makes the P85 tick—where it came from, its features and modifications, and where it's going in the future.

Bill Ruger's policy always has been to supply attractive, durable guns of modern design at the lowest practical price. In the P85's case, the low-end price is due not only to the mass-production advantages of casting and Prescott's extensive use of CNC machining equipment, but also to the pistol's innate design, which exploits the full potential of these manufacturing methods.

Having achieved remarkable success, not only with the 22 pistol but also the 10/22 rifle, single- and double-action revolvers, M77 and Mini-14/30 rifles, Ruger's goals for the P85 were a robust and hard-wearing 9mm semi-auto which would (in the company's words) "meet the functional and reliability criteria of the best 9mm pistols at extremely good value for money." It was to have good ergonomics, unequalled strength and a repeatably high degree of accuracy.

Though the idea was clearly spiced to some degree by the U.S. Army's M9 pistol trials, at the time they took place in 1984 the P85 did not even exist. In fact, the company says its sole motivation was simply what it saw as a potentially high level of domestic demand, particularly from law enforcement—and also in the international market—for "a new generation of 9mm pistols."

Put in context, the move in U.S. law enforcement from revolvers toward the 9mm pistol had already started in the very early '80s, and it was clear that adoption by the U.S. forces would prompt even greater interest, both from police and civil markets. The M9 contract was awarded to Beretta in April, 1985, well before the P85 entered production, but the subsequent Beretta slide-breakage saga only added grist to the Ruger mill.

Bill Ruger had felt from the outset that it was a poor reflection on the U.S. firearms industry that there was only one serious all-American competitor (Smith & Wesson) in the M9 trials; the slide failures of the Italian-made pistols convinced him that (should the competition later be re-opened) next time the P85 also would be there. More of this in due course!

And so to the pistol itself. The various design changes since 1985 (which are detailed in later paragraphs) have mostly been internal; externally the P85 is largely unchanged. In a nutshell, it is a 15-shot, recoil-operated, service-type gun with an alloy frame, double-action trigger and hammer-drop safety, quite similar at first glance to the double-action FN Hi-Power recently relaunched in Belgium. The alloy frame gives the P85 a top-heavy balance, with the center of gravity just behind the trigger; combined with a low bore line, this acts to aid quick shot-to-shot recovery.

The P85 from inception was "designed for casting." Its slide, frame, complete barrel, plus the trigger, hammer, sear and the majority of its other minor components are all cast; and the total parts count is only 56—some 20 percent less than most rival guns. Ruger's aim throughout was to simplify the design while producing an exceptionally strong pistol. As a result, one finds no thin internal sections, overly complex mechanisms or delicate components.

Critics of casting will immediately suggest the robustness of the components and the absence of thin sections are merely functions of the manufacturing methods employed, but Ruger deliberately used the casting technique to improve the pistol's resilience without gratuitously increasing size or weight. The P85 is actually shorter than the Beretta 92F, only a fraction higher and, at 2.06 lbs., weighs a little less. Both pistols, however, fit the Bianchi military holster.

It is true that the frame and slide width of the P85 are unusually generous, but this is intentional, to beef up the design. Casting does have one unexpected bonus internally, in that the slightly rounded edges of parts "as cast" make for mechanisms which require minimal breaking in. The continuing antipathy toward investment casting in some quarters has become something of a hoary old chestnut nowadays. Forging and casting are simply two alternative methods, each of which has its loyal following.

The smooth external contours of the P85 are deliberate (but capitalize on casting), producing a pistol which will not snag on clothing or holsters. It is also kind on the hands when firing. These soft lines may, however, help to explain why (visually at least) the P85 is often described as "chunky" or just plain big. Truth is, it's simply full-sized with few sharp lines to break up the mass. Quality materials are used throughout—the frame on all models is hard-anodized, aircraft-grade aluminum, finished in dark gray for the standard gun and a lighter shade for the stainless model. Slides are 4140 chrome/moly steel on the basic pistol, sandblasted and phosphated to a near-black matte finish.

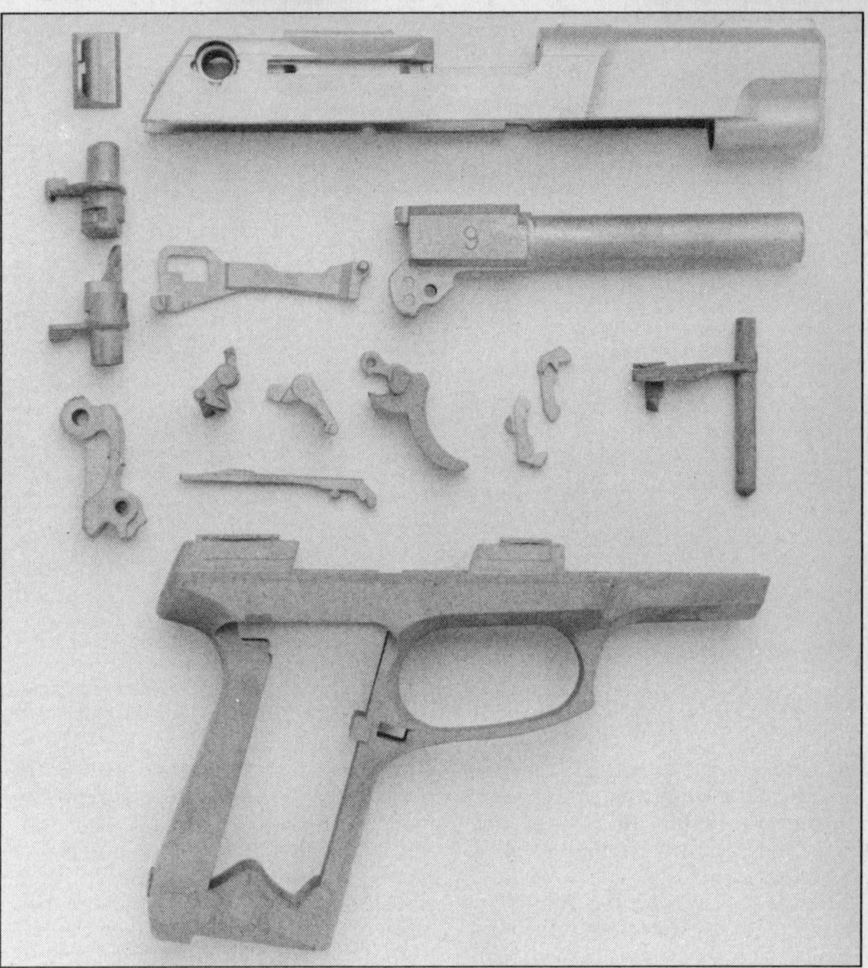

These 15 pieces are the rough cast parts of the P85MKII, prior to being cleaned up on CNC machines. Casting minimizes the amount of heavy machining before final finishing. Total parts count of the gun is 56, about 20 percent less than rival pistols.

Ruger's new stainless-slide pistols have a sandblast finish to the top of the slide and satin-polished sides. In fact, the barrels for all P85s are stainless, as are the hammers and triggers. The company often uses its own proprietary grade of stainless steel, designated "Terhune Anti-Corro" in honor of Stanley Terhune, the metallurgist who has been in charge of Ruger's Pinetree foundry for 30 years. It is difficult to understand why some reviewers have been unenthusiastic about the looks of the standard pistol, since a dulled finish is similarly employed on all U.S. military Berettas and on Glock slides. It is a no-frills approach, but durable, corrosion- and wear-resistant, giving a very businesslike appearance.

Rear curvature of the grip frame adequately prevents any slide contact with the web of the hand, and the grip angle is designed to give a straight-line trigger pull; it also makes the P85 point very naturally. Front- and backstraps are smooth, but the solvent-resistant, synthetic Xenoy grip panels are horizontally grooved. Though the grip material is hard, the grooves prevent any tendency for the hand to slip. The panels clip into the frame at the top, and each is secured by a single large screw near the end of the butt. Current P85s have slightly thinner grip panels than earlier guns to help those with smaller hands, but the frame dimensions remain unchanged. For those who prefer rubber grips, suitable versions are available from specialized companies such as Michaels of Oregon and Pachmayr.

Protruding from the heel of the butt is a lanyard loop, formed in the tip of the hammer spring seat, and in the frontstrap can be seen the seat for the leaf spring of the magazine release catch. All other springs in the P85 are coiled music wire, including the hammer spring. Magazines are blued steel and resemble those of the Hi-Power; they have plastic followers, witness holes at 5, 10 and 15 rounds, and detachable floorplates. Though twin-stack, they taper to a single column at the magazine lips for greater feed reliability. Users who want greater magazine capacity can obtain 18-round after-market versions from Ram-Line, Inc.

The toe of the magazine floorplate extends beyond the butt and can be used to help extract a jammed magazine or (in an emergency) to remove the grip panel screws. For those who find it hard to insert the last few rounds in the magazine, Ruger now provides a loading tool in the complete pistol kit, which comprises a P85, two magazines and a loader, all in a synthetic case with padlock.

The trigger guard is generously sized to allow use with gloves, and the forward edge is slightly recurved, as preferred by many of today's customers (including the U.S. military). The trigger is wide and smooth, and pivots in its own seat in the frame, obviating the need for an axis pin. To the bottom rear of the trigger guard, on both sides of the pistol, is a rectangular magazine-release button. An internal latch

The P85 assembly line is arranged in a horseshoe shape to facilitate efficient parts flow. Slide assembly begins at left, frame assembly at right rear; they meet in the middle for completion. Production of all models is in full swing these days.

is sprung against a cutout in the leading edge of the magazine, and pressure on either release button frees the magazine by pivoting the latch out of engagement.

This release system has been a frequent object of "gun-press" interest, since it requires the button to be pushed forward and inward, unlike other mechanisms where the magazine is secured at the side or corner. The primary purpose of this design was to eliminate the risk of magazines being released accidentally, and in this it succeeds, though it is true that with the earlier grips, at least, those with smaller hands could have difficulty operating the buttons without rolling the hand around the grip. The new grip panels should help here.

Moving toward the slide, the hammer has a knurled-ring spur which allows positive manual cocking. The low-profile "fixed" sights are equipped with instinctive aiming dots, two on the rear, one on the front blade. The rear sight actually can be drifted to zero, and since the front blade is secured by two cross pins, it can be exchanged for others of different heights, if required. The laser-assisted zeroing carried out at the Prescott plant is usually pretty close for most users, though.

Like the magazine release, the decocking/safety lever on the slide also is ambidextrous, though the "safe" marking and colored dots indicating weapon status appear only on the left side. Pushing the lever 85 degrees downward on a cocked gun lowers the hammer and makes the gun safe; pushing it up readies the pistol for firing. The presence of a safety catch (despite the decocking mechanism) is primarily a requirement of the military, though many private purchasers also prefer it. Beneath the catch, on the left side of the gun, a small exposed section of the trigger bar can be seen. Though not ideal, this is not uncommon on modern pistols and does not seem to cause any operating difficulties in adverse conditions.

The safety mechanism itself is quite sophisticated and incorporates a firing-pin blocker, permiting the hammer to contact the firing pin only when the trigger has been pulled through far enough to trip the sear, another stainless component. The P85 still can be loaded, unloaded and the action cycled when the manual safety/decocker is activated, but the trigger and hammer are completely disengaged. And when the hammer is decocked, it contacts not the firing pin but the drum of the safety mechanism. The stainless firing pin is durable enough to be bent through some 300 degrees without snapping.

The latest "decock-only" models of the P85 dispense with the manual safety facility; catches are marked "decock" on the left side of the slide. The double-action only pistol recently introduced has a bare slide with neither decock nor safety-catch provision. Though not ambidextrous (since it remains captive in the frame), the left-mounted slide release is amply sized and easily accessible to the thumb of the firing hand (unlike that on some rival designs). As with most semi-autos, it also does double duty as the stripping catch, but retention in the frame means it cannot be dropped or misplaced when the pistol is disassembled.

Should the P85's magazine be lost or damaged, the pistol is still useable with single rounds since there is no magazine safety disconnect. Some argue that this is a negative point, since so many U.S. police officers are killed with their own guns. The theory goes that a magazine disconnect gives an officer a means of quickly disabling his gun in a struggle. But, to be fair, it would take great presence of mind to try to drop the magazine while fighting off an assailant, and most users would probably prefer to be able to shoot without a magazine. Ruger reports almost zero interest in the disconnect facility from U.S. law enforcement, and the FBI also chose to specify the Smith & Wesson 10mm pistol without its customary magazine safety.

The P85's mechanism is short-recoil along Browning lines, but with a Colt-style swinging link beneath the chamber section of the barrel to cam it out of locking engagement. But there are no locking lugs on the barrel itself—the squared-off chamber section locks directly into the 1¼-inch-long ejection port in the slide, similar to SIG Sauer and Glock pistols. This gives a larger locking engagement surface than Browning-type lugs. The generous ejection port cutout, which extends

P85 pistols have a reputation for reliability and are able to digest almost any brand/type of ammo without stoppages. Indeed, various ammo types are routinely used in testing the pistols at the factory.

across the top and into the left side of the slide, makes for clean ejection and easy clearance of stovepipe jams. It also appears to give a noticeably lower cocking force.

The sturdy P85 extractor also is cast, and when a round is chambered the extractor tip protrudes to the right for visual and tactile confirmation that the gun is loaded. Rounds are presented to the breech well up the feed ramp, to cater for hollowpoint and other non-military bullet profiles. The ejection mechanism is rather unusual, since the ejector is a stamped steel unit which, when stripping the pistol, must first be pushed forward and down into the magazine well before the slide can be removed. However, at that stage the slide already is fully back and locked, and the often-cited risk to the operator's finger when carrying out this maneuver is somewhat overstated. For the faint-hearted, a pencil or other implement can be used instead. Stripping broadly follows Browning principles. The slide is locked back (and the ejector pushed down), then released and eased forward under control until the slide-stop cutout is aligned with the axis pin of the slide stop, whereupon the slide stop can be pushed out from the right. With the slide removed, the barrel and recoil spring with rod are extracted from the slide as per the Hi-Power. The major component of the P85 is the recoil spring with its cast-alloy guide rod, necked toward its tip to allow easy removal from the slide.

The slide rails, wider and deeper than usual, are cast into the frame and comprise four short sections, one pair by the hammer and another ahead of the trigger. Total rail length is much the same as for the Colt M1911, but the split design has the advantage of allowing better clearance of dirt and fouling from the rails in adverse operating conditions. And unlike the U.S. forces' M9 Beretta, the P85's slide is fully enclosed for maximum protection against ingress of sand and dirt.

The full-length slide rails seen on some 9mm pistols are generally thought to improve shot-to-shot consistency by producing a tighter fit between slide and frame. In the case of the P85, this is catered for by the geometry of the barrel/slide interface at the muzzle. No separate barrel bushing is used. This barrel repositioning mechanism was the subject of extensive development work; Ruger believes the P85 offers exceptionally good accuracy potential, and this is borne out by in-house tests which, with one new pistol, produced 15-yard machine-rest grouping of only 1/3-inch with 10 rounds.

It is useful to analyze the key points, positive and otherwise, which so far have emerged from P85 press reviews. As to overall design, most reviewers liked the rounded contours of the pistol, its ambidextrous (and easily accessible) controls, and the absence of a magazine safety. The sights generally have been well received, though there are some who dislike the three-dot system on *any* pistol. Most found the P85 well-zeroed straight out of the box and felt the balance and ergonomics contributed to the low felt recoil and minimal muzzle jump. The large ejection port also was seen as a major bonus for reliability. In particular, it was believed the P85 would be an easy pistol for novices to use, with its simple layout and pleasant shooting characteristics.

The double-action pull on pistols reviewed varied (depending upon the gun) from about 12 to 15 lbs. It was often described as quite long, but most reviewers found it very smooth and easy to handle, due in part to the smooth and wide trigger design. Some felt it was helped by the absence of a half-cock position and magazine disconnect mechanism. Even the FBI (generally a harsh critic) was equally keen on the double action. The DA pressure on the latest P85s is down to only 8½-10½ lbs. from a nominal 12 lbs. on earlier guns.

Above all, the number one favorable comment by all reviewers was about the P85's functional reliability. Most put several hundred rounds of every sort of ammunition through at least one gun, sometimes several. Some even fired the P85 deliberately unlubricated and still had no malfunctions. Taken overall, there were occasional (but very few) instances of the odd failure to fully chamber a round, or the slide not locking back on the last round, plus one or two stovepipe stoppages, but almost always at the end of a heavy firing program or when using the pistol unlubricated. One reviewer reported he had fired over 2000 rounds through one P85 and never cleaned it, but had no malfunctions at all.

Apart from comments on size and appearance, some reviewers felt the grip frame was rather deep from back to front (increasing the length of pull), and that the grip itself (at 1¼ inches) was rather thick, though both aspects now should be settled by the new, thinner grip panels. Most felt the novel magazine-release system was fine, once they had gotten used to it.

Ejector access when stripping was a common point, but more relevant was the question of ejection pattern. With early guns, reviewers complained of occasional cases in the face or down the shirt, but in later guns this has been rectified, following more detailed attention to the configuration of the extractor.

Poor single-action trigger pull was a frequent criticism from many quarters. The SA trigger has a pull the same length as the DA mechanism, commencing with a soft ¼-inch take-up and letting off at about 5 to 6 lbs. On early guns, some complained that the let-off was almost imperceptible, nearly amounting to a "rollover" system, but in later reports with newer guns a number of reviewers were complimentary about the crispness of the pull. It is true the SA pull takes some getting used to, until accustomed to the long take-up. Nominal weight nowadays is 5 lbs.

Accuracy was a continuing theme throughout reviews. Early guns do seem to have been somewhat less accurate than later models, but even those initial P85s were capable of 2½-inch groups at 25 yards from a rest, maybe 4 inches offhand, so the matter is highly subjective. With the passage of time, figures as good as 1¼ inches have been recorded at 20 yards, and the 25-yard average seems to be around 2½ to 3 inches.

No 9mm pistol has ever been seriously designed as a UIT target gun, but the figures above would be perfectly acceptable for any "practical" competitor, and doubtlessly could be tuned with special handloads. Ruger's intention was to exceed the previous accuracy standards for service-type pistols, and at the end of the day the P85 appears to be at least as accurate as any of its leading rivals. Performance is certainly well above that of the military ammunition many users will fire in it. The author, incidentally, found that U.S. military M882 NATO ammunition was a very indifferent product—functioning was fine, but accuracy very average—and noticeably inferior even to Eastern-bloc ball. By contrast, the P85 particularly likes the new Olin 147-grain subsonic OSM cartridge, which inherently seems very accurate.

One must ask, however, if the 25-yard performance of any pistol matters that much, at least from a self-defense viewpoint. The author's own tests with various P85 pistols generally have been at more realistic distances of 7-15 yards, all fired offhand. Firing at 11 yards, even a very early P85 with Eastern-block ammunition grouped to 0.9-inch, spoiled by a self-inflicted flyer 0.3-inch out (the same pistol shot to 2 inches at 25 yards with the aid of a sandbag or two). Another model grouped again to 0.9-inch with five rounds at 8 yards, and even the double-action-only P85 prototype repeatedly shot to an inch at the same range! All in all, the accuracy question seems to be something of a "red herring." If one wants to guarantee a hit on a specific shirt button at 25 yards, use a rifle.

The story of the P85 also is one of continuous product improvement. In the course of developing the first pistols, Ruger took advice from barrel-makers Bar-Sto and J.E. Clark on the whole question of precision barrel design and rates of twist (1:10 was finally adopted). This led to a redesign of the barrel/slide geometry and the slide/frame interface, subsequently incorporated into series production started in 1987. Some minor adjustments also were made to SA trigger pull and the ejector was "tweaked" to produce a less random ejection pattern.

Perhaps the biggest change seen in the production pistols, however, was to the barrels. Up to 1987, a rifled bore section had been welded into the chamber block, but this was superseded by a one-piece casting which was then machined and rifled (by broaching). In late 1987, Ruger provided samples of the P85 to the U.S. Army for the XM10 rerun of the M9 pistol trials, but these were cancelled in March, 1988. The Army competition started again in August, 1988, and included 30 military versions of the P85 with chrome-lined bores and rear sight lockscrews to facilitate zeroing and disassembly. The XM10 story ended with a re-award to Beretta; however Ruger has received a detailed Army report on the performance of its own pistol which, except for minor deficiencies during the mud test, we are told was completely satisfactory.

Fortunately, Ruger's plans for the P85 were in no way dependent upon securing the Army deal, which in any event would have been a low-margin contract. In early 1988, the original long-tapered slide release, which could give problems with certain holsters, was replaced by the slightly shorter and higher-seated version seen on current pistols. Some further refinements to the trigger mechanism were introduced in late 1989 to simplify construction and give a smoother DA pull. First production pistols with the new thinner grip panels also became available at the end of 1989; these now are standard on all models. One group likely to benefit immediately is the growing band of female law enforcement personnel who, like others of us with little hands, have difficulties with many of the double-stack 9mm pistols.

Though Ruger does not supply sights other than the fixed versions which come with the P85, high- and low-profile aftermarket units are available from Millett and MMC. SHOT Show 1990 saw the official launch of the stainless slide and decock-only versions of the P85, and there's more to come.

Many readers already will know something of the torture testing which Ruger has carried out in-house to back up its marketing claims for the P85. The now-famous barrel-obstruction test, in which a round of M882 ammunition was fired behind a full-length plug screwed into the bore, was an early experiment (prompted by the M9 slide failures) to see how the pistol would stand up to long pressure dwell times. Other than the case head giving way and blowing out the extractor, there was only a tiny increase in headspace and some minor gas cutting. The cast extractor was bent through about 35 degrees, but held together. It is worth noting that the bullet had only about 1/100-inch freebore when fired!

In October, 1988, Ruger took a P85 and cut away a 2½-inch-long by ½-inch-wide section of its slide through and forward of the right-hand ejection cutout, effectively leaving the pistol dependent only upon its left slide wall for structural integrity. This test, one could say, is ongoing—5000 rounds of M882 ammunition were fired in two strings (2000 and 3000 rounds), with checks every 1000 rounds, simulating the rated U.S. Army life cycle for the M9. Ruger also wanted to see if the heat from continuous firing would compound the trial. But nothing happened. The gun consumed all the ammunition and the slide (what was left of it after the right side was cut away) remained undistorted. The P85 was not stripped or cleaned during the test. By the time the author fired his quota through it, the pistol had received about 700 more rounds and was still unharmed. A comparison with the fate of the early M9s is unavoidable!

Disassembly of the P85 is begun by locking the slide back, then pushing down the ejector as shown. A fingertip is all that's necessary, but a tool can be used by the faint-of-heart.

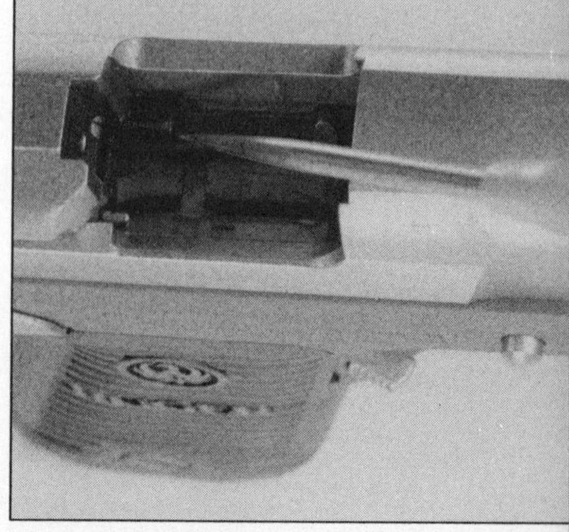

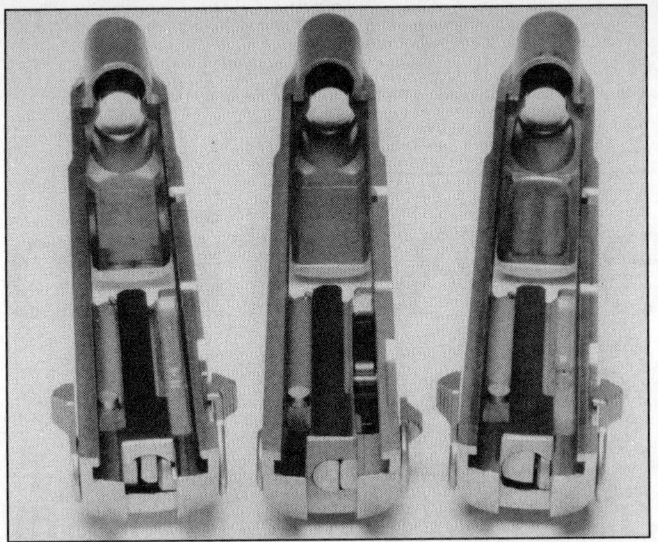

PB5 slide assemblies vary internally according to model and therefore are not interchangeable. Left to right: KP85MKII, KP89DC, KP85. The KP89DC (center) has only the decocking lever. The firing pins are different on all three.

The trigger guard is generously sized to allow shooting with gloves, and the front of the guard has the familiar "hooked" shape for two-handed shooting. Trigger is wide and smooth. Magazine catch is ambidextrous and must be pushed in and forward to release.

Ruger also makes a point of proof-firing each gun with SAAMI-spec proof loads before shipping. In one case, a P85 was still going strong after a thousand of these high-pressure cartridges had been fired through it. The company has a long-term aim of testing a P85 to 100,000 rounds of NATO ammunition, but at last count had only found time to get to 30,000 . . . again, with no adverse results. Ruger, in fact, vouches that it never has had a single slide, frame or barrel fail in testing hundreds of thousands of rounds with various P85s. A bold claim, but one the author has no reason to disbelieve.

More recently, the author prompted (and witnessed) a test in which a P85 was deliberately run over twice by a large pickup truck. This was a repeat of a test originally done by the company to persuade a foreign client that the Xenoy grip panels were as tough as Ruger claimed. In fact, this proved doubly educational, since the truck was standing on coarse gravel, so the whole pistol was potentially at risk. The result? Well, the grip panels not only were intact but virtually unmarked, and the side of the pistol which made intimate contact with the gravel bore only very minor cosmetic markings. Immediately afterward, the pistol was cycled a few times and found to show no evidence of deformation or other damage.

Humidity and salt-water testing of the P85 also reveal some interesting results. In tests done in late 1989, two pistols with an experimental black-oxide slide finish were exposed to salt-water vapor for some time. There was some very minor damage to the slides, and even the stainless barrels were slightly corroded, but there had been no effect at all on the anodized frames with standard finish. In straight 100 percent humidity testing, pistols with the new slide finish which had been exposed for 39 days showed no signs of corrosion at all. These tests speak volumes about the surface coatings used, but mostly about the alloy frames.

In response to criticism of the SA trigger pull on the P85, Ruger has been working for some time on a new mechanism which will give better leverage and half the take-up of the present trigger, resulting in what Bill Ruger describes as "a marvelously crisper pull." It also will have the effect of slightly shortening the DA pull. This "MKII" trigger accompanied by a new safety/decocking lever and firing pin, requires some modifications to the frame, and will result in a new series of model numbers.

The standard pistol simply has become the P85 MKII, but the decock-only version is designated the P89. A 10mm P85 was expected in mid-1990, but has been postponed indefinitely. The 45-caliber P90 version was introduced in June, 1991. The new slide for the 45 pistol is wider and deeper, and the magazine has a synthetic floorplate. A new magazine release also is fitted. A P89 DAO (DA-only) 9mm is scheduled for production in August, 1991. And yes, Ruger has a 40 Auto-caliber P91 decocker on the way, too, scheduled for mid-July, 1991, production. It will be built on the 9mm P89 frame with a "1½-stack" magazine holding 12 rounds.

By now it will be public knowledge that Ruger is currently recalling all 200,000 P85s already shipped, following the discovery that if the firing pin should be broken, there is a possibility that a round could be fired when the hammer is decocked. The Prescott plant intends to modify all the pistols on a rolling program of 20,000 per month. U.S. readers will not need reminding that (liability laws as they are) anything which, however remote the risk, could cause an acccident must be rectified.

But this should be placed in its proper context. It is the first production recall of the P85 (an excellent record nowadays for a new design!) and does not reflect adversely upon Ruger any more than the other big names whose products are recalled in the course of the average year, often for reasons which the author (coming from a less litigious Europe) finds somewhat obscure! Still, better safe than sorry.

Though the Ruger list of handguns is more limited than that of, say, Smith & Wesson, Ruger of course makes a full range of firearms and, based on latest available data, is second only to Remington in total numbers of firearms produced in the USA—some 565,000 in 1988. Perhaps more significantly, nearly every new Ruger entry has been a winner in its own right. The P85 series is right up there with the rest of them, and looks set to stay. And, since the dollar in the wallet is a constant issue in these times of recession and inflation, it is worth paraphrasing one reviewer's comments and reiterating that for the price of some of the competition's pistols you can still buy a brace of P85s and a crate of ammunition to christen them with. ●

An American Pageant

The Lever-Action Legacy

Purely American in design, the lever-action rifle is still a popular choice for hunters who want fast-shooting, handy rifles with a bit of romance to boot.

by WILF E. PYLE

(Below) The Model 94 is probably the most successful Winchester of all time. Below is an early rifle version in 25-35; bottom is a 30-30 carbine.

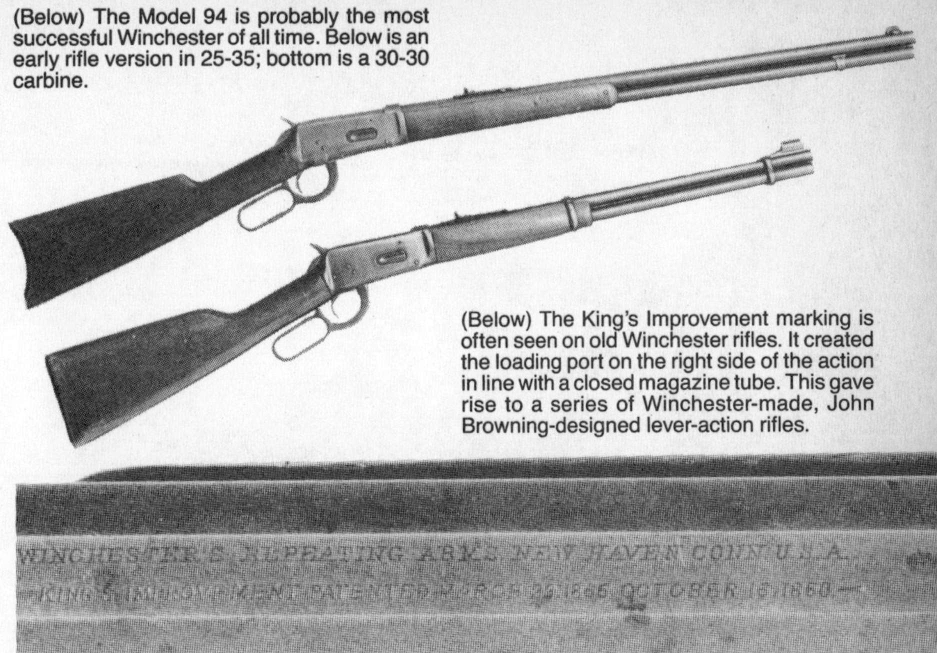

(Below) The King's Improvement marking is often seen on old Winchester rifles. It created the loading port on the right side of the action in line with a closed magazine tube. This gave rise to a series of Winchester-made, John Browning-designed lever-action rifles.

WHEN I STOP and think about it, I realize that I actually like shooting lever-action rifles. It doesn't matter what make or model; I simply like shooting them. Others feel the same way, and they might typically extol the many virtues of the lever gun. They are the first to claim that light weight and fast-handling characteristics are good reasons for a life-long love affair with the levers. I agree, but for me it's also the "shuck-shuck" sound of the action and the "tin-ping" noise of the extracting cartridge that gets my attention. For me, the working sounds of a lever-action rifle are music to my ears.

The lever-action rifle has been a serious part of the American shooting scene since U.S. patent number 30,446 was given to B. Tyler Henry on October 16, 1860. Although his rifles were not generally available for some 3 years, the Henry and its accompanying cartridge, the 44 Henry, went on to set the stage for the lever rifles that followed. Henry was an employee of the New Haven Arms Company which was owned by Oliver F. Winchester.

There were earlier attempts at lever rifle designs. Walter Hunt, a New York machinist, developed a lever-actioned, breech-loading rifle called the "Volitionial Repeater" in 1849. He also developed a primitive cartridge known as the rocket ball. It featured a bullet cavity filled with powder and covered by a disk with a hole in the center that allowed ignition from the primer cap.

Lewis Jennings, a gunsmith who worked for Hunt, further improved the lever rifle by reducing the number of parts and designing the carrier that brought the cartridge up from the magazine. This design was further enhanced by Daniel B. Wesson and Horace Smith. They turned the Hunt-Jennings-Smith firearm into the Smith and Wesson Volcanic repeater. It was a finger-lever-operated pistol with an exposed hammer and an under-barrel magazine. It was here that Oliver Winchester, a shirt maker, entered the firearm business. He acquired a controlling interest in the bankrupt Volcanic Repeating Arms company and renamed it the New Haven Arms Company.

The Henry rifle was developed and sold by the New Haven Arms Company. Civil War soldiers on both sides purchased the Henry for their own use. At a time when the speed and reliability of firearms were critical to personal survival, the Henrys proved effective. Early settlers appreciated the greater firepower and dependability this arm offered. Improvements in the 44 Henry cartridge made the round more trustworthy and powerful. The combination of a fast repeating rifle shooting a hard-hitting, reasonably accurate bullet had the American shooting public clammering for more.

Over 14,000 Henry rifles were sold; thus the New Haven Arms Company prospered and became the Winchester Repeating Arms Company. Further improvements, especially King's patent, which created the loading port on the right side of the action in line with a closed magazine tube, gave rise to a series of Winchester-manufactured, John Browning-designed, lever-action rifles that continues to this day. These models include the 1866, 1871, 1873, 1876, 1886, 1892, 1894 and 1895. Later, the Model 94 would eclipse the Henry many times.

There were other important lever-action developments. The Spencer Patent Repeater was adopted by the U.S. military in carbine and infantry configurations in 1862. It held seven cartridges of 56-caliber. The 350-grain bullets developed a muzzle velocity of 1200 fps and striking energy of 1125 foot pounds. The Spencer beat out the Winchester in military trials, and President Lincoln personally tested the Spencer carbine on the lawn of the White House. That was probably the last time a firearm was legally fired on the steps of the White House. In 1869, the Spencer patent and manufacturing equipment was purchased by the Winchester company and the Spencer slowly disappeared from use, although cartridges were available until 1920.

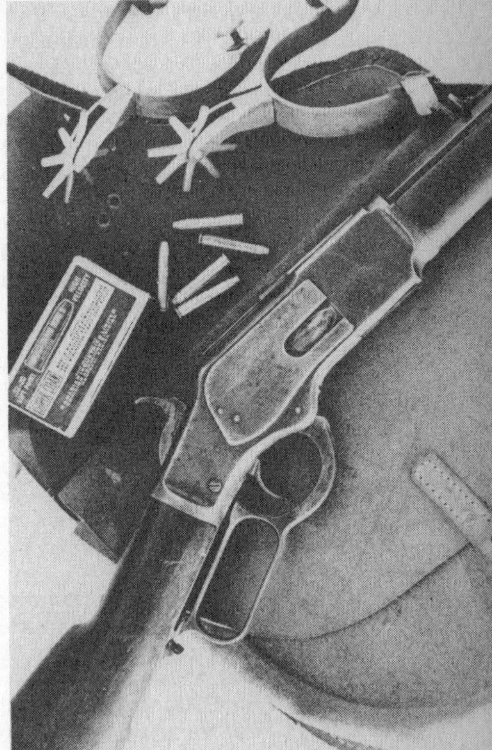

The 1873 Winchester was highly successful as a hunting rifle and self-defense arm. It was chambered for a variety of calibers, including 22 rimfire, and firmly established the Winchester dynasty.

Eli Whitney Jr. also developed a lever-action rifle. Working with patents he acquired from gun designer

(Opposite page) This potpourri of interesting rifles epitomizes the American lever gun pageant. Left to right: Winchester Model 94, Marlin Model 95, Savage Model 99H, Browning BLR, Winchester Model 88, and Winchester Model 71.

John Marlin's greatest contribution to lever-action design is the solid-top receiver that ejects cases out to the right. This gives better protection from dirt and dust, and allows a scope to be mounted directly over the action.

Andrew Burgess, Whitney teamed the lever-action rifle with the then-powerful 45-70 cartridge. This rifle was submitted for military trial but failed due to a poor lifter mechanism. A new lifter design by gunsmith Sam Kennedy made the rifle capable of handling a variety of blackpowder cartridges, and the Whitney-Kennedy achieved enough popularity as a sporting rifle to sell some 25,000 units. Interestingly, Winchester purchased the Whitney Arms Company and soon this rifle also passed into history.

John Marlin contributed to the lever-rifle scene as early as 1881. Much like the Whitney-Kennedy, the Marlin Model 81 featured an external hammer, side port loading and a tubular, under-the-barrel magazine. Like the Winchester and Whitney-Kennedy, ejection was accomplished from the top. Available in sporting rifle and short carbine, the Model 81 was offered in 45-70, 45-85, 38-55 and 32-40. Later, in 1888, a scaled-down version in 32-20, 38-40 and 44-40 was available.

John Marlin's greatest contribution to our lever-action legacy was the Model 1889 lever rifle. This was the first solid-top design that ejected cases out to the right. This, according to advertising literature used to this day, gave better protection from dirt, dust and mud. Later, it allowed for mounting a telescope directly on the receiver. The 1889 spawned many model variations, but it firmly provided an alternative for shooters wanting a rifle that ejected cases to the side rather than out through the sighting plain at the top. Marlin relentlessly advertised this feature, calling it the "Marlin Safety," and all Marlins that followed ejected from the side.

Between introduction and 1892, the lever rifle sold over 2 million of the various makes and models within the United States. This point is even more striking given that the national census showed only 62 million souls. Roughly 3 percent of the population owned a lever rifle, showing that a deep demand for these rifle types existed.

The sales of lever rifles for sporting purposes continued unabated and spawned several decades of renewed rifle design. The thinking in banking circles was that if sport users found favor with lever rifles, perhaps the military would too. Wide acceptance by the American shooting public and the potential for lucrative military contracts weren't missed by the designers, inventors and bankers of the time. Much talent and energy became directed to firearm production, and, in turn, a golden age of firearm design evolved that continued until World War I.

Perhaps the most interesting lever rifle of them all is the Savage Model 99 (left). This is a Model 99H chambered in 30-30. Note the slim forend and butt configuration on this early model.

As the late 1800s approached, interest in firearm manufacture, design and functionality reached a pinnacle. American production techniques were some of the best in the world, and many good financial opportunities were possible from military contracts that supplied everything from rifles to mess tins. As well, overseas governments were anxious to modernize and update their army rifles as better cartridges, improved gun powder, progressive manufacturing techniques and superior steels became available. The turmoil of the last half of the 19th century saw nearly every country going to war at least once. Opportunities for firearm sales and related products were high, and this attracted well-heeled entrepreneurs and businessmen into rifle manufacturing.

It was in this environment that Arthur William Savage was to leave lever users with a fine legacy. Savage was a businessman with an intense interest in firearms. His personal efforts produced a rotary magazine repeater years ahead of its time. As with other lever designs, the Savage 99 would appear in many variations. His first lever rifle was directed at military applications, but in Army trials held at Governor's Island, New York, his design was not selected.

Savage left behind a rotary maga-

zine-fed rifle that allowed the use of more accurate spire-point bullets rather than flat-nosed kinds, featured a solid breech and was of hammerless design. His design transcended the blackpowder era as he was one of the first to recognize the importance future high-power smokeless loads were about to exert on all firearms. The lack of an under-barrel magazine provided improved balance and feel. Accuracy was also better as a one-piece stock and the absence of barrel bands securing the magazine tube reduced interference with the barrel's sine wave created during firing.

The lever-action story contains a single negative, but critical, point. Lever rifles failed miserably as military arms. It is historically correct that several models were picked up in small contracts, but none achieved the extensive acceptance their makers wished. For example, the Winchester Model 73, in musket form, was supplied in small numbers to Spain, and the Model 95, in military configuration, was provided, with much controversy, to the U.S. Army. These, however, never saw service and went to surplus assets in 1906. The Winchester 1876, in full wood military design, saw limited use by the Royal Canadian Mounted Police. The Savage 99, dressed up in full wood with two kinds of bayonets, failed to attract military contracts in America and abroad.

The military found lever rifles difficult to field-strip and clean. It also claimed service problems in the field. Parts required more hand fitting than the average armorer could master without a lot of effort and training. Also, since most military shooting was done from the prone position across trenches and redoubts, the lever got in the way during repeat fire. These criticisms allowed the world's armies to move toward the bolt-action rifle and the lever gun breathed its last as a front-line military firearm.

The lever rifle remained a truly American invention that found its ecological niche in sport hunting. The grand selection of models was in tune with the habitat and gave the hunter what he needed in terms of fast follow-up shots, acceptable accuracy and a lightweight package. These traits translated into an astounding success for the Model 94 Winchester that sold over 5 million pieces. Indeed, the only lever to challenge the American position was the short-lived Sako Finnwolf. This rifle, produced between 1964 and 1972, came with a 23-inch barrel chambered for 243, 244 and 308. At 6¾ pounds, it qualified as a true lightweight. Although the Sako Finnwolf graced the 1963 *Gun Digest* cover, it died on the vine, perhaps because the price was beyond what most of us would pay. Today, a well-used Finnwolf brings over $300.

The lever rifle reached the pinnacle of development with the 1886 Winchester and perhaps somewhat less so with the Marlin 95. The Savage Model 99 did well, but it was the 1886 and later the Model 71, a remade 1886, that typified the best in design, functionality, power and smooth operation. In reality, the 1886 Winchester didn't sell well. It sold best in 1888 and 1895, accumulating production of 160,000 units between 1886 and 1932.

The Model 1886 was a hunter's rifle. Substantial in proportions, available in powerful big game calibers and smooth in operation, it was a rifle built for the outdoors. Immediately the rifle gained popularity in areas of substantial big game hunting—the Rocky Mountain area, northern Canada and, most notably, Alaska. It was available in 45-70, 40-82, 40-65, 38-56, 50-110, 40-70, 38-70, 50-110-450 and 33 Winchester.

The Model 86 Winchester was followed by the Model 71. It shared the hunting gun qualities of the '86, but also introduced the 348 Winchester cartridge to the shooting public. At the time, nobody mentioned that this cartridge was more powerful than the 30-06. It seemed all the firearms press energy was directed toward the inability to center-mount a scope over the receiver. The Model 71 was dismissed in 1958 and the shooting public was deprived of a quality product. This close cousin of the '86 sold 47,000 copies between 1932 and 1958. Fortune smiled on the Model 71, and in 1987, due to a number of patent and favorable legal and management decisions, Browning was in a position to resurrect the gun.

Unlike Marlin, Winchester continued to develop new-style lever-action rifles that recognized the inadequacies of previous generations. The result was the Model 88. Other than a failed attempt to reintroduce the Model 64 Winchester, the Model 88 represented a good effort to regain the prestige and popularity of a high-power lever-action hunting rifle. Early advertisements espoused the 88 as the ready replacement for the 71, and this was an easy claim given the new high-in-

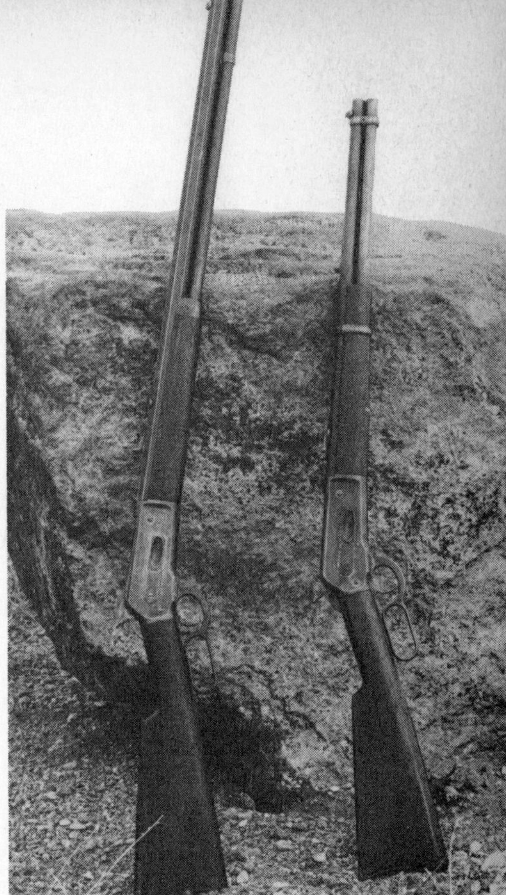

Two very desirable 1886 Winchester rifles. The extra-long, extra-heavy '86 in caliber 45-90 (left), and the rare '86 carbine in 40-82 mark the early high point in lever-action rifle power.

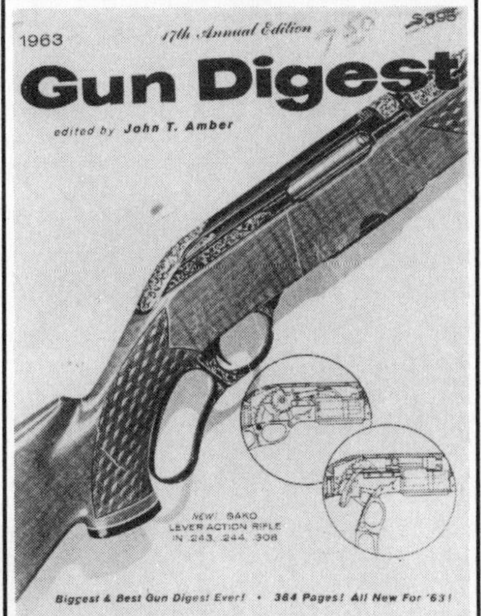

(Left) Lightweight carbines like the old Savage 99 are ideal for young or beginning shooters, but only if they are able to work the action easily and the recoil doesn't punish them.

The Sako Finnwolf (right) was the only overseas attempt to enter the lever-gun market. It lasted only a few years due to high price and limited supply. They're not often seen these days.

The Browning BLR holds the current title of the world's most versatile lever rifle. The upgraded Model 81 version is available in a variety of calibers, including the 284 Winchester, making it, perhaps, the most powerful lever rifle yet.

tensity cartridges of 308, 243, 358 and 284.

For years, the Model 88 remained the high point of lever technology, but the shooting literature claims the 88 was unacceptable to the hunting public. Costs of production, lack of popularity and, get this one, "diverting too much of the plant's effort away from more important projects" were cited by Winchester as reasons for the short 10-year life of the 88. It was and is a pity this rifle was allowed to disappear.

The 88 embodied tradition, ease of use and modern power. The 308 Winchester, the largest seller in the 88 line, even failed to carry the rifle to economies of scale that would keep an assembly line operating. The carbine version featured a barrel band that critics claimed was the source of inaccuracy and a shifting zero. Most important to hunters, the 88 offered a bolt design that locked at the head with three lugs that turned into slots cut into the receiver—just like a bolt action.

Meanwhile, the Savage 99 continued to compete well with all levers. A well thought-out policy of providing what the hunter really wanted kept the venerable 99 in production well beyond Arthur Savage's death in 1941. Stocks were redesigned almost yearly, new intermediate cartridges were frequently available and a clip magazine was introduced along the way. The 99 holds the record for a production lever rifle in the greatest array of cartridges, bar none. Over time, these included the 22 Savage Hi-Power, 22-250, 243, 25-35, 250-3000 (later renamed the 250 Savage), 284 Winchester, 303 Savage, 30-30 Winchester, 32-40, 38-55, 300 Savage, 308, 358 Winchester and the 375 Winchester.

By the way, in 1965 a greater selection of cartridges was available in the Model 99 than in any year previous or since. The knock on the Savage 99, as the cartridge list suggests, was simple. The action length only allowed short cartridges to pass through the rotary magazine and this precluded moving up into the 270 and 30-06 class. This same fact prevented the 99 from being offered in 348 Winchester.

John Browning invented/developed 20 lever-action rifles with production rights for most being sold to Winchester. Only a fraction of his designs were manufactured and made available to the shooting public. However, the lever rifle that today bears the Browning name was not invented by this firearm genius. The Browning BLR, first available in 1971, marked the return of a hunting-quality lever rifle, but by a firm not known for building lever rifles. It also marked a permanent shift away from Winchester as the dominant force in acquiring lever-rifle designs.

The Browning BLR, renamed the Model 81 following a redesign of the clip in 1981, is a thoroughly modern, high-power lever rifle. The action features a set of rotary locking lugs that spin-lock into the receiver as the lever closes. This rifle is a known performer capable of good accuracy with an array of cartridges covering the middle ground of North American hunting. Right now the 81 is available in 222, 223, 22-250, 243, 257 Roberts, 7mm-08, 284 Winchester, 308 and 358. It looks like lengthening the action and four-shot magazine to take 300 Winchester or 7mm Remington Magnum cartridges might be possible. Well, perhaps that's just a dream.

Complaints about the BLR are few. Early models had stocks too thick through the middle, but this is now rectified. The Western look, two-piece stock, prominent lever, short barrel and convenient clip are staples of the Western hunter.

John M. Browning left a legacy of designs and ideas. For now, anyway, the lever shooter has an American-inspired product, although produced in Japan, that meets the ongoing need for a fast-handling rifle that's both powerful and good looking. Inspiration is perhaps the finest legacy in a continuing pageant. There will always be lever rifles for shooters like me, who like the feel and sound of a closing bolt and appreciate performance out in the field. ●

Many hunters favor the detachable box magazine as found on (left to right) the Winchester Model 88, Browning BLR, and Savage Model 99.

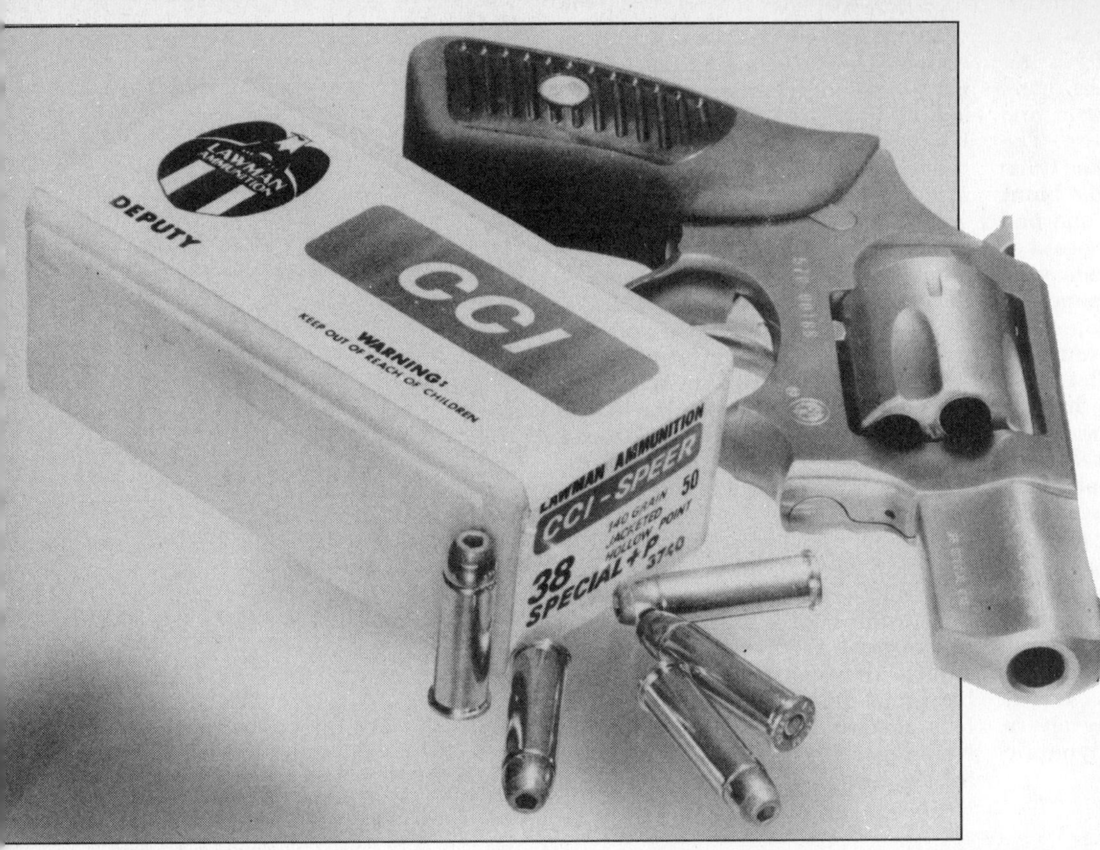

Ruger's 38 Special SP-101 snubby is rated for Plus P use, and teamed with CCI Lawman 140-grain JHP ammo makes an effective combination.

A Short History of Handgun Defense Ammo

Until about 30 years ago, handgun ammo differed little from that of the first cartridge revolvers of 100 years ago.

by TOM FERGUSON

THERE WAS a time, only a few decades back, when ammunition for defense handguns was poor stuff indeed. The situation is changed vastly for the better now, and the ammo is getting better all the time. Today we have respectable performance from cartridges and calibers once deemed puny, and at least one technologically superior projectile that makes bore size almost irrelevant. Most of this progress has taken place in the last 20 years, and some really startling developments have occurred within the last half-decade. To appreciate this superiority of modern ammo we have to go back to 1960.

Until the early 1960s, handgun ammunition differed little from that of the first cartridge revolvers of 100 years ago. Misfires were fewer, of course, and smokeless powder helped, but the projectile was basically the same old round-nose bullet as before.

Ironically, the elongated round-nose bullet was itself the first improved projectile, intended to replace the round ball used in early Colt revolvers, and it pre-dates the cartridge era. The round ball of the first percussion Colts wasn't bad up close due to the blunt shape, but it lacked weight and had poor sectional density. This meant it didn't range well and had inadequate penetration. Combustible paper or skin cartridges were developed for these handguns and these invariably used the "conical ball" or bullet as we know it today. This was the first attempt to increase stopping power, and the idea lasted well into this century. In those long ago days, especially during the Civil War, combatants thought nothing of opening up on one another at ranges of 100 yards and more. Velocity was low in those old revolvers, but momentum and good penetration of the bullet made the practice feasible. The idea of the relatively heavy and long round-nose bullet carried over into the first cartridge revolvers because it had a good aerodynamic configuration.

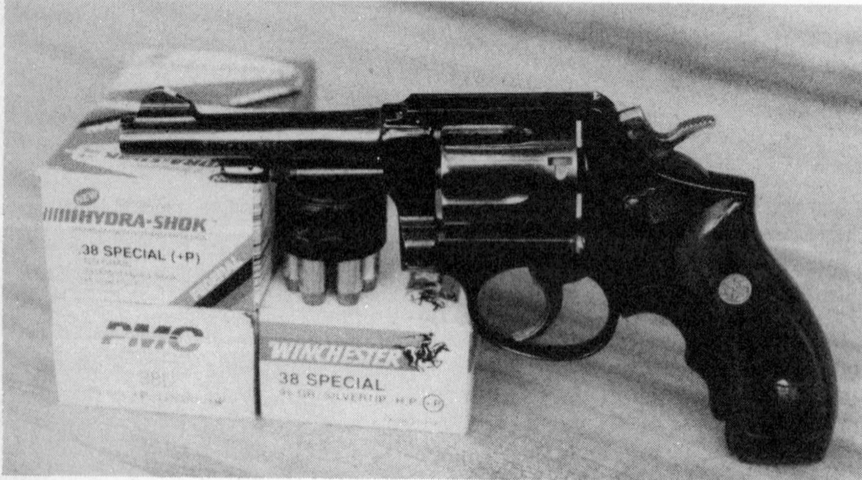

The S&W Model 12 Airweight with alloy frame is an ideal home-defense gun for ladies. The Tyler grip adapter makes the gun handle much better, even in small hands. Best defense ammo is of Plus P persuasion.

Handgunners discovered early on that the pointed or round-nose bullet had poor terminal effect on human adversaries, and may even have been inferior to the round ball. The bullet wounded more often than it killed, unless placed precisely in a vital area. At times, even the much vaunted penetration was compromised.

Whether fired from a 36-caliber percussion Navy Colt or a 38 Special, the round-nose slips easily through flesh and destroys only a minimal amount of tissue. It pushes aside arteries and veins without cutting them cleanly for instant hemorrhaging and it leaves a narrow wound channel which closes behind itself and prevents bleeding. Even an opponent shot through the heart can sometimes live long enough to do great harm. As if this weren't bad enough, the rounded nose often causes the bullet to glance off the skull or other rounded bones without penetrating. There are a great many cases on record where the 38 Special and even the 230-grain FMJ bullet of the 45 ACP have done exactly this. When only soft, fleshy parts are hit, the round-nose bullet tends to diverge from a straight course, failing to give adequate penetration in the intended direction.

If the old round-nose was such a bad design, then why did it last so long? After all, the concept of expanding and hollowpoint rifle bullets was well known from 1880 onward. There are several reasons, actually. To begin, handguns didn't benefit from smokeless powder in the way rifles did. New repeating rifles were designed for the new powder, but there were too many older blackpowder revolvers around for comfort. Even after handgun cartridges began to be loaded with smokeless, pressures were held down to blackpowder levels.

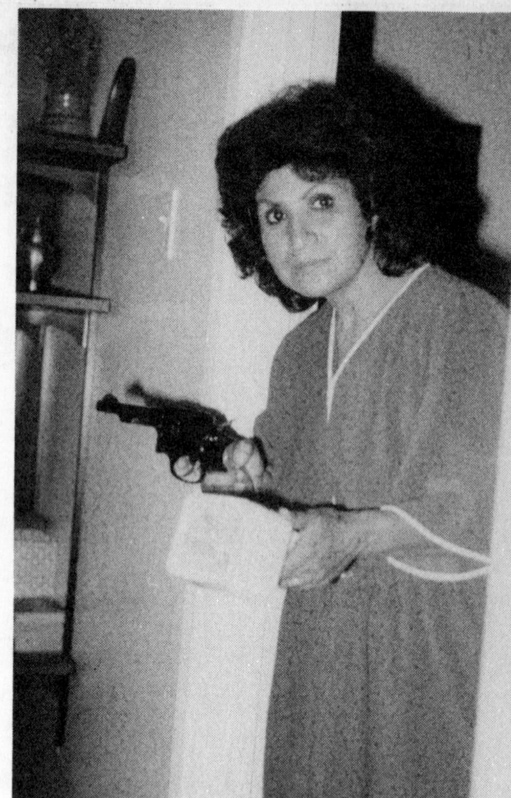
This lady is obviously frightened but nevertheless well-armed with a flashlight and S&W Model 12 Airweight 38 Special loaded with Plus P ammo.

At the velocities produced, around 700 to 900 fps, expansion was unlikely even with the softest lead bullets and the deepest hollowpoints. While rifle velocities leaped ahead enormously under the impetus of smokeless powder, handgun velocities stayed about the same, and so did bullet shape.

Later, as autoloading pistols began to appear, the round-nose design got another vote of confidence. Although the newfangled Luger and Colt autos were designed for smokeless powder and higher velocity, the fully copper-jacketed round-nose was about the only design that would feed reliably through the actions. There is a story that ammo manufacturers produced a few primitive jacketed softpoints and hollowpoints in 380 ACP, 9mm Luger and 38 Super after World War I, but voluntarily discontinued them due to the gangland violence of the Prohibition Era. These cartridges did exist, but more likely they were discontinued because they failed to perform as advertised and were no better than the

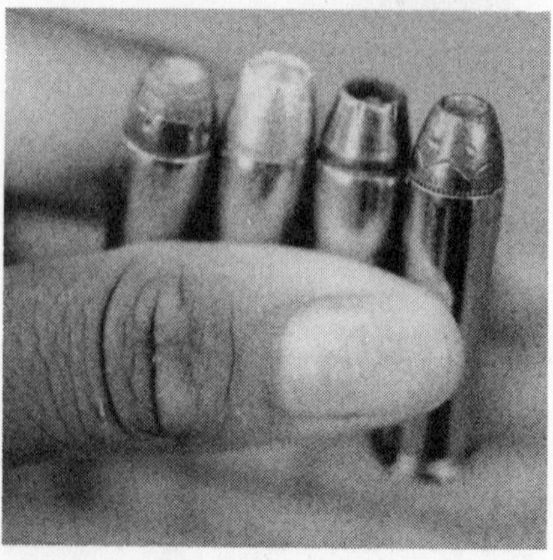
Look for wide, deep hollowpoints and notched or scalloped jackets which help 38 Special ammo expand for greater stopping power.

Good defense ammo includes the 380 ACP MagSafe, Winchester 9mmP Silvertip, Federal Hydra-Shok 38 Special, Remington 357 Magnum, Winchester 41 Magnum Silvertip, Remington 240-grain lead 44 Magnum, 45 ACP Silvertip.

Remington's newest 357 load is a 125-grain JHP rated at only 1220 fps. It's intended for short-barreled revolvers such as this Pachmayr Combat Undercover, and reduces muzzle blast and recoil.

FMJ or lead round-noses. During the same period, the 44-40 and 38-40 revolver cartridges were provided with jacketed softpoint bullets, and apparently caused no sleepless nights for the manufacturers.

The modern jacketed hollowpoint bullets now so common in handgun cartridges had a tough time being born. The first, and some of the best, were produced on home swaging equipment by dedicated handloaders. The goals were to increase effectiveness on game through bullet expansion, and create a cleaner, harder bullet that wouldn't lead the bore. The 357 Magnum was a notorious offender in that respect with the then-current soft lead semi-wadcutter slug. The home experimenters found out several things quickly: Good bullets must have only the thinnest of copper jackets; the lead core must be dead soft; and the velocity must be 1000 fps before expansion could occur. All these rules are still valid. There was a brief flurry of interest in the jacketed softpoint, but expansion was rare, and in any case not as good as the hollowpoint.

During the mid-1960s, ballistician/businessman Lee Jurras got a big jump on the larger ammo makers by establishing the Super Vel cartridge company. Super Vel used thin copper jackets, soft lead, and well designed hollow cavities to promote expansion. Most of all, Jurras ignored traditional bullet weights and produced lighter bullets in all calibers to increase velocity. The Super Vel 38 Special used a 110-grain JHP at about 1000 + fps and it was noted for good expansion and stopping power. The 45 ACP load was given a 190-grain JHP driven to about 1090 fps. This was good news in an era when the usual 38 Special load was a 158-grain round-nose at a nominal 855 fps, true velocity much less than that. The common 45 ACP "combat" load was just as bad. That was nothing more than the G.I. 45 230-grain hardball round at something like 800 fps.

Super Vel's offerings were far superior and found favor with cops and civilians alike. Eventually it was produced in 380 ACP, 9mm Parabellum, 38 Special, 357 Magnum, and 45 ACP. Due to business reasons not related to poor performance, the Super Vel company folded and is now history. However, it set a trend and ammo built on these principles is available from all major ammo companies.

The smallest cartridge now thought suitable for defense use is the 380 ACP. Turn-of-the-century ballistics indicated a round-nosed 95-grain .355-inch bullet at 955 fps, even less in short barrels. In today's cartridges, bullet weight is 85 to 90 grains and is a thin-jacketed hollowpoint designed to expand or deform for greater tissue destruction. Judged by street record, the best seems to be the 85-grain JHP Silvertip from Winchester, which offers one-shot stops about 50 percent of the time. One-shot stops seem to be an obsession with defense experts for no really good reason. A magazine full of 380 Silvertips, well delivered on one opponent, gives about a 100 percent chance of a trip to the cemetery nearly every time and is a better way to fly.

The 38 Special went through even more experimentation because it's the odds-on favorite civilian and police cartridge.

The 38 Special is a blackpowder number, and unfortunately can't be driven much past 1000 fps with any bullet weight. Standard pressure is 18,900 CUP, but ammo makers reluctantly increased this to 22,400 CUP for the first Plus P loads. Bullet expansion was helped by the resulting increase in velocity, however modest. Today, anything that goes into a 38 Special for defense use should be of Plus P persuasion. Bullet weights run from 95 to 140 grains, but the most effective hover around the 125-grain mark. Federal's 129-grain Plus P Hydra-Shok JHP, #P38HS1, is a hard act to follow for other 38 loads. As a rule of thumb, look for notched, pre-weakened jackets and deep cavities which help the bullets expand. It should be noted there are now "Plus P +" 38 Specials which are really low-end 357 Magnum loads. Keep them out of snubbies and alloy-frame guns because it shakes them to pieces.

When good expanding bullets for the 9mm Parabellum finally arrived, this cartridge showed its teeth. It can

The old 45 ACP is still a scary proposition for an intruder when loaded with modern JHP ammunition such as the Remington 185-grain Plus Ps.

be a good stopper with the right ammo. Most JHPs weigh 115 to 124 grains and go 1100+ fps or so, depending on barrel length. Federal and Winchester have long offered a 95-grain loading at over 1300 fps which expands viciously. Thanks to an FBI study which concluded greater penetration was needed, there are now subsonic, 147-grain loads at only 950 fps. They do penetrate well, but the street verdict isn't in yet and true stopping power is dubious. A better bet is the new Remington Plus P load with the 115-grain JHP at 1250 fps.

The 357 Magnum performs well with just about any bullet in that caliber. The 125-grain JHPs from Federal or Remington get 1430 fps in 4-inch barrels, and have the best street record for stopping power, more than any other gun/cartridge combination. As you might expect, it's a bit violent to shoot. Remington recently introduced the R357M11, a 357 load intended for short-barreled defense revolvers. It drives the excellent scalloped jacket JHP to a milder 1220 fps which reduces muzzle blast and recoil, yet retains enough velocity to expand the bullet.

Norma's first 10mm Auto loads used a 170-grain JHP at 1350 fps and a military-style FMJ 200-grain at 1150 fps. This is too hot for defense use. The Winchester 175-grain Silvertip at 1220 fps is milder, yet has ample power for defense. Later, the 10mm got the subsonic treatment also, with a 180-grain JHP at only 950 fps. Humorists say the FBI, which instigated this loading, rediscovered the old 38-40 revolver cartridge of 1880. It may have the horsepower, but the Winchester Silvertip is a better choice.

Smith & Wesson announced the new 40 S&W cartridge in 1990. It's a shortened 10mm with a .850-inch case length, and uses the small pistol primer instead of the large one of the 10mm. It duplicates the 10mm subsonic round but is superior in a couple of ways.

The 40 S&W chronographs a true 950 fps with its 180-grain JHP. The subsonic 10mm Auto should be the same, but averages more like 875 fps. In addition, the 40 S&W is inherently more accurate than the 10mm subsonic due to lesser case capacity, although both are sufficiently accurate for defense. Many police agencies have adopted the 40 S&W because of adequate power combined with mild shooting characteristics.

The 41 Magnum is obsolete in law enforcement but still a fine defense round with the 210-grain lead SWC bullet at 950 fps. The Winchester Silvertip 175-grain JHP gets 1130 fps and should be even better. Don't use the 210-grain JSP at 1250 fps because recoil prevents fast follow-up shots.

Despite an awesome record for stopping power, the 45 ACP 230-grain FMJ hardball round often fails to live up to that reputation. Among better loads are the Winchester 185-grain Silvertip at 950 fps, the Remington 185-grain JHP at 957 fps, and the CCI Lawman 200-grain at 978 fps. All these improve stopping power but have been eclipsed by the newer Remington R45AP6. This Plus P loading sends the 185-grain JHP out at 1150 fps and is the load of choice.

The 44 Magnum is a hunting cartridge, not ideal for defense use. If you have one, use Remington's R44MG4 with the 240-grain lead bullet at 940 fps.

The 45 Colt, 44 Special and 38 Super are proven man-stoppers, but relatively few are in use for that purpose now, and ammunition has not kept up

The new S&W Model 1006 in 10mm Auto is finding favor in police work. Federal loads it with the 180-grain JHP and rates it at a sedate 950 fps. This round is the current "new darling" for law enforcement.

with their capabilities. Winchester markets Silvertip loads for all three, and this is probably the best bet.

Over the last few years the market has filled with so-called "exotic" ammo intended to increase wounding or stopping power. Many of these trick bullets are unreliable at best, and in some the theory is so flawed they are much worse than ordinary JHPs. It's a case of buyer beware, and if you buy any be certain to verify all the claims before carrying it as defense ammo.

Another newcomer to the handgun defense ammo arena is the 40 S&W cartridge, which has already found a home with a number of law enforcement agencies. Its street record is yet to be determined.

The most effective of these exotic loads, from my experience, is MagSafe ammo, available in virtually all handgun calibers. Typically, the MagSafe bullets are driven to very high velocities due to their light weight. The bullet consists of a soft, annealed copper jacket containing carefully layered No. 2 (large) birdshot fixed in an epoxy resin core. On impact the jacket disintegrates to create a large permanent wound cavity, then hurls the birdshot and epoxy fragments forward in shaped charge fashion to penetrate vital organs. Both accuracy and penetration are superior to the well-known Glaser round, and MagSafes have a proven combat record. For a complete list of these lethal defense loads write to MagSafe Ammo Co., 2725 Friendly Grove Rd. NE, Olympia, WA 98506.

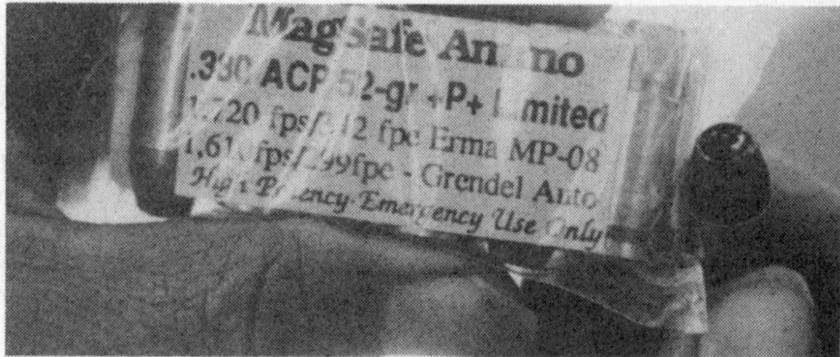

MagSafe ammo in any caliber features ultra-high velocity and fast expansion, as well as deep penetration. Note the velocities given on the package label for specific guns.

In a fairly large nutshell, that's about where we stand today with some very good handgun defense ammunition. It took some time to get things up to snuff, but we are now at a point where the loads are about as effective (and safe to shoot) as they can get with present technology.

A word of advice is in order to those trying to choose the best loads to get the job done, be they uniformed officer or civilian. Even though some of the specialty ammo can be expensive, buy enough rounds to practice with so you know just where the bullets will strike and how you and the gun will react under stressful conditions. Shoot this ammo under as many varied conditions as possible until you are sure of the results. Make absolutely certain that the ammo you choose performs the way you want, then PRACTICE! If brand/type A doesn't cut it, then go on to the next one until you find the one that fits the criteria you've set down for performance parameters.

Then practice some more. ●

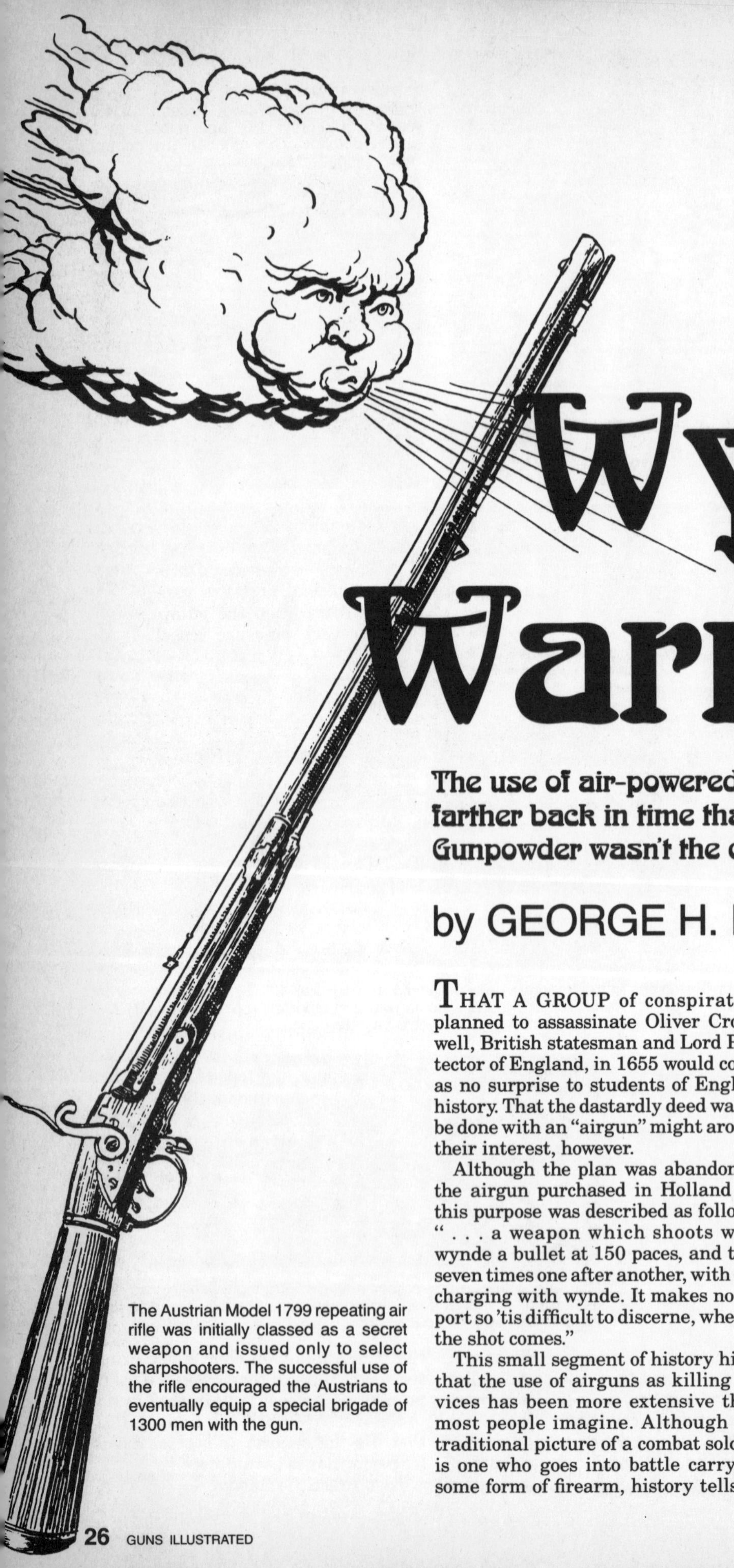

Wynde Warriors

The use of air-powered weapons in warfare goes farther back in time than many would imagine. Gunpowder wasn't the only way to shoot!

by GEORGE H. PADGINTON

The Austrian Model 1799 repeating air rifle was initially classed as a secret weapon and issued only to select sharpshooters. The successful use of the rifle encouraged the Austrians to eventually equip a special brigade of 1300 men with the gun.

THAT A GROUP of conspirators planned to assassinate Oliver Cromwell, British statesman and Lord Protector of England, in 1655 would come as no surprise to students of English history. That the dastardly deed was to be done with an "airgun" might arouse their interest, however.

Although the plan was abandoned, the airgun purchased in Holland for this purpose was described as follows: " . . . a weapon which shoots with wynde a bullet at 150 paces, and that seven times one after another, with one charging with wynde. It makes no report so 'tis difficult to discerne, whence the shot comes."

This small segment of history hints that the use of airguns as killing devices has been more extensive than most people imagine. Although the traditional picture of a combat soldier is one who goes into battle carrying some form of firearm, history tells us that the airgun has played a small but intriguing role in military campaigns of the past.

Apart from native blowguns used in hunting for hundreds of years, historical records seem to indicate that the first attempt to build and use a serious airgun took place in the late 1500s. European gunmakers, in particular, fabricated some very efficient large-bore airguns capable of killing large game or a man at ranges of 100 yards or more. Most of these were pump-up pneumatics, in that it was necessary to pump air into a reservoir which was a part of the gun or secured to the gun after being pressurized. It was truly a test of the gunmakers skill and ingenuity when these early weapons were expected to perform and withstand working pressures of 400 to 1000 pounds per square inch (psi).

Before the advent of the modern cartridge-shooting military rifle, the

This decorated officer's Model 1799 air rifle shows the shoulder-stock pressure reservoir removed from the action. The valve stem can be seen protruding from the lock mechanism.

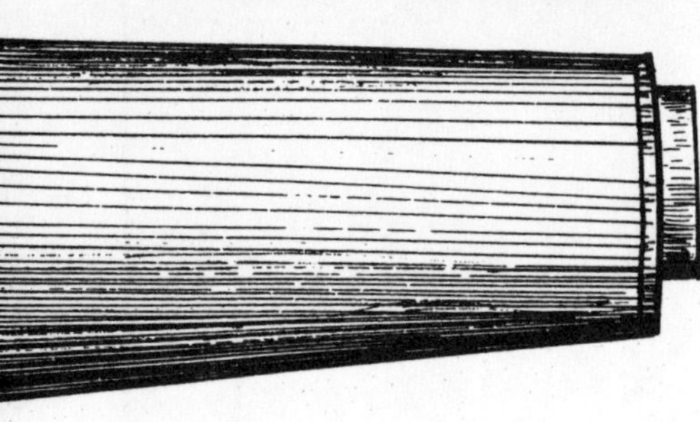

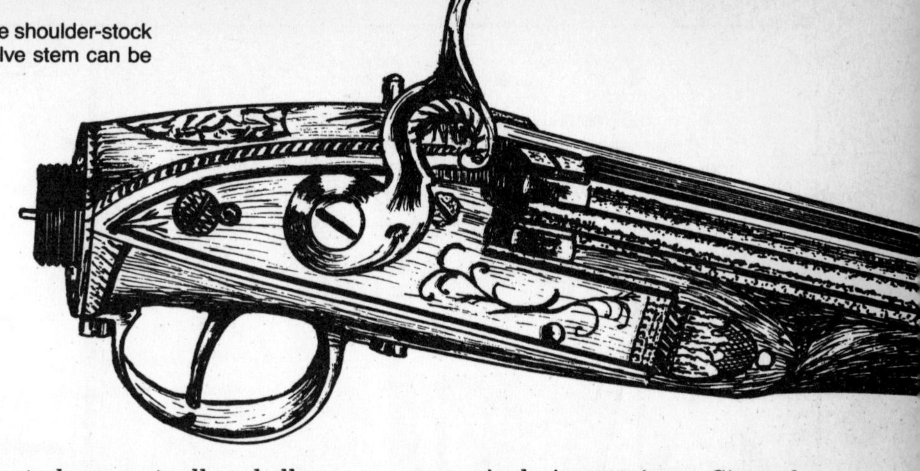

Austrian Army began using successfully a repeating air rifle designed by a B. Girandoni in 1779. A Model 1799 rifle used a detachable buttstock reservoir with enough pressure to allow each soldier, so equipped, to fire 30 to 40 13mm (or 51-caliber) balls with deadly effect. While combatants in the enemy's line of battle were busy stuffing ball and powder down the muzzle of their rifles preparing for the next shot, the Austrian troopers and their air rifles, which were equipped with a unique feed system, were able to get off up to 20 shots per minute. The large 51-caliber ball, traveling at almost 1000 fps could be lethal at up to 150 yards. The early rifles issued to the Austrian troopers were classed as a secret weapon and were employed by only a few select sharpshooters. A brigade of 500 men or more, armed with two or three reserve buttstock air flasks, could lay down a very deadly field of fire. An added advantage of these rifles was that they produced no highly visible cloud of blackpowder smoke which would reveal a shooter's position and obscure his line of fire.

The military air rifle used by the Austrians weighed about 9¼ pounds. The 12-groove rifled barrel measured 32.8 inches in length. The detachable rifle stock was actually a hollow metallic container which was pressurized for the source of power. Indications are that the rear portion of this air-tank stock was covered with leather to allow better shouldering of the weapon, thereby improving the shooter's accuracy. This feature also allowed for more comfortable handling of the gun in cold weather campaigns. Brass was used in the fabrication of the action and valve housing.

On this Austrian rifle a tubular magazine secured to the right-hand side of its receiver held the lead balls. These were loaded from the front and held in place by a spring-loaded cover. Tipping up the muzzle of the rifle allowed a gravity-fed ball to fall into position against a laterally sliding breechblock. When the hammer of the action was drawn to full cock, the sliding breechblock carried the ball into the breech where it would be discharged down the rifled bore. Squeezing the trigger caused a momentary opening of the air valve, which allowed a high-pressure blast of air to propel the round missile to the target. Pressing a breechblock release on the left side of the receiver caused the breechblock to return to the right to receive another ball for the next shot. This same basic concept is used in several repeating airguns manufactured today.

One of the disadvantages of this Austrian rifle was the need for pressurized air containers. Since the depleted containers might have to be re-pressurized during the course of a military engagement, it was necessary to carry pumping equipment into the field in close support of the troops. Each company of soldiers had two special wagons equipped with two pumps and additional pressure vessels. Two men accompanied the pump wagons because each pressure vessel for the rifles required about 2000 pump strokes to fill. Since each Austrian air-gunner carried an extra two to four pressurized containers into battle, this represented a great deal of pumping on the part of the support teams.

An oft told tale, probably apocryphal, concerns Napolean Bonaparte. He was said to have become angered upon learning that some of his troops were being dispatched by Austrian sharpshooters armed with a noiseless and smokeless large-bore air rifle. In his mind, this was considered to be most unsportsmanlike and not to be condoned on the field of battle. He considered this method of dispatching an enemy soldier was truly the work of an assassin and not a soldier. It is reported he gave orders for all Austrian soldiers found equipped with such a device to be executed on the spot.

Historical records reveal that thought was given to supplying the Continental army with air rifles during the American Revolution. Sparse information available on this matter

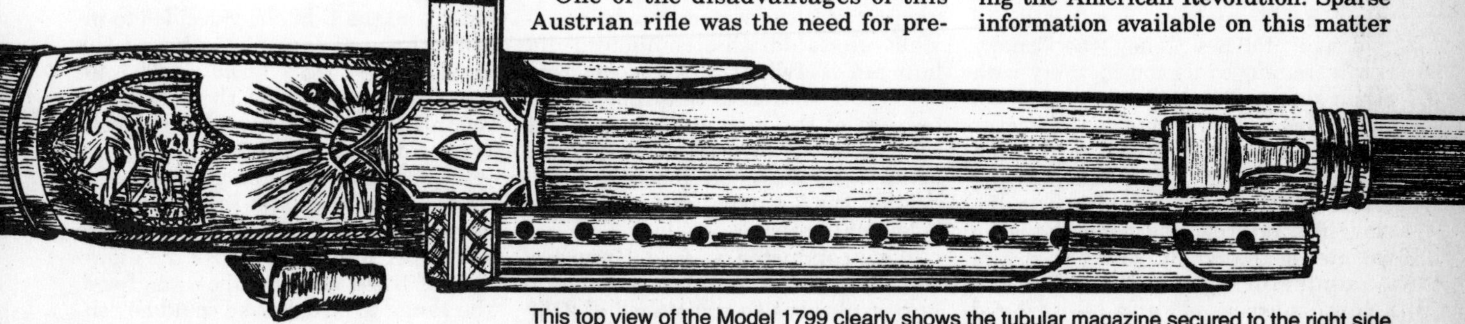

This top view of the Model 1799 clearly shows the tubular magazine secured to the right side of the rifle. The holes in the top of the tube allowed the shooter to see how many balls remained in the magazine. The lateral slide bar which fed the balls from the magazine to the breech is directly behind the tube.

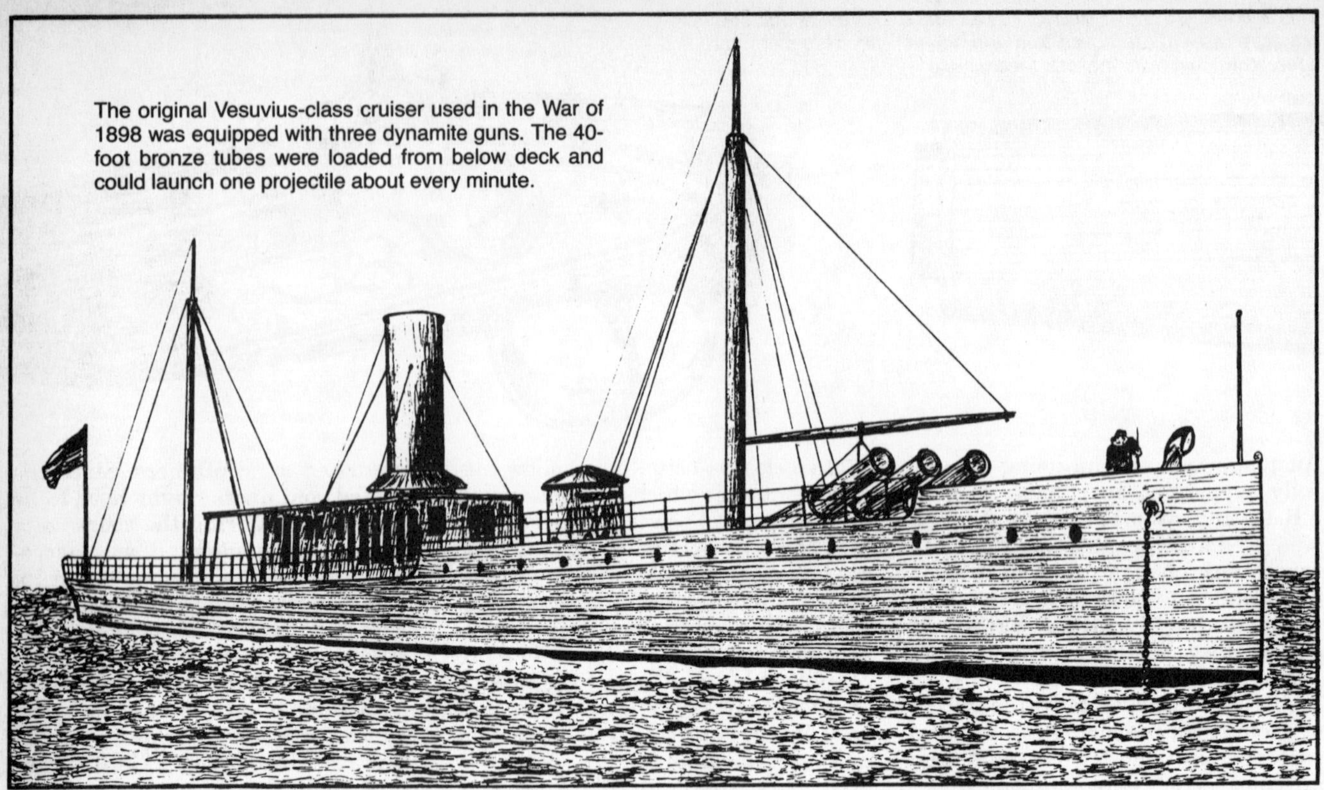
The original Vesuvius-class cruiser used in the War of 1898 was equipped with three dynamite guns. The 40-foot bronze tubes were loaded from below deck and could launch one projectile about every minute.

seems to indicate that they may have seen some use, but only on a trial basis.

Official records from the past also indicate that the air rifle was used as a military weapon on at least one occasion during the American Civil War. During the Battle of Gettysburg, July, 1863, Union troops of the 147th Pennsylvania regiment and the 5th Ohio regiment were being hit by rounds coming into their lines. This occurred in the eastern sector of the battlefield on Culp's Hill on the evening of the second day of the battle. No flashes from rifles could be observed. This air rifle fire was most likely coming from a handful of North Carolina, or more likely Maryland, Confederates who were on the hill at the time.

Writing in the 125-volume "Official Records of the Union and Confederate Armies," Colonel John H. Patrick of the 5th Ohio regiment recalled the incident as follows: "They [the Confederates] annoyed us considerably with their sharpshooters. Some of them had air rifles, and we could not discover their whereabouts. At night the flashes of the regular rifles can be seen, but there is no warning from the air rifle." It is thought that perhaps the armies of the South, with the lack of manufacturing facilities that the North possessed, and being hard pressed to supply their troops with the implements of warfare, seriously considered equipping some of their men with air rifles. It is possible that the rifles used in this incident may well have been some of those Austrian military air rifles first used 70 years earlier.

A variation of the airgun device is the use of an air cannon by the U.S. military in the late 1800s, which hurled dynamite-loaded projectiles great distances. A rather crude device, the first weapon submitted for testing at Fort Hamilton, New York, was 28 feet long and mounted on a heavy tripod. The seamless brass barrel had a bore diameter of 2 inches and a wall thickness of ¼-inch. The 12 cubic feet of compressed air used to fire the projectile was stored in a reservoir at 500 psi. Upon discharge, the pressurized air was directed into the gun breech by a connecting hose. The air cannon hurled a projectile loaded with a then relatively new compound called "Dynamite." Although proven to be somewhat unstable, this compound did have almost twice the explosive power of the gun powders at that time. It was because of this unstable nature that the less violent means of propulsion using compressed air instead of gun powder was felt to present a safer way of launching the projectile.

Tests conducted at Fort Hamilton revealed that this device was able to hurl explosives to a distance of 2100 yards with reasonable accuracy. Similar devices with larger bore diameters were developed requiring launch pressures of 2000 psi. Fifteen-inch bore launch tubes were eventually fabricated and the U.S. Navy decided to install three of the tubes aboard the Navy cruiser *USS Vesuvius.* The 40-foot bronze barrels of these tandem-mounted guns were angled from above the top deck to below decks where the gun crews loaded the long torpedo-like finned projectiles and fired the guns. The rate of fire proved to be about one round per minute. Because the elevation of these launch tubes was fixed, the range to be achieved could be controlled only by regulation of the air pressure fed into the breech behind the projectile.

Fearful of the damage that enemy fire might do to his lightly armored vessel, the commander of the USS Vesuvius approached the fortified Cuban harbor positions only after dusk, and fired one salvo each night.

The first practical use of this naval vessel in combat was at Santiago Harbor, Cuba, during the Spanish-American War. The news media at that time credited the guns with completely devastating the Spanish harbor installations, but this proved to be somewhat of an exaggeration.

One of the biggest problems with this floating cannon battery was that the launch tubes were secured immovably to the ship. The only way they could be aimed at various targets was by manuvering the entire cruiser. Underwater stablizing devices were not yet developed and with the rolling of the vessel, the point of aim and, therefore, the intended impact area was constantly changing.

A dynamite gun emplacement was built at Sandy Hook to help protect the New York harbor. A four-wheeled cart rode on the track circling the gun, which helped the gunners load the large projectiles into the cannon.

It has also been reported that the gun crews serving the air cannons were more fearful of them than were the hostile troops in the target area. The projectiles, each containing a 500-pound charge of dynamite, were not to be handled carelessly.

This same conflict saw the use of a small dynamite gun mounted on a field carriage which was used in the land operations above Santiago.

During the same time period, dynamite guns were built and installed at both San Francisco and Sandy Hook, New York, for protection of their respective harbors. Because of their rather unorthodox external appearance, some observers claimed that the cannons looked more like horizontal drilling rigs, but these harbor guns were capable of launching a 15-inch-diameter finned projectile with a total weight of 1000 pounds to a range of 2400 yards. A smaller 8-inch shell weighing 250 pounds could be lobbed to a maximum range of 6000 yards. For the time in history when these guns were developed, they showed remarkable accuracy, which was far greater than could be obtained with howitzer shells propelled by explosives. At an official range of 5000 yards, or 2.84 miles, 75 percent of the projectiles fired landed in a target area measuring 90 by 360 feet.

In our more modern times, U.S. military forces still find practical application for the occasional use of air as a means of expelling a small projectile. Aerial gunnery candidates during World War II were trained in marksmanship using a fully automatic BB machinegun manufactured by The MacGlashan Air Machine Gun Corporation of Long Beach, California. Built to resemble the air-cooled 30-caliber Browning machinegun, the MacGlashan used compressed air or CO_2 to fire a stream of BBs at a cyclic rate of 400 rounds per minute at a working pressure of 150 psi.

In 1966 and 1967, the U.S. Army began training the principles of instinctive shooting to soldiers slated for duty in Vietnam. Because of the dense undergrowth and concealment opportunities offered the enemy forces, and the suddenness and proximity in which they were encountered, it was felt that the faster U.S. troops could return fire, the less precarious was their own position. Instinctive marksmanship with practice can become quite accurate and the response time from the moment the brain gives the command to "engage target" is considerably less than if one were to use the usual procedure of shouldering a weapon, taking careful aim, and then firing. Under the conditions found in Vietnam, the U.S. Army's use of a lighter weight, larger magazine capacity, rapid-fire weapon, lent itself to this type of quick response.

For this instinctive marksmanship training program, Daisy Manufacturing Co. supplied the Army with BB guns without sights of any kind. In a surprisingly short time, many of the trainees were able to successively hit thrown objects as small as aspirin tablets by looking over the gun barrel and keeping their eyes on the target.

Even today, the U.S. Navy, with all its complex and very expensive weaponry, still relies on the use of air under pressure to discharge torpedoes and launch missles from their submerged undersea vessels.

Records have revealed that in more recent times modern day saboteurs have been known to resort to the ancient blowgun, but not in the usual way. Instead of attempting to dispatch one of the enemy with a poisoned dart, they hope to create food shortages and affect the enemy's morale by setting ripening grain fields aflame. The blowgun, used from a concealed position or perhaps a passing vehicle, is used to launch an ampule of a self-igniting combustible substance.

Despite the passage of time and the technological advances since the blowgun was first developed, modern man still seems to have a practical application for "wynde" weapons in one form or another. ●

A two-wheeled dynamite field gun was used north of Santiago, Cuba, to support Teddy Roosevelt's land campaign. A blank cartridge was fired to generate the air pressure needed to launch the dynamite projectile, directed into the barrel.

The three basic Swedish Mausers tested by the author, top to bottom: Model 1894 Carbine, Model 1896 Long Rifle, and Model 1938 Short Rifle.

Those Sweethearts from Sweden

Initially made in Germany, these military jewels are fascinating to collect and fun to shoot.

by ROBERT T. SHIMEK

The Carl Gustav arsenal made some of the Swedish Mausers, Husqvarna produced the balance. All are marked atop the receiver ring with the factory name and date, as on this Carl Gustav Model 1896.

FEW OF THE CLASSIC military bolt rifles are truly gentle shooters. Their purpose was to kill enemy soldiers on the battlefield—sometimes at a considerable distance—and that job was thought to necessitate a cartridge of middlin'-formidable ballistics. Hence, the turn of the century saw the proliferation of rifles that, with proportionate rearward disturbance of the shooter, dispensed 2500 to 3000 foot pounds of energy at the muzzle.

Not all nations adopted such powerful service weapons, however. Among the countries that didn't was Sweden. The Swedes were impressed with the 6.5x55mm service round that was being developed by Mauser-Werke at Oberndorf, Germany, during the final years of the last century. This cartridge combined a number of virtues: brilliant accuracy, fine long-range performance, and adequate-class power, along with gentleness to the shooter. Sweden adopted the round and Paul Mauser's latest and most advanced (as of 1894) turn-bolt-actioned service rifle. The result remains to this day one of the most accurate, and gentlest, military shooters ever—the legendary 6.5mm Swedish Mauser. Let's examine this rifle/cartridge combo both as an historical entity and as an appliance for modern shooting fun.

The 6.5x55mm round was the result of considerable turn-of-the-century

The Model 1894 Carbine was handy and visually appealing, but the author found it abusive to shoot (see text). Because it printed so high on the target, the Carbine had to be fired from 50 yards. Gun was very accurate as this five-shot .8-inch group attests.

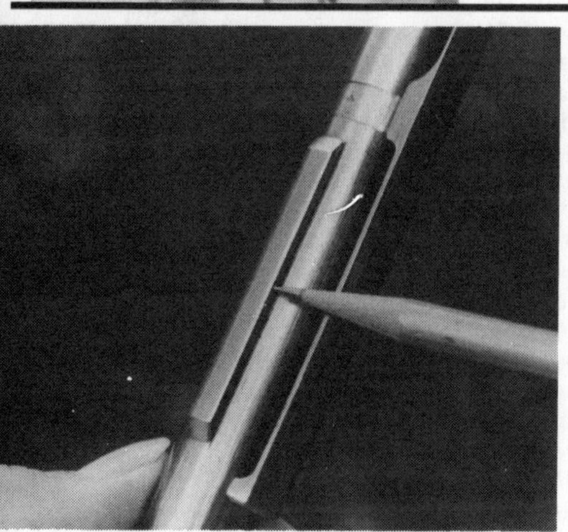

The deepened thumb cut in the Model 1896's receiver necessitated the inclusion of this guide rib on the bolt body to prevent binding.

Mauser-Werke experimentation into small-caliber service rifle cartridges; other experimental centerfire rounds developed had featured bore sizes as small as 5mm caliber, but these had won no adherents. Two nations took the 6.5x55 into service: Sweden and Norway. As adopted by the Swedes, the 6.5x55 initially propelled a 156-grain mil-spec bullet at just under 2400 fps in rifle-length barrels, for about 1 ton of muzzle energy. A later ("M41") loading used a 139-grain bullet at over 2600 fps for 2100 foot pounds of "oomph." The salient virtue of the new round was long-range accuracy; it would prove so good in this regard that Remington would offer its 40XB target rifle in 6.5x55 starting in 1970, despite the total lack of any American-made ammo in this by-then-obsolescent caliber!

The Swedish Mauser action was a derivative of Paul Mauser's already-very-successful 1893 Spanish rifle. As on the '93 action, the receiver was a one-piece forging; there were two opposed locking lugs; the action cocked on closing; the extractor was of non-rotating pattern to prevent double feeds; the magazine was of the rugged and efficient flush-bottom double-column variety; the safety featured three positions—"fire," "intermediate" (striker locked), and "safe" (both striker and bolt locked). The Swedish action featured some improvements over the Spanish action however. Most interesting was a mechanism we *believe* was a decocking feature. This is said to have worked as follows: The cocking piece featured a specially-shaped knurled grasping-projection. When a round was in the chamber, the shooter who wanted to decock the gun without firing it first pointed the muzzle in a safe direction, then rotated the safety to "fire" position, then grasped the cocking piece with one hand and prepared to resist forward spring pressure. The trigger was then pulled and the cocking piece *gently* lowered to the full-down position; accidental discharge was possible if the cocking piece was lowered too forcefully, since the firing pin tip came to rest directly on the primer of the chambered round. Then the safety-lever was rotated 180 degrees clockwise to the "safe" position; this drew the firing pin tip back inside the bolt, held it there, and locked the action closed. It was critically important that the gun be placed "on safe" in this fashion, since otherwise the firing pin tip remained resting on the primer and could easily yield an accidental discharge in the event of even a light blow to the cocking piece. What confuses to this day about this system was that there was no way to *re*-cock the action without cycling the bolt and thus ejecting the chambered round. The cocking piece's special projection could not be grasped once the striker was fully lowered. Hence, here was a decocked mode that required the shooter to sacrifice 20 percent of his mag capacity if re-cocking became necessary. This aspect of the design lends credence to the notions some writers have ventured, to the effect that the "decocking mechanism" wasn't a decocking mechanism at all. At least one scribe has claimed it was a training aid: supposedly, a block of wood could be inserted between projection and bolt sleeve to permit dry-firing without mechanical damage. Another authority has held that the "decocking mechanism" was actually a disassembly aid. We still don't know for sure.

An improvement more useful today was the gas venting system. Most of the German-made Spanish Mausers had shown no gas venting holes at all, which meant that primer or case failures could result in hot gases being driven directly back into the shooter's face. The various Swedish-made Mausers improved upon this to a lesser or greater degree; an 1897-dated Swed-

The ammunition used in shooting the Swedish Mausers was modern commercial fodder from Norma and Hansen. Both 139- and 156-grain FMJ and PSP types were tried.

ish-made M1894 carbine in my possession shows a single venting hole forward of the extractor collar; later Swedish Mausers added one or two more holes elsewhere on the bolt body. I should admit here that I just plain don't know how well vented the earliest German-made Swedish Mausers were, for I have never had opportunity to examine one; nor can I ascertain at what point one port became two or three.

The first Swedish Mauser to materialize was the 1894 Carbine. This 17.4-inch-barreled "shorty" measured just over 37 inches in length and weighed but 7¼ pounds, yet featured a stock that extended very nearly to the muzzle. Sights were of classic European military configuration and consisted of a pyramidal front post accompanied by a smallish V-notch rear; elevation was adjustable from 400 to 1600 meters. The sling passed through a slot in the buttstock. A marking disk was embedded in the stock. Initial examples of this gun were made by Mauser-Werke at Oberndorf and featured the 1894 action. This limited-production predecessor of the 1896 action featured a receiver-wall thumb cut that was a bit too shallow for efficient stripping of cartridges into the action. Accordingly, the 1894 action was soon replaced by the 1896 type, which showed a deepened thumb cut intended to speed up reloading; the deepened thumb cut necessitated placement of a guide-rib on the bolt body to help prevent binding. All carbines made after the introduction of the 1896 action had this improved mechanism. Issue of the Swedish Mauser Carbine was primarily to engineer and artillery units, but the little gun is said to have been less than popular; muzzle blast/report was probably a factor here.

The year 1896 saw not only the introduction of the improved action, but also that of a full-length Swedish Mauser rifle intended for general issue. The gun—the M1896 Long Rifle—was appropriately named, measuring nearly 50 inches with its 29-inch barrel. Weight was over 9 pounds. A distinguishing feature was the straight bolt handle, whereas the carbines utilized a turned down handle. Sights on this arm were adjustable from 300 to 2000 meters. The sling passed through swivels on the underside of the rifle. The Long Rifle performed infantry service. Early M1896s were made by Mauser at Oberndorf, just as 1894 Carbines were, but it soon occurred to the Swedes that it was smarter to build their own guns than to import them, since if Germany became involved in a major war, arms shipments would be a problem. Indigenous manufacture of both the Carbine and the Long Rifle was initiated, and two renowned Swedish firms—Carl Gustav and Husqvarna—were enrolled in the production effort. Dates on surviving Swedish Mausers suggest that the transition to indigenous manufacture was made before the turn of the century. Guns made by these companies were in every sense the qualitative equivalent of the superbly crafted early guns made in Germany. Steel parts were finely fitted and perfectly polished forgings, painstakingly finished either in rust blue or polished natural metal. Some small parts were fire blued. Stocks were of carefully selected walnut. Each gun bore the name of its manufacturer and the date of

Shooting the Short Rifle was more pleasant than the Carbine because of increased weight and the longer barrel. This 2.3-inch group was an average 100-yard effort; the tightest clusters went into about 2 inches.

completion atop its chamber.

Several interesting variations of both Carbine and Long Rifle materialized over the course of production. The Model 94/17 Carbine incorporated an unusual nosecap with a special projection for attachment of a knife-style bayonet. There was an M94 with Model 96-style sling-swivels intended for static defense duty. Long Rifle variations included a shortened gun, cut roughly to Model 1938 Short Rifle specs; this model retained the Model 96-style rear sight. Some of the shortened Long Rifles (and some full-length M96s as well) showed M96-style rear sights modified to target specs, which offered fine adjustments. A muzzle threaded for a flash suppressor was incorporated in some examples. As of 1941, a sniper version of the Long Rifle materialized, the "Model 1941," which made use of any of several 3x and 4x telescopic sights made in Sweden and Germany. The scopes attached to a side mount, and issue was with a leather cheekpiece as well as a cannister container and leather lens covers for the scope. The "sniper-ized" Swedish Mausers are said to represent some of the most accurate battle rifles the world had ever known. This is hardly surprising since the sniper alteration was carried out on examples specially selected for groupability.

The year 1938 saw the final production variation of the Swedish Mauser. This was the Model 38 Short Rifle, which cut barrel length to just under 24 inches and overall length to about 44 inches. The result was a gun handier than the Model 96, though surprisingly, no lighter in weight. Sights on this arm could be adjusted from 100 to

The standard-issue Long Rifle battle sight (above) is set for 300 meters and is sturdily built. The Model 1896 Long Rifle tested has this "target-type" rear sight (below) that allows fine adjustments for windage and elevation.

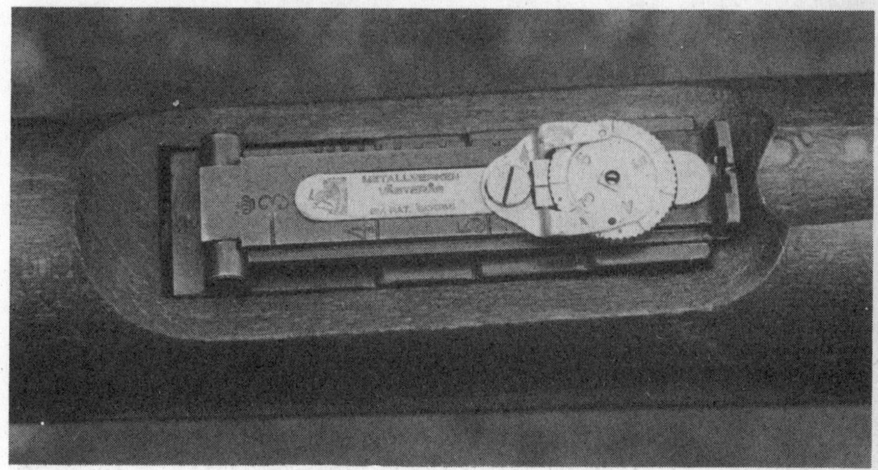

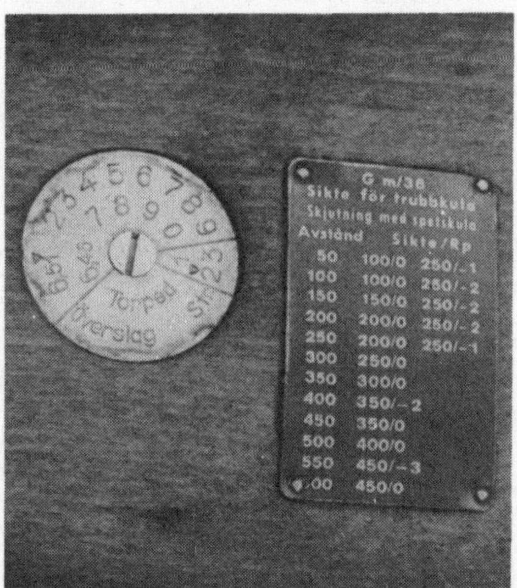

The butt of the Model 1938 Short Rifle has a marking disc that indicates bore dimension, bore condition and the overall condition of the rifle, as well as a sight-setting table to convert ballistics from the original 6.5x55mm loading to the newer M41 cartridge trajectories.

600 meters. The Short Rifle was intended for use by mounted troops, and examples issued for this purpose show a turned-down bolt handle. Some straight-handled Short Rifles are known, which saw infantry service.

The service history of the Swedish Mauser is a long one: The sniper version remained on reserve in Sweden well into the 1980s, and it is known that some Swedish Mauser rifles were rebarreled by service armorers no less than 10 times over their long careers! Surprisingly, because Sweden remained neutral all through WWI and WWII, some Swedish Mausers saw considerable battle use. Examples sold to the Finns performed admirably against the Russians during the Winter War of 1939. And in the post-war era, the gun found a new customer in Denmark, which had lost her service rifles to the invading Germans. Danish guns are identifiable by the Danish coin embedded in the buttstock in place of the Swedish marking disk.

My firing impressions of the Swedish Mauser were gained using one each of the three major M1894/M1896 variants: there was a super-early (single-digit serial number) Carl Gustav-made Carbine, a post-WWI-vintage Carl Gustav-made Long Rifle, and Husqvarna-made WWII-era Short Rifle. All three guns were in excellent or excellent-plus shape, and all showed fine bores. The very desirable low-number Carbine was loaned by a private collector, no Carbines being available presently on our revived surplus arms market. Origin for the Long Rifle and Short Rifle was friend Bill Rogers of Springfield Sporters, Inc. (RD 1, Penn Run, PA 15765). Bill is not presently offering Swedish Mausers for sale, but he does sell a variety of other surplus military rifles. The Long and Short Rifles are, in any event, available from other surplus houses.

This is a good place to point out that before you shoot any Swedish Mauser or other surplus rifle, you *must* have the gun degreased and exhaustively safety-checked by a competent professional gunsmith; this rule holds true no matter how nice the gun looks to the eye!

Ammo used in my shooting represented the two primary commercial brands available in 6.5x55 caliber.

The author checks out a 1.5-inch 100-yard benchrest group fired with the Long Rifle Swedish Mauser. This was a most pleasant rifle to shoot.

From Norma of Sweden came softpoint hunting ammo in 139- and 156-grain weights; Norma fodder is presently being distributed in this country by Federal Cartridge Co. From Hansen Cartridge Co. came 139-grain FMJ mil-spec ammunition and 139-grain softpoint rounds, which are of current Yugoslav manufacture. Both Federal and Hansen advised me that their 6.5x55 offerings employ non-corrosive priming; cases of either brand are Boxer-primed, hence readily reloadable.

The first Swedish Mauser to grab my interest was the cute little M94 Carbine which has always been a visual favorite among Americans. Familiarization handling of this arm revealed predictably pleasant handling and carrying qualities, as well as a smooth action. Sights were configuratively "Period-European"—the shooter got a V-notch rear and a pyramidal front—but the notch and post were a bit larger and visually better than on most other vintage European service rifles I've tried. Noteworthy were the prominent protective "ears" on the front sight. The trigger involved some take-up, but broke clean and was moderately weighted. On the range, some shortcomings were evidenced: The gun's recoil abused my cheek, and now I'm not surprised that Swedish soldiers fell out of love with the Carbine. Group placement was very high. Though I wanted to sample the accuracy at the usual 100 yards, I was limited to 50 yards, since even with rear sight at bottom detent and with 139-grain ammo, the Carbine shot 11 inches high at 50 yards! At 100 yards, impacts would have been off the paper! It is correct safety practice to try out a new firearm at close range and with a high-and-wide backstop before attempting longer-range activity; vintage military rifles especially are wont to print high. The Carbine was extremely accurate as five-shot 50-yard benchrest groups ranged from .8-inch to 1.25 inches center to center, and I'm not sure that *all* loads weren't sub-1-inch groupers in this gun. You'd just need a shooter with a more recoil-resistant cheekbone to find out for certain . . .

The near-50-inches-long Long Rifle was my second shooter. In terms of quality and smoothness, this arm mirrored the M1894 Carbine, and its accuracy was easily as good—from 100 yards, five shots would go into 1.5 inches when the shooter did his part. Regulation was such that bullets impacted 8 inches high at 100 yards. That 1.5-MOA groupability is impressive by the standards even of a modern premium-quality sporting rifle, and by vintage military longarm standards it's spectacular. Such accuracy isn't uncommon among Swedish Mauser Long Rifles either. I've come to *expect* these guns to shoot sub-2 MOA, provided the bore is flawless. Long Rifle shooting qualities were much superior to the Carbine's as the 2-pounds-heavier mass weight led to diminished recoil and virtually no abuse to my cheek. I noticed also, despite my high-quality ear protection, that the muzzle report was less pronounced. The increased sight radius augmented practical accuracy. Sights and trigger were of the same quality as on the Carbine, though the front post was of squared-off Patridge, not pyramidal, configuration and the rear notch was more hemispherical than V-shaped. Of course, the Long Rifle isn't anyone's ideal of what to carry in the field all day—the gun is about as handy as a vaulting pole—but as an item for recreational shooting today, this gun is beyond criticism.

The middlin'-length Short Rifle provided my final shooting impression. At 9-plus pounds, this arm was as gentle as the Long Rifle, yet was substantially handier. Accuracy was again fine: Tightest five-shot 100-yard groups went circa 2 inches center to center. Regulation with my Short Rifle was such that, with the rear sight set for 100 meters, printing was 11 inches high at 100 yards. I never noticed much divergence in point of impact between 139- and 156-grain bullets in these guns. Apparently, the difference at distance *is* significant, though. The Swedes thought enough of the problem that when they changed bullet weights—apparently in 1941—they affixed sighting charts for the new cartridge to the butts. The trigger was especially nice on the Short Rifle, being near match grade in terms of crispness. A single problem—the only one

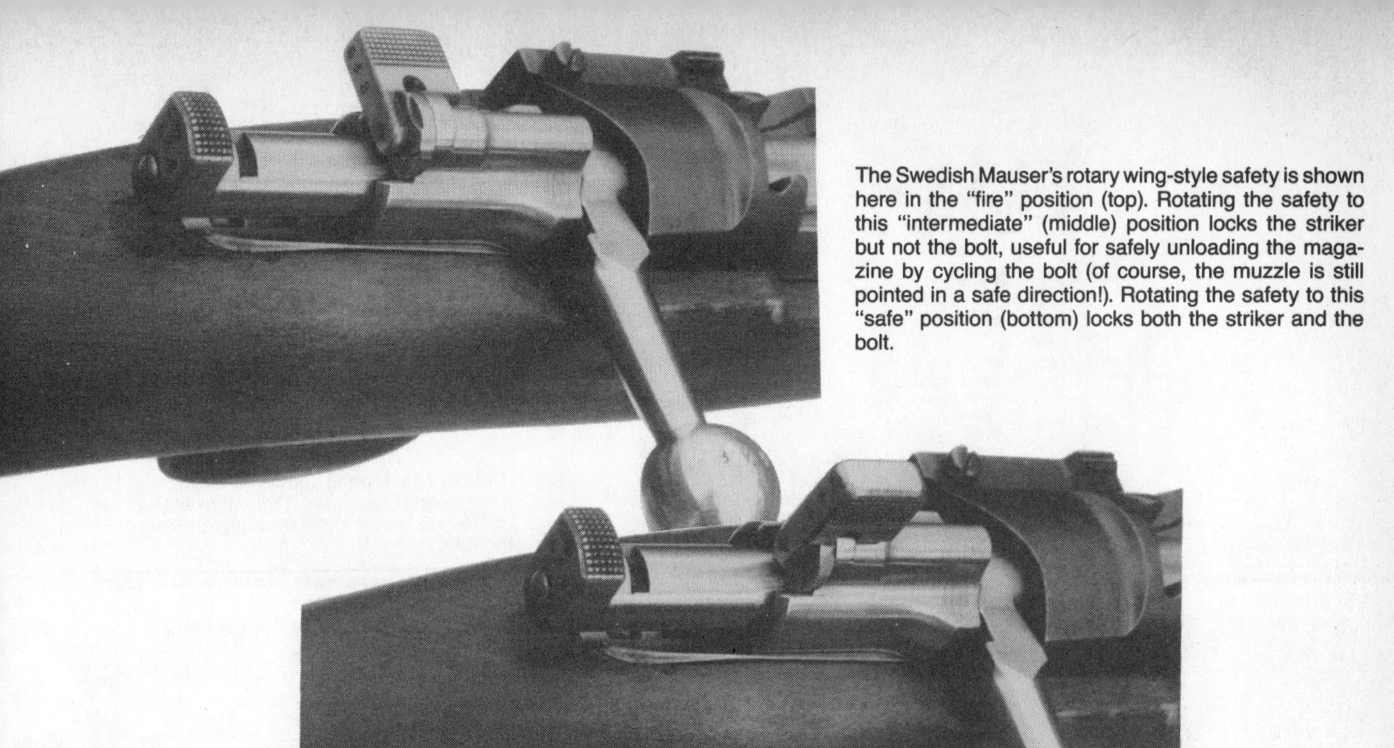

The Swedish Mauser's rotary wing-style safety is shown here in the "fire" position (top). Rotating the safety to this "intermediate" (middle) position locks the striker but not the bolt, useful for safely unloading the magazine by cycling the bolt (of course, the muzzle is still pointed in a safe direction!). Rotating the safety to this "safe" position (bottom) locks both the striker and the bolt.

experienced in all my Swedish Mauser shooting—materialized with this arm. The feed ramp was a trifle rough, so that feeding softpoint cartridges from full magazines could be a problem. I found it best to load up with but two rounds; if this was done, cycling was unimpeded and bullet noses went unmashed.

All three Swedish Mauser variants thus performed well for me. So did both brands of ammunition tried. Which brand was the more accurate, you ask? Having fired both brands only from guns bearing period military sights, I don't feel qualified to answer that question definitively; lighting conditions, fatigue, etc. all play too much havoc with the user of such sights. Most of the time, I seemed to get my best groups with the Norma 156 softpoints. However, the Hansen 139 softpoints could do fine work too: In the Carbine, Norma 156 SPs and Hansen 139 SPs shot identical .8-inch 50-yard clusters. Either brand, and any of the four configurations, was capable of nice groups. Probably the most dramatic way to show this is to report that, in the course of several days' benchrest work firing four different loads from three different guns, the *worst* five-shot group fired at any time with any gun measured 3.5 inches from 100 yards! Some old militaries would be pleased to *average* 3.5 inches at 100 yards!

So here ends my odyssey with the Swedish Mauser rifles. I make no secret of the fact that, along with the 6.5mm Japanese Arisakas, these are my very favorite military shooters in the whole world. I've a bonus doe tag this year, and I had thought about how nice it would be (once I had made my obligatory annual 357 Magnum deer kill) to take a good eatin' whitetail with one of the Swedes. Alas, when my firing trials showed the consistent high printing on the part of all guns, this idea was shelved; I like to be able to zero perfectly for hunting. And one does not, of course, alter the sights on a loaner rifle, much less a collector-grade example.

But the idea of hunting with one of Sweden's vintage tack-drivers sure appeals . . . ●

References and Suggested Readings:

De Haas, Frank. *Bolt Action Rifles.* Northbrook: DBI Books, Inc., 1984.

Ezell, Edward C. *Small Arms of the World.* Harrisburg: Stackpole, 1983.

Hogg, Ian V. and John Weeks. *Military Small Arms of the 20th Century.* Northbrook: DBI Books, Inc., 1981.

Olson, Ludwig. *Mauser Bolt Rifles.* Montezuma: Brownell, 1976.

Tanner, Hans (Editor). *Guns of the World.* Los Angeles: Petersen, 1976.

Walter, John. *The German Rifle.* London: Leventhal, 1979.

(Below) The Jericho shows clean lines and is a handsome handgun. The bulge at the rear of the grip frame looks odd but feels great in the hand.

TWO for the Price of One: The Jericho 941 Pistol

"Among the combat-style pistols there are a couple that are as good. There are none better."

by J. B. WOOD

FOR THE MOST important feature of the Jericho, just separate the numbers into "9" and "41"—because these are the two cartridges it fires, the 9mm Parabellum and the 41 Action Express. Changing from one to the other takes only a few seconds, and involves just three parts: the barrel, magazine, and recoil spring unit.

Probably because it is made by IMI in Israel, the new Jericho pistol from K.B.I., Inc., has a couple of Desert Eagle touches. The shape at the muzzle is similar, and so is the hammer. Otherwise, the design is close to the Italian versions of the Czech CZ75, but with some important differences.

One of these is the shape of the grip frame at the rear. From a deep upper incurve, the backstrap is straight at the center, parallel to the line of the frontstrap. Then, in its lower third, the frame has an outward bulge. When you first look at it, it's a little odd. When you take it in hand, it is exactly right.

Like the CZ75 copies, the Jericho has the slide rails inside the frame. Here, though, the frame extends all the way to the muzzle, and the rails run full length. This gives increased strength and smoothness. Aside from the mechanical advantages, the full-length frame has a clean, lean look.

The medium-high-profile sights have a square post and square notch

The sculptured muzzle of the Jericho bears a slight resemblance to that of the IMI Desert Eagle pistol. Gun has a smooth appearance.

The small dots on each side of the rear sight notch, and one in the front sight, are filled with tritium which glows in low light or darkness.

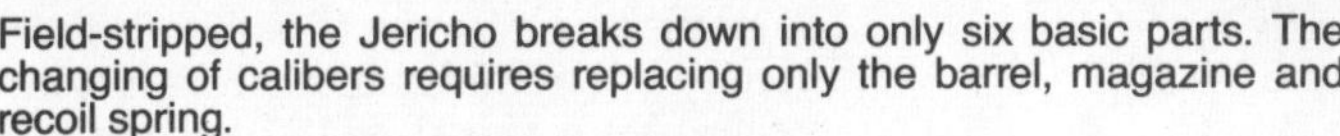

Field-stripped, the Jericho breaks down into only six basic parts. The changing of calibers requires replacing only the barrel, magazine and recoil spring.

picture, and the dovetail-mounted rear sight is laterally adjustable by drifting. The front sight is also in a dovetail slot. The sights have a three-dot system, and the dots are tritium-filled. In low light or in total darkness, they have a green glow that makes them easy to align.

The manual safety is on the slide, with ambidextrous levers. When turned down to on-safe position, the safety draws the firing pin inward and blocks it, then drops the hammer. The slide latch is perfectly located, with its pedal swept downward above the front of the left grip. Both the safety and the slide latch are easily reached without changing the shooting hold.

The trigger has an ergonomically perfect curve, and has no annoying ridges in its finger surface. Like the CZ75, the Jericho has a push-bar double-action system, and the DA pull is smooth and easy. The single-action trigger pull of my pistol is also very good, with minimal slack and no overtravel.

The push-button magazine release is reversible for left-handed operation. The 9mm magazine holds 15 rounds, and has cartridge-count holes at the five, 10, and 15-round levels. In 41 AE, the capacity is 10 rounds. Both of the magazines have floorplates that are removable for cleaning.

The finish is matte blue, and the lower two-thirds of the polymer grips have a pebble-grained surface. A circle at the center contains the cogwheel, sword, and olive branch emblem of Israel Military Industries. The front and back of the grip frame have vertical grooving, and the concave front of the trigger guard is cross-grooved.

The locking system is a falling-barrel type, with the movement precisely controlled by a bent-oblong track in the underlug of the barrel. The rifling in both calibers is polygonal, the first use of this in a pistol since the Heckler & Koch guns. It makes cleaning easier, reduces barrel deposits, and gives a *slight* increase in velocity.

The Jericho comes in a fitted polymer hard case, with recesses for the pistol, accessories, and a box of Uzi-brand ammo in each caliber. Two magazines in each caliber are included, as well as the 41 AE barrel and recoil spring unit. The barrels are plainly marked for each cartridge, and the recoil spring units are coded—blue on the ends of the 9mm, and chrome on the 41 AE unit. The 41 AE magazines are marked for that caliber. Also in the case, in their own recesses, are a Rig-Rod and cleaning brushes to fit each caliber. In the lid of the case is a plastic envelope that contains a well-written and well-illustrated instruction manual. In addition to field-stripping instructions, there is a sequence on disassembly of the magazine for cleaning.

At the range, I tried the pistol with the Uzi-brand cartridges that came with the gun. For the 41 AE, those were the only ones I had on hand. This was a 200-grain FMJ load with a flat nose. Later, with the 9mm system in place, I tried the Jericho with several other 9mm loads, and with all of them, it functioned flawlessly.

The 36-ounce weight of the pistol is perfectly balanced, and this, along with the superb grip, made the felt recoil seem light in 9mm. In 41 AE, the recoil was about like a 38 Super. In both calibers, the fired cases came out clean and undeformed, good news for those who reload.

From a sandbag rest at 50 feet, the 115-grain Uzi 9mm load grouped into 1⅜ by ⅝ inches, well-centered, with all hits in the black of a standard target. Other 9mm loads did as well. With the 41 AE components in place, the

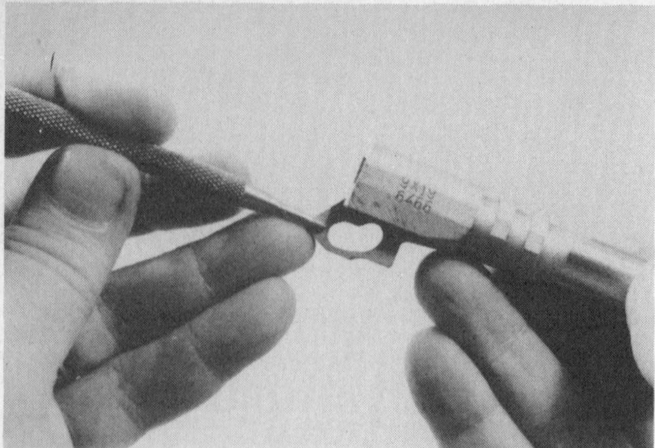

Barrel movement during locking and unlocking is precisely controlled by this oblong track in the underlug. This is the 9mm barrel.

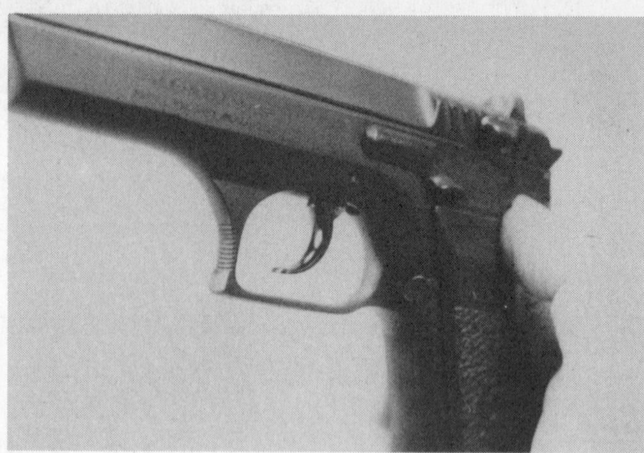

The smooth trigger is perfectly shaped for excellent control. The magazine catch and front of the trigger guard are grooved.

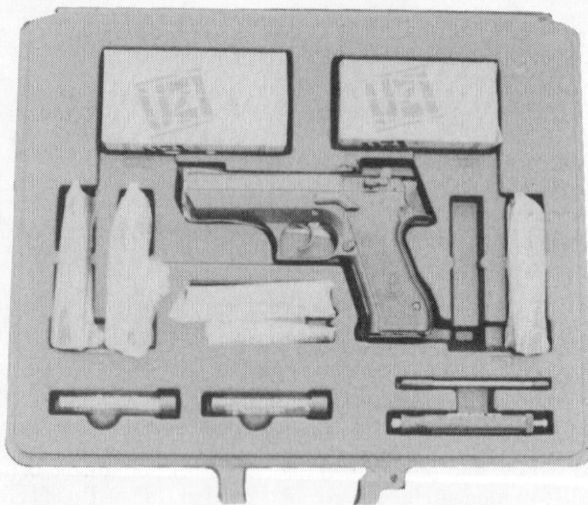

The Jericho Model 941 is delivered with a hard plastic case with compartments for ammunition, conversion barrel, and cleaning gear for both calibers.

best group was 1¼ by ¾ inches, with all five rounds in the 3-inch-diameter black. At closer range, firing double action at combat silhouettes, both calibers put the hits in vital areas.

Takedown for cleaning is easy, and it is exactly the same as the procedure for the Italian CZ75 copies. With the hammer cocked, chamber empty, and magazine removed, the slide is moved rearward until a dot behind the saftey aligns with its mate on the frame. The slide latch can be pushed out toward the left, and the barrel and slide assembly is run forward off the frame.

The recoil spring unit is then detached from the barrel lug and taken out. Its springs are captive—they won't fly away. The barrel is then removed downward and rearward. For reassembly, the process is simply reversed. There are no quirks to cause difficulty.

With the establishment of the 10mm Auto cartridge and the recent arrival of the 40 Smith & Wesson round, there has been some speculation among firearms writers that the 41 Action Express might be eclipsed by these. In power, they point out, the 41 AE is about the same as the 40 S&W, and the latter round has already become an accepted law enforcement cartridge.

But, they are forgetting an important point: If you have a 9mm pistol, and want to make it convertible, both ways, to a "10mm Lite" load, there is only one round that will do it without changing the slide—the rebated-rim 41 Action Express. This factor alone should be enough to keep the 41 AE around for quite a while.

In either mode, as a 9mm Parabellum or a 41 AE, the K.B.I. Jericho 941 is a superb firearm. If you thought, as I did, that the CZ75 and its Italian cousins couldn't be improved upon, you should try the Jericho. Among the combat-style pistols, there are a couple that are as good. There are none better. ●

The ambidextrous manual slide-mounted safety is shown in the on-safe position. The slide latch is well designed and is very easy to reach with the thumb.

Data
Jericho Model 941

Caliber	9mm Para. 41 A.E.
Magazine cap.	15 (9mm) 10 (41 A.E.)
Barrel length	4⅜"
Overall length	8⅛"
Height	5½"
Weight	36.2 oz.
Width	1¼"
Sight radius	6"
Finish	Blue/black
Price	$799
Maker	I.M.I. P.O. Box 1044 Ramat Hasharon Israel
Importer	K.B.I., Inc. P.O. Box 11933 Harrisburg, PA 17108

(Right) Haviland with his "back at the start" 30-06 and a nice Wyoming antelope. The 150-grain Sierra or Barnes X-Bullets at 2955 fps make a good load for open country shooting.

(Above) Some of the cartridges that turned the author's head away from the 30-06 for a few years include the 25-06, 6mm Remington, 7mm Rem. Mag., 338 Winchester Magnum, 270 Winchester and 35 Whelen.

Back at the Start

After trying many different rifles and calibers over the years, the author has reestablished contact with the cartridge he started out with—the good old 30-06.

by JOHN HAVILAND

WHEN I WAS growing up in Western Montana the only big game rifles around were the 30-30 and 30-06. A few cartridges might have strayed in, like the 30-40 Krag or 250-3000, but that was about all.

When I was 12 years old, my father lent me his Remington 30-06 to hunt mule deer. The recoil of that light rifle never bothered me a bit when I shot my first deer. After working the following summer in the hay fields, I had saved enough money to buy my own hunting rifle.

The gun rack was full behind the counter of Hiatt's Sporting Goods. I didn't know one rifle from the next, but I liked looking at and handling each one down the line. Mr. Hiatt handed me a Winchester Model 670 with a Weaver 4x scope in 30-06, and my father said that was the rifle I wanted. I paid the $140 and walked out with the rifle in a rectangular cardboard box, the shape only guns come in.

At the range at the edge of town, the rifle shot everywhere but where I aimed, and after the recoil from a box of shells, my shoulder turned yellow, then black. I went back to Hiatt's, ready to trade for an accurate rifle.

Although Mr. Hiatt had a store to run, he took me back out to the range. He cut a V-shape in opposite sides of a carboard box and set the rifle in the notches, then put up a target at 25 yards.

"But I want it sighted in for 100 yards," I said.

He put up his hand. "Patience," he replied.

Next he took the bolt out of the rifle and looked down the bore at the target. He looked through the scope then fiddled with the scope adjustments, and repeated this procedure a few more times.

"Try this now," Hiatt said.

I shot. The bullet holes were close to center at 25 yards.

We put up a target at 100 yards and I shot three more times. After one more scope adjustment, the rifle hit

The 150-grain bullet in the 30-06 was made for open-country game like antelope. It's a flat-shooting number, and with proper bullet design is an excellent killer.

(Below) A premium bullet like the Speer Grand Slam makes the 30-06 plenty of rifle for North American game. IMR 4831 powder is a favorite for the cartridge.

Haviland started out with a 30-06 as his only deer rifle, and is going back to it with this new Mark X Mauser with Butler Creek synthetic stock, 4x Redfield scope and Weaver rings.

right on the mark.

"We could sight the rifle a couple inches high so you would be on for longer range," Hiatt suggested.

The scope set at 100 yards was what I wanted, though. Everyone I knew sighted their 30-06s "dead-on" at 100. Over the next 5 years all the game I shot with that rifle was in that range.

I shot a mule deer each year with that rifle. Shot through the lungs, the deer fell over or staggered off about 30 yards and died. The first black bear I shot was all of 90 yards away. The 180-grain bullet hit the bear through the shoulder and the animal went down on the spot. I told anyone who would listen the 30-06 was the best big game rifle around. But the first bull elk I shot made me stop and reconsider.

I happened on the bull in the early morning light as it fed with its cows. When the bull turned broadside to me I shot it through the heart. The bull fell to its knees. I took my eyes off the animal to dodge the cows that ran close by on all sides. I looked back at the bull. It was back on its feet and heading out. I shot again and it went down. By the time I put another round in the rifle the elk was back on its feet. I shot him two more times before he stayed down. That made me think maybe my rifle was a bit light for really big game.

When I moved down river to college that fall, the top floor of my dorm was full of hunters from around the country. Expensive rifles stood in the back of their closets. Next door, a fellow from New Jersey had a 270 Weatherby; across the hall a guy from Minnesota had a 7mm Weatherby. Down the hall, two roommates from the Montana prairie hunted with a 270 Winchester and 7mm Remington Magnum. A Pennsylvanian had his reloading press mounted on the study desk in his room, and this was where everyone gathered to talk hunting and guns.

One evening, I edged in a word I had shot a nice mule deer buck with my '06 the weekend before. I compounded the error by saying I had used a *factory-loaded* bullet. Incredulous stares penetrated from around the room.

Shortly after that I purchased some reloading equipment and started reloading the empty 30-06 shells I used to leave on the ground. Everyone at home thought that was an economical move, because they all owned 30-06s and had me reload their shells.

What they couldn't understand, though, was when I bought more hunting rifles.

The first was a 25-06 Remington. My eldest brother looked at the 25-06 case and wondered why anyone would want a light 120-grain bullet for deer hunting when there was also a chance for elk. Of course, I explained, the 25-06 was a rifle for antelope and deer out on the plains. "I don't know," my brother said. "I use my 30-06 for antelope all the time."

I graduated from school before the first chance came along to hunt out on the plains. I took a couple days off work and headed for the flat land. The 25-06 worked fine for the somewhat longer shots than I was used to in the trees. The antelope I shot was 325 level steps away. The mule deer buck I shot was almost as far. I hunted with the

25-06 once in awhile back home in the mountains, but only after my elk tag had been filled.

During the summers the 25-06 was a fun rifle to shoot at gophers and rockchucks. The 75- or 87-grain bullets worked best for varmints. With the scope turned up to 7x, rockchucks were in danger well past 300 yards. For those shots, I loaded the 75-grain bullets up to the maximum of 3650 feet per second. On the much smaller gophers, 250 yards was as far as I could consistently hit. After wasting several pounds of powder shooting full velocity loads, the thought crossed my mind that an 87-grain bullet flying a slow 3100 fps had a flat enough trajectory for shooting out to 250 yards. With these light bullets and the heavier 117s in the 25-06, the varmint and deer end of hunting was covered.

That still left me with the 30-06 for elk and big black bears. A couple elk hunting friends of mine had traded their '06s for 300 and 338 Winchester Magnums. "You need that power for elk," they said. My '06 Winchester was almost 10 years old then, and I rationalized the old rifle was about worn out and I had better trade it in on a new magnum rifle before it fell to pieces. I walked into a hardware store on a September Saturday with the Winchester and walked back out with a Ruger M-77 in 338 Winchester Magnum. Now, I was a serious elk hunter!

Everything was fine until I fired the rifle. My teeth hurt and my shoulder ached. The recoil of the rifle was like a door slamming in my face. Each time I punished myself it cost almost a dollar. I replaced the thin rubber pad on the rifle with a 1-inch pad. A set of RCBS reloading dies came next, and I found a light charge of powder behind a 225-grain Hornady bullet made practice bearable.

That fall only one chance came at a bull elk. When the bull jumped out of its bed in the trees and ran, I missed two somewhat difficult shots as it took off straightaway. He turned and trotted across an opening 60 yards away, and the crosshairs of my scope were still above his body when I shot. The elk stopped at the edge of the open area and looked back, but it didn't matter, because the rifle held only three shells. By the time I had fished a shell out of my pocket, the bull had disappeared into the trees. At least if I had been carrying my 30-06 I'd have had two more shells in the magazine.

In the following years I learned to handle the recoil. A few elk, mule deer, a big black bear and even coyotes fell in front of the 338. One of the elk was a big six-pointer, and when he stood up out of his bed, a 225-grain bullet knocked him back down. The other elk shot with the rifle dropped on the spot when hit through the lungs. Then I drew a cow tag. The cow was at the lead of a bunch of nine elk, and when I shot she ran off without flinching. I found her not far away in the trees, shot through the heart, just like that first elk I had shot so long ago with my 30-06. Since then, I have noticed heart shot game seem to stay on their feet for about a minute, no matter whether they are shot with a 30-06 or 338.

About the time the 338 felt comfortable, I started thinking about a single rifle for all game—a rifle as good for antelope as elk. Looking through the gun catalogs for that perfect rifle was as much fun as buying the rifle itself. The choice narrowed down to three—the 270 Winchester, 7mm Remington Magnum or 300 Winchester. Like a person with a credit card and no sense of tomorrow, I eventually got my hands on all three.

The 270 was easy to shoot. The 130-grain bullet had plenty of speed for the long shots at antelope and mountain goats. For bigger game, though, the 150-grain bullet did not have any more velocity than my old 30-06.

The 7mm magnum shot the 160-grain bullets real fast, until I clocked them on a chronograph. They safely went a maximum of 2925 fps, about the same as a 30-06 with 165-grain bullet. The 7mm bullet did have a flatter trajectory than the 30-caliber, but not enough to matter until past 300 yards.

The 300 magnum had the power of a 338 with the trajectory of a 7 magnum. The 300 also had the recoil of a 338, which made shooting painful from the prone position to take advantage of the flat trajectory from one ridge to the next.

Somewhere in between those rifles odd ones showed up. Rifles in 22-250, 243 Winchester, 6mm Remington, 264 Winchester, 308 Winchester, 35 Whelen, another 270 and even a 30-06 carbine stayed for awhile then quietly struck out. I was like someone looking for the secret of happiness. The farther I looked, the farther I got from the obvious choice.

This past spring a Mark X Mauser barreled action hung by a peg on the wall at the neighborhood gunsmith. "That's my last 30-06 so you'd better grab it," the gunsmith said. "The price will be way up on the next ones I order." The thought of spending money now to save money in the future made sense. On the way home I wondered where the rifle would fit in the gun cabinet.

That evening the thoughts started forming on what type of stock and scope to put on the rifle. An old Redfield 4x scope came out of the drawer. An order went to Butler Creek in Belgrade, Montana, for one of their synthetic stocks. I found the 30-06 reloading dies at the back of the shelf of reloading equipment.

I loaded up a box of 150-grain Barnes X-Bullets with IMR-4320, a box of 165-grain Hornadys and W-760 powder and a box of 180-grain Speer Grand Slams with IMR-4350.

When the Butler Creek stock arrived, I screwed on the barreled action. I liked the fit of the stock. The only care the stock will ever need is to keep it from sitting too close to the campfire so it won't melt. The complete rifle weighs a portable 7.75 pounds.

At the range, I used the same trick Hiatt used those many years before with the cardboard box as a rest to bore-sight the rifle. The chronograph checked the 150s at 2955 fps, the 165s at 2905 and the 180s at 2776. That is good velocity, right up there with a 7 mag. The 150s and 180s grouped consistently at 1-inch. The only problem, one with all the 30-06s I have shot, was when the sights were set for 150-grain bullets at 100 yards, the 180s hit *many* inches higher. I can live with that, though, because one bullet weight is all I take on a hunting trip.

This coming week my wife is going to skip a few days of work. We are going to leave the kids at their grandmother's on our way to the antelope prairie. Gail will shoot the only big game rifle she has ever owned—a 6mm Remington. I will be back where I started—shooting the 30-06. ●

The author's "new" rifle was found as a barreled action in a local gun shop. The Butler Creek synthetic stock fits him (and the action) well and it all makes into a pleasant deer gun for all occasions.

Chuckin' with Thompson/Center

Hunting high-mountain rockchucks is great sport with this pair of Thompson/Center single shots.

by JERRY HORGESHEIMER

High magnification scopes like the Burris 6-24x on the rifle, and the 7x on the Contender, are great for long-range chuck shooting. The Harris bipods are the next best thing to a benchrest and sandbags.

CENTERFIRE 22-caliber rifles have been of great interest to me since I knocked over my first woodchuck with a 22 Hornet about 35 years ago. I was just a kid then, but I had been hit hard by a wonderful malady called varmint hunting. Since then, I have hunted crows, prairie dogs, woodchucks, jackrabbits, rockchucks, foxes and coyotes with a variety of calibers but I keep going back to the 22s.

Although my favorite all-round varmint caliber is without a doubt the 22-250, an interest in the 223 Remington has recently surfaced. It started during a conversation with Tim Pancurak of Thompson/Center at the 1990 SHOT Show in Las Vegas. Tim was showing me the then new Contender Hunter package in 223-caliber. Since I was already intimately familiar with the Contender in larger handgun and rifle calibers, this hunting handgun appeared to have great possibilities for varmint shooting.

My favorite area for hunting western rockchucks offers occasional shots well beyond 300 yards, which is expecting a little too much performance out of the Contender with its 12-inch barrel. For the longer shots, the TCR '87 single shot rifle in the same caliber seemed more appropriate, especially if it was capable of sub-MOA accuracy.

I spent a good part of last winter conjuring up what I thought would be the perfect varmint hunt. Since the terrain of my favorite spot is a flat-topped mountain covered with lava rock outcrops, and shots vary from just off the muzzle to well over ¼-mile away, carrying both a handgun and rifle made sense. I realize the Contender is not the typical handgun, but for what I had in mind, near pinpoint accuracy was a distinct advantage. So, with the March arrival of the Contender and TCR '87, both in 223, my efforts for finding one load that would meet my accuracy requirements for both firearms began in earnest.

The Contender Hunter comes from the factory equipped with a 2.5x scope, a muzzlebrake called the "Muzzle Tamer," a nylon sling and a fleece-lined suede leather carrying case. After shooting this handgun off a benchrest at 100 yards, I could easily see that a more powerful scope would take better advantage of this firearm's accuracy potential. The 2.5x scope is probably ideal for all available calibers except the 223. These other Hunter chamberings are 7-30 Waters, 30-30, 357 Remington Maximum, 35 Remington, 44 Remington Magnum and 45-70 Government.

Three brands of factory ammo, in addition to a variety of handloads, were tested in the Contender and TCR '87 with interesting results.

For hunting rockchucks, I opted for a Burris 7x IER (Intermediate Eye Relief) scope and Burris mounts. Obviously, shooting this combination offhand or short of a very solid rest, was impractical. The solution came in the form of a Harris bipod. With this handy piece of equipment attached just behind the muzzlebrake, I had a built-in benchrest. In fact, I was so impressed with the bipod that I installed a larger model on the rifle. Now I can't figure out how I have gotten along without one for so many years!

The TCR '87 rifle in 223-caliber is available with either light or medium sporter barrel. Since I wanted maximum accuracy, the heavier barrel was selected which is just short of 26 inches in length. This rifle incorporates a monoblock break-open action system, is drilled and tapped for a scope mount and comes with a recoil pad.

One unique aspect of both of these firearms is the availability of interchangeable barrels in a variety of calibers. Although the Contender Hunter comes in only seven calibers, the standard Contender is available in 18 different calibers with barrels that can be field-fitted to the same frame. Accessory barrels for the rifle can be purchased in 10 different calibers, plus 12- and 10-gauge smoothbore shotgun barrels. An accessory barrel rifled for 12-gauge slugs is also available.

John McCarty, president of Burris, suggested I try his new 6-24x Signature Series scope if I was really serious about doing in rockchucks at long range. This scope has a unique feature called a Light Collector which is an aperture adjustment similar to a camera lens. In low light conditions the "twilight" position is dialed in which increases the light transmission. In bright sunlight, especially in the presence of mirage conditions, the "daylight" setting can be used to enhance the crispness of the sight picture.

With everything in place it was time to study performance on the range. Three brands of factory ammo were selected to test against a variety of handloads. Five-shot groups at 100 yards were measured. In addition, the best four shots out of each group were also measured, assuming the widest one was a shooter-induced flyer. Five-shot groups with the Contender ranged from an impressive 1.1-inch group to 2.8 inches. As seen in Table I, the best group with factory loads came from the PMC 55-grain PSP cartridge. The best four out five shots measured an impressive 0.6-inch, center to center.

Shooting the same factory loads in the TCR '87 rifle also produced some interesting results. Two of the six five-shot groups were exactly 1-inch. When considering the best four out of five shots for each of the factory loads, two-thirds of the groups were 1-inch or less, as seen in Table II. The most accurate factory load fired in my rifle was the Federal 40-grain HP followed closely by the PMC 55-grain Ball and the Fed-

Author dons a backpack for a day-long rockchuck hunt in the lava-speckled mountaintops of Utah. Carrying the Contender on the long sling is the only way to go.

The Harris Model BR bipod with number four adapter fits the Contender perfectly and provides a rock-solid rest for shooting small and distant targets.

eral 55-grain SP. Any of these three cartridges were accurate enough for 90 percent of the varmint shooting encountered. However, the PMC load, being a full metal jacket, cannot be considered an ideal rockchuck load because of its non-expanding properties.

A variety of handloads were tested with the objective of finding one load that had acceptable varmint hunting accuracy in both firearms. I arbitrarily decided that satisfactory results would be attained if the rifle would print groups of four out of five shots in less than 1-inch at 100 yards, while the Contender held 1½-inch groups with the same load.

Of the seven factory loads tested, four met the criteria for the TCR '87 rifle but only two passed with the Contender, and none matched both firearms. The latter two were both pointed softpoint bullets by Winchester and PMC. Those meeting the requirement for the rifle were the Federal 40-grain hollowpoint, Federal Premium 55-grain boattail hollowpoint, Federal 55-grain softpoint and the PMC 55-grain ball.

Actually, the results with factory ammo in both firearms was quite impressive. For the shooter who prefers not to reload, a variety of factory ammo generating adequate accuracy for varmint hunting is readily available. However, I found that for maximum accuracy in both my guns, each would require a different load.

Since handloading for me is an end in and of itself, I am prone to testing handloads regardless of the accuracy obtained from factory fodder. Thirteen loads using six different bullets and four powders were run through the TCR '87. Velocities ranged from a low of 2644 feet per second (fps) with a 70-grain bullet to a high of 3561 fps for a 45-grainer. Six of the 13 loads met my accuracy criteria of 1-inch groups for the best four out of five shots. One of the better loads was the Speer 52-grain hollowpoint pushed by 21 grains of H4198 powder. Five consecutive rounds printed 1.1 inches, center-to-center, with the best four grouping at .8-inch. This load generated a muzzle velocity of 2848 fps, which is a mild load in the 223 Remington caliber. Actually, one other load did slightly better than this in the TCR '87. It was the Hornady 53-grain match bullet ahead of 22.5 grains of H322. This load developed 3026 fps and grouped five shots in .9-inch with the best four coming in at .7-inch.

This latter load in the Contender was also quite accurate. Five shots produced a 100-yard group of 2.4 inches but the best four of five shrunk the group size to 1.3 inches. The second most accurate load in the rifle was also very accurate in the handgun. The 52-grain Speer HP in front of 21 grains of H4198 shot within 1.8 inches while the best of four grouped at 1.4 inches. This load in the Contender generated 2517 fps. It is interesting to note that the difference in velocities between the rifle and handgun for this load was 321 fps. The velocity difference for the H322 load, however, was significantly greater at 507 fps.

Whereas the handloads generated somewhat better results in the TCR '87, factory loads were the better performers in the Contender. The average five-shot group was 2.4 inches for the factory loads. Even by excluding the 70-grain reload, the average five-shot group size for the handloads was slightly over 3 inches. The PMC 55-grain PSP factory load at 2606 fps was the outstanding performer in the Contender. Five-shot groups of just over 1-inch were the norm, while the best four out of five were just over ½-inch.

With this limited amount of load testing, it was decision time for selecting a rockchuck hunting load. A two-way compromise was in order since I wanted maximum accuracy in both

The T/C Contender Hunter has a 12-inch barrel with "Muzzle Tamer," sling and swivels and 2.5x scope. Author replaced scope with a Burris 7x. Chucks out to 150 yards were no problem with this rig.

firearms, but I did not want to sacrifice too much velocity. By selecting the handload using the 52-grain Speer HP ahead of 21 grains of H4198 powder, my accuracy criterion was met but velocity was on the low end of the scale.

When varmint hunting, velocity is important for several reasons. First, the faster the bullet is traveling, the flatter the trajectory, which makes precise range estimation less critical. Second, bullet expansion is more predictable and uniform when shot at "typical" velocities. For hollowpoint 22-caliber centerfire bullets, this velocity is probably 3000 to 3200 fps. And third, the faster the bullet is moving, the less effect a crosswind will have at any given distance. I decided that accuracy was more important than velocity for my up-coming chuck hunt and was hoping the mountain breezes would not be too strong.

Since I would be climbing about 1500 feet in elevation after leaving the truck, it was important to go as light as possible but there was still a minimum amount of gear I had to have. When varmint hunting I have now decided that a Harris bipod is mandatory. In fact, I would leave my lunch behind before I would go without the bipod. The Contender is mounted with a Model BR with a number 4 adapter. This rig allows the bipod to swing forward out of the way when not in use. The bore height can be adjusted from 6 to 9 inches, which is ideal when shooting the Contender across a boulder or from the prone position.

A Model 25 Harris bipod was attached to the rifle, which has legs that extend to 25 inches. A solid sitting position with the forend completely supported is then possible. On uneven terrain or when shooting over boulders both bipods are adjustable, one leg at a time, providing great flexibility in shooting positions.

With the Contender zeroed for 100 yards and the TCR '87 for 150, I headed for the top of my favorite chuck mountain. The Contender would be used for those shots out to just past 100 yards; beyond that, the rifle would be pressed into service. The handgun could be held right on out to almost 150 yards on a chuck-size target with reasonable confidence of a hit. At that range, the 52-grain bullet is only 1.7 inches low. At 25 yards the bullet is about a ½-inch low but from 50 to a little beyond 100, it's within a gnats eyebrow of be-

The Model 25 Harris bipod on the TCR '87 rifle extends to 25 inches, making it useful for shooting from the sitting position as well as prone.

Table I
Load Data
T/C Contender 223 "Hunter"

Load	Brass	Bullet Weight (grs.)	Powder	Charge Weight (grs.)	Mean Velocity (fps)	Max. Spread (fps)	Standard Deviation	100-yd. Group (in.) 5/5	100-yd. Group (in.) 4/5
Factory:									
Winchester PSP		55	—	—	2648	37	15	2.1	1.5
PMC PSP		55	—	—	2606	63	23	1.1	0.6
Federal SP		55	—	—	2727	39	17	2.3	1.9
Federal HP		40	—	—	3060	90	32	2.5	2.0
PMC Ball		55	—	—	2990	29	11	2.8	1.9
Olin Ball		55	—	—	2919	60	23	2.7	2.4
PMC PSP		64	—	—	2533	104	40	3.4	2.1
Handloads:									
Speer spire point	PMC	40	H322	24.0	2799	65	23	2.5	2.2
Speer spire point	PMC	40	H322	25.0	2972	161	69	6.2	3.0
Speer spire point	PMC	40	H322	26.0	3107	96	34	4.4	3.4
Speer HP	Federal	52	H4198	21.0	2517	42	17	1.8	1.4
Speer HP	Federal	52	H4198	22.0	2621	64	23	2.6	2.1
Hornady Match	PMC	53	H322	22.5	2519	75	31	2.4	1.3
Hornady Match	Federal	53	H322	23.0	2576	156	58	2.5	2.2
Hornady Match	Federal	53	H322	24.0	2661	132	51	3.6	1.8
Sierra spitzer blitz	Winchester	55	H4198	20.0	2422	81	30	4.3	3.2
Sierra spitzer blitz	Winchester	55	H4198	21.0	2548	50	20	2.3	2.0
Sierra spitzer blitz	Winchester	55	H4198	22.0	2680	78	31	2.4	1.8
Sierra spitzer blitz	Winchester	55	H4198	23.0	2809	80	35	1.9	1.6
Speer semi-spitzer	Winchester	70	H380*	26.0	1954	101	43	7.5	4.9

CCI 400 Primers
*CCI 450 Primers

ing right on.

Table III is a printout from a ballistics software package available from Barnes Bullets, Inc. The second column shows distance of the bullet above or below the line of sight when shooting horizontally. The third column assumes an uphill or downhill angle of 30 degrees. The column labeled "Wind" shows bullet deflection with a 10 mph crosswind. Finally, the last column gives the time of flight for the bullet in seconds. This program provides for adjustments in other factors such as the approximate altitude, temperature and barometric pressure at which you will be shooting. The serious shooter will find the various comparisons interesting and useful.

A variety of components was used in the handload development for the 223-caliber rifle and handgun. Hodgdon powder, bullets by Speer, Sierra and Hornady, CCI primers and Lee dies formed the basis of the process.

With the rifle sighted to hit point of aim at 150 yards, the bullet is about ¾-inch high at 100 and about 2¼ inches low at 200 yards. At 175 yards it is only an inch low so the point-blank range is about 180 yards or so. Table IV is the ballistic table for the rifle using the same load as described for the Contender in the previous table.

Loaded down with two guns, binoculars and a day pack with spotting scope, tripod, ammo, camera, jacket, water and lunch in it, I was ready to decimate the chuck population. Winding up the slope through scattered aspen patches, I would stop occasionally to glass the edges of the meadows, especially when I could see lava outcrops in the vicinity. The first chuck I located was sunning himself on a boulder not far from a large boulder patch just inside the quakies. At a range of about 75 yards I couldn't ask for a better setup for checking out the Contender. I dropped behind a small rise, peeled off the day pack and laid the rifle down. After extending the bipod and chambering a round, I peered over the grassy knoll with the handgun extended so the feet of the bipod were on solid ground past the rise. By resting the butt of the gun on my left fist, I had three-point support that was virtually rock steady. The rockchuck loomed large in the 7x Burris. With the hammer thumbed back, the crosshairs

The accuracy of the TCR '87 in 223 Remington, with its MOA groups, makes a great long-range varmint rifle, especially with the Burris 6-24x scope.

Table II
Barnes Ballistics
Barnes Bullets, Inc.

Description: TCR '87, 223 Rem., 52-gr. Speer HP, 21-H4198
Bullet Weight (grains): 52 — **—Ballistic Coefficient—**
Trajectory Units: yards — **Adjusted Coefficient: .338**
Zero Range: 150 — **Unadjusted B.C.: .225**
Sight Height (inches): 1.50 — **Altitude (ft): 10000**
Crosswind (mph): 10 — **Temperature (F): 70**
Angle (degrees): 30 — **Barometric (in. Hg): 21.80**

Range (yards)	Path (inch) Level	Angle (30)	Velocity (ft/sec)	Energy (ft-lb)	Wind (inch)	TOF (sec)
0	−1.50	0.00	2848	936	0.0	0.0000
25	−0.49	−0.47	2779	891	0.0	0.0264
50	0.24	0.31	2711	849	0.2	0.0539
75	0.67	0.84	2644	807	0.5	0.0819
100	0.79	1.10	2579	768	1.0	0.1109
125	0.59	1.08	2514	730	1.5	0.1402
150	0.00	0.72	2450	693	2.4	0.1714
175	−0.95	0.05	2387	658	3.3	0.2032
200	−2.28	−0.95	2325	624	4.3	0.2354
225	−3.97	−2.25	2264	592	5.4	0.2677
250	−6.11	−3.96	2204	561	6.7	0.3015
275	−8.66	−6.01	2144	531	8.1	0.3356
300	−11.76	−8.54	2086	502	9.8	0.3716

Table III
Barnes Ballistics
Barnes Bullets, Inc.

Description: Contender Hunter, 223 Rem., 52-gr. Speer HP, 21-H4198
Bullet Weight (grains): 52 — **—Ballistic Coefficient—**
Trajectory Units: yards — **Adjusted coefficient: .338**
Zero Range: 100 — **Unadjusted B.C.: .225**
Sight Height (inches): 1.50 — **Altitude (ft): 10000**
Crosswind (mph): 10 — **Temperature (F): 70**
Angle (degrees): 30 — **Barometric (in. Hg): 21.80**

Range (yards)	Path (inch) Level	Angle (30)	Velocity (ft/sec)	Energy (ft-lb)	Wind (inch)	TOF
0	−1.50	0.00	2517	731	0.0	0.0000
25	−0.56	−0.53	2453	695	0.2	0.0311
50	0.01	0.11	2390	659	0.6	0.0628
75	0.20	0.42	2328	626	1.0	0.0950
100	0.00	0.40	2267	593	1.4	0.1274
125	−0.63	0.00	2207	562	2.1	0.1610
150	−1.70	−0.77	2147	532	2.9	0.1952
175	−3.27	−1.98	2089	504	4.0	0.2311
200	−5.31	−3.59	2031	476	5.1	0.2673
225	−7.88	−5.67	1974	450	6.4	0.3048
250	−11.01	−8.23	1919	425	8.0	0.3432
275	−14.73	−11.30	1864	401	9.7	0.3829
300	−19.09	−14.93	1810	378	11.7	0.4239

The TCR '87 and Contender Hunter, both in 223 Remington, make an ideal rockchuck hunting combination.

were centered just aft of the shoulder. I momentarily lost sight of any action with the recoil, but upon closer inspection found the chuck in a heap about 5 feet behind the rock he had been sitting on. The 52-grain Speer HP had performed admirably, even at the reduced velocity through the Contender.

The longest hit with the Contender that day was stepped off at 117 long paces. The only miss with the handgun was at a relatively short range but offhand with all my gear on my back. I had surprised a chuck at about 75 feet, and I knew I had to shoot quickly. Obviously, I shot too fast and missed.

Two military-type factory loads were tried: the PMC 55-grain metal jacket and Olin's 55-grain Ball. The PMC stuff was especially accurate in the TCR '87.

The longest shot with the rifle was at an estimated 275 yards, but since it was across a deep canyon, I couldn't pace it off. Each of the several chucks shot with the rifle were quick one-shot kills, further testifying to the versatility of the Speer bullet. I found the 6-24x Burris scope ideal for this type of hunting. During the day when the sun was at its zenith the scope's aperture was closed to reduce the effect of heat waves off the barrel and ground. In the evening on my way back to the truck, I opened it up to give a brighter field of view. With the sun down behind the mountain I located a rock outcrop about 250 yards away with several old-timers stretched out flat on the warm rocks. Shooting slightly downhill, I held about 3 inches over the back of a big one. At the shot, he flew about 3 feet into the air and dropped stone dead. I duplicated the same performance once more on the same rockpile before calling it a very successful day.

Looking back on that hunt brings many great memories to mind. It was one of those perfect days when everything went just right. The scenery was beautiful, the weather was a delight and my pair of 223s performed flawlessly. ●

Table IV
Load Data
TCR '87 223 Remington

Load	Brass	Bullet Weight (grs.)	Powder	Charge Weight (grs.)	Mean Velocity (fps)	Max. Spread (fps)	Standard Deviation	100-yd. Group (in.) 5/5	100-yd. Group (in.) 4/5
Factory:									
PMC PSP		55	—	—	3122	44	18	2.2	1.5
Federal HP		40	—	—	3655	55	20	1.0	0.6
Federal Premium BTHP		55	—	—	3172	26	11	1.5	1.0
Federal SP		55	—	—	3206	28	10	1.1	0.8
Winchester PSP		55	—	—	3171	34	13	2.2	1.7
Olin Ball		55	—	—	3380	81	31	2.4	1.9
PMC Ball		55	—	—	3415	40	17	1.0	0.8
Handloads:									
Speer HP	Federal	52	H4198	21.0	2848	107	49	1.1	0.8
Speer HP	Federal	52	H4198	22.0	3171	89	41	2.4	2.0
Speer HP	Federal	52	H335*	26.0	3223	94	38	2.3	1.8
Speer HP	Federal	52	BL-C(2)*	27.5	3182	26	12	1.2	0.8
Sierra Blitz	Federal	55	H4198	22.0	3141	62	32	2.0	1.2
Sierra Blitz	Federal	55	H335*	27.0	3318	141	55	2.7	1.7
Sierra Blitz	Winchester	55	H4198	23.0	3290	63	25	1.0	0.5
Speer Spitzer HP	Federal	45	H335*	28.0	3561	101	41	1.3	1.1
Hornady Match	Winchester	53	BL-C(2)*	26.5	2989	32	14	1.3	0.9
Speer Spire SP	Winchester	40	BL-C(2)*	28.0	3411	173	69	1.6	1.3
Speer Semi Spitzer	Winchester	70	BL-C(2)*	23.6	2644	59	26	1.3	1.0
Speer Spire Point	PMC	40	H322	24.0	3401	242	107	1.5	1.1
Hornady Match	PMC	53	H322	22.5	3026	139	52	0.9	0.7

CCI 400 Primers
*CCI 450 Primers

CAST BULLETS in the 6.5 SWEDE

With the large number of these surplus rifles on the market, budget-conscious shooters can have their cake and eat it too!

by MIKE THOMAS

IT IS CERTAINLY no great revelation that there are currently some tremendous bargains available in the area of used military guns. I refrain from calling these arms "surplus" as that's somewhat of a misnomer. Virtually all such firearms are obsolete. The overall condition of the guns varies considerably from new to junk. From what I have observed, many of these guns are pretty tired if the advertised condition is less than very good.

Most excellent-condition guns have near-perfect bores, actions are tight, headspace is correct and safe, and, cosmetically speaking, such pieces are

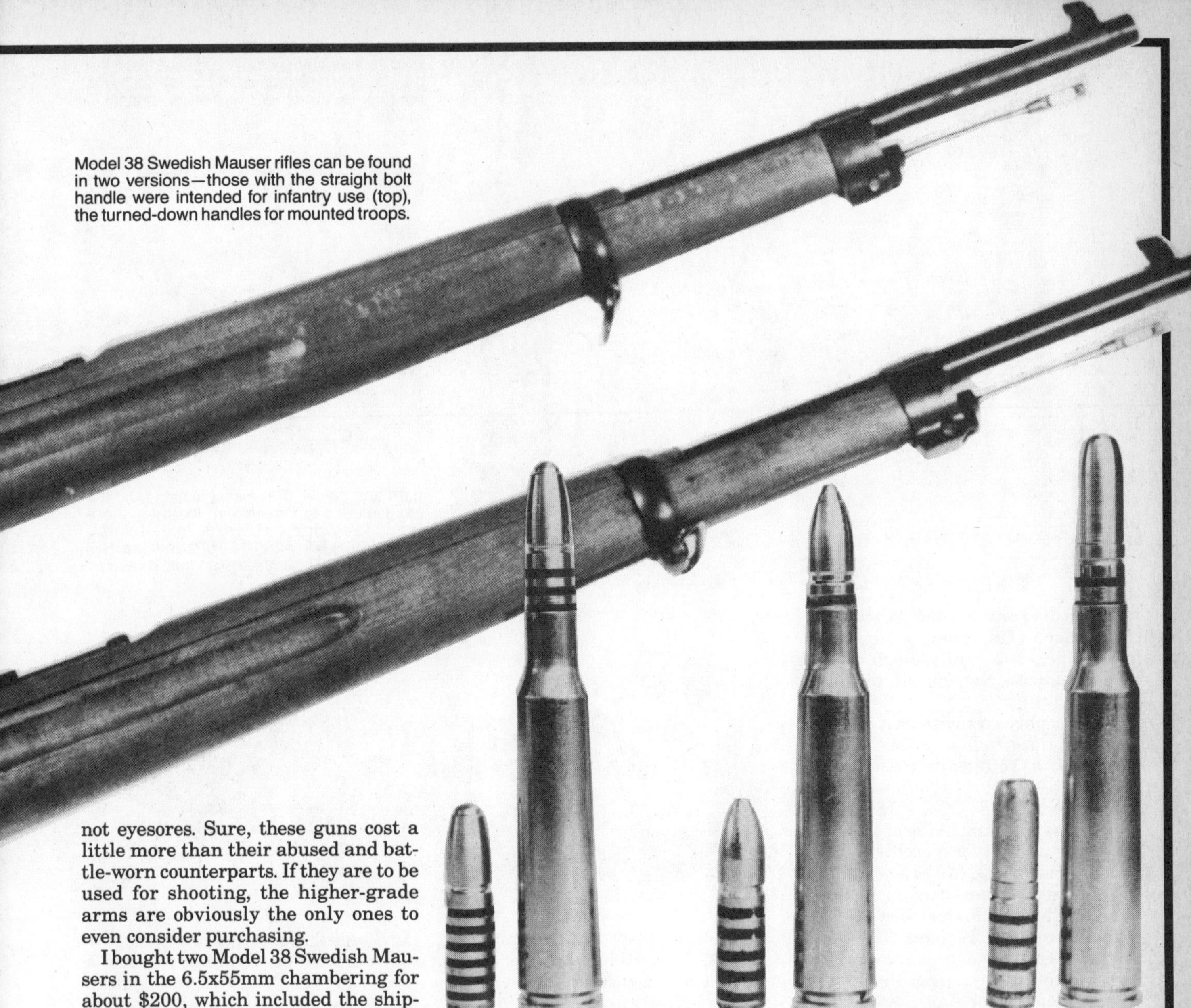
Model 38 Swedish Mauser rifles can be found in two versions—those with the straight bolt handle were intended for infantry use (top), the turned-down handles for mounted troops.

not eyesores. Sure, these guns cost a little more than their abused and battle-worn counterparts. If they are to be used for shooting, the higher-grade arms are obviously the only ones to even consider purchasing.

I bought two Model 38 Swedish Mausers in the 6.5x55mm chambering for about $200, which included the shipping fee. The condition was advertised as "excellent" and I was not disappointed. In fact, the condition was so good that I honestly could not tell whether the rifles had been used at all. There were some handling dings in the stocks, but all metal surfaces were fine and the bores did not even have a trace of copper fouling. Not being a collector, I know little about these guns. *(See "Those Sweethearts from Sweden" in this edition—Editor.)* Nevertheless, there must have been a sizable number produced. There are probably more of these advertised for sale in excellent condition at this time than any other military rifles.

I do a good deal of cast bullet shooting and figured the Swede would be a perfect gun for such use as-is—no customizing, changing sights, trigger, etc. The action itself pre-dates the '98 Mauser and is not quite the equal of the '98 as far as strength goes. That point is often brought up, but it's an academic one at best. The Swede's action is amply strong for the 6.5x55mm cartridge.

Speaking of this foreign round, it has never enjoyed immense popularity in this country. But this situation may turn around somewhat with the easy availability of the rifles now.

Ballistically, the 6.5x55 is about as "all-round" as one could ask for hunting purposes throughout much of our continent. It possesses a relatively flat trajectory and has adequate power for use on game to the size of elk.

The Model 38 rifles have 24-inch barrels and most have the desirable turned-down bolt handles, indicating use by mounted troops; those with straight handles were for infantry. The original Model 96 has a very long 29-inch barrel and a straight bolt handle.

Until recently, about the only 6.5x55 ammunition or empty brass one could find in this country was produced by Norma. Federal Cartridge Co. distributes Norma products in this country. There is certainly no doubt that this is excellent ammunition, and the brass is as durable as any available, regardless of maker. Hansen Cartridge Co. of Southport, Connecticut, is now distributing Yugoslavian-made 6.5x55 ammo. I tried some of this which, by the way, was loaded with a 139-grain full-patch spitzer bullet. Federal sent me some Norma ammunition that was loaded with a similar 139-grain bullet, though of the expanding variety. Both shot accurately in my rifles, but the average 100-yard group size with

(Below) Thomas used Norma brass for all his load development work. Norma has been the only supplier of ammo and brass for quite some time, but other makers are beginning to offer it.

(Left and below) Three cast bullets (and the moulds used to make them) for the author's load development, from left: Lyman #266469, LBT #266-150SP, and the NEI #160-264. All bullets carry an ample amount of lube!

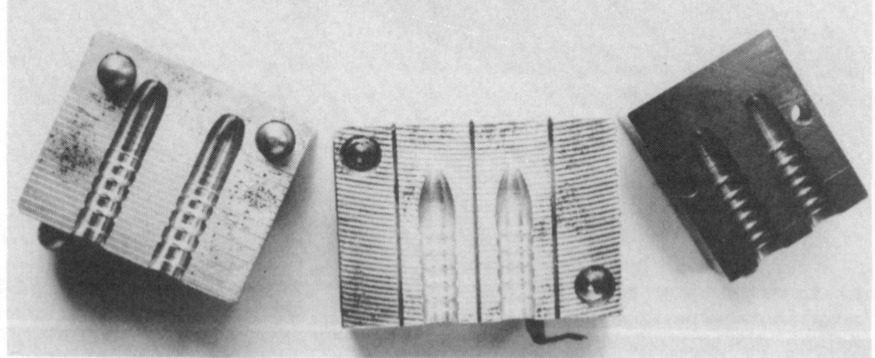

Norma fodder was 2½ inches, whereas the Hansen stuff grouped about an inch larger. Not really much difference, I suppose, considering the open battle sights.

For test purposes with cast bullets, I selected three bullet moulds: Lyman #266469, a 140-grain round-nose; LBT #266-150SP, a 141-grain spitzer; and the NEI #160-264, a 160-grain round-nose. Each mould is of two-cavity design and cut for gas checks.

Let's briefly look at the question of bore diameter. Many loading sources warn that bore diameters vary greatly with these rifles. Perhaps they do; I can't say with any degree of certainty. I used one bullet-sizing die for my work—a Saeco (Redding) .266-inch in my Saeco lubricator/sizer. Bullets sized to this diameter shot well enough in the Swedish Mauser so I saw little point in trying a different size. All bullets were cast of an alloy that measured 16 BHN on my LBT Hardness Tester. That's about midway between wheel weights and linotype as far as hardness goes.

LBT Blue lubricant was used throughout the testing. I won't harp on its merits other than to say that it's an excellent lube for any cast bullet fired at velocities exceeding 1500-1600 fps. Normally, any bore leading experienced with LBT Blue-lubed bullets is only slight surface leading, not the heavy leading that destroys accuracy and is difficult to remove.

Most of the loads developed were not of the "pipsqueak" variety. Low velocity loads have little if any worth as I see it. For very light rifle loads, I have found nothing more suitable than the rimfire 22 Long Rifle cartridge. Many of us cast bullet shooters prefer loads we can effectively use for deer hunting as long as ranges are not beyond 100-125 yards. Such loads have adequate velocities and are reasonably powerful and accurate.

Let me mention the sights on the Swedish Mauser. I can't condemn them as they are perfect for their intended use on a combat rifle, and that's what the Swede is. For target shooting, however, the front post is simply too coarse (wide) and the "V" in the rear sight is far too shallow. My eyes are good and I don't require corrected vision at this time, but two or three successive five-shot groups in a short time would cause eye strain. This sighting problem became evident when I fired one or two fine groups of 2½ to 3 inches but the next group opened to 5 or 6 inches. I repeated this a number of times in my testing and it became quite clear that nothing was wrong with the rifle or load, just the shooter. This should be no problem in a hunting or plinking situation, however. I predict that a scoped Swedish Mauser would provide some rather astonishingly small cast bullet groups.

Thomas used LBT Blue bullet lubricant for his testing, and found it excellent for high-velocity use. Consistency is quite firm and requires heat to flow properly through a lube-sizer.

CCI-200 large rifle primers were used in all loads. Even with slower-burning powders like H4831 there were no indications that magnum primers were needed.

Most cast bullet loading data for the 6.5x55 calls for the use of very fast-burning pistol powders. I just can't imagine the utility of such low-velocity loads. Consequently, my own load development started from scratch. I used several powders which performed well, but one was deemed most useful: Accurate Arms No. 2230. This powder provided good results with all three bullets, combining accuracy and useful muzzle velocities in the 2000 fps range. AA-2230 is often overlooked for cast bullet loads and I fail to see why. I have had excellent results using it in a number of different 30-caliber cast bullet loads.

H4831 might be considered too slow a powder for the 6.5x55, but I was able to consistently get some decent 4-inch

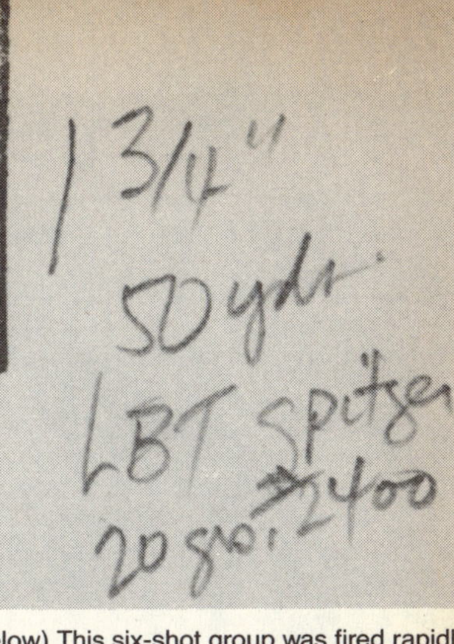

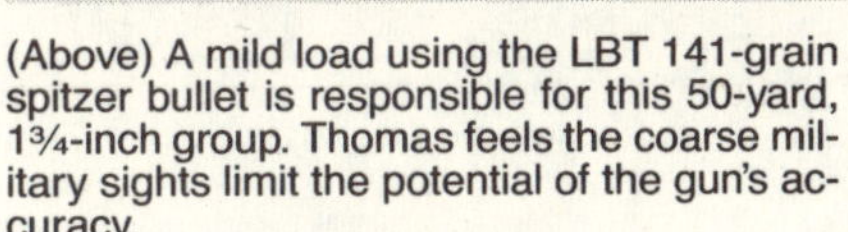

(Above) A mild load using the LBT 141-grain spitzer bullet is responsible for this 50-yard, 1¾-inch group. Thomas feels the coarse military sights limit the potential of the gun's accuracy.

(Below) This six-shot group was fired rapidly from a benchrest, and measures 3½ inches. A considerably tighter group should be possible by allowing the barrel to cool between shots.

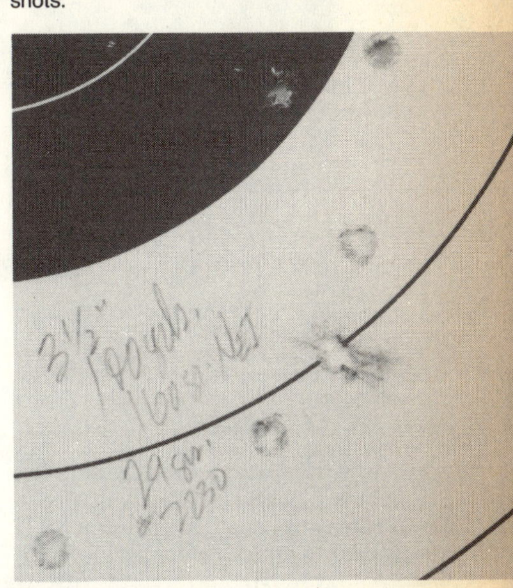

The author found H-414, Hercules 2400 and H4831 to be fine powders for cast bullets in the 6.5x55 Swede, but Accurate Arms 2230 was the single best performer.

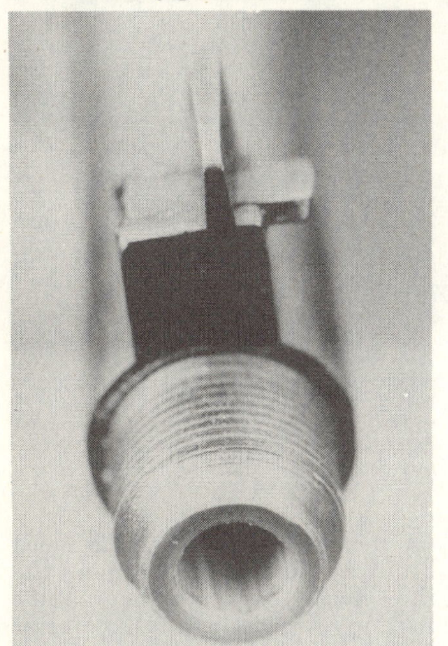

(Above) As can be seen, the front sight is drift-adjustable for windage. The author had to move his sight more than a little for proper 100-yard impact with handloads. The blade is too wide for target shooting.

(Below) Viewed from the front, the very shallow U-notch rear sight is clearly seen. It's fine for combat use, but, like the front blade, is less than ideal for paper punching.

Cast Bullet Load Data
6.5x55 Mauser

Bullet	Powder	Charge (grs.)	O.A.L. (in.)	Vel. (fps)	Group (in.)
140-gr. Lyman #266469	2400	20	2.94	2035	2.75
	H4831	38	2.94	2175	4.00
	AA-2230	29	2.94	2180	4.50
	SR-7625	12	2.94	1545	3.00
141-gr. LBT #266-150SP	AA-2230	27	2.81	2065	3.50
	2400	20	2.81	2005	4.00
160-gr. NEI #160-264	AA-2230	29	3.05	2065	3.00
	H-414	36	3.05	2035	3.50
	H4831	40	3.05	2165	4.00

Notes: All loads are well below listed maximums and were safe in author's test rifle. Ambient temperatures varied from 75 to 95 degrees during testing. All loads used Norma brass and CCI-200 primers. Bullets were seated to just touch the rifling when chambered. O.A.L. may vary from one rifle to another. If any component substitutions are made from those listed, reduce powder charge 5 percent. Bullets were sized to .266-inch. Group size is the average of several five-shot groups fired at 100 yards from a benchrest and rounded to the nearest ¼-inch. Muzzle velocities are rounded to the nearest 5 fps. A PACT PC chronograph was used to record velocities.

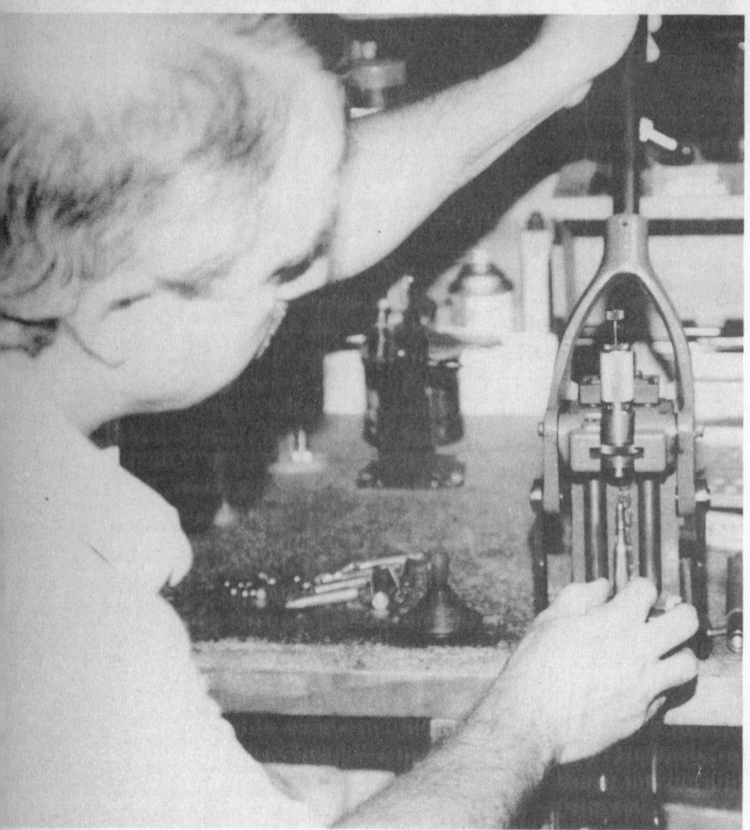

Using his Bonanza Co-Ax press with Redding dies, Thomas prepares to seat the long NEI 160-grain cast bullet in the 6.5 case. These bullets seat deeply in the case, taking up empty space.

Author chronographing cast bullet loads in his Model 38 Swedish Mauser, using a PACT PC chronograph. Recoil was almost nil, as can be expected with the full-dress military rifle.

groups with it when loaded behind the Lyman bullet and the NEI slug. H-414 was somewhat of a disappointment. It showed a distinct compatibility with the 160-grain NEI bullet but with no other. Using 36 grains of H-414 produced a muzzle velocity of 2035 fps with 100-yard groups averaging 3½ inches. Hercules 2400 proved to be outstanding with the Lyman 140-grain bullet. Using 20 grains, this powder propelled the bullet at over 2000 fps and group sizes were often under 3 inches. The LBT spitzer seemed to like 2400 as well.

I tried one fast pistol powder just as a matter of curiosity: SR-7625. Twelve grains launched the Lyman bullet at 1545 fps with an attendant 100-yard group size of 3 inches. Good accuracy, but not a very useful load. Now allow me to mention the powders that did not perform well, i.e., all those which produced 100-yard group sizes larger than 5 inches. IMR-4198 is normally a fine cast bullet powder, but my tests don't bear this out. I also thought IMR-4064 and IMR-4350 would show some promise. Regardless of the bullet or charge weight, suitable loads could not be found using either powder.

As with other rifle cartridges using cast bullet loads, the 6.5x55 often displayed what I refer to as a very narrow tolerance level when powder charges were varied. One grain of powder, more or less, might mean almost nothing in terms of velocity, but group sizes might increase or decrease by 100 percent or more! The loads in the nearby data table may have to be slightly adjusted for use in different rifles to account for this tolerance level phenomenon.

There are probably several other powders that would produce fine results with the 6.5 Swedish cartridge and cast bullets. I doubt that any would do better than AA-2230, but one or two might equal it. Hercules Reloder 7 and Hodgdon's H-322 both come to mind.

The long, 160-grain NEI bullet would appear to be best suited for the 6.5x55 cartridge since it was designed along the same lines as the original military bullet. Though the twist of these bores is a very fast 1:7½, the lighter, shorter bullets seem to perform about as well as the long, heavy bullets. My favorite is the NEI bullet, but only because of weight. With its spitzer design, it is by far more ballistically efficient than the others, but that's a rather moot point in an open-sighted rifle. The LBT bullet has a very long bearing surface for those who find this feature desirable. Apparently, the bearing surface of the NEI and Lyman bullets was adequate for stabilization as there was not much difference in accuracy among the three. Should one encounter a 6.5 rifle with a worn bore, the full-diameter LBT bullet would be the first logical choice. It does seat rather low in the case, but that is not near the hindrance some "knowledgeable" handloaders claim it to be. The Lyman is a most versatile bullet and slightly less finicky than the other two to work with and should perform well in most any 6.5 rifle.

It should go without mentioning that recoil with any of these loads is just short of nonexistent. I thought 30-caliber cast bullet loads were pleasant to shoot until I worked with the Swedish Mauser.

As an added bonus, these loads are easy on old military rifles. With proper cleaning, bore life should be close to indefinite. It's fair to say that case life is very long as well.

The 6.5x55 Swedish Mauser cartridge is a very fine one for use with cast bullets. Many of the rifles chambered for it are truly a bargain at this time and the brass/ammunition is far easier to find than it was just a year ago. Good shooting! ●

Resurrection of a Relic

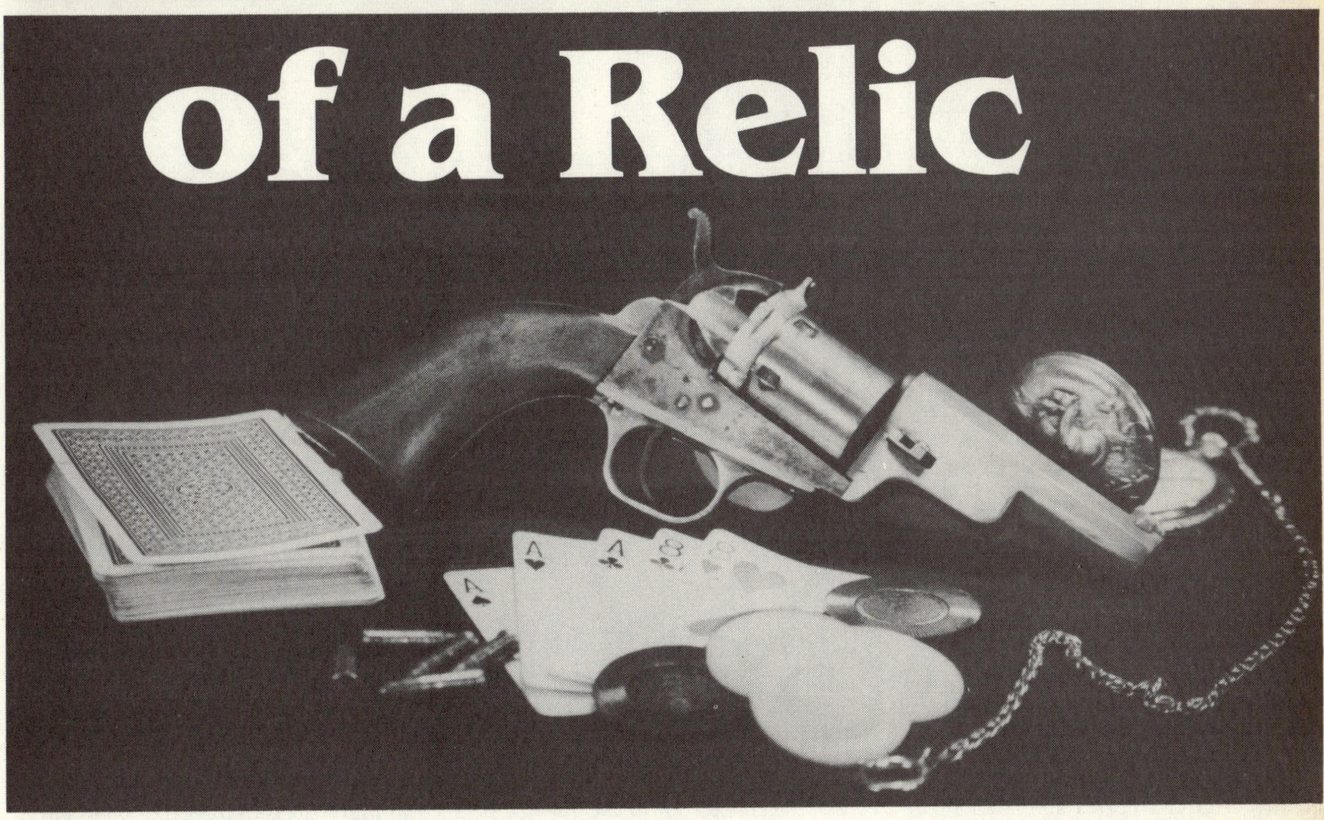

The converted revolver is surrounded by cards, cartridges, poker chips and an antique pocket watch—all authentic recollections of the original's past.

Given to him by an old and close friend, the author had this keepsake 1849 Colt converted to 22 rimfire as a treasured usin' gun.

by JIM McCOSKEY

THROUGH THE curling smoke of one of the cigarettes which probably helped to kill him before his time, our guest grinned somewhat evilly (I thought) over his glass of bourbon. Expansively he began, "I've got a little long standing project in mind which I haven't quite gotten around to. Maybe you'd like to help me with it?"

My old pal, Bill, was always a mischievous kidder and practical joker with an impish sense of humor. Many a time, I had been "had" as a victim of his witticisms. Twenty-five years of association prompted me, therefore, to respond with a warily non-committal grunt.

Undaunted, Bill continued. "I'll tell you the story. As you know, I've never been able to resist tinkering with guns. Well, when I was a kid, our family had a little Colt Model 1849 pocket model revolver which had been converted to 32 rimfire. Supposedly it had belonged to a great uncle of mine, a Civil War veteran, who became kind of a rounder out West after the war. He was not a lawman or a glamorous desperado—just ornery. Definitely the black sheep of our family, this great uncle of mine had drifted around from job to job in the frontier towns. He liked to drink, gamble, chase women, and fight. So the family story went, he eventually got into a serious scrape and killed a man in a fight over a woman in an Omaha saloon with that pistol. Apparently the circumstances of that shooting were questionable enough that my ancestor succeeded in getting out of it without going to jail. In later years he tamed down and returned to Iowa to live with his family and died a farmer. Eventually, the pistol and other things got left with my great-grandfather's family, and had been handed down with other heirlooms. I remember my grandfather, who had known his uncle well, telling the story, and even letting me play a little with the gun. Because he prized

Gunsmith John Gren of Spokane, Washington, does a lot of blackpowder conversions, and is shown here reaming the chambers for author's "new" shooter.

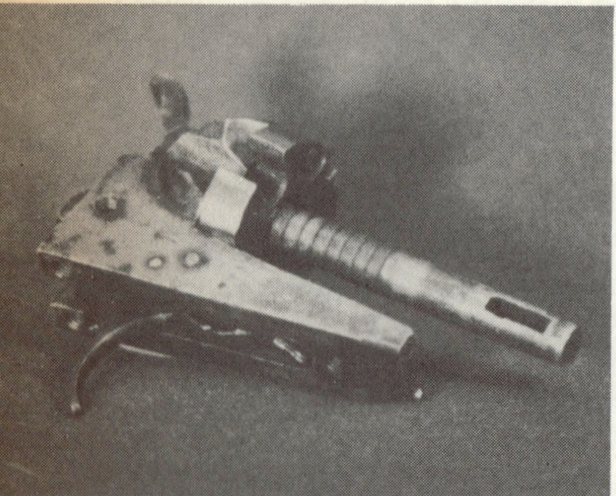

The frame and working parts are all that remained of the 1849 when the author received it from his friend. Gun had been previously converted to 32 rimfire long ago.

it highly, my grandfather frequently oiled the little revolver and kept it carefully wrapped in an oiled rag in an old cigar box along with a few shells, and hid on a shelf in an upstairs bedroom closet.

"One day when I was about 10, I was nosing around where I shouldn't have been, and found that box. I had already learned to shoot a 22 rifle and a shotgun a little, so just couldn't resist testing out this pistol. I stuck the gun under my shirt, and a few of the corroded shells in my pocket, and sneaked off to the woods.

"I got the piece loaded up, cocked the hammer, and cut down on a clod of dirt on the creek bank. The first round failed to fire, but I finally got three of them to go! I didn't hit the clod, but I had a really dirty pistol from that blackpowder! I knew I had to do something about that problem as the old man was a stickler for clean guns in general, and that one in particular! If he found that pistol dirty, I'd be in a trick for sure!"

By this time, Bill had my interest, and I waited a bit impatiently while my compadre lit another cigarette, and took a lustful pull at his glass of snake bite cure.

"Well," he continued, "the upshot of all this is, I decided to take the pistol apart and clean it. I thought it looked simple enough and, if I was careful, I could probably straighten up the whole mess and get it back in the box without getting caught. I had a little combination screwdriver which fit the screws, so I eased out to the garage and got it apart without much trouble. About the time I got the grip straps, barrel and cylinder off, I heard somebody coming! I quickly swept the parts into a handy paper bag and shoved it under the workbench, figuring to finish the job later.

"That next day my grandfather, who had been in failing health, had to enter the hospital. He never returned. Of course, there was a lot of consternation in the family, and I didn't get a chance to get back to the gun for some weeks. When I finally did return, my aunts had done one of those thorough cleaning jobs that maiden ladies are so good at. Despite a desperate search, I couldn't find the bag with the pistol in it. I guess my sense of loss was offset by the fact that my misappropriation of the pistol would not be discovered. So, I put the business out of my mind as one of those sadder, but wiser, lessons learned.

"Well, you know, some 20 years later, while visiting my surviving aunt at the old place, she told me she had something for me, went to the kitchen and brought in the frame and working parts to that little old Colt and gave it to me! She said that when the old garage had been torn down that previous summer, this gun part had been found lying in the dirt down next to one of the sills. She knew I liked guns, so thought I would like to have it. Of course I accepted the piece with mixed emotions. If only I hadn't been so stupid as to take the thing out to start with! On the other hand, I might well not have ever gotten it at all! I have kept the piece for all these years, but just never did anything with it."

Despite my old buddy's penchant for a good story, the tale had a ring of truth; especially since it appeared that he wasn't trying to trade or sell me anything!

At any rate, Bill had kept the frame, intending to round up original parts, if possible, and rebuild the gun. He never got around to it.

My old friend and I had not seen each other for several years prior to that late night bull session. Back in the early 1960s, Bill and I spent many hours trading guns back and forth and shining up our various acquisitions. Some 20 years my senior, Bill was a great mentor with an intense interest in Western and military history.

Because I knew he liked nothing better than to work on gun projects, I remember telling him that he ought to

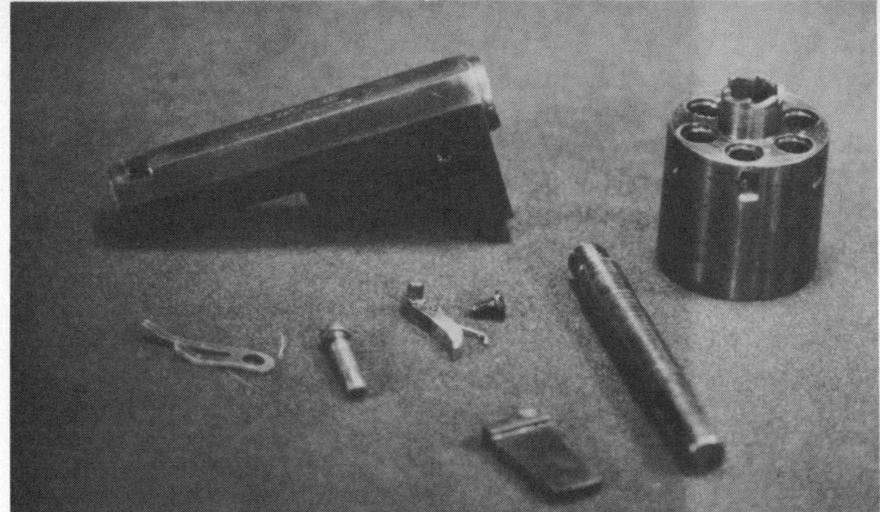

The parts needed to complete the conversion were obtained from a new Italian copy of the Wells Fargo Colt in 31-caliber. The lined 22-caliber cylinder has recessed chambers.

The Gren conversion plate, with loading gate, uses a floating firing pin assembly. The special front sight (right) was an added touch requested by McCoskey.

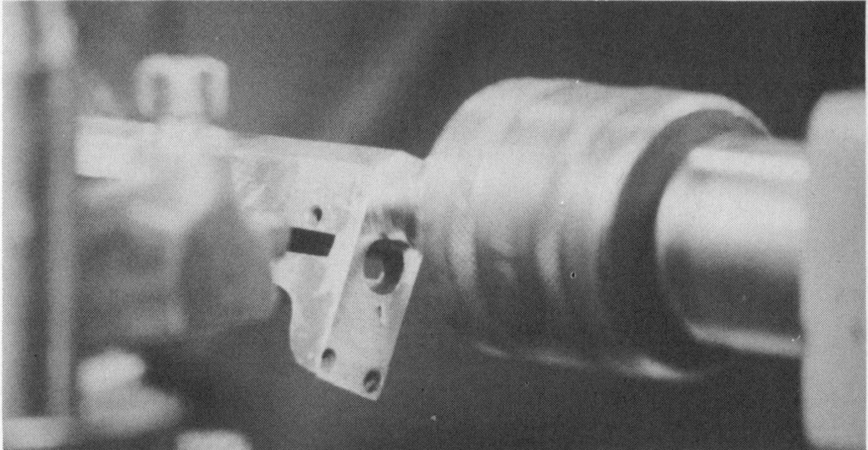

The new percussion barrel was first reamed for the 22-caliber liner. This is a precision operation if the finished barrel is to shoot straight, which this one does!

put that little memento into order himself. But, he seemed to want me to have it and absolutely insisted on sending it to me. When he had come to visit that last time, Bill had brought along some other odds and ends which he bestowed on me, my son and daughter. The past few years had not been kind to him. During the past 2 years, his health had deteriorated sharply. At any rate, we had a great time over that last weekend which he and his lady spent with us. I know we must have replayed every gun trade we'd made over the past two decades. I am proud to count him among the very best loyal friends I have ever been privileged to know.

A few weeks later, the postman delivered a little box. It contained a note saying, "I want you to have this—enjoy fixing it up!" The note was wrapped around that little pistol frame. I called and thanked Bill for it, and we corresponded a couple of times. Last November I returned from a business trip to find that Bill had died. I think he had a premonition, and for that reason insisted that I take the little Colt frame.

The frame, as I received it, was complete as to the working parts. The hammer, trigger, locking bolt and spring were all there and working. Of course, the frame was a bit dirty and a little rusty, but, actually, showed considerable original case-hardening and the "Colt's Patent" markings were deep and clean. The serial number was also clear and deep. A check with the year of manufacture table in R.L. Wilson's Colt book revealed that it was probably made in 1862. As Bill had told me, the pistol had been a conversion from a percussion Model 1849 pocket revolver to 32-caliber rimfire. The frame was indeed a conversion type with a separate breech plate, and the hammer modified to fire a rimfire cartridge.

Such conversions of the various cap and ball revolvers were legion in the period following the Civil War until eventually eclipsed by ready availability of quality handguns designed especially for metallic cartridges. Conversions of the Colts, Remingtons, and other reliable percussion handguns were good, serviceable revolvers, nevertheless. They were carried and used commonly until well after the turn of the century. In my years of gun trading, I have seen and owned many of various descriptions, to include those based on the little Model 1849 pocket.

The original Model 1849 Colt 31-caliber revolver was one of the earliest Colts to become generally popular. It was small, neat, easy to load, accurate, and reliable. The later and larger Model 1851 36-caliber Navy and the Army Model 1860 44 were essentially scaled-up versions of the Model 1849. The little '49 was immensely popular in its original percussion configuration. It was purchased and carried widely during the Civil War though not as an issue weapon. Because of its popularity, the '49 was a natural for conversion to the new metallic cartridges after the war. Colts were converted at the factory most commonly by the Richards or Richards-Mason systems which were similar in nature. Basically, the percussion cylinder was cut off at the rear and a separate breech plate containing a floating firing pin and loading gate fitted. Ejector rod assemblies were also fitted to some models.

The conversion block fitted into my 1849 frame seemed too crude to be an original Colt conversion. I surmised, therefore, that the job had probably been done by a private gunsmith. Anyway, I had on my hands a frame with

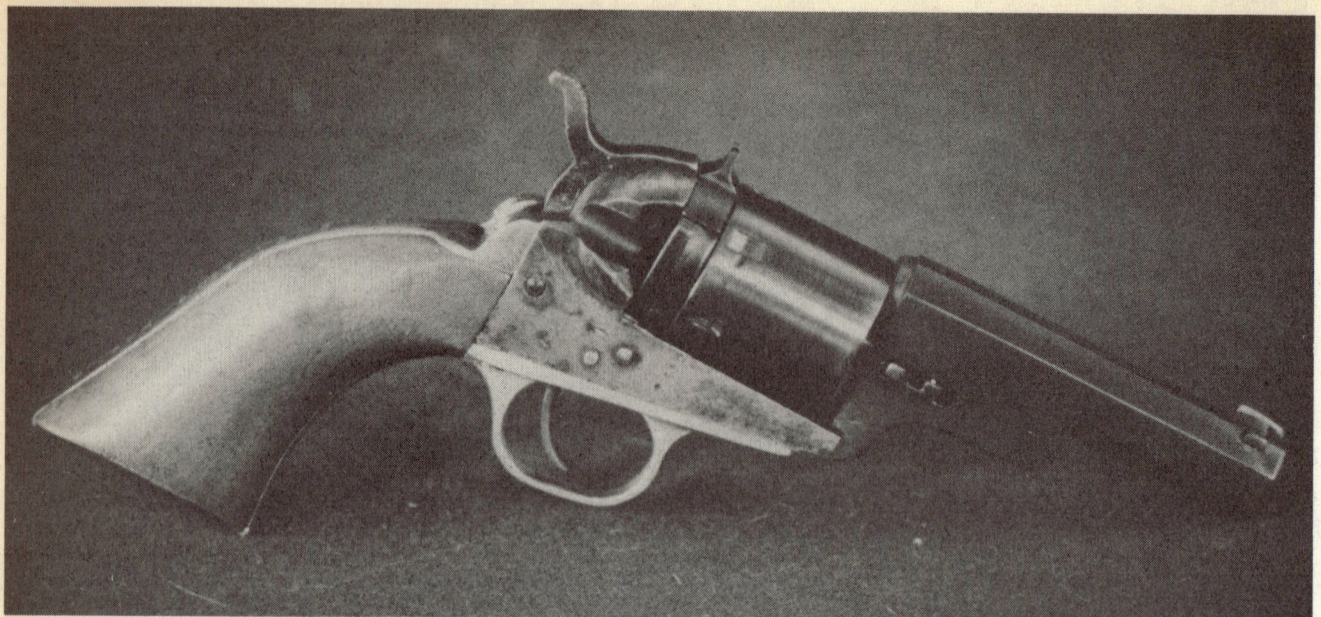

The finished revolver, as rebuilt by John Gren from the original Colt Model 1849. Loading is through the flip-open loading gate. Empties are ejected with a small rod, nail, etc., just as in early post-Civil War conversions.

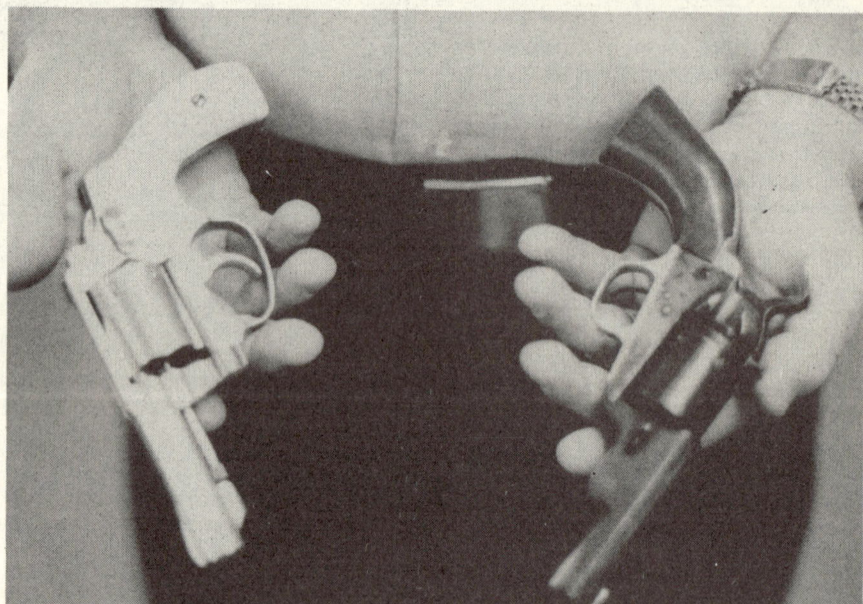

The "relic" 22 conversion is nearly as compact as the S&W 22 WMR, but for single action fanciers the conversion beats the Smith in feel. Both shoot equally well.

working parts, but lacked all the other essentials of a complete revolver: grips and gripstraps, cylinder and barrel. I supposed that possibly somewhere I could find parts enough to put the gun together, but the idea at the time was not at the top of my priority list.

I filed away the little conversion among my keepsakes, vaguely intending to keep on the lookout for '49 Colt parts.

Shortly thereafter, I happened on a letter in the gunsmithing "question and answer" section of one of the major gun magazines. It had been written by a man named John Gren of Spokane, Washington, in response to another reader's query in a past issue about where he could get a '49 Colt pocket percussion pistol converted to 22 rimfire. It developed that John is a custom gunsmith who specializes in converting '49 Colts and other percussion models, original or replica, to 22 Long Rifle.

I contacted John about a pet idea I had about converting a Remington 41-caliber over/under derringer to 22 Long Rifle caliber. He did that job for me and it turned out very well. The conversion functions perfectly, and we were even able to get it to shoot as accurately as most 22 pocket pistols.

Strangely enough, the idea to have John rebuild the '49 pocket conversion didn't hit me until sometime after I got my derringer back. Several weeks later, however, I ran across Bill's '49 pocket conversion frame and the light came on! Here was maybe the way to reclaim the little pistol into a useful but unique item, and yet not destroy the originality of the basic part.

I discussed the idea with John Gren, and while he had mainly been doing such conversion work on replicas, he saw no reason why an original frame could not be fitted with the conversion barrel, cylinder, gripstraps and the rest. He sent me some fine photos of finished work he had done on Colt and Remington guns as well as some handsome photos of restoration work on original antiques. John does other intriguing custom work such as sleeving double-barreled shotguns for 45-70 and even such oddities as 45 Colt. He tells me that he likes projects which run-of-the-mill gunsmiths would not take on.

We decided to undertake the 22 conversion/rebuilding project on my '49 Colt frame.

The system John uses to convert Colt-type percussion revolvers is similar to the Richards. Basically, the process entails cutting off the percussion nipple portion of the cylinder and boring it straight through to take metallic cartridges. Then a plate is fitted just in front of the standing breech which contains a floating firing pin and the loading gate. The nose of the hammer is reconfigured for the new firing pin. Barrels are modified to eliminate the bullet seating lever. The cuts for this part are welded up and finished over, and on some guns a rod ejector, a la Colt single action, is fitted to the right side of the barrel. A new rear sight may be fitted on top the conversion block, or on the barrel itself. With these modifications a basic conversion job on the Richards/Richards-Mason system would be complete.

John lines the barrels and cylinders with precision 22 liners. He is experimenting with 32 and 38 calibers as well.

Because I wanted the finished revolver to be compact, I chose to have it equipped with a short barrel without provision for loading lever or ejector rod. One of the Italian copies of the "Well's Fargo" model very nicely provided the basis for my conversion. I enjoy shooting and using 22 handguns a lot so opted to have my gun made up for the ubiquitous 22 Long Rifle cartridge.

One of Gren's more unusual jobs made from a 36-caliber Navy-type reproduction. Round butt, short barrel, ivory grips and engraving make it distinctive. Caliber is 38 S&W.

In his conversions, Gren uses high quality Italian parts, and each gun converted by him is marked with his company name in accordance with the law. There can be no mistaking one of his conversions for an original.

As it developed, John was able to use all the parts from my original Colt frame except the conversion breechblock. My relic had been set up with a firing pin mounted directly on the hammer. John's system is better and stronger; he uses a floating firing pin, as did the original factory Colt Richards conversions I have seen.

I specified a couple of extra touches. First, in deference to the sentiment involved with the piece, I ordered the backstrap engraved with a presentation legend to me from Bill. Indeed, original Colts were frequently so inscribed. Bill especially liked those presentation Colts so I thought this was appropriate.

Second, I wanted a little brass blade front sight to be dovetailed into the barrel, replacing the pin-type sight normally found on the 1849. I decided to leave the frame in its original finish, with the new parts blued.

After some weeks, my 22 conversion arrived. I must say that it exceeded my expectations. As can be seen from the photos, the gun is sleek, compact, and generally a highly attractive little revolver.

Unfortunately, the day it arrived my Wyoming pasture shooting range was under a waist-deep snowdrift. Nevertheless, even though we had guests on the way for dinner, the first thing I did after arriving home that evening was to test my new acquisition in the basement at my Outers bullet trap! I can get about 30 feet of shooting range down there, which is enough to give a rough idea about how a 22 will shoot.

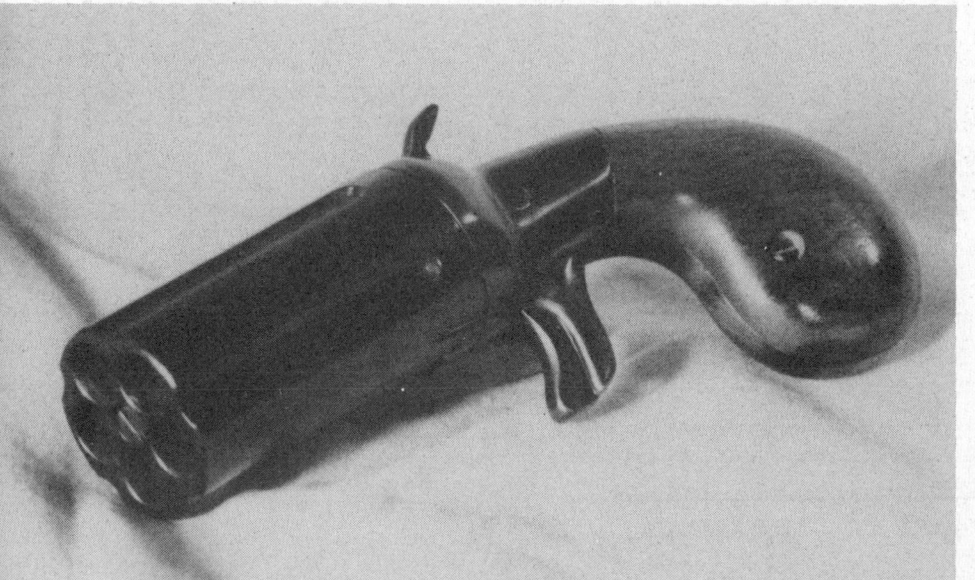

This neat little perrerbox was completely handmade by gunsmith Gren. Caliber is unspecified but appears to be 32.

First, I tried a cylinder full of Winchester T22s. What a pleasant surprise! My little revolver shot a nice tight group in and touching a 1-inch black target paster with two-handed hold! Next, I loaded up with Federal Spitfires, one of the hyper-velocity 22 Long Rifle rounds that I have had consistent good luck with. I got the same tight group, but 2 inches low. A second cylinder full of Spitfires with the entire front sight up in the rear notch centered the group perfectly, and I proceeded to completely shoot away the paster! To say that I was pleased is a real understatement!

Next weekend, the weather permitted outdoor verification of my initial shooting impressions with the little revolver. In testing against three of my modern compact plinking revolvers which I thought were similar enough to provide a realistic comparison, the Gren conversion emerged with great credit. My three comparison pieces are all tried and true field companions: a 4-inch S&W 22 kit gun, 3-inch Model 650 S&W 22 WRM, and an early 1960s vintage S&W 22 kit gun with 2-inch "snub" barrel.

All, to include the Gren conversion, can easily be held into 2 inches or better with a standing two-hand hold at 15 yards, which is about the maximum range I personally would use such a pocket gun on rabbits or squirrels.

Obviously, John Gren knows how to fit up a revolver to shoot accurately with all six chambers. I feel that from a rest, my little conversion will stay under the 2-inch mark out to about 25 yards.

Of course I had a special reason for having my conversion built up. Aside from the keepsake value, however, it is a reliable, practical little 22 of a type one can't buy on the commercial market. For those of us who like the appearance and feel of the percussion-type revolvers, and like to shoot them without the mess and trouble of blackpowder, the Gren conversions are just the ticket. The total cost of my pistol was about what one would have to pay for a new large-caliber Smith & Wesson; most reasonable for a high quality custom handgun, I thought. Now that I have been bitten by the conversion bug, I am thinking of sending John a beat-up, shot-out 38-40 Colt single action to make a 22 out of—but don't tell my wife! ●

BYTES AND BULLETS

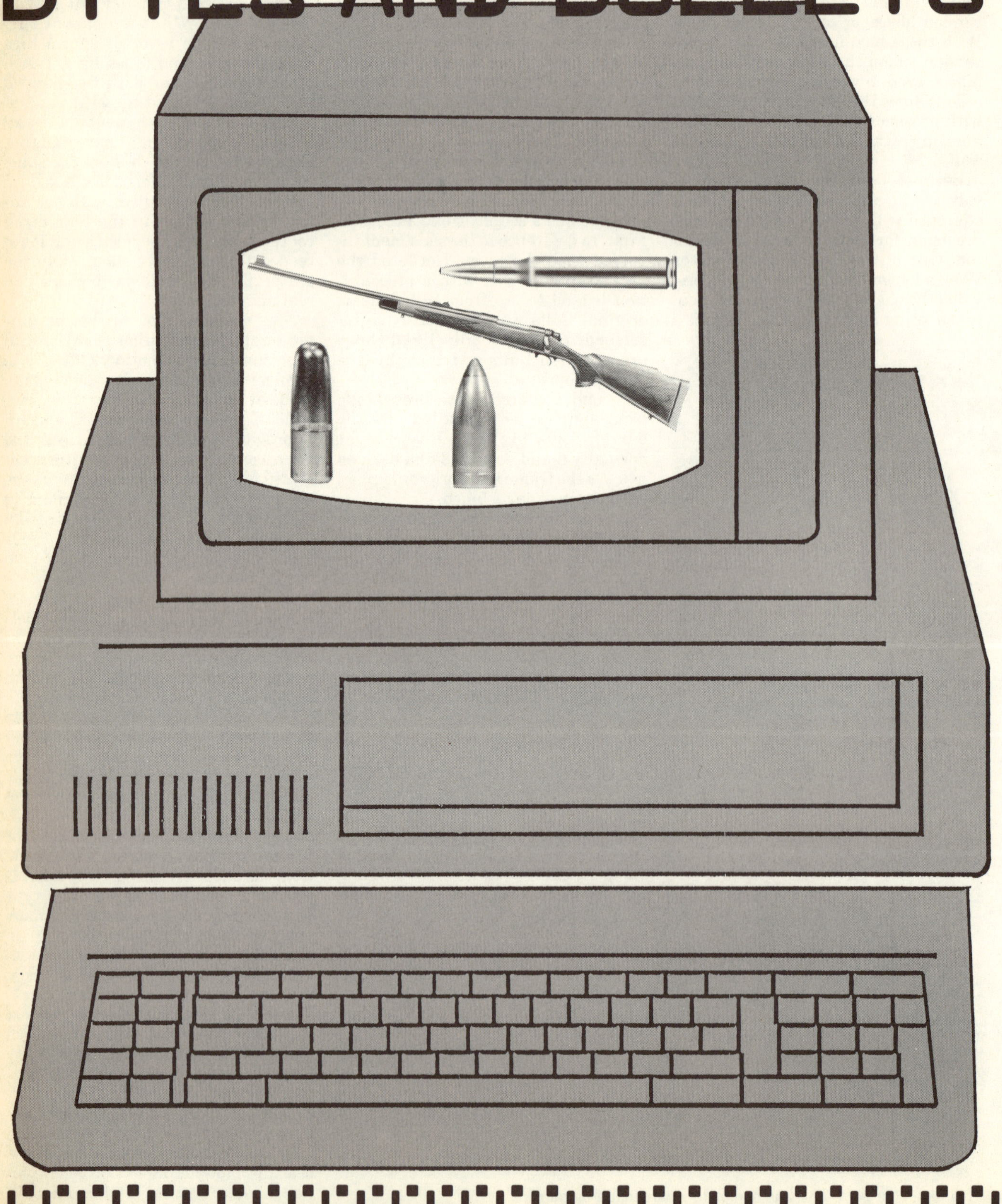

THIS IS THE COMPUTER AGE, NO DOUBT ABOUT IT, AND THE SAVVY RELOADER/HUNTER CAN BENEFIT GREATLY FROM THE VARIOUS BALLISTICS PROGRAMS NOW ON THE MARKET. HERE'S A LOOK AT WHAT THEY DO.

by JIM GOSNELL

AS THE SUN reached its peak, I decided it was time for a short siesta and a little lunch after a long and fruitless morning of searching for a trophy mule deer. It was an unusually warm fall day in western Colorado with the temperature approaching 50 degrees, and I suspect that what most would consider a gorgeous day was working against me. I quickly located a comfortable spot with an excellent view of the valley below me.

Once situated, I glassed the terrain around and below me as I ate, hoping to find the big one. After about 15 minutes, I spotted a hunter below me and to my left a good 700 yards away. He appeared to be stalking something, but I couldn't locate whatever it was. I continued to search the area in the direction he was looking and finally saw what he was after—a beautiful five-point (Western count) mule deer. There was a slight breeze coming almost directly at the hunter and a small rise stood between him and his quarry. Everything was in his favor to fill his tag for this season. It appeared that he would catch sight of the deer again at about 300 yards away.

As the hunter moved into place the deer moved also, but only about 80 yards. As I watched this drama unfold below me I became as excited as if I was the hunter, and the wait was taking its toll on me. Finally, the hunter got into position and prepared to shoot. The big muley was standing in front of a large rock about 350 yards from the hunter, who was still undetected. I watched the recoil of the rifle and an instant later saw the impact of the bullet on the rock well above the deer's back. He was gone in the blink of an eye, giving the hunter no second chance.

Later that afternoon I ran into a hunter and asked if he was the poor soul I had been watching earlier in the day. He was not particularly happy to learn that he had been observed, but we struck up a conservation in spite of his poor spirits. He just couldn't understand how he missed what he thought was such an easy shot. Over the years he said he had taken several deer between 300 and 400 yards with that same rifle and load; this was his first miss.

All this took place several years ago, and at the time I thought the problem was with the hunter, his choice of equipment, or a combination of both. By equipment I mean the 180-grain round-nose bullets he was using in a 308 Winchester. When I questioned him about his choice, he said that was all he had ever used. Now that I have access to some computer ballistic programs, I am able to shed a little more light on the subject. Recalling what I could from that conversation, I plugged the data into my computer and came up with a pretty fair reason why the hunter went home empty-handed that day.

By comparing data from the hunting field to that from the sight-in range, I found that a bullet shot at a target 350 yards away will hit 4.8 inches higher at 8500 feet elevation as opposed to sea level. Yeah, I know, I wouldn't be using round-nose bullets in that type of country; as a matter of fact, I pack a 300 Winchester Magnum when hunting in country where shots of 400 yards are not uncommon. The point is that to get the best use out of your equipment and, therefore, increase your chances of filling the game bag, you must know and understand your firearm's performance.

Until recently, understanding ballistics was at best a headache, and unless you were able to talk shop with someone on the same level as Einstein, you were pretty much left in the dark about what really happened to the bullet after it left the barrel. Now that computers are generally available, they do all the hard work; a basic knowledge of a few terms and the ability to press some keys on the keyboard is all that is needed to open up a whole new world to the average shooter and hunter.

A computer ballistics program can save hours at the range, and probably the best part is that it can pay for itself in ammunition saved in a short time. In the comfort of your home or office you can experiment with hundreds of "what if" situations and never fire a shot. You can calculate the best range for initial sight-in and figure the necessary corrections for your specific hunting area. If you are considering a new rifle, you can compare loads for different bullets in a particular cartridge, or compare different cartridges to find the one that best suits your needs. Worried about recoil? With your computer you can determine recoil energy for any rifle/cartridge combination in a few seconds and not have to suffer a bit. When shooting up or downhill, your point of impact changes significantly. Relatively few people know the proper corrections to make, but the answers are quickly and easily at hand with a computer.

Wind has a tremendous downrange effect on bullets, and you can watch as the computer reveals the exact correction needed for any combination of wind speed, direction and range. It would take years to compile this type of information under actual conditions, as opposed to seconds with a few keyboard strokes. Bullet performance can be reviewed, giving you a pretty good idea which bullet suits your needs best before you ever load a round into the chamber. The Oehler program

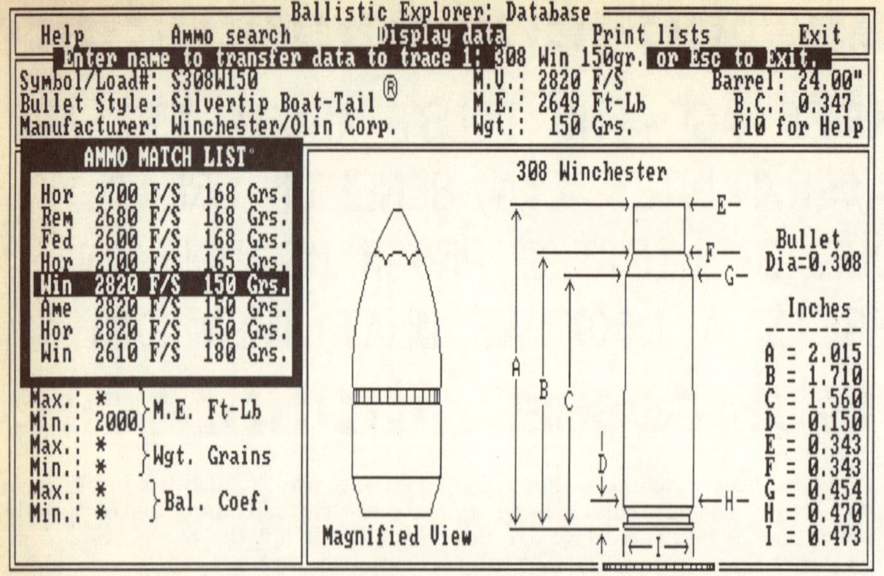

The Database from Oehler's "Ballistic Explorer" program is fun as well as informative. Case and bullet are normally drawn to the same scale, but pressing a key magnifies the bullet so you can get a better look at it. Load data can easily be transferred to the main display for ballistic calculations.

discussed later has a nice feature called "Combined Distance from Center." This graph plots the actual bullet strike at any given downrange point. I was quite surprised to find that when dealing with wind, the bullet can travel outside the vital zone at certain points *before* reaching maximum point-blank range, and then fall back into the vital zone farther down range. Actually, this shortens your true maximum point-blank range. Without this data, and an understanding how to correct for it, your whole hunt can "go south" in a heartbeat. This information can be determined with any of the computer programs, but Oehler makes it easy.

Nothing will ever take the place of actual shooting, but a ballistics program will most certainly reduce the time required to obtain maximum performance from your firearm. I don't know about you, but I can use all the help I can get when getting ready for a deer or elk hunt. And I'm proud to say I have used my computer to its fullest advantage in setting up my Ruger 77 chambered for 7mm Mauser. Originally, I had this rifle zeroed at 200 yards. But I have found that it should be 255 yards with a maximum point-blank range of 300 yards! The same program told me that I need to sight-in 3.48 inches high at 100 yards to obtain a zero at 255 yards.

OK, I know you're asking if all this applies to the real world. Well, I'm here to tell you that it does. Once I sighted in my rifle at 100 yards, printing 3½ inches high, I switched over to a target at 200 yards. According to the computer, it should shoot 2.97 inches high at that range. Things were looking good through the spotting scope, and after five shots and a 200-yard stroll, I found a group just a hair above 3 inches that measured 1.5 inches center-to-center! I'll take it as it is, and I fired only 14 shots including two five-shot groups at 100 and 200 yards, respectively.

Before reviewing the various programs available, let's look at a few terms which will make the understanding of computer ballistics much easier.

Ballistic Coefficient (or BC as it is commonly known): This is a calculated value (or number) which indicates a bullet's ability to overcome air resistance. This number will always be less than 1 (e.g., .485); the closer to 1 the better the bullet's ability to resist air. Don't panic; you don't have to worry about calculating this figure. The bullet manufacturers have done the hard work for you. If you have trouble finding the BC, just drop the manufacturer a note asking for that information.

Muzzle Velocity: This is the actual speed of the bullet as it leaves the barrel. This data is necessary for most ballistic computations and can be obtained several ways. The best is by actually shooting over a chronograph. If you want to be exact, you must convert the chronographed data (known as instrumental velocity) to *muzzle* velocity because the chronograph measures the speed of the bullet some distance (usually about 15 feet) from the actual muzzle. The ballistics programs will make this conversion for you. With the many advances in the field of electronics, as well as relatively low prices, a chronograph is almost an absolute must for the serious shooter.

Another way to obtain muzzle velocity is to use an internal ballistic program which will give you a very close approximation. Finally, you can use the ballistics tables in a reloading manual to get a "ball park" figure for a particular load. The major ammunition makers also publish velocity figures in their catalogs.

Trajectory: This is the actual path the bullet travels once it leaves the muzzle of the firearm. It is important to note that as soon as the bullet departs the barrel it begins to fall due to gravity; it also slows down as a result of air resistance. To overcome this, firearms shoot the bullet slightly above the line of sight allowing it to fall back to the line of sight at the desired zero range. It may sound complicated, but the nearby illustration explains this further.

Maximum Point-Blank Range: Very important to hunters, it is defined as the maximum range a shot can be made holding the sight dead-center on the target and hitting within the vital zone. (See the trajectory illustration nearby.) If you know the maximum point-blank range for a particular load, you do not have to make any range adjustments if the target is within that range.

The correct sight-in adjustments are determined by your computer ballistics program. After the required data has been loaded into the program, it will tell you how much above or below the aiming point your bullet should strike at a given range (i.e., 2.5 inches high at 100 yards, 3.8 inches high at 300 yards, 4.2 inches low at 400 yards, etc.). This is the information you will want to take to the range for sight-in. Keep in mind that the point-blank range will change with the size of game being hunted. It may surprise you to find that many loads have a maximum point-blank range in excess of 300 yards!

Computer programs vary in application and the output they provide. It is up to the purchaser to decide which program meets his needs and is compatible with his computer hardware. For those who like all the "bells and whistles," three of the programs—Barnes, Oehler and Sierra—have graphics output, which is fun to use for comparison but not necessary for analyzing data. The Oehler program also has a graphical data base which provides not only cartridge information, but actual drawings of the cartridge and bullet! Quite honestly, I found this feature a lot of fun, and I spent a considerable amount of time working with it. The current 3.0 version would not support graphics on monochrome, but I just received a test version of the newer 3.2 and the monochrome graphics are great, not to mention the better clarity on my VGA color screen. Version 3.2 has a total of 830 loads stored in the data base!

Interior ballistics is another feature available with three of the programs, specifically Blackwell's *Load From A Disk I*, J.I.T. Ltd. and *The Ballistic Program*. Of great interest to handloaders, they provide surprisingly accurate information on the type and charge weight of powder necessary to obtain desired results from a given cartridge. Here again, hours can be saved both at the loading bench and the range.

If you do not have a computer, the preprogrammed Sharp calculator from J.I.T. Ltd. might be just the ticket. This is actually a mini-computer which calculates interior and exterior ballistics. Lightweight and very portable, it is perfect for use at the range because it provides instant information on loads, allowing you to make the required sight corrections with only one trip to the range. Even if you already have a computer, this makes an excellent addition to any shooter's equipment list. Its small size and incredible output make it an outstanding value.

Documentation comes in all shapes and formats for the ballistic programs. Creating, editing and producing a manual is a very costly venture, and it is no surprise that the more expensive programs have the most extensive manuals. Overall, I found the Barnes manual, which comes in a three-ring binder, to be the leader of the pack with chapters on ballistic history and practical application, along with excellent "how tos" for each of the programs. Oehler provides a first-class bound manual to complement their user-friendly program; Sierra also has a three-ring binder with valuable and easy-to-follow information. Wayne Blackwell provides a computer print-out in a protective cover. Not as fancy as some of the others, it nonetheless provides outstanding instruction and information about his program. *The Ballistic Program* does not have a printed manual, but all the necessary information is on the disk. I spent the extra few minutes to print it out, slipped it into a report cover and found it very complete and helpful.

Once you start using a ballistics program, chances are you will want to find out more on the subject. Books on ballistics are somewhat limited and those written in layman's terms are quite rare. I have found the reference section in the new Sierra reloading manual (both rifle and handgun) to be superb in this respect. The authors, W.T. McDonald and T.C. Almgren, have written a basic review of ballistics in a way that is fairly easy to understand and quite pleasant to read. They also provide all of the calculations for those wishing to cultivate a headache. Another book worth mentioning is *Modern Practical Ballistics* by Arthur J. Pesja, in which the author explains what he calls a new and simplified method for accurate exterior ballistic computations. I found the book informative and, though somewhat technical, intriguing.

Of the programs I tested, each has good qualities as well as limitations and drawbacks. I tried to spend an equal amount of time on each, running similar calculations through them. As I expected, the solutions were not the same from any two programs, but the differences were so small they were not worth concern. Not being a mathematician nor expert in ballistics, I have no way of verifying the obtained results. However, by comparing programs, as well as tables in the reloading manuals, and conducting a couple sessions at the range, I am convinced they are giving me excellent information. Remember that computers are only as good as the information they receive. As the saying goes, "garbage in, garbage out."

Let's take a brief look at each of the programs with which I have been working.

Barnes Ballistic Program

This was written by a guy whose real job is putting rockets into orbit. Very extensive, it has two trajectory programs—"Fastrac," which does quick calculations for both single and dual trajectories; and "Precise," which calculates the changing ballistic coefficient during the flight of the bullet. Multiple BCs can be obtained from the Sierra reloading manual, as well as a complete discussion on how the BC changes with velocity. The usefulness of "Precise" becomes apparent with the considerable time required for the calculations, but the addition of a math co-processor to your computer can really improve speed on this as well as other ballistic programs.

The latest version comes with a graphics program called "Graphem," which allows you to visualize your data from either "Fastrac" or "Precise" and

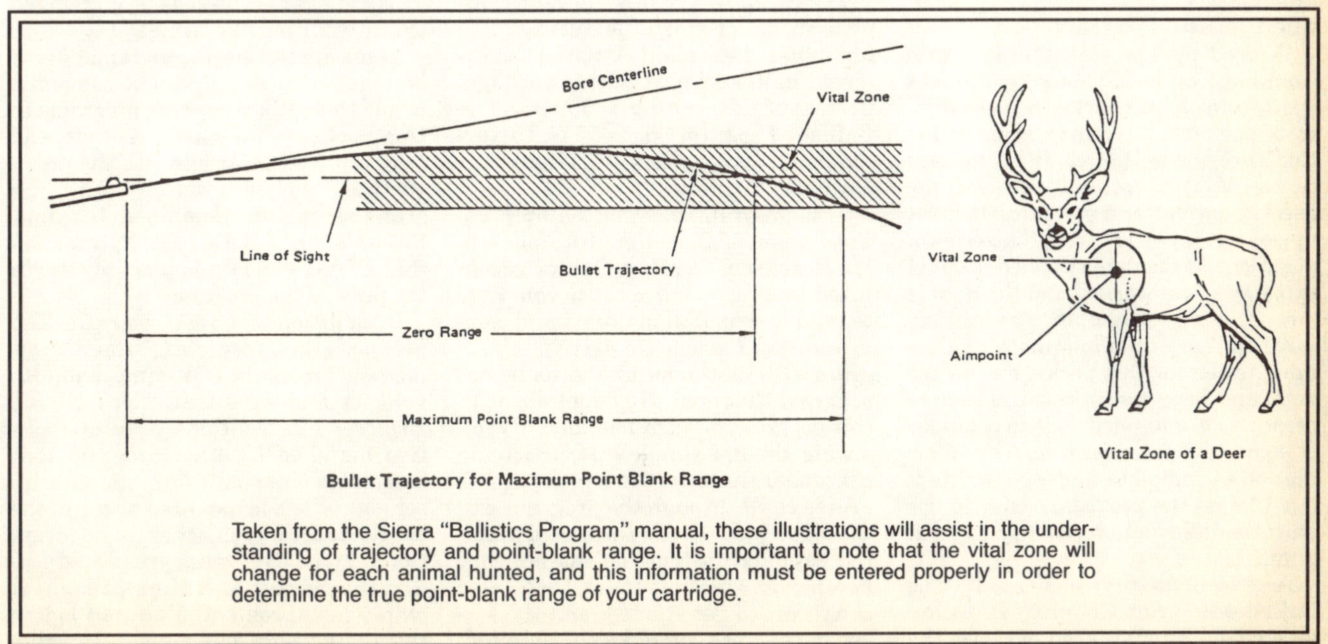

Taken from the Sierra "Ballistics Program" manual, these illustrations will assist in the understanding of trajectory and point-blank range. It is important to note that the vital zone will change for each animal hunted, and this information must be entered properly in order to determine the true point-blank range of your cartridge.

format the graphs, as well as add titles. "Graphem" has a printer driver for laser printers, which I found most useful but not an absolute necessity. In addition to the two ballistics programs and the graphic capabilities, Barnes includes a program called "Barnes Library Program." This is a neat little package which provides information on Barnes bullets, naturally, rifle and handgun cartridges, speed of game, recoil calculations, length of barrel and standard deviation.

This is a top-notch program with the best documentation of any of those tested. Hardware requirements are a minimum of 256K, but 384K makes things much smoother; a graphics card is required for "Graphem." The price is $79.95. (Barnes Bullets, Inc., P.O. Box 215, American Fork, UT 84003.)

Ballistx

Exe, Inc. Software Development makes this program, which is actually three programs in one—internal ballistics, external ballistics and a statistical program. All are menu-driven with on-line help available which has proven to be oustanding. Calculations for the external ballistics can be done in English or metric, a useful option for silhouette shooters. Documentation is in the form of on-line help and is easy to follow.

Internal ballistics programs are most useful to handloaders, allowing experimentation with various loads without ever leaving home. Caution is advised here, as always when handloading, to start out on the *low* end of the loads for actual use. (Exe, Inc., 18830 Partridge Circle, Eden Prairie, MN 55346.)

The Ballistic Program

Offered by The Ballistic Program Company, no less, this program was written by John Clarke. A most complete package, it offers exterior ballistics, interior ballistics, BC computations, BC conversions, case volume determinations and statistics. It is set up so that input is through a series of questions; if the data supplied is out of range, you are warned and the data is not accepted—a simple, straightforward and easy-to-follow program. Documentation for this package is on the disk, and I suggest taking the time to print it out and putting it in a binder of some sort for reference. The information is complete and well written, but I found the program easier to use with the information package close at hand.

An excellent service offered by The Ballistic Program Company is update by modem. Though I did not have the

This target shows the results of an enjoyable day at the range. The Sharp pocket computer was programmed by J.I.T., Inc., and gave the author instant information about the loads he was using. Talk about portable!

opportunity to use this service, it seems a convenient feature. There is no provision for saving files to disk on this program; it is assumed "hard copies" of the various loads will be kept for review. I, for one, have limited space for files and find myself putting as many files on disk as possible for easy storage.

The Ballistic Program is very complete in its offering of features and is fun to use. I especially enjoyed the internal ballistics part of this package. Cost, as of this writing, is $59.95. (The Ballistic Program Co., 2417 N. Patterson St., Thomasville, GA 31792.)

Ballistic Explorer

This program was written by Richard Larsen of Dexadine, Inc. for Oehler Research. Dr. Ken Oehler recognized long ago that most people hate to read instruction manuals and commissioned Larsen to write the program with that in mind. I think he has achieved that goal. No doubt about it, this program is "user friendly." By following the few simple instructions in a box near the top of the screen you can breeze right through the program. For those inclined to read the instructions, the supplied instruction manual has two parts. The first is for those who can't wait to get started, and the second part is very complete and detailed.

This program has several nice features in addition to the normal exterior ballistic information. The most intriguing is the graphic data base which provides actual drawings and dimensions of over 830 factory loads, as well as cartridge information that can be easily transferred to the original program for ballistic calculations. This data can be used as is or changed to suit your particular needs.

There are two graph programs offered and up to six "traces" can be compared at one time. Like the other programs in this package, they are first-rate and easy to use. Oehler also has the previously mentioned program within the graphics called "Combined Distance From Center" (CDFC). The information that CDFC provides is probably worth the price of the program.

In addition to CDFC, you can also produce graphs depicting drop, energy, momentum, path, TOF (time of flight), velocity and winddrift. The *Ballistic Explorer* also contains a unique section found in no other program that calculates sight-in information for laser sights. When mounted on top of the barrel, laser sights act as any conventional sight. But most are placed *under* the barrel and thus present a whole new problem. Mounted below, the sight height has a negative value

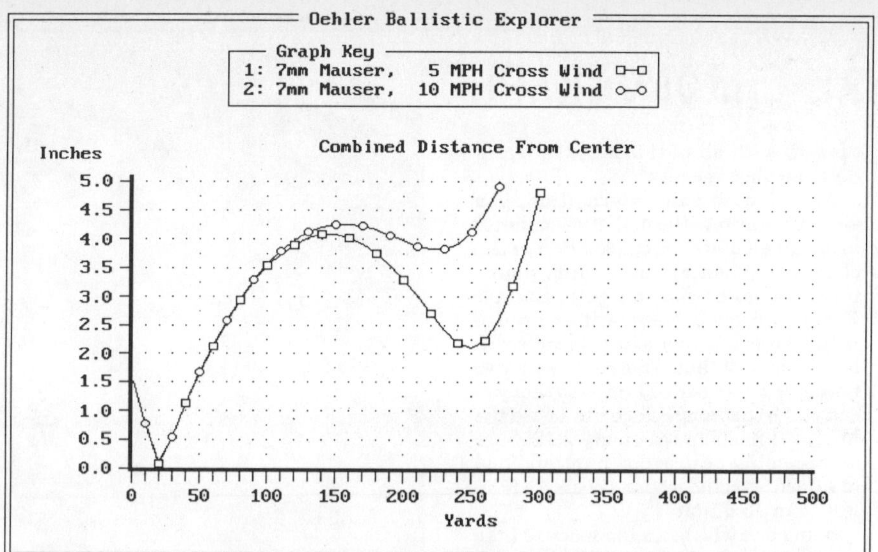

Combined Distance From Center (CDFC) can be a real eye opener. The printout from Oehler's "Ballistic Explorer" shows the effects of a 5- and 10-mph wind on a 7mm Mauser.

and the bullet only crosses the line of the laser once as opposed to twice with conventional mounting. This is a premium program selling for $69.95. (Oehler Research, Inc., P.O. Box 9135, Austin, TX 78766.)

Corbin Software

Corbin Manufacturing Co. has a very interesting list of software for those interested in bullet swaging or the manufacture of bullets, in addition to other applications. I mention Corbin here because I was under the impression they had a ballistics program as well, but they do not. Corbin does have a wonderful program for designing your own swaged bullet, which I hope to report on in the very near future. (Corbin Software, P.O. Box 2171, White City, OR 97503.)

Load From a Disk I & II

This is a series of programs written by W.W. Blackwell of Houston, Texas. Version 7.0 of LFD I offers a "full plate" of features that calculate powder type, charge weight, velocity, pressure, bullet drop, bullet energy, point-blank range, trajectory, recoil, uphill and downhill corrections, and more. I was fascinated with the internal ballistics and worked up quite a number of loads for future use. Although I didn't have the opportunity to test actual results, I did "back fill" some data from several of my favorite loads and found the information very close to my findings.

LFD II contains programs for determining optimum rifling twist, bullet velocity from trajectory, BC from velocity or trajectory, BC from shape, and BC correction. A third Ballistic Coefficient disk provides an incredibly complete list of BCs for most of the major ammunition and bullet manufacturers in the U.S. The LFD programs are user friendly and offer a full range of information for the shooter. Handloaders will definitely appreciate the internal ballistics.

Documentation is provided in the form of a print-out encased in a slip cover and is well written and easy to follow. Although LFD does not offer graphics, it is a complete, well-done, easy-to-use program. LFD I sells for $49.95, LFD II for $25, and the Ballistic Coefficient Disk is $20; or you can get all three for $74.95. (W.W. Blackwell Software, 9826 Sagedale, Houston, TX 77089.)

PC Bullet

From ADC, Inc. of Columbia, Oregon, this program was discovered after I was well into this project. I have not been able to give it equal time, but it does show great promise. It appears to be designed with the reloader in mind, as it has the capability for storing extensive data on each cartridge or load and maintaining that information for future use. The BC data stored in this program is very extensive and easily accessible. Actual shooting conditions can be entered so you can get a true picture of your firearm's performance and, through statistical calculations which are far beyond me, this program will estimate the group size you could expect under perfect conditions at any range.

In addition to storing all the data plugged into *PC Bullet,* it also provides a hard copy on your printer. Graphics are included and give a side view as well as a top view of the bullet's path so the effects of wind can be seen in "living color." Documentation is supplied in a three-ring binder and is well written and easy to follow. I plan to give this program a true workout this winter. (PC Bullet, ADC, Inc., P.O. Box 8, Columbia City, OR 97018.)

Sierra Bullets Exterior Ballistics Program

A straightforward, easy-to-use program, it is based on a mainframe program written by ballisticians W.T. McDonald and T.C. Almgren which was used to calculate the data for the Sierra and Lyman reloading manuals. Version 2.0 comes with graphic capability as well as other improvements, the best of which is the price reduction. It is listed in the 12th edition of *Handloader's Digest* (DBI Books, Inc.) for $199.00 and now carries a much lighter tag of $49.95! That can be further reduced to $39.95 with $5 coupons found in each of the Sierra reloading manuals.

There are three modes of operation in this program: Mode 1 calculates point-blank range; Mode 2 completes the calculation for trajectory; and Mode 3 allows changes in shooting conditions such as altitude, muzzle velocity, wind and angle shooting. Graphics can be viewed on the screen or a hard copy can printed out. This program also contains a library of BCs for Hornady, Speer, Nosler and Sierra bullets. These libraries of BCs are a nice feature because this information is sometimes well hidden in reloading manuals. All in all, this is a fine program with good documentation bound in a three-ring binder. (Sierra Bullets, 1400 W. Henry St., Sedalia, MO 65301.)

J.I.T. Ltd.

I have saved this one for last because it is more than software—it is a small but powerful computer with the software already loaded in. The computer is a Sharp EL 5500III hand-held unit measuring 6.7 inches wide by .375-inch high by 2.9 inches deep and fits nicely in my shirt pocket for trips to the range. Don't let the size fool you as this little puppy is a real powerhouse containing programs for both interior and exterior ballistics!

There are actually two exterior programs, one for field use which calculates time of flight, remaining velocity, drop, remaining energy, wind drift and minute of angle corrections; the other does all of the above but stores pertinent reloading data for future access. There is also a trajectory program which calculates bullet path through 300, 600 or 1000 yards. The interior program does calculations for charge weight, powder type, muzzle velocity and chamber pressure for any cartridge. When not used as a ballistic

PACT PROFESSIONAL CHRONOGRAPH

What's a chronograph doing in an article about computer ballistics? Well, a better question might be, what's a chronograph doing in a ballistic computer? The answer is, quite simply, PACT has come up with a whole new concept for making your range sessions useful, informative and fun. It's kind of a "one-stop shopping center" for those of us who want to know how well our firearms perform.

The new PACT Professional Chronograph has a ballistic computer built right in to give you instant information without ever leaving the range. After shooting a string of shots (or any time during the string, for that matter) over the PACT MK5 Professional Skyscreens, you simply push the review button to analyze your load performance. The first read out, or print out if you choose to print it, is the highest velocity and the lowest velocity with an indication of the shot number in which they occurred. Next comes standard deviation (SD) along with a CV (Coefficient of Variation) percentage, which is, in this case, standard deviation as a percent of your average velocity. Following SD is MAD (Mean Absolute Deviation), which is the average variation of your velocities. CV shows up again and this time it is MAD as a percent to velocity. CV should be used in comparing one load to another, and the smaller the number the better. I won't go into the mechanics of all this due to limited space and the fact that it makes my head hurt. The fourth information readout is average velocity and ES (Extreme Spread) with all of this followed by individual shot velocity.

Armed with this information, you simply enter into the ballistic-computer mode to calculate the trajectory. You can choose to calculate maximum point-blank range or you can go to Specific Range, which will help you if your range is 100 yards but your actual targets will be in excess of that. This mode will give the exact setting at 100 yards so that you can make that long-range hit. I used the MAX PB mode to set up my 22-250 for an upcoming prairie dog hunt and had it zeroed exactly where I wanted it in less than 15 minutes.

Being one who has a tendency to take things to the limits (and sometimes beyond), I pulled out my new Ruger M77 Magnum MKII chambered for 416 Rigby and headed for the range. Probably as a test of the Skyscreens more than anything, I set them up only 8 feet from the muzzle, knowing full well that the Rigby has a muzzleblast that can blow the door off of a bank vault! I am happy to report both the PACT and the Ruger are doing well.

I have to admit that the PACT is not only fun but very useful, and it now sits on my desk running full time. When I need information about ballistics, I no longer have to exit my word processing program—I simply reach for the PACT. To give full details of the PACT Professional Chronograph would take a full article on itself. I suggested you contact PACT at 1-800-722-8462. Price, as of this writing, is $369.95 including Skyscreens.

The new PACT Professional Chronograph will calculate kinetic energy, IPSC Power Factor, the Taylor "Knock Out" Factor, and other useful data, in addition to performing the usual chronograph functions.

PACT
Professional Chronograph
BC: .300 VEL: 2500.0
SIGHT HEIGHT: 1.5
VITAL ZONE: 6.0
MAX P.B. RANGE: 245
MAX P.B. ZERO: 209
2.9 @ 100 YARDS

DIST	PATH	VEL
50	+1.5	2387.4
100	+2.9	2277.7
150	+2.7	2170.7
200	+0.6	2066.3
250	-3.5	1965.1
300	-9.9	1867.2
350	-18.8	1772.4
400	-30.4	1681.1
450	-45.0	1593.5
500	-63.1	1510.7

computer, the Sharp can be used as a scientific/statistical calculator. The supplied manuals also include a business and financial section.

The J.I.T. has accompanied me to the range several times since I received it, and the unit is now part of my standard range gear. Though it hasn't completely replaced my portable NEC 286, it's a damned sight easier to carry around and therefore will see considerable more use in the outdoors. I can even see taking it on hunting trips! Documentation is supplied in the form of stapled sheets, but is complete and easy to follow, and examples of each program's output are supplied. All of this sells for $140 and, for an additional $170, you can get a printer for the Sharp to keep your hard copies on file. This little gem may be just the ticket for those who do not yet have a computer or are looking for increased portability. (J.I.T. Ltd., P.O. Box 749, Glenview, IL 60025.)

OK, for those who skipped to the end to find out which one I like best, you are flat out of luck. Truth is, I like 'em all. I do, however, feel compelled to say at this point that no one program does it all, and in fairness to those who write these programs I doubt there will be such a program in the near future. To write such a program would take more memory than most home computers have and sales would be slim. Each programmer does his best to provide the best overall package he feels the shooting public will need. I'm here to say they do an admirable job of it.

I could probably live with just one or two of these programs, but I still won't say which ones because it all boils down to individual needs, wants and opinions. That would be like me telling you what make of vehicle you should drive, or what breed of hunting dog you need or should be hunting over. I had a lot of fun doing the research for this article and as a result have expanded my knowledge about shooting. I suggest you make a list of your requirements, as well as your wants and budget limitations, and contact each supplier for further information.

This may sound like a strong statement, but anyone who is really serious about shooting and/or hunting should put a computer ballistics program at the top of their "must have" list. If you are among the lucky ones who already have a computer, the price of a program (even the more expensive ones) is a small price to pay for the vast amount of knowledge they provide. Those armed with such information will most certainly help stack the odds in their favor, and that alone is something no computer can calculate.

One note of caution here—once you get started on ballistics programs you're going to get hooked and may find yourself spending more free time at your computer actually learning something as well as having fun. My computer games are collecting a lot of dust now! ●

Ruger Mark II Standard Model, 6-inch barrel, stainless steel.

Ruger Mark II Standard Model, 4-inch barrel, blue finish.

Ruger's Wonderful Standard Autos

In production since 1949, this little pistol keeps on ticking. For plinking or hunting here's a gun that's hard to beat.

by BRAD TOWNSEND

STURM, RUGER & COMPANY, Inc. introduced their first firearm, the 22-caliber autoloading pistol, in 1949. At an unusally low price of $37.50, even for that post-war year, it was an instant success. One reason for its continued popularity over the past 43 years is due to its rugged dependability. Simply stated, it shoots and goes on shooting. Its unique yet simple design is foolproof, as exemplified by the low numbers ever returned to the factory for service.

The original Standard Auto came with a 4¾- or 6-inch barrel and had a rear sight that was adjustable for windage by moving it in its dovetail. The standard magazine had a nine-round capacity. Its German Luger styling, no doubt, helped generate its great popularity.

The Ruger Standard Auto was followed by the Mark I, which was just a refined and more highly machined version of the original. It became a popular target pistol and won many matches for a lot of competitors. It had adjustable target sights and two barrel lengths: 5½-inch bull barrel and 6⅞-inch tapered.

The current production Ruger pistol is designated the Mark II but is not really much different from the original version. The latest model has a bolt-stop mechanism that the earlier models were without, allowing the bolt to remain open after the last shot is fired. In addition, there are shallow scallops cut into the sides of the rear of the receiver, facilitating a better grip on the cocking "ears" of the bolt.

All Mark II models have 10-shot magazines, function with standard and high-velocity 22 Long Rifle ammunition and are available in blued finish and brushed satin stainless steel. Other than the updating noted

These were typical, though not best, groups fired with the three Rugers at 25 yards. The scope on the long-barreled version no doubt helped to shrink the group on top.

above, the standard model is virtually identical to the original with fixed sights and 4¾- and 6-inch barrels and is available in either blue or stainless. The Target Model has a 6⅞-inch button-rifled barrel, adjustable sights and comes in blue or stainless also.

The Bull Barrel model is available in 5½- and 10-inch barrel lengths, has adjustable sights and is finished in blue or stainless, like the other models. The only other Ruger autoloader in the line-up is called the Government Target Model. It is so labeled because of Ruger's contract with the U.S. government to supply this particular version to the Army for handgun training. This pistol is basically the Bull Barrel Model with 6⅞-inch barrel.

Over the past 30 years I have owned, shot or hunted with virtually every type of Ruger firearm made. They have been extremely dependable, often surprisingly accurate and certainly attractive to look at. Of the many firearms in my collection, one of my favorites is an early model Single-Six with flat, non-contoured loading gate. I bought this revolver in 1960 at a local pawn shop for $30, which represented a month's rent at the time for this college student. This handgun has accompanied me on many trail rides, cattle drives, backpacking trips and other outdoor adventures and has always given me a great deal of satisfaction.

For the story at hand, Linda DeProfio, Advertising Production Manager at Ruger, helped me assemble a representative sample of the currently available autoloader models. The 6-inch stainless Standard Model was my choice in the fixed-sight version. Since the Target Model is available in only one barrel length, my only choice was in finish and I opted for the stainless steel.

Finally, regarding the Bull Barrel model, I had a specific objective in mind. One of my favorite off-season activities is hunting western rockchucks and I wanted an accurate pistol/scope combination to try. With this in mind, I selected the 10-inch barrel, again in stainless persuasion. The Burris 2x LER Silver Safari scope was added, using a Burris no-drill no-tap mount. This mount is unique. It has a barrel band that attaches just in front of the receiver and is attached at the rear through the rear sight elevation adjustment screw. Another interesting feature of this design is a vertically mounted stud just in front of the base of the forward ring. I call it a recoil stud, since its purpose is to prevent any scope movement from the continued battering of recoil. For a 22 rimfire, it is probably not so important as for a hard-kicking centerfire pistol or revolver, but there can be some movement. The mount is available in Burris' Safari finish as well as blued.

After assembling a variety of rimfire ammunition, several trips to the pistol range were required to test performance of both the ammo and the handguns. I was also curious to determine the difference in velocity among brands and with different barrel lengths.

As expected, velocities through the 10-inch barrel were considerably higher than with the shorter barrels. The CCI Mini Mag, for example, had a velocity of 1157 fps through the 10-inch barrel. That was 70 fps faster than what the 6⅞-inch barrel generated and 82 fps more than the 6-inch version. The greatest spread in velocity between the shortest and longest barrel length was fired with Winchester Super-X ammunition. The shortest barrel produced 1002 fps while the longest showed 1115 fps for a spread of 113 fps.

At the other extreme is the CCI Pistol Match ammunition. The spread between the extreme barrel lengths is only 8 fps. Of the seven different types of ammunition tested, this one had the lowest average velocity and was the only one designated as pistol ammo. No doubt, the powder type and charge was designed for maximum performance out of a relatively short barrel. The gases generated by the burning powder had pretty much expanded to their maximum within the confines of a 6-inch tube, whereas the gases from the other ammunition were continuing to expand, even after passing through the 10-inch barrel. Since they were designed for rifle-length barrels, it makes sense that the longer pistol barrel would generate more velocity.

As shown in the accompanying table, the CCI Pistol Match ammunition had the lowest average velocity, followed by the CCI Green Tag and the Winchester Super-X. The latter two were about 50 fps faster than the Pistol Match. All three of these bullets weighed within 1½ grains of an even 40 grains. Although the hollowpoint

Ruger Mark II Bull Barrel, 5½-inch barrel, blue finish.

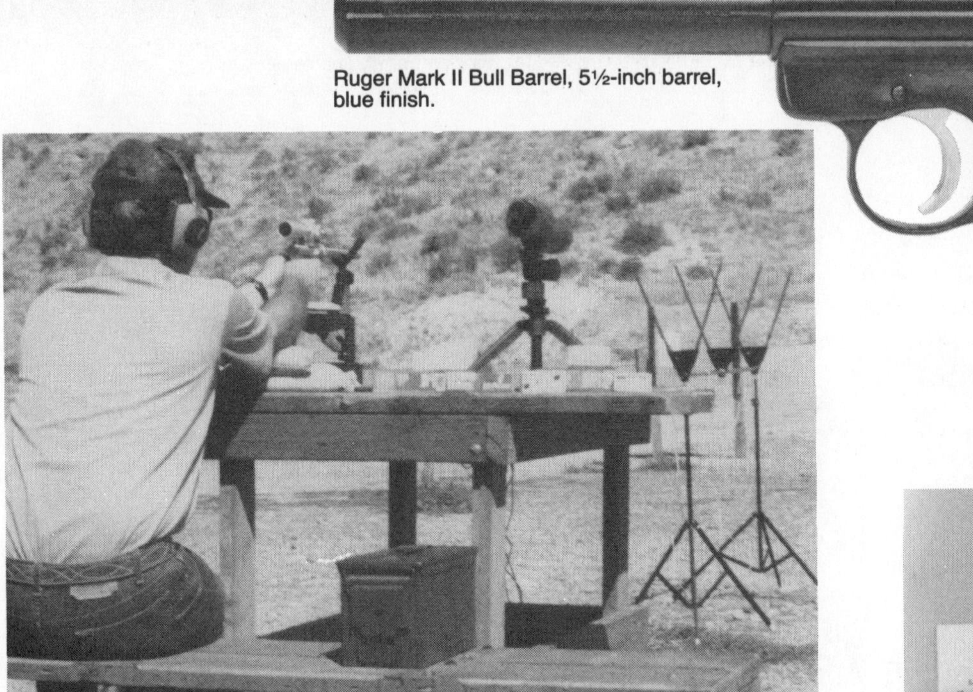

All groups for author's tests were fired from a bench using the Outers Pistol Perch and were chronographed with an Oehler Model 35P with its three Skyscreens.

bullets were lighter than the solids, the Stinger at 30.7 grains was significantly lighter than the others. The Federal Hi-Power, for example, weighs 38 grains and the Mini-Mag is 36.3 grains. The lightweight bullet of the Stinger translates to an impressive velocity of 1402 fps when averaged for the three Ruger pistols.

The accuracy of all three pistols varied with the ammunition used but, overall, was very impressive. The Bull Barrel model with 10-inch barrel produced the tightest groups, as would be expected. Just how tight, however, was quite a pleasant surprise. The best 10-shot group was an impressive .47-inch and was shot with CCI Pistol Match ammunition at 25 yards. The nearby table shows velocities and average group sizes for two 10-shot groups each. Measurements for the best eight out of 10 shots for the average of two groups each is also listed.

The CCI Green Tag Competition was the outstanding performer with the average of two 10-shot groups coming in at .73-inch through the 10-inch gun. In this same pistol, the Winchester Super-X Hollow Point came in second with an average spread for two 10-shot groups at only .78-inch.

The Standard Model and the Target Model, with their open sights and shorter barrels, did not perform quite as well, naturally. Still, most of the groups shot with these two handguns were quite satisfactory for out-of-the-box samples. Based on the human variable involved, I think the groups for the best eight shots out of the string of 10 more closely reflect the true capabilities of these firearms. The likelihood that I caused a couple of flyers in each 10-shot group is fairly high.

The Standard and Bull Barrel models both liked the Winchester Super-X Hollow Point ammo as indicated with groups of under 1-inch. The Target Model performed best with the CCI Pistol Match cartridges, but the Mini-Mags, Blazers and Stingers were not far behind. Remember, though, each firearm is a law unto itself and other samples of these same pistols will probably produce different results.

One variable related to any pistol that contributes significantly to accuracy is the trigger pull. A target pistol generally has a relatively light trigger pull with no creep or backlash. The trigger pulls on my Target and Bull Barrel models were both within ½-ounce of an even 4 pounds. My Standard Model broke at 3 pounds 9½ ounces. All three trigger pulls broke cleanly without any perceptible creep. I like the trigger on a pistol to break like an icicle and all three of these were close to it.

The only criticism I have of the Ruger 22 autoloaders relates to the design of the magazine release. I am used to the thumb release button just be-

The Mark II with 10-inch barrel and Burris scope shot well with a variety of ammunition. The best 10-shot group fired measured .73-inch, center-to-center, at 25 yards.

hind the trigger on most centerfire autoloaders. The release on the Ruger seems awkward, partly due to the requirement of using both hands to release it. I realize that design requirements probably prevent my preferred design.

Returning to the data in the table, the 10-inch-barreled Mark II shoots the Stingers at an impressive 1467 fps. At that velocity, and with its hollow-point bullet, quick and humane kills on small varmints are the rule rather than the exception, if the hunter does his part in proper bullet placement.

Since I am hopelessly addicted to varmint hunting, I was anxious to try the CCI Stingers with the longer barreled Ruger and Burris scope on rock-

Ruger Mark II Bull Barrel Model, 10-inch barrel, stainless steel.

Though the 22 rimfire isn't the ideal rockchuck caliber, the author used it with good results on a high-mountain hunt. Even with hollowpoint Stingers shot placement was critical for quick and humane kills.

The Safari finish on the Burris scope and no-drill no-tap mount closely matches the stainless Ruger. The combination makes a nice hunting package.

chucks. In my adopted home state of Utah, the high alpine meadows of most of the mountain ranges are home to concentrated populations of rockchucks. With a certain amount of stalking, which is great practice, by the way, for big game hunting, ranges can be reduced to under 75 yards. With 10-shot groups from a rest at 25 yards averaging about 1½ inches, with any luck at all I planned on reducing the chuck population with this shooter.

My young hunting companion, Nate Bell, was carrying a custom 22-250 rifle with 6-24x Burris scope. I would carry the Ruger 10-inch Bull Barrel gun with 2x scope. We were ready for any shots out to 400 yards or more but with anything under 75 yards reserved for the pistol.

After setting up the spotting scope at the edge of a mountain meadow, we were anticipating plenty of action. It didn't take long. About 300 yards out we watched a big chuck feeding in the grass about 50 feet from a rock outcrop that, no doubt, hid his lair. A small patch of brush just slightly to our right and fairly close to the varmint would provide cover for a stalk. Since chucks have not only good eyesight, but well developed senses of smell and hearing, the successful hunter uses the same caution as in hunting whitetails.

With a slight breeze quartering toward us from the right, we left the spotting scope and daypacks and on hands and knees worked our way to the cover. Ever so slowly I peered around the edge of the brush, keeping as low as possible. The grass was just high enough that the chuck was still out of sight. I quietly raised to a sitting position so my knees could help support the pistol for a steady shot. Just as I spotted him, he spooked and quickly hightailed it for the rockpile.

He made one fatal mistake. When he reached the rocks, he hesitated at the edge of his burrow for one last look at the source of the disturbance. The crosshairs steadied on his shoulder and the crack of the Stinger shattered the mountain silence. He probably never heard the shot, since the little Stinger bullet zips along at well above the speed of sound.

We paced the distance at 47 yards. The hollowpoint bullet had hit broadside, low on the shoulder, breaking the bone and going into the chest cavity, low enough to pulverize the heart. No exit hole was apparent, indicating that there probably was some expansion of the bullet as it plowed through shoulder bone, a rib and the organs beyond. The quickness of the kill was a testament to the effectiveness of the little fast-moving Stinger bullet.

The results were not quite as good on a 35-yard offhand shot. The chuck, was flattened on a rock down a steep hillside from me. Because of the angle and terrain, I could not get to a rest. At the shot, the chuck rolled off the rock and started scrambling up and over another. My second shot at the moving critter missed, but the third connected and stopped him in his tracks. Upon closer inspection, we determined that the first bullet hit him in about the middle of the back but just to one side of the spinal column. The bullet had gone all the way through and had flattened on the rock.

The third shot caught him well back in the flank and ranged forward into

Ruger Mark II Government Target Model, 6⅞-inch barrel. It's marked "Government Target Model" just below the rear sight.

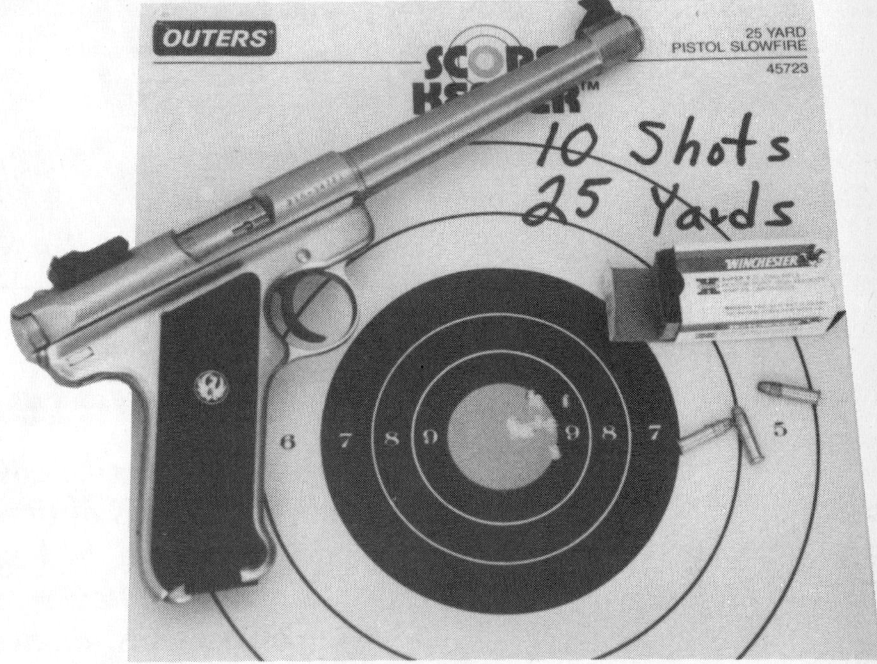

The 6⅞-inch Target Model was very accurate with Winchester Super-X ammo. Best eight out of 10 shots measured an impressive 1.43 inches.

the chest cavity. The third and final chuck taken with the Ruger that day was hit once in the head at about 50 feet. The bullet exited the opposite side, and from the looks of things, the chuck was dead before his head hit the ground.

As a result of that hunt, I have drawn the conclusion, admittedly with limited data, that the 22 rimfire is not even close to the ideal rockchuck caliber. Shot placement was extremely critical with heart and brain shots required for instant kills, even with the fast-moving Stingers. Shooting ranges must be extremely limited to insure near pinpoint accuracy in placing each shot.

Rockchucks have a great tenacity for life and, therefore, require high velocity expanding bullets capable of transmitting a significant amount of shock relative to the body weight of these animals. The 22 Long Rifle just doesn't have it. Close shots on prairie dogs and jackrabbits are a little more predictable but, again, shot placement can still be critical.

What I really learned from this expedition was that the Ruger 10-inch Bull Barrel model topped with the Burris 2x scope is an extremely accurate package. Used within the limitations of the cartridge, this combination is hard to beat. The Standard and Target models are also attractive and accurate examples of what is available today in quality rimfire autoloaders. The stainless steel versions, as my samples were, are nearly maintenance free but even stainless needs cleaning occasionally. Regardless of whether you prefer the traditional blue or the newer stainless, any of the Ruger Mark II models will be top rimfire performers. ●

Ruger Autoloaders

	Standard Model 6″ Barrel 25-yd. Groups			Target Model 6 ⅞″ Barrel 25-yd. Groups			Bull Barrel Model 10″ Barrel 25-yd. Groups		
	Velocity	8/10	10/10	Velocity	8/10	10/10	Velocity	8/10	10/10
CCI Green Tag Competition	1023	1.02	1.47	1044	1.13	1.74	1063	0.53	0.73
CCI Mini-Mag Hollow Point	1075	1.00	2.06	1087	1.20	1.42	1157	0.80	1.30
Federal Hi-Power Hollow Point	1105	1.60	2.23	1150	1.06	1.86	1203	0.93	1.41
CCI Blazer	1126	1.38	1.49	1142	1.10	1.82	1181	0.54	0.97
CCI Pistol Match	990	1.51	1.74	991	0.99	1.45	998	0.57	0.88
CCI Stinger Hollow Point	1367	1.43	2.11	1374	1.48	1.99	1467	1.11	1.55
Winchester Super-X Hollow Point	1002	0.59	0.92	1017	1.43	2.12	1115	0.67	0.78

Velocities were measured 10 feet from the muzzle with an Oehler 35P chronograph.
Groups were fired from a bench using the Outers Pistol Perch.
Two 10-shot groups were fired with each pistol and each ammunition type.
The best eight out of 10 shots as well as each total group were measured and averaged.

by MICHAEL THOMAS

THE 219 ZIPPER

Overlooked, not Obsolete!

Because it was originally chambered in a lever-action rifle, this nifty round was practically doomed from the beginning. In a bolt action or single shot, however, the Zipper can hold its own against modern cartridges.

MOST KNOWLEDGEABLE shooters who have been around for a while are familiar with the fateful demise of the 219 Zipper cartridge. There is little point in a detailed rehashing of the reams of material that have been published during the last 50 years about the Zipper.

For the benefit of the uninformed, let it suffice to make a brief statement as to why the cartridge never gained broad appeal and acceptance by the shooting fraternity. A 1937 Winchester development, the 219 Zipper was chambered in the Model 64 Winchester lever-action rifle. With few changes, this rifle was basically a Model 94. The 219 round, with proper spitzer bullets, was fully a 300-yard varmint cartridge. However, the rifle was sorely lacking as a long-range arm for but one reason—its tubular magazine precluded the use of any bullets except those with a relatively flat or blunt nose. Also, tiny targets at extreme ranges require scope sights, and the 64, with its top ejection design,

A classic "full house" Winchester Hi-Wall varminter in 219 Zipper. Scope is a 10x Unertl, the barrel a Douglas Premium chambered and fitted by Ray Montgomery of Grand Junction, Colorado.

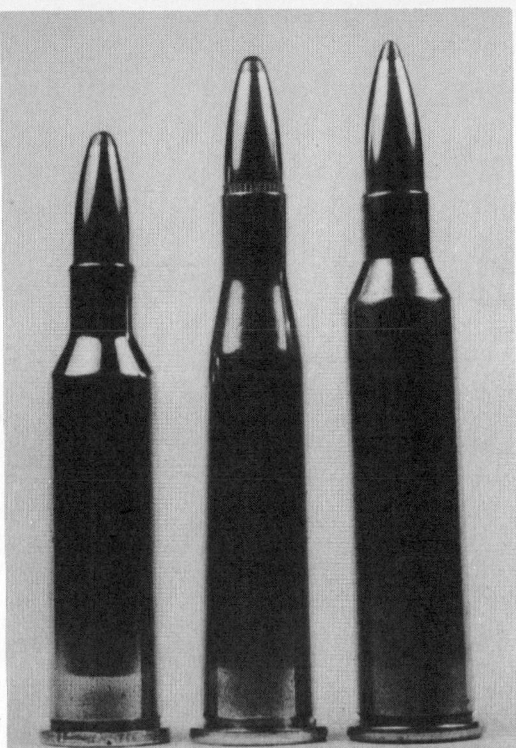

For purposes of comparison, the 219 Zipper is flanked by a pair of 219 Zipper-based wildcats: Left is the 219 Donaldson Wasp, right the 219 Ackley Improved Zipper.

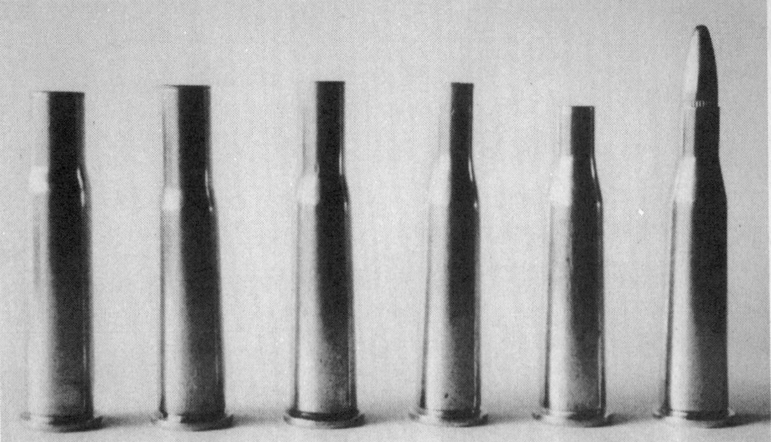

Case forming steps for the 219 Zipper, from left: unaltered 30-30 case; shoulder pushed back with form die number one; neck reduced to about 25-caliber with form die number two; case has been run through the trim die and the neck filed down; case with neck chamfered and sized in 219 full-length sizer; loaded 219 Zipper round.

Zipper dies are not normally found on dealer shelves, but they aren't difficult to obtain from the major die makers. Two excellent 55-grain bullets for the Zipper are (from left) the Winchester "bulk" softpoint and Speer softpoint.

was not the easiest rifle on which to mount a scope. Many years later, Marlin chambered its lever gun for the Zipper. This rifle/cartridge combination set no sales records for Marlin either, but the side-ejection feature did allow for top mounting of a telescopic sight.

As a result of the rifles, the 219 Zipper gained the reputation of being an inaccurate cartridge. It is not my intention to broadly condemn lever-action rifles by saying they are incapable of fine accuracy, but the bolt-action or single shot designs usually have a definite accuracy edge over lever actions for precision long-range shooting.

Winchester ceased production of the Model 64 in 1957 and Marlin followed suit in 1961. No 219 Zipper ammunition has been commercially produced since 1964.

Let us now depart from the lever-action guns and put the Zipper in proper perspective by first looking at the cartridge itself. The case is basically the same as that used for the 22 Savage Hi-Power, 25-35 WCF, 30-30, etc. Chamber pressures for all these rounds are in the 40,000 psi bracket or slightly less, due to the design limits of various rifles in which these cartridges were originally chambered.

From its inception, the 219 Zipper has always required the use of standard .224-inch diameter bullets despite its official Winchester moniker. Compared to more modern 22-caliber centerfires loaded to much higher pressures, the 219 still holds its own. The 1952 edition of *Gun Digest* lists the following ballistics for Winchester (56-grain hollowpoint) and Remington (56-grain softpoint) factory ammunition:

Velocity (fps)		Energy (ft. lbs.)	
Muzzle	3110	Muzzle	1200
100 yds.	2440	100 yds.	740
200 yds.	1940	200 yds.	465
300 yds.	1550	300 yds.	300

Mid-range trajectories at the various ranges are listed respectively as .6, 2.9, and 8.3 inches. Admittedly, the tables are not impressive, but then neither bullet was of a pointed configuration. At one time, a 46-grain bullet was offered by the manufacturers with a reported muzzle velocity of 3390 fps.

Things really improve with judicious (not hot) handloads utilizing spitzer projectiles. To further illustrate the point, the 219 will ballistically beat the 223 Remington on all counts, this still without maximum loads. With stiff yet safe loads in a strong action, the Zipper treads closely on the heels of the 22-250 Remington at 3400 to 3500 fps with 55-grain bullets. That's nothing to sneeze at in terms of performance.

In all fairness, however, case stretching often becomes a problem with these hot-rod loads due to the long and steep taper of the 219's case. Trimming cases after every firing or two is a nuisance most handloaders don't wish to contend with.

After working with the Zipper in a number of rifles, I have found that loading 55-grain bullets to muzzle velocities of 2900 to 3100 fps provides the following advantages: apparent moderate chamber pressures, long case life, greatly decreased bore erosion, and an extreme degree of accu-

While working up loads for his various 219 Zipper rifles, the author has found IMR-4320 to be the single best powder for the cartridge. It works consistently well in a number of guns.

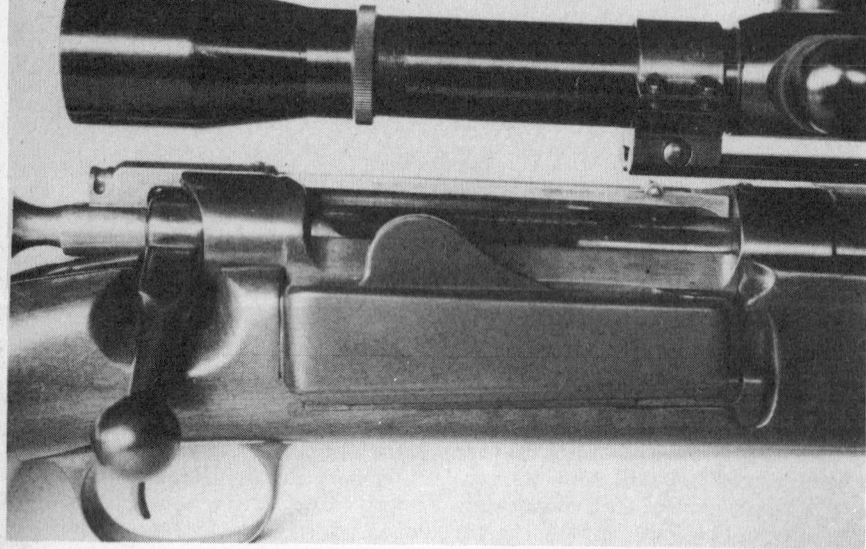

Many 219 Zipper rifles were built-up decades ago using the old 30-40 Krag military action. Though an excellent design, the Krag lacks the strength of many modern bolt actions and maximum loads should be avoided with it. Thomas finds this rig to be just fine for small Texas deer.

racy. In other words, the 219 Zipper is a very practical cartridge.

I have developed many loads for a number of centerfire 22s over the years. Various rifles have been chambered for such oddities as the 22 Long Snapper and the Ackley Improved 22/30-30. Of course, there have been some more conventional cartridges like the 223 Remington and the 22-250 Remington as well. I have never really had a clear understanding of the ambiguous term "inherent accuracy," but if there is such a thing, the Zipper definitely possesses this desirable trait. In short, I find the Zipper to be *the* most accurate 22 centerfire chambering I have had the pleasure to work with thus far.

The standard barrel twist rate for the 219 Zipper is 1:14 (one turn in 14 inches), the same twist used for most of the medium- or large-case 22s. Such a versatile twist rate will provide fine performance with a large percentage of 22 bullets ranging in weight from 45 to 55 grains. I'll qualify that last remark in the interest of practicality. The 45-grain bullets can be pushed to some rather lofty velocities in the Zipper case. Ditto for the 50-grain slugs. However, these lighter bullets don't have the better ballistic coefficients common to those of 55 grains.

Anyone who has done much long-range shooting with a 22 centerfire on a windy day can tell us all about wind drift. At 200 or 300 yards, even the 55-grain bullets are very wind sensitive, although an experienced shooter who can effectively "dope" the wind will often times be able to connect with his target. Not so with the lighter bullets. The estimation factor is just too great. Light bullets lose velocity quite rapidly and, generally speaking, are at least slightly inferior, accuracy-wise, at distances beyond 100 yards.

Some may disagree with my recommendations for bullet selection, but I stand firm on this subject as I prefer to work with that which performs best for me. As a further note, I add that some rifles will handle the heavier bullets of 60 to 70 grains in weight. However, many 1:14 twist barrels will only marginally stabilize these heavyweights. Velocities will be way down as well.

Original 219 Zipper brass or factory-loaded ammunition command collectors' prices these days. Case forming is no problem, though, with the use of

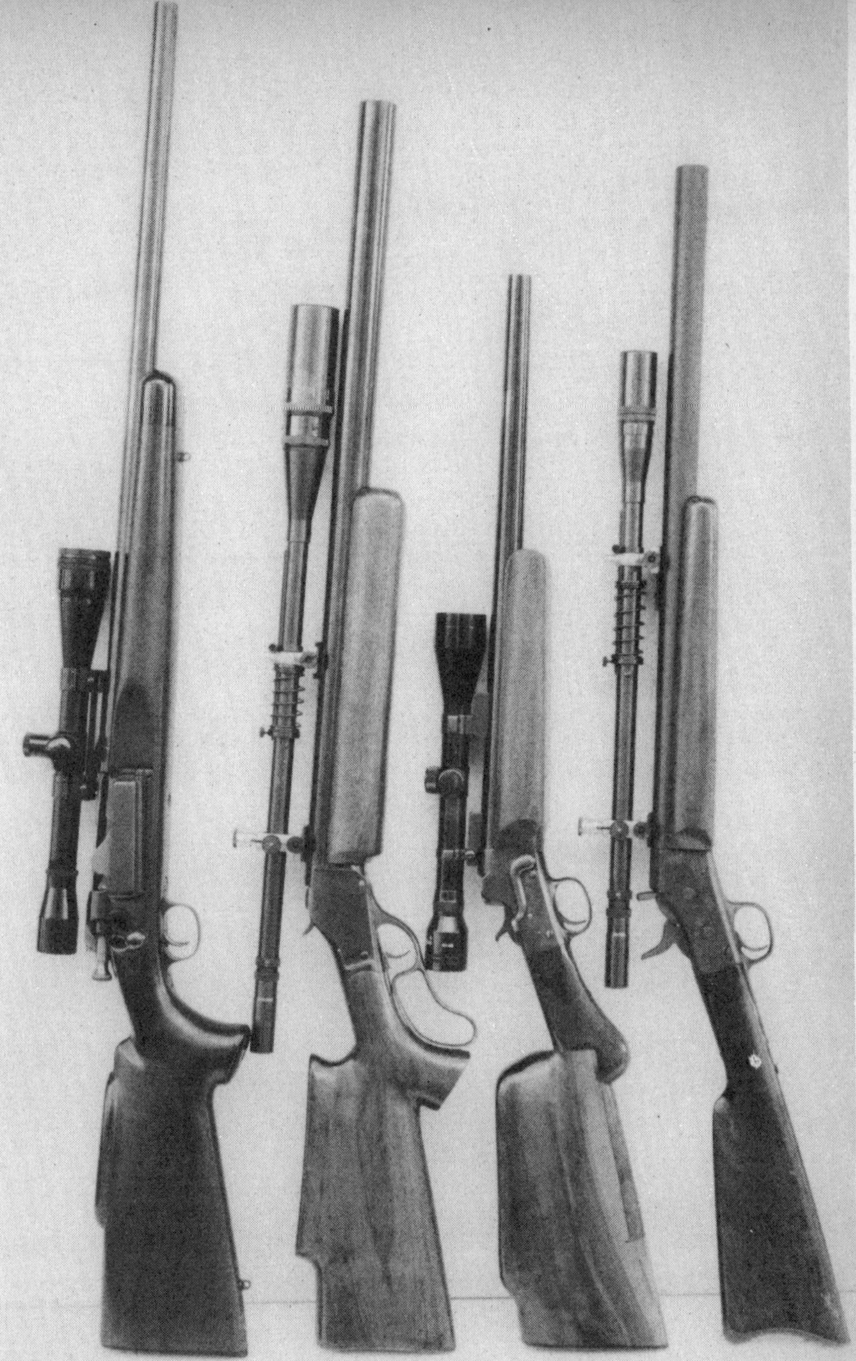

Four of the author's 219 Zipper rifles, from the left: Krag-actioned varminter with 6x Lyman scope, bull-barreled Winchester Hi-Wall with 12x Unertl, Remington-Hepburn with 6x Tasco scope, and a heavy-barreled Remington rolling block with 10x Unertl.

plentiful and inexpensive 30-30 brass. Several of the loading die outfits still produce 219 dies. Case-forming dies are also available and necessary. I ordered a three-die forming set from RCBS and experienced only a short wait before receiving it. The case-forming procedure is not particularly laborious and 100 30-30 hulls can be transformed into Zipper brass in about 2 hours. I see no point in detailing each step in the forming process as excellent instructions are provided by the respective die makers. Carefully used, 100 cases would probably provide a sufficient number of loadings to wear out one barrel.

Depending on the brass used for forming, case necks will likely require outside turning. The maximum neck diameter of a loaded cartridge should never exceed .252-inch, according to industry standards. With all the custom chambers that have been cut over the years, however, this figure may vary somewhat. It's wise to check an individual chamber. I turn my brass so that a loaded round has a clearance of about .003- to .004-inch.

I have gone the usual route in my load development, trying a number of different components along the way. I have yet to find a Zipper rifle that did not have an affinity for IMR-4320 powder. To me, at least, that's somewhat of an irony as I have seldom had better than mediocre results with this powder in other cartridges. (It's a dandy in the 30-40 Krag and the 338-06, though!)

From a practical standpoint, IMR-3031 is the fastest burning powder that should be used in loading the Zipper. The even faster IMR-4198 (or H4198) is recommended in some loadings. In a pinch, these will work, but pressures can skyrocket quickly with its use and accuracy may be less than acceptable. I have done only limited work with Accurate Arms 2230 in the 219 Zipper and was disappointed with overall accuracy. IMR-4064 is a very close second to IMR-4320 from a total performance angle. Hodgdon's H-414 is the slowest powder I have used for Zipper loads. It was tried purely out of curiosity, knowing full well that it would be far from ideal in a case with this capacity. Accuracy was not only excellent, it was on a par with IMR-4320 (sub-MOA groups). All was not roses, however, since the heaviest loads would barely clock 2850 fps at the muzzle with 55-grain bullets—perhaps a trifle slow for all-round use. I have yet to experiment with H-380, the burning rate of which is just a bit faster than H-414. I feel safe in predicting, however, that H-380 would be an excellent propellant for the Zipper, provided that adequate velocity could be attained. H-380 is often the slowest powder recommended for this cartridge.

Only a few of the current loading manuals contain data for the old 219 Zipper. Both Sierra and Hornady books contain a number of loads as does the NRA's manual, *Handloading*. I have a few old loading handbooks that all contain Zipper data, but many of the loads appear to be excessive. Caution should be exercised by those who use such obsolete data for concocting loads. In defense of the old publications, I will say that most, if not all, of the loads were prepared using original Zipper brass, not cases formed from 30-30 hulls. I think it safe to assume that factory Zipper cases had slightly greater powder capacities than our present reformed ones, hence the heavier permissible loads without dangerous pressures.

There are probably many 55-grain

Another of Thomas' Zippers is this Winchester Hi-Wall with bull barrel and 12x Unertl scope. Obviously a heavy rig, it is extremely accurate and fun to shoot.

Formerly a 22 K-Hornet, this Winchester Hi-Wall has been rebarreled to 219 Zipper and wears a 10x Unertl scope. These scopes aren't terribly popular these days, but they have excellent optics. Thomas prefers them for varminting and informal target work, despite their bulk.

bullets that will shoot well in a Zipper-chambered rifle. I have used three types, and there is not an iota's worth of difference among them as far as accuracy goes. In fact, for my purposes, additional testing of bullets would be superfluous.

Whenever I start from scratch working up loads for any centerfire 22 cartridge (excepting those with a very small case like the Hornet), I begin with a bullet with a proven reputation for accuracy—the 55-grain Speer spitzer flat-base. As a general rule of thumb, I have found that a rifle that won't shoot this bullet well probably won't perform with other slugs either.

Lately, I have used a sizable quantity of the Winchester and Remington "bulk" 22-caliber bullets. These are virtually identical 55-grain jacketed softpoint spitzer bullets with a flat base. Random measurements of samples from each brand show them to be slightly undersize in diameter, miking about .2235-inch. Nevertheless, they are as accurate as the Speer bullet as long as velocities are held under 3300 fps. These bulk bullets are inexpensive and are normally sold in lots of 1000.

The 52-grain Sierra hollowpoint boattail match bullet is another highly accurate projectile when loaded in the Zipper hull. My testing, however, shows it to be no better than the other bullets discussed.

Loading data for all of these bullets are interchangeable. Though velocities and points of impact will not be identical, they are fairly close.

Bullet seating depth is less critical with the Zipper cartridge than with many others. I adjust my bullet seating die to give an overall cartridge length of 2.42 inches with the Speer bullet. I do not change the die adjustment when loading the Winchester, Remington or Sierra bullet. The maximum overall length listed in most handloading manuals is 2.26 inches; this length, no doubt, is for lever-action rifle use.

What's my favorite load? Twenty-seven grains of IMR-4320 behind any of those 55-grain bullets is my preference. Depending on the rifle I use, muzzle velocities will run from 2900 to about 3100 fps with the Speer bullet, or from 2875 to 3025 using Remington or Winchester bullets. Sighted 2 inches high at 100 yards, such loads are right on at 200 yards and about 9 inches low at 300. Not 220 Swift trajectory by any means, though this is still flat enough to be very useful.

My own Zipper rifles are all rather old and well used, but do they shoot! I suppose a brief description of each is in order at this point:

1. Winchester Hi-Wall, 26-inch Douglas bull barrel, 12x Unertl scope.

2. Winchester Hi-Wall, 24-inch

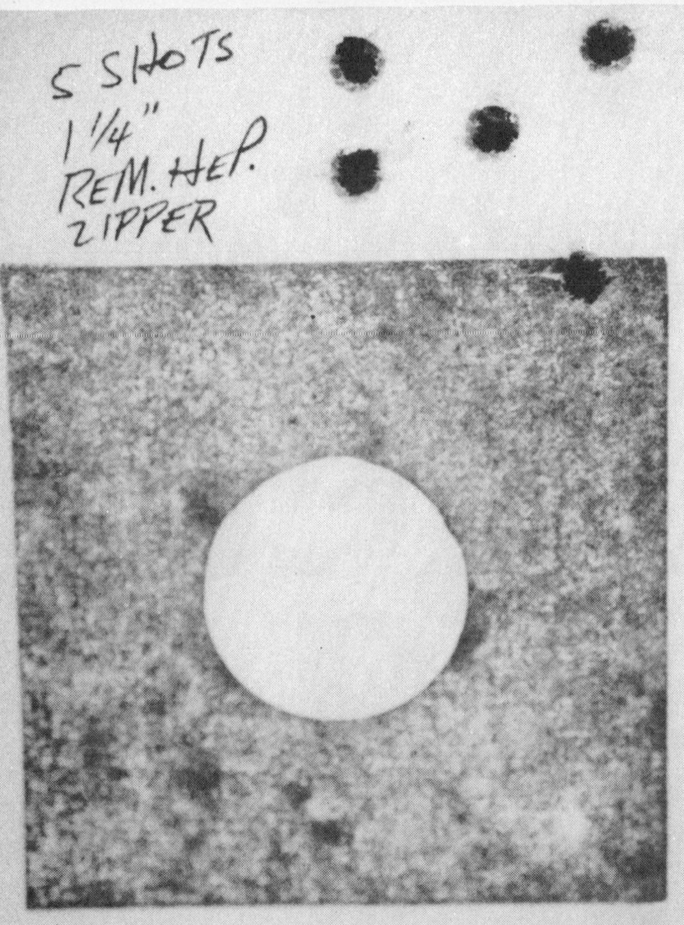

This five-shot group is fairly typical of those fired by the author using his bull-barreled Hi-Wall. Load data is discussed in the text and table nearby.

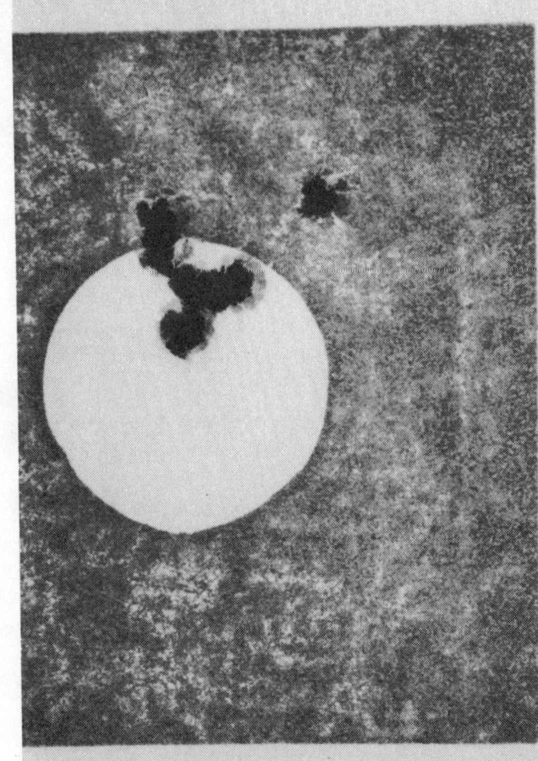

Not all gun writers shoot sub-M.O.A. groups every time! This 1¼-inch, 100-yard group was fired from author's Remington-Hepburn Zipper on a breezy day.

Douglas sporter-weight barrel, 10x Unertl scope.

3. Remington-Hepburn, 22-inch Douglas varmint-weight barrel, 6x Tasco scope.

4. Remington rolling block (#1 action), 25-inch Douglas bull barrel, 10x Unertl scope.

5. U.S. Krag action, 26-inch Douglas varmint-weight barrel, 6x Lyman All-American scope.

I certainly do not expect a lot of readers to run out and scour the used-gun market in search of 219 Zipper rifles, but there are a surprising number of them out there. Easiest to find are the old, converted single shots. Many Winchester Hi-Walls were rebarreled in the '40s and '50s to handle the Zipper cartridge. Slightly less popular for conversion work, but nevertheless fine, were the Remington rolling blocks, Remington-Hepburns and Sharps-Borchardts. Bolt-action enthusiasts may find Zipper-chambered Mausers, '03 Springfields and Krags.

The 219 Zipper is without question one of the finest of the 22 centerfire cartridges. For all-round varmint hunting, it leaves nothing to be desired. Most shooters who consider the 219 obsolete are the same ones who have had no experience with it. As for the versatility factor, the Zipper couples a high degree of accuracy with comparative "middle of the road" ballistic capabilities. And to be realistic, that's all we actually need for virtually 95 percent of our varmint hunting. ●

219 Zipper Data

Bullet	Powder/grs.	Loaded Length (in.)	Velocity (fps)	Comments
45 Hornady Hornet	IMR-4320/28	2.385	3190	Hi-Wall, mild load
52 Sierra BTHP Match	IMR-4320/27	2.42	3090	Hi-Wall, ½-M.O.A.
55 Speer Spitzer	IMR-4320/27	2.42	3080	Hi-Wall, ½-M.O.A.
55 Speer Spitzer	IMR-4320/27	2.42	2995	Krag, ¾-M.O.A.
55 Win. Spitzer	IMR-4320/27	2.42	3000	Hi-Wall, ½-M.O.A.
55 Win. Spitzer	H-414/31	2.42	2855	Hi-Wall, ¾-M.O.A.
55 Win. Spitzer	AAC 2230/25	2.42	2975	Hi-Wall, 1-M.O.A.
55 Rem. Spitzer	IMR-4320/27	2.42	2985	Hi-Wall, ¾-M.O.A.

All muzzle velocities rounded off to the nearest 5 fps. All group sizes rounded to the nearest ¼-inch. Ambient temperatures during testing varied between 55 and 80 degrees Fahrenheit. All test data compiled using CCI-200 Large Rifle primers in cases formed from once-fired Winchester 30-30 brass. A SpeedTach chronograph placed 10 feet from the muzzle was used to record velocity figures. All powder charges should be reduced 10 percent for starting loads. If any components are substituted for those listed in the table, or if the overall cartridge length is changed, powder charges should be further reduced.

A Tyro's Target Rifle

Ever the optimist and innovator, this shooter found the path to target-shooting stardom isn't easy—but it sure is fun!

by WALDO LYDECKER

IT WOULD BE GREAT if I could say it all came about on Pearl Harbor Day, 1980, when a group of fellows I knew enticed me down to the local sandpit to shoot my (self-defense) "house gun" in an informal match . . . and got me hooked on shooting a centerfire rifle.

But I can't. On that day I first hefted a serious long arm (an '03 Springfield, as I recall) and from a prone position over iron sights fired two rounds (the club was a bit short on ammunition that day) at a bullseye target 100 yards away. After a dozen of us had shot for record, we ambled up to the target stands to score our hits, and as the piece of paper with my initials on it was only one of two with a hole in it, I was declared Natural Springs Sportsman's Association fourth annual Military High Power match co-champion, along with the club's President . . . whose rifle we'd all been shooting.

To this day, I have more than a sneaking suspicion that the perforation in the seven ring of my target was someone else's errant shot, and that both my rounds are buried, along with my integrity, in the back wall of the sandpit far wide of the mark.

The fact of the matter is, that on that brisk December Sunday afternoon over a decade ago, I shot competitively for the very first time, and didn't miss another match for almost 10 years.

Mostly what I enjoyed then was shooting a handgun, and my arsenal grew from my father's old WWII Colt 1903 in 32 ACP and a 2-inch Colt Cobra, to a customized Colt Series 70 Gold Cup and a 6-inch S&W 686 with the sweetest action that never went to an NRA/Bianchi Cup match. As the club shot all disciplines, for my shotgun I selected the S&W Model 1000 in 12-gauge, while my rimfires were a pair of Rugers, a Mark II 5½-inch pistol and a 10/22 carbine with a Bushnell 2-7x scope. For the military action matches, I found a sweet stainless Mini-14 and shot that out to 100 yards on sundry silhouette targets.

So my precision centerfire rifle continued to be a loaner from whomever was at the high-power match and was kind enough to let me compete after they'd fired for record. A number of rifles passed through my grip . . . a Remington Mohawk in 308, a Winchester something or other in 30-06, and a Weatherby 224 Magnum . . . but I rarely ever shot the same rifle 2 years running as I invariably scored better with the gun than the owner, thereby causing certain unverbalized anxieties even in Natural Springs' relaxed and gregarious environment, and a resulting unavailability the next time out.

Later, I acquired a used Ruger 44 Magnum carbine upon which I mounted a 4x Tasco scope and some See-Thru rings, and attempted to compete with the little autoloader. Since the magnum rounds were not the most conducive to the necessary sight alignment and trigger control, I once even tried some round-nose Remington 44 Specials and cycled the action by hand.

After that experiment proved less than satisfactory (I noticed the ab-

Now, is this a rifle only a gun nut could love? As originally offered by Remington, the "no frills" stock is hardly a beauty. At its 1967 introduction, the gun sold for $84.95.

The very first day in the "back 40" produced this promising target with Federal's 40-grain loads at 100 yards. Lydecker still has this target stapled to his garage wall.

sence of my name from the list of titlists after having won outright or coheld club trophies in one high-power match or another in 4 out of my first 6 years of competition), I resolved to acquire a precision centerfire rifle of my own, and to make sure I returned home with the hardware again. Though I had done quite well as a handgun competitor, there were too many new young shooters coming along who could run circles around my experience and guile.

So I began to think seriously about what sort of centerfire target rifle I wanted. In making these types of decisions, I read as much as I can on the subject, inquire of those who presumably know more than I . . . and in short order define my needs more clearly.

The basic parameters were thus: A bolt action with a 24-inch varmint-style barrel. The caliber would be 223 Remington for affordability as well as ease of shooting . . . and availability of brass since in the midst of this another fateful decision was made: I would quaveringly stick my big toe into the mysterious waters of reloading!

This was a decision not easily reached, for my sole experience with reloading anything involved an hour in 1982 with a friend's MEC Grabber loading up two boxes of 12-gauge target shells. This fixed in my mind two unshakable perceptions: (A) there was a fair amount of paraphenalia involved; and (B) if I ever decided to take the plunge, I would probably turn into a mushroom in my basement from the amount of time I would happily spend down there adjusting dies, pulling levers, experimenting with charges, etc.

Forcing the issue of handloading onto the back burner of my brain, I concentrated on the rifle I would have.

Although Remingtons were popular, I didn't like the look of the stock, preferring instead the lines of the Ruger Model 77, but which has yet to be chambered in 223. Browning's Stainless A-Bolt Stalker was beautiful but in the wrong calibers, while the lovely Kimber was out of my price range. U.S.R.A. Winchesters were a distinct possibility as the Model 70 met all my requirements, but what I really drew a bead on was a 24-inch heavy-barrel S&W 1500 that was later briefly imported by Mossberg and currently by Interarms. Made in Japan by Howa, it has been described as an Oriental Mauser . . . which sounded pretty good to me.

Problem is that I really wanted just the barreled action, as I had decided that my target gun should have a synthetic stock, and only during the S&W years was just the 24-inch heavy barreled action available. For over a year I dove right to the S&W section of *The Gun List* looking for such an animal, but on those few occasions when one was offered, my phone calls were always met with "Sorry, but that's been sold already."

Not only did this frustrate me, but it served to further convince me that I was on the right track.

Then one day my chum Tony Muscarella stopped by to show me a gun he thought I should take a close look at.

"This is a good one for you," he said with sincerity, "an old Remington 788, a real dandy."

I looked at the ungainly beast and its cheap stock. The lines of the 24-inch semi-heavy barrel were fine, but the rest of the rifle was, uh . . . undistinguished!

"This was a great gun," Tony said. "Remington stopped making the 788s because they competed unfairly with their 700 series. This is a real shooter, and it's only $200."

"Thanks for thinking of me," I responded, "but I think I'll pass on this one. It's not what I really had my heart set on."

A month went by as I continued to

Now serious about this handloading game, the author spent huge amounts of time in the basement with his loading tools—pulling levers, cleaning cases, adjusting this and that—in preparation for his range sessions.

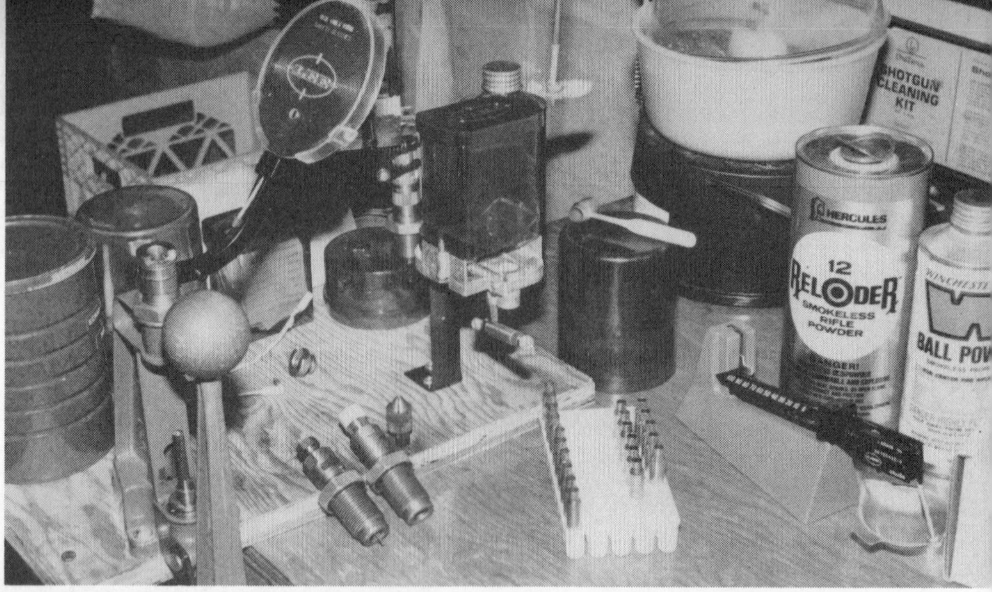

With the Ram-Line synthetic stock bolted up, Lydecker's Remington 788 now looked like a respectable rifle, and he would no longer have to endure snickers and chiding from fellow shooters.

scan the gun ads for used S&W 1500s in 223. At the same time, I noted that Remington 788s were running in the $225-$350 range, although I didn't see any with 24-inch barrels.

Finally Tony returned one day with the 788 under his arm.

"I'm giving you a last chance on this before I take it up to the gun show this weekend and sell it for a lot more," he said. "I know you wanted something else, but I'm telling you this is a shooter."

I spluttered a bit, not only because I still dreamed of the elusive S&W 1500 barreled action, but because I really didn't know anything about 788s . . . and I like to think things through thoroughly when I part with anything greater than $5.95. But then I rationalized that at $200 I wasn't going to get burned with anything I couldn't get my money back out of, and this particular 788 met many of the requirements I'd already decided on. So I forked over a handful of $20 bills and took possession of what quickly evolved into the next great love of my life.

Research revealed that Remington discontinued manufacture of the 788 in 1982, and that when the rifle had been introduced in 1967, it had a suggested retail price of . . . $84.95! Quick, what besides a gull-wing Mercedes appreciates 235 percent in just over 20 years?

As it had no iron sights, I needed a scope just to try the gun out and swapped some ammo for a 12x 40mm Tasco that had once proved too much scope for my Ruger 77/22.

With a Weaver base, some rings and a rough bore-sighting job, I took my ugly duckling out into a pal's back forty and set a target on a cardboard box against a tall berm, and from a rest proceeded to fire my fateful first shots with a box of 60-grain Hornady Spire Points, the maximum weight bullet I felt that the Remington's 1:12 rate of barrel twist would effectively stabilize.

It took three groups of three shots each to find my zero, and then I hunkered down and put 10 into the target. Results were most satisfying—four Xs, another five in the 10-ring and a "flyer" just outside in the 9-ring.

Next I tried out a fistful of 40-grain whizzers which Federal Cartridge was calling its "Blitz" load at the time. After a couple of sighter rounds to identify the changed point of impact, the target was one that I still have stapled on my garage wall.

Although I didn't recognize it at the time, the first twinges of a deep affection—yeah!, passion—were stirring in my bosom.

The first thing to be attended to was the problem of ejecting cases hitting the Tasco's windage knob and deflecting back into the action. Remounting the scope 90 degrees counter-clockwise resolved that, but then gave me fits trying to dope out the proper adjustments, as the elevation knob now set the windage, and vise versa.

That resolution came by the simple expedient of making a little drawing of the scope and the knobs, complete with tiny arrows indicating the directions of adjustment. Turning the sketch 90 degrees to the left, it was at once revealed that clockwise movements would adjust the impact downward and to the right, which notation is affixed in orange plastic marker tape to the left side of the rifle's stock should I ever experience brain fade on the firing line.

Next on the agenda was the 788's drab appearance. The purchase of a Ram-Line synthetic stock took care of that problem handsomely, although a new, longer screw had to be fashioned so I could anchor the rear of the action to the sexy black stock.

Now came the reloading equipment, and as happenstance dictated, Lee Precision was then running an attrac-

During his handloading odyssey, author was sidetracked by the brilliant idea of reseating factory-loaded bullets to optimum depth for his gun. Some reseats (left) worked well compared to the factory-set Remington 60-grain HPs (right).

tive promotion to reintroduce its little single stage C-press. It was just $9.95 with the purchase of any set of dies and a reloading tool. What a deal! Of course, by the time I'd finished my initial purchases, I was running deep into my limited fund of disposable dollars.

In addition to the above cited three basics, I'd decided I required a Lee Safety Powder Scale and funnel; Lyman powder dribbler; primer pocket cleaner; chamfer and bevel tool; case neck cutter, lock stud and gauge holder, etc. While I was awaiting delivery of these items, I poured through close to 5 years worth of carefully hoarded gun magazines, reading previously ignored handloading articles by Bob Milek, Clay Harvey, Ross Seyfried, et al., and taking copious notes on anything to do with the 223 Remington cartridge.

Then, after carefully reading the instructions that accompanied my Lee Collet Die & Dead Length Bullet Seater, I realized that I would also require a full-length sizing die for all that non-fire-formed brass I'd started scrounging from sundry AR-15 and Mini-14 shooters. This not only necessitated the purchase of an RBCS case lube pad, neck brush and lubricant, but Speer's *Reloading Manual Number 11,* for I figured I couldn't afford any more oversights.

With the purchase of 1 pound of Hodgdon BL-C2, some CCI #400 primers and a sampling of 52- and 53-grain bullets from Speer, Nosler, Hornady and Sierra, I was almost ready to launch my quest for the *Perfect 223 Cartridge*, the one tailor-made for my Remington 788 which would give me sub-MOA groups and cause strong manly types in my club to wail and gnash their teeth in frustration at their inability to overcome my superior long-range shooting.

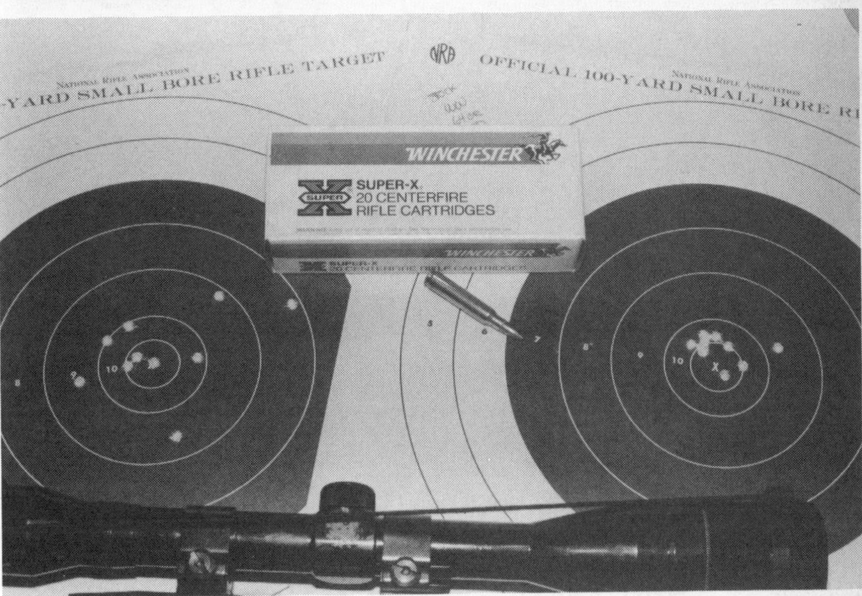

Winchester 64-grain softpoints proved especially erratic when tampered with (left), but gave excellent accuracy in their original form (right). Lydecker figures the ammo makers know what they are doing.

I first placed a call to my chum John Henry, a reloader of long standing, and asked that he guide me through my maiden voyage at the handloading bench, to make certain that I wasn't overlooking anything else that could either injure or embarrass me.

"Gee," John Henry said after surveying all that I had assembled before me, "this is all pretty high-tech stuff! Are you headed off to Wapwallopen after this?"

I was puzzled at the reference.

"That's the range in Pennsylvania where the great benchrest shooters go to shoot ¼-MOA," he told me. "With all this stuff you've got, it looks like you might be headed there someday."

Well, I'd never heard of the place, of course, but little matter. After disposing of the riflery records locally, Wapwallopen seemed like a fine idea.

But first things first—finding the right load for my rifle.

It seemed a relatively easy proposition at the start: Mate a number of like-manufactured cases, resize them full-length if they'd come from another gun or neck-size those previously fired from the 788, scrape the primer pockets clean, check the overall case length and trim if necessary (rarely so), chamfer and debur the case neck opening, carefully prime the cases, charge 20 cases with exactingly measured powder charges, load five of each with four different styles or brands of bullets of the same weight, mark the case heads lightly with different shades of nail polish, and precisely record all the data in my MTM reloader's notebook.

Then repeat that process two or three more times with an additional ½-grain of powder charge each time.

Weekends, I'd take my rifle and several dozen targets off to a corner of the Pine Barrens 100-yard range, and spend hours shooting, cleaning the bore after each 20 rounds, recording results, and discarding obviously substandard component combinations.

Other shooters thought me a madman, but visions of a National Benchrest title danced in my brain, and they soon ignored me. The owners of the Pine Barrens Sportsmen's Range soon built me a good-sized table at the far end of the line with some lumber left over from another project, and I was in heaven.

Weeknights and inclement weekends were spent reloading, and on those glorious days spoiled by neither monsoon nor blizzard, I shot groups with my precisely handcrafted ammunition. John Henry and I had made a joint purchase of 20 pounds of different powders from Hodgdon, Hercules, Accurate Arms, IMR and Winchester, so I had much to work with, enough that the television set upstairs grew cobwebs.

Many combinations were found wanting, as right from the start two components seemed to be consistently superior in their performance in my 788: Winchester's 748 Ball powder and Hornady's 52-grain boattail hollowpoint match bullet. Cases didn't seem to matter as long as I kept them segregated by manufacturer and number of times reloaded. But in the matter of primers, Winchester Small Rifle and CCI's BR-4 quickly went to the head of that particular class.

Every so often I'd get a result that would absolutely confound me, such as when I fired 10 rounds in a string with all components identical except the bullets. The 53-grain Sierra FBHPs performed creditably, giving a 1.29-inch group at 7 o'clock in the 10-ring. The 53-grain Hornadys, though, caused much disorder and uncertainty—one entered the 10-ring at 8 o'clock, while the other four tumbled into the 9-ring at 5 o'clock in a 1.6-inch pattern (outside measurements).

It was weird, like right out of a "Casper the Friendly Ghost" cartoon when a frightened character went through a door without bothering to open it. A nearby photo shows the outlines of the four flat-based bullets striking the target perfectly but sideways.

Needless to say, that recipe was immediately discarded.

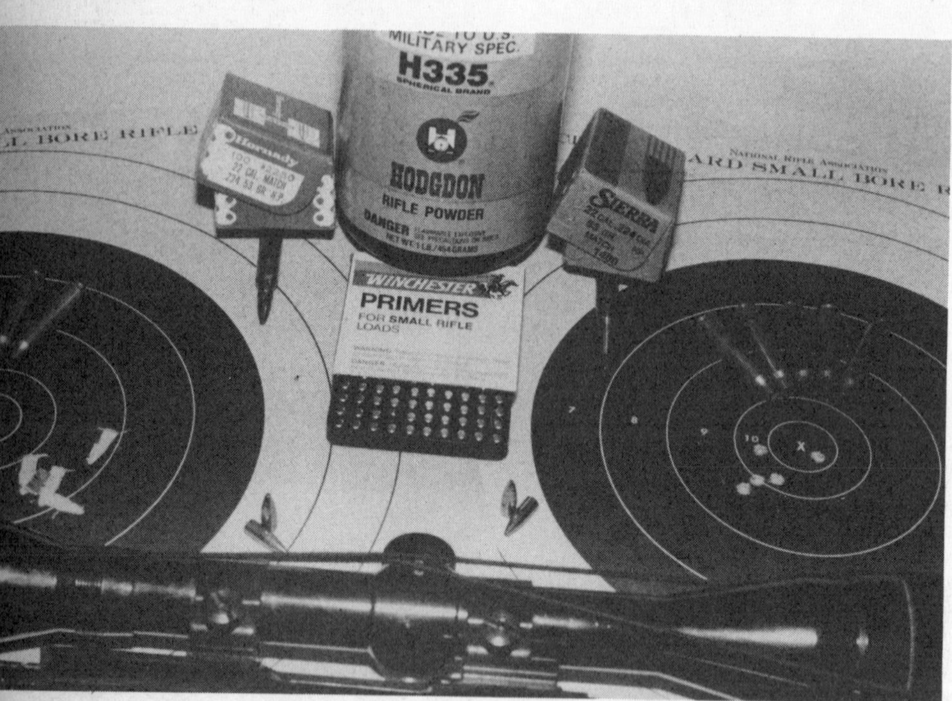

Strange things happen in shooting! Using identical loads except for the bullet's manufacture, left target shows that combination's instability. Hornady's ogive is slightly different than the Sierra bullet.

Along the way other purchases were indicated: A Lee Auto Disk Powder Measure and charging die to speed up that part of the process, and a small Lyman Pop-Top tumbler, as John Henry quickly hit the wall with cleaning my cases every Sunday night.

As my groups grew smaller, I hit the wall also. Having trouble breaking the ¾-inch mark, I decided more reading was in order. Robbie Barrkman (no stranger to precision long guns), of Robar fame, suggested Warren Page's *The Accurate Rifle* (Stoeger Sportsman's Library), and the information contained therein set me back months!

First, any thoughts I ever had of packing up my 788 and heading for Wapwallopen immediately faded. The guys in my centerfire class were shooting 10-shot groups of .3268-inch at 100 yards with .224-inch bullets back in 1953, and by 1973, the book's date of publication, single five-shot groups at 100 yards had shrunk into the mid-.09-inch range. All this was before the vaunted 22 PPC round arrived on the scene and nuked existing records (none of which were set with a 223 Remington, anyway) into oblivion.

Next, the techniques used by some of the hardcore benchresters were well beyond the tolerances of even this dedicated Virgo, like going to the firing line with a single round, a Lee Loader, primers, powder and projectiles, and reloading that same piece of brass after each shot, often seating the bullet gently in the lands of the barrel and carefully slipping the charged case into the upright chamber and mating the elements together with the locking of the bolt.

While Page's dismissal of my cartridge of choice ("The .223 with its short neck has not in standard form drawn much use in the accuracy clan . . .") may have disabused me of the notion of ever competing with the serious benchrest crowd, there was, I decided, no reason why I couldn't be a big fish in a small stream. So, with various dope gleaned from *The Accurate Rifle*, I returned to my basement and set about improving my loads.

The first priority involved discovering the optimum bullet seating depth for my particular rifle, and I took care of that using Page's trial-and-error method of moving the die 1/14th of an inch (coincident with one full turn of a standard seating die) at a time system.

The next plateau was achieved, and my 100-yard groups began to shrink in size.

Somewhere along the line the thought crossed my mind that if factory manufactured rounds must necessarily be seated to a standard for the 223, then, perhaps, I could improve on the performance of commercial cartridges in my 788 by the simple method of reseating to the longer length I'd established. No one, to my knowledge, had ever tried this bold experiment, but it was simple enough to find out if I was onto something hot.

Purchasing a Forster Bullet Puller and .224 collet, plus boxes of miscellaneous loadings from Hornady, Winchester, Remington and Federal, I pulled 10 bullets from each batch and reseated them to as shallow a depth as I could for each manufacturer's particular ogive. After carefully noting the various measurements for each of the four batches, I repaired to the range with rifle, loads, targets and cleaning equipment. MTM's new Portable Maintenance Center, which fit neatly atop my Shooters Box, was a great boon in this, and I marveled at how the various companies in the firearms industry always seemed to come up with just what I required at about the time I discovered I needed it.

The operation was a success, but the patient died!

Shooting alternately one "box-stock" round and one modified round into side-by-side five-shot groups, and then cleaning the barrel after every 20 shots, the simple fact evolved that some groups shot with Federal, Remington and Hornady improved with my custom modifications and others (Winchester, Federal and Hornady) didn't.

Scratch another scathingly brilliant idea!

Back to the basics—tinker with the powder charges, the primers and the bullet seating depths. Shoot, record the results and clean, clean, clean the bore. The "Good Ole Boys" of Outers by this time had become my "Shooting Partners" in their advertising campaign, and the way I went through their bulk bags of 800 cleaning patches, they had plenty of reason to consider me a partner of sorts.

The day I discovered just how good my 788 really was, occurred when I accompanied a friend to a 200-yard range where he was practicing long-distance shots with his M-1A for the annual Soldier of Fortune three-gun match. While he popped off-hand rounds with open iron at an I.P.S.C. target, I sandbagged the 788 and shot various three-shot groups at separate corners of a target. When we inspected our results, he noted that several of my groups were right around the 1-inch mark.

"Damn!" he said earnestly, eye-balling the Remington. "You've got a ½-minute of angle shooter there!"

By the end of our range session, having exhausted the interesting points of aim on the Ram-Line "fun" target, I got his permission for some "head shots" with a handful of miscellaneous 55-grain Remington softpoints rattling the bottom of my MTM Shooter's Box.

When we retrieved our targets, seven of the eight rounds had grouped into 1.89 inches of the upper A-Zone I'd been aiming at, and the entire eight-shot group measured 2.72 inches. I was thrilled.

Eight rounds of miscellaneous Remington 55-grain softpoint ammo, fired at 200 yards, reaffirmed the author's sense that the Model 788 was a real bargain.

"A trigger job should be your next priority," my impressed companion observed. "Six pounds is too heavy for a target gun."

As no one makes "drop-in" triggers for the 788, I approached Powderkeg Gunsmith Ron Bernik of Cape Cod about my project.

"It's easy," Ron assured me. "It's all spelled out in one of the Brownell's *Gunsmith Kinks* volumes."

Two days later my 6-pound pull was now down to a nice crisp 4 pounds, and again my groups improved.

So it was back to the basement for more handloading experimentation. I tried CCI Magnum 450 primers, but WSRs or BR-4s performed the best. Cases didn't seem to be too critical as long as I mated them reasonably well by manufacture and maturity, although personal preference leaned toward the now obsolescent "Frontier" headstamp.

In the matter of propellants, no matter what I used I invariably returned to Winchester's 748. It performed with such significant superiority that others were quickly relegated to the status of surplus use for hacking around reloading older brass with 55-grain PMC FMJs as fodder for my Mini-14.

Only in the area of projectiles did my thinking change. Though the 52-grain

The happy target shooter, relaxed and in search of "The Perfect Load" for his 223 target gun. Author could, and does, spend countless hours trying to make little holes close together at long distance.

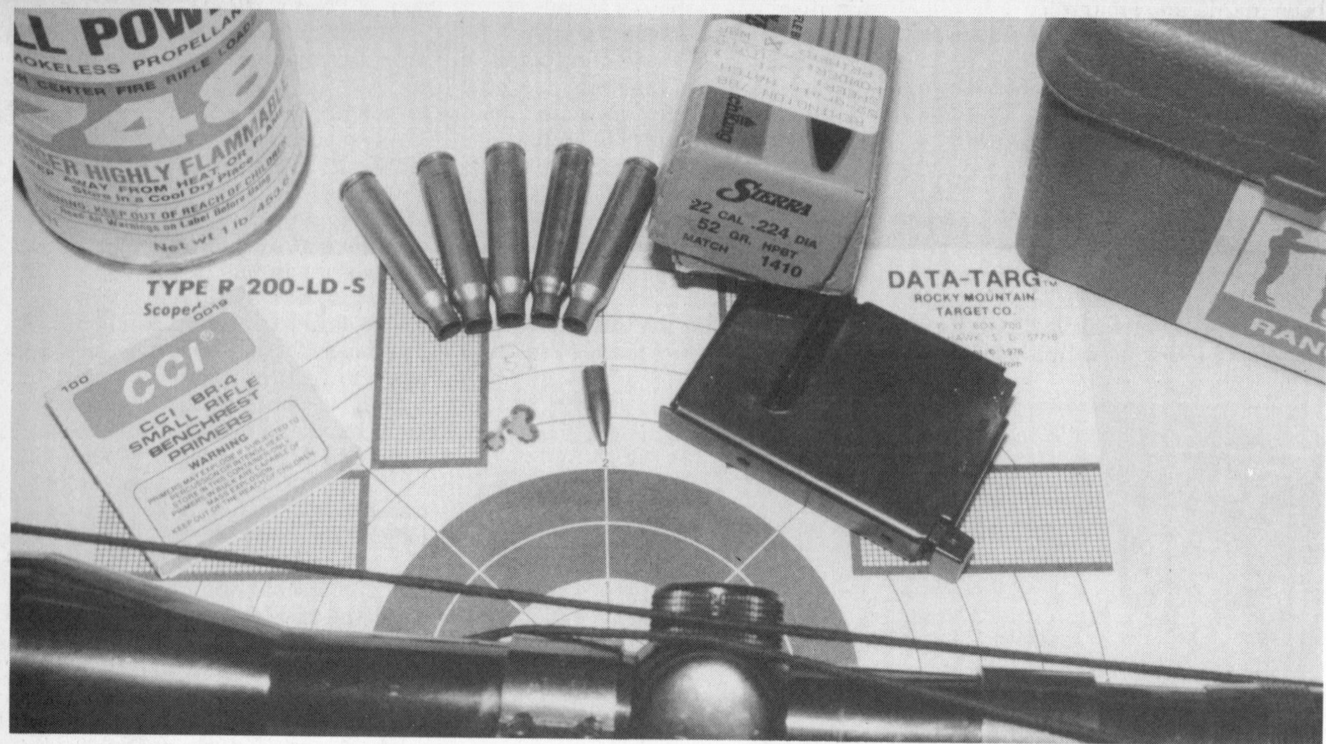

Sometimes everything seems to come together! The greatest single group Lydecker ever shot used the Sierra 52-grain BTHP over 27.5 grains of Winchester 748. It measures .231-inch. Look out, Wapwallopen.

Hornady BTHP match was the early choice for best of the breed, when I upped the charge of W748 from 26.5 to 27.5. grains, the ostensibly identical 52-grain Sierra HPBT emerged as the favorite. Although I have no idea why, I recalled the graphic lesson of the shoot-out between the 53-grain flat-base hollowpoints with H335 and stocked up on the Sierra #1410 bullets.

Temporarily side-tracked while experimenting with some of Speer's new 50-grain "TNT" Spitzers, I returned to the Sierra 52-grain match bullet and achieved my personal pinnacle on November 2, 1990, just 5 weeks shy of the 10-year anniversary of my first success with a long gun.

Unseasonably balmy, it was too nice a day to stay hard at work, so I grabbed my 788 and two dozen rounds I'd loaded the week before, and headed out to the range to shoot some groups over lunch hour.

Setting up one of Stan Enstrom's Data-Targs at 100 yards, I ran a fouling shot through the cold, clean barrel. Now firing for record, I put the crosshair on the center of the bull and pressed the trigger.

Drat! The point of impact was 1-inch to the left of center, but 2¼ inches high. Well, too late to make adjustments for this group, so just keep shooting!

The next four shots went into a single hole just above the first round, and I had to run down to the target stand to confirm that I had just shot the greatest single group of my life.

But there it was, four shots in 0.288-inch, with that first round, probably the second fouling shot I should have fired, "opening" the group up to 0.455-inch, outside measurement. Subtracting the diameter of the caliber, 0.224-inch, I was left with a five-shot group measuring 0.231-inch, center to center.

I submit that this is pretty fair country shootin' for a 23-year-old $85 rifle with an old Tasco scope.

For the record, it was a 52-grain Sierra hollowpoint boattail over 27.5 grains of 748 and a BR-4 primer, in once-fired, neck-sized-only Winchester cases, with an overall length of 2.278 inches.

While I'm having the target encased in Lucite for my den, maybe Wapwallopen may not be such a far-fetched idea! ●

Lydecker's Loads
Remington Model 788
223 Remington

Bullet	Powder/ Charge (grs.)	Primer	Case	Average Velocity[1] (fps)	Best Group[2] (in.)
Speer					
50-gr. TNT	BL-C2/28.0	CCI 450	Fed.	3389	0.455
Sierra					
52-gr. HPBT	748/27.5	BR-4	WW	3032	0.231
Hornady					
53-gr. FBHP	748/26.5	CCI 450	WW	2961	0.675
Sierra					
55-gr. HPBT	H4198/21.0	WSR	WW	2975	0.892
Hornady					
60-gr. SP	748/26.5	WSR	Fron.	3100	0.543

[1]With a PACT Mark III Chronograph and Mark V Skyscreens at 12 feet.
[2]From a sandbag rest at 100 yards.

The Accelerator and I

Author Swiggett was in on the initial testing of this interesting cartridge concept and recently retested the three Accelerators with some eye-opening results.

by HAL SWIGGETT

IT WAS WELDED to the steel/iron turkey silhouette!

Solid!

I could not pry it loose!

At 375 yards!

I'd never seen a bullet jacket do that before; even from my 220 Swift.

Maybe this piece should be titled, "Moose to Prairie Dog, Your 30-06 Can Handle Either."

That's true if you include Accelerator in your ammo case.

We go back a long way, Remington's Accelerator and I. We met almost 2 years before its introduction at the company's annual editors/writers seminar in late 1976. I was working with Neil Oldridge on another project (no salary, just off-the-cuff consulting). Neil was Product Manager of Ammunition along with several other accoutrements, which meant anything new in those fields went through him. My first letter from Neil concerning this endeavor is dated May 5, 1975. It picked up from our January, 1975, meeting and supplied data for their new "Accelerator" in 30-06, 308 and 30-30.

But first an explanation of just what the Accelerator is. The concept: Use of a .224-inch or .243-inch bullet fired from a 30-caliber rifle; bullets to be 55- and 80-grain versions of their Core-Lokt; use of a sabot to hold that bullet. Nothing really new here; sabots have been around for years, but never put to commerical use. Information given me included velocity and foot pounds of energy at the muzzle, 100 and 200 yards. The letter stated, "... accuracy specification is 2.5 inches at 200 yards for extreme spread."

The letter also stated: "We are interested in all performance aspects of this round. Any information you may contribute on accuracy, feed, fire, function, impressions, reactions, etc. will be greatly appreciated. We are particularly interested in performance on light game. Any photographs, recovered bullets, descriptions, etc. would be useful.

"... plan your shooting on your own. We are, naturally, interested in receiving results in a timely manner."

Swiggett used this 30-06 Steyr-Mannlicher rifle for his initial testing of the Accelerator in 1975, and as part of the current tests here, bringing the cartridge up to date.

Velocities given for the two experimental bullets loaded in each of the three calibers were: 30-06 .224-inch at 4050, .243-inch (6mm) 3640; 308 .224-inch at 3720, .243-inch (6mm) 3450; 30-30 .224-inch at 3430, .243-inch (6mm) 3150. These figures were derived from test barrels.

Many cartridges were fired. A good many—up to 100 pounds or so—animals were included in my tests along with many, many rounds fired for ac-

Only three Accelerator chamberings made it to market, and these are the ones shooters see on dealer shelves today. Remington also experimented with the 243 Winchester Accelerator.

curacy. As my primary rifle, I used a much-favored Steyr-Mannlicher 30-06, but in later stages also included a Colt-Sauer. Only 30-06 Accelerators were tested. The two smaller cases were brought out later, but I was not included in these developments.

My first letter to Neil is dated July 11, 1975. The opening paragraph reads: "In case you didn't know it, any taxidermist is going to have an awfully hard time repairing any animal hit with your .224 Accelerator out of a 30-06." Descriptions, in very plain English, of the tissue damage needn't be given here other than to say it was extensive—so much so the word should probably be capitalized. Bullets were almost impossible to recover, but a few fragments here and there were sent back to the factory.

Deep into a letter to Neil dated September 2, 1975, I mentioned the 6mm Accelerator. "Now for my problem . . . did anybody else have any trouble with the 6mm Accelerator load? . . . The 6mm 'Acc' shoots wild, wild, wild." I could not get the accuracy it was supposed to produce. I ended that letter with, "Gosh knows I'm no technician; I just like to shoot and keep records."

The response from Neil was dated September 8, 1975. In part, it read: "Regarding the 6mm Accelerator I am surprised at the results you are receiving. This has been reported to Research and Development who is in the process of running a wide variety of routing (sic) tests."

A year later I wrote to Bill Boettner, who had replaced Neil as Ammunition Products Manager. My subject was twofold. First, I asked about my 44 Magnum 1000 fps load that Remington was about to release and second, commented on my work with the 6mm Accelerator. His response, dated September 23, 1976, was blunt and to the point: "The development of the 44 Magnum 1000 fps load is on schedule, but more work is required on the Accelerator 243 loads."

End of subject. End of correspondence. End of 243 Accelerator loads. I have not seen nor heard of them since.

But, the .224-inch Accelerator is alive and well. The first public announcement from Remington was dated January 1, 1977. It read:

New Remington "Accelerator" Cartridge Converts 30-06 Rifle to Flat-Shooting Small Game Gun

A new and unique development by Remington Arms Company, Inc., called the "Accelerator" cartridge, converts a 30-06 caliber rifle to a flat-shooting, 22 caliber small game gun with the highest bullet velocity ever produced in a factory-loaded round.

The "Accelerator" cartridge involves the use of a .224", 55-grain pointed softpoint bullet inside a 30 caliber sabot casing. The sabot-encased 22 caliber bullet is loaded in a standard 30-06 case and fired in a regular 30-06 rifle.

Ballistics of Remington's "Accelerator" cartridge are outstanding. Muzzle velocity from a 24" barrel is 4080 f.p.s., superior to that of the original 220 Swift in the same barrel length.

Another feature of the "Accelerator" cartridge is its ability to generate such high velocity with a 55-grain bullet. It surpasses by 350 f.p.s. or more the velocity of any current factory-loaded 22 caliber cartridge with a 55-grain bullet. Because the "Accelerator" cartridge's 55-grain bullet has a higher ballistic coefficient than the 48-grain bullet loaded in the original 220 Swift, it is distinctly superior to that round in downrange velocity, energy and trajectory.

Muzzle energy of the "Accelerator" cartridge is 2033 ft-lbs, the highest ever developed for a 22 caliber bullet. In fact, from 0 to 200 yards, it is superior in energy to such heavier cartridges as the 30-30 Win., 35 Remington and 45-70.

Once the "Accelerator" cartridge's sabot encased bullet leaves the muzzle, air resistance peels open the sabot, causing it to drop off the bullet without affecting its accuracy or trajectory. Accuracy of the "Accelerator" cartridge, incidentally, is equal to or better than that of other standard 22 caliber center fire cartridges, depending on the rifle used.

Advantages to the shooter of the "Accelerator" cartridge are twofold. First, it provides the small game

These 1976 Remington factory photos show the Accelerator bullet leaving the muzzle at 4080 fps (left), the bullet separating from the plastic sabot at about 18 inches from the muzzle (middle), and the sabot starting to trail further behind at 24 inches from the muzzle (right).

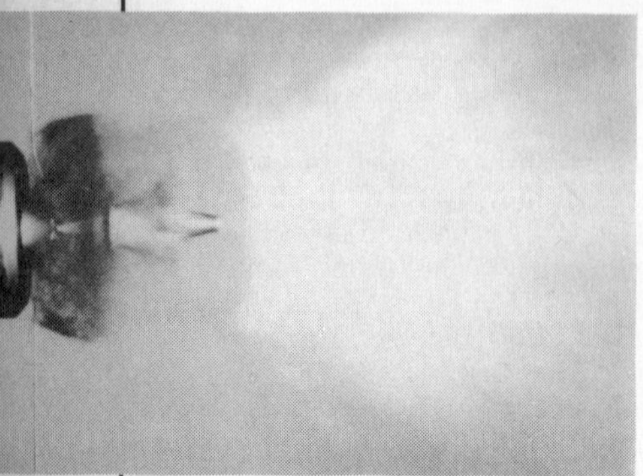

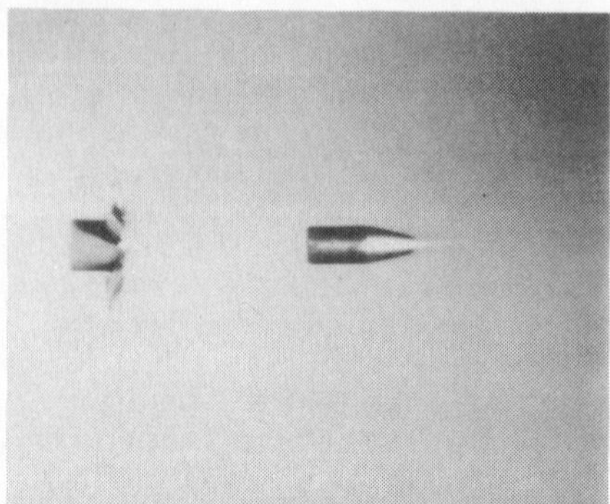

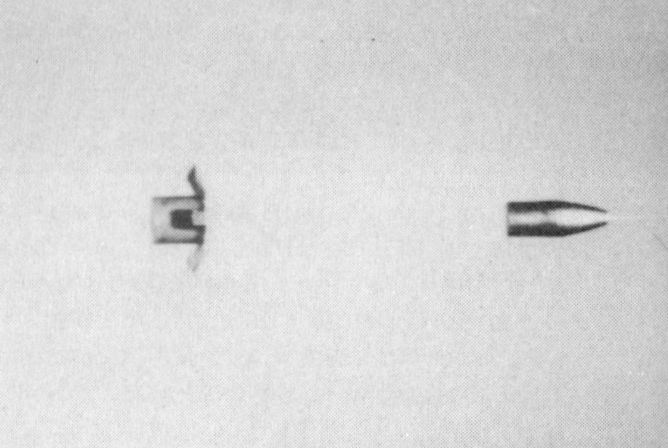

hunter with the highest velocity he has ever had available along with remarkably flat trajectory. Second, it enables the owner of a manually operated (bolt or pump action) 30-06 rifle to have a tight grouping, long-range, small game gun by simply switching ammunition. "Accelerator" cartridges do not operate the action of autoloading rifles but will function in them on a single shot basis.

New 30-06 "Accelerator" cartridges, in both Remington and Peters brand, will be available January 1977."

That is the entire public announcement of Remington's new cartridge. It also included a page of ballistic data providing velocity, energy and bullet drop out to 500 yards. All data was based on 24-inch test barrel results.

The 30-30 version followed by a year and the 308 came later. I don't remember exactly when it made its debut.

The sabot has a hole in its base and weighs a mite short of 5.7 grains. There are a half-dozen "fingers" (for lack of a better word) holding the bullet in place. According to Remington, they separate from the bullet about 14 inches from the muzzle. All I know is that I find them anywhere from 12 or 15 yards on out to sometimes 30 or 35 yards in front of the muzzle. My chronographing is usually done on 25-yard targets with the first screen 8 feet from the muzzle. Never has one of the screens been hit and only rarely has a sabot hit the target. The fingers are always at right angles to the base, opened flat.

Now, 15 years after the Accelerator made its official debut and 17 plus since my introduction, let's see what happens.

Out front, I never was able to come up with the accuracy claimed in that initial release: "Accuracy of the 'Accelerator' cartridge, incidentally, is equal to or better than that of other standard 22-caliber centerfire cartridges, depending on the rifle used." In many, if not most, cases I have found the accuracy to be whatever it is in the barrel with conventional factory-loaded ammo.

I still have my Steyr-Mannlicher 30-06 that I used in those initial tests so, naturally, it was put to work again. The factory listing, from that 24-inch test barrel, is 4080 fps. Using Ken Oehler's great Model 35P chronograph with the start screen at 8 feet, my average of 10 shots showed 3976 fps on the printer. High was 4032 with 3921 as the bottom. Standard deviation was 39. Mighty close.

Accuracy?

All shooting was done at 50 yards and, I must admit this, with ammo that had proved very accurate in these guns—ammo that seemed to bring out the best in each barrel. My Steyr is very fond of Federal's Premium 150-grain boattail softpoint. Three-shot groups were fired. I have never agreed with, nor seen fit to use, five-shot (or, heaven forbid, 10-shot) groups for hunting rifles. My interest is in where that first shot goes. More than three at the same animal and the hunter is already in trouble far beyond anything superior accuracy could help with.

Three of those Federals printed in ¾-inch. Immediately, on the same target, three Accelerator '06s went downrange. They, too, printed in ¾-inch. Not in the same group, however. And therein lies the bugaboo. Accelerator cartridges will not, except in rare cases, print in the same group as the big game bullet. In other words, it *is not* interchangeable in the field. One *cannot* be on a deer stand, see a coyote, switch ammo, and expect to score a center hit. In this case, the group was ⅞-inch right and 2 inches high. Carried out to 150 yards, this would mean 6 inches high—or over his back. The nearly 3 inches right wouldn't cause a miss nor would it cause any concern because of the massive tissue damage delivered through the little 55-grain bullet.

Having access to a friend's 1903-A3 Springfield 30-06 with its two-groove barrel, I had to give it a try. It likes Winchester 165-grain pointed soft-

(Right) Swiggett's current Accelerator testing was done with this sporterized 1903-A3 Springfield (left), and his long-favored Steyr-Mannlicher that was also used in 1975 tests.

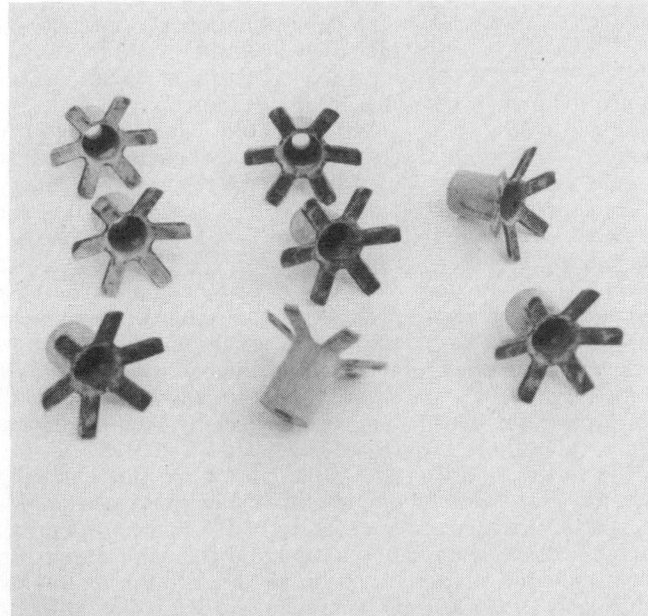

Sabots picked up after Swiggett's tests (above) were found as close as 12 to 15 yards from the gun, and as far as 30 to 35 yards. All show rifling engraving and the petals are folded back at nearly a right angle.

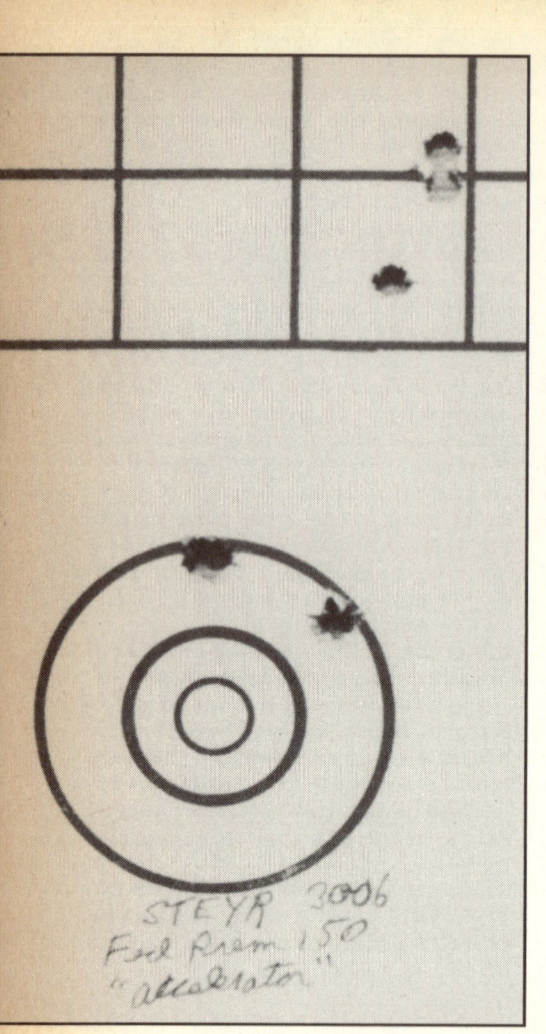

Above: The Steyr target shows two 30-06s went through the left hole; the higher group was printed by the '06 Accelerators. Below: The '03-A3 target, with three conventional-bullet holes in the center. The lower right of those caught one of the Accelerator holes, with the other two high and low right.

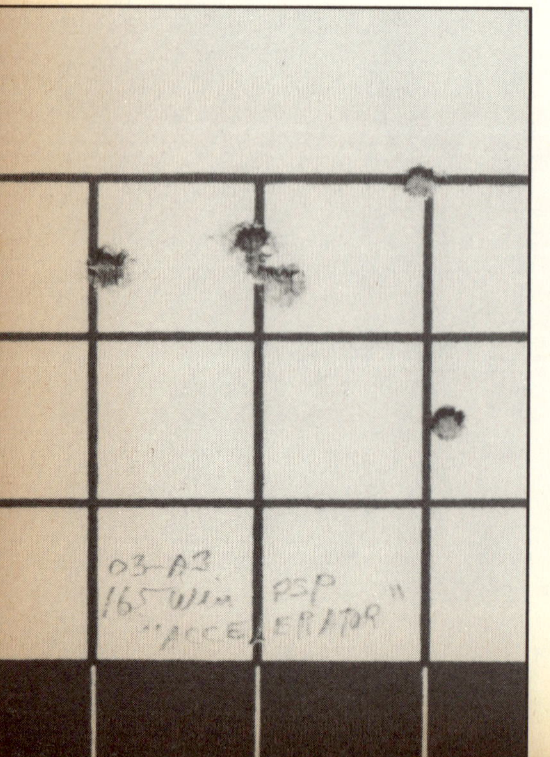

(Above) Swiggett's cute little Remington Model 600 in 308 Winchester used Hansen's 150-grain softpoints as the standard load. Below: The larger holes are from the 308 (a nice group by itself), the smaller from the Accelerators.

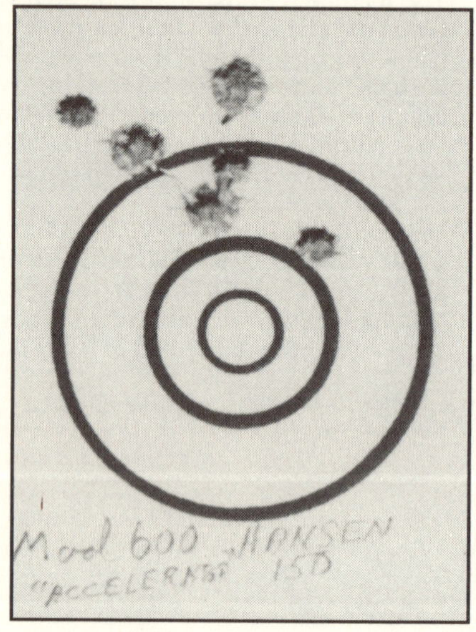

points. Three shots printed in an even 1-inch. Three Accelerator 55-grain bullets centered their 1⅜-inch group 1-inch right with one bullet going through one of the '06 holes.

As stated in the Bible, concerning the coming rapture, one will be taken and one will remain. One 30-06 printed exactly the same group size and the other didn't quite make it—but was still close enough for practical use.

I've not used any Accelerator 308s in the field. All I can relate here is what happened on the range. And it was, to be brutally frank, a bit disconcerting and, maybe better said, embarrassing. Starting off with my cute little Model 600 Remington and a box of Hansen (made in Yugoslavia) 150-grain softpoint bullets (I happened to be field-testing them at that time), my three-shot group measured ⅝-inch. Three Accelerator 55-grain bullets printed, for all practical purposes, in that same group. Actually it was a bit wider, but not sufficient to assure any 200-yard coyote safety or, for that matter, encourage anything beyond immediate departure.

It got worse.

Shooting a sweet, sweet little Remington Model Seven with its Kevlar stock and my long-time favorite 308 whitetail load made up with Speer's 130-grain hollowpoint over 47 grains of 3031 (Ken Oehlered at 2960 fps), the three-shot group was one ragged hole. Looking through my spotting scope after the three Accelerator 308s went downrange, there was no other group on the target. Only a slightly more ragged hole. All six of those bullets had printed in a ⅝-inch group.

It ain't supposed to happen!

Moving on to 30-30 Accelerators, personal experience has been limited, but there has been a little—all in a 14-inch Thompson/Center Contender pistol. A few jackrabbits and two coyotes have felt the sting of 30-30 55-grain Accelerator bullets.

With a listed velocity of 3400 fps from a 24-inch test barrel, the T/C 14-inch produced 3176 fps for a 10-shot average—with a group equaling conventional bullets from that same barrel. Having been a bit involved with Winchester's releasing of their Supreme line of cartridges (an invitee at the first press showing), I opted for two of their 30-caliber offerings—300 Winchester Magnum and 30-30. The oldie was with a specially-built-for-the-cartridge 150-grain Silvertip. My 14-inch T/C liked it a lot. On this particular day, my three-shot group measured ⅝-inch. Exactly 1½ inches higher, the Accelerator did the same thing. One bullet hit so far off to the right it had to be my fault so it was discounted.

Not being the owner of a "modern" 30-30 rifle, a Model 94 in my collection of things not valuable to anyone but myself was brought into action. Three

(Above) Author's slender-barreled Remington Model Seven in 308 fired these 130-grain Speer hollowpoints over 47 grains of 3031, and three .224-inch, 55-grain Accelerators into this one ragged hole (below)!

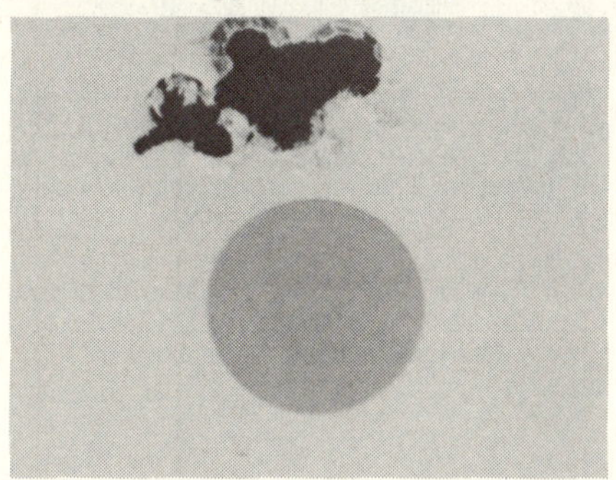

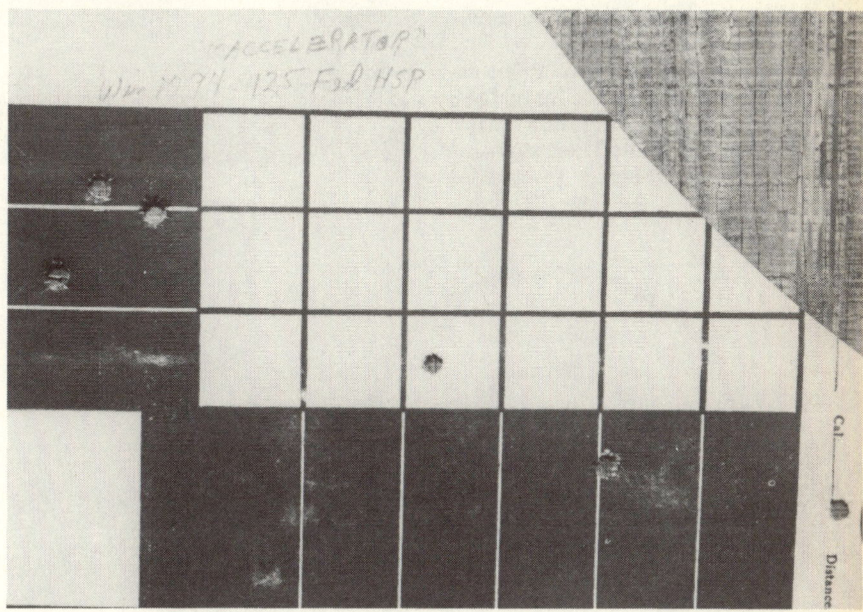

(Top right) Testing of the 30-30 Accelerator was with author's well-used, Ojibway-owned Model 94 Winchester and Thompson/Center's Super 14 Contender. Right: The Winchester used Federal's 125-grain hollowpoint (right), the T/C shot the Winchester Supreme 150-grain Silvertip. Above: The Model 94 did well with the Federal loads but didn't like the Accelerators (three widely spaced holes on the right).

rifles in that collection are authentic Indian firearms. By that I mean I obtained them from Indians I've hunted with and all the use was in their hands. One was a Cooey 22 rimfire single shot from a Cree in northern Saskatchewan; one was from a Mescalero Apache in New Mexico, a 22 WMR; and one was the gun used here, a Model 94, built, according to Winchester records, in 1946. I got it from an Ojibway moose guide in northern Ontario. It is much used and very battle scarred.

A rancher friend carries a Model 94 in his pickup and is convinced Federal 125-grain softpoints are best, so I tried a few in my old Indian rifle. Ten shots of this averaged 2472 fps, less than 100 fps below the factory-listed velocity. Ten 30-30 Accelerator 55-grain bullets averaged 3271 fps, only 129 fps below the factory test barrel figures. With its traditional open sights, my three-shot group with Federal's 125-grain softpoints printed a rather nice triangle measuring $1\frac{1}{8}$ inches across the widest leg. Accelerators? Forget them, at least in this particular rifle. It wasn't a group, but more pattern-like with the center 5 inches right and $2\frac{1}{2}$ inches low. Actually they printed in a line and measured $4\frac{1}{4}$ inches from one end to the other.

So what have I proved?

If nothing else, the validity of Remington's current claim that accuracy for Accelerator cartridges is more or less the accuracy of that particular barrel with conventional bullets.

The Model 94 didn't like them at all, but another carbine might not feel the same way. The T/C Super 14 thought they were delicious and gobbled them up. If anything, this group was a might tighter than with conventional bullets. My 25-plus-year-old Steyr-Mannlicher performed exactly as it did with initial test loads. Those are results that had a hand in getting the cartridge on the market. The military '03-A3, with its two-groove barrel, didn't do all that badly. Its group was a bit larger, but not all that terrible.

The Model 600 in 308 couldn't tell the difference between 150-grain bullets and the little 55-grainers in the Accelerator. And the Model Seven in 308—of course, a favored handload was used, but both it and the Accelerator put all six in one ragged hole.

How the Accelerator will do in your rifle can be determined only one way—try it.

Remington's initial claim about accuracy of normal centerfire cartridges, way back in the beginning, didn't prove out and was dropped. Their current claim of similar accuracy to conven-

(Above) This nice ram is one of several animals dropped with 30-06 Remington, .224-inch, 55-grain Accelerator bullets during the 1975 testing. Tissue damage was extensive.

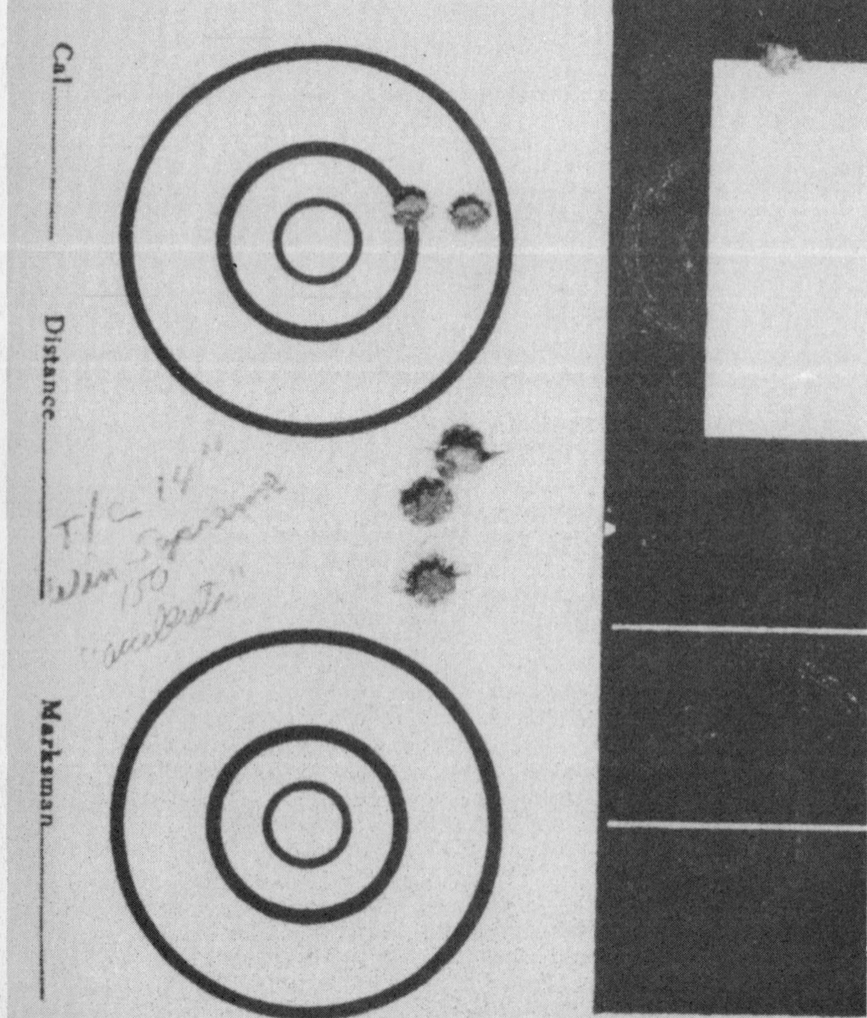

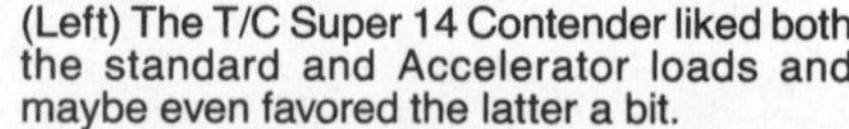

(Left) The T/C Super 14 Contender liked both the standard and Accelerator loads and maybe even favored the latter a bit.

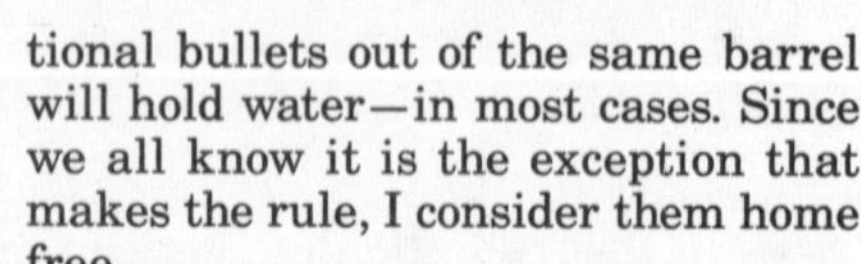

tional bullets out of the same barrel will hold water—in most cases. Since we all know it is the exception that makes the rule, I consider them home free.

And I really do doubt that my findings with the 6mm Accelerator had anything to do with it being dropped. All I know is that when my work with it was reported, the statement ". . . more work is required" was made and then there was total silence from that moment on.

Grouping with these little 55-grain, sabot-held bullets is such, in most cases, that a shooter could, by holding a bit off, interchange them on a hunt. Try a few at 100 yards and 150 yards and then make note of their point of impact. Beyond that, I feel sight adjustments should be made. Only your groups will let you know which way to go.

Accelerator 30-06, 308 and 30-30 cartridges are worth a try; of this I'm sure.

Maybe better put: Yes, your moose, elk, mule deer, whitetail, antelope rifle *can* be a varminter. Of this I am also sure. ●

The New Ram-Line Exactor Pistol

This new "plastic" pistol is a brilliant design at an affordable price. It's high tech and simplicity all in one.

by J. B. WOOD

Exactor pistol has pleasing lines in spite of the odd grip frame shape. Left-handers can shoot the gun easily.

LONG BEFORE the "plastic pistol" furor over the Glock pistol erupted in the media, polymers had been used in pistol frames—Interdynamic (now Intratec) had their KG99, and Heckler & Koch used it in the 9mm VP70Z. Going even further back, there was the High Standard Duramatic. In more recent times, examples would be the Grendel P-10 and P-30.

So, the basic idea is not new. However, the way Gaines Chesnut has done it is a brilliant piece of engineering. The new Ram-Line 22 Long Rifle pistol was first called the Syn-Tech, but was changed to Exactor. Not only is the main grip frame made of polymer, but this tough modern version of plastic is also used for the bolt end piece, the trigger, magazine catch, magazine,

The Exactor pistol field-strips into six easy pieces with only the use of an Allen wrench—no other tools are needed.

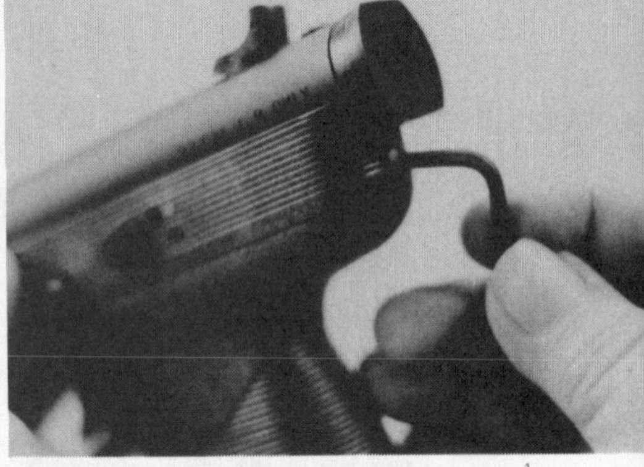

The takedown screw is located at the rear of the frame, and is removed with the supplied Allen wrench.

and the buttons for the bolt latch and the safety.

The barrel is also entirely sheathed in polymer, with flat sides and a vented rib on top. Except for the larger mounting section at the rear, the barrel itself is a slim steel tube. This is one of the features that keeps the weight of this full-sized pistol down to 21 ounces. The receiver is made of aircraft-grade aluminum alloy and, of course, all of the internal parts and springs are steel.

The polymer magazine has one steel part—the constant-force ribbon-coil spring. This feature, found in all Ram-Line magazines, means that the same tension will be supplied to the magazine follower whether there is one round left, or a full magazine. This also makes loading easy, because putting in the 15th round requires the same force as the first one.

A constant-force spring is used in one other location in the pistol. A ribbon-coil powers the sear, and this contributes to a good trigger pull. Another factor that helps is the sear contact point, far from the hammer pivot, giving good leverage. An earlier pistol that I fired had a nice 4-pound trigger pull. The regular-production gun I tested for this article also had a good trigger, with a pull of exactly 1-pound more.

I noticed some other differences between this gun and the early one: The shape of the trigger is better, with less curl at the tip; the trigger and the bolt latch now have separate pivot pins; the grooves that encircle the grip frame appear to have been slightly deepened; the magazine end piece now has a little protrusion at the bottom of the grip, making it easier to assure that the magazine locks in place; and the extractor, which was a pivoting part with a separate V-spring, is now a non-pivoting part that is its own spring.

When you see the Exactor for the first time, you immediately notice the odd shape of the grip frame, which tapers from top to bottom. The Ram-Line people have called this shape "dynamic contour." Some shooters have called it weird, but others have said that the shape gives excellent control of this center-balanced pistol.

Now that I have put quite a few rounds through two of these guns, I have arrived at some very subjective opinions on the shape of the grip frame: It may be perfect for some hands. You can get used to it, and learn to shoot well with it. However, when Ram-Line offers the promised optional grip of conventional shape, I will immediately change to that one.

The early pistol I tried had a fully-adjustable Millett rear sight, and I understand that this will be an extra-cost option. My regular-production gun has a high-profile rear sight with a square notch, dovetail-mounted. The front sight, integral with the barrel sheath, has deep serrations in its slanted rear face.

The manual safety is pushed rearward for on-safe, covering a red dot on the frame. This takes the trigger bar out of engagement with the sear,

The manual safety is shown here in the off-safe position. It requires a conscious effort to manipulate, moving down and forward. When moved back to on-safe, it covers the red dot.

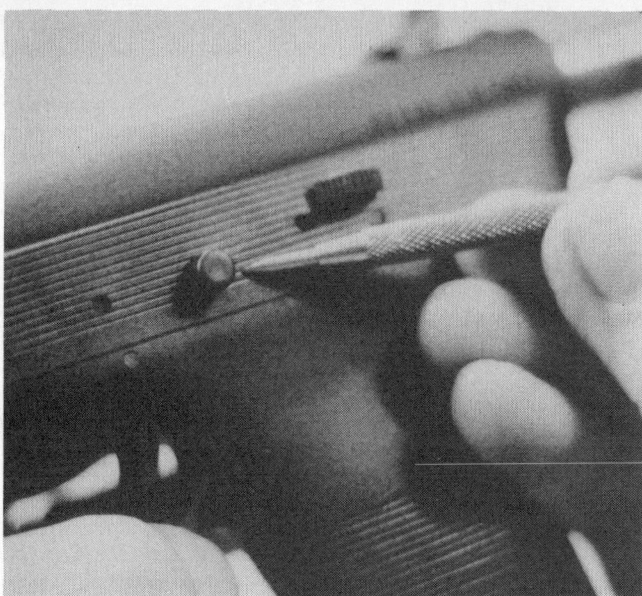

The Exactor bolt latch is located for easy operation. It is pushed downward for release. The safety is shown here in the on-safe position.

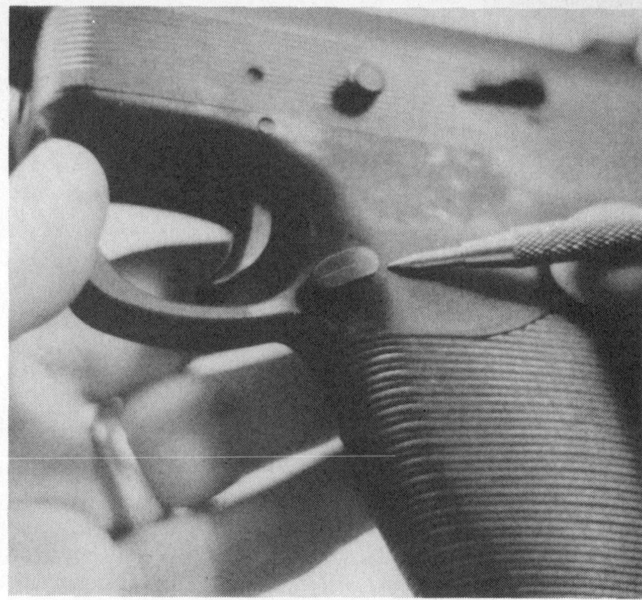

The magazine release is contoured to the curve of the grip. It has minimal side protrusion, is shielded by the grip swell, and is easy to operate.

blocks the sear, and also blocks the trigger bar. If the hammer is in the fired position when the safety is applied, it will also lock the bolt in closed position.

A two-direction movement is required for off-safe. The button must be first pushed downward, then forward. While this movement is easily done, the button can't be inadvertently pushed to off-safe by a tight holster or any other accidental element. The location of the safety is perfect, above the grip on the left side of the pistol.

Just forward of the safety is the bolt latch button, and it is easily reached by the thumb without a change in the shooting hold. The bolt locks open after the last shot. After the magazine is reloaded and reinserted, the bolt can be released by pushing the latch button downward, or by retracting the bolt slightly and letting it go.

The 15-round magazine has a clear body, making it easy to see when it is loaded, and how many rounds are left in it. The follower is red, a good indicator of empty status when seen through the opened action. The catch lug on the magazine is of generous size, and I doubt that it could ever break off.

The interior of this magazine is beautifully engineered. So far, I have fired several hundred assorted rounds through two of these guns, and I have had exactly one malfunction. That was with a target-level load that failed to fully cycle the bolt, and it was not the fault of the Exactor's feed system.

At the range, I found that my regular-production pistol was quite accurate from a casual rest at 25 yards, but it didn't match the target-grade performance of the almost-prototype earlier gun. The best groups, which measured 1-inch, were with Federal Hi-Power and Winchester Target loads.

RWS Target rounds had a best-group reading of 1⅛ inches. The PMC Zappers grouped into 1¼ inches, and the Federal Spitfire went 1¾ inches. All of the initial groups were just a shade to the left, and the rear sight was adjusted accordingly by drifting it in its dovetail mount. The groups were all consistent in configuration, with no stringing and no fliers.

In nonserious target work—bumping cans off a log, firing from belt

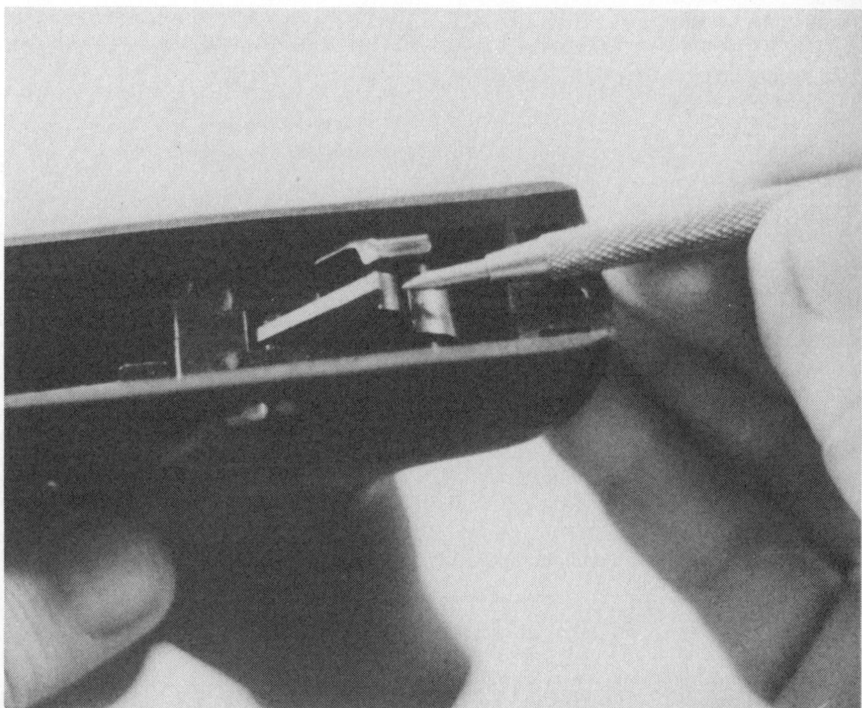

The sear contacts the hammer at upper rear, far from the hammer pivot point. This gives good leverage and contributes to a good trigger pull.

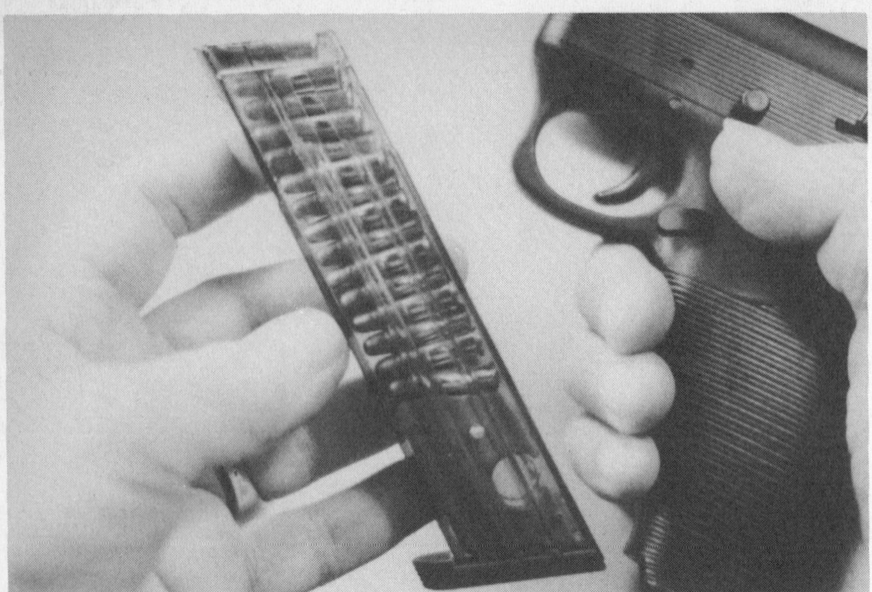

The Exactor magazine is shown with a full load of 15 rounds. The clear body of the magazine makes it easy to check the amount of remaining ammo.

level—the grip shape tended to place my first shots low. Compensating for this was easy, but it required a conscious adjustment in the wrist angle. The pistol feels the same in either hand, and left-handed shooters can operate the controls with a finger instead of the thumb.

Takedown for routine cleaning requires the removal of a single Allen screw at the upper rear of the frame, using the wrench supplied with the gun. The receiver assembly is then lifted up at the rear and taken off. Pushing the bolt pin out upward allows removal of the bolt, and that's it.

In reassembly, you have only to remember that the main screw enters at a slight angle, and the bolt pin has to be oriented for this. No problem—you can't put it together wrong. There is a well-done manual with the gun, and it describes further disassembly, but the simple field-stripping just outlined should be all that is necessary.

The Exactor comes in a nice MTM foam-padded hard plastic case with compartments for ammo and accessories, and the Allen wrench and manual mentioned above are included. A spare magazine is optional, at extra cost, and there is a compartment for it in the case. The largest recess will hold a box or two of ammo, depending on the packaging.

As mentioned earlier, a fully-adjustable rear sight will be an optional accessory. There is also going to be a version with an 8-inch bull-type barrel, for more serious target work. A 25-round magazine is planned, and I've been told that it will not protrude from the bottom of the grip frame.

The light-weight polymer/aluminum construction of the pistol will make it a popular choice for campers, hikers and fishermen. Its flawless functioning and large-capacity magazine make it perfect for plinkers. It would also be a fine survival piece for pilots or anyone who travels in remote areas. I have long been familiar with other Ram-Line products, so I expected the Exactor to work perfectly. It does. ●

Data
Ram-Line Exactor

Caliber	22 Long Rifle
Weight	21 oz.
Length	9¾″
Height	6⅛″
Width	1⅜″
Barrel length	5½″
Sight radius	8⅜″
Magazine capacity	15 rounds
Price	$199.97
Maker	Ram-Line Inc. 10601 W. 48th St. Wheat Ridge, CO 80033

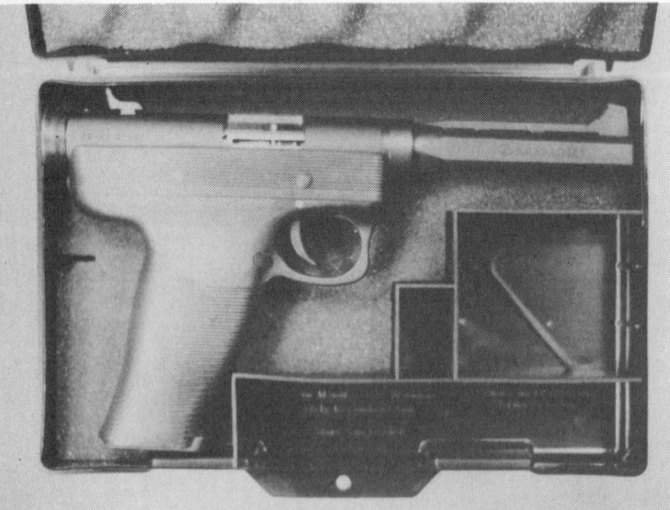

Each Exactor pistol comes in a foam-padded MTM case with compartments for ammunition and small accessories.

A test moulding of the alternate grip frame is shown at the right. It's of a more conventional shape and is to be offered at a later date as an option.

American Arms P98 AUTO PISTOL

Styled after the German Walther P-38, this 22 Long Rifle is a good plinker and trail gun at a reasonable price.

by DICK EADES

AMERICAN ARMS is a relatively new name to the firearms industry, but in the few years they have been around they have made their mark. The owner of American Arms made the shift from the jewelry business to the gun field with scarcely a breath in between. His first efforts involved importation of a line of shotguns manufactured in Spain by the now-defunct Diarm Corporation. He still imports a line of Spanish shotguns, but has added handguns from Germany and now is producing guns in this country.

The most recent introduction by American Arms is a handgun called the P98. At a glance, it is obviously a takeoff on the Walther Model HP or, as it is better known, the P-38. The new gun is available in 22 Long Rifle caliber and is somewhat smaller than its famous look-alike which was chambered for 9mm Parabellum. According to the manufacturer, the gun is a $\frac{7}{8}$-scale model of the P-38, designed by Erma-Werke, Germany. It is, however, manufactured in this country.

A second look at the P98 reveals that its similarity to the P-38 is strictly cosmetic. Functioning is more closely related to another well-known Walther product, the Model PP, which it resembles not at all in appearance.

Overall length of the P98 is 8 inches. It is 5 inches in height, from the magazine release to the top of the rear sight, and $1\frac{3}{8}$ inches at the widest point. The most noticeable feature, dif-

Throughout his tests, Eades found the American Arms P98 to handle and function well. For plinking and small game hunting, it's ideal.

The P-38 (top) and P98 show a definite similarity in outward appearance; internally, however, they are completely different. The P98 is slightly smaller in size and it has a ring-type hammer spur.

ferent from the original P-38, is the ring hammer of the P98 which replaces the rather sharp spurred hammer of the P-38.

Barrel length of the P98 is 4⅞ inches and it is topped by a streamlined front sight identical to that of the P-38. The barrel is actually a steel liner surrounded by an aluminum fairing. Close examination of the barrel sleeve reveals that it and the frame are cast as a single unit! Investment casting has come a long way since it was first used in firearms manufacturing. This pistol also uses a cast slide assembly. Just to make sure everything stays where it should, and to ensure longevity, highly stressed areas are beefed up by the addition of steel inserts where needed. For example, the bolt face is constructed of steel, cleverly dovetailed into the slide. The safety assembly, hammer and slide latch are also steel, as are the recoil spring and guide and all pins required for assembly.

The P98 is, for practical purposes, as close as you can get to a completely non-ferrous handgun. Yes, other makes have used Dural castings for even more parts, but none have produced a handgun as complex as this one with such extensive use of investment castings of a non-ferrous alloy.

The magazine of the P98 (also steel) holds eight rounds of 22 LR ammo. Only high-velocity ammunition is recommended for use. The reason for suggesting only high-velocity ammo is directly related to the slide weight on this little gun. The slide, with safety, bolt face and spring installed, weighs 4.5 ounces. Standard velocity cartridges *may* have enough "oomph" to work this action but would probably cause frequent failures to eject and/or feed.

The grips are contoured to duplicate the appearance of the original P-38, but the frame underneath drops almost straight from top to bottom of the backstrap. The grips are made of an oil-resistant plastic very similar to that used by Walther on original production guns. Unlike the P-38, this 22 lacks a lanyard ring projection at the lower rear of the left grip.

Disassembly of the P98 for cleaning is quick and simple. First, check to see that the pistol is unloaded. Next, move the safety-lever to cover the red dot which renders the pistol "safe." Remove the magazine, rotate the locking lever counterclockwise ¼-turn and pull the front of the trigger guard down. The guard will pivot on a pin located at the rear of the bow. Finally, pull the slide rearward and lift it at the rear to disengage it from the frame. Allow the slide to move forward slowly with spring pressure until it is removed from the frame. The recoil spring and recoil spring guide will remain on the frame and may be lifted from the recess under the left side of the barrel fairing. Further disassembly is not required for routine cleaning and should be avoided since it may void the warranty.

Reassembly is accomplished by reversing the order of the steps outlined. Care must be taken to ensure that the tip of the recoil spring guide is properly seated in a dimple on the left rear of the cross bar at the front of the slide. If this part is not precisely located, reassembly will be impossible.

The manual safety on the P98 permits the hammer and trigger to function normally, but blocks the firing pin from being struck by the hammer. It is quite a simple arrangement, but one that positively prevents accidental discharge once it is engaged.

Sights are a square notch rear and a square post front. This is a distinct improvement over the "U" notch found on original P-38s. The front sight presents a neatly streamlined appearance when viewed from the side but looks like a plain, square post when sighting. The rear sight is adjustable for windage only. Point of impact will vary with different lots of ammunition and the sight picture must be varied to achieve vertically centered hits, depending on the ammo used.

A trigger stop is included to prevent excessive trigger over-travel. The stop is threaded, but I was unable to move it with the tools I had at hand. The factory setting seems about right for either single-action or double-action use. Trigger pull weight is about 4 pounds in single-action mode and 11 pounds in double-action.

Though not in keeping with target requirements, the trigger pull is far above average for 22s of this general type. In single action, the pull is long and soft but without excessive creep. The double-action pull is about what I would expect from a top quality DA revolver and much superior to most DA autoloaders.

Range tests conducted with the P98 were carried out at a maximum distance of 25 yards. The type of shooting for which this pistol was designed will rarely be done at greater range so test-firing was confined to this distance. Conventional bullseye targets were used, as well as a few "casual" targets.

Most shooters who select the P98 will probably use it as a casual plinker rather than as a paper puncher, hence the choice of casual targets. My guess is there are more shots fired from 22s

The American Arms P98 field-stripped. Slide and magazine removal are accomplished in a matter of seconds. Note the recoil spring and guide below the barrel.

at old tin cans, marks on tree stumps and other "targets of opportunity" than are fired formally each year.

Ammunition chosen was a variety of high-velocity Long Rifles from Winchester, Remington, CCI, Federal and PMI. Although the manufacturer's instructions don't mention them either way, a few boxes of hyper-velocity cartridges, such as Remington Yellow Jackets and CCI Stingers, were tossed into the range kit.

Paper targets were set up at 25 yards and first shots were fired from a rest. Good fortune was with us as the group centered on the paper using what I consider a normal hold. The first ammo tried was Remington; next came Federal, and, wonder of wonders, the group printed in the same location! Point of impact shifted slightly with PMI, Winchester and CCI, but no adjustment for windage was required with any ammunition. A minor difference in the amount of front blade shown served to center each different brand of ammunition on the paper. Three shooters tried the gun and all found it surprisingly accurate.

Then the hyper-velocity ammunition was brought out and a magazine loaded with Remington Yellow Jackets. Now we were in a different ball game. They functioned as well as the high-velocity loads but printed about 2½ inches lower on the target. The

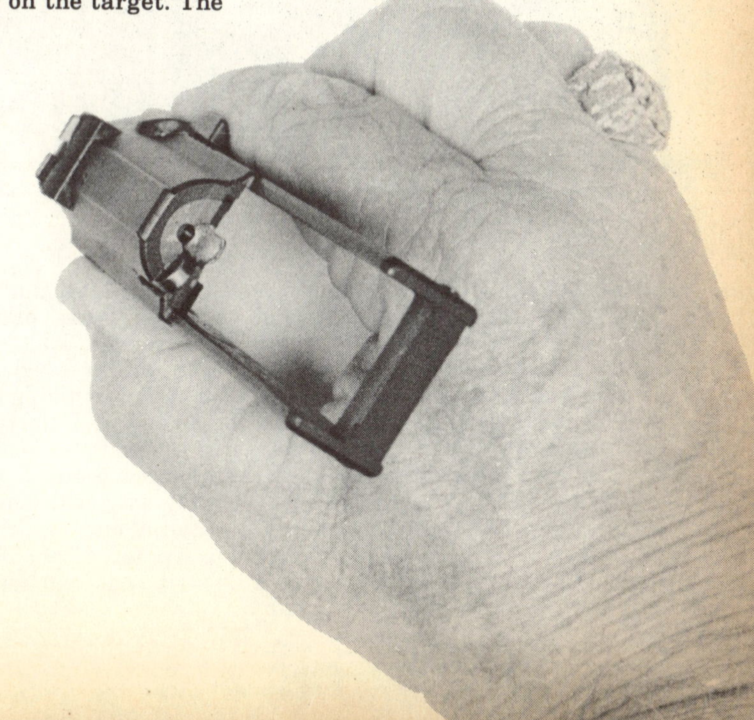

The steel bolt face insert is apparent in this front view of the slide. Steel is used here and other places where shooting stresses would cause problems with the alloy.

The trigger guard of the P98 pivots down at the front for field-stripping. The frame and barrel "housing" are a one-piece non-ferrous casting. The finish is a black paint that is easily repaired.

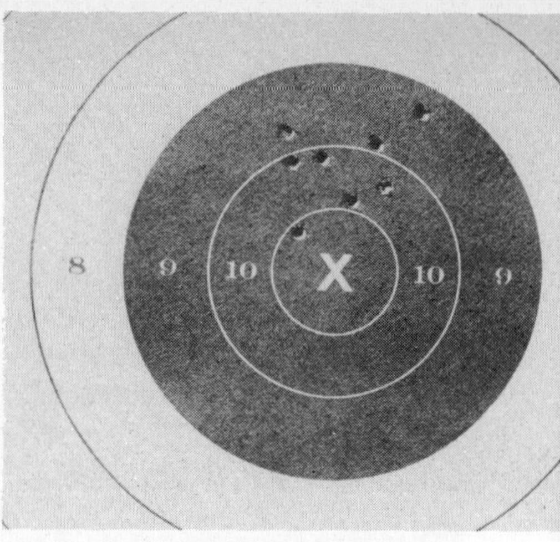

This target was typical of those fired with the P98. Eight shots formed a group between 2 and 3 inches.

Eades found the P98 to suit his shooting style and also discovered its liking for high velocity ammo when used alongside his 22 rifle. One brand/type of ammunition was suitable for both guns.

same held true for CCI's Stinger fodder. Oddly enough, little difference in group size could be detected when shifting from high- to hyper-velocity ammunition. With a single exception, the P98 produced groups within a fraction of an inch of the same size, no matter what load it was presented.

Shifting from the paper bullseyes, we concentrated on a few fierce, wild tin cans. Any of the three of us could successfully roll a can with a series of shots until it managed to hide behind a clump of grass or some other bulletproof screen. We also managed to do away with a few clay targets perched on bushes or hiding in the trees. In my opinion, this is the type of shooting for which the P98 was designed. For such, it has few peers.

My only criticism of the P98 is its external finish which seems to be common paint. After a bit of use and a few tear downs and reassemblies, there were a few spots where the finish had chipped away. Bright metal showed at the rear of the barrel sleeve and at the hinge pin. However, I found this finish can easily be repaired using flat black model airplane lacquer. Maybe there should be no criticism of a painted finish that is as easily repaired as this one.

Possibly, the best thing about the P98 is its price. List is established as $225, but I have seen the gun advertised for less than $200 in several trade papers. Anyone who feels a need for a plinkin' pistol that won't require pawning the family treasures should certainly consider the American Arms P98. It's a winner! ●

Data
American Arms
P98 Pistol

Caliber	22 Long Rifle
Magazine cap.	8 shots
Barrel length	4⅞"
Overall length	8"
Height	5"
Weight	28 oz.
Safeties	Hammer block, magazine
Sights	Fixed front, windage-adj. rear
Stocks	Grooved plastic
Finish	Black
Price	$219
Maker	American Arms 715 E. Armour Rd. N. Kansas City, MO 64116

THE COMPLETE COMPACT CATALOG

GUNDEX®

GUNDEX

A listing of all the guns in the catalog, by name and model, alphabetically and numerically.

E

F

G

H

I

J

K

T

U

V

W

Z

HANDGUNS—AUTOLOADERS, SERVICE & SPORT

Includes models suitable for several forms of competition and other sporting purposes.

A.A. ARMS AP9 AUTO PISTOL
Caliber: 9mm Para., 20-shot magazine.
Barrel: 5".
Weight: 3.5 lbs. **Length:** 11.8" overall.
Stocks: Checkered plastic.
Sights: Adjustable post front in ring, fixed open rear.
Features: Matte blue/black or nickel finish. Lever safety blocks trigger and sear. Fires from closed bolt. Introduced 1988. Made in U.S. by A.A. Arms, Inc.
Price: Matte blue/black **$259.00**
Price: Nickel finish **$294.00**

A.A. Arms AP9

A.A. Arms P95 Auto Pistol
Similar to the AP9 except does not have vented barrel shroud. Comes with 5-shot magazine; 20- and 30-shot magazines available. Introduced 1989.
Price: Matte blue/black finish **$249.99**
Price: Nickel finish **$279.99**

ACCU-TEK MODEL AT-380 AUTO PISTOL
Caliber: 32 ACP, 380 ACP, 5-shot magazine.
Barrel: 2.75".
Weight: 16 oz. **Length:** 5.6" overall.
Stocks: Black combat.
Sights: Blade front, rear adjustable for windage.
Features: External hammer, manual thumb safety with firing pin block and trigger disconnect. Black, chrome or chrome with black slide; also Lady 380 (chrome with gray bleached oak grips). Introduced 1990. Made in U.S. by Accu-Tek.
Price: **$170.00**

Accu-Tek AT-380

AMERICAN ARMS MODEL PX-22/PX-25 AUTO PISTOLS
Caliber: 22 LR or 25 ACP, 7-shot magazine.
Barrel: 2.85".
Weight: 15 oz. **Length:** 5.39" overall.
Stocks: Black checkered plastic.
Sights: Fixed.
Features: Double action; 7-shot magazine. Polished blue finish. Introduced 1989. Made in U.S. From American Arms, Inc.
Price: PX-22 . . . . **$189.00**
Price: PX-25 . . . . **$199.00**

American Arms PX-22

AMERICAN ARMS MODEL CX-22 DA AUTO PISTOL
Caliber: 22 LR, 8-shot magazine.
Barrel: 3⅓".
Weight: 22 oz. **Length:** 6⅓" overall.
Stocks: Checkered black polymer.
Sights: Blade front, rear adjustable for windage.
Features: Double action with manual hammer-block safety, firing pin safety. Alloy frame. Has external appearance of Walther PPK. Blue/black finish. Introduced 1990. Made in U.S. by American Arms, Inc.
Price: **$187.00**

AMERICAN ARMS MODEL P-98 AUTO PISTOL
Caliber: 22 LR, 8-shot magazine.
Barrel: 5".
Weight: 25 oz. **Length:** 8⅛" overall.
Stocks: Grooved black polymer.
Sights: Blade front, rear adjustable for windage.
Features: Double action with hammer-block safety, magazine disconnect safety. Alloy frame. Has external appearance of the Walther P-38 pistol. Introduced 1989. Made in U.S. by American Arms, Inc.
Price: **$219.00**

American Arms P-98

AMERICAN ARMS MODEL PK22 DA AUTO PISTOL
Caliber: 22 LR, 8-shot magazine.
Barrel: 3.3".
Weight: 22 oz. **Length:** 6.3" overall.
Stocks: Checkered plastic.
Sights: Fixed.
Features: Double action. Polished blue finish. Slide-mounted safety. Made in the U.S. by American Arms, Inc.
Price: **$199.00**

AMERICAN ARMS SABRE DA PISTOL

Caliber: 9mm Para., 9-shot; 40 S&W, 8-shot.
Barrel: 3.75".
Weight: 26 oz. **Length:** 6.8" overall.
Stocks: Black polymer composite.
Sights: Blade front, square notch rear adjustable for windage.
Features: Double-action only, short recoil. Left-side safety and magazine catch. Blue or stainless steel. Introduced 1991. Imported from Italy by American Arms, Inc.
Price: Blue **$309.00**
Price: Stainless **$339.00**

American Arms Sabre

AMERICAN ARMS SPECTRE DA PISTOL

Caliber: 9mm Para., 30-shot; 40 S&W, 25-shot magazine.
Barrel: 6".
Weight: 4 lbs., 8 oz. **Length:** 13.75".
Stocks: Black nylon.
Sights: Post front adjustable for windage and elevation, fixed U-notch rear.
Features: Triple action blowback fires from closed bolt; ambidextrous safety and decocking levers; matte black finish; magazine loading tool. For standard velocity ammunition only. From American Arms, Inc.
Price: **$375.00**

AMT Backup

AMT BACKUP AUTO PISTOL

Caliber: 380 ACP, 5-shot magazine.
Barrel: 2½".
Weight: 18 oz. **Length:** 5" overall.
Stocks: Carbon fiber.
Sights: Fixed, open, recessed.
Features: Concealed hammer, blowback operation; manual and grip safeties. All stainless steel construction. Smallest domestically-produced pistol in 380. From AMT.
Price: **$255.95**

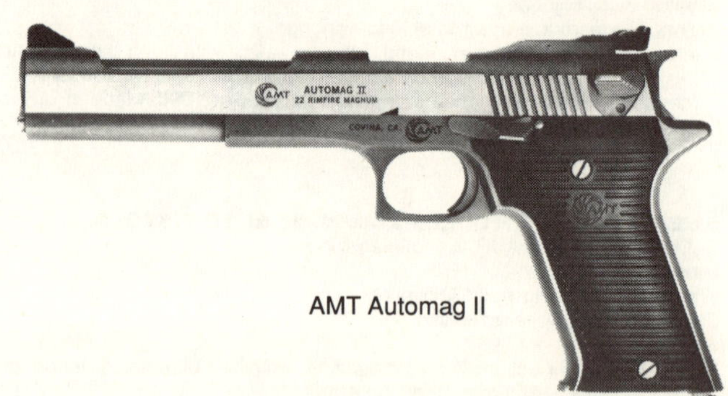

AMT Automag II

AMT AUTOMAG II AUTO PISTOL

Caliber: 22 WMR, 10-shot magazine.
Barrel: 3⅜", 4½", 6".
Weight: About 23 oz. **Length:** 9⅜" overall.
Stocks: Grooved carbon fiber.
Sights: Blade front, Millett adjustable rear.
Features: Made of stainless steel. Gas-assisted action. Exposed hammer. Slide flats have brushed finish, rest is sandblast. Squared trigger guard. Introduced 1986. From AMT.
Price: **$349.99**

AMT 45 ACP HARDBALLER LONG SLIDE

Caliber: 45 ACP.
Barrel: 7". **Length:** 10½" overall.
Stocks: Wrap-around rubber.
Sights: Fully adjustable rear sight.
Features: Slide and barrel are 2" longer than the standard 45, giving less recoil, added velocity, longer sight radius. Has extended combat safety, serrated matte rib, loaded chamber indicator, wide adjustable trigger. From AMT.
Price: **$539.99**

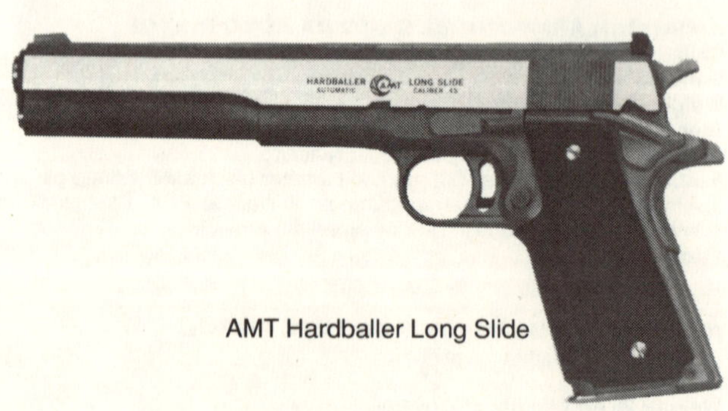

AMT Hardballer Long Slide

AMT 45 ACP HARDBALLER

Caliber: 45 ACP.
Barrel: 5".
Weight: 39 oz. **Length:** 8½" overall.
Stocks: Wrap-around rubber.
Sights: Adjustable.
Features: Extended combat safety, serrated matte slide rib, loaded chamber indicator, long grip safety, beveled magazine well, adjustable target trigger. All stainless steel. From AMT.
Price: **$505.95**
Price: Government model (as above except no rib, fixed sights) . . **$459.99**

AMT Skipper Auto Pistol

Similar to the AMT Government except scaled-down dimensions. Has 4.2" barrel, 7½" overall, weight is 33 oz. Magazine holds 7 shots. Millett adjustable sight. Checkered walnut grips. Chambered for 40 S&W and 45 ACP.
Price: Either caliber **$449.99**

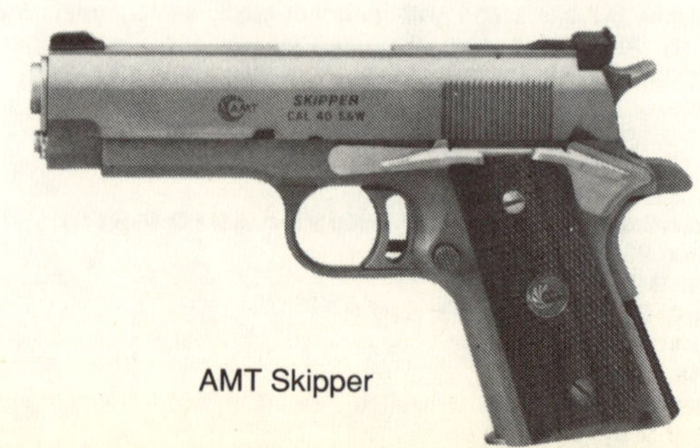

AMT Skipper

AMT Bull's-Eye Target Model
Similar to the AMT 45 ACP Hardballer except chambered for 40 S&W, 8-shot magazine, 5" barrel, weighs 38 oz. Has Millett adjustable sight, long grip safety, wrap-around Neoprene grips, beveled magazine well, wide adjustable trigger. Introduced 1991. From AMT.
Price: **$499.95**

AMT Bull's-Eye Target

AMT ON DUTY DA PISTOL
Caliber: 9mm Para., 40 S&W, 13-shot magazine.
Barrel: 4½".
Weight: 32 oz. **Length:** 7¾" overall.
Stocks: Smooth carbon fiber.
Sights: Blade front, rear adjustable for windage; three-dot system.
Features: Double-action only with inertia firing pin, trigger disconnector safety. Aluminum frame with steel recoil shoulder, stainless steel slide and barrel. Introduced 1991. Made in the U.S. by AMT.
Price: **$505.95**

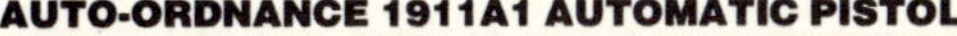

AMT On Duty

AUTO-ORDNANCE 1911A1 AUTOMATIC PISTOL
Caliber: 9mm Para., 38 Super, 9-shot; 10mm, 45 ACP, 7-shot magazine.
Barrel: 5".
Weight: 39 oz. **Length:** 8½" overall.
Stocks: Checkered plastic with medallion.
Sights: Blade front, rear adjustable for windage.
Features: Same specs as 1911A1 military guns—parts interchangeable. Frame and slide blued; each radius has non-glare finish. Made in U.S. by Auto-Ordnance Corp.
Price: 45 cal. **$368.95**
Price: 9mm, 38 Super **$404.25**
Price: 10mm (has three-dot combat sights, rubber wrap-around grips) **$404.25**

Auto-Ordnance ZG-51 Pit Bull Auto
Same as the 1911A1 except has 3½" barrel, weighs 36 oz. and has an over-all length of 7¼". Available in 45 ACP only; 7-shot magazine. Introduced 1989.
Price: **$404.25**

Auto-Ordnance 40 S&W 1911A1
Similar to the standard 1911A1 except has 4½" barrel giving overall length of 7¾", and weighs 37 oz. Has three-dot combat sight system, black rubber wrap-around grips, 8-shot magazine. Introduced 1991.
Price: **$415.95**

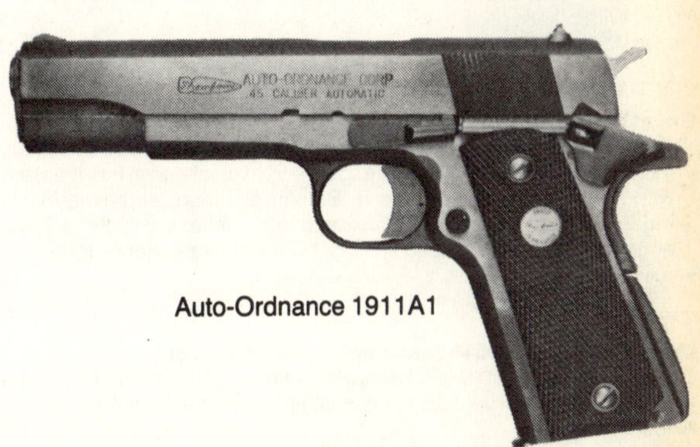

Auto-Ordnance 1911A1

BEEMAN MODEL P-08 AUTO PISTOL
Caliber: 22 LR, 8-shot magazine.
Barrel: 4".
Weight: 25 oz. **Length:** 7¾" overall.
Stocks: Checkered hardwood.
Sights: Fixed.
Features: Has toggle action similar to original "Luger" pistol. Action stays open after last shot. New feeding mechanism. Has magazine and sear disconnect safety systems. Imported from Germany by Beeman.
Price: **$389.50**

BEEMAN MINI P-08 AUTO PISTOL
Caliber: 380 ACP (5-shot).
Barrel: 3.5".
Weight: 22½ oz. **Length:** 7⅜" overall.
Stocks: Checkered hardwood.
Sights: Fixed.
Features: Toggle action similar to original "Luger" pistol. Action stays open after last shot. Has magazine and sear disconnect safety systems. New feeding mechanism. Imported from Germany by Beeman.
Price: **$389.50**

Beeman Mini P-08

BERETTA MODEL 950 BS AUTO PISTOL
Caliber: 22 Short, 6-shot; 25 ACP, 8-shot.
Barrel: 2.5".
Weight: 9.9 oz. (22 Short, 10.2 oz.) **Length:** 4.5" overall.
Stocks: Checkered black plastic.
Sights: Fixed.
Features: Single action, thumb safety; tip-up barrel for direct loading/unloading, cleaning. From Beretta U.S.A.
Price: Blue, 22, 25 . . . . **$175.00**
Price: Nickel, 22, 25 . . . . **$205.00**
Price: Engraved **$250.00**

Beretta Model 21 Pistol
Similar to the Model 950 BS. Chambered for 22 LR and 25 ACP. Both double action. 2.5" barrel, 4.9" overall length. 7-round magazine on 22 cal.; 8-round magazine on 25 cal.; 22 cal. available in nickel finish. Both have walnut grips. Introduced in 1985.
Price: 22-cal. **$225.00**
Price: 22-cal., nickel finish **$250.00**
Price: 25-cal. **$225.00**
Price: 25-cal., nickel finish **$250.00**
Price: EL model, 22 or 25 . . . . **$275.00**

BERETTA MODEL 80 SERIES DA PISTOLS

Caliber: 380 ACP, 13-shot magazine (8-shot for M85F); 22 LR, 7-shot (M87).
Barrel: 3.82".
Weight: About 23 oz. (M84/85); 20.8 oz. (M87). **Length:** 6.8" overall.
Stocks: Glossy black plastic (wood optional at extra cost).
Sights: Fixed front, drift-adjustable rear.
Features: Double action, quick takedown, convenient magazine release. Introduced 1977. Imported from Italy by Beretta U.S.A.
Price: Model 84F (380 ACP) **$495.00**
Price: Model 84F wood grips **$520.00**
Price: Model 84F nickel finish **$560.00**
Price: Model 85F nickel finish, 8-shot **$515.00**
Price: Model 85F plastic grips, 8-shot **$455.00**
Price: Model 85F wood grips, 8-shot **$480.00**
Price: Model 87, 22 LR, 7-shot magazine, wood grips **$460.00**
Price: Model 87 Long Barrel, 22 LR, single action **$480.00**
Price: Model 89 Sport Wood, single action, 22 LR **$685.00**

Beretta Model 84F

Beretta Model 86

Similar to the 380-caliber Model 85 except has tip-up barrel for first-round loading. Barrel length is 4.33", overall length of 7.33". Has 8-shot magazine, walnut or plastic grips. Introduced 1989.
Price: **$530.00**

Beretta Model 86

BERETTA MODEL 92FS PISTOL

Caliber: 9mm Para., 15-shot magazine.
Barrel: 4.9".
Weight: 34 oz. **Length:** 8.5" overall.
Stocks: Checkered black plastic; wood optional at extra cost.
Sights: Blade front, rear adjustable for windage.
Features: Double action. Extractor acts as chamber loaded indicator, squared trigger guard, grooved front- and backstraps, inertia firing pin. Matte finish. Introduced 1977. Made in U.S. and imported from Italy by Beretta U.S.A.
Price: With plastic grips **$630.00**
Price: With wood grips **$635.00**

Beretta Model 92FC Pistol

Similar to the Beretta Model 92F except has cut down frame, 4.3" barrel, 7.8" overall length, 13-shot magazine, weighs 31.5 oz. Introduced 1989.
Price: With plastic grips **$625.00**
Price: With wood grips **$655.00**

Beretta Model 92F-EL Pistol

Same as the standard Model 92FS except has gold trim on the safety levers, trigger, magazine release and grip screws. Top of barrel has the Beretta logo with gold inlay, the slide has P. Beretta signature engraved in gold inlay. Figured walnut grips are contoured and have the Beretta logo deeply engraved. High polish blued finish on barrel, slide and frame. Introduced 1991.
Price: **$700.00**

Beretta Model 92FS

Beretta Model 92SB Compact Type M Pistol

Similar to the Model 92FC except has thinner grip, straight 8-shot magazine. Weighs 30.8 oz., has 1.25" overall width. Introduced 1989.
Price: **$640.00**

BERSA MODEL 23 AUTO PISTOL

Caliber: 22 LR, 10-shot magazine.
Barrel: 3.5".
Weight: 24.5 oz. **Length:** 6.6" overall.
Stocks: Walnut with stippled panels.
Sights: Blade front, notch rear adjustable for windage.
Features: Double action; firing pin and magazine safeties. Available in blue or nickel. Introduced 1989. Imported from Argentina by Eagle Imports, Inc.
Price: Blue **$266.95**
Price: Nickel **$296.95**

BERSA MODEL 85 AUTO PISTOL

Caliber: 380 ACP, 13-shot magazine.
Barrel: 3.5".
Weight: 25.75 oz. **Length:** 6.6" overall.
Stocks: Walnut with stippled panels.
Sights: Blade front, notch rear adjustable for windage.
Features: Double action; firing pin and magazine safeties. Available in blue or nickel. Introduced 1989. Imported from Argentina by Eagle Imports, Inc.
Price: Blue **$314.95**
Price: Nickel **$374.95**
Price: Model 83 (as above, except 7-shot magazine), blue **$266.95**
Price: Model 83, nickel **$296.95**

Bersa Model 85

BRNO CZ 75 AUTO PISTOL
Caliber: 9mm Para., 15-shot magazine.
Barrel: 4.7".
Weight: 35 oz. **Length:** 8" overall.
Stocks: Checkered wood.
Sights: Blade front, rear adjustable for windage.
Features: Double action; blued finish. Imported from Czechoslovakia by T.D. Arms.
Price: $599.00

BRNO CZ 85 Auto Pistol
Same gun as the CZ 75 except has ambidextrous slide release and safety-levers, is available in 9mm Para. and 7.65, contoured composition grips, matte finish on top of slide. Introduced 1986.
Price: $655.00

BROWNING BDM DA AUTO PISTOL
Caliber: 9mm Para., 15-shot magazine.
Barrel: 4.73"
Weight: 31 oz. **Length:** 7.85" overall.
Stocks: Moulded black composition; checkered, with thumbrest on both sides.
Sights: Low profile removable blade front, rear screw adjustable for windage.
Features: Mode selector allows switching from DA pistol to "revolver" mode via a switch on the slide. Decocking lever/safety on the frame. Two redundant, passive, internal safety systems. All steel frame; matte black finish. Introduced 1991. Made in the U.S. From Browning.
Price: $504.95

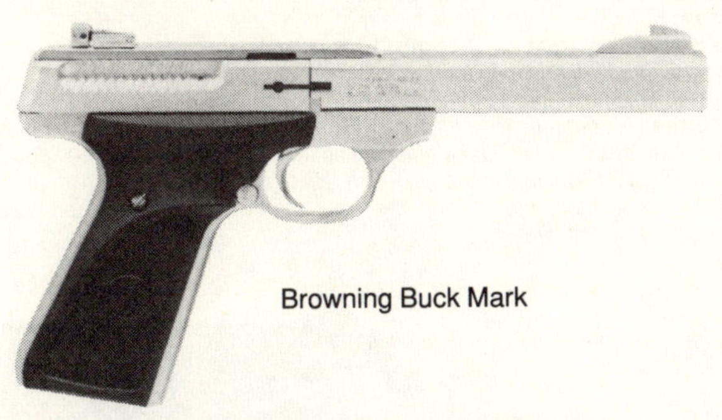
Browning Buck Mark

Browning Buck Mark Varmint

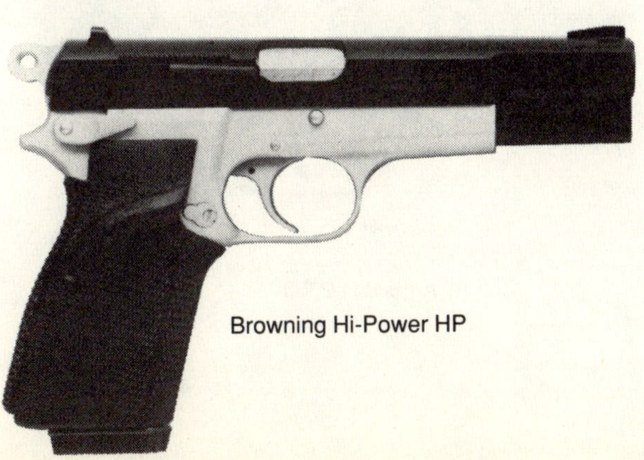
Browning Hi-Power HP

BRNO CZ 83 DOUBLE-ACTION PISTOL
Caliber: 32, 15-shot; 380, 13-shot.
Barrel: 3.7".
Weight: 26.5 oz. **Length:** 6.7" overall.
Stocks: Checkered black plastic.
Sights: Blade front, rear adjustable for windage.
Features: Double action; ambidextrous magazine release and safety. Polished or matte blue. Imported from Czechoslovakia by T.D. Arms.
Price: $425.00

Browning BDM

BROWNING BUCK MARK 22 PISTOL
Caliber: 22 LR, 10-shot magazine.
Barrel: 5½".
Weight: 32 oz. **Length:** 9½" overall.
Stocks: Black moulded composite with skip-line checkering.
Sights: Ramp front, rear adjustable for windage and elevation.
Features: All steel, matte blue finish or nickel, gold-colored trigger. Buck Mark Plus has laminated wood grips. Made in U.S. Introduced 1985. From Browning.
Price: Buck Mark, blue $219.95
Price: Buck Mark, nickel finish with contoured rubber stocks $249.95
Price: Buck Mark Plus $265.95

Browning Buck Mark Varmint
Same as the Buck Mark except has 9⅞" heavy barrel with .900" diameter and full-length scope base (no open sights); black multi-laminated wood grips, with optional forend. Overall length is 14", weight is 48 oz. Introduced 1987.
Price: $334.95

BROWNING HI-POWER 9mm AUTOMATIC PISTOL
Caliber: 9mm Para., 13-shot magazine.
Barrel: 4²¹⁄₃₂".
Weight: 32 oz. **Length:** 7¾" overall.
Stocks: Walnut, hand checkered, or black Polyamide.
Sights: ⅛" blade front; rear screw-adjustable for windage and elevation. Also available with fixed rear (drift-adjustable for windage).
Features: External hammer with half-cock and thumb safeties. A blow on the hammer cannot discharge a cartridge; cannot be fired with magazine removed. Fixed rear sight model available. Ambidextrous safety available only with matte finish, moulded grips. Imported from Belgium by Browning.
Price: Fixed sight model, walnut grips $497.95
Price: 9mm with rear sight adj. for w. and e., walnut grips $543.95
Price: Mark III, standard matte black finish, fixed sight, moulded grips, ambidextrous safety $458.95
Price: Silver chrome, adjustable sight, Pachmayr grips $549.95

Consult our Directory pages for the location of firms mentioned.

Browning Hi-Power HP-Practical Pistol
Similar to the standard Hi-Power except has silver-chromed frame with blued slide, wrap-around Pachmayr rubber grips, round-style serrated hammer and removable front sight, fixed rear (drift-adjustable for windage). Introduced 1991.
Price: $549.95

Browning BDA-380

BROWNING BDA-380 DA AUTO PISTOL
Caliber: 380 ACP, 13-shot magazine.
Barrel: 3 13/16".
Weight: 23 oz. **Length:** 6¾" overall.
Stocks: Smooth walnut with inset Browning medallion.
Sights: Blade front, rear drift-adjustable for windage.
Features: Combination safety and de-cocking lever will automatically lower a cocked hammer to half-cock and can be operated by right- or left-hand shooters. Inertia firing pin. Introduced 1978. Imported from Italy by Browning.
Price: Blue **$522.95**
Price: Nickel **$549.95**

Bryco Model 48

BRYCO MODEL 38 AUTO PISTOLS
Caliber: 22 LR, 32 ACP, 380 ACP, 6-shot magazine.
Barrel: 2.8".
Weight: 15 oz. **Length:** 5.3" overall.
Stocks: Polished resin-impregnated wood.
Sights: Fixed.
Features: Safety locks sear and slide. Choice of satin nickel, bright chrome or black Teflon finishes. Introduced 1988. From Jennings Firearms.
Price: 22 LR, 32 ACP **$109.95**
Price: 380 ACP **$129.95**

BRYCO MODEL 48 AUTO PISTOLS
Caliber: 22 LR, 32 ACP, 380 ACP, 6-shot magazine.
Barrel: 4".
Weight: 19 oz. **Length:** 6.7" overall.
Stocks: Polished resin-impregnated wood.
Sights: Fixed.
Features: Safety locks sear and slide. Choice of satin nickel, bright chrome or black Teflon finishes. Announced 1988. From Jennings Firearms.
Price: 22 LR, 32 ACP **$139.00**
Price: 380 ACP **$139.00**

CALICO MODEL 110 AUTO PISTOL
Caliber: 22 LR, 100-shot magazine.
Barrel: 6".
Weight: 3.7 lbs. (loaded). **Length:** 17.9" overall.
Stocks: Moulded composition.
Sights: Adjustable post front, notch rear.
Features: Aluminum alloy frame; flash suppressor; pistol grip compartment; ambidextrous safety. Uses same helical-feed magazine as M-100 Carbine. Introduced 1986. Made in U.S. From Calico.
Price: **$243.90**

Calico Model 110

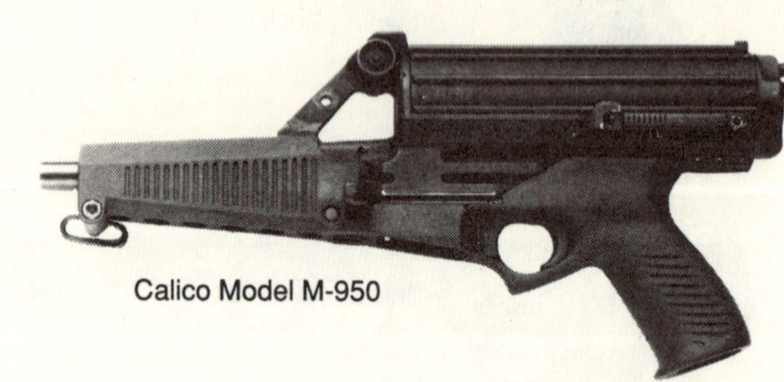
Calico Model M-950

CALICO MODEL M-950 AUTO PISTOL
Caliber: 9mm Para., 50- or 100-shot magazine.
Barrel: 7.5".
Weight: 2.25 lbs. (empty). **Length:** 14" overall (50-shot magazine).
Stocks: Glass-filled polymer.
Sights: Post front adjustable for windage and elevation, fixed notch rear.
Features: Helical feed 50- or 100-shot magazine. Ambidextrous safety, static cocking handle. Retarded blowback action. Glass-filled polymer grip. Introduced 1989. From Calico.
Price: **$596.90**

CLARIDGE HI-TEC S, L
Caliber: 9mm Para., (18-shot); 45 ACP, (10-shot).
Barrel: 5" (S model); 9.5" (L model).
Weight: 3 lbs., 2 oz. (L9 model) **Length:** 15.1" overall.
Stocks: Moulded composition.
Sights: Adjustable post front in ring, open rear adjustable for windage.
Features: Telescoping bolt, floating firing pin. Safety locks the firing pin. Sight radius of 14.1". Made in U.S. From Claridge Hi-Tec, Inc.
Price: S Model (5"), 9mm or 45 . . . . **$720.00**
Price: L model (9.5") 9mm or 45 . . . . **$775.00**

COLT ALL AMERICAN MODEL 2000 DA AUTO
Caliber: 9mm Para., 15-shot magazine.
Barrel: 4.5".
Weight: 29 oz. **Length:** 7.5" overall.
Stocks: Checkered polymer.
Sights: Ramped blade front, rear drift-adjustable for windage. Three dot system.
Features: Double-action only. Moulded polymer frame, blued steel slide. Internal striker block safety. Introduced 1991. Made in U.S. by Colt's Mfg. Co., Inc.
Price: . . . . **NA**

Colt All American 2000

CAUTION: PRICES CHANGE, CHECK AT GUNSHOP.

COLT GOVERNMENT MODEL MK IV/SERIES 80
Caliber: 9mm, 38 Super, 45 ACP, 7-shot.
Barrel: 5".
Weight: 38 oz. **Length:** 8½" overall.
Stocks: Checkered walnut.
Sights: Ramp front, fixed square notch rear.
Features: Grip and thumb safeties and internal firing pin safety, grooved trigger. Accurizor barrel and bushing.
Price: 45 ACP, blue **$639.95**
Price: 45 ACP, stainless **$679.95**
Price: 45 ACP, bright stainless **$749.95**
Price: 9mm, blue **$649.95**
Price: 9mm, stainless **$684.95**
Price: 38 Super, blue **$649.95**
Price: 38 Super, stainless **$684.95**
Price: 38 Super, bright stainless **$754.95**

Colt 10mm Delta Elite
Similar to the Government Model except chambered for 10mm auto cartridge. Has three-dot high profile front and rear combat sights, rubber combat stocks with Delta medallion, internal firing pin safety, and new recoil spring/buffer system. Introduced 1987.
Price: Blue **$704.95**
Price: STS **$714.95**
Price: BSTS **$784.95**

Colt Combat Elite MK IV/Series 80
Similar to the Government Model except in 45 ACP only, has stainless frame with ordnance steel slide and internal parts. High profile front, rear sights with three-dot system, extended grip safety, beveled magazine well, rubber combat stocks. Introduced 1986.
Price: **$774.95**

COLT DOUBLE EAGLE MKII/SERIES 90 DA PISTOL
Caliber: 9mm Para., 38 Super, 9-shot; l0mm, 45 ACP, 8-shot magazine.
Barrel: 5".
Weight: 39 ozs. **Length:** 8½" overall.
Stocks: Black checkered Xenoy thermoplastic.
Sights: Blade front, rear adjustable for windage. High profile three-dot system. Colt Accro adjustable sight optional.
Features: Made of stainless steel with matte finish. Checkered and curved extended trigger guard, wide steel trigger; decocking lever on left side; traditional magazine release; grooved frontstrap; bevelled magazine well; extended grip guard; rounded, serrated combat-style hammer. Announced 1989.
Price: **$695.95**
Price: As above, except Accro adjustable sight **$725.95**
Price: 9mm **$699.95**
Price: 38 Super **$699.95**
Price: 10mm **$715.95**
Price: 10mm, Accro sight **$745.95**
Price: Combat Comm., 45, 4½" bbl. **$695.95**

Colt Double Eagle Officer's ACP
Similar to the regular Double Eagle except 45 ACP only, 3½" barrel, 34 oz., 7¼" overall length. Has 5¼" sight radius. Introduced 1991.
Price: **$679.95**

COLT GOVERNMENT MODEL 380
Caliber: 380 ACP, 7-shot magazine.
Barrel: 3¼".
Weight: 21¾ oz. **Length:** 6" overall.
Stocks: Checkered composition.
Sights: Ramp front, square notch rear, fixed.
Features: Scaled-down version of the 1911A1 Colt G.M. Has thumb and internal firing pin safeties. Introduced 1983.
Price: Blue **$419.95**
Price: Nickel **$469.95**
Price: Stainless **$449.95**
Price: Pocketlite 380, blue **$419.95**

Colt Mustang Plus II
Similar to the 380 Government Model except has the shorter barrel and slide of the Mustang. Introduced 1988.
Price: Blue **$419.95**
Price: Stainless **$448.95**

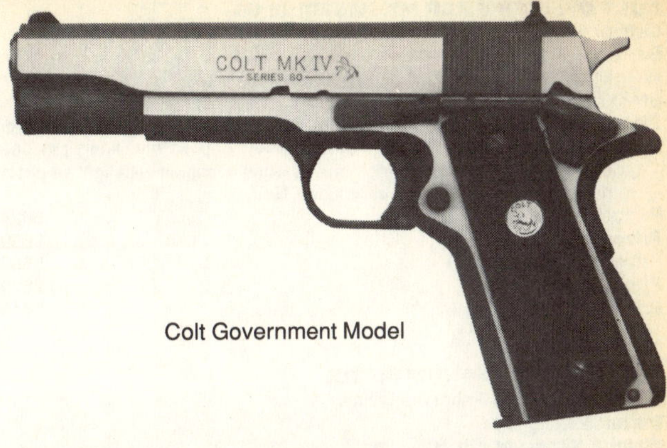

Colt Government Model

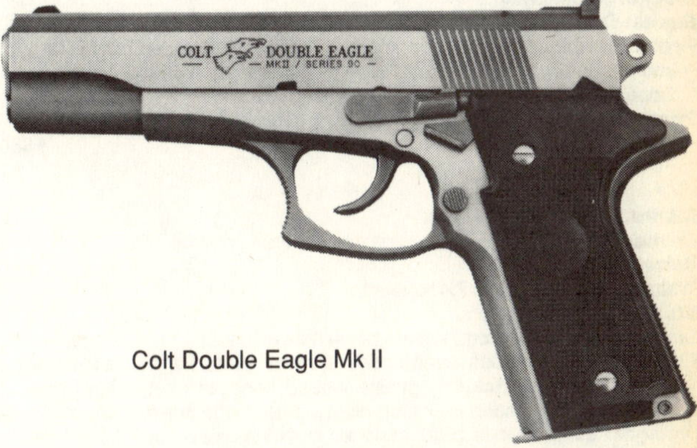

Colt Double Eagle Mk II

Colt Double Eagle Officer's ACP

Colt Government Pocketlite

Colt Mustang 380, Mustang Pocketlite
Similar to the standard 380 Government Model. Mustang has steel frame (18.5 oz.), Pocketlite has aluminum alloy (12.5 oz.). Both are ½" shorter than 380 G.M., have 2¾" barrel. Introduced 1987.
Price: Mustang 380, blue **$419.95**
Price: As above, nickel **$469.95**
Price: As above, stainless **$449.95**
Price: Mustang Pocketlite, blue **$419.95**

COLT OFFICER'S ACP MK IV/SERIES 80

Caliber: 45 ACP, 6-shot magazine.
Barrel: 3½".
Weight: 34 oz. **Length:** 7¼" overall.
Stocks: Checkered walnut.
Sights: Ramp blade front with white dot, square notch rear with two white dots.
Features: Trigger safety lock (thumb safety), grip safety, firing pin safety; grooved trigger; flat mainspring housing. Also available with lightweight alloy frame and in stainless steel. Introduced 1985.
Price: Matte finish **$624.95**
Price: Blue **$639.95**
Price: L.W., matte finish **$639.95**
Price: Stainless **$679.95**
Price: Bright stainless **$749.95**

COONAN 357 MAGNUM PISTOL

Caliber: 357 Mag., 7-shot magazine.
Barrel: 5".
Weight: 42 oz. **Length:** 8.3" overall.
Stocks: Smooth walnut.
Sights: Open, adjustable.
Features: Unique barrel hood improves accuracy and reliability. Many parts interchange with Colt autos. Has grip, hammer, half-cock safeties. From Coonan Arms.
Price: Model B (linkless barrel, interchangeable ramp front sight, new rear sight) **$680.00**

CZ 99 DA AUTO PISTOL

Caliber: 9mm Para., 15-shot magazine; 20-shot optional.
Barrel: 4.25".
Weight: 30 oz. **Length:** 7.4" overall.
Stocks: Checkered walnut.
Sights: Square post front, square notch rear adjustable for windage.
Features: Ambidextrous hammer decock, slide release and slide retainer using one lever; ambidextrous magazine release; firing pin safety; alloy frame, steel slide; chamber loaded indicator; night sights; matte finish. Comes with extra magazine. Introduced 1990. Imported from Yugoslavia by T.D. Arms.
Price: **$650.00**

CZ 40 DA Auto Pistol

Similar to the CZ 99 except chambered for 40 S&W, 11-shot magazine; 7.50" barrel; has slightly modified grip shape. Introduced 1991. Imported from Yugoslavia by T.D. Arms.
Price: . . . . **NA**

Daewoo DP51

D Max Auto

COLT COMBAT COMMANDER AUTO PISTOL

Caliber: 9mm Para., 38 Super, 9-shot; 45 ACP, 7-shot.
Barrel: 4¼".
Weight: 36 oz. **Length:** 7¾" overall.
Stocks: Checkered walnut.
Sights: Fixed, glare-proofed blade front, square notch rear.
Features: Grooved trigger and hammer spur; arched housing; grip and thumb safeties.
Price: 9mm, blue **$649.95**
Price: 45, blue **$639.95**
Price: 45, stainless **$689.95**
Price: 38 Super, blue **$649.95**

Colt Lightweight Commander MK IV/Series 80

Same as Commander except high strength aluminum alloy frame, wood panel grips, weight 27½ oz. 45 ACP only.
Price: Blue **$639.95**

Coonan 357 Magnum

CZ 40

DAEWOO DP51 AUTO PISTOL

Caliber: 9mm Para., 13-shot magazine.
Barrel: 4.1".
Weight: 28.2 oz. **Length:** 7.48" overall.
Stocks: Checkered composition.
Sights: Blade front, square notch rear drift adjustable for windage.
Features: Traditional double-action mechanism. Ambidextrous manual safety and magazine catch, half-cock and firing pin block. Alloy frame, squared trigger guard. Matte black finish. Introduced 1991. Imported from Korea by Davidson's.
Price: **$499.99**

D MAX AUTO PISTOL

Caliber: 9mm Para., 10mm Auto, 40 S&W, 45 ACP, 30-shot magazine.
Barrel: 6" (8", 10" optional).
Weight: 5 lbs. **Length:** 13.75" overall.
Stocks: Smooth walnut grip and forend.
Sights: Post front, open rear adjustable for windage and elevation.
Features: Blowback semi-auto with trigger-block safety. Fires from closed bolt. Side-feed magazine. Max-Coat finish. Drilled and tapped for scope base. Made in the U.S. by D Max Industries.
Price: **$539.00**

CAUTION: PRICES CHANGE, CHECK AT GUNSHOP.

DAVIS P-380 AUTO PISTOL
Caliber: 380 ACP, 5-shot magazine.
Barrel: 2.8".
Weight: 22 oz. **Length:** 5.4" overall.
Stocks: Black composition.
Sights: Fixed.
Features: Choice of chrome or black Teflon finish. Introduced 1991. Made in U.S. by Davis Industries.
Price: $98.00

DAVIS P-32 AUTO PISTOL
Caliber: 32 ACP, 6-shot magazine.
Barrel: 2.8".
Weight: 22 oz. **Length:** 5.4" overall.
Stocks: Laminated wood.
Sights: Fixed.
Features: Choice of black Teflon or chrome finish. Announced 1986. Made in U.S. by Davis Industries.
Price: $87.50

Davis P-32

Desert Eagle Magnum

DESERT EAGLE MAGNUM PISTOL
Caliber: 357 Mag., 9-shot; 41 Mag., 44 Mag., 8-shot; 50 Magnum, 7-shot.
Barrel: 6", 10", 14" interchangeable.
Weight: 357 Mag.—52 oz. (alloy), 62 oz. (steel); 41 Mag., 44 Mag.—56 oz. (alloy), 66.9 oz. (stainless). **Length:** 10¼" overall (6" bbl.).
Stocks: Wraparound soft rubber.
Sights: Blade on ramp front, combat-style rear. Adjustable available.
Features: Rotating three-lug bolt; ambidextrous safety; combat-style trigger guard; adjustable trigger optional. Military epoxy finish. Satin, bright nickel, hard chrome, polished and blued finishes available. Imported from Israel by Magnum Research, Inc.
Price: 357, 6" bbl., standard pistol $789.00
Price: As above, alloy frame $789.00
Price: As above, stainless steel frame $839.00
Price: 41 Mag., 6", standard pistol $799.00
Price: 41 Mag., alloy frame $799.00
Price: 41 Mag., stainless steel frame $849.00
Price: 44 Mag., 6", standard pistol $839.00
Price: As above, alloy frame $839.00
Price: As above, stainless steel frame $889.00
Price: 50 Magnum, 6" bbl., standarad pistol $1,189.00

Desert Industries "Double Deuce"

DESERT INDUSTRIES "DOUBLE DEUCE" PISTOL
Caliber: 22 LR, 6-shot; 25 ACP, 5-shot.
Barrel: 2½".
Weight: 15 oz. **Length:** 5½" overall.
Stocks: Rosewood.
Sights: Fixed.
Features: Double action; stainless steel construction with matte finish; ambidextrous slide-mounted safety. From Desert Industries, Inc.
Price: 22 . . . . $399.95
Price: 25 (Two-Bit Special) $399.95

Consult our Directory pages for the location of firms mentioned.

E.A.A. WITTNESS DA AUTO PISTOL
Caliber: 9mm Para., 16-shot magazine; 40 S&W, 12-shot magazine; 41 Action Express, 11-shot magazine; 45 ACP, 10-shot magazine.
Barrel: 4.72".
Weight: 35.33 oz. **Length:** 8.10" overall.
Stocks: Checkered rubber.
Sights: Undercut blade front, open rear adjustable for windage.
Features: Double-action trigger system; squared-off trigger guard; frame-mounted safety. Introduced 1991. Imported from Italy by European American Armory.
Price: 9mm, blue $305.00
Price: 9mm, satin chrome $329.00
Price: 9mm, blue slide, chrome frame $329.00
Price: 9mm, 5" bbl., ported bbl. and slide, blue $445.00
Price: 9mm Compact, blue, 13-shot $305.00
Price: As above, blue slide, chrome frame, or all-chrome $329.00
Price: 40 S&W or 41 A.E., blue $385.00
Price: As above, blue slide, chrome frame, or all-chrome $405.00
Price: 40 S&W or 41 A.E. Compact, 8-shot, blue $385.00
Price: As above, blue slide, chrome frame, or all-chrome $405.00
Price: 45 ACP, blue $429.00
Price: As above, blue slide, chrome frame, or all-chrome $440.00
Price: 45 ACP Compact, 8-shot, blue $429.00
Price: As above, blue slide, chrome frame or all-chrome $444.00

DESERT INDUSTRIES "WAR EAGLE" PISTOL
Caliber: 9mm Para., 14-shot magazine; 10mm, 13-shot; 45 ACP, 12-shot.
Barrel: 4".
Weight: NA. **Length:** NA.
Stocks: Rosewood.
Sights: Fixed.
Features: Double action; matte-finished stainless steel; ambidextrous safety. Announced 1986. From Desert Industries, Inc.
Price: $795.00

E.A.A. EUROPEAN MODEL AUTO PISTOLS
Caliber: 32 ACP or 380 ACP, 7-shot magazine.
Barrel: 3.88".
Weight: 26 oz. **Length:** 7⅜" overall.
Stocks: European hardwood.
Sights: Fixed blade front; rear drift-adjustable for windage.
Features: Chrome or blue finish; magazine, thumb, and firing pin safeties; external hammer; safety-lever takedown. Imported from Italy by Excam, Inc.
Price: 32-cal., blue $135.00
Price: 32-cal., chrome $149.00
Price: 380-cal., blue $135.00
Price: 380-cal., chrome $149.00

ERMA SPORTING PISTOL MODEL ESP 85A

Caliber: 22 LR, 8-shot; 32 S&W Long, 5-shot.
Barrel: 6".
Weight: 39.9 oz. **Length:** 10" overall.
Stocks: Checkered walnut with thumbrest. Adjustable target stocks optional.
Sights: Interchangeable blade front, micro. rear adjustable for windage and elevation.
Features: Interchangeable caliber conversion kit available; adjustable trigger, trigger stop. Comes with lockable carrying case. Imported from West Germany by Precision Sales Int'l. Introduced 1988.
Price: 22 LR **$1,228.00**
Price: 32 S&W Long **$1,284.00**
Price: 22 LR, chrome **$1,451.00**

Erma ESP 85A

GLOCK 17 AUTO PISTOL

Caliber: 9mm Para., 17-shot magazine.
Barrel: 4.49".
Weight: 21.9 oz. (without magazine). **Length:** 7.21" overall.
Stocks: Black polymer.
Sights: Dot on front blade, white outline rear adjustable for windage and elevation, or fixed.
kFeatures: Polymer frame, steel slide; double-action trigger with "Safe Action" system; mechanical firing pin safety, drop safety; simple takedown without tools; locked breech, recoil operated action. Adopted by Austrian armed forces 1983. NATO approved 1984. Imported from Austria by Glock, Inc.
Price: With extra magazine, magazine loader, cleaning kit **$579.95**
Price: Model 17L (6" barrel) **$963.15**

Glock 22

Grendel P-31

GRENDEL P-30 AUTO PISTOL

Caliber: 22 WMR, 30-shot magazine.
Barrel: 5", 8".
Weight: 21 oz. (5" barrel). **Length:** 8.5" overall (5" barrel).
Stocks: Checkered Zytel.
Sights: Blade front, fixed rear.
Features: Blowback action with fluted chamber; ambidextrous safety, reversible magazine catch. Scope mount available. Introduced 1990.
Price: With 5" barrel **$225.00**
Price: With 8" barrel (Model P-30L) **$280.00**

GRENDEL P-31 AUTO PISTOL

Caliber: 22 WMR, 30-shot magazine.
Barrel: 11".
Weight: 48 oz. **Length:** 17.5" overall.
Stocks: Checkered black Zytel grip and forend.
Sights: Blade front adjustable for windage and elevation, fixed rear.
Features: Blowback action with fluted chamber. Ambidextrous safety. Matte black finish. Muzzlebrake. Scope mount optional. Introduced 1991. Made in the U.S. by Grendel, Inc.
Price: **$345.00**

Glock 19 Auto Pistol

Similar to the Glock 17 except has a 4" barrel, giving an overall length of 6.74" and weight of 20.99 oz. Magazine capacity is 15 rounds. Fixed or adjustable rear sight. Introduced 1988.
Price: **$579.95**

Glock 20 10mm Auto Pistol

Similar to the Glock Model 17 except chambered for 10mm Automatic cartridge. Barrel length is 4.60", overall length is 8.27", and weight is 26.3 oz. (without magazine). Magazine capacity is 15 rounds. Fixed or adjustable rear sight. Comes with an extra magazine, magazine loader, cleaning rod and brush. Introduced 1990. Imported from Austria by Glock, Inc.
Price: **$638.49**

Glock 21 Auto Pistol

Similar to the Glock 17 except chambered for 45 ACP, 13-shot magazine. Overall length is 8.27", weight is 25.2 oz. (without magazine). Fixed or adjustable rear sight. Introduced 1991.
Price: **$638.49**

Glock 22 Auto Pistol

Similar to the Glock 17 except chambered for 40 S&W, 15-shot magazine. Overall length is 7.40", weight is 22.3 oz. (without magazine). Fixed or adjustable rear sight. Introduced 1990.
Price: **$579.95**

Glock 23 Auto Pistol

Similar to the Glock 19 except chambered for 40 S&W, 13-shot magazine. Overall length is 6.97", weight is 20.6 oz. (without magazine). Fixed or adjustable rear sight. Introduced 1990.
Price: **$579.95**

GRENDEL P-10 AUTO PISTOL

Caliber: 380 ACP, 10-shot magazine.
Barrel: 3".
Weight: 15 oz. **Length:** 5.3" overall.
Stocks: Checkered polycarbonate metal composite.
Sights: Fixed.
Features: Double-action only with a low inertia safety hammer system. Magazine loads from the top. Matte black, electroless nickel or green finish. Introduced 1987. From Grendel, Inc.
Price: Black finish **$155.00**
Price: Green finish **$155.00**
Price: Electroless nickel **$170.00**
Price: Nickel-green **$170.00**

Grendel P-30

HAMMERLI MODEL 212 AUTO PISTOL

Caliber: 22 LR, 8-shot magazine.
Barrel: 4.9".
Weight: 31 oz.
Stocks: Checkered walnut.
Sights: Blade front, rear adjustable for windage only.
Features: Polished blue finish. Imported from Switzerland by Beeman and Hammerli Pistols USA.
Price: . . . . **$1,467.00 to 1,662.00**

Heckler & Koch P7M8

Heckler & Koch SP89

IAI JAVELINA 10MM PISTOL

Caliber: 10mm Auto, 8-shot magazine.
Barrel: 5" or 7".
Weight: 40 oz. **Length:** 10½" overall (7" barrel).
Stock: Wraparound rubber.
Sights: Blade front, Millett adjustable rear.
Features: All stainless construction. Brushed finish. Introduced 1989. From Irwindale Arms, Inc.
Price: 5" **$569.99**
Price: 7" **$599.99**

IAI AUTOMAG IV PISTOL

Caliber: 10mm Magnum, 45 Winchester Magnum, 6-shot magazine.
Barrel: 6.5" (45), 8⅝" (10mm).
Weight: 46 oz. **Length:** 10.5" overall with 6.5" barrel.
Stocks: Carbon fiber.
Sights: Blade front, Millett adjustable rear.
Features: Made of stainless steel with brushed finish. Introduced 1990. Made in U.S. by Irwindale Arms, Inc.
Price: **$629.95**

HECKLER & KOCH P7M8 AUTO PISTOL

Caliber: 9mm Para., 8-shot magazine.
Barrel: 4.13".
Weight: 29 oz. **Length:** 6.73" overall.
Stocks: Stippled black plastic.
Sights: Blade front, adjustable rear; three dot system.
Features: Unique "squeeze cocker" in frontstrap cocks the action. Gas-retarded action. Squared combat-type trigger guard. Blue finish. Compact size. Imported from Germany by Heckler & Koch, Inc.
Price: P7M8 . . . . **$949.00**
Price: P7M13 (13-shot capacity, matte black finish, ambidextrous magazine release, forged steel frame) **$1,159.00**

Heckler & Koch P7K3 Auto Pistol

Similar to the P7M8 and P7M13 except chambered for 22 LR or 380 ACP, 8-shot magazine. Uses an oil-filled buffer to decrease recoil. Introduced 1988.
Price: **$949.00**
Price: 22 LR conversion unit **$499.00**

HECKLER & KOCH SP89 AUTO PISTOL

Caliber: 9mm Para., 15- or 30-shot magazine.
Barrel: 4.5".
Weight: 4.4 lbs. **Length:** 12.8" overall.
Stocks: Black high-impact plastic.
Sights: Post front, diopter rear adjustable for windage and elevation.
Features: Semi-auto pistol inspired by the HK94. Has special flash-hider forend. Introduced 1989. Imported from Germany by Heckler & Koch, Inc.
Price: **$1,259.00**

HELWAN "BRIGADIER" AUTO PISTOL

Caliber: 9mm Para., 8-shot magazine.
Barrel: 4.5".
Weight: 32 oz. **Length:** 8" overall.
Stocks: Grooved plastic.
Sights: Blade front, rear adjustable for windage.
Features: Polished blue finish. Single-action design. Cross-bolt safety. Imported by Interarms.
Price: **$275.00**

IAI AUTOMAG III PISTOL

Caliber: 30 Carbine, 9mm Win. Mag., 8-shot magazine.
Barrel: 6⅜".
Weight: 43 oz. **Length:** 10½" overall.
Stocks: Carbon fiber.
Sights: Blade front, Millett adjustable rear.
Features: Stainless steel construction. Hammer-drop safety. Slide flats have brushed finish, rest is sandblasted. Introduced 1989. From Irwindale Arms, Inc.
Price: **$605.95**

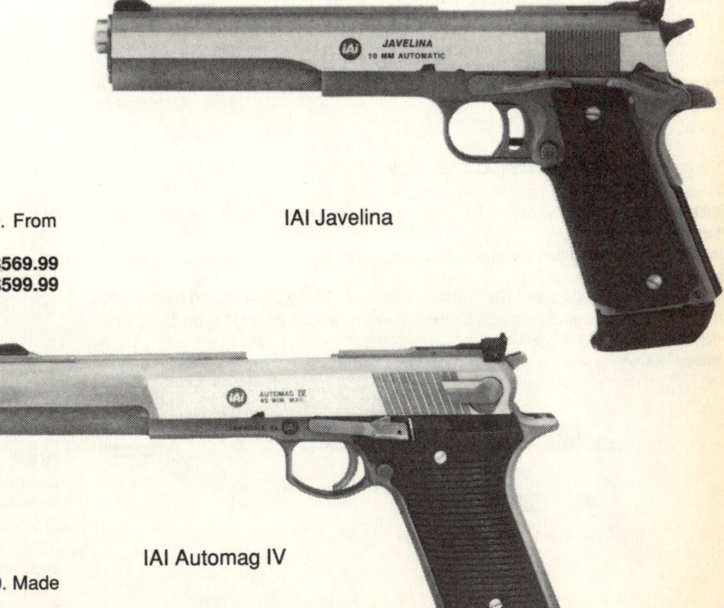

IAI Javelina

IAI Automag IV

INTRATEC TEC-9 AUTO PISTOL
Caliber: 9mm Para., 32-shot magazine.
Barrel: 5".
Weight: 50 oz. **Length:** 12½" overall.
Stock: Moulded composition.
Sights: Fixed.
Features: Semi-auto, fires from closed bolt; firing pin block safety; matte blue finish. From Intratec.
Price: **$266.95**
Price: TEC-9S (as above, except stainless) **$361.95**
Price: TEC-9K (finished with TEC-KOTE) **$300.00**

Intratec TEC-9

Intratec TEC-9M Auto Pistol
Similar to the TEC-9 except smaller. Has 3" barrel, weighs 44 oz.; 20-shot magazine.
Price: **$244.95**
Price: TEC-9MS (as above, stainless) **$337.95**
Price: TEC-9MK (finished with TEC-KOTE) **$280.00**

INTRATEC TEC-22T AUTO PISTOL
Caliber: 22 LR, 30-shot magazine.
Barrel: 4".
Weight: 30 oz. **Length:** 11³⁄₁₆" overall.
Stocks: Moulded composition.
Sights: Protected post front, rear adjustable for windage and elevation.
Features: Ambidextrous cocking knobs and safety. Matte black finish. Accepts any 10/22-type magazine. Introduced 1988. Made in U.S. by Intratec.
Price: **$201.95**
Price: TEC-22TK (as above, TEC-KOTE finish) **$225.95**

Intratec TEC-22T

INTRATEC PROTEC-22, 25 AUTO PISTOLS
Caliber: 22 LR, 10-shot; 25 ACP, 8-shot magazine.
Barrel: 2½".
Weight: 14 oz. **Length:** 5" overall.
Stocks: Wraparound composition in gray, black or driftwood color.
Sights: Fixed.
Features: Double-action only trigger mechanism. Choice of black, satin or TEC-KOTE finish. Announced 1991. From Intratec.
Price: 22 or 25, black finish **$89.00**
Price: 22 or 25, satin or TEC-KOTE finish **$95.00**

Jericho Model 941

JERICHO 941 MULTI-CALIBER PISTOL
Caliber: 9mm, 16-shot; 40 S&W, 41 A.E., 11-shot magazine.
Barrel: 4⅜".
Weight: 33 oz. **Length:** 8⅛" overall.
Stocks: High impact black polymer.
Sights: Blade front, rear adjustable for windage; three tritium dots.
Features: Double action; all steel construction; polygonal rifling; ambidextrous safety. Comes with one box each of 9mm and 41 A.E. ammunition, RIG cleaning kit, four magazines, conversion unit, carrying case. Introduced 1990. Produced in Israel by Israel Military Industries; distributed by K.B.I., Inc.
Price: Blue, dual caliber **$849.00**
Price: Chrome, dual caliber **$949.00**
Price: 9mm only **$599.00**
Price: 40 S&W only **$599.00**

IVER JOHNSON COMPACT 25 ACP
Caliber: 25 ACP.
Barrel: 2".
Weight: 9.3 oz.
Stocks: Checkered composition.
Sights: Fixed.
Features: Ordnance steel construction with bright blue slide, matte blue frame, color case-hardened trigger. Comes in jewelry-type presentation box. Introduced 1991. From Iver Johnson.
Price: **$199.95**

Iver Johnson Compact

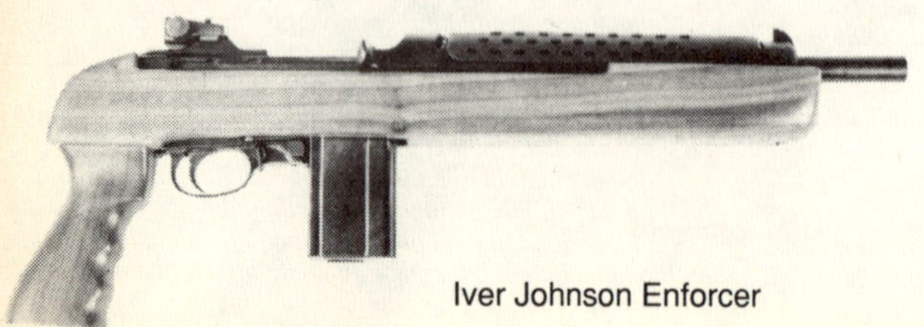
Iver Johnson Enforcer

IVER JOHNSON ENFORCER AUTO
Caliber: 30 M-1 Carbine, 15- or 30-shot magazine, or 9mm Para.
Barrel: 10½".
Weight: 4 lbs. **Length:** 18½" overall.
Stocks: American walnut with metal handguard.
Sights: Gold bead ramp front. Peep rear.
Features: Accepts 15- or 30-shot magazines. From Iver Johnson.
Price: 30 M-1 . . . . **$416.50**
Price: 9mm Para. **$448.95**

Jennings J-25

L.A.R. Grizzly 44 Mag

L.A.R. Grizzly Win Mag 8" & 10"
Similar to the standard Grizzly Win Mag except has lengthened slide and either 8" or 10" barrel. Available in 45 Win. Mag., 45 ACP, 357/45 Grizzly Win. Mag., 10mm or 357 Magnum. Introduced 1987.
Price: 8", 45 ACP, 45 Win. Mag., 357/45 Grizzly Win. Mag. **$1,313.00**
Price: As above, 10" **$1,375.00**
Price: 8", 357 Magnum **$1,337.50**
Price: As above, 10" **$1,400.00**

LLAMA SMALL FRAME AUTO PISTOLS
Caliber: 22 LR, 32, 380.
Barrel: $3\frac{11}{16}$".
Weight: 23 oz. **Length:** 6½" overall.
Stocks: Checkered plastic, thumbrest.
Sights: Fixed front, adjustable notch rear.
Features: Ventilated rib, manual and grip safeties. Imported from Spain by Stoeger Industries.
Price: Blue **$325.00**
Price: Satin chrome, 22 LR or 380 . . . . **$399.00**
Price: Duo-Tone (satin chrome frame, blue slide), 380 only **$385.00**

LLAMA COMPACT FRAME AUTO PISTOL
Caliber: 9mm Para., 9-shot, 45 ACP, 7-shot.
Barrel: $4\frac{5}{16}$".
Weight: 37 oz.
Stocks: Smooth walnut.
Sights: Blade front, rear adjustable for windage.
Features: Scaled-down version of the Large Frame gun. Locked breech mechanism; manual and grip safeties. Introduced 1985. Imported from Spain by Stoeger Industries.
Price: Blue **$385.00**
Price: Satin chrome **$499.00**
Price: Duo-Tone (satin chrome frame, blue slide) **$475.00**

LLAMA LARGE FRAME AUTO PISTOL
Caliber: 38 Super, 45 ACP.
Barrel: 5".
Weight: 40 oz. **Length:** 8½" overall.
Stocks: Checkered walnut.
Sights: Fixed.
Features: Grip and manual safeties, ventilated rib. Imported from Spain by Stoeger Industries.
Price: Blue **$385.00**
Price: Satin chrome, 45 ACP only **$499.00**
Price: Duo-Tone (satin chrome frame, blue slide) **$475.00**

JENNINGS J-22, J-25 AUTO PISTOLS
Caliber: 22 LR, 25 ACP, 6-shot magazine.
Barrel: 2½".
Weight: 13 oz. (J-22). **Length:** $4\frac{15}{16}$" overall (J-22).
Stocks: Walnut on chrome or nickel models; grooved black Cycolac or resin-impregnated wood on Teflon model.
Sights: Fixed.
Features: Choice of bright chrome, satin nickel or black Teflon finish. Introduced 1981. From Jennings Firearms.
Price: J-22, about **$75.00**
Price: J-25, about **$89.95**

L.A.R. GRIZZLY WIN MAG MK I PISTOL
Caliber: 357 Mag., 357/45, 10mm, 40 S&W, 45 Win. Mag., 45 ACP, 7-shot magazine.
Barrel: 5.4", 6.5".
Weight: 51 oz. **Length:** 10½" overall.
Stocks: Checkered rubber, non-slip combat-type.
Sights: Ramped blade front, fully adjustable rear.
Features: Uses basic Browning/Colt 1911A1 design; interchangeable calibers; beveled magazine well; combat-type flat, checkered rubber mainspring housing; lowered and back-chamfered ejection port; polished feed ramp; throated barrel; solid barrel bushings. Available in satin hard chrome, matte blue, Parkerized finishes. Introduced 1983. From L.A.R. Mfg., Inc.
Price: 45 Win. Mag. **$893.00**
Price: 357 Mag. **$920.00**
Price: Conversion units (357 Mag.) **$221.00**
Price: As above, 45 ACP, 10mm, 40 S&W, 45 Win. Mag., 357/45 Win. Mag. **$207.00**

L.A.R. Grizzly 44 Mag MK IV
Similar to the Win. Mag. Mk I except chambered for 44 Magnum, has beavertail grip safety. Matte blue finish only. Has 5.4" or 6.5" barrel. Introduced 1991. From L.A.R. Mfg., Inc.
Price: **$920.00**

Llama Small Frame

Llama M-82

LLAMA M-82 DA AUTO PISTOL
Caliber: 9mm Para., 15-shot magazine.
Barrel: 4¼".
Weight: 39 oz. **Length:** 8" overall.
Stocks: Matte black polymer.
Sights: Blade front, rear drift adjustable for windage. High visibility three-dot system.
Features: Double-action mechanism; ambidextrous safety. Introduced 1987. Imported from Spain by Stoeger Industries.
Price: **$975.00**

LORCIN AUTO PISTOL
Caliber: 25 ACP, 7-shot magazine.
Barrel: 2¼".
Weight: 13.5 oz. **Length:** 4.75" overall.
Stocks: Smooth composition.
Sights: Fixed.
Features: Available in choice of finishes: black and gold, chrome and satin, chrome or black. Introduced 1989. From Lorcin Engineering.
Price: **$79.95**

NEW DETONICS "SERVICEMASTER" DUTY PISTOL
Caliber: 45 ACP, 7-shot magazine.
Barrel: 4½", recessed crown.
Weight: 32 oz. **Length:** 7⅞" overall.
Stocks: Checkered walnut with rubber mainspring housing.
Sights: Ramp front, adjustable rear.
Features: All stainless steel construction; patented self-centering cone barrel system; lengthened and lowered ejection port; beveled magazine well; patented, cushioned, counter-wound dual spring recoil system; hand-fit tolerances; redesigned thumb safety; matte black stainless slide with dual serrations; extended beavertail grip safety; improved magazine release; skeletonized trigger and hammer. Comes with gun rug and two spare magazines. Introduced 1990. From New Detonics Mfg. Corp.
Price: **$998.00**

New Detonics "Combatmaster" Concealable Duty Pistol
Similar to the "Servicemaster" except has 6-shot magazine, 3½" barrel, weighs 28 oz., and measures 4½" overall. Checkered walnut grips with rubber mainspring housing. Ramp front sight, fixed combat rear. Other features same as "Servicemaster." Introduced 1990. From New Detonics Mfg. Corp.
Price: **$920.00**

New Detonics O.S. Backup Pistol
Same as the "Combatmaster" except: no sights; snag-free contours; flat profile safety; short magazine release; flattened slide stop. Satin stainless or black finish. Introduced 1991.
Price: **$895.00**

New Detonics "Ladies' Escort" Auto Pistol
Same as the "Combatmaster" except has reduced grip frame size, shortened trigger reach and space-age color polymer finishes. Introduced 1990. From New Detonics Mfg. Corp.
Price: "Royal Escort" (iridescent purple slide, blackened stainless frame and gold-plated hammer and trigger) **$1,090.00**
Price: "Midnight Escort" (black slide, satin stainless frame, optional gold trigger and hammer) **$990.00**

Norinco Type 54-1

NORINCO TYPE 77B AUTO PISTOL
Caliber: 9mm Para., 8-shot magazine.
Barrel: 5".
Weight: 34 oz. **Length:** 7.5" overall.
Stocks: Checkered wood.
Sights: Blade front, adjustable rear.
Features: Uses trigger guard cocking, gas-retarded recoil action. Front of trigger guard can be used to cock the action with the trigger finger. Introduced 1989. Imported from China by China Sports, Inc.
Price: . . . . **NA**

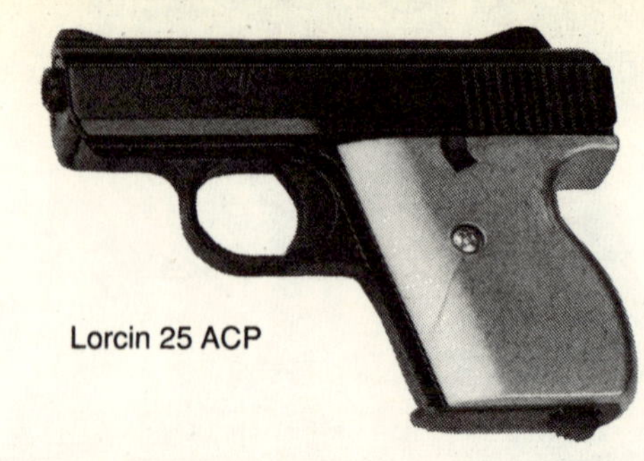
Lorcin 25 ACP

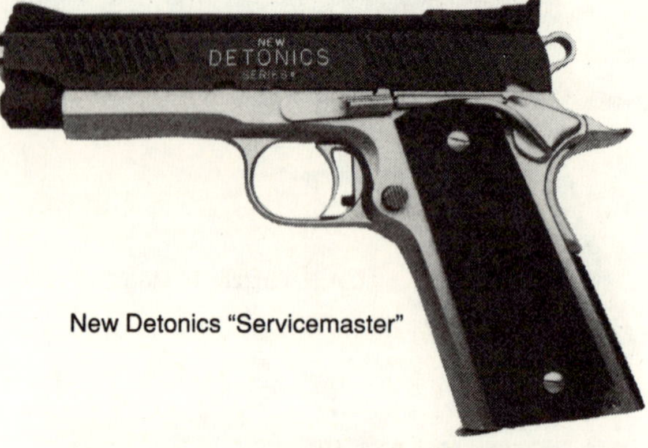

New Detonics "Servicemaster"

New Detonics "Ladies' Escort"

NORINCO TYPE 54-1 TOKAREV AUTO PISTOL
Caliber: 7.62x25mm, 38 Super, 8-shot magazine.
Barrel: 4.5".
Weight: 29 oz. **Length:** 7.7" overall.
Stocks: Grooved black plastic.
Sights: Fixed.
Features: Matte blue finish. Imported from China by China Sports, Inc.
Price: . . . . **NA**

NORINCO TYPE 59 MAKAROV DA PISTOL
Caliber: 9x18mm, 8-shot magazine.
Barrel: 3.5".
Weight: 21 oz. **Length:** 6.3" overall.
Stocks: Checkered plastic.
Sights: Blade front, adjustable rear.
Features: Blue finish. Double action. Introduced 1990. Imported from China by China Sports, Inc.
Price: . . . . **NA**

NORINCO M1911 AUTO PISTOL
Caliber: 45 ACP, 7-shot magazine.
Barrel: 5".
Weight: 39 oz. **Length:** 8.5" overall.
Stocks: Checkered wood.
Sights: Blade front, rear adjustable for windage.
Features: Matte blue finish. Comes with two magazines. Imported from China by China Sports, Inc.
Price: . . . . **NA**

CAUTION: PRICES CHANGE, CHECK AT GUNSHOP.

OMEGA MATCH PISTOL

Caliber: 10mm, 40 S&W, 5-shot; 45 ACP, 7-shot.
Barrel: 6", polygonal rifling.
Weight: 46 oz. **Length:** NA.
Stocks: Rubberized wraparound.
Sights: Removeable ramp front, fully adjustable rear.
Features: Updated version of the original Omega pistol with adjustable breech face, new extractor system. Convertible between calibers. Double serrated slide. Built on 1911A1 frame. Introduced 1991. From Springfield Armory.
Price: **$1,103.00**

Parker Auto

Peregrine Falcon

PARA-ORDNANCE P14.45 AUTO PISTOL

Caliber: 45 ACP, 13-shot magazine.
Barrel: 5".
Weight: 28 oz. (alloy frame). **Length:** 8.5" overall.
Stocks: Textured composition.
Sights: Blade front, rear adjustable for windage. High visibility three-dot system.
Features: Available with alloy, steel or stainless steel frame with black finish (silver or stainless gun). Steel and stainless steel frame guns weigh 38 oz. (P14.45), 35 oz. (P13.45), 33 oz. (P12.45). Grooved match trigger, rounded combat-style hammer. Double column, high-capacity magazine gives 14-shot total capacity (P14.45). Beveled magazine well. Manual thumb, grip and firing pin lock safeties. Solid barrel bushing. Introduced 1990. Made in Canada by Para-Ordnance.
Price: P14.45 . . . . **$716.25**
Price: P13.45 (12-shot magazine, 4¼" bbl., 25 oz., alloy) **$716.25**
Price: P12.45 (11-shot magazine, 3½" bbl., 24 oz., alloy) **$716.25**
Price: Steel frame pistols, as above **$708.75**

QFI MODEL SA25 PISTOL

Caliber: 25 ACP, 6-shot magazine.
Barrel: 2.5".
Weight: 12 oz. **Length:** 4⅝" overall.
Stocks: Smooth walnut.
Sights: Fixed.
Features: External hammer; fast simple takedown. Introduced 1991. Made in U.S.A. by QFI.
Price: Blue **$54.95**
Price: Chrome with pearlite grips **$64.95**
Price: 24K gold and bright blue frame, smooth walnut grips **$104.95**
Price: Tigress 25, blue frame, gold slide, ivory polymer grips, case . **$154.95**

Omega Match

PARKER AUTO PISTOL

Caliber: 9mm Para., 9-shot; 10mm Auto, 8-shot; 40 S&W, 8-shot; 45 ACP, 7-shot; 357 Magnum, 8-shot.
Barrel: 3⅜", 5", 7".
Weight: 29 oz. to 44 oz. **Length:** 6⅜" (3⅜" barrel).
Stocks: Grooved composition.
Sights: Fixed or Millett adjustable.
Features: Single action. Made of stainless steel. Introduced 1990. Made in the U.S. by Wyoming Arms Mfg. Corp.
Price: 3⅜" barrel, fixed sights only **$399.00**
Price: 5" barrel, fixed **$399.00**
Price: 5" barrel, adjustable sights **$424.00**
Price: 7" barrel, adjustable sights, 10mm, 40 S&W, 45 ACP **$449.00**
Price: 7" barrel, adjustable sights, 357 Mag. **$479.00**

PEREGRINE FALCON AUTO PISTOL

Caliber: 10mm, 40 S&W, 10-shot magazine, 45 ACP, 8-shot magazine.
Barrel: 5".
Weight: 37.5 oz. **Length:** 8.5" overall.
Stocks: Black Du Pont Zytel with stipple finish.
Sights: Post front, rear adjustable for windage and elevation; Tri-Square system.
Features: Double-action with passive firing pin lock, decocking lever, ambidextrous thumb safety levers; reversible magazine release; beveled magazine well; stainless steel magazine. Black slide, stainless frame. Announced 1990. Made in U.S. by Peregrine Industries.
Price: 10mm, 40 S&W **$750.00**
Price: 45 ACP **$725.00**

PSP-25 AUTO PISTOL

Caliber: 25 ACP, 6-shot magazine.
Barrel: 2⅛".
Weight: 9.5 oz. **Length:** 4⅛" overall.
Stocks: Checkered black plastic.
Sights: Fixed.
Features: All steel construction with polished finish. Introduced 1990. Made in the U.S. under F.N. license; distributed by K.B.I., Inc.
Price: Blue **$249.00**
Price: Hard chrome **$329.99**

Para-Ordnance P14.45

QFI MODEL LA380 PISTOL

Caliber: 32 ACP, 380 ACP.
Barrel: 3⅛".
Weight: 25 oz. **Length:** 6¼" overall.
Stocks: Smooth European walnut.
Sights: Blade front, rear adjustable for windage.
Features: Single action. External hammer, magazine safety with hammer, trigger and firing pin block. Available in blue, chrome and Lady models. Introduced 1991. Made in U.S. by QFI.
Price: 32 or 380, blue **$146.95**
Price: As above, chrome **$169.95**
Price: Tigress 380, blue frame, gold slide, ivory polymer grips **$239.95**

Ram-Line Exactor

Ram-Line Exactor Target

RANGER G.I. MODEL AUTO PISTOL
Caliber: 45 ACP, 7-shot magazine.
Barrel: 5".
Weight: 38 oz. **Length:** 8½" overall.
Stocks: Checkered plastic.
Sights: Blade front, rear drift adjustable for windage.
Features: Made in U.S. from 4140 steel and other high-strength alloys. Barrel machined from a forged billet. Introduced 1988. From Federal Ordnance, Inc.
Price: Standard model **$439.95**

Ranger Lite Auto Pistol
Similar to the Ranger EXT except has frame of aluminum alloy giving weight of 32 oz. Has wraparound rubber grips, high-profile Millett fixed sights, extended grip and thumb safeties, slide and magazine releases, lightened speed trigger. Black anodized frame, blued steel slide. Introduced 1990. From Federal Ordnance, Inc.
Price: 45 ACP only **$454.95**

Ranger Ten Auto Pistol
Similar to the Ranger EXT except is chambered for 10mm Auto and uses the Peters Stahl linkless barrel system with polygonal rifling. Has extended grip safety, thumb safety, slide and magazine releases, and wraparound rubber grips. Introduced 1990. From Federal Ordnance, Inc.
Price: **$779.95**

RAVEN MP-25 AUTO PISTOL
Caliber: 25 ACP, 6-shot magazine.
Barrel: $2\frac{7}{16}$".
Weight: 15 oz. **Length:** 4¾" overall.
Stocks: Smooth walnut, ivory-colored or black slotted plastic.
Sights: Ramped front, fixed rear.
Features: Available in blue, nickel or chrome finish. Made in U.S. Available from Raven Arms.
Price: **$69.95**

RUGER P85 MARK II AUTOMATIC PISTOL
Caliber: 9mm Para., 15-shot magazine.
Barrel: 4.50".
Weight: 32 oz. **Length:** 7.84" overall.
Stocks: Grooved "Xenoy" composition.
Sights: Square post front, square notch rear adjustable for windage, both with white dot inserts.
Features: Double action with ambidextrous slide-mounted safety which blocks firing pin and disengages firing mechanism. Slide is 4140 chromemoly steel, frame is a lightweight aluminum alloy, both finished matte black. Ambidextrous magazine release. Blue or stainless steel. Introduced 1986; stainless introduced 1990.
Price: P85CMKII, blue, with extra magazine and loader, plastic case **$390.50**
Price: P91DAC, as above, double-action only **$390.50**
Price: KP85CMKII, stainless, with extra magazine and loader, plastic case **$430.50**
Price: KP91DAC, as above, double-action only **$430.50**

RAM-LINE EXACTOR AUTO PISTOL
Caliber: 22 LR, 15-shot magazine (20-shot optional).
Barrel: 5.5".
Weight: 20 oz. **Length:** 9.75" overall.
Stocks: One-piece impact resistant polymer; Dynamic or Conventional style.
Sights: Moulded ramp front with .150" blade, fixed rear.
Features: Injection moulded grip frame, alloy receiver, hybrid composite barrel. Constant force sear spring for smooth trigger pull. Thumb safety isolates the sear and bolt. Semi-transparent magazine. Introduced 1990. Made in U.S. by Ram-Line, Inc.
Price: With either style grip shape **$199.97**
Price: Limited Edition model (receiver finished in choice of gold, blue, red, green or platinum, jeweled bolt) **$229.97**
Price: 20-shot magazine **$24.97**

Ram-Line Exactor Target Model
Same as the standard Exactor except has 8" barrel with dovetail underneath to accept optional weight cavity, weight block, or laser sight. Comes with fully adjustable rear sight, interchangeable post front sight. Target trigger adjusted to 2.5 lbs. Receiver drilled and tapped for scope mounting. Introduced 1991.
Price: With custom carrying case **$279.97**

Ranger EXT Auto Pistol
Similar to the Ranger G.I. model except has Millett high-profile fixed sights, checkered walnut grips, extended grip safety, thumb safety, slide and magazine releases. Introduced 1987. From Federal Ordnance, Inc.
Price: **$459.95**

Ranger AMBO Auto Pistol
Similar to the Ranger EXT except has ambidextrous slide release and safety. Introduced 1987. From Federal Ordnance, Inc.
Price: **$479.95**

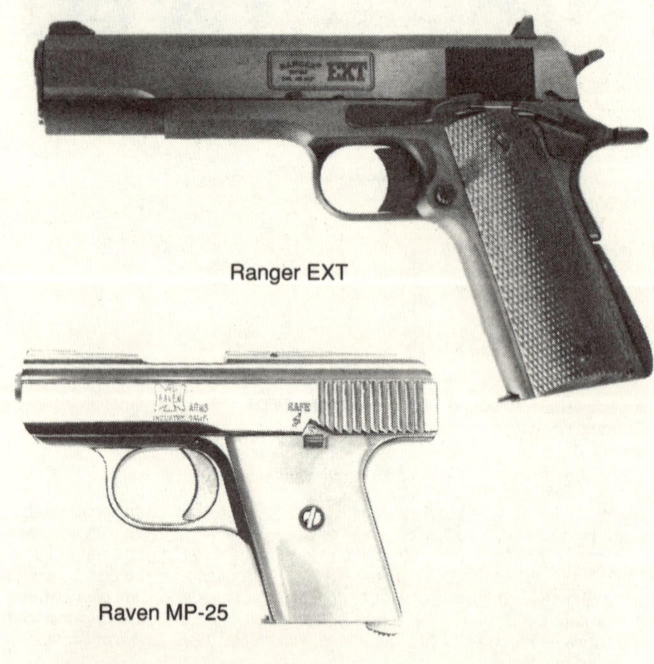

Ranger EXT

Raven MP-25

Ruger P85

CAUTION: PRICES CHANGE, CHECK AT GUNSHOP.

Ruger P85DCC Decocker Automatic Pistol

Similar to the standard P85 except has a decocking lever in place of the regular slide-mounted safety. The decocking lever blocks the hammer from the firing pin while simultaneously blocking the firing pin from forward movement—allows shooter to decock a cocked pistol without manipulating the trigger. Conventional thumb decocking procedures are therefore unnecessary. Blue or stainless steel. Introduced 1990.

Price: P89DCC, blue with extra magazine and loader, plastic case . **$390.50**
Price: KP89DCC, stainless, with extra magazine, plastic case . . . **$430.50**

Ruger P85DCC Decocker

Ruger P89 Double-Action Only Pistol

Same as the KP85 Mk II except operates only in the double-action mode. Has a bobbed, spurless hammer, gripping grooves on each side of the rear of the slide; no external safety or decocking lever. An internal safety prevents forward movement of the firing pin unless the trigger is pulled. Available in 9mm Para., stainless steel only. Introduced 1991.

Price: KP89DAO **$397.50**
Price: With lockable case, extra magazine, magazine loading tool . **$430.50**

Ruger P90 Decocker Pistol

Similar to the P85 Mk II except chambered for 45 ACP, 7-shot single column magazine, and has a manual decocking system. The decocking lever blocks the hammer and prevents forward motion of the firing pin via a separate firing pin block. Available only in stainless steel. Overall length is 7⅞", weight 34 oz. Introduced 1991.

Price: KP90DC **$397.50**
Price: With lockable case, extra magazine, magazine loading tool . **$430.50**

Ruger P91 Decocker Pistol

Similar to the P85 Mk II except chambered for 40 S&W and has a manual decocking system. The decocking lever blocks the hammer and prevents forward motion of the firing pin via a separate firing pin block. Has 12-shot magazine. Stainless steel only. Introduced 1991.

Price: KP91DC **$397.50**
Price: With lockable case, extra magazine, and magazine loading tool **$430.50**

Ruger Mark II Standard

RUGER MARK II STANDARD AUTO PISTOL

Caliber: 22 LR, 10-shot magazine.
Barrel: 4¾" or 6".
Weight: 36 oz. (4¾" bbl.). **Length:** 8 5/16" (4¾" bbl.).
Stocks: Checkered hard rubber.
Sights: Fixed, wide blade front, square notch rear adjustable for windage.
Features: Updated design of the original Standard Auto. Has new bolt hold-open device. 10-shot magazine, magazine catch, safety, trigger and new receiver contours. Introduced 1982.
Price: Blued (MK 4, MK 6) **$224.75**
Price: In stainless steel (KMK 4, KMK 6) **$299.25**

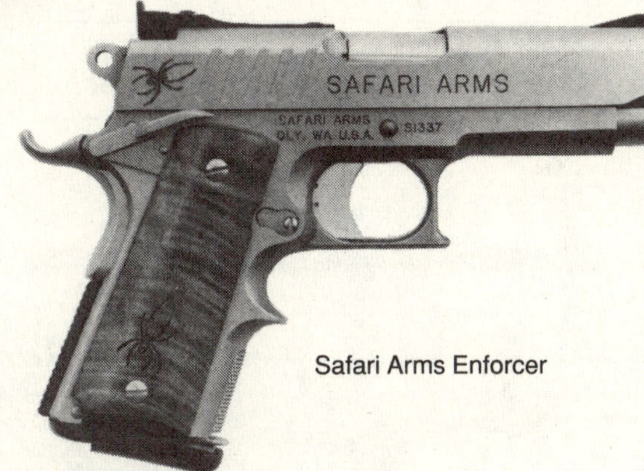

Safari Arms Enforcer

SAFARI ARMS ENFORCER PISTOL

Caliber: 45 ACP, 6-shot magazine.
Barrel: 3.8"
Weight: 35 oz. (standard); 27 oz. (lightweight). **Length:** 7.7" overall.
Stocks: Walnut.
Sights: Ramped blade front, rear adjustable for windage and elevation.
Features: Ambidextrous extended safety, extended slide release; Commander-style hammer; beavertail grip safety; threaded barrel bushing; throated, ported, tuned. Choice of ordnance steel, stainless, or alloy. From Safari Arms, Inc.
Price: **$710.00**

Safari Arms G.I. Safari

Similar to the Enforcer pistol except has G.I. slide and 5" G.I. chrome-lined barrel on a Safari frame unit. Has beavertail grip safety and Commander hammer, double diamond checkered grips. Matte black finish. Introduced 1991. From Safari Arms, Inc.

Price: **$425.00**

SEECAMP LWS 32 STAINLESS DA AUTO

Caliber: 32 ACP Win. Silvertip, 6-shot.
Barrel: 2", integral with frame.
Weight: 10.5 oz. **Length:** 4⅛" overall.
Stocks: Black plastic.
Sights: Smooth, no-snag, contoured slide and barrel top.
Features: Aircraft quality 17-4 PH stainless steel. Inertia-operated firing pin. Hammer fired double-action only. Hammer automatically follows slide down to safety rest position after each shot—no manual safety needed. Magazine safety disconnector. Polished stainless. Introduced 1985. From L.W. Seecamp.
Price: **$350.00**

Seecamp LWS 32

SIG P-210-2 AUTO PISTOL

Caliber: 7.65mm or 9mm Para., 8-shot magazine.
Barrel: 4¾".
Weight: 31¾ oz. (9mm). **Length:** 8½" overall.
Stocks: Checkered black composition.
Sights: Blade front, rear adjustable for windage.
Features: Lanyard loop; matte finish. Conversion unit for 22 LR available. Imported from Switzerland by Mandall Shooting Supplies.
Price: P-210-2 Service Pistol **$2,000.00**

SIG P-210-6 AUTO PISTOL

Caliber: 9mm Para., 8-shot magazine.
Barrel: 4¾".
Weight: 36.2 oz. **Length:** 8½" overall.
Stocks: Checkered black plastic; walnut optional.
Sights: Blade front, micro. adjustable rear for windage and elevation.
Features: Adjustable trigger stop; target trigger; ribbed frontstrap; sandblasted finish. Conversion unit for 22 LR consists of barrel, recoil spring, slide and magazine. Imported from Switzerland by Mandall Shooting Supplies.
Price: P-210-6 . . . . . **$2,500.00**
Price: P-210-5 Target **$2,700.00**

SIG SAUER P220 "AMERICAN" AUTO PISTOL

Caliber: 9mm, 38 Super, 45 ACP, (9-shot in 9mm and 38 Super, 7 in 45).
Barrel: 4⅜".
Weight: 28¼ oz. (9mm). **Length:** 7¾" overall.
Stocks: Checkered black plastic.
Sights: Blade front, drift adjustable rear for windage.
Features: Double action. De-cocking lever permits lowering hammer onto locked firing pin. Squared combat-type trigger guard. Slide stays open after last shot. Imported from Germany by SIGARMS, Inc.
Price: "American," blue (side-button magazine release, 45 ACP only) **$720.00**
Price: "American," blue, 9mm, 38 Super, Siglite night sights **$820.00**
Price: 45 ACP, blue **$720.00**
Price: 45 ACP, blue, Siglite night sights **$750.00**
Price: Nickel **$820.00**
Price: Nickel, Siglite night sights **$920.00**
Price: K-Kote finish **$820.00**
Price: K-Kote, Siglite night sights **$920.00**

SIG SAUER P225 DA AUTO PISTOL

Caliber: 9mm Para., 8-shot magazine.
Barrel: 3.8".
Weight: 26 oz. **Length:** 7³⁄₃₂" overall.
Stocks: Checkered black plastic.
Sights: Blade front, rear adjustable for windage. Optional Siglite night sights.
Features: Double action. De-cocking lever permits lowering hammer onto locked firing pin. Square combat-type trigger guard. Shortened, lightened version of P220. Imported from Germany by SIGARMS, Inc.
Price: **$750.00**
Price: With Siglite night sights **$850.00**
Price: Nickel **$820.00**
Price: Nickel with Siglite night sights **$920.00**
Price: K-Kote finish **$820.00**
Price: K-Kote with Siglite night sights **$920.00**

SIG Sauer P228

SIG Sauer P226 DA Auto Pistol

Similar to the P220 pistol except has 15-shot magazine, 4.4" barrel, and weighs 26½ oz. 9mm only. Imported from Germany by SIGARMS, Inc.
Price: Blue **$780.00**
Price: With Siglite night sights **$880.00**
Price: Blue, double-action only **$780.00**
Price: Blue, double-action only, Siglite night sights **$880.00**
Price: Nickel **$850.00**
Price: Nickel, Siglite night sights **$950.00**
Price: Nickel, double-action only **$850.00**
Price: Nickel, double-action only, Siglite night sights **$950.00**
Price: K-Kote finish **$850.00**
Price: K-Kote, Siglite night sights **$950.00**
Price: K-Kote, double-action only **$850.00**
Price: K-Kote, double-action only, Siglite night sights **$950.00**

SIG Sauer P220 "American"

SIG Sauer P228 DA Auto Pistol

Similar to the P226 except has 3.86" barrel, with 7.08" overall length and 3.35" height. Chambered for 9mm Para. only, 13-shot magazine. Weight is 29.1 oz. with empty magazine. Introduced 1989. Imported from Germany by SIGARMS, Inc.
Price: Blue **$780.00**
Price: Blue, with Siglite night sights **$880.00**
Price: Blue, double-action only **$780.00**
Price: Blue, double-action only, Siglite night sights **$880.00**
Price: Nickel **$850.00**
Price: Nickel, Siglite night sights **$950.00**
Price: Nickel, double-action only **$850.00**
Price: Nickel, double-action only, Siglite night sights **$950.00**
Price: K-Kote finish **$850.00**
Price: K-Kote, Siglite night sights **$950.00**
Price: K-Kote, double-action only **$850.00**
Price: K-Kote, double-action only, Siglite night sights **$950.00**

Consult our Directory pages for the location of firms mentioned.

SIG Sauer P229

SIG Sauer P229 DA Auto Pistol

Similar to the P228 except chambered for 40 S&W with 12-shot magazine. Has 3.86" barrel, 7.08" overall length and 3.35" height. Weight is 30.5 oz. Introduced 1991. Imported from Germany by SIGARMS, Inc.
Price: Blue **$780.00**
Price: P229SL (stainless slide, blue alloy frame) **$850.00**
Price: Blue, double-action only **$780.00**
Price: P229SL (double-action only, stainless slide) **$850.00**

SIG SAUER P230 DA AUTO PISTOL
Caliber: 32 ACP, 8-shot; 380 ACP, 7-shot.
Barrel: 3¾".
Weight: 16 oz. **Length:** 6½" overall.
Stocks: Checkered black plastic.
Sights: Blade front, rear adjustable for windage.
Features: Double action. Same basic action design as P220. Blowback operation, stationary barrel. Introduced 1977. Imported from Germany by SIGARMS, Inc.
Price: Blue **$495.00**
Price: In stainless steel (P230 SL) **$575.00**

SMITH & WESSON MODEL 422, 622 AUTO
Caliber: 22 LR, 10-shot magazine.
Barrel: 4½", 6".
Weight: 22 oz. (4½" bbl.). **Length:** 7½" overall (4½" bbl.).
Stocks: Checkered plastic (Field), checkered walnut (Target).
Sights: Field—serrated ramp front, fixed rear; Target—Patridge front, adjustable rear.
Features: Aluminum frame, steel slide, brushed blue finish; internal hammer. Introduced 1987. Model 2206 introduced 1990.
Price: Blue, 4½", 6", fixed sight **$206.00**
Price: As above, adjustable sight **$257.00**
Price: Stainless (Model 622), 4½", 6", fixed sight **$266.00**
Price: As above, adjustable sight **$316.00**

Smith & Wesson Model 2206 Auto
Similar to the Model 422/622 except made entirely of stainless steel with non-reflective finish. Weight is 35 oz. with 4½" barrel, 39 oz. with 7½" barrel. Other specs are the same. Introduced 1990.
Price: With fixed sight **$299.00**
Price: With adjustable sight **$355.00**

Smith & Wesson Model 2214 Sportsman Auto
Similar to the Model 422 except has 3" barrel, 8-shot magazine; dovetail Patridge front sight with white dot, fixed rear with two white dots; matte blue finish, black composition grips with checkered panels. Overall length 6⅛", weight 18 oz. Introduced 1990.
Price: **$236.00**

SMITH & WESSON MODEL 3913/3914 DOUBLE ACTIONS
Caliber: 9mm Para., 8-shot magazine.
Barrel: 3½".
Weight: 26 oz. **Length:** 6 13/16" overall.
Stocks: One-piece Delrin wraparound, textured surface.
Sights: Post front with white dot, Novak LoMount Carry with two dots, adjustable for windage.
Features: Aluminum alloy frame, stainless slide (M3913) or blue steel slide (M3914). Bobbed hammer with no half-cock notch; smooth .304" trigger with rounded edges. Straight backstrap. Introduced 1989.
Price: Model 3913 . . . . **$568.00**
Price: Model 3914 . . . . **$513.00**

Smith & Wesson Model 3953/3954 DA Pistols
Same as the Models 3913/3914 except double-action only. Model 3953 has stainless slide with alloy frame; Model 3954 has blued steel slide. Overall length 7"; weight 25.5 oz. Introduced 1990.
Price: Model 3953 . . . . **$568.00**
Price: Model 3954 . . . . **$513.00**

Smith & Wesson Model 3913-NL/3914-NL Pistols
Same as the 3913/3914 LadySmith autos except without the LadySmith logo and they have a slightly modified frame design. Right-hand safety only. Model 3913-NL has stainless slide on alloy frame; Model 3914-NL has blued steel. Introduced 1990.
Price: Model 3913-NL **$568.00**
Price: Model 3914-NL **$513.00**

Smith & Wesson Model 3913/3914 LadySmith Autos
Similar to the standard Model 3913/3914 except has frame that is upswept at the front, rounded trigger guard. Comes in either deep blue matte finish with black grips or frosted stainless steel with matching gray grips. Both grips are ergonomically correct for a woman's hand. Both have Novak LoMount Carry rear sight adjustable for windage, smooth edges for snag resistance. Introduced 1990.
Price: Model 3913-LS, stainless **$568.00**
Price: Model 3914-LS, blue **$513.00**

SIG Sauer P230
Smith & Wesson 2214
Smith & Wesson 3913
Smith & Wesson 3954 DA
Smith & Wesson 3913-LS

SMITH & WESSON MODEL 4013/4014, 4053/4054 AUTOS

Caliber: 40 S&W, 7-shot magazine.
Barrel: 3½".
Weight: 26 oz. **Length:** 7" overall.
Stocks: One-piece Xenoy wraparound with straight backstrap.
Sights: Post front with white dot, fixed Novak LoMount Carry rear with two white dots.
Features: Models 4013/4014 are traditional double action; Models 4053/4054 are double-action only; Models 4013, 4053 have stainless slide on alloy frame; 4014, 4054 have blued steel slide. Introduced 1991.
Price: Models 4013, 4053 . . . . **$686.00**
Price: Models 4014, 4054 . . . . **$629.00**

SMITH & WESSON MODEL 4506/4516 AUTOS

Caliber: 45 ACP, 7-shot magazine (M4516), 8-shot magazine (M4506).
Barrel: 3¾" (M4516), 5" (M4506).
Weight: 34½ oz. (4516). **Length:** 7⅛" overall (4516).
Stocks: Delrin one-piece wraparound, arched or straight backstrap on M4506, straight only on M4516.
Sights: Post front with white dot, adjustable or fixed Novak LoMount Carry on M4506, fixed Novak LoMount Carry only on M4516.
Features: M4506 has serrated hammer spur; M4516 has bobbed hammer. Both guns in stainless only. Introduced 1989.
Price: Model 4506, fixed sight **$714.00**
Price: Model 4506, adjustable sight **$743.00**
Price: Model 4516 . . . . **$714.00**
Price: Model 4505 (blue, 5", fixed sight, ambidextrous safety) **$660.00**
Price: As above, adjustable sight **$687.00**
Price: Model 4536 (stainless 3¾"), traditional DA with de-cocking lever) **$740.00**
Price: Model 4556 (stainless, 3¾", DA only) **$714.00**
Price: Model 4526 (stainless, 5", traditional DA with de-cocking lever) **$740.00**
Price: Model 4546 (stainless, 5", DA only) **$714.00**
Price: Model 4566 (stainless, 4¼", traditional DA, ambidextrous safety) **$714.00**
Price: Model 4576 (stainless, 4¼", traditional DA with de-cocking lever) **$740.00**
Price: Model 4586 (stainless, 4¼", DA only) **$714.00**

Smith & Wesson Model 1006 Double-Action Auto

Similar to the Model 4506 except chambered for 10mm auto with 9-shot magazine. Available with either Novak LoMount Carry fixed rear sight with two white dots or adjustable micrometer-click rear with two white dots. All stainless steel construction; one-piece Delrin stocks with straight backstrap; curved backstrap available as option. Has 5" barrel, 8½" overall length, weighs 38 oz. with fixed sight. Rounded trigger guard with knurling. Introduced 1990.
Price: With fixed sight **$747.00**
Price: With adjustable sight **$773.00**

Smith & Wesson Model 1026, 1076 Autos

Same as the Model 1006 except has frame-mounted de-cocking lever, fixed sight only; traditional double-action mechanism. Introduced 1990.
Price: **$755.00**

Smith & Wesson Model 1046, 1086 DA Pistol

Same as the Model 1006 except is double-action only, fixed sight; satin stainless; straight backstrap. Model 1086 has 4¼" barrel. Introduced 1990.
Price: Model 1046 . . . . **$747.00**
Price: Model 1086 . . . . **$730.00**

Smith & Wesson Model 1066 Auto Pistol

Similar to the Model 1006 except has 4¼" barrel, fixed sight, ambidextrous safety. Introduced 1990.
Price: Model 1066 . . . . **$730.00**
Price: Model 1076-NS (as above with night sights) **$825.00**

SMITH & WESSON MODEL 4006 DA AUTO

Caliber: 40 S&W, 11-shot magazine.
Barrel: 4".
Weight: 36 oz. **Length:** 7½" overall.
Stocks: Delrin wraparound with checkered panels.
Sights: Replaceable post front with white dot, Novak LoMount Carry fixed rear with two white dots, or micro. click adjustable rear with two white dots.
Features: Stainless steel construction with non-reflective finish. Straight backstrap. Introduced 1990.
Price: With adjustable sights **$736.00**
Price: With fixed sight **$708.00**

Smith & Wesson 4546 DA

Smith & Wesson Model 4567-NS Pistol

Similar to the Model 4506 except has 4¼" barrel, stainless steel slide and blue steel frame; bobbed hammer; smooth rounded edges; Novak LoMount Carry sights with tritium inserts. Xenoy one-piece wraparound grips with straight backstrap in deep blue color. Overall length is 7⅞", weight 39.4 oz. Introduced 1991. Limited production.
Price: **$735.00**

Smith & Wesson 1006

Smith & Wesson Model 1066-NS 10mm Auto

Similar to the Model 1006 except has 4¼" barrel, .260" bobbed hammer, fixed Novak LoMount Carry rear sight with tritium inserts, black post front with tritium insert. Has Xenoy one-piece wraparound grips with straight backstrap. Matte stainless steel finish. Overall length is 7¾", weight 39.7 oz. Introduced 1990. Limited production.
Price: **$770.00**

Smith & Wesson 4006

Smith & Wesson Model 4046 DA Pistol

Similar to the Model 4006 except is double-action only. Has a semi-bobbed hammer, smooth trigger, 4" barrel; Novak LoMount Carry rear sight, post front with white dot. Overall length is 7½", weight 39 oz. Introduced 1991.
Price: **$708.00**

SMITH & WESSON MODEL 5900 SERIES AUTO PISTOLS
Caliber: 9mm Para., 15-shot magazine.
Barrel: 4".
Weight: 28½ to 37½ oz. (fixed sight); 29 to 38 oz. (adj. sight). **Length:** 7½" overall.
Stocks: Xenoy wraparound with curved backstrap.
Sights: Post front with white dot, fixed or fully adjustable with two white dots.
Features: All stainless, stainless and alloy or carbon steel and alloy construction. Smooth .304" trigger, .260" serrated hammer. Introduced 1989.
Price: Model 5903 (stainless, alloy frame, traditional DA, adjustable sight, ambidextrous safety) . . . **$666.00**
Price: As above, fixed sight . . . **$636.00**
Price: Model 5904 (blue, alloy frame, traditonal DA, adjustable sight, ambidextrous safety) . . . **$620.00**
Price: As above, fixed sight . . . **$592.00**
Price: Model 5906 (stainless, traditonal DA, adjustable sight, ambidextrous safety) . . . **$684.00**
Price: As above, fixed sight . . . **$652.00**
Price: Model 5924 (blue, alloy frame, traditional DA with de-cocking lever, fixed sight . . . **$617.00**
Price: Model 5926 (as above, stainless) . . . **$677.00**
Price: Model 5943 (stainless, alloy frame, DA only, fixed sight) . . . **$636.00**
Price: Model 5944 (as above, blue, alloy frame) . . . **$592.00**
Price: Model 5946 (as above, stainless frame and slide) . . . **$652.00**
Price: Model 5905 (blue frame and slide, fixed sight, ambidextrous safety) . . . **$603.00**
Price: As above with adjustable sight . . . **$632.00**

Smith & Wesson Model 6904/6906 Double-Action Autos
Similar to the Models 5904/5906 except with 3½" barrel, 12-shot magazine (20-shot available), fixed rear sight, .260" bobbed hammer. Introduced 1989.
Price: Model 6904, blue . . . **$561.00**
Price: Model 6906, stainless . . . **$618.00**
Price: Model 6944 (blue, DA only, fixed sight) . . . **$561.00**
Price: Model 6946 (stainless, DA only, fixed sights) . . . **$618.00**
Price: Model 6926 (stainless, traditional DA with de-cocking lever, fixed sight) . . . **$644.00**

SPORTARMS TOKAREV MODEL 213
Caliber: 9mm Para., 8-shot magazine.
Barrel: 4.5".
Weight: 31 oz. **Length:** 7.6" overall.
Stocks: Grooved plastic.
Sights: Fixed.
Features: Blue finish, hard chrome optional. 9mm version of the famous Russian Tokarev pistol. Made in China by Norinco. Imported by Sportarms of Florida. Introduced 1988.
Price: Blue, about . . . **$196.95**
Price: Hard chrome, about . . . **$226.95**

Springfield 1911A1 90s Edition

Springfield Compact

Smith & Wesson 5943 SSV-DA

Smith & Wesson Model 5943-SSV Pistol
Similar to the Model 5903 except has 3½" barrel, short slide and bobbed hammer, and is double-action only. Alloy frame, blued steel slide, slide stop, magazine release, hammer and trigger. Has black post front sight with tritium insert, Novak LoMount Carry fixed rear sight with tritium inserts; black curved backstrap grips. Overall length 7"; weight 28.9 oz. Introduced 1990.
Price: . . . **$690.00**

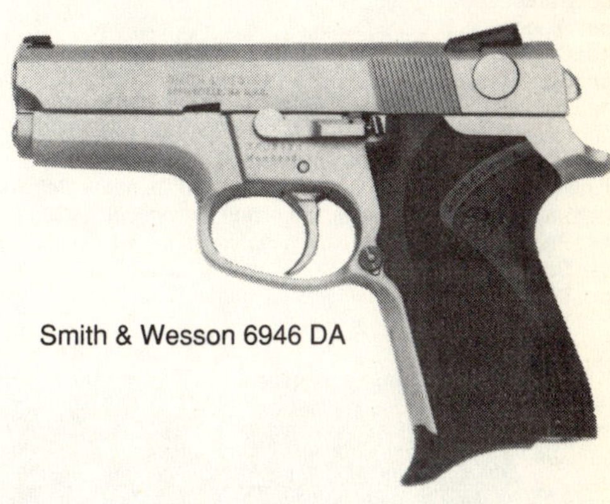
Smith & Wesson 6946 DA

SPRINGFIELD ARMORY 1911A1 90s EDITION PISTOL
Caliber: 9mm Para., 38 Super, 10-shot magazine; 45 ACP, 8-shot.
Barrel: 5".
Weight: 36 oz. **Length:** 8½" overall.
Stocks: Checkered walnut.
Sights: Fixed low-profile combat-style.
Features: Beveled magazine well. All forged parts, including frame, barrel, slide. All new production. Custom slide parts available. Introduced 1990. From Springfield Armory.
Price: Parkerized . . . **$454.00**
Price: Blued . . . **$487.00**
Price: Duotone (blue slide, hard chrome frame) . . . **$532.00**
Price: Stainless . . . **$565.00**

Springfield Armory 1911A1 90s Edition (Linkless)
Similar to the standard 1911A1 90s Edition except uses new linkless lock-up system that eliminates the traditional barrel link and pin. Chambered for 10mm and 40 S&W. Compensated model has 6.5" barrel with polygonal rifling, rubberized wraparound grips, weighs 38 oz., and has dual port compensator system; uncompensated gun has 6" barrel with polygonal rifling, weighs 36 oz., walnut grips. Introduced 1990.
Price: Parkerized . . . **$623.00**
Price: Blued . . . **$662.00**
Price: Duotone . . . **$707.00**

Springfield Armory 1911A1 Compact Pistol
Similar to the Commander model except has a shortened slide with 4.25" barrel, 7.25" overall length. Magazine capacity is 6 shots. Has low-profile three-dot sight system, checkered walnut grips. Available in 45 ACP only. Introduced 1989.
Price: Blued . . . **$545.00**
Price: Parkerized . . . **$514.00**
Price: Duotone . . . **$592.00**

Springfield Armory 1911A1 Defender Pistol

Similar to the 1911A1 Commander except has 4" tapered cone barrel with Dual Port compensator, rubberized grips. Has reverse recoil plug, full-length recoil spring guide, serrated frontstrap, extended thumb safety, Commander-style hammer with modified grip safety to match and a Videki speed trigger. Duotone finish. Introduced 1991.

Price: . . . . **P.O.R.**

Springfield Armory 1911A1 Commander Pistol

Similar to the standard 1911A1 except slide and barrel are ½" shorter. Has low-profile three-dot sight system. Comes with Commander hammer and walnut stocks. Available in 45 ACP only; choice of blue or Parkerized or Duotone finish. Introduced 1989.

Price: Blue **$545.00**
Price: Parkerized **$514.00**
Price: Duotone **$592.00**

SPRINGFIELD ARMORY P9 DA PISTOL

Caliber: 9mm Para., 15-shot magazine; 40 S&W, 45 ACP.
Barrel: 4.72".
Weight: 35.3 oz. **Length:** 8.1" overall.
Stocks: Checkered walnut.
Sights: Blade front, open rear drift-adjustable for windage; three-dot system.
Features: Patterned after the CZ-75. Frame-mounted thumb safety. Magazine catch can be switched to opposite side. Commander hammer. Introduced 1989.
Price: Parkerized **$363.00**
Price: Blued **$376.00**
Price: Duotone **$545.00**
Price: Double-action only . . . . **NA**

Springfield Armory P9 Compact Pistol

Similar to the standard P9 except has 3.66" barrel, 7.24" overall length, and weighs 32.1 oz. Has 13-shot magazine. Introduced 1989.

Price: Parkerized **$376.00**
Price: Blued **$389.00**
Price: Duotone **$563.00**

Springfield P9C Subcompact

STALLARD JS-9MM AUTO PISTOL

Caliber: 9mm Para., 8-shot magazine.
Barrel: 4.5".
Weight: 48 oz. **Length:** 7.72" overall.
Stocks: Textured acetal plastic.
Sights: Fixed, low profile.
Features: Single-action design. Scratch-resistant, non-glare blue finish. Introduced 1990. From MKS Supply, Inc.
Price: **$139.95**

STAR FIRESTAR AUTO PISTOL

Caliber: 9mm Para., 7-shot; 40 S&W, 6-shot.
Barrel: 3.39".
Weight: 30.35 oz. **Length:** 6.5" overall.
Stocks: Checkered rubber.
Sights: Blade front, fully adjustable rear; three-dot system.
Features: Low-profile, combat-style sights; ambidextrous safety. Available in blue or weather-resistant Starvel finish. Introduced 1990. Imported from Spain by Interarms.
Price: Blue, 9mm **$485.00**
Price: Starvel finish 9mm **$515.00**
Price: Blue, 40 S&W **$510.00**
Price: Starvel finish, 40 S&W **$540.00**

Springfield Defender

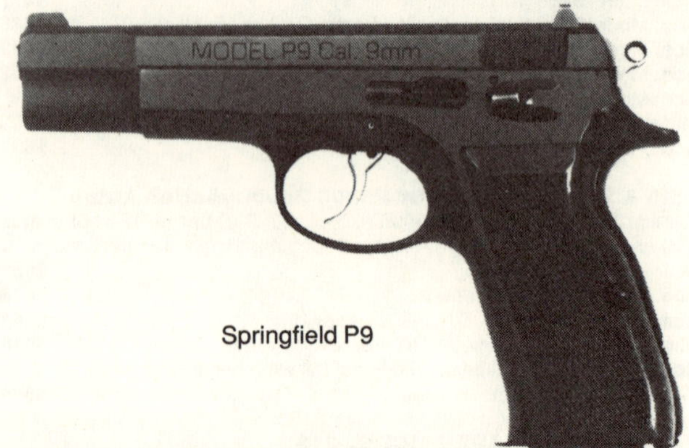

Springfield P9

Springfield Armory P9C Subcompact Pistol

Similar to the standard P9 pistol except has 3½" barrel, weighs 32 oz. and is chambered for 9mm Para. (12-shot magazine) and 40 S&W (9-shot magazine). Traditional double action. Walnut grips, extended magazine floorplate, squared trigger guard. Introduced 1991.

Price: . . . . **P.O.R.**

Springfield Armory P9 LSP Long Slide Pistol

Same as the standard P9 except has 5.03" ported barrel, 8.38" overall length and weighs 38.4 oz. Rubber stocks. Introduced 1990.

Price: Parkerized **$519.00**
Price: Blued **$545.00**
Price: Duotone **$597.00**

Star Firestar

STAR MODEL PD AUTO PISTOL

Caliber: 45 ACP, 6-shot magazine.
Barrel: 3.94".
Weight: 28 oz.k **Length:** 7 7/16" overall.
Stocks: Checkered walnut.
Sights: Ramp front, fully adjustable rear.
Features: Rear sight milled into slide; thumb safety; grooved non-slip frontstrap; nylon recoil buffer; inertia firing pin; no grip or magazine safeties. Imported from Spain by Interarms.
Price: Blue **$475.00**
Price: Starvel **$495.00**

STAR MODEL 30M & 31PK DOUBLE-ACTION PISTOLS
Caliber: 9mm Para., 15-shot magazine.
Barrel: 4.33" (Model M); 3.86" (Model PK).
Weight: 40 oz. (M); 30 oz. (PK). **Length:** 8" overall (M); 7.6" (PK).
Stocks: Checkered black plastic.
Sights: Square blade front, square notch rear click-adjustable for windage and elevation.
Features: Double or single action; grooved front- and backstraps and trigger guard face; ambidextrous safety cams firing pin forward; removable backstrap houses the firing mechanism. Model M has steel frame; Model PK is alloy. Introduced 1984. Imported from Spain by Interarms.
Price: Model 30M, 9mm Para. **$495.00**
Price: Model 31PK, 9mm Para. **$550.00**
Price: Model 31P, steel frame, blue, 40 S&W **$610.00**
Price: As above, Starvel finish **$640.00**
Price: Model 31P, steel frame, blue, 9mm Para. **$550.00**
Price: As above, Starvel finish **$580.00**

Star Model 30M

Star Model BM

STAR MODEL BM, BKM AUTO PISTOLS
Caliber: 9mm Para., 8-shot magazine.
Barrel: 3.9".
Weight: 25 oz.
Stocks: Checkered walnut.
Sights: Fixed.
Features: Blue or chrome finish. Magazine and manual safeties, external hammer. Imported from Spain by Interarms.
Price: Blue, BM **$415.00**
Price: Blue, BKM only **$415.00**
Price: Starvel, BM only **$445.00**

Sundance BOA

SUNDANCE MODEL A-25 AUTO PISTOL
Caliber: 25 ACP, 7-shot magazine.
Barrel: 2".
Weight: 14 oz. **Length:** 4⅞" overall.
Stocks: Grooved black ABS or simulated smooth pearl.
Sights: Fixed.
Features: Rotary safety blocks sear. Bright chrome, satin nickel or black Teflon finish. Introduced 1989. From Sundance Industries, Inc.
Price: **$79.95**

SUNDANCE BOA AUTO PISTOL
Caliber: 25 ACP, 7-shot magazine.
Barrel: 2½".
Weight: 16 oz. **Length:** 4⅞".
Stocks: Grooved composition.
Sights: Fixed.
Features: Grip safety, manual rotary safety; button magazine release; lifetime warranty. Bright chrome, satin nickel or black Teflon finish. Introduced 1991. made in the U.S. by Sundance Industries, Inc.
Price: **$95.00**

TAURUS MODEL PT58 AUTO PISTOL
Caliber: 380 ACP, 12-shot magazine.
Barrel: 4.01".
Weight: 30 oz. **Length:** 7.2" overall.
Stocks: Brazilian hardwood.
Sights: Integral blade on slide front, notch rear adjustable for windage. Three-dot system.
Features: Double action with exposed hammer; inertia firing pin. Introduced 1988. Imported by Taurus International.
Price: Blue **$423.00**
Price: Satin nickel **$454.00**

Taurus PT58

Taurus PT 99 Auto Pistol
Similar to the PT-92 except has fully adjustable rear sight, smooth Brazilian walnut stocks and is available in polished blue or satin nickel. Introduced 1983.
Price: Blue **$512.00**
Price: Blue, Deluxe Shooter's Pak (extra magazine, case) **$540.00**
Price: Nickel **$554.00**
Price: Nickel, Deluxe Shooter's Pak (extra magazine, case) **$583.00**
Price: Stainless steel **$582.00**
Price: Stainless, Deluxe Shooter's Pak (extra magazine, case) . . . **$609.00**

TAURUS MODEL PT 92 AUTO PISTOL
Caliber: 9mm Para., 15-shot magazine.
Barrel: 4.92".
Weight: 34 oz. **Length:** 8.54" overall.
Stocks: Brazilian hardwood.
Sights: Fixed notch rear. Three-dot sight system.
Features: Double action, exposed hammer, chamber loaded indicator. Inertia firing pin. Imported by Taurus International.
Price: Blue **$473.00**
Price: Blue, Deluxe Shooter's Pak (extra magazine, case) **$501.00**
Price: Nickel **$511.00**
Price: Nickel, Deluxe Shooter's Pak (extra magazine, case) **$539.00**
Price: Stainless steel **$538.00**
Price: Stainless, Deluxe Shooter's Pak (extra magazine, case) . . . **$564.00**

Taurus PT 92C Compact Pistol
Similar to the PT-92 except has 4.25" barrel, 13-shot magazine, weighs 31 oz. and is 7.5" overall. Available in blue or satin nickel. Introduced 1991. Imported by Taurus International.
Price: Blue **$473.00**
Price: Blue, Deluxe Shooter's Pak (extra magazine, case) **$501.00**
Price: Nickel **$511.00**
Price: Nickel, Deluxe Shooter's Pak (extra magazine, case) **$539.00**

Taurus PT 92C

Taurus/Laser Aim 9mm Pistol Package
Includes the Taurus Model PT-92 pistol (blue or satin nickel finish) and the Taurus/Laser Aim LA1 laser sight with appropriate mount and rings in matching finish, the LA1C 110-volt charger and LA9C 9-volt field charger, and a sturdy high-impact case. Below-barrel mount allows the use of conventional sights or a scope. Introduced 1990.
Price: Blue **$913.00**
Price: Satin nickel **$951.00**

TAURUS PT 100 AUTO PISTOL
Caliber: 40 S&W, 15-shot magazine.
Barrel: 5".
Weight: 34 oz.
Stocks: Smooth Brazilian hardwood.
Sights: Fixed front, drift-adjustable rear. Three-dot combat.
Features: Double action, exposed hammer. Ambidextrous hammer-drop safety; inertia firing pin; chamber loaded indicator. Introduced 1991. Imported by Taurus International.
Price: Blue . . . . . **NA**
Price: Satin nickel . . . . . **NA**
Price: Stainless steel . . . . . **NA**

Taurus PT 101 Auto Pistol
Same as the PT 100 except has micro-click rear sight adjustable for windage and elevation, three-dot combat-style. Introduced 1991.
Price: Blue . . . . . **NA**
Price: Stain nickel . . . . . **NA**
Price: Stainless steel . . . . . **NA**

UZI® PISTOL
Caliber: 9mm Para.
Barrel: 4.5".
Weight: 3.8 lbs. **Length:** 9.5" overall.
Stocks: Black plastic.
Sights: Post front with white dot, open rear click-adjustable for windage and elevation, two white dots.
Features: Semi-auto blowback action; fires from closed bolt; floating firing pin. Comes in a moulded plastic case with 20-round magazine; 25- and 32-round magazines available. Imported from Israel by Action Arms. Introduced 1984.
Price: **$585.00**

Uzi Pistol

WALTHER PP AUTO PISTOL
Caliber: 32 ACP, 380 ACP, 7-shot.
Barrel: 3.86".
Weight: 23½ oz. **Length:** 6.7" overall.
Stocks: Checkered plastic.
Sights: Fixed, white markings.
Features: Double action; manual safety blocks firing pin and drops hammer; chamber loaded indicator on 32 and 380; extra finger rest magazine provided. Imported from Germany by Interarms.
Price: 32 . . . . . **$1,000.00**
Price: 380 . . . . . **$1,075.00**
Price: Engraved models . . . . . **On Request**

Walther PPK/S American

Walther American PPK/S Auto Pistol
Similar to Walther PP except made entirely in the United States. Has 3.27" barrel with 6.1" length overall. Introduced 1980.
Price: 380 ACP only **$585.00**
Price: As above, stainless **$585.00**

Walther American PPK Auto Pistol
Similar to Walther PPK/S except weighs 21 oz., has 6-shot capacity. Made in the U.S. Introduced 1986.
Price: Stainless, 380 ACP only **$585.00**
Price: Blue, 380 ACP only **$585.00**

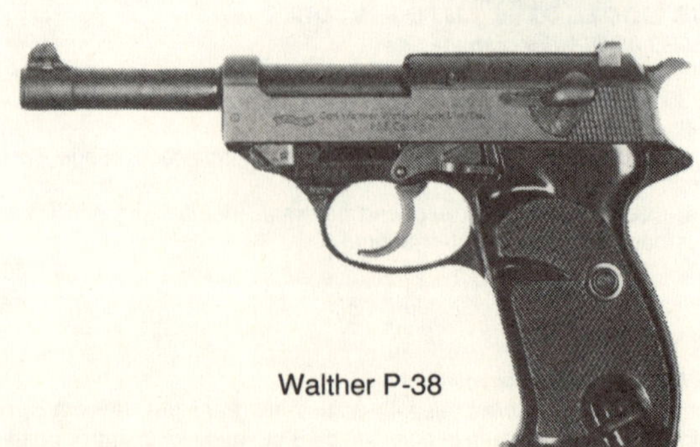
Walther P-38

WALTHER P-38 AUTO PISTOL
Caliber: 9mm Para., 8-shot.
Barrel: 4$^{15}/_{16}$".
Weight: 28 oz. **Length:** 8½" overall.
Stocks: Checkered plastic.
Sights: Fixed.
Features: Double action; safety blocks firing pin and drops hammer. Matte finish standard, polished blue, engraving and/or plating available. Imported from Germany by Interarms.
Price: **$1,065.00**
Price: Engraved models . . . . . **On Request**

Walther P-5 Auto Pistol
Latest Walther design that uses the basic P-38 double-action mechanism. Caliber 9mm Para., barrel length 3½"; weight 28 oz., overall length 7".
Price: **$1,085.00**
Price: P-5 Compact **$1,460.00**

CAUTION: PRICES CHANGE, CHECK AT GUNSHOP.

WALTHER MODEL TPH AUTO PISTOL

Caliber: 22 LR, 6-shot magazine.
Barrel: 2¼".
Weight: 14 oz. **Length:** 5⅜" overall.
Stocks: Checkered black composition.
Sights: Blade front, rear drift-adjustable for windage.
Features: Made of stainless steel. Scaled-down version of the Walther PP/PPK series. Made in U.S. Introduced 1987. From Interarms.
Price: $445.00

Walther TPH

Consult our Directory pages for the location of firms mentioned.

WALTHER P-88 AUTO PISTOL

Caliber: 9mm Para., 15-shot magazine.
Barrel: 4".
Weight: 31½ oz. **Length:** 7⅜" overall.
Stocks: Checkered black composition.
Sights: Blade front, rear adjustable for windage and elevation.
Features: Double action with ambidextrous decocking lever and magazine release; alloy frame; loaded chamber indicator; matte finish. Imported from Germany by Interarms.
Price: $1,550.00

Walther P-88

WILDEY AUTOMATIC PISTOL

Caliber: 30 Wildey Magnum, 10mm Wildey Mag., 11mm Wildey Mag., 45 Win. Mag., 475 Wildey Mag., 357 Peterbuilt.
Barrel: 5", 6", 7", 8", 10", 12", 14" (45 Win. Mag.); 8", 10", 12", 14" (all other cals.). Interchangeable.
Weight: 64 oz. (5" barrel). **Length:** 11" overall (7" barrel).
Stocks: Hardwood.
Sights: Ramp front, fully adjustable rear.
Features: Gas-operated action. Made of stainless steel. Has three-lug rotary bolt. Double action. Polished and matte finish. Made in U.S. by Wildey, Inc.
Price: . . . . $1,175.00 to $1,495.00

Wildey Auto

Wilkinson "Sherry"

Wilkinson "Linda"

WILKINSON "SHERRY" AUTO PISTOL

Caliber: 22 LR, 8-shot magazine.
Barrel: 2⅛".
Weight: 9¼ oz. **Length:** 4⅜" overall.
Stocks: Checkered black plastic.
Sights: Fixed, groove.
Features: Cross-bolt safety locks the sear into the hammer. Available in all blue finish or blue slide and trigger with gold frame. Introduced 1985.
Price: $159.95

WILKINSON "LINDA" AUTO PISTOL

Caliber: 9mm Para., 31-shot magazine.
Barrel: 8$\frac{5}{16}$".
Weight: 4 lbs., 13 oz. **Length:** 12¼" overall.
Stocks: Checkered black plastic pistol grip, maple forend.
Sights: Protected blade front, aperture rear.
Features: Fires from closed bolt. Semi-auto only. Straight blowback action. Cross-bolt safety. Removable barrel. From Wilkinson Arms.
Price: $412.00

Models specifically designed for classic competitive shooting sports.

BF ARMS SINGLE SHOT PISTOL
Caliber: 22 LR, 32-20, 357 Mag., 357 Rem. Mag., 30-30, 7-30 Waters (standard); 22 K Hornet, 222 BFR, 270 Rem., 30 Herrett, 357 Herrett, 375 Super Mag., 7mm Super Mag. (wildcat).
Barrel: 10", 12", 14", 16".
Weight: 46 oz. (10" bbl.).
Stocks: Plain and finger-grooved, ambidextrous; oil-finished walnut.
Sights: Burris Patridge front on ramp, Williams open rear with target knobs, adjustable for windage and elevation. Drilled and tapped for scope mount.
Features: Falling block short-stroke action, automatic case ejection. Wilson or Douglas air-gauged match-grade barrel. Flat black oxide finish. Add $20 for wildcat chamberings. Introduced 1988. Made in U.S. by BF Arms.
Price: 22 LR, 10" barrel, open sights **$450.00**
Price: 10" barrel, standard calibers, open sights **$406.00**
Price: As above, no sights **$345.00**
Price: 12" barrel, standard calibers, open sights **$416.00**
Price: As above, no sights **$355.00**
Price: 14" barrel, standard calibers, open sights **$426.00**
Price: As above, no sights **$365.00**
Price: 16" barrel, standard calibers, open sights **$436.00**
Price: As above, no sights **$375.00**

Beeman/Unique D.E.S. 69

Beeman/Unique 2000-U

BERETTA MODEL 89 TARGET PISTOL
Caliber: 22 LR, 8-shot magazine.
Barrel: 6"
Weight: 41 oz. **Length:** 9.5" overall.
Stocks: Target-type walnut with thumbrest.
Sights: Interchangeable blade front, fully adjustable rear.
Features: Single-action target pistol. Matte blue finish. Imported from Italy by Beretta U.S.A.
Price: **$685.00**

BRNO DRULOV 75 TARGET PISTOL
Caliber: 22 LR, single shot.
Barrel: 10"
Weight: 44 oz. **Length:** 14.75" overall.
Stocks: Walnut.
Sights: Interchangeable blade front, micrometer click-stop rear adjustable for windage and elevation.
Features: Bolt action with adjustable set trigger; all steel construction, blue finish. Introduced 1991. Imported from Czechoslavakia by T.D. Arms.
Price: **$349.00**

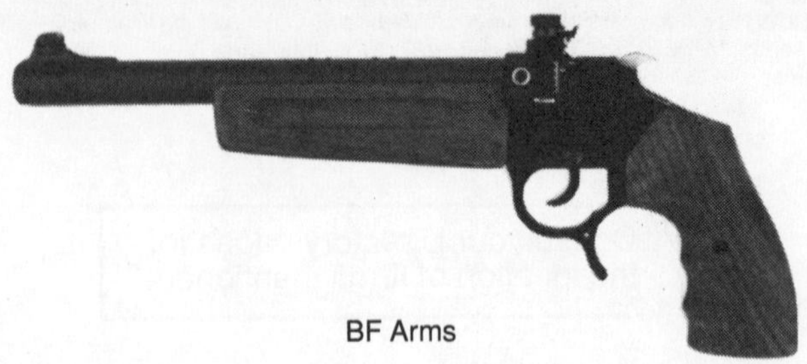
BF Arms

BEEMAN/UNIQUE D.E.S. 32U RAPID FIRE MATCH
Caliber: 32 S&W Long wadcutter.
Barrel: 5.9".
Weight: 40.2 oz.
Stocks: Anatomically shaped, adjustable stippled French walnut.
Sights: Blade front, micrometer click rear.
Features: Trigger adjustable for weight and position; dry firing mechanism; slide stop catch. Optional 120, 220, or 320-gram sleeve weights. Introduced 1990. Imported from France by Beeman.
Price: Right-hand **$1,268.00**

BEEMAN/UNIQUE D.E.S. 69 TARGET PISTOL
Caliber: 22 LR, 5-shot magazine.
Barrel: 5.91".
Weight: 35.3 oz. **Length:** 10.5" overall.
Stocks: French walnut target-style with thumbrest and adjustable shelf; hand-checkered panels.
Sights: Ramp front, micro. adj. rear mounted on frame; 8.66" sight radius.
Features: Meets U.I.T. standards. Comes with 260-gram barrel weight; 100, 150, 350 gram weights available. Fully adjustable match trigger; dry-firing safety device. Imported from France by Beeman.
Price: Right-hand **$1,242.00**
Price: Left-hand **$1,293.00**

BEEMAN/UNIQUE MODEL 2000-U MATCH PISTOL
Caliber: 22 Short, 5-shot magazine.
Barrel: 5.9".
Weight: 43 oz. **Length:** 11.3" overall.
Stocks: Anatomically shaped, adjustable, stippled French walnut.
Sights: Blade front, fully adjustable rear; 9.7" sight radius.
Features: Light alloy frame, steel slide and shock absorber; five barrel vents reduce recoil, three of which can be blocked; trigger adjustable for position and pull weight. Comes with 340-gram weight housing, 160-gram available. Imported from France by Beeman. Introduced 1984.
Price: Right-hand **$1,268.00**
Price: Left-hand **$1,476.00**

Beretta Model 89

BROWNING BUCK MARK SILHOUETTE
Caliber: 22 LR, 10-shot magazine.
Barrel: 9⅞".
Weight: 53 oz. **Length:** 14" overall.
Stocks: Smooth walnut stocks and forend.
Sights: Post-type hooded front adjustable for blade width and height; Millett Gold Cup #360 SIL rear.
Features: Heavy barrel with .900" diameter; 12½" sight radius. Special sighting plane forms scope base. Introduced 1987. Made in U.S. From Browning.
Price: **$379.95**

Browning Buck Mark Silhouette

Browning Buck Mark Unlimited Match
Same as the Buck Mark Silhouette except has 14" heavy barrel. Conforms to IHMSA 15" maximum sight radius rule. Introduced 1991.
Price: **$449.95**

Browning Buck Mark Target 5.5

Browning Buck Mark Target 5.5
Same as the Buck Mark Silhouette except has a 5½" barrel with .900" diameter. Has hooded sights mounted on a scope base that accepts an optical or reflex sight. Rear sight is a Millett Gold Cup #360, front sight is an adjustable post that customizes to different widths, and can be adjusted for height. Contoured walnut grips with thumbrest. Matte blue finish. Overall length is 9⅝", weight is 35½ oz. Has 10-shot magazine. Introduced 1990. From Browning.
Price: **$359.95**
Price: Target 5.5 Gold (as above with gold anodized frame and top rib) **$379.95**

Browning Buck Mark Field 5.5
Same as the Target 5.5 except has hoodless ramp-style front sight and low profile rear sight. Matte blue finish, contoured walnut stocks. Introduced 1991.
Price: **$359.95**

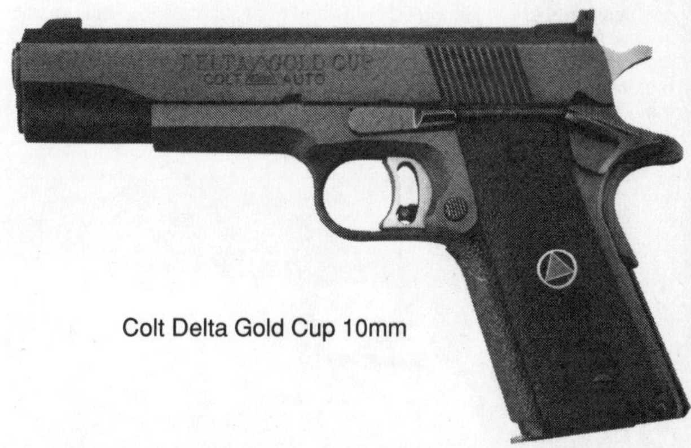

Colt Delta Gold Cup 10mm

COLT GOLD CUP NAT'L MATCH MK IV/Series 80
Caliber: 45 ACP, 7-shot magazine.
Barrel: 5", with new design bushing.
Weight: 39 oz. **Length:** 8½".
Stocks: Blue has checkered walnut, gold-plated medallion; stainless has black walnut.
Sights: Ramp-style front, Colt-Elliason rear adjustable for windage and elevation, sight radius 6¾".
Features: Arched or flat housing; wide, grooved trigger with adjustable stop; ribbed-top slide, hand fitted, with improved ejection port.
Price: Blue **$819.95**
Price: Stainless **$874.95**
Price: Bright stainless **$940.95**
Price: Delta Gold Cup (10mm, stainless) **$899.95**
Price: As above, blue **$869.95**

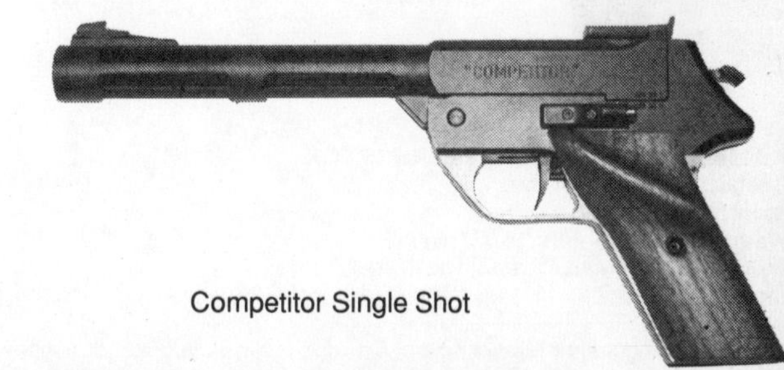

Competitor Single Shot

COMPETITOR SINGLE SHOT PISTOL
Caliber: 22 LR, 223, 7mm TCU, 7mm Int., 30 Herrett, 357 Maximum, 41 Mag., 44 Mag., 454 Casull, 375 Super Mag. Others on special order.
Barrel: 10.5", 14".
Weight: NA **Length:** NA.
Stocks: Smooth walnut with thumbrest.
Sights: Ramp front, open adjustable rear.
Features: Interchangeable barrels of blue ordnance or bright stainless steel; ventilated barrel shroud; receiver has integral scope mount. Introduced 1987. From TMI Products.
Price: With 10.5" bbl. **$562.50**
Price: With 14" bbl. **$578.50**
Price: Extra barrels, 10.5", standard calibers **$93.75**
Price: Special calibers, add **$62.50**

Erma ER Match

ERMA ER MATCH REVOLVERS
Caliber: 22 LR, 32 S&W Long, 6-shot.
Barrel: 6".
Weight: 47.3 oz. **Length:** 11.2" overall.
Stocks: Stippled walnut, adjustable match-type.
Sights: Blade front, micrometer rear adjustable for windage and elevation.
Features: Polished blue finish. Introduced 1989. Imported from Germany by Precision Sales International.
Price: 22 LR or 32 S&W Long **$1,345.00**

E.A.A. MODEL EA22T TARGET AUTO
Caliber: 22 LR, 12-shot.
Barrel: 6".
Weight: 40 oz. **Length:** 9.10" overall.
Stocks: Checkered walnut, with thumbrest.
Sights: Blade on ramp front, rear adjustable for windage and elevation.
Features: Blue finish. Finger-rest magazine. Imported by European American Armory Corp.
Price: **$259.99**

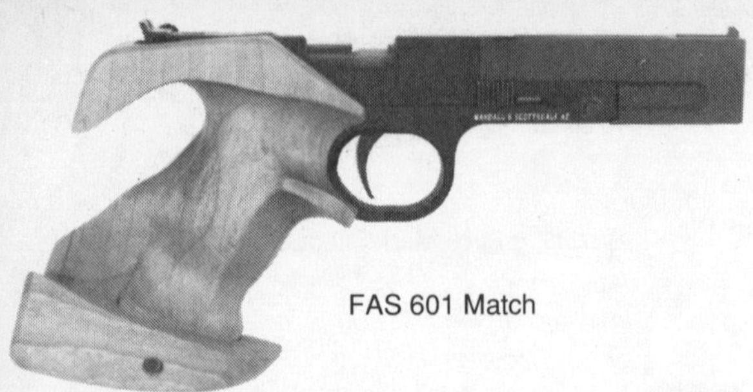
FAS 601 Match

FREEDOM ARMS CASULL MODEL 252 SILHOUETTE
Caliber: 22 LR, 5-shot cyclinder.
Barrel: 9.95".
Weight: 63 oz. **Length:** NA
Stocks: Black micarta, western style.
Sights: 1/8" Patridge front, Iron Sight Gun Works silhouette rear, click adjustable for windage and elevation.
Features: Stainless steel. Built on the 454 Casull frame. Two-point firing pin, lightened hammer for fast lock time. Trigger pull is 3 to 5 lbs. with pre-set overtravel screw. Introduced 1991. From Freedom Arms.
Price: Silhouette Class **$1,295.00**

Freedom Arms Casull Model 252 Varmint
Similar to the Silhouette Class revolver except has 7.5" barrel, weighs 59 oz., has black and green laminated hardwood grips, and comes with brass bead front sight, express shallow V rear sight with windage and elevation adjustments. Introduced 1991. From Freedom Arms.
Price: Varmint Class **$1,248.00**
Price: Extra fitted 22 WMR cylinder **$189.00**

Glock 17L

HAMMERLI MODEL 150 FREE PISTOL
Caliber: 22 LR, single shot.
Barrel: 11.3".
Weight: 43 oz. **Length:** 15.35" overall.
Stocks: Walnut with adjustable palm shelf.
Sights: Sight radius of 14.6". Micro rear sight adjustable for windage and elevation.
Features: Single shot Martini action. Cocking lever on left side of action with vertical operation. Set trigger adjustable for length and angle. Trigger pull weight adjustable between 5 and 100 grams. Guaranteed accuracy of .78", 10 shots from machine rest. Imported from Switzerland by Beeman, Hammerli Pistols USA, and Mandall Shooting Supplies.
Price: About . . . . **$1,895.00 to $2,139.00**

Consult our Directory pages for the location of firms mentioned.

HAMMERLI MODEL 152 MATCH PISTOL
Caliber: 22 LR.
Barrel: 11.2".
Weight: 46.9 oz. **Length:** 16.9" overall.
Stocks: Match.
Sights: Changeable post front, micrometer rear.
Features: Electronic trigger. Introduced 1990. Imported from Switzerland by Beeman, Hammerli Pistols USA, Mandall Shooting Supplies.
Price: About . . . . **$2,105.00 to $2,333.00**

FAS 602 MATCH PISTOL
Caliber: 22 LR, 5-shot.
Barrel: 5.6".
Weight: 37 oz. **Length:** 11" overall.
Stocks: Walnut wraparound; sizes small, medium or large, or adjustable.
Sights: Match. Blade front, open notch rear fully adjustable for windage and elevation. Sight radius is 8.66".
Features: Line of sight is only 11/32" above centerline of bore; magazine is inserted from top; adjustable and removable trigger mechanism; single lever takedown. Full 5-year warranty. Imported from Italy by Mandall Shooting Supplies.
Price: **$1,525.00**

FAS 601 Match Pistol
Similar to SP 602 except has different match stocks with adjustable palm shelf, 22 Short only for rapid fire shooting; weighs 40 oz., 5.6" bbl.; has gas ports through top of barrel and slide to reduce recoil; slightly different trigger and sear mechanisms.
Price: **$1,595.00**

Freedom Casull 252 Varmint

GAUCHER GP SILHOUETTE PISTOL
Caliber: 22 LR, single shot.
Barrel: 10".
Weight: 42.3 oz. **Length:** 15.5" overall.
Stocks: Stained hardwood.
Sights: Hooded post on ramp front, open rear adjustable for windage and elevation.
Features: Matte chrome barrel, blued bolt and sights. Other barrel lengths available on special order. Introduced 1991. Imported by Mandall Shooting Supplies.
Price: **$323.00**

GLOCK 17L COMPETITION AUTO
Caliber: 9mm Para., 17-shot magazine.
Barrel: 6.02".
Weight: 23.3 oz. **Length:** 8.7" overall.
Stocks: Black polymer.
Sights: Blade front with white dot, adjustable rear.
Features: Polymer frame, steel slide; double-action trigger with "Safe Action" system; mechanical firing pin safety, drop safety; simple takedown without tools; locked breech, recoil operated action. Introduced 1989. Imported from Austria by Glock, Inc.
Price: **$963.15**

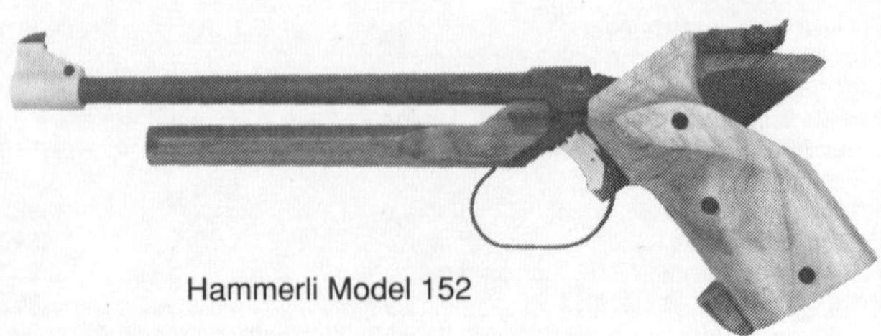
Hammerli Model 152

HAMMERLI MODEL 208s PISTOL
Caliber: 22 LR, 8-shot magazine.
Barrel: 5.9".
Weight: 37.5 oz. **Length:** 10" overall.
Stocks: Walnut, target-type with thumbrest.
Sights: Blade front, open fully adjustable rear.
Features: Adjustable trigger, including length; interchangeable rear sight elements. Imported from Switzerland by Beeman, Hammerli Pistols USA, Mandall Shooting Supplies.
Price: About . . . . **$1,708 to $1,955.00**

Hammerli Model 211

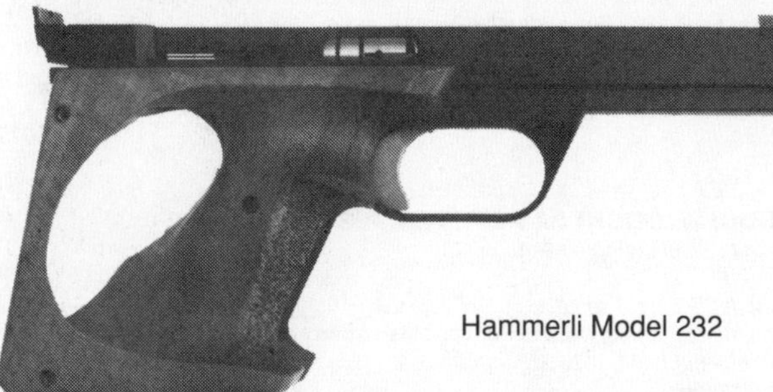
Hammerli Model 232

Hammerli Model 208S

LLAMA M-87 9MM COMP
Caliber: 9mm Para., 14-shot magazine.
Barrel: 6".
Weight: 47 oz. **Length:** 9.5" overall.
Stocks: Polymer composition.
Sights: Patridge front, fully adjustable rear.
Features: A match-ready Comp pistol. Built-in ported compensator, over-size magazine and safety releases, fixed barrel bushing, bevelled magazine well, extended trigger guard. Introduced 1989. Imported by Stoeger Industries.
Price: $1,450.00

NEW DETONICS "SCOREMASTER" TARGET PISTOL
Caliber: 45 ACP, 7-shot magazine.
Barrel: 5" match barrel with recessed crown.
Weight: 36 oz. **Length:** 8⅞" overall.
Stocks: Checkered walnut with rubber mainspring housing.
Sights: Ramp front, positive-click adjustable rear.
Features: All stainless steel construction. Patented self-centering cone barrel system; lengthened and lowered ejection port; beveled magazine well; patented, cushioned counter-wound dual spring recoil system; hand-fitted National Match tolerances; redesigned thumb safety; blackened slide top; dual slide serrations; extended beavertail grip safety; improved magazine release; skeletonized trigger and hammer. Comes with gun rug and two spare magazines. Introduced 1990. From New Detonics Mfg. Corp.
Price: $1,178.00

NEW DETONICS "COMPMASTER" COMPETITION PISTOL
Caliber: 45 ACP, 7-shot magazine.
Barrel: 5.6" compensated match with recessed crown.
Weight: 42 oz. **Length:** 9¾" overall.
Stocks: Pachmayr rubber wraparound.
Sights: Ramp front, positive-click adjustable rear.
Features: Same features as "Scoremaster" pistol. Introduced 1990. From New Detonics Mfg. Corp.
Price: $1,550.00

HAMMERLI MODEL 208, 211, 215 STANDARD
Caliber: 22 LR.
Barrel: 5.9", 6-groove.
Weight: 37.6 oz. (45 oz. with extra heavy barrel weight). **Length:** 10".
Stocks: Walnut. Adjustable palm rest (208), 211 has thumbrest grip.
Sights: Match sights, fully adjustable for windage and elevation (click adjustable). Interchangeable front and rear blades.
Features: Semi-automatic, recoil operated. 8-shot clip. Slide stop. Fully adjustable trigger (2¼ lbs. and 3 lbs.). Extra barrel weight available. Imported from Switzerland by Mandall Shooting Supplies, Beeman.
Price: Model 208, approx. (Mandall) $1,755.00
Price: Model 211, approx. (Mandall) $1,650.00
Price: Model 215, approx. (Mandall) $1,650.00
Price: Model 208 (Beeman) $1,955.00

HAMMERLI MODEL 232 RAPID FIRE PISTOL
Caliber: 22 Short, 6-shot.
Barrel: 5", with six exhaust ports.
Weight: 44 oz. **Length:** 10.4" overall.
Stocks: Stippled walnut; wraparound on Model 232-2, adjustable on 232-1.
Sights: Interchangeable front and rear blades, fully adjustable micrometer rear.
Features: Recoil operated semi-automatic; nearly recoilless design; trigger adjustable from 8.4 to 10.6 oz. with three lengths offered. Wraparound grips available in small, medium and large sizes. Imported from Switzerland by Beeman, Hammerli Pistols USA, Mandall Shooting Supplies. Introduced 1984.
Price: Model 232-1, about . . . . $1,372.00 to $1,800.00
Price: Model 232-1 about $1,545.00
Price: Model 232-2 about $1,800.00

HAMMERLI MODEL 208S TARGET PISTOL
Caliber: 22 LR, 6-shot; 32 S&W Long WC, 5-shot.
Barrel: 4.5".
Weight: 39.1 oz. (32). **Length:** 11.8" overall.
Stocks: Walnut match-type with stippling, adjustable palm shelf.
Sights: Match sights, micrometer adjustable.
Features: Sight radius of 8.8". Comes with barrel weights, spare magazine, loading tool, cleaning rods. Introduced 1990. Imported from Switzerland by Beeman, Hammerli Pistols USA and Mandall Shooting Supplies.
Price: 22-cal., about . . . . $1,448.00 to $1,895.00
Price: 32-cal., about . . . . $1,593.00 to $1,650.00

Llama M-87 Comp

New Detonics "Compmaster"

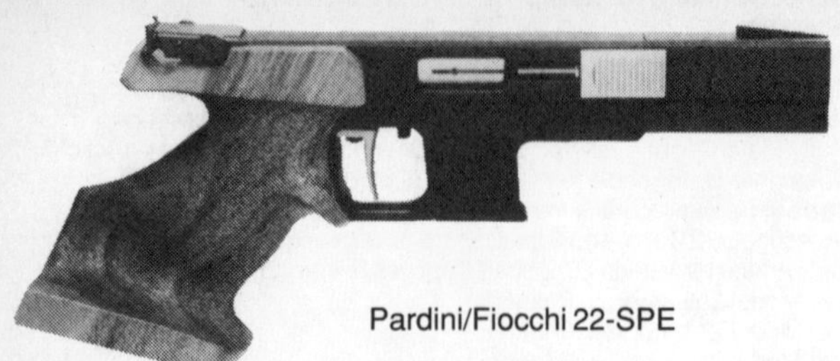

Pardini/Fiocchi 22-SPE

PARDINI/FIOCCHI 32-MP MATCH PISTOL
Caliber: 32 S&W Long, 5-shot magazine.
Barrel: 4.9".
Weight: 38.7 oz. **Length:** 11.7" overall.
Stocks: Anatomical match-type, fixed or adjustable; stippled walnut.
Sights: Match-type undercut blade front, fully adjustable open rear. Two sets of interchangeable front and rear blades.
Features: Fully adjustable match trigger; matte blue finish. Extremely low barrel axis. Comes with locking case, basic tool kit, cleaning kit, extra magazine. Introduced 1991. Imported from Italy by Fiocchi of America, Inc.
Price: **$879.00**

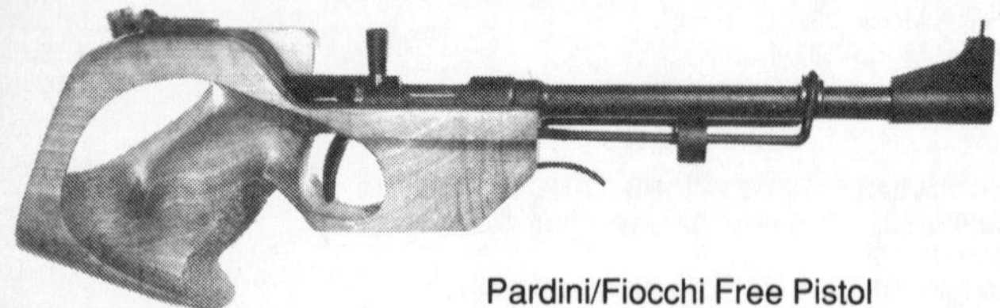

Pardini/Fiocchi Free Pistol

RANGER ALPHA AUTO PISTOL
Caliber: 38 Super, 9-shot; 10mm Auto, 8-shot; 45 ACP, 7-shot.
Barrel: 5", 6", ported or unported.
Weight: 42 oz. **Length:** 8.5" overall.
Stocks: Wraparound rubber.
Sights: Interchangeable front, fully adjustable Peters Stahl rear.
Features: Peters Stahl linkless barrel system, polygonal rifling; extended grip safety, thumb safety, slide release, magazine release. High polish blue finish. Introduced 1990. From Federal Ordnance.
Price: 5" unported, 38 Super, 45 . . . . **$999.95**
Price: 5" ported, 38 Super, 45 . . . . **$1,015.95**
Price: 5" unported, 10mm **$1,015.95**
Price: 5" ported, 10mm **$1,024.95**
Price: 6" unported, 38 Super, 45 . . . . **$1,015.95**
Price: 6" ported, 38 Super, 45 . . . . **$1,024.95**
Price: 6" ported, 10mm **$1,049.95**

PETERS STAHL PSP-07 COMBAT COMPENSATOR PISTOL
Caliber: 45 ACP, 7-shot, or 10mm Auto, 8-shot magazine.
Barrel: 6".
Weight: 45 oz. **Length:** 10" overall.
Stocks: Pachmayr Presenation rubber.
Sights: Interchangeable blade front, fully adjustable Peters Stahl rear.
Features: Linkless barrel with polygonal rifling and integral PS competition compensator; semi-extended PS slide stop and thumb safety; rearward extended magazine release; adjustable Videcki trigger; Wilson stainless beavertail grip safety; Pachmayr rubber mainspring housing. Introduced 1989. Imported from Germany by Federal Ordnance.
Price: 45 ACP **$2,599.95**
Price: 10mm Auto **$2,650.95**

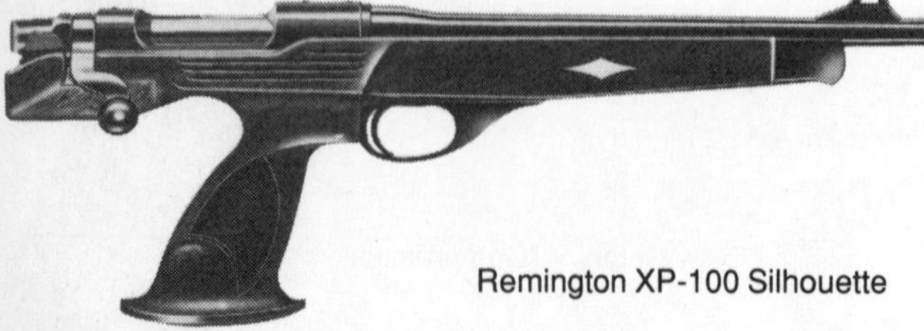

Remington XP-100 Silhouette

PARDINI/FIOCCHI 22-SPE STANDARD PISTOL
Caliber: 22 LR, 5-shot magazine.
Barrel: 4.9".
Weight: 37 oz. **Length:** 11.7" overall.
Stocks: Anatomical match-type stippled walnut; adjustable or fixed.
Sights: Match-type undercut blade front, fully adjustable open rear. Two sets of interchangeable front and rear blades.
Features: Fully adjustable match trigger. Matte blue finish. Comes with locking case, tool and cleaning kits, extra magazine. Imported from Italy by Fiocchi of America, Inc.
Price: **$859.00**

PARDINI/FIOCCHI 22-GPO RAPID FIRE MATCH
Caliber: 22 Short, 5-shot magazine.
Barrel: 5.1".
Weight: 34.5 oz. **Length:** 11.7" overall.
Stocks: Stippled walnut anatomical wraparound, match-type.
Sights: Post front, fully adjustable rear.
Features: Match trigger, matte blue finish. Extremely low barrel axis. Comes with locking case, basic tool kit, cleaning kit, extra magazine. Imported from Italy by Fiocchi of America, Inc.
Price: **$879.00**

PARDINI/FIOCCHI 22-PGP FREE PISTOL
Caliber: 22 LR, single shot.
Barrel: 9".
Weight: 35.3 oz. **Length:** 16.95" overall.
Stocks: Anatomical fixed or adjustable wraparound match-type; stippled walnut.
Sights: Post front, fully adjustable rear. Two sets of interchangeable front and rear blades.
Features: Rotating bolt-action design. Matte blue finish. Fully adjustable match trigger. Imported from Italy by Fiocchi of America, Inc.
Price: **$989.00**

Peters Stahl PSP-07

RANGER SUPERCOMP AUTO PISTOL
Caliber: 10mm Auto, 8-shot; 45 ACP, 7-shot magazine.
Barrel: 6".
Weight: 42 oz. **Length:** 9.4" overall.
Stocks: Wraparound rubber.
Sights: Ramped blade front, fully adjustable, low-profile Ranger rear.
Features: Uses Peters Stahl linkless barrel system with polygonal rifling and integral competition compensator; extended grip safety, thumb safety, slide release, magazine release; lightened speed trigger; full-length recoil spring guide; lowered ejection port; beveled magazine well; ramped and throated barrel. Blued slide, electroless nickel frame. Introduced 1990. From Federal Ordnance.
Price: 10mm **$1,399.95**
Price: 45 ACP **$1,389.95**

REMINGTON XP-100 SILHOUETTE PISTOL
Caliber: 7mm BR Remington, 35 Remington, single shot.
Barrel: 14½".
Weight: 4½ lbs. **Length:** 21¼" overall.
Stocks: Brown nylon, one piece, checkered grip.
Sights: None furnished. Drilled and tapped for scope mounts.
Features: Universal grip fits right or left hand; match-type grooved trigger, two-position thumb safety.
Price: 7mm BR Rem. **$426.00**
Price: 35 Rem. **$440.00**

CAUTION: PRICES CHANGE, CHECK AT GUNSHOP.

Ruger Government Target

Ruger Stainless Government Competition Model 22 Pistol
Similar to the Mark II Government Target Model stainless pistol except has 6⅞" slab-sided bull barrel; the receiver top is drilled and tapped for a Ruger scope base adaptor of blued, chromemoly steel; comes with Ruger 1" stainless scope rings with integral bases for mounting a variety of optical sights; has checkered walnut grip panels with right-hand thumbrest. Has blued open sights with 9¼" radius. Overall length is 11⅛", weight 44 oz. Introduced 1991.
Price: KMK-678GC **$385.25**

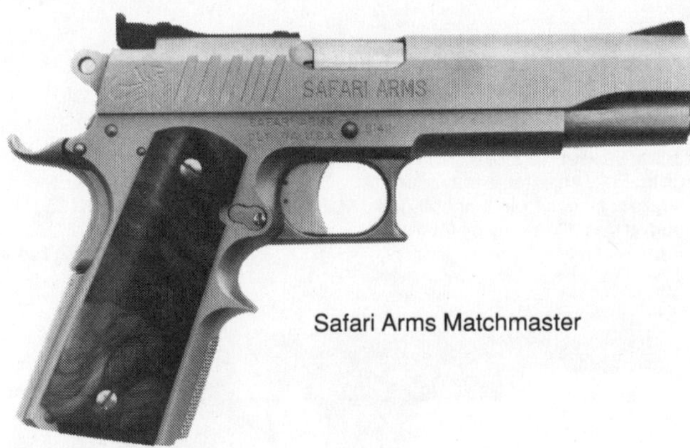

Safari Arms Matchmaster

SMITH & WESSON MODEL 29 SILHOUETTE
Caliber: 44 Magnum, 6-shot.
Barrel: 10⅝".
Weight: 58 oz. **Length:** 16³⁄₁₆" overall.
Stocks: Over-size target-type, checkered Goncalo Alves.
Sights: Four-position front to match the four distances of silhouette targets; micro-click rear adjustable for windage and elevation.
Features: Designed specifically for silhouette shooting. Front sight has click stops for the four pre-set ranges. Introduced 1983.
Price: **$536.00**

SMITH & WESSON MODEL 41 TARGET
Caliber: 22 LR, 10-shot clip.
Barrel: 5½", 7".
Weight: 44 oz. **Length:** 9" overall.
Stocks: Checkered walnut with modified thumbrest, usable with either hand.
Sights: ⅛" Patridge on ramp base; S&W micro-click rear adjustable for windage and elevation.
Features: ⅜" wide, grooved trigger; adjustable trigger stop.
Price: S&W Bright Blue, satin matted top area **$710.00**

SMITH & WESSON MODEL 52 38 MASTER AUTO
Caliber: 38 Special (for mid-range W.C. with flush-seated bullet only), 5-shot magazine.
Barrel: 5".
Weight: 40 oz. with empty magazine. **Length:** 8⅝" overall.
Stocks: Checkered walnut.
Sights: ⅛" Patridge front, S&W micro-click rear adjustable for windage and elevation.
Features: Top sighting surfaces matte finished. Locked breech, moving barrel system; checked for 10-ring groups at 50 yards. Coin-adjustable sight screws. Dry-firing permissible if manual safety on.
Price: S&W Bright Blue **$885.00**

RUGER MARK II TARGET MODEL AUTO PISTOL
Caliber: 22 LR, 10-shot magazine.
Barrel: 5¼", 6⅞".
Weight: 42 oz. **Length:** 11⅛" overall.
Stocks: Checkered hard rubber.
Sights: .125" blade front, micro-click rear, adjustable for windage and elevation. Sight radius 9⅜".
Features: Introduced 1982.
Price: Blued (MK-514, MK-678) **$280.50**
Price: Stainless (KMK-514, KMK-678) **$355.25**

Ruger Mark II Government Target Model
Same gun as the Mark II Target Model except has 6⅞" barrel, higher sights and is roll marked "Government Target Model" on the right side of the receiver below the rear sight. Identical in all aspects to the military model used for training U.S. armed forces except for markings. Comes with factory test target. Introduced 1987.
Price: Blued (MK-678G) **$324.25**
Price: Stainless (KMK-678G) **$411.00**

Ruger Mark II Bull Barrel
Same gun as the Target Model except has 5½" or 10" heavy barrel (10" meets all IHMSA regulations). Weight with 5½" barrel is 42 oz., with 10" barrel, 52 oz.
Price: Blued (MK-512, MK-10) **$280.50**
Price: Stainless (KMK-512, KMK-10) **$355.25**

SAFARI ARMS MATCHMASTER PISTOL
Caliber: 45 ACP, 7-shot magazine.
Barrel: 5".
Weight: 44 oz. **Length:** 8.7" overall.
Stocks: Walnut.
Sights: Combat adjustable.
Features: Beavertail grip safety, ambidextrous extended safety, extended slide release, Commander-style hammer, threaded barrel bushing; throated, ported, tuned. Finishes: Parkerized, matte black, or stainless steel. Available from Safari Arms, Inc.
Price: **$690.00**

Safari Arms Matchmaster Bill of Rights Bicentennial
Same as the Matchmaster except slide and frame are made of beryllium/copper alloy; all other parts are high-polish blue. Serial numbers start at 1791 and end at 1991, with 201 pistols being made. Each is engraved with the Bill of Rights scroll and is cased in an oak presentation case with engraved plaque. Introduced 1991. From Safari Arms, Inc.
Price: **$3,500.00**

Smith & Wesson Model 41

Smith & Wesson Model 52

Thompson/Center Super 14 Contender

THOMPSON/CENTER SUPER 14 CONTENDER
Caliber: 22 LR, 222 Rem., 223 Rem., 7mm TCU, 7-30 Waters, 30-30 Win., 35 Rem., 357 Rem. Maximum, 44 Mag., 10mm Auto, 445 Super Mag., single shot.
Barrel: 14".
Weight: 45 oz. **Length:** 17¼" overall.
Stocks: T/C "Competitor Grip" (walnut and rubber).
Sights: Fully adjustable target-type.
Features: Break-open action with auto safety. Interchangeable barrels for both rimfire and centerfire calibers. Introduced 1978.
Price: **$395.00**
Price: Extra barrels, blued **$185.00**

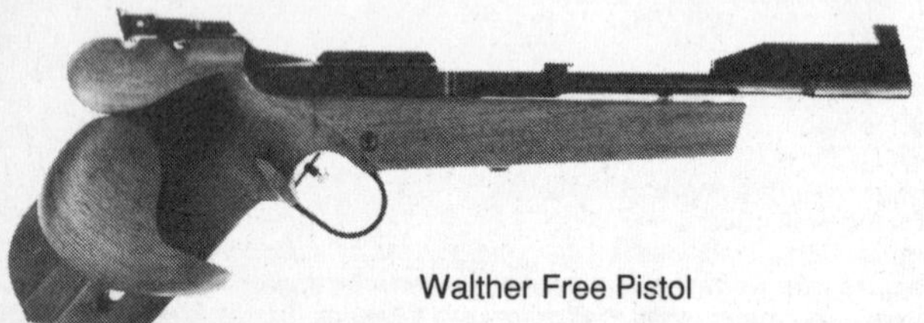
Walther Free Pistol

WALTHER GSP MATCH PISTOL
Caliber: 22 LR, 32 S&W wadcutter (GSP-C), 5-shot.
Barrel: 5¾".
Weight: 44.8 oz. (22 LR), 49.4 oz. (32). **Length:** 11.8" overall.
Stocks: Walnut, special hand-fitting design.
Sights: Fixed front, rear adjustable for windage and elevation.
Features: Available with either 2.2 lb. (1000 gm) or 3 lb. (1360 gm) trigger. Spare mag., bbl. weight, tools supplied in Match Pistol Kit. Imported from Germany by Interarms.
Price: GSP, with case **$1,750.00**
Price: GSP-C, with case **$1,810.00**
Price: 22 LR conversion unit for GSP-C (no trigger unit) **$1,000.00**
Price: 22 Short conversion unit for GSP-C (with trigger unit) **$1,420.00**
Price: 32 S&W conversion unit for GSP-C (no trigger unit) **$1,250.00**

WESSON FIREARMS MODEL 40 SILHOUETTE
Caliber: 357 Maximum, 6-shot.
Barrel: 6", 8", 10".
Weight: 64 oz. (8" bbl.). **Length:** 14.3" overall (8" bbl.).
Stocks: Smooth walnut, target-style.
Sights: ⅛" serrated front, fully adjustable rear.
Features: Meets criteria for IHMSA competition with 8" slotted barrel. Blue or stainless steel.
Price: Blue, 6" **$508.32**
Price: Blue, 8" **$525.19**
Price: Blue, 10" **$543.41**
Price: Stainless, 6" **$568.97**
Price: Stainless, 8" slotted **$595.13**
Price: Stainless, 10" **$609.03**

WESSON FIREARMS MODEL 22 SILHOUETTE REVOLVER
Caliber: 22 LR, 6-shot.
Barrel: 10", regular vent or vent heavy.
Weight: 53 oz.
Stocks: Combat style.
Sights: Patridge-style front, .080" narrow notch rear.
Features: Single action only. Available in blue or stainless. Introduced 1989. From Wesson Firearms Co., Inc.
Price: Blue, regular vent **$430.00**
Price: Blue, vent heavy **$448.42**
Price: Stainless, regular vent **$458.43**
Price: Stainless, vent heavy **$484.53**

SPRINGFIELD ARMORY CUSTOM P9 "WORLD CUP"
Caliber: 9x21, 17-shot; 40 S&W, 12-shot magazine.
Barrel: 5½".
Weight: About 36 oz.
Stocks: Checkered walnut match style.
Sights: Blade front, BoMar adjustable, low mounted.
Features: Match barrel with tapered cone dual-port compensator; full-length recoil rod system; reverse recoil plug; improved custom extractor; extended ambidextrous thumb safety, beavertail grip safety; square trigger guard, checkered front- and backstraps; extended magazine release; aluminum match trigger with overtravel stop, single-action only; match-grade Commander hammer. Comes with three magazines, carrying case. Introduced 1991. From Springfield Armory.
Price: **$2,860.00**

Thompson/Center Super 16 Contender
Same as the T/C Super 14 Contender except has 16¼" barrel. Rear sight can be mounted at mid-barrel position (10¾" radius) or moved to the rear (using scope mount position) for 14¾" radius. Overall length is 20¼". Comes with T/C Competitor Grip of walnut and rubber. Available in 22 LR, 22 WMR, 223 Rem., 7-30 Waters, 30-30 Win., 35 Rem., 44 Mag., 45-70 Gov't. Also available with 16" vent rib barrel with internal choke, caliber 45 Colt/410 shotshell.
Price: **$400.00**
Price: 45-70 Gov't **$420.00**
Price: Extra 16" barrels (blued) **$190.00**
Price: As above, 45-70 . . . . **$205.00**
Price: Super 16 Vent Rib (45-410) **$430.00**
Price: Extra vent rib barrel **$220.00**

WALTHER FREE PISTOL
Caliber: 22 LR, single shot.
Barrel: 11.7".
Weight: 48 oz. **Length:** 17.2" overall.
Stocks: Walnut, special hand-fitting design.
Sights: Fully adjustable match sights.
Features: Special electronic trigger. Matte finish blue. Introduced 1980. Imported from Germany by Interarms.
Price: **$2,140.00**

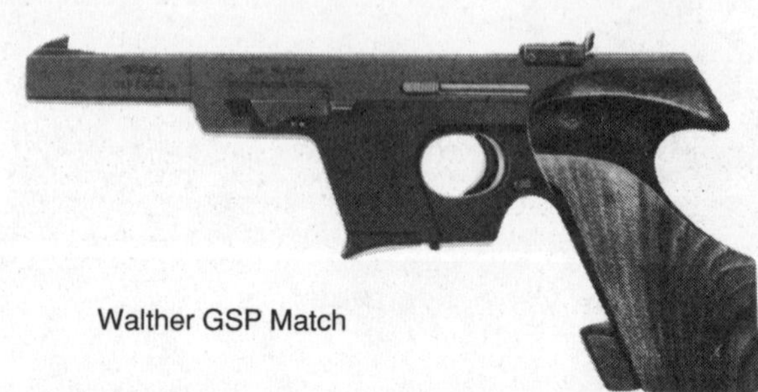
Walther GSP Match

Walther OSP Rapid-Fire Pistol
Similar to Model GSP except 22 Short only, stock has adjustable free-style hand rest.
Price: **$2,085.00**

Wesson Firearms Model 40

Wesson Firearms Model 445 Supermag Revolver
Similar size and weight as the Model 40 revolvers. Chambered for the 445 Supermag cartridge, a longer version of the 44 Magnum. Contact maker for complete price list. Introduced 1989. From Wesson Firearms Co., Inc.
Price: Blue, 6" **$574.55**
Price: Blue, 8" **$605.25**
Price: Blue, 10" **$596.88**
Price: Stainless, 6" **$608.98**
Price: Stainless, 8" **$629.86**
Price: Stainless, 10" **$650.09**

WESSON FIREARMS ACTION CUP/PPC REVOLVERS

Caliber: 38 Spec., 357 Mag., 6-shot.
Barrel: Extra heavy 6" bull shroud with removable underweight.
Weight: 4 lbs., 7 oz. (PPC, with weight).
Stocks: Pachmayr Gripper.
Sights: Tasco Pro Point II on Action Cup; Aristocrat with three-position rear on PPC model.
Features: Competition tuned with narrow trigger, chamfered cylinder chambers. Action Cup available in stainless only, PPC in bright blue or stainless. Introduced 1989.
Price: Action Cup **$913.30**
Price: PPC, blue **$779.83**
Price: PPC, stainless **$857.48**

WICHITA SILHOUETTE PISTOL

Caliber: 308 Win. F.L., 7mm IHMSA, 7mm-308.
Barrel: 14 15/16".
Weight: 4½ lbs. **Length:** 21⅜" overall.
Stock: American walnut with oil finish. Glass bedded.
Sights: Wichita Multi-Range sight system.
Features: Comes with left-hand action with right-hand grip. Round receiver and barrel. Fluted bolt, flat bolt handle. Wichita adjustable trigger. Introduced 1979. From Wichita Arms.
Price: Center grip stock **$1,100.00**
Price: As above except with Rear Position Stock and target-type Lightpull trigger **$1,100.00**

WICHITA INTERNATIONAL PISTOL

Caliber: 22 LR, 22 WMR, 32 H&R Mag., 357 Super Mag., 357 Mag., 7R, 7mm Super Mag., 7-30 Waters, 30-30 Win., single shot.
Barrel: 10", 10½", 14".
Weight: 3 lbs. 2 oz. (with 10", 10½" barrels).
Stocks: Walnut grip and forend.
Sights: Patridge front, adjustable rear.
Features: Made of stainless steel. Break-open action. Grip dimensions same as Colt 45 Auto. Barrel dovetailed to accept Weaver-type rings. Extra barrels are factory fitted. Introduced 1983. Available from Wichita Arms.
Price: International 10" **$510.00**
Price: International 14" **$544.00**
Price: Extra barrels, 10" **$311.00**
Price: Extra barrels, 14" **$343.00**

WICHITA CLASSIC SILHOUETTE PISTOL

Caliber: All standard calibers with maximum overall length of 2.800".
Barrel: 11¼".
Weight: 3 lbs., 15 oz.
Stocks: AAA American walnut with oil finish, checkered grip.
Sights: Hooded post front, open adjustable rear.
Features: Three locking lug bolt, three gas ports; completely adjustable Wichita trigger. Introduced 1981. From Wichita Arms.
Price: **$2,950.00**

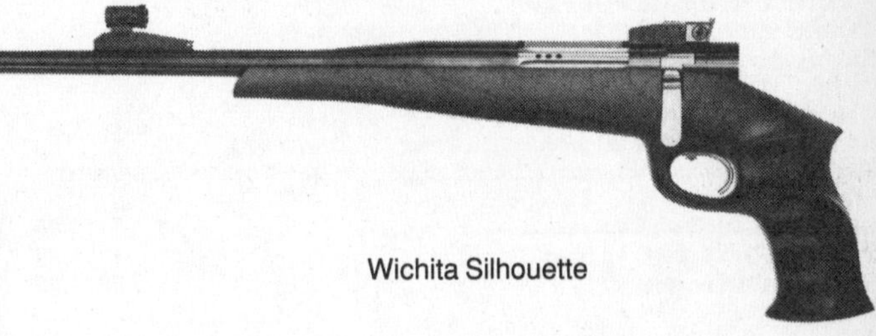

Wichita Silhouette

Wichita International

HANDGUNS—DOUBLE ACTION REVOLVERS, SERVICE & SPORT

Includes models suitable for hunting and competitive courses for fire, both police and international.

Armscor Model 200

ARMSCOR MODEL 200 REVOLVER

Caliber: 22 LR, 22 WMR, 38 Spec., 6-shot.
Barrel: 2½", 4".
Weight: 26 oz. (4" barrel). **Length:** 8⅞" overall (4" barrel).
Stocks: Checkered mahogany or rubber.
Sights: Ramp front, fully adjustable rear on 200TC, fixed rear on 200P.
Features: Blue finish. Introduced 1990. Imported from the Philippines by Armscor.
Price: Model 200P (38 Spec.) **$200.00**
Price: Model 200TC (22 LR or 38 Spec.) **$234.00**

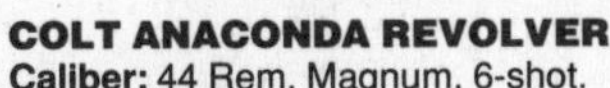

COLT ANACONDA REVOLVER

Caliber: 44 Rem. Magnum, 6-shot.
Barrel: 4", 6", 8".
Weight: 53 oz. **Length:** 11⅝" overall.
Stocks: Combat-style black neoprene with finger grooves.
Sights: Red insert front, adjustable white outline rear.
Features: Stainless steel; full-length ejector rod housing; ventilated barrel rib; offset bolt notches in cylinder; wide spur hammer. Introduced 1990.
Price: **$539.95**

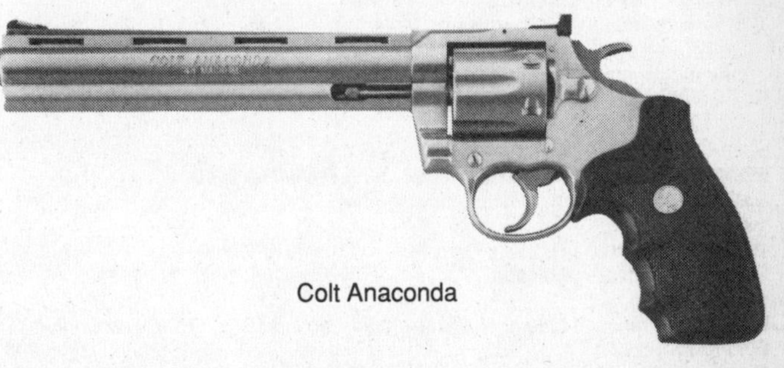

Colt Anaconda

COLT KING COBRA REVOLVER

Caliber: 357 Magnum, 6-shot.
Barrel: 2½", 4", 6", 8" (STS); 2½", 4", 6" (BSTS); 2½", 4", 6" (blue).
Weight: 42 oz. (4" bbl.). **Length:** 9" overall (4" bbl.).
Stocks: Checkered rubber.
Sights: Red insert ramp front, adjustable white outline rear.
Features: Stainless steel; full-length contoured ejector rod housing, barrel rib; matte finish. Introduced 1986.
Price: STS, 2½", 4", 6", 8" **$434.95**
Price: BSTS, 2½", 4", 6", 8" **$469.95**
Price: Blue, 2½", 4", 6" **$409.95**

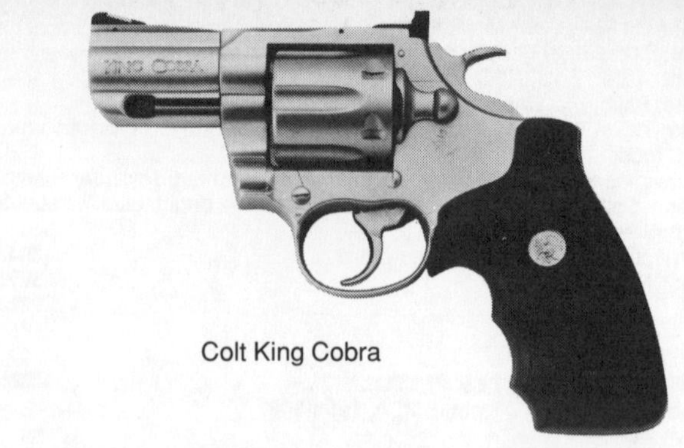

Colt King Cobra

COLT PYTHON REVOLVER

Caliber: 357 Magnum (handles all 38 Spec.), 6-shot.
Barrel: 2½", 4", 6" or 8", with ventilated rib.
Weight: 38 oz. (4" bbl.). **Length:** 9¼" (4" bbl.).
Stocks: Checkered walnut, target-type.
Sights: ⅛" ramp front, adjustable notch rear.
Features: Ventilated rib; grooved, crisp trigger; swing-out cylinder; target hammer.
Price: Blue, 2½", 4", 6", 8" **$775.95**
Price: Stainless, 2½", 4", 6", 8" **$864.95**
Price: Bright stainless, 2½", 4", 6", 8" **$894.95**

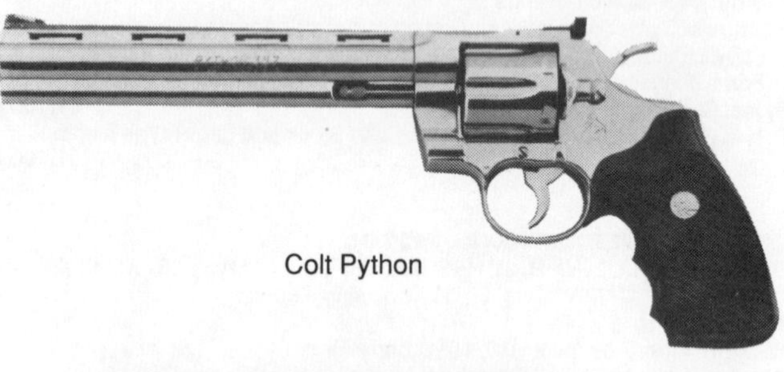
Colt Python

ERMA ER-777 SPORTING REVOLVER

Caliber: 357 Mag., 6-shot.
Barrel: 4", 5½".
Weight: 43.3 oz. **Length:** 9½" overall (4" barrel).
Stocks: Stippled walnut service-type.
Sights: Interchangeable blade front, micro-adjustable rear for windage and elevation.
Features: Polished blue finish. Adjustable trigger. Imported from Germany by Precision Sales Int'l. Introduced 1988.
Price: **$1,200.00**

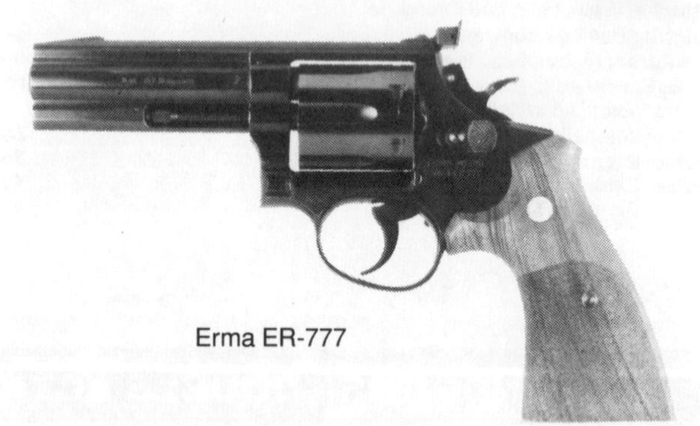
Erma ER-777

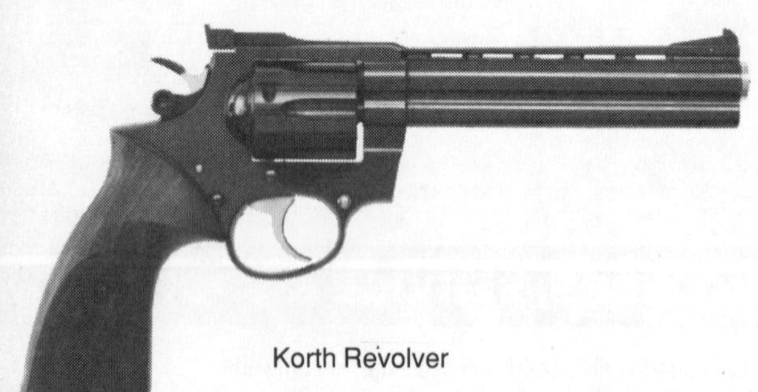
Korth Revolver

KORTH REVOLVER

Caliber: 22 LR, 22 Mag., 32 H&R Mag., 32 S&W Long, 357 Mag., 9mm Parabellum.
Barrel: 3", 4", 6".
Weight: 33 to 38 oz. **Length:** 8" to 11" overall.
Stocks: Checkered walnut, sport or combat.
Sights: Blade front, rear adjustable for windage and elevation.
Features: Four interchangeable cylinders available. Major parts machined from hammer-forged steel; cylinder gap of .002". High polish blue finish. Presentation models have gold trim. Imported from Germany by Mandall Shooting Supplies.
Price: With two cylinders **$3,300.00**

LLAMA COMANCHE III REVOLVERS

Caliber: 357 Mag.
Barrel: 4", 6".
Weight: 28 oz. **Length:** 9¼" (4" bbl.).
Stocks: Checkered walnut.
Sights: Fixed blade front, rear adjustable for windage and elevation.
Features: Ventilated rib, wide spur hammer. Satin chrome finish available. Imported from Spain by Stoeger Industries.
Price: Blue finish **$339.00**
Price: Satin chrome **$395.00**

Llama Super Comanche IV Revolver

Similar to the Comanche except: large frame, 44 Mag. with 6", 8½" barrel, 6-shot cylinder; smooth, extra wide trigger; wide spur hammer; over-size walnut, target-style grips. Weight is 3 lbs., 2 oz. Blue finish only.
Price: 44 Mag. **$440.00**

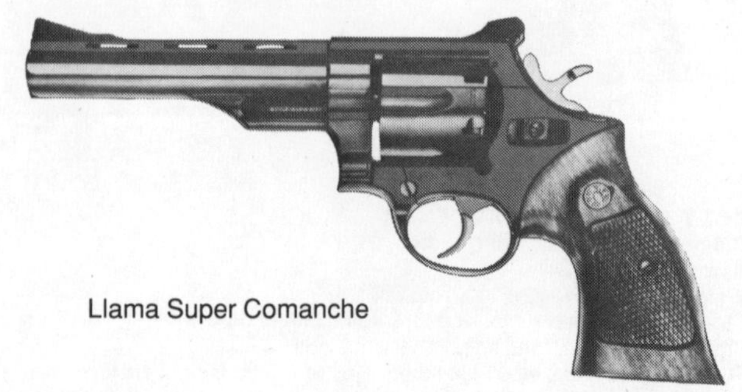
Llama Super Comanche

NEW ENGLAND FIREARMS R92, R73 REVOLVERS

Caliber: 22 LR, 9-shot; 32 H&R Mag., 5-shot.
Barrel: 2½", 4".
Weight: 25 oz. (22 LR, 2½"). **Length:** 7" overall (2½" bbl.).
Stocks: American hardwood.
Sights: Fixed.
Features: Choice of blue or nickel finish. Introduced 1988. From New England Firearms Co.
Price: . . . . **NA**

NEW ENGLAND FIREARMS ULTRA REVOLVER
Caliber: 22 LR, 9-shot.
Barrel: 6".
Weight: 32 oz. **Length:** 8½" overall.
Stocks: Walnut-finished hardwood.
Sights: Blade front, fully adjustable rear.
Features: Blue finish. Bull-style barrel with recessed muzzle, high "Lustre" blue/black finish. Introduced 1989. From New England Firearms.
Price: . . . . **NA**

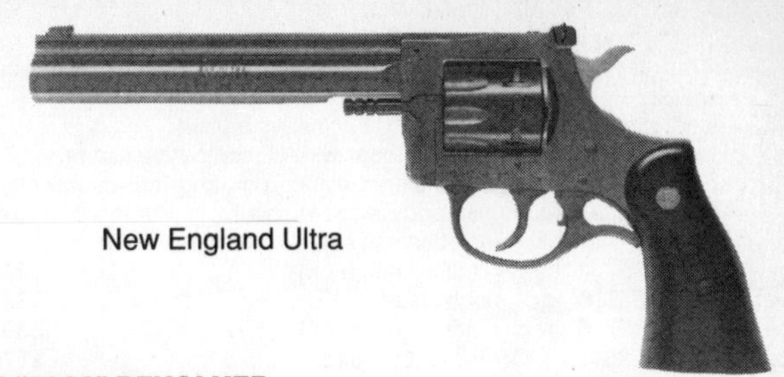
New England Ultra

NEW ENGLAND FIREARMS TOP BREAK REVOLVER
Caliber: 22 LR, 9-shot.
Barrel: 4", 6"; ventilated rib.
Weight: 30 oz. (4" bbl.).
Stocks: Walnut-finished hardwood.
Sights: Elevation-adjustable front, rear for windage.
Features: Top break with auto ejection. Blue finish. Introduced 1991. From New England Firearms.
Price: . . . . **NA**

QFI "ASR" REVOLVERS
Caliber: 38 Special, 357 Mag., 32 S&W, 22 WMR, 22 LR.
Barrel: 4", 6".
Weight: 35 oz. (6" bbl.). **Length:** 11" overall (6" bbl.).
Stocks: Checkered plastic; walnut optional.
Sights: Ramp front, fixed rear on standard models, windage and elevation adjustments on target models.
Features: Thumb-release, swing-out cylinder. Ventilated rib, solid frame. Interchangeable 22 WMR cylinder available with 22 cal. versions. Introduced 1991. Imported by QFI.
Price: . . . . **NA**

Rossi Model 68

ROSSI MODEL 88 STAINLESS REVOLVER
Caliber: 32 S&W, 38 Spec., 5-shot.
Barrel: 2", 3".
Weight: 22 oz. **Length:** 7.5" overall.
Stocks: Checkered wood, service-style.
Sights: Ramp front, square notch rear drift adjustable for windage.
Features: All metal parts except springs are of 440 stainless steel; matte finish; small frame for concealability. Introduced 1983. Imported from Brazil by Interarms.
Price: 3" barrel **$235.00**
Price: M88/2 (2" barrel) **$240.00**

ROSSI MODEL 851 REVOLVER
Caliber: 38 Special, 6-shot.
Barrel: 3" or 4".
Weight: 27.5 oz. (3" bbl.). **Length:** 8" overall (3" bbl.).
Stocks: Checkered Brazilian hardwood.
Sights: Blade front with red insert, rear adjustable for windage.
Features: Medium-size frame; stainless steel construction; ventilated barrel rib. Introduced 1991. Imported from Brazil by Interarms.
Price: **$260.00**

ROSSI MODEL 971 REVOLVER
Caliber: 357 Mag., 6-shot.
Barrel: 4", 6", heavy.
Weight: 36 oz. **Length:** 9" overall.
Stocks: Checkered Brazilian hardwood.
Sights: Blade front, fully adjustable rear.
Features: Full-length ejector rod shroud; matted sight rib; target-type trigger, wide checkered hammer spur. Introduced 1988. Imported from Brazil by Interarms.
Price: 4", stainless **$285.00**
Price: 6", stainless **$285.00**
Price: 4", blue **$260.00**

QFI "5038" REVOLVER
Caliber: 38 Special.
Barrel: 2" solid or 4" vent. rib.
Weight: 27 oz. **Length:** 6¼" overall (2" bbl.).
Stocks: Checkered plastic, Bulldog style. Walnut optional.
Sights: Fixed.
Features: Thumb-release swing-out cylinder, one stroke ejection. Introduced 1991. Made in U.S.A. by QFI.
Price: Blue **$174.95**

QFI "RP SERIES" REVOLVERS
Caliber: 22 LR, 22 WMR, 22 LR/WMR combo, 32 S&W, 32S&W Long, 32 H&R Mag., 38 Spec., 6-shot.
Barrel: 2" or 4".
Weight: 23 oz. (2" barrel). **Length:** 6¼" overall (2" barrel).
Stocks: Magnum-style round butt; checkered plastic.
Sights: Ramp front, fixed square notch rear.
Features: One-piece solid frame; checkered hammer spur, serrated trigger; blue finish. Introduced 1991. Made in U.S. by QFI.
Price: . . . . **$104.95 to $129.95**

ROSSI MODEL 68 REVOLVER
Caliber: 38 Spec.
Barrel: 2", 3".
Weight: 22 oz.
Stocks: Checkered wood.
Sights: Ramp front, low profile adjustable rear.
Features: All-steel frame, thumb latch operated swing-out cylinder. Introduced 1978. Imported from Brazil by Interarms.
Price: 38, blue, 3" **$200.00**
Price: M68/2 (2" barrel) **$205.00**
Price: 3", nickel **$210.00**

Rossi Model 851

Rossi Model 971

RUGER GP-100 REVOLVERS
Caliber: 38 Special, 357 Magnum, 6-shot.
Barrel: 3", 3" heavy, 4", 4" heavy, 6", 6" heavy.
Weight: 3" barrel—35 oz., 3" heavy barrel—36 oz., 4" barrel—37 oz., 4" heavy barrel—38 oz.
Sights: Fixed; adjustable on 4" heavy, 6", 6" heavy barrels.
Stocks: Ruger Cushioned Grip (live rubber with Goncalo Alves inserts).
Features: Uses all new action and frame incorporating improvements and features of both the Security-Six and Redhawk revolvers. Full length and short ejector shroud. Satin blue and stainless steel. Introduced 1988.
Price: GP-141 (357, 4" heavy, adj. sights, blue) . . . **$393.75**
Price: GP-160 (357, 6", adj. sights, blue) . . . **$393.75**
Price: GP-161 (357, 6" heavy, adj. sights, blue) . . . **$393.75**
Price: GPF-330 (357, 3"), GPF-830 (38 Spec.) . . . **$378.00**
Price: GPF-331 (357, 3" heavy), GPF-831 (38 Spec.) . . . **$378.00**
Price: GPF-340 (357, 4"), GPF-840 (38 Spec.) . . . **$378.00**
Price: GPF-341 (357, 4" heavy), GPF-841 (38 Spec.) . . . **$378.00**
Price: KGP-141 (357, 4" heavy, adj. sights, stainless) . . . **$425.25**
Price: KGP-160 (357, 6", adj. sights, stainless) . . . **$425.25**
Price: KGP-161 (357, 6" heavy, adj. sights, stainless) . . . **$425.25**
Price: KGPF-330 (357, 3", stainless), KGPF-830 (38 Spec.) . . . **$409.50**
Price: KGPF-331 (357, 3" heavy, stainless), KGPF-831 (38 Spec.) . **$409.50**
Price: KGPF-340 (357, 4", stainless), KGPF-840 (38 Spec.) . . . **$409.50**
Price: KGPF-341 (357, 4" heavy, stainless), KGPF-841 (38 Spec.) . **$409.50**

RUGER SP-101 REVOLVER
Caliber: 22 LR, 32 H&R Mag., 6-shot, 9mm Para., 38 Special +P, 357 Mag., 5-shot.
Barrel: 2¼", 3 1/16", 4".
Weight: 2¼"—25 oz.; 3 1/16"—27 oz.
Sights: Adjustable on 22, 32, fixed on others.
Stocks: Ruger Cushioned Grip (live rubber with plastic inserts).
Features: Incorporates improvements and features found in the GP-100 revolvers into a compact, small frame, double-action revolver. Full-length ejector shroud. Stainless steel only. Introduced 1988.
Price: KSP-821 (2½", 38 Spec.) . . . **$388.50**
Price: KSP-831 (3 1/16", 38 Spec.) . . . **$388.50**
Price: KSP-221 (2¼", 22 LR) . . . **$388.50**
Price: KSP-240 (4", 22 LR) . . . **$388.50**
Price: KSP-241 (4" heavy bbl., 22 LR) . . . **$388.50**
Price: KSP-3231 (3 1/16", 32 H&R) . . . **$388.50**
Price: KSP-931 (3 1/16", 9mm Para.) . . . **$388.50**
Price: KSP-321 (2¼", 357 Mag.) . . . **$388.50**
Price: KSP-331 (3 1/16", 357 Mag.) . . . **$388.50**

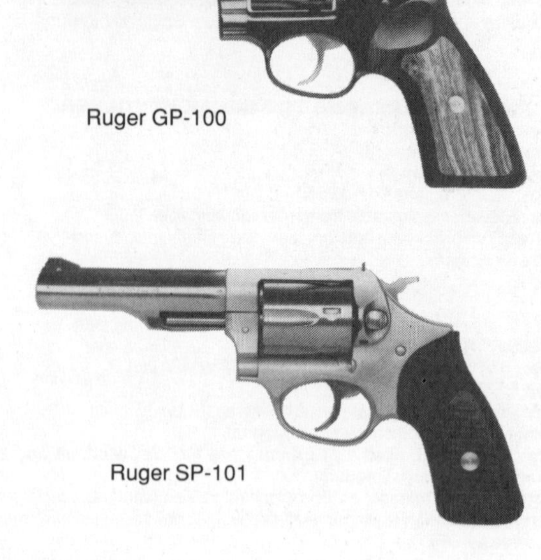

Ruger GP-100

Ruger SP-101

RUGER REDHAWK
Caliber: 41 Mag., 44 Rem. Mag., 6-shot.
Barrel: 5½", 7½".
Weight: About 54 oz. (7½" bbl.). **Length:** 13" overall (7½" barrel).
Stocks: Square butt Goncalo Alves.
Sights: Interchangeable Patridge-type front, rear adjustable for windage and elevation.
Features: Stainless steel, brushed satin finish, or blued ordnance steel. Has a 9½" sight radius. Introduced 1979.
Price: Blued, 41 Mag., 44 Mag., 5½", 7½" . . . **$436.75**
Price: Blued, 41 Mag., 44 Mag., 7½", with scope mount, rings . . . **$473.00**
Price: Stainless, 41 Mag., 44 Mag., 5½", 7½" . . . **$492.25**
Price: Stainless, 41 Mag., 44 Mag., 7½", with scope mount, rings . . **$530.75**

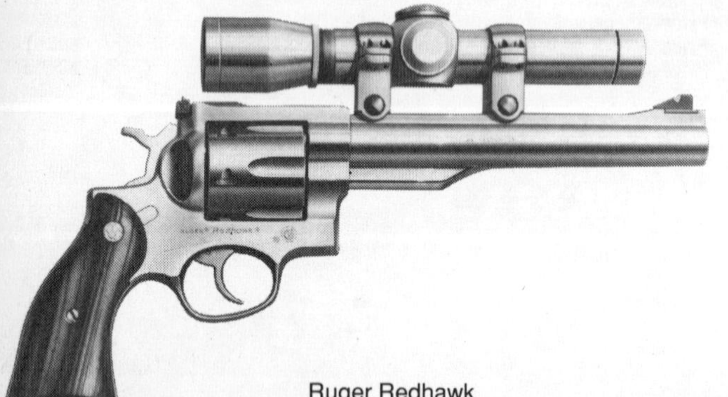

Ruger Redhawk

Ruger Super Redhawk Revolver
Similar to the standard Redhawk except has a heavy extended frame with the Ruger Integral Scope Mounting System on the wide topstrap. The wide hammer spur has been lowered for better scope clearance. Incorporates the mechanical design features and improvements of the GP-100. Choice of 7½" or 9½" barrel, both with ramp front sight base with Redhawk-style Interchangeable Insert sight blades, adjustable rear sight. Comes with Ruger "Cushioned Grip" panels of live rubber and Goncalo Alves wood. Satin polished stainless steel, 44 Magnum only. Introduced 1987.
Price: KSRH-7 (7½"), KSRH-9 (9½") . . . **$561.00**

Ruger Super Redhawk

Smith & Wesson Model 10

SMITH & WESSON Model 10 M&P REVOLVER
Caliber: 38 Special, 6-shot.
Barrel: 2", 4".
Weight: 30½ oz. **Length:** 9¼" overall.
Stocks: Checkered walnut, Service. Round or square butt.
Sights: Fixed, ramp front, square notch rear.
Price: Blue . . . **$333.00**
Price: Nickel . . . **$345.00**

Smith & Wesson Model 10 38 M&P Heavy Barrel
Same as regular M&P except: 4" heavy ribbed bbl. with ramp front sight, square rear, square butt, wgt. 33½ oz.
Price: Blue . . . **$333.00**
Price: Nickel . . . **$345.00**

CAUTION: PRICES CHANGE, CHECK AT GUNSHOP.

SMITH & WESSON MODEL 13 H.B. M&P
Caliber: 357 and 38 Special, 6-shot.
Barrel: 3" or 4".
Weight: 34 oz. **Length:** 9⁵⁄₁₆" overall (4" bbl.).
Stocks: Checkered walnut, Service.
Sights: ⅛" serrated ramp front, fixed square notch rear.
Features: Heavy barrel, K-frame, square butt (4"), round butt (3").
Price: Blue **$339.00**
Price: Model 65, as above in stainless steel **$368.00**

SMITH & WESSON MODEL 14 FULL LUG REVOLVER
Caliber: 38 Special, 6-shot.
Barrel: 6", full lug.
Weight: 47 oz. **Length:** 11⅛" overall.
Stocks: Combat-style Morado with square butt.
Sights: Pinned Patridge front, adjustable micrometer click rear.
Features: Has .500" target hammer, .312" smooth combat trigger. Polished blue finish. Reintroduced 1991. Limited production.
Price: **$425.00**

SMITH & WESSON MODEL 15 COMBAT MASTERPIECE
Caliber: 38 Special, 6-shot.
Barrel: 4", 6".
Weight: 32 oz. **Length:** 9⁵⁄₁₆" (4" bbl.).
Stocks: Checkered walnut. Grooved tangs.
Sights: Front, Baughman Quick Draw on ramp, micro-click rear, adjustable for windage and elevation.
Price: Blued, 4", 6" **$361.00**

SMITH & WESSON MODEL 16 FULL LUG REVOLVER
Caliber: 32 Magnum, 6-shot.
Barrel: 4", 6", 8⅜", full lug.
Weight: 42 oz. **Length:** 9⅛" overall.
Stocks: Square butt Goncalo Alves, combat-style.
Sights: Patridge-style front, adjustable micrometer click rear.
Features: Polished blue finish. Semi-target model has .375" semi-target hammer, .312" smooth combat trigger. Model 16 Target has .500" target hammer, .400" serrated trigger, and is available with either 6" or 8⅜" barrel. Introduced 1990.
Price: Model 16, Semi-target **$368.00**
Price: Model 16 Target, 6" bbl. **$403.00**
Price: Model 16 Target, 8⅜" bbl. **$415.00**

SMITH & WESSON MODEL 17 K-22 FULL LUG
Caliber: 22 LR, 6-shot.
Barrel: 4", 6", 8⅜".
Weight: 39 oz. (6" bbl.). **Length:** 11⅛" overall.
Stocks: Square butt Goncalo Alves, combat-style.
Sights: Patridge front with 6", 8⅜", serrated on 4", S&W micro-click rear adjustable for windage and elevation.
Features: Grooved tang, polished blue finish, full lug barrel. Introduced 1990.
Price: 4", 6" bbl. **$379.00**
Price: 8⅜" bbl. **$427.00**

Smith & Wesson Model 648 K-22 Masterpiece MRF
Similar to the Model 17 except made of stainless steel and chambered for 22 WMR cartridge. Available with 6" full-lug barrel only, combat-style square butt grips, combat trigger and semi-target hammer. Introduced 1991.
Price: **$400.00**

Smith & Wesson Model 617 Full Lug Revolver
Similar to the Model 17 Full Lug except made of stainless steel. Has semi-target .375" hammer, .312" smooth combat trigger on 4"; 6" available with either .312" smooth combat trigger or .400" serrated trigger and .500" target hammer; 8⅜" comes with .500" target hammer and .400" serrated trigger. Introduced 1990.
Price: 4" **$400.00**
Price: 6", semi-target hammer, combat trigger **$400.00**
Price: 6", target hammer, target trigger **$430.00**
Price: 8⅜", target hammer, target trigger **$440.00**

SMITH & WESSON MODEL 19 COMBAT MAGNUM
Caliber: 357 Magnum and 38 Special, 6-shot.
Barrel: 2½", 4", 6".
Weight: 36 oz. **Length:** 9⁹⁄₁₆" (4" bbl.).
Stocks: Checkered Goncalo Alves, target. Grooved tangs.
Sights: Front ⅛" Baughman Quick Draw on 2½" or 4" bbl., Patridge on 6" bbl., micro-click rear adjustable for windagae and elevation.
Features: Also available in nickel finish.
Price: S&W Bright Blue, adj. sights, from **$355.00**
Price: Nickel, 4", 6" only **$375.00**

Smith & Wesson Model 14

Smith & Wesson Model 15

Smith & Wesson Model 16

Smith & Wesson Model 17

Smith & Wesson Model 19

SMITH & WESSON MODEL 25 REVOLVER
Caliber: 45 Colt, 6-shot.
Barrel: 4", 6", 8⅜".
Weight: About 46 oz. **Length:** 11⅜" overall (6" bbl.).
Stocks: Checkered Goncalo Alves, target-type.
Sights: S&W red ramp front, S&W micrometer click rear with white outline.
Features: Available in Bright Blue or nickel finish; target trigger, target hammer. Contact S&W for complete price list.
Price: 4", 6", blue **$429.00**
Price: 8⅜", blue or nickel **$437.00**

Smith & Wesson Model 625-2
Similar to the Model 25 except chambered for 45 ACP, is made of stainless steel. Has pinned black front sight ramp, micrometer rear with plain blade, semi-target hammer, combat trigger, round butt Pachmayr stocks, full lug barrel. Available in 3", 4", 5" barrel lengths. Introduced in 1989.
Price: **$535.00**

Smith & Wesson Model 25

SMITH & WESSON MODEL 27 357 MAGNUM REVOLVER
Caliber: 357 Magnum and 38 Special, 6-shot.
Barrel: 4", 6", 8⅜".
Weight: 45½ oz. (6" bbl.), 44 oz. (4" bbl.).
Length: 11$\frac{5}{16}$" overall (6" bbl.).
Stocks: Checkered walnut, Magna. Grooved tangs and trigger.
Sights: Serrated ramp front, micro-click rear, adjustable for windage and elevation.
Price: S&W Bright Blue, 4" **$451.00**
Price: As above, 6" **$423.00**
Price: 8⅜" bbl., sq. butt, target hammer, trigger, stocks **$431.00**

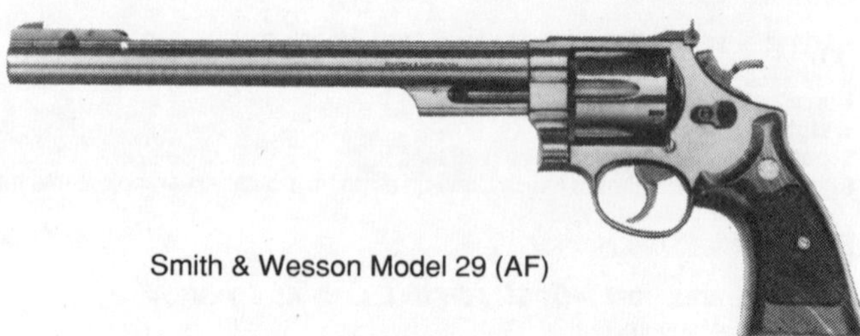
Smith & Wesson Model 29 (AF)

Smith & Wesson Model 27 3½", 5" Revolver
Similar to the standard Model 27 except is a reintroduction of two of the original barrel lengths of 3½" and 5"; pinned black ramp front sight, adjustable micrometer click rear. Has oversize Morado square-butt target stocks. Overall length with 3½" barrel is 9$\frac{1}{16}$", weight is 43½ oz. Reintroduced 1991. Limited production.
Price: **$423.00**

SMITH & WESSON MODEL 29 44 MAGNUM REVOLVER
Caliber: 44 Magnum, 44 Special or 44 Russian, 6-shot.
Barrel: 4", 6", 8⅜", 10⅝".
Weight: 47 oz. (6" bbl.), 44 oz. (4" bbl.). **Length:** 11⅜" overall (6" bbl.).
Stocks: Oversize target-type, checkered Goncalo Alves. Tangs and target trigger grooved, checkered target hammer.
Sights: ⅛" red ramp front, micro-click rear, adjustable for windage and elevation.
Price: S&W Bright Blue, 4", 6" **$482.00**
Price: 8⅜" bbl., blue **$492.00**
Price: 10⅝", blue only (AF) **$536.00**
Price: Model 629 (stainless steel), 4", 6" **$510.00**
Price: Model 629, 8⅜" barrel **$527.00**
Price: As above, nickel **$493.00**
Price: 8⅜" bbl., nickel **$503.00**

Smith & Wesson Model 29, 629 Classic DX Revolvers
Similar to the Classic Hunters except offered only with 6½" or 8⅜" full-lug barrel; comes with five front sights: 50-yard red ramp; 50-yard black Patridge; 100-yard black Patridge with gold bead; 50-yard black ramp; and 50-yard black Patridge with white dot. Comes with Morado combat-type grips with Cornuba wax finish and Hogue combat-style square butt conversion grip. Introduced 1991.
Price: Model 29 Classic DX, 6½" **$686.00**
Price: As above, 8⅜" **$700.00**
Price: Model 629 Classic DX, 6½" **$726.00**
Price: As above, 8⅜" **$750.00**

Consult our Directory pages for the location of firms mentioned.

Smith & Wesson Model 29, 629 Classic Hunters
Similar to the standard Model 29 and 629 except has unfluted cylinder, 6" full-lug barrel; .500" target hammer, .400" serrated target trigger; black pinned ramp front sight, adjustable micrometer click, white outline rear sight; Hogue soft rubber combat grips with square butt. Overall length 11½"; weight 51¾ oz. Reintroduced 1991.
Price: Model 29 Classic Hunter (blue) **$501.00**
Price: Model 629 Classic Hunter (stainless) **$528.00**

Smith & Wesson Model 29, 629 Classic Revolvers
Similar to the standard Model 29 and 629 except has full-lug 5", 6½" or 8⅜" barrel; chamfered front of cylinder; interchangable red ramp front sight with adjustable white outline rear; Hogue square butt Santoprene grips with S&W monogram; the frame is drilled and tapped for scope mounting. Factory accurizing and endurance packages. Overall length with 5" barrel is 10½"; weight is 51 oz. Introduced 1990.
Price: Model 29 Classic, 5", 6½" **$519.00**
Price: As above, 8⅜" **$530.00**
Price: Model 629 Classic (stainless), 5", 6½" **$547.00**
Price: As above, 8 ⅜" **$565.00**

Smith & Wesson Model 629 Classic DX

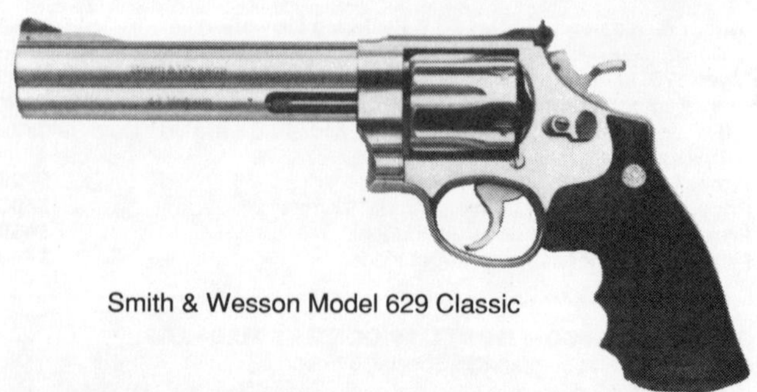
Smith & Wesson Model 629 Classic

SMITH & WESSON MODEL 31 REGULATION POLICE
Caliber: 32 S&W Long, 6-shot.
Barrel: 2", 3".
Weight: 18¾ oz. (3" bbl.). **Length:** 7½" (3" bbl.).
Stocks: Checkered walnut, Magna.
Sights: Fixed, $\frac{1}{10}$" serrated ramp front, square notch rear.
Features: Blued.
Price: **$365.00**

SMITH & WESSON MODEL 34, 22/32 KIT GUN
Caliber: 22 LR, 6-shot.
Barrel: 2", 4".
Weight: 24 oz. (4" bbl.). **Length:** 8⅜" (4" bbl. and round butt).
Stocks: Checkered walnut, round or square butt.
Sights: Front, serrated ramp, micro-click rear, adjustable for windage and elevation.
Price: Blue $366.00
Price: Model 63, as above in stainless $402.00
Price: Model 63, 2" round butt $402.00

Smith & Wesson Model 63

SMITH & WESSON 38 CHIEFS SPECIAL & AIRWEIGHT
Caliber: 38 Special, 5-shot.
Barrel: 2", 3".
Weight: 19½ oz. (2" bbl.); 13½ oz. (Airweight). **Length:** 6½" (2" bbl. and round butt).
Stocks: Checkered walnut, round or square butt.
Sights: Fixed, serrated ramp front, square notch rear.
Price: Blue, standard Model 36, 2", 3" $338.00
Price: As above, nickel, 2" only $349.00
Price: Blue, Airweight Model 37, 2" only $358.00
Price: As above, nickel, 2" only $372.00

Smith & Wesson Model 36 LadySmith

Smith & Wesson Model 36-LS, 60-LS LadySmith
Similar to the standard Model 36. Available with 2" or 3" barrel. The 2" comes with smooth, contoured rosewood grips with the S&W monogram; 3" has smooth, finger-grooved Goncalo Alves grips. Each has a speedloader cutout. Comes in a fitted carry/storage case. Introduced 1989.
Price: Model 36-LS $379.00
Price: Without case $352.00
Price: Model 60-LS (as above except in stainless) $427.00
Price: Without case $400.00

Smith & Wesson Model 60 3"

SMITH & WESSON MODEL 38 BODYGUARD
Caliber: 38 Special, 5-shot.
Barrel: 2".
Weight: 14½ oz. **Length:** 6$\frac{5}{16}$" overall.
Stocks: Checkered walnut.
Sights: Fixed serrated ramp front, square notch rear.
Features: Alloy frame; internal hammer.
Price: Blue $379.00
Price: Nickel $392.00

Smith & Wesson Model 49, 649 Bodyguard Revolvers
Same as Model 38 except steel construction, weight 20½ oz.
Price: Blued, Model 49 . . . . . $359.00
Price: Stainless, Model 649 . . . . . $408.00

SMITH & WESSON MODEL 57 41 MAGNUM REVOLVER
Caliber: 41 Magnum, 6-shot.
Barrel: 4", 6" or 8⅜".
Weight: 48 oz. (6" bbl.). **Length:** 11⅜" (6" bbl.).
Stocks: Oversize target-type checkered Goncalo Alves.
Sights: ⅛" red ramp front, micro-click rear adjustable for windage and elevation.
Price: S&W Bright Blue or nickel, 4", 6" $427.00
Price: 8⅜" bbl. $442.00
Price: Stainless, Model 657, 6" $455.00
Price: As above, 8⅜" $471.00

Smith & Wesson Model 657 Classic Hunter
Similar to the Model 57 except is made of stainless steel, has 6½" full-lug barrel, unfluted cylinder; .500" target hammer, .400" smooth combat trigger; black pinned ramp front sight, adjustable micrometer click rear with white outline; Hogue soft rubber combat grips with round butt. Overall length is 12", weight 52½" overall. Introduced 1991. Limited production.
Price: $471.00

SMITH & WESSON MODEL 64 STAINLESS M&P
Caliber: 38 Special, 6-shot.
Barrel: 2", 3", 4".
Weight: 34 oz. **Length:** 9$\frac{5}{16}$" overall.
Stocks: Checkered walnut, Service style.
Sights: Fixed, ⅛" serrated ramp front, square notch rear.
Features: Satin finished stainless steel, square butt.
Price: $417.00

Smith & Wesson Model 60 Chiefs Special Stainless
Same as Model 36 except: 2" bbl. and round butt only.
Price: Stainless steel $386.00

Smith & Wesson Model 60 3" Full-Lug Revolver
Similar to the Model 60 Chief's Special except has 3" full-lug barrel, adjustable micrometer click black blade rear sight; rubber Uncle Mike's Custom Grade combat grips. Overall length 7½"; weight 24½ oz. Introduced 1991.
Price: $410.00

Smith & Wesson Model 66

SMITH & WESSON MODEL 66 STAINLESS COMBAT MAGNUM
Caliber: 357 Magnum and 38 Special, 6-shot.
Barrel: 2½", 4", 6".
Weight: 36 oz. **Length:** 9$\frac{9}{16}$" overall.
Stocks: Checkered Goncalo Alves target.
Sights: Front, Baughman Quick Draw on ramp, micro-click rear adjustable for windage and elevation.
Features: Satin finish stainless steel.
Price: From . . . . . $404.00 to $450.00

SMITH & WESSON MODEL 586, 686 DISTINGUISHED COMBAT MAGNUMS
Caliber: 357 Magnum.
Barrel: 4", 6", 8⅜", full shroud.
Weight: 46 oz. (6"), 41 oz. (4").
Stocks: Goncalo Alves target-type with speed loader cutaway.
Sights: Baughman red ramp front, four-position click-adjustable front, S&W micrometer click rear (or fixed).
Features: Uses new L-frame, but takes all K-frame grips. Full-length ejector rod shroud. Smooth combat-type trigger, semi-target type hammer. Trigger stop on 6" models. Also available in stainless as Model 686. Introduced 1981.
Price: Model 586, blue, 4", from **$401.00**
Price: Model 586, nickel, from **$413.00**
Price: Model 686, stainless, from **$422.00**
Price: Model 586, 6", adjustable front sight, blue **$436.00**
Price: As above, 8⅜" **$423.00**
Price: Model 686, 6", adjustable front sight **$461.00**
Price: As above, 8⅜" **$479.00**

Smith & Wesson Model 586

Smith & Wesson Model 640 Centennial

SMITH & WESSON MODEL 640, 940 CENTENNIAL
Caliber: 38 Special, 9mm Para., 5-shot.
Barrel: 2", 3".
Weight: 20 oz. **Length:** 6$\frac{5}{16}$" overall.
Stocks: Round butt Goncalo Alves.
Sights: Serrated ramp front, fixed notch rear.
Features: Stainless steel version of the original Model 40 but without the grip safety. Fully concealed hammer, snag-proof smooth edges. Model 640 introduced 1990; Model 940 introduced 1991.
Price: Model 640 (38 Special) **$408.00**
Price: Model 940 (9mm Para., rubber grips) **$429.00**

Smith & Wesson Model 632 Revolver
Similar to the Model 642 Centennial Airweight except chambered for 32 H&R Magnum, with 6-shot cylinder. Has alloy frame, stainless cylinder, yoke and 2" or 3" barrel. Weight with 2" barrel is 15.5 oz. Introduced 1991.
Price: **$410.00**

Smith & Wesson Model 642 Centennial Airweight
Similar to the Model 640 Centennial except has a clear-anodized alloy frame giving weight of 15.8 oz. Chambered for 38 Special, 2" or 3" stainless barrel; stainless cylinder; concealed hammer; Uncle Mike's Custom Grade Santoprene grips. Fixed square notch rear sight, serrated ramp front. Introduced 1990.
Price: **$410.00**

SMITH & WESSON MODEL 651 REVOLVER
Caliber: 22 WMR, 6-shot cylinder.
Barrel: 4".
Weight: 24½ oz. **Length:** 8$\frac{11}{16}$" overall.
Stocks: Checkered service Morado; square butt.
Sights: Red ramp front, adjustable micrometer click rear.
Features: Stainless steel construction with semi-target hammer, smooth combat trigger. Reintroduced 1991. Limited production.
Price: **$412.00**

Smith & Wesson Model 651

SPECTRE FIVE REVOLVER
Caliber: 45 Colt/410 shotshell, 2" and 3"; 5-shot cylinder.
Barrel: 2".
Weight: 48 oz. **Length:** 9" overall.
Stocks: Pachmayr checkered rubber.
Sights: Fixed.
Features: Double action with ambidextrous hammer-block safety; squared trigger guard; internal draw bar safety. Made of chromemoly steel, with matte blue finish. Introduced 1991. From Specialized Weapons, Inc.
Price: **$379.00**

Sportarms HS38S

SPORTARMS MODEL HS38S REVOLVER
Caliber: 38 Special, 6-shot.
Barrel: 3", 4".
Weight: 31.3 oz. **Length:** 8" overall (3" barrel).
Stocks: Checkered hardwood; round butt on 3" model, target-style on 4".
Sights: Blade front, adjustable rear.
Features: Polished blue finish; ventilated rib on 4" barrel. Made in Germany by Herbert Schmidt; Imported by Sportarms of Florida.
Price: About **$150.00**

Taurus Model 73

TAURUS MODEL 73 SPORT REVOLVER
Caliber: 32 H&R Mag., 6-shot.
Barrel: 3", heavy.
Weight: 22 oz. **Length:** 8¼" overall.
Stocks: Checkered Brazilian hardwood.
Sights: Ramp front, notch rear.
Features: Imported by Taurus International.
Price: Blue **$223.00**
Price: Satin nickel **$243.00**

CAUTION: PRICES CHANGE, CHECK AT GUNSHOP.

TAURUS MODEL 66 REVOLVER
Caliber: 357 Magnum, 6-shot.
Barrel: 3", 4", 6".
Weight: 35 oz.
Stocks: Checkered Brazilian hardwood.
Sights: Serrated ramp front, micro-click rear adjustable for windage and elevation. Red ramp front with white outline rear on stainlees models only.
Features: Wide target-type hammer spur, floating firing pin, heavy barrel with shrouded ejector rod. Introduced 1978. Imported by Taurus International.
Price: Blue **$274.00**
Price: Nickel **$289.00**
Price: Stainless steel **$348.00**
Price: Model 65 (similar to M66 except has a fixed rear sight and ramp front), blue, 3" or 4" only **$249.00**
Price: Model 65, satin nickel, 3" or 4" only **$269.00**

Taurus Model 66

TAURUS MODEL 76 REVOLVER
Caliber: 32 H&R Magnum, 6-shot.
Barrel: 6", heavy, solid rib.
Weight: 34 oz.
Stocks: Checkered Brazilian hardwood.
Sights: Patridge-type front, micro-click rear adjustable for windage and elevation.
Features: Traget hammer, adjustable target trigger. Blue only. Introduced 1991. Imported by Taurus International.
Price: **$308.00**

TAURUS MODEL 82 HEAVY BARREL REVOLVER
Caliber: 38 Spec., 6-shot.
Barrel: 3" or 4", heavy.
Weight: 34 oz. (4" bbl.). **Length:** 9¼" overall (4" bbl.).
Stocks: Checkered Brazilian hardwood.
Sights: Serrated ramp front, square notch rear.
Features: Imported by Taurus International.
Price: Blue **$216.00**
Price: Satin nickel **$231.00**

TAURUS MODEL 80 STANDARD REVOLVER
Caliber: 38 Spec., 6-shot.
Barrel: 3" or 4".
Weight: 30 oz. (4" bbl.). **Length:** 9¼" overall (4" bbl.).
Stocks: Checkered Brazilian hardwood.
Sights: Serrated ramp front, square notch rear.
Features: Imported by Taurus International.
Price: Blue **$216.00**
Price: Satin nickel **$231.00**

Taurus Model 85

TAURUS MODEL 83 REVOLVER
Caliber: 38 Spec., 6-shot.
Barrel: 4" only, heavy.
Weight: 34 oz.
Stocks: Oversize checkered Brazilian hardwood.
Sights: Ramp front, micro-click rear adjustable for windage and elevation.
Features: Blue or nickel finish. Introduced 1977. Imported by Taurus International.
Price: Blue **$228.00**
Price: Satin nickel **$241.00**

TAURUS MODEL 85 REVOLVER
Caliber: 38 Spec., 5-shot.
Barrel: 2", 3".
Weight: 21 oz.
Stocks: Checkered Brazilian hardwood.
Sights: Ramp front, square notch rear.
Features: Blue, satin nickel finish or stainless steel. Introduced 1980. Imported by Taurus International.
Price: Blue **$237.00**
Price: Satin nickel, 3" only **$257.00**
Price: Stainless steel **$297.00**

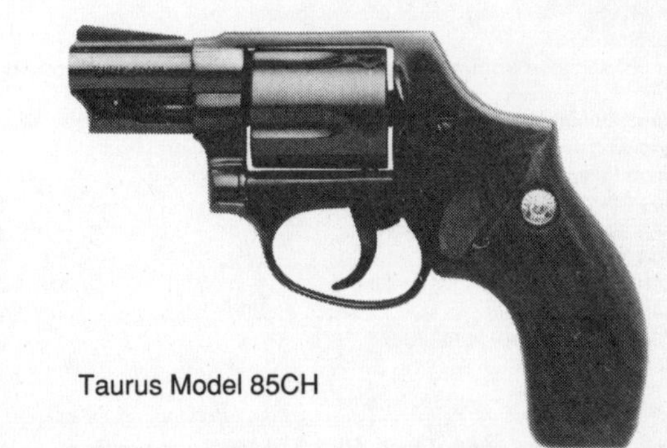
Taurus Model 85CH

Taurus Model 85CH Revolver
Same as the Model 85 except has 2" barrel only and concealed hammer. Smooth Brazilian hardwood stocks. Introduced 1991. Imported by Taurus International.
Price: Blue **$237.00**
Price: Stainless **$297.00**

TAURUS MODEL 86 REVOLVER
Caliber: 38 Spec., 6-shot.
Barrel: 6" only.
Weight: 34 oz. **Length:** 11¼" overall.
Stocks: Oversize target-type, checkered Brazilian hardwood.
Sights: Patridge front, micro-click rear adjustable for windage and elevation.
Features: Blue finish with non-reflective finish on barrel. Imported by Taurus International.
Price: **$308.00**

Taurus Model 86

TAURUS MODEL 669 REVOLVER
Caliber: 357 Mag., 6-shot.
Barrel: 4", 6".
Weight: 37 oz., (4" bbl.).
Stocks: Checkered Brazilian hardwood.
Sights: Serrated ramp front, micro-click rear adjustable for windage and elevation.
Features: Wide target-type hammer, floating firing pin, full-length barrel shroud. Introduced 1988. Imported by Taurus International.
Price: Blue **$284.00**
Price: Stainless **$356.00**

Taurus Model 689 Revolver
Same as the Model 669 except has full-length ventilated barrel rib. Available in blue or stainless steel. Introduced 1990. From Taurus International.
Price: Blue, 4" or 6" **$295.00**
Price: Stainless, 4" or 6" **$370.00**

Taurus/Laser Aim 357 Revolver Package
Includes the Taurus Model 689 revolver (6" barrel, blue or satin nickel finish) and the Taurus/Laser Aim LA1 laser sight with appropriate mount and rings in matching finish, the LA1C 110-volt charger and LA9C 9-volt field charger, and a sturdy high-impact case. Below-barrel mount allows the use of conventional sights or a scope. Introduced 1990.
Price: Blue **$708.00**
Price: Stainless **$783.00**

TAURUS MODEL 94 REVOLVER
Caliber: 22 LR, 9-shot cylinder.
Barrel: 3", 4".
Weight: 25 oz.
Stocks: Checkered Brazilian hardwood.
Sights: Serrated ramp front, click-adjustable rear for windage and elevation.
Features: Floating firing pin, color case-hardened hammer and trigger. Introduced 1989. Imported by Taurus International.
Price: Blue **$249.00**
Price: Stainless **$296.00**

WESSON FIREARMS MODEL 41V, 44V, 45V REVOLVERS
Caliber: 41 Mag., 44 Mag., 45 Colt, 6-shot.
Barrel: 4", 6", 8", 10"; interchangeable.
Weight: 48 oz. (4"). **Length:** 12" overall (6" bbl.).
Stocks: Smooth.
Sights: ⅛" serrated front, white outline rear adjustable for windage and elevation.
Features: Available in blue or stainless steel. Smooth, wide trigger with adjustable over-travel; wide hammer spur. Available in Pistol Pac set also. Contact Wesson Firearms for complete price list.
Price: 41 Mag., 4", vent **$412.80**
Price: As above except in stainless **$461.98**
Price: 44 Mag., 4", blue **$431.45**
Price: As above except in stainless **$507.30**
Price: 45 Colt, 4", vent **$431.45**
Price: As above except in stainless **$507.30**

Wesson Firearms Model 9-2, 15-2 & 32M Revolvers
Same as Models 8-2 and 14-2 except they have adjustable sight. Model 9-2 chambered for 38 Special, Model 15-2 for 357 Magnum. Model 32M is chambered for 32 H&R Mag. Same specs and prices as for 15-2 guns. Available in blue or stainless. Contact Wesson Firearms for complete price list.
Price: Model 9-2 or 15-2, 2½", blue **$337.64**
Price: As above except in stainless **$366.07**

Wesson Firearms Model 15 Gold Series
Similar to the Model 15 except has smoother action to reduce DA pull to 8-10 lbs.; comes with either 6" or 8" vent heavy slotted barrel shroud with bright blue barrel. Shroud is stamped "Gold Series" with the Wesson signature engraved and gold filled. Hammer and trigger are polished bright; rosewood grips. New sights with orange dot Patridge front, white triangle on rear blade. Introduced 1989.
Price: 6" **$543.59**
Price: 8" **$554.26**

Taurus Model 669

Wesson Model 22

Wesson Model 14-2

Wesson Model 32M

WESSON FIREARMS MODEL 8-2 & MODEL 14-2
Caliber: 38 Special (Model 8-2); 357 (14-2), both 6-shot.
Barrel: 2½", 4", 6", 8"; interchangeable.
Weight: 30 oz. (2½"). **Length:** 9¼" overall (4" bbl.).
Stocks: Checkered, interchangeable.
Sights: ⅛" serrated front, fixed rear.
Features: Interchangeable barrels and grips; smooth, wide trigger; wide hammer spur with short double-action travel. Available in stainless or Brite blue. Contact Wesson Firearms for complete price list.
Price: Model 8-2, 2½", blue **$267.15**
Price: As above except in stainless **$311.38**
Price: Model 714-2 Pistol Pac, stainless **$516.68**

WESSON FIREARMS MODEL 22 REVOLVER
Caliber: 22 LR, 22 WMR, 6-shot.
Barrel: 2½", 4", 6", 8", 10"; interchangeable.
Weight: 36 oz. (2½"), 44 oz. (6"). **Length:** 9¼" overall (4" barrel).
Stocks: Checkered; undercover, service or over-size target.
Sights: ⅛" serrated, interchangeable front, white outline rear adjustable for windage and elevation.
Features: Built on the same frame as the Wesson 357; smooth, wide trigger with over-travel adjustment, wide spur hammer, with short double-action travel. Available in Brite blue or stainless steel. Contact Wesson Firearms for complete price list.
Price: 2½" bbl., blue **$337.64**
Price: As above, stainless **$366.07**
Price: With 4", vent. rib, blue **$369.97**
Price: As above, stainless **$398.41**
Price: Stainless Pistol Pac, 22 LR **$689.01**

 CAUTION: PRICES CHANGE, CHECK AT GUNSHOP.

HANDGUNS—SINGLE-ACTION REVOLVERS

Both classic six-shooters and modern adaptations for hunting and sport.

CENTURY GUN DIST. MODEL 100 SINGLE ACTION
Caliber: 30-30, 375 Win., 444 Marlin, 45-70, 50-70.
Barrel: 6½" (standard), 8", 10", 12".
Weight: 6 lbs. (loaded). **Length:** 15" overall (8" bbl.).
Stocks: Smooth walnut.
Sights: Ramp front, Millett adjustable square notch rear.
Features: Highly polished high tensile strength manganese bronze frame, blue cylinder and barrel; coil spring trigger mechanism. Calibers other than 45-70 start at $1,500.00. Contact maker for full price information. Introduced 1975. Made in U.S. From Century Gun Dist., Inc.
Price: 6" barrel, 45-70 . . . . **$850.00**

Century Model 100

CIMARRON U.S. CAVALRY MODEL SINGLE ACTION
Caliber: 45 Colt.
Barrel: 7½".
Weight: 42 oz. **Length:** 13½" overall.
Stocks: Walnut.
Sights: Fixed.
Features: Has "A.P. Casey" markings; "U.S." plus patent dates on frame, serial number on backstrap, trigger guard, frame and cylinder, "APC" cartouche on left grip; color case-hardened frame and hammer, rest charcoal blue. Exact copy of the original. Imported by Cimarron Arms.
Price: **$459.00**

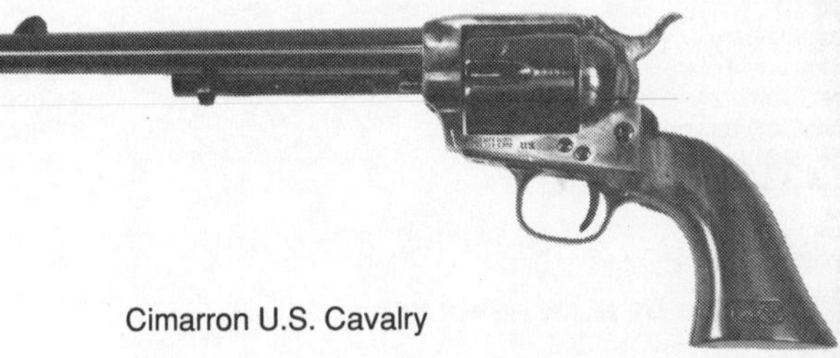
Cimarron U.S. Cavalry

Cimarron Artillery Model Single Action
Similar to the U.S. Cavalry model except has 5½" barrel, weighs 39 oz., and is 11½" overall. U.S. markings and cartouche, case-hardened frame and hammer; 45 Colt only.
Price: **$459.00**

CIMARRON 1873 PEACEMAKER REPRO
Caliber: 22 LR, 22 WMR, 38 WCF, 357 Mag., 44 WCF, 44 Spec., 45 Colt.
Barrel: 4¾", 5½", 7½".
Weight: 39 oz. **Length:** 10" overall (4" barrel).
Stocks: Walnut.
Sights: Blade front, fixed or adjustable rear.
Features: Uses "old model" blackpowder frame with "Bullseye" ejector or New Model frame. Imported by Cimarron Arms.
Price: Peacemaker, 4¾" barrel **$429.00**
Price: Frontier Six Shooter, 5½" barrel **$429.00**
Price: Single Action Army, 7½" barrel **$429.00**

Cimarron 1873 Peacemaker

CIMARRON 1875 REMINGTON
Caliber: 357 Mag., 44-40, 45 Colt, 6-shot.
Barrel: 7½".
Weight: 44 oz. **Length:** 13¾" overall.
Stocks: Smooth walnut.
Sights: Blade front, notch rear.
Features: Replica of the 1875 Remington S.A. Army revolver. Brass trigger guard, color case-hardened frame, rest blued, or nickel finish. Imported by Cimarron Arms.
Price: **$389.95**

Cimarron 1875 Remington

CIMARRON 1890 REMINGTON REVOLVER
Caliber: 357 Mag., 44-40, 45 Colt, 6-shot.
Barrel: 5½".
Weight: 37 oz. **Length:** 12½" overall.
Stocks: American walnut.
Sights: Blade front, groove rear.
Features: Replica of the 1890 Remington single action. Brass trigger guard, rest is blued, or nickel finish. Lanyard ring in butt. Imported by Cimarron Arms.
Price: **$389.95**

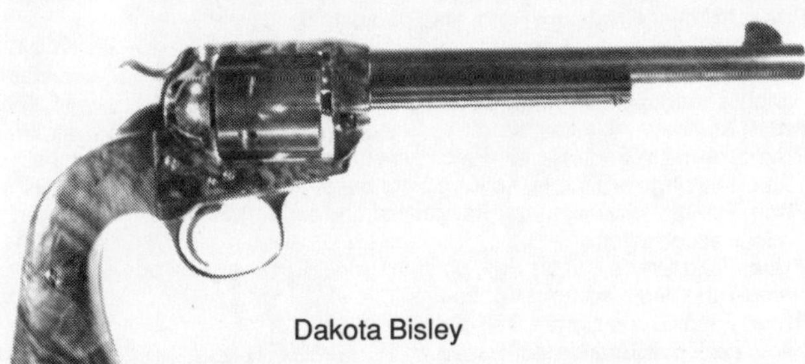
Dakota Bisley

DAKOTA 1894 BISLEY MODEL SINGLE ACTION
Caliber: 357.
Barrel: 4⅝", 5½", 7½".
Weight: 37 oz. **Length:** 10½" overall with 5½" barrel.
Stocks: Smooth walnut.
Sights: Blade front, fixed groove rear.
Features: Colt-type firing pin in hammer; color case-hardened frame, blue barrel, cylinder, steel backstrap and trigger guard. Also available in nickel, factory engraved. Imported by E.M.F.
Price: All calibers, bbl. lengths **$495.00**
Price: Nickel, all cals. **$525.00**
Price: Engraved, all cals., 5½", 7½" lengths **$570.00**
Price: Bisley Target (adjustable sights) **$500.00**

DAKOTA SINGLE-ACTION REVOLVERS
Caliber: 22 LR, 357 Mag., 32-20, 38-40, 44-40, 44 Spec., 45 Colt.
Barrel: 3½", 4¾", 5½", 7½".
Weight: 45 oz. **Length:** 13" overall (7½" bbl.).
Stocks: Smooth walnut.
Sights: Blade front, fixed rear.
Features: Colt-type hammer with firing pin, color case-hardened frame, blue barrel and cylinder, brass grip frame and trigger guard. Available in blue or nickel-plated, plain or engraved. Imported by E.M.F.
Price: 4¾", 5½", 7½" **$450.00**
Price: Engraved **$529.90**
Price: Sheriff Model, 3½" **$600.00**
Price: Dakota Target (adjustable sights) **$550.00**

Dakota Sheriff Model

Dakota Hartford Model Single-Action Revolvers
Similar to the Dakota Single-Action revolvers except available with 5½" barrel (Artillery) or 7½" (Cavalry); or with 4¾" barrel. Identical to the original Colts with inspector cartouche on left grip, original patent dates and U.S. markings. All major parts serial numbered using original Colt-style lettering, numbering. Bullseye ejector head and color case-hardening on frame and hammer. Calibers 22 LR, 32-20, 357, 38-40, 44 Spec., 45 Colt. Introduced 1990. From E.M.F.
Price: **$600.00**
Price: Cavalry or Artillery **$655.00**
Price: Nickel plated **$660.00**
Price: Cattlebrand engraved **$1,000.00**
Price: Cattlebrand engraved nickel **$1,060.00**
Price: Scroll engraved **$840.00**
Price: Scroll engraved nickel **$900.00**

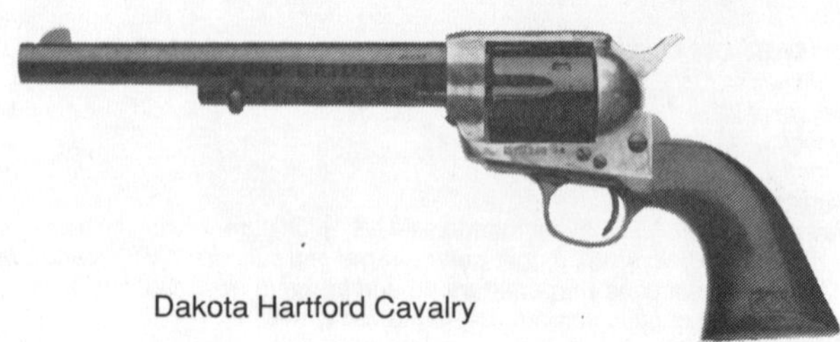

Dakota Hartford Cavalry

DAKOTA 1875 OUTLAW REVOLVER
Caliber: 357, 44-40, 45 Colt.
Barrel: 7½".
Weight: 46 oz. **Length:** 13½" overall.
Stocks: Smooth walnut.
Sights: Blade front, fixed groove rear.
Features: Authentic copy of 1875 Remington with firing pin in hammer; color case-hardened frame, blue cylinder, barrel, steel backstrap and brass trigger guard. Also available in nickel, factory engraved. Imported by E.M.F.
Price: All calibers **$465.00**
Price: Nickel **$525.00**
Price: Engraved **$600.00**
Price: Engraved Nickel **$700.00**

Dakota New Model Single-Action Revolvers
Similar to the standard Dakota except has color case-hardened forged steel frame, black nickel backstrap and trigger guard. Calibers 357 Mag., 44-40, 45 Colt only.
Price: **$490.00**
Price: Nickel **$535.00**

Dakota 1890 Police Revolver
Similar to the 1875 Outlaw except has 5½" barrel, weighs 40 oz., with 12½" overall length. Has lanyard ring in butt. No web under barrel. Calibers 357, 44-40, 45 Colt. Imported by E.M.F.
Price: All calibers **$470.00**
Price: Nickel **$530.00**
Price: Engraved **$620.00**
Price: Engraved nickel **$720.00**

E.A.A. BOUNTY HUNTER REVOLVER
Caliber: 22 LR, 22 WMR, 6-shot cylinder.
Barrel: 4¾", 6", 9".
Weight: 32 oz. **Length:** 10" overall (4¾" barrel).
Stocks: European hardwood.
Sights: Blade front, rear adjustable for windage.
Features: Available in blue, chrome, gold or brass finish. Introduced 1991. From European American Armory Corp.
Price: 4¾", blue **$59.00**
Price: 4¾", blue, 22 LR/22 WMR combo **$69.00**
Price: 4¾", chrome **$69.00**
Price: 4¾", chrome, 22 LR/22 WMR combo **$79.00**
Price: 6", blue **$71.50**
Price: 9", blue **$79.00**
Price: 6", blue and brass finish **$79.00**
Price: 4¾", gold finish **$84.50**

Dakota 1873 Premier Single-Action Revolver
Reproduction of the 1873 Colt revolver with set screw for the cylinder pin release. Most parts interchange with the early Colts. Blue finish, color case-hardened frame. Chambered for 45 Colt only, 4⅝" or 5½" barrel only.
Price: **$550.00**

Freedom 454 Field Grade

FREEDOM ARMS PREMIER 454 CASULL
Caliber: 44 Mag., 45 Colt, 454 Casull, 5-shot.
Barrel: 3", 4¾", 6", 7½", 10".
Weight: 50 oz. **Length:** 14" overall (7½" bbl.).
Stocks: Impregnated hardwood.
Sights: Blade front, notch or adjustable rear.
Features: All stainless steel construction; sliding bar safety system. Hunter Pak includes 7½" gun, sling and studs, aluminum carrying case with tool and cleaning kit. Lifetime warranty. Made in U.S.A.
Price: Field Grade (matte finish, polymer grips), adjustable sights, 4¾", 6", 7½", 10" **$966.00**
Price: Field Grade, fixed sights, 4¾" only **$882.00**
Price: Field Grade, 44 Rem. Mag., adjustable sights, 7½", 10" only . **$966.00**
Price: Premier Grade (brush finish, impregnated hardwood grips) adjustable sights, 4¾", 6", 7½", 10" **$1,242.00**
Price: Premier Grade, fixed sights, 7½" only **$1,133.00**
Price: Premier Grade, no sights (drilled and tapped), 7½" only . . **$1,199.00**
Price: Premier Grade, 44 Rem. Mag., adjustable sights, 7½", 10" only **$1,242.00**
Price: Premier Grade, U.S. Deputy Marshall (3" barrel, no ejector, adjustable sights, medallion in left hardwood grip) **$1,377.00**
Price: As above, fixed sights **$1,257.00**
Price: Premier Grade Hunter Pak, black micarta grips, 2x Leupold scope, Leupold rings and base, no front sight base **$1,728.00**
Price: Premier Grade Hunter Pak, adjustable sight, black micarta grips **$1,504.00**
Price: Field Grade Hunter Pak, polymer grips, 2x Leupold scope, Leupold rings and base, no front sigt base **$1,418.00**
Price: Field Grade Hunter Pak, polymer grips, low-profile adjustable sight **$1,194.00**
Price: Fitted 45 ACP or 45 Colt cylinder, add **$189.00**

MITCHELL SINGLE-ACTION ARMY REVOLVERS
Caliber: 357 Mag., 44-40, 44 Mag., 45 ACP, 45 Colt, 6-shot.
Barrel: 4¾", 5½", 6", 7½", 10", 12", 18".
Weight: NA. **Length:** NA.
Stocks: One-piece walnut.
Sights: Serrated ramp front, fixed or adjustable rear.
Features: Color case-hardened frame, brass or steel backstrap/trigger guard; hammer-block safety. Bright nickel-plated model and dual cylinder models available. Contact importer for complete price list. Imported by Mitchell Arms, Inc.
Price: Cowboy, 4¾", Army 5½", Cavalry 7½", blue, 357, 44-40, 45 Colt, 45 ACP **$349.00**
Price: As above, nickel **$399.00**
Price: 45 Colt/45 ACP dual cyl., blue **$399.00**
Price: As above, nickel **$449.00**
Price: Bat Masterson model, 45 Colt, 4¾", nickel **$399.00**
Price: 1875 Remington, 7½", 357 or 45 Colt **$399.00**
Price: As above, 45 Colt/45 ACP dual cylinder **$450.00**
Price: 1890 Remington, 45 Colt **$399.00**
Price: As above 45 Colt/45 ACP dual cylinder **$450.00**

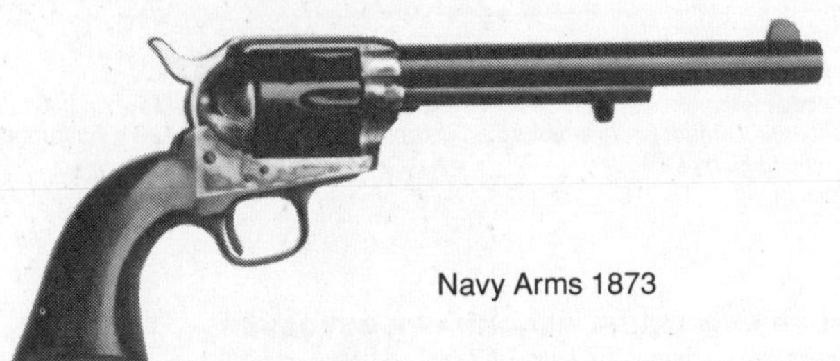

Navy Arms 1873

Navy Arms 1890 Remington-Style Revolver
Similar to the 1875 revolver except does not have the under-barrel web. Available with 5½" barrel only. Has lanyard loop on butt. Blued frame, brass trigger guard. Introduced 1991. Imported by Navy Arms.
Price: **$495.00**

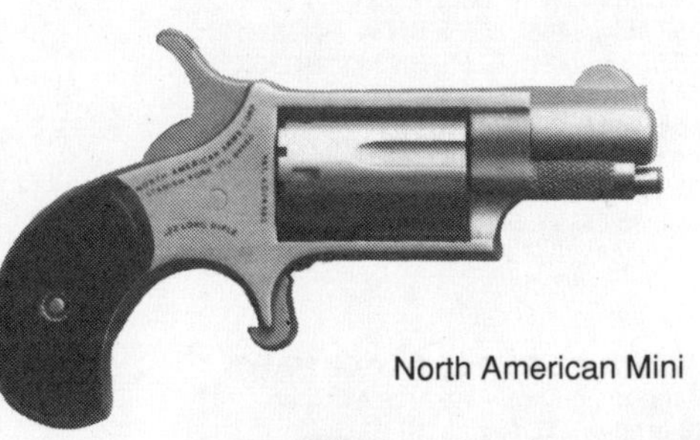

North American Mini

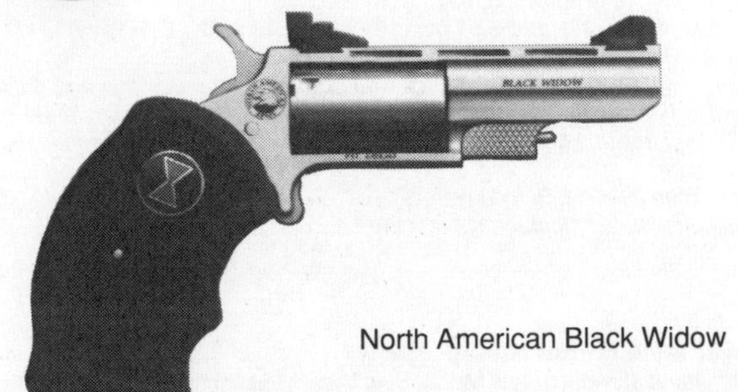

North American Black Widow

Phelps Heritage I

Mitchell Single Action

NAVY ARMS 1873 SINGLE-ACTION REVOLVER
Caliber: 44-40, 45 Colt, 6-shot cylinder.
Barrel: 4¾", 5½", 7½".
Weight: 36 oz. **Length:** 10¾" overall (5½" barrel).
Stocks: Smooth walnut.
Sights: Blade front, groove in topstrap rear.
Features: Blue with color case-hardened frame. Introduced 1991. Imported by Navy Arms.
Price: **$320.00**
Price: 1873 U.S. Cavalry Model (7½", 45 Colt, arsenal markings) . . **$475.00**
Price: 1895 U.S. Artillery Model (as above, 5½" barrel) **$475.00**

NAVY ARMS 1875 REMINGTON-STYLE REVOLVER
Caliber: 44-40, 45 Colt, 6-shot cylinder.
Barrel: 7½".
Weight: 41 oz. **Length:** 13" overall.
Stocks: Smooth walnut.
Sights: Blade front, groove in topstrap rear.
Features: Recreation of gun produced from 1875 to 1889. Color case-hardened frame, brass trigger guard, rest blued. Introduced 1991. Imported by Navy Arms.
Price: **$465.00**

NORTH AMERICAN MINI-REVOLVERS
Caliber: 22 LR, 22 WMR, 5-shot.
Barrel: 1⅛", 1⅝".
Weight: 4 to 6.6 oz. **Length:** 3⅝" to 6⅛" overall.
Stocks: Laminated wood.
Sights: Blade front, notch fixed rear.
Features: All stainless steel construction. Polished satin and matte finish. Engraved models available. From North American Arms.
Price: 22 LR, 1⅛" bbl. **$162.50**
Price: 22 LR, 1⅝" bbl. **$162.50**
Price: 22 WMR, 1⅝" bbl. **$182.50**
Price: 22 WMR, 1⅛" or 1⅝" bbl. with extra 22 LR cylinder **$217.50**

NORTH AMERICAN MINI-MASTER
Caliber: 22 LR, 22 WMR, 5-shot cylinder.
Barrel: 4".
Weight: 10.7 oz. **Length:** 7.75" overall.
Stocks: Checkered hard black rubber.
Sights: Blade front, white outline rear adjustable for elevation, or fixed.
Features: Heavy vent barrel; full-size grips. Non-fluted cylinder. Introduced 1989.
Price: Adjustable sight, 22 WMR or 22 LR **$265.50**
Price: As above with extra WMR/LR cylinder **$300.50**
Price: Fixed sight, 22 WMR or 22 LR **$255.50**
Price: As above with extra WMR/LR cylinder **$290.50**

North American Black Widow Revolver
Similar to the Mini-Master except has 2" Heavy Vent barrel. Built on the 22 WMR frame. Non-fluted cylinder, black rubber grips. Available with either Millett Low Profile fixed sights or Millett sight adjustable for elevation only. Overall length 5⅞", weight 8.8 oz. From North American Arms.
Price: Adjustable sight, 22 LR or 22 WMR **$233.50**
Price: As above with extra WMR/LR cylinder **$268.50**
Price: Fixed sight, 22 LR or 22 WMR **$223.50**
Price: As above with extra WMR/LR cylinder **$258.50**

PHELPS HERITAGE I, EAGLE I REVOLVERS
Caliber: 444 Marlin, 45-70, 6-shot.
Barrel: 8" or 12", 16" (45-70).
Weight: 5½ lbs. **Length:** 19½" overall (12" bbl.).
Stocks: Smooth walnut.
Sights: Ramp front, adjustable rear.
Features: Single action; polished blue finish; safety bar. From Phelps Mfg. Co.
Price: 8", 45-70 or 444 Marlin, about **$865.00**
Price: 12", 45-70 or 444 Marlin, about **$890.00**

QFI PLAINS RIDER SINGLE-ACTION REVOLVER
Caliber: 22 LR, 22 LR/22 WMR, 6-shot.
Barrel: 3¼" or 6½".
Weight: 28 oz. (3¼" barrel).
Stocks: Smooth nylon.
Sights: Blade front, fixed rear.
Features: Floating firing pin, hammer block safety. Available as combo with extra cylinder. Introduced 1991. Made in U.S. by QFI.
Price: 22 LR . . . . **$94.95 to $104.95**
Price: 22 LR/22 WMR combo . . . . **$119.95 to $129.95**

QFI WESTERN RANGER REVOLVER
Caliber: 22 LR, 22 LR/22 WMR.
Barrel: 3¼", 4¾", 6½", 9".
Weight: 31 oz. (4¾" bbl.). **Length:** 10" overall.
Stocks: American walnut.
Sights: Blade front, notch rear.
Features: Single action, blue/black finish. Introduced 1991. Made in the U.S. by QFI.
Price: 22 LR, 3¼" or 4¾" **$104.95**
Price: As above, convertible (22 LR/22 WMR) **$119.95**
Price: 22 LR, 6½" **$104.95**
Price: As above, convertible (22 LR/22 WMR) **$119.95**
Price: 22 LR, 9" **$111.95**
Price: As above, convertible (22 LR/22 WMR) **$131.95**

Ruger N.M. Blackhawk

Ruger N.M. Bisley

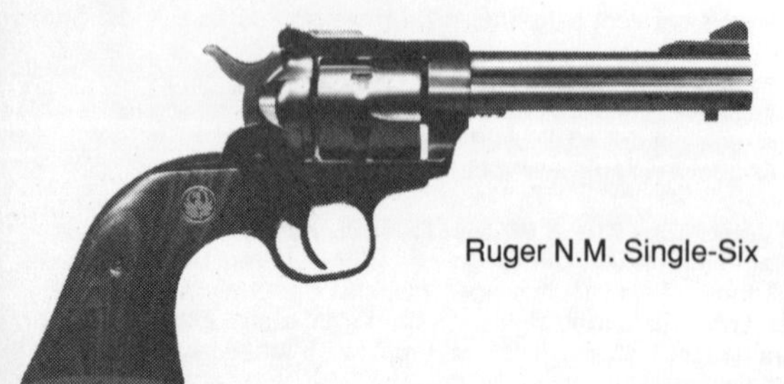
Ruger N.M. Single-Six

RUGER NEW MODEL SUPER SINGLE-SIX CONVERTIBLE
Caliber: 22 LR, 6-shot; 22 WMR in extra cylinder.
Barrel: 4⅝", 5½", 6½", or 9½" (6-groove).
Weight: 34½ oz. (6½" bbl.). **Length:** 11 13/16" overall (6½" bbl.).
Stocks: Smooth American walnut.
Sights: Improved Patridge front on ramp, fully adjustable rear protected by integral frame ribs.
Features: Ruger interlocked mechanism, transfer bar ignition, gate-controlled loading, hardened chromemoly steel frame, wide trigger, music wire springs throughout, independent firing pin.
Price: 4⅝", 5½", 6½", 9½" barrel **$267.75**
Price: 5½", 6½" bbl. only, stainless steel **$337.00**

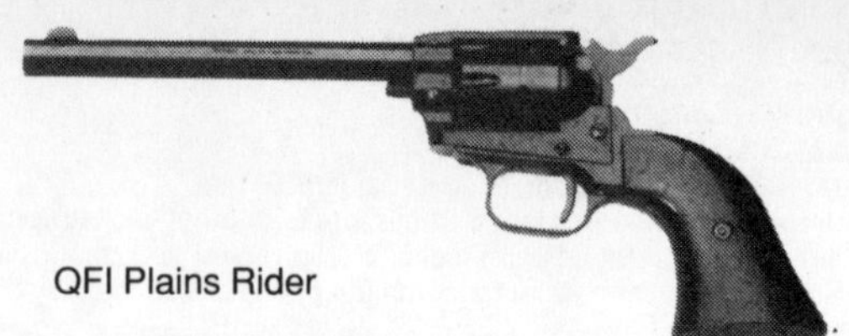
QFI Plains Rider

QFI HORSEMAN SINGLE-ACTION REVOLVER
Caliber: 357 Mag., 44 Mag., 45 Colt.
Barrel: 6" or 7½".
Weight: 45 oz. (6" bbl.).
Stocks: Smooth walnut with medallion; ivory polymer optional.
Sights: Blade front, grooved topstrap (fixed) rear.
Features: Color case-hardened frame. Bright blue finish. Super-smooth action. Introduced 1991. Assembled in the U.S. by QFI.
Price: . . . . **NA**
Price: 24K gold-plated . . . . **NA**

QFI Dark Horseman Single Action
Similar to the "Horseman" revolver except chambered for 44 Mag. and 45 Colt, and has a longer grip frame and adjustable sight. Introduced 1991. Assembled in the U.S. by QFI.
Price: . . . . **NA**

RUGER NEW MODEL BLACKHAWK REVOLVER
Caliber: 30 Carbine, 357 Mag./38 Spec., 41 Mag., 44 Mag., 45 Colt, 6-shot.
Barrel: 4⅝" or 6½", either caliber, 5½" (44 Mag. only); 7½" (30 Carbine, 45 Colt only).
Weight: 42 oz. (6½" bbl.). **Length:** 12¼" overall (6½" bbl.).
Stocks: American walnut.
Sights: ⅛" ramp front, micro-click rear adjustable for windage and elevation.
Features: New Ruger interlocked mechanism, independent firing pin, hardened chromemoly steel frame, music wire springs throughout.
Price: Blue, 30 Carbine (7½" bbl.), BN31 . . . . **$300.25**
Price: Blue, 357 Mag. (4⅝", 6½"), BN34, BN36 . . . . **$312.25**
Price: Blue, 357/9mm (4⅝", 6½"), BN34X, BN36X **$327.25**
Price: Blue, 44 Mag. (5½"), S45N **$360.50**
Price: Stainless, 44 Mag. (5½"), KS45N **$394.00**
Price: Blue, 41 Mag., 44 Mag., 45 Colt (4⅝", 6½"), BN41, BN42, BN44, BN45 . . . . **$312.25**
Price: Stainless, 357 Mag. (4⅝", 6½"), KBN34, KBN36 . . . . **$384.75**

RUGER NEW MODEL SUPER BLACKHAWK
Caliber: 44 Magnum, 6-shot. Also fires 44 Spec.
Barrel: 7½" (6-groove, 20" twist), 10½".
Weight: 48 oz. (7½" bbl.), 51 oz. (10½" bbl.). **Length:** 13⅜" overall (7½" bbl.).
Stocks: Genuine American walnut.
Sights: ⅛" ramp front, micro-click rear adjustable for windage and elevation.
Features: Ruger interlocked mechanism, non-fluted cylinder, steel grip and cylinder frame, square back trigger guard, wide serrated trigger and wide spur hammer.
Price: Blue (S-47N, S-411N) **$360.50**
Price: Stainless (KS-47N, KS-411N) **$394.00**

Ruger New Model Bisley
Similar to standard New Model Blackhawk except the hammer is lower with a smoothly curved, deeply checkered wide spur. The trigger is strongly curved with a wide smooth surface. Longer grip frame has a hand-filling shape. Adjustable rear sight, ramp-style front. Available with an unfluted cylinder and roll engraving, or with a fluted cylinder and no engraving. Fixed or adjustable sights. Chambered for 357, 41, 44 Mags. and 45 Colt; 7½" barrel; overall length of 13". Introduced 1985.
Price: **$372.25**

Ruger New Model Single-Six Revolver
Similar to the Super Single-Six revolver except chambered for 32 H&R Magnum (also handles 32 S&W and 32 S&W Long). Weight is about 34 oz. with 6½" barrel. Barrel lengths: 4⅝", 5½", 6½", 9½". Introduced 1985.
Price: **$257.00**

Ruger New Model Bisley Small Frame

Similar to the New Model Single-Six except frame is styled after the classic Bisley "flat-top." Most mechanical parts are unchanged. Hammer is lower and smoothly curved with a deeply checkered spur. Trigger is strongly curved with a wide smooth surface. Longer grip frame designed with a hand-filling shape, and the trigger guard is a large oval. Dovetail rear sight drift-adjustable for windage; front sight base accepts interchangeable square blades of various heights and styles. Available with an unfluted cylinder and roll engraving, or with a fluted cylinder and no engraving. Weight about 41 oz. Chambered for 22 LR and 32 H&R Mag., 6½" barrel only. Introduced 1985.

Price: **$313.00**

Ruger Small Frame Bisley

SPORTARMS MODEL HS21S SINGLE ACTION

Caliber: 22 LR or 22 LR/22 WMR combo, 6-shot.
Barrel: 5½".
Weight: 33.5 oz. **Length:** 11" overall.
Stocks: Smooth hardwood.
Sights: Blade front, rear drift adjustable for windage.
Features: Available in blue with imitation stag or wood stocks. Made in Germany by Herbert Schmidt; Imported by Sportarms of Florida.
Price: 22 LR, blue, "stag" grips, about **$80.00**
Price: 22 LR/22 WMR combo, blue, wood stocks, about **$110.00**

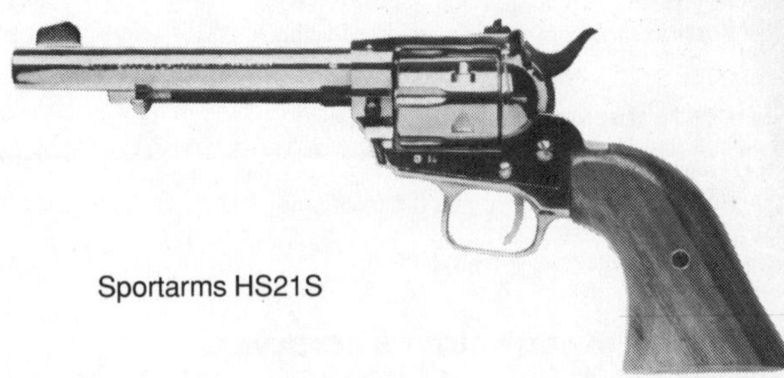

Sportarms HS21S

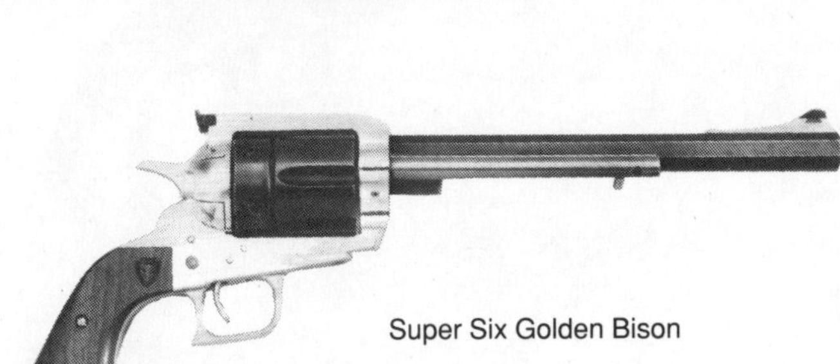

Super Six Golden Bison

SUPER SIX GOLDEN BISON 45-70 REVOLVER

Caliber: 45-70, 6-shot.
Barrel: 6", 10½", octagonal.
Weight: 5 lbs., 12 oz. (6" bbl.) **Length:** 17½" overall (10½" bbl.).
Stocks: Rosewood.
Sights: Blaze orange blade front on ramp, Millett fully adjustable rear.
Features: Cylinder frame and grip frame of high tensile manganese bronze; hammer of manganese bronze with a hardened steel pad for firing pin contact; all coil springs; full-cock, cross-bolt interlocking safety and traveling safeties. Blue/black finish. Lifetime warranty. Leupold scope and strap mount available. Made in the U.S. by Super Six Limited.
Price: Golden Bison (6" bbl.) **$1,895.00**
Price: Golden Bison Bull (10½" bbl.) **$1,895.00**

TEXAS LONGHORN ARMS GROVER'S IMPROVED NO. FIVE

Caliber: 44 Magnum, 6-shot.
Barrel: 5½".
Weight: 44 oz. **Length:** NA.
Stocks: Fancy AAA walnut.
Sights: Square blade front on ramp, fully adjustable rear.
Features: Music wire coil spring action with double locking bolt; polished blue finish. Handmade in limited 1,200-gun production. Grip contour, straps, oversized base pin, lever latch and lockwork identical copies of Elmer Keith design. Lifetime warranty to original owner. Introduced 1988.
Price: **$985.00**

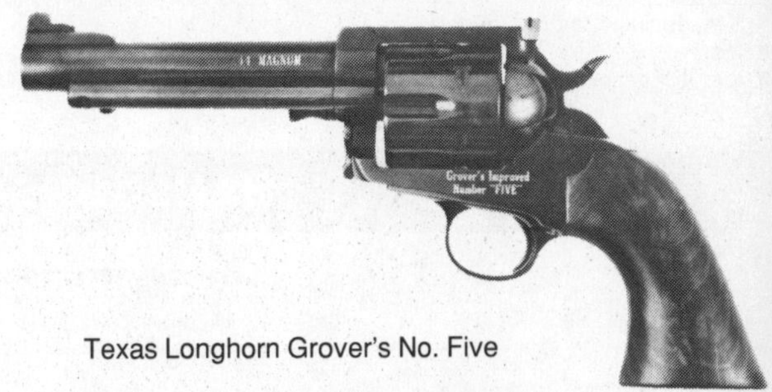

Texas Longhorn Grover's No. Five

TEXAS LONGHORN ARMS RIGHT-HAND SINGLE ACTION

Caliber: All centerfire pistol calibers.
Barrel: 4¾".
Weight: NA. **Length:** NA.
Stocks: One-piece fancy walnut, or any fancy AAA wood.
Sights: Blade front, grooved topstrap rear.
Features: Loading gate and ejector housing on left side of gun. Cylinder rotates to the left. All steel construction; color case-hardened frame; high polish blue; music wire coil springs. Lifetime guarantee to original owner. Introduced 1984. From Texas Longhorn Arms.
Price: South Texas Army Limited Edition—handmade, only 1,000 to be produced; "One of One Thousand" engraved on barrel **$1,500.00**

Texas Longhorn Arms Sesquicentennial Model Revolver

Similar to the South Texas Army Model except has ¾-coverage Nimschke-style engraving, antique golden nickel plate finish, one-piece elephant ivory grips. Comes with handmade solid walnut presentation case, factory letter to owner. Limited edition of 150 units. Introduced 1986.

Price: **$2,500.00**

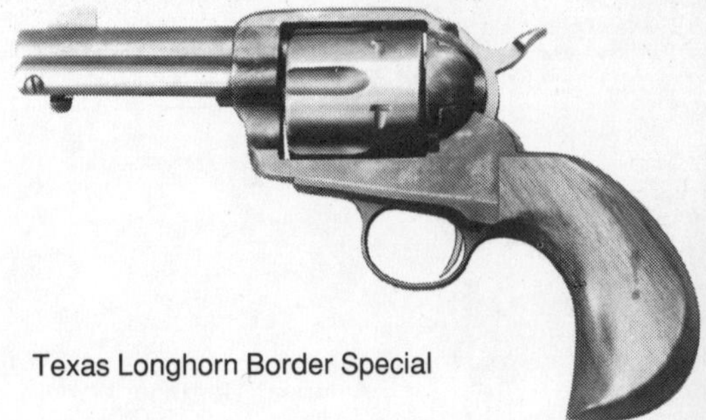

Texas Longhorn Border Special

Texas Longhorn Arms Cased Set

Set contains one each of the Texas Longhorn Right-Hand Single Actions, all in the same caliber, same serial numbers (100, 200, 300, 400, 500, 600, 700, 800, 900). Ten sets to be made (#1000 donated to NRA museum). Comes in hand-tooled leather case. All other specs same as Limited Edition guns. Introduced 1984.

Price: **$5,750.00**
Price: With ¾-coverage "C-style" engraving **$7,650.00**

Texas Longhorn Arms Texas Border Special

Similar to the South Texas Army Limited Edition except has 3½" barrel, bird's-head style grip. Same special features. Introduced 1984.

Price: **$1,500.00**

Texas Longhorn Arms West Texas Flat Top Target

Similar to the South Texas Army Limited Edition except choice of barrel length from 7½" through 15"; flat-top style frame; ⅛" contoured ramp front sight, old model steel micro-click rear adjustable for windage and elevation. Same special features. Introduced 1984.

Price: **$1,500.00**

Texas Longhorn Flat Top

UBERTI 1873 CATTLEMAN SINGLE ACTIONS

Caliber: 38 Spec., 357 Mag., 44 Spec., 44-40, 45 Colt/45 ACP, 6-shot.
Barrel: 4¾", 5½", 7½"; 44-40, 45 Colt also with 3".
Weight: 38 oz. (5½" bbl.). **Length:** 10¾" overall (5½" bbl.).
Stocks: One-piece smooth walnut.
Sights: Blade front, groove rear; fully adjustable rear available.
Features: Steel or brass backstrap, trigger guard; color case-hardened frame, blued barrel, cylinder. Imported from Italy by Uberti USA.
Price: Steel backstrap, trigger guard, fixed sights **$399.00**
Price: Brass backstrap, trigger guard, fixed sights **$350.00**

Uberti Cattleman

Uberti 1873 Buckhorn Single Action

A slightly larger version of the Cattleman revolver. Available in 44 Magnum or 44 Magnum/44-40 convertible, otherwise has same specs.
Price: Steel backstrap, trigger guard, fixed sights **$410.00**
Price: As above, brass **$360.00**
Price: Convertible (two cylinders) add **$40.00**

UBERTI 1875 SA ARMY OUTLAW REVOLVER

Caliber: 357 Mag., 44-40, 45 Colt, 6-shot.
Barrel: 7½".
Weight: 44 oz. **Length:** 13¾" overall.
Stocks: Smooth walnut.
Sights: Blade front, notch rear.
Features: Replica of the 1875 Remington S.A. Army revolver. Brass trigger guard, color case-hardened frame, rest blued. Imported by Uberti USA.
Price: **$355.00**
Price: Nickel-plated **$385.00**

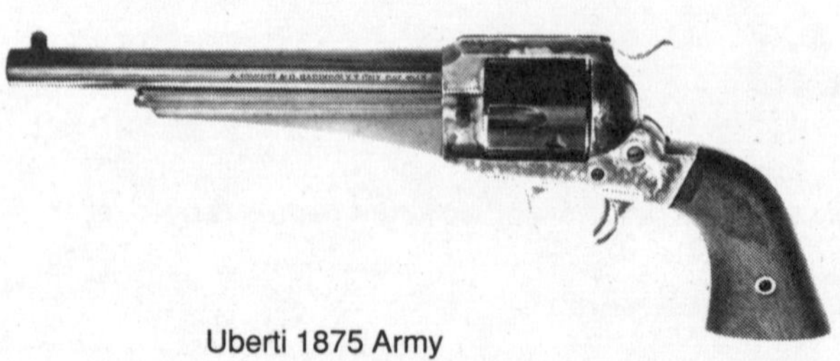

Uberti 1875 Army

UBERTI 1890 ARMY OUTLAW REVOLVER

Caliber: 357 Mag., 44-40, 45 Colt, 6-shot.
Barrel: 5½".
Weight: 37 oz. **Length:** 12½" overall.
Stocks: American walnut.
Sights: Blade front, groove rear.
Features: Replica of the 1890 Remington single action. Brass trigger guard, rest is blued. Imported by Uberti USA.
Price: **$375.00**
Price: Nickel-plated **$420.00**

HANDGUNS—MISCELLANEOUS

Specially adapted single-shot and multi-barrel arms.

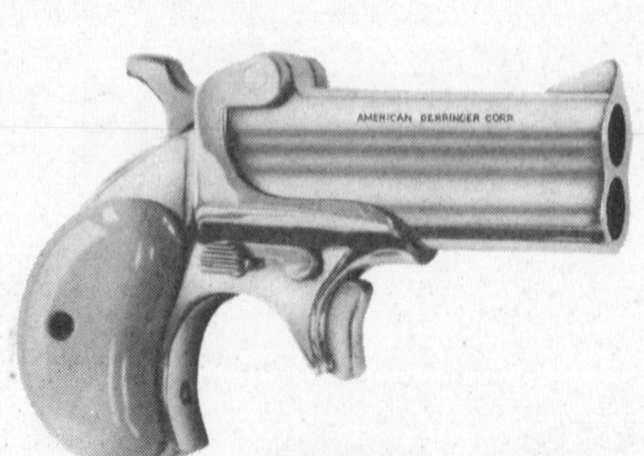

American Derringer Model 1

AMERICAN DERRINGER MODEL 1

Caliber: 22 LR, 22 WMR, 22 Hornet, 223 Rem., 30 Luger, 30-30 Win., 32 ACP, 38 Super, 380 ACP, 38 Spec., 9x18, 9mm Para., 357 Mag., 357 Maximum, 10mm, 40 S&W, 41 Mag., 38-40, 44-40 Win., 44 Spec., 44 American, 44 Mag., 45 Colt, 45 ACP, 410-bore. (2½").
Barrel: 3".
Weight: 15½ oz. (38 Spec.). **Length:** 4.82" overall.
Stocks: Rosewood, Zebra wood.
Sights: Blade front.
Features: Made of stainless steel with high-polish or satin finish. Two-shot capacity. Manual hammer block safety. Introduced 1980. Available in almost any pistol caliber. Contact the factory for complete list of available calibers and prices. From American Derringer Corp.
Price: 22 LR or WMR **$237.50**
Price: 22 Hornet, 223 Rem. **$375.00**
Price: 38 Spec. **$212.00**
Price: 357 Maximum **$265.00**
Price: 357 Mag. **$250.00**
Price: 9x18, 9mm, 380, 38 Super **$210.00**
Price: 10mm, 40 S&W **$250.00**
Price: 44 Spec., 44 American **$320.00**
Price: 44-40 Win., 45 Colt, 45 Auto Rim **$320.00**
Price: 30-30, 41, 44 Mags., 45 Win. Mag. **$387.00**
Price: 45-70, single shot **$312.00**
Price: 45 Colt, 410, 2½" **$320.00**
Price: 45 ACP, 10mm Auto **$250.00**

CAUTION: PRICES CHANGE, CHECK AT GUNSHOP.

American Derringer Lady Derringer
Same as the Model 1 except has tuned action, is fitted with scrimshawed synthetic ivory grips; chambered for 32 H&R Mag. and 38 Spec.; 22 LR, 22 WMR, 380 ACP, 357 Mag., 9mm Para., 45 ACP, 45 Colt/410 shotshell available at extra cost. Deluxe Grade is highly polished; Deluxe Engraved is engraved in a pattern similar to that used on 1880s derringers; 14 karat Gold Engraved is made of about 20 oz. of 14 karat gold and 3 oz. of stainless, engraved, and has a diamond ramp front sight. All come in a French fitted jewelry box. Introduced 1991.
Price: Deluxe Grade **$250.00**
Price: Deluxe Engraved Grade **$695.00**
Price: 14 karat Gold Engraved **$110,000.00**

American Derringer Model 6
Similar to the Model 1 except has 6" barrels chambered for 3" 410 shotshells or 45 Colt, rosewood stocks, 8.2" o.a.l. and weighs 21 oz. Shoots either round for each barrel. Manual hammer block safety. Introduced 1986.
Price: High polish or satin finish **$369.00**
Price: Gray matte finish **$337.50**

American Derringer Model 7
Similar to Model 1 except made of high strength aircraft aluminum. Weighs 7½ oz., 4.82" o.a.l., rosewood stocks. Available in 22 LR, 32 H&R Mag., 380 ACP, 38 Spec., 44 Spec. Introduced 1986.
Price: 22 LR or 38 Spec. **$205.00**
Price: 380 ACP **$205.00**
Price: 32 H&R Mag. **$205.00**
Price: 44 Spec. **$500.00**

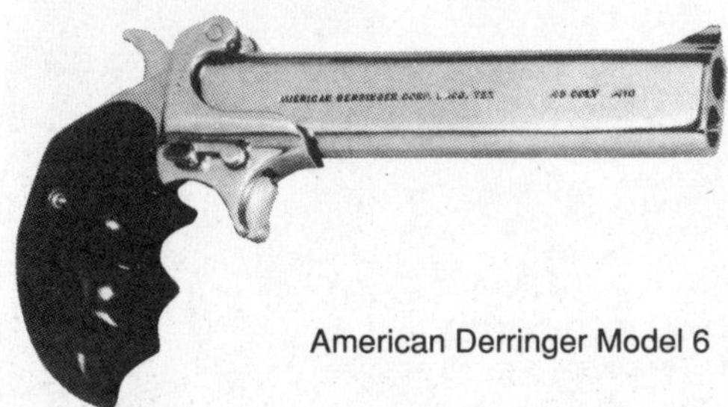

American Derringer Model 6

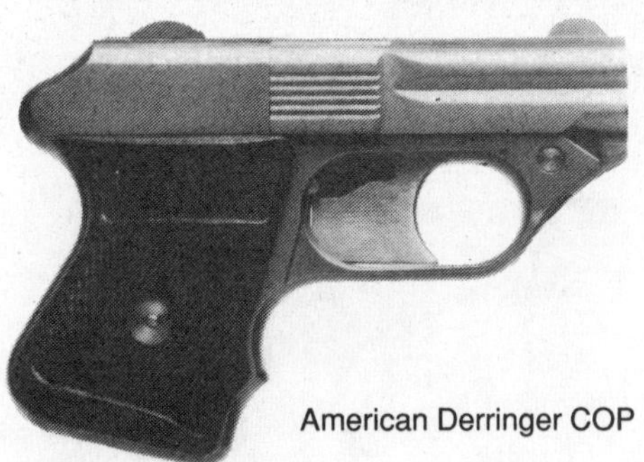

American Derringer COP

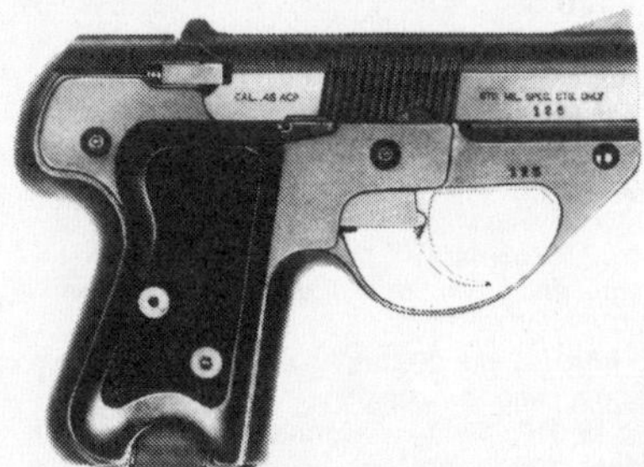

American Derringer Semmerling

American Derringer Texas Commemorative
A Model 1 Derringer with solid brass frame, stainless steel barrel and rosewood grips. Available in 32 H&R Mag., 38 Speical, 44-40 Win., or 45 Colt. Introduced 1987.
Price: 32 Mag. or 38 Spec. **$212.00**
Price: 44-40 or 45 Colt **$320.00**

AMERICAN DERRINGER MODEL 3
Caliber: 38 Special.
Barrel: 2.5".
Weight: 8.5 oz. **Length:** 4.9" overall.
Stocks: Rosewood.
Sights: Blade front.
Features: Made of stainless steel. Single shot with manual hammer block safety. Introduced 1985. From American Derringer Corp.
Price: **$120.00**

American Derringer Model 4
Similar to the Model 1 except has 4.1" barrel, overall length of 6", and weighs 16½ oz.; chambered for 3" 410-bore shotshells or 45 or 44 Magnum Colt. Can be had with 45-70 upper barrel and 3" 410-bore or 45 Colt bottom barrel. Made of stainless steel. Manual hammer block safety. Introduced 1985.
Price: 3" 410/45 Colt (either barrel) **$350.00**
Price: 3" 410/45 Colt or 45-70 (Alaskan Survival model) **$387.50**
Price: 44 Magnum with oversize grips **$422.00**

American Derringer Model 10 Lightweight
Similar to the Model 1 except frame is of aluminum, giving weight of 10 oz. Available in 45 Colt or 45 ACP only. Matte gray finish. Introduced 1989.
Price: 45 Colt **$320.00**
Price: 45 ACP **$250.00**
Price: Model 11 (38 Spec., aluminum bbls., wgt. 11 oz.) **$200.00**

AMERICAN DERRINGER DA 38 MODEL
Caliber: 9mm Para., 38 Spec., 357 Mag.
Barrel: 3".
Weight: 14.5 oz. **Length:** 4.8" overall.
Stocks: Rosewood, walnut or other hardwoods.
Sights: Fixed.
Features: Double-action only; two-shots. Manual safety. Made of satin-finished stainless steel and aluminum. Introduced 1989. From American Derringer Corp.
Price: 38 Spec. **$250.00**
Price: 9mm Para. **$260.00**
Price: 357 Mag. **$369.00**

AMERICAN DERRINGER COP 357 DERRINGER
Caliber: 38 Spec. or 357 Mag., 4-shot.
Barrel: 3.14".
Weight: 16 oz. **Length:** 5.53" overall.
Stocks: Rosewood.
Sights: Fixed.
Features: Double-action only. Four shots. Made of stainless steel. Introduced 1990. Made in U.S. by American Derringer Corp.
Price: **$325.00**

American Derringer Mini COP Derringer
Similar to the COP 357 except chambered for 22 WMR. Barrel length of 2.85", overall length of 4.95", weight is 16 oz. Double action with automatic hammer-block safety. Made of stainless steel. Grips of rosewood, walnut or other hardwoods. Introduced 1990. Made in U.S. by American Derringer Corp.
Price: **$250.00**

AMERICAN DERRINGER SEMMERLING LM-4
Caliber: 9mm Para., 7-shot magazine; 45 ACP, 5-shot magazine.
Barrel: 3.625".
Weight: 24 oz. **Length:** 5.2" overall.
Stocks: Checkered plastic on blued guns, rosewood on stainless guns.
Sights: Open, fixed.
Features: Manually-operated repeater. Height is 3.7", width is 1". Comes with manual, leather carrying case, spare stock screws, wrench. From American Derringer Corp.
Price: Blued **$1,750.00**
Price: Stainless steel **$1,875.00**

ANSCHUTZ EXEMPLAR BOLT-ACTION PISTOL

Caliber: 22 LR, 5-shot; 22 Hornet, 5-shot.
Barrel: 10", 14".
Weight: 3½ lbs. **Length:** 17" overall.
Stock: European walnut with stippled grip and forend.
Sights: Hooded front on ramp, open notch rear adjustable for windage and elevation.
Features: Uses Match 64 action with left-hand bolt; Anschutz #5091 two-stage trigger set at 9.85 oz. Receiver grooved for scope mounting; open sights easily removed. Introduced 1987. Imported from Germany by PSI.
Price: 22 LR **$459.00**
Price: 22 LR, left-hand **$472.00**
Price: 22 LR, 14" barrel **$472.00**
Price: 22 Hornet (no sights, 10" bbl.) **$822.00**

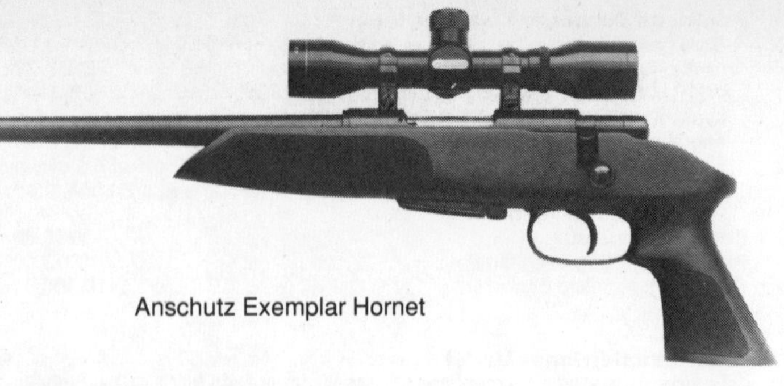

Anschutz Exemplar Hornet

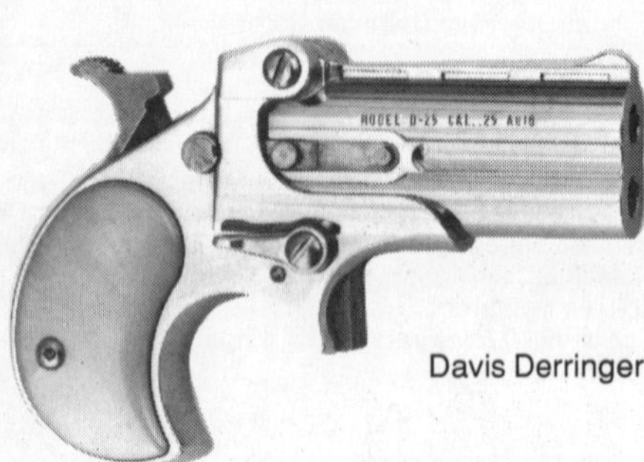

Davis Derringer

DAVIS DERRINGERS

Caliber: 22 LR, 22 WMR, 25 ACP, 32 ACP.
Barrel: 2.4".
Weight: 9.5 oz. **Length:** 4" overall.
Stocks: Laminated wood.
Sights: Blade front, fixed notch rear.
Features: Choice of black Teflon or chrome finish; spur trigger. Introduced 1986. Made in U.S. by Davis Industries.
Price: **$64.90**

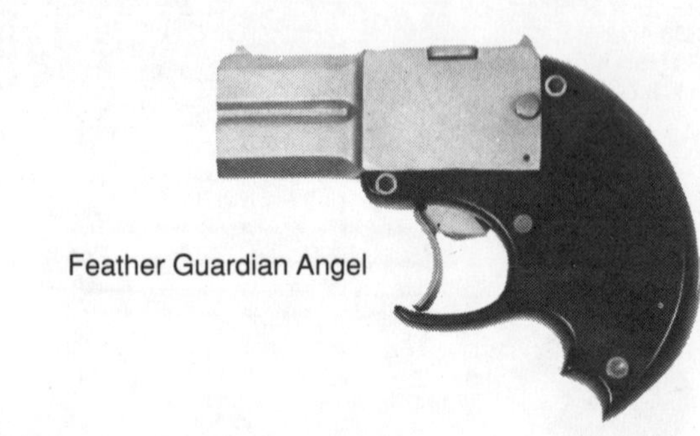

Feather Guardian Angel

FEATHER GUARDIAN ANGEL PISTOL

Caliber: 22 LR/22 WMR.
Barrel: 2".
Weight: 12 oz. **Length:** 5" overall.
Stocks: Black composition.
Sights: Fixed.
Features: Uses a pre-loaded two-shot drop-in "magazine." Stainless steel construction; matte finish. From Feather Industries. Introduced 1988.
Price: **$139.95**

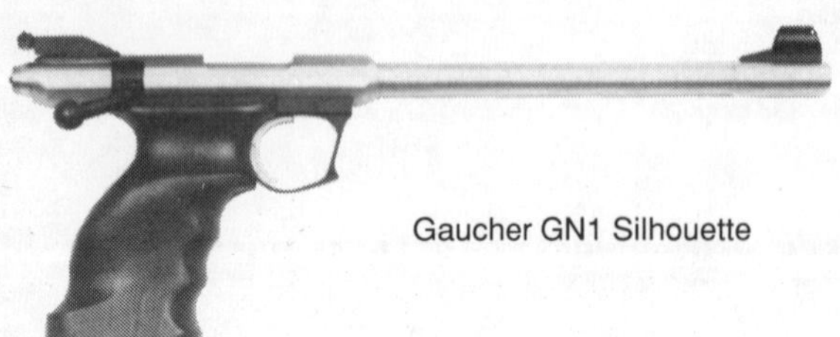

Gaucher GN1 Silhouette

GAUCHER GN1 SILHOUETTE PISTOL

Caliber: 22 LR, single shot.
Barrel: 10".
Weight: 2.4 lbs. **Length:** 15.5" overall.
Stock: European hardwood.
Sights: Blade front, open adjustable rear.
Features: Bolt action, adjustable trigger. Introduced 1990. Imported from France by Mandall Shooting Supplies.
Price: About **$290.00**

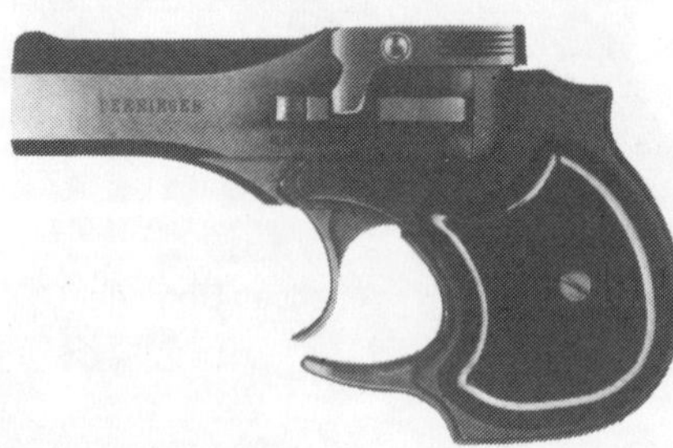

High Standard Derringer

HIGH STANDARD DERRINGER

Caliber: 22 LR, 22 WMR, 2-shot.
Barrel: 3.5".
Weight: 11 oz. **Length:** 5.12" overall.
Stocks: Black composition.
Sights: Fixed.
Features: Double action, dual extraction. Hammer-block safety. Blue finish. Introduced 1990. Made in U.S. by American Derringer Corp.
Price: **$169.95**

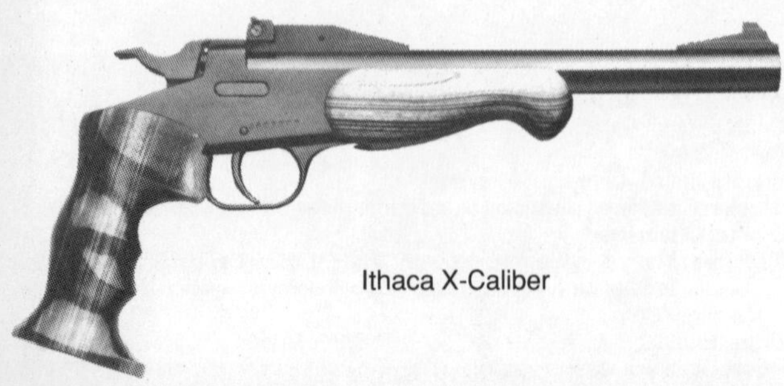

Ithaca X-Caliber

ITHACA X-CALIBER SINGLE SHOT

Caliber: 22 LR, 44 Mag.
Barrel: 10", 15".
Weight: 3¼ lbs. **Length:** 15" overall (10" barrel).
Stocks: Goncalo Alves grip and forend on Model 20; American walnut on Model 30.
Sights: Blade on ramp front; Model 20 has adjustable, removable target-type rear. Drilled and tapped for scope mounting.
Features: Dual firing pin for RF/CF use. Polished blue finish.
Price: 22 LR, 10", 44 Mag., 10" or 15" **$270.00**
Price: 22 LR/44 Mag. combo, 10" and 15" **$365.00**
Price: As above, both 10" barrels **$365.00**

Magnum Research SSP-91

MANDALL/CABANAS PISTOL
Caliber: 177, pellet or round ball; single shot.
Barrel: 9".
Weight: 51 oz. **Length:** 19" overall.
Stock: Smooth wood with thumbrest.
Sights: Blade front on ramp, open adjustable rear.
Features: Fires round ball or pellets with 22 blank cartridge. Automatic safety; muzzlebrake. Imported from Mexico by Mandall Shooting Supplies.
Price: **$125.00**

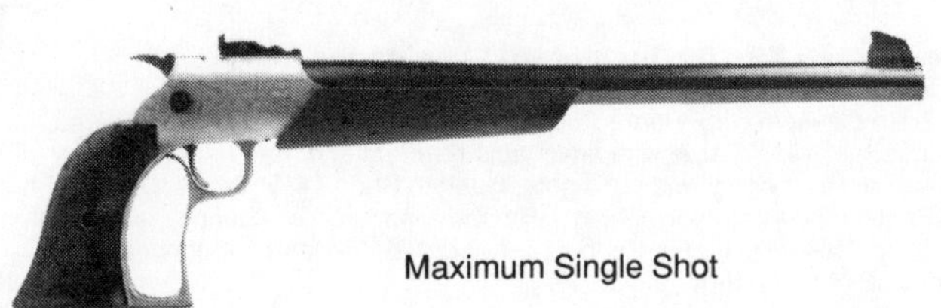
Maximum Single Shot

NEW ENGLAND FIREARMS SINGLE SHOT PISTOL
Caliber: 357 Mag., 357 Rem. Maximum, 44 Mag., 223, 30-30, 7-30 Waters, 35 Rem.
Barrel: 14".
Weight: 49 oz. (synthetic stock); 70 oz. (laminated wood). **Length:** 15⅛" overall.
Stocks: Synthetic or laminated wood.
Sights: Ramp front, adjustable rear.
Features: Rotary cannon-type action cocks on opening. Single stage trigger. Trigger and sliding thumb safeties. Matte blue finish. Made by Competitor Corp. From New England Firearms.
Price: . . . . **NA**

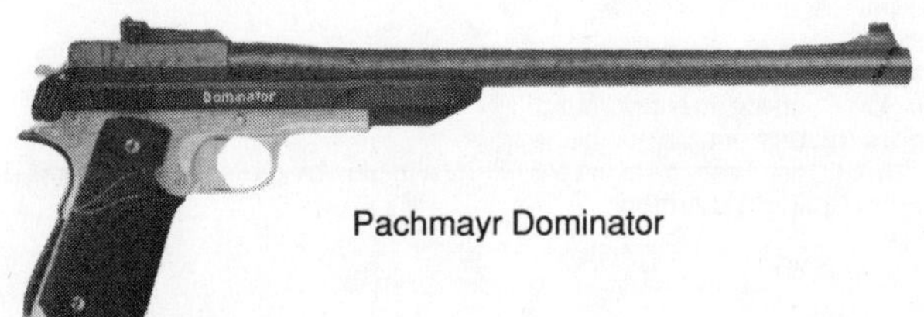

Pachmayr Dominator

RPM XL SINGLE SHOT PISTOL
Caliber: 22 LR, 22 WMR, 225 Win., 25 Rocket, 6.5 Rocket, 32 H&R Mag., 357 Max., 357 Mag., 30-30 Win., 30 Herrett, 357 Herrett, 41 Mag., 44 Mag., 454 Casull, 375 Win., 7mm UR, 7mm Merrill, 30 Merrill, 7mm Rocket, 270 Ren, 270 Rocket, 270 Max., 45-70.
Barrel: 8" slab, 10¾", 12", 14" bull; .450" wide vent. rib, matted to prevent glare.
Weight: About 60 oz. **Length:** 12¼" overall (10¾" bbl.).
Stocks: Smooth Goncalo with thumb and heel rest.
Sights: Front .100" blade, Millett rear adjustable for windage and elevation. Hooded front with interchangeable post optional.
Features: Polished blue finish, hard chrome optional. Barrel is drilled and tapped for scope mounting. Cocking indicator visible from rear of gun. Has spring-loaded barrel lock, positive hammer block thumb safety. Trigger adjustable for weight of pull and over-travel. For complete price list contact RPM.
Price: Regular ¾" frame, right-hand action **$750.00**
Price: As above, left-hand action **$775.00**
Price: Wide ⅞" frame, right-hand action **$800.00**
Price: Extra barrel, 8"-10¾" **$230.00**
Price: Extra barrel, 12"-14" **$300.00**

MAGNUM RESEARCH SSP-91 SINGLE SHOT PISTOL
Caliber: 22 LR, 22 WMR, 22 Hornet, 223, 22-250, 243, 6mm BR, 7mm BR, 7mm-08, 30-30, 308, 30-06, 357 Mag., 35 Rem., 358 Win., 44 Mag., 444 Marlin.
Barrel: 14", interchangable.
Weight: 4lbs., 2 oz. **Length:** 15" overall.
Stocks: Composition, with thumbrest.
Sights: None furnished; drilled and tapped for scope mounting and open sights. Open sights optional.
Features: Cannon-type rotating breech with spring-activated ejector. Ordnance steel with matte blue finish. Cross-bolt safety. External cocking lever on left side of gun. Introduced 1991. Made by Ordnance Technology, Inc. Available from Magnum Research, Inc.
Price: Complete pistol **$299.00**
Price: Barreled action only **$229.00**
Price: Scope base **$12.95**
Price: Adjustable open sights **$29.95**

MAXIMUM SINGLE SHOT PISTOL
Caliber: 22 LR, 22 Hornet, 22 BR, 223 Rem., 22-250, 6mm BR, 6mm-223, 243, 250 Savage, 6.5mm-35, 7mm TCU, 7mm BR, 7mm-35, 7mm INT-R, 7mm-08, 7mm Rocket, 7mm Super Mag., 30 Herrett, 30 Carbine, 308 Win., 7.62 x 39, 32-20, 357 Mag., 357 Maximum, 358 Win., 44 Mag.
Barrel: 8¾", 10½", 14".
Weight: 61 oz. (10½" bbl.); 78 oz. (14" bbl.). **Length:** 15", 18½" overall (with 10½" and 14" bbl., respectively).
Stocks: Smooth walnut stocks and forend.
Sights: Ramp front, fully adjustable open rear.
Features: Falling block action; drilled and tapped for M.O.A. scope mounts; integral grip frame/receiver; adjustable trigger; Douglas barrel (interchangeable); Armoloy finish. Introduced 1983. Made in U.S. by M.O.A. Corp.
Price: Armoloy receiver, blue barrel **$534.00**
Price: Armoloy receiver, stainless steel barrel **$584.00**
Price: Stainless receiver, blue barrel **$566.00**
Price: Stainless receiver, stainless barrel **$616.00**
Price: Extra blued barrel **$149.00**
Price: Extra stainless barrel **$202.00**
Price: Scope mount **$52.00**

NEW ADVANTAGE ARMS DERRINGER
Caliber: 22 LR, 22 WMR, 4-shot.
Barrel: 2½".
Weight: 15 oz. **Length:** 4½" overall.
Stocks: Smooth walnut.
Sights: Fixed.
Features: Double-action mechanism, four barrels, revolving firing pin. Rebounding hammer. Polished blue finish. Reintroduced 1989. From New Advantage Arms Corp.
Price: 22 LR **$199.00**
Price: 22 WMR **$199.00**

PACHMAYR DOMINATOR PISTOL
Caliber: 22 Hornet, 223, 7mm-06, 308, 35 Rem., 44 Mag., single shot.
Barrel: 10½" (44 Mag.), 14" all other calibers.
Weight: 4 lbs. (14" barrel). **Length:** 16" overall (14" barrel).
Stocks: Pachmayr Signature system.
Sights: Optional sights or drilled and tapped for scope mounting.
Features: Bolt-action pistol on 1911A1 frame. Comes as complete gun. Introduced 1988. From Pachmayr.
Price: Either barrel **$524.50**

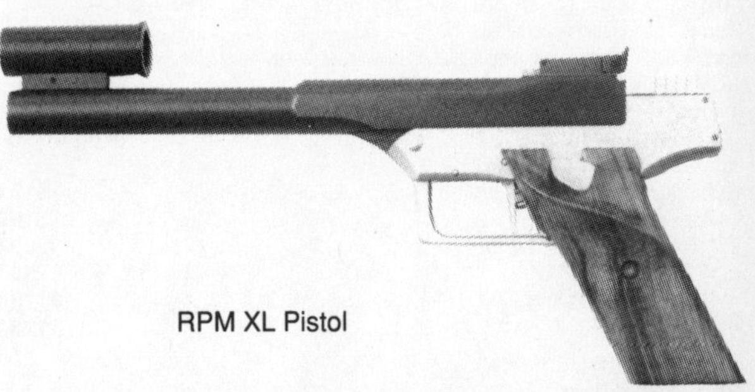
RPM XL Pistol

RANDALL BOLT-ACTION PISTOL
Caliber: 9mm shot, single shot.
Barrel: NA.
Weight: 2.4 lbs. **Length:** 16.5" overall.
Stock: European hardwood.
Sights: Bead front.
Features: Bolt action, blue finish. Introduced 1990. Imported from France by Mandall Shooting Supplies.
Price: **$225.00**

Remington XP-22R

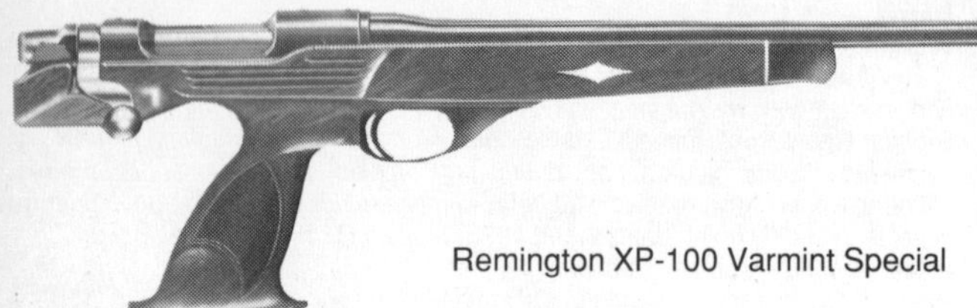
Remington XP-100 Varmint Special

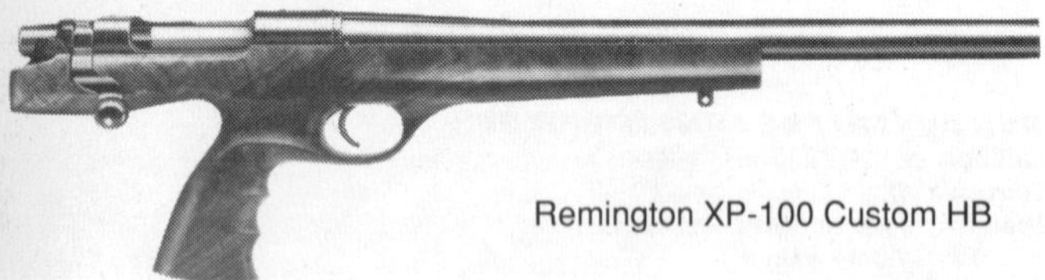
Remington XP-100 Custom HB

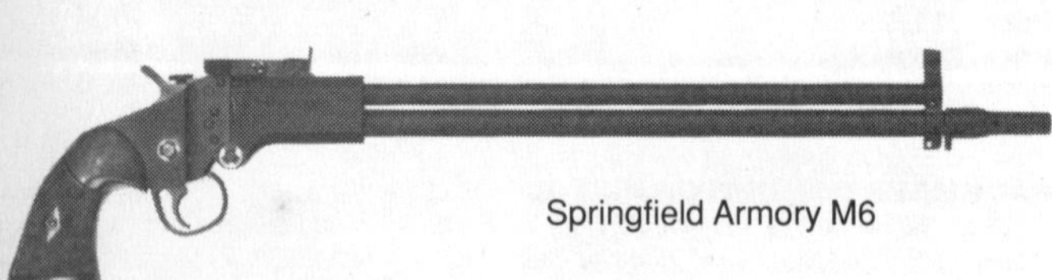
Springfield Armory M6

SPRINGFIELD ARMORY 1911A2 S.A.S.S. PISTOL
Caliber: 22 LR, 223, 243, 7mm BR, 7mm-08, 308, 357 Mag., 358 Win., 44 Mag., single shot.
Barrel: 10¾" or 14.9".
Weight: 4 lbs. 2 oz. (14.9" bbl.). **Length:** 17.2" overall (14.9" bbl.).
Stocks: Rubberized wraparound.
Sights: Blade on ramp front, fully adjustable open rear. Drilled and tapped for scope mounting.
Features: Uses standard 1911A1 frame with a break-open top half interchangeable barrel system. Available as complete gun or as conversion unit only (requires fitting). Introduced 1989.
Price: Complete pistol, 15" bbl. **$519.00**
Price: As above, 10¾" bbl. **$519.00**
Price: Conversion unit, 15" bbl. **$259.00**
Price: As above, 10¾" **$259.00**
Price: Interchangeable barrel, 15" **$128.70**
Price: As above, 10¾" **$128.70**

REMINGTON XP-22R BOLT-ACTION PISTOL
Caliber: 22 LR, 5-shot clip.
Barrel: 14½".
Weight: 4¼ lbs. **Length:** NA.
Stocks: Fiberglass reinforced with Du Pont Kevlar; rear-handled style.
Sights: None furnished; drilled and tapped for scope mounts and iron sights.
Features: Based on Model 541-T rifle action. Stock fitted with front and rear swivel studs. Introduced 1991. Available on special order from Remington Custom Shop.
Price: **$432.00**

REMINGTON XP-100 VARMINT SPECIAL
Caliber: 223 Rem., single shot.
Barrel: 14½".
Weight: 60 oz. **Length:** 21¼" overall.
Stock: Black nylon one-piece, checkered grip with white spacers.
Sights: Tapped for scope mount.
Features: Fits left or right hand, is shaped to fit fingers and heel of hand. Grooved trigger. Rotating thumb safety, cavity in forend permits insertion of up to five 38-cal. 130-gr. metal jacketed bullets to adjust weight and balance. Included is a black vinyl, zippered case.
Price: Including case, about **$418.00**

Remington XP-100 Custom HB Long Range Pistol
Similar to the XP-100 "Varmint Special" except chambered for 223 Rem., 7mm-08 Rem., 35 Rem., 250 Savage, 6mm BR, 7mm BR. Offered with standard 14½" barrel with adjustable rear leaf and front bead sights, or with heavy 15½" barrel without sights. Custom Shop 14½" barrel, Custom Shop English walnut stock in right- or left-hand configuration. Action tuned in Custom Shop. Weight is under 4½ lbs. (heavy barrel, 5½ lbs.). Introduced 1986.
Price: Right- or left-hand **$943.00**

Remington XP-100R KS Repeater Pistol
Similar to the Custom Long Range Pistol except chambered for 223 Rem., 7mm-08 Rem., 250 Savage, 350 Rem. Mag., and 35 Rem., and has a blind magazine holding 5 rounds (7mm-08 and 35), or 6 (223 Rem.). Comes with a rear-handle, synthetic stock of Du Pont Kevlar to eliminate the transfer bar between the forward trigger and rear trigger assembly. Fitted with front and rear sling swivel studs. Has standard-weight 14½" barrel with adjustable leaf rear sight, bead front. The receiver is drilled and tapped for scope mounts. Weight is about 4½ lbs. Introduced 1990. From Remington Custom Shop.
Price: **$798.00**

SPRINGFIELD ARMORY M6 PISTOL
Caliber: 22 rimfire/ 45 Colt.
Barrel: 16".
Weight: 3 lbs.
Stocks: Rubberized wraparound.
Sights: Blade front, adjustable rear.
Features: Pistol version of the M6 rifle. Matte blue/black finish. Introduced 1991. From Springfield Armory.
Price: . . . . **NA**

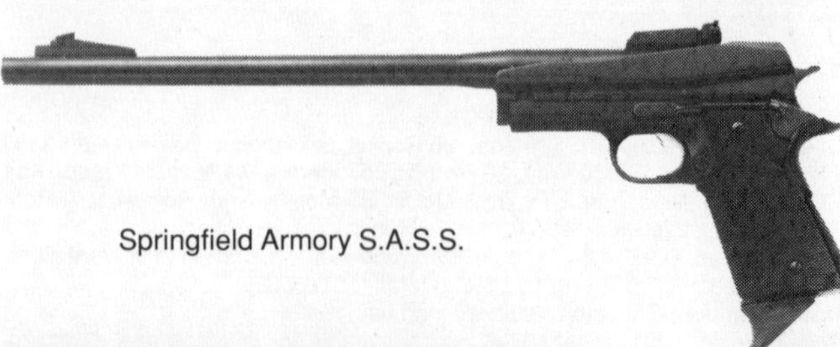
Springfield Armory S.A.S.S.

TEXAS LONGHORN "THE JEZEBEL" PISTOL
Caliber: 22 Short, Long, Long Rifle, single shot.
Barrel: 6".
Weight: 15 oz. **Length:** 8" overall.
Stocks: One-piece fancy walnut grip (right- or left-hand), walnut forend.
Sights: Bead front, fixed rear.
Features: Handmade gun. Top-break action; all stainless steel; automatic hammer block safety; music wire coil springs. Barrel is half-round, half-octagon. Announced 1986. From Texas Longhorn Arms.
Price: About **$250.00**

CAUTION: PRICES CHANGE, CHECK AT GUNSHOP.

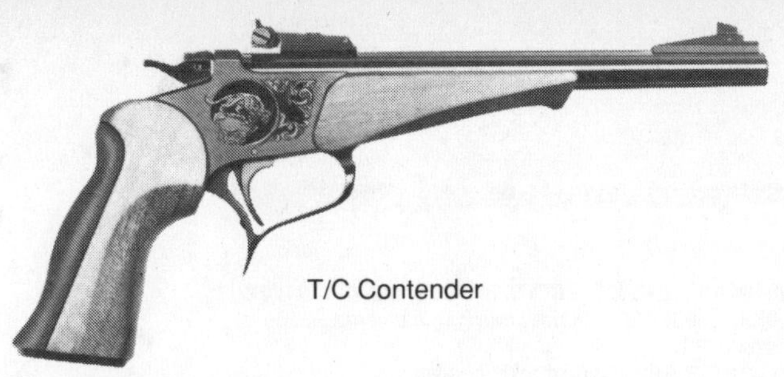
T/C Contender

THOMPSON/CENTER CONTENDER
Caliber: 7mm TCU, 30-30 Win., 22 LR, 22 WMR, 22 Hornet, 223 Rem., 270 Ren, 7-30 Waters, 32-20 Win., 357 Mag., 357 Rem. Max., 44 Mag., 10mm Auto, 445 Super Mag., 45/410, single shot.
Barrel: 10", tapered octagon, bull barrel and vent. rib.
Weight: 43 oz. (10" bbl.). **Length:** 13¼" (10" bbl.).
Stocks: T/C "Competitor Grip." Right or left hand.
Sights: Under-cut blade ramp front, rear adjustable for windage and elevation.
Features: Break-open action with automatic safety. Single-action only. Interchangeable bbls., both caliber (rim & centerfire), and length. Drilled and tapped for scope. Engraved frame. See T/C catalog for exact barrel/caliber availability.
Price: Blued (rimfire cals.) **$385.00**
Price: Blued (centerfire cals.) **$385.00**
Price: Extra bbls. (standard octagon) **$175.00**
Price: 45/410, internal choke bbl. **$195.00**

Thompson/Center Contender Hunter Package
Package contains the Contender pistol in 223, 7-30 Waters, 30-30, 357 Rem. Maximum, 35 Rem., 44 Mag. or 45-70 with 12" barrel with T/C's Muzzle Tamer, a 2.5x Recoil Proof Long Eye Relief scope with lighted reticle, q.d. sling swivels with a nylon carrying sling. Comes with a suede leather case with foam padding and fleece lining. Introduced 1990. From Thompson/Center Arms.
Price: **$665.00**

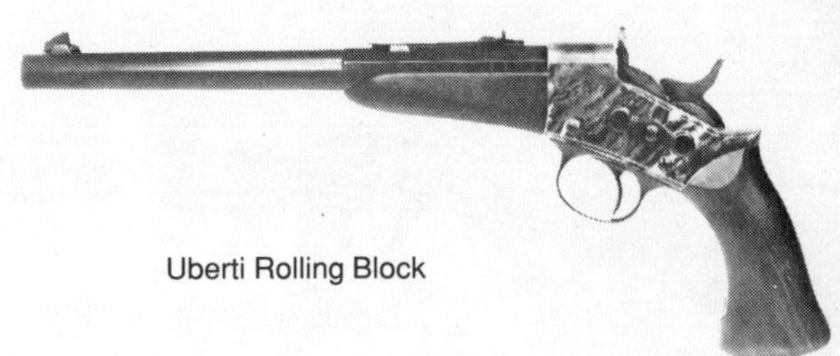
Uberti Rolling Block

UBERTI ROLLING BLOCK TARGET PISTOL
Caliber: 22 LR, 22 WMR, 22 Hornet, 357 Mag., single shot.
Barrel: 9⅞", half-round, half-octagon.
Weight: 44 oz. **Length:** 14" overall.
Stocks: Walnut grip and forend.
Sights: Blade front, fully adjustable rear.
Features: Replica of the 1871 rolling block target pistol. Brass trigger guard, color case-hardened frame, blue barrel. Imported by Uberti USA.
Price: **$370.00**

ULTRA LIGHT ARMS MODEL 20 REB HUNTER'S PISTOL
Caliber: 22-250 thru 308 Win. standard. Most silhouette calibers and others on request. 5-shot magazine.
Barrel: 14", Douglas No. 3.
Weight: 4 lbs.
Stock: Composite Kevlar, graphite reinforced. Du Pont Imron paint in green, brown, black and camo.
Sights: None furnished. Scope mount included.
Features: Timney adjustable trigger; two-position, three-function safety; benchrest quality action; matte or bright stock and metal finish; right- or left-hand action. Shipped in hard case. Introduced 1987. From Ultra Light Arms.
Price: **$1,500.00**

Ultra Light Model 20

CENTERFIRE RIFLES—AUTOLOADERS

Includes models for hunting, adaptable to and suitable for certain competition.

A.A. ARMS AR9 SEMI-AUTOMATIC RIFLE
Caliber: 9mm Para., 20-shot magazine.
Barrel: 16¼".
Weight: 6.5 lbs. **Length:** 33" overall.
Stock: Folding buttstock, checkered plastic grip.
Sights: Adjustable post front in ring, fixed open rear.
Features: Fires from closed bolt; lever safety blocks trigger and sear; vented barrel shroud. Matte blue/black or nickel finish. Introduced 1991. Made in U.S. by A.A. Arms, Inc.
Price: Blue/black finish **$299.00**
Price: Nickel finish **$334.00**

A.A. Arms AR9

Thompson M1

AUTO-ORDNANCE 27 A-1 THOMPSON
Caliber: 45 ACP, 30-shot magazine.
Barrel: 16".
Weight: 11½ lbs. **Length:** About 42" overall (Deluxe).
Stock: Walnut stock and vertical forend.
Sights: Blade front, open rear adjustable for windage.
Features: Recreation of Thompson Model 1927. Semi-auto only. Deluxe model has finned barrel, adjustable rear sight and compensator; Standard model has plain barrel and military sight. From Auto-Ordnance Corp.
Price: Deluxe **$735.00**
Price: 1927A5 Pistol (M27A1 without stock; wgt. 7 lbs.) **$704.00**
Price: Lightweight model **$707.00**

Auto-Ordnance Thompson M1
Similar to the Model 27 A-1 except is in the M-1 configuration with side cocking knob, horizontal forend, smooth unfinned barrel, sling swivels on butt and forend. Matte black finish. Introduced 1985.
Price: **$712.50**

Barrett Model 82 A-1

BARRETT LIGHT-FIFTY MODEL 82 A-1 AUTO
Caliber: 50 BMG, 10-shot detachable box magazine.
Barrel: 29".
Weight: 28.5 lbs. **Length:** 57" overall.
Stock: Composition with Sorbothane recoil pad.
Sights: Open, iron and 12x scope.
Features: Semi-automatic, recoil operated with recoiling barrel. Three-lug locking bolt; muzzlebrake. Self-leveling bipod. Fires same 50-cal. ammunition as the M2HB machinegun. Introduced 1985. From Barrett Firearms.
Price: From **$6,195.00**

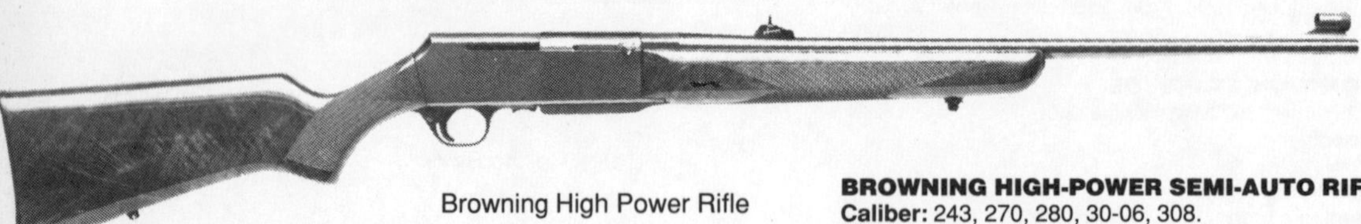

Browning High Power Rifle

BROWNING HIGH-POWER SEMI-AUTO RIFLE
Caliber: 243, 270, 280, 30-06, 308.
Barrel: 22" round tapered.
Weight: 7⅜ lbs. **Length:** 43" overall.
Stock: French walnut p.g. stock and forend, hand checkered.
Sights: Adj. folding-leaf rear, gold bead on hooded ramp front, or no sights.
Features: Detachable 4-round magazine. Receiver tapped for scope mounts. Trigger pull 3½ lbs. Imported from Belgium by Browning.
Price: Grade 1, with sights **$632.95**
Price: Grade 1, no sights **$616.95**

Browning Magnum Semi-Auto Rifle
Same as the standard caliber model, except weighs 8⅜ lbs., 45" overall, 24" bbl., 3-round mag. Cals. 7mm Mag., 300 Win. Mag., 338 Win. Mag.
Price: Grade 1, with sights **$679.95**
Price: Grade 1, no sights **$663.95**

CALICO MODEL M-900 CARBINE
Caliber: 9mm Para., 50- or 100-shot magazine.
Barrel: 16.1".
Weight: 3.7 lbs. (empty). **Length:** 28½" overall (stock collapsed).
Stock: Sliding steel buttstock.
Sights: Post front adjustable for windage and elevation, fixed notch rear.
Feature: Helical feed 50- or 100-shot magazine. Ambidextrous safety, static cocking handle. Retarded blowback action. Glass-filled polymer grip. Introduced 1989. From Calico.
Price: **$628.90**

Calico Model M-900

Calico Model M-951 Tactical Carbine
Similar to the M-900 Carbine except has an adjustable forward grip, long compensator, and 16.1" barrel. 9mm Para., 50- or 100-shot magazine. Introduced 1990. Made in U.S. by Calico.
Price: **$675.90**
Price: M-951-S (as above except fixed buttstock) **$689.90**

Calico Model M-951

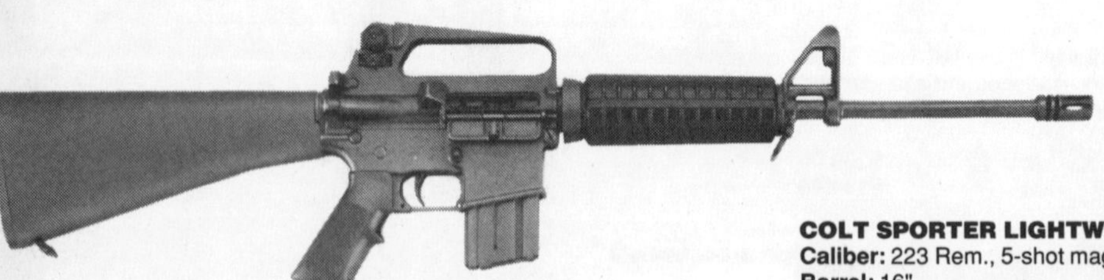

Colt Sporter

COLT SPORTER LIGHTWEIGHT RIFLE
Caliber: 223 Rem., 5-shot magazine.
Barrel: 16".
Weight: 6.7 lbs. **Length:** 34.5" overall extended.
Stock: Composition stock, grip, forend.
Sights: Post front, rear adjustable for windage and elevation.
Features: 5-round detachable box magazine, flash suppressor, sling swivels. Forward bolt assist included. Introduced 1991.
Price: **$859.95**

COLT SPORTER TARGET MODEL RIFLE
Caliber: 223 Rem., 5-shot magazine.
Barrel: 20".
Weight: 7.5 lbs. **Length:** 39" overall.
Stock: Composition stock, grip, forend.
Sights: Post front, aperture rear adjustable for windage and elevation.
Features: Five-round detachable box magazine, standard-weight barrel, flash suppressor, sling swivels. Has forward bolt assist. Military matte black finish. Model introduced 1991.
Price: **$879.95**

Colt Sporter Match Delta HBAR Rifle
Similar to the Sporter Target except has standard stock, heavy barrel, is refined and inspected by the Colt Custom Shop. Comes with a 3-9x rubber armored scope and removable cheekpiece, adjustable scope mount, black leather military-style sling, cleaning kit, and hard carrying case. Pistol grip has Delta medallion. Introduced 1987.
Price: **$1,459.95**

CAUTION: PRICES CHANGE, CHECK AT GUNSHOP.

Colt Match HBAR

Colt Sporter Match HBAR Rifle
Similar to the Sporter Match Delta HBAR except has heavy barrel, 800-meter M-16A2 rear sight adjustable for windage and elevation. Introduced 1991.
Price: **$919.95**

CLARIDGE HI-TEC C CARBINE
Caliber: 9mm Para., 18-shot, 45 ACP, 10-shot.
Barrel: 16.1".
Weight: 4 lbs., 9 oz. **Length:** 31.7" overall.
Stock: Walnut.
Sights: Adjustable post front in ring, open rear adjustable for windage.
Features: Telescoping bolt, floating firing pin. Safety locks the firing pin. Sight radius of 20.1". Accepts same magazines as Claridge Hi-Tec pistols. Can be equipped with scope or Aimpoint sight. Made in U.S. From Claridge Hi-Tec, Inc.
Price: **$895.00**

D MAX AUTO CARBINE
Caliber: 9mm Para., 10mm Auto, 40 S&W, 45 ACP 30-shot magazine.
Barrel: 16.25".
Weight: About 7.5 lbs. **Length:** 38.5".
Stock: Walnut butt, grip, forend.
Sights: Post front, open rear adjustable for windage and elevation. Aperture rear optional.
Features: Blowback semi-auto fires from closed bolt; trigger-block safety. Side-feed magazine. Integral optical sight base. Max-Coat finish. Made in U.S. by D Max Industries.
Price: **$579.00**

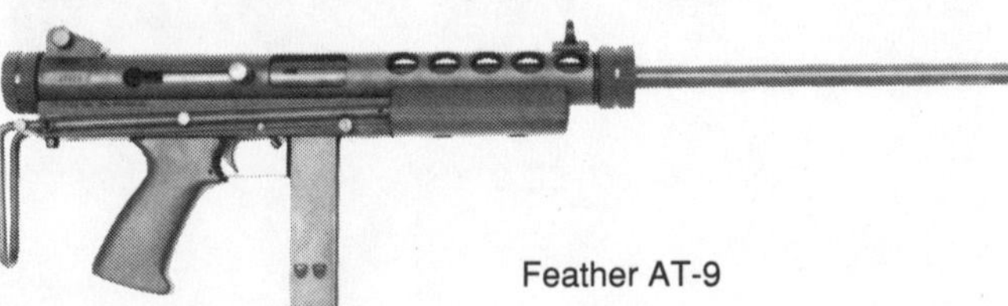
Feather AT-9

FEATHER AT-9 SEMI-AUTO CARBINE
Caliber: 9mm Para., 25-shot magazine.
Barrel: 17".
Weight: 5 lbs. **Length:** 35" overall (stock extended); 26½" (closed).
Stock: Telescoping wire, composition pistol grip.
Sights: Hooded post front, adjustable aperture rear.
Features: Semi-auto only. Matte black finish. From Feather Industries. Announced 1988.
Price: **$499.95**

FEDERAL XC-900/XC-450 AUTO CARBINES
Caliber: 9mm Para., 32-shot magazine; 45 ACP.
Barrel: 16.5" (with flash hider).
Weight: 8 lbs. **Length:** 34½" overall.
Stock: Detachable tube steel; adjustable stock optional.
Sights: Hooded post front, peep rear adjustable for windage and elevation.
Features: Quick takedown for transport, storage. All hell-arc welded steel construction. Made in U.S. by Federal Engineering Corp.
Price: Complete package contains gun, case, extra magazine, sling and q.d. swivels, receiver cap **$636.00**

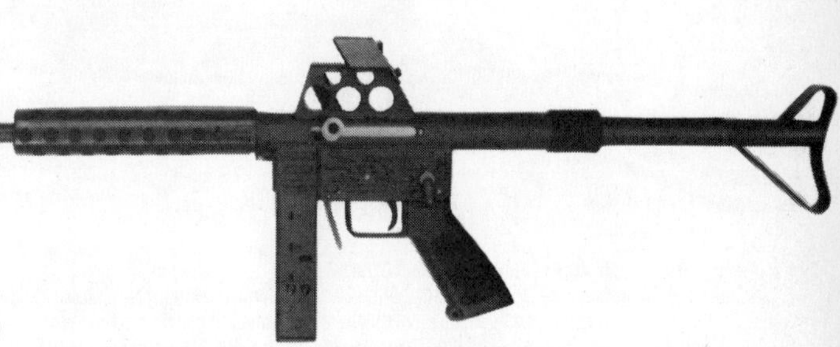
Federal XC-900/XC-450

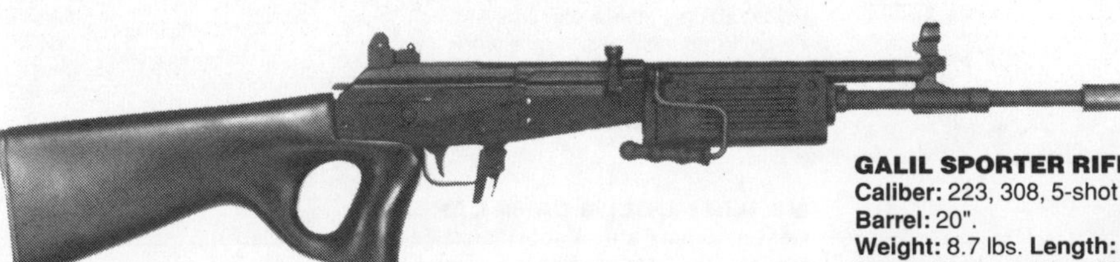
Galil Sporter

GALIL SPORTER RIFLE
Caliber: 223, 308, 5-shot magazine.
Barrel: 20".
Weight: 8.7 lbs. **Length:** 40.5" overall (223).
Stock: Hardwood thumbhole.
Sights: Post front, flip-type adjustable rear.
Features: Black-finished wood and metal. Comes with 5-shot magazine. Introduced 1991. From Springfield Armory.
Price: **$1,423.00**

Heckler & Koch HK-91

HECKLER & KOCH HK-91 AUTO RIFLE
Caliber: 308 Win., 5- or 20-shot magazine.
Barrel: 17.71".
Weight: 9½ lbs. **Length:** 40¼" overall.
Stock: Black high-impact plastic.
Sights: Post front, aperture rear adjustable for windage and elevation.
Features: Delayed roller-lock action. Sporting version of German service rifle. Takes special H&K clamp scope mount. Imported from Germany by Heckler & Koch, Inc. **Law enforcement sales only.**
Price: HK-91 A-2 with plastic stock **$999.00**
Price: HK-91 A-3 with retractable metal stock **$1,199.00**
Price: HK-91/94 scope mount with 1" rings **$357.00**

Heckler & Koch HK-93 Auto Rifle
Similar to HK-91 except in 223 cal., 16.13" barrel, overall length of 35½", weighs 7¾ lbs. Same stock, forend. **Law enforcement sales only.**
Price: HK-93 A-2 with plastic stock **$999.00**
Price: HK-93 A-3 with retractable metal stock **$1,199.00**

Heckler & Koch HK-94

HECKLER & KOCH HK-94 AUTO-CARBINE

Caliber: 9mm Para., 15-shot magazine.
Barrel: 16".
Weight: 6½ lbs. (fixed stock). **Length:** 34¾" overall.
Stock: High-impact plastic butt and forend or retractable metal stock.
Sights: Hooded post front, aperture rear adjustable for windage and elevation.
Features: Delayed roller-locked action; accepts H&K quick-detachable scope mount. Introduced 1983. Imported from Germany by Heckler & Koch, Inc. **Law enforcement sales only.**
Price: HK-94-A2 (fixed stock) **$999.00**
Price: HK-94-A3 (retractable metal stock) **$1,199.00**
Price: 30-shot magazine **$36.00**
Price: Clamp to hold two magazines **$30.00**

Heckler & Koch SR-9

HECKLER & KOCH SR-9 RIFLE

Caliber: 308 Win., 5-shot magazine.
Barrel: 19.7", bull.
Weight: 11 lbs. **Length:** 42.4" overall.
Stock: Kevlar reinforced fiberglass with thumbhole; wood grain finish.
Sights: Post front, aperture rear adjustable for windage and elevation.
Features: A redesigned version of the HK91 rifle. Comes standard with bull barrel with polygonal rifling. Uses HK clawlock scope mounts. Introduced 1990. Imported from Germany by Heckler & Koch, Inc.
Price: **$1,299.00**

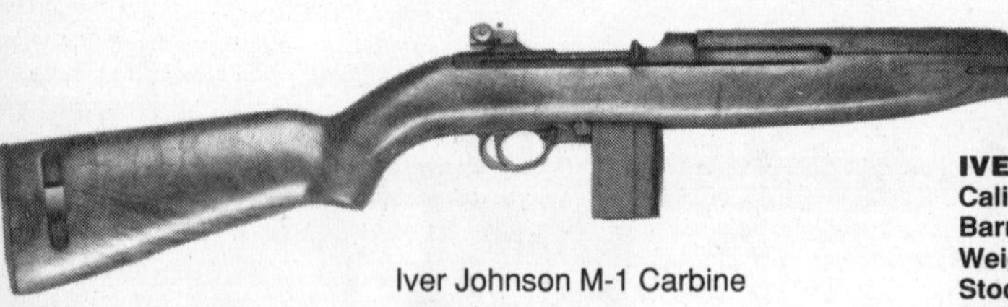

Iver Johnson M-1 Carbine

Iver Johnson 50th Anniversary M-1Carbine

Same as the standard Iver Johnson 30-caliber M-1 Carbine except has deluxe walnut stock with red, white and blue circular enameled American flag embedded in the stock, and gold-filled roll-engraving with the words "50th Anniversary 1941-1991" on the slide. Parkerized finish. Introduced 1991. From Iver Johnson Arms.
Price: **$384.95**

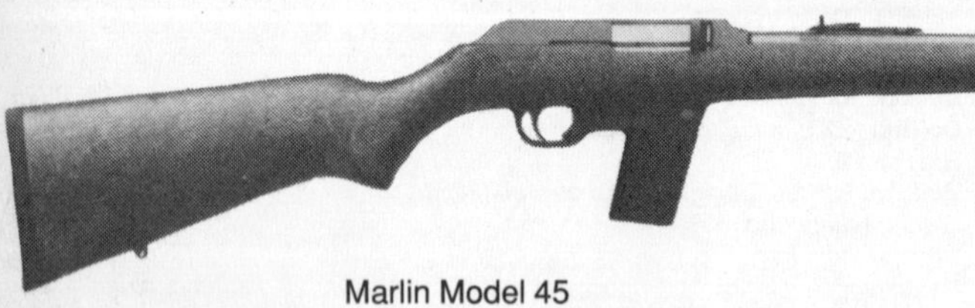

Marlin Model 45

Marlin Model 45 Carbine

Similar to the Model 9 except chambered for 45 ACP, 7-shot magazine. Introduced 1986.
Price: **$346.95**

OLYMPIC ARMS CAR SERIES CARBINES

Caliber: 223, 30-shot; 9mm Para., 34-shot; 45 ACP, 16-shot; 40 S&W, 20-shot; 7.62x39mm, 5-shot.
Barrel: 16".
Weight: 6½ lbs. **Length:** 35" overall (stock extended).
Stock: Telescoping butt.
Sights: Post front, rear adjustable for windage and elevation.
Features: Based on the AR-15 rifle. Has A2 Stowaway pistol grip. Introduced 1975. Made in U.S. by Olympic Arms, Inc.
Price: CAR-15, 223 caliber **$639.95**
Price: CAR-9, 9mm Para. **$709.95**
Price: CAR-45, 45 ACP **$718.95**
Price: CAR-40, 40 S&W **$718.95**
Price: CAR-310, 7.62x39 . . . . **$687.95**

IVER JOHNSON M-1 CARBINE

Caliber: 30 U.S. Carbine, or 9mm Para.
Barrel: 18" four-groove.
Weight: 6½ lbs. **Length:** 35½" overall.
Stock: Glossy-finished hardwood or walnut; or collapsible wire.
Sights: Click-adjustable peep rear.
Features: Gas-operated semi-auto carbine. 15-shot detachable magazine. Made in U.S.A.
Price: 30 cal., Parkerized finish, hardwood stock, metal handguard . **$349.95**
Price: 30 cal., Parkerized finish, walnut stock and handguard **$384.95**
Price: 9mm, hardwood stock, metal handguard **$365.00**
Price: 9mm, walnut stock and handguard **$399.00**
Price: 30 cal., collapsible wire stock **$443.00**
Price: 9mm, collapsible wire stock **$448.95**

MARLIN MODEL 9 CAMP CARBINE

Caliber: 9mm Para., 4-shot magazine (12-shot available).
Barrel: 16½", Micro-Groove® rifling.
Weight: 6¾ lbs. **Length:** 35½" overall.
Stock: Walnut-finished hardwood; rubber buttpad; Mar-Shield® finish; swivel studs.
Sights: Ramp front with orange post, cutaway Wide-Scan™ hood, adjustable open rear.
Features: Manual bolt hold-open; Garand-type safety, magazine safety; loaded chamber indicator; receiver drilled, tapped for scope mounting. Introduced 1985.
Price: **$346.95**
Price: Model 9N (nickel-Teflon finish) **$390.95**

Consult our Directory pages for the location of firms mentioned.

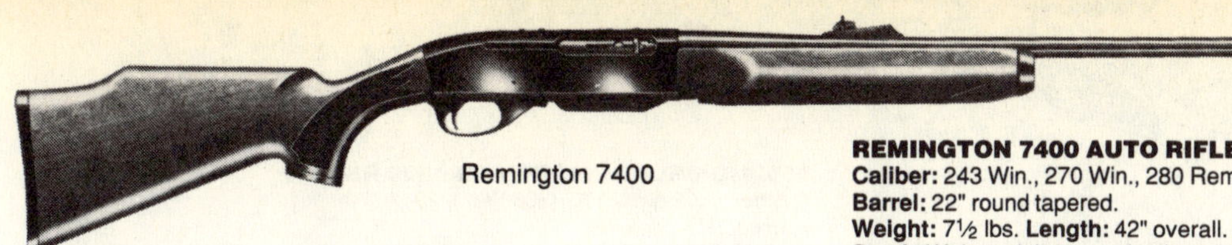

Remington 7400

REMINGTON 7400 AUTO RIFLE

Caliber: 243 Win., 270 Win., 280 Rem., 308 Win. and 30-06, 4-shot magazine.
Barrel: 22" round tapered.
Weight: 7½ lbs. **Length:** 42" overall.
Stock: Walnut, deluxe cut checkered p.g. and forend. Satin or high-gloss finish.
Sights: Gold bead front sight on ramp; step rear sight with windage adjustable.
Features: Redesigned and improved version of the Model 742. Positive cross-bolt safety. Receiver tapped for scope mount. 4-shot clip mag. Introduced 1981.
Price: About $501.00
Price: Carbine (18½" bbl., 30-06 only) $501.00

Remington 7400 175th Anniversary Rifle

Same as the standard Model 7400 except receiver is engraved with Remington's 175th anniversary scroll design with an American eagle, high-gloss finish walnut stock with deep-cut checkering. Available in 30-06 only. Introduced 1991.
Price: $515.00

Ruger Mini-14/5R

RUGER MINI-14/5R RANCH RIFLE

Caliber: 223 Rem., 5-shot detachable box magazine.
Barrel: 18½".
Weight: 6.4 lbs. **Length:** 37¼" overall.
Stock: American hardwood, steel reinforced.
Sights: Ramp front, fully adjustable rear.
Features: Fixed piston gas-operated, positive primary extraction. New buffer system, redesigned ejector system. Ruger S100RH scope rings included. 20-, 30-shot magazine available to police departments and government agencies only.
Price: Mini-14/5R, blued $504.50
Price: K-Mini-14/5R, stainless $552.50
Price: Mini-14/5, blued, no scope rings $468.00
Price: K-Mini-14/5, stainless, no scope rings $516.00

Ruger Mini Thirty Rifle

Similar to the Mini-14 Ranch Rifle except modified to chamber the 7.62x39 Russian service round. Weight is about 7 lbs., 3 oz. Has 6-groove barrel with 1-10" twist, Ruger Integral Scope Mount bases and folding peep rear sight. Detachable 5-shot staggered box magazine. Blued finish. Introduced 1987.
Price: Blue $504.50
Price: Stainless $552.50

SPRINGFIELD ARMORY BM-59

Caliber: 7.62mm NATO (308 Win.), 20-shot box magazine.
Barrel: 19.3".
Weight: 9¼ lbs. **Length:** 43.7" overall.
Stock: Walnut, with trapped rubber buttpad.
Sights: Military square blade front, click adjustable peep rear.
Features: Full military-dress Italian service rifle. Available in selective fire or semi-auto only. Refined version of the M-1 Garand. Accessories available include: folding Alpine stock, muzzlebrake/flash suppressor/grenade launcher combo, bipod, winter trigger, grenade launcher sights, bayonet, oiler. Extremely limited quantities. Introduced 1981.
Price: Standard Italian model, about $1,950.00
Price: Alpine model, about $2,275.00
Price: Alpine Paratrooper model, about $2,275.00
Price: Nigerian Mark IV model, about $2,340.00

Springfield DR-200

SPRINGFIELD ARMORY DR-200 SPORTER RIFLE

Caliber: 223, 5-shot magazine.
Barrel: 18.3".
Weight: 7.5 lbs. **Length:** NA.
Stock: Walnut thumbhole.
Sights: Post front, adjustable aperture rear.
Features: Matte blue finish. Introduced 1991. Imported from Korea by Springfield Armory.
Price: $687.00

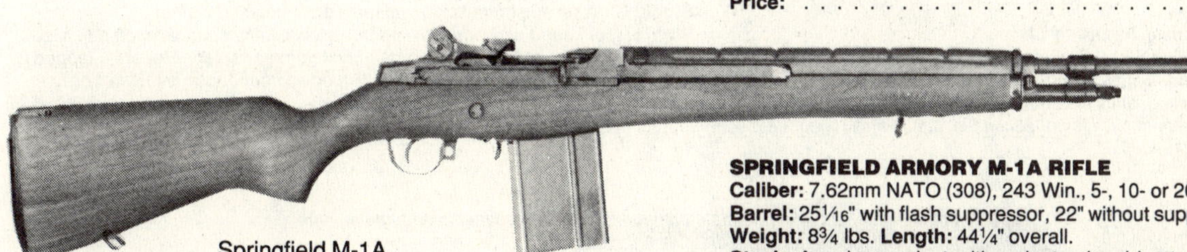

Springfield M-1A

SPRINGFIELD ARMORY M-1A RIFLE

Caliber: 7.62mm NATO (308), 243 Win., 5-, 10- or 20-shot box magazine.
Barrel: 25$\frac{1}{16}$" with flash suppressor, 22" without suppressor.
Weight: 8¾ lbs. **Length:** 44¼" overall.
Stock: American walnut with walnut colored heat-resistant fiberglass handguard. Matching walnut handguard available. Also available with fiberglass stock.
Sights: Military, square blade front, full click-adjustable aperture rear.
Features: Commercial equivalent of the U.S. M-14 service rifle with no provision for automatic firing. From Springfield Armory. Military accessories available including 3x-9x56 ART scope and mount. Optional accurizing packages available.
Price: Standard M-1A rifle, about $1,078.00
Price: National Match about $1,269.00
Price: Super Match (heavy premium barrel) about $1,689.00
Price: M1A-A1 Bush Rifle, walnut stock, about $1,143.00

SPRINGFIELD ARMORY SAR-8 SPORTER RIFLE

Caliber: 308 Win., 20-shot magazine.
Barrel: 18".
Weight: 8.7 lbs. **Length:** 40.3" overall.
Stock: Black or green composition forend, wood thumbhole butt.
Sights: Protected post front, rotary-style adjustable rear.
Features: Delayed roller-lock action, fluted chamber; matte black finish. Introduced 1990. From Springfield Armory.
Price: $1,164.00

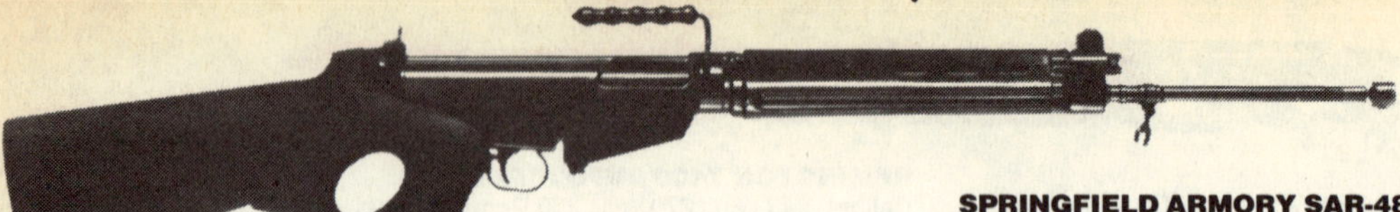
Springfield SAR-4800

STEYR A.U.G. AUTOLOADING RIFLE

Caliber: 223 Rem.
Barrel: 20".
Weight: 8½ lbs. **Length:** 31" overall.
Stock: Synthetic, green. One-piece moulding houses receiver group, hammer mechanism and magazine.
Sights: 1.5x scope only; scope and mount form the carrying handle.
Features: Semi-automatic, gas-operated action; can be converted to suit right- or left-handed shooters, including ejection port. Transparent 30- or 42-shot magazines. Folding vertical front grip. Introduced 1983. Imported from Austria by Gun South, Inc. **Available on limited basis only to law enforcement officers.**
Price: Right- or left-handed model **$1,375.00**

Uzi Carbine

SPRINGFIELD ARMORY SAR-4800 RIFLE

Caliber: 7.62mm NATO (308 Win.), 20-shot magazine.
Barrel: 21".
Weight: 9.5 lbs. **Length:** 43.3" overall.
Stock: Fiberglass forend, wood thumbhole butt.
Sights: Protected post, adjustable peep rear.
Features: New production. Introduced 1990. Optional accurizing packages available. From Springfield Armory.
Price: Standard Sporter model **$1,286.00**
Price: "Bush" Sporter rifle, 18" barrel **$1,286.00**

WILKINSON TERRY CARBINE

Caliber: 9mm Para., 31-shot magazine.
Barrel: 16³⁄₁₆".
Weight: 6 lbs., 3 oz. **Length:** 30" overall.
Stock: Maple stock and forend.
Sights: Protected post front, aperture rear.
Features: Semi-automatic blowback action fires from a closed breech. Bolt-type safety and magazine catch. Ejection port has automatic trap door. Receiver equipped with dovetail for scope mounting. Made in U.S. From Wilkinson Arms.
Price: **$485.92**

UZI CARBINE

Caliber: 9mm Para.
Barrel: 16.1".
Weight: 8.4 lbs. **Length:** 24.4" overall (stock folded).
Stock: Folding metal. Wood stock available as an accessory.
Sights: Post-type front, "L" flip-type rear adjustable for 100 meters and 200 meters. Both click-adjustable for windage and elevation.
Features: Adapted to meet BATF regulations, this semi-auto has the same qualities as the famous submachine gun. Made by Israel Military Industries. Comes in moulded carrying case with sling, magazine, sight adjustment key. From Springfield Armory.
Price: . . . . **P.O.R.**

CENTERFIRE RIFLES—LEVER & SLIDE

Both classic arms and recent designs in American-style repeaters for sport and field shooting.

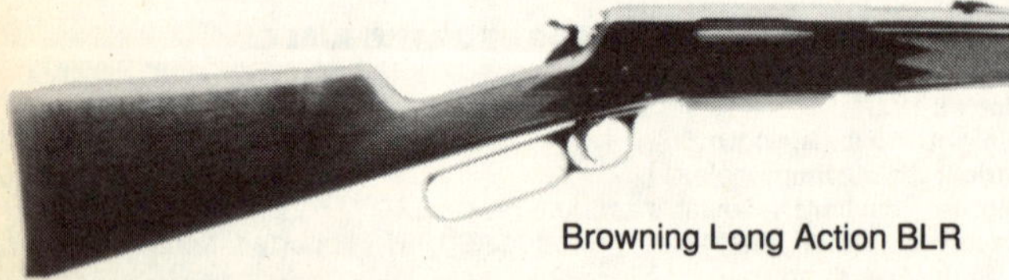
Browning Long Action BLR

Browning Model 81 Long Action BLR

Similar to the standard Model 81 BLR except has long acton to accept 30-06, 270 and 7mm Rem. Mag. Barrel lengths are 22" for 30-06 and 270, 24" for 7mm Rem. Mag. Has six-lug rotary bolt; bolt and receiver are full-length fluted. Fold-down hammer at half-cock. Weight about 8½ lbs., overall length 42½" (22" barrel). Introduced 1991.
Price: **$529.95**

BROWNING MODEL 81 BLR LEVER-ACTION RIFLE

Caliber: 222, 223, 22-250, 243, 257 Roberts, 7mm-08, 308 Win. or 358 Win., 4-shot detachable magazine.
Barrel: 20" round tapered.
Weight: 6 lbs., 15 oz. **Length:** 39¾" overall.
Stock: Checkered straight grip and forend, oil-finished walnut.
Sights: Gold bead on hooded ramp front; low profile square notch adj. rear.
Features: Wide, grooved trigger; half-cock hammer safety. Receiver tapped for scope mount. Recoil pad installed. Imported from Japan by Browning.
Price: With sights **$486.95**

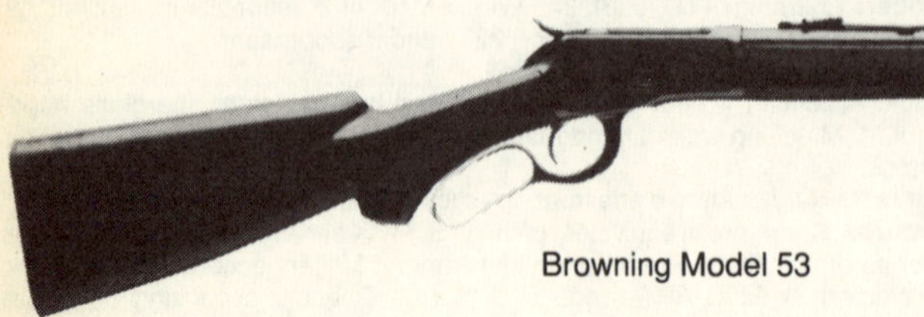
Browning Model 53

BROWNING MODEL 53 LEVER-ACTION RIFLE

Caliber: 32-20, 7-shot magazine.
Barrel: 22", round, tapered.
Weight: 6 lbs., 8 oz. **Length:** 39½" overall.
Stock: Full pistol grip with semi-beavertail forend of select walnut with high gloss finish. Cut checkering on grip and forend. Metal grip cap.
Sights: Post bead front, adjustable open rear.
Features: Based on the Model 92 Winchester with half-length magazine. Blue finish, including trigger. Limited to 5000 guns. Introduced 1990. Imported from Japan by Browning.
Price: **$675.00**

 CAUTION: PRICES CHANGE, CHECK AT GUNSHOP.

CIMARRON 1860 HENRY REPLICA
Caliber: 44 WCF, 13-shot magazine.
Barrel: 24¼" (rifle), 22" (carbine).
Weight: 9½lbs. **Length:** 43" overall (rifle).
Stock: European walnut.
Sights: Bead front, open adjustable rear.
Features: Brass receiver amd buttplate. Uses original Henry loading system. Faithful to the original rifle. Introduced 1991. Imported by Cimarron Arms.
Price: **$799.95**

CIMARRON 1866 WINCHESTER REPLICAS
Caliber: 22 LR, 22 WMR, 38 Spec., 44 WCF.
Barrel: 24¼" (rifle), 19" (carbine).
Weight: 9 lbs. **Length:** 43" overall (rifle).
Stock: European walnut.
Sights: Bead front, open adjustable rear.
Features: Solid brass receiver, buttplate, forend cap. Octagonal barrel. Faithful to the original Winchester '66 rifle. Introduced 1991. Imported by Cimarron Arms.
Price: Rifle **$689.95**
Price: Carbine **$649.95**

Cimarron 1873 Short

CIMARRON 1873 SHORT RIFLE
Caliber: 22 LR, 22 WMR, 357 Magnum, 44-40, 45 Colt.
Barrel: 20" tapered octagon.
Weight: 7.5 lbs. **Length:** 39" overall.
Stock: Walnut.
Sights: Bead front, adjustable semi-buckhorn rear.
Features: Has half "button" magazine. Original-type markings, including caliber, on barrel and elevator and "Kings" patent. From Cimarron Arms.
Price: **$799.95**

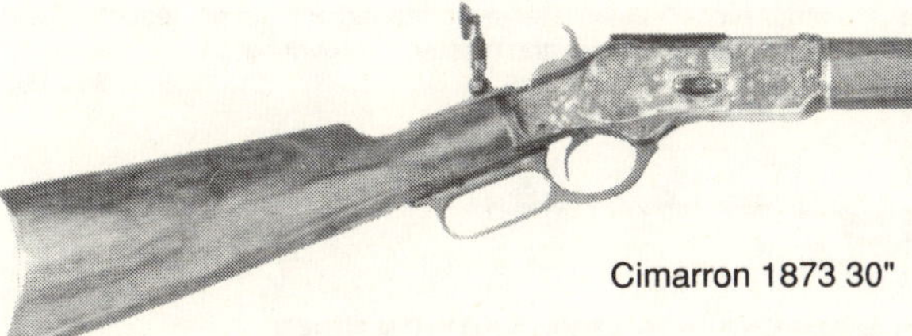
Cimarron 1873 30"

CIMARRON 1873 30" EXPRESS RIFLE
Caliber: 22 LR, 22 WMR, 357 Mag., 38-40, 44-40, 45 Colt.
Barrel: 30", octagonal.
Weight: 8½ lbs. **Length:** 48" overall.
Stock: Walnut.
Sights: Blade front, semi-buckhorn ramp rear. Tang sight optional.
Features: Color case-hardened frame; choice of modern blue-black or charcoal blue for other parts. Barrel marked "Kings improvement." From Cimarron Arms.
Price: **$819.95**

Cimarron 1873 Sporting Rifle
Similar to the 1873 Express except has 24" barrel with half-magazine.
Price: **$799.95**
Price: 1873 Saddle Ring Carbine, 19" barrel **$729.95**

Dixie 1873

DIXIE 1873 RIFLE
Caliber: 44-40, 11-shot magazine.
Barrel: 20", round.
Weight: 7¾ lbs. **Length:** 39" overall.
Stock: Walnut.
Sights: Blade front, adjustable rear.
Features: Engraved and case-hardened frame. Duplicate of Winchester 1873. Made in Italy. From Dixie Gun Works.
Price: **$995.00**
Price: Plain, blued carbine **$875.00**

E.M.F. 1866 YELLOWBOY LEVER ACTIONS
Caliber: 38 Spec., 44-40.
Barrel: 19" (carbine), 24" (rifle).
Weight: 9 lbs. **Length:** 43" overall (rifle).
Stock: European walnut.
Sights: Bead front, open adjustable rear.
Features: Solid brass frame, blued barrel, lever, hammer, buttplate. Imported from Italy by E.M.F.
Price: Rifle **$835.00**
Price: Carbine **$805.00**

Consult our Directory pages for the location of firms mentioned.

E.M.F. MODEL 73 LEVER-ACTION RIFLE
Caliber: 357 Mag., 44-40, 45 Colt.
Barrel: 24".
Weight: 8 lbs. **Length:** 43¼" overall.
Stock: European walnut.
Sights: Bead front, rear adjustable for windage and elevation.
Features: Color case-hardened frame (blue on carbine). Imported by E.M.F.
Price: Rifle **$1,010.00**
Price: Carbine, 19" barrel **$980.00**

E.M.F. HENRY CARBINE
Caliber: 44-40 or 44 rimfire.
Barrel: 21".
Weight: About 9 lbs. **Length:** About 39" overall.
Stock: Oil-stained American walnut.
Sights: Blade front, rear adjustable for elevation.
Features: Reproduction of the original Henry carbine with brass frame and buttplate, rest blued. From E.M.F.
Price: Standard **$1,100.10**

MARLIN MODEL 444SS LEVER-ACTION SPORTER
Caliber: 444 Marlin, 5-shot tubular magazine.
Barrel: 22" Micro-Groove®.
Weight: 7½ lbs. **Length:** 40½" overall.
Stock: American black walnut, capped p.g. with white line spacers, rubber rifle buttpad. Mar-Shield® finish; swivel studs.
Sights: Hooded ramp front, folding semi-buckhorn rear adjustable for windage and elevation.
Features: Hammer-block safety. Receiver tapped for scope mount; offset hammer spur.
Price: **$453.95**

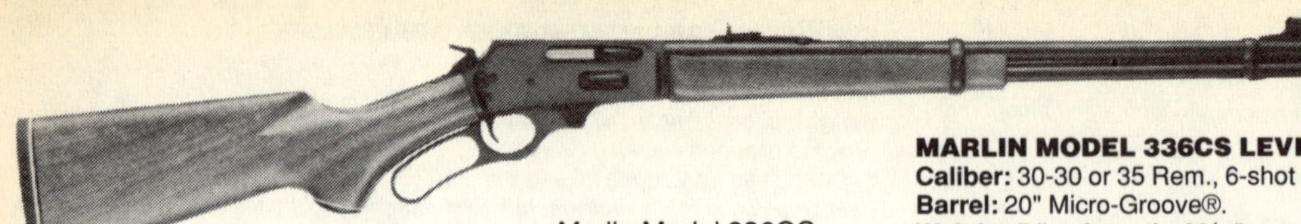

Marlin Model 336CS

MARLIN MODEL 336CS LEVER-ACTION CARBINE
Caliber: 30-30 or 35 Rem., 6-shot tubular magazine.
Barrel: 20" Micro-Groove®.
Weight: 7 lbs. **Length:** 38½" overall.
Stock: Select American black walnut, capped p.g. with white line spacers. Mar-Shield® finish; rubber buttpad.
Sights: Ramp front with Wide-Scan™ hood, semi-buckhorn folding rear adjustable for windage and elevation.
Features: Hammer-block safety. Receiver tapped for scope mount, offset hammer spur; top of receiver sand blasted to prevent glare.
Price:$374.95

Marlin Model 30AS Lever-Action Carbine
Same as the Marlin 336CS except has walnut-finished hardwood p.g. stock, 30-30 only, 6-shot. Hammer-block safety. Adjustable rear sight, brass bead front.
Price: **$318.95**

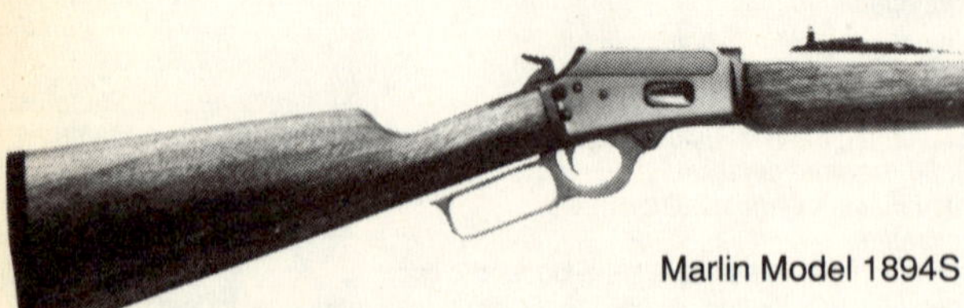

Marlin Model 1894S

MARLIN MODEL 1894S LEVER-ACTION CARBINE
Caliber: 44 Special/44 Magnum, 10-shot tubular magazine.
Barrel: 20" Micro-Groove®.
Weight: 6 lbs. **Length:** 37½" overall.
Stock: American black walnut, straight grip and forend. Mar-Shield® finish. Rubber rifle buttpad.
Sights: Wide-Scan™ hooded ramp front, semi-buckhorn folding rear adjustable for windage and elevation.
Features: Hammer-block safety. Receiver tapped for scope mount, offset hammer spur, solid top receiver sand blasted to prevent glare.
Price: **$420.95**

Marlin Model 1894CS Carbine
Similar to the standard Model 1894S except chambered for 38 Special/357 Magnum with full-length 9-shot magazine, 18½" barrel, hammer-block safety, brass bead front sight. Introduced 1983.
Price: **$420.95**

Marlin Model 1894CL

MARLIN MODEL 1895SS LEVER-ACTION RIFLE
Caliber: 45-70, 4-shot tubular magazine.
Barrel: 22" round.
Weight: 7½ lbs. **Length:** 40½" overall.
Stock: American black walnut, full pistol grip. Mar-Shield® finish; rubber buttpad; q.d. swivel studs.
Sights: Bead front with Wide-Scan™ hood, semi-buckhorn folding rear adjustable for windage and elevation.
Features: Hammer-block safety. Solid receiver tapped for scope mounts or receiver sights; offset hammer spur.
Price: **$453.95**

Marlin Model 1894CL Classic
Similar to the 1894CS except chambered for 218 Bee, 25-20 and 32-20 Win. Has 6-shot tubular magazine. 22" barrel with 6-groove rifling, brass bead front sight, adjustable semi-buckhorn folding rear. Hammer-block safety. Weighs 6¼ lbs., overall length of 38¾". Introduced 1988.
Price: **$451.95**

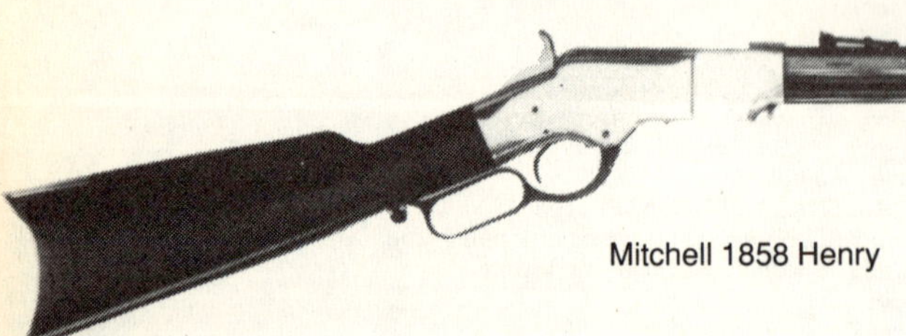

Mitchell 1858 Henry

MITCHELL 1858 HENRY REPLICA
Caliber: 44-40, 13-shot magazine.
Barrel: 24¼" (rifle), 22" (carbine).
Weight: 9.5 lbs. **Length:** 43" overall (rifle).
Stock: European walnut.
Sights: Bead front, open adjustable rear.
Features: Brass receiver and buttplate. Uses original Henry loading system. Faithful to the original rifle. Introduced 1990. Imported by Mitchell Arms, Inc.
Price: **$875.00**

MITCHELL 1866 WINCHESTER REPLICA
Caliber: 22 LR, 19-shot; 38 Spec., 44-40, 13-shot.
Barrel: 24¼" (rifle); 19" (carbine).
Weight: 9 lbs. **Length:** 43" overall (rifle).
Stock: European walnut.
Sights: Bead front, open adjustable rear.
Features: Solid brass receiver, buttplate, forend cap. Octagonal barrel. Faithful to the original Winchester '66 rifle. Introduced 1990. Imported by Mitchell Arms, Inc.
Price: **$699.00**

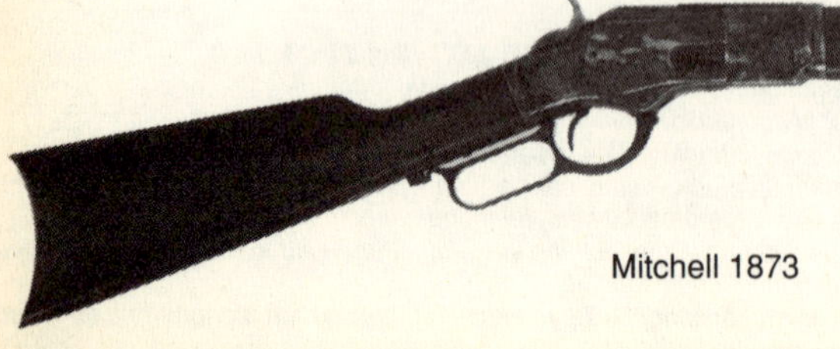

Mitchell 1873

MITCHELL 1873 WINCHESTER REPLICA
Caliber: 22 LR, 19-shot; 44-40, 45 Colt, 13-shot.
Barrel: 24¼" (rifle), 19" (carbine).
Weight: 9.5 lbs. **Length:** 43" overall (rifle).
Stock: European walnut.
Sights: Bead front, open adjustable rear.
Features: Color case-hardened steel receiver. Faithful to the original Model 1873 rifle. Introduced 1990. Imported by Mitchell Arms, Inc.
Price: **$795.00**

CENTERFIRE RIFLES—LEVER & SLIDE

NAVY ARMS MILITARY HENRY RIFLE
Caliber: 44-40, 12-shot magazine.
Barrel: 24¼".
Weight: 9 lbs., 4 oz.
Stock: European walnut.
Sights: Blade front, adjustable ladder-type rear.
Features: Brass frame, buttplate, rest blued. Recreation of the model used by cavalry units in the Civil War. Has full-length magazine tube, sling swivels; no forend. Introduced 1991. Imported from Italy by Navy Arms.
Price: **$875.00**

Navy Arms Iron Frame Henry
Similar to the Military Henry Rifle except receiver is blued or color case-hardened steel. Introduced 1991. Imported by Navy Arms.
Price: **$895.00**

Navy Arms Henry Trapper
Similar to the Military Henry Rifle except has 16½" barrel, weighs 7½ lbs. Brass frame and buttplate, rest blued. Introduced 1991. Imported from Italy by Navy Arms.
Price: **$875.00**

NAVY ARMS 1866 YELLOWBOY RIFLE
Caliber: 44-40, 12-shot magazine.
Barrel: 24", full octagon.
Weight: 8½ lbs. **Length:** 42½" overall.
Stock: European walnut.
Sights: Blade front, adjustable ladder-type rear.
Features: Brass frame, forend tip, buttplate, blued barrel, lever, hammer. Introduced 1991. Imported from Italy by Navy Arms.
Price: **$675.00**
Price: Carbine. 19" barrel **$660.00**

NAVY ARMS 1873 WINCHESTER-STYLE RIFLE
Caliber: 44-40, 45 Colt, 12-shot magazine.
Barrel: 24".
Weight: 8¼ lbs. **Length:** 43" overall.
Stock: European walnut.
Sights: Blade front, buckhorn rear.
Features: Color case-hardened frame, rest blued. Full-octagon barrel. Introduced 1991. Imported by Navy Arms.
Price: **$825.00**
Price: Carbine, 19" barrel **$800.00**

Remington 7600

REMINGTON 7600 SLIDE ACTION
Caliber: 243, 270, 280, 30-06, 308, 35 Whelen.
Barrel: 22" round tapered.
Stock: Cut-checkered walnut p.g. and forend, Monte Carlo with full cheekpiece. Satin or high-gloss finish.
Sights: Gold bead front sight on matted ramp, open step adjustable sporting rear.
Feature: Redesigned and improved version of the Model 760. Detachable 4-shot clip. Cross-bolt safety. Receiver tapped for scope mount. Also available in high grade versions. Introduced 1981.
Price: About **$484.00**
Price: Carbine (18½" bbl., 30-06 only) **$484.00**

Rossi Carbine

ROSSI M92 SRC SADDLE-RING CARBINE
Caliber: 38 Spec./357 Mag., 44 Spec./44-40, 44 Mag., 10-shot magazine.
Barrel: 20".
Weight: 5¾ lbs. **Length:** 37" overall.
Stock: Walnut.
Sights: Blade front, buckhorn rear.
Features: Recreation of the famous lever-action carbine. Handles 38 and 357 interchangeably. Has high-relief puma medallion inlaid in the receiver. Introduced 1978. Imported by Interarms.
Price: **$350.00**
Price: 44 Spec./44 Mag. (Model 65) **$370.00**

Rossi M92 SRS Puma Short Carbine
Similar to the standard M92 except has 16" barrel, overall length of 33", in 38/357 only. Puma medallion on side of receiver. Introduced 1986.
Price: **$350.00**

Savage 99C

SAVAGE 99C LEVER-ACTION RIFLE
Caliber: 243 or 308 Win., detachable 4-shot magazine.
Barrel: 22", chromemoly steel.
Weight: 8 lbs. **Length:** 41¾" overall.
Stock: Walnut with checkered p.g. and forend, Monte Carlo comb.
Sights: Hooded ramp front, adjustable ramp rear sight. Tapped for scope mounts.
Features: Grooved trigger, top tang slide safety locks trigger and lever. Brown rubber buttpad, q.d. swivel studs, push-button magazine release.
Price: **$620.00**

Timber Wolf Pump

TIMBER WOLF PUMP RIFLE
Caliber: 38 Spec./357 Mag., 10-shot magazine; 44 Mag., 10-shot magazine.
Barrel: 18.5".
Weight: 5.5 lbs. **Length:** 36.5" overall.
Stock: Walnut.
Sights: Blade front, adjustable rear.
Features: Push-button safety on trigger guard; integral scope mount on receiver. Blue finish. Introduced 1989. Imported from Israel by Action Arms Ltd. and Springfield Armory.
Price: 357 Mag., about **$425.00**
Price: 44 Mag., about **$445.00**

CENTERFIRE RIFLES—LEVER & SLIDE

UBERTI HENRY RIFLE
Caliber: 44-40.
Barrel: 24¼", half-octagon.
Weight: 9.2 lbs. **Length:** 43¾" overall.
Stock: American walnut.
Sights: Blade front, rear adjustable for elevation.
Features: Frame, elevator, magazine follower, buttplate are brass, balance blue (also available in polished steel). Imported by Uberti USA.
Price: **$899.00**
Price: Henry Carbine (22¼" bbl.) **$850.00**
Price: Henry Trapper (16", 18" bbl.) **$850.00**

UBERTI 1866 SPORTING RIFLE
Caliber: 22 LR, 22 WMR, 38 Spec., 44-40, 45 Colt.
Barrel: 24¼", octagonal.
Weight: 8.1 lbs. **Length:** 43¼" overall.
Stock: Walnut.
Sights: Blade front adjustable for windage, rear adjustable for elevation.
Features: Frame, buttplate, forend cap of polished brass, balance charcoal blued. Imported by Uberti USA.
Price: **$750.00**
Price: Yellowboy Carbine (19" round bbl.) **$685.00**
Price: Yellowboy "Indian" Carbine (engraved receiver, "nails" in wood) **$780.00**
Price: 1866 "Red Cloud Commemorative" Carbine **$760.00**
Price: 1866 "Trapper's Model" Carbine (16" bbl.) **$685.00**

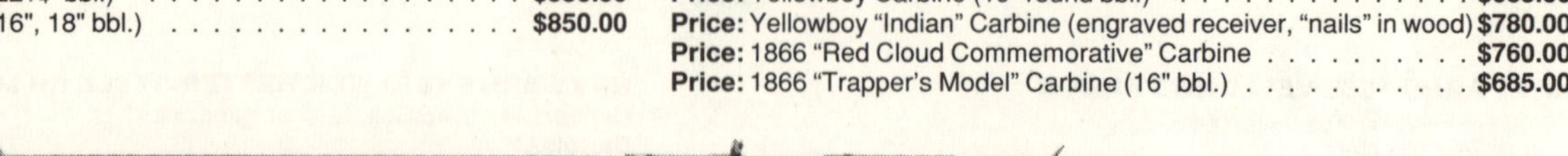

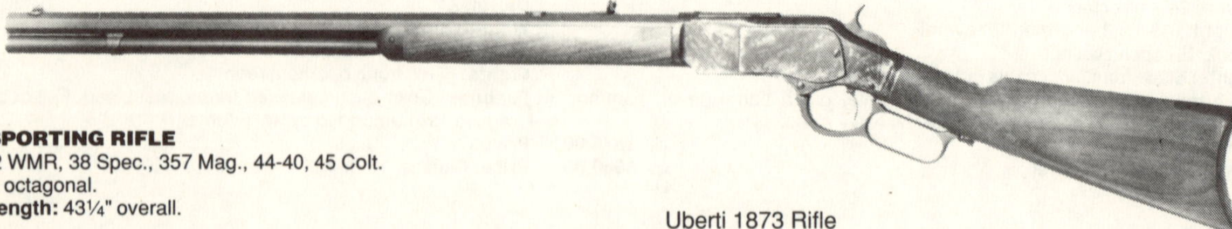

Uberti 1873 Rifle

UBERTI 1873 SPORTING RIFLE
Caliber: 22 LR, 22 WMR, 38 Spec., 357 Mag., 44-40, 45 Colt.
Barrel: 24¼", 30", octagonal.
Weight: 8.1 lbs. **Length:** 43¼" overall.
Stock: Walnut.
Sights: Blade front adjustable for windage, open rear adjustable for elevation.
Features: Color case-hardened frame, blued barrel, hammer, lever, buttplate, brass elevator. Also available with pistol grip stock ($100.00 extra). Imported by Uberti USA.
Price: **$899.00**
Price: 1873 Carbine (19" round bbl.) **$850.00**
Price: 1873 "Trapper's Model" Carbine (16" bbl.) **$850.00**

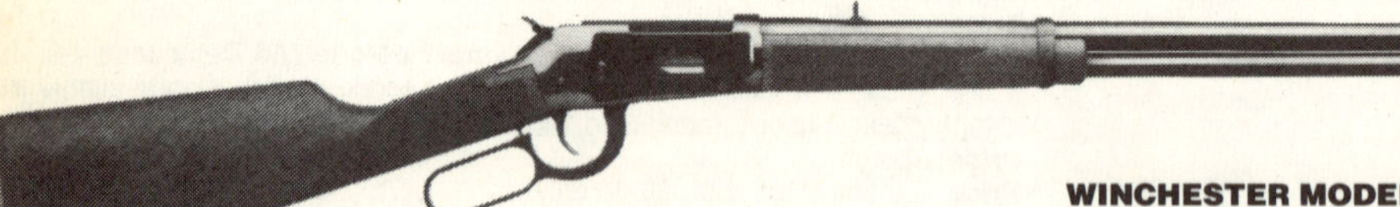

Winchester Model 94 Big Bore

WINCHESTER MODEL 94 BIG BORE SIDE EJECT
Caliber: 307 Win., 356 Win., 6-shot magazine.
Barrel: 20".
Weight: 7 lbs. **Length:** 38⅝" overall.
Stock: American walnut. Satin finish.
Sights: Hooded ramp front, semi-buckhorn rear adjustable for windage and elevation.
Features: All external metal parts have Winchester's deep blue finish. Rifling twist 1:12". Rubber recoil pad fitted to buttstock. Introduced 1983. From U.S. Repeating Arms Co.
Price: Walnut **$325.00**

Winchester Model 94 Ranger Side Eject Lever-Action Rifle
Same as Model 94 Side Eject except has 5-shot magazine, American hardwood stock and forend, post front sight. Introduced 1985.
Price: **$277.00**
Price: With 4x32 Bushnell scope, mounts **$325.00**

WINCHESTER MODEL 94 SIDE EJECT LEVER-ACTION RIFLE
Caliber: 30-30, 7x30 Waters, 6-shot tubular magazine.
Barrel: 16", 20".
Weight: 6½ lbs. **Length:** 37¾" overall.
Stock: Straight grip walnut stock and forend.
Sights: Hooded blade front, semi-buckhorn rear. Drilled and tapped for scope mount. Post front sight on Trapper model.
Features: Solid frame, forged steel receiver; side ejection, exposed rebounding hammer with automatic trigger-activated transfer bar. Introduced 1984.
Price: 30-30, checkered walnut **$325.00**
Price: 30-30, no checkering, walnut **$309.00**
Price: With 1.5-4.5x Bushnell scope, mounts, walnut **$388.00**
Price: Trapper model (16" bbl.), 30-30, walnut **$309.00**
Price: As above, 45 Colt, 44 Mag./44 Spec., walnut **$325.00**
Price: With WinTuff laminated hardwood stock **$335.00**

CENTERFIRE RIFLES—BOLT ACTION

Includes models for a wide variety of sporting and competitive purposes and uses.

Alpine Rifle

ALPINE BOLT-ACTION RIFLE
Caliber: 22-250, 243 Win., 270, 30-06, 308, 7mm Rem. Mag., 8mm, 5-shot magazine (3 for magnum).
Barrel: 23" (std. cals.), 24" (mag.).
Weight: 7½ lbs.
Stock: European walnut. Full p.g. and Monte Carlo; checkered p.g. and forend; rubber recoil pad; white line spacers; sling swivels.
Sights: Ramp front, open rear adjustable for windage and elevation.
Features: Made by Firearms Co. Ltd. in England. Imported by Mandall Shooting Supplies.
Price: Standard Grade **$395.00**
Price: Supreme Grade **$425.00**

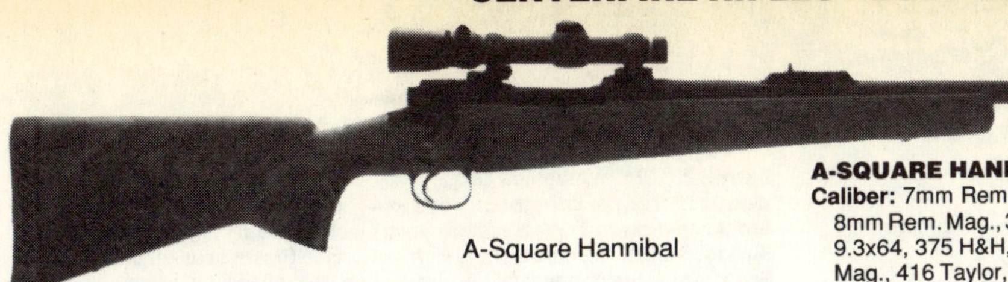

A-Square Hannibal

A-SQUARE CAESAR BOLT-ACTION RIFLE

Caliber: 7mm Rem. Mag., 30-06, 300 Win. Mag., 300 H&H, 300 Wea. Mag., 8mm Rem. Mag., 338 Win. Mag., 340 Wea. Mag., 9.3x62, 9.3x64, 375 Wea. Mag., 375 H&H, 375 JRS, 416 Hoffman, 416 Rem. Mag., 416 Taylor, 425 Express, 458 Win. Mag., 458 Lott, 450 Ackley, 470 Capstick.
Barrel: 20" to 26" (no-cost customer option).
Weight: 8½ to 11 lbs.
Stock: Claro walnut with hand-rubbed oil finish; classic style with A-Square Coil-Chek® features for reduced recoil; flush detachable swivels. Customer choice of length of pull.
Sights: Choice of three-leaf express, forward or normal-mount scope, or combination (at extra cost).
Features: Matte non-reflective blue, double cross-bolts, steel and fiberglass reinforcement of wood from tang to forend tip; three-position positive safety; three-way adjustable trigger; expanded magazine capacity. Right- or left-hand. Introduced 1984. Made in U.S. by A-Square Co., Inc.
Price: **$1,900.00**

A-SQUARE HANNIBAL BOLT-ACTION RIFLE

Caliber: 7mm Rem. Mag., 30-06, 300 Win. Mag., 300 H&H, 300 Wea. Mag., 8mm Rem. Mag., 338 Win. Mag., 340 Wea. Mag., 338 A-Square Mag., 9.3x62, 9.3x64, 375 H&H, 375 Wea. Mag., 375 JRS, 375 A-Square Mag., 378 Wea. Mag., 416 Taylor, 416 Rem. Mag., 416 Hoffman, 416 Rigby, 416 Wea. Mag., 404 Jeffery, 425 Express, 458 Win. Mag., 458 Lott, 450 Ackley, 460 Short A-Square Mag., 460 Wea. Mag., 470 Capstick, 495 A-Square Mag., 500 A-Square Mag.
Barrel: 20" to 26" (no-cost customer option).
Weight: 9 to 11¾ lbs.
Stock: Claro walnut with hand-rubbed oil finish; classic style with A-Square Coil-Chek® features for reduced recoil; flush detachable swivels. Customer choice of length of pull. Available with synthetic stock.
Sights: Choice of three-leaf express, forward or normal-mount scope, or combination (at extra cost).
Features: Matte non-reflective blue, double cross-bolts, steel and fiberglass reinforcement of wood from tang to forend tip; Mauser-style claw extractor; expanded magazine capacity; two-position safety; three-way target trigger. Right-hand only. Introduced 1983. Made in U.S. by A-Square Co., Inc.
Price: Walnut stock **$1,860.00**
Price: Synthetic stock **$1,900.00**

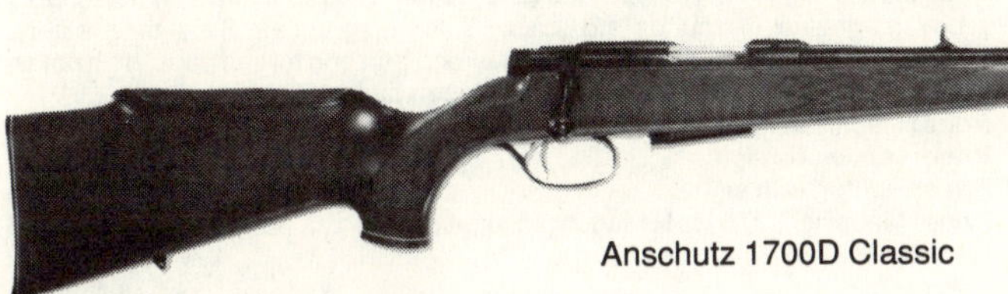

Anschutz 1700D Classic

Anschutz 1700D Custom Rifles

Similar to the Classic models except have roll-over Monte Carlo cheekpiece, slim forend with Schnabel tip, Wundhammer palm swell on pistol grip, rosewood grip cap with white diamond insert. Skip-line checkering on grip and forend. Introduced 1988. Imported from Germany by PSI.
Price: **$1,229.00**
Price: Meistergrade (select stock, gold engraved trigger guard) . . **$1,424.00**

BARRETT MODEL 90 BOLT-ACTION RIFLE

Caliber: 50 BMG, 5-shot magazine.
Barrel: 29".
Weight: 22 lbs. **Length:** 35" overall.
Stock: Sorbothane recoil pad.
Sights: Scope optional.
Features: Bolt-action, bullpup design. Disassembles without tools; extendable bipod legs; match-grade barrel; high efficiency muzzlebrake. Introduced 1990. From Barrett Firearms Mfg., Inc.
Price: From **$3,350.00**

ANSCHUTZ 1700D CLASSIC RIFLES

Caliber: 22 Hornet, 5-shot clip; 222 Rem., 2-shot clip.
Barrel: 23½", 13/16" dia. heavy.
Weight: 7¾ lbs. **Length:** 42½" overall.
Stock: Select European walnut with checkered pistol grip and forend.
Sights: None furnished, drilled and tapped for scope mounting.
Features: Adjustable single stage trigger. Receiver drilled and tapped for scope mounting. Introduced 1988. Imported from Germany by Precision Sales International.
Price: **$1,350.00**
Price: Meistergrade (select stock, gold engraved trigger guard) . . **$1,545.00**

ANSCHUTZ 1700D BAVARIAN BOLT-ACTION RIFLE

Caliber: 22 Hornet, 222 Rem., detachable clip.
Barrel: 24".
Weight: 7¼ lbs. **Length:** 43" overall.
Stock: European walnut with Bavarian cheek rest. Checkered p.g. and forend.
Sights: Hooded ramp front, folding leaf rear.
Features: Uses the improved 1700 Match 54 action with adjustable trigger. Drilled and tapped for scope mounting. Introduced 1988. Imported from Germany by Precision Sales International.
Price: **$1,379.00**
Price: Meistergrade (select stock, gold engraved trigger guard) . . **$1,574.00**

Beeman/HW 60J

BEEMAN/HW 60J BOLT-ACTION RIFLE

Caliber: 222 Rem.
Barrel: 22.8".
Weight: 6.5 lbs. **Length:** 41.7" overall.
Stock: Walnut with cheekpiece; cut checkered p.g. and forend.
Sights: Hooded blade on ramp front, open rear.
Features: Polished blue finish; oil-finished wood. Imported from Germany by Beeman. Introduced 1988.
Price: **$889.50**

BRNO ZKB 680 FOX BOLT-ACTION RIFLE

Caliber: 22 Hornet, 222 Rem., 5-shot magazine.
Barrel: 23½".
Weight: 5 lbs., 12 oz. **Length:** 42½" overall.
Stock: Turkish walnut, with Monte Carlo.
Sights: Hooded front, open adjustable rear.
Features: Detachable box magazine; adjustable double-set triggers. Imported from Czechoslovakia by T.D. Arms.
Price: **$499.00**

BRNO ZKK 600, 601, 602 BOLT-ACTION RIFLES

Caliber: 30-06, 270 (M600); 223, 243 (M601); 300 Win. Mag., 375 H&H (M602), 5-shot magazine.
Barrel: 23½" (M600, 601); 25" (M602).
Weight: 6 lbs., 3 oz. to 9 lbs., 4 oz. **Length:** 43" overall (M601).
Stock: Walnut.
Sights: Hooded ramp front, open folding leaf adjustable rear.
Features: Adjustable set-trigger (standard trigger included); easy-release floorplate; sling swivels. Imported from Czechoslovakia by T.D. Arms.
Price: ZKK 600 Standard **$599.00**
Price: As above, Monte Carlo stock **$649.00**
Price: ZKK 601 Standard **$549.00**
Price: As above, Monte Carlo stock **$599.00**
Price: ZKK 602, Monte Carlo stock **$749.00**
Price: As above, Standard stock **$689.00**

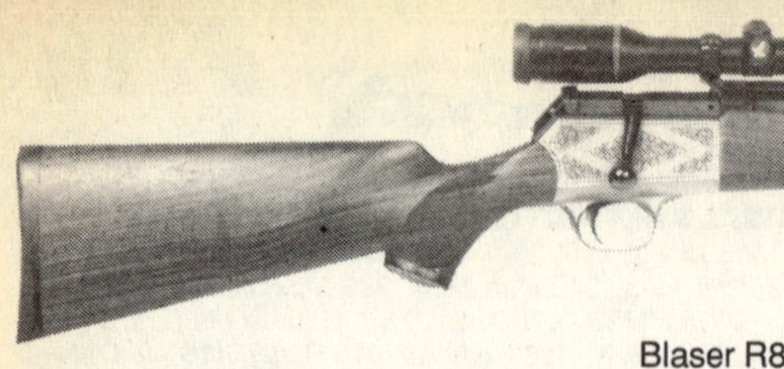

Blaser R84

BLASER R84 BOLT-ACTION RIFLE

Caliber: Std. cals.—22-250, 243, 6mm Rem., 25-06, 270, 280, 30-06; magnum cals.—257 Wea., 264 Win. Mag., 7mm Rem. Mag., 300 Win. Mag., 300 Wea.,

Barrel: 23" (24" in magnum cals.).

Weight: 7-7¼ lbs. **Length:** Std. cals.—41" overall (23" barrel).

Stock: Two-piece Turkish walnut. Solid black buttpad.

Sights: None furnished. Comes with low-profile Blaser scope mountings.

Features: Interchangeable barrels (scope mountings on barrel), and magnum/standard caliber bolt assemblies. Left-hand models available in all calibers. Imported from Germany by Autumn Sales, Inc.

Price: Right-hand, standard or magnum calibers **$1,850.00**
Price: Left-hand, standard or magnum calibers **$1,900.00**
Price: Interchangeable barrels, standard or magnum calibers **$545.00**

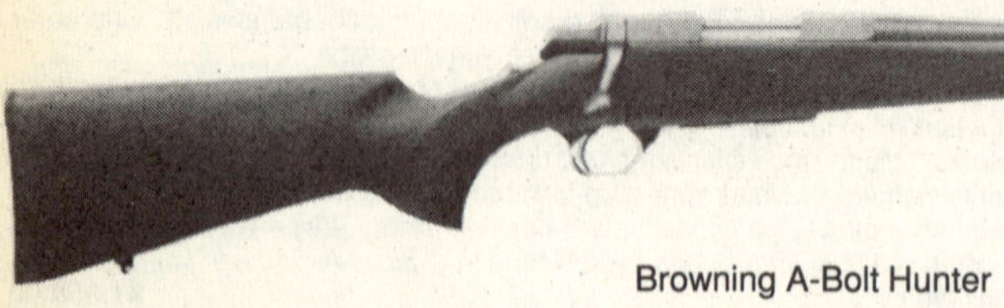

Browning A-Bolt Hunter

BROWNING A-BOLT RIFLE

Caliber: 25-06, 270, 30-06, 280, 7mm Rem. Mag., 300 Win. Mag., 338 Win. Mag., 375 H&H Mag.

Barrel: 22" medium sporter weight with recessed muzzle; 26" on mag. cals.

Weight: 6½ to 7½ lbs. **Length:** 44¾" overall (magnum and standard); 41¾" (short action).

Stock: Classic style American walnut; recoil pad standard on magnum calibers.

Features: Short-throw (60°) fluted bolt, three locking lugs, plunger-type ejector; adjustable trigger is grooved and gold-plated. Hinged floorplate, detachable box magazine (4 rounds std. cals., 3 for magnums). Slide tang safety. Medallion has glossy stock finish, rosewood grip and forend caps, high polish blue. Introduced 1985. Imported from Japan by Browning.

Price: Medallion, no sights **$571.95**
Price: Hunter, no sights **$492.95**
Price: Hunter, with sights **$555.95**
Price: Medallion, 375 H&H Mag., with sights **$668.95**

Browning A-Bolt Short Action

Similar to the standard A-Bolt except has short action for 22 Hornet, 223, 22-250, 243, 257 Roberts, 7mm-08, 284 Win., 308 chamberings. Available in Hunter or Medallion grades. Weighs 6½ lbs. Other specs essentially the same. Introduced 1985.

Price: Medallion, no sights **$571.95**
Price: Hunter, no sights **$492.95**
Price: Hunter, with sights **$555.95**

Browning A-Bolt Stainless Stalker

Browning A-Bolt Stainless Stalker

Similar to the Hunter model A-Bolt except receiver is made of stainless steel; the rest of the exposed metal surfaces are finished with a durable matte silver-gray. Graphite-Fiberglass composite textured stock. No sights are furnished. Available in 270, 30-06, 7mm Rem. Mag., 375 H&H. Introduced 1987.

Price: **$639.95**
Price: Composite Stalker (as above, checkered stock) **$492.95**
Price: Left-hand, no sights **$659.95**
Price: 375 H&H, with sights **$734.95**
Price: 375 H&H, left-hand, with sights **$757.95**

Browning A-Bolt Left Hand

Same as the Medallion model A-Bolt except has left-hand action and is available only in 270, 30-06, 7mm Rem. Mag. Introduced 1987.

Price: **$596.95**

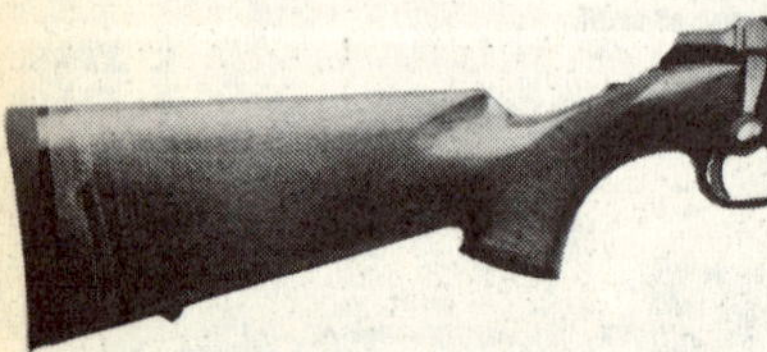

Browning Micro Medallion

Browning A-Bolt Gold Medallion

Similar to the standard A-Bolt except has select walnut stock with brass spacers between rubber recoil pad and between the rosewood grip cap and forend tip; gold-filled barrel inscription; palm-swell pistol grip, Monte Carlo comb, 22 lpi checkering with double borders; engraved receiver flats. In 270, 30-06, 7mm Rem. Mag. only. Introduced 1988.

Price: **$774.95**

Browning A-Bolt Micro Medallion

Similar to the standard A-Bolt except is a scaled-down version. Comes with 20" barrel, shortened length of pull (13$\frac{5}{16}$"); three-shot magazine capacity; weighs 6 lbs., 1 oz. Available in 243, 308, 7mm-08, 257 Roberts, 223, 22-250. Introduced 1988.

Price: No sights **$571.95**

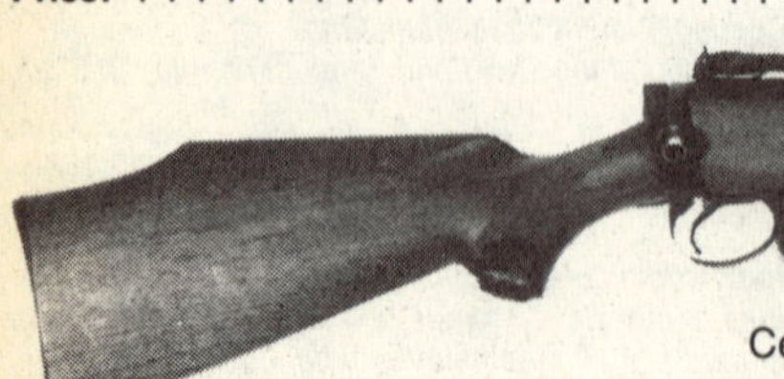

Century Enfield #4

CENTURY ENFIELD SPORTER #4

Caliber: 303 British, 10-shot magazine.

Barrel: 25.2".

Weight: NA. **Length:** 44.5" overall.

Stock: Beechwood with checkered p.g. and forend, Monte Carlo comb.

Sights: Blade front, adjustable aperture rear.

Features: Uses Lee-Enfield action; blue finish. Introduced 1987. From Century International Arms.

Price: **$185.95**
Price: Jungle Sporter (20½" bbl.) **$212.95**

Century Centurion 14

CENTURY CENTURION 14 SPORTER
Caliber: 303 British, 7mm Rem. Mag., 300 Win. Mag., 5-shot magazine.
Barrel: 24".
Weight: NA. **Length:** 43.3" overall.
Stock: Walnut-finished European hardwood. Checkered p.g. and forend. Monte Carlo comb.
Sights: None furnished.
Features: Uses modified Pattern 14 Enfield action. Drilled and tapped for scope mounting. Blue finish. From Century International Arms.
Price: 303, about **$225.95**
Price: Magnum calibers, about **$251.95**

Century Swedish #38

CENTURY SWEDISH SPORTER #38
Caliber: 6.5x55 Swede, 5-shot magazine.
Barrel: 24".
Weight: NA. **Length:** 44.1" overall.
Stock: Walnut-finished European hardwood with checkered p.g. and forend; Monte Carlo comb.
Sights: Blade front, adjustable rear.
Features: Uses M38 Swedish Mauser action; comes with Holden Ironsighter see-through scope mount. Introduced 1987. From Century International Arms.
Price: About **$212.95**

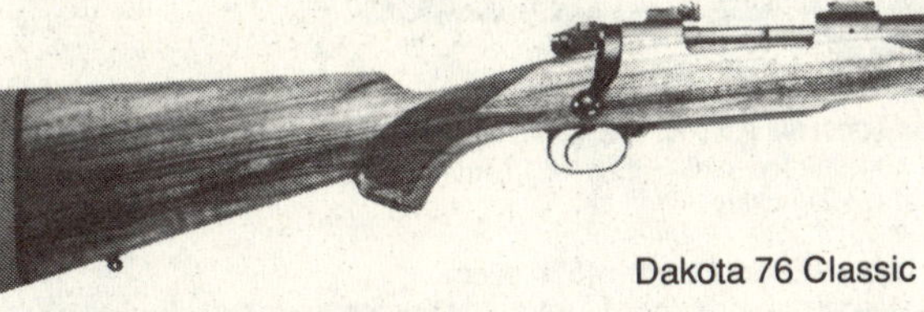

Dakota 76 Classic

DAKOTA 76 CLASSIC BOLT-ACTION RIFLE
Caliber: 257 Roberts, 270, 280, 30-06, 7mm Rem. Mag., 338 Win. Mag., 300 Win. Mag., 375 H&H, 458 Win. Mag.
Barrel: 23".
Weight: 7½ lbs. **Length:** NA.
Stock: Medium fancy grade walnut in classic style. Checkered p.g. and forend; solid buttpad.
Sights: None furnished; drilled and tapped for scope mounts.
Features: Has many features of the original Model 70 Winchester. One-piece rail trigger guard assembly; steel grip cap. Adjustable trigger. Many options available. Left-hand rifle available at same price. Introduced 1988. From Dakota Arms, Inc.
Price: **$2,150.00**

Dakota 76 Short Action Rifles
A scaled-down version of the standard Model 76. Standard chamberings are 22-250, 243, 6mm Rem., 250-3000, 7mm-08, 308, others on special order. Short Classic Grade has 21" barrel; Alpine Grade is lighter (6½ lbs.), has a blind magazine and slimmer stock. Introduced 1989.
Price: Short Classic **$2,150.00**
Price: Alpine **$1,995.00**

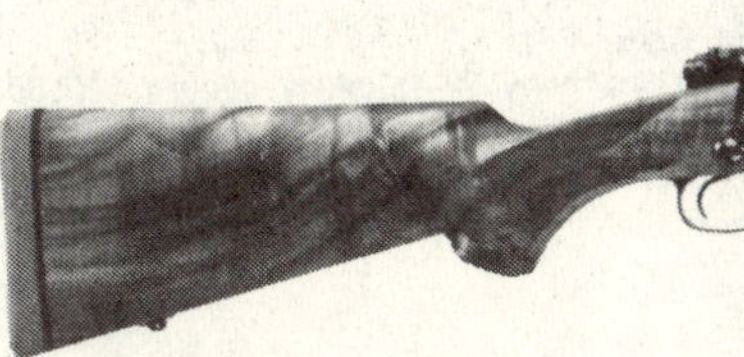

Dakota 76 Safari

DAKOTA 76 SAFARI BOLT-ACTION RIFLE
Caliber: 338 Win. Mag., 300 Win. Mag., 375 H&H, 458 Win. Mag.
Barrel: 23".
Weight: 8½ lbs. **Length:** NA.
Stock: Fancy walnut with ebony forend tip; point-pattern with wraparound forend checkering.
Sights: Ramp front, standing leaf rear.
Features: Has many features of the original Model 70 Winchester. Barrel band front swivel, inletted rear. Cheekpiece with shadow line. Steel grip cap. Introduced 1988. From Dakota Arms, Inc.
Price: Wood stock **$2,950.00**

Dakota 416 Rigby African
Similar to the 76 Safari except chambered for 416 Rigby, four-round magazine, select wood, two stock cross-bolts. Has 24" barrel, weight of 9.4 lbs. Ramp front sight, standing leaf rear. Introduced 1989.
Price: **$3,500.00**

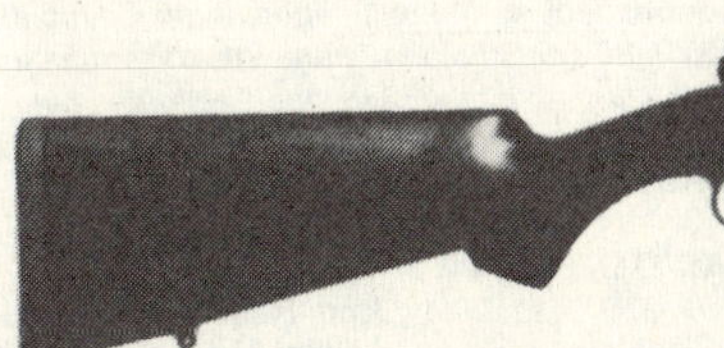

Auguste Francotte

AUGUSTE FRANCOTTE BOLT-ACTION RIFLES
Caliber: 243, 270, 7x64, 30-06, 308, 300 Win. Mag., 338, 7mm Rem. Mag., 375 H&H, 458 Win. Mag.; others on request.
Barrel: 23½" to 26½".
Weight: 8 to 10 lbs.
Stock: Fancy European walnut. To customer specs.
Sights: To customer specs.
Features: Basically a custom gun, Francotte offers many options. Imported from Belgium by Armes de Chasse.
Price: **$10,179.00**

AUGUSTE FRANCOTTE RIMAG BOLT-ACTION RIFLE
Caliber: 358 Norma Mag., 375 H&H, 378 Wea. Mag., 404 Jeffery, 416 Rigby, 450 Watts, 460 Wea. Mag., 458 Win. Mag., 505 Gibbs; others on request.
Barrel: 23.6" to 26", heavy round.
Weight: 9 to 10 lbs.
Stock: Deluxe European walnut, to customer specs. Standard checkering, oil finish, steel grip cap.
Sights: Ring-mounted front blade, fixed leaf rear.
Features: Uses A. Francotte Rimag action with three-position safety, round or square bridge. Imported from Belgium by Armes de Chasse.
Price: From about **$14,068.00**

CAUTION: PRICES CHANGE, CHECK AT GUNSHOP.

HEYM SR 20 TROPHY SERIES RIFLE

Caliber: 243, 7x57, 270, 308, 30-06, 7mm Rem. Mag., 338 Win. Mag., 375 H&H; other calibers on request.

Barrel: 22" (standard cals.); 24" (magnum cals.).

Weight: About 7 lbs.

Stock: AAA-grade European walnut with cheekpiece, solid rubber buttpad, checkered grip and forend, oil finish, rosewood grip cap.

Sights: German silver bead ramp front, open rear on quarter-rib. Drilled and tapped for scope mounting.

Features: Octagonal barrel, barrel-mounted q.d. swivel, standard q.d. rear swivel. Imported from Germany by Heckler & Koch, Inc.

Price: **$2,450.00**

Price: For left-hand rifle, add **$450.00**

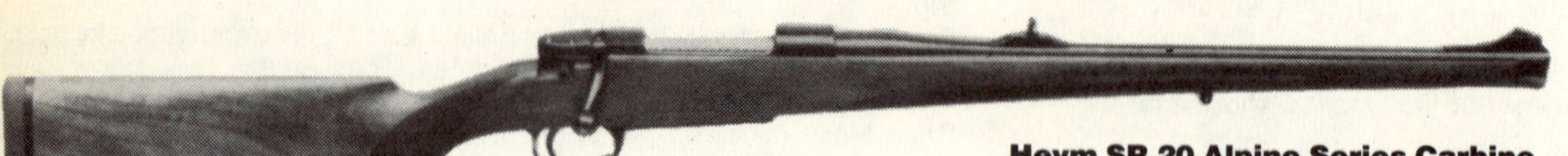

Heym SR 20 Alpine

Heym SR 20 Alpine Series Carbine

Similar to the Trophy Series except available in 243, 270, 7x57, 308, 30-06, 6.5x55, 7x64, 8x57JS with 20" barrel, open sights; full-length "Mountain rifle" stock with steel forend cap, steel grip cap. Introduced 1989. Imported from Germany by Heckler & Koch, Inc.

Price: **$2,335.00**

Heym SR 20 Classic Sportsman Series Rifle

Similar to the Trophy Series except has round barrel without sights. Imported from Germany by Heckler & Koch, Inc. Introduced 1989.

Price: Standard calibers **$2,285.00**

Price: Magnum calibers **$2,415.00**

Heym SR 20 Classic Safari Rifle

Similar to the Trophy Series except in 404 Jeffery, 425 Express, 458 Win. Mag. 24" barrel; has large post front sight, three-leaf express rear; barrel-mounted ring-type front q.d. swivel, q.d. rear; double-lug recoil bolt in stock. Introduced 1989. Imported from Germany by Heckler & Koch, Inc.

Price: **$2,725.00**

Price: For left-hand rifle, add **$450.00**

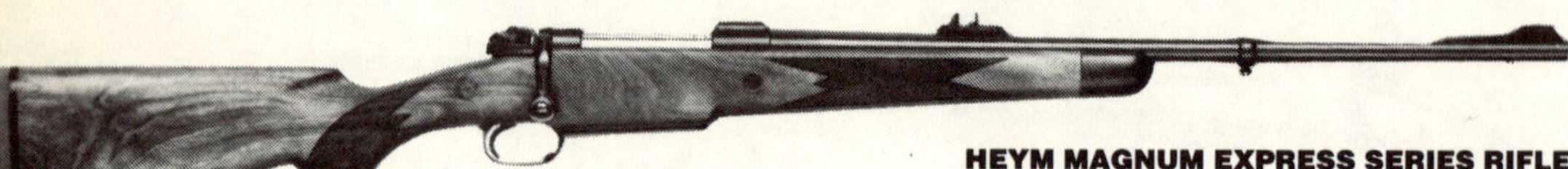

Heym Express

HEYM MAGNUM EXPRESS SERIES RIFLE

Caliber: 404 Jeffery, 416 Rigby, 500 Nitro Express 3", 460 Wea. Mag., 500 A-Square, 450 Ackley.

Barrel: 24".

Weight: About 9.9 lbs. **Length:** 45¼" overall.

Stock: Classic English design of AAA-grade European walnut with cheekpiece, solid rubber buttpad, steel grip cap.

Sights: Adjustable post front on ramp, three-leaf express rear.

Features: Modified magnum Mauser action, Timney single trigger; special hinged floorplate; barrel-mounted q.d. swivel, q.d. rear; vertical double recoil lug in rear of stock. Introduced 1989. Imported from Germany by Heckler & Koch, Inc.

Price: **$6,500.00**

Price: For left-hand rifle, add **$575.00**

HOWA M1500 TROPHY BOLT-ACTION RIFLE

Caliber: 223, 22-250, 243, 270, 30-06, 308, 7mm Rem. Mag., 300 Win. Mag., 338 Win. Mag.

Barrel: 22" (24" in magnum calibers).

Weight: 7½-7¾ lbs. **Length:** 42" overall (42½" for 270, 30-06, 7mm).

Stock: American walnut with Monte Carlo comb and cheekpiece; 18 lpi checkering on p.g. and forend.

Sights: Hooded ramp gold bead front, open round-notch rear adjustable for windage and elevation. Drilled and tapped for scope mounts.

Features: Trigger guard and magazine box are a single unit with a hinged floorplate. Comes with q.d. swivel studs. Composition non-slip buttplate with white spacer. Magnum models have rubber recoil pad. Introduced 1979. Imported from Japan by Interarms.

Price: **$539.00**

Price: 7mm Rem. Mag., 300 Win. Mag., 338 Win. Mag. **$559.00**

Howa Heavy Barrel Varmint Rifle

Similar to the Trophy model except has heavy 24" barrel, available in 223, 308 and 22-250 only, Parkerized finish. No sights furnished; drilled and tapped for scope mounts. Introduced 1989. Imported from Japan by Interarms.

Price: **$579.00**

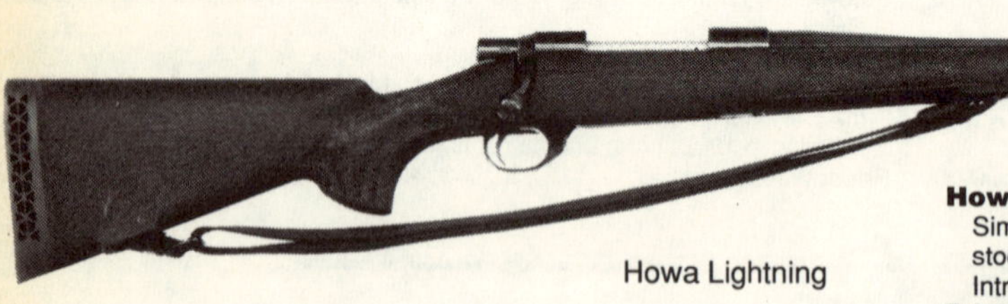

Howa Lightning

Howa Lightning Rifle

Similar to the Howa Trophy model except comes with lightweight Carbolite stock; weighs 7 lbs. Available in 270, 30-06, 300 Win. Mag., 7mm Rem. Mag. Introduced 1988.

Price: 270, 30-06 . . . . **$539.00**

Price: 7mm Rem. Mag., 300 Win. Mag. **$559.00**

Consult our Directory pages for the location of firms mentioned.

IVER JOHNSON MODEL 5100A1 LONG-RANGE RIFLE

Caliber: 50 BMG.

Barrel: 29", fully fluted, free-floating.

Weight: 36 lbs. **Length:** 51.5" overall.

Stocks: Composition. Adjustable drop and comb.

Sights: Comes with Leupold Ultra M1 20x scope.

Features: Bolt-action long-range rifle. Comes with Automatic Ranging Scope Base. Adjustable trigger. Rifle breaks down for transport, storage. From Iver Johnson.

Price: **$5,000.00**

KDF K15 AMERICAN BOLT-ACTION RIFLE

Caliber: 25-06, 257 Wea. Mag., 270, 270 Wea. Mag., 7mm Rem. Mag., 30-06, 300 Win. Mag., 300 Wea. Mag., 338 Win. Mag., 340 Wea. Mag., 375 H&H, 411 KDF Mag., 416 Rem. Mag., 458 Win. Mag.; 4-shot magazine for standard calibers, 3-shot for magnums.

Barrel: 22" standard, 24" optional.

Weight: About 8 lbs. **Length:** 44" overall (24" barrel).

Stock: Laminated standard; Kevlar composite or AAA walnut in classic, schnabel or thumbhole styles optional.

Sights: None furnished; optional. Drilled and tapped for scope mounting.

Features: Three-lug locking design with 60° bolt lift; ultra-fast lock time; fully adjustable trigger. Options available. Introduced 1991. Made in U.S. by KDF, Inc.

Price: From **$2,300.00**

KRICO MODEL 700 BOLT-ACTION RIFLES
Caliber: 17 Rem., 222, 222 Rem. Mag., 223, 5.6x50 Mag., 243, 308, 5.6x57 RWS, 22-250, 6.5x55, 6.5x57, 7x57, 270, 7x64, 30-06, 9.3x62, 6.5x68, 7mm Rem. Mag., 300 Win. Mag., 8x68S, 7.5 Swiss, 9.3x64, 6x62 Freres.
Barrel: 23.6" (std. cals.); 25.5" (mag. cals.).
Weight: 7 lbs. **Length:** 43.3" overall (23.6" bbl.).
Stock: European walnut, Bavarian cheekpiece.
Sights: Blade on ramp front, open adjustable rear.
Features: Removable box magazine; sliding safety. Drilled and tapped for scope mounting. Imported from Germany by Mandall Shooting Supplies.
Price: Model 700 . . . . . **$995.00**
Price: Model 700 Deluxe S **$1,495.00**
Price: Model 700 Deluxe **$1,025.00**
Price: Model 700 Stutzen (full stock) **$1,295.00**

KRICO MODEL 600 BOLT-ACTION RIFLE
Caliber: 222, 223, 22-250, 243, 308, 5.6x50 Mag., 4-shot magazine.
Barrel: 23.6".
Weight: 7.9 lbs. **Length:** 43.7" overall.
Stock: European walnut with Monte Carlo comb.
Sights: None furnished; drilled and tapped for scope mounting.
Features: Rubber recoil pad, sling swivels, checkered grip and forend. Polished blue finish. Imported from Germany by Mandall Shooting Supplies.
Price: **$1,250.00**

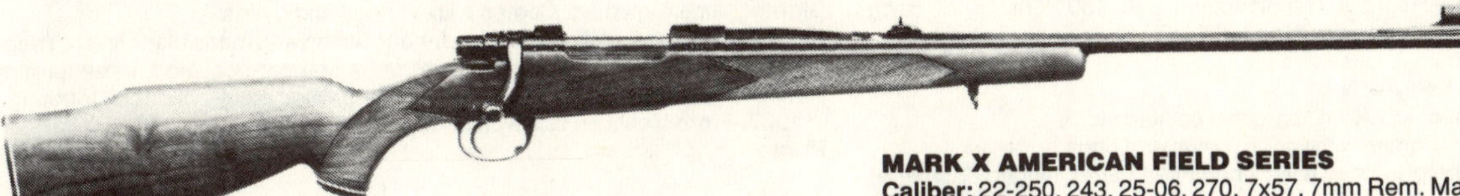

Mark X Viscount

Mark X Viscount Rifle
Same gun and features as the Mark X American Field except has stock of European hardwood. Imported from Yugoslavia by Interarms. Reintroduced 1987.
Price: **$539.00**
Price: 7mm Rem. Mag., 300 Win. Mag. **$559.00**

MARK X AMERICAN FIELD SERIES
Caliber: 22-250, 243, 25-06, 270, 7x57, 7mm Rem. Mag., 308 Win., 30-06, 300 Win. Mag.
Barrel: 24".
Weight: 7 lbs. **Length:** 45" overall.
Stock: Genuine walnut stock, hand checkered with 1" sling swivels.
Sights: Ramp front with removable hood, open rear sight adjustable for windage and elevation.
Features: Mauser-system action. One-piece trigger guard with hinged floorplate, drilled and tapped for scope mounts and receiver sight, hammer-forged chrome vanadium steel barrel. Imported from Yugoslavia by Interarms.
Price: With adj. trigger, sights **$665.00**
Price: 7mm Rem. Mag., 300 Win. Mag. **$685.00**

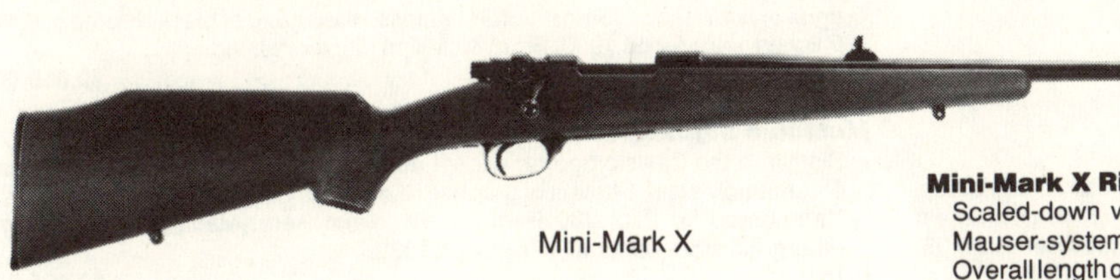

Mini-Mark X

Mini-Mark X Rifle
Scaled-down version of the Mark X American Field. Uses miniature M98 Mauser-system action, chambered for 223 Rem. and 7.62x39; 20" barrel. Overall length of 39¾", weight 6.35 lbs. Drilled and tapped for scope mounting. Checkered hardwood stock. Adjustable trigger. Introduced 1987. Imported from Yugoslavia by Interarms.
Price: **$500.00**

Mauser Model 66

MAUSER MODEL 66 BOLT-ACTION RIFLE
Caliber: 243, 270, 308, 30-06, 5.6x57, 6.5x57, 7x64, 9.3x62, 7mm Rem. Mag., 300 Wea. Mag., 300 Win. Mag., 6.5x68, 8x68S, 9.3x64, 375 H&H, 458 Win. Mag. Three-shot magazine.
Barrel: 21" (Stutzen); 24" (standard cals.); 26" (magnum cals.).
Weight: 7.5 to 9.3 lbs. **Length:** 39" overall (std. cals.).
Stock: Hand-checkered European walnut, hand-rubbed oil finish. Rosewood forend and grip caps.
Sights: Blade front on ramp, open rear adjustable for windage and elevation.
Features: Telescopic short-stroke action; interchangeable, free-floated, medium-heavy barrels. Mini-claw extractor; adjustable single-stage trigger; internal magazine. Introduced 1989. Imported from Germany by Precision Imports, Inc.
Price: With Monte Carlo stock **$1,998.00**
Price: Stutzen (full-length stock) **$2,104.00**
Price: Safari model**$2,332.00**

Mauser Model 99

MAUSER MODEL 99 BOLT-ACTION RIFLE
Caliber: 243, 25-06, 270, 308, 30-06, 5.6x57, 6.5x57, 7x57, 7x64 (standard cals.); 7mm Rem. Mag., 257 Wea. Mag., 270 Wea. Mag., 300 Wea. Mag., 300 Win. Mag., 338 Win. Mag., 375 H&H, 8x68S, 9.3x64 (magnum cals.); removable 4-shot magazine (std. cals.), 3-shot (magnum cals.).
Barrel: 24" (std.), 26" (mag.).
Weight: About 8 lbs. **Length:** 44" overall (std. cals.).
Sights: None furnished. Drilled and tapped for scope mounting.
Features: Accuracy bedding with free-floated barrel, three front-locking bolt lugs, 60° bolt throw. Fastest lock time of any sporting rifle. Adjustable single-stage trigger. Silent safety locks bolt, sear, trigger. Introduced 1989. Imported from Germany by Precision Imports, Inc.
Price: Classic stock, oil finish, std. cals. **$1,267.00**
Price: As above, magnum cals. **$1,320.00**
Price: Classic stock, high luster finish, std. cals. **$1,426.00**
Price: As above, magnum cals. **$1,479.00**
Price: Monte Carlo stock, oil finish, std. cals. **$1,267.00**
Price: As above, magnum cals. **$1,320.00**
Price: Monte Carlo stock, high luster, std. cals. **$1,426.00**
Price: As above, magnum cals. **$1,479.00**

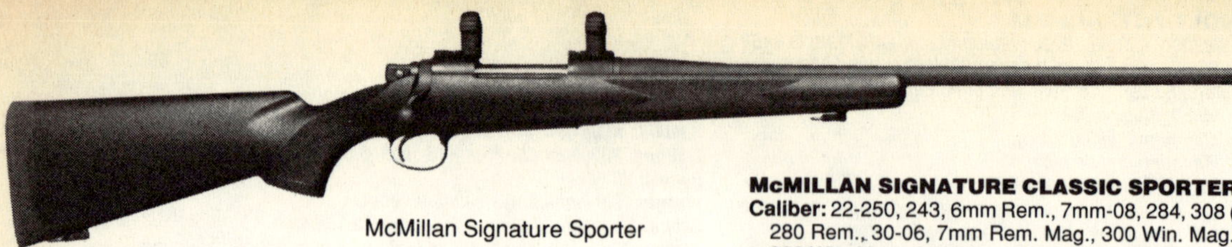

McMillan Signature Sporter

McMILLAN STANDARD SPORTER
Caliber: 6.5x55, 7mm-08 Rem., 308 (short action); 270, 280 Rem., 30-06 (long action); 7mm Rem. Mag., 300 Win. Mag., 338 Win. Mag. (magnum action).
Barrel: 24".
Weight: About 7½ lbs. **Length:** NA.
Stock: Choice of walnut or McMillan fiberglass painted stock.
Sights: None furnished. Comes with scope mount and rings.
Features: Uses chromemoly action and button-rifled barrel; hinged floorplate; Shilen trigger. Guaranteed 1 MOA accuracy. Introduced 1991. Sold through authorized McMillan dealers only. From McMillan Gunworks, Inc.
Price: **$1,250.00**

McMILLAN SIGNATURE CLASSIC SPORTER
Caliber: 22-250, 243, 6mm Rem., 7mm-08, 284, 308 (short action); 25-06, 270, 280 Rem., 30-06, 7mm Rem. Mag., 300 Win. Mag., 300 Wea. (long action); 338 Win. Mag., 340 Wea., 375 H&H (magnum action).
Barrel: 22", 24", 26".
Weight: 7 lbs. (short action).
Stock: McMillan fiberglass in green, beige, brown or black. Recoil pad and 1" swivels installed. Length of pull up to 14¼".
Sights: None furnished. Comes with 1" rings and bases.
Features: Uses McMillan right- or left-hand action with matte black finish. Trigger pull set at 3 lbs. Four-round magazine for standard calibers; three for magnums. Aluminum floorplate. Fibergrain and wood stocks optional. Introduced 1987. From McMillan Gunworks, Inc.
Price: **$1,900.00**

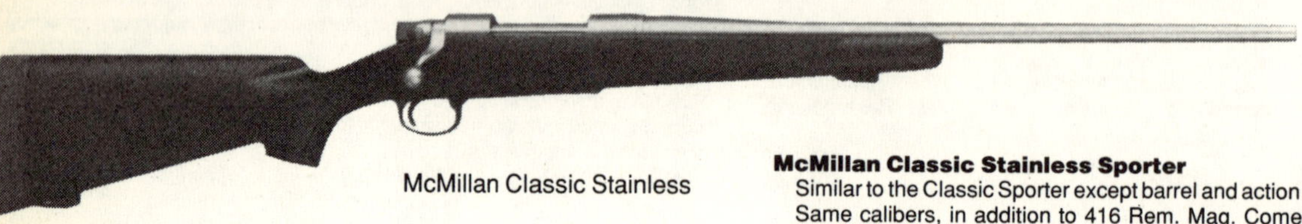

McMillan Classic Stainless

McMillan Classic Stainless Sporter
Similar to the Classic Sporter except barrel and action made of stainless steel. Same calibers, in addition to 416 Rem. Mag. Comes with fiberglass stock, right- or left-hand action in natural stainless, glass bead or black chrome sulfide finishes. Introduced 1990. From McMillan Gunworks, Inc.
Price: **$2,050.00**

McMillan Signature Super Varminter
Similar to the Classic Sporter except has heavy contoured barrel, adjustable trigger, field bipod and special hand-bedded fiberglass stock (Fibergrain optional). Chambered for 223, 22-250, 220 Swift, 243, 6mm Rem., 25-06, 7mm-08 and 308. Comes with 1" rings and bases. Introduced 1989.
Price: **$1,950.00**

McMillan Signature Titanium Mountain Rifle
Similar to the Classic Sporter except action made of titanium alloy, barrel of chromemoly steel. Stock is of graphite reinforced fiberglass. Weight is 5½ lbs. Chambered for 270, 280 Rem., 30-06, 7mm Rem. Mag., 300 Win. Mag. Fibergrain stock optional. Introduced 1989.
Price: **$2,495.00**

McMillan Alaskan

McMillan Signature Alaskan
Similar to the Classic Sporter except has match-grade barrel with single leaf rear sight, barrel band front, 1" detachable rings and mounts, steel floorplate, electroless nickel finish. Has wood Monte Carlo stock with cheekpiece, palm-swell grip, solid buttpad. Chambered for 270, 280 Rem., 30-06, 7mm Rem. Mag., 300 Win. Mag., 300 Wea., 358 Win., 340 Wea., 375 H&H. Introduced 1989.
Price: **$2,750.00**

McMILLAN TALON SPORTER RIFLE
Caliber: 25-06, 270, 280 Rem., 30-06 (Long Action); 7mm Rem. Mag., 300 Win. Mag., 300 Wea. Mag., 300 H&H, 338 Win. Mag., 340 Wea. Mag., 375 H&H, 416 Rem. Mag.
Barrel: 24" (standard).
Weight: About 7½ lbs. **Length:** NA.
Stock: Choice of walnut or McMillan fiberglass.
Sights: None furnished; comes with rings and bases. Open sights optional.
Features: Uses pre-'64 Model 70-type action with cone breech, controlled feed, claw extractor and three-position safety. Barrel and action are of stainless steel; chromemoly optional. Introduced 1991. From McMillan Gunworks, Inc.
Price: **$2,100.00**

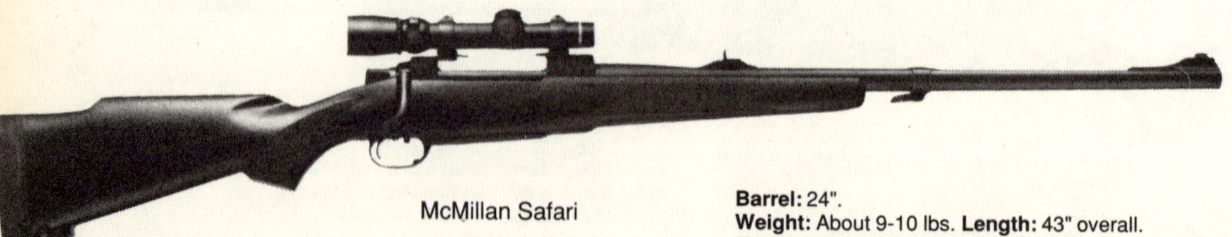

McMillan Safari

McMILLAN TALON SAFARI RIFLE
Caliber: 300 Win. Mag., 300 Wea. Mag., 338 Win. Mag., 300 H&H, 340 Wea. Mag., 375 H&H, 404 Jeffery, 416 Rem. Mag., 458 Win. Mag. (Safari Magnum); 378 Wea. Mag., 416 Rigby, 416 Wea. Mag., 460 Wea. Mag. (Safari Super Magnum).
Barrel: 24".
Weight: About 9-10 lbs. **Length:** 43" overall.
Stock: McMillan fiberglass Safari.
Sights: Barrel band front ramp, multi-leaf express rear.
Features: Uses McMillan Safari action. Has q.d. 1" scope mounts, positive locking steel floorplate, barrel band sling swivel. Match-grade barrel. Matte black finish standard. Introduced 1989. From McMillan Gunworks, Inc.
Price: Talon Safari Magnum **$2,950.00**
Price: Talon Safari Super Magnum**$3,405.00**

Parker-Hale 81 Classic

PARKER-HALE MODEL 81 CLASSIC RIFLE
Caliber: 22-250, 243, 6mm Rem., 270, 6.5x55, 7x57, 7x64, 308, 30-06, 300 Win. Mag., 7mm Rem. Mag., 4-shot magazine.
Barrel: 24".
Weight: About 7¾ lbs. **Length:** 44½" overall.
Stock: European walnut in classic style with oil finish, hand-cut checkering; palm-swell pistol grip, rosewood grip cap.
Sights: Drilled and tapped for open sights and scope mounting. Scope bases included.
Features: Uses Mauser-style action; one-piece steel, Oberndorf-style trigger guard with hinged floorplate; rubber buttpad; quick-detachable sling swivels. Introduced 1984. Available through Navy Arms.
Price: **$860.00**

Parker-Hale Model 1100 Lightweight Rifle
Similar to the Model 81 Classic except has slim barrel profile, hollow bolt handle, alloy trigger guard/floorplate. The Monte Carlo stock has a schnabel forend, hand-cut checkering, swivel studs, palm-swell pistol grip. Comes with hooded ramp front sight, open Williams rear adjustable for windage and elevation. Same calibers as Model 81. Overall length is 43", weight 6½ lbs., with 22" barrel. Introduced 1984. Available through Navy Arms.
Price: **$595.00**

Parker-Hale Model 81 Classic African Rifle
Similar to the Model 81 Classic except chambered only for 375 H&H and 9.3x62. Has adjustable trigger, barrel band front swivel, African express rear sight, engraved receiver. Classic-style stock has a solid buttpad, checkered pistol grip and forend. Introduced 1986. Available through Navy Arms.
Price: **$1,100.00**

Consult our Directory pages for the location of firms mentioned.

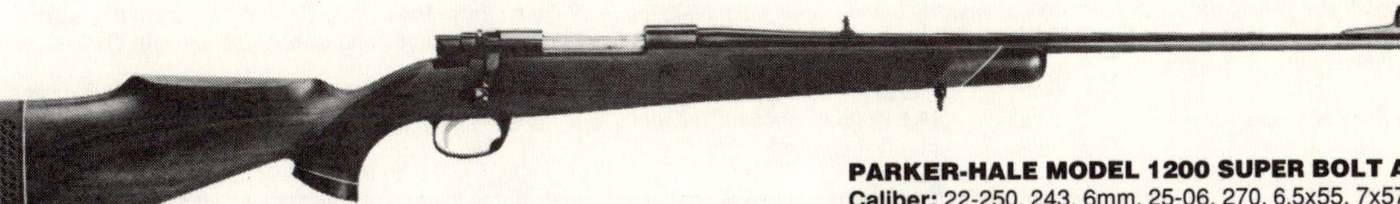
Parker-Hale 1200 Super

PARKER-HALE MODEL 1200 SUPER BOLT ACTION
Caliber: 22-250, 243, 6mm, 25-06, 270, 6.5x55, 7x57, 7x64, 308, 30-06, 8mm Mauser (standard action); 7mm Rem. Mag., 300 Win. Mag. (1200M Super Magnum).
Barrel: 24".
Weight: About 7½ lbs. **Length:** 44½" overall.
Stock: European walnut, rosewood grip and forend tips, hand-cut checkering; roll-over cheekpiece; palm-swell pistol grip; ventilated recoil pad; wraparound checkering.
Sights: Hooded post front, open rear.
Features: Uses Mauser-style action with claw extractor; gold-plated adjustable trigger; silent side safety locks trigger, sear and bolt; aluminum trigger guard. Introduced 1984. Available through Navy Arms.
Price: **$680.00**

Parker-Hale Model 1200 Super Clip Rifle
Same as the Model 1200 Super except has a detachable steel box magazine and steel trigger guard. Introduced 1984. Available through Navy Arms.
Price: **$740.00**

PARKER-HALE MODEL 2100 MIDLAND RIFLE
Caliber: 22-250, 243, 6mm, 270, 6.5x55, 7x57, 7x64, 308, 30-06, 300 Win. Mag., 7mm Rem. Mag.
Barrel: 22".
Weight: About 7 lbs. **Length:** 43" overall.
Stock: European walnut, cut-checkered pistol grip and forend; sling swivels.
Sights: Hooded post front, flip-up open rear.
Features: Mauser-type action has twin front locking lugs, rear safety lug, and claw extractor; hinged floorplate; adjustable single-stage trigger; silent side safety. Introduced 1984. Available through Navy Arms.
Price: **$365.00**

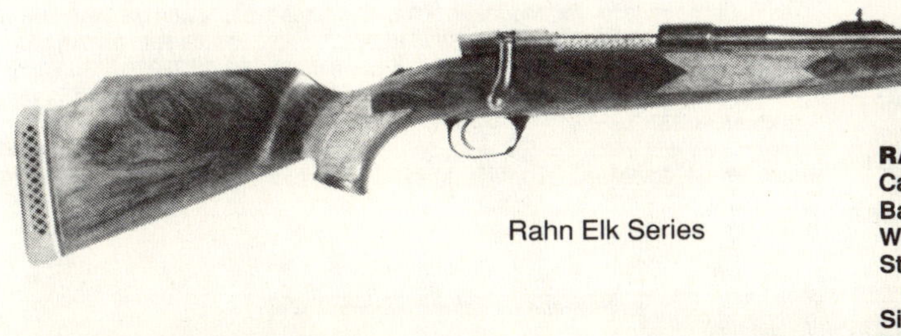
Rahn Elk Series

RAHN DEER SERIES BOLT-ACTION RIFLE
Caliber: 25-06, 308, 270.
Barrel: 24".
Weight: NA. **Length:** NA.
Stock: Circassian walnut with rosewood forend and grip caps, Monte Carlo cheekpiece, semi-schnabel forend; hand checkered.
Sights: Bead front, open adjustable rear. Drilled and tapped for scope mount.
Features: Free-floating barrel; rubber recoil pad; one-piece trigger guard with hinged, engraved floorplate; 22 rimfire conversion insert available. Introduced 1986. From Rahn Gun Works, Inc.
Price: **$1,250.00**
Price: With custom stock made to customer specs **$1,300.00**

Rahn Himalayan Series Rifle
Similar to the "Deer Series" except chambered for 5.6x57 or 6.5x68S, short stock of walnut or fiberglass, and floorplate engravings of a yak with scroll border. Introduced 1986.
Price: **$1,375.00**
Price: With walnut stock made to customer specs **$1,450.00**

Rahn Safari Series Rifle
Similar to the "Deer Series" except chambered for 308 Norma Mag., 300 Win. Mag., 8x68S, 9x64. Choice of Cape buffalo, rhino or elephant engraving. Gold oval nameplate with three initials. Introduced 1986.
Price: **$1,500.00**
Price: With stock made to customer specs **$1,575.00**

Rahn Elk Series Rifle
Similar to the "Deer Series" except chambered for 6x56, 30-06, 7mm Rem. Mag. and has elk head engraving on floorplate. Introduced 1986.
Price: **$1,350.00**
Price: With stock made to customer specs **$1,425.00**

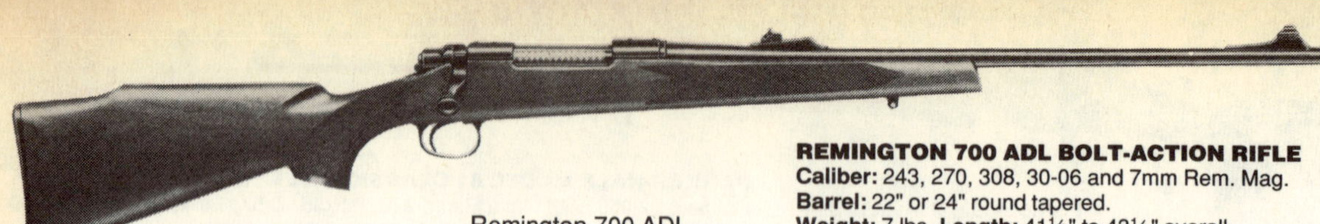
Remington 700 ADL

REMINGTON 700 ADL BOLT-ACTION RIFLE
Caliber: 243, 270, 308, 30-06 and 7mm Rem. Mag.
Barrel: 22" or 24" round tapered.
Weight: 7 lbs. **Length:** 41½" to 43½" overall.
Stock: Walnut. Satin-finished p.g. stock with fine-line cut checkering, Monte Carlo.
Sights: Gold bead ramp front; removable, step-adj. rear with windage screw.
Features: Side safety, receiver tapped for scope mounts.
Price: About **$431.00**
Price: 7mm Rem. Mag., about **$458.00**
Price: Model 700 ADL/LS (laminated stock, 243, 270, 30-06 only) . . **$484.00**
Price: As above, 7mm Rem. Mag. **$505.00**

Remington 700 BDL Left Hand
Same as 700 BDL except mirror-image left-hand action, stock. Available in 22-250, 243, 308, 270, 30-06 only.
Price: About **$568.00**
Price: 7mm Rem. Mag., 338 Win. Mag., about **$592.00**

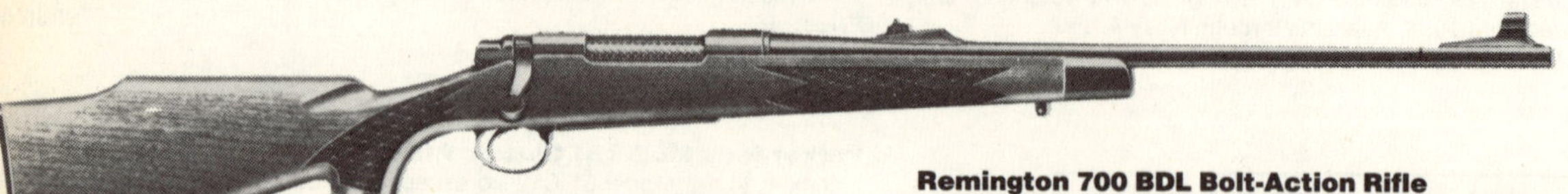
Remington 700 BDL

Remington 700 BDL Bolt-Action Rifle
Same as the 700 ADL except chambered for 222, 223 (short action, 24" barrel), 22-250, 25-06, 6mm Rem. (short action, 22" barrel), 243, 270, 7mm-08, 280, 30-06, 308; skip-line checkering; black forend tip and grip cap with white line spacers. Matted receiver top, quick-release floorplate. Hooded ramp front sight; q.d. swivels.
Price: About **$509.00**
Also available in 17 Rem., 7mm Rem. Mag., 300 Win. Mag. (long action, 24" barrel), 338 Win. Mag., 35 Whelen (long action, 22" barrel). Overall length 44½", weight about 7½ lbs.
Price: About **$535.00**
Price: Custom Grade, about **$2,181.00**

Remington 700 Safari
Similar to the 700 BDL except custom finished and tuned. In 8mm Rem. Mag., 375 H&H, 416 Rem. Mag. or 458 Win. Magnum calibers only with heavy barrel. Hand checkered, oil-finished stock in classic or Monte Carlo style with recoil pad installed. Delivery time is about 5 months.
Price: About **$951.00**
Price: Safari Custom KS (Kevlar stock) **$1,096.00**

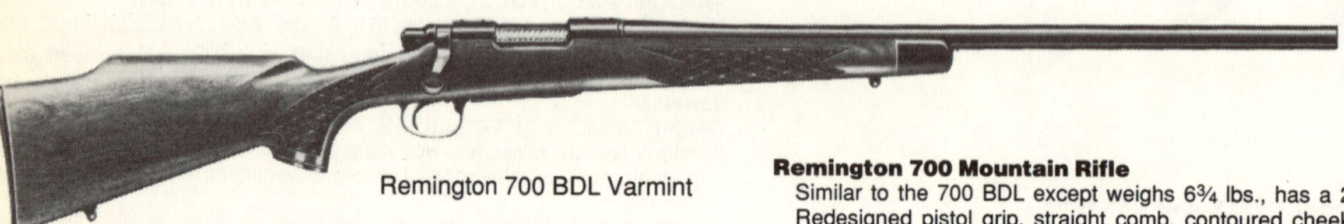
Remington 700 BDL Varmint

Remington 700 Mountain Rifle
Similar to the 700 BDL except weighs 6¾ lbs., has a 22" tapered barrel. Redesigned pistol grip, straight comb, contoured cheekpiece, satin stock finish, fine checkering, hinged floorplate and magazine follower, two-position thumb safety. Chambered for 243, 257 Roberts, 270 Win., 7x57, 7mm-08, 280 Rem., 30-06, 308, 4-shot magazine. Overall length is 42½". Introduced 1986.
Price: About **$517.00**

Remington 700 BDL Varmint Special
Same as 700 BDL, except 24" heavy bbl., 43½" overall, weighs 9 lbs. Cals. 222, 223, 22-250, 243, 6mm Rem., 7mm-08 Rem. and 308. No sights.
Price: About **$543.00**

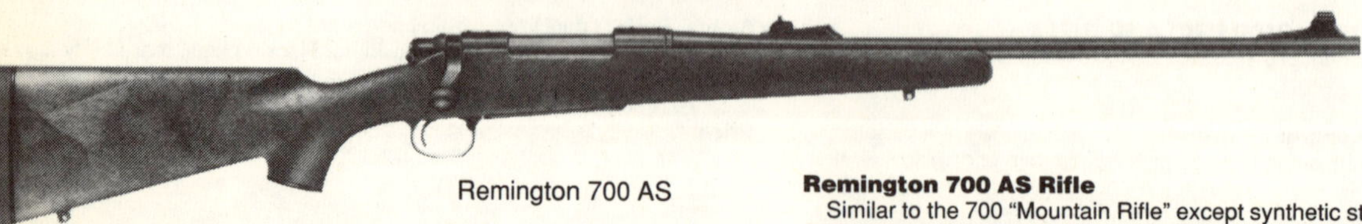
Remington 700 AS

Remington 700 AS Rifle
Similar to the 700 "Mountain Rifle" except synthetic stock is of thermoplastic resin. Same style as the "Mountain Rifle," available in black with lightly textured finish (cheekpiece left smooth). Solid buttpad, grip cap with Remington logo. Right-hand action only with hinged floorplate in 22-250, 243, 270, 280 Rem., 308, 30-06, 7mm Rem. Mag., 300 Wea. Mag., 22" barrel, weight 6¾ lbs. Introduced 1989.
Price: **$528.00**
Price: 7mm Rem. Mag., 300 Wea. Mag. **$549.00**

Remington 700 Custom KS Mountain Rifle
Similar to the 700 "Mountain Rifle" except custom finished with Kevlar reinforced resin synthetic stock. Available in both left- and right-hand versions. Chambered for 270 Win., 280 Rem., 30-06, 7mm Rem. Mag., 300 Win. Mag., 300 Wea. Mag., 35 Whelen, 338 Win. Mag., 8mm Rem. Mag., 375 H&H, all with 24" barrel only. Weight is 6 lbs., 6 oz. Introduced 1986.
Price: About **$947.00**

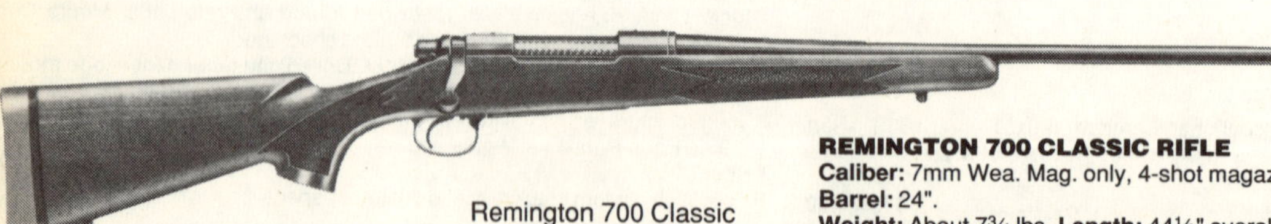
Remington 700 Classic

REMINGTON 700 CLASSIC RIFLE
Caliber: 7mm Wea. Mag. only, 4-shot magazine.
Barrel: 24".
Weight: About 7¾ lbs. **Length:** 44½" overall.
Stock: American walnut, 20 lpi checkering on p.g. and forend. Classic styling. Satin finish.
Sights: None furnished. Receiver drilled and tapped for scope mounting.
Features: A "classic" version of the M700 ADL with straight comb stock. Fitted with rubber recoil pad. Sling swivel studs installed. Hinged floorplate. Limited production in 1991 only.
Price: About **$535.00**

CAUTION: PRICES CHANGE, CHECK AT GUNSHOP.

Remington Model Seven

REMINGTON MODEL SEVEN BOLT-ACTION RIFLE

Caliber: 223 Rem. (5-shot); 243, 7mm-08, 6mm, 308 (4-shot).
Barrel: 18½".
Weight: 6¼ lbs. **Length:** 37½" overall.
Stock: Walnut, with modified schnabel forend. Cut checkering.
Sights: Ramp front, adjustable open rear.
Features: New short-action design; silent side safety; free-floated barrel except for single pressure point at forend tip. Introduced 1983.
Price: About $517.00

Remington Model Seven Custom KS

Similar to the standard Model Seven except has custom finished stock of lightweight Kevlar aramid fiber and chambered for 223 Rem., 7mm-08, 308, 35 Rem. and 350 Rem. Mag. Barrel length is 20", weight 5¾ lbs. Comes with iron sights and is drilled and tapped for scope mounting. Special order through Remington Custom Shop. Introduced 1987.
Price: $947.00

Ruger Magnum Rifle

RUGER M77 MARK II MAGNUM RIFLE

Caliber: 375 H&H (4-shot magazine); 416 Rigby (3-shot magazine).
Barrel: NA.
Weight: 9.25 lbs. (375); 10.25 lbs. (416). **Length:** NA.
Stock: Circassian walnut.
Sights: Ramp front, three leaf express on serrated rib. Rib also serves as base for front scope ring.
Features: Uses an enlarged Mark II action, safety, trigger mechanism, trigger guard, floorplate. Introduced 1989.
Price: M77RSM MKII $1,550.00

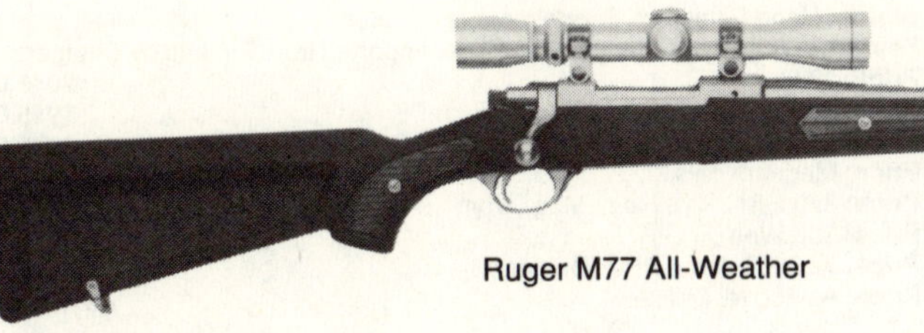

Ruger M77 All-Weather

RUGER M77 MARK II RIFLE

Caliber: 223, 243, 6mm Rem., 270, 308, 30-06, 7mm Rem. Mag., 300 Win. Mag., 4-shot magazine.
Barrel: 20", 22", 24".
Weight: About 7 lbs. **Length:** 39¾" overall.
Stock: American walnut.
Sights: None furnished. Receiver has Ruger integral scope mount base, comes with Ruger 1" rings.
Features: Short action with new trigger and three-position safety. New trigger guard with redesigned floorplate latch. Left-hand model available. Introduced 1989.
Price: M77MKIIR (no sights, 243, 6mm Rem., 308) $531.25
Price: M77MKIIRS (open sights, 243, 308) $587.00
Price: M77MKIIRL (short action, 6 lbs., 223, 243, 308) $564.25
Price: M77MKIILR (long action, left-hand, 270, 30-06, 7mm Rem. Mag., 300 Win. Mag.) $546.25

Ruger M77 Mark II All-Weather Stainless Rifle

Similar to the wood-stock M77 Mark II except all metal parts are of stainless steel, and has an injection-moulded, glass-fiber-reinforced Du Pont Zytel stock. Chambered for 223, 243, 270, 308, 30-06, 7mm Rem. Mag., 300 Win. Mag. Has the fixed-blade-type ejector, three-position safety, and new trigger guard with patented floorplate latch. Comes with Integral Scope Base Receiver and 1" Ruger scope rings, built-in sling swivel loops. Introduced 1990.
Price: KM77MKIIRP $531.25

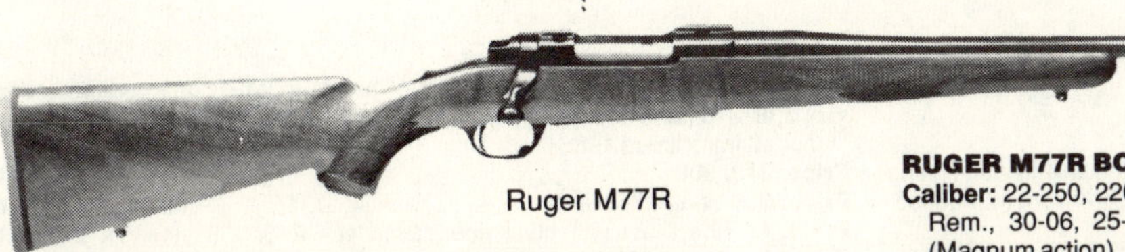

Ruger M77R

RUGER M77R BOLT-ACTION RIFLE

Caliber: 22-250, 220 Swift (Short Stroke action); 270, 7x57, 257 Roberts, 280 Rem., 30-06, 25-06, 7mm Rem. Mag., 300 Win. Mag., 338 Win. Mag. (Magnum action).
Barrel: 22" round tapered (24" in 220 Swift and magnum action calibers).
Weight: 6¾ lbs. **Length:** 42" overall (22" barrel).
Stock: Hand checkered American walnut, p.g. cap, sling swivel studs and recoil pad.
Sights: None supplied; comes with scope rings.
Features: Integral scope mount bases, diagonal bedding system, hinged floorplate, adjustable trigger, tang safety.
Price: With Ruger steel scope rings, no sights (M77R) $531.25

Ruger M77RS Magnum Rifle

Similar to Ruger 77 except magnum-size action. Calibers 270, 30-06, 25-06, 7mm Rem. Mag., 300 Win. Mag., 338 Win. Mag., 35 Whelen, with 24" barrel. Weight about 7 lbs. Integral-base receiver, Ruger 1" rings and open sights.
Price: $587.00

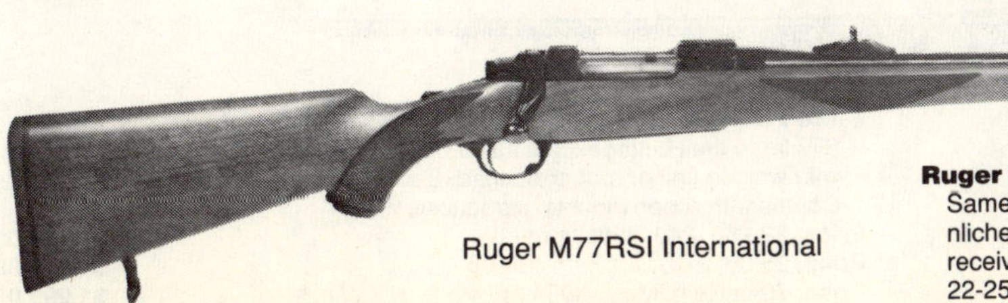

Ruger M77RSI International

Ruger M77RSI International Rifle

Same as the standard Model 77 except has 18½" barrel, full-length Mannlicher-style stock, with steel forend cap, loop-type sling swivel. Integral-base receiver, open sights, Ruger 1" steel rings. Improved front sight. Available in 22-250, 250-3000, 308, 270, 30-06. Weighs 7 lbs. Length overall is 38⅜".
Price: $593.75

Ruger M77RL Ultra Light
Similar to the standard Model 77 except weighs only 6 lbs., chambered for 270, 30-06, 257, 22-250; barrel tapped for target scope blocks; has 20" Ultra Light barrel. Overall length 40". Ruger's steel 1" scope rings supplied. Introduced 1983.
Price: $564.25

Ruger M77RLS Ultra Light Carbine
Similar to the Model 77RL Ultra Light except has 18½" barrel, Ruger Integral Scope Mounting System, iron sights, and hinged floorplate. Available in 270, 30-06 (Magnum action). Weight is 6 lbs., overall length 38⅞". Introduced 1987.
Price: $564.25

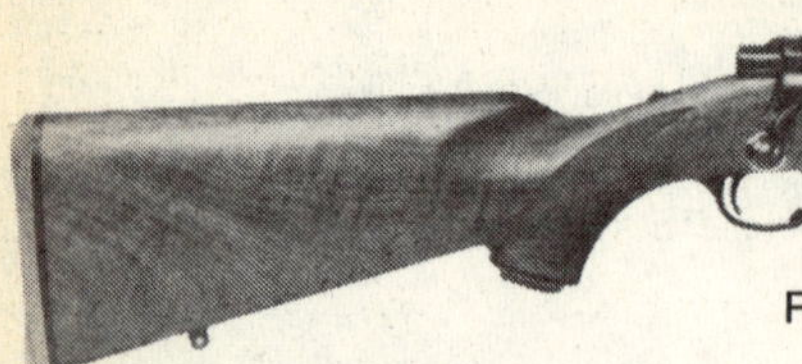
Ruger M77V Varmint

RUGER M77V VARMINT
Caliber: 22-250, 220 Swift, 243, 6mm, 25-06, 308.
Barrel: 24" heavy straight tapered, 24" in 220 Swift.
Weight: Approx. 9 lbs. **Length:** Approx. 44" overall (24" barrel).
Stock: American walnut, similar in style to Magnum Rifle.
Sights: Barrel drilled and tapped for target scope blocks. Integral scope mount bases in receiver.
Features: Ruger diagonal bedding system. Ruger steel 1" scope rings supplied. Fully adjustable trigger. Barreled actions available in any of the standard calibers and barrel lengths.
Price: $546.25

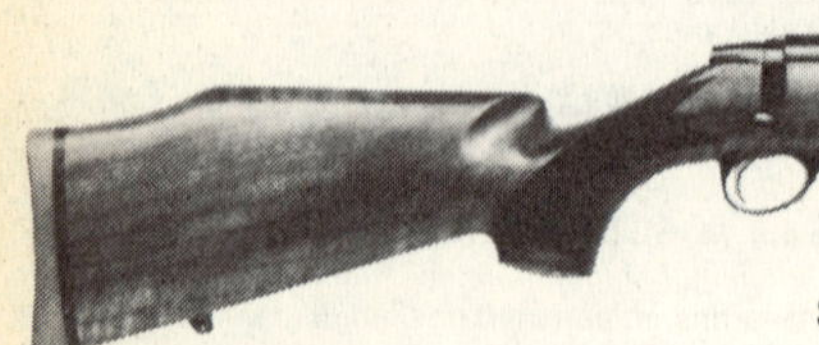
Sako Hunter

SAKO HUNTER RIFLE
Caliber: 17 Rem., 222 PPC, 222, 223, 6mm PPC (short action); 22-250, 243, 7mm-08, 308 (medium action); 25-06, 270, 30-06, 7mm Rem. Mag., 300 Win. Mag., 338 Win. Mag., 375 H&H Mag., 300 Wea. Mag., 416 Rem. Mag. (long action).
Barrel: 22" to 24" depending on caliber.
Weight: 5¾ lbs. (short); 6¼ lbs. (med.); 7¼ lbs. (long).
Stock: Hand-checkered European walnut.
Sights: None furnished. Scope mounts included.
Features: Adj. trigger, hinged floorplate. Imported from Finland by Stoeger.
Price: 17 Rem. $945.00
Price: 222, 223, 22-250, 243, 308, 7mm-08 . . . . $945.00
Price: Long action cals. (except magnums) $975.00
Price: Magnum cals. $995.00
Price: 375 H&H, 416 Rem. Mag., from $1,010.00
Price: 300 Wea. $1,010.00
Price: 22 PPC, 6mm PPC, Hunter $1,185.00
Price: As above, Deluxe $1,485.00

Sako Hunter Left-Hand Rifle
Same gun as the Sako Hunter except has left-hand action, stock with dull finish. Available in long action and magnum calibers only. Introduced 1987.
Price: Standard calibers $1,055.00
Price: Magnum calibers $1,070.00
Price: 375 H&H, 416 Rem. Mag. $1,085.00
Price: Deluxe, standard calibers $1,385.00
Price: Deluxe, magnum calibers $1,400.00
Price: Deluxe, 375 H&H, 416 Rem. Mag. $1,415.00

Sako Mannlicher-Style Carbine
Same as the Hunter except has full "Mannlicher" style stock, 18½" barrel, weighs 7½ lbs., chambered for 243, 25-06, 270, 308 and 30-06, 7mm Rem. Mag., 300 Win. Mag., 338 Win. Mag., 375 H&H. Introduced 1977. From Stoeger.
Price: 243, 308 . . . . $1,095.00
Price: 25-06, 270, 30-06 . . . . $1,130.00
Price: 7mm Rem. Mag., 300 Win. Mag., 338 Win. Mag.,375 H&H $1,150.00

Sako Safari Grade Bolt Action
Similar to the Hunter except available in long action, calibers 338 Win. Mag. or 375 H&H Mag. or 416 Rem. Mag. only. Stocked in French walnut, checkered 20 lpi, solid rubber buttpad; grip cap and forend tip; quarter-rib "express" rear sight, hooded ramp front. Front sling swivel band-mounted on barrel.
Price: $2,710.00

Sako Carbine

Sako Hunter LS Rifle
Same gun as the Sako Hunter except has laminated stock with dull finish. Chambered for same calibers. Also available in left-hand version. Introduced 1987.
Price: Medium action $1,080.00
Price: Long action, from $1,125.00
Price: Magnum cals., from $1,140.00
Price: 375 H&H, 416 Rem. Mag., from $1,156.00
Price: Left-hand, long action, 270, 280 Rem., 30-06 . . . . $1,185.00
Price: Left-hand, long action, 7mm Rem. Mag., 300 Win. Mag., 338 Win. Mag. $1,200.00
Price: Left-hand, long action, 375 H&H, 416 Rem. Mag. $1,215.00

Sako Carbine
Similar to the Hunter except with 18½" barrel, in 243, 308 (medium action), or 338, 375 (long action) and with conventional oil-finished stock of the Hunter model. Introduced 1986.
Price: 243, 308 . . . . $945.00
Price: 338 Win., 375 H&H . . . . $995.00 to $1,010.00
Price: As FiberClass with black fiberglass stock, 243, 308 . . . . . $1,239.00
Price: As above, 338 Win., 375 H&H . . . . $1,290.00 to $1,299.00

Consult our Directory pages for the location of firms mentioned.

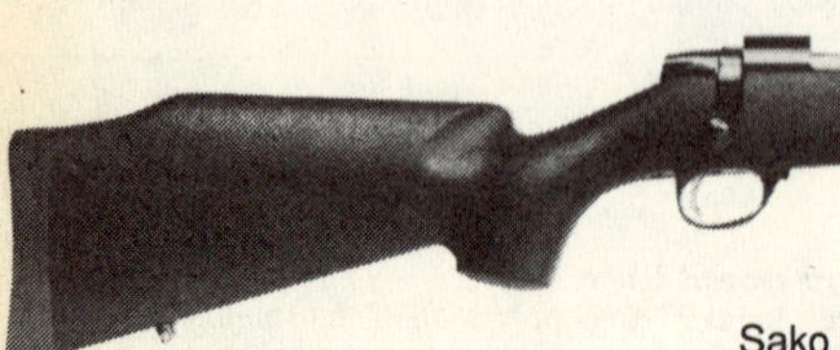
Sako FiberClass

Sako FiberClass Sporter
Similar to the Hunter except has a black fiberglass stock in the classic style, with wrinkle finish, rubber buttpad. Barrel length is 23", weight 7 lbs., 2 oz. Comes with scope mounts. Introduced 1985.
Price: 22-250, 243, 308, 7mm-08 . . . . $1,235.00
Price: 25-06, 270, 280 Rem., 30-06 . . . . $1,275.00
Price: 7mm Rem. Mag., 300 Win. Mag., 338 Win. Mag. $1,290.00
Price: 375 H&H, 416 Rem. Mag. $1,299.00

Sako Heavy Barrel

Sako Deluxe Lightweight
Same action as Hunter except has select wood, rosewood p.g. cap and forend tip. Fine checkering on top surfaces of integral dovetail bases, bolt sleeve, bolt handle root and bolt knob. Vent. recoil pad, skip-line checkering, mirror finish bluing.
Price: 17 Rem., 222, 223, 22-250, 243, 308, 7mm-08 . . . . **$1,285.00**
Price: 25-06, 270, 280 Rem., 30-06 . . . . **$1,325.00**
Price: 7mm Rem. Mag., 300 Win. Mag., 338 Win. Mag. **$1,340.00**
Price: 300 Wea., 375 H&H, 416 Rem. Mag. **$1,355.00**

Sako Varmint Heavy Barrel
Same as std. Super Sporter except has beavertail forend; available in 17 Rem., 222, 223 (short action), 22 PPC, 6mm PPC (single shot), 22-250, 243, 308, 7mm-08 (medium action). Weight from 8¼ to 8½ lbs., 5-shot magazine capacity.
Price: 17 Rem., 222, 223 (short action) **$1,080.00**
Price: 22-250, 243, 308 (medium action) **$1,080.00**
Price: 22 PPC, 6mm PPC (single shot) **$1,265.00**

Sako Super Deluxe Sporter
Similar to Deluxe Sporter except has select European walnut with high- gloss finish and deep-cut oak leaf carving. Metal has super high polish, deep blue finish. Special order only.
Price: **$2,710.00**

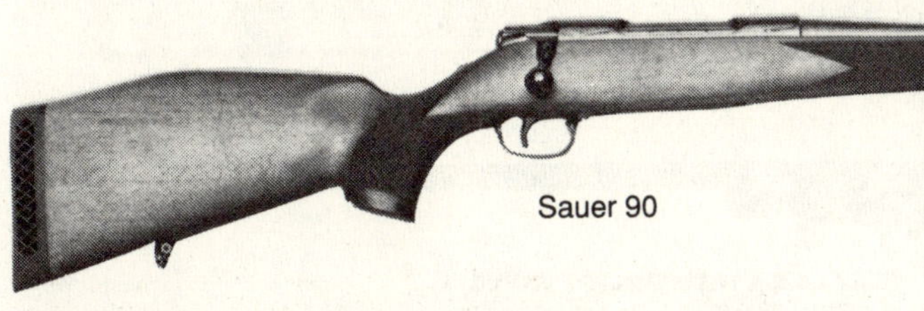
Sauer 90

SAUER 90 BOLT-ACTION RIFLE
Caliber: 270, 25-06, 30-06, 7mm Rem. Mag., 300 Win. Mag., 300 Wea. Mag., 338 Win., 375 H&H, 4-shot magazine for standard calibers, 3-shot for magnums.
Barrel: 24" (standard calibers), 26" (magnum calibers).
Weight: 7.25 to 8 lbs. **Length:** 44" overall (24" barrel).
Stock: Monte Carlo style with sculptured cheekpiece, hand-checkered grip and forend, rosewood grip cap and forend tip. Lux is European walnut with oil finish, Supreme is American walnut with high-gloss lacquer finish.
Sights: None furnished; drilled and tapped for scope mount.
Features: Rear bolt cam activated locking lug action with 65° bolt lift, fully adjustable gold-plated trigger, chamber-loaded signal pin, cocking indicator, tang-mounted slide safety. Detachable box magazine. Introduced 1986. Imported from Germany by Guns Unlimited, Inc.
Price: Lux or Supreme **$1,495.00**
Price: With engraving LVL I **$2,495.00**
Price: With engraving LVL II **$3,095.00**
Price: With engraving LVL III **$3,395.00**
Price: With engraving LVL IV **$3,995.00**

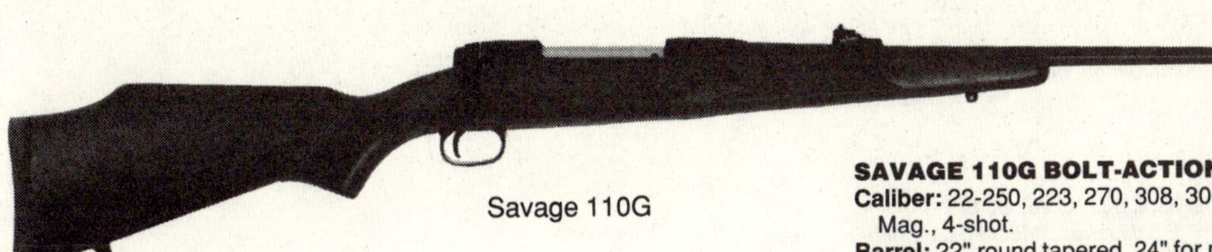
Savage 110G

Savage 110GXP3 Bolt-Action Rifle
Similar to the 110G except comes with 3-9x32 scope, Kwik-Site rings and bases, Savage/Pathfinder leather sling, Uncle Mike's swivels, gun lock, ear plugs, safety glasses and sight-in target. Available in 243, 270, 30-06, 7mm Rem. Mag., 300 Win. Mag. Introduced 1991.
Price: **$340.00**

Savage 110CY Youth/Ladies Rifle
Similar to the Savage 110G except has walnut-finished hardwood stock with 12½" length of pull, and is chambered for 243 and 300 Savage. Comes with gun lock, ear plugs, sight-in target and shooting glasses. Introduced 1991.
Price: **$350.00**

Savage 112FV Varmint Rifle
Similar to the Savage 110G except has 26" heavy barrel, chambered for 223 and 22-250, and comes with a DuPont Rynite stock. Drilled and tapped for scope mounts. Weight is 9 lbs. Included are gun lock, ear plugs, sight-in target and shooting glases. Reintroduced 1991.
Price: **$360.00**

SAVAGE 110G BOLT-ACTION RIFLE
Caliber: 22-250, 223, 270, 308, 30-06, 243, 5-shot; 7mm Rem. Mag., 300 Win. Mag., 4-shot.
Barrel: 22" round tapered, 24" for magnum.
Weight: 6¾ lbs. **Length:** 42⅜" (22" barrel).
Stock: Walnut-finished checkered hardwood with Monte Carlo; hard rubber buttplate.
Sights: Ramp front, step adjustable rear.
Features: Top tang safety, receiver tapped for scope mount. Full-floating barrel; adjustable trigger. Introduced 1989.
Price: **$340.00**
Price: Left-hand, 30-06, 270, 7mm Rem. Mag. only, M110GLNS . . **$400.00**
Price: Model 110GNS (no sights) **$340.00**

Savage 110WLE Limited Edition Rifle
Similar to the Savage 110G except is chambered for 250-3000 and 300 Savage only, and comes with high-luster #2 fancy-grade American walnut stock with cut checkering, swivel studs, and recoil pad. Highly polished barrel; the bolt has a laser-etched Savage logo. Included are gun lock, ear plugs, sight-in target and shooting glasses. Introduced 1991.
Price: About **$475.00**

Savage 114CU Classic Ultra Rifle
Similar to the Savage 110G except comes with a straight American walnut stock with high-gloss finish, cut checkering, grip cap and recoil pad. Removable box magazine hold five rounds (four for magnums). Chambered for 270, 30-06, 7mm Rem. Mag. and 300 Win. Mag. Introduced 1991.
Price: **$520.00**

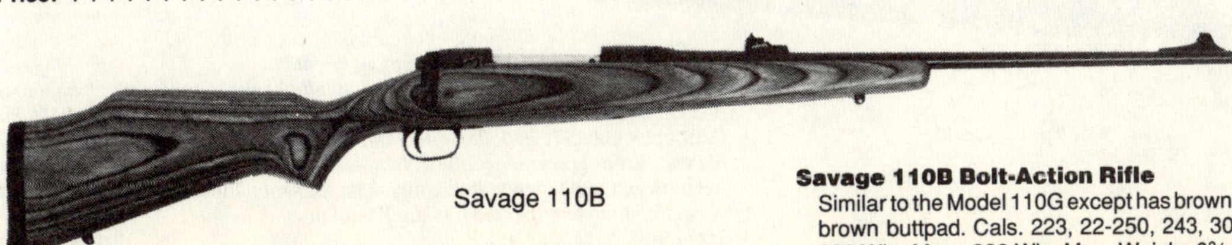
Savage 110B

Savage 110B Bolt-Action Rifle
Similar to the Model 110G except has brown laminated Monte Carlo stock with brown buttpad. Cals. 223, 22-250, 243, 308, 270, 30-06, 7mm Rem. Mag., 300 Win. Mag., 338 Win. Mag. Weighs 6¾ lbs. Introduced 1989.
Price: **$400.00**

CAUTION: PRICES CHANGE, CHECK AT GUNSHOP.

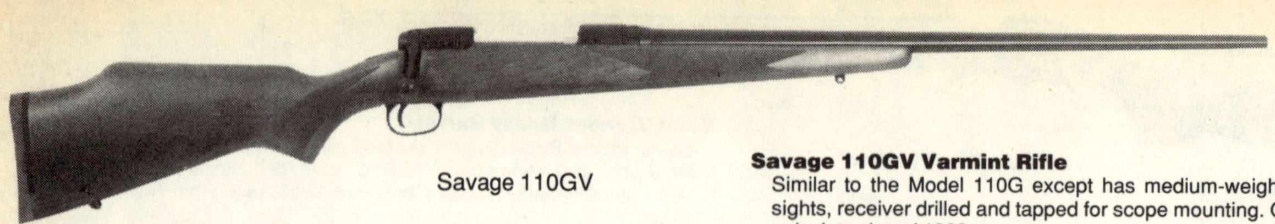

Savage 110GV

Savage 110GV Varmint Rifle

Similar to the Model 110G except has medium-weight varmint barrel, no sights, receiver drilled and tapped for scope mounting. Calibers 22-250, 223 only. Introduced 1989.

Price: **$400.00**

Savage 110F Bolt-Action Rifle

Similar to the Model 110G except has a black Du Pont Rynite® stock with black buttpad, swivel studs, removable open sights. Same calibers as the 110G except also in 338 Win. Mag. Introduced 1988.

Price: Right-hand only **$400.00**
Price: Model 110FNS (no sights, integral Weaver-type bases) . . . **$390.00**

Savage 116FSS Bolt-Action Rifle

Similar to the Savage 110F except made of stainless steel. Has black DuPont Rynite stock. Drilled and tapped for scope mounts; no open sights supplied. In 30-06, 270, 7mm Rem. Mag., 300 Win. Mag., 338 Win. Mag.; 22" barrel for 30-06, 270; 24" for magnums. Introduced 1991.

Price: **$500.00**

Savage 110FXP3 Bolt-Action Rifle

Same as the Savage 110F except comes with a 3-9x32 scope, Kwik-Site rings and bases, Savage/Pathfinder leather sling, Uncle Mike's swivels, gun lock, ear plugs, shooting glasses and sight-in target. Chambered for 243, 30-06, 270, 7mm Rem. Mag., 300 Win. Mag. Introduced 1991.

Price: **$450.00**

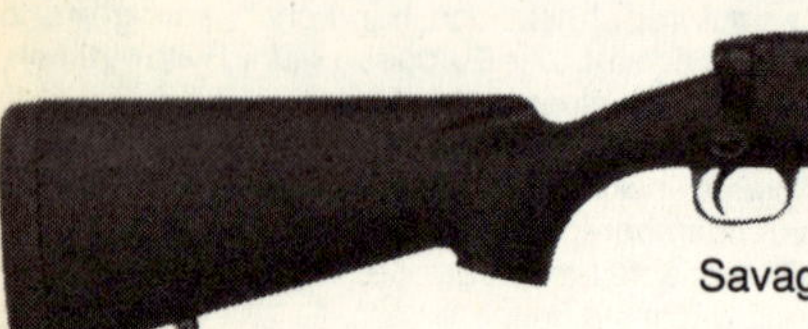

Savage 110FP Police

SAVAGE 110FP POLICE RIFLE

Caliber: 223, 308, 4-shot magazine.
Barrel: 24", heavy.
Weight: 9 lbs. **Length:** 45.5" overall.
Stock: Black Rynite composition.
Sights: None furnished. Receiver drilled and tapped for scope mounting.
Features: Matte finish on all metal parts. Double swivel studs on the forend for sling and/or bipod mount. Introduced 1990. From Savage Arms.
Price: **$500.00**

Steyr Model M

STEYR-MANNLICHER SPORTER MODELS SL, L, M, S, S/T

Caliber: 222 Rem., 222 Rem. Mag., 223 Rem., 5.6x50 Mag. (Model SL); 5.6x57, 243, 308, 22-250, 6mm Rem. (Model L); 6.5x57, 270, 7x64, 30-06, 9.3x62, 6.5x55, 7.5 Swiss, 7x57, 8x57 JS (Model M); 6.5x68, 7mm Rem. Mag., 300 Win. Mag., 8x68S, 9.3x64, 375 H&H, 458 Win. Mag. (Model S).
Barrel: 20" (full-stock), 23.6" (half-stock), 26" (magnums).
Weight: 6.8 to 7.5 lbs. **Length:** 39" (full-stock), 43" (half-stock).
Stock: Hand-checkered European walnut. Full Mannlicher or standard half-stock with Monte Carlo comb and rubber recoil pad. Classic American-style stock available on all but Varmint, Models S, S/T at no extra cost.
Sights: Ramp front, open adjustable rear.
Features: Choice of single- or double-set triggers. Detachable 5-shot rotary magazine. Drilled and tapped for scope mounting. Model M actions available in left-hand models; S (magnum) actions available in half-stock only. Imported by Gun South, Inc.
Price: Models SL, L, M, half-stock **$1,618.00**
Price: As above, full-stock **$1,743.00**
Price: Models SL, L Varmint, 26" heavy barrel **$1,743.00**
Price: Model M left-hand, half-stock **$1,743.00**
Price: As above, full-stock (270, 7x57, 7x64, 30-06) **$1,868.00**
Price: Model S Magnum **$1,743.00**
Price: Model S/T, 26" heavy barrel (375 H&H, 9.3x64, 458 Win. Mag.) **$1,868.00**

Consult our Directory pages for the location of firms mentioned.

Steyr-Mannlicher Model M Professional Rifle

Similar to the Sporter series except has black ABS Cycolac stock, Parkerized finish. Chambered for 6.5x57, 270, 7x64, 30-06, 9.3x62, 6.5x55, 7.5 Swiss, 7x57 and 8x57 JS. Has 23.6" barrel, weighs 7.5 lbs. Also available in left-hand version. Imported by Gun South, Inc.

Price: **$1,368.00**

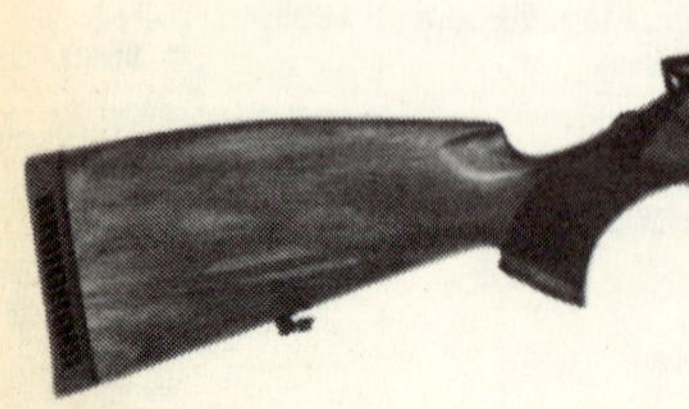

Steyr Luxus M

Steyr-Mannlicher Luxus Model L, M, S

Similar to the Sporter series except has single set trigger, detachable steel 3-shot, in-line magazine, rear tang slide safety. Calibers: 5.6x57, 243, 308 (Model L); 6.5x57, 270, 7x64, 30-06, 9.3x62, 6.5x55, 7.5 Swiss (Model M); 6.5x68, 7mm Rem. Mag., 300 Win. Mag., 8x68S (Model S). S (magnum) calibers available in half-stock only. Classic American-style stock available at no extra charge. Imported by Gun South, Inc.

Price: Model L, M, half-stock **$2,118.00**
Price: As above, full-stock **$2,243.00**
Price: Model S (magnum) **$2,243.00**

Tikka Rifle

TIKKA BOLT-ACTION RIFLE

Caliber: 22-250, 223, 243, 270, 308, 30-06, 7mm Rem. Mag., 300 Win. Mag., 338 Win. Mag.
Barrel: 22½" (std. cals.), 24½" (magnum cals.).
Weight: 7⅛ lbs. **Length:** 43" overall (std. cals.).
Stock: European walnut with Monte Carlo comb, rubber buttpad, checkered grip and forend.
Sights: None furnished.
Features: Detachable four-shot magazine (standard calibers), three-shot in magnums. Receiver dovetailed for scope mounting. Introduced 1988. Imported from Finland by Stoeger Industries.
Price: Standard calibers **$795.00**
Price: Magnum calibers **$820.00**

Tikka Premium Grade Rifles

Similar to the standard grade Tikka except has stock with roll-over cheekpiece, select walnut, rosewood grip and forend caps. Hand-checkered grip and forend. Highly polished and blued barrel. Introduced 1990. Imported from Finland by Stoeger.
Price: Standard calibers **$980.00**
Price: Magnum calibers **$1,015.00**

Tikka Whitetail/Battue Rifle

Similar to the standard Tikka rifle except has 20½" barrel with raised quarter-rib with wide V-shaped sight for rapid sighting. Chambered for 308, 270, 30-06, 7mm Rem. Mag., 300 Win. Mag., 338 Win. Mag. Made in Finland by Sako. Introduced 1991. Imported by Stoeger.
Price: 308, 270, 30-06 . . . . **$820.00**
Price: 7mm Rem. Mag., 300 Win. Mag., 338 Win. Mag. **$850.00**

Tikka Varmint/Continental Rifle

Similar to the standard Tikka rifle except has heavy barrel, extra-wide forend. Chambered for 22-250, 223, 243, 308. Introduced 1991. Made in Finland by Sako. Imported by Stoeger.
Price: **$1,035.00**

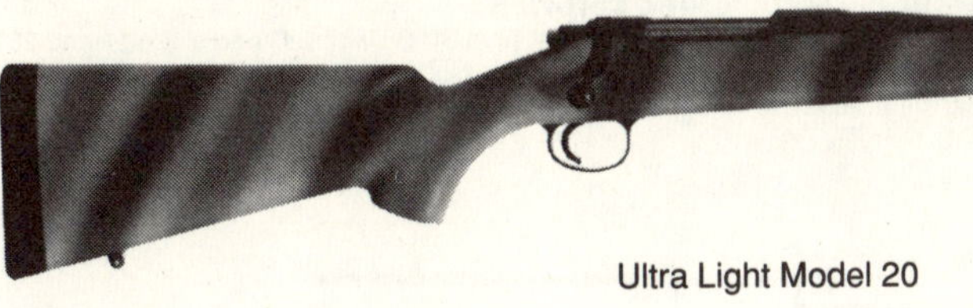

Ultra Light Model 20

ULTRA LIGHT ARMS MODEL 20 RIFLE

Caliber: 17 Rem., 22 Hornet, 222 Rem., 223 Rem. (Model 20S); 22-250, 6mm Rem., 243, 257 Roberts, 7x57, 7x57 Ackley, 7mm-08, 284 Win., 308 Savage. Improved and other calibers on request.
Barrel: 22" Douglas Premium No. 1 contour.
Weight: 4½ lbs. **Length:** 41½" overall.
Stock: Composite Kevlar, graphite reinforced. Du Pont imron paint colors—green, black, brown and camo options. Choice of length of pull.
Sights: None furnished. Scope mount included.
Features: Timney adjustable trigger; two-position three-function safety. Benchrest quality action. Matte or bright stock and metal finish. 3" magazine length. Shipped in a hard case. From Ultra Light Arms, Inc.
Price: Right-hand **$2,400.00**
Price: Model 20 Left Hand (left-hand action and stock) **$2,500.00**
Price: Model 24 (25-06, 270, 280 Rem., 30-06, 3⅜" magazine length) **$2,500.00**
Price: Model 24 Left Hand (left-hand action and stock) **$2,600.00**

Ultra Light Arms Model 28 Rifle

Similar to the Model 20 except in 264, 7mm Rem. Mag., 300 Win. Mag., 338 Win. Mag. Uses 24" Douglas Premium No. 2 contour barrel. Weighs 5½ lbs., 45" overall length. KDF or ULA recoil arrestor built in. Any custom feature available on any ULA product can be incorporated.
Price: Right-hand **$2,900.00**
Price: Left-hand **$3,000.00**

VOERE MODEL 2155, 2165 BOLT-ACTION RIFLE

Caliber: 22-250, 270, 308, 243, 30-06, 7x64, 5.6x57, 6.5x55, 8x57 JRS, 7mm Rem. Mag., 300 Win. Mag., 8x68S, 9.3x62, 9.3x64, 6.5x68.
Stock: European walnut, hog-back style; checkered pistol grip and forend.
Sights: Ramp front, open adjustable rear.
Features: Mauser-type action with 5-shot detachable box magazine; double-set or single trigger; drilled and tapped for scope mounting. Imported from Austria by L. Joseph Rahn. Introduced 1984.
Price: M2165, standard calibers, single trigger **$970.00**
Price: As above, double-set triggers **$1,023.00**
Price: M2165, magnum calibers, single trigger **$1,045.00**
Price: As above, double-set triggers **$1,098.00**
Price: M2165, classic stock, single trigger **$970.00**
Price: As above, double-set triggers **$876.00**
Price: M2155 (as above, no jeweling, military safety, single trigger) . **$798.00**
Price: As above, double triggers **$876.00**

Weatherby Mark V

WEATHERBY MARK V BOLT-ACTION RIFLE

Caliber: All Weatherby cals., plus 22-250 and 30-06.
Barrel: 24" or 26" round tapered.
Weight: 6½-10½ lbs. **Length:** 43¼"-46½" overall.
Stock: Walnut, Monte Carlo with cheekpiece, high luster finish, checkered p.g. and forend, recoil pad.
Sights: Optional (extra).
Features: Cocking indicator, adjustable trigger, hinged floorplate, thumb safety, quick detachable sling swivels.
Price: Cals. 224 and 22-250, std. bbl., right-hand only **$1,060.00**
Price: With 26" semi-target bbl., right-hand only **$1,088.00**
Price: Cals. 240, 257, 270, 7mm, 30-06 and 300 (24" bbl.) right- or left-hand **$1,081.00**
Price: With 26" No. 2 contour bbl., right-hand or 300 W.M. left only **$1,106.00**
Price: Cal. 340 (26" bbl.), right- or left-hand **$1,106.00**
Price: Cal. 378 (26" bbl.), right- or left-hand **$1,269.00**
Price: 416 W.M., 24", right- or left-hand **$1,381.00**
Price: As above, 26" **$1,406.00**
Price: 460 W.M., 24", right- or left-hand **$1,456.00**
Price: As above, 26" **$1,481.00**

Weatherby Lazermark V Rifle

Same as standard Mark V except stock has extensive laser carving under cheekpiece on butt, p.g. and forend. Introduced 1981.
Price: 22-250, 224 Wea., 24" bbl., right-hand only **$1,181.00**
Price: As above, 26" bbl., right-hand only **$1,213.00**
Price: 240 Wea. thru 300 Wea., 24" bbl., right- or left-hand **$1,206.00**
Price: As above, 26" bbl., right-hand or 300 W.M. left-hand **$1,231.00**
Price: 340 Wea., right- or left-hand **$1,231.00**
Price: 378 Wea., right- or left-hand **$1,394.00**
Price: 416 W.M., 24", right- or left-hand **$1,513.00**
Price: As above, 26" **$1,538.00**
Price: 460 W.M., 24" right- or left-hand **$1,588.00**
Price: As above, 26" **$1,613.00**

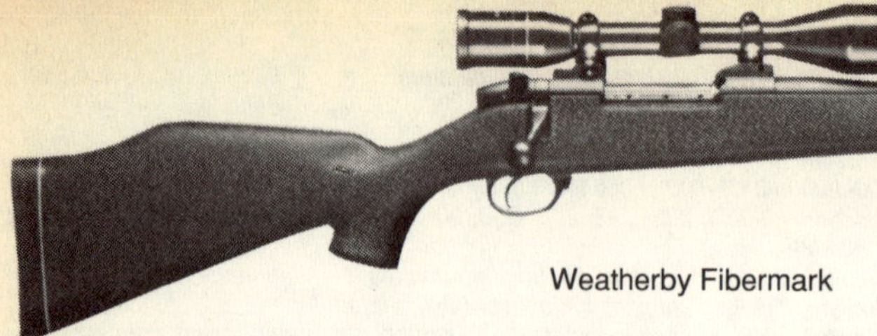

Weatherby Fibermark

Weatherby Mark V Safari Grade Custom Rifles

Uses the Mark V barreled action. Stock is of European walnut with satin oil finish, rounded ebony tip and cap, black presentation recoil pad, no white spacers, and pattern #16 fine-line checkering. Matte finish bluing, floorplate is engraved "Weatherby Safari Grade"; 24" barrel. Standard rear stock swivel, barrel band front swivel. Has quarter-rib rear sight with a stationary leaf and one folding shallow V leaf. Front sight is a hooded ramp with brass bead. Right- or left-hand. Allow 8-10 months delivery. Introduced 1985.

Price: 300 W.M. **$3,064.00**
Price: 340 W.M. **$3,076.00**
Price: 378 W.M. **$3,224.00**
Price: 416 W.M. **$3,308.00**
Price: 460 W.M. **$3,308.00**

Weatherby Mark V Alaskan Rifle

Similar to the Weatherby Fibermark rifle except all metal parts are plated with electroless nickel for corrosion resistance. Available in 270 Wea. Mag., 7mm Wea. Mag., 300 Wea. Mag., 340 Wea. Mag. Introduced 1991.

Price: . . . . **NA**

Weatherby Fibermark Rifle

Same as the standard Mark V except the stock is of fiberglass; finished with a non-glare black wrinkle finish and black recoil pad; receiver and floorplate have low luster blue finish; fluted bolt has a satin finish. Available in left- or right-hand, 24" or 26" barrel, 240 Wea. Mag. through 340 Wea. Mag. calibers. Introduced 1983.

Price: 240 W.M. through 300 W.M., 24" bbl. **$1,225.00**
Price: 240 W.M. through 340 W.M., 26" bbl., right-hand or 300, 340, W.M. left-hand only **$1,250.00**

Weatherby Mark V Crown Custom Rifles

Uses hand-honed, engraved Mark V barreled action with fully-checkered bolt knob, damascened bolt and follower. Floorplate is engraved "Weatherby Custom." Super fancy walnut stock with inlays and stock carving. Gold monogram with name or initials. Right-hand only. Available in 240, 257, 270, 7mm, 300 Wea. Mag. or 30-06. Introduced 1989.

Price: From . . . . **$3,400.00** to **$4,534.00**
Price: For 340 W.M., add **$16.00**

Weatherby Mark V Rifle Left-Hand

Available in all Weatherby calibers, plus 30-06 with 24" barrel. Left-hand 26" barrel available in 300 and 340 calibers. Not available in 224 W.M. and 22-250 Varmintmaster.

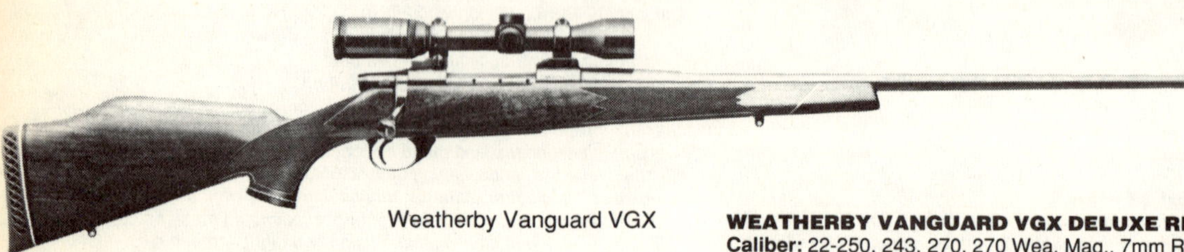

Weatherby Vanguard VGX

WEATHERBY EUROMARK BOLT-ACTION RIFLE

Caliber: All Weatherby calibers except 224, 22-250.
Barrel: 24" or 26" round tapered.
Weight: 6½ to 10½ lbs. **Length:** 44¼" overall (24" bbl.).
Stock: Walnut, Monte Carlo with extended tail, fine-line hand checkering, satin oil finish, ebony forend tip and grip cap with maple diamond, solid buttpad.
Sights: Optional (extra).
Features: Cocking indicator; adjustable trigger; hinged floorplate; thumb safety; q.d. sling swivels. Introduced 1986.
Price: With 24" barrel (240, 257, 270, 7mm, 30-06, 300), right- or left-hand **$1,131.00**
Price: 26" No. 2 contour barrel, right- or left-hand (300 only) . . . **$1,156.00**
Price: 340 W.M., 26", right- or left-hand **$1,156.00**
Price: 378 W.M., right- or left-hand **$1,322.00**
Price: 416 W.M., 24", right- or left-hand **$1,438.00**
Price: As above, 26" **$1,469.00**
Price: 460 W.M., 24", right- or left-hand **$1,513.00**
Price: As above, 26" **$1,538.00**

WEATHERBY VANGUARD VGX DELUXE RIFLE

Caliber: 22-250, 243, 270, 270 Wea. Mag., 7mm Rem. Mag., 30-06, 300 Win. Mag., 300 Wea. Mag., 338 Win. Mag.; 5-shot magazine (3-shot for magnums).
Barrel: 24", No. 2 contour.
Weight: 7⅞-8½ lbs. **Length:** 44½" overall (22-250, 243 are 44").
Stock: Walnut with high luster finish; rosewood grip cap and forend tip.
Sights: Optional, available at extra cost.
Features: Fully adjustable trigger; side safety; rubber recoil pad. Introduced 1989. Imported from Japan by Weatherby.
Price: **$656.00**

Weatherby Vanguard Weatherguard Rifle

Has a forest green or black wrinkle-finished synthetic stock. All metal is matte blue. Has a 24" barrel, weighs 7½ lbs., measures 44½". In 223, 243, and 308; 40½" in 270, 7mm-08, 7mm Rem. Mag., 30-06. Accepts same scope mount bases as Mark V action. Introduced 1989.

Price: Right-hand only **$450.00**

Weatherby Vanguard Classic I

Weatherby Vanguard Classic II Rifle

Similar to the Classic I except has rounded forend with black tip, black grip cap with walnut diamond inlay, 20 lpi checkering. Solid black recoil pad. Oil-finished stock. Available in 22-250, 243, 270, 7mm Rem. Mag., 30-06, 300 Win. Mag., 338 Win. Mag., 270 Wea. Mag., 300 Wea. Mag. Introduced 1989.

Price: **$656.00**

Weatherby Vanguard Classic I Rifle

Similar to the Vanguard VGX Deluxe except has a "classic" style stock without Monte Carlo comb, no forend tip. Has distinctive Weatherby grip cap. Satin finish on stock. Available in 223, 243, 270, 7mm-08, 7mm Rem. Mag., 30-06, 308; 24" barrel. Introduced 1989.

Price: **$506.00**

Whitworth Express Rifle

WHITWORTH SAFARI EXPRESS RIFLE
Caliber: 375 H&H, 458 Win. Mag.
Barrel: 24".
Weight: 7½-8 lbs. **Length:** 44".
Stock: Classic English Express rifle design of hand checkered, select European walnut.
Sights: Three-leaf open sight calibrated for 100, 200, 300 yards on ¼-rib, ramp front with removable hood.
Features: Solid rubber recoil pad, barrel-mounted sling swivel, adjustable trigger, hinged floorplate, solid steel recoil cross bolt.
Price: 375, 458, with express sights **$835.00**

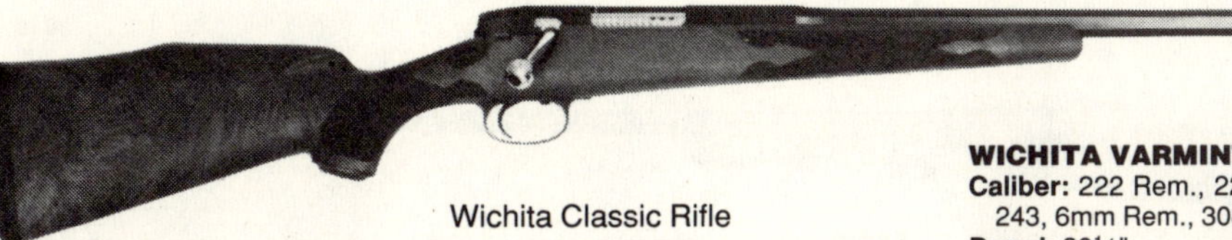

Wichita Classic Rifle

WICHITA CLASSIC RIFLE
Caliber: 17-222, 17-222 Mag., 222 Rem., 222 Rem. Mag., 223 Rem., 6x47; other calibers on special order.
Barrel: 21⅛".
Weight: 8 lbs. **Length:** 41" overall.
Stock: AAA Fancy American walnut. Hand-rubbed and checkered (20 lpi). Hand-inletted, glass bedded, steel grip cap. Pachmayr rubber recoil pad.
Sights: None. Drilled and tapped for scope mounting.
Features: Available as single shot or repeater. Octagonal barrel and Wichita action, right- or left-hand. Checkered bolt handle. Bolt is hand-fitted, lapped and jeweled. Adjustable trigger is set at 2 lbs. Side thumb safety. Firing pin fall is 3/16". Non-glare blue finish. From Wichita Arms.
Price: Single shot **$2,950.00**

WICHITA VARMINT RIFLE
Caliber: 222 Rem., 222 Rem. Mag., 223 Rem., 22 PPC, 6mm PPC, 22-250, 243, 6mm Rem., 308 Win.; other calibers on special order.
Barrel: 20⅛".
Weight: 9 lbs. **Length:** 40⅛" overall.
Stock: AAA Fancy American walnut. Hand-rubbed finish, hand checkered, 20 lpi pattern. Hand-inletted, glass bedded, steel grip cap. Pachmayr rubber recoil pad.
Sights: None. Drilled and tapped for scope mounts.
Features: Right- or left-hand Wichita action with three locking lugs. Available as a single shot or repeater with 3-shot magazine. Checkered bolt handle. Bolt is hand fitted, lapped and jeweled. Side thumb safety. Firing pin fall is 3/16". Non-glare blue finish. From Wichita Arms.
Price: Single shot **$2,250.00**

Winchester Model 70 Ranger

Winchester Ranger Rifle
Similar to Model 70 Lightweight except chambered only for 243, 270, 30-06, with 22" barrel. American hardwood stock, no checkering, composition buttplate. Metal has matte blue finish. Introduced 1985.
Price: **$423.00**
Price: Ranger Ladies/Youth, 243, 308 only, scaled-down stock . . . **$423.00**

WINCHESTER MODEL 70 LIGHTWEIGHT RIFLE
Caliber: 270, 280, 30-06 (standard action); 22-250, 223, 243, 308 (short action), both 5-shot magazine, except 6-shot in 223.
Barrel: 22".
Weight: 6¼ lbs. **Length:** 40½" overall (std.), 40" (short).
Stock: American walnut with satin finish, deep-cut checkering.
Sights: None furnished. Drilled and tapped for scope mounting.
Features: Three position safety; stainless steel magazine follower; hinged floorplate; sling swivel studs. Introduced 1984.
Price: Walnut **$447.00**
Price: With WinTuff laminated stock, 270, 30-06 only **$447.00**
Price: With WinCam green laminated stock, 270, 30-06 only **$447.00**

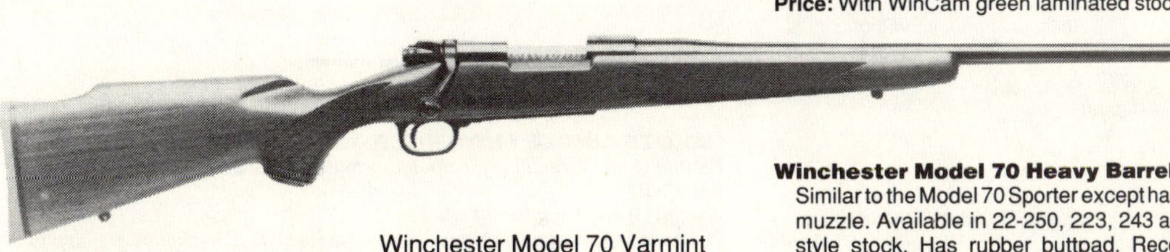

Winchester Model 70 Varmint

Winchester Model 70 Heavy Barrel Varmint
Similar to the Model 70 Sporter except has heavy 26" barrel with counter-bored muzzle. Available in 22-250, 223, 243 and 308. Receiver bedded in sporter-style stock. Has rubber buttpad. Receiver drilled and tapped for scope mounting. Weight about 9 lbs., overall length 46". Introduced 1989.
Price: **$531.00**

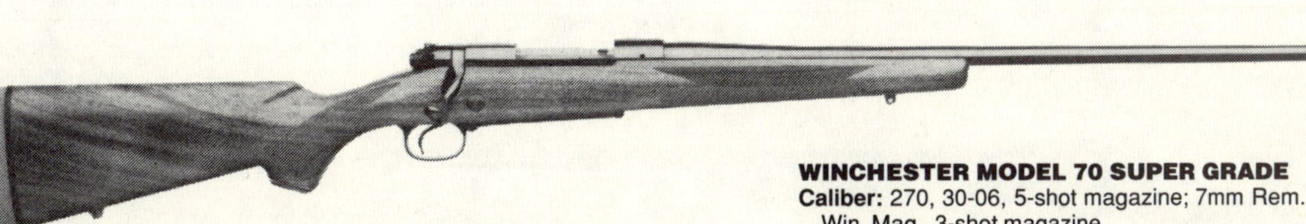

Winchester Model 70 Super Grade

WINCHESTER MODEL 70 SUPER GRADE
Caliber: 270, 30-06, 5-shot magazine; 7mm Rem. Mag., 300 Win. Mag., 338 Win. Mag., 3-shot magazine.
Barrel: 24".
Weight: About 7¾ lbs. **Length:** 44½" overall.
Stock: Walnut with straight comb, sculptured cheekpiece, wraparound cut checkering, tapered forend, solid rubber buttpad.
Sights: None furnished; comes with scope bases and rings.
Features: Controlled round feeding with stainless steel claw extractor, bolt guide rail, three-position safety; all steel bottom metal, hinged floorplate, stainless magazine fcllower. Introduced 1990. From U.S. Repeating Arms Co.
Price: **$997.00**

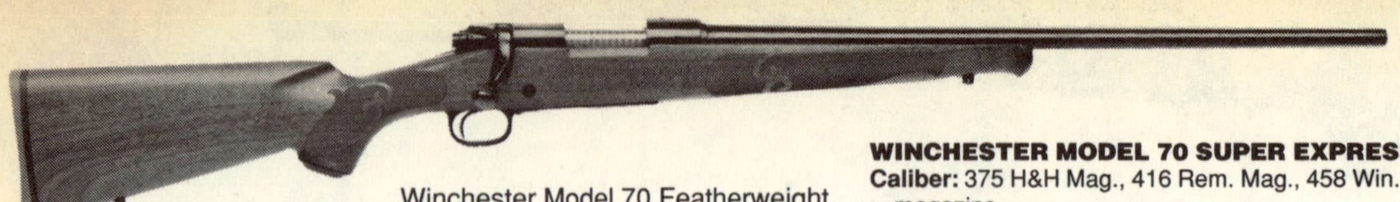

Winchester Model 70 Featherweight

Winchester Model 70 Featherweight
Available with standard action in 270 Win., 280 Rem., 30-06, 7mm Rem. Mag., 300 Win. Mag., short action in 22-250, 223, 243, 6.5x55, 308; 22" tapered. Featherweight barrel; classic-style American walnut stock with Schnabel forend, wraparound checkering fashioned after early Model 70 custom rifle patterns. Red rubber buttpad, sling swivel studs. Weighs 6¾ lbs. (standard action), 6½ lbs. (short action). Introduced 1984.
Price: **$510.00**

WINCHESTER MODEL 70 SUPER EXPRESS MAGNUM
Caliber: 375 H&H Mag., 416 Rem. Mag., 458 Win. Mag., 470 Capstick, 3-shot magazine.
Barrel: 24" (375); 22" (458).
Weight: 8½ lbs.
Stock: American walnut with Monte Carlo cheekpiece. Wraparound checkering and finish.
Sights: Hooded ramp front, open rear.
Features: Two steel cross bolts in stock for added strength. Front sling swivel stud mounted on barrel. Contoured rubber buttpad. From U.S. Repeating Arms Co.
Price: About **$816.00**

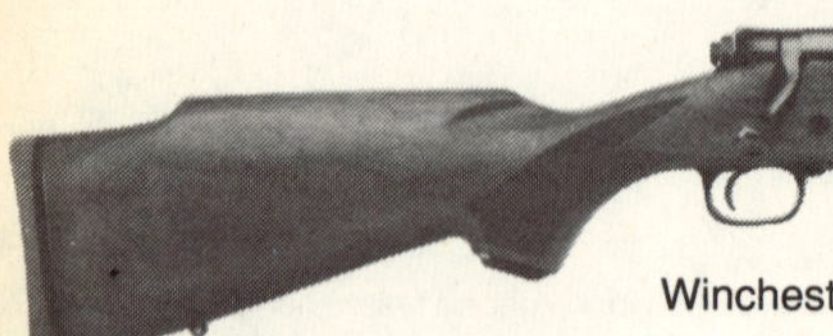

Winchester Model 70 Sporter

WINCHESTER MODEL 70 SPORTER
Caliber: 22-250, 223, 243, 25-06, 270, 270 Wea., 30-06, 264 Win. Mag., 7mm Rem. Mag., 300 H&H, 300 Win. Mag., 300 Wea. Mag., 338 Win. Mag., 3-shot magazine.
Barrel: 24".
Weight: 7¾ lbs. **Length:** 44½" overall.
Stock: American walnut with Monte Carlo cheekpiece. Cut checkering and satin finish.
Sights: Optional hooded ramp front, adjustable folding leaf rear. Drilled and tapped for scope mounting.
Features: Three-position safety, stainless steel magazine follower; rubber buttpad, epoxy bedded receiver recoil lug. From U.S. Repeating Arms Co.
Price: With sights **$510.00**
Price: Without sights **$510.00**

CENTERFIRE RIFLES—SINGLE SHOT

Classic and modern designs for sporting and competitive use.

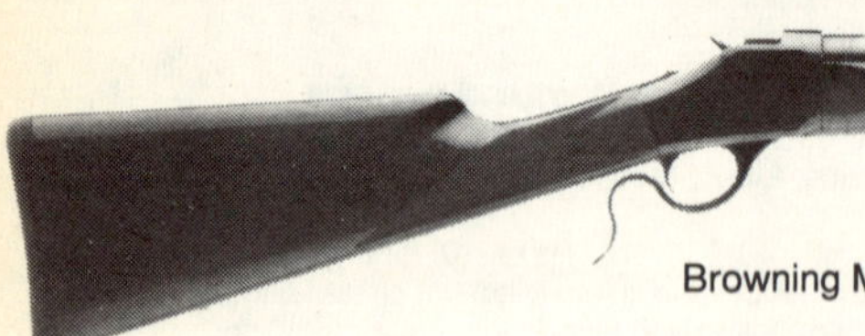

Browning Model 1885

BROWNING MODEL 1885 SINGLE SHOT RIFLE
Caliber: 223, 22-250, 30-06, 270, 7mm Rem. Mag., 45-70.
Barrel: 28".
Weight: About 8½ lbs. **Length:** 43½" overall.
Stock: Walnut with straight grip, schnabel forend.
Sights: None furnished; drilled and tapped for scope mounting.
Features: Replica of J.M. Browning's high-wall falling block rifle. Octagon barrel with recessed muzzle. Imported from Japan by Browning. Introduced 1985.
Price: **$771.95**

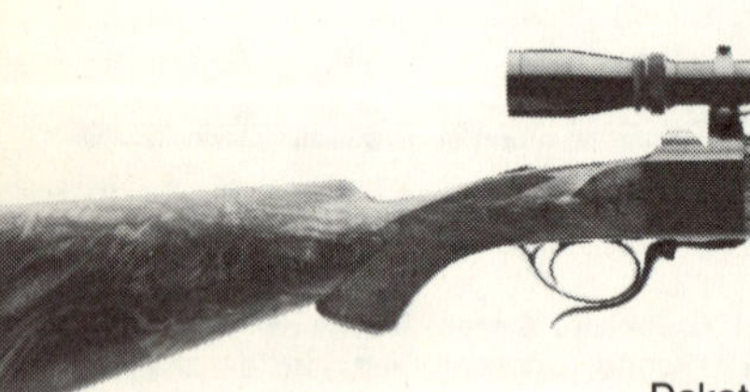

Dakota Single Shot

DAKOTA SINGLE SHOT RIFLE
Caliber: Most rimmed and rimless commercial calibers.
Barrel: 23".
Weight: 6 lbs. **Length:** 39½" overall.
Stock: Medium fancy grade walnut in classic style. Checkered grip and forend.
Sights: None furnished. Drilled and tapped for scope mounting.
Features: Falling block action with under-lever. Top tang safety. Removable trigger plate for conversion to single set trigger. Introduced 1990. Made in U.S. by Dakota Arms.
Price: **$1,950.00**
Price: Barreled action **$1,450.00**
Price: Action only **$1,200.00**

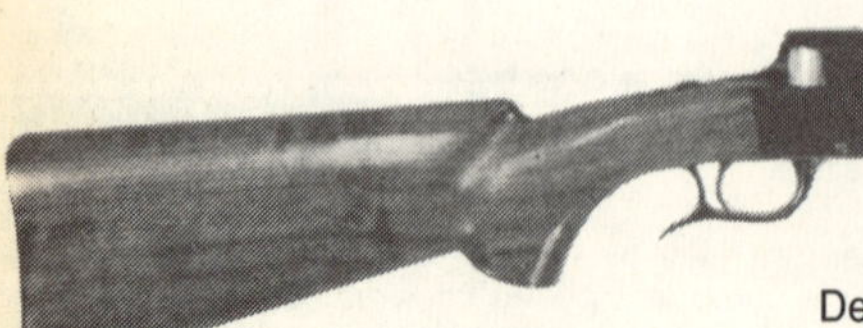

Desert Industries G-90

DESERT INDUSTRIES G-90 SINGLE SHOT RIFLE
Caliber: All popular calibers.
Barrel: 20" to 26", interchangeable.
Weight: About 7.5 lbs.
Stock: Walnut.
Sights: None furnished. Drilled and tapped for scope mounting.
Features: Cylindrical falling block action. All steel construction. Blue finish. Announced 1990. From Desert Industries, Inc.
Price: **$525.00**

CAUTION: PRICES CHANGE, CHECK AT GUNSHOP.

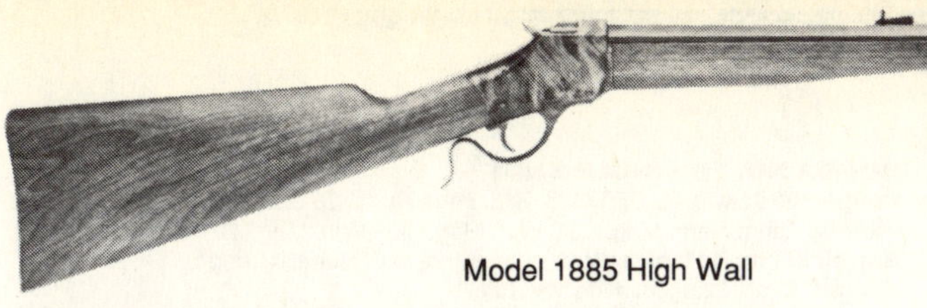

Model 1885 High Wall

AUGUSTE FRANCOTTE CARPATHE MOUNTAIN RIFLE
Caliber: 243, 270, 308, 30-06, 7x65R, 7x57R, 5.6x52R, 5.6x57R, 6.5x57R, 6.5x68R, 7mm Rem. Mag., 300 Win. Mag.
Barrel: 23.5" to 26".
Weight: NA. **Length:** NA.
Stock: Deluxe walnut to customer specs; oil finish, fine checkering.
Sights: None furnished; scope mount extra.
Features: Single-barrel rifle with sidelock action, third fastener, extractor, manual safety, splinter forend. Many options available. Imported from Belgium by Armes de Chasse.
Price: Boxlock, from about $14,482.00
Price: Sidelock, from about $26,275.00

MODEL 1885 HIGH WALL RIFLE
Caliber: 30-40 Krag, 32-40, 38-55, 40-65 WCF, 45-70.
Barrel: 26" (30-40), 28" all others. Douglas Premium #3 tapered octagon.
Weight: NA. **Length:** NA.
Stock: Premium American black walnut.
Sights: Marble's standard ivory bead front, #66 long blade flat top rear with reversible notch and elevator.
Features: Recreation of early octagon top, thick-wall High Wall with coil spring action. Tang drilled, tapped for High Wall tang sight. Receiver, lever, hammer and breechblock color case-hardened. Introduced 1991. Available from Montana Armory, Inc.
Price: $1,095.00

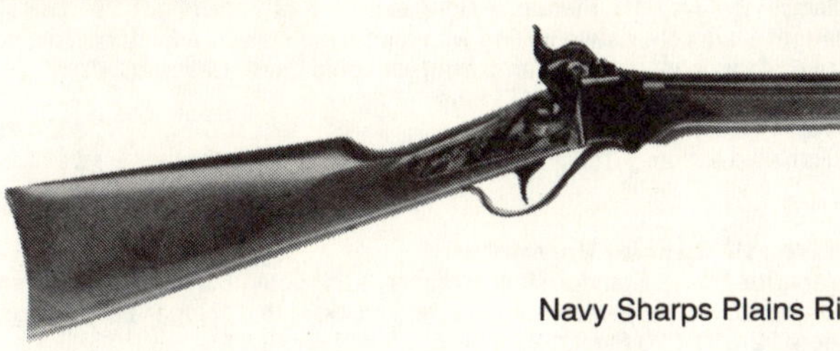

Navy Sharps Plains Rifle

NAVY ARMS SHARPS PLAINS RIFLE
Caliber: 45-70.
Barrel: 28½".
Weight: 8 lbs., 10 oz. **Length:** 45¾" overall.
kStock: Checkered walnut butt and forend.
Sights: Blade front, open rear adjustable for windage.
Features: Color case-hardened action, rest blued. Introduced 1991. Imported by Navy Arms.
Price: $650.00

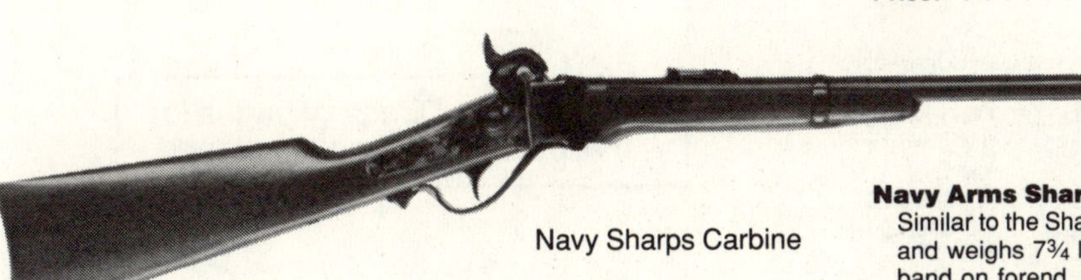

Navy Sharps Carbine

Navy Arms Sharps Cavalry Carbine
Similar to the Sharps Plains Rifle except has 22" barrel, overall length of 39", and weighs 7¾ lbs. Has blade front sight, military ladder-style rear, barrel band on forend. Color case-hardened action, rest blued. Introduced 1991. Imported by Navy Arms.
Price: $650.00

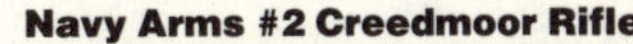

Navy Buffalo Rifle

NAVY ARMS ROLLING BLOCK BUFFALO RIFLE
Caliber: 45-70.
Barrel: 26".
Stocks: Walnut.
Sights: Blade front, adjustable rear.
Features: Reproduction of classic rolling block action. Available with full-octagon or half-octagon-half-round barrel. Color case-hardened action. From Navy Arms.
Price: $485.00

Navy Arms #2 Creedmoor Rifle
Similar to the Navy Arms Buffalo Rifle except has 30" tapered octagon barrel, checkered full-pistol grip stock, blade front sight, open adjustable rear sight and Creedmoor tang sight. Introduced 1991. Imported by Navy Arms.
Price: $640.00

New England Handi-Rifle

NEW ENGLAND FIREARMS HANDI-RIFLE
Caliber: 22 Hornet, 223, 30-30, 45-70.
Barrel: 22".
Weight: 6½ lbs.
Stock: Walnut-finished hardwood.
Sights: Ramp front, folding rear. Drilled and tapped for scope mount; 223 Rem. has no open sights, comes with scope mounts.
Features: Break-open action with side-lever release. Blue finish. Introduced 1989. From New England Firearms.
Price: . . . . NA

REMINGTON-STYLE ROLLING BLOCK CARBINE
Caliber: 45-70.
Barrel: 30", octagonal.
Weight: 11¾ lbs. **Length:** 46½" overall.
Stock: Walnut.
Sights: Blade front, adjustable rear.
Features: Color case-hardened receiver, brass trigger guard, buttplate and barrel band, blued barrel. Imported from Italy by E.M.F.
Price: $820.00

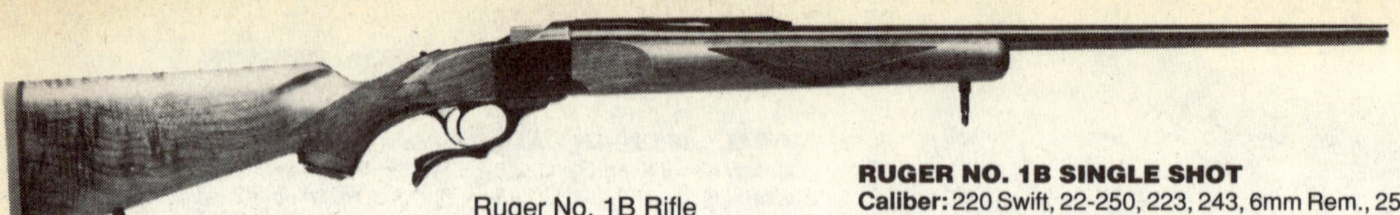

Ruger No. 1B Rifle

RUGER NO. 1B SINGLE SHOT

Caliber: 220 Swift, 22-250, 223, 243, 6mm Rem., 25-06, 257 Roberts, 270, 280, 30-06, 7mm Rem. Mag., 300 Win. Mag., 338 Win. Mag., 270 Wea., 300 Wea.
Barrel: 26" round tapered with quarter-rib; with Ruger 1" rings.
Weight: 8 lbs. **Length:** 43⅜" overall.
Stock: Walnut, two-piece, checkered p.g. and semi-beavertail forend.
Sights: None, 1" scope rings supplied for integral mounts.
Features: Under-lever, hammerless falling block design has auto ejector, top tang safety.
Price: **$603.75**
Price: Barreled action **$409.00**

Ruger No. 1A Light Sporter

Similar to the No. 1B Standard Rifle except has lightweight 22" barrel, Alexander Henry-style forend, adjustable folding leaf rear sight on quarter-rib, dovetailed ramp front with gold bead. Calibers 243, 30-06, 270 and 7x57. Weight about 7¼ lbs.
Price: No. 1A **$603.75**
Price: Barreled action **$409.00**

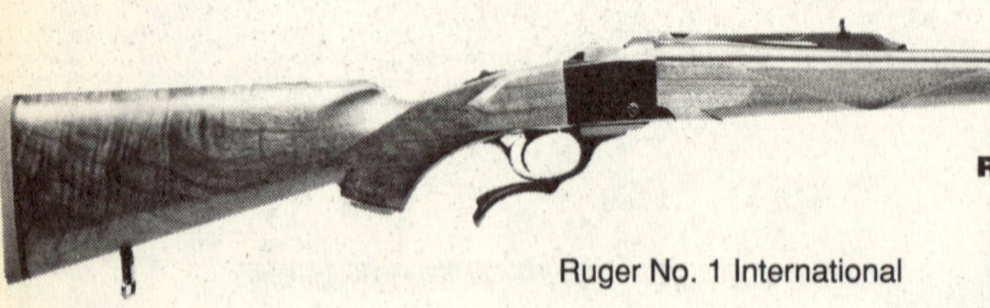

Ruger No. 1 International

Ruger No. 1 RSI International

Similar to the No. 1B Standard Rifle except has lightweight 20" barrel, full-length Mannlicher-style forend with loop sling swivel, adjustable folding leaf rear sight on quarter-rib, ramp front with gold bead. Calibers 243, 30-06, 270 and 7x57. Weight is about 7¼ lbs.
Price: No. 1 RSI **$624.75**
Price: Barreled action **$409.00**

Ruger No. 1H Tropical Rifle

Similar to the No. 1B Standard Rifle except has Alexander Henry forend, adjustable folding leaf rear sight on quarter-rib, ramp front with dovetail gold bead, 24" heavy barrel. Calibers 375 H&H (weight about 8¼ lbs.), 416 Rem. Mag. and 458 Win. Mag. (weight about 9 lbs.).
Price: No. 1H **$603.75**
Price: Barreled action **$409.00**

Ruger No. 1V Special Varminter

Similar to the No. 1B Standard Rifle except has 24" heavy barrel. Semi-beavertail forend, barrel tapped for target scope block, with 1" Ruger scope rings. Calibers 22-250, 220 Swift, 223, 25-06. Weight about 9 lbs.
Price: No. 1V **$603.75**
Price: Barreled action **$409.00**

Ruger No. 1S Medium Sporter

Similar to the No. 1B Standard Rifle except has Alexander Henry-style forend, adjustable folding leaf rear sight on quarter-rib, ramp front sight base and dovetail-type gold bead front sight. Calibers 7mm Rem. Mag., 338 Win. Mag., 300 Win. Mag. with 26" barrel, 45-70 with 22" barrel. Weight about 7½ lbs. In 45-70.
Price: No. 1S **$603.75**
Price: Barreled action **$409.00**

Consult our Directory pages for the location of firms mentioned.

C. Sharps 1875 Sporting

C. SHARPS ARMS NEW MODEL 1875 RIFLE

Caliber: 22LR, 32-40 & 38-55 Ballard, 38-56 WCF, 40-65 WCF, 40-90 3¼", 40-90 2⅝", 40-70 2¹⁄₁₀", 40-70 2¼", 40-70 2½", 40-50 1¹¹⁄₁₆", 40-50 1⅞", 45-90, 45-70, 45-100, 45-110, 45-120. Also available on special order only in 50-70, 50-90, 50-140.
Barrel: 24", 26", 30" (standard); 32", 34" optional.
Weight: 8-12 lbs.
Stocks: Walnut, straight grip, shotgun butt with checkered steel buttplate.
Sights: Silver blade front, Rocky Mountain buckhorn rear.
Features: Recreation of the 1875 Sharps rifle. Production guns will have case colored receiver. Available in Custom Sporting and Target versions upon request. Announced 1986. From C. Sharps Arms Co. and Montana Armory, Inc.
Price: 1875 Carbine (24" tapered round bbl.) **$725.00**
Price: 1875 Saddle Rifle (26" tapered oct. bbl.) **$825.00**
Price: 1875 Sporting Rifle (30" tapered oct. bbl.) **$850.00**
Price: 1875 Business Rifle (28" tapered round bbl.) **$775.00**

C. Sharps Arms 1875 Classic Sharps

Similar to the New Model 1875 Sporting Rifle except has 26", 28" or 30" full octagon barrel, crescent buttplate with toe plate, Hartford-style forend with cast German silver nose cap. Blade front sight, Rocky Mountain buckhorn rear. Weight is 10 lbs. Introduced 1987. From C. Sharps Arms Co. and Montana Armory, Inc.
Price: **$1,075.00**

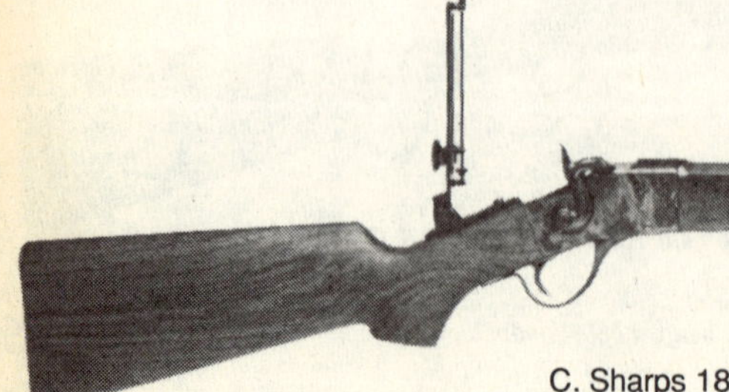

C. Sharps 1875 Long Range

C. Sharps Arms New Model 1875 Target & Long Range

Similar to the New Model 1875 except available in all listed calibers except 22 LR; 34" tapered octagon barrel; globe with post front sight, Long Range Vernier tang sight with windage adjustments. Pistol grip stock with cheek rest; checkered steel buttplate. Introduced 1991. From C. Sharps Arms Co. and Montana Armory, Inc.
Price: **$1,165.00**

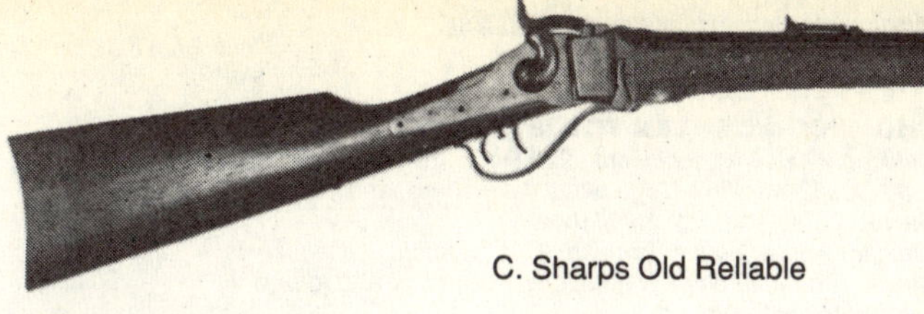

C. Sharps Old Reliable

SHARPS 1874 OLD RELIABLE
Caliber: 45-70.
Barrel: 28", octagonal.
Weight: 9¼ lbs. **Length:** 46" overall.
Stock: Checkered walnut.
Sights: Blade front, adjustable rear.
Features: Double set triggers on rifle. Color case-hardened receiver and buttplate, blued barrel. Imported from Italy by E.M.F.
Price: Rifle or carbine **$950.00**

C. SHARPS ARMS NEW MODEL 1874 OLD RELIABLE
Caliber: 40-50, 40-70, 40-90, 45-70, 45-90, 45-100, 45-110, 45-120, 50-70, 50-90, 50-140.
Barrel: 26", 28", 30" tapered octagon.
Weight: About 10 lbs. **Length:** NA.
Stock: American black walnut; shotgun butt with checkered steel buttplate; straight grip, heavy forend with schnabel tip.
Sights: Blade front, buckhorn rear. Drilled and tapped for tang sight.
Features: Recreation of the Model 1874 Old Reliable Sharps Sporting Rifle. Double set triggers. Reintroduced 1991. Made in U.S. by C. Sharps Arms. Available from Montana Armory, Inc.
Price: **$995.00**

Shiloh Long Range Express

Shiloh Sharps 1874 Business Rifle
Similar to No. 3 Rifle except has 28" heavy round barrel, military-style buttstock and steel buttplate. Weight about 9½ lbs. Calibers 40-50 BN, 40-70 BN, 40-90 BN, 45-70 ST, 45-90 ST, 50-70 ST, 50-100 ST, 32-40, 38-55, 40-70 ST, 40-90 ST.
Price: **$765.00**
Price: 1874 Carbine (similar to above except 24" round bbl., single trigger—double set avail.) **$765.00**
Price: 1874 Saddle Rifle (similar to Carbine except has 26" octagon barrel, semi-fancy shotgun butt) **$830.00**

Shiloh Sharps 1874 Military Carbine
Has 22" round barrel with blade front sight and full buckhorn ladder-type rear. Military-style buttstock with barrel band on military-style forend. Steel buttplate, saddle bar and ring. Standard supreme grade only. Weight is about 8½ lbs. Calibers 40-70 BN, 45-70, 50-70. Introduced 1989.
Price: **$795.00**

Shiloh Sharps 1874 Military Rifle
Has 30" round barrel. Iron block front sight and Lawrence-style rear ladder sight. Military butt, buttplate, patchbox assembly optional; three barrel bands; single trigger (double set available). Calibers 40-50x1$^{11}/_{16}$" BN, 40-70x2$^{1}/_{10}$" BN, 40-90 BN, 45-70x2$^{1}/_{10}$" ST, 50-70 ST.
Price: **$895.00**

SHILOH SHARPS 1874 LONG RANGE EXPRESS
Caliber: 40-50 BN, 40-70 BN, 40-90 BN, 45-70 ST, 45-90 ST, 45-110 ST, 50-70 ST, 50-90 ST, 50-110 ST, 32-40, 38-55, 40-70 ST, 40-90 ST.
Barrel: 34" tapered octagon.
Weight: 10½ lbs. **Length:** 51" overall.
Stock: Oil-finished semi-fancy walnut with pistol grip, shotgun-style butt, traditional cheek rest and accent line. Schnabel forend.
Sights: Globe front, sporting tang rear.
Features: Recreation of the Model 1874 Sharps rifle. Double set triggers. Made in U.S. by Shiloh Rifle Mfg. Co.
Price: **$895.00**
Price: Sporting Rifle No. 1 (similar to above except with 30" bbl., blade front, buckhorn rear sight) **$860.00**
Price: Sporting Rifle No. 3 (similar to No. 1 except straight-grip stock, standard wood) **$765.00**
Price: 1874 Hartford model **$925.00**

Shiloh Sharps 1874 Montana Roughrider
Similar to the No. 1 Sporting Rifle except available with half-octagon or full-octagon barrel in 24", 26", 28", 30", 34" lengths; standard supreme or semi-fancy wood, shotgun, pistol grip or military-style butt. Weight about 8½ lbs. Calibers 30-40, 30-30, 40-50x1$^{11}/_{16}$" BN, 40-70x2$^{1}/_{10}$" BN, 45-70x2$^{1}/_{10}$" ST. Globe front and tang sight optional.
Price: Standard supreme **$765.00**
Price: Semi-fancy **$850.00**

Shiloh Sharps The Jaeger
Similar to the Montana Roughrider except has half-octagon 26" lightweight barrel, 30-30 only. Standard supreme black walnut.
Price: **$835.00**

T/C Contender Carbine

Thompson/Center Contender Carbine Youth Model
Same as the standard Contender Carbine except has 16¼" barrel, shorter buttstock with 12" length of pull. Comes with fully adjustable open sights. Overall length is 29", weight about 4 lbs., 9 oz. Available in 22 LR, 22 WMR, 223 Rem., 7x30 Waters, 30-30, 35 Rem., 44 Mag. Also available with 16¼", rifled vent. rib barrel chambered for 45/410.
Price: **$395.00**
Price: With 45/410 barrel **$425.00**
Price: Extra barrels **$180.00**
Price: Extra 45/410 barrel **$220.00**
Price: Extra 45-70 barrel **$205.00**

THOMPSON/CENTER CONTENDER CARBINE
Caliber: 22 LR, 22 Hornet, 223 Rem., 7mm T.C.U., 7x30 Waters, 30-30 Win., 357 Rem. Maximum, 35 Rem., 44 Mag., 410, single shot.
Barrel: 21".
Weight: 5 lbs., 2 oz. **Length:** 35" overall.
Stock: Checkered American walnut with rubber buttpad. Also with Rynite stock and forend.
Sights: Blade front, open adjustable rear.
Features: Uses the T/C Contender action. Eleven interchangeable barrels available, all with sights, drilled and tapped for scope mounting. Introduced 1985. Offered as a complete Carbine only.
Price: Rifle calibers **$430.00**
Price: Extra barrels, rifle calibers, each **$195.00**
Price: 410 shotgun **$450.00**
Price: Extra 410 barrel **$220.00**
Price: Rynite stock, forend **$395.00**
Price: As above, 21" vent. rib smoothbore 410 bbl. **$420.00**

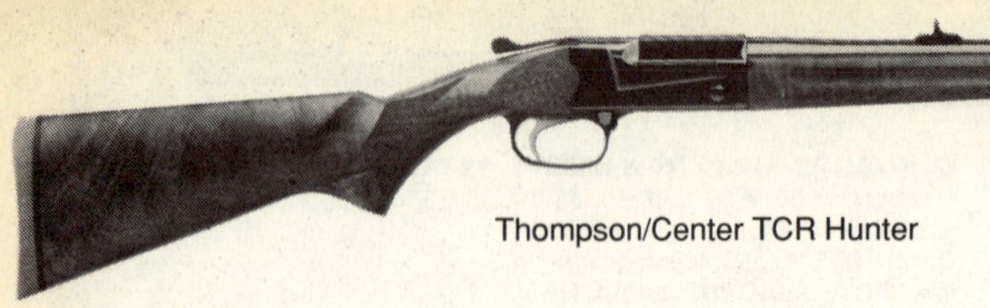

Thompson/Center TCR Hunter

Thompson/Center Contender Carbine Survival System
Combines the Rynite-stocked Contender Carbine with two 16¼" barrels—one chambered for 223 Rem., the other for 45 Colt/410 bore. The frame/buttstock assembly store in the camouflage Cordura case, measuring 25½"x6¾". Introduced 1991.
Price: **$589.00**

THOMPSON/CENTER TCR '87 SINGLE SHOT RIFLE
Caliber: 22 Hornet, 222 Rem., 223 Rem., 22-250, 243 Win., 270, 308, 7mm-08, 30-06, 32-40 Win., 12-ga. slug. Also 10-ga. and 12-ga. field barrels.
Barrel: 23" (standard), 25⅞" (heavy).
Weight: About 6¾ lbs. **Length:** 39½" overall.
Stock: American black walnut, checkered p.g. and forend.
Sights: None furnished.
Features: Break-open design with interchangeable barrels. Single-stage trigger. Cross-bolt safety. Made in U.S. by T/C. Introduced 1983.
Price: With Medium Sporter barrel (223, 22-250, 7mm-08, 308, 32-40 Win.) **$550.00**
Price: With Light Sporter barrel (22 Hornet, 222, 223, 22-250, 243, 270, 7mm-08, 308, 30-06) **$550.00**
Price: 12-ga. slug barrel **$250.00**
Price: Extra Medium or Light Sporter barrel **$250.00**
Price: 10-, 12-ga. field barrels **$250.00**

UBERTI ROLLING BLOCK BABY CARBINE
Caliber: 22 LR, 22 WMR, 22 Hornet, 357 Mag., single shot.
Barrel: 22".
Weight: 4.8 lbs. **Length:** 35½" overall.
Stock: Walnut stock and forend.
Sights: Blade front, fully adjustable open rear.
Features: Resembles Remington New Model No. 4 carbine. Brass trigger guard and buttplate; color case-hardened frame, blued barrel. Imported by Uberti USA.
Price: **$430.00**

Uberti Rolling Block

DRILLINGS, COMBINATION GUNS, DOUBLE RIFLES

Designs for sporting and utility purposes worldwide.

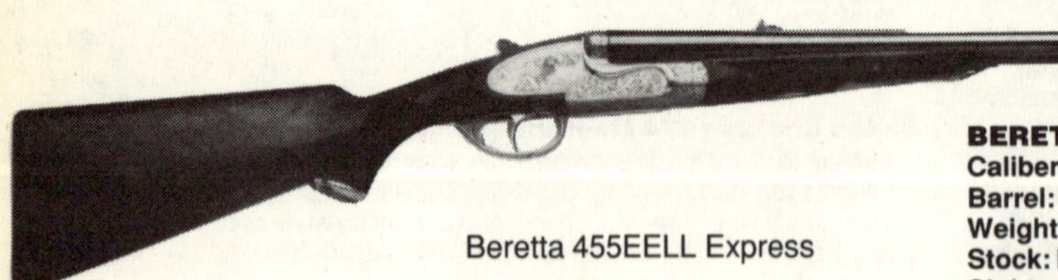

Beretta 455EELL Express

BERETTA MODEL 455 SxS EXPRESS RIFLE
Caliber: 375 H&H, 458 Win. Mag., 470 NE, 500 NE 3", 416 Rigby.
Barrel: 23½" or 25½".
Weight: 11 lbs.
Stock: European walnut with hand-checkered grip and forend.
Sights: Blade front, folding leaf V-notch rear.
Features: Sidelock action with easily removable sideplates; color case-hardened finish (455), custom big game or floral motif engraving (455EELL). Double triggers, recoil pad. Introduced 1990. Imported from Italy by Beretta U.S.A.
Price: Model 455 . . . . **$34,350.00**
Price: Model 455EELL **$44,000.00**

BERNARDELLI EXPRESS VB DOUBLE RIFLE
Caliber: 9.3x74R.
Barrel: 25½".
Weight: About 7.9 lbs.
Stock: Select walnut with cheekpiece, long beavertail-schnabel forend; hand checkered grip and forend. Pistol grip or straight English.
Sights: Bead on ramp front, quarter-rib with leaf rear.
Features: Coin-finished or color case-hardened boxlock action with automatic ejectors, double or single trigger; hand-cut rib. Introduced 1990. Imported from Italy by Magnum Research.
Price: **$7,033.00**
Price: With single trigger **$7,240.00**

BERETTA EXPRESS SSO DOUBLE RIFLES
Caliber: 375 H&H, 458 Win. Mag., 9.3x74R.
Barrel: 25.5".
Weight: 11 lbs.
Stock: European walnut with hand-checkered grip and forend.
Sights: Blade front on ramp, open V-notch rear.
Features: Sidelock action with color case-hardened receiver (gold inlays on SSO6 Gold). Ejectors, double triggers, recoil pad. Introduced 1990. Imported from Italy by Beretta U.S.A.
Price: SSO6 . . . . **$19,000.00**
Price: SSO6 Gold **$21,550.00**

BERNARDELLI COMB 2000 COMBINATION GUN
Caliber/Gauge: 12- or 16-ga. over 22 Hornet, 222 Rem., 5.6x50R Mag., 243, 6.5x55, 6.5x57R, 270, 7x57R, 308, 30-06, 8x57JRS, 9.3x74R.
Barrel: 23½".
Weight: 6¾ lbs.
Stock: Select walnut with Bavarian cheekpiece, hand checkered, oil finish.
Sights: Blade front, quarter-rib with open rear. Rib accepts rail-type scope mount.
Features: Silvered and engraved boxlock action; double-set trigger; automatic ejectors. Rifle barrel partially free floating. Introduced 1990. Imported from Italy by Magnum Research.
Price: **$2,441.00**
Price: With extra set of shotgun barrels **$3,062.00**

BRNO SUPER EXPRESS O/U DOUBLE RIFLE
Caliber: 7x65R, 9.3x74R, 375 H&H, 458 Win. Mag.
Barrel: 23½".
Weight: 8½ to 9 lbs. **Length:** 40" overall.
Stock: European walnut with raised cheekpiece, skip-line checkering.
Sights: Bead on ramp front, quarter-rib with open rear.
Features: Sidelock action with engraved sideplates; double-set triggers; selective automatic ejectors; rubber recoil pad. Barrels regulated for 100 meters. Imported from Czechoslovakia by T.D. Arms.
Price: **$3,900.00**

CAUTION: PRICES CHANGE, CHECK AT GUNSHOP.

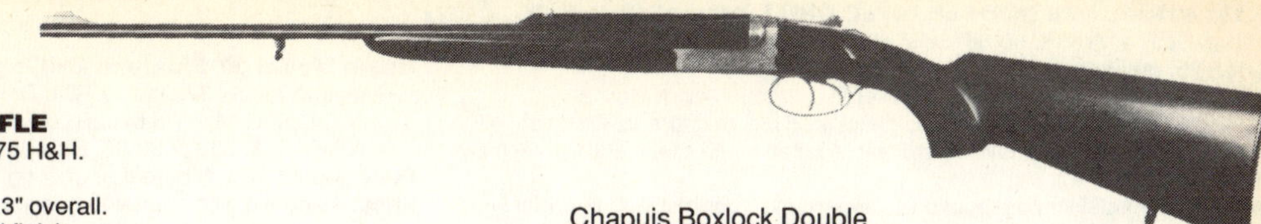

Chapuis Boxlock Double

CHAPUIS BOXLOCK DOUBLE RIFLE
Caliber: 7x65R, 8x57 JRS, 9.3x74R, 375 H&H.
Barrel: 23.6".
Weight: About 8 lbs., 6 oz. **Length:** 40.3" overall.
Stock: French walnut with pistol grip, oil finish.
Sights: Bead on ramp front, adjustable express rear on quarter-rib.
Features: Boxlock action; engraved, coin-finish receiver. Automatic ejectors, double triggers, double hook barrels. Imported from France by Armes de Chasse.
Price: About **$9,500.00**

CHAPUIS RGEXPRESS DOUBLE RIFLE
Caliber: 30-06, 7x65R, 8x57 JRS, 9.3x74R.
Barrel: 23.6".
Weight: 8-9 lbs. **Length:** NA.
Stock: Deluxe walnut with Monte Carlo comb, oil finish.
Sights: Bead on ramp front, adjustable express rear on quarter-rib.
Features: Boxlock action with long trigger guard, automatic ejectors, double hook Blitz system action with coil springs; coin metal finish; trap grip cap for extra front sight. Imported from France by Armes de Chasse.
Price: About . . . . **$7,000.00 to $8,500.00**

AUGUSTE FRANCOTTE BOXLOCK DOUBLE RIFLE
Caliber: 243, 270, 30-06, 7x64, 7x65R, 8x57JRS, 9.3x74R, 375 H&H, 470 N.E.; other calibers on request.
Barrel: 23.5" to 26".
Weight: NA. **Length:** NA.
Stock: Deluxe European walnut to customer specs; pistol grip or straight grip with Francotte cheekpiece; checkered butt; oil finish.
Sights: Bead front on long ramp, quarter-rib with fixed V rear.
Features: Side-by-side barrels; Anson & Deeley boxlock action with double triggers (front hinged), manual safety, floating firing pins and gas vent safety screws. Splinter or beavertail forend. English scroll engraving; coin finish or color case-hardening. Many options available. Imported from Belgium by Armes de Chasse.
Price: From about **$20,900.00**

HEYM MODEL 33 BOXLOCK DRILLING
Caliber/Gauge: 5.6x50R Mag., 5.6x52R, 6.5x55, 6.5x57R, 7x57R, 7x65R, 8x57JRS, 9.3x74R, 243, 308, 30-06; 16x16 (2¾"), 20x20 (3").
Barrel: 25" (Full & Mod.).
Weight: About 6½ lbs. **Length:** 42" overall.
Stock: Dark European walnut, checkered p.g. and forend; oil finish.
Sights: Silver bead front, folding leaf rear. Automatic sight positioner. Available with scope and Suhler claw mounts.
Features: Boxlock action with Greener-type cross bolt and safety, double under lugs. Double-set triggers. Plastic or steel trigger guard. Engraving coverage varies with model. Imported from Germany by Heckler & Koch, Inc.
Price: Model 33 Standard **$7,900.00**
Price: Model 33 Deluxe (hunting scene engraving) **$8,300.00**

HEYM MODEL 88B SIDE-BY-SIDE DOUBLE RIFLE
Caliber: 30-06, 8x57JRS, 9.3x74R, 375 H&H.
Barrel: 25".
Weight: 7½ lbs. (std. cals.), 8½ lbs. (mag.). **Length:** 42" overall.
Stock: Fancy French walnut, classic North American design.
Sights: Silver bead post on ramp front, fixed or three-leaf express rear.
Features: Action has complete coverage hunting scene engraving. Available as boxlock or with q.d. sidelocks. Imported from Germany by Heckler & Koch, Inc.
Price: Boxlock . . . . **$12,230.00 to 15,000.00**
Price: Sidelock, Model 88B-SS, from **$15,400.00**

Heym Model 55BF O/U Combo Gun
Similar to Model 55B O/U rifle except chambered for 12-, 16-, or 20-ga. (2¾" or 3") over 5.6x50R, 222 Rem., 223 Rem., 5.6x52R, 243, 6.5x57R, 270, 7x57R, 7x65R, 308, 30-06, 8x57JRS, 9.3x74R. Has solid rib barrel. Available with interchangeable shotgun and rifle barrels.
Price: Model 55BF boxlock **$6,600.00**

BRNO ZH 300 SERIES COMBINATION GUN
Caliber/Gauge: 5.6x52R/12-ga., 5.6x50R Mag./12, 7x57R/12, 7x57R/16.
Barrel: 23½" (Full).
Weight: 7.9 lbs. **Length:** 40½" overall.
Stock: Walnut.
Sights: Bead on blade front, folding leaf rear.
Features: Boxlock action; 8-barrel set for combination calibers and O/U shotgun barrels in 12-ga. (Field, Trap, Skeet) and 16-ga. (Field). Imported from Czechoslovakia by T.D. Arms.
Price: **$3,500.00**

AUGUSTE FRANCOTTE SIDELOCK DOUBLE RIFLES
Caliber: 243, 7x64, 7x65R, 8x57JRS, 270, 30-06, 9.3x74R, 375 H&H, 470 N.E.; others on request.
Barrel: 23½" to 26".
Weight: 7.61 lbs. (medium calibers), 11.1 lbs. (mag. calibers).
Stock: Fancy European walnut; dimensions to customer specs. Straight or pistol grip style. Checkered butt, oil finish.
Sights: Bead on ramp front, leaf rear on quarter-rib; to customer specs.
Features: Custom made to customer's specs. Special extractor for rimless cartridges; back-action sidelocks; double trigger with hinged front trigger. Automatic or free safety. Wide range of options available. Imported from Belgium by Armes de Chasse.
Price: **$36,620.00**

Consult our Directory pages for the location of firms mentioned.

HEYM MODEL 22S SAFETY COMBO GUN
Caliber/Gauge: 16- or 20-ga. (2¾", 3"), 12-ga. (2¾") over 22 Hornet, 22 WMR, 222 Rem., 223, 243 Win., 5.6x50R, 5.6x52R, 6.5x55, 6.5x57R, 7x57R, 8x57 JRS.
Barrel: 24", solid rib.
Weight: About 5½ lbs.
Stock: Dark European walnut, hand-checkered p.g. and forend. Oil finish.
Sights: Silver bead ramp front, folding leaf rear.
Features: Tang-mounted cocking slide, floating rifle barrel, single-set trigger. Base supplied for quick-detachable scope mounts. Patented rocker-weight system automatically uncocks gun if accidentally dropped or bumped hard. Imported from Germany by Heckler & Koch, Inc.
Price: Model 22SZ **$3,995.00**

Heym Model 88B

HEYM MODEL 55B/55SS O/U DOUBLE RIFLE
Caliber: 7x65R, 308, 30-06, 8x57JRS, 9.3x74R.
Barrel: 25".
Weight: About 8 lbs., depending upon caliber. **Length:** 42" overall.
Stock: Dark European walnut, hand-checkered p.g. and forend. Oil finish.
Sights: Silver bead ramp front, open V-type rear.
Features: Boxlock or full sidelock; Kersten double cross bolt, cocking indicators; hand-engraved hunting scenes. Options available include interchangeable barrels, Zeiss scopes in claw mounts, deluxe engravings and stock carving, etc. Imported from Germany by Heckler & Koch, Inc.
Price: Model 55B boxlock **$9,450.00**
Price: Model 55SS sidelock **$15,000.00**
Price: Interchangeable shotgun barrels, add **$3,500.00**
Price: Interchangeable rifle barrels, add **$5,200.00**

DRILLINGS, COMBINATION GUNS, DOUBLE RIFLES

HEYM MODEL 37B DOUBLE RIFLE DRILLING

Caliber/Gauge: 7x65R, 30-06, 8x57JRS, 9.3x74R; 20-ga. (3").
Barrel: 25" (shotgun barrel choked Full or Mod.).
Weight: About 8½ lbs. **Length:** 42" overall.
Stock: Dark European walnut, hand-checkered p.g. and forend. Oil finish.
Sights: Silver bead front, folding leaf rear. Available with scope and Suhler claw mounts.
Features: Full sidelock construction. Greener-type cross bolt, double under lugs, cocking indicators. Imported from Germany by Heckler & Koch, Inc.
Price: Model 37B double rifle drilling **$14,275.00**
Price: Model 37B Deluxe (hunting scene engraving) **$16,700.00**

Heym Model 37 Sidelock Drilling

Similar to Model 37 Double Rifle Drilling except has 12x12, 16x16 or 20x20 over 5.6x50R Mag., 5.6x52R, 6.5x55, 6.5x57R, 7x57R, 7x65R, 8x57JRS, 9.3x74R, 243, 308 or 30-06. Rifle barrel is manually cocked and uncocked.
Price: Model 37 with border engraving **$11,285.00**
Price: As above with engraved hunting scenes **$17,325.00**

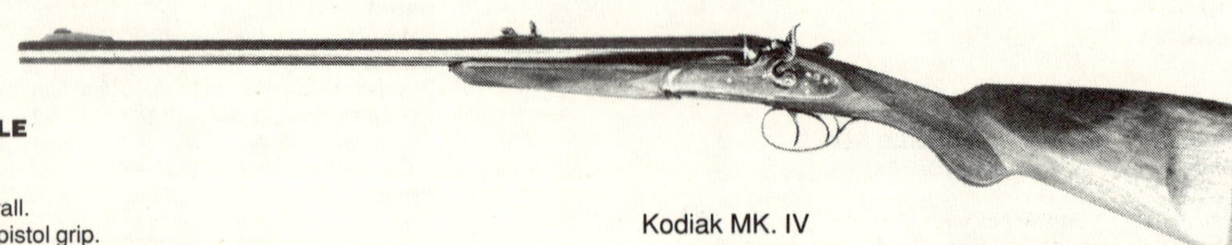

Kodiak MK. IV

KODIAK MK. IV DOUBLE RIFLE

Caliber: 45-70.
Barrel: 24".
Weight: 10 lbs. **Length:** 42½" overall.
Stock: European walnut with semi-pistol grip.
Sights: Ramp front with bead, adjustable two-leaf rear.
Features: Exposed hammers, color case-hardened locks. Rubber recoil pad. Comes cased. Introduced 1988. Imported from Italy by Trail Guns Armory.
Price: About **$1,495.00**

KRIEGHOFF TECK O/U COMBINATION GUN

Caliber/Gauge: 12, 16, 20/22 Hornet, 222, 243, 270, 30-06, 308 and standard European calibers. O/U rifle also available in 458 Win. on special order.
Barrel: 25" on double rifle combo, 28" on O/U shotgun. Optional free-floating rifle barrel available.
Weight: 7-7½ lbs.
Stock: Hand-checkered European walnut with German-style grip and cheekpiece.
Sights: White bead front on shotgun, open or folding on rifle or combo.
Features: Boxlock action with non-selective single trigger or optional single/double trigger. Greener cross bolt. Ejectors standard on all but O/U rifle. Top tang safety. Light scroll engraving. Imported from Germany by Krieghoff International, Inc.
Price: From . . . . **$7,995.00** to **$9,500.00**
Price: Ulm (full sidelock model), from . . . . **$13,500.00 to 16,985.00**

Krieghoff Trumpf

KRIEGHOFF TRUMPF DRILLING

Caliber/Gauge: 12, 16, 20/22 Hornet, 222 Rem., 243, 270, 30-06, 308. Standard European calibers also available.
Barrel: 25". Shot barrels choked Imp. Mod. & Full. Optional free-floating rifle barrel available.
Weight: About 7½ lbs.
Stock: Hand-checkered European walnut with German-style grip and cheekpiece. Oil finish.
Sights: Bead front, automatic pop-up open rear.
Features: Boxlock action with double or optional single trigger, top tang shotgun safety. Fine, light scroll engraving. Imported from Germany by Krieghoff International, Inc.
Price: **$11,995.00**
Price: Neptun (full sidelock drilling), from **$15,500.00**

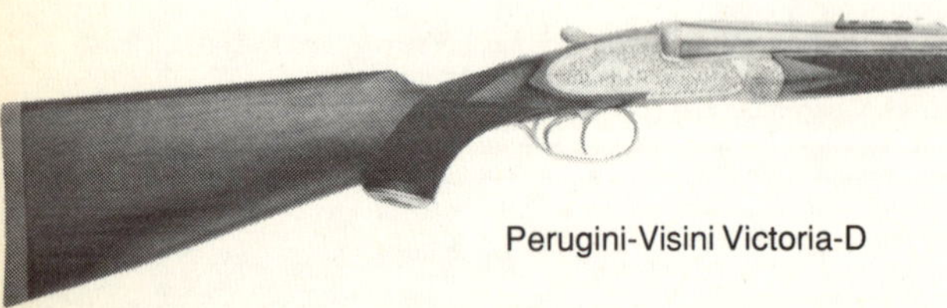

Perugini-Visini Victoria-D

Perugini-Visini Victoria Double Rifles

A boxlock double rifle which shares many of the same features of the Selous model. Calibers 7x65R, 30-06, 9.3x74R, 375 H&H Mag., 458 Win. Mag., 470; double triggers; automatic ejectors. Many options available, including an extra 20-ga. barrel set.
Price: Victoria-M (7x65R, 30-06, 9.3x74R), from about **$6,800.00**
Price: Victoria-D (375, 458, 470), from about **$12,500.00**

PERUGINI-VISINI MODEL SELOUS SIDELOCK DOUBLE RIFLE

Caliber: 30-06, 7mm Rem. Mag., 7x65R, 9.3x74R, 270 Win., 300 H&H, 338 Win., 375 H&H, 458 Win. Mag., 470 Nitro.
Barrel: 22"-26".
Weight: 7¼ to 10½ lbs., depending upon caliber. **Length:** 41" overall (24" bbl.).
Stocks: Oil-finished walnut, checkered grip and forend; cheekpiece.
Sights: Bead on ramp front, express rear on quarter-rib.
Features: True sidelock action with ejectors; sideplates are hand detachable; comes with leather trunk case. Introduced 1983. Imported from Italy by Wm. Larkin Moore.
Price: **$24,000.00**

Savage 24F

Savage 24F-12T Turkey Gun

Similar to Model 24F except has camouflage Rynite stock and Full, Imp. Cyl., Mod. choke tubes. Available only in 22 Hornet or 223 over 12-gauge with 3" chamber. Introduced 1989.
Price: **$420.00**

SAVAGE 24F O/U

Caliber/Gauge: 22 Hornet, 223, 30-30 over 12 (24F-12) or 22 LR, 22 Hornet, 223, 30-30 over 20-ga. (24F-20); 3" chambers.
Action: Takedown, low rebounding visible hammer. Single trigger, barrel selector spur on hammer.
Barrel: 24" separated barrels; 12-ga. has Full, Mod., Imp. Cyl. choke tubes, 20-ga. has fixed Mod. choke.
Weight: 7 lbs. **Length:** 40½" overall.
Stock: Black Rynite composition.
Sights: Ramp front, rear open adjustable for elevation. Grooved for tip-off scope mount.
Features: Removable butt cap for storage and accessories. Introduced 1989.
Price: 24F-12 . . . . **$400.00**
Price: 24F-20 . . . . **$400.00**

CAUTION: PRICES CHANGE, CHECK AT GUNSHOP.

Springfield M6 Scout

SPRINGFIELD ARMORY M6 SCOUT RIFLE/SHOTGUN
Caliber: 22 LR over 410-bore.
Barrel: 18".
Weight: 4 lbs. **Length:** 31½" overall.
Stock: Steel, folding, with magazine for 15 22 LR, four 410 shells.
Sights: Blade front, military aperture for 22; V-notch for 410.
Features: All-metal construction. Designed for quick disassembly and minimum maintenance. Folds for compact storage. Introduced 1982; reintroduced 1991. Made in U.S. by Springfield Armory.
Price: **$193.00**

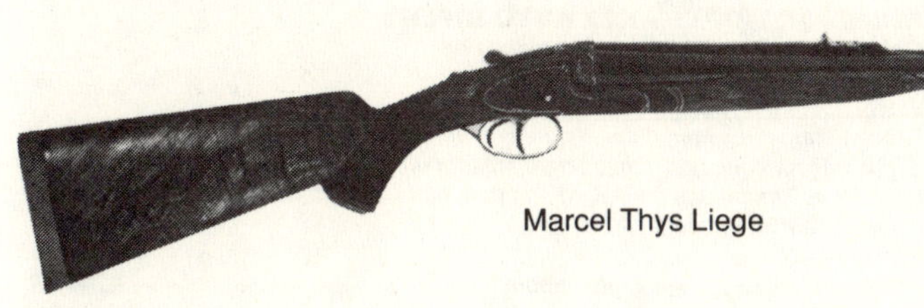
Marcel Thys Liege

MARCEL THYS LIEGE DOUBLE RIFLE
Caliber: 22 LR, 22 Hornet, 30-06, 375 H&H, 450 #2, 458 Win. Mag., 470 Nitro, 500 3", 577, 600 Nitro.
Barrel: 24" to 27".
Weight: 6 lbs. to 14 lbs.
Stock: Dark full-grain European walnut with oil finish.
Sights: Bead on ramp front, quarter-rib rear with one standing leaf, two folding leaves.
Features: Sidelock action with hand detachable locks, reinforced Holland-style frame, chopper lump barrels, reinforced top tang extension; full-coverage game scene engraving. Introduced 1990. Imported from Belgium by Cape Outfitters.
Price: Royal LUX (standard game scene engraving, coin finish or color case-hardened action) **$19,500.00**
Price: King Royal (gold inlaid game scenes)**$20,750.00**

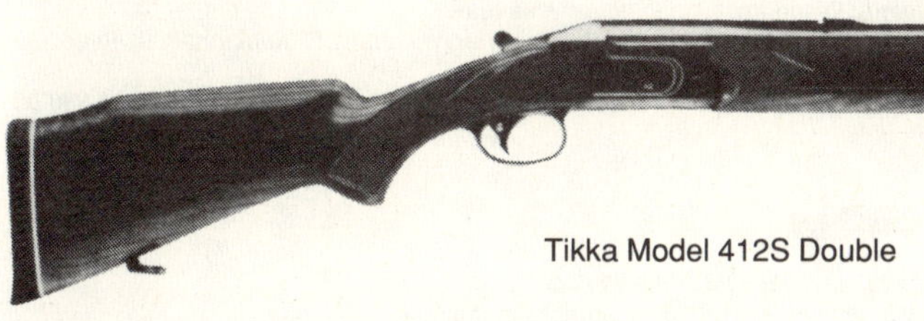
Tikka Model 412S Double

TIKKA MODEL 412S DOUBLE RIFLE
Caliber: 9.3x74R.
Barrel: 24".
Weight: 8⅝ lbs.
Stock: American walnut with Monte Carlo style.
Sights: Ramp front, adjustable open rear.
Features: Barrel selector mounted in trigger. Cocking indicators in tang. Recoil pad. Valmet scope mounts available. Introduced 1980. Imported from Italy by Valmet.
Price: With ejectors, 9.3x74R **$1,365.00**

TIKKA MODEL 412S COMBINATION GUN
Caliber/Gauge: 12 over 222, 308.
Barrel: 24" (Imp. Mod.).
Weight: 7⅝ lbs.
Stock: American walnut, with recoil pad. Monte Carlo style. Standard measurements 14"x1⅗"x2"x2⅗".
Sights: Blade front, flip-up-type open rear.
Features: Barrel selector on trigger. Hand-checkered stock and forend. Barrels are screw-adjustable to change bullet point of impact. Barrels are interchangeable. Introduced 1980. Imported from Italy by Valmet.
Price: **$1,195.00**
Price: Extra barrels, from **$685.00**

A. ZOLI RIFLE-SHOTGUN O/U COMBO
Caliber/Gauge: 12-ga. over 222, 308 or 30-06.
Barrel: Combo—24"; shotgun—28" (Mod. & Full).
Weight: About 8 lbs. **Length:** 41" overall (24" bbl.).
Stock: European walnut.
Sights: Blade front, flip-up rear.
Features: Available with German claw scope mounts on rifle/shotgun barrels. Comes with set of 12/12 (Mod. & Full) barrels. Imported from Italy by Mandall Shooting Supplies.
Price: With two barrel sets **$1,695.00**
Price: As above with claw mounts, scope **$2,495.00**

RIMFIRE RIFLES—AUTOLOADERS

Designs for hunting, utility and sporting purposes, including training for competition.

AMT Lightning 25/22

AMT Lightning Small-Game Hunting Rifle
Same as the Lightning 25/22 except has conventional stock of black fiberglass-filled nylon, checkered at the grip and forend, and fitted with Uncle Mike's swivel studs. Removable recoil pad provides storage for ammo, cleaning rod and survival knife. No iron sights—receiver grooved for scope mounting. Has a 22" target weight barrel, weighs 6¾ lbs., overall length of 40½". Introduced 1987. From AMT.
Price: **$269.99**

AMT LIGHTNING 25/22 RIFLE
Caliber: 22 LR, 30-shot magazine.
Barrel: 18", tapered or bull.
Weight: 6 lbs. **Length:** 26½" (folded), 37" (open).
Stock: Folding stainless steel.
Sights: Ramp front, rear adjustable for windage.
Features: Made of stainless steel with matte finish. Receiver dovetailed for scope mounting. Extended magazine release. Standard or "bull" barrel. Youth stock available. Introduced 1984. From AMT.
Price: **$279.99**

Anschutz 525

ANSCHUTZ 525 DELUXE AUTO
Caliber: 22 LR, 10-shot clip.
Barrel: 24".
Weight: 6½ lbs. **Length:** 43" overall.
Stock: European hardwood; checkered pistol grip, Monte Carlo comb, beavertail forend.
Sights: Hooded ramp front, folding leaf rear.
Features: Rotary safety, empty shell deflector, single stage trigger. Receiver grooved for scope mounting. Introduced 1982. Imported from Germany by PSI.
Price: **$514.00**

ARMSCOR MODEL 20P AUTO RIFLE
Caliber: 22 LR, 15-shot magazine.
Barrel: 20½".
Weight: 6 lbs. **Length:** 40⅝" overall.
Stock: Walnut-finished mahogany.
Sights: Hooded front, rear adjustable for elevation.
Features: Receiver grooved for scope mounting. Blued finish. Introduced 1990. Imported from the Philippines by Armscor.
Price: About **$91.19**
Price: Model 20C (carbine-style stock, steel barrel band, buttplate) . **$118.69**
Price: Model 2000SC (as above except has checkered stock, fully adjustable sight, rubber buttpad, forend tip), about **$243.69**
Price: Model 50S (similar to Model 20P except has ventilated barrel shroud, and 30-shot magazine) **$146.19**

ARMSCOR MODEL AK22 AUTO RIFLE
Caliber: 22 LR, 15- and 30-shot magazine.
Barrel: 18¼".
Weight: 7.4 lbs. **Length:** 37⅞" overall.
Stock: Plain mahogany.
Sights: Post front, open rear adjustable for windage and elevation.
Features: Resembles the AK-47. Matte black finish. Introduced 1987. Imported from the Philippines by Armscor.
Price: About **$162.44**
Price: With folding steel stock, about **$206.19**

ARMSCOR MODEL 1600 AUTO RIFLE
Caliber: 22 LR, 15-shot magazine.
Barrel: 20".
Weight: 7½ lbs. **Length:** 40" overall.
Stock: Black fiberglass or wood.
Sights: Post front, aperture rear.
Features: Resembles Colt AR-15. Matte black finish. Introduced 1987. Imported from the Philippines by Armscor.
Price: About **$118.69**
Price: M1600R (as above except has retractable buttstock, ventilated forend), about **$129.94**

BERNARDELLI SEMI-AUTOMATIC 9MM FLOBERT CARBINE
Caliber: 9mm Flobert, 3- or 4-shot magazine.
Barrel: 20.8".
Weight: 5 lbs., 6 oz.
Stock: European walnut with Monte Carlo comb.
Sights: Blade front, open adjustable rear.
Features: Push-button safety in rear of trigger guard. Blue/black finish. Imported from Italy by Magnum Research.
Price: **$438.00**

Auto-Ordnance 1927A-3

AUTO-ORDNANCE 1927A-3
Caliber: 22 LR, 10-, 30- or 50-shot magazine.
Barrel: 16", finned.
Weight: About 7 lbs.
Stock: Walnut stock and forend.
Sights: Blade front, open rear adjustable for windage and elevation.
Features: Recreation of the Thompson Model 1927, only in 22 Long Rifle. Alloy receiver, finned barrel.
Price: **$487.50**

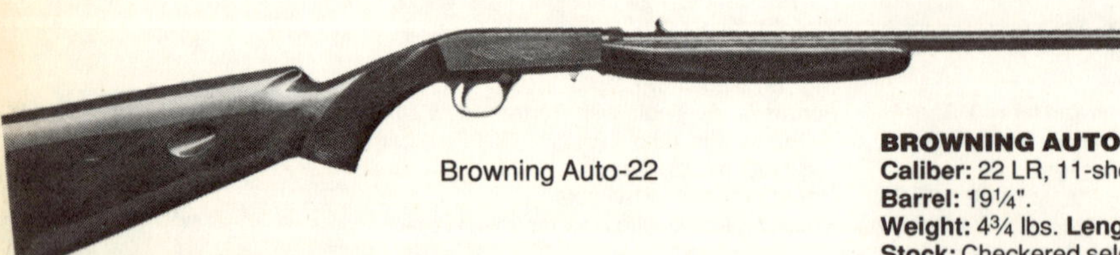
Browning Auto-22

BROWNING AUTO-22 RIFLE
Caliber: 22 LR, 11-shot.
Barrel: 19¼".
Weight: 4¾ lbs. **Length:** 37" overall.
Stock: Checkered select walnut with p.g. and semi-beavertail forend.
Sights: Gold bead front, folding leaf rear.
Features: Engraved receiver with polished blue finish; cross-bolt safety; tubular magazine in buttstock; easy takedown for carrying or storage. Imported from Japan by Browning.
Price: Grade I **$344.95**

Browning Auto-22 Grade VI
Same as the Grade I Auto-22 except available with either grayed or blued receiver with extensive engraving with gold-plated animals: right side pictures a fox and squirrel in a woodland scene; left side shows a beagle chasing a rabbit. On top is a portrait of the beagle. Stock and forend are of high-grade walnut with a double-bordered cut checkering design. Introduced 1987.
Price: Grade VI, blue or gray receiver **$708.95**

CALICO MODEL M-100 CARBINE
Caliber: 22 LR, 100-shot magazine.
Barrel: 16".
Weight: 5.7 lbs. (loaded). **Length:** 35.8" overall (stock extended).
Stock: Folding steel.
Sights: Post front adjustable for elevation, notch rear adjustable for windage.
Features: Uses alloy frame and helical-feed magazine; ambidextrous safety; removable barrel assembly; pistol grip compartment; flash suppressor; bolt stop. Made in U.S. From Calico.
Price: **$344.90**
Price: M-101 (as above with fixed buttstock) **$349.90**

Calico Model M-105 Sporter

Calico Model M-105 Sporter
Similar to the M-100 except has hand-rubbed wood buttstock and forend. Weight is 4¾ lbs. Introduced 1987.
Price: **$373.90**

Feather AT-22

FEATHER AT-22 SEMI-AUTO CARBINE
Caliber: 22 LR, 20-shot magazine.
Barrel: 17".
Weight: 3.25 lbs. **Length:** 35" overall (stock extended).
Stock: Telescoping wire; composition pistol grip.
Sights: Protected post front, adjustable aperture rear.
Features: Removable barrel. Length when folded is 26". Matte black finish. From Feather Industries. Introduced 1986.
Price: **$249.95**

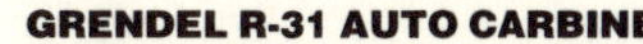

Grendel R-31

GRENDEL R-31 AUTO CARBINE
Caliber: 22 WMR, 30-shot magazine.
Barrel: 16".
Weight: 4 lbs. **Length:** 23.5" overall (stock collapsed).
Stock: Telescoping tube, Zytel forend.
Sights: Post front adustable for windage and elevation, aperture rear.
Features: Blowback action with fluted chamber; ambidextrous safety. Steel receiver. Matte black finish. Muzzle brake. Scope mount optional. Introduced 1991. Made in U.S. by Grendel, Inc.
Price: **$385.00**

Kintrek Model KBP-1

KINTREK MODEL KBP-1 AUTO RIFLE
Caliber: 22 LR, 17-shot magazine.
Barrel: 25".
Weight: 5.5 lbs. **Length:** 31½" overall.
Stock: Solid black synthetic with smooth pebble finish.
Sights: Post front, fully adjustable aperture rear. Drilled and tapped for scope mount.
Features: Bullpup design. Has grip safety and trigger-blocking safeties. Ejects empties out through bottom of stock. Bolt hold-open operated by grip safety. Matte black finish. Introduced 1991. Made in U.S. by Kintrek, Inc.
Price: **$249.00**

KRICO MODEL 260 AUTO RIFLE
Caliber: 22 LR, 5-shot magazine.
Barrel: 19.6".
Weight: 6.6 lbs. **Length:** 38.9" overall.
Stock: Beech.
Sights: Blade on ramp front, open adjustable rear.
Features: Receiver grooved for scope mounting. Sliding safety. Imported from Germany by Mandall Shooting Supplies.
Price: **$700.00**

Lakefield Model 64B

LAKEFIELD ARMS MODEL 64B AUTO RIFLE
Caliber: 22 LR, 10-shot magazine.
Barrel: 20".
Weight: 5½ lbs. **Length:** 40" overall.
Stock: Walnut-finished hardwood with Monte Carlo-type comb, checkered grip and forend.
Sights: Bead front, open adjustable rear. Receiver grooved for scope mounting.
Features: Thumb-operated rotating safety. Blue finish. Side ejection, bolt hold-open device. Introduced 1990. Made in Canada by Lakefield Arms Ltd.
Price: About **$129.95**

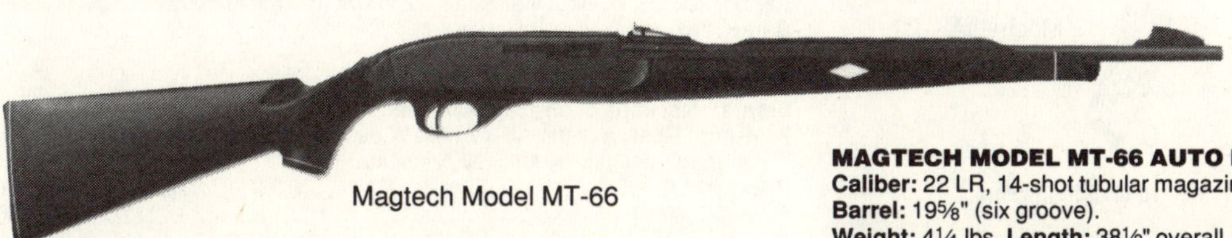

Magtech Model MT-66

MAGTECH MODEL MT-66 AUTO RIFLE
Caliber: 22 LR, 14-shot tubular magazine.
Barrel: 19⅝" (six groove).
Weight: 4¼ lbs. **Length:** 38½" overall.
Stock: Moulded black nylon with checkered pistol grip and forend.
Sights: Blade front, open adjustable rear.
Features: Tube magazine loads through buttplate; top tang safety; receiver grooved for scope mounts. Introduced 1991. Imported from Brazil by Magtech Recreational Products, Inc.
Price: About **$109.95**

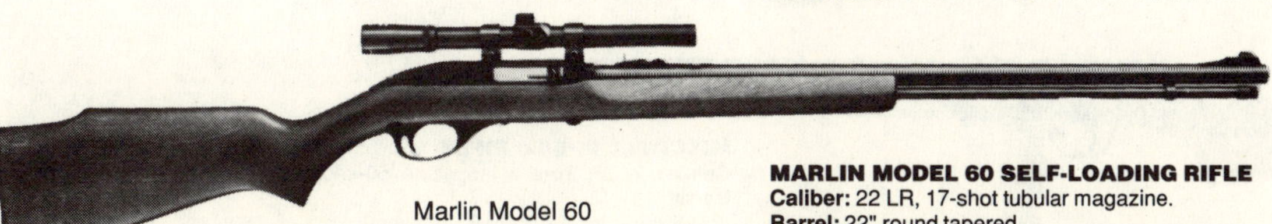

Marlin Model 60

MARLIN MODEL 60 SELF-LOADING RIFLE
Caliber: 22 LR, 17-shot tubular magazine.
Barrel: 22" round tapered.
Weight: About 5½ lbs. **Length:** 40½" overall.
Stock: Walnut-finished Monte Carlo, full pistol grip; Mar-Shield® finish.
Sights: Ramp front, open adjustable rear.
Features: Matted receiver is grooved for scope mount. Manual bolt hold-open; automatic last-shot bolt hold-open.
Price: **$137.95**

Marlin Model 70 HC

MARLIN MODEL 70 HC AUTO
Caliber: 22 LR, 15-shot clip magazine.
Barrel: 18" (16-groove rifling).
Weight: 5 lbs. **Length:** 36¾" overall.
Stock: Walnut-finished hardwood with Monte Carlo, full p.g. Mar-Shield® finish.
Sights: Ramp front, adjustable open rear. Receiver grooved for scope mount.
Features: Receiver top has serrated, non-glare finish; cross-bolt safety; manual bolt hold-open.
Price: $154.95

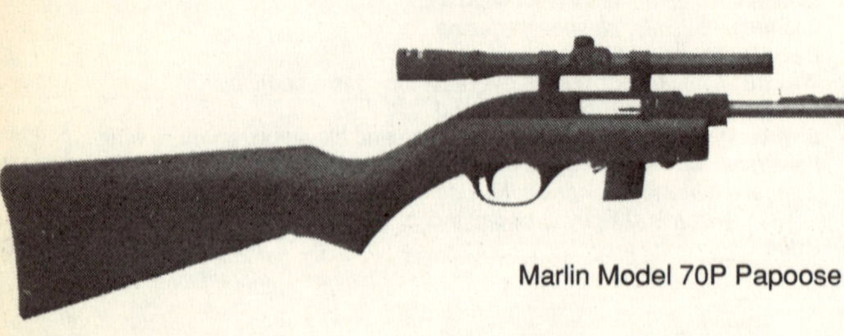
Marlin Model 70P Papoose

Marlin Model 70P Papoose
Similar to the Model 70 HC except is a takedown model with easily removable barrel—no tools needed. Has 16¼" Micro-Groove® barrel, walnut-finished hardwood stock, ramp front, adjustable open rear sights, cross-bolt safety. Takedown feature allows removal of barrel without tools. Overall length is 35¼", weight is 3¼ lbs. Receiver grooved for scope mounting. Comes with zippered case. Introduced 1986.
Price: $172.95

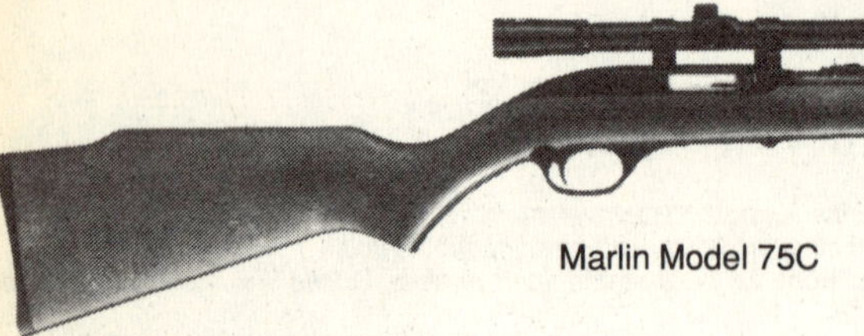
Marlin Model 75C

MARLIN MODEL 75C SELF-LOADING RIFLE
Caliber: 22 LR, 13-shot tubular magazine.
Barrel: 18".
Weight: 5 lbs. **Length:** 36½" overall.
Stock: Walnut-finished hardwood; Monte Carlo with full p.g.
Sights: Ramp front, adjustable open rear.
Features: Manual bolt hold-open; automatic last-shot bolt hold-open; cross-bolt safety; receiver grooved for scope mounting.
Price: $137.95

MARLIN MODEL 995 SELF-LOADING RIFLE
Caliber: 22 LR, 7-shot clip magazine.
Barrel: 18" Micro-Groove®.
Weight: 5 lbs. **Length:** 36¾" overall.
Stock: American black walnut, Monte Carlo-style, with full pistol grip. Checkered p.g. and forend; white buttplate spacer; Mar-Shield® finish.
Sights: Ramp bead front with Wide-Scan™ hood; adjustable folding semi-buckhorn rear.
Features: Receiver grooved for scope mount; bolt hold-open device; cross-bolt safety. Introduced 1979.
Price: $183.95

Consult our Directory pages for the location of firms mentioned.

Mitchell AK-22

MITCHELL AK-22 SEMI-AUTO RIFLE
Caliber: 22 LR, 20-shot magazine; 22 WMR, 10-shot magazine.
Barrel: 18".
Weight: 6½ lbs. **Length:** 36" overall.
Stock: European walnut.
Sights: Post front, open adjustable rear.
Features: Replica of the AK-47 rifle. Wide magazine to maintain appearance. Imported from Italy by Mitchell Arms, Inc.
Price: 22 LR $325.00
Price: 22 WMR $349.00

MITCHELL GALIL/22 AUTO RIFLE
Caliber: 22 LR, 20-shot magazine; 22 WMR, 10-shot magazine.
Barrel: 18".
Weight: 6.5 lbs. **Length:** 36" overall.
Stock: European walnut butt, grip, forend.
Sights: Post front adjustable for elevation, rear adjustable for windage.
Features: Replica of the Israeli Galil rifle. Introduced 1987. Imported by Mitchell Arms, Inc.
Price: 22 LR $325.00
Price: 22 WMR $349.00

Mitchell PPS/50

MITCHELL PPS/50 RIFLE
Caliber: 22 LR, 20-shot magazine (50-shot drum optional).
Barrel: 16½".
Weight: 5½ lbs. **Length:** 33½" overall.
Stock: Walnut.
Sights: Blade front, adjustable rear.
Features: Full-length perforated barrel shroud. Matte finish. Introduced 1989. Imported by Mitchell Arms, Inc.
Price: With 20-shot "banana" magazine $325.00
Price: With 50-shot drum magazine $394.00

CAUTION: PRICES CHANGE, CHECK AT GUNSHOP.

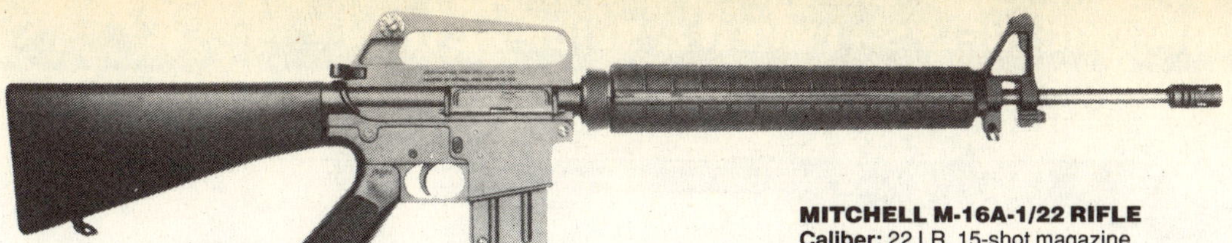

Mitchell M-16A-1/22

MITCHELL M-16A-1/22 RIFLE
Caliber: 22 LR, 15-shot magazine.
Barrel: 20.5".
Weight: 7 lbs. **Length:** 38.5" overall.
Stock: Black composition.
Sights: Adjustable post front, adjustable aperture rear.
Features: Replica of the AR-15 rifle. Full width magazine. Comes with military-type sling. Introduced 1990. Imported by Mitchell Arms, Inc.
Price: 22 LR **$325.00**

Mitchell CAR-15/22 Semi-Auto Rifle
Similar to the M-16 A-1/22 rifle except has 16¾" barrel, telescoping butt, giving an overall length of 32" when collapsed. Adjustable post front sight, adjustable aperture rear. Scope mount available. Has 15-shot magazine. Replica of the CAR-15 rifle. Introduced 1990. Imported by Mitchell Arms, Inc.
Price: **$349.00**

MITCHELL MAS/22 AUTO RIFLE
Caliber: 22 LR, 20-shot magazine.
Barrel: 18".
Weight: 7½ lbs. **Length:** 28.5" overall.
Stock: Walnut butt, grip and forend.
Sights: Adjustable post front, flip-type aperture rear.
Features: Bullpup design resembles French armed forces rifle. Top cocking lever, flash hider. Introduced 1987. Imported by Mitchell Arms, Inc.
Price: 22 LR **$325.00**

Norinco 22 ATD

NORINCO MODEL 22 ATD RIFLE
Caliber: 22 LR, 11-shot magazine.
Barrel: 19.4".
Weight: 4.6 lbs. **Length:** 36.6" overall.
Stock: Checkered hardwood.
Sights: Blade front, open adjustable rear.
Features: Browning-design takedown action for storage, transport. Cross-bolt safety. Tube magazine loads through buttplate. Blue finish with engraved receiver. Introduced 1987. Imported from China by Interarms.
Price: **$165.00**
Price: Camouflage case **$16.00**

Remington 552BDL

REMINGTON 552BDL SPEEDMASTER RIFLE
Caliber: 22 S (20), L (17) or LR (15) tubular mag.
Barrel: 21" round tapered.
Weight: About 5¾ lbs. **Length:** 40" overall.
Stock: Walnut. Checkered grip and forend.
Sights: Bead front, step open rear adjustable for windage and elevation.
Features: Positive cross-bolt safety, receiver grooved for tip-off mount.
Price: About **$213.00**

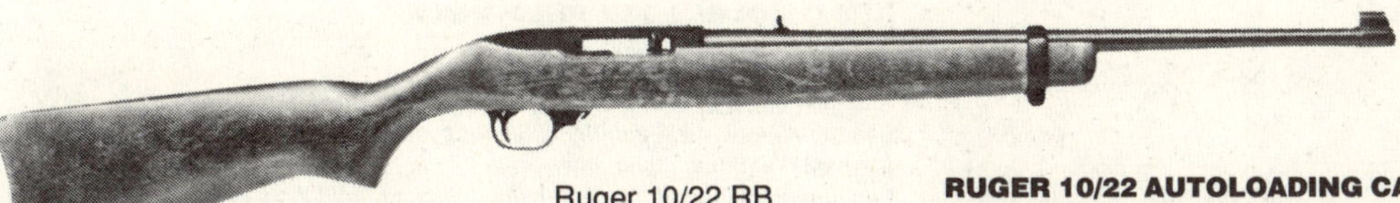

Ruger 10/22 RB

RUGER 10/22 AUTOLOADING CARBINE
Caliber: 22 LR, 10-shot rotary magazine.
Barrel: 18½" round tapered.
Weight: 5 lbs. **Length:** 37¼" overall.
Stock: American hardwood with p.g. and bbl. band.
Sights: Gold bead front, folding leaf rear adjustable for elevation.
Features: Detachable rotary magazine fits flush into stock, cross-bolt safety, receiver tapped and grooved for scope blocks or tip-off mount. Scope base adaptor furnished with each rifle.
Price: Model 10/22 RB (birch stock) **$192.00**

Ruger 10/22 Auto Sporter
Same as 10/22 Carbine except walnut stock with hand checkered p.g. and forend; straight buttplate, no barrel band, has sling swivels.
Price: Model 10/22 DSP **$242.50**

VOERE MODEL 2115 AUTO RIFLE
Caliber: 22 LR, 8- or 15-shot magazine.
Barrel: 18.1".
Weight: 5.75 lbs. **Length:** 37.7" overall.
Stock: Walnut-finished beechwood with cheekpiece; checkered pistol grip and forend.
Sights: Post front with hooded ramp, leaf rear.
Features: Clip-fed autoloader with single stage trigger, wing-type safety. Imported from Austria by L. Joseph Rahn. Introduced 1984.
Price: Model 2115 . . . . **$475.00**
Price: Model 2114S (as above except no cheekpiece, checkering or white line spacers at grip, buttplate) **$410.00**

TEXAS REMINGTON REVOLVING CARBINE
Caliber: 22 LR.
Barrel: 21".
Weight: 5¾ lbs. **Length:** 36" overall.
Stock: Smooth walnut.
Sights: Blade front, rear adjustable for windage and elevation.
Features: Brass frame, buttplate and trigger guard, blued cylinder and barrel. Introduced 1991. Imported from Italy by E.M.F.
Price: **$420.00**

RIMFIRE RIFLES—LEVER & SLIDE ACTION

Classic and modern models for sport and utility, including training.

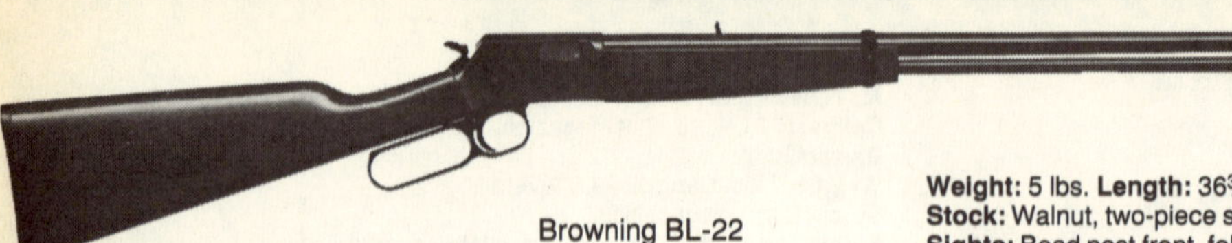
Browning BL-22

BROWNING BL-22 LEVER-ACTION RIFLE
Caliber: 22 S (22), L (17) or LR (15), tubular magazine.
Barrel: 20" round tapered.
Weight: 5 lbs. **Length:** 36¾" overall.
Stock: Walnut, two-piece straight grip Western style.
Sights: Bead post front, folding-leaf rear.
Features: Short throw lever, half-cock safety, receiver grooved for tip-off scope mounts. Imported from Japan by Browning.
Price: Grade I **$301.50**
Price: Grade II (engraved receiver, checkered grip and forend) **$343.50**

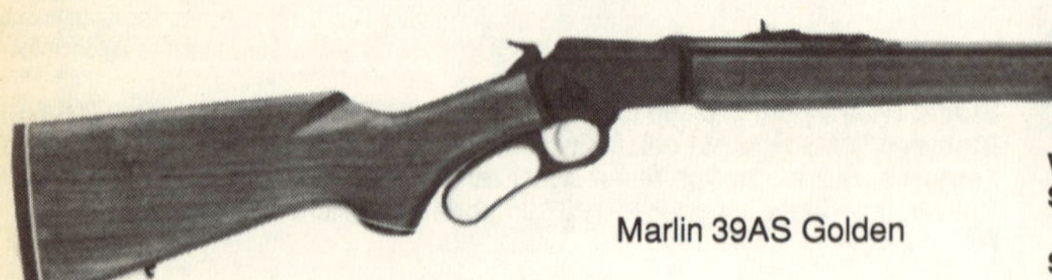
Marlin 39AS Golden

MARLIN MODEL 39AS GOLDEN LEVER-ACTION RIFLE
Caliber: 22 S (26), L (21), LR (19), tubular magazine.
Barrel: 24" Micro-Groove®.
Weight: 6½ lbs. **Length:** 40" overall.
Stock: American black walnut with white line spacers at p.g. cap and buttplate; Mar-Shield® finish. Swivel studs; rubber buttpad.
Sights: Bead ramp front with detachable Wide-Scan™ hood, folding rear semi-buckhorn adjustable for windage and elevation.
Features: Hammer-block safety; rebounding hammer. Takedown action, receiver tapped for scope mount (supplied), offset hammer spur; gold-plated steel trigger.
Price: **$375.95**

MARLIN 39TDS CARBINE
Caliber: 22 S (16), 22 L (12), 22 LR (11).
Barrel: 16½" Micro-Groove®.
Weight: 5¼ lbs. **Length:** 32⅝" overall.
Stock: American black walnut with straight grip; short forend with blued tip. Mar-Shield® finish.
Sights: Ramp front with Wide-Scan™ hood, adjustable semi-buckhorn folding rear.
Features: Takedown style, comes with carrying case. Hammer-block safety, rebounding hammer; blued metal, gold-plated steel trigger. Introduced 1988.
Price: With case **$418.95**

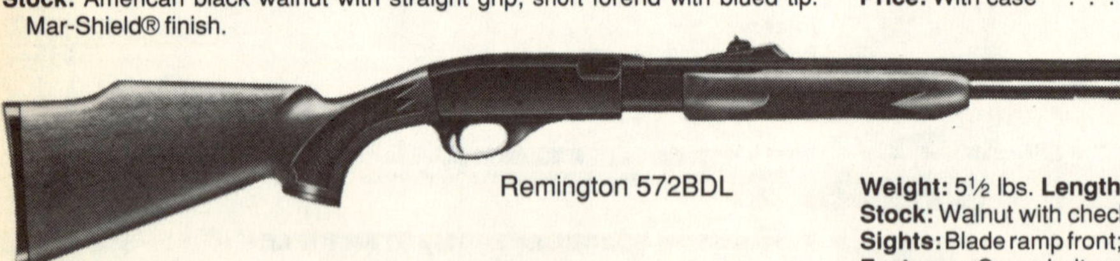
Remington 572BDL

REMINGTON 572BDL FIELDMASTER PUMP RIFLE
Caliber: 22 S (20), L (17) or LR (14), tubular magazine.
Barrel: 21" round tapered.
Weight: 5½ lbs. **Length:** 42" overall.
Stock: Walnut with checkered p.g. and slide handle.
Sights: Blade ramp front; sliding ramp rear adjustable for windage and elevation.
Features: Cross-bolt safety; removing inner magazine tube converts rifle to single shot; receiver grooved for tip-off scope mount.
Price: About **$223.00**

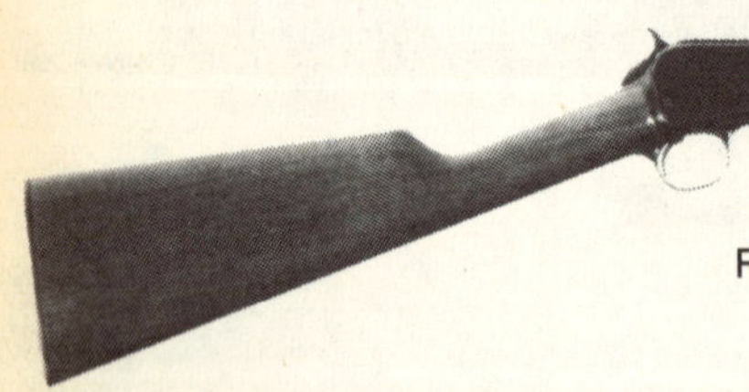
Rossi Model 62 SAC

ROSSI MODEL 62 SA PUMP RIFLE
Caliber: 22 LR, 22 WMR.
Barrel: 23", round or octagonal.
Weight: 5¾ lbs. **Length:** 39¼" overall.
Stock: Walnut, straight grip, grooved forend.
Sights: Fixed front, adjustable rear.
Features: Capacity 20 Short, 16 Long or 14 Long Rifle. Quick takedown. Imported from Brazil by Interarms.
Price: Blue **$225.00**
Price: Nickel **$240.00**
Price: Blue, with octagonal barrel **$250.00**
Price: 22 WMR, as Model 59 . . . . **$275.00**

Rossi Model 62 SAC Carbine
Same as standard model except 22 LR only, has 16¼" barrel. Magazine holds slightly fewer cartridges.
Price: Blue **$225.00**
Price: Nickel **$240.00**

Winchester Model 9422

WINCHESTER MODEL 9422 LEVER-ACTION RIFLE
Caliber: 22 S (21), L (17), LR (15), tubular magazine.
Barrel: 20½".
Weight: 6¼ lbs. **Length:** 37⅛" overall.
Stock: American walnut, two-piece, straight grip (no p.g.).
Sights: Hooded ramp front, adjustable semi-buckhorn rear.
Features: Side ejection, receiver grooved for scope mounting, takedown action. From U.S. Repeating Arms Co.
Price: Walnut **$342.00**
Price: With WinTuff laminated stock, about **$342.00**

Winchester Model 9422 Magnum Lever-Action Rifle
Same as the 9422 except chambered for 22 WMR cartridge, has 11-round mag. capacity.
Price: Walnut **$357.00**
Price: With WinCam green stock, about **$357.00**
Price: With WinTuff brown laminated stock, about **$357.00**

CAUTION: PRICES CHANGE, CHECK AT GUNSHOP.

Includes models for a variety of sports, utility and competitive shooting.

Anschutz Achiever

ANSCHUTZ ACHIEVER BOLT-ACTION RIFLE
Caliber: 22 LR, 5-shot clip.
Barrel: 19½".
Weight: 5 lbs. **Length:** 35½" to 36⅔" overall.
Stock: Walnut-finished hardwood with adjustable buttplate, vented forend, stippled pistol grip. Length of pull adjustable from 11⅞" to 13".
Sights: Hooded front, open rear adjustable for windage and elevation.
Features: Uses Mark 2000-type action with adjustable two-stage trigger. Receiver grooved for scope mounting. Designed for training in junior rifle clubs and for starting young shooters. Introduced 1987. Imported from Germany by Precision Sales International.
Price: **$395.00**
Price: Sight Set #1 . . . . **$59.50**

ANSCHUTZ 1449D YOUTH BOLT-ACTION RIFLE
Caliber: 22 LR, 5-shot clip.
Barrel: 16¼".
Weight: 3½ lbs. **Length:** 32½" overall.
Stock: Walnut-finished European hardwood.
Sights: Hooded ramp front, open adjustable rear.
Features: Uses the Anschutz Mark 2000 action which is grooved for scope mounting. Comes with 5-shot magazine; single shot clip adaptor and 10-shot clip available as accessories. Introduced 1990. Imported from Germany by Precision Sales International.
Price: **$249.00**

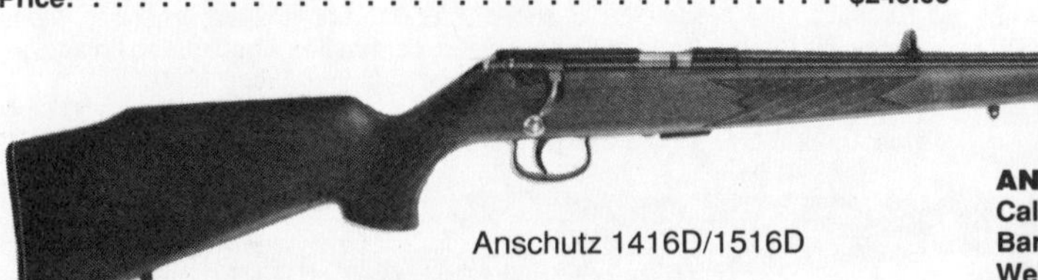

Anschutz 1416D/1516D

ANSCHUTZ 1416D/1516D DELUXE RIFLES
Caliber: 22 LR (1416D), 5-shot clip; 22 WMR (1516D), 4-shot clip.
Barrel: 22½".
Weight: 6 lbs. **Length:** 41" overall.
Stock: European walnut; Monte Carlo with cheekpiece, schnabel forend, checkered pistol grip and forend.
Sights: Hooded ramp front, folding leaf rear.
Features: Uses Model 1403 target rifle action. Adjustable single stage trigger. Receiver grooved for scope mounting. Imported from Germany by Precision Sales International.
Price: 1416D, 22 LR **$624.00**
Price: 1516D, 22 WMR **$685.00**
Price: 1416D Classic left-hand **$726.00**

Anschutz 1418D/1518D Deluxe Rifles
Similar to the 1416D/1516D rifles except has full-length Mannlicher-style stock, shorter 19¾" barrel. Weighs 5½ lbs. Stock has buffalo horn schnabel tip. Double-set trigger available on special order. Model 1418D chambered for 22 LR, 1518D for 22 WMR. Imported from Germany by Precision Sales International.
Price: 1418D **$979.00**
Price: 1518D **$998.00**

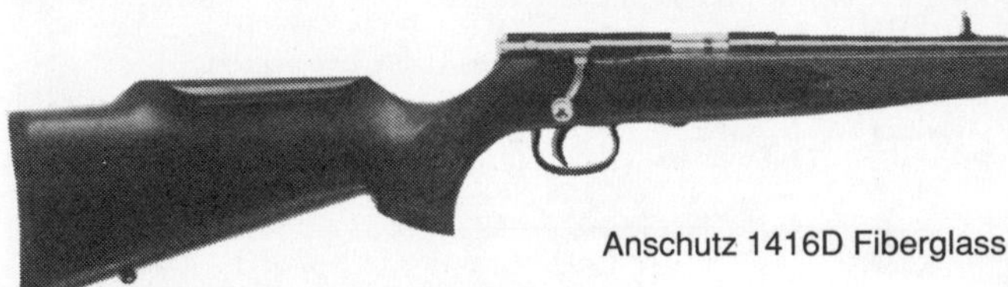

Anschutz 1416D Fiberglass

ANSCHUTZ 1416D FIBERGLASS
Caliber: 22 LR, 5-shot magazine.
Barrel: 22½".
Weight: 5¼ lbs. **Length:** 40¼" overall.
Stock: McMillan fiberglass Monte Carlo with roll-over cheekpiece, Wundhammer grip swell, schnabel forend tip.
Sights: Hooded front ramp, folding leaf rear.
Features: Match 64 takedown action with removable firing pin; adjustable trigger; slide safety; 10-shot magazine and single shot adaptor available. Introduced 1991. Imported from Germany by Precision Sales International, Inc.
Price: **$842.00**

ANSCHUTZ 1700D CLASSIC RIFLES
Caliber: 22 LR, 5-shot clip; 22 WMR, 4-shot clip.
Barrel: 23½", 13/16" dia. heavy.
Weight: 7¾ lbs. **Length:** 42½" overall.
Stock: Select European walnut with checkered pistol grip and forend.
Sights: None furnished, drilled and tapped for scope mounting.
Features: Adjustable single stage trigger. Receiver drilled and tapped for scope mounting. Introduced 1988. Imported from Germany by Precision Sales International.
Price: 22 LR **$1,199.00**
Price: 22 WMR **$1,199.00**
Price: As above, Meistergrade (select walnut, gold engraved trigger guard), add **$195.00**

Consult our Directory pages for the location of firms mentioned.

Anschutz 1700D Custom Rifles
Similar to the Classic models except have roll-over Monte Carlo cheekpiece, slim forend with schnabel tip, Wundhammer palm swell on pistol grip, rosewood grip cap with white diamond insert. Skip-line checkering on grip and forend. Introduced 1988. Imported from Germany by Precision Sales International.
Price: 22 LR **$1,229.00**
Price: 22 WMR **$1,229.00**
Price: Custom 1700 Meistergrade (select walnut, gold engraved trigger guard), add **$195.00**

Anschutz 1700 FWT Bolt-Action Rifle
Similar to the Anschutz Custom except has McMillan fiberglass stock with Monte Carlo, roll-over cheekpiece, Wundhammer swell, and checkering. Comes without sights but the receiver is drilled and tapped for scope mounting. Has 24" barrel, single stage #5095 trigger. Introduced 1989.
Price: With fiberglass stock **$1,174.00**
Price: As above, with Fibergrain stock **$1,384.00**

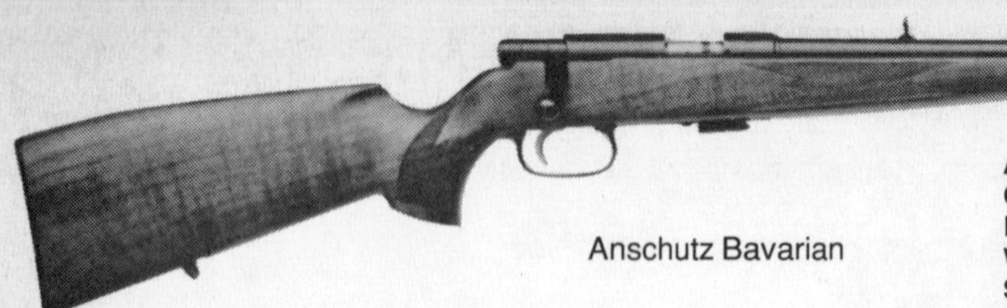
Anschutz Bavarian

ARMSCOR MODEL 14P BOLT-ACTION RIFLE
Caliber: 22 LR, 10-shot magazine.
Barrel: 22⅞".
Weight: 6 lbs. **Length:** 41" overall.
Stock: Walnut-finished mahogany.
Sights: Bead front, rear adjustable for elevation.
Features: Receiver grooved for scope mounting. Blued finish. Introduced 1987. Imported from the Philippines by Armscor.
Price: About **$96.19**
Price: Model 14D Deluxe (checkered stock) **$108.69**
Price: Model 1400LW Classic Lightweight (straight stock, schnabel forend, checkered walnut) **$199.94**
Price: As above, 22 WMR (Model 1500LW) **$218.69**

Armscor Model 1500S Rifle
Similar to the Model 14P except chambered for 22 WMR. Has 21.5" barrel, double lug bolt, checkered stock, weighs 6.5 lbs. Introduced 1987.
Price: About **$133.69**

BEEMAN/HW 60J-ST BOLT-ACTION RIFLE
Caliber: 22 LR.
Barrel: 22.8".
Weight: 6.5 lbs. **Length:** 41.7" overall.
Stock: Walnut with cheekpiece, cut checkered p.g. and forend.
Sights: Hooded blade on ramp front, open rear.
Features: Polished blue finish; oil-finished walnut. Imported from Germany by Beeman. Introduced 1988.
Price: **$585.00**

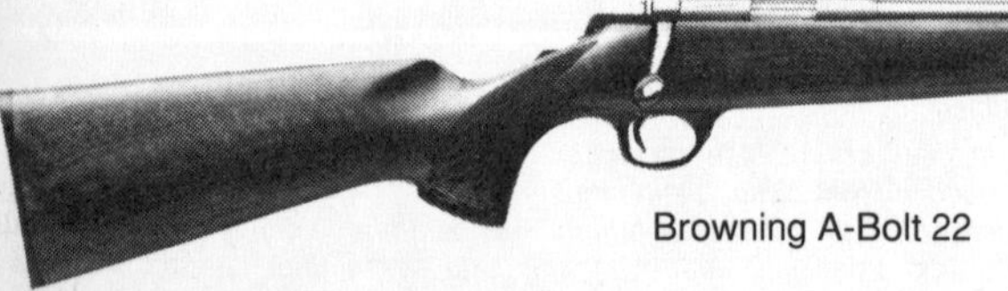
Browning A-Bolt 22

Browning A-Bolt Gold Medallion
Similar to the standard A-Bolt except stock is of high-grade walnut with brass spacers between stock and rubber recoil pad and between the rosewood grip cap and forend. Medallion-style engraving covers the receiver flats, and the words "Gold Medallion" are engraved and gold filled on the right side of the barrel. High gloss stock finish. Introduced 1988.
Price: No sights **$496.95**

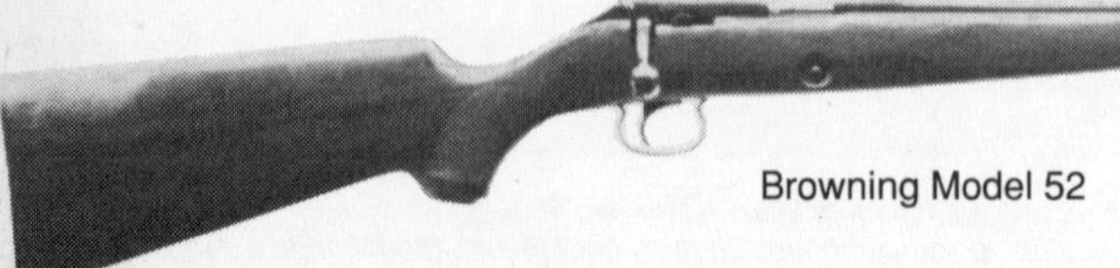
Browning Model 52

BROWNING MODEL 52 BOLT-ACTION RIFLE
Caliber: 22 LR, 5-shot magazine.
Barrel: 24".

ANSCHUTZ 1700D BAVARIAN BOLT-ACTION RIFLE
Caliber: 22 LR, 22 WMR, 5-shot clip.
Barrel: 24".
Weight: 7¼ lbs. **Length:** 43" overall.
Stock: European walnut with Bavarian cheek rest. Checkered p.g. and forend.
Sights: Hooded ramp front, folding leaf rear.
Features: Uses the Improved 1700 Match 54 action with adjustable 5096 trigger. Drilled and tapped for scope mounting. Introduced in 1988. Imported from Germany by Precision Sales International.
Price: 22 LR **$1,229.00**
Price: 22 WMR **$1,229.00**
Price: Custom 1700D Meistergrade (select walnut, gold engraved trigger guard), add **$195.00**

Anschutz 1700D Graphite Custom Rifle
Similar to the Model 1700D Custom except has McMillan graphite reinforced stock with roll-over cheekpiece. Comes with embroidered sling, Michael's quick-detachable swivels. Introduced 1991.
Price: **$1,205.00**

Armscor Model 1500 SC Super Classic
Similar to the Model 1500S except has hand-checkered American walnut stock with Monte Carlo and cheekpiece, contrasting wood forend tip and grip cap, red rubber recoil pad, engine-turned bolt. Introduced 1990.
Price: **$262.44**
Price: In 22 LR, as Model 1400 SC **$241.19**

Beeman/HW 60J-ST

BRNO ZKM 452 BOLT-ACTION RIFLE
Caliber: 22 LR, 5- or 10-shot magazine.
Barrel: 25".
Weight: 6 lbs., 10 oz. **Length:** 43½" overall.
Stock: Beechwood.
Sights: Hooded bead front, open rear adjustable for elevation.
Features: Blue finish; oiled stock with checkered p.g. Imported from Czechoslovakia by T.D. Arms.
Price: **$399.00**

BROWNING A-BOLT 22 BOLT-ACTION RIFLE
Caliber: 22 LR, 22 WMR, 5-shot magazines standard.
Barrel: 22".
Weight: 5 lbs., 9 oz. **Length:** 40¼" overall.
Stock: Walnut with cut checkering, rosewood grip cap and forend tip.
Sights: Offered with or without open sights. Open sight model has ramp front and adjustable folding leaf rear.
Features: Short 60-degree bolt throw. Top tang safety. Grooved for 22 scope mount. Drilled and tapped for full-size scope mounts. Detachable magazines. Gold-colored trigger preset at about 4 lbs. Imported from Japan by Browning. Introduced 1986.
Price: A-Bolt 22, no sights **$374.95**
Price: A-Bolt 22, with open sights **$384.95**
Price: A-Bolt 22 WMR, no sights **$429.95**
Price: As above, with sights **$439.95**

Weight: 7 lbs. **Length:** NA.
Stock: High-grade walnut with oil-like finish. Cut-checkered grip and forend, metal grip cap, rosewood forend tip.
Sights: None furnished. Drilled and tapped for scope mounting or iron sights.
Features: Recreation of the Winchester Model 52C Sporter with minor safety improvements. Duplicates the adjustable Micro-Motion trigger system. Button release magazine. Introduced 1991. Imported from Japan by Browning.
Price: **$499.95**

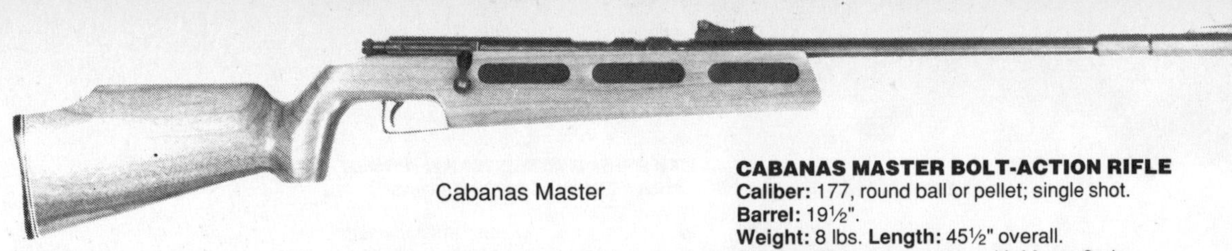
Cabanas Master

CABANAS MASTER BOLT-ACTION RIFLE
Caliber: 177, round ball or pellet; single shot.
Barrel: 19½".
Weight: 8 lbs. **Length:** 45½" overall.
Stocks: Walnut target-type with Monte Carlo.
Sights: Blade front, fully adjustable rear.
Features: Fires round ball or pellet with 22-cal. blank cartridge. Bolt action. Imported from Mexico by Mandall Shooting Supplies. Introduced 1984.
Price: **$150.00**
Price: Varmint model (has 21½" barrel, 4½ lbs., 41" o.a.l., varmint-type stock) **$109.95**

Cabanas Leyre Bolt-Action Rifle
Similar to Master model except 44" overall, has sport/target stock.
Price: **$134.95**
Price: Model R83 (17" barrel, hardwood stock, 40" o.a.l.) **$79.95**
Price: Mini 82 Youth (16½" barrel, 33" o.a.l., 3½ lbs.) **$69.95**
Price: Pony Youth (16" barrel, 34" o.a.l., 3.2 lbs.) **$79.95**
Price: Safari **$99.95**

Cabanas Espronceda IV Bolt-Action Rifle
Similar to the Leyre model except has full sporter stock, 18¾" barrel, 40" overall length, weighs 5½ lbs.
Price: **$119.95**

CABANAS RIFLE
Caliber: 177.
Barrel: 19".
Weight: 6 lbs., 12 oz. **Length:** 42" overall.
Stock: Target-type thumbhole.
Sights: Blade front, open fully adjustable rear.
Features: Fires round ball or pellets with 22 blank cartridge. Imported from Mexico by Mandall Shooting Supplies.
Price: **$159.95**

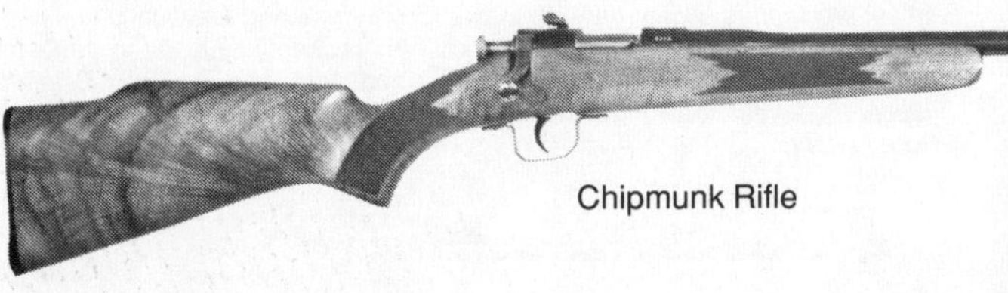
Chipmunk Rifle

CHIPMUNK SINGLE SHOT RIFLE
Caliber: 22, S, L, LR, single shot.
Barrel: 16⅛".
Weight: About 2½ lbs. **Length:** 30" overall.
Stocks: American walnut, or camouflage.
Sights: Post on ramp front, peep rear adjustable for windage and elevation.
Features: Drilled and tapped for scope mounting using special Chipmunk base ($9.95). Made in U.S. Introduced 1982. From Oregon Arms.
Price: Standard **$149.95**
Price: Deluxe (better wood, checkering) **$199.95**

Cooper Model 36

COOPER ARMS MODEL 36, 38 SPORTER RIFLES
Caliber: 22 LR, 22 Cooper Magnum Centerfire, 5-shot magazine.
Barrel: 22".
Weight: 8 lbs. **Length:** 41¾" overall.
Stock: AA Claro walnut, hand-checkered (Standard grade); AA fancy French walnut or AAA Claro walnut with beaded Monte Carlo cheekpiece, hand-checkering (Custom grade).
Sights: None furnished; optional.
Features: Action has three front locking lugs, 45-degree bolt rotation; fully adjustable single stage trigger; Wiseman/McMillan competition barrel; swivel studs, Pachmayr buttpad, oil-finished wood. Introduced 1991. Made in U.S. by Cooper Arms.
Price: Model 36 Custom (22 LR) **$795.00**
Price: Model 36 Standard (22 LR) **$695.00**
Price: Model 38 Custom (22 Cooper Centerfire Magnum) **$995.00**
Price: Model 38 Standard (22 Cooper Centerfire Magnum) **$895.00**

CZ 99 PRECISION 22 BOLT-ACTION RIFLE
Caliber: 22 LR, 5-shot magazine; 10-shot optional.
Barrel: 22".
Weight: 6.1 lbs. **Length:** 41" overall.
Stock: European walnut with checkered grip and forend.
Sights: Hooded bead on ramp front, folding rear adjustable for windage and elevation.
Features: Sliding safety locks trigger and bolt; receiver grooved for scope mounting. Polished blue finish. Introduced 1990. Imported from Yugoslavia by T.D. Arms.
Price: **$259.00**

KRICO MODEL 300 BOLT-ACTION RIFLES
Caliber: 22 LR, 22 WMR, 22 Hornet.
Barrel: 19.6" (22 RF), 23.6" (Hornet).
Weight: 6.3 lbs. **Length:** 38.5" overall (22 RF).
Stock: Walnut-stained beech.
Sights: Blade on ramp front, open adjustable rear.
Features: Double triggers, sliding safety. Checkered grip and forend. Imported from Germany by Mandall Shooting Supplies.
Price: Model 300 Standard **$700.00**
Price: Model 300 Deluxe **$795.00**
Price: Model 300 Stutzen (walnut full-length stock) **$825.00**
Price: Model 300 SA (walnut Monte Carlo stock) **$750.00**

LAKEFIELD ARMS MARK I BOLT-ACTION RIFLE
Caliber: 22 LR, single shot.
Barrel: 20½".
Weight: 5½ lbs. **Length:** 39½" overall.
Stock: Walnut-finished hardwood with Monte Carlo-type comb, checkered grip
Sights: Bead front, open adjustable rear. Receiver grooved for scope mounting.
Features: Thumb-operated rotating safety. Blue finish. Introduced 1990. Made in Canada by Lakefield Arms Ltd.
Price: About **$109.95**
Price: Mark I-Y (Youth), 19" barrel, 37" overall, 5 lbs. **$109.95**

Lakefield Mark II

LAKEFIELD ARMS MARK II BOLT-ACTION RIFLE
Caliber: 22 LR, 10-shot magazine.
Barrel: 20½".
Weight: 5½ lbs. **Length:** 39½" overall.
Stock: Walnut-finished hardwood with Monte Carlo-type comb, checkered grip and forend.
Sights: Bead front, open adjustable rear. Receiver grooved for scope mounting.
Features: Thumb-operated rotating safety. Blue finish. Introduced 1990. Made in Canada by Lakefield Arms Ltd.
Price: About **$119.95**
Price: Mark II-Y (Youth), 19" barrel, 37" overall, 5 lbs. **$119.95**

Magtech MT-22C

MAGTECH MODEL MT-22C BOLT-ACTION RIFLE
Caliber: 22 S, L, LR, 6-shot magazine.
Barrel: 21" (six-groove).
Weight: 5¾ lbs. **Length:** 39" overall.
Stock: Brazilian hardwood.
Sights: Blade front, open rear adjustable for windage and elevation.
Features: Sliding wing-type safety; double extractors; red cocking indicator; receiver grooved for scope mount. Introduced 1991. Imported from Brazil by Magtech Recreational Products, Inc.
Price: About **$119.95**

Magtech Model MT-22T Bolt-Action Rifle
Similar to the MT-22C except has 15-shot tubular magazine. Introduced 1991. Imported from Brazil by Magtech Recreational Products, Inc.
Price: About **$119.95**

Marlin 880

MARLIN MODEL 880 BOLT-ACTION RIFLE
Caliber: 22 LR; 7-shot clip magazine.
Barrel: 22" Micro-Groove®.
Weight: 5½ lbs. **Length:** 41".
Stock: Monte Carlo American black walnut with checkered p.g. and forend. Rubber buttpad, swivel studs. Mar-Shield® finish.
Sights: Wide-Scan™ ramp front, folding semi-buckhorn rear adjustable for windage and elevation.
Features: Receiver grooved for scope mount. Introduced 1989.
Price: **$201.95**

Marlin Model 25N Bolt-Action Repeater
Similar to Marlin 880, except walnut-finished p.g. stock, adjustable open rear sight, ramp front.
Price: **$145.95**

Marlin 25MN

Marlin Model 25MN Bolt-Action Rifle
Similar to the Model 25N except chambered for 22 WMR. Has 7-shot clip magazine, 22" Micro-Groove® barrel, walnut-finished hardwood stock. Introduced 1989.
Price: **$166.95**

Marlin Model 881 Bolt-Action Rifle
Same as the Marlin 880 except tubular magazine, holds 17 Long Rifle, 19 Long, 25 Short cartridges. Weighs 6 lbs.
Price: **$209.95**

Marlin Model 882 Bolt-Action Rifle
Same as the Marlin 880 except 22 WMR cal. only with 7-shot clip magazine; weight about 6 lbs. Comes with swivel studs.
Price: **$221.95**

Marlin Model 883 Bolt-Action Rifle
Same as Marlin 882 except tubular magazine holds 12 rounds of 22 WMR ammunition.
Price: **$230.95**
Price: Model 883N (nickel-Teflon finish) **$254.95**

Marlin 15YN

MARLIN MODEL 15YN "LITTLE BUCKAROO"
Caliber: 22 S, L, LR, single shot.
Barrel: 16¼" Micro-Groove;rm.
Weight: 4¼ lbs. **Length:** 33¼" overall.
Stock: One-piece walnut-finished hardwood with Monte Carlo; Mar-Shield® finish.
Sights: Ramp front, adjustable open rear.
Features: Beginner's rifle with thumb safety, easy-load feed throat, red cocking indicator. Receiver grooved for scope mounting. Introduced 1989.
Price: **$140.95**

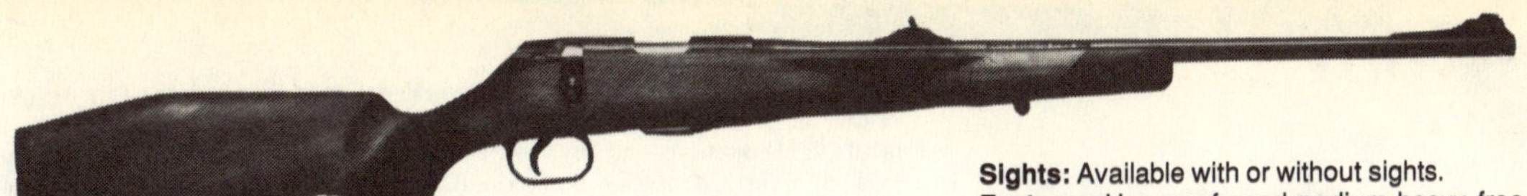

Mauser Model 201

MAUSER MODEL 201 BOLT-ACTION RIFLE
Caliber: 22 LR, 22 WMR, 5-shot magazine.
Barrel: 21".
Weight: About 6.5 lbs. **Length:** 40" overall.
Stock: Walnut-stained beech with Monte Carlo comb and cheekpiece. Checkered grip and forend.
Sights: Available with or without sights.
Features: Hammer forged medium-heavy, free-floated barrel. Bolt has two front locking lugs, dual extractors. Adjustable trigger. Safety locks bolt, sear and trigger. Receiver accepts rail mounts and is drilled and tapped for scope mounting. Introduced 1989. Imported from Germany by Precision Imports, Inc.
Price: 22 LR with sights **$472.00**
Price: As above, no sights **$445.00**
Price: 22 WMR with sights **$520.00**
Price: As above, no sights **$493.00**
Price: Luxus, 22 LR with sights **$631.00**
Price: As above, no sights **$604.00**
Price: Luxus, 22 WMR with sights **$679.00**
Price: As above, no sights **$652.00**

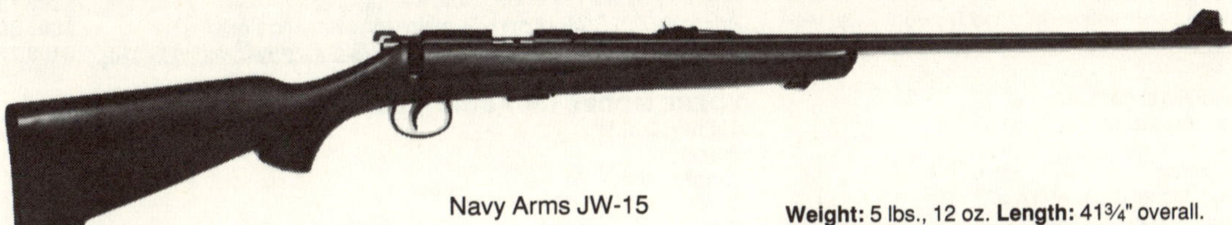

Navy Arms JW-15

NAVY ARMS JW-15 BOLT-ACTION RIFLE
Caliber: 22 LR, 5-shot detachable magazine.
Barrel: 24".
Weight: 5 lbs., 12 oz. **Length:** 41¾" overall.
Stock: Walnut-stained hardwood.
Sights: Hooded blade front, open rear drift adjustable for windage.
Features: Polished blue finish; sling swivels; wing-type safety. Introduced 1991. Imported by Navy Arms.
Price: **$115.00**

Navy Arms TU-KKW

NAVY ARMS TU-KKW TRAINING RIFLE
Caliber: 22 LR, 5-shot detachable magazine.
Barrel: 26".
Weight: 8 lbs. **Length:** 44" overall.
Stock: Walnut-stained hardwood.
Sights: Blade front, open rear adjustable for elevation; military style.
Features: Replica of the German WWII training rifle. Polished blue metal. Bayonet lug, cleaning rod, takedown disk in butt. Introduced 1991. Imported by Navy Arms.
Price: **$250.00**

NORINCO JW-15 BOLT-ACTION RIFLE
Caliber: 22 LR, 5-shot detachable magazine.
Barrel: 23.8".
Weight: 5.5 lbs. **Length:** 41.5" overall.
Stock: Walnut-finished hardwood.
Sights: Ramp front, rear drift adjustable for windage.
Features: Grooved receiver for scope mounting; Model 70-type safety locks firing pin and bolt. Introduced 1991. Imported from China by Interarms.
Price: **$115.00**

NORINCO TYPE EM-332 BOLT-ACTION RIFLE
Caliber: 22 LR, 5-shot magazine.
Barrel: 18.5".
Weight: 4.5 lbs. **Length:** 41.5" overall.
Stock: Hardwood.
Sights: Blade front on ramp, open adjustable rear.
Features: Has magazine holder on side of butt that holds two extra magazines. Blue finish. Introduced 1990. Imported from China by China Sports, Inc.
Price: . . . . **NA**

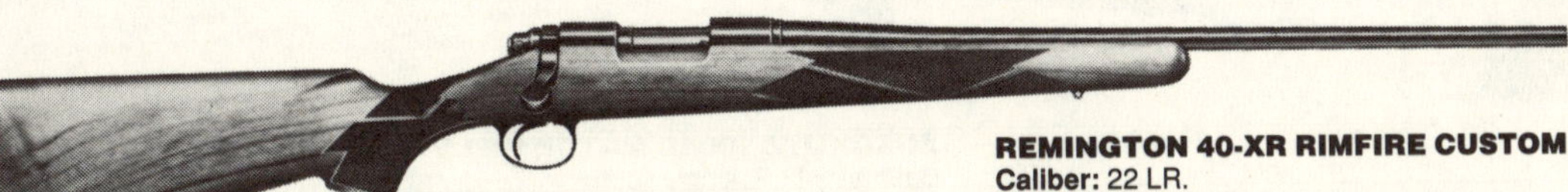

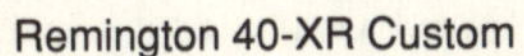

Remington 40-XR Custom

REMINGTON 40-XR RIMFIRE CUSTOM SPORTER
Caliber: 22 LR.
Barrel: 24".
Weight: 10 lbs. **Length:** 42½" overall.
Stock: Full-sized walnut, checkered p.g. and forend.
Sights: None furnished; drilled and tapped for scope mounting.
Features: Custom Shop gun. Duplicates Model 700 centerfire rifle.
Price: Grade I **$2,181.00**

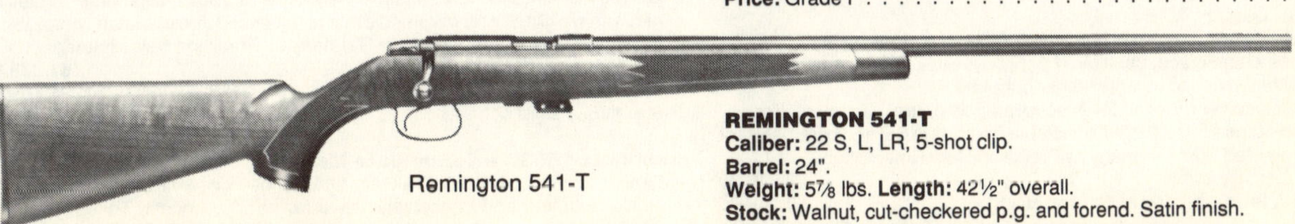

Remington 541-T

REMINGTON 541-T
Caliber: 22 S, L, LR, 5-shot clip.
Barrel: 24".
Weight: 5⅞ lbs. **Length:** 42½" overall.
Stock: Walnut, cut-checkered p.g. and forend. Satin finish.
Sights: None. Drilled and tapped for scope mounts.
Features: Clip repeater. Thumb safety. Reintroduced 1986.
Price: About **$355.00**

Ruger 77/22

RUGER 77/22 RIMFIRE BOLT-ACTION RIFLE
Caliber: 22 LR, 10-shot rotary magazine; 22 WMR, 9-shot rotary magazine.
Barrel: 20".
Weight: About 5¾ lbs. **Length:** 39¾" overall.
Stock: Checkered American walnut or Injection-moulded Du Pont Zytel reinforced with nylon.
Sights: Gold bead front, adjustable folding leaf rear or plain barrel with 1" Ruger rings.
Features: Mauser-type action uses Ruger's 10-shot rotary magazine. Three-position safety, simplified bolt stop, patented bolt locking system. Uses the dual screw barrel attachment system of the 10/22 rifle. Integral scope mounting system with 1" Ruger rings. Blued model introduced in 1983. Stainless steel model and blued model with the synthetic stock introduced in 1989.
Price: 77/22R (no sights, rings, walnut stock) **$382.75**
Price: 77/22S (open sights, walnut stock) **$382.75**
Price: 77/22RS (open sights, rings, walnut stock) **$403.75**
Price: 77/22RP (no sights, rings, synthetic stock) **$315.00**
Price: 77/22SP (open sights, synthetic stock) **$315.00**
Price: 77/22RSP (open sights, rings, synthetic stock) **$336.00**
Price: K77/22RP (stainless, no sights, rings, synthetic stock) **$378.00**
Price: K77/22SP (stainless, open sights, synthetic stock) **$378.00**
Price: K77/22RSP (stainless, open sights, rings, synthetic stock) . . **$399.00**
Price: 77/22RM (22 WMR, blue, walnut stock) **$382.75**
Price: K77/22RMP (22 WMR, stainless, synthetic stock) **$399.00**
Price: 77/22RSM (22 WMR, blue, open sights, rings, walnut stock) . **$403.75**

REMINGTON 581-S SPORTSMAN RIFLE
Caliber: 22 S, L or LR, 5-shot clip magazine.
Barrel: 24" round.
Weight: 4¾ lbs. **Length:** 42⅜" overall.
Stock: Walnut-finished hardwood, Monte Carlo with p.g.
Sights: Bead post front, screw adjustable open rear.
Features: Sliding side safety, wide trigger, receiver grooved for tip-off scope mounts. Comes with single shot adaptor. Reintroduced 1986.
Price: About **$196.00**

VOERE MODEL 1007 BOLT-ACTION RIFLE
Caliber: 22 LR.
Barrel: 18".
Weight: About 5½ lbs.
Stock: Oil-finished beechwood.
Sights: Hooded front, open adjustable rear.
Features: Military-look stock; sling swivels. Convertible to single shot. Imported from Austria by L. Joseph Rahn. Introduced 1984.
Price: 1007 Biathlon **$430.00**

COMPETITION RIFLES—CENTERFIRE & RIMFIRE

Includes models for classic American and ISU target competition and other sporting and competitive shooting.

ANSCHUTZ 64-MS, 64-MS LEFT SILHOUETTE
Caliber: 22 LR, single shot.
Barrel: 21½", medium heavy; ⅞" diameter.
Weight: 8 lbs. **Length:** 39½" overall.
Stock: Walnut-finished hardwood, silhouette-type.
Sights: None furnished. Receiver drilled and tapped for scope mounting.
Features: Uses Match 64 action. Designed for metallic silhouette competition. Stock has stippled checkering, contoured thumb groove with Wundhammer swell. Two-stage #5091 trigger. Slide safety locks sear and bolt. Introduced 1980. Imported from Germany by Precision Sales International.
Price: 64-MS **$885.00**
Price: 64-MS Left **$948.00**

ANSCHUTZ 1403B BIATHLON RIFLE
Caliber: 22 LR, 5-shot magazine.
Barrel: 21½".
Weight: 8½ lbs. **Length:** 42½" overall.
Stock: Blonde-finished European hardwood. Stippled pistol grip.
Sights: Globe front with snow cap and muzzle cover, optional micrometer peep rear with spring-hinged snow cap.
Features: Uses Match 64 Target action with three-way adjustable two-stage trigger; slide safety. Comes with five magazines. Adjustable buttplate. Introduced 1991. Imported from Germany by Precision Sales International.
Price: **$997.50**

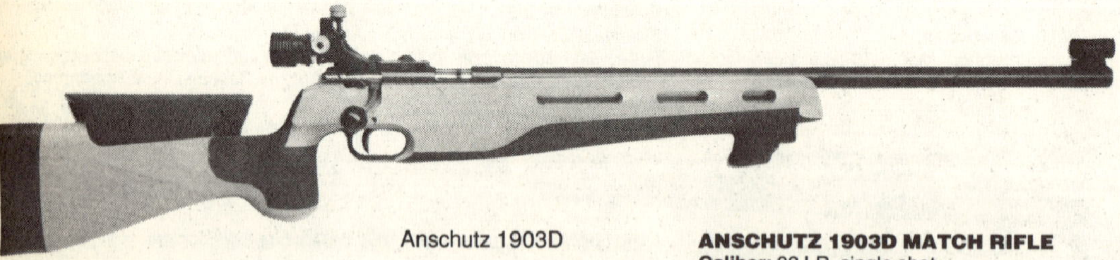

Anschutz 1903D

ANSCHUTZ 1911 MATCH RIFLE
Caliber: 22 LR, single shot.
Barrel: 27¼" round (1" dia.).
Weight: 11 lbs. **Length:** 46" overall.
Stock: Walnut-finished European hardwood; American prone style with Monte Carlo, cast-off cheekpiece, checkered p.g., beavertail forend with swivel rail and adjustable swivel, adjustable rubber buttplate.
Sights: None. Receiver grooved for Anschutz sights (extra). Scope blocks.
Features: Two-stage #5018 trigger adjustable from 2.1 to 8.6 oz. Extremely fast lock time. Imported from Germany by Precision Sales International.
Price: Right-hand, no sights **$2,026.00**
Price: M1911-L (true left-hand action and stock) **$2,146.00**

ANSCHUTZ 1903D MATCH RIFLE
Caliber: 22 LR, single shot.
Barrel: 25", ¾" diameter.
Weight: 8.6 lbs. **Length:** 43¾" overall.
Stock: Walnut-finished hardwood with adjustable cheekpiece; stippled grip and forend.
Sights: None furnished.
Features: Uses Anschutz Match 64 action and #5091 two-stage trigger. A medium weight rifle for intermediate and advanced Junior Match competition. Introduced 1987. Imported from Germany by Precision Sales International.
Price: Right-hand **$1,039.00**
Price: Left-hand **$1,105.00**
Price: #6823 sight set **$246.00**

Anschutz 1803D Intermediate Match
Similar to the Model 1903D except has blonde-finished European hardwood stock, buttplate and cheekpiece have fewer adjustments. Takes Anschutz #6825 sight set (optional). Weight is 9.5 lbs. Introduced 1991.
Price: **$1,012.00**
Price: #6825 sight set **$227.00**

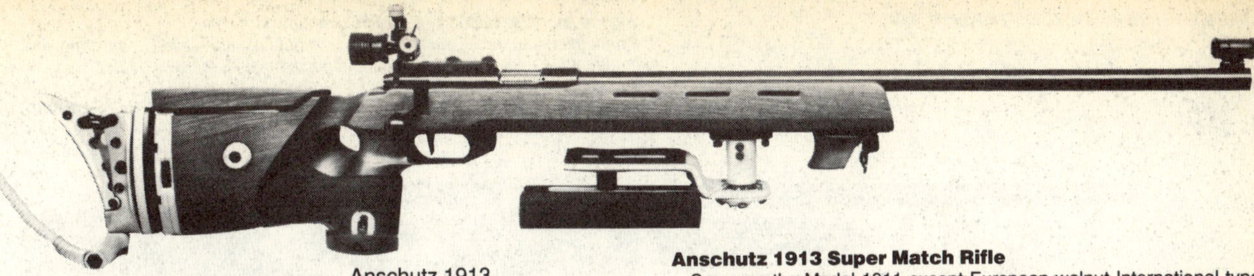

Anschutz 1913

Anschutz 1910 Super Match II
Similar to the Super Match 1913 rifle except has a stock of European hardwood with tapered forend and deep receiver area. Hand and palm rests not included. Uses Match 54 action. Adjustable hook buttplate and cheekpiece. Sights not included. Introduced 1982. Imported from Germany by Precision Sales International.
Price: Right-hand **$2,585.00**
Price: Left-hand **$2,733.00**

Anschutz 1907 Match Rifle
Same action as Model 1913 but with 7/8" diameter 26" barrel. Length is 44½" overall, weight 10 lbs. Blonde wood finish with vented forend. Designed for ISU requirements; suitable for NRA matches.
Price: Right-hand, no sights **$1,729.00**
Price: M1907-L (true left-hand action and stock) **$1,834.00**

Anschutz 1913 Super Match Rifle
Same as the Model 1911 except European walnut International-type stock with adjustable cheekpiece, adjustable aluminum hook buttplate, adjustable hand stop, weight 15½ lbs., 46" overall. Imported from Germany by Precision Sales International.
Price: Right-hand, no sights **$2,895.00**
Price: M1913-L (left-hand action and stock) **$3,059.00**

Anschutz 54.18MS Silhouette Rifle
Same basic features as Anschutz 1913 Super Match but with special metallic silhouette European hardwood stock and two-stage trigger. Has 22" barrel; receiver drilled and tapped.
Price: **$1,449.00**
Price: 54.18MSL (true left-hand version of above) **$1,521.00**

Anschutz 54.18MS REP

ANSCHUTZ 1827B BIATHLON RIFLE
Caliber: 22 LR, 5-shot magazine.
Barrel: 21½".
Weight: 8½ lbs. with sights. **Length:** 42½" overall.
Stock: Walnut-finished hardwood; cheekpiece, stippled pistol grip and forend.
Sights: Globe front specially designed for Biathlon shooting, micrometer rear with hinged snow cap.
Features: Uses Match 54 action and nine-way adjustable trigger; adjustable wooden buttplate, Biathlon butthook, adjustable hand-stop rail. **Special Order Only.** Introduced 1982. Imported from Germany by Precision Sales International.
Price: Right-hand **$2,256.00**
Price: With Fortner straight-pull bolt **$3,498.00**
Price: Left-hand **$3,768.00**

Anschutz 54.18MS REP Deluxe Silhouette Rifle
Same basic action and trigger specifications as the Anschutz 1913 Super Match but with removable 5-shot clip magazine, 22" barrel extendable to 30" using optional extension and weight set. Receiver drilled and tapped for scope mounting. Silhouette stock with thumbhole grip is of fiberglass with walnut wood Fibergrain finish. Introduced 1990. Imported from Germany by Precision Sales International.
Price: 54.18MS REP Deluxe **$2,079.00**
Price: 54.18MS Standard with fiberglass stock **$1,788.00**

ANSCHUTZ 1808D RT SUPER MATCH 54 TARGET
Caliber: 22 LR, single shot.
Barrel: 32½".
Weight: 9.4 lbs. **Length:** 50½" overall.
Stock: Walnut-finished European hardwood. Heavy beavertail forend; adjustable cheekpiece and buttplate. Stippled grip and forend.
Sights: None furnished. Grooved for scope mounting.
Features: Designed for Running Target competition. Nine-way adjustable single-stage trigger, slide safety. Introduced 1991. Imported from Germany by Precision Sales International.
Price: Right-hand **$1,631.00**
Price: Left-hand **$1,681.00**

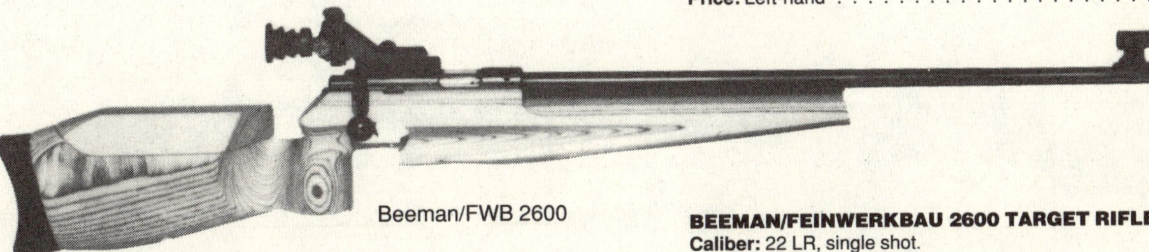

Beeman/FWB 2600

BEEMAN/HW 660 MATCH RIFLE
Caliber: 22 LR.
Barrel: 26".
Weight: 10.7 lbs. **Length:** 45.3" overall.
Stock: Match-type walnut with adjustable cheekpiece and buttplate.
Sights: Globe front, match aperture rear.
Features: Adjustable match trigger; stippled p.g. and forend; forend accessory rail. Imported from Germany by Beeman. Introduced 1988.
Price: **$889.50**

BEEMAN/FEINWERKBAU 2600 TARGET RIFLE
Caliber: 22 LR, single shot.
Barrel: 26.3".
Weight: 10.6 lbs. **Length:** 43.7" overall.
Stock: Laminated hardwood and hard rubber.
Sights: Globe front with Interchangeable Inserts; micrometer match aperture rear.
Features: Identical smallbore companion to the Beeman/FWB 600 air rifle. Free floating barrel. Match trigger has fingertip weight adjustment dial. Introduced 1986. Imported from Germany by Beeman.
Price: Right-hand **$1,398.00**
Price: Left-hand **$1,575.00**
Price: Free rifle, right-hand **$1,998.00**
Price: Free rifle, left-hand **$2,150.00**

BEEMAN/WEIHRAUCH HW 60 TARGET RIFLE
Caliber: 22 LR, single shot.
Barrel: 26.8".
Weight: 10.8 lbs. **Length:** 45.7" overall.
Stock: Walnut with adjustable buttplate. Stippled p.g. and forend. Rail with adjustable swivel.
Sights: Hooded ramp front, match-type aperture rear.
Features: Adjustable match trigger with push-button safety. Left-hand version also available. Introduced 1981. Imported from Germany by Beeman.
Price: Right-hand **$798.00**
Price: Left-hand **$878.95**

Cooper Model TRP-1

COOPER ARMS MODEL TRP-1 ISU STANDARD RIFLE
Caliber: 22 LR, single shot.
Barrel: 24".
Weight: 8.5 lbs. **Length:** 40.5" overall.
Stock: Walnut, competition style with adjustable cheekpiece and buttpad.
Sights: None furnished; accepts Anschutz sight packages.
Features: Action has three front locking lugs, 45-degree bolt rotation; fully adjustable single stage trigger; hand-lapped match grade Wiseman/McMillan barrel. Introduced 1991. Made in U.S. by Cooper Arms.
Price: **$795.00**

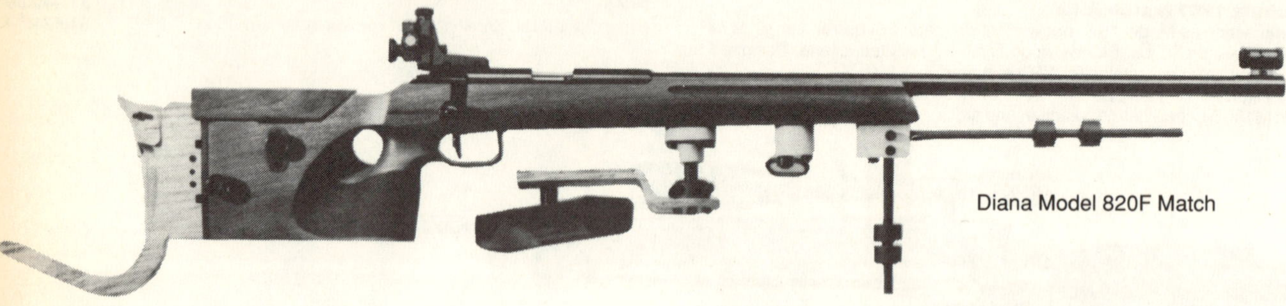
Diana Model 820F Match

DIANA MODEL 820F MATCH RIFLE
Caliber: 22 LR, single shot.
Barrel: 27.1".
Weight: 15.4 lbs. **Length:** 44.4" overall.
Stock: Walnut.
Sights: Tunnel front, fully adjustable match rear.
Features: Designed for free rifle events. Adjustable hook buttplate, adjustable cheekpiece, hand stop. Stock stabilizer and palm rest optional. Trigger adjustable from 1.4 to 8.8 oz. Introduced 1990. Imported from Germany by Dynamit Nobel-RWS, Inc.
Price: Right-hand only **$2,000.00**

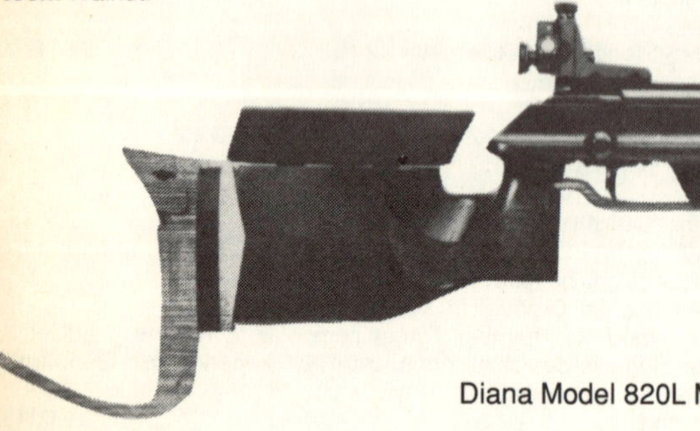
Diana Model 820L Match

DIANA MODEL 820L MATCH RIFLE
Caliber: 22 LR, single shot.
Barrel: 25.9".
Weight: 10.5 lbs. **Length:** 44.4" overall.
Stock: Walnut.
Sights: Tunnel front, fully adjustable match rear.
Features: Designed for three-position match shooting. Adjustable cheekpiece. Trigger adjustable from 1.4 to 8.8 oz. Accessory buttplate available. Introduced 1990. Imported from Germany by Dynamit Nobel-RWS, Inc.
Price: Right-hand only **$1,500.00**

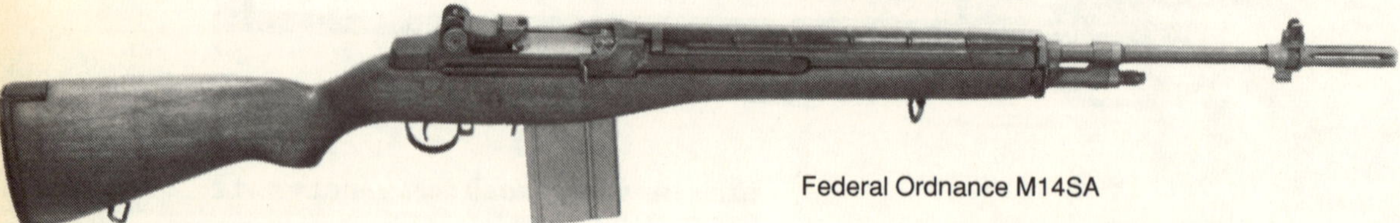
Federal Ordnance M14SA

FINNISH LION STANDARD TARGET RIFLE
Caliber: 22 LR, single shot.
Barrel: 27⅝".
Weight: 10½ lbs. **Length:** 44⁹⁄₁₆" overall.
Stock: French walnut, target style.
Sights: Globe front, International micrometer rear.
Features: Optional accessories: palm rest, hook buttplate, forend stop and swivel assembly, buttplate extension, five front sight aperture inserts, three rear sight apertures, Allen wrench. Adjustable trigger. Imported from Finland by Mandall Shooting Supplies.
Price: **$695.00**

FEDERAL ORDNANCE M14SA TARGET RIFLE
Caliber: 7.62mm NATO (308 Win.).
Barrel: 22".
Weight: 9 lbs., 8 oz. **Length:** 48" overall.
Stock: Fiberglass or wood.
Sights: G.I., fully adjustable for windage and elevation.
Features: Civilian version of the M-14 service rifle. All metal has Parkerized finish. Introduced 1988. From Federal Ordnance.
Price: With fiberglass stock **$749.95**
Price: With walnut stock, forend **$839.95**
Price: With black textured stock **$749.95**

Heckler & Koch PSG-1

HECKLER & KOCH PSG-1 MARKSMAN RIFLE
Caliber: 308, 5- and 20-shot magazines.
Barrel: 25.6", heavy.
Weight: 17.8 lbs. **Length:** 47.5" overall.
Stock: Matte black high impact plastic, adjustable for length, pivoting butt cap, vertically-adjustable cheekpiece; target-type pistol grip with adjustable palm shelf.
Sights: Hendsoldt 6x42 scope.
Features: Uses HK-91 action with low-noise bolt closing device; special forend with T-way rail for sling swivel or tripod. Gun comes in special foam-fitted metal transport case with tripod, two 20-shot and two 5-shot magazines, cleaning rod. Imported from Germany by Heckler & Koch, Inc. Introduced 1986.
Price: **$8,859.00**

Krico Model 360S Biathlon

KRICO MODEL 360S BIATHLON RIFLE
Caliber: 22 LR, 5-shot magazine.
Barrel: 21.25".
Weight: 9.26 lbs. **Length:** 40.55" overall.
Stock: Walnut with high comb, adjustable buttplate.
Sights: Globe front, fully adjustable Diana 82 match peep rear.
Features: Straight-pull action with 17.6-oz. match trigger. Comes with five magazines (four stored in stock recess), muzzle/sight snow cap. Introduced 1991. Imported from Germany by Mandall Shooting Supplies.
Price: **$1,695.00**

KRICO MODEL 500 KRICOTRONIC MATCH RIFLE
Caliber: 22 LR, single shot.
Barrel: 23.6".
Weight: 9.4 lbs. **Length:** 42.1" overall.
Stock: European walnut, match type with adjustable butt.
Sights: Globe front, match micrometer aperture rear.
Features: Electronic ignition system for fastest possible lock time. Completely adjustable trigger. Barrel has tapered bore. Imported from Germany by Mandall Shooting Supplies.
Price: **$3,950.00**

KRICO MODEL 360 S2 BIATHLON RIFLE
Caliber: 22 LR, 5-shot magazine.
Barrel: 21.25".
Weight: 9 lbs., 15 oz. **Length:** 40.55" overall.
Stock: Biathlon design of black epoxy-finished walnut with pistol grip.
Sights: Globe front, fully adjustable Diana 82 match peep rear.
Features: Pistol-grip-activated action. Comes with five magazines (four stored in stock recess), muzzle/sight snow cap. Introduced 1991. Imported from Germany by Mandall Shooting Supplies.
Price: **$1,595.00**

KRICO MODEL 400 MATCH RIFLE
Caliber: 22 LR, 22 Hornet, 5-shot magazine.
Barrel: 23.2" (22 LR), 23.6" (22 Hornet).
Weight: 8.8 lbs. **Length:** 42.1" overall (22 RF).
Stock: European walnut, match type.
Sights: None furnished; receiver grooved for scope mounting.
Features: Heavy match barrel. Double-set or match trigger. Imported from Germany by Mandall Shooting Supplies.
Price: **$950.00**

KRICO MODEL 600 SNIPER RIFLE
Caliber: 222, 223, 22-250, 243, 308, 4-shot magazine.
Barrel: 23.6".
Weight: 9.2 lbs. **Length:** 45.2" overall.
Stock: European walnut with adjustable rubber buttplate.
Sights: None supplied; drilled and tapped for scope mounting.
Features: Match barrel with flash hider; large bolt knob; wide trigger shoe. Parkerized finish. Imported from Germany by Mandall Shooting Supplies.
Price: **$2,645.00**
Price: As Model 600 Single Shot (match stock) **$950.00**

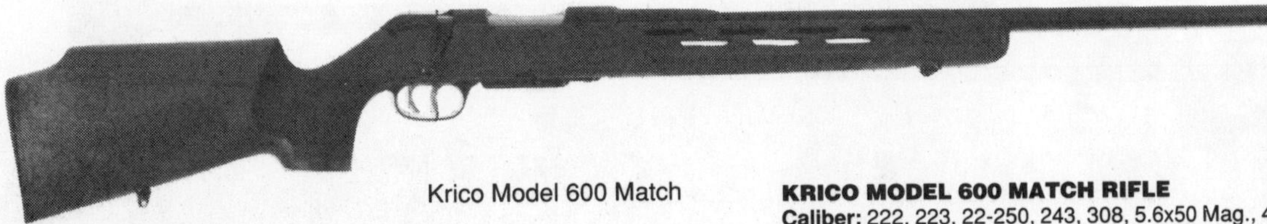
Krico Model 600 Match

LAKEFIELD ARMS MODEL 91T TARGET RIFLE
Caliber: 22 LR, single shot.
Barrel: 25".
Weight: 8 lbs. **Length:** 43⅝" overall.
Stock: Target-type, walnut-finished hardwood.
Sights: Target front with inserts, peep rear with ¼-minute click adjustments.
Features: Comes with shooting rail and hand stop. Also available as 5-shot repeater as Model 91-TR. Introduced 1991. Made in Canada by Lakefield Arms.
Price: Model 91T **$389.95**
Price: Model 91-TR (repeater) **$409.95**

KRICO MODEL 600 MATCH RIFLE
Caliber: 222, 223, 22-250, 243, 308, 5.6x50 Mag., 4-shot magazine.
Barrel: 23.6".
Weight: 8.8 lbs. **Length:** 43.3" overall.
Stock: Match stock of European walnut with cheekpiece.
Sights: None furnished; drilled and tapped for scope mounting.
Features: Match stock with vents in forend for cooling, rubber recoil pad, sling swivels. Imported from Germany by Mandall Shooting Supplies.
Price: **$1,025.00**

Lakefield Model 90B

LAKEFIELD ARMS MODEL 90B TARGET RIFLE
Caliber: 22 LR, 5-shot magazine.
Barrel: 21".
Weight: 8¼ lbs. **Length:** 39⅝" overall.
Stock: Natural finish hardwood with clip holder, carrying and shooting rails, butt hook, hand stop.
Sights: Target front with inserts, peep rear with ¼-minute click adjustments.
Features: Biathlon-style rifle with snow cap muzzle protector. Comes with five magazines. Introduced 1991. Made in Canada by Lakefield Arms.
Price: About **$479.95**

Magtech MT-52-T

MAGTECH MODEL MT-52-T TARGET RIFLE
Caliber: 22 LR, 6- or 10-shot magazine.
Barrel: 26.2" (8 groove).
Weight: 9.2 lbs. **Length:** 43.3" overall.
Stock: Brazilian hardwood with stippled grip, fully adjustable rubber buttplate, aluminum forend rail with sling support.
Sights: Globe front with inserts, match-type aperture rear.
Features: Fully adjustable trigger, free-floating barrel, receiver grooved for scope mounting. Introduced 1991. Imported from Brazil by Magtech Recreational Products, Inc.
Price: About **$389.99**

Marlin Model 2000

MARLIN MODEL 2000 TARGET RIFLE
Caliber: 22 LR, single shot.
Barrel: 22" heavy, Micro-Groove® rifling, match chamber, recessed muzzle.
Weight: 8 lbs. **Length:** 41" overall.
Stock: High-comb fiberglass/Kevlar with stipple finish grip and forend.
Sights: Hooded Lyman front with seven aperture inserts, fully adjustable Lyman target rear peep.
Features: Stock finished with royal blue enamel. Buttplate adjustable for length of pull, height and angle. Aluminum forend rail with stop and quick-detachable swivel. Two-stage target trigger; red cocking indicator. Five-shot adaptor kit available. Introduced 1991. From Marlin.
Price: **$509.95**

MAUSER MODEL 86-SR SPECIALTY RIFLE
Caliber: 308 Win., 9-shot detachable magazine.
Barrel: 25.6", fluted, 1:12 twist.
Weight: About 10.8 lbs. **Length:** 47.7" overall.
Stock: Laminated wood, fiberglass, or special match thumbhole wood. All have rail in forend and adjustable recoil pad.
Sights: None furnished. Competition metallic sights or scope mount optional.
Features: Match barrel with muzzlebrake. Action has two front bolt locking lugs. Action bedded in stock with free-floated barrel. Match trigger adjustable as single or two-stage; fully adjustable for weight, slack, and position. Silent safety locks bolt, firing pin. Introduced 1989. Imported from Germany by Precision Imports, Inc.
Price: With fiberglass stock **$4,400.00**
Price: With match thumbhole stock **$4,650.00**

McMILLAN NATIONAL MATCH RIFLE
Caliber: 308, 5-shot magazine.
Barrel: 24", stainless steel.
Weight: About 11 lbs. (std. bbl.). **Length:** 43" overall.
Stock: Modified ISU fiberglass with adjustable buttplate.
Sights: Barrel band and Tompkins front; no rear sight furnished.
Features: McMillan repeating action with clip slot, Canjar trigger. Match-grade barrel. Available in right-hand only. Fibergrain stock, sight installation, special machining and triggers optional. Introduced 1989. From McMillan Gunworks, Inc.
Price: **$2,147.00**

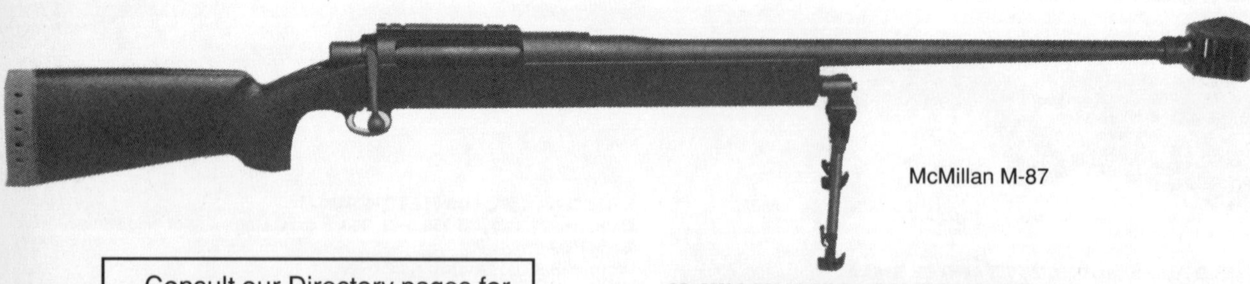
McMillan M-87

Consult our Directory pages for the location of firms mentioned.

McMILLAN M-87 50-CALIBER RIFLE
Caliber: 50 BMG, single shot.
Barrel: 29", with muzzlebrake.
Weight: About 21½ lbs. **Length:** 53" overall.
Stock: McMillan fiberglass.
Sights: None furnished.
Features: Right-handed McMillan stainless steel receiver, chromemoly barrel with 1:15 twist. Introduced 1987. From McMillan Gunworks, Inc.
Price: **$3,395.00**
Price: M-87R (5-shot repeater) "Combo" **$3,890.00**

McMILLAN M-88 50-CALIBER RIFLE
Similar to the M-87 except has a fully adjustable fiberglass stock, single shot shellholder bolt receiver. Uses McMillan Quick Takedown system. Weight is about 21 lbs. Introduced 1988.
Price: **$3,525.00**

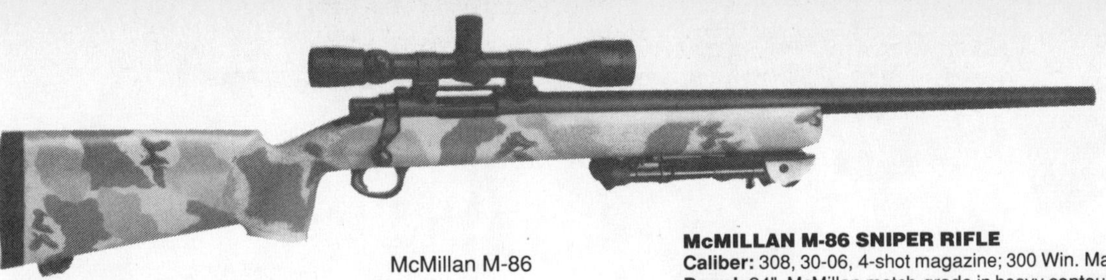

McMillan M-86

McMILLAN M-89 SNIPER RIFLE
Caliber: 308 Win., 5-shot magazine.
Barrel: 28" (with suppressor).
Weight: 15 lbs., 4 oz.
Stock: McMillan fiberglass; adjustable for length; recoil pad.
Sights: None furnished. Drilled and tapped for scope mounting.
Features: Uses McMillan repeating action. Comes with bipod. Introduced 1990. From McMillan Gunworks, Inc.
Price: Standard (non-suppressed) **$1,950.00**

McMILLAN M-86 SNIPER RIFLE
Caliber: 308, 30-06, 4-shot magazine; 300 Win. Mag., 3-shot magazine.
Barrel: 24", McMillan match-grade in heavy contour.
Weight: 11¼ lbs. (308), 11½ lbs. (30-06, 300). **Length:** 43½" overall.
Stock: Specially designed McHale fiberglass stock with textured grip and forend, recoil pad.
Sights: None furnished.
Features: Uses McMillan repeating action. Comes with bipod. Matte black finish. Sling swivels. Introduced 1989. From McMillan Gunworks, Inc.
Price: **$1,695.00**

McMillan Long Range

McMILLAN LONG RANGE RIFLE
Caliber: 300 Win. Mag., single shot.
Barrel: 26", stainless steel, match-grade.
Weight: 14 lbs. **Length:** 46½" overall.
Stock: Fiberglass with adjustable buttplate and cheekpiece. Adjustable for length of pull, drop, cant and cast-off.
Sights: Barrel band and Tompkins front; no rear sight furnished.
Features: Uses McMillan solid bottom single shot action and Canjar trigger. Barrel twist 1:12. Introduced 1989. From McMillan Gunworks, Inc.
Price: **$2,147.00**

Olympic Multimatch

OLYMPIC ARMS MULTIMATCH RIFLE
Caliber: 223, 30-shot magazine.
Barrel: 16" Ultramatch; free-floated with aluminum handguard.
Weight: 7½ lbs. **Length:** 35½" overall.
Stock: Composition AR-15A2 butt.
Sights: None furnished; scope mount.
Features: Built on AR-15-type action. Has stainless steel free-floating barrel with aluminum handguard. Introduced 1991. Made in U.S. by Olympic Arms, Inc.
Price: **$915.95**

Olympic Ultramatch

OLYMPIC ARMS ULTRAMATCH RIFLE
Caliber: 223, 30-shot magazine.
Barrel: 20", stainless steel, 1:10 twist.
Weight: 9 lbs. (add 1¾ lbs for steel handguard). **Length:** 39½" overall.
Stock: Black composition; match aluminum or steel handguard.
Sights: None supplied; includes scope mounts.
Features: Uses international match AR-15-type receiver, set trigger; Max-hard surfacing on upper and lower receivers. Introduced 1987. Made in U.S. by Olympic Arms, Inc.
Price: **$1,152.95**

Olympic International

Olympic Arms International Match Rifle
Similar to the Ultramatch Rifle except comes with globe front sight, fully adjustable aperture rear, standard trigger set at 4.5 to 5 lbs pull. Introduced 1991. Made in U.S. by Olympic Arms, Inc.
Price: **$1,179.95**

CAUTION: PRICES CHANGE, CHECK AT GUNSHOP.

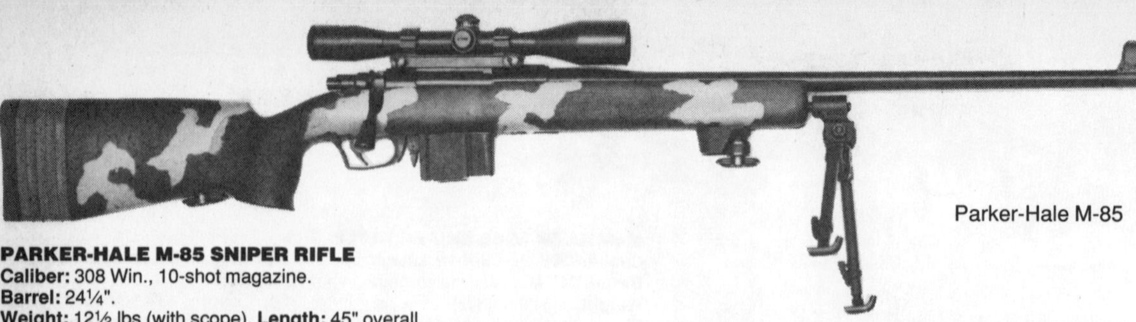
Parker-Hale M-85

PARKER-HALE M-85 SNIPER RIFLE
Caliber: 308 Win., 10-shot magazine.
Barrel: 24¼".
Weight: 12½ lbs (with scope). **Length:** 45" overall.
Stock: McMillan fiberglass (several color patterns available).
Sights: Post front adjustable for windage, fold-down rear adjustable for elevation.
Features: Comes with quick-detachable bipod, palm stop with rail; sling swivels; matte finish. Available through Navy Arms.
Price: Less scope **$1,975.00**

PARKER-HALE M-87 TARGET RIFLE
Caliber: 308 Win., 243, 6.5x55, 308, 30-06, 300 Win. Mag. (other calibers on request), 5-shot detachable box magazine.
Barrel: 26" heavy.
Weight: About 10 lbs. **Length:** 45" overall.
Stock: Walnut target-style, adjustable for length of pull; solid buttpad; accessory rail with hand-stop. Deeply stippled grip and forend.
Sights: None furnished. Receiver dovetailed for Parker-Hale "Roll-Off" scope mounts.
Features: Mauser-style action with large bolt knob. Parkerized finish. Introduced 1987. Available through Navy Arms.
Price: **$1,525.00**

OLYMPIC ARMS SERVICE MATCH RIFLE
Caliber: 223, 30-shot magazine.
Barrel: 20" Ultramatch.
Weight: 8¾ lbs. **Length:** 39½" overall.
Stock: Black composition A2 standard stock.
Sights: Post front, fully adjustable aperture rear.
Features: Conforms to all DCM standards. Uses Olympic Arms E2 upper receiver, lined A2-style handguards, standard trigger, choice of A1 or A2 flash suppressor. Introduced 1989. Made in U.S. by Olympic Arms, Inc.
Price: **$899.95**

REMINGTON 40-XC KS NATIONAL MATCH COURSE RIFLE
Caliber: 7.62 NATO, 5-shot.
Barrel: 24", stainless steel.
Weight: 11 lbs. without sights. **Length:** 43½" overall.
Stock: Kevlar, position-style, with palm swell, handstop.
Sights: None furnished.
Features: Designed to meet the needs of competitive shooters firing the national match courses. Position-style stock, top loading clip slot magazine, anti-bind bolt and receiver, bright stainless steel barrel. Meets all ISU Army Rifle specifications. Adjustable buttplate, adjustable trigger.
Price: About **$1,278.00**

Remington 40-XR KS

REMINGTON 40-XR KS RIMFIRE POSITION RIFLE
Caliber: 22 LR, single shot.
Barrel: 24", heavy target.
Weight: 10 lbs. **Length:** 43" overall.
Stock: Kevlar. Position-style with front swivel block on forend guide rail.
Sights: Drilled and tapped. Furnished with scope blocks.
Features: Meets all ISU specifications. Deep forend, buttplate vertically adjustable, wide adjustable trigger.
Price: About **$1,202.00**

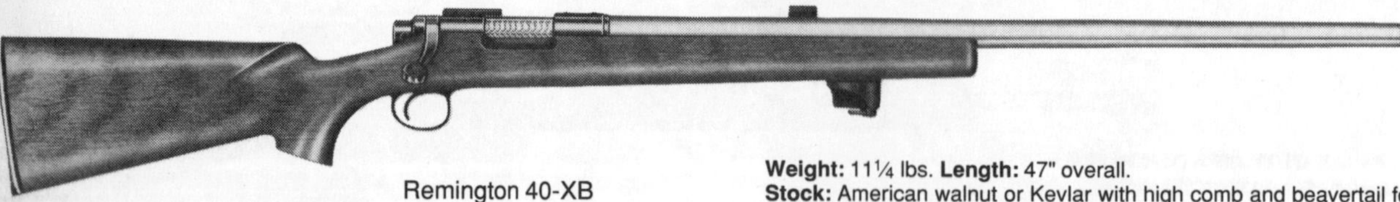
Remington 40-XB

REMINGTON 40-XB RANGEMASTER TARGET CENTERFIRE
Caliber: 222 Rem., 222 Rem. Mag., 223, 220 Swift, 22-250, 6mm Rem., 243, 25-06, 7mm BR Rem., 7mm Rem. Mag., 30-338 (30-7mm Rem. Mag.), 300 Win. Mag., 7.62 NATO (308 Win.), 30-06, single shot.
Barrel: 27¼".
Weight: 11¼ lbs. **Length:** 47" overall.
Stock: American walnut or Kevlar with high comb and beavertail forend stop. Rubber non-slip buttplate.
Sights: None. Scope blocks installed.
Features: Adjustable trigger pull. Receiver drilled and tapped for sights.
Price: Standard s.s., stainless steel barrel, about **$1,053.00**
Price: Model 40-XB KS **$1,202.00**
Price: Extra for repeater model (KS) **$88.00**
Price: Extra for 2-oz. trigger **$146.00**

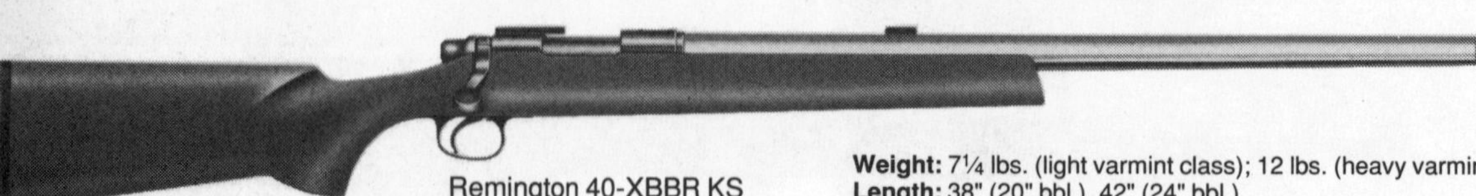
Remington 40-XBBR KS

REMINGTON 40-XBBR KS
Caliber: 22 BR Rem., 222 Rem., 222 Rem. Mag., 223, 6mmx47, 6mm BR Rem., 7.62 NATO (308 Win.).
Barrel: 20" (light varmint class), 24" (heavy varmint class).
Weight: 7¼ lbs. (light varmint class); 12 lbs. (heavy varmint class).
Length: 38" (20" bbl.), 42" (24" bbl.).
Stock: Kevlar.
Sights: None. Supplied with scope blocks.
Features: Unblued stainless steel barrel, trigger adjustable from 1½ lbs. to 3½ lbs. Special 2-oz. trigger at extra cost. Scope and mounts extra.
Price: With Kevlar stock **$1,278.00**
Price: Extra for 2-oz. trigger, about **$146.00**

Springfield M-1A Match

SPRINGFIELD ARMORY M-21 LAW ENFORCEMENT
Caliber: 308 Win.
Barrel: 22", Douglas heavy, air-gauged.
Weight: 15.25 lbs. (with bipod, scope mount). **Length:** 44¼" overall.
Stock: Heavy walnut with adjustable comb, ventilated recoil pad. Glass bedded.
Sights: National Match front and rear.
Features: Refinement of the standard M-1A rifle. Has specially knurled shoulder for new figure-eight operating rod guide. New style folding and removable bipod. Guaranteed to deliver MOA accuracy. Comes with six 20-round magazines, leather military sling, cleaning kit. Introduced 1987. From Springfield Armory, Inc.
Price: **$2,163.00**

SPRINGFIELD ARMORY M-1A SUPER MATCH
Caliber: 308 Win.
Barrel: 22", heavy Douglas Premium, or Hart stainless steel.
Weight: About 10 lbs. **Length:** 44½" overall.
Stock: Heavy walnut competition stock with longer pistol grip, contoured area behind the rear sight, thicker butt and forend, glass bedded.
Sights: National Match front and rear.
Features: Has new figure-eight style operating rod guide, new stock design. Introduced 1987. From Springfield Armory, Inc.
Price: About **$1,689.00**

Steyr-Mannlicher SSG P-1

STEYR-MANNLICHER SSG P-1 RIFLE
Caliber: 243, 308 Win.
Barrel: 25.6".
Weight: 8.6 lbs. **Length:** 44.5" overall.
Stock: Choice of ABS "Cycolac" synthetic half-stock or walnut. Removable spacers in butt adjusts length of pull from 12¾" to 14".
Sights: Hooded blade front, folding leaf rear.
Features: Parkerized finish. Choice of interchangeable single- or double-set triggers. Detachable 5-shot rotary magazine (10-shot optional). Drilled and tapped for scope mounts. Imported from Austria by Gun South, Inc.
Price: Synthetic half-stock **$1,634.00**
Price: Walnut half-stock **$2,082.00**
Price: SSG-PII (as above except has large bolt knob, heavy bbl., no sights, forend rail). **$1,783.00**
Price: SSG-PII with walnut stock **$2,231.00**

Steyr-Mannlicher SSG Match
Same as Model SSG Marksman except has heavy barrel, match bolt, Walther target peep sights and adjustable rail in forend to adjustable sling travel. Weight is 11 lbs.
Price: Synthetic half-stock **$2,306.00**
Price: Walnut half-stock **$2,743.00**

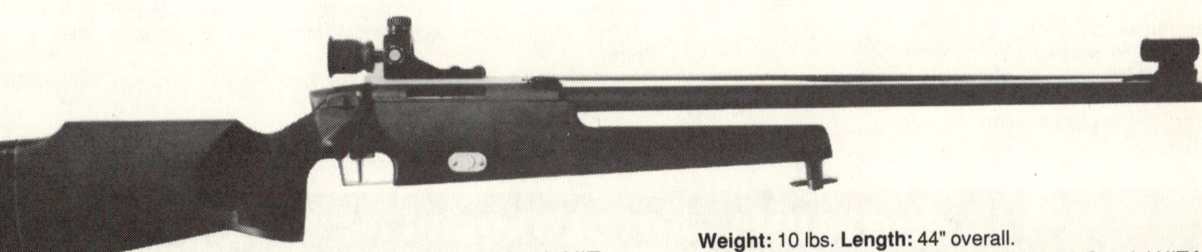
Steyr-Mannlicher Match UIT

STEYR-MANNLICHER MATCH UIT RIFLE
Caliber: 308 Win., 10-shot magazine.
Barrel: 25.5".
Weight: 10 lbs. **Length:** 44" overall.
Stock: Walnut with stippled grip and forend. Special UIT Match design.
Sights: Walther globe front, Walther peep rear.
Features: Double-pull trigger adjustable for let-off point, slack, weight of first-stage pull, release force and length; buttplate adjustable for height and length. Meets UIT specifications. Introduced 1984. Imported from Austria by Gun South, Inc.
Price: **$4,562.00**

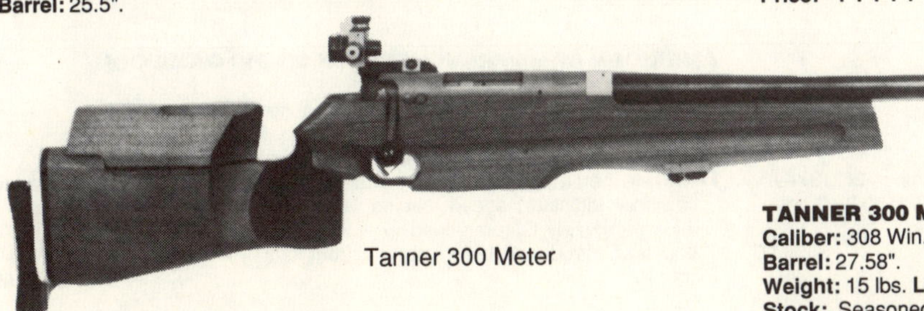
Tanner 300 Meter

TANNER 300 METER FREE RIFLE
Caliber: 308 Win., 7.5 Swiss, single shot.
Barrel: 27.58".
Weight: 15 lbs. **Length:** 45.3" overall.
Stock: Seasoned walnut, thumbhole style, with accessory rail, palm rest, adjustable hook butt.
Sights: Globe front with interchangeable inserts, Tanner-design micrometer-diopter rear with adjustable aperture.
Features: Three-lug revolving-lock bolt design; adjustable set trigger; short firing pin travel; supplied with 300-meter test target. Imported from Switzerland by Mandall Shooting Supplies. Introduced 1984.
Price: About **$4,900.00**

Consult our Directory pages for the location of firms mentioned.

TANNER STANDARD UIT RIFLE
Caliber: 308, 7.5mm Swiss, 10-shot.
Barrel: 25.9".
Weight: 10.5 lbs. **Length:** 40.6" overall.
Stock: Match style of seasoned nutwood with accessory rail; coarsely stippled pistol grip; high cheekpiece; vented forend.
Sights: Globe front with interchangeable inserts, Tanner micrometer-diopter rear with adjustable aperture.
Features: Two locking lug revolving bolt encloses case head. Trigger adjustable from ½ to 6½ lbs.; match trigger optional. Comes with 300-meter test target. Imported from Switzerland by Mandall Shooting Supplies. Introduced 1984.
Price: About **$4,700.00**

TANNER 50 METER FREE RIFLE
Caliber: 22 LR, single shot.
Barrel: 27.7".
Weight: 13.9 lbs. **Length:** 44.4" overall.
Stock: Seasoned walnut with palm rest, accessory rail, adjustable hook buttplate.
Sights: Globe front with interchangeable inserts, Tanner micrometer-diopter rear with adjustable aperture.
Features: Bolt action with externally adjustable set trigger. Supplied with 50-meter test target. Imported from Switzerland by Mandall Shooting Supplies. Introduced 1984.
Price: About **$3,900.00**

Walther UIT Match

Walther UIT Match
Same specifications and features as standard GX-1 Match rifle but has scope mount bases. Forend has new tapered profile, fully stippled. Imported from Germany by Interarms.
Price: **$1,400.00**

WALTHER GX-1 MATCH RIFLE
Caliber: 22 LR, single shot.
Barrel: 25½".
Weight: 16.5 lbs. **Length:** 46" overall.
Stock: Walnut, adjustable for length and drop; forend guide rail for sling or palm rest.
Sights: Globe-type front, fully adjustable aperture rear.
Features: Conforms to both NRA and UIT requirements. Fully adjustable trigger. Left-hand stock available on special order. Imported from Germany by Interarms.
Price: **$2,350.00**

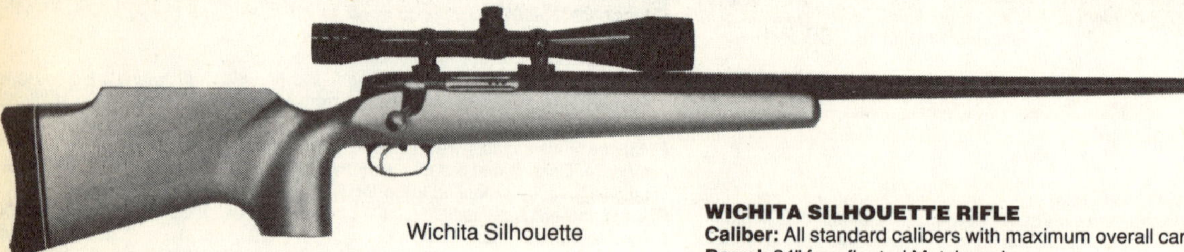

Wichita Silhouette

WALTHER KK/MS SILHOUETTE RIFLE
Caliber: 22 LR, single shot.
Barrel: 25.5".
Weight: 8.75 lbs. **Length:** 44.75" overall.
Stock: Walnut with thumbhole, stippled grip and forend.
Sights: None furnished. Receiver grooved for scope mounting.
Features: Over-size bolt knob. Adjustable trigger. Rubber buttpad. Introduced 1989. Imported from Germany by Interarms.
Price: **$1,175.00**

WICHITA SILHOUETTE RIFLE
Caliber: All standard calibers with maximum overall cartridge length of 2.800".
Barrel: 24" free-floated Matchgrade.
Weight: About 9 lbs.
Stock: Metallic gray fiberthane with ventilated rubber recoil pad.
Sights: None furnished. Drilled and tapped for scope mounts.
Features: Legal for all NRA competitions. Single shot action. Fluted bolt, 2-oz. Canjar trigger; glass-bedded stock. Introduced 1983. From Wichita Arms.
Price: **$2,250.00**
Price: Left-hand **$2,400.00**

SHOTGUNS—AUTOLOADERS

Includes a wide variety of sporting guns and guns suitable for various competitions.

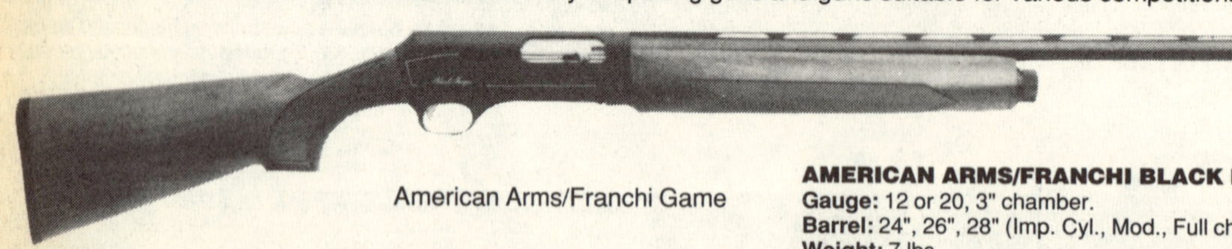

American Arms/Franchi Game

American Arms/Franchi Black Magic Skeet Gun
Similar to the Black Magic Game Gun except has 2¾" chamber, 26" (Skeet), ported barrel; weight 7¼ lbs. Stock dimensions of 14½"x1½"x2¼". Introduced 1989.
Price: **$699.00**

AMERICAN ARMS/FRANCHI BLACK MAGIC 48/AL
Gauge: 12 or 20, 2¾" chamber.
Barrel: 24", 26", 28" (Mod. choke tube). Vent. rib.
Weight: 5.2 lbs. (20-gauge). **Length:** NA
Stock: 14¼"x1⅝"x2½". Walnut with checkered grip and forend.
Features: Recoil-operated action. Chrome-lined bore; cross-bolt safety. Imported from Italy by American Arms, Inc.
Price: **$529.00**

AMERICAN ARMS/FRANCHI BLACK MAGIC GAME GUN
Gauge: 12 or 20, 3" chamber.
Barrel: 24", 26", 28" (Imp. Cyl., Mod., Full choke tubes).
Weight: 7 lbs.
Stock: 14¼"x1½"x2⅜". Walnut, checkered grip and forend.
Features: Inertia recoil system with rotary locking bolt; magazine cut-off; loaded chamber indicator; speed loading feature; shoots all 2¾" and 3" shells interchangeably. Chrome-lined bores; cross-bolt safety locks trigger, firing pin and sear. Introduced 1989. Imported from Italy by American Arms, Inc.
Price: **$659.00**

American Arms/Franchi Black Magic Trap Gun
Similar to the Black Magic Game Gun except 30" barrel with 2¾" chamber, Mod., Imp. Mod., Full choke tubes. Walnut stock and forend with cut checkering; stock dimensions of 14½"x1¼"x1⅜". Weighs 7½ lbs. Introduced 1989. Imported from Italy by American Arms, Inc.
Price: **$739.00**

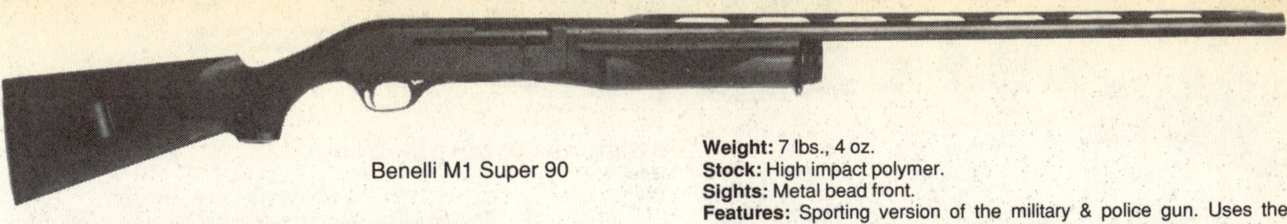

Benelli M1 Super 90

BENELLI M1 SUPER 90 FIELD AUTO SHOTGUN
Gauge: 12, 3" chamber.
Barrel: 21", 24", 26", 28" (choke tubes).
Weight: 7 lbs., 4 oz.
Stock: High impact polymer.
Sights: Metal bead front.
Features: Sporting version of the military & police gun. Uses the rotating Montefeltro bolt system. Ventilated rib; blue finish. Comes with set of five choke tubes. Imported from Italy by Heckler & Koch, Inc.
Price: **$729.00**

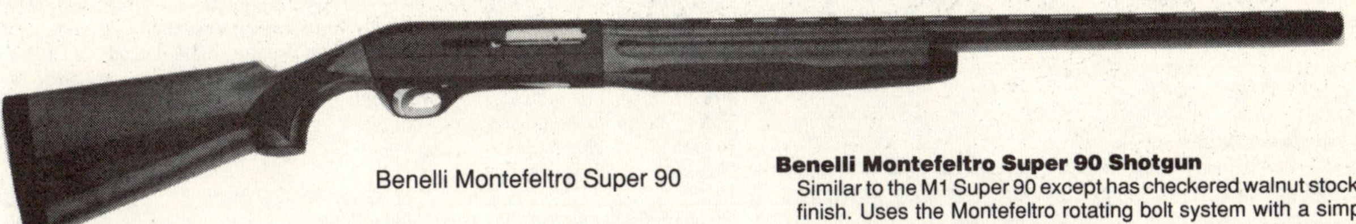

Benelli Montefeltro Super 90

Benelli M1 Super 90 Slug Shotgun
Similar to the M1 Super 90 Field except comes with 19¾" barrel (Cyl. choke) giving 41" overall length and weight of 6 lbs., 13 oz. Has 3" chamber, 7-shot magazine capacity, matte black finish. Standard buttstock of high-impact polymer. Rifle sights standard, ghost ring sighting system available. Imported from Italy by Hecker & Koch, Inc.
Price: With rifle sights **$659.00**
Price: With ghost ring sight system **$714.00**

Benelli Montefeltro Super 90 Shotgun
Similar to the M1 Super 90 except has checkered walnut stock with high-gloss finish. Uses the Montefeltro rotating bolt system with a simple inertia recoil design. Full, Imp. Mod, Mod., Imp. Cyl. choke tubes. Weight is 7-7½ lbs. Finish is matte black. Introduced 1987.
Price: Standard Hunter, 26", 28" **$729.00**
Price: Left-hand, 26", 28" **$799.00**
Price: Uplander, 21" or 24" bbl. **$729.00**
Price: Smoothbore Slug with scope mount, rifle sights **$729.00**

Benelli Black Eagle Competition

BENELLI BLACK EAGLE COMPETITION AUTO SHOTGUN
Gauge: 12, 3" chamber.
Barrel: 26", 28" (Full, Mod., Imp. Cyl., Imp. Mod., Skeet choke tubes). Mid-bead sight.
Weight: 7.1 to 7.6 lbs. **Length:** 49⅝" overall (26" barrel).
Stock: European walnut with high-gloss finish. Special competition stock comes with drop adjustment kit.
Features: Uses the Montefeltro rotating bolt inertia recoil operating system with a two-piece steel/aluminum etched receiver (bright on lower, blue upper). Drop adjustment kit allows the stock to be custom fitted without modifying the stock. Black lower receiver finish, blued upper. Introduced 1989. Imported from Italy by Heckler & Koch, Inc.
Price: **$995.00**

Benelli Black Eagle Slug

Benelli Black Eagle Slug Gun
Similar to the Black Eagle except has 24" (Cyl.) rifled barrel without rib, weighs 7 lbs., 2 oz. Uses the Montefeltro inertia recoil rotating bolt system with two-piece steel and alloy receiver. Top steel receiver drilled and tapped for scope mount (included). Introduced 1990. Imported from Italy by Heckler & Koch, Inc.
Price: With scope mount **$859.00**

Benelli Super Black Eagle

BENELLI MONTEFELTRO SUPER 90 SLUG GUN
Gauge: 12, 3" chamber, 4-shot magazine.
Barrel: 24" (Cyl.), smoothbore.
Weight: 7 lbs. **Length:** 45.5" overall.
Stock: European walnut with matte finish; comes with drop adjustment kit.
Sights: Open iron sights and scope mount.
Features: Uses Montefeltro inertia recoil rotating bolt system. Comes with scope mount. Introduced 1990. Imported from Italy by Heckler & Koch, Inc.
Price: **$729.00**

BENELLI SUPER BLACK EAGLE SHOTGUN
Gauge: 12, 3½" chamber.
Barrel: 26", 28" (Imp. Cyl., Mod., Imp. Mod., Full choke tubes).
Weight: 7 lbs., 5 oz. **Length:** 49⅝" overall (28" barrel).
Stock: European walnut with satin or gloss finish. Adjustable for drop.
Sights: Bead front.
Features: Uses Montfeltro inertia recoil bolt system. Fires all 12-gauge shells from 2¾" to 3½" magnums. Introduced 1991. Imported from Italy by Heckler & Koch, Inc.
Price: **$989.00**

Beretta A-303 Skeet

Beretta A-303 Matte Finish
Similar to the standard A-303 except has non-reflective finish on all wood and metal surfaces, and comes with studs and sling swivels. Available in 24", 26", 28", 30" barrel lengths with Mobilchoke choke tubes, 3" chamber. Introduced 1991.
Price: **$665.00**

Beretta A-303 Upland Model
Similar to the 12-gauge field A-303 except has 24" vent. rib barrel with Mobilchoke choke tubes, 2¾" chamber, straight English-style stock. Introduced 1989.
Price: **$665.00**

BERETTA A-303 AUTO SHOTGUN
Gauge: 12 or 20, 2¾" or 3" chamber.
Barrel: 12-ga., 3"—24", 26", 28", 30", 32"; 12-ga., 2¾"—26", 28", 30"; 20-ga., 2¾" or 3"—26", 28". All equipped with Mobilchoke choke tubes. Slug model has 22" (Cyl.) barrel.
Weight: About 6½ lbs., 20-gauge; about 7½ lbs., 12-gauge.
Stock: American walnut; hand-checkered grip and forend.
Features: Gas-operated action, alloy receiver, magazine cut-off, push-button safety. Mobilchoke models come with three interchangeable flush-mounted screw-in choke tubes. Imported from Italy by Beretta U.S.A. Introduced 1983.
Price: Mobilchoke, 12-ga. or 20-ga. **$665.00**
Price: 12-ga. trap with Monte Carlo stock **$725.00**
Price: 12-ga. trap with standard trap stock **$685.00**
Price: 12- or 20-ga., Skeet **$685.00**
Price: Slug, 12-ga. only **$665.00**
Price: A-303 Youth Gun, 20-ga., 2¾" chamber, 24" barrel **$680.00**
Price: A-303 Sporting Clays with Mobilchoke **$745.00**
Price: A-303 Sporting Clays 20-ga. **$745.00**

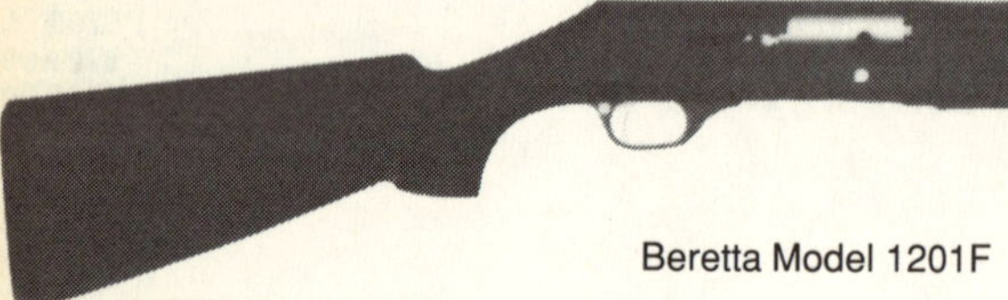

Beretta Model 1201F

BERETTA MODEL 1201F AUTO SHOTGUN
Gauge: 12, 3" chamber.
Barrel: 28" vent. rib with Mobilchoke choke tubes.
Weight: 7 lbs., 4 oz.
Stock: Special strengthened technopolymer, matte black finish. Adjustable butt and recoil pad.
Features: Resists abrasion and adverse effects of water, salt and other damaging materials associated with tough field conditions. Imported from Italy by Beretta U.S.A. Introduced 1988.
Price: **$540.00**

BRI/BENELLI 123-SL-80 RIFLED SHOTGUN
Gauge: 12, 2¾" chamber.
Barrel: 24⅛", rifled.
Weight: 9 lbs.
Length: 45½" overall.
Stock: European walnut with checkered p.g. and forend.
Sights: None furnished. Drilled and tapped for scope mounting.
Features: Rifled bore. Quick interchangeable barrels; cross-bolt safety; engraved receiver; recoil pad. From Ballistic Research Industries.
Price: **$995.00**

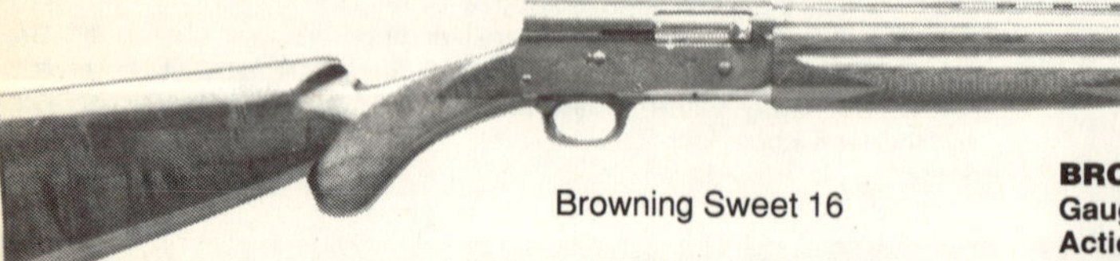

Browning Sweet 16

Browning Auto-5 Magnum 12
Same as standard Auto-5 except chambered for 3" magnum shells (also handles 2¾" magnum and 2¾" HV loads). 28" Mod., Full; 30" and 32" (Full) bbls. Comes with Invector choke tubes. 14"x1⅝"x2½" stock. Recoil pad. Wgt. 8¾ lbs.
Price: With Invector choke tubes **$742.95**
Price: Extra Invector barrel **$249.95**

Browning Auto-5 Magnum 20
Same as Magnum 12 except 26" or 28" barrel with Invector choke tubes. With ventilated rib, 7½ lbs.
Price: Invector only **$742.95**
Price: Extra Invector barrel **$249.95**

BROWNING AUTO-5 LIGHT 12 AND 20, SWEET 16
Gauge: 12, 16, 20, 5-shot; 3-shot plug furnished; 2¾" or 3" chamber.
Action: Recoil operated autoloader; takedown.
Barrel: 26", 28", 30" Invector (choke tube) barrel; also available with Light 20-ga. 28" (Mod.) or 26" (Imp. Cyl.) barrel.
Weight: 12-, 16-ga. 7¼ lbs.; 20-ga. 6⅜ lbs.
Stock: French walnut, hand checkered half-p.g. and forend. 14¼"x1⅝"x2½".
Features: Receiver hand engraved with scroll designs and border. Double extractors, extra bbls. Interchangeable without factory fitting; mag. cut-off; cross-bolt safety. Imported from Japan by Browning.
Price: Light 12, 20, Sweet 16, vent. rib., Invector **$719.95**
Price: Extra Invector barrel **$249.95**
Price: Light 12 Buck Special **$724.95**
Price: 3" Magnum Buck Special **$747.95**
Price: Extra fixed-choke barrel (Light 20 only) **$194.95**
Price: 12, 16, 20 Buck Special barrel **$254.95**

Browning A-500G

BROWNING A-500G AUTO SHOTGUN
Gauge: 12, 3" chamber.
Barrel: 26", 28", 30", Invector choke tubes. Ventilated rib.
Weight: 7 lbs., 14 oz. (26" bbl.). **Length:** 47½" overall.
Stock: 14⅜"x1½"x2". Select walnut with gloss finish, rounded pistol grip. Recoil pad standard.
Features: Gas-operated action with four-lug rotary bolt, cross-bolt safety. Interchangeable barrels. High-polish blue finish with light engraving on receiver and "A-500G" in gold color. Patented gas metering system to handle all loads. Built-in buffering system to absorb recoil, reduce stress on internal parts. Introduced 1990. Imported by Browning.
Price: **$639.95**
Price: Extra Invector barrels **$249.95**
Price: A-500G Buck Special **$672.95**
Price: 24" Buck Special barrel **$282.95**

BROWNING A-500R AUTO SHOTGUN
Gauge: 12 only, 3" chamber.
Barrel: 24" Buck Special, 26", 28", 30" with Invector choke tubes.
Weight: 7 lbs., 7 oz. (30" bbl.).
Length: 49½" overall (30" bbl.).
Stock: 14¼"x1½"x2½"; select walnut with gloss finish; checkered p.g. and forend; black vent., recoil pad.
Sights: Metal bead front.
Features: Uses a short-recoil action with four-lug rotary bolt and composite and coil spring buffering system. Shoots all loads without adjustment. Has a magazine cut-off, Invector chokes. Introduced 1987. Imported from Belgium by Browning.
Price: $559.95
Price: A-500R Buck Special $559.95
Price: Extra Invector barrel $199.95
Price: 24" Buck Special barrel $232.95

Churchill Automatic

CHURCHILL AUTOMATIC SHOTGUN
Gauge: 12, 2¾" or 3" chamber, 5-shot magazine.
Barrel: 24", 25", 26", 28" (choke tubes).
Weight: NA. **Length:** NA.
Stock: Walnut with satin finish, hand checkering.
Features: Gas-operated action, magazine cut-off, non-glare metal finish. Gold-colored trigger. Introduced 1990. Imported by Ellett Bros.
Price: $549.95
Price: Turkey, 25" bbl. $569.95

COSMI AUTOMATIC SHOTGUN
Gauge: 12 or 20, 2¾" or 3" chamber.
Barrel: 22" to 34". Choke (including choke tubes) and length to customer specs. Boehler steel.
Weight: About 6¼ lbs. (20-ga.).
Stock: Length and style to customer specs. Hand-checkered exhibition grade circassian walnut standard.
Features: Hand-made, essentially a custom gun. Recoil-operated auto with tip-up barrel. Made completely of stainless steel (lower receiver polished); magazine tube in buttstock holds 7 rounds. Double ejectors, double safety system. Comes with fitted leather case. Imported from Italy by Incor, Inc.
Price: From $7,400.00

Mossberg 5500 MKII

MOSSBERG MODEL 5500 MKII SEMI-AUTO SHOTGUN
Gauge: 12, 2¾" and 3" chamber.
Barrel: 26", 28" (2¾" chamber, ACCU-II tubes—Imp. Cyl., Mod., Full); 24", 28" (3" chamber, ACCU-II tubes—Imp. Cyl., Mod., Full (both vent. rib).
Weight: 7½ lbs. **Length:** 48" overall with 28" barrel.
Stock: 14"x1½"x2½". Walnut-stained hardwood.
Features: Combo or single barrel versions available. Gas-operated action. Blue or camo finish. Mossberg Cablelock included. Introduced 1988.
Price: From about $425.00
Price: Camo, 28", from about $468.00

Remington SP-10

REMINGTON SP-10 MAGNUM AUTO SHOTGUN
Gauge: 10, 3½" chamber, 3-shot magazine.
Barrel: 26", 30" (Full and Mod. Rem Chokes).
Weight: 11 to 11¼ lbs. **Length:** 47½" overall (26" barrel).
Stock: Walnut with satin finish. Checkered grip and forend.
Sights: Metal bead front.
Features: Stainless steel gas system with moving cylinder; ⅜" ventilated rib. Receiver and barrel have matte finish. Brown recoil pad. Comes with padded Cordura nylon sling. Introduced 1989.
Price: $1,265.00

Remington SP-10 Magnum Turkey Combo
Combines the SP 10 with 26" or 30" vent. rib barrel, plus extra 22" rifle-sighted barrel with Mod., Full, Extra-Full Turkey Rem Choke tubes. Comes with camo sling, swivels. Introduced 1991.
Price: $1,363.00

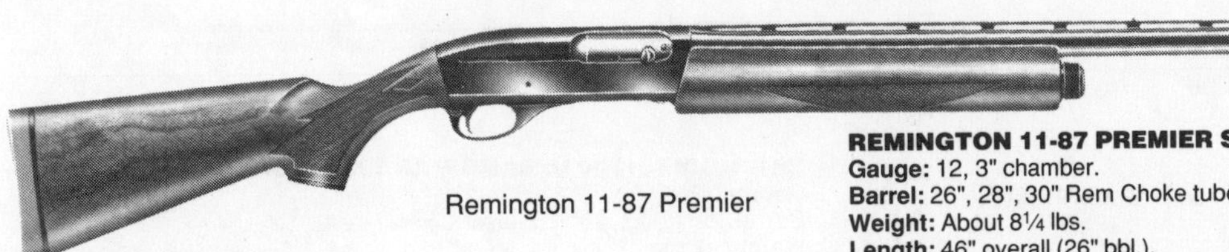
Remington 11-87 Premier

REMINGTON 11-87 PREMIER SHOTGUN
Gauge: 12, 3" chamber.
Barrel: 26", 28", 30" Rem Choke tubes.
Weight: About 8¼ lbs.
Length: 46" overall (26" bbl.).
Stock: Walnut with satin or high-gloss finish; cut checkering; solid brown buttpad; no white spacers.
Sights: Bradley-type white-faced front, metal bead middle.
Features: Pressure compensating gas system allows shooting 2¾" or 3" loads interchangeably with no adjustments. Stainless magazine tube; redesigned feed latch, barrel support ring on operating bars; pinned forend. Introduced 1987.
Price: $605.00
Price: Left-hand $664.00
Price: Premier Cantilever Deer Barrel, scope rings, sling, swivels, Monte Carlo stock $645.00

Remington 11-87 175th Anniversary Shotgun
Same as the Model 11-87 Premier except receiver is engraved with Remington's 175th anniversary scroll design with an American eagle, walnut wood with high-gloss finish. Comes with 28" vent. rib barrel and Rem Choke tubes; 12-ga. only. Introduced 1991.
Price: $618.00

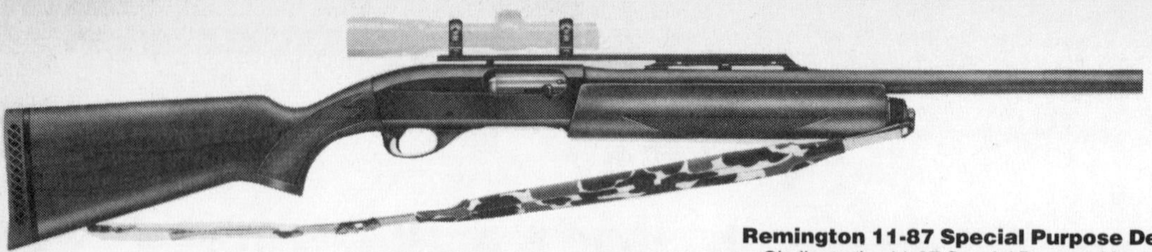

Remington 11-87 Deer

Remington 11-87 Special Purpose Magnum

Similar to the 11-87 Premier except has dull stock finish, Parkerized exposed metal surfaces. Bolt and carrier have dull blackened coloring. Comes with 26" or 28" barrel with Rem Chokes, padded Cordura nylon sling and q.d. swivels. Introduced 1987.

Price: $605.00
Price: With synthetic stock and forend (SPS) $605.00
Price: Magnum-Turkey with synthetic stock (SPS-T) $618.00

Remington 11-87 Special Purpose Deer Gun

Similar to the 11-87 Special Purpose Magnum except has 21" barrel with rifle sights, rifled and Imp. Cyl. choke tubes. Gas system set to handle all 2¾" and 3" slug, buckshot, high velocity field and magnum loads. Not designed to function with light 2¾" field loads. Introduced 1987.

Price: $585.00
Price: With cantilever scope mount, rings $638.00

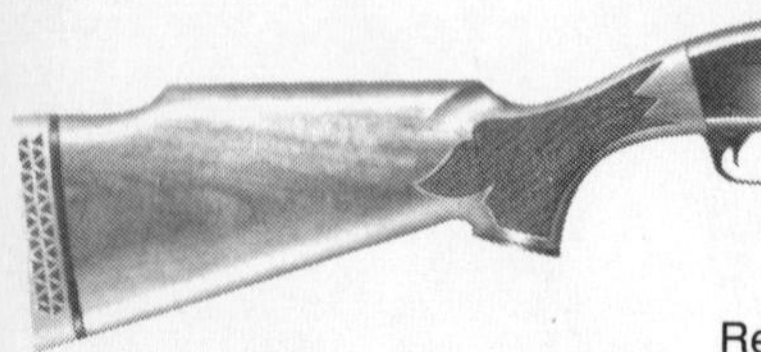

Remington 11-87 Trap

Remington 11-87 Premier Skeet

Similar to 11-87 Premier except Skeet dimension stock with cut checkering, satin finish, two-piece buttplate; 26" barrel with Skeet or Rem Chokes (Skeet, Imp. Skeet). Gas system set for 2¾" shells only. Introduced 1987.

Price: $661.00
Price: Left-hand $726.00

Remington 11-87 Premier Trap

Similar to 11-87 Premier except trap dimension stock with straight or Monte Carlo combs; select walnut with satin finish and Tournament-grade cut checkering; 30" barrel with Rem Chokes (Trap Full, Trap Extra Full, Trap Super Full). Gas system set for 2¾" shells only. Introduced 1987.

Price: With straight stock, Rem Choke $669.00
Price: With Monte Carlo stock $684.00
Price: Left-hand, straight stock $735.00
Price: Left-hand, Monte Carlo stock $751.00

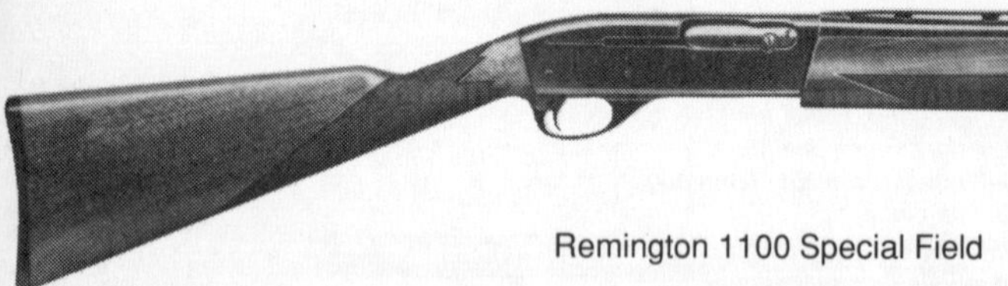

Remington 1100 Special Field

Remington 1100 20-Ga. Deer Gun

Same as 1100 except 20-ga. only, 21" barrel (Imp. Cyl.), rifle sights adjustable for windage and elevation; recoil pad with white spacer. Weight 7¼ lbs.

Price: About $531.00

Remington 1100 Special Field

Similar to standard Model 1100 except 12- and 20-ga. only, comes with 21" Rem Choke barrel. LT-20 version 6½ lbs.; has straight-grip stock, shorter forend, both with cut checkering. Comes with vent. rib only; matte finish receiver without engraving. Introduced 1983.

Price: 12- and 20-ga., 21" Rem Choke, about $588.00

REMINGTON 1100 LT-20 AUTO

Gauge: 20, 28, 410.
Barrel: 25" (Full, Mod.), 26", 28" with Rem Chokes.
Weight: 7½ lbs.
Stock: 14"x1½"x2½". American walnut, checkered p.g. and forend.
Features: Quickly interchangeable barrels. Matted receiver top with scroll work on both sides of receiver. Cross-bolt safety.
Price: With Rem Chokes, 20-ga. about $588.00
Price: 28 and 410 . . . . $632.00
Price: Youth Gun LT-20 (21" Rem Choke) $575.00
Price: 20-ga., 3" magnum $588.00

Remington 1100 LT-20 Tournament Skeet

Same as the 1100 except 26" barrel, special Skeet boring, vent. rib, ivory bead front and metal bead middle sights. 14"x1½"x2½" stock. 20-, 28-, 410-ga. Weight 7½ lbs., cut checkering, walnut, new receiver scroll.

Price: Tournament Skeet (28, 410), about $669.00
Price: Tournament Skeet (20), about $669.00

SKB Model 1900 Field

SKB Model 1900 Trap

Similar to the Model 1900 Field except in 12-gauge only (2¾" chamber), 30" barrel with Inter Choke tubes and 9.5mm wide raised rib. Introduced 1988.

Price: $545.00

SKB Model 1900 Auto Shotgun

Similar to the Model 1300 except has engraved bright-finish receiver, grip cap, gold-plated trigger. Introduced 1988.

Price: Field $545.00
Price: Slug (22" barrel, rifle sights) $545.00

SKB MODEL 1300 UPLAND MAG SHOTGUN

Gauge: 12, 2¾" or 3"; 20, 3".
Barrel: 22" (Slug), 26", 28" (Inter Choke tubes).
Weight: 6½ to 7¼ lbs.
Length: 48¼" overall (28" barrel).
Stock: 14½"x1½"x2½". Walnut, with hand-checkered grip and forend.
Sights: Metal bead front.
Features: Gas operated with Universal Automatic System. Blued receiver. Magazine cut-off system. Introduced 1988. Imported from Japan by Guns Unlimited, Inc.
Price: Field $495.00
Price: Slug (22" bbl., rifle sights) $495.00

Winchester Model 1400 Walnut

WINCHESTER MODEL 1400 AUTO SHOTGUN

Gauge: 12 and 20, 2¾" chamber.
Barrel: 22", 26", 28" vent. rib with Winchoke tubes (Imp. Cyl., Mod., Full).
Weight: 7¾ lbs.
Length: 48⅝" overall.
Stock: Walnut-finished hardwood, finger-grooved forend with deep cut checkering. Also available with walnut stock.
Sights: Metal bead front.
Features: Cross-bolt safety, front-locking rotary bolt, black serrated buttplate, gas-operated action. From U.S. Repeating Arms Co., Inc.
Price: Ranger, vent. rib with Winchoke, about **$358.00**
Price: As above with walnut stock (1400 Walnut) **$398.00**
Price: Deer barrel combo, about **$440.00**
Price: Deer gun, about **$349.00**

Winchester Model 1400 Custom Auto Shotgun
Same as the standard Model 1400 except has hand-engraved receiver, semi-fancy walnut butt with recoil pad and forend. Comes with 28" vent. rib barrel with Winchoke Imp. Cyl., Mod. and Full choke tubes. Built in Winchester Custom Shop. Options available. Introduced 1991.
Price: From **$1,695.00**

Winchester Model 1400 Walnut "Slug Hunter"
Similar to the Model 1400 except in 12-ga. only with smooth bore 22" barrel, with adjustable open sights. Comes with Imp. Cyl. and Sabot choke tubes. Receiver is drilled and tapped for scope mounting, has threaded steel inserts and comes with bases. Walnut stock and forend with cut checkering. Introduced 1990. From U.S. Repeating Arms Co., Inc.
Price: **$442.00**

SHOTGUNS—SLIDE ACTIONS

Includes a wide variety of sporting guns and guns suitable for competitive shooting.

ARMSCOR MODEL 30 D/IC PUMP SHOTGUN

Gauge: 12, 5-shot magazine.
Barrel: 26", 28" (Imp. Cyl., Mod., Full tubes).
Weight: 7.4 lbs.
Length: 47" overall. (28").
Stock: Checkered mahogany.
Sights: Metal bead front.
Features: Double action bars; blue finish; grooved forend. Introduced 1987. Imported from the Philippines by Armscor.
Price: **$266.19**
Price: With rifle sights (Model 30 R/DG/K) **$193.69**

BRI SPECIAL RIFLED PUMP SHOTGUN

Gauge: 12, 3" chamber.
Barrel: 24" (Cyl.) rifled.
Weight: 7½ lbs.
Length: 44" overall.
Stock: Walnut with high straight comb. Rubber recoil pad.
Sights: None. Comes with scope mount on barrel.
Features: Uses Mossberg Model 500 Trophy Slugster action; double slide bars, twin extractors, dual shell latches; top receiver safety. From Ballistic Research Industries. Introduced 1988.
Price: About **$695.00**

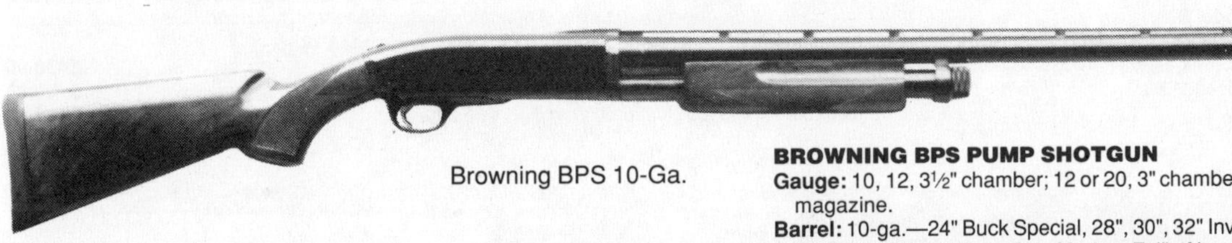
Browning BPS 10-Ga.

BROWNING BPS PUMP SHOTGUN

Gauge: 10, 12, 3½" chamber; 12 or 20, 3" chamber (2¾" in target guns), 5-shot magazine.
Barrel: 10-ga.—24" Buck Special, 28", 30", 32" Invector; 12-, 20- ga.—22", 24", 26", 28", 30", 32" (Imp. Cyl., Mod. or Full). Also available with Invector choke tubes, 12- or 20-ga.; Upland Special has 22" barrel with Invector tubes. BPS 3½" has back-bored barrel.
Weight: 7 lbs., 8 oz. (28" barrel). **Length:** 48¾" overall (28" barrel).
Stock: 14¼"x1½"x2½". Select walnut, semi-beavertail forend, full p.g. stock.
Features: Bottom feeding and ejection, receiver top safety, high post vent. rib. Double action bars eliminate binding. Vent. rib barrels only. All 12- and 20-gauge guns with 3" chamber available with fully engraved receiver flats at no extra cost. Each gsuge has its own unique game scene. Introduced 1977. Imported from Japan by Browning.
Price: 10-ga., Hunting, Invector **$572.95**
Price: 12-ga., 3½" Mag., Hunting, Invector PLUS **$572.95**
Price: 12-ga., Hunting **$442.95**
Price: 12-, 20-ga., Upland Special, Invector **$442.95**
Price: 10-ga. and 3½" 12-ga. Mag., Buck Special **$577.95**
Price: 12-ga. Buck Special **$448.95**

Browning BPS Pump Shotgun (Ladies and Youth Model)
Same as BPS Upland Special except 20-ga. only, 22" Invector barrel, stock has pistol grip with recoil pad. Length of pull is 13¼". Introduced 1986.
Price: **$442.95**

Browning BPS Stalker Pump Shotgun
Same gun as the standard BPS except all exposed metal parts have a matte blued finish and the stock has a durable black finish with a black recoil pad. Available in 10-ga. (3½") and 12-ga. with 3" or 3½" chamber, 22", 28", 30" barrel with Invector choke system. Introduced 1987.
Price: 12-ga., 3" chamber **$442.95**
Price: 10-, 12-ga., 3½" chamber **$572.95**

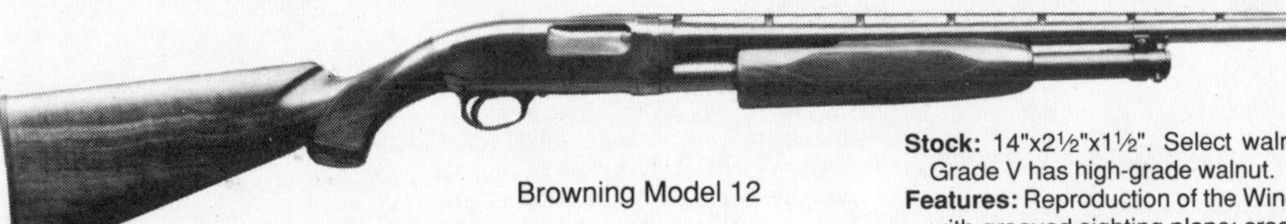
Browning Model 12

BROWNING MODEL 12 PUMP SHOTGUN

Gauge: 28, 2¾" chamber; 410-bore, 3" chamber.
Barrel: 26" (Mod.).
Weight: 7 lbs., 1 oz. **Length:** 45" overall.
Stock: 14"x2½"x1½". Select walnut with cut checkering, semi-gloss finish; Grade V has high-grade walnut.
Features: Reproduction of the Winchester Model 12. Has high post floating rib with grooved sighting plane; cross-bolt safety in trigger guard; polished blue finish. Limited to 8500 Grade I and 4000 Grade V guns. Introduced 1988. Imported from Japan by Browning.
Price: Grade I, 28-ga. **$771.95**
Price: Grade V, 28-ga. **$1,246.00**
Price: Model 42 120-bore, Grade I **$799.95**
Price: Model 42 410-bore, Grade V **$1,360.00**

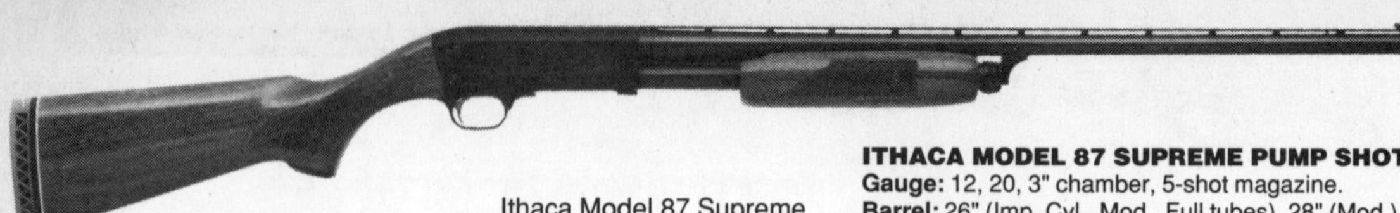

Ithaca Model 87 Supreme

ITHACA MODEL 87 SUPREME PUMP SHOTGUN
Gauge: 12, 20, 3" chamber, 5-shot magazine.
Barrel: 26" (Imp. Cyl., Mod., Full tubes), 28" (Mod.), 30" (Full). Vent. rib.
Weight: 6¾ to 7 lbs.
Stock: 14"x1½"x2¼". Full fancy-grade walnut, checkered p.g. and slide handle.
Sights: Raybar front.
Features: Bottom ejection, cross-bolt safety. Polished and blued engraved receiver. Reintroduced 1988. From Ithaca Acquisition Corp.
Price: $819.00
Price: M87 Camo Vent. (28", Mod. choke tube, camouflage finish) . $524.00
Price: M87 Field $458.00

Ithaca Model 87 Deluxe Pump Shotgun
Similar to the Model 87 Supreme Vent. Rib except comes with choke tubes in 25", 26", 28" (Mod.), 30" (Full). Standard-grade walnut.
Price: $495.00

Ithaca Model 87 Turkey Gun
Similar to the Model 87 Supreme except comes with 24" (fixed Full or Full choke tube) barrel, either Camoseal camouflage or matte blue finish, oiled wood, blued trigger.
Price: With fixed choke, blue $409.00
Price: With choke tube, blue $420.00
Price: With fixed choke, Camoseal $514.00
Price: With choke tube, Camoseal $525.00

ITHACA MODEL 87 DEERSLAYER SHOTGUN
Gauge: 12, 20, 3" chamber.
Barrel: 20", 25" (Special Bore), or rifled bore.
Weight: 6 to 6¾ lbs.
Stock: 14"x1½"x2¼". American walnut. Checkered p.g. and slide handle.
Sights: Raybar blade front on ramp, rear adjustable for windage and elevation, and grooved for scope mounting.
Features: Bored for slug shooting. Bottom ejection, cross-bolt safety. Reintroduced 1988. From Ithaca Acquisition Corp.
Price: $391.00
Price: Ultra Deerslayer (20-ga. only, 2¾", 5 lbs.) $444.00
Price: Deluxe Combo (12- and 20-ga. barrels) $549.00
Price: Deluxe $429.00
Price: Field Deerslayer $391.00

Ithaca Deerslayer II Rifled Shotgun
Similar to the Deerslayer except has rifled 25" barrel and checkered American walnut stock and forend with high-gloss finish and Monte Carlo comb. Solid frame construction. Introduced 1988.
Price: 12 or 20 . . . . . $525.00

Ithaca Model 87 Basic Field Combo
Similar to the Model 87 Supreme except comes with 28" (choke tubes) and 20" or 25" (Deer, Special Bore) barrels. Oil-finished wood, no checkering, blued trigger.
Price: $427.00
Price: As above except with rifled barrel $459.99

Ithaca Model 87 Ultra Field Pump Shotgun
Similar to the Model 87 Supreme except the receiver is made of aircraft-quality aluminum. Available in 12-ga., 2¾" chamber or 20-ga., 2¾" chamber, 25" (Mod.) with choke tube. Weight is 5 lbs. (20-ga.), 6 lbs. (12-ga.). Reintroduced 1988.
Price: $481.00
Price: Ultra Deluxe $514.00

MOSSBERG MODEL 835 ULTI-MAG PUMP
Gauge: 12, 3½" chamber.
Barrel: 24", 28", Accu-Mag with four choke tubes for steel or lead shot.
Weight: 7¾ lbs.
Length: 48½" overall.
Stock: 14"x1½"x2½". Walnut-stained hardwood or camo synthetic; both have recoil pad.
Sights: White bead front, brass mid-bead.
Features: Shoots 2¾", 3" or 3½" shells. Backbored barrel to reduce recoil, improve patterns. Ambidextrous thumb safety, twin extractors, dual slide bars. Mossberg Cablelock included. Introduced 1988.
Price: Blue, wood stock $430.00
Price: Camo finish, synthetic stock $460.00
Price: National Wild Turkey Federation 1991 Edition (Realtree camo) $498.00

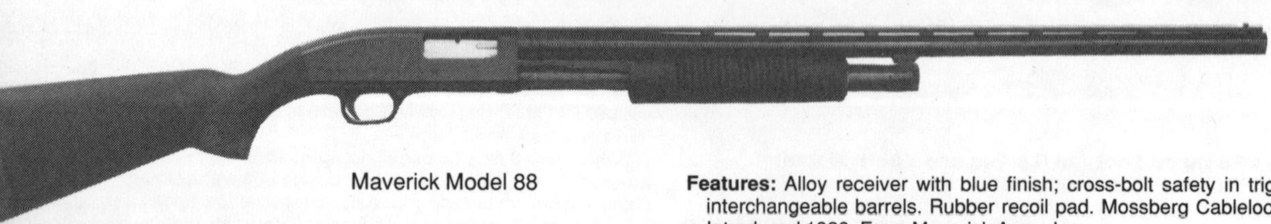

Maverick Model 88

MAVERICK MODEL 88 PUMP SHOTGUN
Gauge: 12, 3" chamber.
Barrel: 28" (Mod.), plain or vent. rib; 30" (Full), plain or vent. rib.
Weight: 7¼ lbs. **Length:** 48" overall with 28" bbl.
Stock: Black synthetic with ribbed synthetic forend.
Sights: Bead front.
Features: Alloy receiver with blue finish; cross-bolt safety in trigger guard; interchangeable barrels. Rubber recoil pad. Mossberg Cablelock included. Introduced 1989. From Maverick Arms, Inc.
Price: 28" or 30", plain barrel $196.00
Price: As above, vent. rib $218.00
Price: 24" bbl. (Cyl.), rifle sights $218.00
Price: 28", vent., with one Full steel shot choke tube $237.00
Price: Model 91, 28" plain bbl., 3½" chamber $316.00
Price: Combo, 18½" (Cyl.) and 28" (Mod.), plain bbl. $240.00
Price: Combo, 18½" (Cyl., plain) and 28" (Mod., Vent.) $266.00

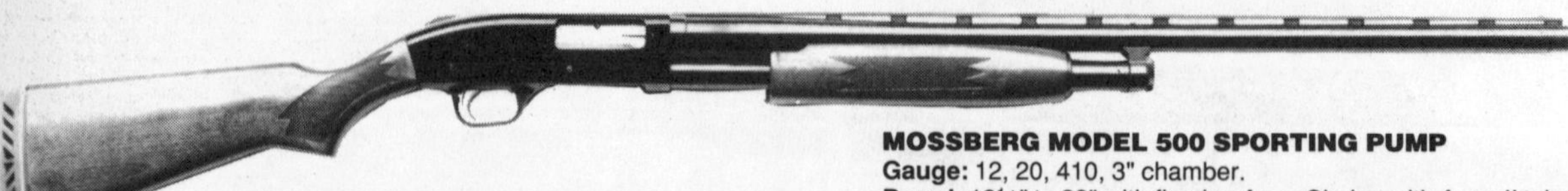

Mossberg Model 500 Sporting

MOSSBERG MODEL 500 SPORTING PUMP
Gauge: 12, 20, 410, 3" chamber.
Barrel: 18½" to 28" with fixed or Accu-Choke, with Accu-II tubes or Accu-Steel tubes for steel shot, plain or vent. rib.
Weight: 6¼ lbs. (410), 7¼ lbs. (12).
Length: 48" overall (28" barrel).
Stock: 14"x1½"x2½". Walnut-stained hardwood. Checkered grip and forend.
Sights: White bead front, brass mid-bead.
Features: Ambidextrous thumb safety, twin extractors, disconnecting safety, dual action bars. Mossberg Cablelock included. From Mossberg.
Price: From about $326.00
Price: Sporting Combos (field barrel and Slugster barrel), from . . . $326.00

Mossberg Model 500 Camo Pump
Same as the Model 500 Sporting Pump except 12-gauge only and entire gun is covered with special camouflage finish. Receiver drilled and tapped for scope mounting. Comes with q.d. swivel studs, swivels, camouflage sling, Mossberg Cablelock.
Price: From about $355.00
Price: Camo Combo (as above with extra Slugster barrel), from about $390.00

Mossberg 500 Trophy

MOSSBERG MODEL 500 TROPHY SLUGSTER
Gauge: 12, 3" chamber.
Barrel: 24", rifled bore. Plain (no rib).
Weight: 7¼ lbs. **Length:** 44" overall.
Stock: 14" pull, 1⅜" drop at heel. Walnut-stained hardwood; Dual comb design for proper eye positioning with or without scoped barrels. Recoil pad and q.d. swivel studs.
Features: Ambidextrous thumb safety, twin extractors, dual slide bars. Comes with scope mount. Mossberg Cablelock included. Introduced 1988.
Price: Rifled bore, with scope mount $379.00
Price: Rifled bore, rifle sights $349.00

NEW ENGLAND FIREARMS PUMP SHOTGUN
Gauge: 12, 3" chamber, 6-shot magazine.
Barrel: 26", 28", screw-in choke tubes. Vent. rib.
Weight: About 7 lbs. **Length:** NA.
Stocks: Walnut-finished hardwood.
Features: Bottom ejection; dual action bars; cross-bolt safety; takedown action. Blue finish. Introduced 1991. From New England Firearms Co., Inc.
Price: . . . . NA

New England Firearms Slug Gun
Same as the Pump Shotgun except has 20" barrel, Cyl. bore, ramp-type front sight and fully adjustable rear. Receiver drilled and tapped for scope mounts. Blue finish. Introduced 1991.
Price: . . . . NA
Price: Police Riot Gun (18½", Cyl. bore, bead sight) . . . . NA

Remington 870 Wingmaster

REMINGTON 870 WINGMASTER
Gauge: 12, 3" chamber.
Barrel: 26", 28", 30" (Rem Chokes).
Weight: 7¼ lbs.
Length: 46½" overall (26" bbl.).
Stock: 14"x2½"x1". American walnut with satin or high-gloss finish, cut-checkered p.g. and forend. Rubber buttpad.
Sights: Ivory bead front, metal mid-bead.
Features: Double action bars; cross-bolt safety; blue finish. Available in right- or left-hand style. Introduced 1986.
Price: $450.00
Price: Left-hand (28" only) $519.00
Price: Deer Gun (rifle sights, 20" bbl., fixed choke) $411.00
Price: Deer Gun, left-hand, Monte Carlo stock $493.00
Price: LW-20 20-ga., vent. rib, 26", 28" (Rem Choke) $450.00

Remington 870 Wingmaster Small Gauges
Same as the standard Model 870 Wingmaster except chambered for 20-ga. (2¾" and 3"), 28-ga., and 410-bore. The 20-ga. available with 26", 28" vent. rib barrel with Rem Choke tubes, high-gloss or satin wood finish; 28 and 410 available with 25" Full or Mod. fixed choke, satin finish only.
Price: 20-ga. $450.00
Price: 20-ga. Deer Gun, rifle sights $411.00
Price: Cantilever Deer Barrel with sling, swivels, scope rings, Monte Carlo stock $496.00
Price: 28 and 410 . . . . $497.00

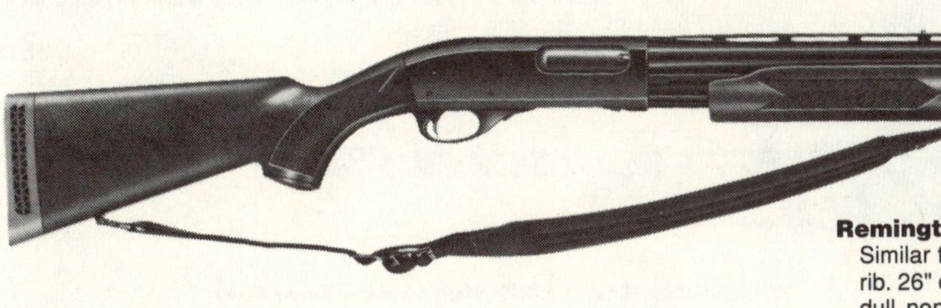
Remington 870 SPS-T Turkey

Remington 870 TC Trap
Same as the Model 870 except 12-ga. only, 30" Rem Choke, vent. rib barrel, Ivory front and white metal middle beads. Special sear, hammer and trigger assembly. 14⅜"x1½"x1⅞" stock with recoil pad. Hand fitted action and parts. Weight 8 lbs.
Price: Model 870TC Trap, Rem Choke, about $612.00
Price: TC Trap with Monte Carlo stock, about $626.00

Remington 870 Special Purpose Magnum
Similar to the Model 870 except chambered only for 12-ga., 3" shells, vent. rib. 26" or 28" Rem Choke barrel. All exposed metal surfaces are finished in dull, non-reflective black. Wood has an oil finish. Comes with padded Cordura 2" wide sling, quick-detachable swivels. Chrome-lined bores. Dark recoil pad. Introduced 1985.
Price: About $450.00
Price: With synthetic stock, forend (SPS) $344.00
Price: Magnum-Turkey (synthetic stock, forend) SPS-T $358.00

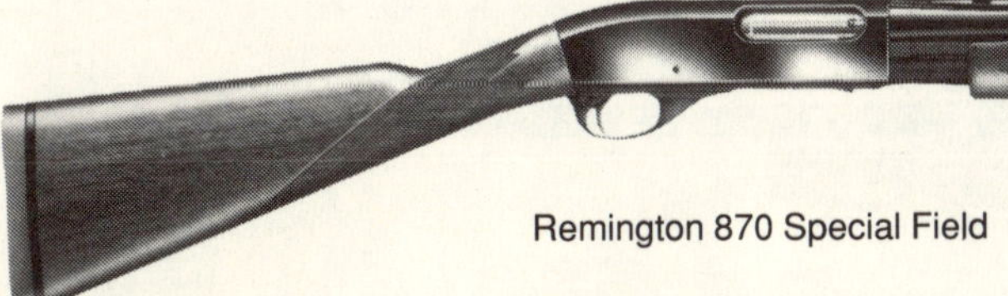
Remington 870 Special Field

Remington 870 Special Field
Similar to the standard Model 870 except comes with 21" barrel only, 3" chamber, choked Imp. Cyl., Mod., Full and Rem Choke; 12-ga. weighs 6¾ lbs., LW-20 weighs 6 lbs.; has straight-grip stock, shorter forend, both with cut checkering. Vent. rib barrel only. Introduced 1984.
Price: 12- or 20-ga., Rem Choke, about $450.00

Remington 870 Special Purpose Deer Gun
Similar to the 870 Wingmaster except available with 20" barrel with rifled and Imp. Cyl. choke tubes; rifle sights or cantilever scope mount with rings. Metal has black, non-glare finish, satin finish on wood. Recoil pad, detachable sling of camo Cordura nylon. Introduced 1989.
Price: With rifle sights, Monte Carlo stock $438.00
Price: With scope mount and rings, Monte Carlo stock $496.00

Remington 870 High Grades
Same as 870 except better walnut, hand checkering. Engraved receiver and barrel. Vent. rib. Stock dimensions to order.
Price: 870D, about $2,383.00
Price: 870F, about $4,910.00
Price: 870F with gold inlay, about $7,364.00

Remington 870 Express Turkey

Remington 870 Express

Similar to the 870 Wingmaster except has a walnut-toned hardwood stock with solid, black recoil pad and pressed checkering on grip and forend. Outside metal surfaces have a black oxide finish. Comes with 26" or 28" vent. rib barrel with a Mod. Rem Choke tube. Introduced 1987.

Price: **$263.00**
Price: Express Combo (with extra 20" Deer barrel) **$358.00**
Price: Express 20-ga., 28" with Mod. Rem Choke tubes **$263.00**

Remington 870 Express Turkey

Same as the Model 870 Express except comes with 3" chamber, 21" vent. rib turkey barrel and Extra-Full Rem Choke Turkey tube; 12-ga. only. Introduced 1991.

Price: **$277.00**

Remington Model 870 Express Youth Gun

Same as the Model 870 Express except comes with 12½" length of pull, 21" barrel with Mod. Rem Choke tube. Hardwood stock with low-luster finish. Introduced 1991.

Price: **$263.00**

Remington 870 Cantilever

Remington 870 Express Rifle-Sighted Deer Gun

Same as the Model 870 Express except comes with 20" barrel with fixed Imp. Cyl. choke, open iron sights, Monte Carlo stock. Introduced 1991.

Price: **$255.00**

Remington 870 Express Cantilever Deer Gun

Same as the Model 870 Express except comes with 20" barrel with rifled and Imp. Cyl. Rem Choke tubes designed for slugs or buckshot. Includes barrel-mounted cantilever scope mount, scope rings, sling and swivels, Monte Carlo stock. Introduced 1991.

Price: **$333.00**

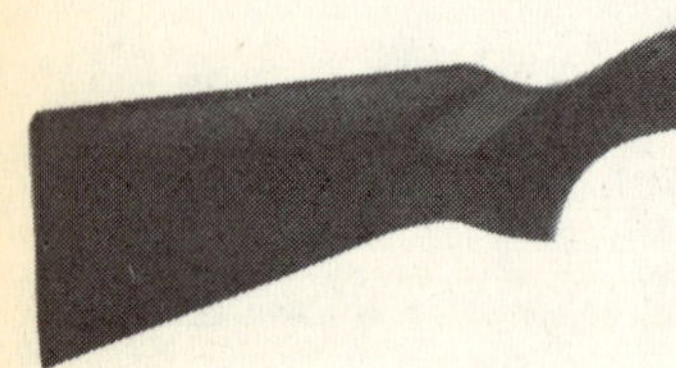

Winchester Model 1300

Winchester Model 1300 Waterfowl Pump

Similar to the 1300 Featherweight except in 3" 12-ga. only, 28" vent. rib barrel with Winchoke system; stock and forend of walnut with low-luster finish. All metal surfaces have special non-glare matte finish. Comes with sling. Introduced 1985.

Price: Walnut stock **$367.00**
Price: With brown laminated stock **$367.00**

WINCHESTER MODEL 1300 FEATHERWEIGHT PUMP

Gauge: 12 and 20, 3" chamber, 5-shot capacity.
Barrel: 22", 26", 28", vent. rib, with Full, Mod., Imp. Cyl. Winchoke tubes.
Weight: 6⅜ lbs.
Length: 42⅝" overall.
Stock: American walnut, with deep cut checkering on pistol grip, traditional ribbed forend; high luster finish.
Sights: Metal bead front.
Features: Twin action slide bars; front-locking rotary bolt; roll-engraved receiver; blued, highly polished metal; cross-bolt safety with red indicator. Introduced 1984. From U.S. Repeating Arms Co., Inc.

Price: About **$355.00**
Price: Model 1300 Ladies/Youth, 22" vent. rib **$338.00**

Winchester Model 1300 Rifled Slug

Winchester Model 1300 Turkey Gun

Similar to the standard Model 1300 Featherweight except 12-ga. only, 30" barrel with Mod., Full and Extra Full Winchoke tubes, matte finish wood and metal. Comes with recoil pad, Cordura sling and swivels.

Price: With WinCam green camo laminated stock, about **$391.00**
Price: National Wild Turkey Federation #2 edition **$411.00**

Winchester Model 1300 Slug Hunter Deer Gun

Same as the Model 1300 except has rifled 22" barrel, WinTuff laminated stock or walnut, rifle-type sights. Introduced 1990.

Price: Walnut stock **$403.00**
Price: Laminated stock **$403.00**
Price: Whitetails Unlimited model **$423.00**

Winchester Model 1300 Slug Hunter

Winchester Model 1300 Slug Hunter

Similar to the Model 1300 except in 12-ga. only with smooth bore 22" barrel, with adjustable open sights. Comes with Imp. Cyl. and Sabot choke tubes. Receiver is drilled and tapped for scope mounting, and comes with bases. Walnut stock and forend with cut checkering. Introduced 1990. From U.S. Repeating Arms Co., Inc.

Price: **$413.00**

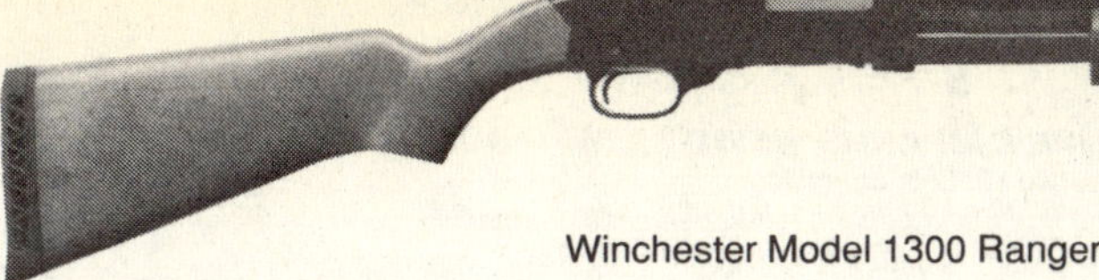
Winchester Model 1300 Ranger

Winchester Model 1300 Ranger Pump Gun Combo & Deer Gun
Similar to the standard Ranger except comes with two barrels: 22" (Cyl.) deer barrel with rifle-type sights and an interchangeable 28" vent. rib Winchoke barrel with Full, Mod. and Imp. Cyl. choke tubes. Drilled and tapped; comes with rings and bases. Available in 12- and 20-gauge 3" only, with recoil pad. Introduced 1983.
Price: With two barrels **$333.00**
Price: 12- or 20-ga., 22" (Cyl.) **$281.00**
Price: 12-ga., 22" rifled barrel **$305.00**
Price: 12-ga., 22" (Imp. Cyl., rifled sabot tubes) **$316.00**
Price: Combo 12-ga. with 18" (Cyl.) and 28" (Mod. tube) **$346.00**

WINCHESTER MODEL 1300 RANGER PUMP GUN
Gauge: 12 or 20, 3" chamber, 5-shot magazine.
Barrel: 26", 28" vent. rib with Full, Mod., Imp. Cyl. Winchoke tubes.
Weight: 7 to 7¼ lbs.
Length: 48⅝" to 50⅝" overall.
Stock: Walnut-finished hardwood with ribbed forend.
Sights: Metal bead front.
Features: Cross-bolt safety, black rubber recoil pad, twin action slide bars, front-locking rotating bolt. From U.S. Repeating Arms Co., Inc.
Price: Vent. rib barrel, Winchoke, about **$277.00**

Winchester Model 1300 Ranger Ladies/Youth Pump Gun
Similar to the standard Ranger except chambered only for 3" 20-ga., 22" vent. rib barrel with Winchoke tubes (Full, Mod., Imp. Cyl.). Weighs 6½ lbs., measures 41⅝" o.a.l. Stock has 13" pull length and gun comes with discount certificate for full-size stock. Introduced 1983. From U.S. Repeating Arms Co., Inc.
Price: Vent. rib barrel, Winchoke **$294.00**
Price: With walnut stock **$338.00**
Price: National Wild Turkey Federation #1 . . . . **$411.00**

SHOTGUNS—OVER/UNDERS

Includes a variety of game guns and guns for competitive shooting.

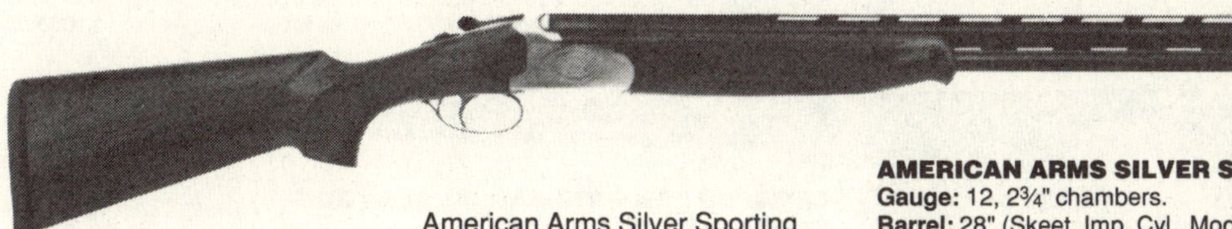
American Arms Silver Sporting

AMERICAN ARMS SILVER I O/U
Gauge: 12, 20, 28, 410, 3" chamber (28 has 2¾").
Barrel: 26" (Imp. Cyl. & Mod., all gauges), 28" (Mod. & Full, 12, 20).
Weight: About 6¾ lbs.
Stock: 14⅛"x1⅜"x2⅜". Checkered walnut.
Sights: Metal bead front.
Features: Boxlock action with scroll engraving, silver finish. Single selective trigger, extractors. Chrome-lined barrels. Manual safety. Rubber recoil pad. Introduced 1987. Imported from Italy and Spain by American Arms, Inc.
Price: 12- or 20-gauge **$489.00**
Price: 28 or 410 . . . . **$549.00**

AMERICAN ARMS SILVER SPORTING O/U
Gauge: 12, 2¾" chambers.
Barrel: 28" (Skeet, Imp. Cyl., Mod., Full choke tubes).
Weight: 7⅜ lbs. **Length:** 45½" overall.
Stock: 14⅜"x1½"x2⅜". Figured walnut, cut checkering; Sporting Clays quick-mount buttpad.
Sights: Target bead front.
Features: Boxlock action with single selective trigger, automatic selective ejectors; special broadway channeled rib; vented barrel rib; chrome bores. Chrome-nickel finish on frame, with engraving. Introduced 1990. Imported from Spain by American Arms, Inc.
Price: **$819.00**

American Arms Silver Lite O/U
Similar to the Silver I except has lightweight alloy receiver with blue finish and engraving. Available in 12- or 20-gauge only. Single selective trigger, automatic selective ejectors. Comes with 26" barrel with Imp. Cyl., Mod., Full choke tubes. Introduced 1990. Imported by American Arms, Inc.
Price: **$699.00**

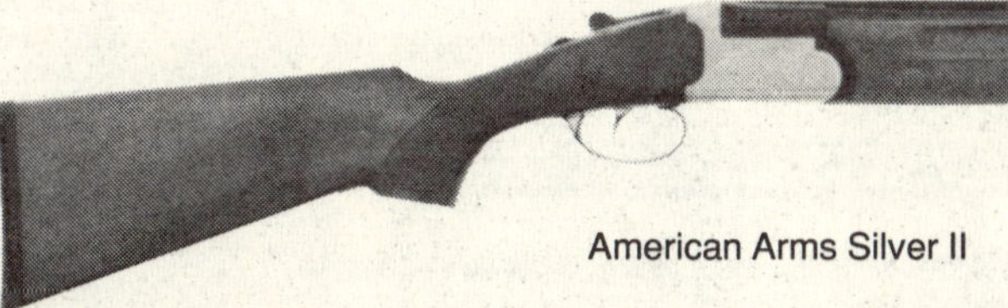
American Arms Silver II

AMERICAN ARMS/FRANCHI SPORTING HUNTER O/U SHOTGUN
Gauge: 12, 3" chambers.
Barrel: 28" (Skeet, Imp. Cyl., Mod., Full choke tubes).
Weight: 7 lbs.
Stock: 14¼"x1½"x2⅜". Figured walnut with cut checkering, semigloss finish; schnabel forend tip. Solid black recoil pad.
Features: Boxlock action with polished blue finish, gold accents. Single selective trigger, automatic selective ejectors, automatic safety. Introduced 1989. Imported from Italy by American Arms, Inc.
Price: **$1,249.99**

American Arms Silver II Shotgun
Similar to the Silver I except 26" barrel (Imp. Cyl., Mod., Full choke tubes, 12- and 20-ga.), 28" (Imp. Cyl., Mod., Full choke tubes, 12-ga. only), 26" (Imp. Cyl. & Mod. fixed chokes, 28 and 410), 26" two-barrel set (Imp. Cyl. & Mod., fixed, 28 and 410); automatic selective ejectors. Weight is about 6 lbs., 15 oz. (12-ga., 26").
Price: **$629.00**
Price: Two-barrel set (28, 410) **$998.00**

American Arms/Franchi Lightweight Hunter
Similar to the Sporting Hunter except comes in 12- or 20-gauge (2¾" chambers), 26" barrels with four Franchoke choke tubes. Weighs 6 lbs. Introduced 1989. Imported from Italy by American Arms, Inc.
Price: 12 or 20 . . . . **$1,209.00**

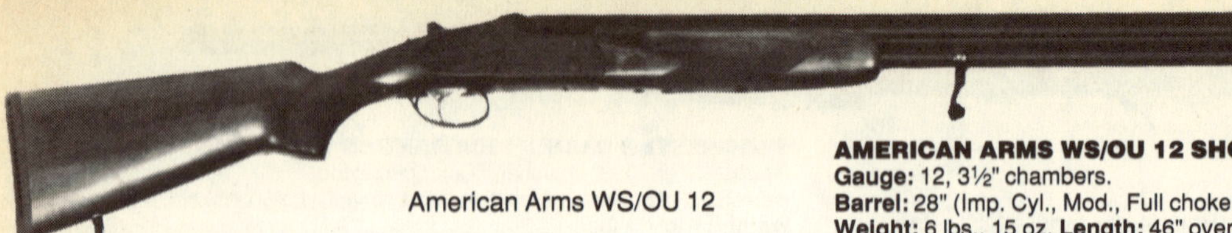
American Arms WS/OU 12

AMERICAN ARMS WS/OU 12 SHOTGUN

Gauge: 12, 3½" chambers.
Barrel: 28" (Imp. Cyl., Mod., Full choke tubes).
Weight: 6 lbs., 15 oz. **Length:** 46" overall.
Stock: 14⅛"x1⅛"x2⅜". European walnut with cut checkering, black vented recoil pad, matte finish.
Features: Boxlock action with single selective trigger, automatic selective ejectors; chrome bores. Matte metal finish. Imported by American Arms, Inc.
Price: **$639.00**

American Arms WT/OU 10 Shotgun

Similar to the WS/OU 12 except chambered for 10-gauge 3½" shell, 26" (Full & Full, choke tubes) barrel. Single selective trigger, extractors. Non-reflective finish on wood and metal. Imported by American Arms, Inc.
Price: **$859.00**

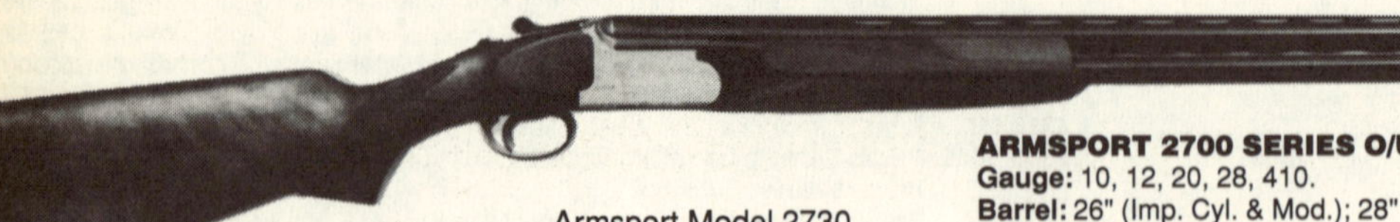
Armsport Model 2730

ARMSPORT 2700 SERIES O/U

Gauge: 10, 12, 20, 28, 410.
Barrel: 26" (Imp. Cyl. & Mod.); 28" (Mod. & Full); vent. rib.
Weight: 8 lbs.
Stock: European walnut, hand-checkered p.g. and forend.
Features: Single selective trigger, automatic ejectors, engraved receiver. Imported by Armsport. Contact Armsport for complete list of models.
Price: M2733/2735 (Boss-type action, 12, 20, extractors) **$750.00**
Price: M2741 (as above with ejectors) **$810.00**
Price: M2730/2731 (as above with single trigger, screw-in chokes) **$1,010.00**
Price: M2705 (410 bore, 26" Imp. & Mod., double triggers) **$750.00**
Price: M2742 Sporting Clays (12-ga., 28", choke tubes) **$900.00**
Price: M2744 Sporting Clays (20-ga., 26", choke tubes) **$900.00**
Price: M2750 Sporting Clays (12-ga., 28", choke tubes, sideplates) **$1035.00**
Price: M2751 Sporting Clays (20-ga., 26", choke tubes, sideplates) **$1035.00**

ARMSPORT 2700 O/U GOOSE GUN

Gauge: 10, 3½" chambers.
Barrel: 32" (Full & Full).
Weight: About 9.8 lbs.
Stock: European walnut.
Features: Boss-type action; double triggers; extractors. Introduced 1986. Imported from Italy by Armsport.
Price: Fixed chokes **$1,175.00**

Armsport 2900 Tri-Barrel

ARMSPORT 2900 TRI-BARREL SHOTGUN

Gauge: 12, 3" or 3½" chambers.
Barrel: 28" (Imp., Mod., Full on 3"; Mod., Full, Full on 3½").
Weight: 7¾ lbs.
Stock: European walnut.
Features: Has three barrels. Top-tang barrel selector; double triggers; silvered, engraved frame. Introduced 1986. Imported from Italy by Armsport.
Price: **$3,400.00**

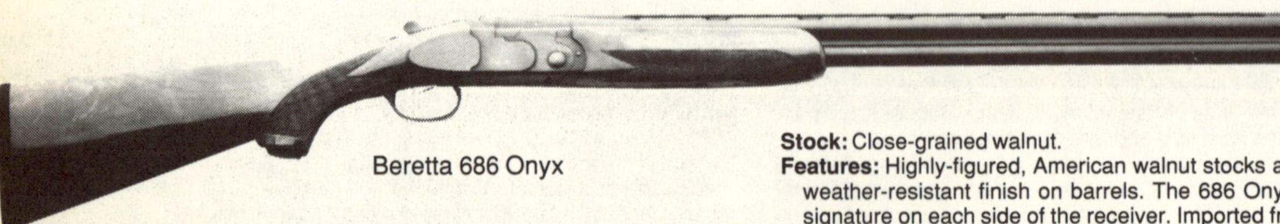
Beretta 686 Onyx

BERETTA OVER/UNDER FIELD SHOTGUNS

Gauge: 12, 20, 28, and 410 bore, 2¾", 3" and 3½" chambers.
Barrel: 26" and 28" (fixed chokes or Mobilchoke tubes).
Stock: Close-grained walnut.
Features: Highly-figured, American walnut stocks and forends, and a unique, weather-resistant finish on barrels. The 686 Onyx bears a gold P. Beretta signature on each side of the receiver. Imported from Italy by Beretta U.S.A.
Price: 686 Onyx **$1,225.00**
Price: 686 two bbl. set **$1,840.00**
Price: 686 Field **$1,225.00**
Price: 687L Field **$1,655.00**
Price: 687 EL **$2,740.00**
Price: 687 EELL . . . . **$4,015.00** to **$4,455.00**

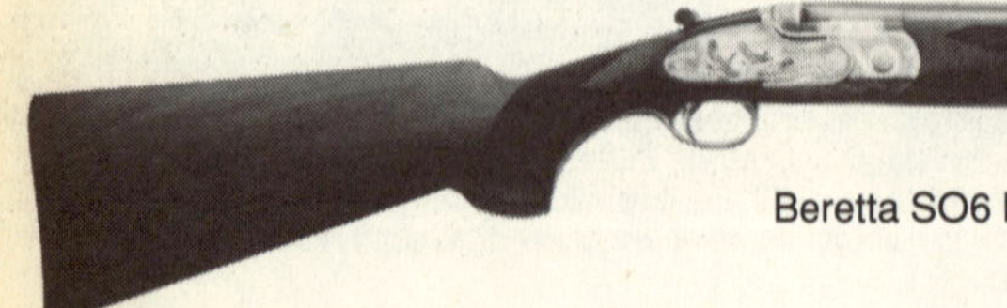
Beretta SO6 EELL

BERETTA MODEL SO5, SO6, SO9 SHOTGUNS

Gauge: 12, 2¾" chambers.
Barrel: To customer specs.
Stock: To customer specs.
Features: SO5—Trap, Skeet and Sporting Clays models SO5 and SO5 EELL; SO6—SO6 and SO6 EELL are field models. SO6 has a case-hardened or silver receiver with contour hand engraving. SO6 EELL has hand-engraved receiver in a fine floral or "fine English" pattern or game scene, with bas-relief chisel work and gold inlays. SO6 and SO6 EELL are available with sidelocks removable by hand. Imported from Italy by Beretta U.S.A.
Price: SO5 Trap, Skeet, Sporting **$11,500.00**
Price: SO5 Combo, two-bbl. set **$14,800.00**
Price: SO6 Trap, Skeet, Sporting **$15,500.00**
Price: SO6 EELL Field, custom specs **$25,550.00**
Price: SO9 (12, 20, 28, 410, 26", 28", 30", any choke) **$27,350.00**

Consult our Directory pages for the location of firms mentioned.

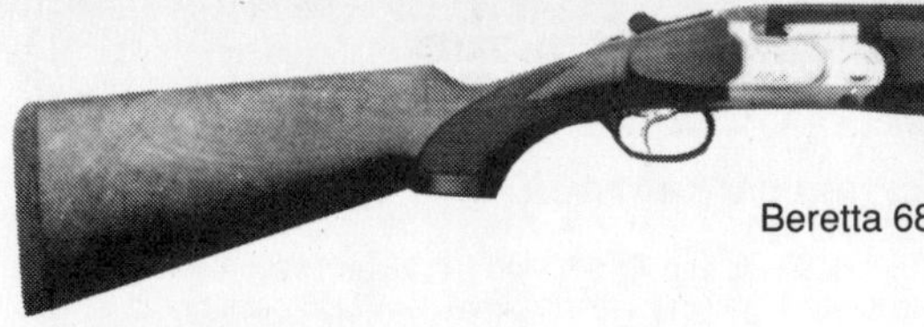

Beretta 682 Sporting

BERETTA SPORTING CLAYS SHOTGUNS
Gauge: 12 and 20, 2¾" chambers.
Barrel: 28", 30", Mobilchoke.
Stock: Close-grained walnut.
Sights: Luminous front sight and center bead.
Features: Equipped with Beretta Mobilchoke flush-mounted screw-in choke tube system. Models vary according to grade, from field-grade Beretta 686 Sporting with its floral engraving pattern, to competition-grade Beretta 682 Sporting with its brushed satin finish and adjustable length of pull to the 687 Sporting with intricately hand-engraved game scenes, fine line, deep-cut checkering. Imported from Italy by Beretta U.S.A.
Price: 686 Sporting **$1,735.00**
Price: 682 Sporting, 30" **$2,260.00**
Price: 682 Super Sport, 28", 30", tapered rib **$2,400.00**
Price: 687 Sporting **$2,285.00**
Price: 687 Sporting (20-gauge) **$2,285.00**
Price: 687 EELL Sporter (hand engraved sideplates, deluxe wood) **$4,200.00**
Price: 686 English Course Sporting, 2¾" chambers, 28" **$1,800.00**
Price: 687 English Course Sporting, 2¾" chambers, 28" **$2,355.00**
Price: 682 Sporting Combo, 28" and 30" **$3,025.00**
Price: 686 Sporting Combo, 28" and 30" **$2,320.00**
Price: 687 Sporting Combo, 28" and 30" **$3,060.00**

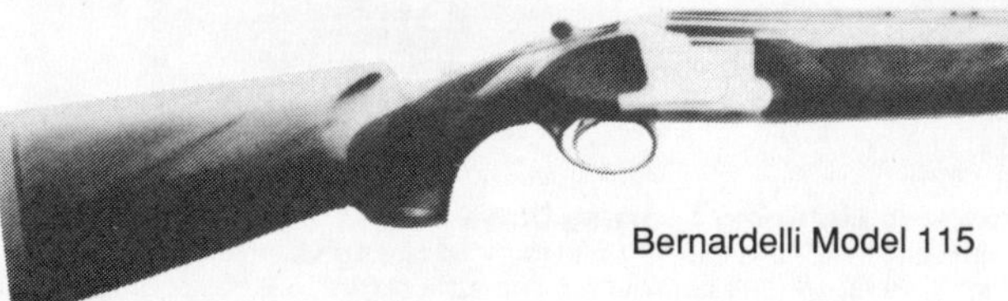

Bernardelli Model 115

Bernardelli Model 115 Over/Under Shotgun
Similar to the Model 192 except designed for competition shooting with thicker barrel walls, specially designed stock with anatomical grip. Leather-faced recoil pad and schnabel forend on Sporting Clays and Skeet guns. Concave top rib, ventilated middle rib. Imported from Italy by Magnum Research.
Price: Model 115 S (inclined-plane locking, ejectors, selective or non-selective trigger, Multichoke standard on Sporting Clays) **$3,920.00**

BABY BRETTON OVER/UNDER SHOTGUN
Gauge: 12 or 20, 2¾" chambers.
Barrel: 27½" (Cyl., Imp. Cyl., Mod., Full choke tubes).
Weight: About 5 lbs.
Stock: Walnut, checkered pistol grip and forend, oil finish.
Features: Receiver slides open on two guide rods, is locked by a large thumb lever on the right side. Extractors only. Light alloy barrels. Imported from France by Mandall Shooting Supplies.
Price: **$895.00**

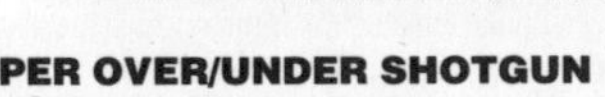

BRNO SUPER OVER/UNDER SHOTGUN
Gauge: 12, 2¾" or 3" chambers.
Barrel: 27½" (Full & Mod.).
Weight: 7 lbs., 4 oz. (Field). **Length:** 44" overall.
Stock: Walnut, with raised cheekpiece.
Features: Sidelock action with double safety interceptor sears; double triggers on Field model; automatic selective ejectors; engraved sideplates. Trap and Skeet models available. Imported from Czechoslovakia by T.D. Arms.
Price: **$899.00**

BRNO ZH 301 OVER/UNDER SHOTGUN
Gauge: 12, 2¾" or 3" chambers.
Barrel: 27½" (Full & Mod.).
Weight: 7 lbs. **Length:** 44½" overall.
Stock: Walnut.
Features: Boxlock action with acid-etch engraving; double triggers. Imported from Czechoslovakia by T.D. Arms.
Price: **$599.00**

BERETTA SERIES 682 COMPETITION OVER/UNDERS
Gauge: 12, 2¾" chambers.
Barrel: Skeet—26" and 28"; trap—30" and 32", Imp. Mod. & Full and Mobilchoke; trap mono shotguns—32" and 34" Mobilchoke; trap top single guns—32" and 34" Full and Mobilchoke; trap combo sets—from 30" O/U, 32" unsingle to 32" O/U, 34" top single.
Stock: Close-grained walnut, hand checkered.
Sights: Luminous front sight and center bead.
Features: Trap Monte Carlo stock has deluxe trap recoil pad. Various grades available; contact Beretta U.S.A. for details. Imported from Italy by Beretta U.S.A.
Price: 682 Skeet **$2,180.00**
Price: 682 Trap **$2,160.00**
Price: 682 Trap Mono shotguns **$2,965.00**
Price: 682 Trap Top Single shotguns **$2,300.00**
Price: 682 Trap Combo sets . . . . **$2,915.00** to **$2,965.00**
Price: 682 Pigeon Silver **$2,400.00**
Price: 687 EELL Trap . . . . **$4,045.00** to **$5,120.00**
Price: 687 EELL Skeet (4-bbl. set) **$7,105.00**
Price: 682 Super Skeet (adjustable comb and butt pads, bbl. porting) **$2,535.00**
Price: 682 Super Trap (adjustable comb and butt pad, bbl. porting) . . . . **$2,505.00** to **$3,380.00**

BERNARDELLI MODEL 192 MS-MC O/U SHOTGUN
Gauge: 12, 2¾" or 3" chambers.
Barrel: 25½" (Imp. Cyl. & Imp. Mod., Cyl. & Mod.), 26¾" (Imp. Cyl. & Imp. Mod., Mod. & Full), 28" (Mod. & Full), 29½" (Imp. Mod. & Full); or with Multichoke tubes.
Weight: About 7 lbs.
Stock: 14"x1⅜"x2⅜". Hand checkered European walnut. English or pistol grip style.
Features: Boxlock action; single selective trigger. Silvered, engraved action. Imported from Italy by Magnum Research.
Price: With Multichokes **$1,833.00**
Price: Model 192 Waterfowler (3½" chambers, three Multichoke tubes) **$1,958.00**
Price: Model 192 MS (Sporting Clays, non-selective or selective trigger) **$2,307.00**
Price: Model 220 MS (similar to M192 except 20-ga., different frame style) **$1,812.00**

BRNO CZ 581 OVER/UNDER SHOTGUN
Gauge: 12, 2¾" or 3" chambers.
Barrel: 28" (Full & Mod.).
Weight: 7 lbs., 6 oz. **Length:** 45½" overall.
Stock: Turkish walnut with raised cheekpiece.
Features: Boxlock action; automatic selective ejectors; automatic safety; sling swivels; vent. rib; double triggers. Imported from Czechoslovakia by T.D. Arms.
Price: **$649.00**

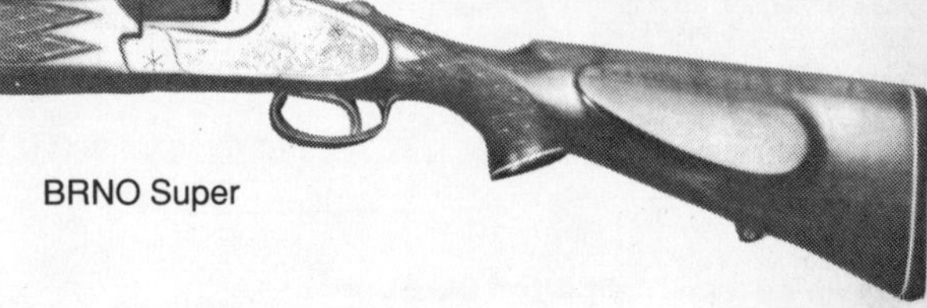

BRNO Super

BRNO 500 OVER/UNDER SHOTGUN
Gauge: 12, 2¾" chambers.
Barrel: 27½" (Full & Mod.).
Weight: 7 lbs. **Length:** 44½" overall.
Stock: Walnut, with raised cheekpiece.
Features: Boxlock action with ejectors; double triggers; acid-etched engraving. Imported from Czechoslovakia by T.D. Arms.
Price: **$629.00**

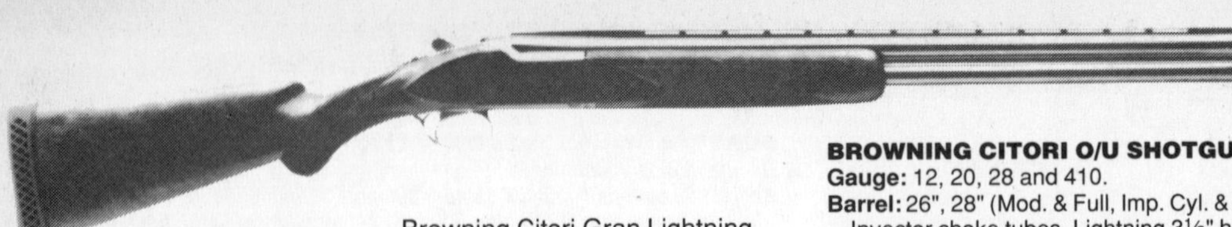

Browning Citori Gran Lightning

Browning Micro Citori Lightning
Similar to the standard Citori 20-ga. Lightning except scaled down for smaller shooter. Comes with 24" barrels with Invector choke system, 13¾" length of pull. Weighs about 6 lbs., 3 oz. Introduced 1991.
Price: **$1,120.00**

Browning Citori O/U Trap Models
Similar to standard Citori except 12 gauge only; 30", 32" ported or non-ported (Full & Full, Imp. Mod. & Full, Mod. & Full) or Invector PLUS, 34" single barrel in Combo Set (Full, Imp. Mod., Mod.), or Invector model; Monte Carlo cheek piece (14⅜"x1⅜"x1⅜"x2"); fitted with trap-style recoil pad; conventional target rib and high post target rib.
Price: Grade I, Invector PLUS, ported bbls., with hard case **$2,035.00**
Price: As above, non-ported bbls., with hard case **$2,010.00**
Price: Grade I, Invector, high post target rib **$1,195.00**
Price: Grade III, Invector, high post target rib **$1,700.00**
Price: Grade VI, Invector, high post target rib **$2,400.00**

BROWNING CITORI O/U SHOTGUN
Gauge: 12, 20, 28 and 410.
Barrel: 26", 28" (Mod. & Full, Imp. Cyl. & Mod.), in 28 and 410. Also offered with Invector choke tubes. Lightning 3½" has Invector PLUS back-bored barrels.
Weight: 6 lbs., 8 oz. (26" 410) to 7 lbs., 13 oz. (30" 12-ga.).
Length: 43" overall (26" bbl.).
Stock: Dense walnut, hand checkered, full p.g., beavertail forend. Field-type recoil pad on 12-ga. field guns and trap and Skeet models.
Sights: Medium raised beads, German nickel silver.
Features: Barrel selector integral with safety, automatic ejectors, three-piece takedown. Imported from Japan by Browning. Contact Browning for complete list of models and prices.
Price: Grade I, Hunting, Invector, 12 and 20 . . . . **$1,065.00**
Price: Grade III, Invector, 12 and 20 . . . . **$1,565.00**
Price: Grade VI, Hunting, Invector, 12 and 20 . . . . **$2,250.00**
Price: Grade I, Hunting, 28 and 410, fixed chokes **$1,055.00**
Price: Grade III, Lightning, 28 and 410, fixed chokes **$1,740.00**
Price: Grade VI, 28 and 410, high post rib, fixed chokes **$2,435.00**
Price: Grade I, Lightning, Invector, 12, 16, 20 . . . . **$1,095.00**
Price: Grade I, Hunting, 28", 30" only, 3½", Invector PLUS **$1,135.00**
Price: Grade III, Lightning, Invector, 12, 16, 20 . . . . **$1,595.00**
Price: Grade VI, Lightning, Invector, 12, 16, 20 . . . . **$2,285.00**
Price: Gran Lightning, 26", 28", Invector **$1,485.00**

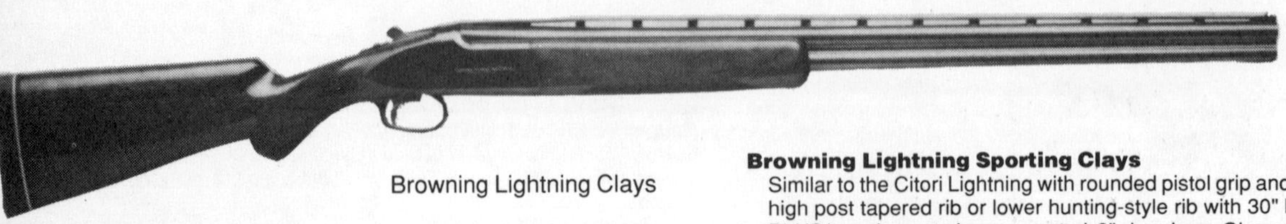

Browning Lightning Clays

Browning Citori O/U Skeet Models
Similar to standard Citori except 26", 28" (Skeet & Skeet) only; stock dimensions of 14⅜"x1½"x2", fitted with Skeet-style recoil pad; conventional target rib and high post target rib.
Price: Grade I Invector (high post rib) **$1,200.00**
Price: Grade I, 28 and 410 (high post rib) **$1,210.00**
Price: Grade III, 12 and 20 (high post rib) **$1,700.00**
Price: Grade VI, 12 and 20 (high post rib) **$2,400.00**
Price: Four barrel Skeet set—12, 20, 28, 410 barrels, with case, Grade I only **$4,000.00**
Price: Grade III, four-barrel set (high post rib) **$4,550.00**
Price: Grade VI, four-barrel set (high post rib) **$5,100.00**
Price: Grade I, three-barrel set **$2,780.00**
Price: Grade III, three-barrel set **$3,200.00**
Price: Grade VI, three-barrel set **$3,925.00**

Browning Lightning Sporting Clays
Similar to the Citori Lightning with rounded pistol grip and classic forend. Has high post tapered rib or lower hunting-style rib with 30" back-bored Invector PLUS barrels, ported or non-ported, 3" chambers. Gloss stock finish, radiused recoil pad. Has "Lightning Sporting Clays Edition" engraved and gold filled on receiver. Introduced 1989.
Price: Low-rib, ported **$1,225.00**
Price: High-rib, ported **$1,280.00**
Price: Low-rib, non-ported **$1,170.00**
Price: High-rib, non-ported **$1,225.00**

Browning Special Sporting Clays
Similar to the GTI except has full pistol grip stock with palm swell, gloss finish, 28", 30" or 32" barrels with back-bored Invector PLUS chokes (ported or non-ported); high post tapered rib. Also available as 28" and 30" two-barrel set. Introduced 1989.
Price: With ported barrels **$1,280.00**
Price: With non-ported barrels **$1,225.00**

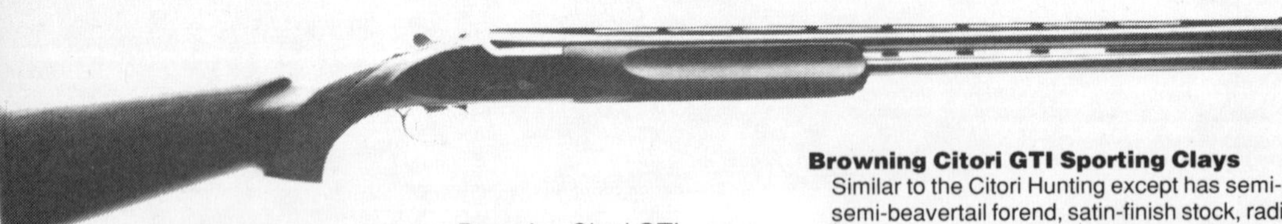

Browning Citori GTI

Browning Superlight Citori Over/Under
Similar to the standard Citori except available in 12, 20 with 24", 26" or 28" Invector barrels, 28 or 410 with 26" barrels choked Imp. Cyl. & Mod. or 28" choked Mod. & Full. Has straight grip stock, schnabel forend tip. Superlight 12 weighs 6 lbs., 9 oz. (26" barrels); Superlight 20, 5 lbs., 12 oz. (26" barrels). Introduced 1982.
Price: Grade I only, 28 or 410 . . . . **$1,115.00**
Price: Grade III, Invector, 12 or 20 . . . . **$1,600.00**
Price: Grade III, 28 or 410 . . . . **$1,750.00**
Price: Grade VI, Invector, 12 or 20 . . . . **$2,300.00**
Price: Grade VI, 28 or 410 . . . . **$2,450.00**
Price: Grade I Invector, 12 or 20 . . . . **$1,100.00**
Price: Grade I Invector, Upland Special (24" bbls.), 12 or 20 . . . **$1,100.00**

Browning Citori GTI Sporting Clays
Similar to the Citori Hunting except has semi-pistol grip with slightly grooved, semi-beavertail forend, satin-finish stock, radiused rubber buttpad. Has three interchangeable trigger shoes, trigger has three length of pull adjustments. Wide 13mm vent. rib, 28" or 30" barrels (ported or non-ported) with Invector PLUS choke tubes. Ventilated side ribs. Introduced 1989.
Price: With ported barrels **$1,295.00**
Price: With non-ported barrels **$1,240.00**

Browning Citori PLUS Trap Gun
Similar to the Grade I Citori Trap except comes only with 30" barrels with .745" over-bore, Invector PLUS choke system with Full, Imp. Mod. and Mod. choke tubes; high post, ventilated, tapered, target rib for adjustable impact from 3" to 12" above point of aim. Available with or without ported barrels. Select walnut stock has high-gloss finish, Monte Carlo comb, modified beavertail forend and is fully adjustable for length of pull, drop at comb and drop at Monte Carlo. Has Browning Recoil Reduction System. Comes with hard case. Introduced 1989.
Price: Grade I, with ported barrel **$2,035.00**
Price: Grade I, non-ported barrel **$2,010.00**

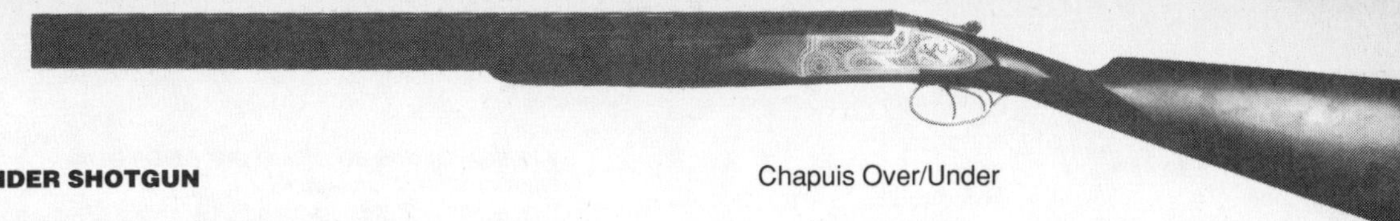

Chapuis Over/Under

CHAPUIS OVER/UNDER SHOTGUN

Gauge: 12, 16, 20.

Barrel: 22", 23.6", 26.8", 27.6", 31.5", chokes to customer specs.

Weight: 5 to 10 lbs. **Length:** NA.

Stock: French walnut, straight English or pistol grip.

Features: Double hook blitz system center sidelock action with notched action zone, automatic ejectors or extractors. Long trigger guard (most models), choice of raised solid rib, vent. rib or ultra light rib. Imported from France by Armes de Chasse.

Price: About **$4,000.00**

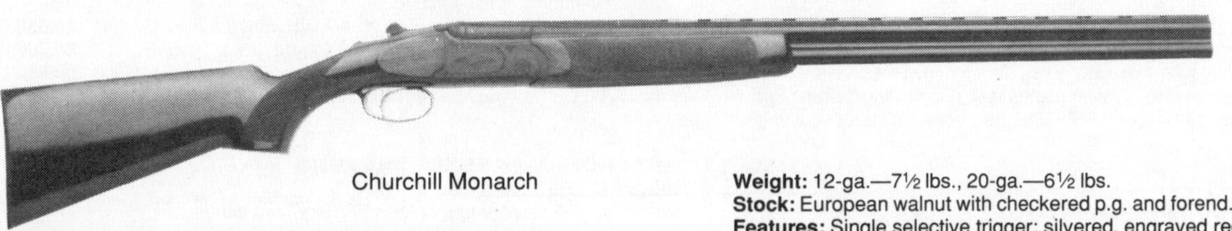

Churchill Monarch

CHURCHILL MONARCH OVER/UNDER SHOTGUNS

Gauge: 12 or 20, 28, 410, 3" chambers.

Barrel: 26" (410, Mod. & Full), 26" (Imp. Cyl. & Mod.), 28" (Mod. & Full). Chrome-lined.

Weight: 12-ga.—7½ lbs., 20-ga.—6½ lbs.

Stock: European walnut with checkered p.g. and forend.

Features: Single selective trigger; silvered, engraved receiver; vent. rib. Introduced 1986. Imported by Ellett Bros.

Price: 12- or 20-ga., silvered receiver **$549.95**

Price: 28-ga., silvered receiver **$599.95**

Price: 410-bore, 26" (Mod. & Full) **$609.95**

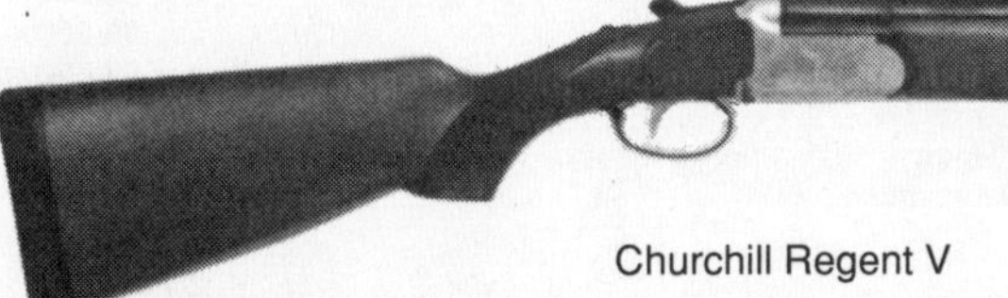

Churchill Regent V

Churchill Regent Competition Over/Under Shotguns

Similar to the Churchill Regent V except available with trap and Skeet stock dimensions. Trap available in 12-gauge with 30" barrels, choked Imp. Mod. & Full. Skeet is 12-gauge with 26" barrels choked Skeet & Skeet. Both have European walnut wood with schnabel forend, oil finish, silvered, engraved receiver, selective automatic ejectors, single selective trigger, 2¾" chambers. Introduced 1991.

Price: Trap **$999.95**

Price: Skeet **$969.95**

CHARLES DALY FIELD GRADE O/U

Gauge: 12 or 20, 3" chambers.

Barrel: 12- and 20- ga.—26" (Imp. Cyl. & Mod.), 12-ga.—28" (Mod. & Full).

Weight: 6 lbs., 15 oz. (12-ga.); 6 lbs., 10 oz. (20-ga.). **Length:** 43½" overall (26" bbl.).

Stock: 14⅛"x1⅜"x2⅜". Walnut with cut-checkered grip and forend. Black, vent. rubber recoil pad. Semi-gloss finish.

Features: Boxlock action with manual safety; extractors; single selective trigger. Color case-hardened receiver with engraving. Introduced 1989. Imported from Europe by Outdoor Sports Headquarters.

Price: **$475.00**

CHURCHILL WINDSOR IV OVER/UNDER SHOTGUNS

Gauge: 12, 20, 28, 410, 3" chambers.

Barrel: 26" (Skeet & Skeet, Imp. Cyl. & Mod.), 28" (Mod. & Full), 30" (Mod. & Full, Full & Full), 12-ga.; 26" (Skeet & Skeet, Imp. Cyl. & Mod.), 28" (Mod. & Full), 20-ga.; 25", 26" (Imp. Cyl. & Mod.), 28" (Mod. & Full), 28-ga.; 24", 26" (Full & Full), 410 bore; or 27", 30" ICT choke tubes.

Stock: European walnut, checkered pistol grip, oil finish.

Features: Boxlock action with silvered, engraved finish; single selective trigger; automatic ejectors. Imported from Italy by Ellett Bros. Introduced 1984.

Price: Windsor IV, 12 and 20 . . . . **$849.95**

Price: Windsor IV, 28 and 410 . . . . **$799.95**

Churchill Regent V Over/Under Shotguns

Similar to the Windsor except better engraving; available only in 12- or 20-gauge (3" chambers), 28" barrels, with ICT interchangeable choke tubes (Imp. Cyl., Mod., Full). Dummy sideplates. Introduced 1984.

Price: Regent V, 12- or 20-ga. **$919.95**

Charles Daly Lux Over/Under

Similar to the Field Grade except available in 12, 20, 28, 410-bore, has automatic selective ejectors, antique silver finish on frame, and has choke tubes for Imp. Cyl., Mod. and Full. Introduced 1989.

Price: **$699.95**

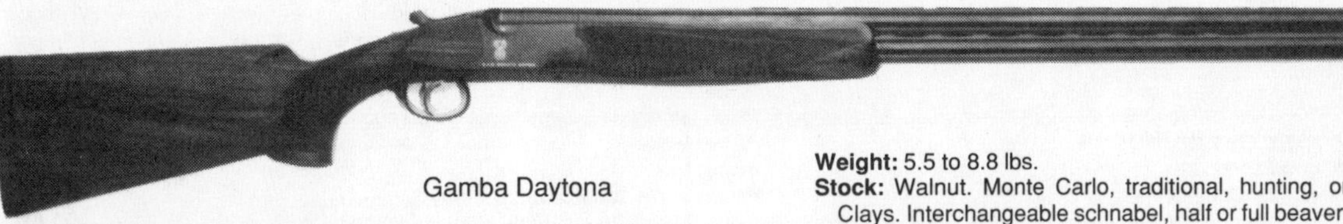

Gamba Daytona

GAMBA DAYTONA, DAYTONA TRAP O/U

Gauge: 12 and 20, 2¾" chambers.

Barrel: 26¾" (Cyl. & Cyl.), 28" (Mod. & Full), 29" (Mod. & Full, Imp. Mod. & Full), 32" (Full & Full).

Weight: 5.5 to 8.8 lbs.

Stock: Walnut. Monte Carlo, traditional, hunting, or special Skeet/Sporting Clays. Interchangeable schnabel, half or full beavertail.

Features: Boxlock action with shallow frame, automatic ejectors. Release trigger and interchangeable barrel sets available. SL models have engraved sideplates. Introduced 1990. Imported from Italy by Heckler & Koch, Inc.

Price: **$5,725.00**

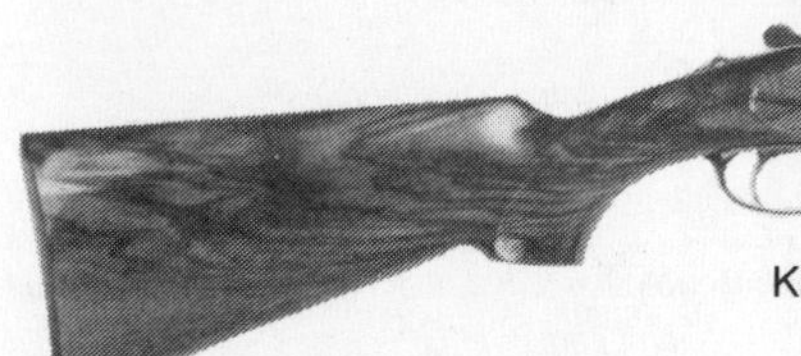

Kassnar Grade I

KASSNAR GRADE I O/U SHOTGUN

Gauge: 12, 20, 28, 410, 3" chambers.

Barrel: 26" (Imp. Cyl. & Mod.), 28" (Mod. & Full), 28" (choke tubes).

Weight: 6.5 to 7.5 lbs.

Stock: European walnut with checkered grip and forend.

Features: Boxlock action with single selective trigger; blued and engraved receiver; vent. rib. Imported by K.B.I., Inc.

Price: . . . . **$500.00** to **$750.00**

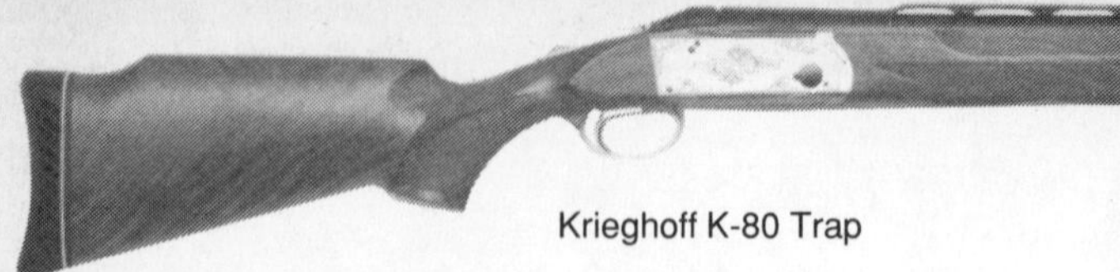
Krieghoff K-80 Trap

KRIEGHOFF K-80 LIVE BIRD SHOTGUN

Gauge: 12, 2¾" chambers.
Barrel: 28", 30" (Imp. Mod. & Super Full or choke tubes), 29" optional (Imp. Mod. & Special Full).
Weight: About 8 lbs.
Stock: Four stock dimensions available. Checkered walnut.
Features: Steel receiver with satin gray finish, engraving. Selective mechanical trigger adjustable for position. Ventilated step rib. Free-floating barrels. Comes with aluminum case. Introduced 1980. Imported from Germany by Krieghoff International, Inc.
Price: Standard grade **$5,950.00**

Krieghoff K-80 Four-Barrel Skeet Set
Similar to the Standard Skeet except comes with barrels for 12, 20, 28, 410. Comes with fitted aluminum case.
Price: Standard grade **$12,890.00**

Krieghoff K-80 International Skeet
Similar to the Standard Skeet except has ½" ventilated Broadway-style rib, special Tula chokes with gas release holes at muzzle. International Skeet stock. Comes in fitted aluminum case.
Price: Standard grade **$6,250.00**

Krieghoff K-80/RT Shotguns
Same as the standard K-80 shotguns except has a removable internally selective trigger mechanism. Can be considered an option on all K-80 guns of any configuration. Introduced 1990.
Price: RT (removable trigger) option on K-80 guns, add **$1,850.00**
Price: Extra trigger mechanisms **$1,450.00**

KRIEGHOFF K-80 O/U TRAP SHOTGUN

Gauge: 12, 2¾" chambers.
Barrel: 30", 32" (Imp. Mod. & Full or choke tubes).
Weight: About 8½ lbs.
Stock: Four stock dimensions or adjustable stock available; all have palm-swell grips. Checkered European walnut.
Features: Satin nickel receiver. Selective mechanical trigger, adjustable for position. Ventilated step rib. Introduced 1980. Imported from Germany by Krieghoff International, Inc.
Price: K-80 O/U (30", 32", Imp. Mod. & Full), from **$5,950.00**
Price: K-80 Unsingle (32", 34", Full), Standard, from **$6,700.00**
Price: K-80 Topsingle (34", Full), Standard, from **$6,550.00**
Price: K-80 Combo (two-barrel set), Standard, from **$8,595.00**

KRIEGHOFF K-80 SKEET SHOTGUN

Gauge: 12, 2¾" chambers.
Barrel: 28" (Skeet & Skeet, optional Tula or choke tubes).
Weight: About 7¾ lbs.
Stock: American Skeet or straight Skeet stocks, with palm-swell grips. Walnut.
Features: Satin gray receiver finish. Selective mechanical trigger adjustable for position. Choice of ventilated 8mm parallel flat rib or ventilated 8-12mm tapered flat rib. Introduced 1980. Imported from Germany by Krieghoff International, Inc.
Price: Standard, Skeet chokes **$5,880.00**
Price: As above, Tula chokes **$6,250.00**
Price: Lightweight model (weighs 7 lbs.), Standard **$5,650.00**
Price: Two-Barrel Set (tube concept), 12-ga., Standard **$9,990.00**
Price: Skeet Special (28", tapered flat rib, Skeet & Skeet choke tubes) **$5,995.00**

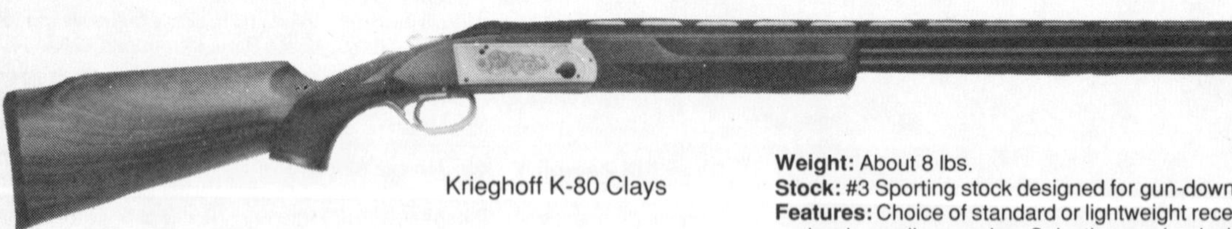
Krieghoff K-80 Clays

KRIEGHOFF K-80 SPORTING CLAYS O/U

Gauge: 12, 2¾" chambers.
Barrel: 28" or 30" with choke tubes.
Weight: About 8 lbs.
Stock: #3 Sporting stock designed for gun-down shooting.
Features: Choice of standard or lightweight receiver with satin nickel finish and classic scroll engraving. Selective mechanical trigger adjustable for position. Choice of tapered flat, 8mm parallel flat, or step-tapered barrel rib. Free-floating barrels. Aluminum case. Imported from Germany by Krieghoff International, Inc.
Price: Standard grade with five choke tubes **$6,350.00**

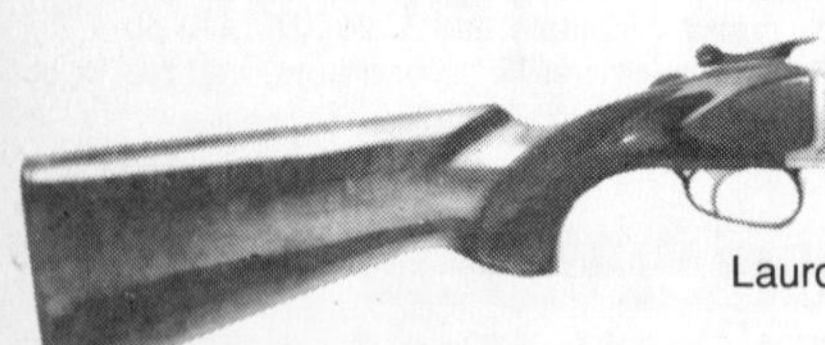
Laurona Super 85 MS

LAURONA SUPER MODEL OVER/UNDERS

Gauge: 12, 20, 2¾" or 3" chambers.
Barrel: 26", 28" (Multichoke), 29" (Multichokes and Full).
Weight: About 7 lbs.
Stock: European walnut. Dimensions vary according to model. Full pistol grip.
Features: Boxlock action, silvered with engraving. Automatic selective ejectors; choke tubes available on most models; single selective or twin single triggers; black chrome barrels. Has 5-year warranty, including metal finish. Imported from Spain by Galaxy Imports.
Price: Model 83 MG, 12- or 20-ga. **$1,540.00**
Price: Model 84S Super Trap (fixed chokes) **$1,920.00**
Price: Model 85 Super Game, 12- or 20-ga. **$1,575.00**
Price: Model 85 MS Super Trap (Full/Multichoke) **$1,970.00**
Price: Model 85 MS Super Pigeon **$1,890.00**
Price: Model 85 S Super Skeet, 12-ga. **$1,810.00**
Price: Model 85 MS Spec. Sporting, 12-ga. **$1,850.00**

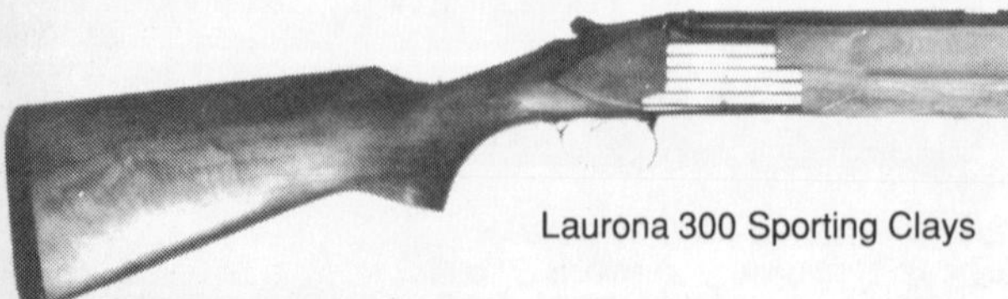
Laurona 300 Sporting Clays

Laurona Silhouette 300 Trap
Same gun as the Silhouette 300 Sporting Clays except has 29" barrels, trap stock dimensions of 14⅜"x1⁷⁄₁₆"x1⅝", weighs 7 lbs., 15 oz. Available with flush or knurled Multichokes.
Price: **$1,790.00**

LAURONA SILHOUETTE 300 SPORTING CLAYS

Gauge: 12, 2¾" or 3" chambers.
Barrel: 28", 29" (Multichoke tubes, flush-type or knurled).
Weight: 7 lbs., 12 oz.
Stock: 14⅜"x1⅜"x2½". European walnut with full pistol grip, beavertail forend. Rubber buttpad.
Features: Selective single trigger, automatic selective ejectors. Introduced 1988. Imported from Spain by Galaxy Imports.
Price: **$1,760.00**
Price: Silhouette Ultra-Magnum, 3½" chambers **$1,760.00**

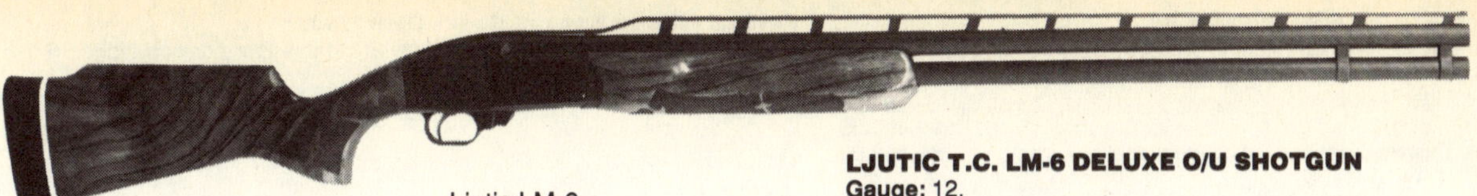
Ljutic LM-6

Ljutic Four-Barrel Skeet Set
LM-6 over/under 12-ga. frame with matched set of four 28" barrels in 12, 20, 28 and 410. Ljutic Paternator chokes and barrel are integral. Stock is to customer specs, of fine American or French walnut with EX (or Extra) Fancy checkering.
Price: Four-barrel set **$26,995.00**

LJUTIC T.C. LM-6 DELUXE O/U SHOTGUN
Gauge: 12.
Barrel: 28" to 34", choked to customer specs for live birds, trap, International Trap.
Weight: To customer specs.
Stock: To customer specs. Oil finish, hand checkered.
Features: Custom-made gun. Hollow-milled rib, pull or release trigger, pushbutton opener in front of trigger guard. From Ljutic Industries.
Price: Super Deluxe LM-6 O/U **$9,995.00**
Price: Over/under Combo (interchangeable single barrel, two trigger guards, one for single trigger, one for doubles) **$16,995.00**
Price: Extra over/under barrel sets, 29"-32" **$5,995.00**

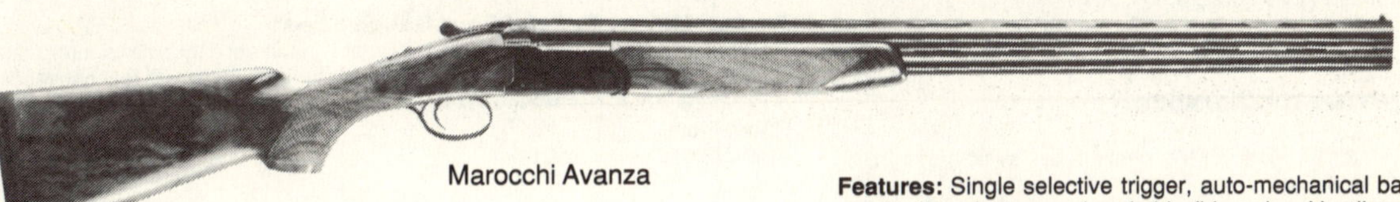
Marocchi Avanza

MAROCCHI AVANZA O/U SHOTGUN
Gauge: 12 and 20, 3" chambers.
Barrel: 26" (Imp. Cyl. & Mod. or Imp. Cyl., Mod., Full Interchokes); 28" (Mod. & Full or Imp. Cyl. Mod., Full Interchokes).
Weight: 6 lbs., 6 oz. to 6 lbs., 13 oz.
Stock: 14"x2¼"x1½". Select walnut with cut checkering. Recoil pad.
Features: Single selective trigger, auto-mechanical barrel cycling, automatic selective ejectors, unbreakable firing pins. Ventilated top and middle ribs. Automatic safety. Introduced 1990. Imported from Italy by Precision Sales International.
Price: 12-ga., 26" or 28", fixed chokes **$999.00**
Price: As above, with Interchokes **$1,099.00**
Price: 20-ga., 26" or 28", fixed chokes **$1,019.00**
Price: As above, with Interchokes **$1,119.00**
Price: Sporting Clays (12-ga. only, 28" Interchokes, trigger adj. for length) **$1,189.00**

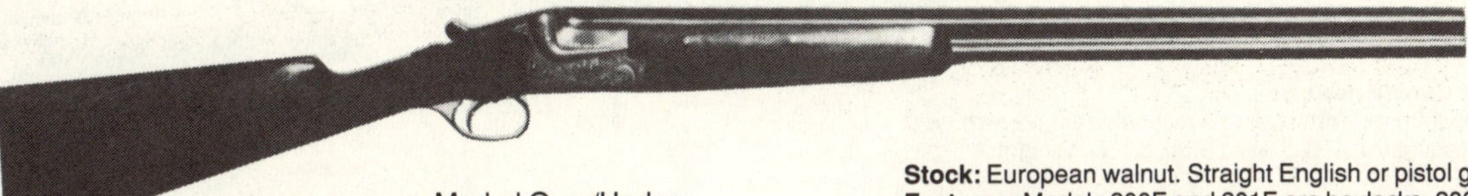
Merkel Over/Under

MERKEL OVER/UNDER SHOTGUNS
Gauge: 12, 16, 20, 28, 410, 2¾", 3" chambers.
Barrel: 26", 26¾", 28" (standard chokes).
Weight: 6 to 7 lbs.
Stock: European walnut. Straight English or pistol grip.
Features: Models 200E and 201E are boxlocks, 203E and 303E are sidelocks. All have auto. ejectors, articulated front triggers. Auto. safety, selective and non-selective triggers optional. Imported from Germany by Armes de Chasse.
Price: 200E, about **$3,700.00**
Price: 201E, about **$4,800.00**
Price: 203E (sidelock), about **$9,500.00**
Price: 303E (sidelock), about**$16,500.00**

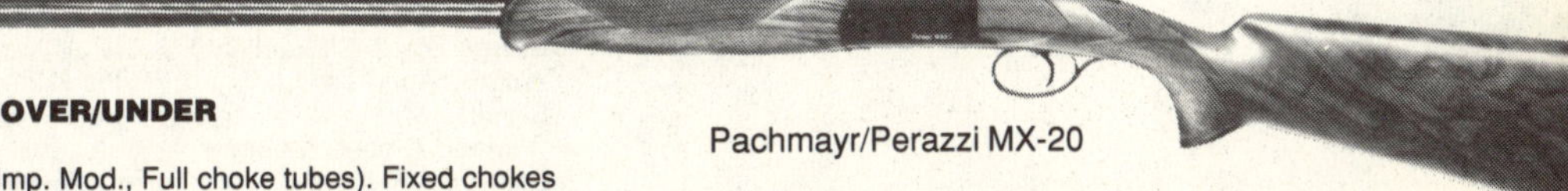
Pachmayr/Perazzi MX-20

PACHMAYR/PERAZZI MX-20 OVER/UNDER
Gauge: 20, 3" chambers.
Barrel: 26" (Cyl., Imp. Cyl., Mod., Imp. Mod., Full choke tubes). Fixed chokes available.
Weight: 6 lbs., 8 oz.
Stock: 14½"x1⅜"x2¼"x1½"; select European walnut with 26 lpi checkering, checkered butt.
Sights: Nickel silver front bead.
Features: Boxlock action, uses special 20-gauge frame. Carved schnabel-type forend. Single selective trigger, automatic selective ejectors, manual safety. Comes with lockable fitted case. Introduced 1986. From Pachmayr, Ltd.
Price: **$5,600.00**

Perazzi Grand American 88 Special
Similar to the MX8 except has tapered 7/16"x5/16" high ramped rib. Choked Imp. Mod. & Full, 29½" barrels.
Price: From **$6,700.00**
Price: Special Single (32" or 34" single barrel), from **$6,400.00**
Price: DB81 Special, from **$6,700.00**

PERAZZI MX8/MX8 SPECIAL TRAP, SKEET
Gauge: 12, 2¾" chambers.
Barrel: Trap—29½" (Imp. Mod. & Extra Full), 31½" (Full & Extra Full). Choke tubes optional. Skeet—27⅝" (Skeet & Skeet).
Weight: About 8½ lbs. (Trap); 7 lbs., 15 oz. (Skeet).
Stock: Interchangeable and custom made to customer specs.
Features: Has detachable and interchangeable trigger group with flat V springs. Flat 7/16" ventilated rib. Many options available. Imported from Italy by Perazzi U.S.A., Inc.
Price: From **$6,700.00**
Price: MX8 Special (adj. four-position trigger), from **$6,400.00**
Price: MX8 Special Single (32" or 34" single barrel, step rib), from **$6,400.00**
Price: MX8 Special Combo (o/u and single barrel sets), from . . . **$9,150.00**

Perazzi MX3 Special

Perazzi MX3 Special Single, Over/Under
Similar to the MX8 Special except has an adjustable four-position trigger, high 7/16"x5/16" rib, weighs 8½ lbs. Choked Mod. & Full.
Price: From **$6,000.00**
Price: MX3 Special Single (32" or 34" single barrel), from **$5,650.00**
Price: MX3 Special Combo (o/u and single barrel sets), from . . . **$7,950.00**

CAUTION: PRICES CHANGE, CHECK AT GUNSHOP.

Perazzi MX1, MX1B Special Over/Under

Similar to the MX8 except has ramped, tapered rib, interchangeable trigger assembly with leaf hammer springs, $27\frac{5}{8}$" barrels choked Imp. Mod. & Extra Full. Weight is 7 lbs., 12 oz.

Price: MX1, from **$6,400.00**
Price: MX1B (as above except has flat conventional rib), from . . **$6,400.00**

Perazzi Mirage Special Skeet Over/Under

Similar to the MX8 Skeet except has adjustable four-position trigger, Skeet stock dimensions.

Price: From **$6,700.00**

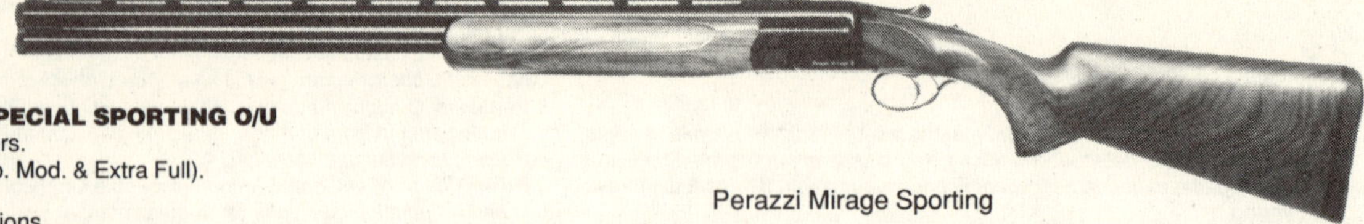

Perazzi Mirage Sporting

PERAZZI MIRAGE SPECIAL SPORTING O/U

Gauge: 12, $2\frac{3}{4}$" chambers.
Barrel: $27\frac{5}{8}$", $28\frac{3}{8}$" (Imp. Mod. & Extra Full).
Weight: 7 lbs., 12 oz.
Stock: Special specifications.
Features: Has single selective trigger; flat $\frac{7}{16}$"x$\frac{5}{16}$" vent. rib. Many options available. Imported from Italy by Perazzi U.S.A., Inc.
Price: **$8,050.00**

Perazzi Mirage Special Four-Gauge Skeet

Similar to the Mirage Sporting model except has Skeet dimensions, interchangeable, adjustable four-position trigger assembly. Comes with four barrel sets in 12, 20, 28, 410, flat $\frac{5}{16}$"x$\frac{5}{16}$" rib.

Price: From **$15,600.00**
Price: MX3 Special Set, from **$13,900.00**

PERAZZI MX12 HUNTING OVER/UNDER

Gauge: 12, $2\frac{3}{4}$" chambers.
Barrel: 26", $27\frac{5}{8}$", $28\frac{3}{8}$", $29\frac{1}{2}$" (Mod. & Full); choke tubes available in $27\frac{5}{8}$", $29\frac{1}{2}$" only (MX12C).
Weight: 7 lbs., 4 oz.
Stock: To customer specs; Interchangeable.
Features: Single selective trigger; coil springs used in action; schnabel forend tip. Imported from Italy by Perazzi U.S.A., Inc.
Price: From **$6,400.00**
Price: MX12C (with choke tubes), from **$6,750.00**

Consult our Directory pages for the location of firms mentioned.

Perazzi MX20C

Perazzi MX20 Hunting Over/Under

Similar to the MX12 except 20-ga. frame size. Available in 20, 28, 410 with $2\frac{3}{4}$" or 3" chambers. 26" standard, and choked Mod. & Full. Weight is 6 lbs., 6 oz.

Price: From **$6,800.00**
Price: MX20C (as above, 20-ga. only, choke tubes), from **$7,150.00**

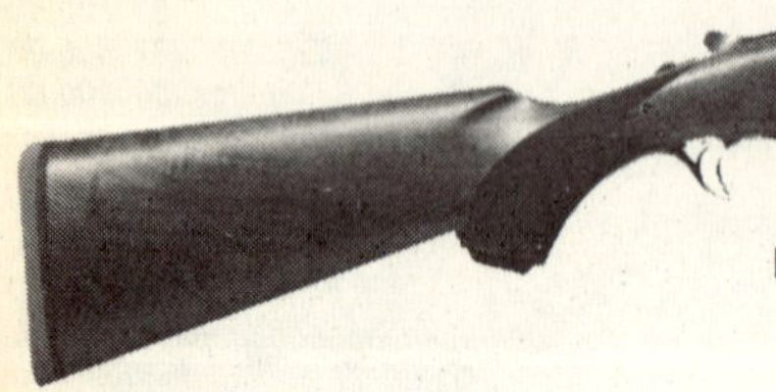

Ruger Red Label

RUGER RED LABEL O/U SHOTGUN

Gauge: 12 and 20, 3" chambers.
Barrel: 26", 28" (Skeet, Imp. Cyl., Full, Mod. Screw-in choke tubes).
Weight: About 7 lbs. (20-ga.); $7\frac{1}{2}$ lbs. (12-ga.). **Length:** 43" overall (26" barrels).
Stock: 14"x$1\frac{1}{2}$"x$2\frac{1}{2}$". Straight grain American walnut. Checkered p.g. and forend, rubber recoil pad.
Features: Automatic safety/barrel selector, stainless steel trigger and receiver. Patented barrel side spacers may be removed if desired. Available only with stainless receiver. 20-ga. introduced 1977; 12-ga. introduced 1982.
Price: **$1,102.50**

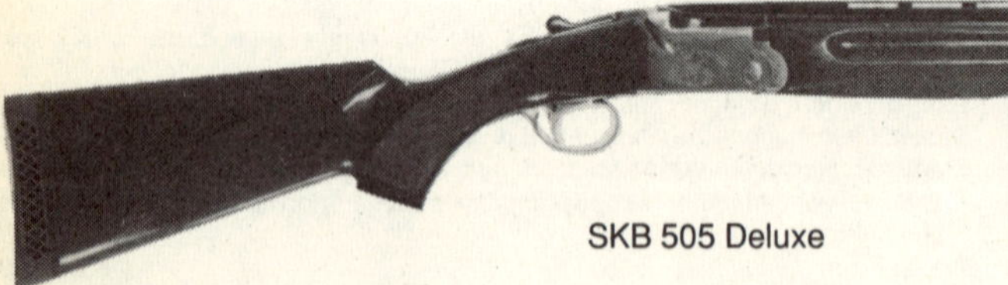

SKB 505 Deluxe

SKB MODEL 505 DELUXE OVER/UNDER SHOTGUN

Gauge: 12, $2\frac{3}{4}$" or 3"; 20, 3"; 28, $2\frac{3}{4}$"; 410, 3".
Barrel: 12-ga.—26", 28", 30", 32", 34" (Inter-Choke tube); 20-ga.—26", 28" (Inter-Choke tube); 28—26", 28" (Inter-Choke tube); 410—26", 28" (Imp. Cyl. & Mod., Mod. & Full).
Weight: 6.6 to 8.5 lbs.
Length: 43" to $51\frac{3}{8}$" overall.
Stock: $14\frac{1}{8}$"x$1\frac{1}{2}$"x$2\frac{3}{16}$". Hand checkered walnut with high-gloss finish. Target stocks available in standard and Monte Carlo.
Sights: Metal bead front (field), target style on Skeet, trap, Sporting Clays.
Features: Boxlock action; silver nitride finish with game scene engraving; manual safety, automatic ejectors, single selective trigger. Introduced 1987. Imported from Japan by G.U., Inc.
Price: Field **$995.00**
Price: Two-barrel Field Set (12 & 20 or 28 & 410) **$1,495.00**
Price: Trap, Skeet **$995.00**
Price: Two-barrel trap combo **$1,395.00**
Price: Sporting Clays model **$1,045.00**
Price: Skeet Set (20, 28, 410) **$2,195.00**

SKB Model 605 Over/Under Shotgun

Similar to the Model 505 Deluxe except has gold-plated trigger, semi-fancy American walnut stock, jeweled barrel block and fine engraving in silvered receiver, top lever, and trigger guard.

Price: Field **$1,195.00**
Price: Two-barrel Field Set (12 & 20 or 28 & 410) **$1,695.00**
Price: Trap, Skeet **$1,195.00**
Price: Two-barrel trap combo **$1,595.00**
Price: Sporting Clays **$1,245.00**
Price: Skeet Set (20, 28, 410) **$2,395.00**

SKB Model 885 Over/Under Trap, Skeet, Sporting Clays
Similar to the Model 605 except has engraved sideplates, top lever and trigger guard, semi-fancy American walnut stock.
Price: Field, Skeet/Trap $1,595.00
Price: Skeet Set (20, 28, 410) $2,995.00
Price: Trap Combo $2,195.00
Price: Field Set $2,195.00
Price: Sporting Clays $1,645.00

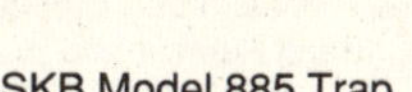

SKB Model 885 Trap

San Marco 12-Gauge

San Marco Field Special O/U Shotgun
Similar to the 12-ga. Wildfowler except in 12-, 20- and 28-gauge with 3" chambers, 26" (Imp. Cyl. & Mod.) or 28" (Full & Mod.) barrels. Stock dimensions of 14¼"x1½"x1½". Weight of 5½ to 6 lbs. Engraved, silvered receiver, vented top and middle ribs, single trigger. Introduced 1990. Imported from Italy by Cape Outfitters.
Price: $695.00

SAN MARCO 12-GA. WILDFOWLER SHOTGUN
Gauge: 12, 3½" chambers.
Barrel: 28" (Mod. & Mod., Full & Mod.), vented top and middle ribs.
Weight: 7 lbs., 12 oz.
Stock: 15"x1½"x2¼". Walnut, with checkered grip and forend.
Features: Chrome-lined bores with long forcing cones; single non-selective trigger; extractors on Standard, automatic ejectors on Deluxe; silvered, engraved action. Waterproof wood finish. Introduced 1990. Imported from Italy by Cape Outfitters.
Price: Standard $595.00
Price: Deluxe $695.00

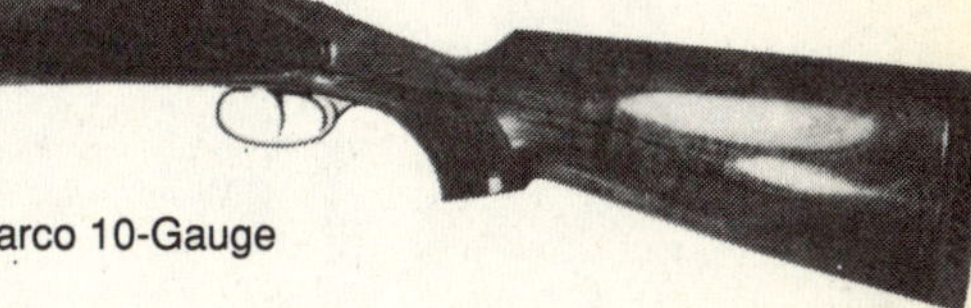

San Marco 10-Gauge

SAN MARCO 10-GAUGE O/U SHOTGUN
Gauge: 10, 3½" chambers.
Barrel: 28" (Mod. & Mod.), 32" (Mod. & Full). Chrome lined.
Weight: 9 to 9½ lbs.
Stock: 15"x1⅜"x2⅛". Walnut.
Features: Solid ⅜" barrel rib. Long forcing cones. Double triggers, extractors; Deluxe grade has automatic ejectors. Engraved receiver with game scenes, matte finish. Waterproof finish on wood. Introduced 1990. Imported from Italy by Cape Outfitters.
Price: Standard grade $795.00
Price: Deluxe grade $895.00

SAVAGE 312 FIELD O/U SHOTGUN
Gauge: 12, 3".
Barrel: 26", 28" (Imp. Cyl., Mod., Full choke tubes).
Weight: 7 lbs. **Length:** 43" overall (26" barrel).
Stock: Checkered walnut with ventilated recoil pad.
Features: Single trigger; satin chrome finished frame. Ventilated top and middle ribs. Introduced 1990. From Savage Arms.
Price: $680.00

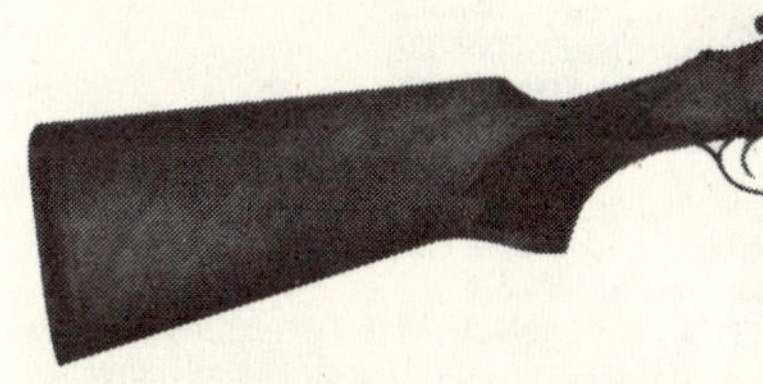

Savage 312 Clays

Savage 312SC Sporting Clays Shotgun
Similar to the Model 312F Field gun except has 28" barrels (Skeet 1, Skeet 2, Mod., Imp. Cyl., Mod., Full choke tubes), curved target-type recoil pad. Receiver marked with "Sporting Clays" on each side. Introduced 1990. From Savage Arms.
Price: $720.00

Savage 312T Trap Over/Under Shotgun
Similar to the Model 312 Field gun, except has 30" barrels (Full, Mod. choke tubes), measures 47" overall, weighs 7¼ lbs., and has checkered walnut Monte Carlo stock with rubber recoil pad. Introduced 1990. From Savage Arms.
Price: $700.00

Savage 320 Over/Under Shotgun
Similar to the Savage 312 except chambered for 20-gauge, 3" shells, has 26" barrels with Imp. Cyl., Mod. and Full choke tubes. Stock is high-gloss walnut with cut checkering, recoil pad. Weight is 6¾ lbs. Comes with gun lock, ear plugs, shooting glasses. Introduced 1991.
Price: . . . . NA

Techni-Mec SPL 640

STOEGER/IGA OVER/UNDER SHOTGUN
Gauge: 12, 20, 3" chambers.
Barrel: 26" (Full & Full, Imp. Cyl. & Mod.), 28" (Mod. & Full).
Weight: 6¾ to 7 lbs.
Stock: 14½"x1½"x2½". Oil-finished hardwood with checkered pistol grip and forend.
Features: Manual safety, single trigger, extractors only, ventilated top rib. Introduced 1983. Imported from Brazil by Stoeger Industries.
Price: $495.00

TECHNI-MEC MODEL SPL 640 FOLDING O/U
Gauge: 12, 16, 20, 28, 2¾" chambers; 410, 3" chambers.
Barrel: 26" (Mod. & Full).
Weight: 5½ lbs.
Stock: European walnut.
Features: Gun folds in half for storage, transportation. Chrome-lined barrels; ventilated rib; photo-engraved silvered receiver. Imported from Italy by L. Joseph Rahn, Mandall (double triggers only). Introduced 1984.
Price: Double triggers . . . . $389.00 to $500.00
Price: Single trigger $399.00
Price: Model SPL 642, double triggers (Rahn) $429.00
Price: Model SPL 642M, as above, single trigger (Rahn) $433.00

TECHNI-MEC MODEL SR 692 EM OVER/UNDER

Gauge: 12, 16, 20, 2¾" or 3" chambers.
Barrel: 26", 28", 30" (Mod., Full, Imp. Cyl., Cyl.).
Weight: 6½ lbs.
Stock: 14½"x1½"x2½". European walnut with checkered grip and forend.
Features: Boxlock action with dummy sideplates, fine game scene engraving; single selective trigger; automatic ejectors available. Contact importer for data on complete line. Imported from Italy by L. Joseph Rahn. Introduced 1984.
Price: **$1,086.00**
Price: Slug gun **$925.00**
Price: SR 690 Trap, Skeet **$988.00**
Price: SRL 694 Trap, Skeet **$1,428.00**
Price: SRL 695 Trap, Skeet **$1,322.00**
Price: SRL 702 Trap, Skeet **$1,765.00**
Price: SRL 802 Trap, Skeet **$1,171.00**

TECHNI-MEC MODEL 610 OVER/UNDER

Gauge: 10, 3½" chambers.
Barrel: 32" (Imp. Mod. & Full).
Stocks: Hand-checkered walnut.
Features: Single selective trigger; silvered engraved frame, blued barrels. Rubber recoil pad. Introduced 1991. Imported from Italy by Mandall Shooting Supplies.
Price: **$1,050.00**

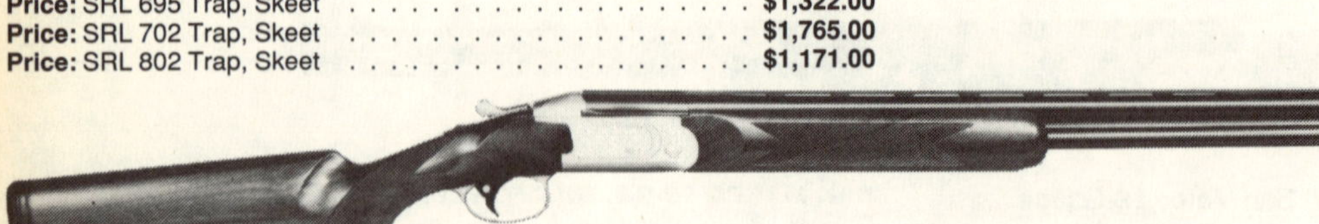

Tikka 412S Skeet

TIKKA MODEL 412S FIELD GRADE OVER/UNDER

Gauge: 12, 20, 3" chambers.
Barrel: 24", 26", 28", 30" with stainless steel screw-in chokes (Imp. Cyl, Mod., Imp. Mod., Full); 20-ga., 28" only.
Weight: About 7¼ lbs.
Stock: American walnut. Standard dimensions—13⁹⁄₁₀"x1½"x2⅖". Checkered p.g. and forend.
Features: Free interchangeability of barrels, stocks and forends into double rifle model, combination gun, etc. Barrel selector in trigger; auto. top tang safety; barrel cocking indicators. Introduced 1980. Imported from Italy by Valmet.
Price: Model 412S (ejectors) **$1,060.00**

Weatherby Athena V

WEATHERBY ATHENA O/U SHOTGUNS

Gauge: 12, 20, 28, 410, 3" chambers; 2¾" on Trap gun.
Action: Boxlock (simulated sidelock) top lever break-open. Selective auto ejectors, single selective trigger (selector inside trigger guard).
Barrel: Fixed choke, 12-, 20-ga.—26", 28" (Skeet & Skeet); IMC Multi-Choke tubes, 12, 20, 410, Field models—26" (Skeet, Imp. Cyl., Mod.), 28" (Imp. Cyl., Mod., Full), 30" (12-ga. only. Full, Mod., Full); O/U Trap models—30", 32" (Mod., Imp. Mod., Full).
Weight: 12-ga., 7⅜ lbs.; 20-ga. 6⅞ lbs.
Stock: American walnut, checkered p.g. and forend (14¼"x1½"x2½").
Features: Mechanically operated trigger. Top tang safety, Greener cross bolt, fully engraved receiver, recoil pad installed. IMC models furnished with three interchangeable flush-fitting choke tubes. Imported from Japan by Weatherby. Introduced 1982.
Price: Skeet, fixed choke **$1,750.00**
Price: 12- or 20-ga., IMC Multi-Choke, Field **$1,736.00**
Price: IMC Multi-Choke Trap **$1,756.00**
Price: Athena Grade V (more elaborate engraving), 12 and 20 . . **$2,175.00**
Price: Extra IMC Multi-Choke tubes **$18.50**
Price: Master Skeet Tube set
(12-ga. gun with six Briley tubes in 20, 28, 410) **$3,486.00**

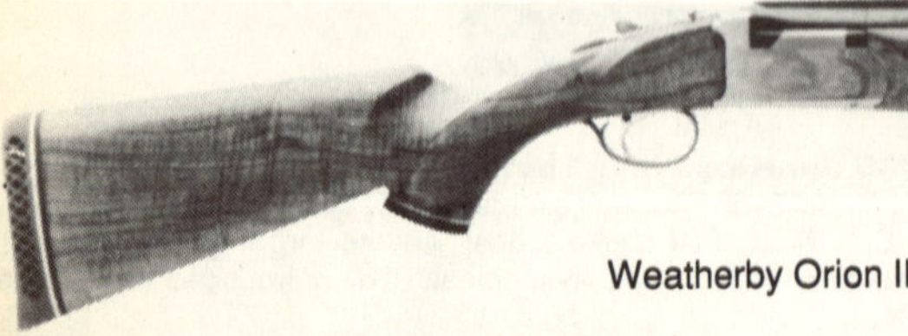

Weatherby Orion III

WEATHERBY ORION O/U SHOTGUNS

Gauge: 12, 20, 410, 3" chambers; 28, 2¾" chambers.
Barrel: Fixed choke, 12, 20, 28, 410—26", 28", 30" (Imp. Cyl. & Mod., Full & Mod., Skeet & Skeet); IMC Multi-Choke, 12, 20, Field models—26" (Imp. Cyl., Mod., Full, Skeet), 28" (Imp. Cyl., Mod., Full), 30" (Mod., Full); O/U Trap models—30", 32" (Imp. Mod., Mod., Full); Single bbl. Trap—32", 34" (Imp. Mod., Mod., Full).
Weight: 6½ to 9 lbs.
Stock: American walnut, checkered grip and forend. Rubber recoil pad. Dimensions for Field and Skeet models, 14¼"x1½"x2½".
Features: Selective automatic ejectors, single selective mechanical trigger. Top tang safety, Greener cross bolt. Orion I has plain blued receiver, no engraving; Orion II has engraved, blued receiver; Orion III has silver-gray receiver with engraving. Imported from Japan by Weatherby.
Price: Orion I, Field, 12 or 20, IMC **$938.00**
Price: Orion II, Field, 12 or 20, IMC **$1,094.00**
Price: Orion II, Field, 28 or 410, fixed chokes **$1,094.00**
Price: Orion II, Skeet, 12 or 20, fixed chokes **$1,106.00**
Price: Orion II, Trap, 12, IMC **$1,150.00**
Price: Orion III, Field, 12 or 20, IMC **$1,200.00**

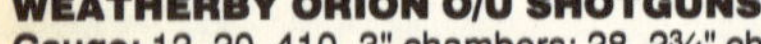

Weatherby Orion Clays

Weatherby Orion Sporting Clays

Similar to the standard Orion except in 12-gauge only with 28" barrels, IMC choke tubes with elongated forcing cones. Blued receiver with two 24 karat gold clay targets on the bottom of the receiver. Has a raised rib with center and front beads. Special stock dimensions of 14¼"x2¼"x1½"; rounded buttpad. Introduced 1991.
Price: . . . . **NA**

PIETRO ZANOLETTI MODEL 2000 FIELD O/U

Gauge: 12 only.
Barrel: 28" (Mod. & Full).
Weight: 7 lbs.
Stock: European walnut, checkered grip and forend.
Sights: Gold bead front.
Features: Boxlock action with auto ejectors, double triggers; engraved receiver. Imported from Italy by Mandall Shooting Supplies. Introduced 1984.
Price: **$895.00**

SHOTGUNS—SIDE BY SIDES

Variety of models for utility and sporting use, including some competitive shooting.

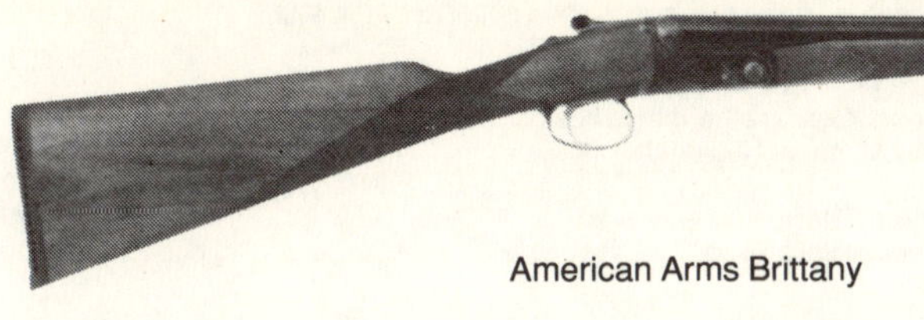

American Arms Brittany

AMERICAN ARMS BRITTANY SHOTGUN

Gauge: 12, 20, 3" chambers.
Barrel: 12-ga.—27"; 20-ga.—25" (Imp. Cyl., Mod., Full choke tubes).
Weight: 6 lbs., 7 oz. (20-ga.).
Stock: 14⅛"x1⅜"x2⅜". Hand-checkered walnut with oil finish, straight English-style with semi-beavertail forend.
Features: Boxlock action with case-color finish, engraving; single selective trigger, automatic selective ejectors; rubber recoil pad. Introduced 1989. Imported from Spain by American Arms, Inc.
Price: **$669.00**

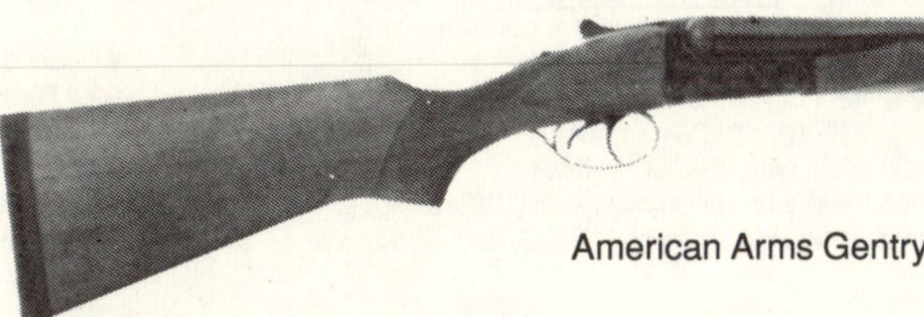

American Arms Gentry

AMERICAN ARMS GENTRY DOUBLE SHOTGUN

Gauge: 12, 20, 28, 410, 3" chambers except 16, 28, 2¾".
Barrel: 26" (Imp. Cyl. & Mod., all gauges), 28" (Mod., & Full, 12 and 20 gauges).
Weight: 6¼ to 6¾ lbs.
Stock: 14⅛"x1⅜"x2⅜". Hand-checkered walnut with semi-gloss finish.
Sights: Metal bead front. .
Features: Boxlock action with English-style scroll engraving, color case-hardened finish. Double triggers, extractors. Independent floating firing pins. Manual safety. Five-year warranty. Introduced 1987. Imported from Spain by American Arms, Inc.
Price: 12, 16 or 20 . . . . **$549.00**
Price: 28 or 410 . . . . **$579.00**

American Arms Derby Side-by-Side

Has sidelock action with English-style engraving on the sideplates. Straight-grip, hand-checkered walnut stock with splinter forend, hand-rubbed oil finish. Single non-selective trigger, automatic selective ejectors. Same chokes, rib, barrel lengths as the Gentry. Has 5-year warranty. From American Arms, Inc.
Price: **$929.00**
Price: 28 and 410 . . . . **$949.00**

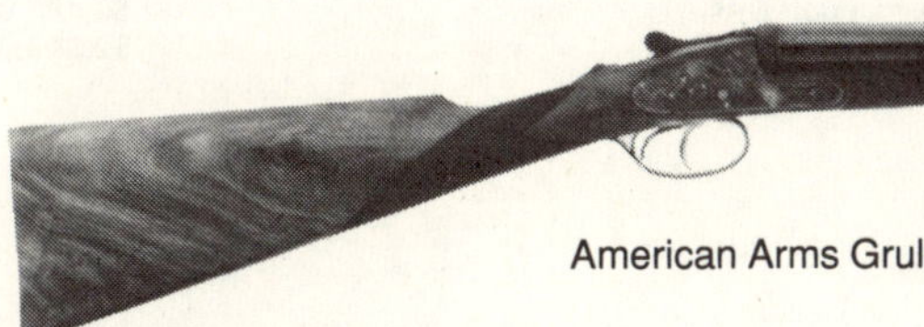

American Arms Grulla

AMERICAN ARMS GRULLA #2 DOUBLE SHOTGUN

Gauge: 12, 20, 28, 410.
Barrel: 12-ga.—28" (Mod. & Full); 26" (Imp. Cyl. & Mod.), all gauges.
Weight: 5 lbs., 13 oz. to 6 lbs., 4 oz.
Stock: Select walnut with straight English grip, splinter forend; hand-rubbed oil finish; checkered grip, forend, butt.
Features: True sidelock action with double triggers, detachable locks, automatic selective ejectors, cocking indicators, gas escape valves. Color case-hardened receiver with scroll engraving. English-style concave rib. Introduced 1989. Imported from Spain by American Arms, Inc.
Price: 12, 20, 28, 410 . . . . **$2,798.00**
Price: Two-barrel sets **$3,679.00**

AMERICAN ARMS WS/SS 10

Gauge: 10, 3½" chambers.
Barrel: 32" (Full & Full). Flat rib.
Weight: 10 lbs., 13 oz.
Stock: 14$\frac{5}{16}$"x1⅜"x2⅜". Hand-checkered walnut with beavertail forend, full pistol grip, dull finish, rubber recoil pad.
Features: Boxlock action with double triggers and extractors. All metal has Parkerized finish. Comes with camouflaged sling, sling swivels, 5-year warranty. Introduced 1987. Imported from Spain by American Arms, Inc.
Price: **$589.00**

American Arms TS/SS 10 Double Shotgun

Similar to the WS/SS 10 except has 26" (Full & Full choke tubes) barrels, raised solid rib. Double triggers, extractors. All metal and wood has matte finish. Imported by American Arms, Inc.
Price: **$619.00**

American Arms TS/SS 12 Side-by-Side

Similar to the WS/SS 10 except in 12-ga. with 3½" chambers, 26" barrels with Imp. Cyl., Mod., Full choke tubes, single selective trigger, extractors. Comes with camouflage sling, swivels, 5-year warranty. From American Arms, Inc.
Price: **$589.00**

Armsport Double

ARMSPORT 1050 SERIES DOUBLE SHOTGUNS

Gauge: 12, 20, 410, 28, 3" chambers.
Barrel: 12-ga.—28" (Mod. & Full); 20-ga.—26" (Imp. & Mod.); 410—26" (Full & Full); 28-ga.—26" (Mod. & Full).
Weight: About 6¾ lbs.
Stock: European walnut.
Features: Chrome-lined barrels. Boxlock action with engraving. Imported from Italy by Armsport.
Price: 12, 20 . . . . **$760.00**
Price: 28, 410 . . . . **$860.00**

ARIZAGA MODEL 31 DOUBLE SHOTGUN

Gauge: 12, 16, 20, 28, 410.
Barrel: 26", 28" (standard chokes).
Weight: 6 lbs., 9 oz. **Length:** 45" overall.
Stock: Straight English style or pistol grip.
Features: Boxlock action with double triggers; blued, engraved receiver. Imported by Mandall Shooting Supplies.
Price: **$450.00**

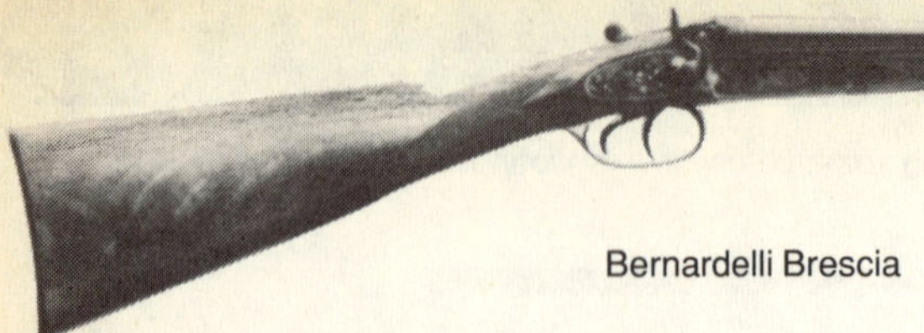

Bernardelli Brescia

BERNARDELLI SERIES S. UBERTO DOUBLES
Gauge: 12, 20, 28, 2¾" or 3" chambers.
Barrel: 25⅝", 26¾", 28", 29½" (Mod. & Full).
Weight: 6 to 6½ lbs.
Stock: 14³⁄₁₆"x2⅜"x1⁹⁄₁₆" standard dimensions. Select walnut with hand checkering.
Features: Anson & Deeley boxlock action with Purdey locks, choice of extractors or ejectors. Uberto 1 has color case-hardened receiver, Uberto 2 and F.S. silvered and differ in amount and quality of engraving. Custom options available. Imported from Italy by Magnum Research.
Price: S. Uberto 2E **$1,924.00**
Price: As above with single trigger **$2,005.00**

Bernardelli System Holland H. Side-by-Side
True sidelock action. Available in 12-gauge only, reinforced breech, three round Purdey locks, automatic ejectors, folding right trigger. Model VB Liscio has color case-hardened receiver and sideplates with light engraving. VB and VB Tipo Lusso are silvered and engraved.
Price: VB Liscio **$10,757.00**
Price: VB Lusso **$14,377.00**
Price: VB Gold **$57,992.00**

BERETTA MODEL 452 SIDELOCK SHOTGUN
Gauge: 12, 2¾" or 3" chambers.
Barrel: 26", 28", 30", choked to customer specs.
Weight: 6 lbs., 13 oz.
Stock: Dimensions to customer specs. Highly figured walnut; Model 452 EELL has walnut briar.
Features: Full sidelock action with English-type double bolting; automatic selective ejectors, manual safety; double triggers, single or single non-selective trigger on request. Essentially custom made to specifications. Model 452 is coin finished without engraving; 452 EELL is fully engraved. Imported from Italy by Beretta U.S.A.
Price: 452 . . . . **$21,000.00**
Price: 452 EELL **$28,625.00**

BERNARDELLI BRESCIA HAMMER DOUBLE SHOTGUN
Gauge: 12, 20, 2¾" or 3"; 16, 2¾".
Barrel: 25½" (Cyl. & Mod., Imp. Cyl. & Imp. Mod.), 26¾" (Imp. Cyl. & Imp. Mod., Mod. & Full), 28" (Mod. & Full), 29½" (Imp. Mod. & Full).
Weight: About 7 lbs.
Stock: Straight English grip. Checkered European walnut.
Features: Color case-hardened boxlock action. Introduced 1990. Imported from Italy by Magnum Research.
Price: **$2,482.00**
Price: Model Italia, fully engraved **$2,844.00**
Price: Model Italia Extra **$7,861.00**

Bernardelli Series Roma Shotguns
Similar to the Series S. Uberto Models except with dummy sideplates to simulate sidelock action. In 12-, 16-, 20-, 28-gauge, 25½", 26¾", 28", 29" barrels. Straight English or pistol grip stock. Chrome-lined barrels, boxlock action, double triggers, ejectors, automatic safety. Checkered butt. Special choke combinations, barrel lengths optional.
Price: Roma 3E, about **$1,986.00**
Price: Roma 4E (12, 20, 28), about **$2,276.00**
Price: Roma 6E (12, 20, 28), about **$2,482.00**
Price: Roma 3EM with ejectors, about **$2,067.00**
Price: Roma 4EM with ejectors (12, 20, 28), about **$2,354.00**
Price: Roma 6EM with ejectors (12, 20, 28), about **$2,563.00**

BERNARDELLI HEMINGWAY LIGHTWEIGHT DOUBLES
Gauge: 12, 20, 2¾" or 3"; 16, 2¾".
Barrel: 23½" to 28" (Cyl. & Imp. Cyl. to Mod. & Full).
Weight: 6¼ lbs.
Stock: Straight English grip of checkered European walnut.
Features: Silvered and engraved boxlock action. Folding front trigger on double-trigger models. Ejectors. Imported from Italy by Magnum Research.
Price: Hemingway, 12 or 20 . . . . **$2,172.00**
Price: With single trigger **$2,253.00**
Price: Deluxe, with sideplates **$2,482.00**
Price: As above, single trigger **$2,563.00**

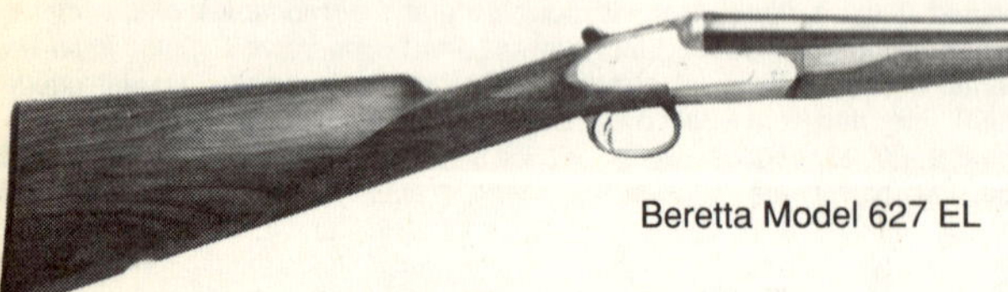

Beretta Model 627 EL

BRNO ZP149, ZP349 SIDE-BY-SIDE
Gauge: 12, 2¾" or 3" chambers.
Barrel: 28½" (Full & Mod.).
Weight: 7 lbs., 3 oz. **Length:** 45" overall.
Stock: Turkish or Yugoslavian walnut with raised cheekpiece.
Features: Sidelock action with double triggers, automatic ejectors, barrel indicators, auto safety. Imported from Czechoslovakia by T.D. Arms.
Price: ZP149, standard **$589.00**
Price: As above, engraved **$609.00**
Price: ZP349, extractors, standard **$629.00**
Price: As above, engraved **$649.00**

BERETTA SIDE-BY-SIDE FIELD SHOTGUNS
Gauge: 12 and 20, 3", 3½" chambers.
Barrel: 26" and 28" (Mobilchoke tubes).
Stock: Close-grained American walnut.
Features: Front and center beads on a raised ventilated rib. Has P. Beretta signature on each side of the receiver, while a gold gauge marking is inscribed atop the rib. Imported from Italy by Beretta U.S.A.
Price: 626 Onyx **$1,640.00**
Price: 627 EL **$2,785.00**
Price: 627 EELL (pistol grip or straight English stock) **$4,735.00**

Consult our Directory pages for the location of firms mentioned.

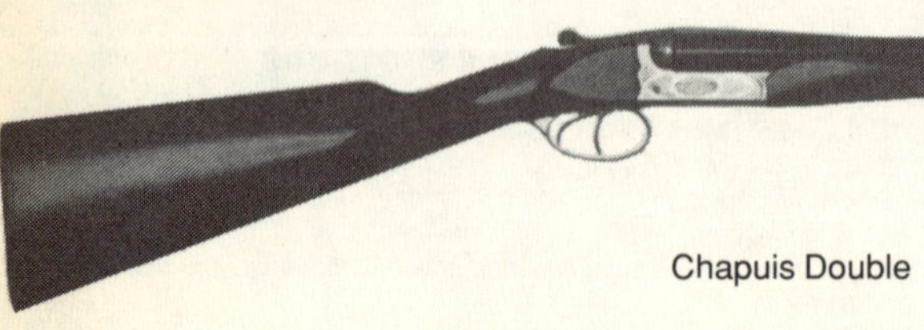

Chapuis Double

CHAPUIS SIDE-BY-SIDE SHOTGUN
Gauge: 12, 16, 20.
Barrel: 22", 23.6", 26.8", 27.6", 31.5", chokes to customer specs.
Weight: 5 to 10 lbs. **Length:** NA.
Stock: French walnut, straight English or pistol grip.
Features: Double hook Blitz system center sidelock action with notched action zone, automatic ejectors or extractors. Long trigger guard (most models), choice of raised solid rib, vent. rib or ultra light rib. Imported from France by Armes de Chasse.
Price: About **$4,000.00**

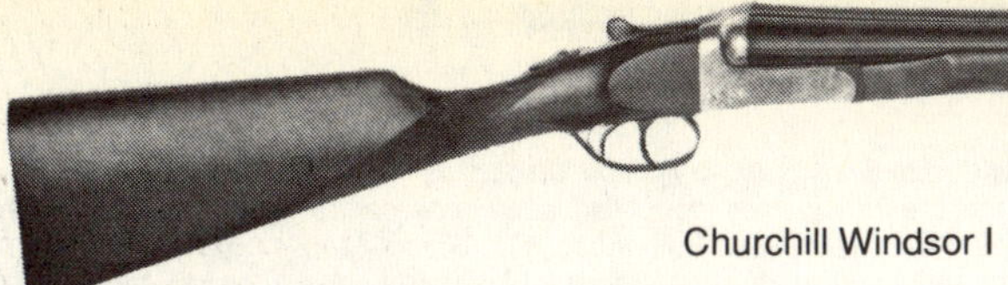

Churchill Windsor I

CHURCHILL ROYAL SIDE-BY-SIDE SHOTGUN

Gauge: 10 (3½"), 12 (3"), 20, 28, 410 (3").
Barrel: 12-ga.—26" (Imp. Cyl. & Mod.), 28" (Mod. & Full); 20-ga.—26", 28" (Imp. Cyl. & Mod., Mod. & Full); 28, 410—26" (Full & Full).
Weight: 5¾ to 6½ lbs.
Stock: Straight-grip style of checkered European walnut.
Features: Color case-hardened boxlock action with double triggers, extractors; chromed barrels with concave rib. Introduced 1988. Imported by Ellett Bros.
Price: 10-ga. **$819.95**
Price: 12- and 20-ga. **$609.95**
Price: 28-ga. **$639.95**
Price: 410-bore **$699.95**

CRUCELEGUI HERMANOS MODEL 150 DOUBLE

Gauge: 12, 16 or 20, 2¾" chambers.
Action: Greener triple cross bolt.
Barrel: 20", 26", 28", 30", 32" (Cyl. & Cyl., Full & Full, Mod. & Full, Mod. & Imp. Cyl., Imp. Cyl. & Full, Mod. & Mod.).
Weight: 5 to 7¼ lbs.
Stock: Hand-checkered walnut, beavertail forend.
Features: Double triggers; color case-hardened receiver; sling swivels; chrome-lined bores. Imported from Spain by Mandall Shooting Supplies.
Price: **$450.00**

CHURCHILL WINDSOR I SIDE-BY-SIDE SHOTGUNS

Gauge: 12, 16, 20 (16 ga. 2¾" ; others 3").
Barrel: 12-ga.—26" (Imp. Cyl. & Mod.), 28" (Mod. & Full); 16-ga.—28" (Mod. & Full); 20-ga.—26" (Imp. Cyl. & Mod.), 28" (Mod. & Full).
Weight: About 8 lbs. (12-ga.).
Stock: Hand-checkered European walnut with rubber buttpad.
Features: Anson & Deeley boxlock action with silvered and engraved finish; automatic top tang safety; double triggers; beavertail forend; extractors only. Imported from Spain by Ellett Bros. Introduced 1984.
Price: 12-ga., 28" bbl. **$659.95**
Price: 12-ga., (26"), 16-, 20-ga. **$659.95**

CHARLES DALY MODEL DSS DOUBLE

Gauge: 12, 20, 3" chambers.
Barrel: 26", choke tubes.
Weight: 6 lbs., 13 oz. (12-ga.). **Length:** 44.5" overall.
Stock: 14⅛"x1⅜"x2⅜". Figured walnut; pistol grip; cut checkering; black rubber recoil pad; semi-beavertail forend.
Features: Boxlock action with automatic selective ejectors, automatic safety, gold single trigger. Engraved, silvered frame. Introduced 1990. Imported by Outdoor Sports Headquarters.
Price: **$675.00**

Ferlib F VII

FERLIB MODEL F VII DOUBLE SHOTGUN

Gauge: 12, 16, 20, 28, 410.
Barrel: 25" to 28".
Weight: 5½ lbs. (20-ga.).
Stock: Oil-finished walnut, checkered straight grip and forend.
Features: Boxlock action with fine scroll engraving, silvered receiver. Double triggers standard. Introduced 1983. Imported from Italy by Wm. Larkin Moore.
Price: F.VI **$5,000.00**
Price: F.VII **$5,700.00**
Price: F.VII SC **$7,200.00**
Price: F.VII SP Sideplate **$10,100.00**

Francotte Boxlock

AUGUSTE FRANCOTTE BOXLOCK SHOTGUN

Gauge: 12, 16, 20, 28 and 410-bore, 2¾" or 3" chambers.
Barrel: 26" to 29", chokes to customer specs.
Weight: NA. **Length:** NA.
Stock: Deluxe European walnut to customer specs. Straight or pistol grip; checkered butt; oil finish; splinter or beavertail forend.
Sights: Bead front.
Features: Anson & Deeley boxlock action with double locks, double triggers (front hinged), manual or automatic safety, Holland & Holland ejectors. English scroll engraving, coin finish or color case-hardening. Many options available. Imported from Belgium by Armes de Chasse.
Price: From about **$17,172.00**

GAMBA LONDON SIDE-BY-SIDE SHOTGUN

Gauge: 12 or 20.
Barrel: 26" (Imp. Cyl. & Imp. Mod.), 28" (Mod. & Full).
Weight: 6.25 to 6.75 lbs.
Stock: Turkish or French walnut with straight English grip.
Features: Holland & Holland sidelock action with automatic ejectors, chopper lump barrels; double or single triggers. Introduced 1990. Imported from Italy by Heckler & Koch, Inc.
Price: From **$9,200.00**

AUGUSTE FRANCOTTE SIDELOCK SHOTGUN

Gauge: 12, 16, 20, 28 and 410-bore, 2¾" or 3" chambers.
Barrel: 26" to 29", chokes to customer specs.
Weight: NA. **Length:** NA.
Stock: Deluxe European walnut to customer specs. Straight or pistol grip; checkered butt; oil finish; splinter or beavertail forend.
Sights: Bead front.
Features: True Holland & Holland sidelock action with double locks, double triggers (front hinged), manual or automatic safety, Holland & Holland ejectors. English scroll engraving, coin finish or color case-hardening. Many options available. Imported from Belgium by Armes de Chasse.
Price: From about **$30,041.00**

Gamba Principessa

GAMBA PRINCIPESSA SIDE-BY-SIDE

Gauge: 12 and 20, 2¾" chamber.
Barrel: 26", 28" (Mod. & Full or Imp. Cyl., & Mod.)
Weight: 6.18 lbs. (20-ga.).
Stock: Walnut, straight English grip with standard forend.
Features: Boxlock action with automatic ejectors; double or single triggers by request. Introduced 1990. Imported from Italy by Heckler & Koch, Inc.
Price: With double triggers **$2,250.00**
Price: With single trigger **$2,610.00**

Gamba Oxford 90

Gamba Oxford 90 Side-by-Side Shotgun
Similar to the Principessa model except has cosmetic sideplates. Comes with 26" or 28" barrels (Mod. & Full or Imp. Cyl. & Imp. Mod.); weight is 5.5 to 6.8 lbs. depending upon gauge. Introduced 1990. Imported from Italy by Heckler & Koch, Inc.
Price: With double triggers $2,700.00
Price: With single trigger $3,050.00

Garbi Model 100

GARBI MODEL 100 DOUBLE
Gauge: 12, 16, 20, 28.
Barrel: 26", 28", choked to customer specs.
Weight: 5½ to 7½ lbs.
Stock: 14½"x2¼"x1½". European walnut. Straight grip, checkered butt, classic forend.
Features: Sidelock action, automatic ejectors, double triggers standard. Color case-hardened action, coin finish optional. Single trigger; beavertail forend, etc. optional. Five other models are available. Imported from Spain by Wm. Larkin Moore.
Price: From $3,900.00

Garbi Model 101 Side-by-Side
Similar to the Garbl Model 100 except is hand engraved with scroll engraving, select walnut stock. Better overall quality than the Model 100. Imported from Spain by Wm. Larkin Moore.
Price: $4,500.00

Garbi Model 103A, B Side-by-Side
Similar to the Garbl Model 100 except has Purdey-type fine scroll and rosette engraving. Better overall quality than the Model 101. Model 103B has nickel-chrome steel barrels, H&H-type easy opening mechanism; other mechanical details remain the same. Imported from Spain by Wm. Larkin Moore.
Price: Model 103A, from $6,100.00
Price: Model 103B, from $8,300.00

Garbi Model 200 Side-by-Side
Similar to the Garbl Model 100 except has heavy-duty locks, magnum proofed. Very fine Continental-style floral and scroll engraving, well figured walnut stock. Other mechanical features remain the same. Imported from Spain by Wm. Larkin Moore.
Price: $8,400.00

Hatfield Uplander

HATFIELD UPLANDER SHOTGUN
Gauge: 20, 3" chambers.
Barrel: 26" (Imp. Cyl. & Mod.).
Weight: 5¾ lbs.
Stock: Straight English style, special select XXX fancy maple. Hand-rubbed oil finish. Splinter forend.
Features: Double locking under-lug boxlock action; color case-hardened frame; single non-selective trigger. Grades differ in engraving, finish, gold work. Introduced 1988. From Hatfield.
Price: Grade II Uplander $2,500.00
Price: Grade III Uplander Super Pigeon $3,500.00
Price: Grade IV Uplander Golden Quail $5,500.00
Price: Grade V Uplander Woodcock $6,900.00
Price: Grade VI Uplander Black Widow $7,900.00
Price: Grade VII Uplander Royale $7,900.00
Price: Grade VIII Uplander Top Hat $17,500.00

BILL HANUS BIRDGUN DOUBLES
Gauge: 16, 20, 28.
Barrel: 26" (Skeet & Skeet).
Weight: About 6¼ lbs. (16-ga.).
Stock: Hand-checkered walnut; straight grip, semi-beavertail forend.
Features: Color case-hardened boxlock action; raised Churchill rib; single non-selective trigger; auto ejectors, auto safety. Introduced 1991. Imported by Precision Sports.
Price: 16-, 20-ga. $1,269.95
Price: 28-ga. $1,399.95

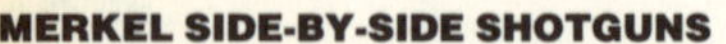
Merkel Double

MERKEL SIDE-BY-SIDE SHOTGUNS
Gauge: 12, 16, 20, 2¾" or 3" chambers.
Barrel: 26", 26¾", 28" (standard chokes).
Weight: 6 to 7 lbs.
Stock: European walnut. Straight English or pistol grip.
Features: Models 8, 47E, 147E, 76E are boxlocks; others are sidelocks. All have double triggers, double lugs and Greener cross-bolt locking and automatic ejectors. Choking and patterning for steel shot (by importer). Upgraded wood, engraving, etc. optional. Imported from Germany by Armes de Chasse.
Price: Model 8, about $1,500.00
Price: Model 47E, about $2,000.00
Price: Model 147E, about $2,500.00
Price: Model 76E $3,500.00
Price: Model 47S, about $4,500.00
Price: Model 147S, about $5,000.00
Price: Model 247S about $5,500.00
Price: Model 347S, about $6,000.00
Price: Model 447S, about $7,000.00

PARKER REPRODUCTION SIDE-BY-SIDE SHOTGUN
Gauge: 12, 20, 28, 2¾" or 3" chambers.
Barrel: 26" (Imp. Cyl. & Mod., 2¾" chambers), Skeet & Skeet available, 28" (Mod. & Full).
Weight: About 6¾ lbs. (12-ga.), 6½ lbs. (20-ga.), 5½ lbs. (28-ga.).
Stock: Fancy American walnut, checkered grip and forend. Straight stock or pistol grip, splinter or beavertail forend; 28 lpi checkering.
Features: Reproduction of the original Parker—parts interchangeable with original. Double or single selective trigger; checkered skeleton buttplate; selective ejectors; bores hard chromed, excluding choke area. Two-barrel sets available. Hand engraved scroll and scenes on case-hardened frame. Fitted leather trunk included. Limited production. Introduced 1984. Made by Winchester in Japan. Imported by Parker Div. of Reagent Chemical.
Price: D Grade, one-barrel set $3,370.00
Price: A-1 Special, two-barrel set $11,200.00

CAUTION: PRICES CHANGE, CHECK AT GUNSHOP.

Piotti Model Piuma

PIOTTI KING NO. 1 SIDE-BY-SIDE
Gauge: 12, 16, 20, 28, 410.
Barrel: 25" to 30" (12-ga.), 25" to 28" (16, 20, 28, 410). To customer specs. Chokes as specified.
Weight: 6½ lbs. to 8 lbs. (12-ga. to customer specs.).
Stock: Dimensions to customer specs. Finely figured walnut; straight grip with checkered butt with classic splinter forend and hand-rubbed oil finish standard. Pistol grip, beavertail forend, satin luster finish optional.
Features: Holland & Holland pattern sidelock action, automatic ejectors. Double trigger with front trigger hinged standard; non-selective single trigger optional. Coin finish standard; color case-hardened optional. Top rib; level, file-cut standard; concave, ventilated optional. Very fine, full coverage scroll engraving with small floral bouquets, gold crown in top lever, name in gold, and gold crest in forend. Imported from Italy by Wm. Larkin Moore.
Price: $17,500.00

Piotti Lunik Side-by-Side
Similar to the Piotti King No. 1 except better overall quality. Has Renaissance-style large scroll engraving in relief, gold crown in top lever, gold name and gold crest in forend. Best quality Holland & Holland-pattern sidelock ejector double with chopper lump (demi-bloc) barrels. Other mechanical specifications remain the same. Imported from Italy by Wm. Larkin Moore.
Price: $18,700.00

PIOTTI PIUMA SIDE-BY-SIDE
Gauge: 12, 16, 20, 28, 410.
Barrel: 25" to 30" (12-ga.), 25" to 28" (16, 20, 28, 410).
Weight: 5½ to 6¼ lbs. (20-ga.).
Stock: Dimensions to customer specs. Straight grip stock with walnut checkered butt, classic splinter forend, hand-rubbed oil finish are standard; pistol grip, beavertail forend, satin luster finish optional.
Features: Anson & Deeley boxlock ejector double with chopper lump barrels. Level, file-cut rib, light scroll and rosette engraving, scalloped frame. Double triggers with hinged front standard, single non-selective optional. Coin finish standard, color case-hardened optional. Imported from Italy by Wm. Larkin Moore.
Price: $10,700.00

Piotti King Extra Side-by-Side
Similar to the Piotti King No. 1 except highest quality wood and metal work. Choice of either bulino game scene engraving or game scene engraving with gold inlays. Engraved and signed by a master engraver. Exhibition grade wood. Other mechanical specifications remain the same. Imported from Italy by Wm. Larkin Moore.
Price: $27,300.00

Consult our Directory pages for the location of firms mentioned.

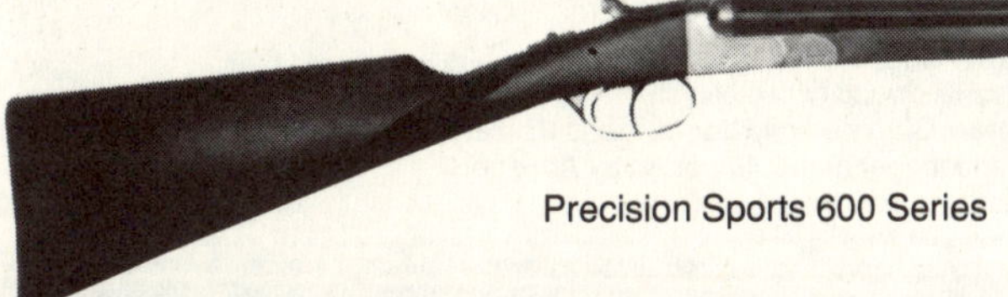

Precision Sports 600 Series

PRECISION SPORTS MODEL 600 SERIES DOUBLES
Gauge: 10, 3½" chambers; 12, 16, 20, 2¾" chambers; 28, 410, 3" chambers.
Barrel: 25", 26", 27", 28" (Imp. Cyl. & Mod., Mod. & Full).
Weight: 12-ga., 6¾-7 lbs.; 20-ga., 5¾-6 lbs.
Stock: 14½"x1½"x2½". Hand-checkered walnut with oil finish. "E" (English) models have straight grip, splinter forend, checkered butt. "A" (American) models have p.g. stock, beavertail forend, buttplate.
Features: Boxlock action; silvered, engraved action; automatic safety; ejectors or extractors. E-models have double triggers, concave rib (XXV models have Churchill-type rib); A-models have single, non-selective trigger, raised matte rib. Made in Spain by Ugartechea. Imported by Precision Sports. Introduced 1986.

Price: 640E (12, 16, 20; 26", 28"), extractors $849.95
Price: 640E (28, 410 only), extractors $939.95
Price: 640A (12, 16, 20; 26", 28"), extractors $964.95
Price: 640A (28, 410 only), ejectors $1,109.95
Price: 640M "Big Ten" (10-ga. 26", 30", 32", Full & Full) $999.95
Price: 640 Slug Gun (12, 25", Imp. Cyl. & Imp. Cyl.) $1,229.95
Price: 645E (12, 16, 20; 26", 28"), with ejectors $1,089.95
Price: 645E (28, 410), with ejectors $1,219.95
Price: 645A (12, 16, 20; 26", 28"), with ejectors $1,219.95
Price: 645A (28, 410), ejectors $1,389.95
Price: 645E-XXV (12, 16, 20; 25"), with ejectors $1,119.95
Price: 645E-XXV (28, 410), with ejectors $1,249.95
Price: 645E Bi-Gauge (20/28), ejectors $1,730.95
Price: 645A Bi-Gauge (20/28), ejectors $1,889.95
Price: 670E (12, 16, 20; 26", 28") sidelock, with ejectors $4,269.95
Price: 670E (28, 410) sidelock, with ejectors $5,039.95
Price: 680E-XXV (12, 16, 20; 25") sidelock, ejectors, case-color action $4,069.95
Price: 680E-XXV (28, 410; 25") sidelock, ejectors, case-color action $4,469.95

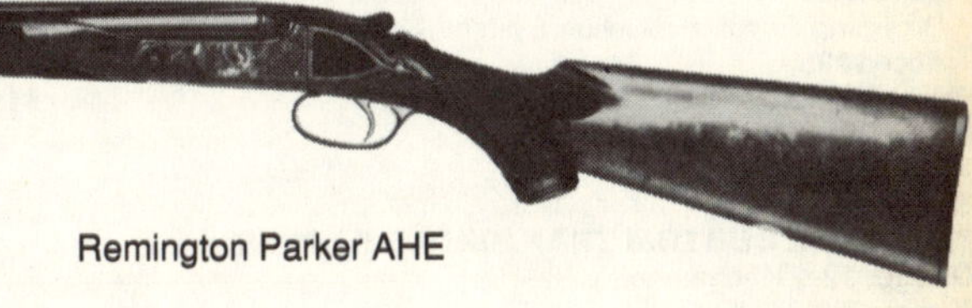

Remington Parker AHE

REMINGTON PARKER AHE SIDE-BY-SIDE
Gauge: 20, 2¾" chambers.
Barrel: 28" (any combination of Skeet, Imp. Cyl., Mod., Full chokes).
Weight: About 6½ lbs.
Stock: Circassian or American walnut; straight or pistol grip; beavertail or splinter forend; rubber recoil pad, Parker buttplate or engraved skeleton steel buttplate. Checkered 28 lpi.
Features: Custom-made gun. Single selective trigger, automatic ejectors; scroll-engraved color case-hardened receiver. Limited production. Reintroduced 1988. From Remington.
Price: From $17,000.00

RIZZINI BOXLOCK SIDE-BY-SIDE
Gauge: 12, 20, 28, 410.
Barrel: 25" to 30" (12-ga.), 25" to 28" (20, 28, 410).
Weight: 5½ to 6¼ lbs. (20-ga.).
Stock: Dimensions to customer specs. Straight grip stock with checkered butt, classic splinter forend, hand-rubbed oil finish are standard; pistol grip, beavertail forend, satin luster finish optional.
Features: Anson & Deeley boxlock ejector double with chopper lump barrels. Level, file-cut rib, light scroll and rosette engraving, scalloped frame. Double triggers with hinged front standard, single non-selective optional. Coin finish standard, color case-hardened optional. Imported from Italy by Wm. Larkin Moore.
Price: 12-, 20-ga., from $19,900.00
Price: 28, 410 bore, from $22,000.00

RIZZINI SIDELOCK SIDE-BY-SIDE
Gauge: 12, 20, 28, 410.
Barrel: 25" to 30" (12-ga.), 25" to 28" (20, 28, 410). To customer specs. Chokes as specified.
Weight: 6½ lbs. to 8 lbs. (12-ga. to customer specs).
Stock: Dimensions to customer specs. Finely figured walnut; straight grip with checkered butt with classic splinter forend and hand-rubbed oil finish standard. Pistol grip, beavertail forend, satin luster finish optional.
Features: Holland & Holland pattern sidelock action, auto ejectors. Double triggers with front trigger hinged standard; non-selective single trigger optional. Coin finish standard; color case-hardened optional. Top rib level, file cut standard; concave, ventilated optional. Very fine, full coverage scroll engraving with small floral bouquets, gold crown in top lever, name in gold, and gold crest in forend. Imported from Italy by Wm. Larkin Moore.
Price: 12-, 20-ga., from $31,500.00
Price: 28, 410 bore, from $35,300.00

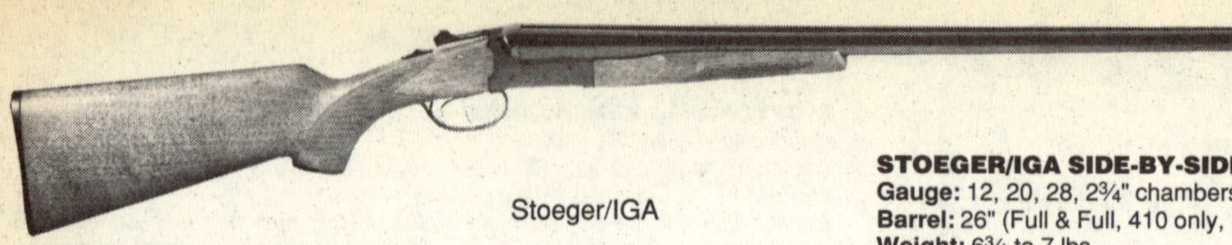
Stoeger/IGA

UGARTECHEA 10-GAUGE MAGNUM SHOTGUN
Gauge: 10, 3½" chambers.
Action: Boxlock.
Barrel: 32" (Full).
Weight: 11 lbs.
Stock: 14½"x1½"x2⅝". European walnut, checkered at pistol grip and forend.
Features: Double triggers; color case-hardened action, rest blued. Front and center metal beads on matted rib; ventilated rubber recoil pad. Forend release has positive Purdey-type mechanism. Imported from Spain by Mandall Shooting Supplies.
Price: $599.95

STOEGER/IGA SIDE-BY-SIDE SHOTGUN
Gauge: 12, 20, 28, 2¾" chambers; 410, 3" chambers.
Barrel: 26" (Full & Full, 410 only, Imp. Cyl. & Mod.), 28" (Mod. & Full).
Weight: 6¾ to 7 lbs.
Stock: 14½"x1½"x2½". Oil-finished hardwood. Checkered pistol grip and forend.
Features: Automatic safety, extractors only, solid matted barrel rib. Double triggers only. Introduced 1983. Imported from Brazil by Stoeger Industries.
Price: $357.00
Price: Coach Gun, 12, 20, 410, 20" bbls. $340.00

SHOTGUNS—BOLT ACTIONS & SINGLE SHOTS

Variety of designs for utility and sporting purposes, as well as for competitive shooting.

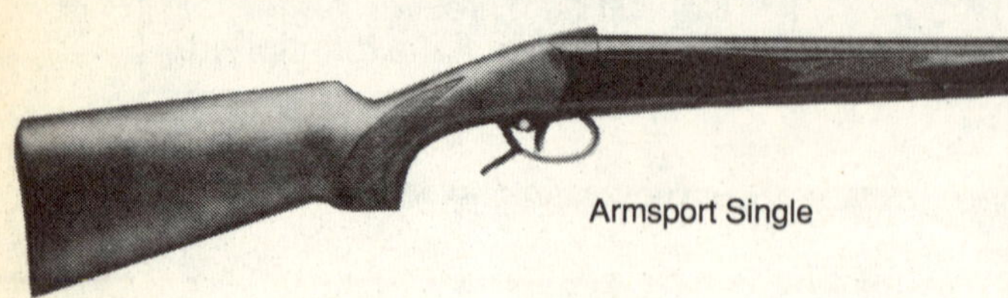
Armsport Single

ARMSPORT SINGLE BARREL SHOTGUN
Gauge: 20, 3" chamber.
Barrel: 26" (Mod.).
Weight: About 6½ lbs.
Stock: Hardwood with oil finish.
Features: Chrome-lined barrel, manual safety, cocking indicator. Opening lever behind trigger guard. Imported by Armsport.
Price: $90.00

Browning BT-99 PLUS

Browning BT-99 PLUS Trap Gun
Similar to the Grade I BT-99 except comes only with 34" barrel with .745" over bore, Invector PLUS choke system with Full, Imp. Mod. and Mod. choke tubes; high post, ventilated, tapered, target rib adjustable from 3" to 12" above point of aim. Available with or without ported barrel. Select walnut stock has high-gloss finish, Monte Carlo comb, modified beavertail forend and is fully adjustable for length of pull, drop at comb and drop at Monte Carlo. Has Browning Recoil Reduction System. Comes with Travel Vault case. Introduced 1989.
Price: Grade I, with ported barrel $1,900.00
Price: Grade I, non-ported barrel $1,875.00

ITHACA 5E CUSTOM TRAP SINGLE BARREL
Gauge: 12, 2¾" chamber.
Barrel: 32", 34" (Full).
Weight: 8½ lbs.
Stock: 14⅜"x1⅜"x1⅜". AA Fancy American walnut.
Sights: White bead front, brass middle bead.
Features: Frame, top lever, trigger guard extensively engraved and gold inlaid. Reintroduced 1988. From Ithaca Acquisition Corp.
Price: 5E $7,500.00
Price: Dollar Grade Trap $10,000.00

BROWNING BT-99 COMPETITION TRAP SPECIAL
Gauge: 12, 2¾" chamber.
Action: Top lever break-open, hammerless.
Barrel: 32" or 34" with 11/32" wide high post floating vent. rib. Comes with Invector choke tubes or fixed Full, Imp. Mod.
Weight: 8 lbs. (32" bbl.).
Stock: French walnut; hand-checkered, full pistol grip, full beavertail forend; recoil pad. Trap dimensions with M.C. 14⅜"x1⅜"x1⅜"x2".
Sights: Ivory front and middle beads.
Features: Gold-plated trigger with 3½-lb. pull, deluxe trap-style recoil pad, automatic ejector, no safety. Available with either Monte Carlo or standard stock. Imported from Japan by Browning.
Price: Grade I Invector $1,070.00
Price: As above, non-Invector $1,045.00

Browning BT-99 PLUS Micro
Similar to the standard BT-99 PLUS except scaled down for smaller shooters. Comes with 30" barrel with adjustable rib system and buttstock with adjustable length of pull range of 13½" to 14". Also has Browning's recoil reducer system, ported barrels, Invector PLUS choke system and back-bored barrel. Weight is about 8 lbs., 6 oz. Introduced 1991.
Price: With ported barrel, Travel Vault case $1,900.00
Price: With non-ported barrel, Travel Vault case $1,875.00

Desert Industries

DESERT INDUSTRIES BIG TWENTY SHOTGUN
Gauge: 20, 2¾" chamber.
Barrel: 19" (Cyl.).
Weight: 4¾ lbs. **Length:** 31¾" overall.
Stock: Fixed wire, with buttplate. Walnut forend and grip.
Stock: Bead front.
Features: Single shot action of all steel construction. Blue finish. Announced 1990. From Desert Industries, Inc.
Price: $189.95

Krieghoff KS-5 Trap

KRIEGHOFF KS-5 TRAP GUN
Gauge: 12, 2¾" chamber.
Barrel: 32", 34"; Full choke or choke tubes.
Weight: About 8½ lbs.
Stock: Choice of high Monte Carlo (1½"), low Monte Carlo (1⅜") or factory adjustable stock. European walnut.
Features: Ventilated tapered step rib. Adjustable trigger or optional release trigger. Choice of blue or nickeled receiver. Comes with fitted aluminum case. Introduced 1988. Imported from Germany by Krieghoff International, Inc.
Price: Fixed choke, cased **$3,250.00**
Price: With choke tubes **$3,630.00**

Krieghoff KS-5 Special
Same as the KS-5 except the barrel has a fully adjustable rib and adjustable stock. Rib allows shooter to adjust point of impact from 50%/50% to nearly 90%/10%. Introduced 1990.
Price: **$4,150.00**

KRIEGHOFF K-80 SINGLE BARREL TRAP GUN
Gauge: 12, 2¾" chamber.
Barrel: 32" or 34" Unsingle; 34" Top Single. Fixed Full or choke tubes.
Weight: About 8¾ lbs.
Stock: Four stock dimensions or adjustable stock available. All hand-checkered European walnut.
Features: Satin nickel finish with K-80 logo. Selective mechanical trigger adjustable for finger position. Tapered step vent. rib. Adjustable point of impact on Unsingle.
Price: Standard grade full Unsingle **$6,700.00**
Price: Standard grade full Top Single **$6,550.00**
Price: RT (removable trigger) option, add **$1,850.00**

LAURONA GRAND TRAP GTO COMBO
Gauge: 12, 2¾" chamber.
Barrel: 34" (top single barrel), 29" (O/U barrels); Multichokes.
Weight: NA. **Length:** NA.
Stock: European walnut with Monte Carlo comb, orthopedic grip, curved trap recoil pad, full beavertail forend with finger grooves.
Sights: Bead front.
Features: Has 10mm steel rib designed for 40-yard interception. Special elongated forcing cone with flush choke tubes. Bottom chamber area fitted with buffered recoil system. Introduced 1990. Imported from Spain by Galaxy Imports, Ltd.
Price: With both barrel sets **$2,660.00**

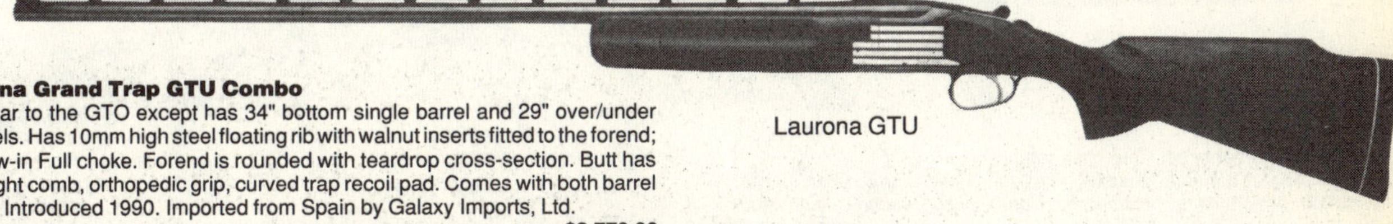

Laurona GTU

Laurona Grand Trap GTU Combo
Similar to the GTO except has 34" bottom single barrel and 29" over/under barrels. Has 10mm high steel floating rib with walnut inserts fitted to the forend; screw-in Full choke. Forend is rounded with teardrop cross-section. Butt has straight comb, orthopedic grip, curved trap recoil pad. Comes with both barrel sets. Introduced 1990. Imported from Spain by Galaxy Imports, Ltd.
Price: **$2,770.00**

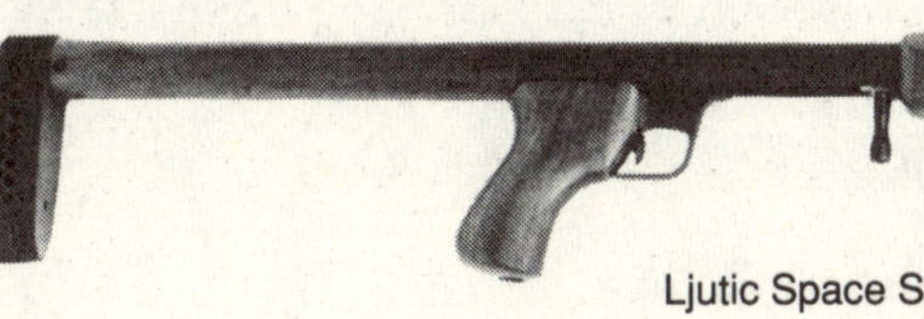

Ljutic Mono Gun

LJUTIC MONO GUN SINGLE BARREL
Gauge: 12 only.
Barrel: 34", choked to customer specs; hollow-milled rib, 35½" sight plane.
Weight: Approx. 9 lbs.
Stock: To customer specs. Oil finish, hand checkered.
Features: Totally custom made. Pull or release trigger; removable trigger guard contains trigger and hammer mechanism; Ljutic pushbutton opener on front of trigger guard. From Ljutic Industries.
Price: With standard, medium or Olympic rib, custom 32"-34" bbls. **$3,895.00**
Price: As above with screw-in choke barrel **$3,995.00**

Ljutic LTX Super Deluxe Mono Gun
Super Deluxe version of the standard Mono Gun with high quality wood, extra-fancy checkering pattern in 24 lpi, double recessed choking. Available in two weights: 8¼ lbs. or 8¾ lbs. Extra light 33" barrel; medium-height rib. Introduced 1984. From Ljutic Industries.
Price: **$4,995.00**
Price: With three screw-in choke tubes **$5,595.00**

Ljutic Space Shotgun

LJUTIC RECOILLESS SPACE GUN SHOTGUN
Gauge: 12 only, 2¾" chamber.
Barrel: 30" (Full). Screw-in or fixed-choke barrel.
Weight: 8½ lbs.
Stock: 14½" to 15" pull length; universal comb; medium or large p.g.
Sights: Vent. rib.
Features: Pull trigger standard, release trigger available; anti-recoil mechanism. Revolutionary new design. Introduced 1981. From Ljutic Industries.
Price: From **$3,995.00**

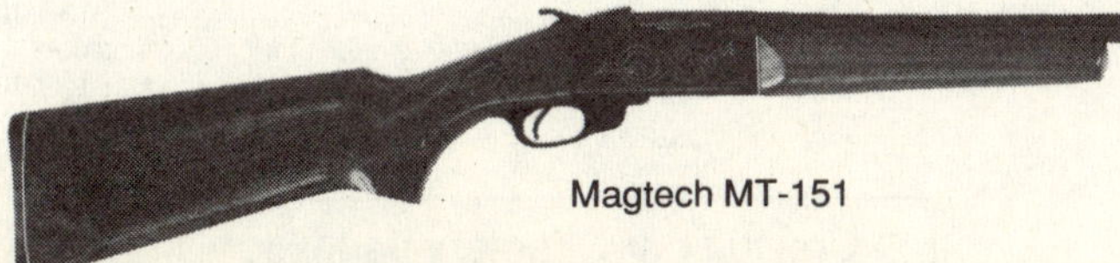

Magtech MT-151

MAGTECH MODEL MT-151 SINGLE SHOT SHOTGUN
Gauge: 12, 20, 410, 3" chamber; 16, 2¾" chamber.
Barrel: 12-ga.—28" (Mod.), 30" (Full); 16-ga.—28" (Mod.); 20-ga.—26" (Mod.), 28" (Full); 410—25", 28" (Full).
Weight: About 5¾ lbs.
Stock: Brazilian hardwood, beavertail forend.
Features: Trigger guard opener button. Exposed hammer. Three-piece takedown. Introduced 1991. Imported from Brazil by Magtech Recreational Products, Inc.
Price: About **$99.95**

Marlin Model 55

MARLIN MODEL 55 GOOSE GUN BOLT ACTION
Gauge: 12 only, 2¾" or 3" chamber.
Action: Bolt action, thumb safety, detachable two-shot clip. Red cocking indicator.
Barrel: 36" (Full).
Weight: 8 lbs. **Length:** 56¾" overall.
Stock: Walnut-finished hardwood, p.g., ventilated recoil pad. Swivel studs, MarShield® finish.
Features: Brass bead front sight, U-groove rear sight.
Price: **$254.95**

New England Pardner

NEW ENGLAND FIREARMS PARDNER SHOTGUN
Gauge: 12, 16 (2¾"), 20, 410, 3" chamber.
Barrel: 12-ga.—24" (Cyl.), rifle sights, 28" (Mod., Full); 16-ga.—28" (Full); 20-ga.—26" (Mod., Full); 410 bore—26" (Full).
Weight: About 5½ lbs. **Length:** 43" overall (28" barrel).
Stock: Walnut-finished hardwood; 13¾" pull length (12½" youth).
Features: Transfer-bar ignition; side-lever action release. Blued receiver, blued barrel. Youth model available with 22" barrel. Introduced 1987. From New England Firearms Co.
Price: . . . . **NA**
Price: Deluxe Pardner (as above except has Double Back-up buttstock holding two extra shells) . . . . **NA**

Perazzi TMX

PERAZZI TM1 SPECIAL SINGLE TRAP
Gauge: 12, 2¾" chambers.
Barrel: 32" or 34" (Extra Full).
Weight: 8 lbs., 6 oz.
Stock: To customer specs; interchangeable.
Features: Tapered and stepped high rib; adjustable four-position trigger. Also available with choke tubes. Imported from Italy by Perazzi U.S.A., Inc.
Price: From **$5,100.00**
Price: TMX Special Single (as above except special high rib), from **$5,100.00**

Remington Model 90-T

REMINGTON 90-T SUPER SINGLE SHOTGUN
Gauge: 12, 2¾" chamber.
Barrel: 30", 32", 34", fixed choke or Rem Choke tubes; ported or non-ported. Medium-high tapered, ventilated rib; white Bradley-type front bead, stainless center bead.
Weight: About 8¾ lbs.
Stock: 14⅜"x1⅜" (or 1½" or 1¼")x1½". Choice of drops at comb, pull length available plus or minus 1". Figured American walnut with low-luster finish, checkered 18 lpi; black vented rubber recoil pad. Cavity in forend and buttstock for added weight.
Features: Barrel is over-bored with elongated forcing cones. Removable sideplates can be ordered with engraving; drop-out trigger assembly. Metal has non-glare matte finish. Available with extra barrels in different lengths, chokes, extra trigger assemblies and sideplates, porting, stocks. Introduced 1990. From Remington.
Price: Depending on options **$2,595.00**

Snake Charmer II

SNAKE CHARMER II SHOTGUN
Gauge: 410, 3" chamber.
Barrel: 18¼".
Weight: About 3½ lbs. **Length:** 28⅝" overall.
Stock: ABS grade impact resistant plastic.
Features: Thumbhole-type stock holds four extra rounds. Stainless steel barrel and frame. Reintroduced 1989. From Sporting Arms Mfg., Inc.
Price: **$139.00**
Price: New Generation Snake Charmer (as above except with black carbon steel bbl.) **$129.00**

STOEGER/IGA SINGLE BARREL SHOTGUN
Gauge: 12, 2¾" chamber; 20, 410, 3" chamber.
Barrel: 12-ga.—26" (Imp. Cyl.), 28" (Full); 20-ga.—26" (Full); 410 bore—26" (Full).
Weight: 5¼ lbs.
Stock: 14"x1½"x2½". Brazilian hardwood.
Sights: Metal bead front.
Features: Exposed hammer with half-cock safety; extractor; blue finish. Introduced 1987. Imported from Brazil by Stoeger Industries.
Price: **$105.00**

Consult our Directory pages for the location of firms mentioned.

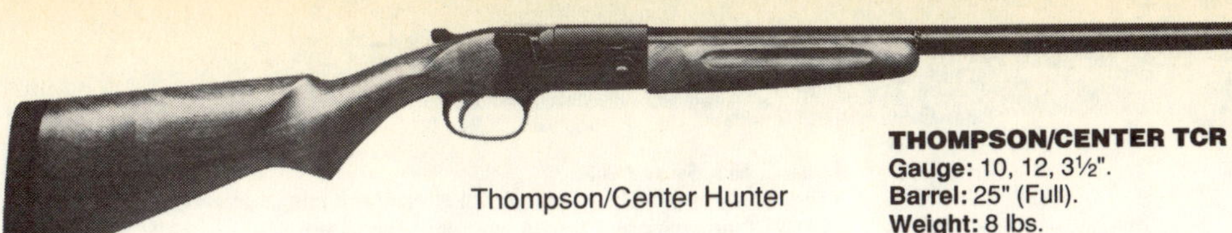

Thompson/Center Hunter

THOMPSON/CENTER TCR '87 HUNTER SHOTGUN
Gauge: 10, 12, 3½".
Barrel: 25" (Full).
Weight: 8 lbs.
Stock: Uncheckered walnut.
Sights: Bead front.
Features: Uses same receiver as TCR '87 rifle models, and stock has extra 7/16" drop at heel. Choke designed for steel shot. Introduced 1989. From Thompson/Center.
Price: **$550.00**

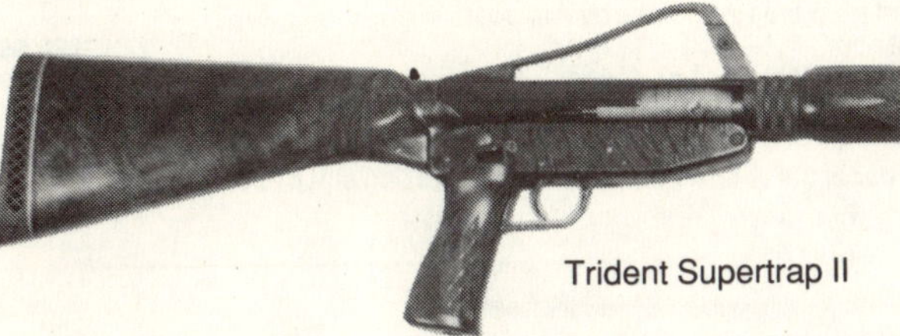

Trident Supertrap II

TRIDENT SUPERTRAP II TRAP SHOTGUN
Gauge: 12, 2¾" chamber.
Barrel: 30" standard, other lengths to order. Screw-in chokes.
Weight: About 9 lbs.
Stock: English or Claro walnut. Hand-checkered grip and forend. Standard pull is 14¼", other lengths to order.
Sights: White bead front on adjustable short rib, adjustable rear rib.
Features: Trigger can be converted to pull or release by one turn of a screw. Very light recoil. Long forcing cone, .750" bore, ported. Introduced 1990. Made in U.S. by Trident Ltd.
Price: **$2,500.00**

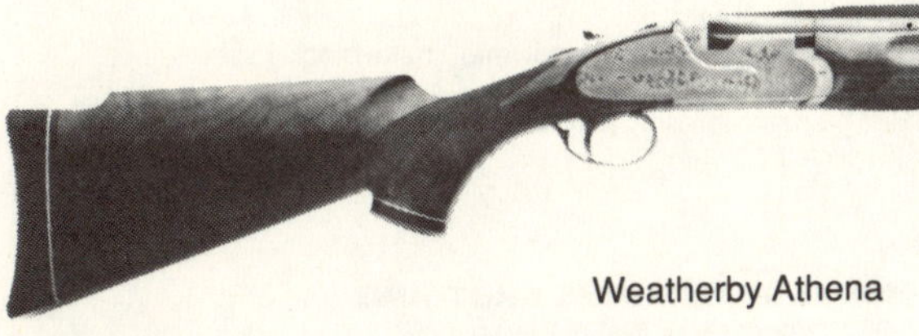

Weatherby Athena

WEATHERBY ATHENA SINGLE BARREL TRAP
Gauge: 12, 2¾" chamber.
Barrel: 32", 34" (Full, Mod., Imp. Mod., Multi-Choke tubes).
Weight: About 8½ lbs. **Length:** 49½" overall with 32" barrel.
Stock: 14⅜"x1⅜"x2⅛"x1¾". American walnut with checkered p.g. and forend.
Sights: White front, brass middle bead.
Features: Engraved, silvered sideplate receiver; ventilated rubber recoil pad. Can be ordered with an extra over/under barrel set. Introduced 1988. Imported from Japan by Weatherby.
Price: **$1,756.00**
Price: Combo **$2,325.00**

SHOTGUNS—MILITARY & POLICE

Designs for utility, suitable for and adaptable to competitions and other sporting purposes.

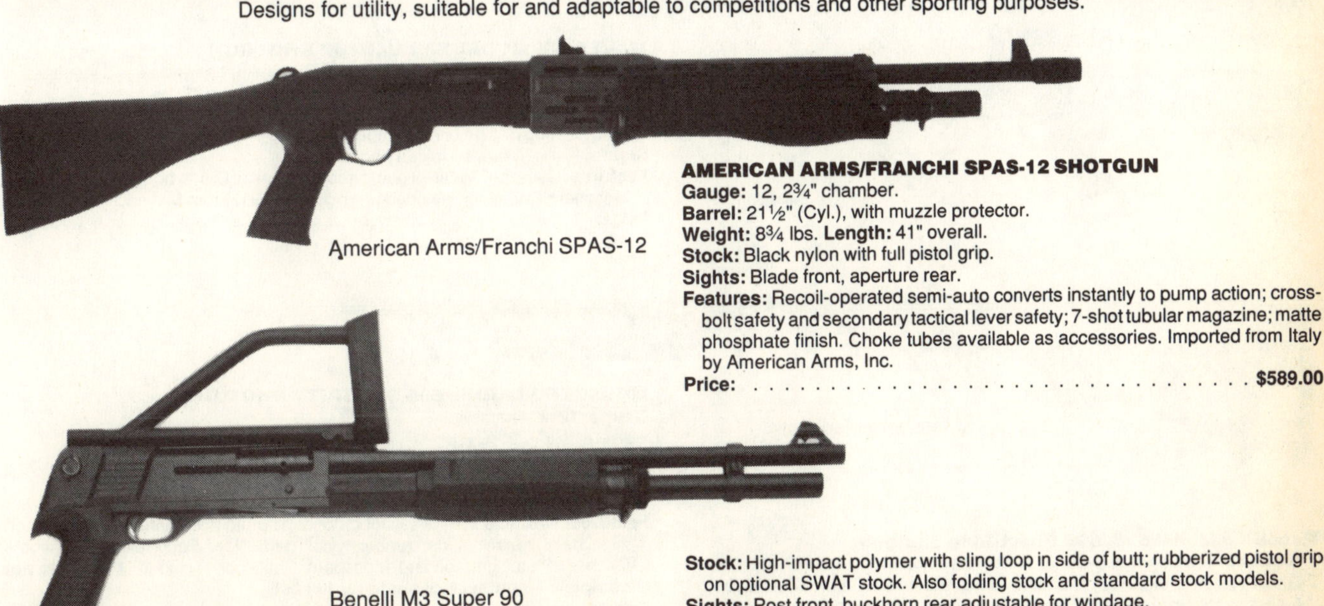

American Arms/Franchi SPAS-12

AMERICAN ARMS/FRANCHI SPAS-12 SHOTGUN
Gauge: 12, 2¾" chamber.
Barrel: 21½" (Cyl.), with muzzle protector.
Weight: 8¾ lbs. **Length:** 41" overall.
Stock: Black nylon with full pistol grip.
Sights: Blade front, aperture rear.
Features: Recoil-operated semi-auto converts instantly to pump action; cross-bolt safety and secondary tactical lever safety; 7-shot tubular magazine; matte phosphate finish. Choke tubes available as accessories. Imported from Italy by American Arms, Inc.
Price: **$589.00**

Benelli M3 Super 90

BENELLI M3 SUPER 90 PUMP/AUTO SHOTGUN
Gauge: 12, 3" chamber, 7-shot magazine.
Barrel: 19¾" (Cyl.).
Weight: 7 lbs., 8 oz. **Length:** 41" overall.
Stock: High-impact polymer with sling loop in side of butt; rubberized pistol grip on optional SWAT stock. Also folding stock and standard stock models.
Sights: Post front, buckhorn rear adjustable for windage.
Features: Combination pump/auto action. Alloy receiver with inertia recoil rotating locking lug bolt; matte finish; automatic shell release lever. Introduced 1989. Imported by Heckler & Koch, Inc.
Price: **$859.00**
Price: With Ghost Ring sight system **$914.00**
Price: With folding stock **$959.00**

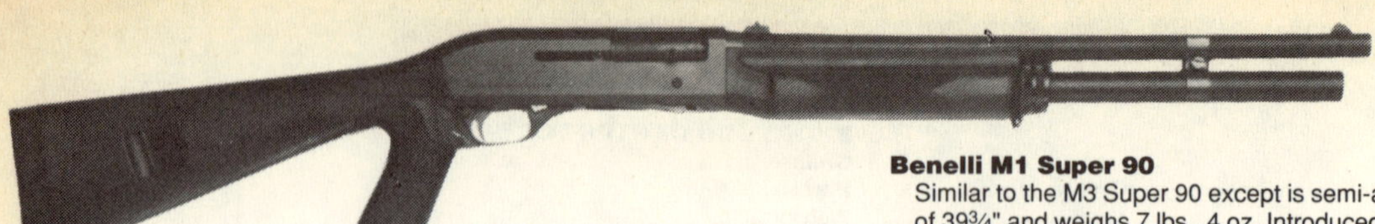

Benelli M1 Super 90

Benelli M1 Super 90

Similar to the M3 Super 90 except is semi-automatic only, has overall length of 39¾" and weighs 7 lbs., 4 oz. Introduced 1986.

Price: Slug Gun with standard stock **$659.00**
Price: With pistol grip stock (Defense) **$714.00**
Price: With ghost ring sight system **$714.00**

ARMSCOR MODEL 30R RIOT GUN

Gauge: 12, 5- or 7-shot capacity.
Barrel: 20" (Cyl.).
Weight: 7.2 lbs. **Length:** 40" overall.
Stock: Plain mahogany.
Sights: Metal bead front.
Features: Double action bars; blue finish; grooved forend. Introduced 1987. Imported from the Philippines by Armscor.

Price: About **$193.69**
Price: Model 30K (21" bbl., 7-shot, olive green butt and forend) . . . **$193.69**
Price: Model 30C (20" bbl., 5-shot, combo black removable butt with pistol grip) **$199.94**
Price: Model 30FS (20" bbl., 5-shot, black folding stock and pistol grip) **$208.69**

Beretta 1201FP3

BERETTA MODEL 1201FP3 AUTO SHOTGUN

Gauge: 12, 3" chamber.
Barrel: 20" (Cyl.).
Weight: 7.3 lbs. **Length:** NA
Stock: Special strengthened technopolymer, matte black finish.
Stock: Fixed rifle type.
Features: Has 6-shot magazine. Introduced 1988. Imported from Italy by Beretta U.S.A.
Price: **$575.00**

CROSSFIRE MODEL 88P RIFLE/SHOTGUN

Caliber/Gauge: 243, 308 Win./12-ga., 2¾" chamber.
Barrel: 20".
Weight: 9.5 lbs. **Length:** 39.75" overall.
Stock: Lightweight composite.
Sights: Optional. Adjustable open or optical battle sight.
Features: Combination pump/semi-auto action; each can be independently reloaded while the other is in operation. Has two barrels. Uses 20-shot M-14 magazine for 308, 7-shot box magazine for 12-ga. First round chambered by pump action, fires semi-auto thereafter. Announced 1989. From Special Service Arms.
Price: Less sights **$1,399.00**

Ithaca Model 87 Hand Grip Shotgun

Similar to the Model 87 M&P except has black polymer pistol grip and slide handle with nylon sling. In 12- or 20-gauge, 18½" barrel (Cyl.), 5-shot magazine. Reintroduced 1988.

Price: **$391.00**

ITHACA MODEL 87 M&P DSPS SHOTGUNS

Gauge: 12, 3" chamber, 5- or 8-shot magazine.
Barrel: 20" (Cyl.).
Weight: 7 lbs.
Stock: Walnut.
Sights: Bead front on 5-shot, rifle sights on 8-shot.
Features: Parkerized finish; bottom ejection; cross-bolt safety. Reintroduced 1988. From Ithaca Acquisition Corp.
Price: M&P, 5-shot **$407.00**
Price: DSPS, 8-shot **$407.00**

Maverick Bullpup

MAVERICK MODEL 88 BULLPUP SHOTGUN

Gauge: 12, 3" chamber; 6-shot magazine.
Barrel: 18½" (Cyl.).
Weight: 9½ lbs. **Length:** 26½" overall.
Stock: Bullpup design of high-impact plastics.
Sights: Fixed, mounted in carrying handle.
Features: Uses the Model 88 pump shotgun action. Cross-bolt and grip safeties. Mossberg Cablelock included. Introduced 1991. From Maverick Arms.
Price: **$313.00**

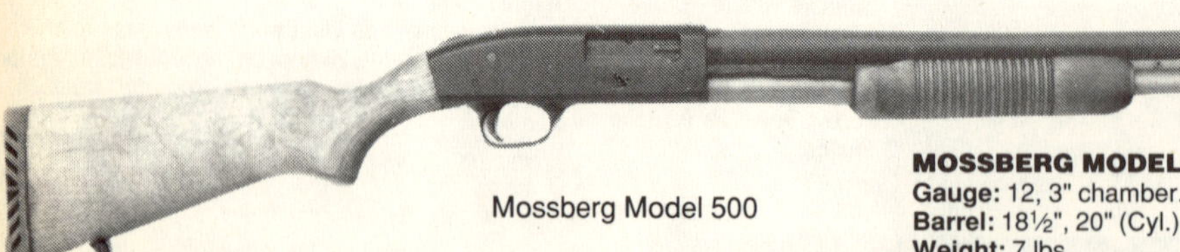

Mossberg Model 500

MOSSBERG MODEL 500 SECURITY SHOTGUNS

Gauge: 12, 3" chamber.
Barrel: 18½", 20" (Cyl.).
Weight: 7 lbs.
Stock: Walnut-finished hardwood or synthetic field.
Sights: Metal bead front.
Features: Available in 6- or 8-shot models. Top-mounted safety, double action slide bars, swivel studs, rubber recoil pad. Blue, Parkerized, Marinecote finishes. Pistol grip kit and Mossberg Cablelock included. **Price list not complete—contact Mossberg for full list.**
Price: From about **$276.00**
Price: Mini Combo (as above except also comes with a handguard and pistol grip kit), from about **$284.00**
Price: Maxi Combo (as above except also comes with an extra field barrel), from about **$302.00**
Price: With Ghost-Ring sight, from about **$334.00**
Price: As above, Parkerized, from about **$386.00**

Mossberg Model 500, 590 Ghost-Ring Shotguns

Similar to the Model 500 Security except has adjustable blade front, adjustable Ghost-Ring rear sight with protective "ears." Model 500 has 18.5" (Cyl.) barrel, 6-shot capacity; Model 590 has 20" (Cyl.) barrel, 9-shot capacity. Both have synthetic field stock. Mossberg Cablelock included. Introduced 1990. From Mossberg.

Price: Model 500, blue **$345.00**
Price: As above, Parkerized **$398.00**
Price: Model 590, blue **$410.00**
Price: As above, Parkerized **$461.00**

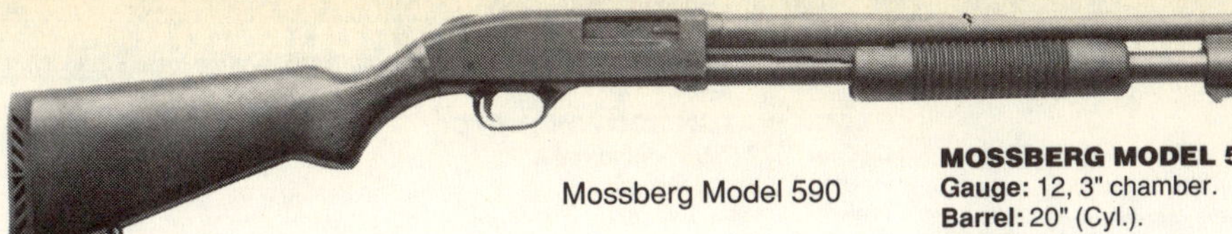
Mossberg Model 590

MOSSBERG MODEL 590 SHOTGUN
Gauge: 12, 3" chamber.
Barrel: 20" (Cyl.).
Weight: 7¼ lbs.
Stock: Synthetic field or Speedfeed.
Sights: Metal bead front.
Features: Top-mounted safety, double slide action bars. Comes with heat shield, bayonet lug, swivel studs, rubber recoil pad. Blue, Parkerized or Marinecote finish. Mossberg Cablelock included. From Mossberg.
Price: Blue, synthetic stock **$350.00**
Price: Parkerized, synthetic stock **$400.00**
Price: Blue, Speedfeed stock **$367.00**
Price: Parkerized, Speedfeed stock **$417.00**

Mossberg Model 500, 590 Intimidator Shotguns
Similar to the Model 500 or 590 Security with synthetic stock except has integral Laser Sight built into the forend. Mossberg Cablelock included. Introduced 1990.
Price: Model 500, blue, 6-shot **$635.00**
Price: Model 500, Parkerized, 6-shot **$688.00**
Price: Model 590, blue, 9-shot **$703.00**
Price: Model 590, Parkerized, 9-shot **$755.00**

Mossberg Model 500, 590 Mariner Pump
Similar to the Model 500 or 590 Security except all metal parts finished with Marinecote, a Teflon and metal coating to resist rust and corrosion. Synthetic field stock; pistol grip kit included. Mossberg Cablelock included.
Price: 6-shot **$385.00**
Price: 9-shot **$456.00**

Mossberg Model HS 410 Shotgun
Similar to the Model 500 Security pump except chambered for 410, 3" shells; has pistol grip forend, thick recoil pad, muzzle brake and has special spreader choke on the 18.5" barrel. Overall length is 37.5", weight is 6.25 lbs. Blue finish; synthetic field stock. Also available with integral Laser Sight forend. Mossberg Cablelock included. Introduced 1990.
Price: HS 410 . . . . **$388.00**
Price: HS 410 Laser **$699.00**

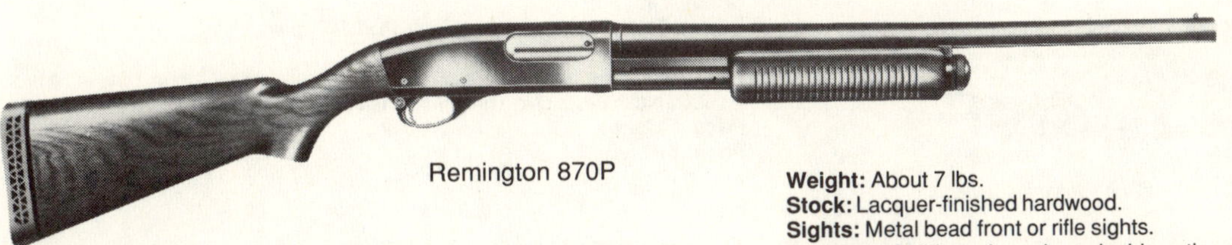
Remington 870P

REMINGTON 870P POLICE SHOTGUN
Gauge: 12, 3" chamber.
Barrel: 18", 20" (Police Cyl.), 20" (Imp. Cyl.).
Weight: About 7 lbs.
Stock: Lacquer-finished hardwood.
Sights: Metal bead front or rifle sights.
Features: Solid steel receiver, double action slide bars. Blued or Parkerized finish.
Price: 18" or 20", bead sight, about **$355.00**
Price: 20", rifle sights, about **$382.00**

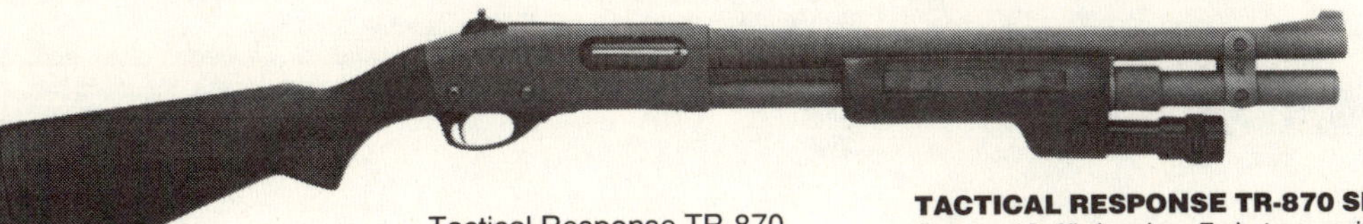
Tactical Response TR-870

TACTICAL RESPONSE TR-870 SHOTGUN
Gauge: 12, 3" chamber, 7-shot magazine.
Barrel: 18" (Cyl.).
Weight: NA. **Length:** NA.
Stock: Davis Speed Feed II. Fiberglass filled polypropolene with recoil absorbing buttplate. Laser Products nylon forend houses flashlight.
Sights: Ramp front with Trijicon tritium insert, Williams adjustable Ghost- Ring rear.
Features: Highly modified Remington 870P with Parkerized finish. Comes with nylon adjustable action sling, Uncle Mike's Jumbo Head safety, and Adventurers Outpost 6-shot Side Saddle ammo holder on left side of receiver. Introduced 1991. From Automatic Weaponry.
Price: **$695.00**

TRIDENT MODEL 12 PUMP SHOTGUN
Gauge: 12, 2¾" chamber, 10-shot magazine.
Barrel: 18¼".
Weight: 8 lbs. **Length:** 38" overall.
Stock: Synthetic butt grip pump handle; 13" length of pull.
Sights: Blade front, square notch rear.
Features: Fast takedown. Blue or camo finish. Introduced 1991. Made in U.S. by Trident Ltd.
Price: **$550.00**

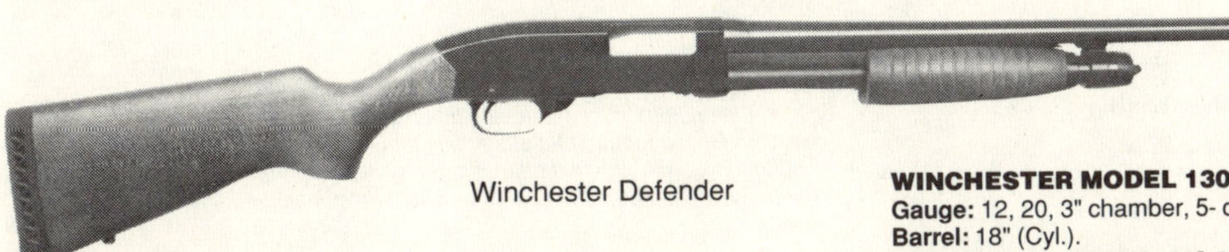
Winchester Defender

WINCHESTER MODEL 1300 DEFENDER PUMP GUN
Gauge: 12, 20, 3" chamber, 5- or 8-shot capacity.
Barrel: 18" (Cyl.).
Weight: 6¾ lbs. **Length:** 38⅝" overall.
Stock: Walnut-finished hardwood stock and ribbed forend, or synthetic; or pistol grip.
Sights: Metal bead front.
Features: Cross-bolt safety, front-locking rotary bolt, twin action slide bars. Black rubber buttpad. From U.S. Repeating Arms Co.
Price: 8-shot, wood or synthetic stock **$243.00**
Price: 5-shot, wood stock **$243.00**

Winchester Model 1300 Stainless Marine Pump Gun
Same as the Defender except has bright chrome finish, stainless steel barrel, rifle-type sights only. Phosphate coated receiver for corrosion resistance.
Price: About **$423.00**

Winchester 8-Shot Pistol Grip Pump Security Shotguns
Same as regular Defender Pump but with pistol grip and forend of high-impact resistant ABS plastic with non-glare black finish. Introduced 1984.
Price: Pistol Grip Defender, about **$243.00**

BLACKPOWDER SINGLE SHOT PISTOLS—FLINT & PERCUSSION

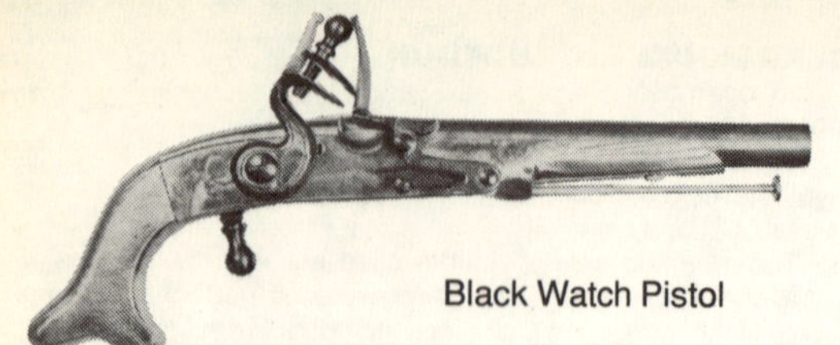
Black Watch Pistol

BLACK WATCH SCOTCH PISTOL
Caliber: 577 (.500" round ball).
Barrel: 7", smoothbore.
Weight: 1½ lbs. **Length:** 12" overall.
Stock: Brass.
Sights: None.
Features: Faithful reproduction of this military flintlock. From Dixie Gun Works, E.M.F.
Price: . . . . **$148.00 to $310.00**

Dixie Charleville

CHARLEVILLE FLINTLOCK PISTOL
Caliber: 69 (.680" round ball).
Barrel: 7½".
Weight: 48 oz. **Length:** 13½" overall.
Stock: Walnut.
Sights: None.
Features: Brass frame, polished steel barrel, iron belt hook, brass buttcap and backstrap. Replica of original 1777 pistol. Imported by Dixie Gun Works, E.M.F., Navy Arms.
Price: **$325.00**

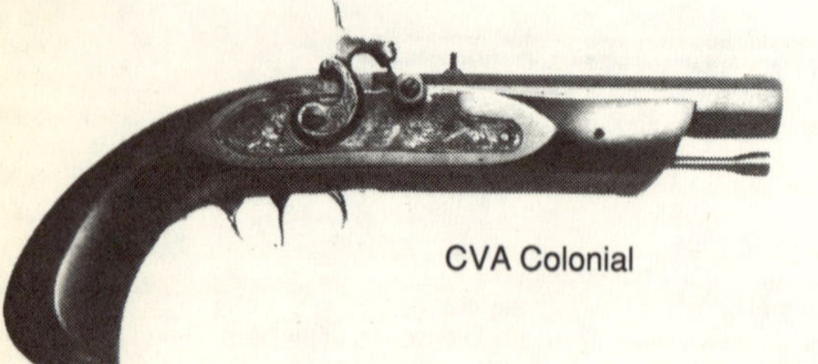
CVA Colonial

CVA COLONIAL PISTOL
Caliber: 45.
Barrel: 6¾", octagonal, rifled. **Length:** 12¾" overall.
Stock: Selected hardwood.
Features: Case-hardened lock, brass furniture, fixed sights. Steel ramrod. Available in percussion only. Imported by CVA.
Price: Finished **$149.95**
Price: Kit **$109.95**

CVA Hawken

CVA HAWKEN PISTOL
Caliber: 50.
Barrel: 9¾"; 1" flats.
Weight: 50 oz. **Length:** 16½" overall.
Stock: Select hardwood.
Sights: Beaded blade front, fully adjustable open rear.
Features: Color case-hardened lock, polished brass wedge plate, nose cap, ramrod thimbles, trigger guard, grip cap. Hooked breech. Imported by CVA.
Price: **$214.95**
Price: Kit **$139.95**

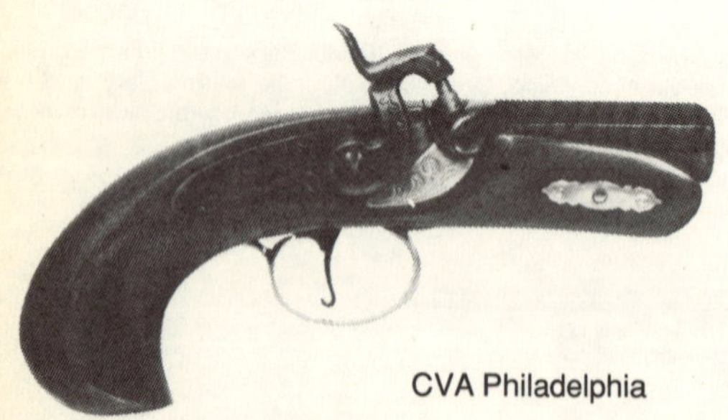
CVA Philadelphia

CVA PHILADELPHIA DERRINGER PISTOL
Caliber: 45.
Barrel: 3⅛".
Weight: 16 oz. **Length:** 7" overall.
Stock: Select hardwood.
Sights: Fixed.
Features: Engraved wedge holder and barrel. Imported by CVA.
Price: **$119.95**
Price: Kit form **$99.95**

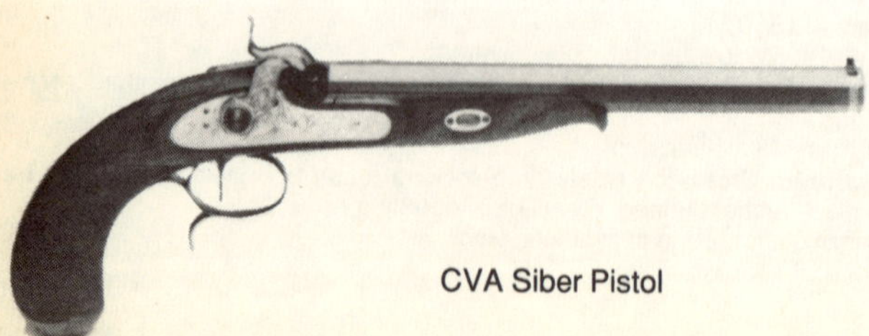
CVA Siber Pistol

CVA SIBER PISTOL
Caliber: 45.
Barrel: 10½".
Weight: 34 oz. **Length:** 15½" overall.
Stock: High-grade French walnut, checkered grip.
Sights: Barleycorn front, micro-adjustable rear.
Features: Reproduction of pistol made by Swiss watchmaker Jean Siber in the 1800s. Precise lock and set-trigger give fast lock time. Has engraving, blackened stainless barrel, trigger guard. Imported by CVA.
Price: **$578.95**

CVA VEST POCKET DERRINGER
Caliber: 44.
Barrel: 2½", brass.
Weight: 7 oz.
Stock: Two-piece walnut.
Features: All brass frame with brass ramrod. A muzzle-loading version of the Colt No. 3 derringer. Imported by CVA.
Price: Finished **$79.95**
Price: Kit **$76.95**

CAUTION: PRICES CHANGE, CHECK AT GUNSHOP.

Dixie Brass Frame

Dixie Lincoln Derringer

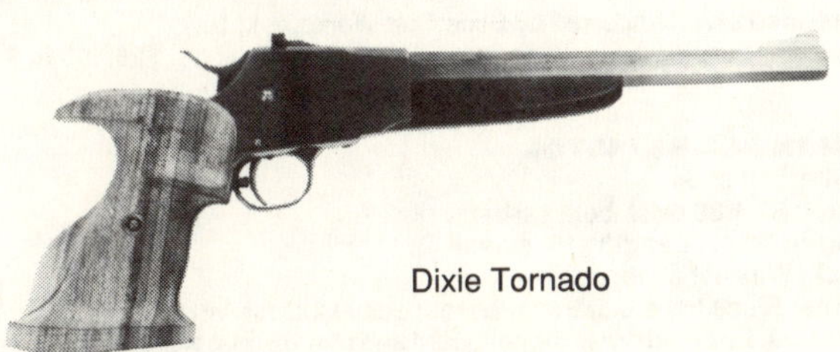
Dixie Tornado

DIXIE TORNADO TARGET PISTOL
Caliber: 44 (.430" round ball).
Barrel: 10", octagonal, 1:22 twist.
Stocks: Walnut, target-style. Left unfinished for custom fitting. Walnut forend.
Sights: Blade on ramp front, micro-type open rear adjustable for windage and elevation.
Features: Grip frame style of 1860 Colt revolver. Improved model of the Tingle and B.W. Southgate pistol. Trigger adjustable for pull. Frame, barrel, hammer and sights in the white, brass trigger guard. Comes with solid brass, walnut-handled cleaning rod with jag and nylon muzzle protector. Introduced 1983. From Dixie Gun Works.
Price: **$215.50**

Dixie Harper's Ferry

HAWKEN PERCUSSION PISTOL
Caliber: 54.
Barrel: 9", octagonal.
Weight: 40 oz. **Length:** 14" overall.
Stock: Checkered walnut.
Sights: Blade front, fixed notch rear.
Features: German silver trigger guard, blued barrel. Imported from Italy by E.M.F.
Price: **$370.00**

DIXIE ABILENE DERRINGER
Caliber: 41.
Barrel: 2½", six-groove rifling.
Weight: 8 oz. **Length:** 6½" overall.
Stock: Walnut.
Features: All steel version of Dixie's brass-framed derringers. Blued barrel, color case-hardened frame and hammer. Shoots .395" patched ball. Comes with wood presentation case. From Dixie Gun Works.
Price: **$81.50**
Price: Kit form **$51.95**

DIXIE BRASS FRAME DERRINGER
Caliber: 41.
Barrel: 2½".
Weight: 7 oz. **Length:** 5½" overall.
Stock: Walnut.
Features: Brass frame, color case-hardened hammer and trigger. Shoots .395" round ball. Engraved model available. From Dixie Gun Works.
Price: Plain model **$69.95**
Price: Engraved model **$95.50**
Price: Kit form, plain model **$53.95**

DIXIE LINCOLN DERRINGER
Caliber: 41.
Barrel: 2", 8 lands, 8 grooves.
Weight: 7 oz. **Length:** 5½" overall.
Stock: Walnut finish, checkered.
Sights: Fixed.
Features: Authentic copy of the "Lincoln Derringer." Shoots .400" patched ball. German silver furniture includes trigger guard with pineapple finial, wedge plates, nose, wrist, side and teardrop inlays. All furniture, lockplate, hammer, and breech plug engraved. Imported from Italy by Dixie Gun Works.
Price: With wooden case **$285.95**
Price: Kit (not engraved) **$89.95**

DIXIE PENNSYLVANIA PISTOL
Caliber: 44 (.430" round ball).
Barrel: 10" (⅞" octagon).
Weight: 2½ lbs.
Stock: Walnut-stained hardwood.
Sights: Blade front, open rear drift-adjustable for windage; brass.
Features: Available in flint only. Brass trigger guard, thimbles, nosecap, wedgeplates; high-luster blue barrel. Imported from Italy by Dixie Gun Works.
Price: Finished **$134.95**
Price: Kit **$119.95**

DIXIE SCREW BARREL PISTOL
Caliber: .445".
Barrel: 2½".
Weight: 8 oz. **Length:** 6½" overall.
Stock: Walnut.
Features: Trigger folds down when hammer is cocked. Close copy of the originals once made in Belgium. Uses No. 11 percussion caps. From Dixie Gun Works.
Price: **$89.00**
Price: Kit **$64.95**

FRENCH-STYLE DUELING PISTOL
Caliber: 44.
Barrel: 10".
Weight: 35 oz. **Length:** 15¾" overall.
Stock: Carved walnut.
Sights: Fixed.
Features: Comes with velvet-lined case and accessories. Imported by Mandall Shooting Supplies.
Price: **$295.00**

HARPER'S FERRY 1806 PISTOL
Caliber: 58 (.570" round ball).
Barrel: 10".
Weight: 40 oz. **Length:** 16" overall.
Stock: Walnut.
Sights: Fixed.
Features: Case-hardened lock, brass-mounted browned barrel. Replica of the first U.S. Gov't.-made flintlock pistol. Imported by Navy Arms, Dixie Gun Works, E.M.F.
Price: . . . . **$225.00 to $325.00**
Price: Kit (Dixie) **$184.95**

BLACKPOWDER SINGLE SHOT PISTOLS—FLINT & PERCUSSION

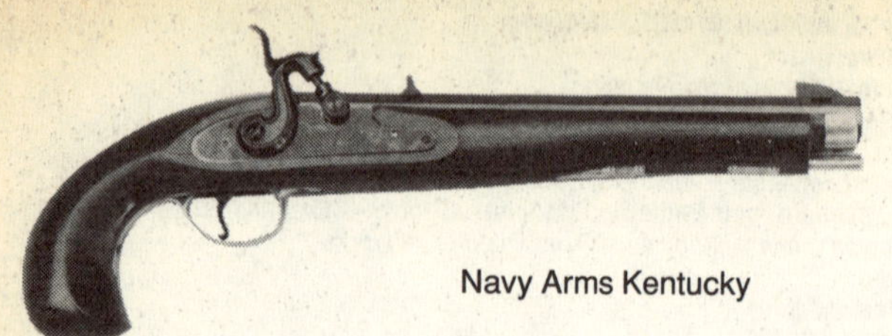

Navy Arms Kentucky

Kentucky Percussion Pistol

Similar to flint version but percussion lock. Imported by Cabela's, The Armoury, E.M.F., Navy Arms, CVA (50-cal.).

Price: . . . . **$141.95** to **$250.00**
Price: Brass barrel (E.M.F.) **$275.00**
Price: In kit form (CVA, Armoury) **$97.95**
Price: Single cased set (Navy Arms) **$205.00**
Price: Double cased set (Navy Arms) **$330.00**

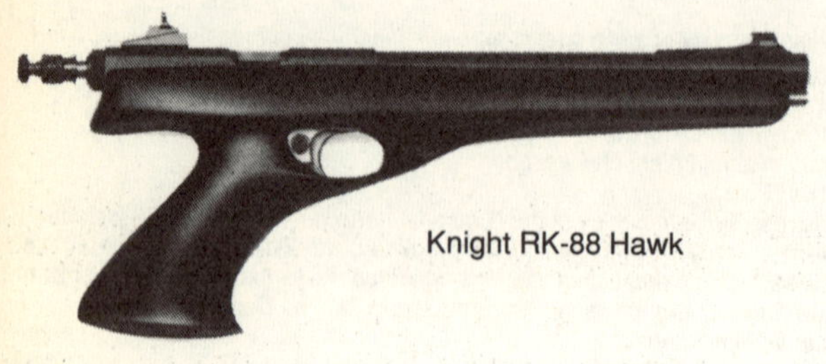

Knight RK-88 Hawk

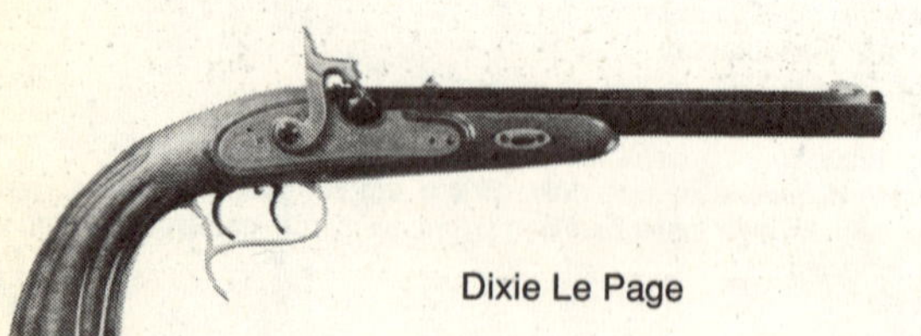

Dixie Le Page

Lyman Plains Pistol

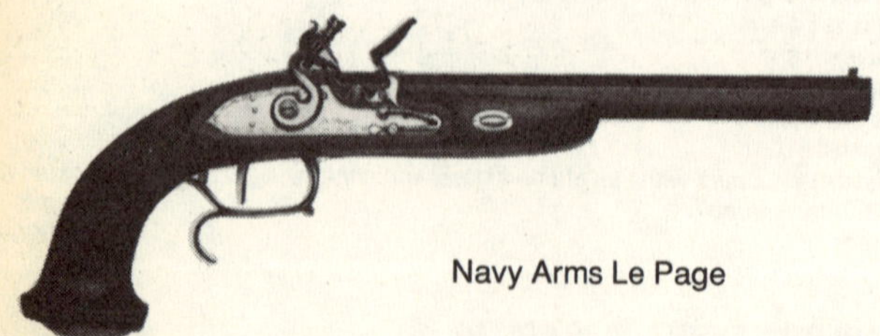

Navy Arms Le Page

WILLIAM MOORE FLINTLOCK PISTOL

Caliber: 45.
Barrel: 10", octagonal.
Weight: 36 oz. **Length:** 15" overall.
Stock: Checkered hardwood.
Sights: Blade front, fixed notch rear.
Features: German silver trigger guard, rest blued. Imported from Italy by E.M.F.
Price: **$400.00**

KENTUCKY FLINTLOCK PISTOL

Caliber: 44, 45.
Barrel: 10⅛".
Weight: 32 oz. **Length:** 15½" overall.
Stock: Walnut.
Sights: Fixed.
Features: Specifications, including caliber, weight and length may vary with importer. Case-hardened lock, blued barrel; available also as brass barrel flint Model 1821. Imported by Cabela's (44, 50), Navy Arms (44 only), The Armoury, E.M.F.
Price: . . . . **$145.00** to **$207.00**
Price: Brass barrel (E.M.F.) **$225.00**
Price: In kit form, from . . . . **$90.00** to **$112.00**
Price: Single cased set (Navy Arms) **$230.00**
Price: Double cased set (Navy Arms) **$350.00**

KNIGHT RK-88 HAWK PISTOL

Caliber: 45, 50, 54.
Barrel: 10"; 1:16 twist.
Weight: 32 oz. **Length:** NA.
Stock: Black composite.
Sights: Bead on blade front, open rear adjustable for windage.
Features: In-line percussion ignition system. The Double Safety System has an ambidextrous trigger safety and screw-type hammer safety. Drilled and tapped for scope mounting. Introduced 1991. From Modern Muzzle Loading.
Price: **$429.95**

LE PAGE PERCUSSION DUELING PISTOL

Caliber: 45.
Barrel: 10", rifled.
Weight: 40 oz. **Length:** 16" overall.
Stock: Walnut, fluted butt.
Sights: Blade front, notch rear.
Features: Double-set triggers. Blued barrel; trigger guard and buttcap are polished silver. Imported by Dixie Gun Works, E.M.F.
Price: . . . . **$259.95 to $400.00**

LYMAN PLAINS PISTOL

Caliber: 50 or 54.
Barrel: 8", 1:30 twist, both calibers.
Weight: 50 oz. **Length:** 15" overall.
Stock: Walnut half-stock.
Sights: Blade front, square notch rear adjustable for windage.
Features: Polished brass trigger guard and ramrod tip, color case-hardened coil spring lock, spring-loaded trigger, stainless steel nipple, blackened iron furniture. Hooked patent breech, detachable belt hook. Introduced 1981. From Lyman Products.
Price: Finished **$209.95**
Price: Kit **$174.95**

Consult our Directory pages for the location of firms mentioned.

MOORE & PATRICK FLINT DUELING PISTOL

Caliber: 45.
Barrel: 10", rifled.
Weight: 32 oz. **Length:** 14½" overall.
Stock: European walnut, checkered.
Sights: Fixed.
Features: Engraved, silvered lockplate, blue barrel. German silver furniture. Imported from Italy by Dixie Gun Works.
Price: **$335.00**

NAVY ARMS LE PAGE DUELING PISTOL

Caliber: 44.
Barrel: 9", octagon, rifled.
Weight: 34 oz. **Length:** 15" overall.
Stock: European walnut.
Sights: Adjustable rear.
Features: Single-set trigger. Polished metal finish. From Navy Arms.
Price: Percussion **$355.00**
Price: Single cased set, percussion **$540.00**
Price: Double cased set, percussion **$930.00**
Price: Flintlock, rifled **$435.00**
Price: Flintlock, smoothbore (45-cal.) **$435.00**
Price: Flintlock, single cased set **$625.00**
Price: Flintlock, double cased set **$1,100.00**

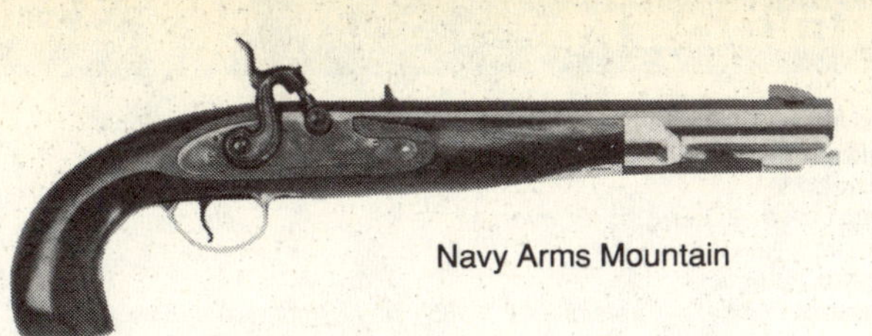
Navy Arms Mountain

NAVY ARMS MOUNTAIN PISTOL
Caliber: 50.
Barrel: 10", octagonal, rifled.
Weight: 36 oz. **Length:** 15½" overall.
Stock: European walnut.
Sights: Blade front, notch rear adjustable for windage.
Features: Color case-hardened lock, blued barrel, brass furniture. Imported by Navy Arms.
Price: Flintlock **$155.00**
Price: Percussion **$145.00**

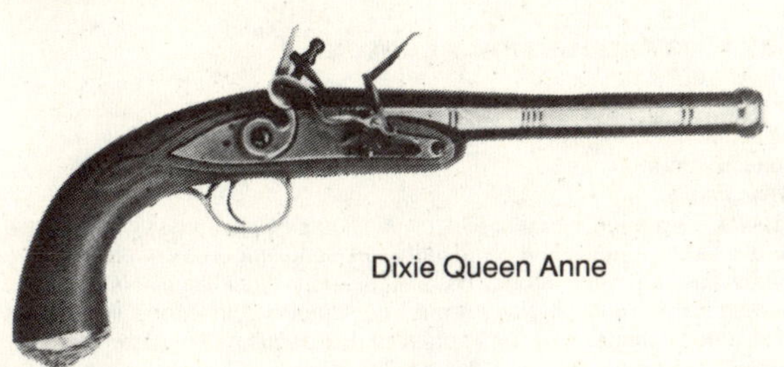
Dixie Queen Anne

QUEEN ANNE FLINTLOCK PISTOL
Caliber: 50 (.490" round ball).
Barrel: 7½", smoothbore.
Stock: Walnut.
Sights: None.
Features: Browned steel barrel, fluted brass trigger guard, brass mask on butt. Lockplate left in the white. Made by Pedersoli in Italy. Introduced 1983. Imported by Dixie Gun Works, Navy Arms.
Price: From Dixie **$166.50**
Price: From Navy Arms **$145.00**
Price: Kit (Dixie Gun Works only) **$138.50**

THOMPSON/CENTER SCOUT PISTOL
Caliber: 50 and 54.
Barrel: 12", interchangeable.
Weight: 4 lbs., 6 oz. **Length:** NA.
Stocks: American black walnut stocks and forend.
Sights: Blade on ramp front, fully adjustable Patridge rear.
Features: Patented in-line ignition system with special vented breech plug. Patented trigger mechanism consists of only two moving parts. Interchangeable barrels. Wide grooved hammer. Brass trigger guard assembly. Introduced 1990. From Thompson/Center.
Price: 50- or 54-cal **$275.00**
Price: Extra barrel, 50- or 54-cal **$140.00**

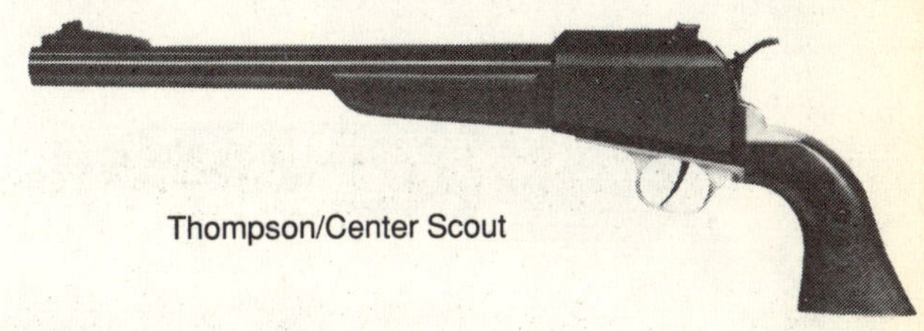
Thompson/Center Scout

Traditions William Parker

TRADITIONS WILLIAM PARKER PISTOL
Caliber: 45.
Barrel: 10⅜", 15/16" flats.
Weight: 40 oz. **Length:** 17½" overall.
Stock: Walnut with checkered grip.
Sights: Blade front, fixed rear.
Features: Replica dueling pistol with 1:18 twist, hooked breech. Polished steel barrel, lock. From Traditions, Inc.
Price: **$240.00**

Traditions Pioneer

TRADITIONS PIONEER PISTOL
Caliber: 45.
Barrel: 9⅝", 13/16" flats.
Weight: 36 oz. **Length:** 15" overall.
Stock: Beech.
Sights: Blade front, fixed rear.
Features: V-type mainspring; hooked breech; 1:18 twist. Single trigger. German silver furniture, blackened hardware. From Traditions, Inc.
Price: **$160.00**
Price: Kit **$114.00**

TRADITIONS TRAPPER PISTOL
Caliber: 45, 50.
Barrel: 9¾", ⅞" flats.
Weight: 2¾ lbs. **Length:** 16" overall.
Stock: Beech.
Sights: Blade front, adjustable rear.
Features: Double-set triggers; brass buttcap, trigger guard, wedge plate, forend tip, thimble. From Traditions, Inc.
Price: **$162.00**
Price: Kit **$124.00**

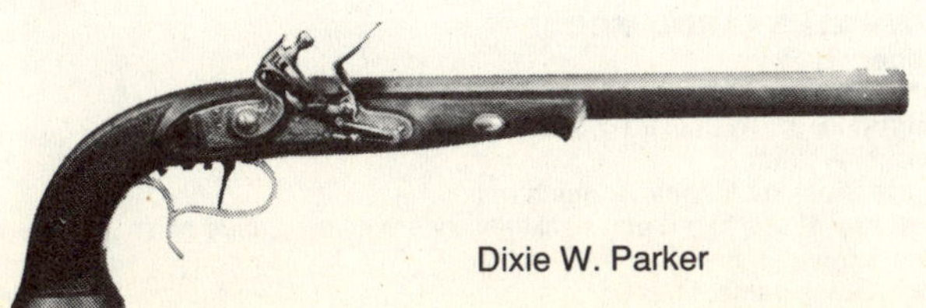
Dixie W. Parker

W. PARKER FLINTLOCK PISTOL
Caliber: 45.
Barrel: 11", rifled.
Weight: 40 oz. **Length:** 16½" overall.
Stock: Walnut.
Sights: Blade front, notch rear.
Features: Browned barrel, silver-plated trigger guard, finger rest, polished and engraved lock. Double-set triggers. Imported by Dixie Gun Works, Traditions, Inc.
Price: . . . . **$208.00** to **$310.00**

BLACKPOWDER REVOLVERS

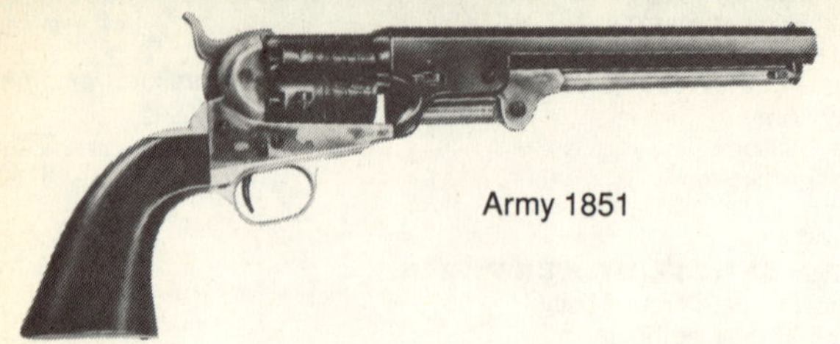

Army 1851

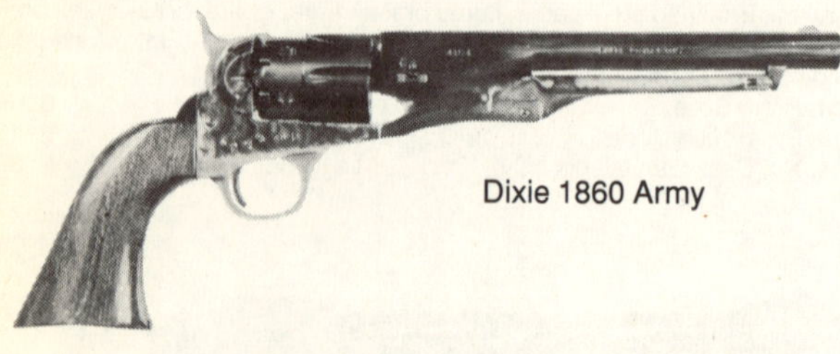

Dixie 1860 Army

Dixie 1849 Pocket

CABELA'S PATERSON REVOLVER
Caliber: 36, 5-shot cylinder.
Barrel: 7½".
Weight: 24 oz. **Length:** 11½" overall.
Stocks: One-piece walnut.
Sights: Fixed.
Features: Recreation of the 1836 gun. Color case-hardened frame, steel backstrap; roll-engraved cylinder scene. Imported by Cabela's.
Price: $199.95

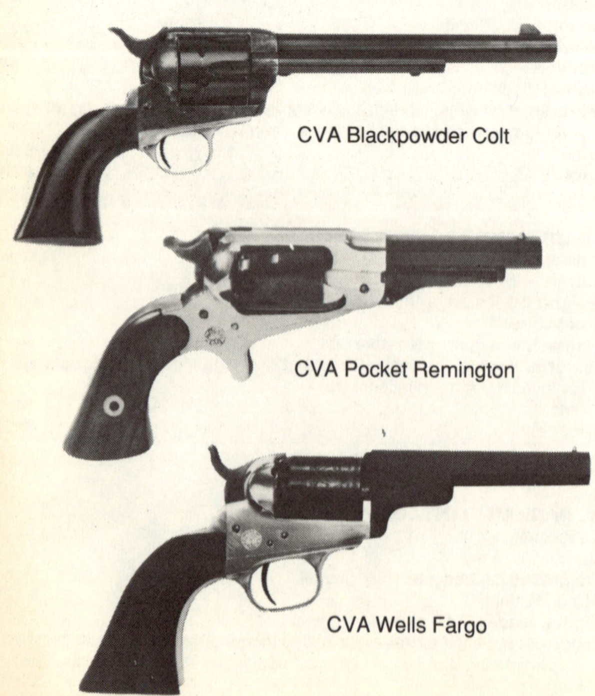

CVA Blackpowder Colt

CVA Pocket Remington

CVA Wells Fargo

ARMY 1851 PERCUSSION REVOLVER
Caliber: 44, 6-shot.
Barrel: 7½".
Weight: 45 oz. **Length:** 13" overall.
Stocks: Walnut finish.
Sights: Fixed.
Features: 44-caliber version of the 1851 Navy. Imported by The Armoury.
Price: $129.00

ARMY 1860 PERCUSSION REVOLVER
Caliber: 44, 6-shot.
Barrel: 8".
Weight: 40 oz. **Length:** 13⅝" overall.
Stocks: Walnut.
Sights: Fixed.
Features: Engraved Navy scene on cylinder; brass trigger guard; case-hardened frame, loading lever and hammer. Some importers supply pistol cut for detachable shoulder stock, have accessory stock available. Imported by Cabela's, E.M.F., CVA, Navy Arms, The Armoury, Cimarron, Dixie Gun Works (half-fluted cylinder, not roll engraved), Euroarms of America (brass or steel model), Armsport, Mitchell, Uberti USA.
Price: About . . . . **$92.95** to **$235.00**
Price: Single cased set (Navy Arms) **$240.00**
Price: Double cased set (Navy Arms) **$365.00**
Price: 1861 Navy: Same as Army except 36-cal., 7½" bbl., wgt. 41 oz., cut for shoulder stock; round cylinder (fluted avail.), from E.M.F., CVA (brass frame), Cabela's, Mitchell . . . . **$99.95** to **$249.00**
Price: Steel frame kit (E.M.F., Mitchell, Navy, Euroarms) **$125.00 to $146.00**
Price: Colt Army Police, fluted cyl. (Cabela's) **$96.95**

BABY DRAGOON 1848, 1849 POCKET, WELLS FARGO
Caliber: 31.
Barrel: 3", 4", 5"; seven-groove, RH twist.
Weight: About 21 oz.
Stock: Varnished walnut.
Sights: Brass pin front, hammer notch rear.
Features: No loading lever on Baby Dragoon or Wells Fargo models. Unfluted cylinder with stagecoach holdup scene; cupped cylinder pin; no grease grooves; one safety pin on cylinder and slot in hammer face; straight (flat) mainspring. From Dixie Gun Works, Uberti USA, Cabela's.
Price: 6" barrel, with loading lever (Dixie Gun Works) **$185.00**
Price: 3", 4", 5½", 6" (Uberti USA) **$295.00**
Price: As above, silver-plated (Uberti USA) **$240.00**
Price: 1849 Pocket (Cabela's) **$189.95**

CVA BLACKPOWDER SINGLE ACTION COLT
Caliber: 44, 6-shot.
Barrel: 7".
Weight: 45 oz. **Length:** 13" overall.
Stocks: One-piece walnut.
Sights: Blade front, notch rear in topstrap.
Features: Blue finish with color case-hardened frame, brass backstrap and trigger guard. Cylinder has recessed nipples for percussion caps, safety notches. Introduced 1991. Imported by CVA.
Price: **$419.95**

CVA POCKET REMINGTON
Caliber: 31.
Barrel: 4", octagonal.
Weight: 15½ oz. **Length:** 7½" overall.
Stocks: Two-piece walnut.
Sights: Post front, grooved topstrap rear.
Features: Spur trigger, brass frame with blued barrel and cylinder. Available finished or in kit form. Introduced 1984. Imported by CVA.
Price: Finished **$164.95**
Price: Kit **$162.95**

CVA WELLS FARGO MODEL
Caliber: 31.
Barrel: 4", octagonal.
Weight: 28 oz. (with extra cylinder). **Length:** 9" overall.
Stocks: Walnut.
Sights: Post front, hammer notch rear.
Features: Brass frame and backstrap or steel frame; blue finish. Comes with extra cylinder. Imported by CVA.
Price: Brass frame, finished **$164.95**
Price: As above, kit **$139.95**
Price: Steel frame, finished **$248.95**

CAUTION: PRICES CHANGE, CHECK AT GUNSHOP.

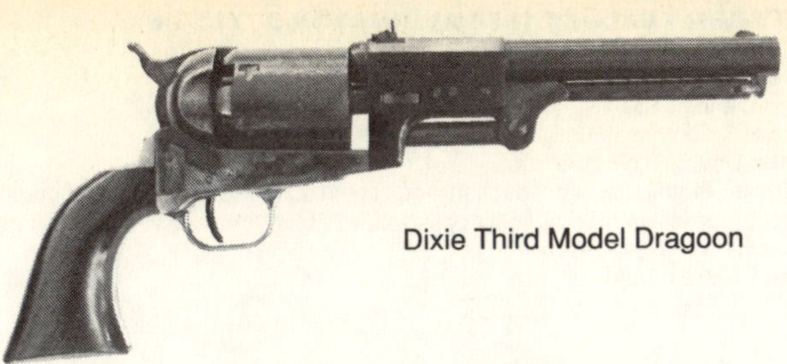
Dixie Third Model Dragoon

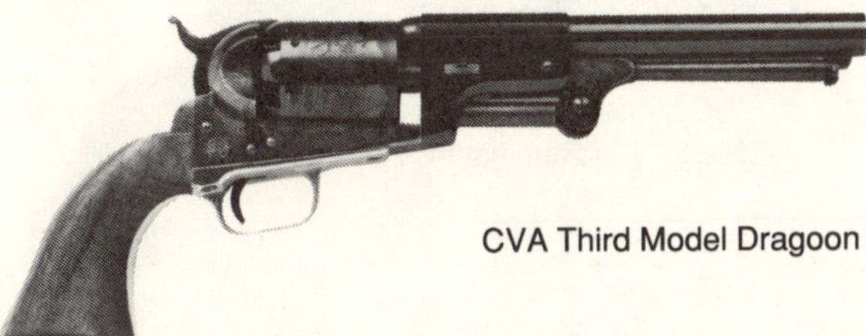
CVA Third Model Dragoon

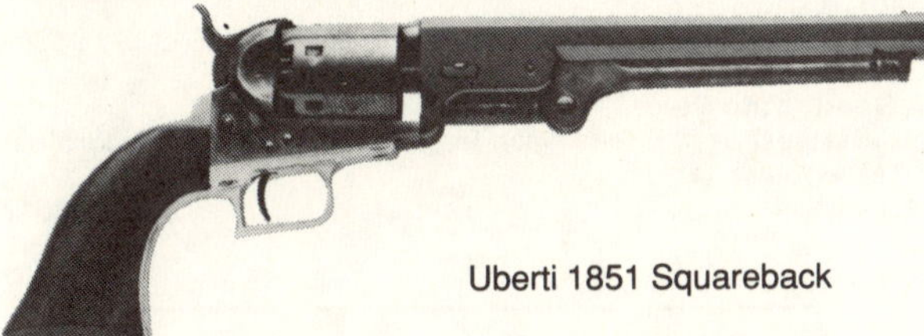
Uberti 1851 Squareback

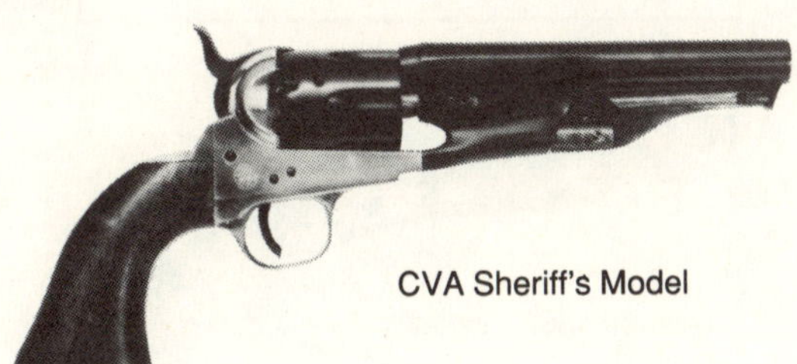
CVA Sheriff's Model

Uberti 1861 Navy Percussion Revolver
Similar to 1851 Navy except has round 7½" barrel, rounded trigger guard, German silver blade front sight, "creeping" loading lever. Available with fluted or round cylinder. Imported by Uberti USA.
Price: Steel backstrap, trigger guard, cut for stock **$299.00**

CVA Colt Sheriff's Model
Similar to the Uberti 1861 Navy except has 5½" barrel, brass or steel frame, semi-fluted cylinder. In 36-caliber only.
Price: Brass frame, finished **$199.95**
Price: As above, kit **$172.95**
Price: Steel frame, finished **$229.95**
Price: 1861 Navy, steel frame, 36-cal. **$279.95**
Price: As above, brass frame, 44-cal. **$185.95**
Price: As above, kit **$163.95**

LE MAT CAVALRY MODEL REVOLVER
Caliber: 44/65.
Barrel: 6¾" (revolver); 4⅞" (single shot).
Weight: 3 lbs., 7 oz.
Stocks: Hand-checkered walnut.
Sights: Post front, hammer notch rear.
Features: Exact reproduction with all-steel construction; 44-cal. 9-shot cylinder, 65-cal. single barrel; color case-hardened hammer with selector; spur trigger guard; ring at butt; lever-type barrel release. From Navy Arms.
Price: Cavalry model (lanyard ring, spur trigger guard) **$595.00**
Price: Army model (round trigger guard, pin-type barrel release) . . **$595.00**
Price: Naval-style (thumb selector on hammer) **$595.00**

DIXIE THIRD MODEL DRAGOON
Caliber: 44 (.454" round ball).
Barrel: 7⅜".
Weight: 4 lbs., 2½ oz.
Stocks: One-piece walnut.
Sights: Brass pin front, hammer notch rear, or adjustable folding leaf rear.
Features: Cylinder engraved with Indian fight scene. This is the only Dragoon replica with folding leaf sight. Brass backstrap and trigger guard; color case-hardened steel frame, blue-black barrel. Imported by Dixie Gun Works.
Price: **$195.00**

CVA Third Model Colt Dragoon
Similar to the Dixie Third Dragoon except has 7½" barrel, weighs 4 lbs., 6 oz., blade front sight. Overall length of 14". 44-caliber, 6-shot.
Price: **$278.95**

DIXIE WYATT EARP REVOLVER
Caliber: 44.
Barrel: 12" octagon.
Weight: 46 oz. **Length:** 18" overall.
Stocks: Two-piece walnut.
Sights: Fixed.
Features: Highly polished brass frame, backstrap and trigger guard; blued barrel and cylinder; case-hardened hammer, trigger and loading lever. Navy-size shoulder stock ($45) will fit with minor fitting. From Dixie Gun Works.
Price: **$130.00**

GRISWOLD & GUNNISON PERCUSSION REVOLVER
Caliber: 36 or 44, 6-shot.
Barrel: 7½".
Weight: 44 oz. (36-cal.). **Length:** 13" overall.
Stocks: Walnut.
Sights: Fixed.
Features: Replica of famous Confederate pistol. Brass frame, backstrap and trigger guard; case-hardened loading lever; rebated cylinder (44-cal. only). Rounded Dragoon-type barrel. Imported by Navy Arms (as Reb Model 1860), E.M.F.
Price: About **$229.00**
Price: Kit (E.M.F.) **$95.00**
Price: Single cased set (Navy Arms) **$190.00**
Price: Double cased set (Navy Arms) **$300.00**
Price: Reb 1860 (Navy Arms) **$100.00**
Price: As above, kit **$80.00**

NAVY MODEL 1851 PERCUSSION REVOLVER
Caliber: 36, 44, 6-shot.
Barrel: 7½".
Weight: 44 oz. **Length:** 13" overall.
Stocks: Walnut finish.
Sights: Post front, hammer notch rear.
Features: Brass backstrap and trigger guard; some have 1st Model squareback trigger guard, engraved cylinder with navy battle scene; case-hardened frame, hammer, loading lever. Imported by The Armoury, Cabela's, Mitchell, Navy Arms, E.M.F., Dixie Gun Works, Euroarms of America, Armsport, CVA (36-cal. only), Uberti USA.
Price: Brass frame . . . . **$95.00** to **$229.00**
Price: Steel frame . . . . **$130.00** to **$285.00**
Price: Silver-plated backstrap, trigger guard (Uberti USA) **$249.00**
Price: Kit form . . . . **$110.00** to **$123.95**
Price: Engraved model (Dixie Gun Works) **$139.95**
Price: Single cased set, steel frame (Navy Arms) **$225.00**
Price: Double cased set, steel frame (Navy Arms) **$325.00**
Price: Confederate Navy (Cabela's) **$59.88**

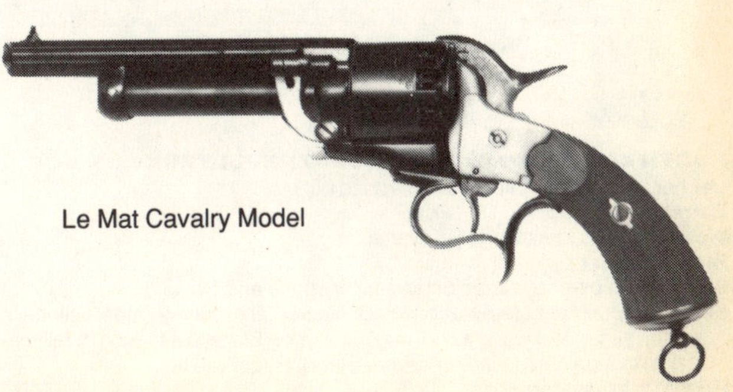
Le Mat Cavalry Model

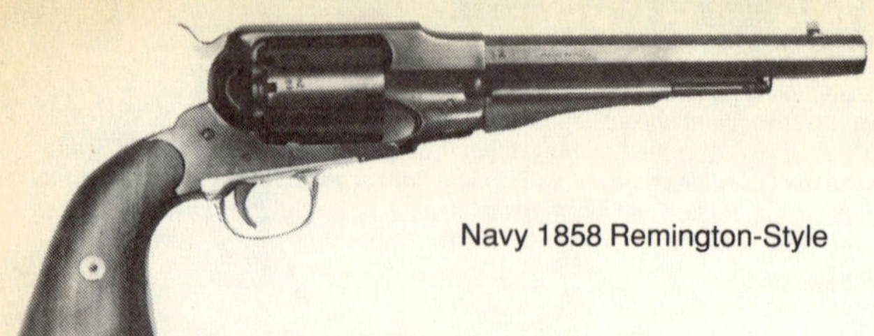
Navy 1858 Remington-Style

NEW MODEL 1858 ARMY PERCUSSION REVOLVER
Caliber: 36 or 44, 6-shot.
Barrel: 6½" or 8".
Weight: 40 oz. **Length:** 13½" overall.
Stocks: Walnut.
Sights: Blade front, groove-in-frame rear.
Features: Replica of Remington Model 1858. Also available from some importers as Army Model Belt Revolver in 36-cal., a shortened and lightened version of the 44. Target Model (Uberti USA, Navy Arms) has fully adjustable target rear sight, target front, 36 or 44. Imported by Cabela's, CVA (as 1858 Remington Army), Dixie Gun Works, Navy Arms, The Armoury, E.M.F., Euroarms of America (engraved, stainless and plain), Armsport, Mitchell, Uberti USA.
Price: Steel frame, about . . . . **$140.00** to **$180.00**
Price: Steel frame kit (Euroarms, Navy Arms) . . . . . . **$115.95** to **$150.00**
Price: Single cased set (Navy Arms) **$220.00**
Price: Double cased set (Navy Arms) **$365.00**
Price: Stainless steel Model 1858 (Euroarms, Uberti USA, Cabela's, Navy Arms, Armsport, E.M.F.) . . . . **$220.00** to **$325.00**
Price: Target Model, adjustable rear sight (Cabela's, CVA, Euroarms, Uberti USA, Navy Arms, E.M.F.) . . . . **$95.95** to **$239.00**
Price: Brass frame (CVA, Cabela's, Navy Arms) . . . . . **$97.95** to **$212.95**
Price: As above, kit (CVA, Dixie Gun Works, Navy Arms) . **$94.75** to **$188.95**
Price: Remington "Texas" (Mitchell) **$199.00**

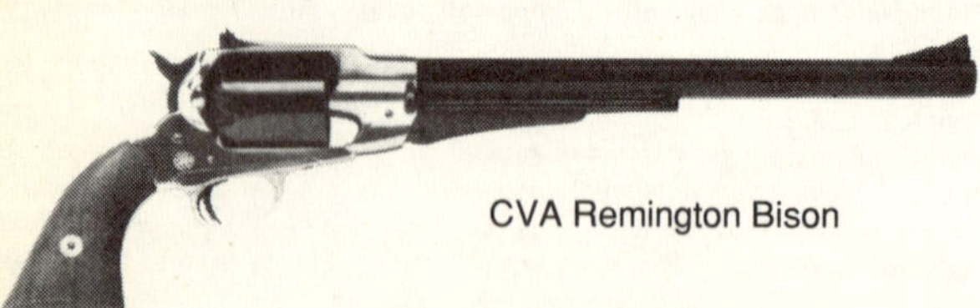
CVA Remington Bison

POCKET POLICE 1862 PERCUSSION REVOLVER
Caliber: 36, 5-shot.
Barrel: 4½", 5½", 6½", 7½".
Weight: 26 oz. **Length:** 12" overall (6½" bbl.).
Stocks: Walnut.
Sights: Fixed.
Features: Round tapered barrel; half-fluted and rebated cylinder; case-hardened frame, loading lever and hammer; silver or brass trigger guard and backstrap. Imported by CVA (5½" only), Navy Arms (5½" only), Uberti USA (5½", 6½" only).
Price: About . . . . **$143.95** to **$279.00**
Price: Single cased set with accessories (Navy Arms) **$260.00**
Price: Kit (CVA) **$155.95**
Price: With silver-plated backstrap, trigger guard (Uberti USA) **$245.00**

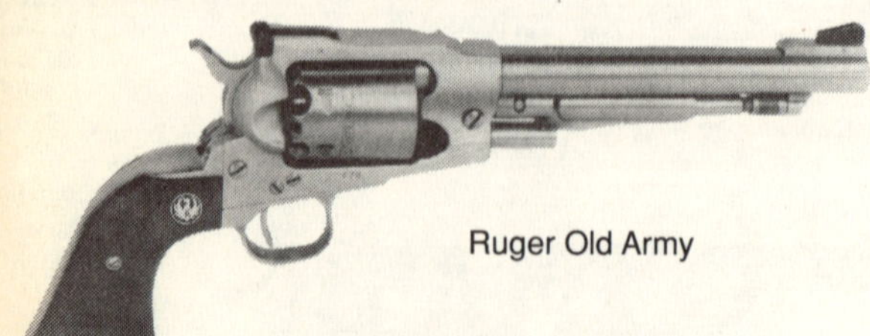
Ruger Old Army

RUGER 44 OLD ARMY PERCUSSION REVOLVER
Caliber: 44, 6-shot. Uses .457" dia. lead bullets.
Barrel: 7½" (6-groove, 16" twist).
Weight: 46 oz. **Length:** 13¾" overall.
Stocks: Smooth walnut.
Sights: Ramp front, rear adjustable for windage and elevation.
Features: Stainless steel standard size nipples, chromemoly steel cylinder and frame, same lockwork as in original Super Blackhawk. Also available in stainless steel. Made in USA. From Sturm, Ruger & Co.
Price: Stainless steel (Model KBP-7) **$407.50**
Price: Blued steel (Model BP-7) **$319.50**

NAVY ARMS DELUXE 1858 REMINGTON-STYLE REVOLVER
Caliber: 44.
Barrel: 8".
Weight: 2 lbs., 13 oz.
Stocks: Smooth walnut.
Sights: Dovetailed blade front.
Features: First exact reproduction—correct in size and weight to the original, with progressive rifling; highly polished with blue finish, silver-plated trigger guard. From Navy Arms.
Price: Deluxe model **$325.00**

Uberti 1858 Remington

CVA 1858 Remington Target
Similar to the New Model 1858 Remington except has ramped blade front sight, adjustable rear.
Price: **$308.95**

CVA Remington Bison
Similar to the CVA 1858 Remington Target except has 10¼" octagonal barrel, 44-caliber, brass frame.
Price: Finished **$317.95**

Consult our Directory pages for the location of firms mentioned.

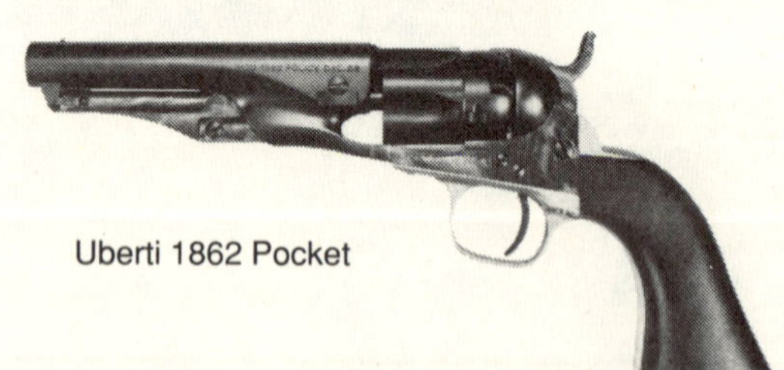
Uberti 1862 Pocket

Euroarms Rogers & Spencer

ROGERS & SPENCER PERCUSSION REVOLVER
Caliber: 44.
Barrel: 7½".
Weight: 47 oz. **Length:** 13¾" overall.
Stocks: Walnut.
Sights: Cone front, integral groove in frame for rear.
Features: Accurate reproduction of a Civil War design. Solid frame; extra large nipple cut-out on rear of cylinder; loading lever and cylinder easily removed for cleaning. From Euroarms of America (standard blue, engraved, burnished, target models), Navy Arms.
Price: . . . . **$160.00** to **$240.00**
Price: Nickel-plated **$215.00**
Price: Engraved (Euroarms) **$286.00**
Price: Kit version **$95.00**
Price: Target version (Euroarms) **$234.00**
Price: Brushed satin chrome (Navy Arms) **$230.00**
Price: Burnished London Gray (Euroarms) **$234.00**

CAUTION: PRICES CHANGE, CHECK AT GUNSHOP.

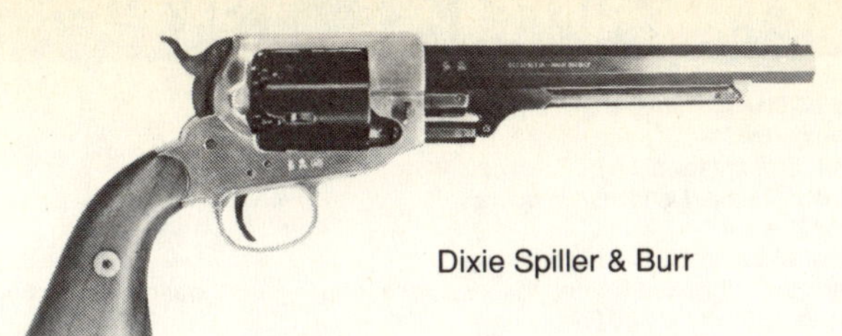
Dixie Spiller & Burr

Texas Paterson

UBERTI 1862 POCKET NAVY PERCUSSION REVOLVER
Caliber: 36, 5-shot.
Barrel: 5½", 6½", octagonal, 7-groove, LH twist.
Weight: 27 oz. (5½" barrel). **Length:** 10½" overall (5½" bbl.).
Stocks: One-piece varnished walnut.
Sights: Brass pin front, hammer notch rear.
Features: Rebated cylinder, hinged loading lever, brass or silver-plated backstrap and trigger guard, color-cased frame, hammer, loading lever, plunger and latch, rest blued. Has original-type markings. From Uberti USA.
Price: With brass backstrap, trigger guard **$278.00**

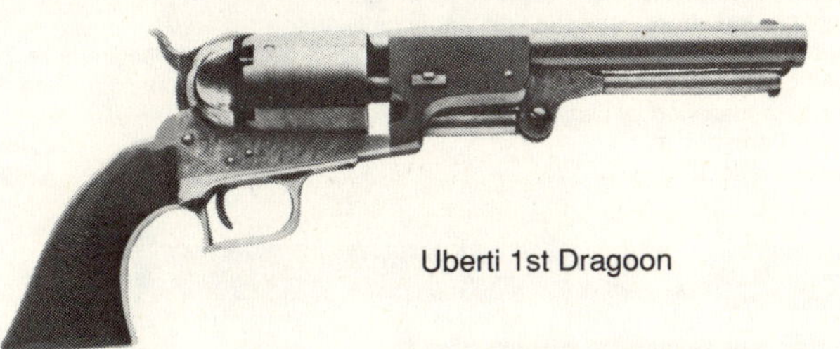
Uberti 1st Dragoon

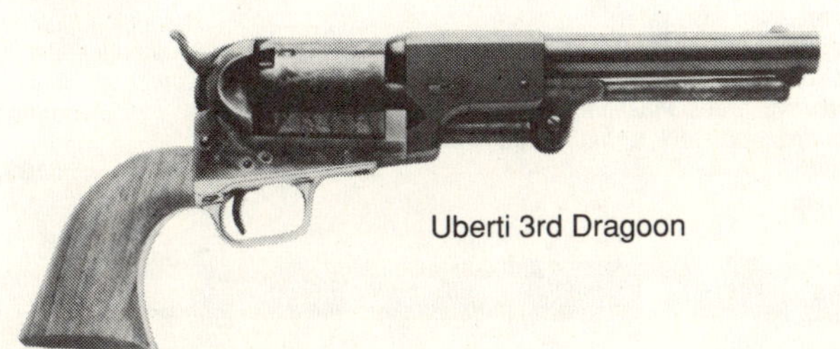
Uberti 3rd Dragoon

Uberti 3rd Model Dragoon Revolver
Similar to the 2nd Model except for oval trigger guard, long trigger, modifications to the loading lever and latch. Imported by Uberti USA.
Price: Military model (frame cut for shoulder stock, steel backstrap) **$320.00**
Price: Civilian (brass backstrap, trigger guard) **$299.00**
Price: Western (silver-plated backstrap, trigger guard) **$340.00**
Price: Shoulder stock **$125.00**

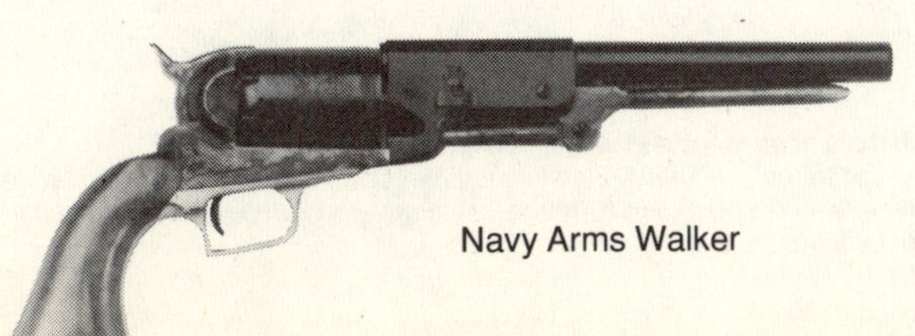
Navy Arms Walker

SHERIFF MODEL 1851 PERCUSSION REVOLVER
Caliber: 36, 44, 6-shot.
Barrel: 5".
Weight: 40 oz. **Length:** 10½" overall.
Stocks: Walnut.
Sights: Fixed.
Features: Brass backstrap and trigger guard; engraved navy scene; case-hardened frame, hammer, loading lever. Imported by E.M.F.
Price: Steel frame **$180.00**
Price: Brass frame **$140.00**

NAVY-SHERIFF 1851
Same as 1851 Sheriff model except has 4" barrel. Imported by Uberti USA, Mitchell.
Price: About . . . . **$169.95** to **$229.00**
Price: Stainless steel (Uberti USA) **$295.00**

SPILLER & BURR REVOLVER
Caliber: 36 (.375" round ball).
Barrel: 7", octagon.
Weight: 2½ lbs. **Length:** 12½" overall.
Stocks: Two-piece walnut.
Sights: Fixed.
Features: Reproduction of the C.S.A. revolver. Brass frame and trigger guard. Also available as a kit. From Dixie Gun Works, Mitchell, Navy Arms.
Price: . . . . **$89.95** to **$199.00**
Price: Kit form **$65.00**
Price: Single cased set (Navy Arms) **$215.00**
Price: Double cased set (Navy Arms) **$325.00**

TEXAS PATERSON 1836 REVOLVER
Caliber: 36 (.376" round ball).
Barrel: 7½".
Weight: 42 oz.
Stocks: One-piece walnut.
Sights: Fixed.
Features: Copy of Sam Colt's first commercially-made revolving pistol. Has no loading lever but comes with loading tool. From Dixie Gun Works, Navy Arms, Uberti USA.
Price: About . . . . **$310.00 to $385.00**
Price: With loading lever (Uberti USA) **$399.00**
Price: Engraved (Navy Arms) **$450.00**

UBERTI 1st MODEL DRAGOON
Caliber: 44.
Barrel: 7½", part round, part octagon.
Weight: 64 oz.
Stocks: One-piece walnut.
Sights: German silver blade front, hammer notch rear.
Features: First model has oval bolt cuts in cylinder, square-back flared trigger guard, V-type mainspring, short trigger. Ranger and Indian scene roll-engraved on cylinder. Color case-hardened frame, loading lever, plunger and hammer; blue barrel, cylinder, trigger and wedge. Available with old-time charcoal blue or standard blue-black finish. Polished brass backstrap and trigger guard. From Uberti USA.
Price: **$299.00**

Uberti 2nd Model Dragoon Revolver
Similar to the 1st Model except distinguished by rectangular bolt cuts in the cylinder.
Price: **$299.00**
Price: As Confederate Tucker & Sherrard, with 3rd Model loading lever and special cylinder engraving **$299.00**

WALKER 1847 PERCUSSION REVOLVER
Caliber: 44, 6-shot.
Barrel: 9".
Weight: 84 oz. **Length:** 15½" overall.
Stocks: Walnut.
Sights: Fixed.
Features: Case-hardened frame, loading lever and hammer; iron backstrap; brass trigger guard; engraved cylinder. Imported by Cabela's, CVA, Navy Arms, Dixie Gun Works, Uberti USA, E.M.F., Cimarron.
Price: About . . . . **$195.00** to **$359.95**
Price: Single cased set (Navy Arms) **$330.00**

ARMOURY R140 HAWKEN RIFLE
Caliber: 45, 50 or 54.
Barrel: 29".
Weight: 8¾ to 9 lbs. **Length:** 45¾" overall.
Stock: Walnut, with cheekpiece.
Sights: Dovetail front, fully adjustable rear.
Features: Octagon barrel, removable breech plug; double set triggers; blued barrel, brass stock fittings, color case-hardened percussion lock. From Armsport, The Armoury.
Price: . . . . **$225.00** to **$280.00**

BOSTONIAN PERCUSSION RIFLE
Caliber: 45.
Barrel: 30", octagonal
Weight: 7¼ lbs. **Length:** 46" overall.
Stock: Walnut.
Sights: Blade front, fixed notch rear.
Features: Color case-hardened lock, brass trigger guard, buttplate, patchbox. Imported from Italy by E.M.F.
Price: **$305.00**

Cabela's Accura 9000

CABELA'S ACCURA 9000 MUZZLELOADER
Caliber: 50, 54.
Barrel: 27"; 1:54 twist.
Weight: About 7½ lbs. **Length:** 44" overall.
Stock: European walnut with Monte Carlo cheeckpiece, checkered grip and forend.
Sights: Hooded front with interchangeable blades, open rear adjustable for windage and elevation.
Features: In-line ignition system with removable breech plug. Automatic safety and half-cock. Quick detachable sling swivels, schnabel forend tip, recoil pad. From Cabela's.
Price: Right or left-hand **$399.95**

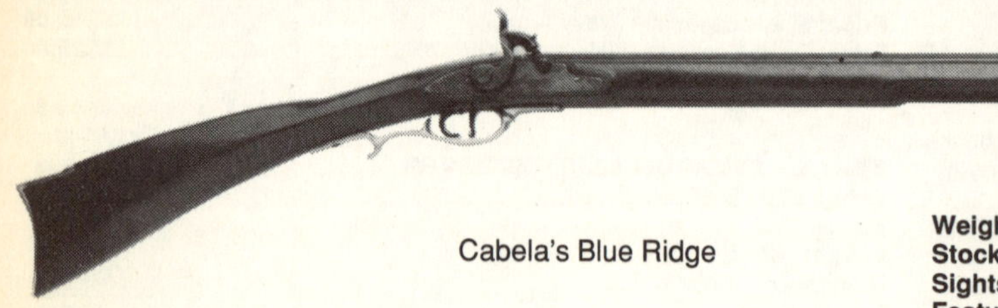
Cabela's Blue Ridge

CABELA'S BLUE RIDGE RIFLE
Caliber: 36, 45, 50.
Barrel: 39".
Weight: 7¾ lbs. **Length:** 55⅛" overall.
Stock: European walnut or tiger striped maple.
Sights: Blade front, rear drift adjustable for windage.
Features: Brown-finished octagonal barrel; adjustable double-set triggers. Trigger guard and buttplate of polished brass, lock and fittings are color case-hardened. Imported by Cabela's.
Price: Percussion **$249.95**
Price: Flintlock **$269.95**

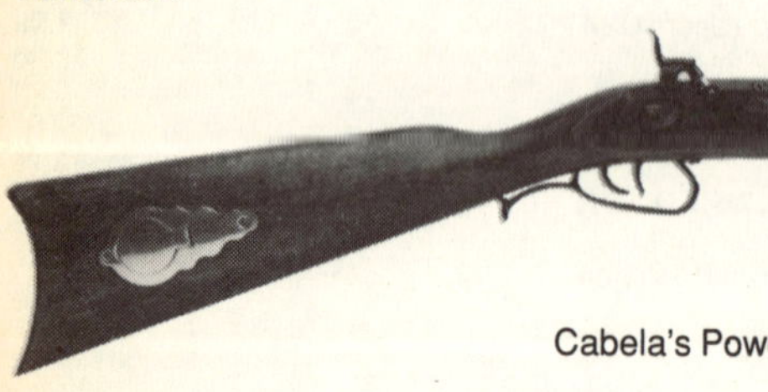
Cabela's Powder River

CABELA'S POWDER RIVER RIFLE
Caliber: 45, 50, 54.
Barrel: 32"; 1:66 twist.
Stock: Hard maple.
Sights: German silver blade front, adjustable buckhorn rear.
Features: Uses Masslin-style lock, double-set triggers with oversized trigger guard. Iron stock furniture. Made in the U.S. From Cabela's.
Price: **$199.95**

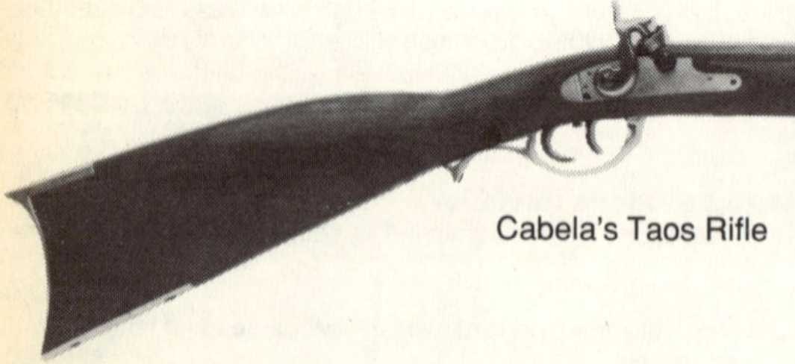
Cabela's Taos Rifle

CABELA'S TAOS RIFLE
Caliber: 45, 50.
Barrel: 28¼".
Weight: 6 lbs., 11 oz. **Length:** 43¼" overall.
Stock: Oil-finished walnut.
Sights: Blade front, rear adjustable for windage.
Features: Carbine version of the Pennsylvania rifle. Adjustable double-set triggers. Imported by Cabela's.
Price: **$199.95**

CABELA'S TRADITIONAL HAWKEN'S
Caliber: 45, 50, 54, 58.
Barrel: 29".
Weight: About 9 lbs.
Stock: Walnut.
Sights: Blade front, open adjustable rear.
Features: Flintlock or percussion. Adjustable double-set triggers. Polished brass furniture, color case-hardened lock. Imported by Cabela's.
Price: Percussion, right-hand **$159.95**
Price: Percussion, right-hand, kit **$134.95**
Price: Percussion, left-hand **$164.95**
Price: Flintlock, right-hand **$189.95**
Price: Flintlock kit **$164.95**

Cabela's Hawken's Hunter Rifle
Similar to the Traditional Hawken's except has more modern stock style with rubber recoil pad, blued furniture, sling swivels. Percussion only, in 45-, 50-, 54- or 58-caliber.
Price: Right-hand **$184.95**
Price: Left-hand **$189.95**

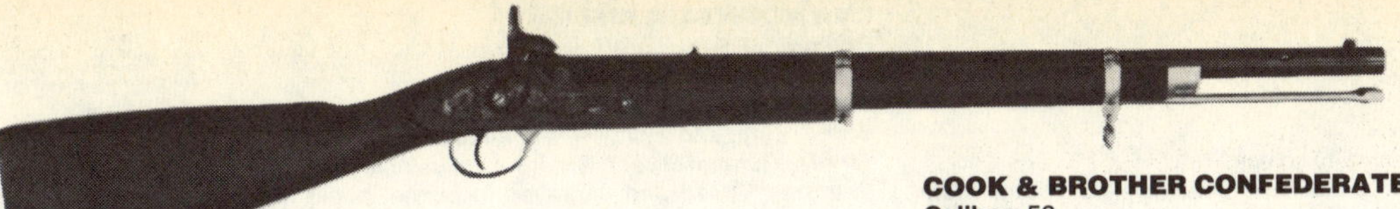
Cook & Brother

COOK & BROTHER CONFEDERATE CARBINE
Caliber: 58.
Barrel: 24".
Weight: 7½ lbs. **Length:** 40½" overall.
Stock: Select walnut.
Features: Recreation of the 1861 New Orleans-made artillery carbine. Color case-hardened lock, browned barrel. Buttplate, trigger guard, barrel bands, sling swivels and nose cap of polished brass. From Euroarms of America.
Price: **$366.00**

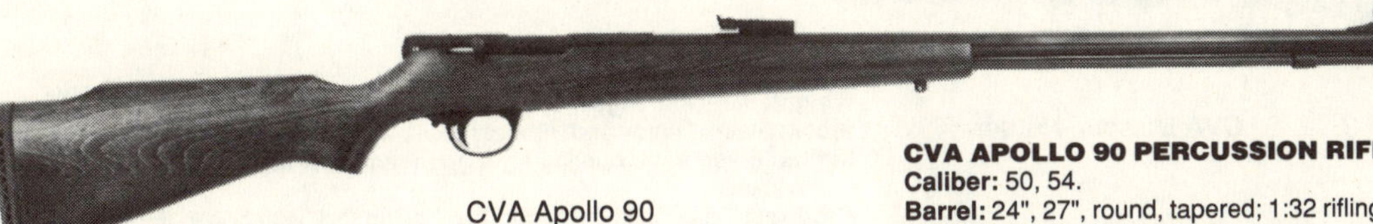
CVA Apollo 90

CVA APOLLO 90 PERCUSSION RIFLE
Caliber: 50, 54.
Barrel: 24", 27", round, tapered; 1:32 rifling. Chrome bore.
Weight: 7½ lbs. **Length:** 45" overall.
Stock: Select hardwood. Monte Carlo comb with flutes, beavertail cheekpiece; ventilated rubber recoil pad, sling swivel studs.
Stock: Removable brass bead on ramp front, removable hunting-style open rear adjustable for windage and elevation.
Features: In-line percussion system with push-pull bolt block safety system. One-piece blued barrel and receiver. Receiver drilled and tapped for scope mounting, has loading window and spark protector cover. Vented for gas escape. Introduced 1990. Imported by CVA.
Price: Standard Grade **$449.95**
Price: Carbine, 24" **$449.95**

CVA Apollo 90 Premier Grade Rifle
Similar to the Apollo 90 Standard Grade except has walnut stock, chromed bore. Introduced 1990. Imported by CVA.
Price: **$538.95**
Price: With laminated stock, swivels and sling **$598.95**

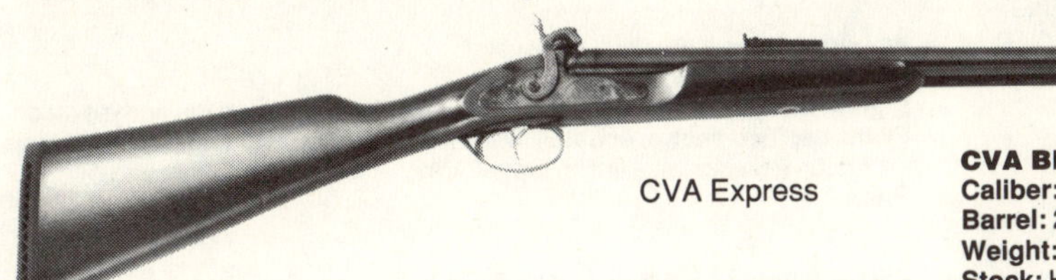
CVA Express

CVA EXPRESS RIFLE
Caliber: 50, 54.
Barrel: 28", round.
Weight: 9 lbs.
Stock: Walnut-stained hardwood.
Sights: Bead and post front, adjustable rear.
Features: Double rifle with twin percussion locks and triggers, adjustable barrels. Hooked breech. Introduced 1989. From CVA.
Price: Finished **$649.95**

CVA BLAZER RIFLE
Caliber: 50 (.490" ball).
Barrel: 28", octagon.
Weight: 6 lbs., 13 oz.
Stock: Hardwood.
Sights: Brass blade front, fixed semi-buckhorn rear.
Features: Straight-line percussion with straight stock of modern design. From CVA.
Price: Finished **$209.95**
Price: Kit **$173.95**

CVA FRONTIER CARBINE
Caliber: 50.
Barrel: 24" octagon; 15/16" flats.
Weight: 6½ lbs. **Length:** 40" overall.
Stock: Selected hardwood.
Sights: Brass blade front, fixed open rear.
Features: Color case-hardened lockplate, screw-adjustable sear engagement, V-type mainspring. Early style brass trigger with tension spring. Brass buttplate, trigger guard, wedge plate, nose cap, thimble. From CVA.
Price: **$259.95**
Price: Kit **$188.95**

Consult our Directory pages for the location of firms mentioned.

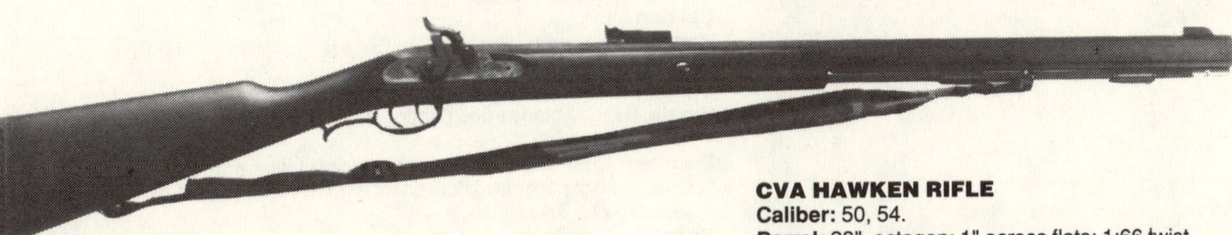
CVA Hunter Hawken

CVA HAWKEN RIFLE
Caliber: 50, 54.
Barrel: 28", octagon; 1" across flats; 1:66 twist.
Weight: 8 lbs. **Length:** 44" overall.
Stock: Select walnut.
Sights: Beaded blade front, fully adjustable open rear.
Features: Fully adjustable double-set triggers; brass patch box, wedge plates, nosecap, thimbles, trigger guard and buttplate; blued barrel; color case-hardened, engraved lockplate. V-type mainspring. Percussion only. Hooked breech, chrome bore. Introduced 1981. From CVA.
Price: Finished rifle, percussion **$439.95**
Price: St. Louis Hawken (as above, except does not have chrome bore; hardwood stock), finished **$338.95**
Price: As above, combo kit (50-, 54-cal. bbls.) **$339.95**
Price: 50-cal./12-ga. combo, finished **$418.95**

CVA Hunter Hawken Rifle, Carbine
Similar to the CVA Hawken except has select hardwood stock with dark color, non-glare finish, vented rubber recoil pad, sling swivels, and adjustable rear sight. Carbine has 24" barrel, 40" overall length. Black nosecap, trigger guard, thimbles and wedge plates. Available in 50- or 54- caliber. Introduced 1990. Imported by CVA.
Price: Either caliber, rifle or carbine, finished **$329.95**
Price: 50-cal. rifle kit **$249.95**

CVA KENTUCKY RIFLE
Caliber: 50.
Barrel: 33½", rifled, octagon; ⅞" flats.
Weight: 7½ lbs. **Length:** 48" overall.
Stock: Select hardwood.
Sights: Brass Kentucky blade-type front, fixed open rear.
Features: Available in percussion only. Stainless steel nipple included. From CVA.
Price: Percussion **$329.95**
Price: Percussion kit **$249.95**
Price: Kentucky Hunter (half-stock) **$319.95**

CVA MOUNTAIN RIFLE
Caliber: 50, 54.
Barrel: 32" octagon; 15⁄16" flats.
Weight: 9 lbs. **Length:** 48" overall.
Stock: European walnut with cheekpiece.
Sights: German silver blade front, adjustable open rear.
Features: Blued and engraved lockplate; bridle, fly, screw-adjustable sear engagement. Double-set triggers. Pewter nose cap, trigger guard, buttplate. From CVA.
Price: Chrome bore **$439.95**
Price: Standard (not chromed) **$359.95**

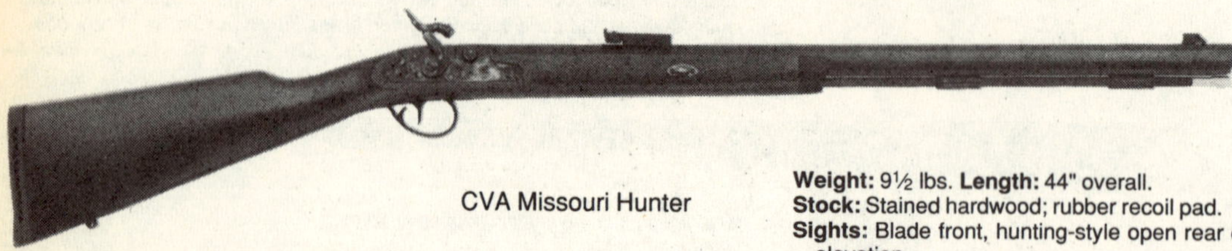

CVA Missouri Hunter

CVA MISSOURI HUNTER RIFLE
Caliber: 50.
Barrel: 28" octagon; 15⁄16" flats.
Weight: 9½ lbs. **Length:** 44" overall.
Stock: Stained hardwood; rubber recoil pad.
Sights: Blade front, hunting-style open rear click adjustable for windage and elevation.
Features: Color case-hardened percussion lock with bridle, fly, V-type mainspring. Single trigger. Blackened nose cap and wedge plate, blued thimble and wedge. From CVA.
Price: **$299.95**

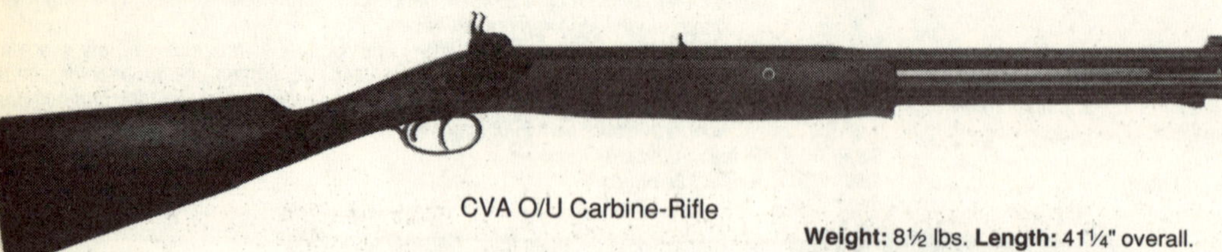

CVA O/U Carbine-Rifle

CVA O/U CARBINE-RIFLE
Caliber: 50.
Barrel: 24".
Weight: 8½ lbs. **Length:** 41¼" overall.
Stock: Checkered walnut.
Sights: Blade front with gold bead, near adjustable for windage and elevation.
Features: Two-shot over/under with two hammers, two triggers. Adjustable barrels. Polished blue finish. From CVA.
Price: **$797.95**

CVA SQUIRREL RIFLE
Caliber: 36, 36/50 Combo.
Barrel: 25", octagonal; ⅞" flats.
Weight: 6 lbs. **Length:** 40¾" overall.
Stock: Hardwood.
Sights: Beaded blade front, fully adjustable hunting-style rear.
Features: Color case-hardened lockplate, brass buttplate, trigger guard, wedge plates, thimbles; double-set triggers; hooked breech; authentic V-type mainspring. From CVA.
Price: Finished, percussion, 36-cal. **$329.95**
Price: Kit, percussion, 36-cal. **$249.95**
Price: As above, with 36- and 50-cal. bbls. **$329.95**

CVA PENNSYLVANIA LONG RIFLE
Caliber: 50.
Barrel: 40", octagonal; ⅞" flats.
Weight: 8 lbs., 3 oz. **Length:** 55¾" overall.
Stock: Select walnut.
Sights: Brass blade front, fixed semi-buckhorn rear.
Features: Color case-hardened lockplate, brass buttplate, toe plate, patchbox, trigger guard, thimbles, nosecap; blued barrel, double-set triggers; authentic V-type mainspring. Introduced 1983. From CVA.
Price: Finished, percussion **$698.95**
Price: Finished, flintlock **$698.95**

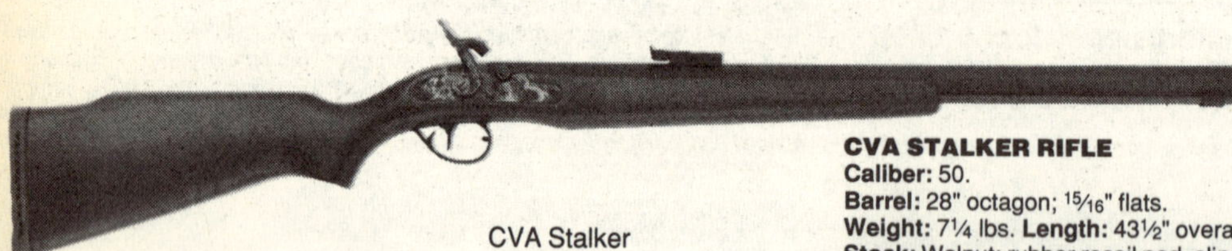

CVA Stalker

CVA PLAINSMAN RIFLE
Caliber: 50.
Barrel: 24" octagonal, 15⁄16" flats; 1:48 rifling.
Weight: 6 lbs., 9 oz. **Length:** 40" overall.
Stock: Select hardwood.
Sights: Brass blade front, fixed semi-buckhorn rear.
Features: Color case-hardened lock plate; screw-adjustable sear engagement, V-type mainspring; single trigger with large guard; black trigger guard, wedge plate and thimble. Introduced 1990. Imported by CVA.
Price: Finished **$229.95**

CVA STALKER RIFLE
Caliber: 50.
Barrel: 28" octagon; 15⁄16" flats.
Weight: 7¼ lbs. **Length:** 43½" overall.
Stock: Walnut; rubber recoil pad, sling swivels and sling.
Sights: Beaded blade front, hunting-style open rear click adjustable for windage and elevation.
Features: Color case-hardened percussion lock with bridle, fly, V-type mainspring. Single trigger. Blackened trigger guard, blued thimble, wedge and wedge plate. From CVA.
Price: Premier Grade **$398.95**
Price: Standard Grade (hardwood stock, no sling or swivels) **$280.95**

DIXIE 1863 SPRINGFIELD MUSKET
Caliber: 58 (.570" patched ball or .575" Minie).
Barrel: 50", rifled.
Stocks: Walnut stained.
Sights: Blade front, adjustable ladder-type rear.
Features: Bright-finish lock, barrel, furniture. Reproduction of the last of the regulation muzzleloaders. Imported from Japan by Dixie Gun Works.
Price: Finished **$475.00**
Price: Kit **$330.00**

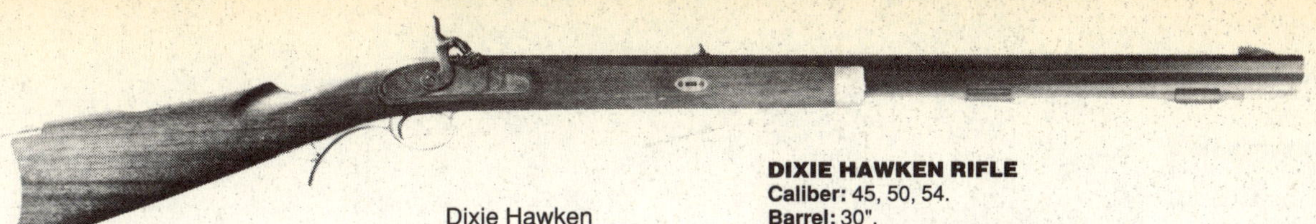

Dixie Hawken

DIXIE HAWKEN RIFLE
Caliber: 45, 50, 54.
Barrel: 30".
Weight: 8 lbs. **Length:** 46½" overall.
Stock: Walnut.
Sights: Blade front, adjustable rear.
Features: Blued barrel, double-set triggers, steel crescent buttplate. Imported by Dixie Gun Works.
Price: Finished **$225.00**
Price: Kit **$185.00**

DIXIE DELUX CUB RIFLE
Caliber: 40.
Barrel: 28".
Weight: 6½ lbs.
Stock: Walnut.
Sights: Fixed.
Features: Short rifle for small game and beginning shooters. Brass patchbox and furniture. Flint or percussion. From Dixie Gun Works.
Price: Finished **$315.00**
Price: Kit **$205.00**

DIXIE INDIAN GUN
Caliber: 75.
Barrel: 31", round tapered.
Weight: About 9 lbs. **Length:** 47" overall.
Stock: Hardwood.
Sights: Blade front.
Features: Modified Brown Bess musket; brass furniture, browned lock and barrel. Lock is marked "GRICE 1762" with crown over "GR." Serpent-style sideplate. Introduced 1983. From Dixie Gun Works.
Price: Complete **$485.00**
Price: As above, in kit form **$435.00**

Dixie Tennessee

DIXIE TENNESSEE MOUNTAIN RIFLE
Caliber: 32 or 50.
Barrel: 41½", 6-groove rifling, brown finish. **Length:** 56" overall.
Stock: Walnut, oil finish; Kentucky-style.
Sights: Silver blade front, open buckhorn rear.
Features: Recreation of the original mountain rifles. Early Schultz lock, interchangeable flint or percussion with vent plug or drum and nipple. Tumbler has fly. Double-set triggers. All metal parts browned. From Dixie Gun Works.
Price: Flint or percussion, finished rifle, 50-cal. **$395.00**
Price: Kit, 50-cal. **$345.00**
Price: Left-hand model, flint or percussion **$395.00**
Price: Left-hand kit, flint or perc., 50-cal. **$345.00**
Price: Squirrel Rifle (as above except in 32-cal. with 13/16" barrel flats), flint or percussion **$395.00**
Price: Kit, 32-cal., flint or percussion **$345.00**

Dixie 1861

DIXIE U.S. MODEL 1861 SPRINGFIELD
Caliber: 58.
Barrel: 40".
Weight: About 8 lbs. **Length:** 55 13/16" overall.
Stock: Oil-finished walnut.
Sights: Blade front, step adjustable rear.
Features: Exact recreation of original rifle. Sling swivels attached to trigger guard bow and middle barrel band. Lockplate marked "1861" with eagle motif and "U.S. Springfield" in front of hammer; "U.S." stamped on top of buttplate. From Dixie Gun Works.
Price: **$450.00**
Price: Kit **$420.00**

EUROARMS BUFFALO CARBINE
Caliber: 58.
Barrel: 26", round.
Weight: 7¾ lbs. **Length:** 42" overall.
Stock: Walnut.
Sights: Blade front, open adjustable rear.
Features: Shoots .575" round ball. Color case-hardened lock, blue hammer, barrel, trigger; brass furniture. Brass patchbox. Imported by Euroarms of America.
Price: **$407.00**

Gonic GA-87

GONIC GA-87 M/L RIFLE
Caliber: 30, 45, 50.
Barrel: 24" (Carbine), 26" (Rifle).
Weight: 6 to 6½ lbs. **Length:** 41" overall (Carbine).
Stock: American walnut with checkered grip and forend, or laminated stock.
Sights: Bead front, open rear adjustable for windage and elevation; drilled and tapped for scope bases.
Features: Closed-breech action with straight-line ignition. Modern trigger mechanism with ambidextrous safety. Satin blue finish on metal, satin stock finish. Carbine available only in 30-, 45-cal. Introduced 1989. From Gonic Arms, Inc.
Price: Standard Rifle or Carbine, no sights **$479.24**
Price: As above, with sights **$521.82**
Price: Deluxe Rifle or Carbine, no sights **$511.93**
Price: As above, with sights **$554.91**

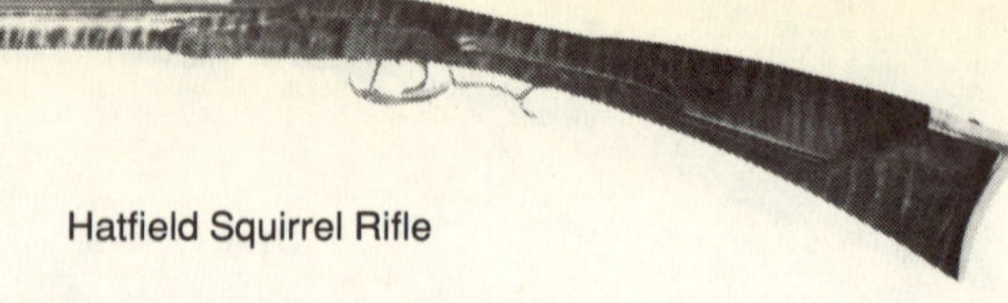
Hatfield Squirrel Rifle

HATFIELD SQUIRREL RIFLE
Caliber: 36, 45, 50.
Barrel: 39½", octagon, 32" on half-stock.
Weight: 7½ lbs. (32-cal.).
Stock: American fancy maple.
Sights: Silver blade front, buckhorn rear.
Features: Recreation of the traditional squirrel rifle. Available in flint or percussion with brass trigger guard and buttplate. From Hatfield Rifle Works. Introduced 1983.
Price: Full stock, percussion, Grade II **$598.00**
Price: As above, flintlock **$620.00**
Price: As above, Grade III, flint or percussion **$700.00**
Price: Mountain Rifle **$665.00**

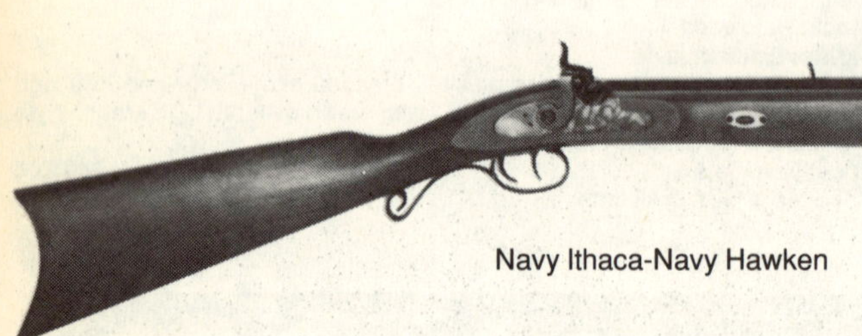
Navy Ithaca-Navy Hawken

ITHACA-NAVY HAWKEN RIFLE
Caliber: 50.
Barrel: 32" octagonal, 1" dia.
Weight: About 9 lbs.
Stocks: Walnut.
Sights: Blade front, rear adjustable for windage.
Features: Hooked breech, 1⅞" throw percussion lock. Attached twin thimbles and under-rib. German silver barrel key inlays, Hawken-style toe and buttplates, lock bolt inlays, barrel wedges, entry thimble, trigger guard, ramrod and cleaning jag, nipple and nipple wrench. Introduced 1977. From Navy Arms.
Price: Complete, percussion **$365.00**
Price: Kit, percussion **$325.00**

KENTUCKY FLINTLOCK RIFLE
Caliber: 44, 45, or 50.
Barrel: 35".
Weight: 7 lbs. **Length:** 50" overall.
Stock: Walnut stained, brass fittings.
Sights: Fixed.
Features: Available in carbine model also, 28" bbl. Some variations in detail, finish. Kits also available from some importers. Imported by Navy Arms, The Armoury.
Price: About . . . . **$217.95** to **$324.00**
Price: Percussion, 45 or 50-cal. (Navy Arms) **$240.00**

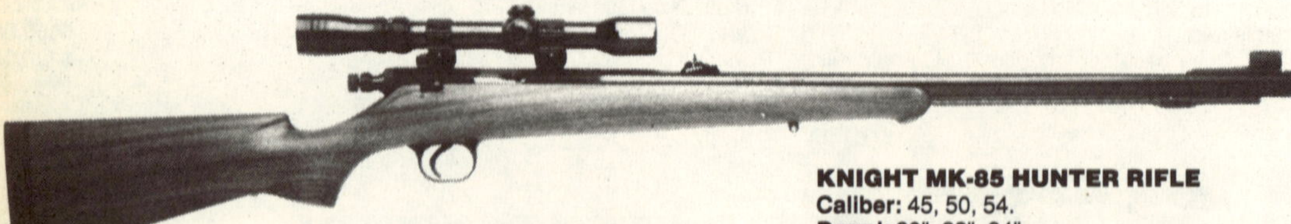
Knight MK-85

Knight BK-89 Squirrel Rifle
Similar to the MK-85 except in 36-caliber only with 24" barrel, and weighs 5½ lbs. Barrel twist is 1:24.
Price: **$499.95**

HARPER'S FERRY 1803 FLINTLOCK RIFLE
Caliber: 54 or 58.
Barrel: 35".
Weight: 9 lbs. **Length:** 59½" overall.
Stock: Walnut with cheekpiece.
Sights: Brass blade front, fixed steel rear.
Features: Brass trigger guard, sideplate, buttplate; steel patch box. Imported by Euroarms of America, Navy Arms (54-cal. only).
Price: **$512.00**
Price: 54-cal. (Navy Arms) **$475.00**

HAWKEN RIFLE
Caliber: 45, 50, 54 or 58.
Barrel: 28", blued, 6-groove rifling.
Weight: 8¾ lbs. **Length:** 44" overall.
Stock: Walnut with cheekpiece.
Sights: Blade front, fully adjustable rear.
Features: Coil mainspring, double-set triggers, polished brass furniture. From Armsport, Ellett Bros., Navy Arms, E.M.F.
Price: . . . . **$245.00** to **$345.00**
Price: 50-, 54-cal., right-hand, percussion (Ellett Bros.) **$289.95**
Price: 50-, 54-cal., left-hand, percussion (Ellett Bros.) **$299.95**
Price: 50-cal., right-hand, flintlock (Ellett Bros.) **$309.95**
Price: 50-cal., left-hand, flintlock (Ellett Bros.) **$339.95**

KENTUCKIAN RIFLE & CARBINE
Caliber: 44.
Barrel: 35" (Rifle), 27½" (Carbine).
Weight: 7 lbs. (Rifle), 5½ lbs. (Carbine). **Length:** 51" overall (Rifle), 43" (Carbine).
Stock: Walnut stain.
Sights: Brass blade front, steel V-ramp rear.
Features: Octagon barrel, case-hardened and engraved lockplates. Brass furniture. Imported by Dixie Gun Works.
Price: Rifle or carbine, flint, about **$259.95**
Price: As above, percussion, about **$249.95**

Kentucky Percussion Rifle
Similar to flintlock except percussion lock. Finish and features vary with importer. Imported by Navy Arms (45-cal.), The Armoury, CVA.
Price: About **$259.95**
Price: 50-cal. (Navy Arms) **$240.00**
Price: Kit, 50-cal. (CVA) **$143.95**

KNIGHT MK-85 HUNTER RIFLE
Caliber: 45, 50, 54.
Barrel: 20", 22", 24".
Weight: 7 lbs.
Stock: Classic, walnut; recoil pad; swivel studs.
Sights: Hooded blade front on ramp, open adjustable rear.
Features: One-piece in-line bolt assembly with straight through Sure-Fire ignition system. Adjustable Timney Featherweight trigger. Drilled and tapped for scope mounting. Made in U.S. From Modern Muzzle Loading, Inc.
Price: **$519.95**
Price: Stalker (laminated, colored stock), 50 or 54 . . . . **$579.95**
Price: Predator (stainless steel, composition stock), 50 or 54 . . . . **$649.95**
Price: Back Country Carbine (50, 54, 20", premium grade walnut) . . **$519.95**
Price: Grizzly PLB (50, 54, integral muzzle brake, brown laminated stock) **$649.95**
Price: T-5 Woodsman (50, 54, 22" barrel, matte blue, hardwood stock) **$229.95**

CAUTION: PRICES CHANGE, CHECK AT GUNSHOP

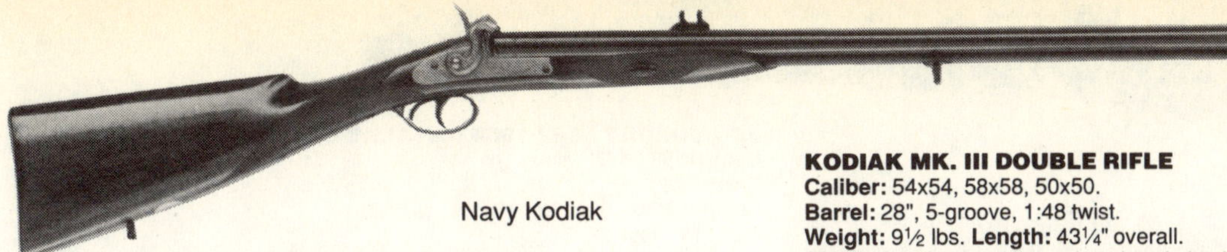

Navy Kodiak

LONDON ARMORY 3-BAND 1853 ENFIELD
Caliber: 58 (.577" Minie, .575" round ball, .580" maxi ball).
Barrel: 39".
Weight: 9½ lbs. **Length:** 54" overall.
Stock: European walnut.
Sights: Inverted "V " front, traditional Enfield folding ladder rear.
Features: Recreation of the famed London Armory Company Pattern 1862 Enfield Musket. One-piece walnut stock, brass buttplate, trigger guard and nose cap. Lockplate marked "London Armoury Co. " and with a British crown. Blued Baddeley barrel bands. From Dixie Gun Works, Euroarms of America, Navy Arms.
Price: About . . . . **$350.00** to **$427.00**
Price: Assembled kit (Euroarms of America) **$380.00**

LONDON ARMORY ENFIELD MUSKETOON
Caliber: 58, Minie ball.
Barrel: 24", round.
Weight: 7-7½ lbs. **Length:** 40½" overall.
Stock: Walnut, with sling swivels.
Sights: Blade front, graduated military-leaf rear.
Features: Brass trigger guard, nose cap, buttplate; blued barrel, bands, lockplate, swivels. Imported by Euroarms of America, Navy Arms.
Price: . . . . **$300.00 to $350.00**
Price: Kit **$250.00**

KODIAK MK. III DOUBLE RIFLE
Caliber: 54x54, 58x58, 50x50.
Barrel: 28", 5-groove, 1:48 twist.
Weight: 9½ lbs. **Length:** 43¼" overall.
Stock: Czechoslovakian walnut, hand-checkered.
Sights: Adjustable bead front, adjustable open rear.
Features: Hooked breech allows interchangeability of barrels. Comes with sling and swivels, adjustable powder measure, bullet mould and bullet starter. Engraved lockplates, top tang and trigger guard. Locks and top tang polished, rest blued. Introduced 1976. Imported from Italy by Trail Guns Armory, Inc., Navy Arms.
Price: 50-, 54-, 58-cal. SxS **$550.00**
Price: Spare barrels, all calibers **$294.25**
Price: Spare barrels, 12-ga.x12-ga. **$195.00**

LONDON ARMORY 2-BAND ENFIELD 1858
Caliber: .577" Minie, .575" round ball.
Barrel: 33".
Weight: 10 lbs. **Length:** 49" overall.
Stock: Walnut.
Sights: Folding leaf rear adjustable for elevation.
Features: Blued barrel, color case-hardened lock and hammer, polished brass buttplate, trigger guard, nosecap. From Navy Arms, Euroarms of America, Dixie Gun Works.
Price: . . . . **$399.00** to **$450.00**
Price: Assembled kit (Euroarms of America) **$364.00**

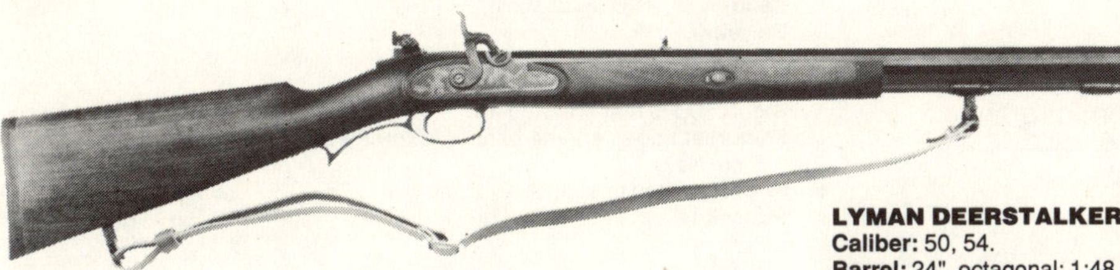

Lyman Deerstalker

Lyman Deerstalker Custom Carbine
Similar to the Deerstalker rifle except in 50-caliber only with 21" stepped octagon barrel; 1:24 twist for optimum performance with conical projectiles. Comes with Lyman 37MA front sight, Lyman 16A folding rear. Weighs 6¾ lbs., measures 38½" overall. Percussion or flintlock. Comes with Delrin ramrod, modern sling and swivels. Introduced 1991.
Price: **$320.00**

LYMAN DEERSTALKER RIFLE
Caliber: 50, 54.
Barrel: 24", octagonal; 1:48 rifling.
Weight: 7½ lbs.
Stock: Walnut with black rubber buttpad.
Sights: Lyman #37MA beaded front, fully adjustable fold-down Lyman #16A rear.
Features: Stock has less drop for quick sighting. All metal parts are blackened, with color-case-hardened lock; single trigger. Comes with sling and swivels. Available in flint or percussion. Introduced 1990. From Lyman.
Price: 50- or 54-cal., percussion **$329.95**
Price: 50- or 54-cal., flintlock **$349.95**

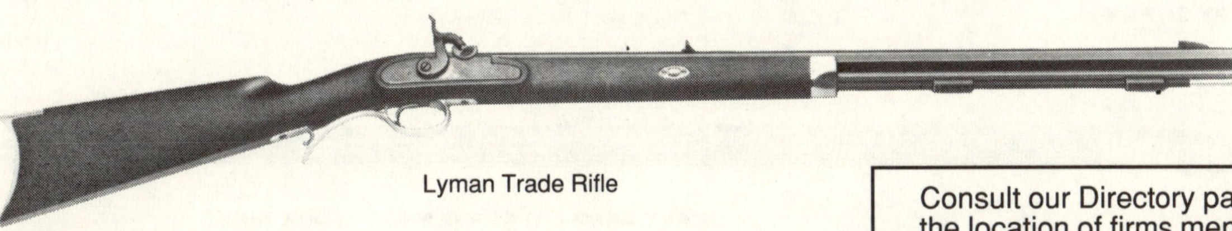

Lyman Trade Rifle

Consult our Directory pages for the location of firms mentioned.

LYMAN TRADE RIFLE
Caliber: 50 or 54.
Barrel: 28" octagon, 1:48 twist.
Weight: 8¾ lbs. **Length:** 45" overall.
Stock: European walnut.
Sights: Blade front, open rear adjustable for windage or optional fixed sights.
Features: Fast twist rifling for conical bullets. Polished brass furniture with blue steel parts, stainless steel nipple. Hook breech, single trigger, coil spring percussion lock. Steel barrel rib and ramrod ferrules. Introduced 1980. From Lyman.
Price: Percussion **$299.95**
Price: Kit, percussion **$239.95**
Price: Flintlock **$329.95**
Price: Kit, flintlock **$274.95**

LYMAN GREAT PLAINS RIFLE
Caliber: 50- or 54-cal.
Barrel: 32", 1:66 twist.
Weight: 9 lbs.
Stock: Walnut.
Sights: Steel blade front, buckhorn rear adjustable for windage and elevation and fixed notch primitive sight included.
Features: Blued steel furniture. Stainless steel nipple. Coil spring lock, Hawken-style trigger guard and double-set triggers. Round thimbles recessed and sweated into rib. Steel wedge plates and toe plate. Introduced 1979. From Lyman.
Price: Percussion **$389.95**
Price: Flintlock **$419.95**
Price: Percussion kit **$314.95**
Price: Flintlock kit **$334.95**

J.P. Murray

J.P. MURRAY 1862-1864 CAVALRY CARBINE
Caliber: 58 (.577" Minie).
Barrel: 23".
Weight: 7 lbs., 9 oz. **Length:** 39" overall.
Stock: Walnut.
Sights: Blade front, rear drift adjustable for windage.
Features: Browned barrel, color case-hardened lock, blued swivel and band springs, polished brass buttplate, trigger guard, barrel bands. From Navy Arms, Euroarms of America.
Price: . . . . **$300.00** to **$358.00**

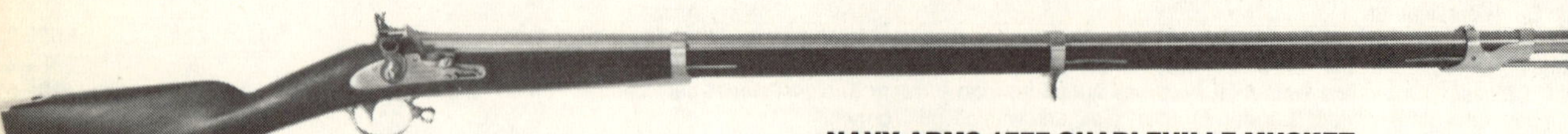

Navy 1763 Charleville

NAVY ARMS 1777 CHARLEVILLE MUSKET
Caliber: 69.
Barrel: 44⅝".
Weight: 10 lbs., 4 oz. **Length:** 59¾" overall.
Stock: Walnut.
Sights: Brass blade front.
Features: Exact copy of the musket used in the French Revolution. All steel is polished, in the white. Brass flashpan. Introduced 1991. Imported by Navy Arms.
Price: **$595.00**
Price: 1763 Standard Charleville Musket, finished **$550.00**
Price: As above, kit **$450.00**
Price: 1816 M.T. Wickham Musket **$595.00**

NAVY ARMS CUB RIFLE
Caliber: 36.
Barrel: 26".
Weight: 5¾ lbs. **Length:** 41½" overall.
Stock: Walnut.
Sights: Blade front, open rear adjustable for windage and elevation.
Features: Octagonal barrel; color case-hardened percussion lock. Imported by Navy Arms.
Price: **$175.00**

Consult our Directory pages for the location of firms mentioned.

NAVY ARMS 1863 SPRINGFIELD
Caliber: 58, uses .575" Minie.
Barrel: 40", rifled.
Weight: 9½ lbs. **Length:** 56" overall.
Stock: Walnut.
Sights: Open rear adjustable for elevation.
Features: Full-size three-band musket. Polished bright metal, including lock. From Navy Arms.
Price: Finished rifle **$550.00**
Price: Kit **$450.00**

Navy Country Boy

NAVY ARMS COUNTRY BOY RIFLE
Caliber: 32, 36, 45, 50.
Barrel: 26".
Weight: 5½ lbs.
Stock: Walnut.
Sights: Blade front, adjustable rear.
Features: Octagonal rifled barrel; blue finish; hooked breech; Mule Ear lock for fast ignition. From Navy Arms.
Price: **$165.00**
Price: Kit (50-cal. only) **$145.00**

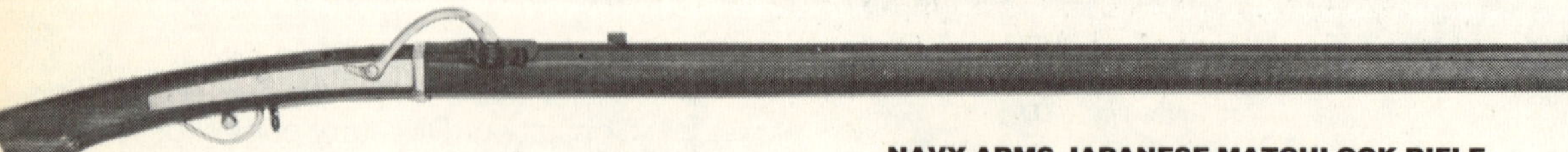

Navy Japanese Matchlock

NAVY ARMS JAPANESE MATCHLOCK RIFLE
Caliber: 50.
Barrel: 41".
Weight: 8½ lbs. **Length:** 54¼" overall.
Stock: Stained hardwood.
Sights: Blade front, rear adjustable for windage.
Features: Replica of the matchlocks used by the Samurai. Brass lock, serpentine and trigger guard. Introduced 1991. Imported by Navy Arms.
Price: **$495.00**

NAVY ARMS MORTIMER FLINTLOCK RIFLE
Caliber: 54.
Barrel: 36".
Weight: 9 lbs. **Length:** 52¼" overall.
Stock: Checkered walnut.
Sights: Bead front, rear adjustable for windage.
Features: Waterproof pan, roller frizzen; sling swivels; browned barrel; external safety. Introduced 1991. Imported by Navy Arms.
Price: **$535.00**

NAVY ARMS PIONEER FLINTLOCK RIFLE
Caliber: 45.
Barrel: 26" octagon.
Weight: 5¾ lbs. **Length:** 41½" overall.
Stock: Walnut.
Sights: Blade front, fully adjustable rear.
Features: Hooked breech; color case-hardened lock; blued barrel and furniture. Imported by Navy Arms.
Price: **$190.00**

CAUTION: PRICES CHANGE, CHECK AT GUNSHOP.

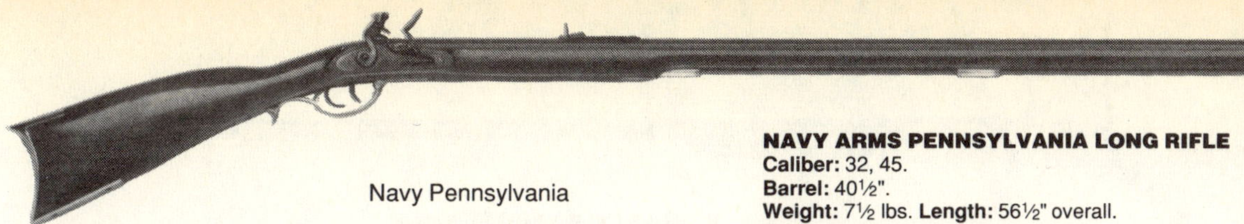

Navy Pennsylvania

NAVY ARMS PENNSYLVANIA LONG RIFLE
Caliber: 32, 45.
Barrel: 40½".
Weight: 7½ lbs. **Length:** 56½" overall.
Stock: Walnut.
Sights: Blade front, fully adjustable rear.
Features: Browned barrel, brass furniture, polished lock with double-set triggers. Introduced 1991. Imported by Navy Arms.
Price: Percussion **$280.00**
Price: Flintlock **$300.00**

NAVY ARMS SHARPS PERCUSSION CARBINE
Caliber: 54.
Barrel: 22".
Weight: 7¾ lbs. **Length:** 39" overall.
Stock: Walnut.
Sights: Blade front, military ladder-type rear.
Features: Color case-hardened action, blued barrel. Has saddle ring. Introduced 1991. Imported from Navy Arms.
Price: **$650.00**

Navy Smith Carbine

NAVY ARMS SMITH CARBINE
Caliber: 50.
Barrel: 21½".
Weight: 7¾ lbs. **Length:** 39" overall.
Stock: American walnut.
Sights: Brass blade front, folding ladder-type rear.
Features: Replica of the breech-loading Civil War carbine. Color case-hardened receiver, rest blued. Cavalry model has saddle ring and bar, Artillery model has sling swivels. Introduced 1991. Imported by Navy Arms.
Price: Cavalry model **$595.00**
Price: Artillery model **$595.00**

PARKER-HALE ENFIELD 1853 MUSKET
Caliber: .577".
Barrel: 39", 3-groove cold-forged rifling.
Weight: About 9 lbs. **Length:** 55" overall.
Stock: Seasoned walnut.
Sights: Fixed front, rear step adjustable for elevation.
Features: Three-band musket made to original specs from original gauges. Solid brass stock furniture, color hardened lockplate, hammer; blued barrel, trigger. Available through Navy Arms.
Price: **$475.00**

Consult our Directory pages for the location of firms mentioned.

PARKER-HALE ENFIELD PATTERN 1858 NAVAL RIFLE
Caliber: .577".
Barrel: 33".
Weight: 8½ lbs. **Length:** 48½" overall.
Stock: European walnut.
Sights: Blade front, step adjustable rear.
Features: Two-band Enfield percussion rifle with heavy barrel. Five-groove progressive depth rifling, solid brass furniture. All parts made exactly to original patterns. Available through Navy Arms.
Price: **$550.00**

PARKER-HALE VOLUNTEER RIFLE
Caliber: .451".
Barrel: 32".
Weight: 9½ lbs. **Length:** 49" overall.
Stock: Walnut, checkered wrist and forend.
Sights: Globe front, adjustable ladder-type rear.
Features: Recreation of the type of gun issued to volunteer regiments during the 1860s. Rigby-pattern rifling, patent breech, detented lock. Stock is glass bedded for accuracy. Available through Navy Arms.
Price: **$750.00**
Price: Three-band Volunteer **$815.00**

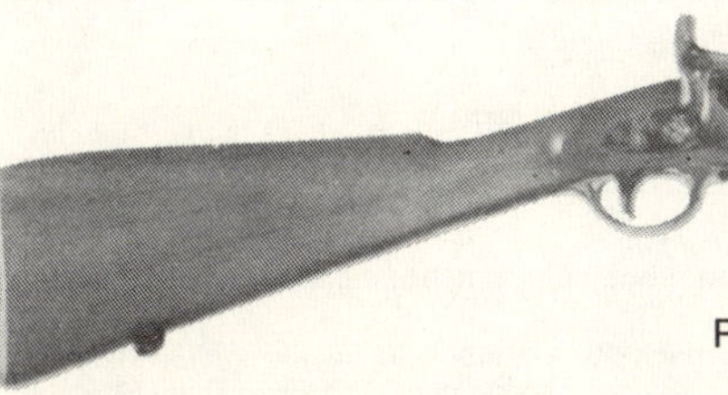

Parker-Hale 1861

PARKER-HALE ENFIELD 1861 MUSKETOON
Caliber: 58.
Barrel: 24".
Weight: 7 lbs. **Length:** 40½" overall.
Stock: Walnut.
Sights: Fixed front, adjustable rear.
Features: Percussion muzzleloader, made to original 1861 English patterns. Available through Navy Arms.
Price: **$450.00**

Parker-Hale Whitworth

PARKER-HALE WHITWORTH MILITARY TARGET RIFLE
Caliber: 45.
Barrel: 36".
Weight: 9¼ lbs. **Length:** 52½" overall.
Stock: Walnut. Checkered at wrist and forend.
Sights: Hooded post front, open step-adjustable rear.
Features: Faithful reproduction of the Whitworth rifle, only bored for 45-cal. Trigger has a detented lock, capable of being adjusted very finely without risk of the sear nose catching on the half-cock bent and damaging both parts. Introduced 1978. Available through Navy Arms.
Price: **$815.00**

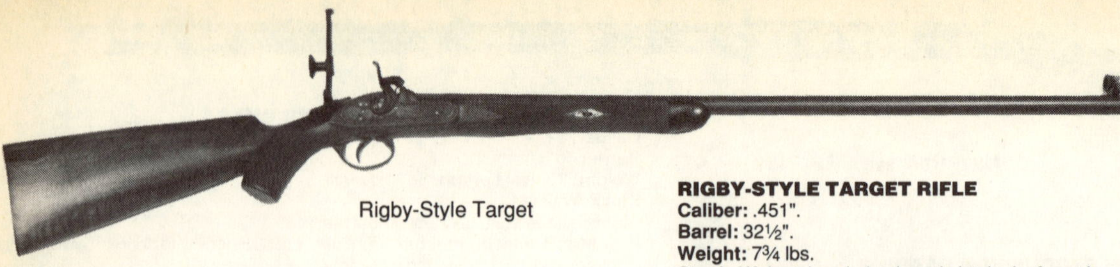
Rigby-Style Target

PENNSYLVANIA FULL-STOCK RIFLE
Caliber: 45 or 50.
Barrel: 32" rifled, 15/16" dia.
Weight: 8½ lbs.
Stock: Walnut.
Sights: Fixed.
Features: Available in flint or percussion. Blued lock and barrel, brass furniture. Offered complete or in kit form. From The Armoury.
Price: Flint **$250.00**
Price: Percussion **$225.00**

RIGBY-STYLE TARGET RIFLE
Caliber: .451".
Barrel: 32½".
Weight: 7¾ lbs.
Stock: Walnut; hand-checkered pistol grip, forend.
Stock: Target front with micrometer adjustment; adjustable Vernier peep rear.
Features: Comes with loading accessories—bullet starter, bullet sizer, special ramrod. Introduced 1985. From Navy Arms.
Price: **$645.00**

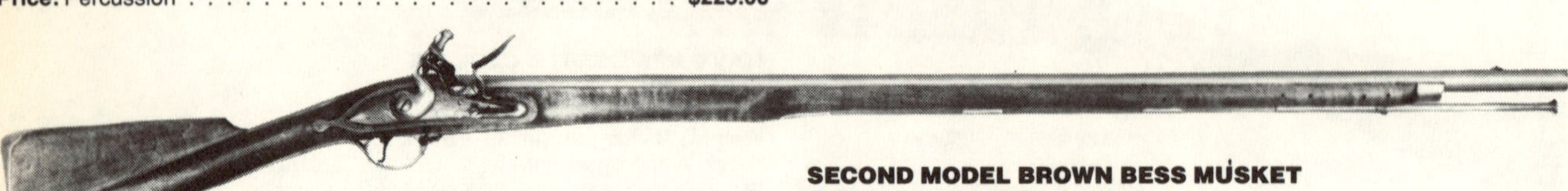
Navy Brown Bess

SECOND MODEL BROWN BESS MUSKET
Caliber: 75, uses .735" round ball.
Barrel: 42", smoothbore.
Weight: 9½ lbs. **Length:** 59" overall.
Stock: Walnut (Navy); walnut-stained hardwood (Dixie).
Sights: Fixed.
Features: Polished barrel and lock with brass trigger guard and buttplate. Bayonet and scabbard available. From Navy Arms, Dixie Gun Works, E.M.F.
Price: Finished . . . . **$475.00** to **$850.00**
Price: Kit (Dixie Gun Works, Navy Arms) . . . . **$400.00** to **$430.00**
Price: Carbine (Navy Arms) **$520.00**

SAN FRANCISCO COMMEMORATIVE PERCUSSION RIFLE
Caliber: 45.
Barrel: 35", octagonal.
Weight: 7½ lbs. **Length:** 50" overall.
Stock: Walnut.
Sights: Blade front, fixed notch rear.
Features: Brass trim, buttplate, patchbox with engraving. Imported from Italy by E.M.F.
Price: **$395.00**

SHARPS PERCUSSION RIFLES
Caliber: 54.
Barrel: 28".
Weight: 9 lbs. **Length:** 46" overall.
Stock: Checkered walnut.
Sights: Blade front, ladder-type adjustable rear.
Features: Blued barrel, color case-hardened receiver and buttplate. Imported from Italy by E.M.F.
Price: Rifle or carbine **$950.00**

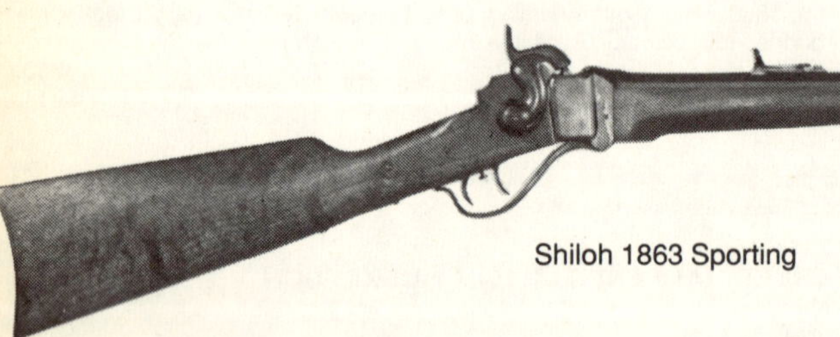
Shiloh 1863 Sporting

Shiloh Sharps Model 1863 Sporting Rifle
Similar to the Military Carbine except has 30" octagon barrel, blade front and sporting rear sights, shotgun butt available, steel buttplate, schnabel forend. Standard-grade wood (semi-fancy available).
Price: **$785.00**

SHILOH SHARPS 1863 MILITARY RIFLE
Caliber: 54.
Barrel: 30", round.
Weight: 8 lbs., 12 oz.
Stock: Military-style butt, steel buttplate; patchbox optional. Standard-grade walnut.
Sights: Iron block front, Lawrence-style ladder rear.
Features: Recreation of the 1863 percussion rifle. Made in U.S. by Shiloh Rifle Mfg. Co.
Price: **$895.00**
Price: 1863 Military Carbine (as above except has 22" round bbl., band on military-style forend, saddle bar and ring) **$795.00**

T/C Big Boar

THOMPSON/CENTER BIG BOAR RIFLE
Caliber: 58.
Barrel: 26" octagon; 1:48 twist.
Weight: 7¾ lbs. **Length:** 42½" overall.
Stock: American black walnut; rubber buttpad; swivels.
Sights: Bead front, fullt adjustable open rear.
Features: Percussion lock; single trigger with wide bow trigger guard. Comes with soft leather sling. Introduced 1991. From Thompson/Center.
Price: **$330.00**

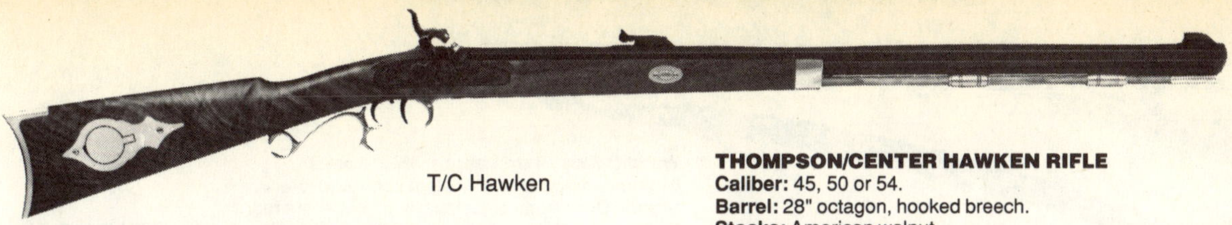
T/C Hawken

THOMPSON/CENTER CHEROKEE RIFLE
Caliber: 32, 45.
Barrel: 24", 13⁄16" across flats.
Weight: About 6 lbs.
Stock: American walnut.
Sights: Open hunting style; round notch rear fully adjustable for windage and elevation.
Features: Single trigger only. Interchangeable barrels. Brass buttplate, trigger guard, forend escutcheons and lockplate screw bushing. Introduced 1984. From Thompson/Center
Price: 32-, 45-caliber **$320.00**

THOMPSON/CENTER HAWKEN RIFLE
Caliber: 45, 50 or 54.
Barrel: 28" octagon, hooked breech.
Stocks: American walnut.
Sights: Blade front, rear adjustable for windage and elevation.
Features: Solid brass furniture, double-set triggers, button rifled barrel, coil-type mainspring. From Thompson/Center.
Price: Percussion model (45-, 50- or 54-cal.) **$365.00**
Price: Flintlock model (50-cal.) **$380.00**
Price: Percussion kit **$265.00**
Price: Flintlock kit **$285.00**

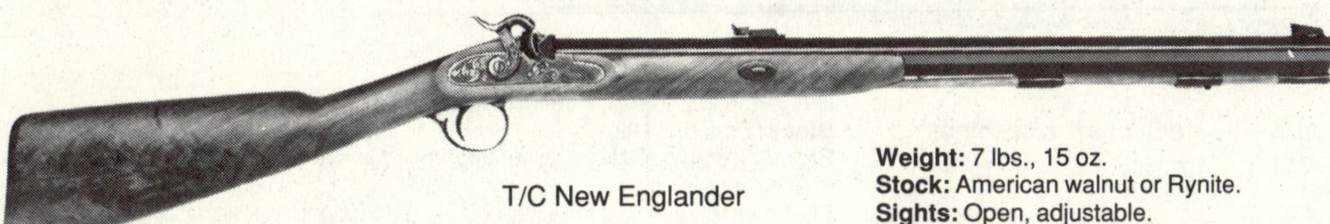
T/C New Englander

THOMPSON/CENTER NEW ENGLANDER RIFLE
Caliber: 50, 54.
Barrel: 28", round.
Weight: 7 lbs., 15 oz.
Stock: American walnut or Rynite.
Sights: Open, adjustable.
Features: Color case-hardened percussion lock with engraving, rest blued. Also accepts 12-ga. shotgun barrel. Introduced 1987. From Thompson/Center.
Price: Right-hand model **$260.00**
Price: As above, Rynite stock **$245.00**
Price: Left-hand model **$280.00**
Price: Accessory 12-ga. barrel, right-hand **$120.00**

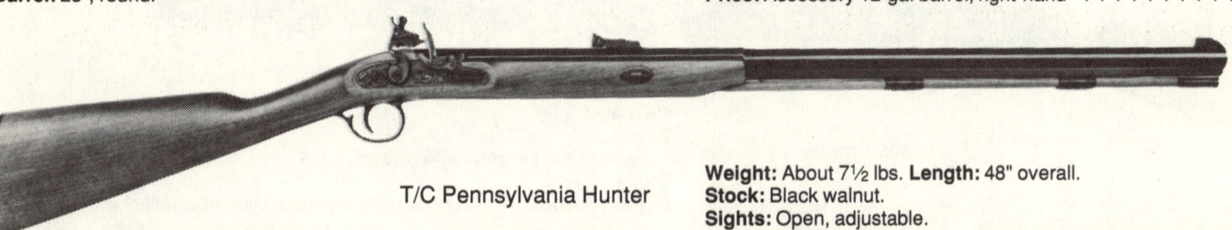
T/C Pennsylvania Hunter

THOMPSON/CENTER PENNSYLVANIA HUNTER RIFLE
Caliber: 50.
Barrel: 31", half-octagon, half-round.
Weight: About 7½ lbs. **Length:** 48" overall.
Stock: Black walnut.
Sights: Open, adjustable.
Features: Rifled 1:66 for round ball shooting. Available in flintlock or percussion. From Thompson/Center.
Price: Percussion **$310.00**
Price: Flintlock **$325.00**

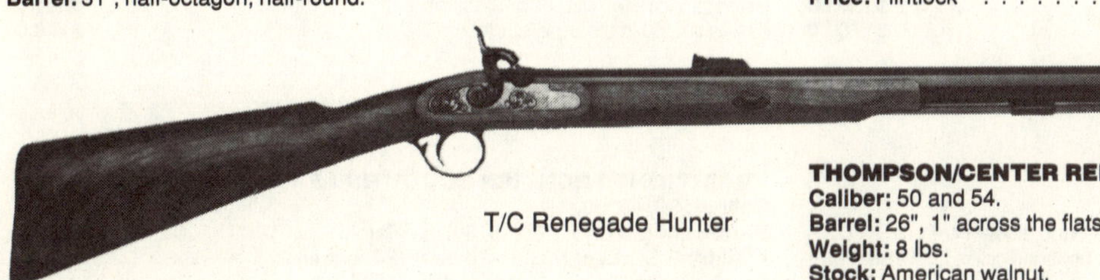
T/C Renegade Hunter

THOMPSON/CENTER RENEGADE RIFLE
Caliber: 50 and 54.
Barrel: 26", 1" across the flats.
Weight: 8 lbs.
Stock: American walnut.
Sights: Open hunting (Patridge) style, fully adjustable for windage and elevation.
Features: Coil spring lock, double-set triggers, blued steel trim. From Thompson/Center.
Price: Percussion model **$325.00**
Price: Flintlock model, 50-cal. only **$335.00**
Price: Percussion kit **$235.00**
Price: Flintlock kit **$250.00**
Price: Left-hand percussion, 50- or 54-cal. **$335.00**

Thompson/Center Renegade Hunter
Similar to standard Renegade except has single trigger in a large-bow shotgun-style trigger guard, no brass trim. Available in 50- or 54-caliber. Color case-hardened lock, rest blued. Introduced 1987. From Thompson/Center.
Price: **$300.00**

T/C White Mountain

THOMPSON/CENTER WHITE MOUNTAIN CARBINE
Caliber: 45, 50 and 54.
Barrel: 21", half-octagon, half-round.
Weight: 6½ lbs. **Length:** 38" overall.
Stock: American black walnut.
Sights: Open hunting (Patridge) style, fully adjustable rear.
Features: Percussion or flintlock. Single trigger, large trigger guard; rubber buttpad; rear q.d. swivel, front swivel mounted on thimble; comes with sling. Introduced 1989. From Thompson/Center.
Price: Percussion **$325.00**
Price: Flintlock **$345.00**

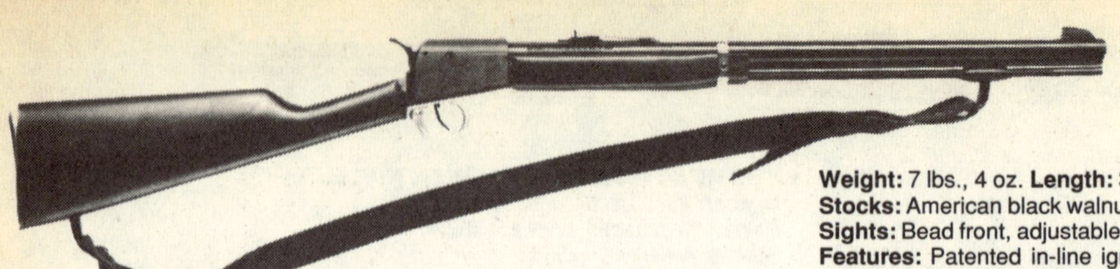

T/C Scout

THOMPSON/CENTER SCOUT RIFLE
Caliber: 50 and 54.
Barrel: 21", interchangeable, 1:20 twist.
Weight: 7 lbs., 4 oz. **Length:** 38⅝" overall.
Stocks: American black walnut stock and forend.
Sights: Bead front, adjustable semi-buckhorn rear.
Features: Patented in-line ignition system with special vented breech plug. Patented trigger mechanism consists of only two moving parts. Interchangeable barrels. Wide grooved hammer. Brass trigger guard assembly, brass barrel band and buttplate. Ramrod has blued hardware. Comes with q.d. swivels and suede leather carrying sling. Drilled and tapped for standard scope mounts. Introduced 1990. From Thompson/Center.
Price: 50- or 54-cal. **$370.00**
Price: Extra barrel, 50- or 54-cal. **$160.00**

Traditions Buckskinner

TRADITIONS BUCKSKINNER CARBINE
Caliber: 50.
Barrel: 21", 15/16" flats, half octagon, half round.
Weight: 6 lbs. **Length:** 36¼" overall.
Stock: Beech.
Sights: Beaded blade front, hunting-style open rear click adjustable for windage and elevation.
Features: Uses V-type mainspring, single trigger. Non-glare hardware. Comes with leather sling. From Traditions, Inc.
Price: Percussion **$259.00**
Price: Flintlock **$284.00**

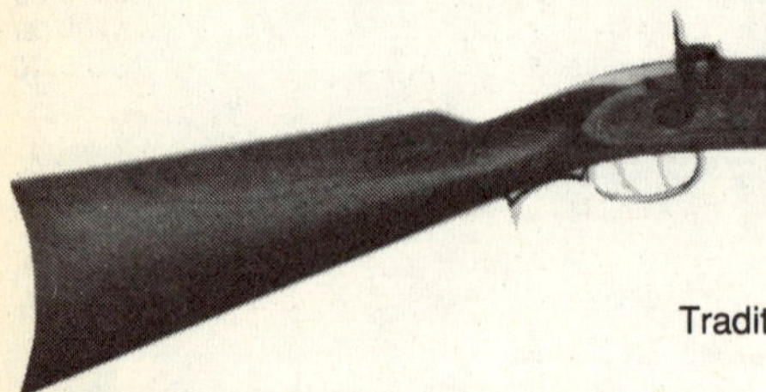

Traditions Frontier

Traditions Frontier Carbine
Similar to the Frontier Rifle except has 24" barrel, is 40½" overall, weighs 6½ lbs. Available in 50-caliber percussion only. From Traditions, Inc.
Price: **$230.00**
Price: Kit **$170.00**

TRADITIONS FRONTIER RIFLE
Caliber: 45, 50.
Barrel: 28", 15/16" flats.
Weight: 8 lbs. **Length:** 44¾" overall.
Stock: Beech.
Sights: Beaded blade front, hunting-style rear click adjustable for windage and elevation.
Features: Adjustable sear engagement with fly and bridle, V-type mainspring; double-set triggers. Brass furniture. From Traditions, Inc.
Price: 45-caliber, percussion **$230.00**
Price: 50-caliber, flint or percussion **$251.00**
Price: Kit, 50-caliber percussion **$170.00**

TRADITIONS HAWKEN RIFLE
Caliber: 50, 54.
Barrel: 32¼"; 1" flats.
Weight: 9 lbs. **Length:** 50" overall.
Stock: Walnut with cheekpiece.
Sights: Hunting style, click adjustable for windage and elevation.
Features: Fiberglass ramrod, double-set triggers, polished brass furniture. From Traditions, Inc.
Price: Percussion **$394.00**

Traditions Hunter Rifle
Similar to the Hawken except has blackened and German silver furniture. Has 28¼" barrel with 1" flats.
Price: Percussion only, 50- or 54-cal. **$404.00**
Price: Hawken Woodsman (50- or 54-cal.) **$259.00**
Price: As above, kit **$200.00**

TRADITIONS FRONTIER SCOUT RIFLE
Caliber: 36, 45, 50.
Barrel: 24" (36-cal.), 26" (45, 50); ⅞" flats.
Weight: 6 lbs. **Length:** 39⅛" overall (24" barrel).
Stock: Beech.
Sights: Blade Front, primitive-style adjustable rear.
Features: Scaled-down version of the Frontier rifle for smaller shooters. Percussion only. Color case-hardened lock plate. Introduced 1991. From Traditions, Inc.
Price: **$215.00**

Traditions Pennsylvania

TRADITIONS PENNSYLVANIA RIFLE
Caliber: 45, 50.
Barrel: 40¼", ⅞" flats.
Weight: 9 lbs. **Length:** 57½" overall.
Stock: Walnut.
Sights: Blade front, adjustable rear.
Features: Brass patchbox and ornamentation. Double-set triggers. From Traditions, Inc.
Price: Flintlock **$473.00**
Price: Percussion **$446.00**

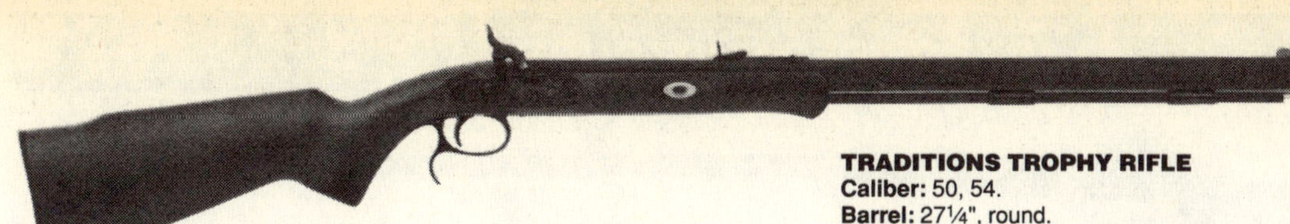

Traditions Pioneer

TRADITIONS PIONEER RIFLE
Caliber: 50, 54.
Barrel: 27¼"; 15⁄16" flats.
Weight: 7 lbs. **Length:** 44" overall.
Stock: Beech with pistol grip, recoil pad.
Sights: German silver blade front, buckhorn rear with elevation ramp.
Features: V-type mainspring, adjustable single trigger; blackened furniture; color case-hardened lock; large trigger guard. From Traditions, Inc.
Price: Percussion only **$202.00**

TRYON TRAILBLAZER RIFLE
Caliber: 50.
Barrel: 32", 1" flats.
Weight: 9 lbs. **Length:** 48" overall.
Stock: European walnut with cheekpiece.
Sights: Blade front, semi-buckhorn rear.
Features: Reproduction of a rifle made by George Tryon about 1820. Double-set triggers, back action lock, hooked breech with long tang. From Navy Arms.
Price: **$375.00**

TRADITIONS TROPHY RIFLE
Caliber: 50, 54.
Barrel: 27¼", round.
Weight: 7 lbs. **Length:** 44¾" overall.
Stock: Walnut with full pistol grip and cheekpiece.
Sights: Patridge-style blade front, hunting-style rear click adjustable for windage and elevation.
Features: Engraved, color case-hardened lock with bridle, claw mainspring; single trigger adjustable for weight. Sling swivels; fiberglass ramrod; recoil pad. From Traditions, Inc.
Price: Percussion only **$404.00**

TRYON RIFLE
Caliber: 50, 54.
Barrel: 34", octagon; 1:63 twist.
Weight: 9 lbs. **Length:** 49" overall.
Stock: European walnut with steel furniture.
Sights: Blade front, fixed rear.
Features: Reproduction of an American plains rifle with double-set triggers and back-action lock. Imported from Italy by Dixie Gun Works.
Price: **$390.00**
Price: Kit **$375.00**

Navy Arms Tryon Creedmoor Target Model
Similar to the standard Tryon rifle except 45-caliber only, 33" octagon barrel, globe front sight with inserts, fully adjustable match rear. Has double-set triggers, sling swivels. Imported by Navy Arms.
Price: **$495.00**

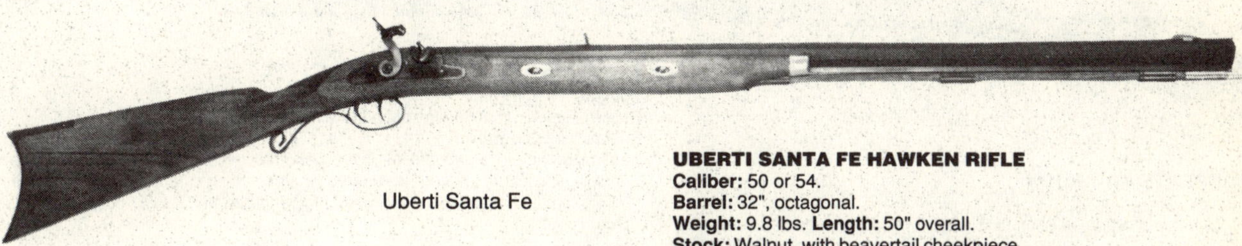

Uberti Santa Fe

UBERTI SANTA FE HAWKEN RIFLE
Caliber: 50 or 54.
Barrel: 32", octagonal.
Weight: 9.8 lbs. **Length:** 50" overall.
Stock: Walnut, with beavertail cheekpiece.
Sights: German silver blade front, buckhorn rear.
Features: Browned finish, color case-hardened lock, double triggers, German silver ferrule, wedge plates. Imported by Uberti USA.
Price: **$480.00**

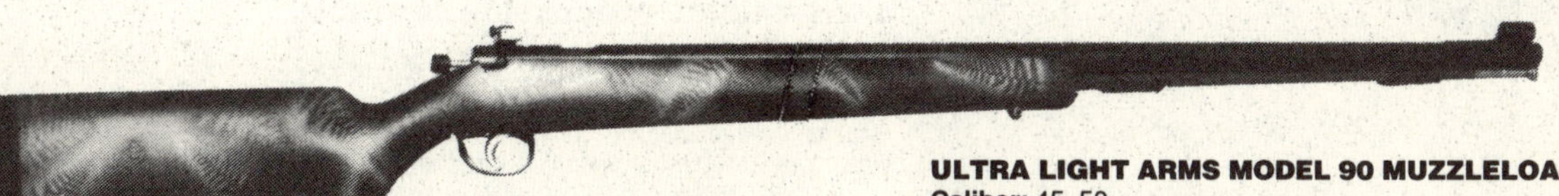

Ultra Light Model 90

ULTRA LIGHT ARMS MODEL 90 MUZZLELOADER
Caliber: 45, 50.
Barrel: 28", button rifled; 1:48 twist.
Weight: 6 lbs.
Stock: Kevlar/graphite, colors optional.
Sights: Hooded blade front on ramp, Williams aperture rear adjustable for windage and elevation.
Features: In-line ignition system with top loading port. Timney trigger; integral side safety. Comes with recoil pad, sling swivels and hard case. Introduced 1990. Made in U.S. by Ultra Light Arms.
Price: **$950.00**

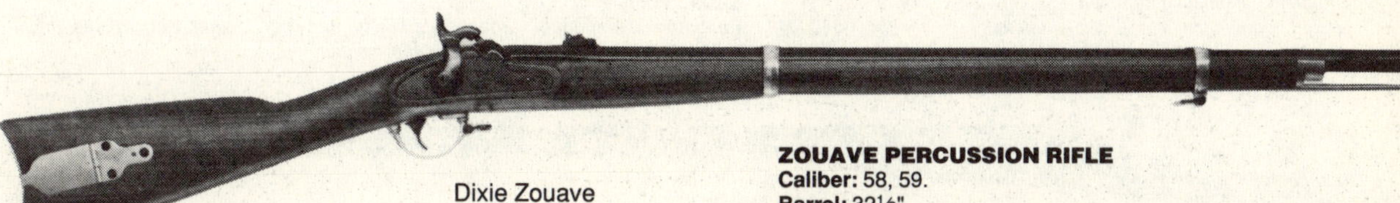

Dixie Zouave

Mississippi Model 1841 Percussion Rifle
Similar to Zouave rifle but patterned after U.S. Model 1841. Imported by Dixie Gun Works, Euroarms of America, Navy Arms.
Price: . . . . **$430.00** to **$463.00**

ZOUAVE PERCUSSION RIFLE
Caliber: 58, 59.
Barrel: 32½".
Weight: 9½ lbs. **Length:** 48½" overall.
Stock: Walnut finish, brass patchbox and buttplate.
Sights: Fixed front, rear adjustable for elevation.
Features: Color case-hardened lockplate, blued barrel. From CVA, Navy Arms, Dixie Gun Works, Euroarms of America (M1863), E.M.F.
Price: About . . . . **$325.00** to **$540.00**
Price: CVA, 58-cal. **$416.95**
Price: Kit (Euroarms 58-cal. only) **$263.00**

BLACKPOWDER SHOTGUNS

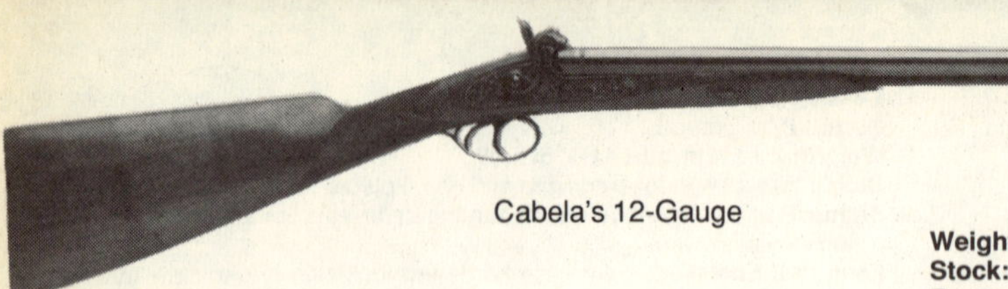
Cabela's 12-Gauge

CABELA'S 12-GAUGE SHOTGUN

Gauge: 12.
Barrel: 28".
Weight: 7½ lbs. **Length:** 44.1" overall.
Stock: Hand-checkered European walnut.
Features: Recreates an English muzzleloader. Color case-hardened lock, blued chrome-lined barrels. Imported by Cabela's.
Price: **$339.95**
Price: 10-gauge (30" barrels, engraved lockplates) **$389.95**

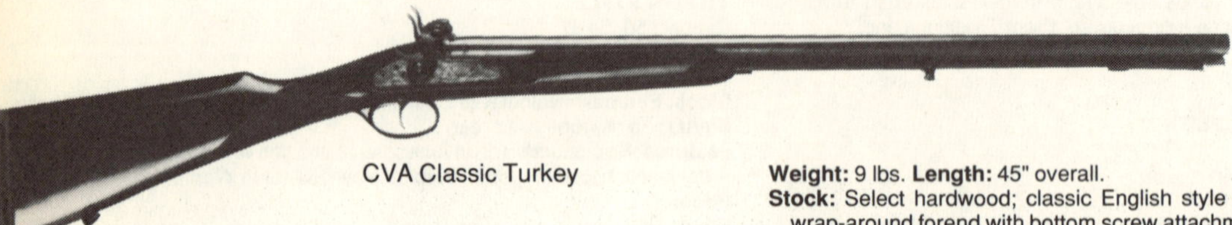
CVA Classic Turkey

CVA CLASSIC TURKEY DOUBLE SHOTGUN

Gauge: 12.
Barrel: 28" (Imp. & Imp.).
Weight: 9 lbs. **Length:** 45" overall.
Stock: Select hardwood; classic English style with checkered straight grip, wrap-around forend with bottom screw attachment.
Sights: Bead front.
Features: Hinged double triggers; color case-hardened and engraved lockplates, trigger guard and tang. Rubber recoil pad. Not suitable for steel shot. Introduced 1990. Imported by CVA.
Price: **$578.95**

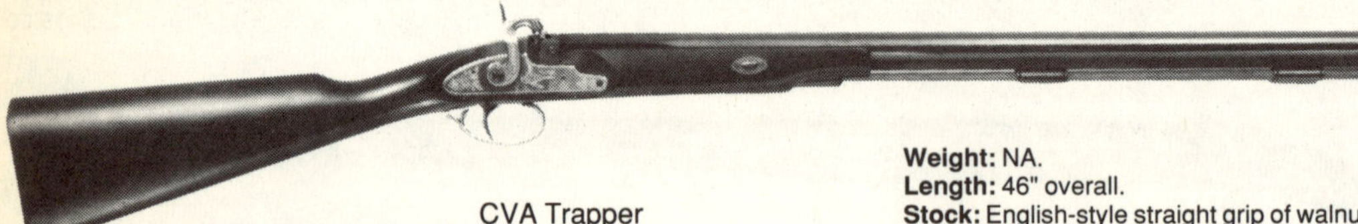
CVA Trapper

CVA TRAPPER PERCUSSION

Gauge: 12.
Barrel: 28". Choke tubes (Mod., Imp., Full).
Weight: NA.
Length: 46" overall.
Stock: English-style straight grip of walnut-finished hardwood.
Sights: Brass bead front.
Features: Single blued barrel; color case-hardened lockplate and hammer; screw adjustable sear engagements, V-type mainspring; brass wedge plates; color case-hardened and engraved trigger guard and tang. From CVA.
Price: Finished **$428.95**

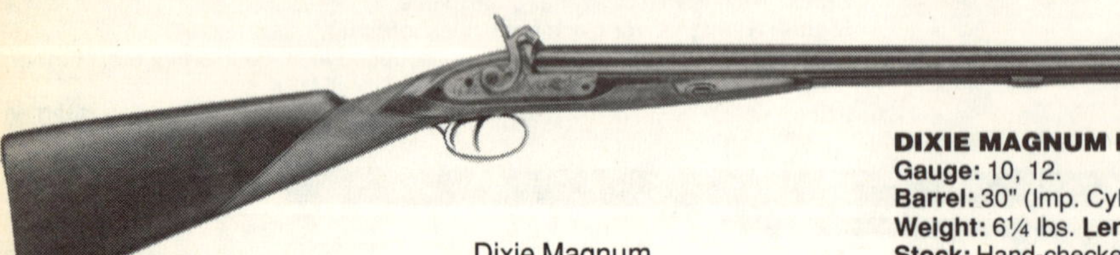
Dixie Magnum

DIXIE MAGNUM PERCUSSION SHOTGUN

Gauge: 10, 12.
Barrel: 30" (Imp. Cyl. & Mod.) in 10-ga.; 28" in 12-ga.
Weight: 6¼ lbs. **Length:** 45" overall.
Stock: Hand-checkered walnut, 14" pull.
Features: Double triggers, light hand engraving. Case-hardened locks in 12-ga.; polished steel in 10-ga. with sling swivels. From Dixie Gun Works.
Price: Upland **$357.00**
Price: 12-ga. kit **$280.00**
Price: 10-ga. **$399.00**
Price: 10-ga. kit **$335.00**

E.M.F. PERCUSSION O/U SHOTGUN

Gauge: 12.
Barrel: 30".
Weight: 7¼ lbs. **Length:** 46" overall.
Stock: Walnut.
Features: Color case-hardened action, buttplate and barrel bands, blue barrels; double triggers. Imported from Italy by E.M.F.
Price: **$640.00**

EUROARMS DUCK SHOTGUN

Gauge: 8, 10, 12.
Barrel: 33".
Weight: 8½ lbs. **Length:** 49" overall.
Stock: Walnut.
Features: Color case-hardened lock; blue hammer, trigger, barrel; brass furniture. Imported by Euroarms of America.
Price: **$407.00**

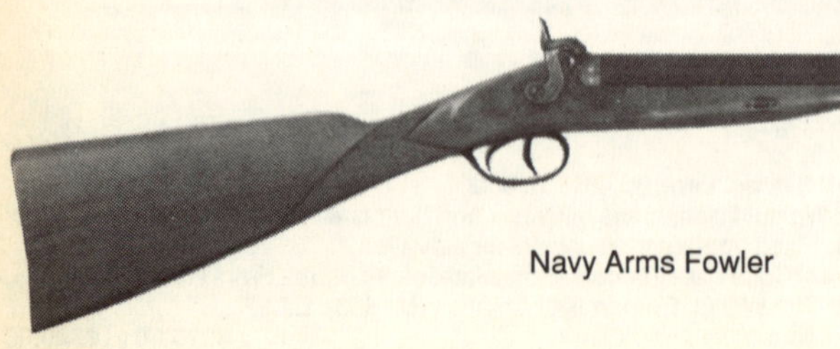
Navy Arms Fowler

NAVY ARMS FOWLER SHOTGUN

Gauge: 12.
Barrel: 28".
Weight: 7 lbs., 12 oz. **Length:** 45" overall.
Stock: Walnut-stained hardwood.
Features: Color case-hardened lockplates and hammers; checkered stock. Imported by Navy Arms.
Price: Fowler model, 12-ga. only **$295.00**

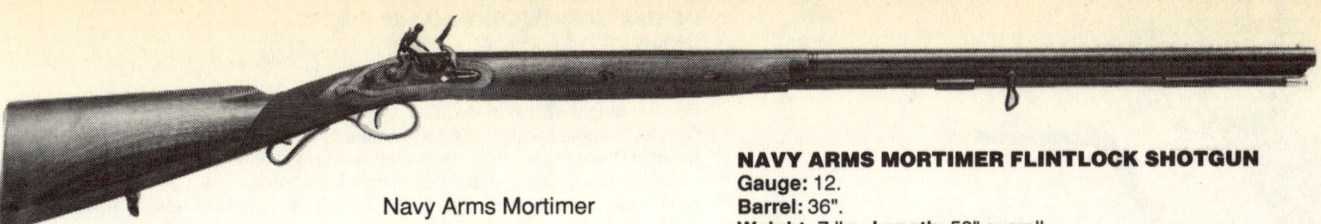
Navy Arms Mortimer

NAVY ARMS MORTIMER FLINTLOCK SHOTGUN
Gauge: 12.
Barrel: 36".
Weight: 7 lbs. **Length:** 53" overall.
Stock: Walnut, with cheekpiece.
Features: Waterproof pan, roller frizzen, external safety. Color case-hardened lock, rest blued. Introduced 1991. Imported by Navy Arms.
Price: **$535.00**

NAVY ARMS STEEL SHOT MAGNUM SHOTGUN
Gauge: 10.
Barrel: 28" (Cyl. & Cyl.).
Weight: 7 lbs., 9 oz. **Length:** 45½" overall.
Stock: Walnut, with cheekpiece.
Features: Designed specifically for steel shot. Engraved, polished locks; sling swivels; blued barrels. Introduced 1991. Imported by Navy Arms.
Price: **$400.00**

Consult our Directory pages for the location of firms mentioned.

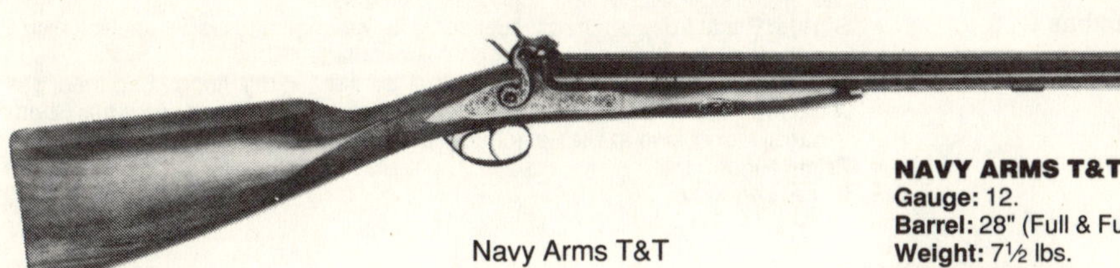
Navy Arms T&T

NAVY ARMS T&T SHOTGUN
Gauge: 12.
Barrel: 28" (Full & Full).
Weight: 7½ lbs.
Stock: Walnut.
Sights: Bead front.
Features: Color case-hardened locks, double triggers, blued steel furniture. From Navy Arms.
Price: **$375.00**

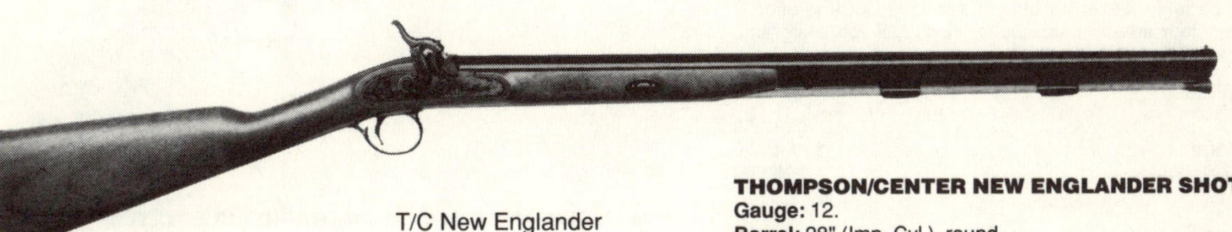
T/C New Englander

TRAIL GUNS KODIAK 10-GAUGE DOUBLE
Gauge: 10.
Barrel: 20", 30¾" (Cyl. bore).
Weight: About 9 lbs. **Length:** 47⅛" overall.
Stock: Walnut, with cheek rest. Checkered wrist and forend.
Features: Chrome-plated bores; engraved lockplates, brass bead front and middle sights; sling swivels. Introduced 1980. Imported from Italy by Trall Guns Armory, Inc.
Price: **$425.00**

THOMPSON/CENTER NEW ENGLANDER SHOTGUN
Gauge: 12.
Barrel: 28" (Imp. Cyl.), round.
Weight: 5 lbs., 2 oz.
Stock: Select American black walnut with straight grip.
Features: Percussion lock is color case-hardened, rest blued. Also accepts 26" round 50- and 54-cal. rifle barrel. Introduced 1986. From Thompson/Center.
Price: Right-hand **$260.00**
Price: Right-hand, Rynite stock **$245.00**
Price: Left-hand **$280.00**
Price: Accessory rifle barrel, right-hand, 50 or 54 . . . . **$120.00**
Price: As above, left-hand **$130.00**

AIRGUNS—HANDGUNS

BEEMAN P1 MAGNUM AIR PISTOL
Caliber: 177, 20, 22, single shot.
Barrel: 8.4".
Weight: 2.5 lbs. **Length:** 11" overall.
Power: Top lever cocking; spring piston.
Stocks: Checkered walnut.
Sights: Blade front, square notch rear with click micrometer adjustments for windage and elevation. Grooved for scope mounting.
Features: Dual power for 177 and 20-cal.: low setting gives 350-400 fps; high setting 500-600 fps. Rearward expanding mainspring simulates firearm recoil. All Colt 45 auto grips fit gun. Dry-firing feature for practice. Optional wooden shoulder stock. Introduced 1985. Imported by Beeman.
Price: 177, 22-cal. **$329.50**
Price: 5mm **$339.50**
Price: 177, 22, stainless finish **$365.00**
Price: 5mm, stainless finish **$375.00**

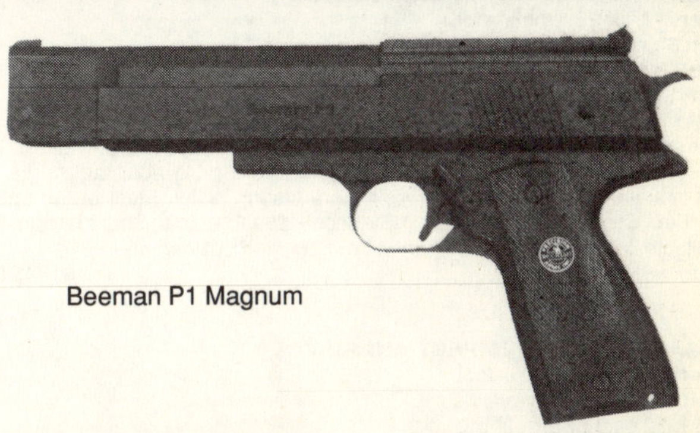
Beeman P1 Magnum

Beeman P2 Match Air Pistol
Similar to the Beeman P1 Magnum except shoots only 177 or 5mm pellets; completely recoilless single-stroke pnuematic action. Weighs 2.2 lbs. Choice of thumbrest match grips or standard style. Introduced 1990.
Price: 177, standard grip **$375.00**
Price: 177, match grip **$399.95**
Price: 5mm, standard grip **$385.00**
Price: 5mm, match grip **$409.95**

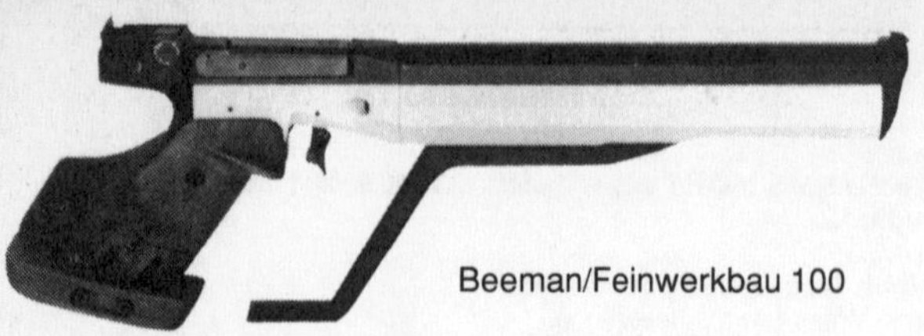
Beeman/Feinwerkbau 100

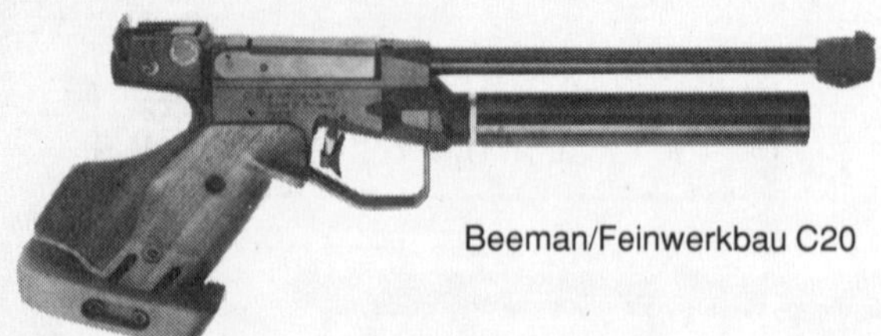
Beeman/Feinwerkbau C20

BEEMAN/FEINWERKBAU 65 MKII AIR PISTOL
Caliber: 177, single shot.
Barrel: 6.1" or 7.5", removable bbl. wgt. available.
Weight: 42 oz. **Length:** 13.3" or 14.1" overall.
Power: Spring, sidelever cocking.
Stocks: Walnut, stippled thumbrest; adjustable or fixed.
Sights: Front, interchangeable post element system, open rear, click adjustable for windage and elevation and for sighting notch width. Scope mount available.
Features: New shorter barrel for better balance and control. Cocking effort 9 lbs. Two-stage trigger, four adjustments. Quiet firing, 525 fps. Programs instantly for recoil or recoilless operation. Permanently lubricated. Steel piston ring. Special switch converts trigger from 17.6-oz. pull to 42-oz. let-off. Imported by Beeman.
Price: Right-hand $998.50
Price: Left-hand, 6.1" barrel $1,045.00
Price: Model 65 Mk. I (7.5" bbl.) $965.00

Beeman/Feinwerkbau C5

BEEMAN/WEBLEY HURRICANE PISTOL
Caliber: 177 or 22, single shot.
Barrel: 8", rifled.
Weight: 2.4 lbs. **Length:** 11½" overall.
Power: Spring piston.
Stocks: Thumbrest, checkered high-impact synthetic.
Sights: Hooded front; micro-click rear adjustable for windage and elevation.
Features: Velocity of 470 fps (177-cal.). Single stroke cocking, adjustable trigger pull, manual safety. Rearward recoil like a firearm pistol. Steel piston and cylinder. Scope base included; 1.5x scope **$54.97** extra. Shoulder stock available. Introduced 1977. Imported from England by Beeman.
Price: $189.98

BEEMAN/WEBLEY TEMPEST AIR PISTOL
Caliber: 177 or 22, single shot.
Barrel: 6.75", rifled ordnance steel.
Weight: 32 oz. **Length:** 9" overall.
Power: Spring piston.
Stocks: Checkered black epoxy with thumbrest.
Sights: Post front; rear has sliding leaf adjustable for windage and elevation.
Features: Adjustable trigger pull, manual safety. Velocity 470 fps (177-cal.). Steel piston in steel liner for maximum performance and durability. Unique rearward spring simulates firearm recoil. Shoulder stock available. Introduced 1979. Imported from England by Beeman.
Price: $159.98

BEEMAN/FEINWERKBAU 100 PISTOL
Caliber: 177, single shot.
Barrel: 10.1", 12-groove rifling.
Weight: 2.5 lbs. **Length:** 16.5" overall.
Power: Single-stroke pneumatic, sidelever cocking.
Stocks: Stippled walnut with adjustable palm shelf.
Sights: Blade front, open rear adjustable for windage and elevation. Notch size adjustable for width. Interchangeable front blades.
Features: Velocity 460 fps. Fully adjustable trigger. Cocking effort 12 lbs. Introduced 1988. Imported by Beeman.
Price: Right-hand $898.50
Price: Left-hand $950.00

BEEMAN/FEINWERKBAU C20 CO_2 PISTOL
Caliber: 177, single shot.
Barrel: 10.1", 12-groove rifling.
Weight: 2.5 lbs. **Length:** 16" overall.
Power: Special CO_2 cylinder.
Stock: Stippled walnut with adjustable palm shelf.
Sights: Blade front, open rear adjustable for windage and elevation. Notch size adjustable for width. Interchangeable front blades.
Features: Fully adjustable trigger; can be set for dry firing. Separate gas chamber for uniform power. Cylinders interchangeable even when full. Short-barrel model also available. Introduced 1988. Imported by Beeman.
Price: Right-hand $965.00
Price: Left-hand $1,025.00

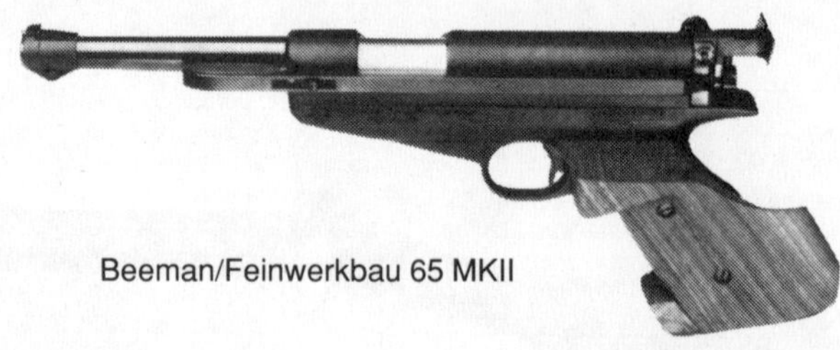
Beeman/Feinwerkbau 65 MKII

BEEMAN/FEINWERKBAU C5 CO_2 RAPID FIRE PISTOL
Caliber: 177.
Barrel: 7.25".
Weight: 2.42 lbs.
Power: NA.
Stocks: Anatomical match.
Sights: Match.
Features: Velocity 510 fps. Has special trigger shape with swivel action, longitudinal positioning. Introduced 1990. Imported by Beeman.
Price: Right-hand $1,350.00
Price: Left-hand $1,425.00

Beeman/Webley Hurricane

Beeman/Webley Tempest

 CAUTION: PRICES CHANGE, CHECK AT GUNSHOP.

Benjamin/Sheridan CO_2

Benjamin/Sheridan Pneumatic

BSA SCORPION AIR PISTOL
Caliber: 177 or 22, single shot.
Barrel: 7¾".
Weight: 3½ lbs. **Length:** 15¾" overall.
Power: Spring piston, barrel cocking.
Stocks: Moulded synthetic with thumbrest.
Sights: Globe front, adjustable open rear.
Features: Velocity to 600 fps (177); 400 fps (22). Two-stage trigger. Barrel extension to ease cocking effort. Polished blue finish. Imported from England by Air Rifle Specialists.
Price: **$190.00**

CROSMAN AUTO AIR II PISTOL
Caliber: BB, 17-shot magazine, 177 pellet, single shot.
Barrel: 8⅝" steel, smoothbore.
Weight: 13 oz. **Length:** 10¾" overall.
Power: CO_2 Powerlet.
Stocks: Grooved plastic.
Sights: Blade front, adjustable rear; three-dot system.
Features: Velocity to 390 fps (BBs), 325 fps (pellets). Semi-automatic action with BBs, single shot with pellets. Silvered finish. Introduced 1991. From Crosman.
Price: About **$39.99**

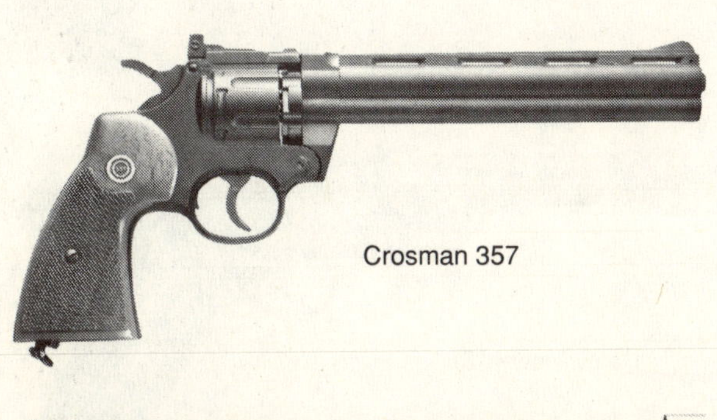
Crosman 357

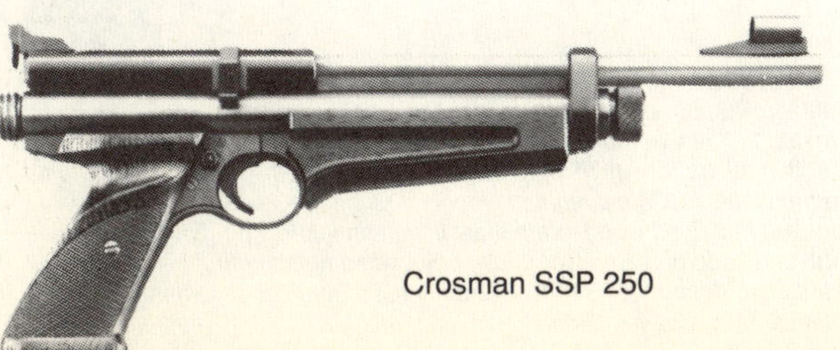
Crosman SSP 250

BEEMAN/WEIHRAUCH HW70 AIR PISTOL
Caliber: 177, single shot.
Barrel: 6¼", rifled.
Weight: 38 oz. **Length:** 12¾" overall.
Power: Spring, barrel cocking.
Stocks: Plastic, with thumbrest.
Sights: Hooded post front, square notch rear adjustable for windage and elevation.
Features: Adjustable trigger, 24-lb. cocking effort, 410 fps MV; automatic barrel safety. Imported by Beeman.
Price: **$169.98**

BENJAMIN/SHERIDAN CO_2 PELLET PISTOLS
Caliber: 177, 20, 22, single shot.
Barrel: 6⅜", rifled brass.
Weight: 28 oz. **Length:** 9" overall.
Power: 12-gram CO_2 cylinder.
Stocks: Walnut on nickeled model, simulated walnut on black guns.
Sights: High ramp front, fully adjustable notch rear.
Features: Velocity to 400 fps. Turn-bolt action wiht cross-bolt safety. Gives about 40 shots per CO_2 cylinder. Introduced 1991. Made in U.S. by Benjamin Air Rifle Co.
Price: Black finish, EB17 (177), EB20 (20), EB22 (22) **$97.95**
Price: Nickel finish, E17 (177), E20 (20), E22 (22) **$105.95**

BENJAMIN/SHERIDAN PNEUMATIC PELLET PISTOLS
Caliber: 177, 20, 22, single shot.
Barrel: 9⅜", rifled brass.
Weight: 40 oz. **Length:**12¼" overall.
Power: Under-lever pnuematic, hand pumped.
Stocks: Walnut stocks and pump handle.
Sights: High ramp front, fully adjustable notch rear.
Features: Velocity to 400 fps (variable). Bolt action with cross-bolt safety. Choice of black or nickel finish. Made in U.S. by Benjamin Air Rifle Co.
Price: Black finish, HB17 (177), HB20 (20), HB22 (22) **$107.95**
Price: Nickel finish, H17 (177), H20 (20), H22 (22) **$113.95**

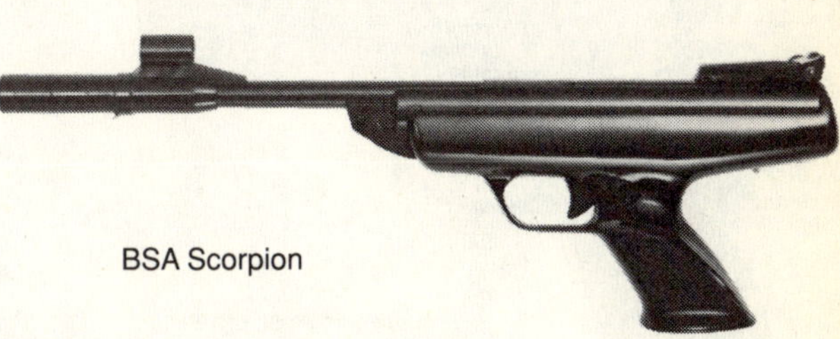
BSA Scorpion

CROSMAN MODEL 357 AIR PISTOL
Caliber: 177, 6- or 10-shot.
Barrel: 4" (Model 357-4), 6" (Model 357-6), rifled steel; 8" (Model 357-8), rifled brass.
Weight: 32 oz. (6"). **Length:** 11⅜" overall.
Power: CO_2 Powerlet.
Stocks: Checkered wood-grain plastic.
Sights: Ramp front, fully adjustable rear.
Features: Average 430 fps (Model 357-6). Break-open barrel for easy loading. Single or double action. Vent. rib barrel. Wide, smooth trigger. Two speed loaders come with each gun. Model 357-8 has matte gray finish, black grips. From Crosman.
Price: 4" or 6", about **$55.00**
Price: 8", about **$62.00**
Price: Model 1357 (same gun as above, except shoots BBs, has 6-shot clip), about **$55.00**

Crosman Model 3357 Spot Marker
Same specs as 8" Model 357 but shoots 50-cal. paint balls. Has break-open action for quick loading 6-shot clip of paint balls. CO_2 power allows repeater firing; hammer-block safety; adjustable rear sight, blade front.
Price: About **$89.00**

CROSMAN MODEL SSP 250 PISTOL
Caliber: 177, 20, 22, single shot.
Barrel: 9⅞", rifled steel.
Weight: 3 lbs., 1 oz. **Length:** 14" overall.
Power: CO_2 Powerlet.
Stocks: Composition; black, with checkering.
Sights: Hooded front, fully adjustable rear.
Features: Velocity about 460 fps. Interchangeable accessory barrels. Two-stage trigger. High/low power settings. From Crosman.
Price: About **$47.00**

CROSMAN MODEL 1322 AIR PISTOL
Caliber: 22, single shot.
Barrel: 8", button rifled.
Weight: 37 oz. **Length:** 13⅝".
Power: Hand pumped.
Sights: Blade front, rear adjustable for windage and elevation.
Features: Moulded plastic grip, hand size pump forearm. Cross-bolt safety. Also available in 177/BB cal. as Model 1377. From Crosman.
Price: About **$50.00**
Price: 1377, about **$50.00**

Crosman Model 1322/1377

Crosman Skanaker

CROSMAN/SKANAKER MATCH AIR PISTOL
Caliber: 177.
Barrel: 9.94".
Weight: 37 oz. **Length:** 16.38" overall.
Power: Refillable CO_2 cylinders.
Stocks: Hardwood, adjustable for thickness; adjustable palm shelf.
Sights: Three-way adjustable post front, open rear with three interchangeable leaves.
Features: Velocity of 550 fps. Angled, adjustable match trigger can be aligned to fit the natural position of the trigger finger. Barrel is hinged near the muzzle for loading. Introduced 1987. From Crosman.
Price: About **$650.00**

DAISY/POWER LINE MODEL 45 AIR PISTOL
Caliber: 177, 13-shot clip.
Barrel: 5", rifled steel.
Weight: 1.25 lbs. **Length:** 8.5" overall.
Power: CO_2.
Stocks: Checkered plastic.
Sights: Fixed.
Features: Velocity 400 fps. Semi-automatic repeater with double-action trigger. Manually operated lever-type trigger block safety; magazine safety. Introduced 1990. From Daisy Mfg. Co.
Price: About **$69.00**

DAISY/POWER LINE MODEL 44 REVOLVER
Caliber: 177 pellets, 6-shot.
Barrel: 6", rifled steel; interchangeable 4" and 8".
Weight: 2.7 lbs.
Power: CO_2.
Stocks: Moulded plastic with checkering.
Sights: Blade on ramp front, fully adjustable notch rear.
Features: Velocity up to 400 fps. Replica of 44 Magnum revolver. Has swingout cylinder and interchangeable barrels. Introduced 1987. From Daisy Mfg. Co.
Price: **$49.00**

Daisy/Power Line 93

DAISY/POWER LINE 93 PISTOL
Caliber: 177, BB, 15-shot clip.
Barrel: 5", steel.
Weight: 17 oz. **Length:** NA.
Power: CO_2.
Stocks: Checkered plastic.
Sights: Fixed.
Features: Velocity to 400 fps. Semi-automatic repeater. Manual lever-type trigger-block safety. Introduced 1991. From Daisy Mfg. Co.
Price: About **$60.00**
Price: Model 693 (nickel-chrome plated), about **$65.00**

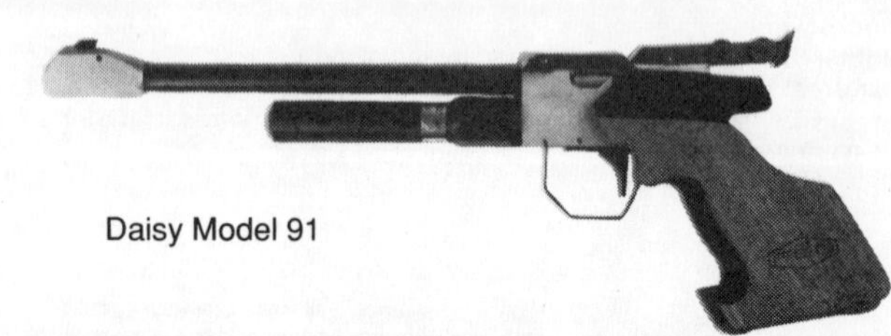

Daisy Model 91

DAISY MODEL 91 MATCH PISTOL
Caliber: 177, single shot.
Barrel: 10.25", rifled steel.
Weight: 2.5 lbs. **Length:** 16.5" overall.
Power: CO_2, 12-gram cylinder.
Stocks: Stippled hardwood; anatomically shaped and adjustable.
Sights: Blade and ramp front, changeable-width rear notch with full micrometer adjustments.
Features: Velocity to 476 fps. Gives 55 shots per cylinder. Fully adjustable trigger. Introduced 1991. Imported by Daisy Mfg. Co.
Price: About **$500.00**

Consult our Directory pages for the location of firms mentioned.

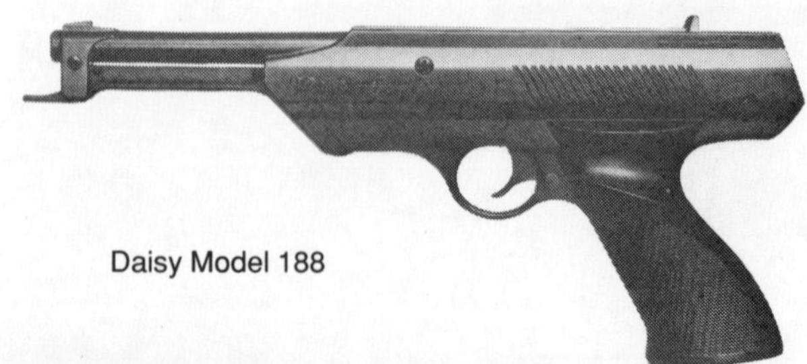

Daisy Model 188

DAISY MODEL 188 BB PISTOL
Caliber: BB.
Barrel: 9.9", steel smoothbore.
Weight: 1.67 lbs. **Length:** 11.7" overall.
Stocks: Copolymer; checkered with thumbrest.
Sights: Blade and ramp front, open fixed rear.
Features: 24-shot repeater. Spring action with under-barrel cocking lever. Grip and receiver of Nylafil-copolymer material. Introduced 1979. From Daisy Mfg. Co.
Price: About **$25.00**

DAISY/YOUTH LINE MODEL 1500 PISTOL
Caliber: BB, 60-shot reservoir.
Barrel: 1.5", smoothbore.
Weight: 22 oz. **Length:** 11.1" overall.
Power: Daisy CO_2 cylinder.
Stocks: Moulded wood-grain plastic with checkering.
Sights: Blade on ramp front, fully adjustable notch rear.
Features: Velocity of 340 fps. Gravity feed magazine. Cross-bolt safety. From Daisy Mfg. Co.
Price: About **$38.00**

DAISY/POWER LINE 717 PELLET PISTOL
Caliber: 177, single shot.
Barrel: 9.61".
Weight: 2.8 lbs. **Length:** 13½" overall.
Stocks: Moulded wood-grain plastic, with thumbrest.
Sights: Blade and ramp front, micro-adjustable notch rear.
Features: Single pump pneumatic pistol. Rifled steel barrel. Cross-bolt trigger block. Muzzle velocity 385 fps. From Daisy Mfg. Co. Introduced 1979.
Price: About **$68.00**

DAISY/POWER LINE MATCH 777 PELLET PISTOL
Caliber: 177, single shot.
Barrel: 9.61" rifled steel by Lothar Walther.
Weight: 32 oz. **Length:** 13½" overall.
Power: Sidelever, single pump pneumatic.
Stocks: Smooth hardwood, fully contoured with palm and thumbrest.
Sights: Blade and ramp front, match-grade open rear with adjustable width notch, micro. click adjustments.
Features: Adjustable trigger; manual cross-bolt safety. MV of 385 fps. Comes with cleaning kit, adjustment tool and pellets. From Daisy Mfg. Co.
Price: About **$236.00**

DAISY/POWER LINE CO_2 1200 PISTOL
Caliber: BB, 177.
Barrel: 10½", smooth.
Weight: 1.6 lbs. **Length:** 11.1" overall.
Power: Daisy CO_2 cylinder.
Stocks: Contoured, checkered moulded wood-grain plastic.
Sights: Blade ramp front, fully adjustable square notch rear.
Features: 60-shot BB reservoir, gravity feed. Cross-bolt safety. Velocity of 420-450 fps for more than 100 shots. From Daisy Mfg. Co.
Price: About **$39.00**

"GAT" AIR PISTOL
Caliber: 177, single shot.
Barrel: 7½" cocked, 9½" extended.
Weight: 22 oz.
Power: Spring piston.
Stocks: Cast checkered metal.
Sights: Fixed.
Features: Shoots pellets, corks or darts. Matte black finish. Imported from England by Stone Enterprises, Inc.
Price: **$21.95**

MARKSMAN 17 AIR PISTOL
Caliber: 177, single shot.
Barrel: 7.5".
Weight: 46 oz. **Length:** 14.5" overall.
Power: Spring-air, barrel-cocking.
Stocks: Checkered composition with right-hand thumbrest.
Sights: Tunnel front, fully adjustable rear.
Features: Velocity of 360-400 fps. Introduced 1986. Imported from Spain by Marksman Products.
Price: **$56.00**

MARKSMAN 1010 REPEATER PISTOL
Caliber: 177, 18-shot repeater.
Barrel: 2½", smoothbore.
Weight: 24 oz. **Length:** 8¼" overall.
Power: Spring.
Features: Velocity to 200 fps. Thumb safety. Black finish. Uses BBs, darts or pellets. Repeats with BBs only. From Marksman Products.
Price: Matte black finish **$24.95**
Price: Model 1010X (as above except nickel-plated) **$32.95**
Price: Model 1015 (brown grips with commemorative medallion) . . . **$26.95**

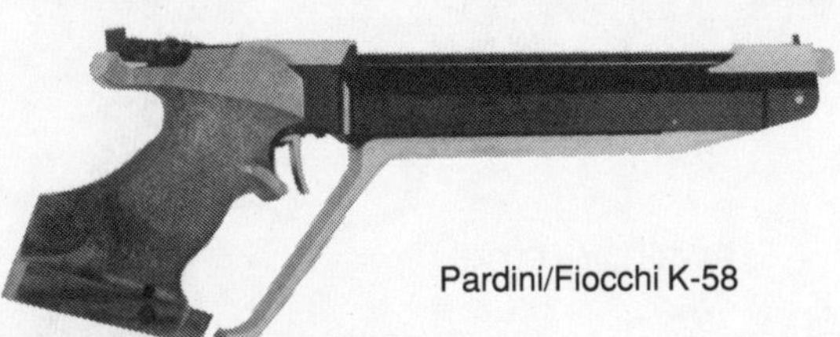
Pardini/Fiocchi K-58

Daisy/Power Line 747 Pistol
Similar to the 717 pistol except has a 12-groove rifled steel barrel by Lothar Walther. Velocity of 360 fps. Manual cross-bolt safety.
Price: About **$109.00**

Daisy/Power Line 777

GAMO CENTER AIR PISTOL
Caliber: 177, single shot.
Barrel: 7.08", rifled.
Weight: 2.8 lbs. **Length:** 13.8" overall.
Power: Spring-air, underlever cocking.
Stocks: Checkered synthetic; adjustable to four angles.
Sights: Blade front, open rear adjustable for windage and elevation.
Features: Velocity to 400 fps. Blued finish. Imported by Great Lakes Airguns.
Price: **$129.95**

Marksman 17

MARKSMAN PLAINSMAN 1049 CO_2 PISTOL
Caliber: BB, 100-shot repeater.
Barrel: 5⅞", smooth.
Weight: 28 oz. **Length:** 9½" overall.
Stock: Simulated walnut with thumbrest.
Power: 12-gram CO_2 cylinders.
Features: Velocity of 400 fps. Three-position power switch. Automatic ammunition feed. Positive safety. From Marksman Products.
Price: **$47.95**

Marksman 1010

PARDINI/FIOCCHI K-58 AIR PISTOL
Caliber: 177, single shot.
Barrel: 9".
Weight: 37.7 oz. **Length:** 15.5" overall.
Power: CO_2.
Stocks: Anatomical fixed or adjustable match type; stippled walnut.
Sights: Post front, fully adjustable match rear. Two sets of interchangeable front and rear blades included.
Features: Alloy construction; adjustable match trigger. Comes with locking case. Introduced 1990. Imported from Italy by Fiocchi of America, Inc.
Price: **$659.00**
Price: Model K-60 (similar to K-58 except has 9.6" barrel with 36.7-oz. weight, 16" overall length, constant velocity double pre-chambered gas feed) **$659.00**

RECORD CHAMPION AIR PISTOL
Caliber: 177, 12-shot repeater.
Barrel: 7.6", rifled.
Weight: 2.8 lbs. **Length:** 10.2" overall.
Power: Spring-air, sidelever cocking.
Stocks: Smooth walnut. Contoured target style available.
Sights: Post front, fully adjustable rear.
Features: Velocity to 420 fps. Magazine loads into bottom of grip. Ambidextrous grips. Introduced 1987. Imported from Germany by Great Lakes Airguns.
Price: **$149.50**

Record Champion

RECORD JUMBO DELUXE AIR PISTOL
Caliber: 177, single shot.
Barrel: 6", rifled.
Weight: 1.9 lbs. **Length:** 7.25" overall.
Power: Spring-air, lateral cocking lever.
Stocks: Smooth walnut.
Sights: Blade front, fully adjustable open rear.
Features: Velocity to 322 fps. Thumb safety. Grip magazine compartment for extra pellet storage. Introduced 1983. Imported from Germany by Great Lakes Airguns.
Price: **$95.50**

Record Jumbo

RWS/DIANA MODEL 5G AIR PISTOL
Caliber: 177, single shot.
Barrel: 7".
Weight: 2¾ lbs. **Length:** 16" overall.
Power: Spring-air, barrel cocking.
Stocks: Plastic, thumbrest design.
Sights: Tunnel front, micro-click open rear.
Features: Velocity of 410 fps. Two-stage trigger with automatic safety. Imported from Germany by Dynamit Nobel-RWS, Inc.
Price: **$175.00**

RWS/Diana Model 5GS Air Pistol
Same as the Model 5G except comes with 1.5x15 pistol scope with ramp-style mount, muzzlebrake/weight. No open sights supplied. Introduced 1983.
Price: **$260.00**

RWS/Diana 5G

RWS/DIANA MODEL 6M MATCH AIR PISTOL
Caliber: 177, single shot.
Barrel: 7".
Weight: 3 lbs. **Length:** 16" overall.
Power: Spring-air, barrel cocking.
Stocks: Walnut-finished hardwood with thumbrest.
Sights: Adjustable front, micro. click open rear.
Features: Velocity of 410 fps. Recoilless double piston system, movable barrel shroud to protect from sight during cocking. Imported from Germany by Dynamit Nobel-RWS, Inc.
Price: Right-hand **$390.00**
Price: Left-hand **$410.00**

RWS/Diana Model 6G, 6GS Air Pistols
Similar to the Model 6M except does not have the movable barrel shroud. Has click micrometer rear sight, two-stage adjustable trigger, interchangeable tunnel front sight. Available in right- or left-hand models.
Price: Right-hand **$285.00**
Price: Left-hand **$310.00**
Price: Model 6GS (with 1.5x15 scope, bbl. wgt., right-hand) **$370.00**
Price: As above, left-hand **$390.00**

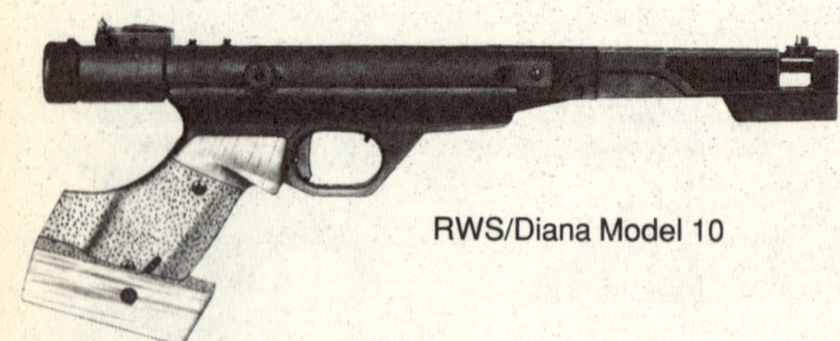
RWS/Diana Model 10

RWS/Diana Model 10 Match Air Pistol
Refined version of the Model 6M. Has special adjustable match trigger, oil-finished and stippled match grips, barrel weight. Also available in left-hand version, and with fitted case.
Price: Model 10 . . . . **$670.00**
Price: Model 10, left-hand **$735.00**
Price: Model 10, with case **$720.00**
Price: Model 10, left-hand, with case **$765.00**

RWS GAMO PR-45 AIR PISTOL
Caliber: 177, single shot.
Barrel: 8.3".
Weight: 25 oz. **Length:** 11" overall.
Power: Pre-compressed air.
Stocks: Composition.
Sights: Blade front, adjustable rear.
Features: Velocity to 430 fps. Recoilless and vibration free. Manual safety. Imported from Spain by Dynamit Nobel-RWS, Inc.
Price: **$125.00**
Price: Compact model (adjustable walnut grips, adjustable trigger, swiveling trigger shoe) **$190.00**

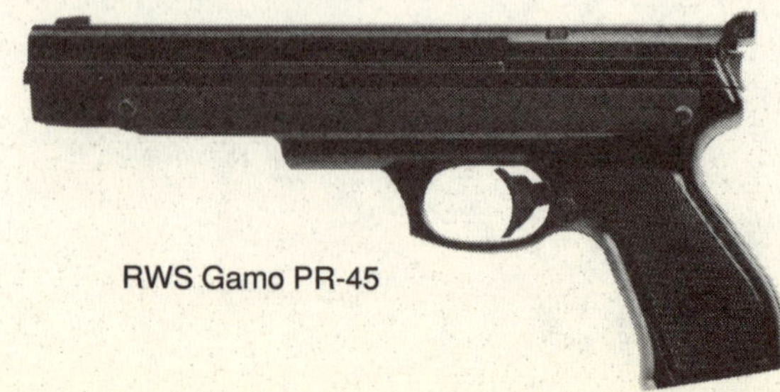
RWS Gamo PR-45

RWS GAMO FALCON AIR PISTOL
Caliber: 177, single shot.
Barrel: 7.1".
Weight: 2.8 lbs. **Length:** 14.9" overall.
Power: Underlever cocking, spring piston.
Stocks: Composition.
Sights: Blade front, adjustable open rear.
Features: Velocity to 430 fps. Cocking effort of 27 lbs. Manual safety; two-stage adjustable trigger. Imported from Spain by Dynamit Nobel-RWS, Inc.
Price: $85.00

RWS Gamo Falcon

WALTHER CP 3 AIR PISTOL
Caliber: 177, single shot.
Barrel: 9".
Weight: 40 oz. **Length:** 14¾" overall.
Power: CO_2.
Stocks: Full target-type stippled wood with adjustable hand shelf.
Sights: Target post front, fully adjustable target rear.
Features: Velocity of 520 fps, CO_2 powered; target-quality trigger; comes with adaptor for charging with standard CO_2 air tanks, case, and accessories. Introduced 1983. Imported from Germany by Interarms.
Price: $960.00
Price: Model CP-5 Match $1,650.00

AIRGUNS—LONG GUNS

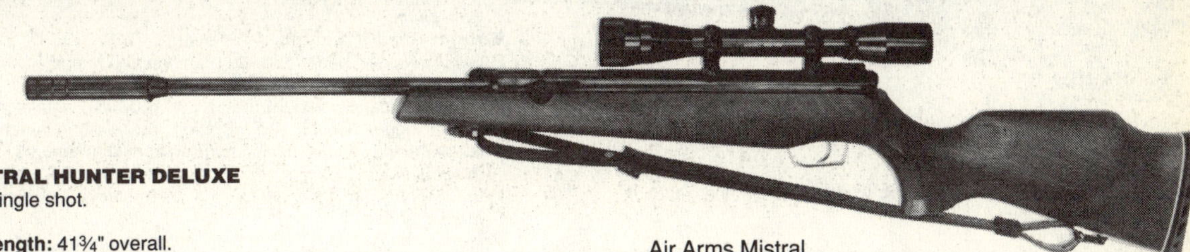
Air Arms Mistral

AIR ARMS MISTRAL HUNTER DELUXE
Caliber: 177, 22, single shot.
Barrel: 15", rifled.
Weight: 8.7 lbs. **Length:** 41¾" overall.
Power: Spring-air, sidelever cocking.
Stock: Oil-finished, stained hardwood with cut checkered grip. Ventilated rubber buttplate.
Sights: Comes with 4x air rifle scope with focusing objective lens. Scope anti-slip block supplied.
Features: Velocity to 930 fps (177). Comes with 6-oz. muzzle weight, leather sling, quick-detachable swivels. Brass trigger and trigger guard. Introduced 1987. Imported from England by Great Lakes Airguns.
Price: 177 or 22 . . . . $410.40

Air Arms Model Bora Hunter Deluxe
Similar to the Mistral model except has 11" barrel, weighs 8 lbs. and has 37¾" overall length. Velocity up to 930 fps (177-cal.). Imported from England by Great Lakes Airguns.
Price: 177 or 22 . . . . $410.46

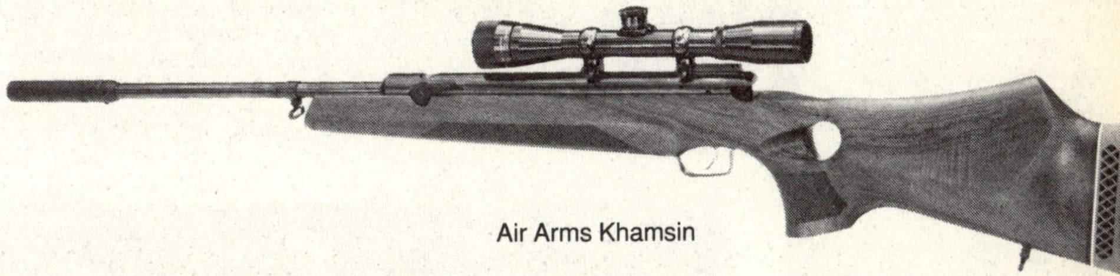
Air Arms Khamsin

AIR ARMS MODEL KHAMSIN
Caliber: 177, 22; single shot.
Barrel: 15", rifled.
Weight: 8 lbs., 2 oz. **Length:** 39¾" overall.
Power: Spring-air, sidelever cocking.
Stock: Oil-finished French walnut thumbhole-style, with cut checkering on p.g. and forend. Ventilated rubber buttplate and sling swivels.
Sights: None furnished. Comes with scope anti-slip block.
Features: Velocity up to 940 fps (177-cal.). Polished brass trigger and trigger guard. Introduced 1987. Imported from England by Great Lakes Alrguns.
Price: Either caliber $573.77

Air Arms SE-90

AIR ARMS SM 100 AIR RIFLE
Caliber: 177, 22, single shot.
Barrel: 22", 12-groove Lothar Walther.
Weight: 8½ lbs. **Length:** 39½" overall.
Power: Pre-charged compressed air from diving tank.
Stock: Walnut-finished beech.
Sights: None furnished.
Features: Velocity to 1000 fps (177), 800 fps (22). PFTE-coated lightweight striker for consistent shots. Blued barrel and air chamber. Imported from England by Air Rifle Specialists.
Price: $870.00
Price: For left-hand stock add $60.00
Price: Model XM 100 (same as SM100 except walnut stock) . . . $1,060.00
Price: For left-hand stock add $60.00

AIR ARMS SE-90 AIR RIFLE
Caliber: 177, 22, single shot.
Barrel: 15", rifled steel by Walther.
Weight: 8 lbs., 4 oz. **Length:** 42¾" with muzzle weight.
Power: Spring-air, sidelever cocking.
Stock: Hardwood with checkered grip and forend, high cheekpiece.
Sights: None furnished. Comes with anti-slip scope block.
Features: Velocity of 943 fps (177), 730 (22). Uses same action as the Mistral rifle. Blue/black finish on metal parts. Comes with muzzle shroud/weight, brass trigger and trigger guard. Introduced 1990. Imported from England by Great Lakes Airguns.
Price: $370.00

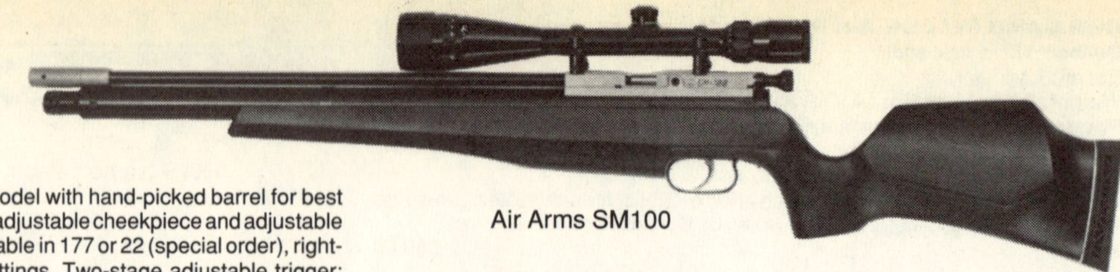
Air Arms SM100

Air Arms TM 100 Air Rifle
Similar to the SM 100 except is target model with hand-picked barrel for best accuracy. Target-type walnut stock with adjustable cheekpiece and adjustable buttplate. Stippled grip and forend. Available in 177 or 22 (special order), right- or left-hand models. Variable power settings. Two-stage adjustable trigger; 22" barrel. Imported from England by Air Rifle Specialists.
Price: **$1,300.00**
Price: Left-hand **$1,360.00**

Air Arms NJR 100 Air rifle
Similar to the TM 100 except designed for Field Target competition. Hand-picked Walther barrel for best accuracy. Walnut Field Target thumbhole stock has adjustable forend, cheekpiece and buttpad. Has lever-type bolt, straight-blade trigger. Imported from England by Air Rifle Specialists.
Price: **$1,800.00**
Price: Left-hand **$1,860.00**

Anschutz 2001

ANSCHUTZ 2001 MATCH AIR RIFLE
Caliber: 177, single shot.
Barrel: 26".
Weight: 10½ lbs. **Length:** 44½" overall.
Stock: European hardwood; stippled grip and forend.
Sights: Globe front, #6824 Micro Peep rear.
Features: Balance, weight match the 1907 ISU smallbore rifle. Uses #5019 match trigger. Recoil and vibration free. Fully adjustable cheekpiece and buttplate. Introduced 1988. Imported from Germany by Precision Sales International.
Price: Right-hand **$1,799.00**
Price: Left-hand **$1,889.00**
Price: Model 2001D RT (Running Target) **$1,889.00**

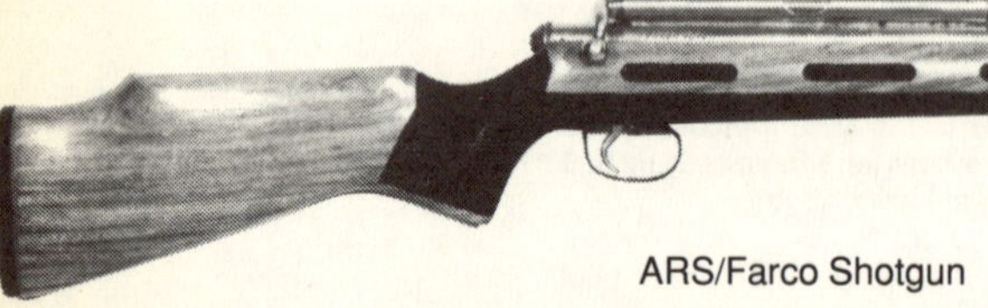
ARS/Farco Shotgun

ARS/FARCO CO_2 AIR SHOTGUN
Caliber: 51 (28-gauge).
Barrel: 30".
Weight: 7 lbs. **Length:** 48½" overall.
Power: 10-oz. refillable CO_2 tank.
Stock: Hardwood.
Sights: Bead front, fixed dovetail rear.
Features: Gives over 100 ft. lbs. energy for taking small game. Imported by Air Rifle Specialists.
Price: **$395.00**

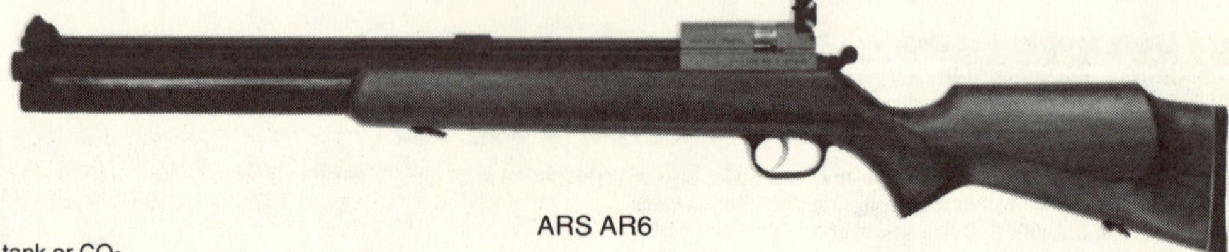
ARS AR6

ARS AR6 REPEATING AIR RIFLE
Caliber: 22, 6-shot repeater.
Barrel: 23¼".
Weight: 6¾ lbs. **Length:** 38¼" overall.
Power: Pre-compressed air from diving tank or CO_2.
Stock: Walnut with checkered grip; rubber buttpad.
Sights: Blade front, adjustable peep rear.
Features: Velocity to 1100 fps with 25-grain pellet. Receiver grooved for scope mounting. Imported from Korea by Air Rifle Specialists.
Price: **$550.00**

Beeman/Feinwerkbau 300-S

BEEMAN/FEINWERKBAU 300-S SERIES MATCH RIFLE
Caliber: 177, single shot.
Barrel: 19.9", fixed solid with receiver.
Weight: Approx. 10 lbs. with optional bbl. sleeve. **Length:** 42.8" overall.
Power: Single stroke sidelever, spring piston.
Stock: Match model—walnut, deep forend, adjustable buttplate.
Sights: Globe front with interchangeable inserts. Click micro. adjustable match aperture rear. Front and rear sights move as a single unit.
Features: Recoilless, vibration free. Five-way adjustable match trigger. Grooved for scope mounts. Permanent lubrication, steel piston ring. Cocking effort 9 lbs. Optional 10-oz. barrel sleeve. Available from Beeman.
Price: Right-hand **$869.00**
Price: Left-hand **$950.00**
Price: Tyrolean, right-hand **$1,295.00**
Price: Tyrolean, left-hand **$1,310.00**

BEEMAN/FEINWERKBAU 300-S MINI-MATCH

Caliber: 177, single shot.
Barrel: 17⅛".
Weight: 8.8 lbs. **Length:** 40" overall.
Power: Spring piston, single stroke sidelever cocking.
Stock: Walnut. Stippled grip, adjustable buttplate. Scaled-down for youthful or slightly built shooters.
Sights: Globe front with interchangeable inserts, micro. adjustable rear. Front and rear sights move as a single unit.
Features: Recoilless, vibration free. Grooved for scope mounts. Steel piston ring. Cocking effort about 9½ lbs. Barrel sleeve optional. Left-hand model available. Introduced 1978. Imported by Beeman.
Price: Right-hand **$1,095.00**
Price: Left-hand **$1,198.00**

BEEMAN/FEINWERKBAU MODEL 601 AIR RIFLE

Caliber: 177, single shot.
Barrel: 16.6".
Weight: 10.8 lbs. **Length:** 43" overall.
Power: Single stroke pneumatic.
Stock: Special laminated hardwoods and hard rubber for stability.
Sights: Tunnel front with interchangeable inserts, click micrometer match apperture rear.
Features: Recoilless action; double supported barrel; special, short rifled area frees pellet from barrel faster so shooter's motion has minimum effect on accuracy. Fully adjustable match trigger. Trigger and sights blocked when loading latch is open. Imported by Beeman. Introduced 1984.
Price: Right-hand **$1,495.00**
Price: Left-hand **$1,635.00**
Price: Right-hand, walnut stock **$1,495.00**

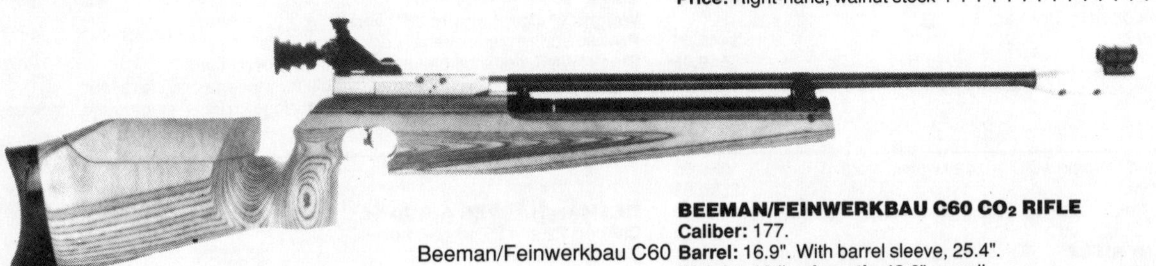

Beeman/Feinwerkbau C60

Beeman/Feinwerkbau 601 Running Target

Similar to the standard Model 601. Has 16.9" barrel (33.7" with barrel sleeve); special match trigger, short loading gate which allows scope mounting. No sights—built for scope use only. Introduced 1987.
Price: Right-hand **$1,935.00**
Price: Left-hand **$1,595.00**
Price: Running target scope mounts **$159.95**

BEEMAN/FEINWERKBAU C60 CO_2 RIFLE

Caliber: 177.
Barrel: 16.9". With barrel sleeve, 25.4".
Weight: 10 lbs. **Length:** 42.6" overall.
Stock: Laminated hardwood and hard rubber.
Sights: Tunnel front with interchangeable inserts, quick release micro. click match aperture rear.
Features: Similar features, performance as Beeman/FWB 601. Virtually no cocking effort. Right- or left-hand. Running target version available. Introduced 1987. Imported from Germany by Beeman.
Price: Right-hand **$1,390.00**
Price: Left-hand **$1,530.00**

Beeman/HW30

BEEMAN/HW30 AIR RIFLE

Caliber: 177, 22, single shot.
Barrel: 17" (177), 16.9" (20); 12-groove rifling.
Weight: 5.5 lbs.
Power: Spring piston; single-stroke barrel cocking.
Stock: Walnut-finished hardwood.
Sights: Blade front, adjustable rear.
Features: Velocity about 660 fps (177). Double-jointed cocking lever. Cast trigger guard. Synthetic non-drying breech and piston seals. Introduced 1990. Imported by Beeman.
Price: 177 . . . . **$179.98**
Price: 20 . . . . **$185.98**

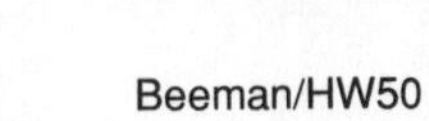

Beeman/HW50

BEEMAN/HW50 LIGHT/SPORTER TARGET RIFLE

Caliber: 177, single shot.
Barrel: 18.4"; 12-groove rifling.
Weight: 6.9 lbs. **Length:** 43.1" overall.
Power: Spring piston; single-stroke barrel cocking.
Stock: Walnut-finished hardwood.
Sights: Blade front, adjustable rear.
Features: Velocity about 705 fps. Synthetic non-drying breech and piston seals. Double-jointed cocking lever. Introduced 1990. Imported by Beeman.
Price: **$199.98**

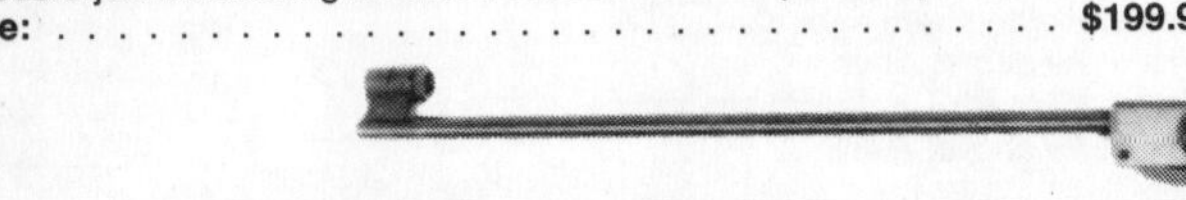

Beeman/HW55T

BEEMAN/HW55 TARGET RIFLES

Model	**55SM**	**55MM**	**55T**
Caliber:	177	177	177
Barrel:	18½"	18½"	18½"
Length:	43½"	43½"	43½"
Wgt. lbs.:	7.8	7.8	7.8
Rear sight:	All aperture		
Front sight:	All with globe and four interchangeable inserts.		
Power:	All spring (barrel cocking). 660-700 fps.		
Price:	**$479.50**	**$559.50**	**$619.50**

Features: Trigger fully adjustable and removable. Micrometer rear sight adjusts for windage and elevation in all. Pistol grip high comb stock with beavertail forend, walnut finish stock on 55SM. Walnut stock on 55MM, Tyrolean stock on 55T. Nylon piston seals in all. Imported by Beeman.

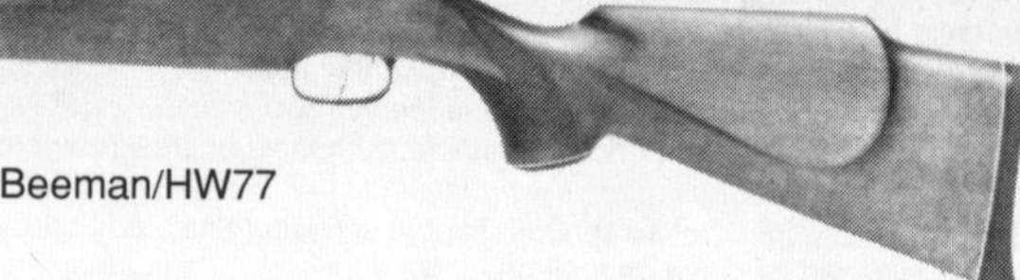
Beeman/HW77

BEEMAN/HW77 AIR RIFLE & CARBINE
Caliber: 177, 20 or 22, single shot.
Barrel: 14.5" or 18.5", 12-groove rifling.
Weight: 8.9 lbs. **Length:** 39.7" or 43.7" overall.
Power: Spring-piston; under-lever cocking.
Stocks: Walnut-stained beech; rubber buttplate, cut checkering on grip; cheekpiece.
Sights: Blade front, open adjustable rear.
Features: Velocity 830 fps. Fixed-barrel with fully opening, direct loading breech. Extended under-lever gives good cocking leverage. Adjustable trigger. Grooved for scope mounting. Carbine has 14.5" barrel, weighs 8.7 lbs., and is 39.7" overall. Imported by Beeman.
Price: Right-hand, 177 . . . . . . **$449.95**
Price: Left-hand, 177 . . . . . . **$519.95**
Price: Right-hand, 20 . . . . . . **$479.95**
Price: Left-hand, 20 . . . . . . **$529.95**
Price: Right-hand, 22 . . . . . . **$479.95**
Price: Left-hand, 22 . . . . . . **$519.95**
Price: 177 Deluxe and Carbine with Tyrolean walnut stock **$589.95**
Price: As above, 5mm **$599.95**

BEEMAN FX-1 AIR RIFLE
Caliber: 177, single shot.
Barrel: 18", rifled.
Weight: 6.6 lbs. **Length:** 43" overall.
Power: Spring-piston, barrel cocking.
Stock: Walnut-stained hardwood.
Sights: Tunnel front with interchangeable inserts; rear with rotating disc to give four sighting notches.
Features: Velocity 680 fps. Match-type adjustable trigger. Receiver grooved for scope mounting. Imported by Beeman.
Price: **$169.50**

BEEMAN CARBINE MODEL C1
Caliber: 177 or 22, single shot.
Barrel: 14", 12-groove rifling.
Weight: 6¼ lbs. **Length:** 38" overall.
Power: Spring-piston, barrel cocking.
Stock: Walnut-stained beechwood with rubber buttpad.
Sights: Blade front, rear click-adjustable for windage and elevation.
Features: Velocity 830 fps. Adjustable trigger. Receiver grooved for scope mounting. Imported by Beeman.
Price: **$249.95**

BEEMAN/HARPER AIRCANE
Caliber: 22 and 25, single shot.
Barrel: 31½", rifled.
Weight: 1 lb. **Length:** 34" overall.
Features: Walking cane also acts as an airgun. Solid walnut handle with polished brass ferrule. Available in various hand-carved models. Intricate deep engraving on the ferrule. Uses rechargeable air "cartridges" loaded with pellets. Kit includes separate pump, extra cartridges and fitted case. Introduced 1987. Imported by Beeman.
Price: Basic set **$595.95**
Price: Goose, Labrador, Spaniel sets **$655.00**

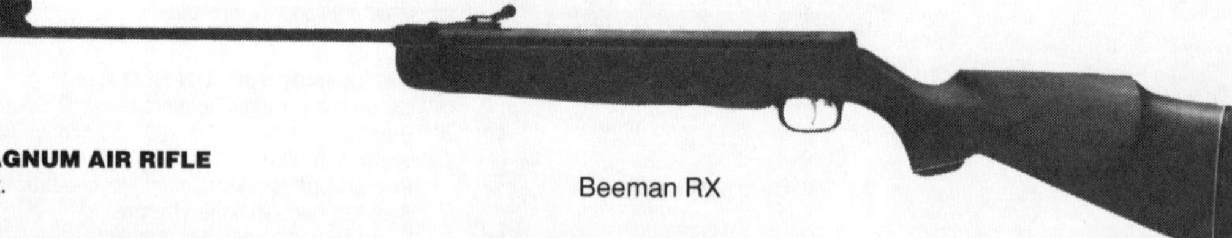
Beeman RX

BEEMAN RX GAS-SPRING MAGNUM AIR RIFLE
Caliber: 177, 20, 22, 25, single shot.
Barrel: 19.6"; 12-groove rifling.
Weight: 8.8 lbs.
Power: Gas-spring piston air; single stroke barrel cocking.
Stock: Walnut-finished hardwood, hand checkered, with cheekpiece. Adjustable cheekpiece and buttplate.
Sights: Tunnel front, click-adjustable rear.
Features: Velocity adjustable to about 1200 fps. Uses special sealed chamber of air as a mainspring. Gas-spring cannot take a set. Introduced 1990. Imported by Beeman.
Price: 177 or 22 . . . . . . **$469.95**
Price: 20 or 25 . . . . . . **$479.95**

BEEMAN R1 CARBINE
Caliber: 177, 20, 22, 25, single shot.
Barrel: 16.1".
Weight: 8.6 lbs. **Length:** 41.7" overall.
Power: Spring-piston, barrel cocking.
Stock: Stained beech; Monte Carlo comb and checkpiece; cut checkered p.g.; rubber buttpad.
Sights: Tunnel front with interchangeable inserts, open adjustable rear; receiver grooved for scope mounting.
Features: Velocity up to 1050 fps (177). Non-drying nylon piston and breech seals. Adjustable metal trigger. Machined steel receiver end cap and safety. Right- or left-hand stock. Imported by Beeman.
Price: 177 or 22, right-hand **$439.98**
Price: As above, left-hand **$489.98**
Price: 20- or 25-cal., right-hand **$449.98**
Price: As above, left-hand **$499.98**

Beeman R7 Air Rifle
Similar to the R8 model except has lighter ambidextrous stock, match-grade trigger block; velocity of 680-700 fps; barrel length 17"; weight 5.8 lbs. Milled steel safety. Imported by Beeman.
Price: 177 . . . . . . **$269.98**
Price: 20 . . . . . . **$279.98**

BEEMAN R1 AIR RIFLE
Caliber: 177, 20 or 22, single shot.
Barrel: 19.6", 12-groove rifling.
Weight: 8.5 lbs. **Length:** 45.2" overall.
Power: Spring-piston, barrel cocking.
Stock: Walnut-stained beech; cut-checkered pistol grip; Monte Carlo comb and cheekpiece; rubber buttpad.
Sights: Tunnel front with interchangeable inserts, open rear click-adjustable for windage and elevation. Grooved for scope mounting.
Features: Velocity of 940-1050 fps (177), 860 fps (20), 800 fps (22). Non-drying nylon piston and breech seals. Adjustable metal trigger. Milled steel safety. Right- or left-hand stock. Available with adjustable cheekpiece and buttplate at extra cost. Custom and Super Laser versions available. Imported by Beeman.
Price: Right-hand, 177 or 22 . . . . . . **$439.98**
Price: Left-hand, 177 or 22 . . . . . . **$489.98**
Price: Right-hand, 20 . . . . . . **$449.98**
Price: Left-hand, 20 . . . . . . **$499.98**
Price: Field Target, right-hand, 177 . . . . . . **$599.95**
Price: As above, 5mm **$619.95**
Price: 177 with Tyrolean walnut stock **$589.95**
Price: As above, 5mm **$599.95**

BEEMAN R1 LASER AIR RIFLE
Caliber: 177, 20, 22, 25, single shot.
Barrel: 16.1" or 19.6".
Weight: 8.4 lbs. **Length:** 41.7" overall (16.1" barrel).
Power: Spring-piston, barrel cocking.
Stock: Laminated wood with Monte Carlo comb and cheekpiece; checkered p.g. and forend; rubber buttpad.
Sights: Tunnel front with interchangeable inserts, open adjustable rear.
Features: Velocity up to 1150 fps (177). Special powerplant components. Built from the Beeman R1 rifle by Beeman.
Price: 177 or 22-cal. **$889.50**
Price: 20-cal. **$899.50**
Price: 25-cal. **$899.50**

Beeman R8

BEEMAN R8 AIR RIFLE
Caliber: 177, single shot.
Barrel: 18.3".
Weight: 7.2 lbs. **Length:** 43.1" overall.
Power: Barrel cocking, spring-piston.
Stock: Walnut with Monte Carlo cheekpiece; checkered pistol grip.
Sights: Globe front, fully adjustable rear; interchangeable inserts.
Features: Velocity of 735 fps. Similar to the R1. Nylon piston and breech seals. Adjustable match-grade, two-stage, grooved metal trigger. Milled steel safety. Rubber buttpad. Imported by Beeman.
Price: **$349.98**

BEEMAN/WEBLEY ECLIPSE AIR RIFLE
Caliber: 177, 22, 25, single shot.
Barrel: 17.5".
Weight: 8.25 lbs. **Length:** 44.5" overall.
Power: Under-lever cocking.
Stock: Lacquer-finished beechwood with high relief cheekpiece, checkered grip with palm swell.
Sights: Blade front, adjustable rear.
Features: Two-stage trigger, ambidextrous safety catch. Receiver grooved for scope mounting, with arrestor grooves. Fitted with Webley's patent mainspring damper to eliminate vibration. Introduced 1990. Imported from England by Beeman.
Price: **$459.95**

BEEMAN R10 AIR RIFLES
Caliber: 177, 20, 22, single shot.
Barrel: 16.1" and 19.7"; 12-groove rifling.
Weight: 7.9 lbs. **Length:** 46" overall.
Power: Spring-piston, barrel cocking.
Stock: Standard—walnut-finished hardwood with Monte Carlo comb, rubber buttplate; Deluxe has white spacers at grip cap, buttplate, checkered grip, cheekpiece, rubber buttplate.
Sights: Tunnel front with interchangeable inserts, open rear click adjustable for windage and elevation. Receiver grooved for scope mounting.
Features: Over 1000 fps in 177-cal. only; 26-lb. cocking effort; milled steel safety and body tube. Right- and left-hand models. Introduced 1986. Imported by Beeman.
Price: 177 or 22 Standard **$349.98**
Price: 5mm Standard **$359.98**
Price: 177 Deluxe, right-hand **$399.98**
Price: 177 Deluxe, left-hand **$449.98**
Price: 5mm Deluxe, right-hand **$409.98**
Price: 5mm Deluxe, left-hand **$459.98**
Price: 22 Deluxe, right-hand **$399.98**
Price: 22 Deluxe, left-hand **$449.95**

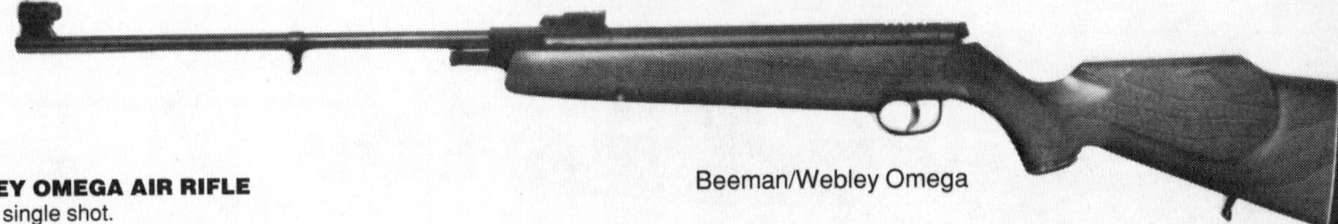

Beeman/Webley Omega

BEEMAN/WEBLEY OMEGA AIR RIFLE
Caliber: 177 or 22, single shot.
Barrel: 19¼", rifled.
Weight: 7.8 lbs. **Length:** 43½" overall.
Power: Spring-piston air; barrel cocking.
Stock: Walnut-stained beech with cut-checkered grip; cheekpiece; rubber buttpad.
Features: Special quick-snap barrel latch; self-lubricating piston seal; receiver grooved for scope mounting. Introduced 1985. Imported from England by Beeman.
Price: **$429.95**

Consult our Directory pages for the location of firms mentioned.

BEEMAN/WEBLEY VULCAN III DELUXE
Caliber: 177 or 22, single shot.
Barrel: 17", rifled.
Weight: 7.6 lbs. **Length:** 43.7" overall.
Power: Spring-piston air, barrel cocking.
Stock: Walnut. Cut checkering, rubber buttpad, cheekpiece. Standard version has walnut-stained beech.
Sights: Hooded front, micrometer rear.
Features: Velocity of 830 fps (177), 675 fps (22). Single-stage adjustable trigger; receiver grooved for scope mounting. Self-lubricating piston seal. Introduced 1983. Imported by Beeman.
Price: Standard **$249.95**
Price: Deluxe **$329.95**

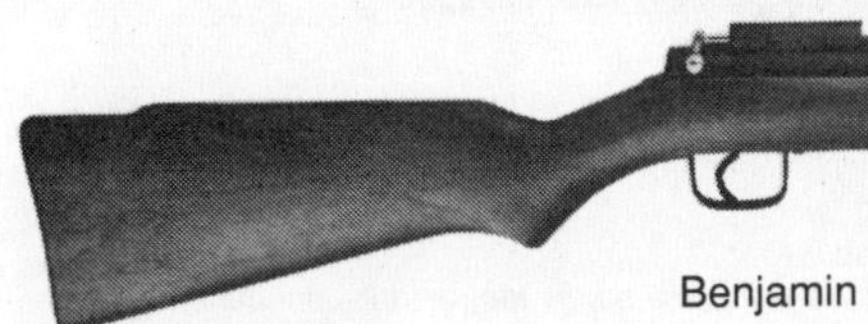

Benjamin CO_2

BENJAMIN CO_2 AIR RIFLES
Caliber: 177 or 22, single shot.
Barrel: 19⅜", rifled brass.
Weight: 5 lbs. **Length:** 36½" overall.
Power: 12-gram CO_2 cylinder.
Stock: Walnut with Monte Carlo comb.
Sights: High ramp front, fully adjustable notch rear or Williams peep.
Features: Velocity to 600 fps (177). Bolt action with ambidextrous push-pull safety. Gives about 40 shots per cylinder. Black or nickel finish. Introduced 1991. Made in the U.S. by Benjamin Air Rifle Co.
Price: Black finish, open sight, Model G397 (177), Model G392 (22) . **$99.95**
Price: As above with Williams peep, Model G397W (177), Model G392W (22) **$126.95**
Price: Nickel finish, open sight, Model GS397 (177), Model GS392 (22) **$106.95**
Price: As above with Williams peep, Model GS397W (177), GS392W (22) **$133.95**

Benjamin Pneumatic

BENJAMIN PNEUMATIC (PUMP-UP) AIR RIFLES
Caliber: 177 or 22, single shot.
Barrel: 19⅜", rifled brass.
Weight: 5½ lbs. **Length:** 36¼" overall.
Power: Under-lever pneumatic, hand pumped.
Stock: Walnut Monte Carlo stock and forend.
Sights: High ramp front, choice of fully adjustable notch rear or Williams peep.
Features: Variable velocity to 750 fps. Bolt action with ambidextrous push-pull safety. Black or nickel finish. Introduced 1991. Made in the U.S. by Benjamin Air Rifle Co.
Price: Black finish, open sight, Model 397 (177), Model 392 (22) . . **$110.95**
Price: As above with Williams peep sight, Model 397W (177), Model 392W (22) **$137.95**
Price: Nickel finish, open sight, Model S397 (177), Model S392 (22) **$117.95**
Price: As above with Williams peep sight, Model S397W (177), Model S392W (22) **$144.95**

BSA Supersport

BSA SUPERSPORT AIR RIFLE
Caliber: 177, 22 or 25, single shot.
Barrel: 18½".
Weight: 7 lbs. **Length:** 41¾" overall.
Power: Spring piston or optional sealed gas Ram.
Stock: Walnut-stained European beech.
Sights: Globe front, adjustable open rear.
Features: Velocity up to 1010 fps (177); 830 fps (22); 700 fps (25). Adjustable two-stage trigger. Polished blue finish. Checkered pistol grip, rubber buttpad. Introduced 1991. Imported from England by Air Rifle Specialists.
Price: Spring piston model **$275.00**
Price: With sealed gas Ram **$374.00**

CROSMAN MODEL 66 POWERMASTER
Caliber: 177 (single shot) or BB.
Barrel: 20", rifled, solid steel.
Weight: 3 lbs. **Length:** 38½" overall.
Stock: Wood-grained plastic; checkered p.g. and forend.
Sights: Ramp front, fully adjustable open rear.
Features: Velocity about 675 fps. Bolt action, cross-bolt safety. Introduced 1983. From Crosman.
Price: About **$42.00**
Price: Model 664X (as above, with 4x scope) **$47.00**

BSA SUPERSTAR AIR RIFLE
Caliber: 177 or 22, single shot.
Barrel: 18½".
Weight: 7¾ lbs. **Length:** 42½" overall.
Power: Under-lever cocking spring piston or optional sealed gas Ram.
Stock: Walnut-stained European beech; checkered grip, rubber buttpad.
Sights: Globe front, open adjustable rear.
Features: Velocity up to 1000 fps (177); 800 fps (22). Adjustable two-stage trigger. Polished blue finish. Introduced 1991. Imported from England by Air Rifle Specialists.
Price: Spring piston model **$395.00**
Price: With sealed gas Ram **$494.00**

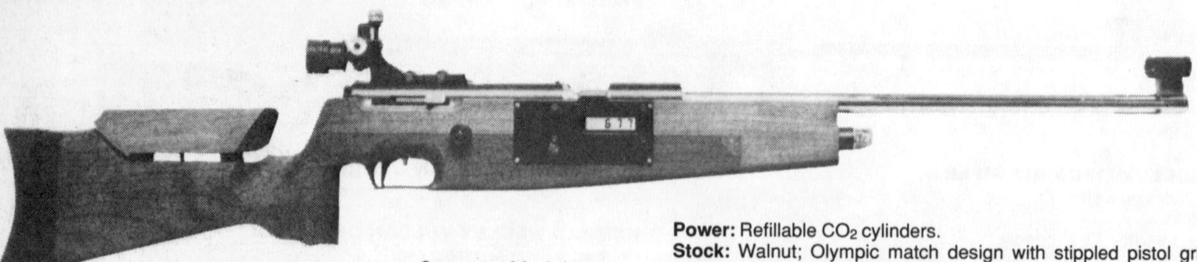
Crosman Model 84

CROSMAN MODEL 84 CO_2 MATCH RIFLE
Caliber: 177, single shot.
Barrel: 21". Barrel has a chrome shroud to give extra sight radius.
Power: Refillable CO_2 cylinders.
Stock: Walnut; Olympic match design with stippled pistol grip and forend, adjustable buttplate and comb.
Sights: Match sights—globe front, micrometer adjustable rear.
Features: A CO_2 pressure regulated rifle with adjustable velocity up to 720 fps. Each CO_2 cylinder has more than enough power to complete a 60-shot Olympic match course. Each gun can be custom fitted to the shooter. Made in U.S.A. Introduced 1984. From Crosman.
Price: About **$1,379.00**

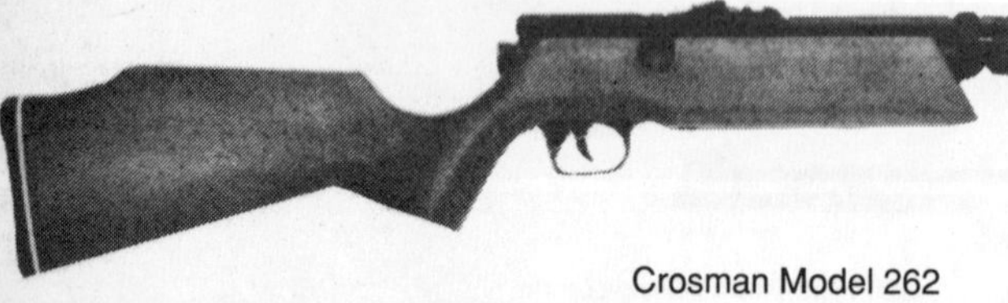
Crosman Model 262

CROSMAN MODEL 262 SPORTER AIR RIFLE
Caliber: 177 pellet, single shot.
Barrel: 21.75", rifled steel.
Weight: 4 lbs. 14 oz.
Power: CO_2 Powerlet.
Stock: Hardwood.
Sights: Fixed front, adjustable rear.
Features: Easy-loading pellet port, two-stage trigger. Introduced 1990. From Crosman.
Price: About **$69.00**

Crosman Model 760

CROSMAN MODEL 781 SINGLE PUMP
Caliber: 177, 5-shot pellet clip; 195-shot BB magazine.
Barrel: 19½".
Weight: 2 lbs., 14 oz. **Length:** 34¾" overall.
Power: Pneumatic, single pump.
Stock: Wood-grained plastic; checkered p.g. and forend.
Sights: Blade front, open adjustable rear.
Features: Velocity of 350-400 fps (pellets). Uses only one pump. Hidden BB reservoir holds 195 shots; pellets loaded via 4-shot clip. Introduced 1984. From Crosman.
Price: About **$29.00**

CROSMAN MODEL 760 PUMPMASTER
Caliber: 177 pellets or BB, 200-shot.
Barrel: 19½", rifled steel.
Weight: 3 lbs., 1 oz. **Length:** 36" overall.
Power: Pneumatic, hand pumped.
Features: Short stroke, power determined by number of strokes. Walnut-finished plastic checkered stock and forend. Post front sight and adjustable rear sight. Cross-bolt safety. Introduced 1983. From Crosman.
Price: About **$30.00**

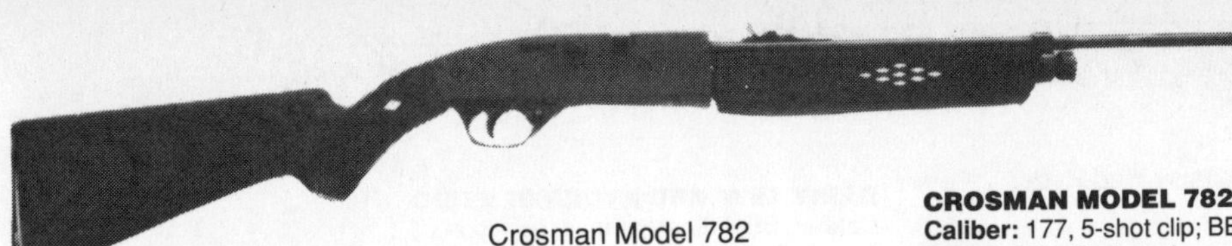
Crosman Model 782

CROSMAN MODEL 788 BB SCOUT RIFLE

Caliber: BB only, 20-shot magazine.
Barrel: 14", steel.
Weight: 2 lbs. 7 oz. **Length:** 31½" overall.
Stock: Wood-grained ABS plastic, checkered p.g. and forend.
Sights: Blade on ramp front, open adjustable rear.
Features: Variable pump power—three pumps give MV of 330 fps, six pumps 437 fps, 10 pumps 450 fps (BBs, average). Steel barrel, cross-bolt safety. Introduced 1978. From Crosman.
Price: About $29.00

CROSMAN MODEL 782 BLACK DIAMOND AIR RIFLE

Caliber: 177, 5-shot clip; BB, 195-shot magazine.
Barrel: 18", rifled steel.
Weight: 2 lbs., 14 oz.
Power: CO_2 Powerlet.
Stock: Wood-grained plastic; checkered grip and forend.
Sights: Blade front, open adjustable rear.
Features: Velocity up to 545 fps (pellets), 590 fps (BB). Black finish with white diamonds. Introduced 1990. From Crosman.
Price: About $39.95

Crosman Model 790

CROSMAN MODEL 790 OUTBACKER AIR RIFLE

Caliber: 177, 5-shot clip; BB, 195-shot magazine.
Barrel: 16$\frac{3}{16}$", steel, smooth.
Weight: 2 lbs., 14 oz.
Power: Pneumatic, single pump.
Stock: Textured plastic with Alligator grain checkering on grip and forend.
Sights: Pinpoint sight tube looks like real scope, but no magnification.
Features: Velocity up to 400 fps (177), 450 fps (BB). Includes canteen that fits in stock, compass in pistol grip and adventure guide shooting game. Introduced 1990. From Crosman.
Price: About $40.00

Crosman Backpacker

CROSMAN MODEL 1389 BACKPACKER RIFLE

Caliber: 177, single shot.
Barrel: 14", rifled steel.
Weight: 3 lbs. 3 oz. **Length:** 31" overall.
Power: Hand pumped, pneumatic.
Stock: Composition, skeletal type.
Sights: Blade front, rear adjustable for windage and elevation.
Features: Velocity to 560 fps. Detachable stock. Receiver grooved for scope mounting. Metal parts blued. From Crosman.
Price: About $54.00

CROSMAN MODEL 2100 CLASSIC AIR RIFLE

Caliber: 177 pellets or BBs, 200-shot BB magazine.
Barrel: 21", rifled.
Weight: 4 lbs., 13 oz. **Length:** 39¾" overall.
Power: Pump-up, pneumatic.
Stock: Wood-grained checkered ABS plastic.
Features: Three pumps give about 450 fps, 10 pumps about 795 fps. Cross-bolt safety; concealed reservoir holds over 180 BBs. From Crosman.
Price: About $54.00

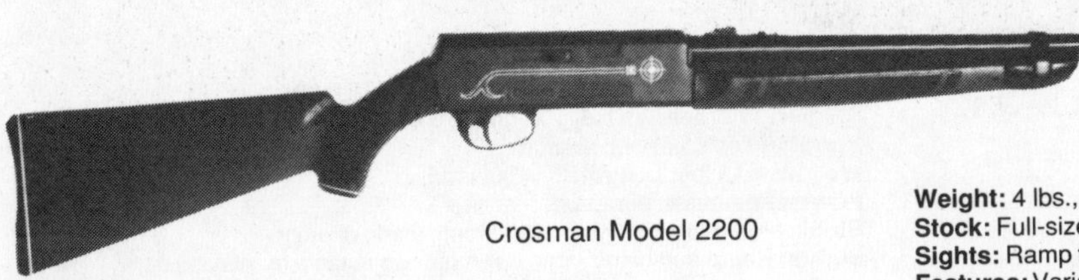
Crosman Model 2200

CROSMAN MODEL 2200 MAGNUM AIR RIFLE

Caliber: 22, single shot.
Barrel: 19", rifled steel.
Weight: 4 lbs., 12 oz. **Length:** 39" overall.
Stock: Full-size, wood-grained plastic with checkered p.g. and forend.
Sights: Ramp front, open step-adjustable rear.
Features: Variable pump power—three pumps give 395 fps, six pumps 530 fps, 10 pumps 620 fps (average). Full-size adult air rifle. Has white line spacers at pistol grip and buttplate. Introduced 1978. From Crosman.
Price: About $54.00

Daisy Model 840

DAISY MODEL 840

Caliber: 177 pellet single shot; or BB 350-shot.
Barrel: 19", smoothbore, steel.
Weight: 2.7 lbs. **Length:** 36.8" overall.
Stock: Moulded wood-grain stock and forend.
Sights: Ramp front, open, adjustable rear.
Features: Single pump pneumatic rifle. Muzzle velocity 335 fps (BB), 300 fps (pellet). Steel buttplate; straight pull bolt action; cross-bolt safety. Forend forms pump lever. Introduced 1978. From Daisy Mfg. Co.
Price: About $38.00

Daisy Red Ryder

DAISY/POWER LINE 130 AIR RIFLE
Caliber: 177, single shot.
Barrel: 18", rifled steel.
Weight: 5.9 lbs. **Length:** 41" overall.
Power: Spring-air, barrel cocking.
Stock: European-style hardwood.
Sights: Hooded front with blade on ramp, micrometer adjustable open rear.
Features: Velocity up to 800 fps. Introduced 1990. Imported from Spain by Daisy Mfg. Co.
Price: About **$155.00**

DAISY 1938 RED RYDER CLASSIC
Caliber: BB, 650-shot repeating action.
Barrel: Smoothbore steel with shroud.
Weight: 2.2 lbs. **Length:** 35.4" overall.
Stock: Walnut stock burned with Red Ryder lariat signature.
Sights: Post front, adjustable V-slot rear.
Features: Walnut forend. Saddle ring with leather thong. Lever cocking. Gravity feed. Controlled velocity. One of Daisy's most popular guns. From Daisy Mfg. Co.
Price: About **$41.00**

Daisy/Power Line 753

DAISY/POWER LINE 853
Caliber: 177 pellets.
Barrel: 20.9"; 12-groove rifling, high-grade solid steel by Lothar Walther™, precision crowned; bore size for precision match pellets.
Weight: 5.08 lbs. **Length:** 38.9" overall.
Power: Single-pump pneumatic.
Stock: Full-length, select American hardwood, stained and finished; black buttplate with white spacers.
Sights: Globe front with four aperture inserts; precision micrometer adjustable rear peep sight mounted on a standard ⅜" dovetail receiver mount.
Features: Single shot. From Daisy Mfg. Co.
Price: About **$200.00**

DAISY/POWER LINE 753 TARGET RIFLE
Caliber: 177, single shot.
Barrel: 20.9", Lothar Walther.
Weight: 6.4 lbs. **Length:** 39.75" overall.
Power: Recoilless pneumatic, single pump.
Stock: Walnut with adjustable cheekpiece and buttplate.
Sights: Globe front with interchangeable inserts, diopter rear with micro. click adjustments.
Features: Includes front sight reticle assortment, web shooting sling. From Daisy Mfg. Co.
Price: About **$325.00**

DAISY/POWER LINE 856 PUMP-UP AIRGUN
Caliber: 177 (pellets), BB, 100-shot BB magazine.
Barrel: Rifled steel with shroud.
Weight: 2¾ lbs. **Length:** 37.4" overall.
Power: Pneumatic pump-up.
Stock: Moulded wood-grain plastic.
Sights: Ramp and blade front, open rear adjustable for elevation.
Features: Velocity from 315 fps (two pumps) to 650 fps (10 pumps). Finger grooved forend. Cross-bolt trigger-block safety. Introduced 1985. From Daisy Mfg. Co.
Price: About **$39.00**

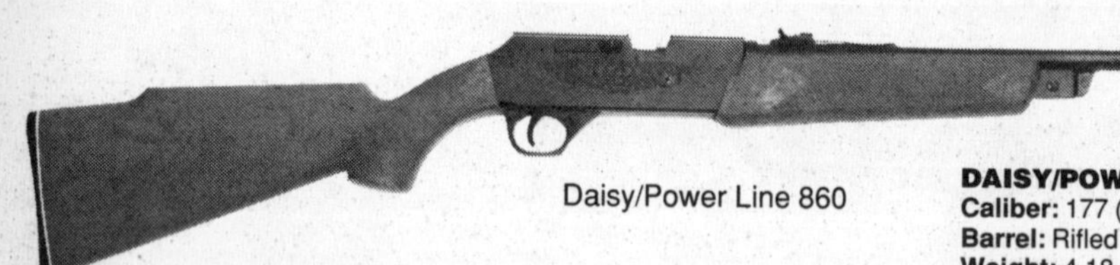

Daisy/Power Line 860

DAISY/POWER LINE 880 PUMP-UP AIRGUN
Caliber: 177 pellets, BB.
Barrel: Rifled steel with shroud.
Weight: 4.5 lbs. **Length:** 37¾" overall.
Power: Pneumatic pump-up.
Stock: Wood-grain moulded plastic with Monte Carlo cheekpiece.
Sights: Ramp front, open rear adjustable for elevation.
Features: Crafted by Daisy. Variable power (velocity and range) increase with pump strokes. 10 strokes for maximum power. 100-shot BB magazine. Cross-bolt trigger safety. Positive cocking valve. From Daisy Mfg. Co.
Price: About **$54.00**

DAISY/POWER LINE 860 PUMP-UP AIRGUN
Caliber: 177 (pellets), BB, 100-shot BB magazine.
Barrel: Rifled steel with shroud.
Weight: 4.18 lbs. **Length:** 37.4" overall.
Power: Pneumatic pump-up.
Stock: Moulded wood-grain with Monte Carlo cheekpiece.
Sights: Ramp and blade front, open rear adjustable for elevation.
Features: Velocity from 315 fps (two pumps) to 650 fps (10 pumps). Shoots BBs or pellets. Heavy die-cast metal receiver. Cross-bolt trigger-block safety. Introduced 1984. From Daisy Mfg. Co.
Price: About **$52.00**

DAISY/POWER LINE 922
Caliber: 22, 5-shot clip.
Barrel: Rifled steel with shroud.
Weight: 4.5 lbs. **Length:** 37¾" overall.
Stock: Moulded wood-grained plastic with checkered p.g. and forend, Monte Carlo cheekpiece.
Sights: Ramp front, fully adjustable open rear.
Features: Muzzle velocity from 270 fps (two pumps) to 530 fps (10 pumps). Straight-pull bolt action. Separate buttplate and grip cap with white spacers. Introduced 1978. From Daisy Mfg. Co.
Price: About **$65.00**
Price: Models 970/920 (same as Model 922 except with hardwood stock and forend), about **$100.00**

Daisy Model 95

"GAT" AIR RIFLE

Caliber: 177, single shot.
Barrel: 17¼" cocked, 23¼" extended.
Weight: 3 lbs.
Power: Spring piston.
Stock: Composition.
Sights: Fixed.
Features: Velocity about 450 fps. Shoots pellets, darts, corks. Imported from England by Stone Enterprises, Inc.
Price: $34.95

DAISY/YOUTH LINE RIFLES

Model:	**95**	**111**	**105**
Caliber:	BB	BB	BB
Barrel:	18"	18"	13½"
Length:	35.2"	34.3"	29.8"
Power:	Spring	Spring	Spring
Capacity:	700	650	400
Price: About	**$37.00**	**$30.00**	**$25.00**

Features: Model 95 stock and forend are wood; 105 and 111 have plastic stocks. From Daisy Mfg. Co.

FAMAS SEMI-AUTO AIR RIFLE

Caliber: 177, 10-shot magazine.
Barrel: 19.2".
Weight: About 8 lbs. **Length:** 29.8" overall.
Power: 12 gram CO_2.
Stock: Synthetic bullpup design.
Sights: Adjustable front, aperture rear.
Features: Velocity of 425 fps. Duplicates size, weight and feel of the centerfire MAS French military rifle in caliber 223. Introduced 1988. Imported from France by Century International Arms.
Price: $432.95

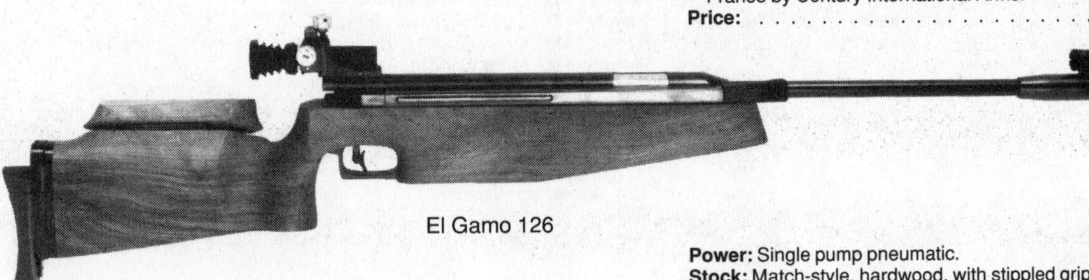

El Gamo 126

EL GAMO 126 SUPER MATCH TARGET RIFLE

Caliber: 177, single shot.
Barrel: Match grade, precision rifled.
Weight: 10.6 lbs. **Length:** 43.8" overall.
Power: Single pump pneumatic.
Stock: Match-style, hardwood, with stippled grip and forend.
Sights: Hooded front with interchangeable elements, fully adjustable match rear.
Features: Velocity of 590 fps. Adjustable trigger; easy loading pellet port; adjustable buttpad. Introduced 1984. Imported from Spain by Daisy Mfg. Co.
Price: About $650.00

Marksman/Anschutz 380

MARKSMAN 28 INTERNATIONAL AIR RIFLE

Caliber: 177, single shot.
Barrel: 17".
Weight: 5¾ lbs.
Power: Spring-air, barrel cocking.
Stock: Hardwood.
Sights: Hooded front, adjustable rear.
Features: Velocity of 580-620 fps. Introduced 1989. Imported from Germany by Marksman Products.
Price: $186.00

MARKSMAN 40 INTERNATIONAL AIR RIFLE

Caliber: 177, single shot.
Barrel: 18⅜".
Weight: 7⅓ lbs.
Power: Spring-air, barrel cocking.
Stock: Hardwood.
Sights: Hooded front, adjustable rear.
Features: Velocity of 700-720 fps. Introduced 1989. Imported from Germany by Marksman Products.
Price: $242.00

MARKSMAN/ANSCHUTZ MODEL 380 MATCH AIR RIFLE

Caliber: 177, single shot.
Barrel: 20.75".
Weight: 10.75 lbs.
Power: Spring piston, sidelever cocking.
Stock: Match-style, walnut, with adjustable cheekpiece, adjustable buttplate.
Sights: Tunnel front with interchangeable inserts, match diopter rear.
Features: Velocity of 600-640 fps. Fully adjustable trigger. Recoilless and vibration free. Introduced 1990. Imported from Germany by Marksman Products.
Price: Right-hand $1,000.00
Price: Left-hand $1,050.00

Consult our Directory pages for the location of firms mentioned.

MARKSMAN 56-FTS FIELD TARGET RIFLE

Caliber: 177, single shot.
Barrel: 19⅝".
Weight: 8.8 lbs.
Power: Spring-air, barrel cocking.
Stock: Hardwood with stippled grip; ambidextrous, with adjustable cheekpiece, adjustable buttplate.
Sights: None furnished.
Features: Velocity of 910-940 fps. Introduced 1989. Imported from Germany by Marksman Products.
Price: $415.00

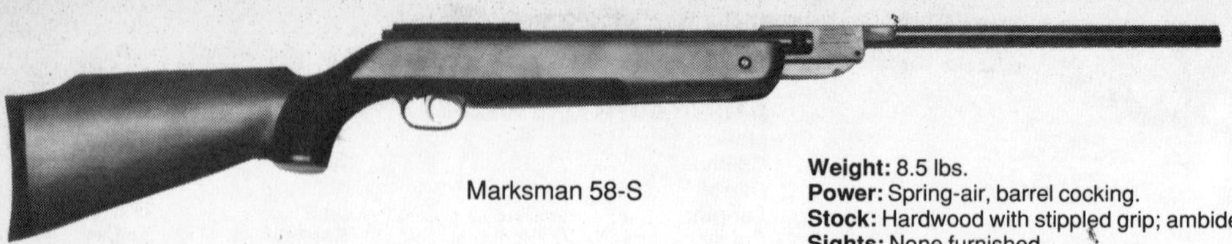

Marksman 58-S

MARKSMAN 58-S SILHOUETTE RIFLE
Caliber: 177, single shot.
Barrel: 16".
Weight: 8.5 lbs.
Power: Spring-air, barrel cocking.
Stock: Hardwood with stippled grip; ambidextrous.
Sights: None furnished.
Features: Velocity 910-940 fps. Adjustable Rekord trigger. Removable full-length barrel sleeve. Introduced 1989. Imported from Germany by Marksman Products.
Price: **$357.00**

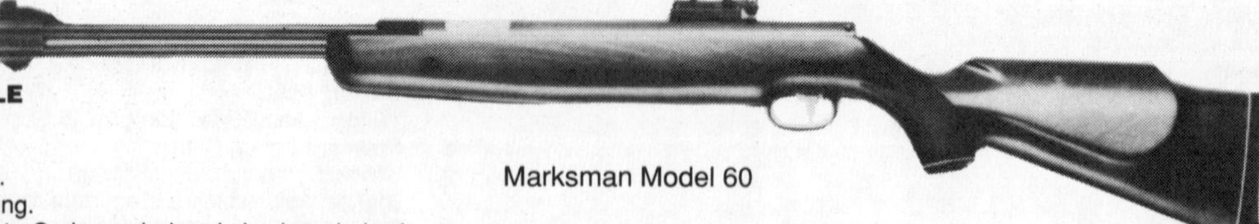

Marksman Model 60

MARKSMAN MODEL 60 AIR RIFLE
Caliber: 177, single shot.
Barrel: 18.5", rifled.
Weight: 8.9 lbs. **Length:** 44.75" overall.
Power: Spring piston, under-lever cocking.
Stock: Walnut-stained beech with Monte Carlo comb, hand-checkered pistol grip, rubber butt pad.
Sights: Blade front, open, micro. adjustable rear.
Features: Velocity of 810-840 fps. Automatic button safety on rear of receiver. Receiver grooved for scope mounting. Fully adjustable Rekord trigger. Introduced 1990. Imported from Germany by Marksman Products.
Price: **$399.00**
Price: Model 61 Carbine (14.5" barrel) **$399.00**

MARKSMAN 70T AIR RIFLE
Caliber: 177, 20 or 22, single shot.
Barrel: 19.75".
Weight: 8 lbs. **Length:** 45.5" overall.
Power: Spring air, barrel cocking.
Stock: Stained hardwood with Monte Carlo cheekpiece, rubber buttpad, cut checkered p.g.
Sights: Hooded front, open fully adjustable rear.
Features: Velocity of 910-940 fps (177), 810-840 fps (20), 740-780 fps (22); adjustable Rekord trigger. Introduced 1988. Imported from Germany by Marksman Products.
Price: 177 (Model 70T) **$299.00**
Price: 20 (Model 72) **$299.00**
Price: (Model 71) **$299.00**

MARKSMAN 1740 AIR RIFLE
Caliber: 177 or 18-shot BB repeater.
Barrel: 15½", smoothbore.
Weight: 5 lbs., 1 oz. **Length:** 36½" overall.
Power: Spring, barrel cocking.
Stock: Moulded high-impact ABS plastic.
Sights: Ramp front, open rear adjustable for elevation.
Features: Velocity about 450 fps. Automatic safety; fixed front, adjustable rear sight; positive feed BB magazine; shoots 177-cal. BBs, pellets and darts. From Marksman Products.
Price: **$45.95**
Price: Model 1780 (deluxe sights, rifled barrel, shoots only pellets) . . **$58.95**

Marksman 55T Air Rifle
Similar to the Model 70T except has uncheckered hardwood stock, no cheekpiece, plastic buttplate. Adjustable Rekord trigger. Overall length is 45.25", weight is 7½ lbs. Available in 177-caliber only.
Price: **$257.00**
Price: Model 59T (as above, carbine) **$257.00**

Marksman 1790

MARKSMAN 1750 BB BIATHLON REPEATER RIFLE
Caliber: BB, 18-shot magazine.
Barrel: 15", smoothbore.
Weight: 4.7 lbs.
Power: Spring piston, barrel cocking.
Stock: Moulded composition.
Sights: Tunnel front, open adjustable rear.
Features: Velocity of 450 fps. Automatic safety. Positive Feed System loads a BB each time gun is cocked. Introduced 1990. From Marksman Products.
Price: **$50.95**

RWS/Diana Model 26 Air Rifle
Similar to the Model 24 except weighs 6.25 lbs., gives velocity of 750 fps (177), 500 fps (22). Automatic safety, scope rail, synthetic seals.
Price: 177 or 22 . . . . **$175.00**

RWS/Diana Model 28 Air Rifle
Similar to the Model 26 except has Monte Carlo stock with cheekpiece, rubber recoil pad and two-stage trigger. Velocity of 750 fps (177), 500 fps (22).
Price: 177 or 22 . . . . **$190.00**

MARKSMAN 1790 BIATHLON TRAINER
Caliber: 177, single shot.
Barrel: 15", rifled.
Weight: 4.7 lbs.
Power: Spring-air, barrel cocking.
Stock: Synthetic.
Sights: Hooded front, match-style diopter rear.
Features: Velocity of 450 fps. Endorsed by the U.S. Biathlon Team. Introduced 1989. From Marksman Products.
Price: **$69.95**

RWS/DIANA MODEL 24 AIR RIFLE
Caliber: 177, 22, single shot.
Barrel: 17", rifled.
Weight: 6 lbs. **Length:** 42" overall.
Power: Spring air, barrel cocking.
Stock: Beech.
Sights: Hooded front, adjustable rear.
Features: Velocity of 700 fps (177). Easy cocking effort; blue finish. Imported from Germany by Dynamit Nobel-RWS, Inc.
Price: **$145.00**
Price: Model 24J (13.5" bbl., 177 only) **$110.00**
Price: Model 24C **$145.00**

RWS/Diana Model 34 Air Rifle
Similar to the Model 24 except has 19" barrel, weighs 7.5 lbs. Gives velocity of 1000 fps (177), 800 fps (22). Adjustable trigger, synthetic seals. Comes with scope rail.
Price: 177 or 22 . . . . **$205.00**

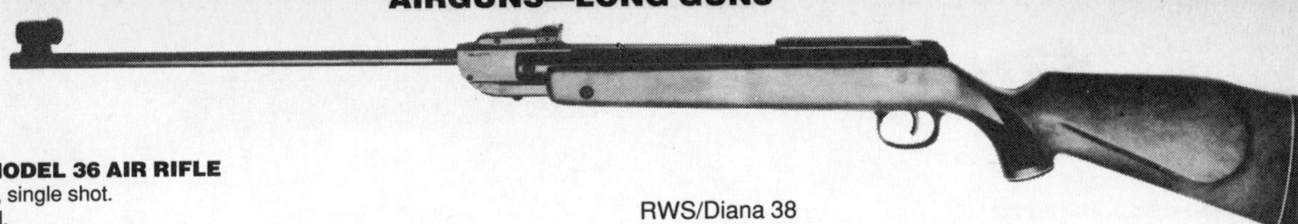
RWS/Diana 38

RWS/DIANA MODEL 36 AIR RIFLE
Caliber: 177, 22, single shot.
Barrel: 19", rifled.
Weight: 8 lbs. **Length:** 45" overall.
Power: Spring air, barrel cocking.
Stock: Beech.
Sights: Hooded front (interchangeable inserts avail.), adjustable rear.
Features: Velocity of 1000 fps (177-cal.). Comes with scope mount; two-stage adjustable trigger. Imported from Germnay by Dynamit Nobel-RWS, Inc.
Price: $295.00
Price: Model 38 (as above, walnut stock) $345.00
Price: Model 36S (as above except comes with sling, swivels, barrel weight, 4x20 scope) $345.00
Price: Model 36 Muzzlebrake (same as Model 36 except no sights, has muzzlebrake/barrel weight) $275.00
Price: Model 36 Carbine (same as Model 36 except has 15" barrel) $295.00

RWS/DIANA MODEL 45 AIR RIFLE
Caliber: 177, single shot.
Weight: 7¾ lbs. **Length:** 46" overall.
Power: Spring air, barrel cocking.
Stock: Walnut-finished hardwood with rubber recoil pad.
Sights: Globe front with interchangeable inserts, micro. click open rear with four-way blade.
Features: Velocity of 820 fps. Dovetail base for either micrometer peep sight or scope mounting. Automatic safety. Imported from Germany by Dynamit Nobel-RWS, Inc.
Price: $225.00

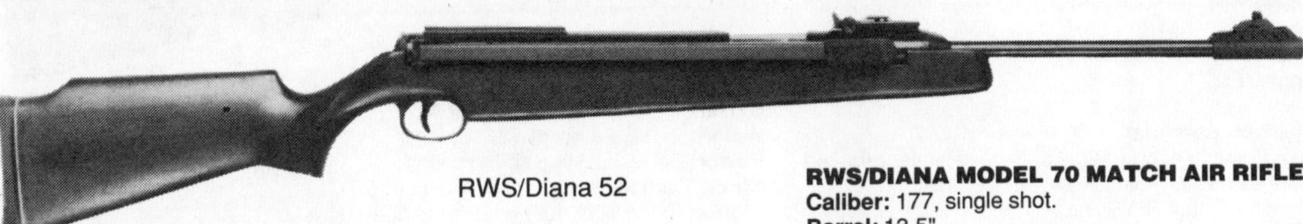
RWS/Diana 52

RWS/DIANA MODEL 52 AIR RIFLE
Caliber: 177, 22, single shot.
Barrel: 17", rifled.
Weight: 8½ lbs. **Length:** 43" overall.
Power: Spring air, sidelever cocking.
Stock: Beech, with Monte Carlo, cheekpiece, checkered grip and forend.
Sights: Ramp front, adjustable rear.
Features: Velocity of 1100 fps (177). Blue finish. Solid rubber buttpad. Imported from Germany by Dynamit Nobel-RWS, Inc.
Price: $385.00
Price: Model 48 (same as Model 52 except no Monte Carlo, cheekpiece or checkering) $345.00

RWS/DIANA MODEL 70 MATCH AIR RIFLE
Caliber: 177, single shot.
Barrel: 13.5".
Weight: 4.5 lbs. **Length:** 33" overall.
Power: Spring air, barrel cocking.
Stock: Beech, match-type.
Sights: Tunnel front with interchangeable inserts, fully adjustable peep rear.
Features: Velocity of 450 fps. Adjustable trigger. Designed and scaled for junior shooters. Introduced 1990. Imported from Germany by Dynamit Nobel-RWS, Inc.
Price: $190.00

RWS/Diana Model 72 Air Rifle
Similar to the Model 70 except has recoilless action. Introduced 1990.
Price: $340.00

RWS/Diana 75 T01

RWS/Diana Model 75S T01 Air Rifle
Similar to the Model 75 T01 except has beech stock specially shaped for standing and three-position shooting. Buttplate is vertically adjustable with curved and straight spacers for individual fit, adjustable cheekpiece. Introduced 1990.
Price: Right-hand $935.00
Price: Left-hand $975.00

RWS/DIANA MODEL 75 T01 MATCH AIR RIFLE
Caliber: 177, single shot.
Barrel: 19".
Weight: 11 lbs. **Length:** 43.7" overall.
Power: Spring air, sidelever cocking.
Stock: Oil-finished beech with stippled grip, adjustable buttplate, accessory rail. Conforms to ISU rules.
Sights: Globe front with five inserts, fully adjustable match peep rear.
Features: Velocity of 574 fps. Fully adjustable trigger. Model 75 HV has stippled forend, adjustable cheekpiece. Uses double opposing piston system for recoilless operation. Imported from Germany by Dynamit Nobel-RWS, Inc.
Price: Model 75 T01 . . . . $850.00

RWS/Diana 100

RWS/DIANA MODEL 100 MATCH AIR RIFLE
Caliber: 177, single shot.
Barrel: 19".
Weight: 11 lbs. **Length:** 43" overall.
Power: Spring air, sidelever cocking.
Stock: Walnut.
Sights: Tunnel front, fully adjustable match rear.
Features: Velocity of 580 fps. Single-stroke cocking; cheekpiece adjustable for height and length; recoilless operation. Cocking lever secured against rebound. Introduced 1990. Imported from Germany by Dynamit Nobel-RWS, Inc.
Price: Right-hand only $850.00

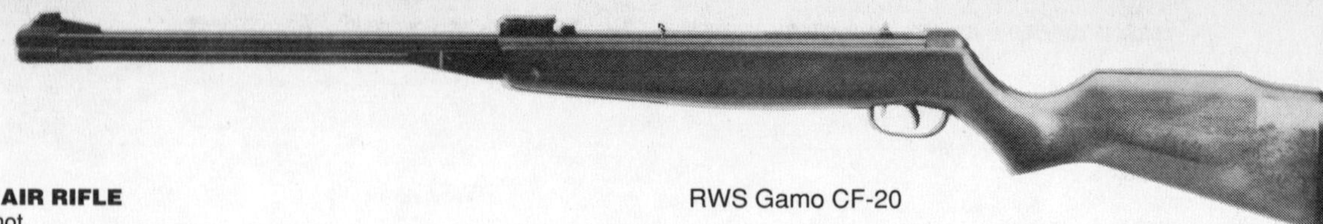
RWS Gamo CF-20

RWS GAMO CF-20 AIR RIFLE
Caliber: 177, single shot.
Barrel: 17.7".
Weight: 6.6 lbs. **Length:** 43.3" overall.
Power: Barrel cocking, spring piston.
Stock: Hardwood.
Sights: Blade on ramp front, fully adjustable open rear.
Features: Velocity to 800 fps. Cocking effort of 33 lbs. Grooved receiver, synthetic seals, dual safeties; sdjustable two-stage trigger. Imported from Spain by Dynamit Nobel-RWS, Inc.
Price: **$190.00**

RWS Gamo Delta

RWS GAMO EXPOMATIC 2000 AIR RIFLE
Caliber: 177, 25-shot magazine.
Barrel: 17.7".
Weight: 5.5 lbs. **Length:** 40.9" overall.
Power: Barrel cocking, spring piston.
Stock: Hardwood.
Sights: Blade front, fully adjustable open rear.
Features: Velocity to 600 fps. Cocking effort of 20 lbs. Dual safeties, grooved receiver, synthetic seals. Magazine tube holds 25 pellets, loads automatically. Imported from Spain by Dynamit Nobel-RWS, Inc.
Price: **$150.00**

RWS GAMO DELTA AIR RIFLE
Caliber: 177.
Barrel: 15.73".
Weight: 5.3 lbs. **Length:** 37" overall.
Power: Barrel cocking, spring piston.
Stock: Carbon fiber.
Sights: Blade front, fully adjustable open rear.
Features: Velocity to 565 fps. Has 20-lb. cocking effort. Synthetic seal; dual safeties; grooved for scope mounting. Imported from Spain by Dynamit Nobel-RWS, Inc.
Price: **$105.00**

RWS Gamo Gamatic

RWS GAMO GAMATIC 85 AIR RIFLE
Caliber: 177, 25-shot magazine.
Barrel: 17.7".
Weight: 6.18 lbs. **Length:** 37.8" overall.
Power: Barrel cocking, spring piston.
Stock: Carbon fiber.
Sights: Hooded blade front, fully adjustable open rear.
Features: Velocity to 565 fps. Cocking effort of 20 lbs. Grooved receiver; manual safety. Imported from Spain by Dynamit Nobel-RWS, Inc.
Price: **$160.00**

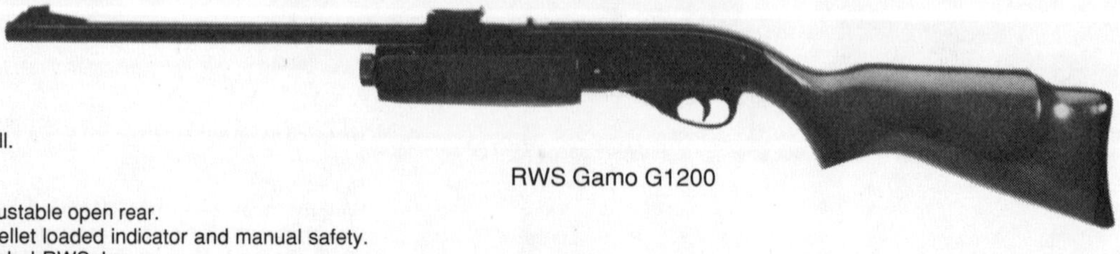

RWS Gamo G1200

RWS GAMO G1200 CO_2 RIFLE
Caliber: 177, 12-shot magazine.
Barrel: 17.7".
Weight: 6.4 lbs. **Length:** 38.1" overall.
Power: CO_2.
Stock: Hardwood.
Sights: Blade on ramp front, fully adjustable open rear.
Features: Velocity to 560 fps. Has pellet loaded indicator and manual safety. Imported from Spain by Dynamit Nobel-RWS, Inc.
Price: **$185.00**

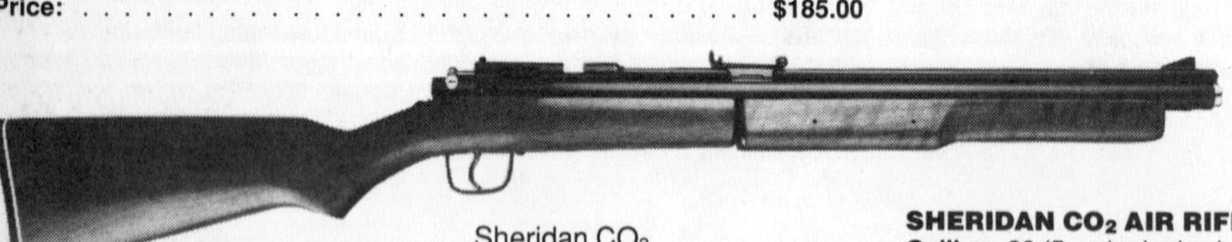
Sheridan CO_2

SHERIDAN PNEUMATIC (PUMP-UP) AIR RIFLES
Caliber: 20 (5mm), single shot.
Barrel: 19⅜", rifled brass.
Weight: 6 lbs. **Length:** 36½" overall.
Power: Under-lever pneumatic, hand pumped.
Stock: Walnut with buttplate and sculpted forend.
Sights: High ramp front, fully adjustable notch rear or Williams peep.
Features: Variable velocity to 700 fps. Bolt action with ambidextrous push-pull safety. Blue finish (Blue Streak) or nickel finish (Silver Streak). Introduced 1991. Made in the U.S. by Sheridan Div., Benjamin Air Rifle Co.
Price: Blue Streak, open sight, Model CB9 . . . . . . **$123.95**
Price: As above with Williams peep, Model CBW9 . . . . . . **$150.95**
Price: Silver streak, open sight, Model C9 . . . . . . **$129.95**
Price: As above with Williams peep, Model CW9 . . . . . . **$156.95**

SHERIDAN CO_2 AIR RIFLES
Caliber: 20 (5mm), single shot.
Barrel: 19⅜", rifled brass.
Weight: 5 lbs. **Length:** 36½" overall.
Power: 12-gram CO_2 cylinder.
Stock: Walnut, with buttplate.
Sights: High ramp front, fully adjustable notch rear or Williams peep.
Features: Velocity to 550 fps. Gives about 40 shots per cylinder. Bolt action with ambidextrous push-pull safety. Blue finish (Blue Streak) or nickel finish (Sliver Streak). Introduced 1991. Made in the U.S. by Sheridan Div., Benjamin Air Rifle Co.
Price: Blue Streak, open sight, Model FB9 . . . . . . **$109.95**
Price: As above with Williams peep, Model FBW9 . . . . . . **$136.95**
Price: Silver Streak, open sight, Model F9 . . . . . . **$116.95**
Price: As above with Williams peep, Model FW9 . . . . . . **$143.95**

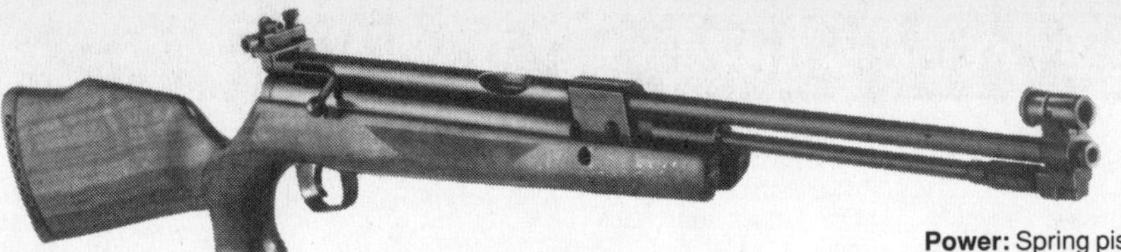
Sterling HR83

STERLING SPRING PISTON AIR RIFLES
Caliber: 177, 20, 22, single shot.
Barrel: 18½", Lothar Walther, steel.
Weight: 9½ lbs. (HR81), 9¾ lbs. (HR83). **Length:** 42½" overall. (HR81).
Power: Spring piston with under-barrel lever.
Stock: American walnut (HR81); HR83 has walnut with checkpiece and hand-checkered grip. Rubber buttpad.
Features: Velocity to 700 fps (177). Spring-loaded bolt action with adjustable single stage match trigger. Introduced 1983. Made in the U.S. by Benjamin Air Rifle Co.
Price: Standard models, HR81-17 (177), HR81-20 (20), HR81-22 (22) $299.95
Price: Deluxe models, HR83-17 (177), HR83-20 (20), HR83-22 (22) $423.95

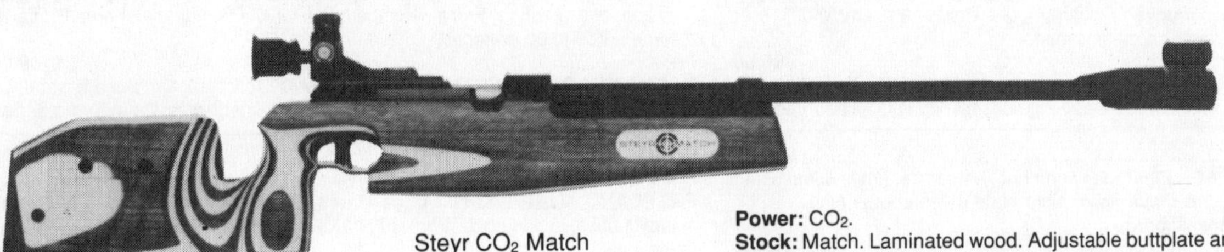

Steyr CO_2 Match

STEYR CO_2 MATCH AIR RIFLE
Caliber: 177, single shot.
Barrel: 23¾", (13¾" rifled).
Weight: 10½ lbs. **Length:** 44½" overall.
Power: CO_2.
Stock: Match. Laminated wood. Adjustable buttplate and cheekpiece.
Sights: Match. Globe front, aperture rear.
Features: Velocity 577 fps. CO_2 cylinders are refillable; about 250 shots per cylinder. Designed for 10-meter shooting. Introduced 1990. Imported from Austria by Gun South, Inc.
Price: $925.00
Price: Left-hand $995.00
Price: Running Target Rifle, right-hand $1,175.00
Price: As above, left-hand $1,250.00

Theoben Classic

THEOBEN CLASSIC AIR RIFLE
Caliber: 177 or 22, single shot.
Barrel: 19½".
Weight: 7¾ lbs. **Length:** 44" overall.
Power: Gas ram piston. Variable power.
Stock: Walnut with checkered grip and forend.
Sights: None furnished. Comes with scope mount.
Features: Velocity to 1100 fps (177) and 900 fps (22). Barrel-cocking action. Polished blue finish on metal, oil-finished stock. Adjustable trigger. Imported from England by Air Rifle Specialists.
Price: $960.00
Price: For left-hand stock add $60.00
Price: Grand Prix model (same as Classic except has thumbhole stock with adjustable buttplate) $1,070.00
Price: For left-hand stock add $60.00

Theoben Eliminator Air Rifle
Similar to the Theoben Classic except has a longer, more sturdily built action with longer piston stroke for more power. Has walnut thumbhole stock with adjustable buttplate and comes with sling. Imported from England by Air Rifle Specialists.
Price: $1,650.00
Price: Left-hand stock, add $60.00

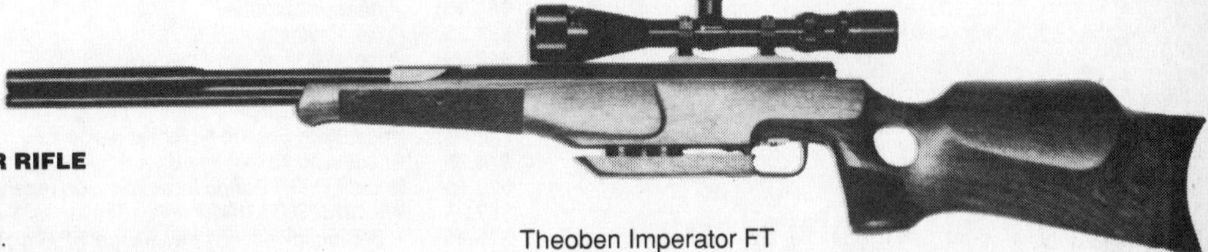
Theoben Imperator FT

THEOBEN IMPERATOR FT AIR RIFLE
Caliber: 177, single shot.
Barrel: 16".
Weight: 8½ lbs. **Length:** 42" overall.
Power: Under-lever cocking gas Ram piston. Variable power.
Stock: Hand-checkered European walnut, thumbhole design with adjustable forend block, roll-over cheekpiece, adjustable rubber buttpad.
Sights: None furnished. Comes with scope mount.
Features: Velocity up to 900 fps. Stippled grip and forend panels. Adjustable match-grade trigger. Imported from England by Air Rifle Specialists.
Price: $1,500.00

Theoben Imperator SLR 88 Air Rifle
Sporter version of the Theoben Imperator FT in 22-caliber only. Has conventional sporter stock of oil-finished walnut with checkered grip and forend. Has 7-shot clip. Velocity up to 725 fps. Imported from England by Air Rifle Specialists.
Price: $1,680.00

WALTHER LGR UNIVERSAL MATCH AIR RIFLE
Caliber: 177, single shot.
Barrel: 25.5".
Weight: 13 lbs. **Length:** 44¾" overall.
Power: Spring air, barrel cocking.
Stock: Walnut match design with stippled grip and forend, adjustable cheekpiece, rubber buttpad.
Features: Has the same weight and contours as the Walther U.I.T. rimfire target rifle. Comes complete with sights, accessories and muzzle weight. Imported from Germany by Interarms.
Price: $1,250.00

WALTHER CG90 AIR RIFLE
Caliber: 177, single shot.
Barrel: 18.9".
Weight: 10.2 lbs. **Length:** 44" overall.
Power: CO_2 cartridge.
Stock: Match type of European walnut; stippled grip.
Sights: Globe front, fully adjustable match rear.
Features: Uses tilting-block action. Introduced 1989. Imported from Germany by Interarms.
Price: $1,300.00

METALLIC SIGHTS

Sporting Leaf and Open Sights

BURRIS SPORTING REAR SIGHT Made of spring steel, supplied with multi-step elevator for coarse adjustments and notch plate with lock screw for finer adjustments.
Price: $14.95

LYMAN No. 16 Middle sight for barrel dovetail slot mounting. Folds flat when scope or peep sight is used. Sight notch plate adjustable for elevation. White triangle for quick aiming. 3 heights: A—.400" to .500", B—.345" to .445", C—.500" to .600".
Price: $12.50

MARBLE FALSE BASE #72, #73, #74 New screw-on base for most rifles replaces factory base. 3⁄8" dovetail slot permits installation of any folding rear sight. Can be had in sweat-on models also.
Price: $6.50

MARBLE CONTOUR RAMP #14R For late model Rem. 725, 740, 760, 742 rear sight mounting. 9⁄16" between mounting screws. Accepts all sporting rear sights.
Price: $13.95

MARBLE FOLDING LEAF Flat-top or semi-buckhorn style. Folds down when scope or peep sights are used. Reversible plate gives choice of "U" or "V" notch. Adjustable for elevation.
Price: $12.50
Price: Also available with both windage and elevation adjustment . . . $18.50

MARBLE SPORTING REAR With white enamel diamond, gives choice of two "U" and two "V" notches or different sizes. Adjustment in height by means of double step elevator and sliding notch piece. For all rifles; screw or dovetail installation.
Price: . . . . $12.50-$14.20

MARBLE #20 UNIVERSAL New screw or sweat-on base. Both have .100" elevation adjustment. In five base sizes. Three styles of U-notch, square notch, peep. Adjustable for windage and elevation.
Price: Screw-on $19.25
Price: Sweat-on $17.65

MILLETT RIFLE SIGHT Open, fully adjustable rear sight fits standard 3⁄8" dovetail cut in barrel. Choice of white outline or target rear blades, .360". Front with white or orange bar, .343", .400", .430", .460", .500", .540".
Price: Rear sight $52.95
Price: Front sight $11.75

MILLETT SCOPE-SITE Open, adjustable or fixed rear sights dovetail into a base integral with the top scope-mounting ring. Blaze orange front ramp sight is integral with the front ring half. Rear sights have white outline aperture. Provides fast, short-radius, Patridge-type open sights on the top of the scope. Can be used with all Millett rings, Weaver-style bases, Ruger 77 (also fits Redhawk), Ruger Ranch Rifle, No. 1, No. 3, Rem. 870, 1100; Burris, Leupold and Redfield bases.
Price: Angle-Loc for Weaver-style bases, windage adjustable, low, medium, high $44.95
Price: Angle-Loc for Weaver-style bases, fully adj., low, med., high . . $77.95
Price: For Ruger 77 (also Redhawk), windage only, medium $44.95
Price: As above, fully adjustable $77.95
Price: For Ruger 77, No. 1, 3 (also Redhawk), windage only $44.95
Price: As above, fully adjustable $77.95
Price: For Rem. 870, 1100 shotguns, windage only $43.95
Price: As above, fully adjustable $76.95
Price: For Millett, Burris, Leupold, Redfield bases, windage only, low, medium, high $43.95
Price: As above, fully adjustable $76.95
Price: Scope-Site top only, windage only $29.65
Price: As above, fully adjustable $62.95
Price: Scope-Site Hi-Turret, fully adjustable, low, medium, high $76.95
Price: As above, Tops only (.410" rear blade, .540" rifle front) $62.95
Price: For Colt Python, Peacekeeper, Diamondback, fully adjustable . $80.25
Price: For Dan Wesson (through 357 Mag., fully adj., two rings) $80.25
Price: As above, 41/44 Mag., three rings $96.20
Price: For Ruger Redhawk, windage only, medium $44.95
Price: As above, fully adjustable $77.95

WICHITA MULTI RANGE SIGHT SYSTEM Designed for silhouette shooting. System allows you to adjust the rear sight to four repeatable range settings, once it is pre-set. Sight clicks to any of the settings by turning a serrated wheel. Front sight is adjustable for weather and light conditions with one adjustment. Specify gun when ordering.
Price: Rear sight $88.00
Price: Front sight $66.00

WILLIAMS DOVETAIL OPEN SIGHT (WDDS) Open rear sight with windage and elevation adjustment. Furnished with "U" notch or choice of blades. Slips into dovetail and locks with gib lock. Heights from .281" to .531".
Price: With blade $13.00
Price: Less Blade $8.55

WILLIAMS GUIDE OPEN SIGHT (WGDS) Open rear sight with windage and elevation adjustment. Bases to fit most military and commercial barrels. Choice of square "U" or "V" notch blade, 3⁄16", 1⁄4", 5⁄16", or 3⁄8" high.
Price: With blade $15.70
Price: Extra blades, each $4.45
Price: Less blade $11.25

Micrometer Receiver Sights

BEEMAN/WEIHRAUCH MATCH APERTURE SIGHT Micrometer 1⁄4-minute click adjustment knobs with settings indicated on scales.
Price: $89.95

BEEMAN/FEINWERKBAU MATCH APERTURE SIGHTS Locks into one of four eye-relief positions. Micrometer 1⁄4-minute click adjustments; may be set to zero at any range. Extra windage scale visible beside eyeshade. Primarily for use at 5 to 20 meters.
Price: $169.95

BEEMAN SPORT APERTURE SIGHT Positive click micrometer adjustments. Standard units with flush surface screwdriver adjustments. Deluxe version has target knobs. For air rifles with grooved receivers.
Price: Standard $34.98
Price: Deluxe $44.98

FREELAND TUBE SIGHT Uses Unertl 1" micrometer mounts. For 22-cal. target rifles, including 52 Win., 37, 40X Rem. and BSA Martini.
Price: $150.00

LYMAN No. 57 1⁄4-minute clicks. Stayset knobs. Quick release slide, adjustable zero scales. Made for almost all modern rifles.
Price: $61.00

LYMAN No. 66 Fits close to the rear of flat-sided receivers, furnished with Stayset knobs. Quick release slide, 1⁄4-min. adjustments. For most lever or slide action or flat-sided automatic rifles.
Price: $61.00

LYMAN No. 66U Light weight, designed for most modern shotguns with a flat-sided, round-top receiver. 1⁄4-minute clicks. Requires drilling, tapping. Not for Browning A-5, Rem. M11.
Price: $61.00

LYMAN 90MJT RECEIVER SIGHT Mounts on standard Lyman and Williams FP bases. Has 1⁄4-minute audible micrometer click adjustments, target knobs with direction indicators. Adjustable zero scales, quick release slide. Large 7⁄8" diameter aperture disk.
Price: $69.95

MILLETT ASSAULT RIFLE SIGHTS Fully adjustable, heat-treated nickel steel peep aperture receiver sights for AR-15, Mini-14. AR-15 rear sight has windage and elevation adjustments; non-glare replacement ramp-style front also available. Mini-14 sight has fine windage and elevation adjustments; replaces original.
Price: Rear sight for above guns $51.45
Price: Front and rear combo for AR-15 . . . . $62.65
Price: Front sight for AR-15 . . . . $12.25
Price: Front and rear combo for Mini-14 . . . . $68.25
Price: Front sight for Mini-14 . . . . $17.85

WILLIAMS FP Internal click adjustments. Positive locks. For virtually all rifles, T/C Contender, Heckler & Koch HK-91, Ruger Mini-14, plus Win., Rem. and Ithaca shotguns.
Price: From $47.90
Price: With Twilight Aperture $49.37
Price: With Target Knobs $56.90
Price: With Target Knobs & Twilight Aperture $58.37
Price: With Square Notched Blade $50.42
Price: With Target Knobs & Square Notched Blade $59.53
Price: FP-GR (for dovetail-grooved receivers, 22s and air guns) $47.90

WILLIAMS TARGET FP Similar to the FP series but developed for most bolt-action rimfire rifles. Target FP High adjustable from 1.250" to 1.750" above centerline of bore; Target FP Low adjustable from .750" to 1.250". Attaching bases for Rem. 540X, 541-S, 580, 581, 582 (#540); Rem. 510, 511, 512, 513-T, 521-T (#510); Win. 75 (#75); Savage/Anschutz 64 and Mark 12 (#64). Some rifles require drilling, tapping.
Price: High or Low, with Base $75.75
Price: As above, less Base $64.85
Price: Base only $10.90

WILLIAMS 5-D SIGHT Low cost sight for shotguns, 22s and the more popular big game rifles. Adjustment for windage and elevation. Fits most guns without drilling or tapping. Also for British SMLE.
Price: $27.16
Price: With Twilight Aperture $28.63
Price: With Shotgun Aperture $27.16

WILLIAMS GUIDE (WGRS) Receiver sight for 30 M1 Carbine, M1903A3 Springfield, Savage 24s, Savage-Anschutz rifles and Weatherby XXII. Utilizes military dovetail; no drilling. Double-dovetail windage adjustment, sliding dovetail adjustment for elevation.
Price: $25.79
Price: With Twilight Aperture $27.26
Price: With Open Sight Blade $23.69

Front Sights

LYMAN HUNTING SIGHTS Made with gold or white beads 1/16" to 3/32" wide and in varying heights for most military and commercial rifles. Dovetail bases.
Price: **$8.95**

MARBLE STANDARD Ivory, red, or gold bead. For all American-made rifles, 1/16" wide bead with semi-flat face which does not reflect light. Specify type of rifle when ordering.
Price: **$7.50**

MARBLE-SHEARD "GOLD" Shows up well even in darkest timber. Shows same color on different colored objects; sturdily built. Medium bead. Various models for different makes of rifles so specify type of rifle when ordering.
Price: **$9.50**

MARBLE CONTOURED Same contour and shape as Marble-Sheard but uses standard 1/16" or 3/32" bead, ivory, red or gold. Specify rifle type.
Price: **$8.65**

MARBLE PATRIDGE Gold-faced Patridge front sight is available in .250" or .34" widths and heights from .260" to .538".
Price: **$9.50**

POLY-CHOKE Rifle front sights available in six heights and two widths. Model A designed to be inserted into the barrel dovetail; Model B is for use with standard .350" ramp; both have standard 3/8" dovetails. Gold or ivory color 1/16" bead. From Marble Arms.
Price: **$6.00**

WILLIAMS RISER BLOCKS For adding .250" height to front sights when using a receiver sight. Two widths available: .250" for Williams Streamlined Ramp or .340" on all standard ramps having this base width. Uses standard 3/8" dovetail.
Price: **$4.60**

Globe Target Front Sights

FREELAND SUPERIOR Furnished with six 1" plastic apertures. Available in 4½"-6½" lengths. Made for any target rifle.
Price: **$48.50**
Price: With six metal insert apertures **$51.60**
Price: Front base **$12.50**

FREELAND TWIN SET Two Freeland Superior Front Sights, long or short, allow switching from 50 yd. to 100 yd. ranges and back again without changing rear sight adjustment. Sight adjustment compensation is built into the set; just interchange and you're "on" at either range. Set includes six plastic apertures.
Price: **$67.00**
Price: With six metal apertures **$70.00**

FREELAND MILITARY Short model for use with high-powered rifles where sight must not extend beyond muzzle. Screw-on base; six plastic apertures.
Price: **$48.50**
Price: With six metal apertures **$51.60**
Price: Front base **$12.50**

LYMAN 20 MJT TARGET FRONT Has 7/8" diameter, one-piece steel globe with 3/8" dovetail base. Height is .700" from bottom of dovetail to center of aperture. Comes with seven Anschutz-size steel inserts—two posts and five apertures .126" through .177".
Price: **$29.95**

LYMAN No. 17A TARGET Includes seven interchangeable inserts: four apertures, one transparent amber and two posts .50" and .100" in width.
Price: **$27.00**
Price: Insert set **$7.95**

Ramp Sights

LYMAN SCREW-ON RAMP Used with 8-40 screws but may also be brazed on. Heights from .10" to .350". Ramp without sight.
Price: **$15.50**

MARBLE FRONT RAMPS Available in either screw-on or sweat-on style, five heights: 3/16", 5/16", 3/8", 7/16", 9/16". Standard 3/8" dovetail slot.
Price: **$14.95**
Price: Hoods for above ramps **$3.25**

WILLIAMS SHORTY RAMP Companion to "Streamlined" ramp, about ½" shorter. Screw-on or sweat-on. It is furnished in 1/8", 3/16", 9/32", and 3/8" heights without hood only.
Price: **$11.25**
Price: With dovetail lock **$13.25**

WILLIAMS STREAMLINED RAMP Hooded style in screw-on or sweat-on models. Furnished in 9/16", 7/16", 3/8", 5/16", 3/16" heights.
Price: With hood **$17.80**
Price: Without hood **$14.70**

Handgun Sights

BO-MAR DELUXE BMCS Gives 3/8" windage and elevation adjustment at 50 yards on Colt Gov't 45; sight radius under 7". For GM and Commander models only. Uses existing dovetail slot. Has shield-type rear blade.
Price: **$65.95**

BO-MAR LOW PROFILE RIB & ACCURACY TUNER Streamlined rib with front and rear sights; 7⅛" sight radius. Brings sight line closer to the bore than standard or extended sight and ramp. Weight 5 oz. Made for Colt Gov't 45, Super 38, and Gold Cup 45 and 38.
Price: **$123.00**

BO-MAR COMBAT RIB For S&W Model 19 revolver with 4" barrel. Sight radius 5¾", weight 5½ oz.
Price: **$110.00**

BO-MAR FAST DRAW RIB Streamlined full-length rib with integral Bo-Mar micrometer sight and serrated fast draw sight. For Browning 9mm, S&W 39, Colt Commander 45, Super Auto and 9mm.
Price: **$110.00**

BO-MAR WINGED RIB For S&W 4" and 6" length barrels—K-38, M10, HB 14 and 19. Weight for the 6" model is about 7¼ oz.
Price: **$123.00**

BO-MAR COVER-UP RIB Adjustable rear sight, winged front guards. Fits right over revolver's original front sight. For S&W 4" M-10HB, M-13, M-58, M-64 & 65, Ruger 4" models SDA-34, SDA-84, SS-34, SS-84, GF-34, GF-84.
Price: **$117.00**

C-MORE SIGHTS Replacement front sight blades offered in two types and five styles. Made of Du Pont Acetal, they come in a set of five high-contrast colors: blue, green, pink, red and yellow. Easy to install. Patridge style for Colt Python (all barrels), Ruger Super Blackhawk (7½"), Ruger Blackhawk (4⅝"); ramp style for Python (all barrels), Blackhawk (4⅝"), Super Blackhawk (7½" and 10½"). From Mag-na-port Int'l.
Price: Per set **$19.95**

MMC COMBAT FIXED REAR SIGHT (Colt 1911-Type Pistols) This veteran MMC sight is well known to those who prefer a true combat sight for "carry" guns. Steel construction for long service. Choose from a wide variety of front sights.
Price: Combat Fixed Rear, plain **$18.45**
Price: As above, white outline **$23.65**
Price: Combat Front Sight for above, six styles, from **$5.15**

MMC M/85 ADJUSTABLE REAR SIGHT Designed to be compatible with the Ruger P-85 front sight. Fully adjustable for windage and elevation.
Price: M/85 Adjustable Rear Sight, plain **$52.45**
Price: As above, white outline **$57.70**

MMC STANDARD ADJUSTABLE REAR SIGHT Available for Colt 1911 type, Ruger Standard Auto, and now for S&W 469, and 659 pistols. No front sight change is necessary, as this sight will work with the original factory front sight.
Price: Standard Adjustable Rear Sight, plain leaf **$46.05**
Price: Standard Adjustable Rear Sight, white outline **$51.15**

MMC MINI-SIGHT Miniature size for carrying, fully adjustable, for maximum accuracy with your pocket auto. MMC's Mini-Sight will work with the factory front sight. No machining is necessary; easy installation. Available for Walther PP, PPK, and PPK/S pistols. Will also fit fixed sight Browning Hi-Power (P-35).
Price: Mini-Sight, plain **$58.45**
Price: Mini-Sight, white bar **$63.45**

MEPROLIGHT SIGHTS Replacement open sights for popular handguns and Uzi carbine, AR-15/M-16 rifles. Both front and rear sights have tritium inserts for illumination in low-light conditions. Inserts give constant non-glare green light for 5 years, even in cold weather. For most popular auto pistols, revolvers, some rifles and shotguns. From Hesco, Inc.
Price: Universal front for revolvers **$24.95**
Price: Front and rear sights **$89.95**
Price: Shotgun bead **$24.95**

MILLETT 3-DOT SYSTEM SIGHTS The 3-Dot System sights use a single white dot on the front blade and two dots flanking the rear notch. Fronts available in Dual-Crimp and Wide Stake-On styles, as well as special applications. Adjustable rear sight available for most popular auto pistols and revolvers.
Price: Front, from **$15.25**
Price: Adjustable rear, from . . . . **$46.96** to **$68.25**

MILLETT SERIES 100 ADJUSTABLE SIGHTS Replacement sights for revolvers and auto pistols. Positive click adjustments for windage and elevation. Designed for accuracy and ruggedness. Made to fit S&W, Colt, Beretta, SIG Sauer P220, P225, P226, Ruger P-85, Ruger GP-100 (and others), Glock 17, CZ-75, TZ-75, Dan Wesson, Browning, AMT Hardballer. Rear blades are available in white outline or positive black target. All steel construction and easy to install.
Price: . . . . **$46.95** to **$75.35**

MILLETT MARK SERIES PISTOL SIGHTS Mark I and Mark II replacement combat sights for government-type auto pistols, including H&K P7. Mark I is high profile, Mark II low profile. Both have horizontal light deflectors.
Price: Mark I, front and rear **$32.95**
Price: Mark II, front and rear **$46.95**
Price: For H&K P7 . . . . **$46.95**

MILLETT REVOLVER FRONT SIGHTS All-steel replacement front sights with either white or orange bar. Easy to install. For Ruger GP-100, Redhawk, Security-Six, Police-Six, Speed-Six, Colt Trooper, Diamondback, King Cobra, Peacemaker, Python, Dan Wesson 22 and 15-2.
Price: **$15.25**

MILLETT DUAL-CRIMP FRONT SIGHT Replacement front sight for automatic pistols. Dual-Crimp uses an all-steel two-point hollow rivet system. Available in eight heights and four styles. Has a skirted base that covers the front sight pad. Easily installed with the Millett Installation Tool Set. Available in Blaze Orange Bar, White Bar, Serrated Ramp, Plain Post.
Price: **$15.25**

MILLETT STAKE-ON FRONT SIGHT Replacement front sight for automatic pistols. Stake-On sights have skirted base that covers the front sight pad.

Easily installed with the Millet Installation Tool Set. Available in seven heights and four styles—Blaze Orange Bar, White Bar, Serrated Ramp, Plain Post.
Price: **$15.25**

OMEGA OUTLINE SIGHT BLADES Replacement rear sight blades for Colt and Ruger single action guns and the Interarms Virginian Dragoon. Standard Outline available in gold or white notch outline on blue metal. From Omega Sales, Inc.
Price: **$8.95**

OMEGA MAVERICK SIGHT BLADES Replacement "peep-sight" blades for Colt, Ruger SAs, Virginian Dragoon. Three models available—No. 1, Plain; No. 2, Single Bar; No. 3, Double Bar Rangefinder. From Omega Sales, Inc.
Price: Each **$6.95**

TRIJICON SELF-LUMINOUS SIGHTS Three-dot sighting system uses self luminous inserts in the sight blade and leaf. Tritium "lamps" are mounted in a metal cylinder and protected by a polished crystal sapphire. For most popular handguns, fixed or adjustable sights, and some rifles. From Trijicon, Inc.
Price: . . . . **$28.95** to **$175.00**

THOMPSON/CENTER "ULTIMATE" SIGHTS Replacement front and rear sights for the T/C Contender. Front sight has four interchangeable blades (.060", .080", .100", .120"), rear sight has four notch widths of the same measurements for a possible 16 combinations. Rear sight can be used with existing soldered front sights.
Price: Front sight **$35.00**
Price: Rear sight **$65.00**

WICHITA SERIES 70/80 SIGHT Provides click windage and elevation adjustments with precise repeatability of settings. Sight blade is grooved and angled back at the top to reduce glare. Available in Low Mount Combat or Low Mount Target styles for Colt 45s and their copies, S&W 645, Hi-Power, CZ 75 and others.
Price: **$62.50**

WICHITA 45 SIGHT SYSTEMS For 45 auto pistols. Target and Combat styles available. Designed by Ron Power. All-steel construction, click adjustable. Each sight has two traverse pins, a large hinge pin and two elevation return springs. Sight blade is serrated and mounted on an angle to deflect light. Patridge front for target, ramp front for combat. Both are legal for ISPC and NRA competitions.
Price: Rear sight, target or combat **$62.50**
Price: Front sight, Patridge or ramp **$9.85**

WICHITA GRAND MASTER DELUXE RIBS Ventilated rib has wings machined into it for better sight acquisition. Made of stainless steel, sights blued. Uses Wichita Multi-Range rear sight, adjustable front sight. Made for revolvers with 6" barrel.
Price: Model 301 (adj. sight K-frames with custom bbl. of 1.000"-1.032" dia., L- and N-frames with 1.062"-1.100" bbl.) **$143.00**
Price: Model 302 (fixed sight K-frames; M10, 65, 13 with 1.000" bbl., N-frame with 1.062" bbl.) **$143.00**
Price: Model 303 (Model 29, 629 with factory bbl., adj. sight K-, L-, N-frames) **$143.00**

WICHITA DOUBLE MASTER RIB Ventilated rib has wings machined on either side of fixed front post sight for better acquisition and is relieved for Mag-na-ports. Milled to accept Weaver See-Thru-style rings. Made of blued steel. Has Wichita Multi-Range rear sight system. Made for Model 29/629 with factory barrel, and all adjustable-sight K-, L- and N-frames.
Price: Model 403 . . . . **$128.95**

Shotgun Sights

ACCURA-SITE For shooting shotgun slugs. Three models to fit most shotguns—"A" for vent. rib barrels, "B" for solid ribs, "C" for plain barrels. Rear sight has windage and elevation provisions. Easily removed and replaced. Includes front and rear sights.
Price: . . . . **$27.95** to **$34.95**

FIRE FLY EM-109 SL SHOTGUN SIGHT Made of aircraft-grade aluminum, this ¼-oz. "channel" sight has a thick, sturdy hollowed post between the side rails to give a Patridge sight picture. All shooting is done with both eyes open, allowing the shooter to concentrate on the target, not the sights. The hole in the sight post gives reduced-light shooting capability and allows for fast, precise aiming. For sport or combat shooting. For all shotguns with or without vent. rib. From JAS, Inc. Add $3 postage.
Price: **$29.95**

LYMAN Three sights of over-sized ivory beads. No. 10 Front (press fit) for double barrel or ribbed single barrel guns...**$4.50**; No. 10D Front (screw fit) for non-ribbed single barrel guns (comes with wrench)...**$5.50**; No. 11 Middle (press fit) for double and ribbed single barrel guns..**$4.50**.

MMC M&P COMBAT SHOTGUN SIGHT SET A durable, protected ghost ring aperture, combat sight made of steel. Fully adjustable for windage and elevation.
Price: M&P Sight Set (front and rear) **$73.45**
Price: As above, installed **$83.95**

MARBLE SHOTGUN BEAD SIGHTS No. 214—Ivory front bead, 11/64", tapered shank...**$3.70**; No. 223—Ivory rear bead, .080", tapered shank...**$3.75**; No. 217—Ivory front bead, 11/64", threaded shank...**$4.00**; No. 223-T—Ivory rear bead, .080", threaded shank...**$5.30**. Reamers, taps and wrenches available from Marble Arms.

MILLET SHURSHOT SHOTGUN SIGHT A sight system for shotguns with ventilated rib. Rear sight attaches to the rib, front sight replaces the front bead. Front has an orange face, rear has two orange bars. For 870, 1100 or other models.
Price: Front and rear **$20.95**
Price: Adjustable front and rear **$27.40**

POLY-CHOKE Replacement front shotgun sights in four styles—Xpert, Poly Bead, Xpert Mid Rib sights, and Bev-L-Block. Xpert Front available in 3x56, 6x48 thread, 3/32" or 5/32" shank length, gold, ivory...**$4.50**; or Sun Spot orange bead...**$4.50**; Poly Bead is standard replacement ⅛" bead, 6x48...**$2.40**; Xpert Mid Rib in tapered carrier (ivory only) or 3x56 threaded shank (gold only)...**$3.50**; Hi and Lo Blok sights with 6x48 thread, gold or ivory...**$3.50** or Sun Spot Orange...**$4.50**. From Marble Arms.

SLUG SIGHTS Made of non-marring black nylon, front and rear sights stretch over and lock onto the barrel. Sights are low profile with blaze orange front blade. Adjustable for windage and elevation. For plain-barrel (non-ribbed) guns in 12-, 16- and 20-gauge, and for shotguns with 5/16" and ⅜" ventilated ribs. From Innovision Ent.
Price: **$11.95**

WILLIAMS GUIDE BEAD SIGHT Fits all shotguns, ⅛" ivory, red or gold bead. Screws into existing sight hole. Various thread sizes and shank lengths.
Price: **$4.50**

WILLIAMS SLUGGER SIGHTS Removable aluminum sights attach to the shotgun rib. High profile front, fully adjustable rear. Fits 15/16" ribs.
Price: **$34.95**

Sight Attachments

FREELAND LENS ADAPTER Fits 1⅛" O.D. prescription ground lens to all standard tube and receiver sights for shooting without glasses.
Price: Without lens **$66.50**
Price: Clear lens ground to prescription **$24.00**
Price: Yellow or green prescription lens **$24.00**

MERIT IRIS SHUTTER DISC Eleven clicks give 12 different apertures. No. 3 Disc and Master, primarily target types, 0.22" to .125"; No. 4, ½" dia. hunting type, .025" to .155". Available for all popular sights. The Master Deluxe, with flexible rubber light shield, is particularly adapted to extension, scope height, and tang sights. All Merit Deluxe models have internal click springs; are hand fitted to minimum tolerance.
Price: Master Deluxe **$63.00**
Price: No. 3 Disc **$52.00**
Price: No. 4 Hunting Disc **$45.00**

MERIT LENS DISC Similar to Merit Iris Shutter (Model 3 or Master) but incorporates provision for mounting prescription lens integrally. Lens may be obtained locally from your optician. Sight disc is 7/16" wide (Model 3), or ¾" wide (Master). Model 3 Target.
Price: **$65.00**
Price: Master Deluxe **$75.00**

MERIT OPTICAL ATTACHMENT For revolver and pistol shooters, instantly attached by rubber suction cup to regular or shooting glasses. Any aperture .020" to .156".
Price: Deluxe (swings aside) **$63.00**

WILLIAMS APERTURES Standard thread, fits most sights. Regular series ⅜" to ½" O.D., .050" to .125" hole. "Twilight" series has white reflector ring. .093" to .125" inner hole.
Price: Regular series **$4.05**
Price: Twilight series **$5.55**
Price: Wide open 5/16" aperture for shotguns fits 5-D an Foolproof sights **$7.15**

SCOPES & MOUNTS
HUNTING, TARGET & VARMINT SCOPES

Maker and Model	Magn.	Field at 100 Yds. (feet)	Relative Bright-ness	Eye Relief (in.)	Length (in.)	Tube Dia. (in.)	W&E Adjust-ments	Weight (ozs.)	Price	Other Data
ACTION ARMS										
Micro-Dot										
1.5-4.5x LER Pistol	1.5-4.5	80-26	—	12-24	8.8	1	Int.	9.5	**$189.00**	[1]56mm objective. Variable intensity LED red aiming dot. Average battery life 20 to 4500 hours. Waterproof, nitrogen-filled aluminum tube. Fits most standard 1" rings. Imported by Action Arms Ltd.
1.5-4.5x Rifle	1.5-4.5	80-26	—	3	9.8	1	Int.	10.5	**189.00**	
2-7x32	2-7	54-18	—	3	11	1	Int.	12.1	**189.00**	
3-9x40	3-9	40-14	—	3	12.2	1	Int.	13.3	**189.00**	
4x-12x[1]	4-12	—	—	3	14.3	1	Int.	18.3	**299.00**	
Ultra-Dot 1x	—	—	—	—	5.1	1	Int.	4.0	**160.00**	
ADCO										
Mirage	0	—	—	—	5.5	1	Int.	4.5	**159.00**	Dot covers 1.5" at 100 yards. Black finish; nickel finish **$159.00**. Uses long-life lithium wafer battery that fits into the sight body—no battery appendage. From ADCO.
AIMPOINT										
AP 1000[1]	0	—	—	—	6	—	Int.	7.8	**189.95**	Illuminates red dot in field of view. Noparallax (dot does not need to be centered). Unlimited field of view and eye relief. On/off, adj. intensity. Dot covers 3" @ 100 yds. Mounts avail. for all sights and scopes. [1]Clamps to Weaver-type bases. Available in blue (AP1000-B) or stainless (AP1000-S) finish. 3x scope attachment (for rifles only), **$109.95**. [2]Requires 1" rings. Black or stainless finish. 3x scope attachment (for rifles only), **$129.95**. [3]Projects red dot of visible laser light onto target. Black finish (LSR-2B) or stainless (LSR-2S); or comes with rings and accessories. Optional toggle switch, **$34.95**. Lithium battery life up to 15 hours. [4]Black finish (AP 5000-B) or stainless (AP 5000-S); avail. with regular 3-min. or 10-min. Mag Dot as B2 or S2. [5]Black finish (AP2P) or stainless (AP2P-S); 2x magnification scope with floating dot. From Aimpoint. Made in Sweden.
Series 3000 Short[2]	0	—	—	—	5.5	1	Int.	5.5	**249.95**	
Series 3000 Long[2]	0	—	—	—	6⅞	1	Int.	5.8	**259.95**	
Laserdot[3]	—	—	—	—	4	1	Int.	4.0	**329.95**	
AP 5000[4]	0	—	—	—	5.5	30mm	Int.	5.8	**309.95**	
AP 2P[5]	2	—	—	—	8.5	1	Int.	8.3	**324.95**	
ARMSON										
O.E.G.	0	—	—	—	5⅛	1	Int.	4.3	**183.90**	Shows red dot aiming point. No batteries needed. Standard model fits 1" ring mounts (not incl.). Other models available for many popular shotguns, para-military rifles and carbines. [1]Daylight Only Sight with ⅜" dovetail mount for 22s. Does not contain tritium. Also avail. as 22 D/N (Day-Night) with tritium, **$144.90**. From Trijicon, Inc.
22 DOS[1]	0	—	—	—	3¾	—	Int.	3.0	**105.90**	
BAUSCH & LOMB										
2x Handgun	2	22.5	—	10-24	8.4	1	Int.	6.7	**346.95**	All except Target scopes have ¼-minute click adjustments; Target scopes have ⅛-minute adjustments with standard turrets and expanded turret knobs. Target scopes come with sunshades, screw-on lens caps. Contact Bushnell for details.
4x Handgun	4	25	—	10-20	8.4	1	Int.	7.0	**359.95**	
4x Balfor Compact	4	25	—	3.3	10.0	1	Int.	10.0	**362.95**	
1.5-6x	1.5-6	75-18	294-18.4	3.3	10.6	1	Int.	10.5	**593.95**	
2-8x Balvar Compact	2-8	51-13	—	3.5	10.0	1	Int.	11.5	**479.95**	
3-9x40	3-9	36-12	—	3.2	13.0	1	Int.	16.2	**570.95**	
2.5-10x Balvar	2.5-10	43.5-11	—	3.3	13.8	1	Int.	13	**652.95**	
6-24x Varmint	6-24	18-4.5	66.1-4.2	3.1	16.6	1	Int.	20.1	**719.95**	
12x-32x40	12-32	—	—	3.2	13.5	1	Int.	18.9	**822.95**	
24x Target	24	4.7	—	3.2	15.2	1	Int.	15.7	**665.95**	
36x Target	36	3.5	—	3.2	15.2	1	Int.	15.7	**719.95**	
Scope Chief	4	37.3	96	3½	12	1	Int.	12	**306.95**	
Scope Chief	3-9	39-13	267-30	3.3	12.6	1	Int.	13.9	**354.95**	
Scope Chief	1½-4½	73.7-24.5	267-30	3.5-3.5	9.6	1	Int.	10	**335.95**	
Scope Chief	4-12	29-10	150-17	3.2	13.5	1	Int.	15.9	**397.95**	
BEEMAN										
Blue Ring 20[1]	1.5	14	150	11-16	8.3	¾	Int.	3.6	**59.95**	All scopes have 5-pt. reticle, all glass, fully coated lenses. [1]Pistol scope; cast mounts included. [2]Pistol scope; silhouette knobs. [3]Rubber armor coating; built-in double adj. mount, parallax-free setting. [4]Objective focus, built-in double-adj. mount; matte finish. [5]Objective focus. [6]Also available with color reticle. [7]Includes cast mounts. [8]Objective focus; silhouette knobs; matte finish. [9]Also in "L" models with reticle lighted by ambient light or tiny add-on illuminator. Lighted models slightly higher priced. Imported by Beeman.
Blue Ribbon 25[2]	2	19	150	10-24	9 1/16	1	Int.	7.4	**154.95**	
SS-1[3,7]	2.5	30	61	3.25	5½	1	Int.	7	**198.50**	
SS-2[4,6,7,8,9]	3	34.5	74	3.5	6.8	1.38	Int.	13.6	**265.00**	
Blue Ribbon 50R[5]	2.5	33	245	3.5	12	1	Int.	11.8	**198.95**	
Blue Ring 10	4	27	69	3.0	10.6	1	Int.	9.5	**99.95**	
Blue Ribbon 66R[6,8,9]	2-7	62-16	384-31	3	11.4	1	Int.	14.9	**269.95**	
Blue Ring 49R[5]	4	30	64	3	11.8	1	Int.	11.3	**99.50**	
Blue Ring 12	3-9	39-13	172-20	3.0	12.8	1	Int.	12.7	**119.95**	
SS-3[3,4]	1.5-4	44.6-24.6	172-24	3	5.75	⅞	Int.	8.5	**279.95**	
Blue Ribbon 67R	3-9	435-15	265-29	3	14.4	1	Int.	15.2	**395.00**	
Blue Ribbon 68R	4-12	30.5-11	150-13.5	3	14.4	1	Int.	15.2	**419.95**	
Blue Ribbon 54R[5]	4	29	96	3.5	12	1	Int.	12.3	**198.95**	
SS-2[4,6,8]	4	24.6	41	5	7	1.38	Int.	13.7	**285.00**	
B-SQUARE										
BSL-1	—	—	—	—	2.75	.75	Int.	2.25	**439.95**	Blue or stainless finish. From B-Square Co.
BURRIS										
Fullfield										
1½x	1.6	62	—	3¼	10¼	1	Int.	9.0	**200.00**	
2½x	2.5	55	—	3¼	10¼	1	Int.	9.0	**211.95**	
4x[1,2,3]	3.75	36	—	3¼	11¼	1	Int.	11.5	**224.95**	
6x[1,3]	5.8	23	—	3¼	13	1	Int.	12.0	**242.95**	
10x[1,4,6,7,8]	9.8	12	—	3¼	15	1	Int.	15	**296.95**	

Maker and Model	Magn.	Field at 100 Yds. (feet)	Relative Bright-ness	Eye Relief (in.)	Length (in.)	Tube Dia. (in.)	W&E Adjust-ments	Weight (ozs.)	Price	Other Data
BURRIS (cont.)										
12x[1,4,6,7,8]	11.8	10.5	—	3¼	15	1	Int.	15	**305.95**	All scopes avail. in Plex reticle. Steel-on-steel click adjustments. [1]Dot reticle $13 extra. [2]Post crosshair reticle $13 extra. [3]Matte satin finish $20 extra. [4]Available with parallax adjustment $28 extra (standard on 10x, 12x, 4-12x, 6-12x, 6-18x, 6x HBR and 3-12x Signature). [5]Silver Safari finish $30 extra. [6]Target knobs $20 extra, standard on silhouette models, LER and XER with P.A., 6x HBR. [7]Sunshade avail. [8]Avail. with Fine Plex reticle. [9]Available with German three-post reticle.
1¾-5x[1,2]	1.7-4.6	66-25	—	3¼	10⅞	1	Int.	13	**269.95**	
2-7x[1,2,3]	2.5-6.8	47-18	—	3¼	12	1	Int.	14	**298.95**	
3-9x[1,2,3]	3.3-8.7	38-15	—	3¼	12⅝	1	Int.	15	**314.95**	
4-12x[1,4,8]	4.4-11.8	27-10	—	3¼	15	1	Int.	18	**382.95**	
6-18x[1,4,6,7,8]	6.5-17.6	16-7	—	3¼	15.8	1	Int.	18.5	**382.95**	
Mini Scopes										
4x[4,5]	3.6	24	—	3¾-5	8¼	1	Int.	7.8	**182.95**	
6x[1,4]	5.5	17	—	3¾-5	9	1	Int.	8.2	**200.95**	
6x HBR P.A.[1]	6.0	13	—	4.5	11¼	1	Int.	13.0	**269.95**	
2-7x	2.5-6.9	32-14	—	3¾-5	12	1	Int.	10.5	**249.95**	
3-9x[5]	3.6-8.8	25-11	—	3¾-5	12⅝	1	Int.	11.5	**254.95**	
4-12x[1,4,6]	4.5-11.6	19-8	—	3¾-4	15	1	Int.	15	**337.95**	
Signature Series										LER=Long Eye Relief; IER=Intermediate Eye Relief; XER=Extra Eye Relief. From Burris.
1.5-6x[2,3,5,9]	1.7-5.8	70-20	—	3½-4	10.8	1	Int.	13.0	**346.95**	
4x	4.0	30	—	3	12⅛	1	Int.	14	**325.95**	
6x	6.0	20	—	3	12⅛	1	Int.	14	**340.95**	
3-9x	3.3-8.8	36-14	—	3	12⅞	1	Int.	15.5	**412.95**	
3-12x	3.3-11.7	34-9	—	3	14¼	1	Int.	21	**517.95**	
6-24x[1,3,5,6,8]	6.6-23.8	17-6	—	3-2½	16.0	1	Int.	22.7	**571.95**	
Handgun										
1½-4x LER[1,5]	1.6-3.8	16-11	—	11-25	10¼	1	Int.	11	**278.95**	
2½-7x LER[4,5]	2.7-6.7	12-7.5	—	11-28	12	1	Int.	12.5	**289.95**	
3-9x LER[4,5]	3.4-8.4	12-5	—	22-14	11	1	Int.	14	**327.95**	
1x LER[1]	1.1	27	—	10-24	8¾	1	Int.	6.8	**170.95**	
2x LER[4,5,6]	1.7	21	—	10-24	8¾	1	Int.	6.8	**175.95**	
3x LER[4,6]	2.7	17	—	10-20	8⅞	1	Int.	6.8	**192.95**	
4x LER[1,4,5,6]	3.7	11	—	10-22	9⅝	1	Int.	9.0	**199.95**	
5x LER[1,4,6]	4.5	8.7	—	12-22	10⅞	1	Int.	9.2	**215.95**	
7x IER[1,4,5,6]	6.5	6.5	—	10-16	11¼	1	Int.	10	**233.95**	
10x IER[1,4,6]	9.5	4	—	8-12	13½	1	Int.	14	**287.95**	
Scout Scope										
1½x XER[3,9]	1.5	22	—	7-18	9	1	Int.	7.3	**175.95**	
2¾x XER[3,9]	2.7	15	—	7-14	9⅜	1	Int.	7.5	**182.95**	
BUSHNELL										
Sportview Rangemaster 4-12x	4-12	27-9	—	3.2	13.5	1	Int.	14	**157.95**	All Scope Chief, Banner and Custom models come with Multi-X reticle. [1]Also in 40mm. **Only selected models shown.** Contact Bushnell for complete details.
Sportview Standard 4x	4	28	—	4	11.75	1	Int.	9.5	**63.95**	
Sportview Standard 3-9x	3-9	38-12	—	3.5	11.75	1	Int.	10	**79.95**	
Banner 22 Rimfire 4x	4	28	—	3	11.9	1	Int.	8	**83.95**	
Banner 22 Rimfire 3-7x	3-7	29-13	—	2.5	10	¾	Int.	6.5	**93.95**	
Banner 3-9x56	3-9	39-12.5	—	3.5	14.4	1	Int.	18.4	**290.95**	
Banner 10x	10	12	—	3	14.7	1	Int.	14.3	**263.95**	
Banner Lite-Site 3-9x[1]	3-9	36-12	—	3.3	13.6	1	Int.	14	**370.95**	
Banner Shotgun 2.5x	2.5	45	—	3.5	10.9	1	Int.	8	**105.95**	
Banner Standard 6x[1]	6	19.5	—	3	13.5	1	Int.	11.5	**194.95**	
Banner Standard 3-9x	3-9	43-14	—	3	12.1	1	Int.	14	**160.95**	
Trophy WA 1.75-5x	1.75-5	73-24.5	—	3.2	10.8	1	Int.	10.2	**220.95**	
Trophy WA 4x	4	34.2	—	3.4	12.4	1	Int.	11.9	**173.95**	
Trophy WA 3-9x	3-9	40-13	—	3.3	11.8	1	Int.	12.9	**226.95**	
CHARLES DALY										
4x32	4	28	—	3.25	11.75	1	Int.	9.5	**70.00**	[1]Pistol scope. [2]Adj. obj. From Outdoor Sports Headquarters.
4x32[2]	4	28	—	3	9	1	Int.	8.5	**129.00**	
4x40 WA	4	36	—	3.25	13	1	Int.	11.5	**98.00**	
2.5x20[1]	2.5	17	—	3	7.3	1	Int.	7.25	80.00	
2.5x32	2.5	47	—	3	12.25	1	Int.	10	**80.00**	
2-7x32 WA	2-7	56-17	—	3	11.5	1	Int.	12	**125.00**	
3-9x40	3-9	35-14	—	3	12.5	1	Int.	11.25	**77.00**	
3-9x40 WA	3-9	36-13	—	3	12.75	1	Int.	12.5	**125.00**	
4-12x40 WA	4-12	30-11	—	3	13.75	1	Int.	14.5	**133.00**	
2x20[1]	2	16	—	16-25	8.75	1	Int.	6.5	**107.00**	
INTERAIMS										
Mark V	0	—	—	—	5	1	Int.	6	**129.95**	Mark V for rifles, handguns, shotguns. Projects red dot aiming point. Dot size 1½" @ 100 yds. One V intended for handguns. Comes with rings. Dot size less than 1½" @ 100 yds. Both waterproof. Battery life 50-10,000 hours. Black or nickel finish on One V. Imported by Stoeger.
One V	0	—	—	—	4.5	1	Int.	4	**139.95**	
AUS JENA										
ZF4x32-M	4	32	—	3.5	10.8	26mm	Int.	10	**475.00**	Fixed power scopes have 26mm alloy tubes, variables, 30mm alloy; rings avail. from importer. Also avail. with rail mount. Multi-coated lenses. Waterproof and fogproof. ⅓-min. clicks. Choice of nine reticles. Imported from Germany by Europtik, Ltd.
ZF6x42-M	6	22	—	3.5	12.6	26mm	Int.	13	**510.00**	
ZF8x56-M	8	17	—	3.5	14	26mm	Int.	17	**580.00**	
VZF1.5-6x42-M	1.5-6	67.8-22	—	3.5	12.6	30mm	Int.	14	**635.00**	
UZF3-12x56-M	3-12	30-11	—	3.5	15	30mm	Int.	18	**710.00**	
KASSNAR VISTASCOPES										
HI0405	4	26	—	4	12	1	Int.	9.1	**NA**	Waterproof, fogproof, shockproof. Four-post reticle. From K.B.I.
HI0413	3-9	28-12	—	3.4-2.9	12	1	Int.	9.8	**NA**	
HI0448	3-9	40-14	—	3.4-2.8	12.6	1	Int.	12.7	**NA**	
HI0480 Compact	4	21	—	4.1	9.9	1	Int.	9.1	**NA**	
HI0499 Pistol	4	9	—	14.5	9.5	1	Int.	9.5	**NA**	
HI0502 Pistol	2.5	12.6	—	13	8.9	1	Int.	9.1	**NA**	

CAUTION: PRICES CHANGE, CHECK AT GUNSHOP.

Maker and Model	Magn.	Field at 100 Yds. (feet)	Relative Brightness	Eye Relief (in.)	Length (in.)	Tube Dia. (in.)	W&E Adjustments	Weight (ozs.)	Price	Other Data
KILHAM										
Hutson Handgunner II	1.7	8	—	—	5½	⅞	Int.	5.1	**119.95**	Unlimited eye relief; internal click adjustments; crosshair reticle. Fits Thompson/Center rail mounts, for S&W K, N, Ruger Blackhawk, Super, Super Single-Six, Contender.
Hutson Handgunner	3	8	—	10-12	6	⅞	Int.	5.3	**119.95**	
LASER AIM										
LA1[1]	—	—	—	—	3.50	.812	Int.	4	**239.00**	[1]LA1 Magnum has adjustable dot size, 1000-yard range, **$259.00.** [2]Mounts on top of scope; separate power module. [3]LA5 Magnum has 2.75" length, 1000-yard range. [4]For shotguns. Range 300 yards, 2" dot at 100 yards; LA6 Magnum has 2.75" length, 1000-yard range, **$259.00.** [5]Variable dot intensity, long battery life; includes battery, extender tube, fitter, eyepiece. [6]Intense red dot at crosshair intersection, adjustable intensity; electronic fiber optic lens system. Projects high intensity beam of laser light up to 300 yards. Dot size at 100 yards is 1". Adjustable for w. & e. Includes rings to mount on scope rail, battery charger plugs into cigarette lighter. Optional 110V charger, **$19.00**. From Emerging Technologies, Inc.
LA3[2]	—	—	—	—	1.15	1.94	Int.	1.5	**259.00**	
LA5[3]	—	—	—	—	1.9	.75	Int.	1.19	**219.00**	
LA6[4]	—	—	—	—	1.9	.75	Int.	1.19	**239.00**	
LA99 Illusion D.O.T.[5]	—	—	—	—	5.1	1	Int.	3.9	**129.00**	
LA27 Powerdot[6]	2-7	48.2-13.8	—	3-4	11.1	1	Int.	12	**219.00**	
LA39 Powerdot	3-9	37-12.5	—	2.7-3.2	12.3	1	Int.	13.4	**219.00**	
LA412 Powerdot	4-12	28.1-9.2	—	3	14.4	1	Int.	21	**319.00**	
LASER DEVICES										
He Ne FA-6	—	—	—	—	6.2	—	Int.	11	**229.50**	Projects high intensity beam of laser light onto target as an aiming point. Adj. for w. & e. [1]Diode laser system. From Laser Devices, Inc.
He Ne FA-9	—	—	—	—	12	—	Int.	16	**299.00**	
He Ne FA-9P	—	—	—	—	9	—	Int.	14	**299.00**	
FA-4[1]	—	—	—	—	4.5	—	Int.	3.5	**299.00**	
LASERSIGHT										
LS45	0	—	—	—	7.5	—	Int.	8.5	**245.00**	Projects a highly visible beam of concentrated laser light onto the target. Adjustable for w.& e. Visible up to 500 yds. at night. For handguns, rifles, shotguns. Uses two standard 9V batteries. From Imatronic Lasersight.
LS25	0	—	—	—	6	¾	Int.	3.5	**270.00**	
LS55	0	—	—	—	7	1	Int.	7	**299.00**	
LEATHERWOOD										
ART II	3.0-8.8	31-12	—	3.5	13.9	1	Int.	42	**750.00**	Compensates for bullet drop via external circular cam. Matte gray finish. Designed specifically for the M1A/M-14 rifle. Quick Detachable model for rifles with Weaver-type bases. From North American Specialties.
LEUPOLD										
Alaskan 2.5x	2.5	34.4	—	4.2	10.1	⅞	Int.	9.9	**241.10**	Constantly centered reticles, choice of Duplex, tapered CPC, Leupold Dot, Crosshair and Dot. CPC and Dot reticles extra. [1]2x and 4x scopes have from 12"-24" of eye relief and are suitable for handguns, top ejection arms and muzzleloaders. [2]3x9 Compact, 6x Compact, 12x, 3x9, 3.5x10 and 6.5x20 come with adjustable objective. [3]Target scopes have 1-min. divisions with ¼-min. clicks, and adjustable objectives. 50-ft. Focus Adaptor available for indoor target ranges, **$48.00**. Sunshade available for all adjustable objective scopes, **$16.10**. [4]Also available in matte finish for about **$20.00** extra. [5]Dot or Duplex; focused at 300 yds. with A.O., **$405.40**. [6]Silver finish about $20 extra. [7]Matte finish with Multicoat 4, **$373.20**. [8]Also avail. without target adjustments, matte finish, Multicoat 4, **$605.40**. [9]Matte finish. [10]Multicoat 4; also non-A.O., matte finish, **$516.10**. From Leupold.
Alaskan 4x	3.7	24	—	3.9	9.9	⅞	Int.	10.7	**258.90**	
Alaskan 6x	5.8	15.2	—	3.8	10.8	⅞	Int.	11.4	**276.80**	
Vari-X III 3.5x10 STD Police[9]	3.5-10	29.5-10.7	—	3.6-4.6	12.5	1	Int.	13.5	**587.50**	
M8-2X EER[1]	1.7	21.2	—	12-24	7.9	1	Int.	6.0	**223.20**	
M8-2X EER Silver[1]	1.7	21.2	—	12-24	7.9	1	Int.	6.0	**244.60**	
M8-4X EER[1]	3.7	9	—	12-24	8.4	1	Int.	7.0	**283.90**	
M8-4X EER Silver[1]	3.7	9	—	12-24	8.4	1	Int.	7.0	**305.40**	
M8-2.5X Compact	2.3	39.5	—	4.9	8.0	1	Int.	6.5	**248.20**	
M8-4X Compact	3.6	25.5	—	4.5	9.2	1	Int.	7.5	**266.10**	
2-7x Compact	2.5-6.6	41.7-16.5	—	5-3.7	9.9	1	Int.	8.5	**337.50**	
6x Compact	5.7	16.2	—	3.9	10.7-11.0	1	Int.	10.0	**283.90**	
3-9x Compact	3.2-8.6	34-13.5	—	4.0-3.0	11-11.3	1	Int.	11.0	**355.40**	
M8-4X[4]	4.0	24	—	4.0	10.7	1	Int.	9.3	**266.10**	
M8-6X[7]	5.9	17.7	—	4.3	11.4	1	Int.	10.0	**283.90**	
M8-6x 42mm	6.0	17	—	4.5	12	1	Int.	11.3	**355.40**	
M8-8X[2]	7.8	14.3	—	3.9	12.4	1	Int.	13.0	**383.90**	
M8-12X[2]	11.6	9.1	—	4.2	13.0	1	Int.	13.5	**392.90**	
M8-8x A.O. Varmint	7.8	14.3	—	3.9	12.4	1	Int.	13.0	**460.00**	
M8-12x A.O. Varmint	11.6	9.1	—	4.2	13.0	1	Int.	13.5	**480.00**	
6.5x20 Target A.O.[9]	6.5-19.2	14.2-5.5	—	5.3-3.6	14.2	1	Int.	17.5	**658.90**	
BR-24X[3]	24.0	4.7	—	3.2	13.8	1	Int.	15.3	**766.10**	
BR-36X[3]	36.0	3.2	—	3.4	14.1	1	Int.	15.6	**801.80**	
Vari-X-II 1x4	1.6-4.2	70.5-28.5	—	4.3-3.8	9.2	1	Int.	9.0	**301.80**	
Vari-X-II 2x7[4]	2.5-6.6	42.5-17.8	—	4.9-3.8	11.0	1	Int.	10.5	**353.60**	
Vari-X-II 3x9[1,4,6]	3.3-8.6	32.3-14.0	—	4.1-3.7	12.3	1	Int.	13.5	**355.40**	
Vari-X-II 3-9x50mm[4]	3.3-8.6	32.3-14	—	4.7-3.7	12	1	Int.	13.6	**426.80**	
Vari-X-II 4-12 A.O. Matte	4.4-11.6	22.8-11.0	—	5.0-3.3	12.3	1	Int.	13.5	**480.40**	
Vari-X-III 1.5x5	1.5-4.5	66.0-23.0	—	5.3-3.7	9.4	1	Int.	9.5	**444.60**	
Vari-X-III 2.5x8[4]	2.6-7.8	37.0-13.5	—	4.7-3.7	11.3	1	Int.	11.5	**480.40**	
Vari-X-III 3.5-10x50 A.O.[10]	3.3-9.7	29.5-10.7	—	4.6-3.6	12.4	1	Int.	13.0	**535.70**	
Vari-X-III 3.5-10x50[2,4]	3.3-9.7	29.5-10.7	—	4.6-3.6	12.4	1	Int.	14.4	**605.40**	
Vari-X-III 3.5-10 A.O. Varmint	3.3-9.7	29.5-10.7	—	4.6-3.6	12.4	1	Int.	14.4	**624.00**	
Vari-X-III 6.5-20 A.O. Varmint[8]	6.5-19.2	14.2-5.5	—	5.3-3.6	14.2	1	Int.	17.5	**698.00**	
Mark 4 M1-10x[9]	10	11.1	—	3.6	13⅛	1	Int.	21	**1,339.30**	
Mark 4 M1-16x[9]	16	6.6	—	4.1	12⅞	1	Int.	22	**1,339.30**	
Mark 4 M3-10x[9]	10	11.1	—	3.6	13⅛	1	Int.	21	**1,339.30**	
Vari-X-III 6.5x20[2]	6.5-19.2	14.2-5.5	—	5.3-3.6	14.2	1	Int.	16.0	**587.50**	
Rimfire										
Vari-X-II 2-7x RF Special	3.6	25.5	—	4.5	9.2	1	Int.	7.5	**355.40**	
Shotgun										
M8 2x EER	1.7	21.2	—	12-24	7.9	1	Int.	6.0	**258.00**	
M8 2.5x Compact	2.3	39.5	—	12-24	8.0	1	Int.	6.5	**278.00**	

HUNTING, TARGET & VARMINT SCOPES

Maker and Model	Magn.	Field at 100 Yds. (feet)	Relative Bright-ness	Eye Relief (in.)	Length (in.)	Tube Dia. (in.)	W&E Adjust-ments	Weight (ozs.)	Price	Other Data
LEUPOLD (cont.)										
M8 4x	3.7	9.0	—	12-24	8.4	1	Int.	6.0	**298.00**	
Vari-X-II 1x4	1.6-4.2	70.5-28.5	—	4.3-3.8	9.2	1	Int.	9.0	**338.00**	
Vari-X-II 2x7	2.5-6.6	42.5-17.8	—	4.9-3.8	11.0	1	Int.	9.0	**396.00**	
MIRADOR										
RXW 4x40[1]	4	37	—	3.8	12.4	1	Int.	12	**179.95**	[1]Wide Angle scope. Multi-coated objective lens. Nitrogen filled; waterproof; shockproof. From Mirador Optical Corp.
RXW 1.5-5x20[1]	1.5-5	46-17.4	—	4.3	11.1	1	Int.	10	**188.95**	
RXW 3-9x40	3-9	43-14.5	—	3.1	12.9	1	Int.	13.4	**251.95**	
NICHOLS										[1]Matte finish; also avail. with high gloss. [2]Adj. obj. [3]Stainless; also 3-9x40, blue, **$144.00**. [4]50-yd. parallax, with 22 rings; also with adj. obj., **$130.00**. [5]Also in stainless. [6]50-yd. parallax, **$90.00**. [7]Also 3-9x40, **$124.00**. Imported by G.U., Inc.
"Light" Series										
1.5-5x20 WA	1.5-5	80.8-24.2	—	3.2-3.7	—	1	Int.	—	**264.00**	
2-7x32 WA	2-7	60.4-17.5	—	3.3-3.9	—	1	Int.	—	**280.00**	
3-9x40 WA	3-9	40.2-13.3	—	3.2-3.6	—	1	Int.	—	**290.00**	
3-10x44 WA	3-10	40.2-12.1	—	3.1-3.6	—	1	Int.	—	**310.00**	
4-12x44 WA A.O.	4-12	30.1-10	—	3.1-3.6	—	1	Int.	—	**320.00**	
6.5-20x45 WA A.O.	6.5-20	18.5-6.2	—	3.1-3.5	—	1	Int.	—	**380.00**	
"Magnum Target"										
12x44[2]	12	8.7	—	3.1	14.3	1	Int.	19.1	**525.00**	
24x44[2]	24	4.3	—	2.9	14.3	1	Int.	18.4	**525.00**	
6-20x44[2]	6-20	17.4-5.4	—	3.1-3.0	14.4	1	Int.	19.8	**577.00**	
"Classic"										
4x40 WA	4	37.0	—	3.8	13.0	1	Int.	11.6	**140.00**	
6x40 WA	6	24.5	—	3.3	13.0	1	Int.	11.6	**142.00**	
1.5-4.5x WA	1.5-4.5	54.0-22.0	—	3.4-3.3	11.5	1	Int.	10.9	**163.00**	
2-7x32 WA	2-7	36.7-15.8	—	2.8-2.6	11.7	1	Int.	10.9	**163.00**	
3-9x32 WA[3]	3-9	39.3-13.1	—	3.4-2.9	11.4	1	Int.	10.5	**163.00**	
4-12x40	4-12	30.0-11.0	—	3.9-3.2	12.3	1	Int.	12.3	**170.00**	
"Air Gun/Rimfire"										
4x32[4]	4	28.5	—	3.1	12.2	1	Int.	10.7	**105.00**	
2-7x32 WA A.O.	2-7	36.7-15.7	—	2.8-2.6	11.8	1	Int.	10.5	**187.00**	
"Classic Handgun"										
2x20[5]	2	17.0	—	8.6-19.5	7.4	1	Int.	7.5	**135.00**	
2-7x28[5]	2-7	40.0-9.7	—	8.9-19.5	9.0	1	Int.	9.0	**260.00**	
"Bullet"										
4x32[6]	4	28.5	—	3.1	12.2	1	Int.	10.7	**82.00**	
3-9x32[7]	3-9	34.5-23.6	—	3.1-3.0	12.6	1	Int.	11.2	**118.00**	
NIKON										
4x40	4	26.7	—	3.5	11.7	1	Int.	11.7	**263.00**	Super multi-coated lenses and blackening of all internal metal parts for maximum light gathering capability; positive ¼-MOA; fogproof; waterproof; shockproof; luster and matte finish. From Nikon, Inc.
1.5-4.5x20	1.5-4.5	67.8-22.5	—	3.7-3.2	10.1	1	Int.	9.5	**324.00**	
1.5-4.5x24 EER	1.5-4.4	13.7-5.8	—	24-18	8.9	1	Int.	9.3	**324.00**	
2-7x32	2-7	46.7-13.7	—	3.9-3.3	11.3	1	Int.	11.3	**384.00**	
3-9x40	3-9	33.8-11.3	—	3.6-3.2	12.5	1	Int.	12.5	**404.00**	
4-12x40 A.O.	4-12	25.7-8.6	—	3.6-3.2	14	1	Int.	16.6	**507.00**	
6.5-20x44	6.5-19.4	16.2-5.4	—	3.5-3.1	14.8	1	Int.	19.6	**565.00**	
2x20 EER	2	22	—	26.4	8.1	1	Int.	6.3	**204.00**	
PENTAX										
1.5-5x	1.5-5	66-25	—	3-3¼	11	1	Int.	13	**330.00**	Multi-coated lenses, fogproof, waterproof, nitrogen-filled. Penta-Plex reticle. Click ¼-MOA adjustments. Matte finish **$20.00** extra. [1]Also in matte chrome, **$260.00**. [2]Also in matte chrome, **$390.00**. [3]Gloss finish only. [4]ProFinish (matte), **$530.00**. [5]Chrome-Matte finish, **$400.00**. Imported by Pentax Corp.
4x	4	35	—	3¼	11.6	1	Int.	12.2	**280.00**	
6x	6	20	—	3¼	13.4	1	Int.	13.5	**310.00**	
2-7x	2-7	42.5-17	—	3-3¼	12	1	Int.	14	**360.00**	
3-9x	3-9	33-13.5	—	3-3¼	13	1	Int.	15	**380.00**	
3-9x Lightseeker[4]	3-9	36-14	—	3	12.7	1	Int.	15	**485.00**	
3-9x Mini	3-9	26.5-10.5	—	3¾	10.4	1	Int.	13	**320.00**	
4-12x Mini[3]	4-12	19-8	—	3.75-4	11.3	1	Int.	11.3	**410.00**	
6-18x[3]	6-18	16-7	—	3-3.25	15.8	1	Int.	15.8	**460.00**	
Pistol										
2x LER[1]	2	21	—	10-24	8¾	1	Int.	6.8	**240.00**	
1.5-4x LER[2]	1.5-4	16-11	—	11-25	10	1	Int.	11	**360.00**	
2½-7x[5]	2.5-7	12.0-7.5	—	11-28	12	1	Int.	12.5	**380.00**	
RWS										
100	4	—	—	8	10½	¾	Int.	7	**60.00**	Air gun scopes. All have Dyna-Plex reticle. Model 800 is for air pistols. Imported from Japan by Dynamit Nobel-RWS.
300	4	—	—	8	12¾	1	Int.	11	**130.00**	
350	4	—	—	8	10	1	Int.	10	**110.00**	
400	2-7	—	—	8	12¾	1	Int.	12	**135.00**	
800	1.5	—	—	28	8¾	1	Int.	6	**125.00**	
CS-10	2.5	—	—	8	5¾	1	Int.	7	**120.00**	
REDFIELD										
Ultimate Illuminator 3-9x	3.4-9.1	27-9	—	3-3.5	15.1	30mm	Int.	20.5	**626.95**	*Accutrac feature avail. on these scopes at extra cost. Traditionals have round lenses. 4-Plex reticle is standard. [1]"Magnum Proof." Specially designed for magnum and auto pistols. Uses "Double Dovetail" mounts. Also in nickel-plated finish, 2½x, **$232.95**, 4x, **$244.95**. [2]With matte finish, **$523.95**. [3]Also available with matte finish at extra cost. [4]All Golden Five Star scopes come with Butler Creek flip-up lens covers. [5]Black anodized finish. Also in nickel finish, **$293.95**. [6]56mm adj. objective; European #4 or 4-Plex reticle; comes with 30mm steel rings with Rotary Dovetail System. ¼-min. click adj. Also in matte finish, **$725.95**. [7]Also available nickel-plated, **$316.95**.
Ultimate Illuminator 3-12x[6]	2.9-11.7	27-10.5	—	3-3½	15.4	30mm	Int.	23	**716.95**	
Illuminator Trad. 3-9x	2.9-8.7	33-11	—	3½	12¾	1	Int.	17	**465.95**	
Illuminator Widefield 4x	4.2	28	—	3-3.5	11.7	1	Int.	13.5	**359.95**	
Illuminator Widefield 2-7x	2.0-6.8	56-17	—	3-3.5	11.7	1	Int.	13.5	**458.95**	
Illuminator Widefield 3-9x*[2]	2.9-8.7	38-13	—	3½	12¾	1	Int.	17	**515.95**	
Tracker 4x[3]	3.9	28.9	—	3½	11.02	1	Int.	9.8	**154.95**	
Tracker 6x[3]	6.2	18	—	3.5	12.4	1	Int.	11.1	**174.95**	
Tracker 2-7x[3]	2.3-6.9	36.6-12.2	—	3½	12.20	1	Int.	11.6	**200.95**	
Tracker 3-9x[3]	3.0-9.0	34.4-11.3	—	3½	14.96	1	Int.	13.4	**224.95**	
Traditional 4x ¾"	4	24½	27	3½	9⅜	¾	Int.	—	**153.95**	
Traditional 2½x	2½	43	64	3½	10¼	1	Int.	8½	**153.95**	
Golden Five Star 4x[4]	4	28.5	58	3.75	11.3	1	Int.	9.75	**216.95**	

CAUTION: PRICES CHANGE, CHECK AT GUNSHOP.

Maker and Model	Magn.	Field at 100 Yds. (feet)	Relative Bright-ness	Eye Relief (in.)	Length (in.)	Tube Dia. (in.)	W&E Adjust-ments	Weight (ozs.)	Price	Other Data
REDFIELD (cont.)										
Golden Five Star 6x[4]	6	18	40	3.75	12.2	1	Int.	11.5	**236.95**	
Golden Five Star 2-7x[4]	2.4-7.4	42-14	207-23	3-3.75	11.25	1	Int.	12	**279.95**	
Golden Five Star 3-9x[4,7]	3.0-9.1	34-11	163-18	3-3.75	12.50	1	Int.	13	**297.95**	
Golden Five Star 4-12x A.O.*[4]	3.9-11.4	27-9	112-14	3-3.75	13.8	1	Int.	16	**382.95**	
Golden Five Star 6-18x A.O.*[4]	6.1-18.1	18.6	50-6	3-3.75	14.3	1	Int.	18	**403.95**	
Compact Scopes										
Golden Five Star Compact 4x	3.8	28	—	3.5	9.75	1	Int.	8.8	**207.95**	
Golden Five Star Compact 6x	6.3	17.6	—	3.5	10.70	1	Int.	9.5	**232.95**	
Golden Five Star Compact 2-7x	2.4-7.1	40-16	—	3-3.5	9.75	1	Int.	9.8	**274.95**	
Golden Five Star Compact 3-9x	3.3-9.1	32-11.25	—	3-3.5	10.7	1	Int.	10.5	**293.95**	
Golden Five Star Compact 4-12x	4.1-12.4	22.4-8.3	—	3-3.5	12	1	Int.	13	**369.95**	
Pistol Scopes										
2½xMP[1]	2.5	9	64	14-19	9.8	1	Int.	10.5	**216.95**	
4xMP[1]	3.6	9	—	12-22	9 11/16	1	Int.	11.1	**230.95**	
2-6x[5]	2-5.5	25-7	—	10-18	10.4	1	Int.	11	**273.95**	
Widefield Low Profile Compact										
Widefield 4xLP Compact	3.7	33	—	3.5	9.35	1	Int.	10	**254.95**	
Widefield 3-9x LP Compact	3.3-9	37.0-13.7	—	3-3.5	10.20	1	Int.	13	**326.95**	
Low Profile Scopes										
Widefield 2¾xLP	2¾	55½	69	3½	10½	1	Int.	8	**239.95**	
Widefield 4xLP	3.6	37½	84	3½	11½	1	Int.	10	**267.95**	
Widefield 6xLP	5.5	23	—	3½	12¾	1	Int.	11	**289.95**	
Widefield 1¾x-5xLP	1¾-5	70-27	136-21	3½	10¾	1	Int.	11½	**329.95**	
Widefield 2x-7xLP*	2-7	49-19	144-21	3½	11¾	1	Int.	13	**337.95**	
Widefield 3x-9xLP*	3-9	39-15	112-18	3½	12½	1	Int.	14	**373.95**	
SCHMIDT & BENDER										[1]All steel. 30-year warranty. All have ⅓-min. click adjustment, centered reticles, nitrogen filling. Most models avail. in aluminum with mounting rail. Imported from Germany by Paul Jaeger, Inc.
Vari-M 1¼-4x20[1]	1¼-4	96-16	—	3¼	10.4	30mm	Int.	12.3	**619.99**	
Vari-M 1½-6x42	1½-6	60-19.5	—	3¼	12.2	30mm	Int.	17.5	**684.99**	
Vari-M 2½-10x56	2½-10	37.5-12	—	3¼	14.6	30mm	Int.	21.9	**804.99**	
All Steel 4-12x42	4-12	34.7-12	—	3¼	13.25	30mm	Int.	23	**736.99**	
SHEPHERD										[1]Also avail. as 310-1, 310-E, **$413.60**. [2]Also avail. as 310-P1, 310-P2, 310-P3 with matte finish, click adj., **$413.60**. [3]Also avail. as 310-M1, 310-M2, 310-M3 with matte finish, click adj., no A.O., **$403.60**. [4]Also avail. as 27-4 with 9" stadia circles, traj. for 22 rifles, **$345.00** [5]Matte finish, click adj. for shotgun, carbine, blackpowder. All have Dual Reticle System with rangefinder-bullet drop compensation; multi-coated lenses, waterproof, shockproof, nitrogen filled. From Shepherd Scope, Ltd.
3940-E	3-9	43.5-15	178-20	3.3	13	1	Int.	17	**497.28**	
310-2[1,2,3]	3-10	35.3-11.6	178-16	3-3.75	12.8	1	Int.	18	**413.60**	
27-2[4]	2.5-7.5	42-14	164-18	2.5-3	11.6	1	Int.	16.3	**349.00**	
CBS[5]	1.5-5	82.5-27.5	45.5-40.9	2.5-3.25	11	1	Int.	14.9	**409.75**	
SIMMONS										
44 Mag										[1]Matte; also polished finish. [2]Silver; also black matte or polished. [3]32mm; also 40mm, **$145.95**. [4]Granite finish. [5]Camouflage. [6]Black Polish. [7]With ring mounts. Imported by Simmons Outdoor Corp.
M-1043	2-7	56-16	—	3.3	11.8	1	Int.	13	**256.95**	
M-1044	3-10	38-12	—	3	12.8	1	Int.	16.9	**268.95**	
M-1045	4-12	27-9	—	3	12.6	1	Int.	19.5	**268.95**	
Prohunter										
7700[1]	2-7	58-17	—	3.25	11.6	1	Int.	12.4	**131.95**	
7705	3-9	39-14	—	3.25	12.6	1	Int.	11.6	**131.95**	
7710[2]	3-9	40-15	—	3	12.6	1	Int.	14	**142.95**	
7720	6-18	17.6-5.8	—	3	14.3	1	Int.	16	**168.95**	
7725	4.5	26	—	3	11.9	1	Int.	9.9	**82.95**	
Whitetail Series										
WT01	4	27	—	3	12.3	1	Int.	12	**94.95**	
WT02[3]	3-9	33-12.3	—	3.1-3	12.6	1	Int.	14	**129.95**	
Whitetail Classic										
WTC10[4]	4	35	—	4	12	1	Int.	11	**134.95**	
WTC11[4]	1.5-5	80-23.5	—	3.4-3.2	9.3	1	Int.	9.7	**169.95**	
WTC12[4]	2.5-8	49.5-15	—	3.2-3	12.2	1	Int.	14	**185.95**	
WTC13[4]	3.5-10	35-12	—	3.2-3	12.8	1	Int.	16.2	**204.95**	
WTC14[4]	2-10	50-11	—	3	12.8	1	Int.	16.9	**256.95**	
Deerfield										
21006	4	29	—	3	11.8	1	Int.	12	**66.95**	
21010	3-9	35.5-12	—	2.75	12.75	1	Int.	14	**91.95**	
21029	3-9	36-12	—	2.75	12.8	1	Int.	16	**104.95**	
21031	4-12	28-11	—	3	13	1	Int.	18	**144.95**	
21060[5]	4	26	—	4	12	1	Int.	9.1	**87.95**	
21061[5]	3-9	38-12	—	3.4-2.9	12	1	Int.	9.8	**115.95**	
21062[5]	3-9	38-11	—	3.4-2.9	12.6	1	Int.	12.3	**125.95**	
Gold Medal Silhouette										
23000	12	10	—	3.1-3	14.5	1	Int.	21	**616.95**	
23001	24	5	—	3	14.5	1	Int.	21	**627.95**	
23002	6-20	17.5-6	—	3	14.7	1	Int.	23	**680.95**	
Gold Medal Handgun										
22007[6]	1.5-4	17.5-7	—	10-25.75	8.8	1	Int.	10	**314.95**	
22002[6]	2.5-7	11-4.3	—	14-27	9.25	1	Int.	11	**324.95**	
22004[6]	2	16.5	—	12-23	8	1	Int.	9	**168.95**	

HUNTING, TARGET & VARMINT SCOPES

Maker and Model	Magn.	Field at 100 Yds. (feet)	Relative Bright-ness	Eye Relief (in.)	Length (in.)	Tube Dia. (in.)	W&E Adjust-ments	Weight (ozs.)	Price	Other Data
SIMMONS (cont.)										
22006[6]	4	6.5	—	11-18	9.4	1	Int.	10	**224.95**	
Shotgun										
21005	2.5	26	—	5	7.4	1	Int.	7	**85.95**	
7790	4	16	—	5.5	8.8	1	Int.	9.2	**117.95**	
Rimfire										
1001[7]	4	17.5	—	2.75	8.3	¾	Int.	4	**34.95**	
1002[7]	4	19	—	3.5	10.75	¾	Int.	4	**13.95**	
1004[7]	3-7	26-12.5	—	2.5	11.4	¾	Int.	6	**45.95**	
1022[7]	4	33	—	3	12.1	¾	Int.	12	**74.95**	
21007[7]	4	29	—	3.75	11.8	¾	Int.	14	**108.95**	
STEINER										
Penetrator										
6x42	6	20.4	—	3.1	14.8	26mm	Int.	14	**889.00**	Waterproof, fogproof, nitrogen filled, accordion-type eye cup. From Pioneer Marketing & Research, Inc.
1.5x6x42	1.5-6	64-21	—	3.1	12.8	30mm	Int.	17	**1,099.00**	
3-12x56	3-12	29-10	—	3.1	14.8	30mm	Int.	21	**1,299.00**	
SWAROVSKI HABICHT										
4x32	4	33	—	3¼	11.3	1	Int.	15	**585.00**	All models offered in either steel or lightweight alloy tubes. Weights shown are for lightweight versions. Choice of nine constantly centered reticles. Eyepiece recoil mechanism and rubber ring shield to protect face. Imported by Swarovski Optik North America Ltd.
6x42	6	23	—	3¼	12.6	1	Int.	17.9	**635.00**	
8x56	8	17	—	3¼	14.4	1	Int.	23	**740.00**	
1.5-4.5x20	1.4-4.5	74-25.5	—	3.5	9.5	1	Int.	11.3	**525.00**	
1.5-6x42	1.5-6	61-21	—	3¼	12.6	30mm	Int.	16	**810.00**	
2.2-9x42	2.2-9	39.5-15	—	3¼	13.3	30mm	Int.	15.5	**955.00**	
3-12x56	3-12	30-11	—	3¼	15.25	1	Int.	18	**1,045.00**	
Cobra 1.5-14	1.5	50	—	3.9	7.87	1	Int.	10	**550.00**	
AL Scopes										
4x32A	4	30	—	3.2	11.5	1	Int.	10.8	**450.00**	
6x36A	6	21	—	3.2	11.9	1	Int.	11.5	**480.00**	
1.5-4.5x20A	1.5-4.5	75-25.8	—	3.5	9.53	1	Int.	10.6	**525.00**	
3-9x36	3-9	39-13.5	—	3.3	11.9	1	Int.	13	**565.00**	
SWIFT										
600 4x15	4	16.2	—	2.4	11	¾	Int.	4.7	**19.75**	All Swift scopes, with the exception of the 4x15, have Quadraplex reticles and are fogproof and waterproof. The 4x15 has crosshair reticle and is non-waterproof. [1]Available in black or silver finish—same price.
601 3-7x20	3-7	25-12	—	3-2.9	11	1	Int.	5.6	**48.50**	
650 4x32	4	29	—	3.5	12	1	Int.	9	**75.00**	
653 4x40WA	4	35.5	—	3.75	12.25	1	Int.	12	**96.50**	
654 3-9x32	3-9	35.75-12.75	—	3	12.75	1	Int.	13.75	**94.50**	
656 3-9x40WA	3-9	42.5-13.5	—	2.75	12.75	1	Int.	14	**103.50**	
657 6x40	6	18	—	3.75	13	1	Int.	10	**99.50**	
660 4x20	4	25	—	4	11.8	1	Int.	9	**79.50**	
664 4-12x40	4-12	27-9	—	3-2.8	13.3	1	Int.	14.8	**140.00**	
665 1.5-4.5x21	1.5-4.5	69-24.5	—	3.5-3	10.9	1	Int.	9.6	**102.75**	
666 Shotgun 1x20	1	113	—	3.2	7.5	1	Int.	9.6	**98.00**	
Pistol Scopes										
661 4x32	4	90	—	10-22	9.2	1	Int.	9.5	**108.50**	
662 2.5x32	2.5	14.3	—	9-22	8.9	1	Int.	9.3	**102.50**	
663 2x20[1]	2	18.3	—	9-21	7.2	1	Int.	8.4	**103.50**	
TASCO										
World Class										[1]Water, fog & shockproof; fully coated optics; ¼-min. click stops; haze filter caps; lifetime warranty. [2]30/30 range finding reticle. [3]World Class Wide Angle; Supercon multi-coated optics; Opti-Centered® 30/30 range finding reticle; lifetime warranty. [4]⅓ greater zoom range. [5]Trajectory compensating scopes, Opti-Centered® stadia reticle. [6]Anodized finish. [7]True one-power scope. [8]Coated optics; crosshair reticle; ring mounts included to fit most 22, 10mm receivers. [9]Fits Remington 870, 1100, 11-87. [10]Electronic dot reticle with rheostat; coated optics; adj. for windage and elevation; waterproof, shockproof, fogproof; Lithium battery; 3x power booster avail.; matte black or matte aluminum finish; dot or T-3 reticle. [11]TV view. [12]Also matte aluminum finish. [13]Also 40mm, **\$86.00**. [14]Also 40mm, **\$102.00**. [15]Also 40mm, **\$101.00**. [16]Also with crosshair reticle. [17]Also 30/30 reticle. [18]Dot size 1.5" at 100 yds.; waterproof. **Contact Tasco for details on complete line.**
DWC4x40	4	36	—	3	13	1	Int.	11.5	**144.00**	
WA4x40	4	36	100.0	3	13	1	Int.	11.5	**144.00**	
WA6x40	6	23	—	3	12.75	1	Int.	11.5	**152.00**	
WA13.5x20[1,3,10]	1-3.5	115-31	400.0-32.4	3.5	9.75	1	Int.	10.2	**196.00**	
WA1.75-5x20[1,3]	1.75-5	72-24	129.9-16.0	3	10⅝	1	Int.	9.8	**206.00**	
WA27x32[1,3,9]	2-7	56-17	256.0-20.2	3.25	11.5	1	Int.	12	**176.00**	
WA39x40[1,3,6,11]	3-9	43.5-15	176.8-19.3	3⅛	12.75	1	Int.	12.5	**168.00**	
World Class Compact										
CW4x32LE	4	25	64	5	10.0	1	Int.	9.5	**159.00**	
CW28x32	2-8	55-16	—	3	10.5	1	Int.	11.5	**188.00**	
World Class Airgun										
AG4x40A	4	36	—	3	13	1	Int.	14	**200.00**	
AG39x50WA	3-9	41-14	—	3	15	1	Int.	17.5	**336.00**	
World Class Electronic										
ER39x40WA	3-9	41-14	176.8-19.3	3	12.75	1	Int.	16	**368.00**	
World Class Mag IV-44										
WC2510x44[6]	2.5-10	41-11	—	3.5	12.5	1	Int.	14.4	**224.00**	
World Class TS										
TS24x44	24	4.5	—	3	14	1	Int.	17.9	**344.00**	
TS36x44	36	3	—	3	14	1	Int.	17.9	**368.00**	
TS624x44	6-24	15-4.5	—	3	14	1	Int.	18.5	**408.00**	
TS832x44	8-32	11-3.5	—	3	14	1	Int.	19.5	**440.00**	
World Class TR										
TR39x40WA	3-9	41-14	—	3	12.75	1	Int.	12.5	**224.00**	
World Class Pistol										
PWC2x22[12]	2	25	—	11-20	8.75	1	Int.	7.3	**147.00**	
PWC4x28[12]	4	8	—	12-19	9.45	1	Int.	7.9	**190.00**	
P1.254x28[12]	1.25-4	23-9	—	15-23	9.25	1	Int.	8.2	**220.00**	
Mag IV										
W312x40[1,2,4]	3-12	33-11	176.8-10.8	3	12⅛	1	Int.	12	**136.00**	
W416x40[1,2,4]	4-16	25.5-7	100.0-6.2	3	14.25	1	Int.	16.75	**176.00**	
W624x40	6-24	17-4	—	3	15.25	1	Int.	16.8	**232.00**	
Traditional										
W2.5x20V	2.5	43	—	3.75	10	1	Int.	7.1	**64.00**	
W4x20V	4	30	—	3.5	11.5	1	Int.	8.2	**64.00**	

Maker and Model	Magn.	Field at 100 Yds. (feet)	Relative Bright-ness	Eye Relief (in.)	Length (in.)	Tube Dia. (in.)	W&E Adjust-ments	Weight (ozs.)	Price	Other Data
TASCO (cont.)										
W4x32V[11,13]	4	32	—	3	12	1	Int.	12.5	**59.00**	
W6x40V	6	20	—	3	12.5	1	Int.	11.5	**89.00**	
W39x32V[11,14]	3-9	39-13	—	3	12	1	Int.	11	**76.00**	
Standard										
WS2.5x32	2.5	42	—	3.25	11	1	Int.	10	**67.00**	
WS4x32	4	29	—	3	11.5	1	Int.	10.2	**58.00**	
WS39x32[15]	3-9	35-12	—	3	11.75	1	Int.	11	**73.00**	
Rubber Armored										
RC4x40A	4	27	—	3.25	12.5	1	Int.	14.2	**160.00**	
RC39x40A	3-9	35-12	—	3.25	12.5	1	Int.	14.3	**176.00**	
TR Scopes										
TR39x40WA	3-9	41-14	—	3	13	1	Int.	12.5	**224.00**	
TR416x40	4-16	26-7	—	3	14.25	1	Int.	16.8	**248.00**	
TR624x40	6-24	17-4	—	3	15.5	1	Int.	17.5	**272.00**	
Shotgun Scopes										
SG2.5x32[9]	2.5	42	163.8	3.25	11.75	1	Int.	15.7	**98.00**	
WA1.75-5x20[9]	1.75-5	74-24	—	3	10.5	1	Int.	10	**206.00**	
WA13.5x20[9]	1-3.5	103-31	—	3	9	1	Int.	12	**196.00**	
Airgun										
AG4x20	4	20	—	2.5	10.75	.75	Int.	5	**38.00**	
AG4x32	4	28	—	3	12	1	Int.	13	**176.00**	
AG4x40WA	4	36	—	3	13	1	Int.	14	**200.00**	
AG39x50WA	3-9	27-9	—	3	15	1	Int.	17.5	**336.00**	
Rimfire										
RF4x15[8]	4	22.5	13.6	2.5	11	.75	Int.	4	**15.00**	
RF4x20DS[8]	4	20	25.0	2.5	10.5	.75	Int.	3.8	**23.00**	
RF4x32	4	31	—	3	12.5	1	Int.	12.6	**70.00**	
RF37x20	3-7	24-11	—	2.5	11.5	.75	Int.	5.7	**39.00**	
P1.5x15	1.5	22.5	—	9.5-20.75	8.75	.75	Int.	3.25	**30.00**	
Propoint										
PDP2[10,12]	1	25-12	—	—	5	30mm	Int.	5.5	**245.00**	
PDP3[10,12]	1	40	—	—	5	30mm	Int.	5.5	**294.00**	
PB1[16]	3	35	—	3	5.5	30mm	Int.	6.3	**171.00**	
PB3	2	30	—	—	1.25	30mm	Int.	2.6	**196.00**	
Proclass										
P1x22S[17]	1	43-22	—	8-28	6.5	30mm	Int.	7.8	**183.00**	
P2x22S[17]	2	23-18	—	10-24	6.5	30mm	Int.	7.7	**196.00**	
P3x22[12,17]	3	13-6	—	12-24	8.25	30mm	Int.	8.5	**220.00**	
ER2x22P	2	25-15	—	8-20	8.75	30mm	Int.	9.4	**245.00**	
ER4x30P	4	7-6	—	12-24	9.75	30mm	Int.	12	**269.00**	
P1.25-4x22	1.25-4	23-9	—	12-28	9.25	30mm	Int.	9.5	**330.00**	
World Class Plus										
WCP6x44	6	21	—	3.25	12.75	1	Int.	13.6	**248.00**	
WCP39x44	3-9	39-14	—	3.5	12.75	1	Int.	15.8	**296.00**	
LaserPoint[18]	—	—	—	—	2	⅝	Int.	.75	**389.00**	
THOMPSON/CENTER RECOIL PROOF PISTOL SCOPES										[1]Also silver finish, **$265.00** (#8316); with rail mount, black, **$257.00** (#8317); with lighted reticle, black, **$295.00** (#8326); with rail, lighted reticle, black, **$300.00** (#8327). [2]With lighted reticle, **$225.00** (#8322); silver, **$235.00** (#8323); with lighted reticle, rail mount, black, **$235.00** (#8320). [3]With lighted reticle, **$295.00** (#8626). [4]With rail mount, lighted reticle, **$170** (#8640). From Thompson/Center.
8312 Compact Rail[2]	2.5	15	64	9-21	7.25	1	Int.	6.6	**160.00**	
8315 Compact[1]	2.5-7	15-5	125-16	8-21	9.25	1	Int.	9.2	**250.00**	
Rifle Scopes										
8621 Compact	1.5-5	61-20	177-16	3	10	1	Int.	8.5	**190.00**	
8623 Compact WA[3]	3-9	33-11	113-13	3	10.75	1	Int.	9.9	**210.00**	
8624 Compact[4]	4	26	64	3	10	1	Int.	8.2	**155.00**	
TRIJICON SPECTRUM										[1]Self-luminous low-light reticle glows in poor light; allows choice of red, amber or green via a selector ring on objective end. [2]Advanced Combat Optical Gunsight for AR-15, M-16, with integral mount. [3]Reticle glows only red in poor light. From Trijicon, Inc.
4x40[1]	4	38	—	3.0	12.2	1	Int.	15.0	**513.00**	
6x56[1]	6	24	—	3.0	14.1	1	Int.	20.3	**575.00**	
1-3x20[1]	1-3	94-33	—	3.7-4.9	9.6	1	Int.	13.2	**594.00**	
3-9x40[1]	3-9	35-14	—	3.3-3.0	13.1	1	Int.	16.0	**569.00**	
3-9x56[1]	3-9	35-14	—	3.3-3.0	14.2	1	Int.	21.5	**649.00**	
ACOG[2]	4	37	—	1.5	5.8	—	Int.	9.7	**695.00**	
4x32 Red[3]	4	29	—	3.3	11.6	1	Int.	10.2	**298.00**	
UNERTL										[1]Dural ¼-MOA click mounts. Hard coated lenses. Non-rotating objective lens focusing. [2]¼-MOA click mounts. [3]With target mounts. [4]With calibrated head. [5]Same as 1" Target but without objective lens focusing. [6]Price with ¼-MOA click mounts. [7]With new Posa mounts. [8]Range focus unit near rear of tube. Price is with Posa or standard mounts. Magnum clamp. From Unertl.
1" Target	6,8,10	16-10	17.6-6.25	2	21½	¾	Ext.	21	**233.00**	
1¼" Target[1]	8,10,12,14	12-16	15.2-5	2	25	¾	Ext.	21	**302.00**	
1½" Target	8,10,12,14, 16,18,20	11.5-3.2	—	2¼	25½	¾	Ext.	31	**326.00**	
2" Target[2]	8,10,12,14, 16,18,24, 30,36	8	22.6-2.5	2¼	26¼	1	Ext.	44	**431.00**	
Varmint, 1¼"[3]	6,8,10,12	1-7	28-7.1	2½	19½	⅞	Ext.	26	**296.00**	
Ultra Varmint, 2"[4]	8,10,12,15	12.6-7	39.7-11	2½	24	1	Ext.	34	**420.00**	
Small Game[5]	4,6	25-17	19.4-8.4	2¼	18	¾	Ext.	16	**175.00**	
Vulture[6]	8	11.2	29	3-4	15⅝	1	Ext.	15½	**333.00**	
	10	10.9	18½	—	16⅛	1				
Programmer 200[7]	8,10,12,14, 16,18,20, 24,30,36	11.3-4	39-1.9	—	26½	1	Ext.	45	**532.00**	
BV-20[8]	20	8	4.4	4.4	17⅞	1	Ext.	21¼	**390.00**	
WEATHERBY										Lumiplex reticle in all models. Blue-black, nonglare finish. From Weatherby.
Supreme 1¾-5x20	1.7-5	66.6-21.4	—	3.4	10.7	1	Int.	11	**248.00**	
Supreme 2-7x34	2.1-6.8	59-16	—	3.4	11¼	1	Int.	10.4	**256.00**	
Supreme 4x44	3.9	32	—	3	12½	1	Int.	11.6	**256.00**	
Supreme 3-9x44	3.1-8.9	36-13	—	3.5	12.7	1	Int.	11.6	**300.00**	

HUNTING, TARGET & VARMINT SCOPES

Maker and Model	Magn.	Field at 100 Yds. (feet)	Relative Bright-ness	Eye Relief (in.)	Length (in.)	Tube Dia. (in.)	W&E Adjust-ments	Weight (ozs.)	Price	Other Data
WEAVER										
K2.5	2.5	35	—	3.7	9.5	1	Int.	7.3	**99.84**	Micro-Trac adjustment system with ¼-minute clicks on all models. All have Dual-X reticle. One-piece aluminum tube, satin finish, nitrogen filled, multi-coated lenses, waterproof. From Weaver.
K4	3.7	26.5	—	3.3	11.3	1	Int.	10	**108.31**	
K6	5.7	18.5	—	3.3	11.4	1	Int.	10	**117.97**	
V3	1.1-2.8	88-32	—	3.9-3.7	9.2	1	Int.	8.5	**130.95**	
V9	2.8-8.7	33-11	—	3.5-3.4	12.1	1	Int.	11.1	**141.29**	
V10	2.2-9.6	38.5-9.5	—	3.4-3.3	12.2	1	Int.	11.2	**150.04**	
KT15	14.6	7.5	—	3.2	12.9	1	Int.	14.7	**236.29**	
WILLIAMS										
Twilight Crosshair TNT	1½-5	57¾-21	177-16	3½	10¾	1	Int.	10	**196.30**	[1]Matte or glossy black finish. TNT models from Williams Gunsight Co.
Twilight Crosshair TNT	2½	32	64	3¾	11¼	1	Int.	8½	**138.95**	
Twilight Crosshair TNT	4	29	64	3½	11¾	1	Int.	9½	**145.25**	
Twilight Crosshair TNT	2-6	45-17	256-28	3	11½	1	Int.	11½	**196.30**	
Twilight Crosshair TNT	3-9	36-13	161-18	3	12¾	1	Int.	13½	**206.30**	
Guideline II										
4x[1]	4	29	64	3.6	11¾	1	Int.	9½	**199.95**	
1.5-5x[1]	1.5-5	57¾-21	177-16	3.5	10¾	1	Int.	10	**239.95**	
2-6x[1]	2-6	45½-10¾	256-28	3	11½	1	Int.	11½	**239.95**	
3-9x[1]	3-9	36½-12¾	161.2-17.6	3.1-2.9	12¾	1	Int.	13½	**266.60**	
Pistol Scopes										
Twilight 1.5x TNT	1.5	19	177	18-25	8.2	1	Int.	6.4	**143.70**	
Twilight 2x TNT	2	17.5	100	18-25	8.5	1	Int.	6.4	**145.80**	
WILLIAMS OPTICS										
30mm Superb Series WA										
1.5x20	1.5	78.73	69.64	3.9	9.4	1.18	Int.	12.3	**300.53**	30mm Superb Series: All models can be ordered with target or external knobs, magnifying reticle (European style), objective adjustment (O.A.), and choice of six reticles. Variables—IPC, extra-heavy construction of 6061 T-6 alloy. Fogproof, recoil-proof coated optics.
4x42	4	31.16	43.40	4.5	12.2	1.18	Int.	14.6	**374.78**	
6x42	6	19	19.29	3.7	12.2	1.18	Int.	14.6	**385.39**	
8x56	8	13.12	19.29	3.7	13.5	1.18	Int.	19.0	**424.28**	
15x56[1]	15	8.5	5.38	3.3	15.9	1.18	Int.	25.7	**601.07**	
30mm Variables										
1-4x20	1-4	101-30.1	157-9.8	4.3-3.3	9.4	1.18	Int.	11.1	**434.89**	
2-8x42	2-8	46.9-16	173-11	4.5-3.5	13.3	1.18	Int.	17.4	**493.23**	
2.5-10	2.5-10	42.6-13	111.1-69	4.3-3.3	13.3	1.18	Int.	17.4	**510.91**	
3-12x56	3-12	37.7-10.8	137-16	3.9-3.3	14.3	1.18	Int.	25.7	**601.07**	
4-20x42	4-20	26-6	40-4	3.3-3.0	17.7	1.18	Int.	23.8	**664.71**	
American 1" Series WA										
Adirondack 1x20	1	—	—	—	—	1	Int	—	**159.10**	American Series: Special reticles (12), target knobs, BDC objective lens adjustment feature can be added to any scope at extra cost. Sunshades also avail. 12x thru 24x can be made on special order. German-type speed focus avail. as option on all American Series scopes. Waterproof, fogproof, recoil-proof, fully coated.
Raton 2.5x32	2.5	33.0	161	3.5	11.7	1	Int.	9.2	**160.00**	
Las Vegas 4x32[2]	4	29.0	64	3.3	11.7	1	Int.	9.2	**162.64**	
Kalispell 6x40[3]	6	18.5	45	3.2	13.0	1	Int.	10.2	**187.07**	
Pecos 8x40 O.A.	8	13.5	25	3.0	13.0	1	Int.	10.2	**239.46**	
San Antonio 10x40 O.A.	10	12.5	16	3.0	13.0	1	Int.	10.4	**242.67**	
Variables										
Abeline 1-3x20	1-3	—	—	—	—	1	Int.	—	**224.51**	
Shiloh 1.5-4.5x20	1.5-4.5	—	—	—	—	1	Int.	—	**228.05**	
Denver 2-7x32[4]	2-7	—	—	—	—	1	Int.	—	**213.91**	
Santa Fe 3-9x32[5]	3-9	43.5-15	114-13	3.3-3.0	12.2	1	Int.	12.0	**210.37**	
Sutter's Creek 4-12x40 O.A.	4-12	30.5-11	100-12.3	3.0	15.8	1	Int.	15.0	**284.63**	
European 1" Series										European 1": All wide angle with choice of 12 reticless, obj. adj. avail. on some models. BDC and target knobs avail. on all as options. Sunshades, locking lens covers, speed focus also optional. **Partial listing of models shown.** Contact Williams Optics for full details. [1]With adj. obj.; [2]Also 4x40, 4x40 with adj. obj.; [3]Also with adj. obj.; [4]Also 2-7x40, 2-7x40 with adj. obj.; [5]Also 3-9x40, 3-9x40 with adj. obj.; [6]Also 4x30, 4x40; [7]Also 10x40.
Jutland 4x20[6]	4	33	25	3.2	11.0	1	Int.	10.5	**197.00**	
Grenoble 6x40	6	26	43.56	3	13.2	1	Int.	13.7	**230.46**	
Rhineland 8x56	8	20	49	3.2	13.5	1	Int.	17.2	**292.50**	
Hamburg 10x56 O.A.[7]	10	—	—	3.2	13.5	1	Int.	17.2	**354.21**	
Brunswick 15x56 O.A.	15	—	—	3.1	13.5	1	Int.	17.6	**390.85**	
ZEISS										
Diatal C 4x32	4	30	—	3.5	10.6	1	Int.	11.3	**575.00**	All scopes have ¼-minute click-stop adjustments. Choice of Z-Plex or fine crosshair reticles. Rubber armored objective bell, rubber eyepiece ring. Lenses have T-Star coating for highest light transmission. Z-Series scopes offered in non-rail tubes with duplex reticles only; 1" and 30mm. Imported from Germany by Carl Zeiss Optical, Inc.
Diatal C 6x32	6	20	—	3.5	10.6	1	Int.	11.3	**620.00**	
Diatal C 10x36	10	12	—	3.5	12.7	1	Int.	14.1	**740.00**	
Diatal Z 6x42	6	22.9	—	3.5	12.7	1.02 (26mm)	Int.	13.4	**785.00**	
Diatal Z 8x56	8	18	—	3.5	13.8	1.02 (26mm)	Int.	17.6	**915.00**	
Diavari C 1.5-4.5	1.5-4.5	72-27	—	3.5	11.8	1	Int.	13.4	**795.00**	
Diavari C 3-9x36	3-9	36-13	—	3.5	11.2	1	Int.	15.2	**830.00**	
Diavari ZA 1.5-6x42	1.5-6	65.5-22.9	—	3.5	12.4	1.18 (30mm)	Int.	18.5	**1,060.00**	
Diavari Z 3-12x56	3-12	27.6-9.9	—	3.2	15.3	1.18 (30mm)	Int.	25.8	**1,210.00**	
ZERO MAG										
Zero Mag	0	—	—	—	5	—	Int.	7	**59.95**	Has optional indirect lighting element to illuminate crosshairs (**$79.95**). For vent. rib, Rem. slug barrel, std. Weaver base, std. 22 dovetail, Hastings slug barrel mounts. From Autumn Tracker Design.

Hunting scopes in general are furnished with a choice of reticle—crosshairs, post with crosshairs, tapered or blunt post, or dot crosshairs, etc. The great majority of target and varmint scopes have medium or fine crosshairs but post or dot reticles may be ordered. W—Windage E—Elevation MOA—Minute of angle or 1" (approx.) at 100 yards, etc.

CAUTION: PRICES CHANGE, CHECK AT GUNSHOP.

SCOPE MOUNTS

Maker, Model, Type	Adjust.	Scopes	Price	Suitable for
ACTION ARMS	No	1" split rings	**From $16.00**	For UZI, Ruger Mk. II, Mini-14, Win. 94, AR-15, Rem. 870, Ithaca 37, and many other popular rifles, handguns. From Action Arms.
AIMPOINT	No	1"	**39.95-79.95**	Mounts/rings for all Aimpoint sights and 1" scopes. For many popular revolvers, auto pistols, shotguns, military-style rifles/carbines, sporting rifles. Most require no gunsmithing. [1]Mounts Aimpoint Laser-dot below barrel; many popular handguns, military-style rifles. Contact Aimpoint.
Laser Mounts[1]	No	1", 30mm	**51.95-59.95**	
AIMTECH				
Handguns				
AMT Auto Mag II, III	No	1"	**50.95-59.95**	Mount scopes, lasers, electronic sights using Weaver-style base. All mounts allow use of iron sights; no gunsmithing. Available in satin black or satin stainless finish. From L&S Technologies, Inc.
Auto Mag IV	No	1"	**59.95**	
Astra revolvers	No	1"	**59.95**	
Beretta/Taurus auto	No	1"	**59.95**	
Browning Buck Mark/Challenger II	No	1"	**50.95**	
Browning Hi-Power	No	1"	**50.95**	
Colt Woodsman/Match Target	No	1"	**50.95**	
Colt Double Eagle	No	1"	**59.95**	
Glock 17, 17L, 19, 22, 23	No	1"	**59.95**	
Govt. 45 Auto	No	1"	**50.95**	
Para-Ordnance 45	No	1"	**59.95**	
Rossi revolvers	No	1"	**59.95**	
Ruger Blackhawk/Super	No	1"	**59.95**	
Ruger Mk I, Mk II	No	1"	**39.95**	
S&W K,L,N frame	No	1"	**59.95**	
S&W Model 41 Target	No	1"	**50.95**	
S&W Model 52 Target	No	1"	**50.95**	
S&W 45, 9mm autos	No	1"	**50.95**	
S&W 422/622/2206	No	1"	**50.95**	
Taurus revolvers	No	1"	**59.95**	
TZ/CZ/P9 9mm	No	1"	**59.95**	
Rifles				
AR-15	No	1"	**21.95**	
Knight MK85	No	1"	**21.95**	
Shotguns				
Benelli Super 90	No	1"	**41.95**	
Ithaca 37	No	1"	**31.95**	
Mossberg 500	No	1"	**31.95**	
Mossberg 835 Ultimag	No	1"	**31.95**	
Mossberg 5500	No	1"	**31.95**	
Remington 870/1100	No	1"	**31.95**	
Winchester 1300/1400	No	1"	**31.95**	
A.R.M.S.				
Beretta AR-70	No	—	**59.00**	From A.R.M.S., Inc.
FN FAL LAR	No	Weaver-type rail	**98.00**	
FN FAL LAR Para.	No	—	**120.00**	
M16A1/A2/AR-15	No	Weaver-type rail	**49.95**	
Swan G-3	No	Weaver-type	**165.00**	
ARMSON				
AR-15[1]	No	O.E.G.	**35.95**	[1]Fastens with one nut. [2]Models 181, 182, 183, 184, etc. [3]Claw mount. [4]Claw mount, bolt cover still easily removable. From Trijicon, Inc.
Mini-14[2]	No	O.E.G.	**49.95**	
H&K[3]	No	O.E.G.	**67.95**	
UZI[4]	No	O.E.G.	**67.95**	
ARMSPORT				
100 Series[1]	No	1" rings. Low, med., high	**12.50**	[1]Weaver-type rings. [2]Weaver-type base; most poular rifles. Made in U.S. From Armsport.
104 22-cal.	No	1"	**12.50**	
201 See-Thru	No	1"	**16.00**	
1-Piece Base[2]	No	—	**6.30**	
2-Piece Base[2]	No	—	**3.15**	
B-SQUARE				
Pistols				[1]Clamp-on, blue finish; stainless finish **$59.95.** [2]Blue finish; stainless finish **$59.95.** [3]Clamp-on, blue; stainless finish **$59.95.** [4]Dovetail; stainless finish **$59.95.** [5]No gunsmithing, no sight removal; blue; stainless finish **$79.95.** [6]Weaver-style rings. Rings not included with Weaver-type bases; stainless finish add $10. [7]NATO Stanag dovetail model, **$99.50.** [8]Blue; stainless **$69.95.** [9]Blue; stainless **$59.95.** [10]Handguard mounts. [11]Receiver mounts. [12]Stainless finish add $10. [13]Under-barrel mount, no gunsmithing. [14]Ejector rod mount. [15]Guide rod mount. [16]Used with B-Square BSL-1 Laser Sight only. Mounts for many shotguns, airguns, military and law enforcement guns also available. **Partial listing of mounts shown here. Contact B-Square for more data.** B-Square makes mounts for the following military rifles: AK47/AKS, Egyptian Hakim, French MAS 1936, M91 Argentine Mauser, Model 98 Brazilian and German Mausers, Model 93, Spanish Mauser (long and short), Model 1916 Mauser, Model 38 and 96 Swedish Mausers, Model 91 Russian (round and octagon receivers), Chinese SKS 56, SMLE No. 1, Mk. III, 1903 Springfield, U.S. 30-cal. Carbine, and others. Those following replace gun's rear sight: AK47/AKS, P14/1917 Enfield, FN49, M1 Garand, M1-A/M14 (no sight removal), SMLE No. 1, Mk III/No. 4 & 5, Mk. 1, 1903/1903-A3 Springfield, Beretta AR 70 (no sight removal).
Beretta/Taurus 92/99[6]	—	1"	**69.95**	
Browning Buck Mark[6]	No	1"	**49.95**	
Colt 45 Auto	E only	1"	**69.95**	
Colt Python/MkIV, 4",6",8"[1,6]	E	1"	**49.95**	
Daisy 717/722 Champion	No	1"	**39.95**	
Dan Wesson Clamp-On[2,6]	E	1"	**49.95**	
Ruger 22 Auto Mono-Mount[3]	No	1"	**49.95**	
Ruger Single-Six[4]	No	1"	**49.95**	
Ruger Blackhawk, Super B'hwk[8]	W&E	1"	**59.95**	
Ruger GP-100[9]	No	1"	**49.95**	
Ruger Redhawk[8]	W&E	1"	**59.95**	
S&W 422[9]	No	1"	**49.95**	
Taurus 66[9]	No	1"	**49.95**	
S&W K, L, N frame[2,6]	No	1"	**49.95**	
T/C Contender (Dovetail Base)	W&E	1"	**39.95**	
Rifles				
Charter AR-7	No	1"	**39.95**	
Mini-14 (dovetail/NATO Stanag)[5,6]	W&E	1"	**69.95**	
M-94 Side Mount	W&E	1"	**49.95**	
RWS, Beeman/FWB Air Rifles	E only	—	**69.95**	
Ruger 77[6]	W&E	1"	**49.95**	
Ruger Ranch/Mini Thirty[6]	W&E	1"	**49.95**	

CAUTION: PRICES CHANGE, CHECK AT GUNSHOP.

SCOPE MOUNTS

Maker, Model, Type	Adjust.	Scopes	Price	Suitable for
B-SQUARE (cont.)				
SMLE Side Mount	W&E	1"	**49.95**	
Rem. Model Seven, 600, 660, etc.[6]	No	1" One-piece base	**9.95**	
Military				
AK-47/AKM/AKS/SKS-56[10]	No	1"	**49.95**	
AK-47, SKS-56[11]	No	1"	**69.95**	
M1-A[7]	W&E	1"	**99.50**	
AR-15/16[7]	W&E	1"	**59.95**	
FN-LAR/FAL[6,7]	E only	1"	**149.50**	
HK-91/93/94[6,7]	E only	1"	**99.50**	
Shotguns[6]				
Browning A-5[6]	No	1"	**49.95**	
Franchi 48/AL[6]	No	1"	**49.95**	
Franchi Elite, Prestige, SPAS[6]	No	1"	**49.95**	
Ithaca 37[6]	No	1"	**39.95**	
Mossberg 500, 712, 5500[6]	No	1"	**39.95**	
Rem. 870/1100 (12 & 20 ga.)[6]	No	1"	**39.95**	
Rem. 870, 1100 (and L.H.)[6]	No	1"	**39.95**	
BSL Laser Mounts				
Scope Tube Clamp[12,13,16]	No	—	**39.95**	
45 Auto[12,13,16]	No	—	**69.95**	
SIG P226[12,13,16]	No	—	**69.95**	
Beretta 92F/Taurus PT99[12,13,16]	No	—	**69.95**	
Browning Hi-Power[13,16]	No	—	**69.95**	
Colt King Cobra, Python, MkV[12,13,16]	No	—	**39.95**	
S&W L Frame[13,16]	No	—	**39.95**	
Taurus 66/69[12,14,16]	No	—	**69.95**	
S&W K,L,N Frames[12,14,16]	No	—	**69.95**	
Beretta 92F/Taurus PT99[12,15,16]	No	—	**79.95**	
Glock 17[15,16]	No	—	**79.95**	
Ruger P85[12,15,16]	No	—	**79.95**	
S&W 4006, 1006[15,16]	No	—	**89.95**	
S&W 5904[15,16]	No	—	**79.95**	
S&W 5906[15,16]	No	—	**89.95**	
BAUSCH & LOMB	No	1"	**62.95**	Rem. 700, 7400/7600, Ruger 77, Browning A-Bolt, Browning BBR, Savage 110, Win. 70, Marlin 336. Contact Bushnell for details.
BEEMAN				All grooved receivers and scope bases on all known air rifles and 22-cal. rimfire rifles (½" to ⅝"—6mm to 15mm).
Double Adjustable	W&E	1"	**29.98**	
Deluxe Ring Mounts	No	1"	**29.98**	
Professional Mounts	W&E	1"	**149.95**	
BOCK				[1]Q.D.; pivots right for removal. For Steyr-Mannlicher, Win. 70, Rem. 700, Mauser 98, Dakota, Sako, Sauer 80, 90. Magnum has extra-wide rings, same price. [2]Heavy-duty claw-type; reversible for front or rear removal. For Steyr-Mannlicher rifles. [3]True claw mount for bolt-action rifles. Also in extended model. For Steyr-Mannlicher, Win. 70, Rem. 700. Also avail. as Gunsmith Bases—bases not drilled or contoured—same price. [4]Extra-wide rings. [5]Fit most 22 rimfires with dovetail receivers. Imported from Germany by Gun South, Inc.
Swing ALK[1]	W&E	1", 26mm, 30mm	**224.00**	
Safari KEMEL[2]	W&E	1", 26mm, 30mm	**149.00**	
Claw KEMKA[3]	W&E	1", 26mm, 30mm	**224.00**	
ProHunter Fixed[4]	No	1", 26mm, 30mm	**95.00**	
Dovetail 22[5]	No	1", 26mm	**59.00**	
BUEHLER				
One Piece (T)[1]	W only	1" split rings, 3 heights	**Complete—83.00**	[1]Most popular models. [2]Sako dovetail receivers. [3]15 models. [4]No drilling & tapping. [5]Aircraft alloy, dyed blue or to match stainless; for Colt Diamondback, Python, Trooper, Ruger Blackhawk, Single-Six, Security-Six, S&W K-frame, Dan Wesson.
		1" split rings, engraved	**Rings only—112.00**	
		26mm split rings, 2 heights	**Rings only—59.00**	
		30mm split rings, 1 height	**Rings only—71.00**	
One Piece Micro Dial (T)[1]	W&E	1" split rings	**Complete—106.00**	
Two Piece (T)[1]	W only	1" split rings	**Complete—83.00**	
Two Piece Dovetail (T)[2]	W only	1" split rings	**Complete—101.75**	
One Piece Pistol (T)[3]	W only	1" split rings	**Complete—83.00**	
One Piece Pistol Stainless (T)[1]	W only	1" stainless rings	**Complete—106.75**	
One Piece Ruger Mini-14 (T)[4]	W only	1" split rings	**Complete—101.75**	
One Piece Pistol M83 Blue[4,5]	W only	1" split rings	**Complete—94.50**	
One Piece Pistol M83 Silver[4,5]	W only	1" stainless rings	**Complete—109.50**	
BURRIS				
Supreme One Piece (T)[1]	W only	1" split rings, 3 heights	**1 piece base—24.95**	[1]Most popular rifles. Universal rings, mounts fit Burris, Universal, Redfield, Leupold and Browning bases. Comparable prices. [2]Browning Standard 22 Auto rifle. [3]Grooved receivers. [4]Universal dovetail; accept Burris, Universal, Redfield, Leupold rings. For Dan Wesson, S&W, Virginian, Ruger Blackhawk, Win. 94. [5]Medium standard front, extension rear, per pair. Low standard front, extension rear, per pair. [6]Mini scopes, scopes with 2" bell, for M77R. [7]Selected rings and bases available with matte Safari or silver finish. [8]For S&W K,L,N frames, Colt Python, Dan Wesson with 6" or longer barrels. [9]For long scope tubes; Rem. 700, Win. 70A, FN.
Trumount Two Piece (T)	W only	1" split rings, 3 heights	**2 piece base—22.95**	
Trumount Two Piece Ext.[9]	W only	1" split rings	**27.95**	
Browning Auto Mount[2]	No	1" split rings	**18.95**	
Rings Mounts[3]	No	1" split rings	**1" rings—17.95**	
L.E.R. Mount Bases[4]	W only	1" split rings	**22.95**	
L.E.R. No Drill-No Tap Bases[4,7,8]	W only	1" split rings	**37.00-41.75**	
Extension Rings[5]	No	1" scopes	**38.95**	
Ruger Ring Mount[6]	W only	1" split rings	**43.95**	
Std. 1"Rings	—	Low, medium, high heights	**31.95**	
Zee Rings	—	Fit Weaver bases; medium and high heights	**26.95**	
BUSHNELL				
Detachable (T) mounts only[1]	W only	1" split rings, uses Weaver base	**Rings—21.95**	[1]Most popular rifles. Includes windage adjustment.
22 mount	No	1" only	**Rings—9.95**	

Maker, Model, Type	Adjust.	Scopes	Price	Suitable for
CAPE OUTFITTERS				
Quick Detachable	No	1" split rings, lever quick detachable	**99.95**	Double rifles; Sauer, Win. Model 70, Rem. 700, Browning Safari, Mauser 98, grooved receiver 22s. All steel; returns to zero. From Cape Outfitters.
CLEARVIEW				
Universal Rings (T)[1]	No	1" split rings	**21.95**	[1]All popular rifles including Sav. 99. Uses Weaver bases. [2]Allows use of open sights. [3]For 22 rimfire rifles with grooved receivers or bases. [4]Fits 13 models. Broadest view area of the type. [5]Side mount for both M94 and M94-375 Big Bore.
Mod. 101, 336[2]	No	1" split rings	**21.95**	
Broad-View[4]	No	1"	**21.95**	
Model 22[3]	No	3/4", 7/8", 1"	**13.95**	
94 Winchester[5]	No	1"	**21.95**	
CONETROL				
Huntur[1]	W only	1", 26mm, 26.5mm solid or split rings, 3 heights	**59.91**	[1]All popular rifles, including metric-drilled foreign guns. Price shown for base, two rings. Matte finish. [2]Gunnur grade has mirror-finished rings, satin-finish base. Price shown for base, two rings. [3]Custum grade has mirror-finished rings and mirror-finished, streamlined base. Price shown for base, two rings. [4]Win. 94, Krag, older split-bridge Mannlicher-Schoenauer, Mini-14, etc. Prices same as above. [5]For all popular guns with integral mounting provision, including Sako, BSA, Ithacagun, Ruger, Tikka, H&K, BRNO—**$29.97-$44.97**—and many others. Also for grooved-receiver rimfires and air rifles. Prices same as above. [6]For XP-100, T/C Contender, Colt SAA, Ruger Blackhawk, S&W. [7]Sculptured two-piece bases as found on fine custom rifles. Price shown is for base alone. Also available unfinished—**$74.91.** [8]30mm rings made in projectionless style, medium height only. Three-ring mount available for T/C Contender pistol in Conetrol's three grades.
Gunnur[2]	W only	1", 26mm, 26.5mm solid or split rings, 3 heights	**74.91**	
Custum[3]	W only	1", 26mm, 26.5mm solid or split rings, 3 heights	**89.91**	
One Piece Side Mount Base[4]	W only	1", 26mm, 26.5mm solid or split rings, 3 heights	—	
Daptar Bases[5]	W only	1", 26mm, 26.5mm solid or split rings, 3 heights	—	
Pistol Bases, 2 or 3-ring[6]	W only	1" scopes	—	
Fluted Bases[7]	W only	Standard Conetrol rings	**99.99**	
30mm Rings[8]	W only	30mm	**49.98-69.96**	
COOPER ARMS RINGS				
Rings for grooved receivers	No	1"	**79.95**	[1]For grooved receivers. [2]30mm **$95.95**; 30mm Double Lever rings for bases **$124.95**. [3]For Kimber and many popular rifles. High and low semi-detachable rings for Kimber grooved receivers or Kimber 89 Squarebridge. Rings fit other popular rifles by using Kimber-style two-piece screw-on bases. Double Lever Q.D. rings in medium height for same applications. All avail. in bright blue, matte blue or stainless. From Cooper Arms.
Double Lever Q.D.[1]	No	1"	**109.95**	
Rings for bases[2]	No	1"	**79.95**	
Scope Mount Bases[3]	No	—	**9.50**	
EAW				
Quick Detachable Top Mount	W&E	1",26mm	**259.99**	Also 30mm rings to fit Burris, Redfield or Leupold-type bases, low and high, **$112.00**; 1" or 26mm rings only, **$85.00** Most popular rifles. Elevation adjusted with variable-height sub-bases for rear ring. Imported by Paul Jaeger, Inc.
	W&E	1"/26mm with front extension ring	**259.99**	
	W&E	30mm	**279.99**	
	W&E	30mm with front extension ring.	**279.99**	
GENTRY				
Feather-Light Rings	No	1", 30mm	**75.00**	One-piece rings in matte blue or matte stainless. Price shown for 1"; 30mm **$100.00.** From David Gentry.
GRIFFIN & HOWE				
Standard Double Lever (S)	No	1" or 26mm split rings.	**305.00**	All popular models (Garand **$215**). All rings **$75.** Top ejection rings available. Price installed for side mount.
HOLDEN				
Wide Ironsighter™	No	1" split rings	**26.95**	[1]Most popular rifles, including Ruger Mini-14, H&R M700, and muzzleloaders. Rings have oval holes to permit use of iron sights. [2]For 1" dia. scopes. [3]For 3/4" or 7/8" dia. scopes. [4]For 1" dia. extended eye relief scopes. [5]702—Browning A-Bolt; 709—Marlin 39A. [6]732—Ruger 77/22 R&RS, No. 1, Ranch Rifle; 777 fits Ruger 77R, RS. Both 732, 777 fit Ruger integral bases. [7]Fits most popular blackpowder rifles; one model for Holden Ironsighter mounts, one for Weaver rings. Adj. rear sight is integral.
Ironsighter Center Fire[1]	No	1" split rings	**26.95**	
Ironsighter S-94	No	1" split rings	**31.95**	
Ironsighter 22-Cal. Rimfire				
Model #500[2]	No	1" split rings	**14.95**	
Model #600[3]	No	7/8" split rings also fits 3/4"	**14.95**	
Series #700[5]	No	1" split rings	**26.95**	
Model 732, 777[6]	No	1" split rings	**56.95**	
Ironsighter Handguns[4]	No	1" split rings	**31.95-56.95**	
Blackpowder Mount[7]	No	1"	**26.95-56.95**	
KRIS MOUNTS				
Side-Saddle[1]	No	1", 26mm split rings	**12.98**	[1]One-piece mount for Win. 94. [2]Most popular rifles and Ruger. [3]Blackhawk revolver. Mounts have oval hole to permit use of iron sights.
Two Piece (T)[2]	No	1", 26mm split rings	**8.98**	
One Piece (T)[3]	No	1", 26mm split rings	**12.98**	
KWIK MOUNT				
Shotgun Mount	No	1", laser or red dot device	**49.95**	Wrap-around design; no gunsmithing required. Models for Browning BPS, A-5 12-ga., Sweet 16, 20, Rem. 870/1100 (LTW and L.H.), S&W 916, Mossberg 500, Ithaca 37 & 51 12-ga., S&W 1000/3000, Win. 1400. From KenPatable Ent.
KWIK-SITE				
KS-See-Thru[1]	No	1"	**21.95**	[1]Most rifles. Allows use of iron sights. [2]22-cal. rifles with grooved receivers. Allows use of iron sights. [3]Model 94, 94 Big Bore. No drilling or tapping. Also in adjustble model **$49.95.** [4]Most rifles. One-piece solid construction. Use on Kwik-Site bases. 32mm obj. lens or larger. [5]Non-see-through model; for grooved receivers. [6]Allows Mag Lite or C or D, Mini Mag Lites to be mounted atop See-Thru mounts. [7]Fits any Redfield, Tasco, Weaver or universal-style Kwik-Site dovetail base. Bright blue, black matte or satin finish. Standard, high heights.
KS-22 See-Thru[2]	No	1"	**18.95**	
KS-W94[3]	No	1"	**30.95**	
Imperial Bench Rest	No	1"	**30.95**	
KSM Bench Rest[4]	No	1"	**30.95**	
KS-WEV	No	1"	**21.95**	
KS-WEV-HIGH	No	1"	**21.95**	
KS-T22 1"[5]	No	1"	**18.95**	
KS-FL Flashlite[6]	No	Mini or C cell flashlight	**49.95**	
KS-T88[7]	No	1", 30mm	**9.75**	
Combo Bases & Rings	No	1"	**26.75**	

SCOPE MOUNTS

Maker, Model, Type	Adjust.	Scopes	Price	Suitable for
LASER AIM	No	Laser Aim	**29.00-69.00**	Mounts Laser Aim above or below barrel. Avail. for most popular handguns, rifles, shotguns, including militaries. From Emerging Technologies, Inc.
LASERSIGHT	No	LS45 only	**29.95-149.00**	For the LS45 Lasersight. Allows LS45 to be mounted alongside any 1" scope. Universal adapter attaches to any full-length Weaver-type base. For most popular military-type rifles, Mossberg, Rem. shotguns, Python, Desert Eagle, S&W N frame, Colt 45ACP. From Imatronic Lasersight.
LEUPOLD				
Alaskan Rings[10]	—	7/8"	**32.00**	[1]Rev. front and rear combinations; matte finish **$24**. [2]Avail. polished, matte or silver (low, med. only) finish. [3]Base and two rings; Casull, Ruger, S&W, T/C; add $5.00 for silver finish. [4]Rem. 700, Win. 70-type actions. [5]For Ruger No. 1, 77, 77/22; interchangeable with Ruger units. [6]For dovetailed rimfire rifles. [7]Sako; high, medium, low. [8]Must be drilled, tapped for each action. [9]Unfinished bottom, top completed; sold singly. [10]Fit all Leupold STD one-, two-piece bases. [11]Most dovetail-receiver 22s. Matte finish **$32.00**.
STD Bases[1]	W only	One- or two-piece bases	**22.10**	
STD Rings[2]	—	1" super low, low, medium, high	**32.00**	
STD Handgun mounts[3]	No	—	**56.40**	
Dual Dovetail Bases[1,4]	No	—	**22.10**	
Dual Dovetail Rings[11]	—	1", super low, low	**32.00**	
Ring Mounts[5,6,7]	No	7/8", 1"	**81.10**	
22 Rimfire[11]	No	7/8", 1"	**60.00**	
Gunmaker Base[8]	W only	1"	**14.60**	
Gunmaker Ring Blanks[9]	—	1"	**21.10**	
LEATHERWOOD				
Bridge Bases[1]	No	ART II or all dovetail rings	**15.00**	[1]Many popular bolt actions. Mounts accept Weaver or dovetail-type rings. From North American Specialties.
M1A/M-14 Q.D.	No	ART II or all dovetail rings	**105.00**	
AR-15/M-16 Base	No	ART II or all dovetail rings	**25.00**	
FN-FAL Base	No	ART II or all dovetail rings	**100.00**	
FN Para. Base	No	ART II or all dovetail rings	**110.00**	
Steyr SSG Base	No	ART II or all dovetail rings	**55.00**	
MARLIN				
One Piece QD (T)	No	1" split rings	**14.95**	Most Marlin lever actions.
MILLETT				
Black Onyx Smooth	—	1", low, medium, high	**29.65**	Rem. 40X, 700, 722, 725, Ruger 77 (round top), Weatherby, FN Mauser, FN Brownings, Colt 57, Interarms Mark X, Parker-Hale, Sako (round receiver), many others. [1]Fits Win. M70, 70XTR, 670, Browning BBR, BAR, BLR, A-Bolt, Rem. 7400/7600, Four, Six, Marlin 336, Win. 94 A.E., Sav. 110. [2]To fit Weaver-type bases. [3]Engraved. Smooth **$30.65**. [4]For Rem. 870, 1100; smooth. [5]Two and three-ring sets for Colt Python, Trooper, Diamondback, Peacekeeper, Dan Wesson, Ruger Redhawk, Super Redhawk. [6]Turn-in bases and Weaver-style for most popular rifles and T/C Contender, XP-100 pistols. [7]Both Weaver and turn-in styles; three heights. [8]Med. or high; ext. front—std. rear, ext. rear—std. front, ext. front—ext. rear; **$38.95** for double extension. From Millett Sights.
Chaparral Engraved	—	engraved	**43.95**	
One-Piece Bases[6]	Yes	1"	**23.95**	
Universal Two-Piece Bases				
700 Series	W only	Two-piece bases	**23.95**	
FN Series	W only	Two-piece bases	**23.95**	
70 Series[1]	W only	1", two-piece bases	**23.95**	
Angle-Loc Rings[2]	W only	1", low, medium, high	**30.65-44.95**	
Ruger 77 Rings[3]	—	1"	**44.95**	
Shotgun Rings[4]	—	1"	**26.95**	
Handgun Bases, Rings[5]	—	1"	**32.95-61.35**	
30mm Rings[7]	—	30mm	**35.95**	
Extension Rings[8]	—	1"	**33.95**	
RAM-LINE				
Mini-14 Mount	Yes	1"	**24.97**	No drilling or tapping. Use std. dovetail rings. Has built-in shell deflector. Made of solid black polymer. From Ram-Line, Inc.
REDFIELD				
JR-SR (T)[1]	W only	3/4", 1", 26mm, 30mm	**JR—22.95-52.95** **SR—22.95-23.95**	[1]Low, med & high, split rings. Reversible extension front rings for 1". 2-piece bases for Sako. Colt Sauer bases **$39.85**. Med. Top Access JR rings nickel-plated, **$29.95**. SR two-piece ABN mount nickel-plated, **$23.95**. [2]Split rings for grooved 22s. See-Thru mounts **$16.95**. [3]Used with MP scopes for: S&W K, L or N frame, XP-100, T/C Contender, Ruger receivers. [4]For Ruger Model 77 rifles, medium and high; medium only for M77/22. [5]For Model 77. Also in matte finish, **$44.95**. [6]Nickel-plated, **$33.95**. [7]For 22 rifles with grooved receivers. Fits all radius dovetails.
Ring (T)[2]	No	3/4" and 1"	**27.95**	
Three-Ring Pistol System SMP[3]	No	1" split rings (three)	**58.95-65.95**	
Midline Base & Rings[4]	No	1", low, medium, high	**13.95**	
Widefield See-Thru Mounts	No	1"	**16.95**	
Ruger Rings[4]	No	1", med., high	**35.95**	
Ruger 30mm[5]	No	1"	**46.95**	
Midline Ext. Rings	No	1"	**18.95**	
Steel "WS" Rings[6]	W	1", 30mm	**26.95**	
Steel 22 Ring Mount, Base[7]	No	3/4", 1"	**13.95-29.95**	
S&K				
Insta-Mount (T) bases and rings[1]	W only	Use S&K rings only	**25.00-99.00**	[1]1903, A3, M1 Carbine, Lee Enfield #1, Mk. III, #4, #5, M1917, M98 Mauser, FN Auto, AR-15, AR-180, M-14, M-1, Ger. K-43, Mini-14, M1-A, Krag, AKM, AK-47, Win. 94, SKS Type 56, Daewoo, H&K. [2]Most popular rifles already drilled and tapped. Horizontally and vertically split rings, matte or high gloss.
Conventional rings and bases[2]	W only	1" split rings	**From 50.00**	
Skulptured Bases, Rings[2]	W only	1", 26mm, 30mm	**From 50.00**	
SSK INDUSTRIES				
T'SOB	No	1"	**55.00-145.00**	Custom installation using from two to four rings (included). For T/C Contender, most 22 auto pistols, Ruger and other S.A. revolvers, Ruger, Dan Wesson, S&W, Colt DA revolvers. Black or white finish. Uses Kimber rings in two- or three-ring sets. In blue or SSK Khrome. For T/C Contender or most popular revolvers. Standard, non-detachable model also available, from **$125.00**.
Quick Detachable	No	1"	**From 160.00**	
SAKO				
QD Dovetail	W only	1" only	**46.50-54.50**	Sako, or any rifle using Sako action, 3 heights available. Stoeger, importer.
SIMMONS				
1460[1]	No	1"	**17.95**	
1462[2]	No	1"	**17.95**	

CAUTION: PRICES CHANGE, CHECK AT GUNSHOP.

SCOPE MOUNTS

Maker, Model, Type	Adjust.	Scopes	Price	Suitable for
SIMMONS (cont.)				
1465[3]	No	1"	17.95	[1]Browning Auto. [2]Marlin 336, 444, 36, 62, Glenfield 30. [3]Rem. 700 SA/Seven. [4]Rem. 700 L.A. [5]Win. 70A. [6]Sav. 110. [7]Rem. 870, 1100, 11-87. [8]Rem. Seven, 700 LA/SA; two-piece, med. rings. [9]Rem. Four, Six, 7400/7600, two-piece, med. rings. [10]Win. 70A LA/SA, two-piece, med. rings. [11]Sav. 110, two-piece, med. rings. Contact Simmons Outdoor Corp. for complete list of applications.
1466[4]	No	1"	17.95	
1469[5]	No	1"	17.95	
1471[6]	No	1"	17.95	
21000[7]	No	1"	38.95	
SRB01[8]	No	1"	43.95	
SRB02[9]	No	1"	43.95	
SRB04[10]	No	1"	43.95	
SRB08[11]	No	1"	43.95	
TASCO				
World Class				[1]Steel; low, high only; also high-profile see-through; fit Tasco, Weaver, other universal bases; black gloss or satin chrome. [2]Low, high only; for Redhawk and Super, No.1, Mini-14 & Thirty, 77, 77/22; blue or stainless. [3]Low, med., high; ⅜" grooved receivers; black or satin chrome. [4]Low, med., high; for Tasco W.C. bases, some dovetail; black gloss only. [5]For Desert Eagle pistols, 22s, air rifles with deep dovetails. [6]Low, med., high; black gloss, matte satin chrome; also Traditional Ringsets **$31.00** (1"), **$42.00** (26mm), **$53.00** (30mm). [7]For popular rifles and shotguns; one-piece, two-piece, Q.D., long and short action, extension. Handgun bases have w&e adj. [8]For many popular handguns, blue or stainless. From Tasco.
Universal "W" Ringmount[1]	No	1", 30mm	34.00-64.00	
Ruger[2]	No	1", 30mm	38.00-58.00	
22, Air Rifle[3]	No	1", 30mm	16.00-32.00	
Center-Fire Ringmount[4]	No	1", 26mm, 30mm	18.40-38.80	
Desert Eagle Ringmount[5]	No	1", 30mm	25.60-36.00	
Ringsets[6]	No	1", 26mm, 30mm	26.00-50.00	
Bases[7]	Yes	—	26.00-40.00	
Pro-Mount Handgun Base[8]	No	—	11.00-37.00	
THOMPSON/CENTER				
Contender 9746[1]	No	T/C Lobo	17.00	[1]All Contenders except vent. rib. [2]T/C rail mount scopes; all Contenders except vent. rib. [3]All S&W K and Combat Masterpiece, Hi-Way Patrolman, Outdoorsman, 22 Jet, 45 Target 1955. Requires drilling, tapping. [4]Blackhawk, Super Blackhawk, Super Single-Six. Requires drilling, tapping. [5]45 or 50 cal.; replaces rear sight. [6]Rail mount scopes; 54-cal. Hawken, 50, 54, 56-cal. Renegade. Replaces rear sight. [7]Cherokee 32 or 45 cal., Seneca 36 or 45 cal. Replaces rear sight. Carbine mount #9743 for Short Tube scope #8640, **$13.75**. [8]For T/C "Short Tube" scope #8630; matte blue; also #9710 base for std. scope; no gunsmithing. [9]Also silver finish, **$46.50**. [10]For Contender Carbine, pistol, Scout; silver finish, **$38.00**. [11]For Contender pistol, Carbine, Scout, all M/L long guns.
Contender 9741[2]	No	2½, 4 RP	17.00	
Contender 7410	No	Bushnell Phantom, 1.3-2.5x	17.00	
S&W 9747[3]	No	Lobo or RP	17.00	
Ruger 9748[4]	No	Lobo or RP	17.00	
Hawken 9749[5]	No	Lobo or RP	17.00	
Hawken/Renegade 9754[6]	No	Lobo or RP	17.00	
Cherokee/Seneca 9756[7]	No	Lobo or RP	17.00	
New Englander 9757	No	Lobo or RP	17.00	
TCR '87 Base 9760[8]	Yes	—	38.00	
Detachable Rings[9]	—	1"	46.50	
T/C Base[10]	Yes	1"	38.00	
Quick Release System[11]	No	1"	Rings 48.00 Base 24.50	
UNERTL				
¼ Click[1]	Yes	¾", 1" target scopes	Per set 115.00	[1]Unertl target or varmint scopes. Posa or standard mounts, less bases.
WEAVER				[1]Nearly all modern rifles. Low, med., high. 1" extension **$30.96**. 1" med. stainless steel **$40.53**. [2]Nearly all modern rifles, shotguns. [3]Most modern big bore rifles; std., high. [4]22s with ⅜" grooved receivers. [5]Nearly all modern rifles. 1" See-Thru extension **$30.96**. [6]Most modern big bore rifles. [7]No drilling, tapping. For Colt Python, Trooper, 357, Officer's Model, Ruger Blackhawk & Super, Mini-14, Security-Six, 22 auto pistols, Redhawk, Blackhawk SRM 357, S&W current K, L with adj. sights. [8]For Rem. 870, 1100, 11-87, Browning A-5, BPS, Ithaca 37, 87, Beretta A303, Winchester 1200-1500, Mossberg 500. [9]For some popular sporting rifles. [10]Dovetail design mount for Rem. 700, Win. 70, FN Mauser, low, med., high rings; std., extension bases. From Weaver.
Detachable Mounts				
Top Mount[1]	No	⅞",, 1"	25.49-26.51	
Side Mount[2]	No	1", 1" Long	28.02-33.13	
Pivot Mount[3]	No	1"	35.91	
Tip-Off Mount[4]	No	⅞", 1"	20.40-26.00	
		1"	26.00	
See-Thru Mount				
Traditional[6]	No	1"	NA	
Symmetrical[6]	No	1"	NA	
Detachable[5]	No	1"	26.51	
Tip-Off[4]	No	1", ⅞"	26.51	
Pro View[6]	No	1"	NA	
Mount Base System[7]				
Blue Finish	No	1"	68.93	
Stainless Finish	No	1"	96.44	
Shotgun Converta-Mount System[8]	No	1"	68.93	
Rifle Mount System[9]	No	1"	30.58	
Paramount Mount Systems[10]				
Bases, pair	Yes	1"	23.69	
Rings, pair	No	1"	30.76	
WIDEVIEW				
Premium 94 Angle Eject	No	1"	24.00	[1]For Weaver-type bases. Models for many popular rifles. Low ring, high ring and grooved receiver types. From Wideview Scope Mount Corp.
Premium See-Thru	No	1"	22.00	
22 Premium See-Thru	No	¾", 1"	16.00	
Universal Ring Angle Cut	No	1"	24.00	
Universal Ring Straight Cut	No	1"	22.00	
Solid Mounts				
Lo Ring Solid[1]	No	1"	16.00	
Hi Ring Solid[1]	No	1"	16.00	
22 Grooved Receiver	No	1"	16.00	
94 Side Mount	No	1"	26.00	
WILLIAMS				
Sidemount with HCO Rings[1]	No	1", split or extension rings.	62.40	[1]Most rifles, Br. S.M.L.E. (round rec.) **$7.80** extra. [2]Most rifles including Win. 94 Big Bore. [3]Many modern rifles. [4]No drilling, tapping required; heat treated alloy. For Ruger Blackhawk, Super Blackhawk, Redhawk; S&W N frame, M29 with 10⅝" barrel (**$52.60**); Colt Python, King Cobra; Ruger MkII Bull Barrel; Streamline Top Mount for T/C Contender (**$26.05**), High Top Mount with sub-base (**$43.70**).
Sidemount, offset rings[2]	No	Same	51.40	
Sight-Thru Mounts[3]	No	1", ⅞" sleeves	21.00	
Streamline Mounts	No	1" (bases form rings).	21.00	
Guideline Handgun[4]	No	1" split rings.	63.95	
YORK				
M-1 Garand	Yes	1"	39.95	Centers scope over the action. No drilling, tapping or gunsmithing. Uses standard dovetail rings. From York M-1 Conversions.

(S)—Side Mount (T)—Top Mount; 22mm=.866"; 25.4mm=1.024"; 26.5mm=1.045"; 30mm=1.81"

DIRECTORY OF THE ARMS TRADE

The **Product Directory** contains the same product categories as in past editions of Guns Illustrated, plus two new ones: **Computer Software—Ballistics** and **Shooting/Training Schools.** Each category lists the manufacturers' names in alphabetical order.

The **Manufacturers' Directory** lists alphabetically the manufacturers, their addresses and phone numbers.

INDEX TO THE DIRECTORY OF THE ARMS TRADE

PRODUCT DIRECTORY

AMMUNITION (Commercial)

Action Ammo Ltd.
ACTIV Industries, Inc.
AFSCO Ammunition
A&M Waterfowl, Inc.
A-Square Co., Inc.
American Ballistics Company, Inc. (9mm subsonic, ball ammo)
Atlanta Discount Ammo
Black Hills Ammunition
Blount Sporting Equipment Division
CBC
CCI
Cor-Bon Bullet and Ammo Co.
Crosman Airguns
Daisy Manufacturing Co.
Denver Bullets, Inc.
Dynamit Nobel-RWS, Inc.
Eldorado Cartridge Corp.
Eley Ltd.
Elite Ammunition
Estate Cartridge, Inc.
kFederal Cartridge Co.
Frontier Cartridge Division
Hansen Cartridge Co.
Horizons Unlimited
Hornady Manufacturing Co.
ICI-America
Israel Military Industries Ltd. (IMI)
Kent Cartridge Mfg. Co. Ltd., The
Lapua Ltd.
M&D Munitions Ltd.
Maionchi - L.M.I.
Men - Metallwerk Elisenhuete GmbH
New England Ammunition Company
Omark Industries
Palcher Ammunition
Pony Express Reloaders
P.P.C. Corp.
Precision Prods. of Wash., Inc.
Pro Load Ammunition, Inc.
Prometheus/Titan Black
Remington Arms Co.
Rocky Fork Enterprises (obsolete & hard to find)
RWS
Southern Ammunition Co., Inc.
Speer
Star Reloading Co., Inc.
3-D Ammunition & Bullets
United States Ammunition Co., Inc.
Weatherby, Inc.
Winchester Div., Olin Corp.
Zero Ammunition Co., Inc.

AMMUNITION (Custom)

AFSCO Ammunition
Allred Bullet Co.
A-Square Co., Inc.
Atlanta Discount Ammo
Ballistica Maximus North
Ballistica Maximus South
BE, Inc.
B.E.L.L.
Black Mountain Bullets
Buffalo Bullet Co., Inc. (muzzle-loading bullets)
Cartridge Co., C.W.
Cartridges Unlimited (British Express; metric; U.S.)
Cor-Bon, Inc. (bullets)
Country Armourer, The
Cumberland Arms
Custom Hunting Ammo & Arms
Custom Tackle & Ammo
Eldorado Cartridge Corp.
Elite Ammunition
Elko Arms
Ellis Sport Shop, E.W.
Epps (Orillia) Northern Ltd., Ellwood
Estate Cartridge, Inc. (shotshell)
First Distributors, Inc., Jack
Freedom Arms, Inc.
Gammog, Gregory B. Gally
Gonzalez, Ramon B.
"Gramps" Antique Cartridges
Grizzly Bullets
Hardin Specialty Distributors
Hindman, Ace
Jensen's Custom Ammunition
Jett & Co., Inc.
Keeler, R.H. (armor piercing for police and military only)
Kent Cartridge Mfg. Co. Ltd., The
L.A.R. Manufacturing, Inc.
Lindsley Arms Cartridge Co., Inc.
Lomont Precision Bullets (cast only)
Mack's Sport Shop
MagSafe Ammo Co.
Markell Incorporated
McConnellstown Reloading & Cast Bullets, Inc.
McMurdo, Lynn (custom 50-cal. bullets)
M&D Munitions Ltd.
Mountain Arms
Mountain South
NAI/Ballistek (cases for 25-20 Win. single shot)
North American Arms
Palcher Ammunition
Patriot Mfg. & Sales
Personal Protection Systems, Ltd. (high-performance handgun loads)
Pony Express Reloaders
Precision Munitions, Inc. (reloaded ammo)
Professional Hunter Supplies
R.I.S. Co., Inc. (custom match bullets 50-cal. BMG)
Sailer, Anthony F.
Sanders Custom Gun Service
Spence, George W. (boxer-primed cartridges)
SSK Industries
State Arms Gun Co.
3-D Ammunition & Bullets (reloaded police ammo)
3-Ten Corp. (44 magnum bulleted shot loads; handgun)
Thunderbird Cartridge Co., Inc.
Trophy Bonded Bullets, Inc.
Vitt/Boos
Wardrop, R.A.
Widener's Reloading & Shooting Supply, Inc.
Wildey, Inc.
Worthy Products, Inc.
Zero Ammunition Co., Inc.

AMMUNITION (Foreign)

Action Arms Ltd.
AFSCO Ammunition
Atlanta Discount Ammo
Beeman Precision Arms, Inc. (air)
Brenneke KG, Wilhelm
Champion's Choice, Inc. (Lapua ammo)
Cheddite France S.A.
ChinaSports, Inc.
CBC
Dynamit Nobel-RWS, Inc. (RWS, Geco, Rottweil)
Eley Ltd.
Fabrique Nationale Nouvelle Herstal S.A.
Fiocchi of America, Inc.
Hansen Cartridge Co.
Hirtenberger Patronen-, Zundhutchen- & Metallwarenfabrik
Israel Military Industries Ltd. (IMI)
Jager, Inc., Paul (RWS centerfire ammo)
Kent Cartridge Mfg. Co. Ltd., The
Lapua Ltd.
Maionchi - L.M.I.
PMC-Eldorado Cartridge Co.
Pragotrade
PTK International
RWS
Samco Global Arms, Inc.

AMMUNITION COMPONENTS—BULLETS, POWDER, PRIMERS

Accuracy Unlimited (Game Buster Bullet)
Accurate Arms Co., Inc. (powders)
Acme Custom Bullets
Allred Bullet Co. (custom bullets)
American Bullets
A-Square Co., Inc. (custom bullets; brass)
American Products Co. (12-ga. shot wad)
Armfield Custom Bullets
Atlanta Discount Ammo
Ballard Built Custom Bullets
Ballistic Prods., Inc. (shotgun powders, primers)
Barnes Bullets, Inc.
B.E.L.L.
Berger Bullets (custom 22, 6mm benchrest bullets)
Bergman and Williams (copper tube 308 custom bullets; lead wire in all sizes)
Bertram Bullet Co.
Bitterroot Bullet Co.
Black Mountain Bullets (custom Fluid King match bullets)
Blount Sporting Equipment Division
Blue Mountain Bullets (custom)
Bor-Clear Bullets
Brenneke KG, Wilhelm
Bruno Bullets Shooters Supply (22, 6mm benchrest bullets)
Buffalo Bullet Co., Inc.
Buffalo Rock Shooters Supply
Bull-X, Inc.
Calhoon Mfg., James
Cartridges Unlimited (obsolete cast bullets)
CCI
CFVentures ("soft gas checks": wax wads for metallic cartridges)
Cheddite France S.A. (primed cartridges and cases)
CheVron Bullets
Colorado Sutlers Arsenal
CBC
Competition Bullets, Inc.
Cooper-Woodward
Corbin Mfg. & Supply, Inc. (bullets)
Cor-Bon, Inc. (375, 44, 45 solid brass partition bullets)
Creative Cartridge Co.
Denver Bullets, Inc. (hardcast bullets)
DKT, Inc. (bullets)
DuPont
Dynamit Nobel-RWS, Inc. (RWS percussion caps)
Eldorado Cartridge Corp.
Eldorado Custom Shop
Excaliber Wax, Inc. (wax bullets)
Federal Cartridge Co. (primers)
Fiocchi of America, Inc. (primers; shotshell cases)
Fowler Bullets (benchrest bullets)
Freedom Arms, Inc.
Glaser Safety Slug, Inc.
GOEX, Inc. (blackpowder)
Golden Powder International Sales, Inc. (Golden Powder/blackpowder)
Green Bay Bullets (cast lead bullets)
Grizzly Bullets (custom)
Gun City
Hardin Specialty Distr. (casings, 7.63mm/44 Automag)
Harris Enterprises (cust. bullets)
Harrison Bullet Works, (custom swaged 41 magnum bullets)
Hart & Son, Inc., Robert W.
Hawk Laboratories, Inc. (jacketed bullets—all calibers)
Hercules, Inc. (smokeless powder)
Hodgdon Powder Co., Inc. (smokeless, Pyrodex and blackpowder)
Hornady Mfg. Co.
Hull, Lynn E.
Huntington Die Specialties
IMR Powder Co. (smokeless powders only)
Israel Military Industries Ltd. (IMI)
Jensen Bullets
Jaro Manuf. (bullets)
Jensen's Custom Ammunition
Kent Cartridge Mfg. Co. Ltd., The
Kodiak Custom Bullets
Lage Uniwad, Inc.
Lane Bullets (custom cast handgun bullets)
Lachaussee S.A.
Lapua Ltd.
Lindsley Arms Cartridge Co., Inc. (brass)
Ljutic Industries, Inc. (Mono-wads)
Lomont Precision Bullets (custom cast bullets)
Mack's Sport Shop (custom bullets)
Magnus Bullet Co., Inc.
MagSafe Ammo Co. (controlled core bullets for reloading)
Maionchi - L.M.I.
Marple & Associates, Dick (hulls only)
Mayville Engineering Co. (non-toxic steel shot kits)
McConnellstown Reloading & Cast Bullets, Inc.
McMurdo, Lynn (50-cal. custom bullets)
M&D Munitions Ltd.
Metallic Casting & Copper Corp. (MCC) (cast bullets)
Michael's Antiques (Balle Blondeau)
Midway Arms, Inc.
MoLoc Bullets
Mountain Arms
Mushroom Express Bullet Co. (ML bullets only)
Necromancer Industries, Inc.
NORMA
Northern Precision Custom Swaged Bullets (.416)
Nosler Bullets, Inc.
O'Connor Rifle Products Co., Ltd. (steelhead cartridge cases)
Old Western Scrounger, Inc.
Omark
Orion Bullets (partitioned, bonded bullets)
Patriot Manufacturing & Sales (custom bullets)
Pattern Control (plastic wads)
PMC-Eldorado Cartridge Co.
Polywad, Inc. (Spred-Rs for shotshells)
Pomeroy, Robert (formed cases, obsolete cases, bullets)
Pony Express Reloaders
Precision Components & Guns
Precision Munitions, Inc. (cast bullets)
Precision Reloading, Inc.
Professional Hunter Supplies (408, 375, 308, 510 custom bullets)
Pyrodex (blackpowder substitute)
Reardon Products (dry-lube powder)
Remington Arms Co.
Renner Co., R.J. (rubber bullets)
Rolston, Fred, Jr. (cast bullets only)
Rossi S.A. Metalurgica E Municoes, Amadeo
Rubright Bullets (custom 22 & 6mm benchrest bullets)
Sandia Die & Cartridge
Scot Powder Co. (smokeless powder)
Shappy Bullets (swaged and cast lead bullets)
Sierra Bullets, Inc. (jacketed rifle and handgun bullets)
Southern Ammunition Co., Inc.
Speer Products
Sport Flite Mfg., Inc. (zinc bases, lead wire)

SSK Industries
Star Reloading Co., Inc. (bullets)
Stevi Machine, Inc. (cases)
Swift Bullet Co. (375 big game, 224 custom)
Taracorp Industries (Lawrence Brand lead shot)
3-D Ammunition & Bullets
Thompson Bullet Lube
Thompson Precision (bullets)
Thunderbird Cartridge Co., Inc. (powder)
TMI Products
Trophy Bonded Bullets, Inc. (big game 458, 308, 375 bonded cust. bullets only)
True Flight Bullet Co. (Tru Flight bullets)
Tucson Mold, Inc.
United States Ammunition Co. (bullets)
Vihtavuori Oy
Vitt/Boos (Aerodynamic shotgun slug, 12-ga. only)
Warren Muzzleloading Co., Inc.
Watson Trophy Match Bullets, Ed (22, 6mm custom benchrest bullets)
Widener's Reloading & Shooting
Wildey, Inc.
Winchester Div., Olin Corp.
Windjammer Tournament Wads, Inc. (shotshell wads)
Woodland Bullets (bullets)
Worthy Products, Inc. (slug loads)
X-Ring Rubber Bullets
Zero Ammunition, Inc.

ANTIQUE ARMS DEALERS

Ad Hominem
Air Rifle Center (airguns only)
Ammunition Consulting Services, Inc.
Antique Arms Co.
Aplan, James O.
Beeman Precision Arms, Inc. (airguns only)
Bondini Paolo
Boggs, Wm.
British Arms Co. Ltd.
Buckskin Machine Works
Can Am Enterprises
Cannavaro, Brian V.
Cape Outfitters
Century Intl. Arms, Inc.
Clements Handicrafts Unltd., Chas
Colonial Repair (mainly restorations)
Condon, Inc., David
Corry, John (English guns)
Dixie Gun Works, Inc.
Dixon Muzzleloading Shop, Inc.
Dyson & Son Ltd., Peter (accoutrements for ant. gun coll.; custom- and machine-made)
Ed's Gun House
Epps (Orillia) Northern Ltd., Ellwood
Fagan & Co., William
First Distributors, Inc., Jack
Flayderman & Co., N.
Flintlock Muzzle Loading Gun Shop, The
Frielich, Robert S.
Fulmer Antique Firearms, Chet
Glass, Herb
Goergen, James
Griffin's Guns & Antiques
Guncraft Sports, Inc.
Hallowell & Co.
Hansen & Co.
Hansen Cartridge Company
Kelley's
Kopec Ent., John A.
Lever Arms Serv. Ltd.
Liberty Antique Gunworks
Log Cabin Sport Shop
Lone Pine Trading Post
Markell Incorporated
McKee, Arthur (Rem. double shotguns)
Mendez, John A.
Michael's Antiques
Museum of Historical Arms
Muzzleloaders Etc., Inc.
Navy Arms Co.
New Orleans Arms Co.
Old Western Scrounger, Inc.
Pioneer Guns
Pony Express Sport Shop, Inc.
Retting, Inc., Martin B.
Rutgers Gun & Boat Center
San Francisco Gun Exch.
Safari Outfitters Ltd.
Semmer, Charles
Sherwood Intl. Export Corp.
S&S Firearms
Steves House of Guns
Stott's Creek Armory, Inc.
Track of the Wolf, Inc.
Trail Guns Armory
Ward & Van Valkenburg
Wayne, James
Wiest, M.C.
Yearout, Lewis

APPRAISERS, GUNS, ETC.

Ad Hominem
Ahlman's, Inc.
Air Rifle Center (airguns only)
Ammunition Consulting Serv., Inc.
Aplan, James O.
Armoury, Inc., The
Arms
Beeman Precision Arms, Inc. (airguns only)
Bess, Gordon
Betz, Harold A.
Busani, Leo
Butterfield & Butterfield
Camilli, Lou
Chadick's Ltd.
Cape Outfitters
Christie's East
Christopher Firearms Co., Inc., E.
Clements, Chas
Condon, Inc., David
Custom Tackle & Ammo
Dilliott Gunsmithing, Inc.
Dixon Muzzleloading Shop, Inc.
D.O.C. Specialists
Ed's Gun House
Ellis Sport Shop, E.W.
Epps (Orillia) Northern Ltd., Ellwood
Eversull & Co., Inc., K.
Fagan & Co., W.
Flayderman & Co., Inc., N.
Forgett, Valmore J., Jr.
Frederick Gun Shop
Goergen, James
Gonzalez, Ramon B.
Goodwin, Fred
"Gramps" Antique Cartridges
Greenwald, Leon E."Bud"
Griffin & Howe
Guncraft Sports, Inc.
Hallowell & Co.
Hansen & Co.
Hansen Cartridge Company
Holland, Dick
Hughes, Steven Dodd
Idaho Ammunition Service (ammunition)
Irwin, Campbell H.
Jonas, Jack H. (animal trophies)
Kelley's
Kopec Ent., John A. (SA Colt only)
Liberty Antique Gunworks
Lone Pine Trading Post
Markell Incorporated
Martin, Elwyn H.
Mazur Restoration, Pete
Miller Trading Co.
Museum of Historical Arms, Inc., The
New England Arms Co.
Orvis Co., Inc., The
Paragon Sales, Inc.
Perazzi USA, Inc.
Pioneer Guns
Pony Express Sport Shop, Inc.
Rahn Gun Works, Inc.
Richards, John
Riggs, Jim
Sarco, Inc.
Shooting Gallery, The
Storey, Dale
Ten-Ring Precision, Inc.
Ulrich, Doc & Bud
Tillinghast, James C.
Unick's Gunsmithing
Wayne, James
Wells Ltd., R.A.
Whildin & Sons, Ltd., E.H.
Wiest, M.C.
Winchester Sutler, Inc.
Wisner's Gun Shop, Inc.
Yearout, Lewis

AUCTIONEERS, GUNS, ETC.

Ammunition Consulting Serv., Inc.
Bourne Co., Inc., Richard A.
Butterfield & Butterfield
Christie's East
Fagan & Co., W.
Goodwin, Fred (Silver Ridge Gun Shop)
Kelley's
"Little John's" Antique Arms
Parke-Bernet
Sotheby's
Tillinghast, James C.

BOOKS (ARMS), Publishers and Dealers

Armory Publications
Arms & Armour Press Ltd.
Beeman Precision Arms, Inc. (airguns only)
Blacksmith Corp.
Blacktail Mountain Books
Brownells, Inc.
DBI Books, Inc.
DeHaas, Mark
Flores Publications, J.
Fortress Publications, Inc.
Guncraft Books
Gun Hunter Books
Gun Room Press, The
Gunnerman Books
Handgun Press
Ironside International Publishers, Inc.
Kopec Ent., John A. (SA Colts)
Kopp Publishing Co.
Lyman Products, Corp.
Madis, David
Matthews, Inc., Bill
McKee Publications
Outdoorsman's Bookstore, The
Paladin Press
Petersen Publishing Company
Pettinger Arms Books, Gerald
Pranger, Ed
Riling Arms Books Co., Ray
Rutgers Book Center (bookseller)
Stackpole Books
Stoeger Publishing Co.
Threat Management Institute
Trafalgar Square
Trotman, Ltd., Ken
Wahl Corp., Paul
Winchester Press
Wolfe Publishing Co.

BULLET AND CASE LUBRICANTS

American Gas & Chemical Co., Ltd.
Blackhawk West, R.L. Hough
Blount Sporting Equipment Division
Camp-Cap Products
C-H Tool & Die Corp.
Clenzoil Corp.
Cooper-Woodward (Perfect Lube)
Corbin Mfg. & Supply, Inc.
Green Bay Bullets (EZE-Size case lube)
Guardsman Products
Hornady Manufacturing Co.
Huntington Die Specialties
Javelina Products (Alox beeswax; bullet lubricant)
LeClear Industries
Lee Precision, Inc.
Lighthouse Mfg. Co., Inc.
Lithi Bee Bullet Lube
Lyman Products Corp. (Size-Ezy)
Magma Engineering Co.
Micro-Lube
Midway Arms, Inc.
M&M Engineering (case lubes)
M&N Bullet Lube
NEI (Ten X-Lube; mould prep.)
Northeast Industrial, Inc.
Pacific Tool Co.
Redding, Inc.
Rooster Laboratories (Zambini and HVR bullet lubes; case lubes & polish)
SAECO
Sandia Die & Cartridge Co.
Shooters Accessory Supply
Shootin' Accessories Ltd.
Slipshot MTS Group
Tamarack Prods., Inc. (bullet lube)
Thompson Bullet Lube
Watson Trophy Match Bullets, Ed
TDP Industries, Inc.

BULLET SWAGE DIES AND TOOLS

Bullet Swaging Supply, Inc.
C-H Tool & Die Corp.
Clerke Co., J.A. (moulds)
Coats, Mrs. Lester (lead wire core cutter)
Corbin Mfg. & Supply, Inc.
Fremont Tool Works
Hanned Precision (cast bullet tools)
Hawk Laboratories, Inc. (jackets and tubes for swaging)
Hollywood Loading Tools
Huntington Die Specialties
Javelina Products
Lachaussee S.A.
M&M Engineering
Necromancer Industries, Inc.
Rorschach Precision Products
SAS Dies
Seneca Run Iron Works, Inc. (muzzle-loading round ball)
Sport Flite Mfg., Inc.

CARTRIDGES FOR COLLECTORS

Ad Hominem
Ammunition Consulting Serv., Inc.
Cameron's
Campbell, Dick
Cape Outfitters
Cartridges Unlimited
Duffy, Chas. E.
Dunn, Tom M.
Eldorado Custom Shop (antique brass)
Epps (Orillia) Northern Ltd., Ellwood
Excaliber Wax, Inc.
Fiocchi of America
First Distributors, Inc., Jack
Forty Five Ranch Enterprises
Furr Arms
Glaser Safety Slug, Inc.
"Gramps" Antique Cartridges
Griffin's Guns & Antiques
Hansen Cartridge Company
Idaho Ammunition Service (ammunition)
Kelley's
Kopp, Terry K.
M&D Munitions Ltd.
Metallic Casting & Copper Corp. (MCC)
Muzzleloaders Etcetera, Inc.
Old Western Scrounger, Inc.
PMC-Eldorado Cartridge Co.
Ramos, Jesse
San Francisco Gun Exchange
Spence, George W.
Tillinghast, James C.
Ward & Van Valkenburg
Yearout, Lewis

CASES, CABINETS AND RACKS—GUN

A&B Industries, Inc. (cases: Top-Line Prods.)
Abel Safe & File Co.
Airmold/W.R. Grace & Co.-Conn.

Alco Carrying Cases (aluminum)
Allen Co., Bob (carrying cases)
Allen Co., Inc.
American Import Co., The
American Security Products Co.
Americase
API Outdoors, Inc. (racks)
Arizona Custom Case
Arkfield Mfg. & Dist. Co., Inc. (security steel cabinets)
Art Jewel Enterprises Ltd. (cases)
Ashby, Isaac
Beeman Precision Arms, Inc.
Big Sky Racks, Inc.
Big Spring Enterprise "Bore Stores" (synthetic cases)
Black Sheep Brand
Boyt Co., Div. of Welsh Sporting Goods (cases)
Browning, (Gen. Off.)
Bush Master
Cannon Safe, Inc.
Cascade Fabrication (aluminum cases)
Chipmunk
Crane & Crane, Inc.
Dara-Nes, Inc.
Deepeeka Exports Pvt. Ltd. (cases & racks)
Detroit-Armor Corp. (Saf-Gard steel gun safe)
Doskocil Mfg. Co., Inc. (Gun Guard carrying)
DTM International, Inc. (cases)
East Enterprises, Inc.
Elk River, Inc. (cases)
English Sales Co., A.G. (gun safes)
Enhanceo Presentations, Inc. (hardwood and leather cases)
Epps (Orillia) Northern Ltd., Ellwood (custom gun cases)
Eversull & Co., Inc., K
Flambeau Products Corp.
Fort Knox Security Products (safes)
Galati International (cases)
Gun-Ho Sports Cases
Gun Parts Corp. (cases)
Gusdorf Corp. (gun cabinets)
Hafner Enterprises, Inc. (cases)
Hall Plastics, Inc., John (cases)
Hansen Cartridge Co.
Harrison-Hurtz Enterprises, Inc. (cust. hardwood cases)
Hogue Grips
Huey Gun Cases, Marvin (handbuilt leather cases)
Hugger Hooks Co.
Hunting Classics Ltd.
Impact Case Company
Jumbo Sports Prods.
Kalispel Metal Prods. (aluminum boxes)
Kane Products, Inc.
KLP Mfg. (Cordura nylon carry cases)
Knock on Wood Antiques (gun & security cabinets)
Kolpin Mfg., Inc.
Lakewood Products, Inc.
Marple & Associates, Dick
McGuire, Bill (custom)
National Security Safe Company, Inc.
Nesci Enterprises, Inc. (firearms security chests)
Oregon Arms, Inc. (soft cases)
Otto, Tim (custom cases)
Palmer Metal Products (firearms storage boxes)
Penguin Industries, Inc.
Perazzi USA, Inc.
Protecto Plastics (carrying cases)
Rahn Gun Works, Inc. (leather trunk cases)
Red Head, Inc.
Russwood Custom Pistol Grips
San Angelo Sports Products, Inc.
Schulz Industries (carrying cases)
Security Gun Chest
Sonderman, Robert B. (walnut handgun cases)
Sports Support Systems, Inc.
SSK Co. (wooden cases)
Sweet Home Inc.
Tread Corp. (security gun chest)
Unick's Gunsmithing
Waller & Son, Inc., W.
WAMCO, Inc. (wooden display cases)
Weather Shield Sports Equipment, Inc.
Wilson Case Co. (cases)
Ziegel Engineering (aluminum cases)

CHOKE DEVICES, RECOIL ABSORBERS & RECOIL PADS

Action Products, Inc. (recoil shock eliminator)
Arms Ingenuity Co. (Jet-Away)
Armsport, Inc. (choke devices)
Baker, Stan (shotgun specialist)
Briley Mfg. Co. (choke tubes)
C&H Research (Mercury recoil suppressor)
Cellini, Vito, Francesca, Inc. (recoil reducer; muzzlebrake)
Clinton River Gun Serv., Inc. (Reed Choke)
Cody Trading Post, Inc. (choke tubes)
Colonial Arms, Inc. (invector-style screw-in choke tubes)
Cubriel, Reggie (leather recoil pads)
Delta Vectors, Inc. (Techni-Port recoil compensation)
Edwards Recoil Reducer
E&L Mfg., Inc.
Fabian Bros. Sptg. Goods, Inc. (DTA Muzzle Mizer rec. abs.; MIL/brake)
Gentry Custom Gunmaker, David (muzzlebrakes)
Griggs Products (recoil director)
Gun Parts Corp.
Harper, William E.
Hastings
I.N.C., Inc. (Kick-Eez recoil pad)
Intermountain Arms (Gunner's Choice muzzlebrake)
Jenkins Recoil Pads, Inc.
KDF, Inc. (muzzlebrake)
Lyman Products Corp. (Cutts Comp.)
Mag-na-port International, Inc. (muzzlebrake system)
Mag-Na-Port of Canada
Marble Arms Corp. (Poly Choke)
Meadow Industries
Nelson/Weather-rite
Pachmayr Ltd. (recoil pads)
P.A.S.T. Corp. (recoil reducer shield)
Poly Choke
Pro-Port Ltd.
Protektor Model Co. (shoulder recoil pad)
Reed Choke
Shell Shack
Shootin' Accessories Ltd.
Shotguns Unlimited (custom shotgun choke work)
Silhouette Arms Custom 45 Shop, Inc.
Sipes Gun Shop
Tank's Rifle Shop
Upper Missouri Trading Co.
Walker Arms Co., Inc.

CHRONOGRAPHS AND PRESSURE TOOLS

Canons Delcour
Competition Electronics, Inc.
Custom Chronograph, Inc.
D&H Precision Tooling (pressure testing receiver)
H-S Precision, Inc. (pressure barrels)
Jaeger, Inc., Paul
Lachaussee S.A.
Oehler Research, Inc.
P.A.C.T., Inc. (Precision chronogr.)
Quartz-Lok
Shooting Chrony
Su-Press-On, Inc. (chronographs)
Tepeco (Tepeco Speed-Meter)

CLEANING AND REFINISHING SUPPLIES

Acculube II, Inc. (lubricants/cleaners)
Accupro Gun Care (chemical bore cleaner)
Accuracy Products (solvent gun cleaner)
Adco Sales, Inc.
All's
Alsa Corp., The (ALLGUN Universal gun care kit)
American Gas & Chemical Co., Ltd. (TSI gun lube)
Anderson Mfg. Co. (stock finishes)
Armite Labs. (pen oiler)
Armoloy Co. of Ft. Worth (refinishing)
Beeman Precision Arms, Inc. (airguns only)
Belltown, Ltd. (gun cleaning cloth kit)
Beretta, Dr. Franco
Big 45 Frontier Gun Shop
Birchwood-Casey
Blount Sporting Equipment Division
Blue and Gray Prods., Inc.
Bondini Paolo
Break-Free (lubricants)
Brobst, Jim (J-B Cleaning Compound)
Brownells, Inc.
Browning (Gen. Off.)
Chopie Mfg., Inc. (Black Solve gun cleaner)
Clenzoil Corp.
Crouse's Country Cover (Masking Gun Oil)
Deepeeka Exports Pvt. Ltd. (cleaning kits)
Delhi Gun House
Dem-Bart Checkering Tools, Inc.
Dewey Mfg. Co., J. (one-piece gun cleaning rod)
DMG Technologies, Inc.
Dri-Slide, Inc.
Du-Lite Corp.
Dutchman's Firearms, Inc., The
Eezox, Inc. (cleaner, rust preventative)
E&L Mfg., Inc.
Flex Gun Rods Co., Inc.
Flouramics, Inc. (lubricant-gun coat)
Force 10, Inc. (anti-rust protectant)
Forster Products, Inc.
Fountain Products
Forty-Five Ranch Enterprises
FTI
Grace Metal Products, Inc.
Guardsman Products
Gun Parts Corp. (gun blue)
Hafner Enterprises, Inc.
Heatbath Corp.
Hoppe's Division, Penguin Ind., Inc.,
Hydrosorbent Products (silica gel dehumidifier)
Iosso Marine Products
Jantz Supply, Ken
J-B Bore Cleaner
Johnston Brothers
Jonad Corp. (lubricators)
Kellog's Professional Prods., Inc.
Kent Cartridge Mfg. Co. Ltd., The
Kleen-Bore, Inc.
Kleinendorst, K.W. (rifle cleaning cables)
Kopp, Terry K. (stock rubbing compound; rust preventative grease)
Lee, Mark (rust blue solution)
LEM Gun Specialties (Lewis Lead Remover)
LPS Chemical Prods.
LT Industries, Inc. (airguns—flexible cleaning rods/felt cleaning pellets)
Lynx-Line
Marble Arms Co.
Markell Incorporated
Marsh, Mike (gun accessories)
Micro Sight Co. (stock bedding compound)
Mountain View Sports, Inc.
Muscle Products Corp./Firepower Lubricants
Nesci Enterprises, Inc.
Old World Oil Products (gun stock finish)
Omark
Outers Laboratories, Div. of Blount
Ox-Yoke Originals, Inc. (dry lubrication patches)
Pease Accuracy, Bob
P&M Sales and Service
Precision Sports
R&S Industries Corp. (Miracle All Purpose polishing cloth)
Reardon Products (Dry-Lube)
Red Star Target Co.
Rice Protective Gun Coatings
Richards Classic Oil Finish (gunstock oils, wax)
RIG Products
Rooster Laboratories (cartridge/case cleaner, polish, protectant)
Rusteprufe Labs
Rust Guardit
Rusty Duck Premium Gun Care Products
Sandia Die & Cartridge
Scott, Inc., Tyler (muzzle-loading black solvent; patch lube)
Seacliff International, Inc. (portable parts washer)
Shooter's Choice
Shootin' Accessories Ltd.
Slipshot MTS Group
Sports Suppot Systems, Inc.
Su-Press-On, Inc.
Taylor & Robbins (Throat Saver, cleaning rod guide)
TDP Industries, Inc.
Texas Platers Supply Co.
Totally Dependable Products
Treso, Inc. (Durango Gun Rod)
United States Products Co. (Gold Medallion bore cleaner/conditioner)
Van Gorden, C.S. (Van's Instant Blue)
Venco Industries, Inc. (Shooter's Choice bore cleaner and conditioner)
Watson Trophy Match Bullets, Ed
WD-40 Co.
Williams Gun Sight Co. (finish kit)
Williams Shootin' Iron Service (Lynx Line)
Wisconsin Platers Supply Co.
Z-Coat Co.
Zip Aerosol Prods.

COMPUTER SOFTWARE—BALLISTICS

ADC, Inc.
Arms
Ballistics Program Co., Inc., The
DBASE
Blackwell, W.W. (Load from a Disk)
Canons Delcour
Corbin Applied Technology
Country Armourer, The
Destination North Software
HomeCraft Software
Hutton Rifle Ranch
Lachaussee S.A.
Magma Engineering Company
Maionchi - L.M.I.
Pejsa Ballistics
Sierra Bullets
Vancini, Carl A.

CUSTOM GUNSMITHS

Accuracy Gun Shop
Accuracy Unlimited
Accurate Plating & Weaponry, Inc.
Adair, Bill
Ahlman's, Inc.
Aldis, Richard L.
Alpine's Precision Gunsmithing
American Custom Gunmakers Guild
Amrine's Gun Shop
Answer Products Co.
Antique Arms Co.
Apel, Dietrich
Armament Gunsmithing Co., Inc.
Arms Craft Gunsmithing (rebluing, restorations)
Arms Ingenuity Co.
Armurier, Hiptmayer
Atzigen, Ed von
A&W Repair (stock restoration)
Baer Custom Guns (rifles)

Bain & Davis, Inc.
Baity's Custom Gunworks
Balickie Custom Stocks, Joe J.
Barnes Custom Shop
Barta's Gunsmithing
Bartlett, Donald
Behlert Precision (custom)
Beitzinger, George
Belding's Custom Gun Shop
Bell's Custom Shop (handguns)
Bellm Contenders
Benchmark Guns
Beretta, Dr. Franco
Bergmann & Williams
Bess, Gordon
Betz, Harold A.
Biesen, Al
Biesen, Roger
Billeb, Stephen L.
Billings Gunsmiths, Inc.
Billingsley, Ross (custom rifles)
Bill's Gun Repair
Bishop & Son, Inc., E.C.
Bob's Mexican Market (bluing)
Bolden, Duane (rust bluing)
Border Guns & Leather
Borovnik KG, Ludwig
Bowen Classic Arms Corp.
Bowerly, Kent
Brace, Larry D.
Brazos Arms Co. (gunsmithing)
Brgoch, Frank
Briganti Custom Gunsmith
Brown Precision, Inc. (rifles)
Bruno Bullets/Shooters Supply
Buckskin Machine Works
Budin, Dave
Burgess and Son, Robert W.
Burkhart, Don (rifles)
Bustani, Leo
Cache La Poudre Rifleworks (muzzleloaders)
CAM Enterprises
Camilli, Lou (muzzleloaders)
Campbell, Dick
Carter, Ralph L.
Champlin Firearms, Inc.
Champlin, R. MacDonald (muzzle-loading rifles and pistols)
Christopher Firearms Co., Inc., E.
Chuck's Gun Shop
Classic Arms Corp.
Clinton River Gun Serv., Inc.
Cloward's Gun Shop
Coffin, Charles H.
Coffin, Jim
Colonial Repair
Conrad, C.A.
Corkys Gun Clinic
Costa, David
Cox, C. Ed
Creekside Gun Shop, Inc. (color case hardening, bone charcoal bluing)
Cumberland Arms
Cumberland Knife & Gun Works (muzzleloaders)
Custom Gun Guild
Custom Gun Products
Custom Gun Stocks
Dangler, Homer L. (Kentucky rifles)
Darlington Gun Works, Inc.
Davis Service Center, Bill
D&D Gunsmiths, Ltd.
Delorge, Ed
Dever, Jack
Devereaux, R.H.
Dilliott Gunsmithing, Inc.
DiStefano, Dominic
Dixon, William
Donnelly-Siskiyou Gun Works, C.P.
Dowtin Gunworks (DGW)
Dressel, Paul G., Jr.
Duffy, Charles E.
Duncan's Gunworks, Inc.
Echols, D'Arcy A.
Eggleston, Jere
Elko Arms
Emmons, Bob
Erhardt, Dennis
Eversull & Co., Inc., K.
Eyster, Ken

Farmer-Dressel, Sharon
Fautheree, Andy
Fellowes, Ted (muzzleloaders)
FERLIB, Armi di Ferraglio Libero
Ferris Firearms
Fiberpro, Inc. (rifles)
First Distributors, Inc., Jack
Fish, Marshall F.
Fisher, Jerry A.
Flaig's
Flint Creek Arms Co. (bluing, repairs)
Flynn's Cust. Guns
Fogle, James W.
Forster, Larry L.
Forthofer's Gunsmithing, Pete
Forty-Niner Trading Co.
Fountain Products
Francesca Stabilizer's, Inc.
Frank Custom Guns, Ron
Frazier Brothers Sporting Goods
Fredrick Gun Shop
Freeland's Scope Stands, Inc.
Frontier Arms Co.
Furr, Karl J.
Gander Mountain, Inc.
Garrett Accur-Lt. D.F.S. Co.
Gator Guns & Repair
Genecco Gun Works, K.
Gentry Custom Gunmaker, David (custom Montana Mtn. Rifle)
Gillman, Edwin
Gilman-Mayfield
Giron, Robert E.
Goens, Dale W.
Gonzalez, Ramon B.
Goode, A.R.
Goodling's Gunsmithing
Goodwin, Fred, Goodwin's Gunshop
Grace, Charles E.
Granger, Georges
Graybill, Gene
Green, Roger M.
Greg Gunsmithing Repair
Greider Precision Products
Griffin & Howe
Guncraft, Inc.
Guncraft Sports, Inc.
Gun Doctor, The
Gun Shop, The
Guns
Gunsite Gunsmithy
Gunsmithing Ltd.
Gun Works, The (muzzleloaders)
Gutridge, Inc.
Hagn Rifles & Actions (s.s. actions & rifles)
Hammans, Charles E.
Hanson's Gun Center, Dick
Hardison, Charles
Hart & Son, Inc., Robert W. (actions, stocks)
Hartmann & Weiss GmbH
Hecht, Hubert J., Waffen-Hecht
Heilmann, Stephen
Heppler, Keith
High Bridge Arms, Inc.
Highsmith, M.V.
Hiptmayer, Klaus
Hoag, James W.
Hobaugh, Wm.
Hobbie Gunsmithing, Duane A.
Hodgson, Richard
Hoenig & Rodman
Hofer, Peter
Holland, Dick
Hollis Gun Shop
Horst, Alan K. (custom)
H-S Precision, Inc.
Huebner, Corey O.
Hughes, Steven Dodd (muzzleloaders)
Hunkeler, Al (muzzleloaders)
Hyper-Single, Inc.,(precision single shot rifles)
Intermountain Arms
Irwin, Campbell H.
Ivanoff, Thomas G.
Jackalope Gun Shop
Jaeger, Inc., Paul
Jamison, R.L., Jr.
Jarrett Rifles, Inc. (rifles)
Jim's Gun Shop
Johnson, Neal G.

Johnson, Peter S., c/o Orvis Co.
Juenke, Vern
Jurras, L.E.
Kartak Gun Works
KDF, Inc.
Ken's Gun Specialties
Kesselring Gun Shop
Kilham, Benjamin
Klein, Don,
Kleinendorst, K.W.
Kneiper, Jim (rifles)
KOGOT
Kopp, Terry K.
Korzinek, J. (riflesmith)
LaFrance Specialties
Lair, Sam (single shots)
Lampert, Ron L.
Larkin Moore & Co., Wm.
Lawson Co., Harry
Lawson, John G.
Lebeau - Courally S.A.
Lee, Mark
LeFever & Sons, Inc., Frank
Liberty Antique Gunworks
Lilja Precision Rifle Barrels, Inc.
Lind, Al
Linebaugh Custom Sixguns, John
Ljutic Industries, Inc. (shotguns)
Lofland, James W. (single shot rifles)
Logan, Harry M.
London Guns Ltd.
Long Island Gunsmith, Ltd. (Carriage Trade Shotgun)
MacDonald, R. Champlin
Mag-na-port International, Inc.
Makinson, Nicholas (English guns; repairs & renovations)
Mandarino, Monte (Penn. rifles)
Manley Shooting Supplies, Lowell
Marquart Precision Co.
Martin, Elwyn H.
Masker, Seely, Custom Rifles (benchrest)
Mathews & Son, Inc., Geo. E.
Matthews, Larry
Mazur Restoration, Pete (double-barrel rifles & shotguns)
McCament, Jay
McCann's Muzzle-Gun Works (ML)
McCormick's Custom Gun Bluing
McFarland, Stan (custom rifles)
McGowen Rifle Barrels
McGuire, Bill
McMurdo, Lynn
Mercer, R.M.
Mid-America Recreation, Inc.
Miller Arms, Inc.
Miller Co., David (rifles)
Miller, S.A., Point Roberts Sports Ltd.
Miller, Tom
Milliron Custom Guns & Stocks, Earl
Mills, Hugh B., Jr.
Moeller, Steve
Monell Custom Guns
Mountain Bear Rifle Works, Inc.
Morrison Custom Rifles, J.W.
Morrow, Bud
Moschetti, Mitch
Mountain Bear Rifle Works, Inc.
MPI Stocks
Mrock, Larry
Mulholland, Gordon
Mustra's Custom Guns, Inc., Carl
Neighbor, William
Nelson, Stephen E.
Nettestad, Bruce A.
New England Arms Co.
New England Custom Gun Service
Newman Gunshop (muzzleloaders)
Nickels, Paul R.
Nicklas, Ted
Noreen, Peter H.
Norman, Jim
North Fork Custom Gunsmithing
Nu-Line Guns
Oakland Custom Arms, Inc.
Old World Gunsmithing
Olson, Vic
Orvis Co., Inc., The
Ottmar, Maurice
Pachmayr Ltd.

Pagel Gun Works (custom gunmaking and refinishing)
Pasadena Gun Center
Paterson Gunsmithing
Pell, John T.
Pence Precision Barrels
Penrod Precision
Pentheny de Pentheny
Peterson Gun Shop, A.W. (muzzleloaders)
Pevear, John C.
Plante, Eugene T.
Powell & Son (Gunmakers) Ltd., William
Power Custom, Inc.
Precision Specialties
Professional Gunsmiths of America
Pro-Port, Ltd.
P&S Gun Service
R&J Gunshop
Ries, Chuck
Rifle Shop
Rizzini Battista
Robar Co's, Inc., The
Roberts, J.J.
Roberts, Wm. A., Jr. (muzzleloaders)
Robinson, Don (airrifle stocks)
Rocky Mountain Rifle Works, Ltd.
Rogers Gunsmithing, Bob
Royal Arms
Russell's Rifle Shop
Ryan, Chad
Sanders Custom Gun Serv.
Sandy's Custom Gunshop
Schaefer, Roy V.
Schiffman, Curt (rifle builder)
Schumakers Gun Shop
Schwartz Custom Guns, Wayne E.
Schwartz Custom Guns, David W.
Scott Fine Guns, Inc., Thad
Scott (Gunmakers) Ltd., W&C
Scott/McDougall Custom Gunsmiths
Shane's Gunsmithing
Shaw, Inc., E.R.
Shaw's
Shell Shack (muzzleloaders)
Sheridan Gunshop
Sherk, Dan A.
Shilen Rifles, Inc.
Shiloh Rifle Mfg. Co., Inc.
Shockley, Harold H. (hot bluing & plating)
Shootin' Shack ('smithing services)
Shooting Gallery, The
Shootist Supply
Silhouette Arms Custom 45 Shop, Inc.
Silver Shields, Inc.
Sipes Gun Shop
Siskiyou Gun Works
Skinner, John R.
Sklany, Steve (Ferguson rifle)
Slezak, Jerome F.
Smith, Art
Smith, John
Snapp's Gunshop
Speiser, Fred D.
Spencer Reblue Service (electroless nickel plating)
Sports Shack
Sportsmen's Equip. Co.
Sportsmen's Exchange & Western Gun Traders, Inc.
Springfield Armory, Inc.
SSK Industries
Starnes, Ken
Steelman's Gun Shop
Steffens, Ron
Storey, Dale A.
Stott's Creek Armory, Inc. (single shot and muzzle-loading work/restoration only)
Strawbridge, Victor W.
Stroup, Earl R. (rifles)
Strutz, W.C.
Sunora Gun Shop
Swann, D.J. (makers of falling block rifle)
Swenson's 45 Shop, A.D.
Swift River Gunworks
Szweda, Robert
300 Gunsmith Service, Inc.
Talmage, William G.
Tank's Rifle Shop
Taylor & Robbins
Tennessee Valley Mfg.
Tertin, James A.

Thompson, Larry R.
Thurston Sports Center
Titus Shooting Specialties, Daniel
Tom's Gunshop
Trapper Gun, Inc.
Trevallion Gunstocks, David
Trident Ltd.
Tucker, James C.
Ulrich, Dennis A.
Unick's Gunsmithing
Upper Missouri Trading Co.
Vais Arms
Van Epps, Milton
Van Horn, Gil (safari rifles)
Van Patten, J.W.
Vest, John
Vic's Gun Refinishing
Vintage Arms, Inc. (single shot rifles & pistols)
Volquartsen Custom Ltd.
Walker Arms Co., Inc.
Wallace, R.D.
Wardell Precision Handguns Ltd.
Wardrop, R.A.
Weatherby, Inc.
Weaver Arms Corp.
Weaver's Gun Shop
Weber, Chris/Waffen-Weber
Weems, Cecil
Wells, Fred
Wells Ltd., R.A.
Wessinger Custom Guns & Engraving
West, Robert G.
Western Design
Western Gunstock Mfg. Co.
Western Ordnance Int'l Corp.
White Rock Tool & Die, Keith Rice
Wiebe, Duane
Wiest, M.C.
Williams Gun Sight Co.
Williams Shootin' Iron Service
Williamson-Pate Gunsmith Service
Wilson's Gun Shop
Winter, Robert M.
Wisner's Gun Shop, Inc.
Womack, Lester
Yankee Gunsmith
Yee, Mike
Zeeryp, Russ

CUSTOM METALSMITHS

Accuracy Unlimited
Ahlman's, Inc.
Alley Supply Co.
Apel, Dietrich
Armament Gunsmithing Co., Inc.
Baer Custom Guns
Baron Technology, Inc.
Barta's Gunsmithing
Behlert Precision
Beitzinger, George
Bellm Contenders
Benchmark Guns
Biesen Gunmaker, Al
Billingsley, Ross (rifle)
Bishop & Son, Inc., E.C.
Brace, Larry D.
Briganti Custom Gunsmith
Bustani, Leo
Campbell, Dick
Cannavaro, Brian V. (patchboxes, inlays)
Carter, Ralph L.
Champlin Firearms, Inc.
Checkmate Guns Custom Refinishing (electroplating)
Cloward's Gun Shop
Clinton River Gun Serv., Inc.
Colonial Repair
Condor Mfg. Co.
Costa, David
Craftguard (bluing, plating, Parkerizing)
Crandall Tool & Machine Co.
Cullity Restoration, Daniel
Custom Gun Guild
Custom Gun Products
D&D Gunsmiths, Ltd.
de Pentheny O'Kelly, Hugh P.
Dever, Jack
D&H Precision Tooling
Dilliott Gunsmithing, Inc.
DiStefano, Dominic
Duncan's Gunworks, Inc.
Echols, D'Arcy A.
Eyster Heritage Gunsmiths, Inc., Ken
Farmer-Dressel, Sharon
Fish, Marshall F.
Flaig's
Fountain Products
Francesca Stabilizer's, Inc.
Fredrick Gun Shop (engine turning)
Fullmer, Geo. M. (precise chambering—300 cals.)
Genecco Gun Works, K.
Gentry Custom Gunmaker, David
Giron, Robert E.
Goens, Dale W.
Goodwin, Fred
Gordie's Gun Shop
Green, Roger M.
Griffin & Howe
Gun Doctor, The
Guns
Gunsmithing Ltd.
Gutridge, Inc.
Hagn Rifles & Actions
Hart & Son, Inc., Robert W.
Hecht, Hubert J., Waffen-Hecht
Heilmann, Stephen
Heinie, Richard
Heppler, Keith
Heppler's Machining
Hiptmayer, Klaus
Hobaugh, Wm. H.
Hollis Gun Shop
H-S Precision, Inc.
Hyper-Single, Inc.
Intermountain Arms
Ivanoff, Thomas G.
Jaeger, Inc., Paul
Jamison, R.L., Jr.
Jantz Supply, Ken
Jones Custom Products, Neil A.
Jurras, L.E.
Kartak Gun Works
Kilham, Benjamin
Klein, Don
Kleinendorst, K.W.
Kopp, Terry K.
Lampert, Ron L.
Lee Supplies, Mark
Lilja Precision Rifle Barrels, Inc.
Logan, Harry M.
Matthews, Larry
Mazur Restoration, Pete (traditional metal finishing)
McCament, Jay
McFarland, Stan
Mid-America Recreation, Inc.
Miller Arms, Inc.
Morrison Custom Rifles, J.W.
Morrow, Bud
Mountain Bear Rifle Works, Inc.
Mullis Guncraft
Nelson, Stephen
Nettestad, Bruce A.
New England Custom Gun Service
Noreen, Peter H.
Oakland Custom Arms, Inc.
Olson, Vic
Pagel Gun Works
Pasadena Gun Center
Penrod Precision
Pevear, John C.
Precise Chambering Co.
Precise Metalsmithing Enterprises
Precision Specialties, Ltd.
P&S Gun Service
Rogers Gunsmithing, Bob
Schwartz Custom Guns, Wayne E.
Sheridan Gunshop
Shirley & Co. Riflemakers, J.A.
Shockley, Harold H.
Silhouette Arms Custom 45 Shop, Inc.
Silver Shields, Inc.
Sipes Gun Shop
Snapp's Gunshop
Sportsmen's Exchange & Western Gun Traders, Inc.
Steffens, Ron (bluing barrels w/o bluing bore)
Storey, Dale A.
Talley, Dave
Unick's Gunsmithing
Van Patten, J.W.
Vic's Gun Refinishing
Waldron, Herman
Wallace, R.D.
Wardell Precision Handguns Ltd.
Wells, Fred
Werth, Terry
Wessinger Custom Guns & Engraving
West, Robert G.
Western Design
White Rock Tool & Die, Keith Rice (rebarreling action mods.)
Wiebe, Duane
Williamson-Pate Gunsmith Service
Westrom, John

DECOYS

A&M Waterfowl, Inc. (motorized ducks, geese)
Baekgaard Ltd.
Burnham Bros, Inc.
Carry-Lite, Inc.
Deer Me Products Co. (anchors)
Fair Game International (Enticer duck decoys)
Farm Form, Inc. (goose)
Feather Flex Decoys
Flambeau Prods. Corp.
G&H Decoys, Inc.
Klingler, Kenneth J.
North Wind Decoys Co. (goose, duck windsock)
Penn's Woods Products, Inc.
Quack Decoy Corp.
Royal Arms (wooden, duck)
Skaggs, Ron E.
Sports Innovations, Inc.
Waterfield Sports, Inc.
Woods Wise Products

ENGRAVERS, ENGRAVING TOOLS

Adair, Bill
Adams, John J.
Alfano, Sam
Allard, Gary
Anthony & George, Ltd.
Baron Technology
Bates, Billy R.
Bell Originals, Inc., Sid
Bledsoe, Weldon
Bleile, C. Roger
Boessler, Erich
Bone, Ralph P.
Bonham, Henry "Hank"
Bratcher, Dan
Brgoch, Frank
Brooker, Dennis B.
Brownells, Inc. (engraving tools)
Burgess, Byron
Burt, Robert B.
CAM Enterprises
Cannavaro, Brian V.
Christopher Firearms Co., Inc., E.
Churchill, Winston
Clark Firearms Engraving
Clark, Frank
Coffey, Barbara
Davidson, Jere
Delorge, Ed
Drain, Mark
Dubber, Michael W.
Evans, Robert
Eyster Heritage Gunsmiths, Inc., Ken
Fanzoj, John
Favre, Jacqueline
FERLIB, Armi di Ferraglio Libero
Firearms Engravers Guild of America
Flannery Engraving Co., Jeff W.
Floatstone Mfg. Co.
Fogle, James W.
Fountain Products
Frank, Henry
Francolini, Leonard
Gene's Custom Guns
George, Tim and Christy
Glendo
Glimm, Jerome C.
Gournet, Geoffroy R.
Grant, Howard V.
Griffin & Howe
GRS Corp. (Gravermeister tool)
Gurney Engraving Method
Gwinnell, Bryson J.
Hale, Peter
Hand Engravers Supply Co.
Harris Hand Engraving, Paul A.
Harwood, Jack O.
Hendricks, Frank E.
Hiptmayer, Heidemarie
Horst, Alan K.
Ingle, Ralph W., Master Engraver
Jaeger, Inc., Paul
Jantz Supply, Ken (tools)
Johns, Bill
Kamyk, Steven
Kehr, Roger
Kelly, Lance
Klingler, Kenneth J. (gun stocks)
Koevenig Engraving Service, E.J.
Kudlas, John
Largent, Nelson H.
Lebeau - Courally S.A.
Leibowitz, Leonard (etcher)
Letschnig, Franz, Master-Engraver
Lindsay, Steve
London Guns Ltd.
Mains, Wm. H.
Maki, Robert E.
Marek, George
McDonald, Dennis
McKenzie, Lynton S.M.
Mele, Frank
Miller, S.A.
Mittermeier, Frank (tool)
Moschetti, Mitch
Nelson, Gary K.
New Orleans Arms Co.
New Orleans Jewelers Supply (engraving tool)
NgraveR Co. (MagnaGraver tool)
Oker's Engraving
Old Dominion Engravers
Pachmayr Ltd.
Pedersen & Son, C.R.
Pilkington, Scott
Piquette, Paul R.
Plante, Eugene T.
Potts, Wayne E.
Pranger, Ed
Puccinelli Design, Leonard
Rabeno, Martin
Reno, Wayne & Karen (scrimshanders)
Riggs, Jim (handguns)
Roberts, J.J.
Rohner, John R. and Hans
Rosser, Bob
Rundell, Joe
Runge, Robert P.
Sampson, Roger
Schiffman, Mike
Schuck, Clay
Shaw's
Sherwood, George
Shostle, Ben
Sinclair, W.P.
Skaggs, Ron E.
Smith, Mark A.
Smith, Ron
Theis, Terry
Thiewes, George W.
Thirion, Denise
Valade, Robert B.
Vest, John
Viramontez, Ray
Vorhes, David
Wagoner, Vernon G.
Wallace, R.D.
Wallace, Terry
Warenski, Julie
Warren, Kenneth W.
Welch, Sam

Wells, Rachel
Wessinger Custom Guns & Engraving
Willig, Claus
Wolfe, Bernie (engraving, plating, scrimshawing)
Wood, Mel

GAME CALLS

Adventure Game Calls
Arkansas Mallard Duck Calls
Ashby, Isaac (turkey)
Baekgaard Ltd.
Blakemore Game Calls, Jim
Bostick Wildlife Calls, Inc.
Burnham Bros.
Carter's Wildlife Calls, Inc., Garth
Cedar Hill Game Call Co.
D-Boone Ent., Inc.
Deepeeka Exports Pvt. Ltd.
Dr. O's Products, Ltd.
Duck Call Specialists
Faulk's Game Call Co., Inc.
Fibron Products, Inc.
Flow-Rite of Tennessee, Inc.
Green Head Corp.
Hall's Shooting Products, Inc., Joe
Haydel's Game Calls, Inc.
Hunter's Specialties, Inc.
Keowee Game Calls
Kingyon, Paul L.
Knight & Hale Game Calls
Lohman Mfg. Co.
Mallardtone Game Calls
Marsh, Johnny (duck & goose calls)
Moss Double Tone, Inc.
Mountain Hollow Game Calls
Newman Gun Shop (custom, slate, turkey calls)
Oakman Turkey Calls
Olt Co., Phil S.
Penn's Woods Products, Inc.
Preston Pittman Game Calls, Inc. (diaphragm turkey calls)
Primos Wild Game Calls, Inc.
Quaker Boy, Inc.
Rickard, Inc., Pete
Salter Calls, Inc., Eddie
San Angelo Sports Products, Inc.
Sceery Company, E.J.
Scobey Duck & Goose Calls, Glynn
Scotch Hunting Products Co., Inc.
Scrugg's Game Calls, Stanley
Stewart Game Calls, Inc., Johnny
Tink's Safariland Hunting Corp.
Woods Wise Products
Wyant's Premium Outdoor Products, Inc., Roger

GUN PARTS, U.S. AND FOREIGN

AMT
Action Ammo, Ltd.
Amherst Arms (U.S. Military)
Armes de Chasse
Armsport, Inc.
Aztec International Ltd.
B&D Trading Co., Inc.
Badger Shooter's Supply
Behlert Custom Guns, Inc. (handgun parts)
Bob's Gun Shop
Border Guns & Leather
Cadre Supply
Can Am Enterprises
Caspian Arms
Century Intl. Arms, Inc.
Cherokee Gun Accessories
Concorde Arms, Inc.
Delta Arms Ltd.
Duffy, Charles E.
Eagle International, Inc.
Essex Arms (45 1911A1 frames & slides)
Fabian Bros. Sporting Goods, Inc.
Federal Ordnance, Inc.
First Distributors, Inc., Jack
Galati International
Greider Precision Products
Gun Parts Corp.
Gun-Tec (Win. mag. tubing; Win. 92 conversion parts)
Hansen Cartridge Company
Hastings
Kopp, Terry K.
Kopec Ent., John A. (SA Colts only)
Kriegeskorte GmbH, A.
L.A.R. Manufacturing, Inc.
Liberty Antique Gunworks (S&W only)
Lodewick, Walter H. (Winchester parts)
Martz, John V. (parts for Luger and P-38s)
Masen Co., John
McKee, Arthur (micrometer receiver sights)
Olympic Arms, Inc.
Pacific Intl. Merch. Corp. (Vega 45 Colt mag.)
Para-Ordnance Mfg., Inc. (frames only)
Perazzi USA, Inc.
Pre-64 Winchester Parts Co.
Quality Parts Co.
Ranch Products
Retting, Inc., Martin B.
Rizzini Battista
Royal Ordnance Works Ltd.
Sarco, Inc.
Sherwood Intl. Export Corp.
Smires, Clifford L. (Mauser rifle parts)
Springfield Armory, Inc.
Springfield Sporters, Inc.
Tank's Rifle Shop
Taurus S.A., Forjas
Triple-K Mfg. Co. (magazines, gun parts)
T&S Industries, Inc.
Twin Pine Armory
Weisz Antique Gun Parts
W.C. Wolff Co. (springs only)
Zoli U.S.A., Inc., Antonio

GUNS (Air)

Air Rifle Specialists
Beeman Precision Arms, Inc. (Feinwerkbau, Weihrauch, Webley)
Benjamin Air Rifle Co.
Brass Eagle, Inc. (paintball guns)
ChinaSports, Inc.
Component Concepts, Inc. (paintball)
Crosman Airguns (a Coleman Co.)
Crosman Products of Canada Ltd.
Daisy Mfg. Co.
Dynamit Nobel-RWS, Inc. (Dianawerk)
Feinwerkbau Westinger & Altenburger GmbH & Co. KG
Fiocchi of America, Inc.
Ford Ltd., J. and J.
GFR Corp.
Great Lakes Airguns
Hebard Guns, Gil
Interarms (Walther)
I.S.S. International Shooters Service
Mac-1 Airgun Distributors
Marksman Products
McMurray & Son
National Survival Game, Inc. (paintball guns)
Nationwide Airgun Repairs (airgun repairs/restoration)
N.S.G., Inc.
Phoenix Arms Co., Ltd. (Jackal)
Precision Sales International, Inc.
Pursuit Marketing, Inc. (PMI) (paintball)
S.G.S. Sporting Guns Srl
Sheridan Products, Inc.
Stone Enterprises Ltd.
Taurus S.A., Forjas
Tippman Pneumatics, Inc.
Weihrauch KG, Hermann

GUNS (Foreign)

Action Arms Ltd.
American Arms, Inc.
Anschutz
Armes de Chasse (Merkel)
Armi San Pacio Srl
Armscor Precision
Arms Corp. of America, Inc.
Arms Corp. of the Philippines
Armsport, Inc.
Arrieta, S.L.
Autumn Sales, Inc.
Ballistic Research Industries (BRI)
Beeman Precision Arms, Inc. (FWB, Weihrauch, FAS, Unique, Korth, Hammerli firearms)
Benelli Armi, S.p.A.
Beretta U.S.A.
Bondini Paolo (blackpowder)
Bretton
British Arms Co. Ltd.
BRI
BRNO
Browning (Gen. offices)
Browning (Parts & Service)
Cape Outfitters
Century Intl. Arms, Inc.
Chadick's Ltd.
Chapuis Armes
ChinaSports, Inc.
Cimarron Arms (Uberti)
Connecticut Valley Arms Co.
Cosmi Americo & F.
Daly, Charles
Davidson's
Dixie Gun Works, Inc. (ML guns)
Dynamit Nobel-RWS, Inc. (Diana)
Eagle Imports, Inc.
Elko Arms
Ellett Bros. (Churchill shotguns)
EMF Co., Inc. (early and modern firearms)
Euroarms of America, Inc. (ML)
Fabrique Nationale Nouvelle Herstal S.A.
Fanzoj, John
FERLIB, Armi di Ferraglio Libero
Fiocchi of America, Inc.
Francotte, Auguste & Cie, S.A.
Frankonia Jagd, Hofmann & Co.
Galaxy Imports, Ltd., Inc.
Gamba, Renato, S.p.A.
Garbi, Armas (shotguns)
Glock, Inc.
Griffin & Howe (Purdey, Holland & Holland)
G.U., Inc.
GSI, Inc. (Steyr, FN, Mannlicher)
Hallowell & Co. (agents for John Rigby & Co.)
Hammerli, USA
Heckler & Koch, Inc.
Heym, Friedrich Wilh.
Incor, Inc. (Cosmi auto shotgun)
Industria de la Escopeta S.A.L. (shotguns)
Interarmco
Interarms Ltd.
Israel Military Industries Ltd. (IMI)
I.S.S. International Shooters Service
Jaeger, Inc., Paul
K.B.I., Inc. (Baikal shotguns)
Kimel Industries
Kriegeskorte GmbH, A.
Korth GmbH
Krieghoff International, Inc.
Lakefield Arms Ltd.
Laurona Shotguns
Lebeau - Courally S.A.
Llama
Magnum Research, Inc. (Desert Eagle)
MAGTECH Recreational Products, Inc.
Mandall Shooting Supplies
Mannlicher
Manufacture D'Armes Des Pyrenees Francaises - Unique
Mauser-Werke Oberndorf
Merkuria, FTC (BRNO)
Midwest Gun Sport (E. Dumoulin)
Mitchell Arms, Inc.
Moore & Co., Wm. Larkin (Garbi, FERLIB, Piotti, Perugini-Visini)
Navy Arms Co.
Norinco
Outdoor Sports Headquarters, Inc. (Charles Daly shotguns)
Pachmayr Ltd.
Parker Reproductions (shotguns)
Perazzi U.S.A., Inc.
Perugini-Visini & Co.
Poly Technologies, Inc.
Powell & Son (Gunmakers) Ltd., William (custom made)
Pragotrade (BRNO rifles, CZ pistols)
Precision Imports, Inc. (Mauser)
Precision Sales Intl., Inc., PSI (Anschutz)
Precision Sports
PTK International, Inc.
Puccinelli, Leonard
Quality Arms, Inc. (Bernardelli; FERLIB; Bretton shotguns)
Rahn Gun Works, Inc.
Rossi S.A. Metalurgica E Municoes, Amadeo
Samco Global Arms
Sardius Industries Ltd. (handguns)
Sauer
Scott Fine Guns, Inc., Thad (Perugini Visini; Bertuzzi; Mario Beschi shotguns)
S.G.S. Sporting Guns Srl
Sigarms, Inc.
Sile Distributors
Simmons Enterprises, Ernie (Sauer rifles; SKB shotguns)
Sodia Jagdgewehrfabrik, Franz
Sportarms of Florida
Springfield Armory, Inc.
Star Bonifacio Echeverria S.A. (handguns)
State Arms Gun Co. (.50 bolt-action rifle)
Steyr-Daimler-Puch (rifles)
Stoeger Industries
Taurus International Mfg., Inc.
T.D. Arms
T.F.C. Spa (shotguns)
Tradewinds, Inc.
Uberti USA, Inc.
Ugartechea, Ignacio
Valmet
Verney-Carron
Voere (rifles)
Waffen-Frankonia
Weatherby, Inc.
Weihrauch KG, Hermann
Westley Richards & Co.
Zabala Hermanos S.A. (shotguns)
Zavodi Crvena Zastava
Zoli USA, Inc., Antonio

GUNS (U.S.-made)

A.A. Arms, Inc.
Accu-Tek
AMAC
American Arms, Inc.
American Derringer Corp.
AMT
Armament Systems and Procedures, Inc. (ASP pistol)
A-Square Co., Inc.
Auto-Ordnance Corp.
Automatic Weaponry
Barrett Firearms Mfg., Inc. (Light Fifty)
Beretta U.S.A.
BF Arms (single shot pistol)
Browning
Bryco Arms (Distributed by Jennings Firearms)
Calico Light Weapons Systems
Century Gun Dist., Inc. (Century Model 100 SA rev.)
Chadick's Ltd.
Chipmunk
Claridge Hi-Tec, Inc.
Colonial Repair
Colt Firearms
Competition Limited
Competitor Corp., Inc.
Coonan Arms, Inc. (357 Mag. auto.)
Cooper Arms
Dakota Arms, Inc. (bolt-action rifles)
Davis Industries (derringers; 32 auto pistol)
Desert Industries, Inc.
D Max Industries
Eagle Arms, Inc.
EMF Co., Inc.
Essex Arms

European American Armory Corp.
Falling Block Works
Feather Industries, Inc.
Federal Eng. Corp.
Freedom Arms, Inc. (mini and Casull revolvers)
FTL Marketing/Auto Nine Corp.
Gilbert Equipment Co.
Gonic Arms, Inc.
Grendel, Inc.
Hanus, Bill
Hatfield International, Inc. (squirrel rifle)
Horton Dist. Co., Inc., Lew (sporting firearms wholesaler)
IAI (Irwindale Arms, Inc.)
Intratec
Ithaca Aquisition Corp./Ithaca Gun Co.
Jennings Firearms, Inc.
Johnson, Iver
K.B.I., Inc.
KDF, Inc.
Kimel Industries
Kintrek, Inc.
L.A.R. Manufacturing, Inc.
Ljutic Industries, Inc. (Mono-Gun)
Lorcin Engineering Co., Inc. (L-25 pistol)
Magnum Research, Inc.
Marlin Firearms Co.
Maverick Arms, Inc.
McMillan Gunworks, Inc.
Merrill Pistol
MK Arms, Inc. (semi-auto carbines)
M.O.A. Corp. (Maximum pistol)
Modern Muzzleloading, Inc.
Montana Armory, Inc.
Mossberg & Sons, O.F.
Navy Arms Co.
New Advantage Arms Corp.
New Detonics Mfg. Corp. (auto pistol)
New England Firearms Co., Inc.
North American Arms
North American Specialties
Olympic Arms, Inc.
Oregon Arms, Inc.
Pachmayr Ltd.
Parker-Hale
Peregrine Industries, Inc.
Phelps Mfg. Co. (Heritage I in 45-70)
Precision Small Parts, Inc.
Quality Firearms, Inc.
Rahn Gun Works, Inc.
Ram-Line, Inc.
Raven Arms (P-25 pistols)
Remington Arms Co.
RPM (R&R Sporting Arms, Inc.) (XL pistol; formerly Merrill)
Safari Arms/SGW
SAM, Inc.
Savage Arms, Inc.
Seecamp Co., Inc., L.W.
Sharps Arms Co., Inc., C.
Shiloh Rifle Mfg. Co., Inc.
Smith & Wesson
Special Service Arms Mfg., Inc.
Specialized Weapons, Inc.
Sporting Arms, Mfg. (Night Charmer/Snake Charmer II)
Springfield Armory, Inc.
Sturm, Ruger & Co., Inc.
Sundance Industries, Inc. (Model A-25 pistol)
Super Six Limited
Taurus International, Inc.
Texas Longhorn Arms, Inc. (single-action sixgun)
Thompson/Center Arms
TMI Products
Trail Guns Armory (muzzleloaders)
Trident Ltd.
Ultra Light Arms, Inc.
U.S. Arms Corp.
U.S. Repeating Arms Co. (Win.)
Weatherby, Inc.
Wesson Firearms Co., Inc.
Western Ordnance Int'l Corp.
Wichita Arms, Inc.
Wildey, Inc.
Wilkinson Arms
Wyoming Armory, Inc.
Wyoming Arms Mfg. Corp.

GUNS AND GUN PARTS, REPLICA AND ANTIQUE

Antique Arms Co.
Armi San Paolo
Armsport, Inc.
Beeman Precision Arms, Inc.
Border Guns & Leather
British Arms Co. Ltd.
Buckskin Machine Works
Burgess & Son, Robert W.
Cache La Poudre Rifleworks
Champlin, R. MacDonald
Day & Sons, Inc., Leonard
Delhi Gun House
Dixie Gun Works, Inc.
Dwyer, Dan (manufacturer of obsolete and antique parts)
Federal Ordnance, Inc.
First Distributors, Inc., Jack
Goodwin, Fred (Win. rings & studs)
Gun Parts Corp.
Hansen Cartridge Company
Hopkins & Allen Arms (parts only)
House of Muskets, Inc., The (ML supplies)
Kopp, Terry K. (restoration and parts 1890 and 1906 Win.)
Liberty Antique Gunworks (S&W only)
Log Cabin Sport Shop
Lucas, Edw. E. (45/70 Springfield parts; some Sharps, Spencer parts)
Lyman Products Corp.
McKee, Arthur
Munsch Gunsmithing, Tommy (Win. obsolete and Marlin parts only)
October Country
OMR Feinmechanik, Jagd-u. Sportwaffen GmbH
Ram-Line, Inc.
Sarco, Inc.
Shiloh Rifle Mfg. Co., Inc. (Sharps)
Sklany, Steve
South Bend Replicas, Inc.
S&S Firearms
Taylor's & Co., Inc.
Track of the Wolf, Inc.
Traditions, Inc.
Trail Guns Armory
Twin Pine Armory
Upper Missouri Trading Co.
Weisz Antique Gun Parts
Wescombe (Rem. rolling block parts)
Winchester Sutler, Inc.

GUNS, SURPLUS—PARTS AND AMMUNITION

Aztec International Ltd.
Ballistica Maximus North
Ballistica Maximus South
Braun, M.
Can Am Enterprises (Enfield rifles)
Century Intl. Arms, Inc.
Concorde Arms, Inc.
Federal Ordnance, Inc.
Garcia National Gun Traders, Inc.
Gun Parts Corp.
Hansen Cartridge Company
Keng's Firearms Specialty, Inc.
Kimel Industries
Lever Arms Service Ltd.
Paragon Sales, Inc. (ammunition)
Raida Intertraders S.A. (surplus guns)
Samco Global Arms, Inc.
Sarco, Inc. (military surplus ammo)
Sherwood Intl. Export Corp.
Southern Ammunition Co., Inc.
Southern Armory (modern military parts)
Springfield Sporters, Inc.
Su-Press-On, Inc. (parts)
U.S. Arms Corp.

GUNSMITHS, CUSTOM (see Custom Gunsmiths)

GUNSMITHS, HANDGUN (see Pistolsmiths)

GUNSMITH SCHOOLS

Colorado School of Trades
Forster Products, Inc.
Lassen Community College
Modern Gun Repair School (correspondence school only)
Montgomery Technical College (also 1-yr. engraving school)
Murray State College
North American Correspondence Schools
Pennsylvania Gunsmith School
Piedmont Community College
Pine Technical Institute
Professional Gunsmiths of America (Technical training ctr.)
Shenandoah School of Gunsmithing
Southeastern Community College
Trinidad State Junior College
Yavapai College

GUNSMITH SUPPLIES, TOOLS, SERVICES

Adair, Bill
Alley Supply Co. (JET line lathes, mills, etc.; Sweany Site-A-Line Optical bore collimator)
All's, The Jim J. Tembilis Co., Inc.
Armite Labs. (pen oiler)
Atlantic Mills, Inc. (gun cleaners, patches, shop wipes)
Baiar, Jim (hex screws)
Baron Technology (chemical etching, plating)
Behlert Precision
Bell Design Gun Services (Accusorb bedding system)
Bell Originals, Inc., Sid (floorplate decoration)
Bellm Contenders (rifles only)
Biesen, Al (grip caps, buttplates)
Biesen, Roger
Birchwood-Casey
Blue Ridge Machinery and Tools, Inc. (gunsmithing lathe, mills and shop supplies)
Briganti Custom Gunsmith (cold rust bluing, hand polishing, metal work)
Brownells, Inc.
Brownell Checkering Tools, W.E.
B-Square Co.
Buehler Scope Mounts
Canjar Co., M.H. (triggers, etc.)
Chapman Mfg. Co.
Choate Machine & Tool (tools)
Chopie Mfg., Inc.
Classic Arms Corp. (floorplates, grip caps)
Clymer Mfg. Co., Inc. (reamers)
Cook, Dave (metalsmithing only)
Crouse's Country Cover (Masking Gun Oil)
Custom Gun Products
Davidson Products For Shooters
Dayton Traister Co. (triggers; safeties)
Decker Shooting Products
Defense Moulding Enterprises (magazines)
Dem-Bart Hand Checkering Tools, Inc.
Dremel Mfg. Co. (grinders)
Duffy, Charles E.
Du-Lite Corp.
The Dutchman's Firearms, Inc.
Dyson & Son Ltd., Peter (accessories for antique gun collectors)
Edmund Scientific Co.
First, Distributors, Inc., Jack
Fisher, Jerry
Flashette Co. (bore illuminator gun cleaning aid)
Flex Gun Rods Co., Inc.
Foredom Electric Co.
Forster Products, Inc.
Garrett Accur-Lt. D.F.S. Co.
Grace Metal Products (screwdrivers, drifts)
GRS Corp. (Gravermeister; Grave Max tools)
Gunline Tools
Gun Parts Corp.
Gun-Tec (files)
Gutridge, Inc. (pin takedown tool, S&W action tool)
Half Moon Rifle Shop (hex screws)
Henriksen Tool Co., Inc. (reamers)
Huey Gun Cases, Marvin (high-grade English ebony tools)
Iosso Marine Products
Jantz Supply, Ken
JGS Precision Tool Mfg.
Jim's Gun Shop ("Belgian Blue" rust blues; stock fillers)
Kasenit Co., Inc. (surface hardening compound)
Kopp, Terry K. (stock rubbing compound; rust preventive grease)
Korzinek, J. (stainless steel bluing)
Lawson, John G.
Lea Mfg. Co.
Lee Supplies, Mark
Lee's Red Ramps
Liberty Antique Gunworks (spl. S&W tools)
Lock's Phila. Gun Exch.
Lortone, Inc.
Marsh, Mike (gun accessories)
Masen Co., John
McMillan Rifle Barrels (services)
MDS, Inc. (bore lights)
Meier Works (European accessories)
Metalife Industries (Metalife refinishing services)
Michaels of Oregon Co.
Millenium
Miniature Machine Co. (MMC) (screwdriver grinding fixtures)
Mittermeier, Frank
Moreton/Fordyce Enterprises
Nitex, Inc. (custom metal finish)
N&J Sales Co. (screwdrivers)
Novak's .45 Shop
Nowlin Custom Guns/Manufacturing
Palmgren Steel Prods. (vises, etc.)
Panavise Prods., Inc.
Pendleton Royal
Pilkington Gun Co. (Q.D. scope mount)
Power Custom, Inc.
Redman's Rifling & Reboring (22 rimfire liners)
Robar Co's, Inc., The
Roto/Carve (tool)
Russell Co., A.G. (Arkansas oilstones)
Rusteprufe Laboratories
Scott/McDougall Custom Gunsmiths
Seacliff International Inc. (portable parts washer)
Shaw's
Silhouette Arms Custom 45 Shop, Inc.
Slipshot MTS Group (metal treatment system)
Sports Support Systems, Inc. (Present Arms trade name)
Starrett Co., L.S.
Stuart Products, Inc. (Sight-Vise)
Sure Shot of L.A., Inc.
Texas Platers Supply Co. (plating kit)
Timney Mfg., Inc. (triggers)
Treville, Stan de (checkering patterns)
Van Gorden & Son, Inc., C.S. (Instant Blue)
Walker Arms Co., Inc. (tools)
Washita Mountain Whetstone Co.
Weaver Arms Corp. (action wrenches & transfer punches)
Weaver's Gun Shop (tools)
White Rock Tool & Die (rental chambering tools)
Will-Burt Co. (vises)
Williams Gun Sight Co.
Williams Shootin' Iron Service
Wilson Arms Co.
Wolff Co., W.C. (springs)

HANDGUN ACCESSORIES

AA Arms, Inc.
Action Ammo Ltd.

Adco Sales, Inc.
Ajax Custom Grips, Inc.
Allen Companies, Bob
American Gas & Chemical Co. Ltd. (cleaning lube)
American Gripcraft (exotic wood)
AMT
Answer Products Co. (Accu-Comfort Magnum Pistol Glove)
Armsport, Inc.
Baker's Leather Goods, Ray
Baramie Corp. (Hip-Grip)
Bar-Sto Precision Machine (barrels)
Behlert Precision
Brauer Bros. Mfg. Co.
Brown Products, Ed
Centaur Systems, Inc. (Quadra-Lok barrels)
Central Specialties Co. (trigger locks only)
Cobra Gunskin
Dade Screw Machine Products (Dade speed loaders)
Detonics
Dibble, Derek A. (magazines)
Doskocil Mfg. Co., Inc (Gun Guard cases)
Eagle International, Inc.
Essex Arms (45 Auto frames)
Feminine Protection, Inc. (holster handbags)
Frielich Police Equipment (cases)
Frielich, R.S. (cases)
Galati International
Glock, Inc.
Gremmel Enterprises (conversion units)
Gunfitters
Gun-Ho Sports Cases
Gun Parts Corp.
Hafner Enterprises, Inc.
Hebard Guns, Gil
Hill Speed Leather, Ernie
H.K.S. Products (revolver speed loaders)
Intratec
Jett & Co., Inc.
Keller Co., The
King's Gun Works
K&K Ammo Wrist Band
Kopp, Terry K.
Lakewood Products, Inc.
La Prade (full moon clips)
Lee's Red Ramps (ramp insert, spring kits)
Lee Precision, Inc. (pistol rest holders)
Liberty Antique Gunworks (shims for S&W revolvers)
Lighthouse Mfg. Co., Inc.
Loch Leven
Lomont Precision Bullets, Kent (Auto Mag only)
Lone Star Gunleather
Magnum Research, Inc.
Mag-Pack
Mahony, Philip Bruce
M.A.M. Products, Inc. (free standing brass catcher for all auto pistols and/or semi-auto rifles)
Markell Incorporated
Masen Co., John
Millett Industries
MTM Molded Prods. Co.
Mustra's Custom Guns, Inc., Carl
Noble Co., Jim
No-Sho Mfg. Co.
Nowlin Custom Guns/Manufacturing
Owen, Harry
Pachmayr Ltd.(cases)
Pacific Intl. Merch. Corp. (Vega 45 Colt combination magazine)
Pflumm Gun Mfg. Co. (pistol cases)
Poly Choke Div. (handgun ribs)
Ranch Products (third-moon clips)
Ransom Intl. Corp.
Rattlers Brand
Rupert's Gun Shop
Russwood Custom Pistol Grips
Safariland Ltd., Inc.
Sile Distributors
Sonderman, Robert (solid walnut fitted handgun cases; other woods)
Southwind Sancions
Sport Specialties (22 rimfire adapters; 22 insert barrels for T/C Contender, automatic pistols)
Sportsmen's Equipment Co.
SSK Industries
Taurus S.A., Forjas
Triple K Manufacturing Co. (mags. for semi-auto handguns)
Tyler Mfg.-Dist., Melvin (grip adaptor)
Volquartsen Custom Ltd.
Wardell Precision Handguns Ltd. (grip adaptor)
Wilson's Gun Shop

HANDGUN GRIPS

Ahrends, Kim (exotic wood grips for 1911-frame pistols)
Ajax Custom Grips, Inc.
Altamont Mfg. Co.
Art Jewel Enterprises Ltd. (Eagle Grips)
Barami Corp.
Bear Hug Grips, Inc. (custom)
Beeman Precision Arms, Inc. (airguns only)
Behlert Precision
Boone's Custom Ivory Grips, Inc.
Boyd's Gunstock Industries, Inc.
Cobra Gunskin
Cole-Grip
Davis Service Center, Bill
Eagle Grips
Fish, Marshall F.
Fishpaw, Roy C. (custom wood & ivory)
Fitz Pistol Grip Co.
Gun Parts Corp.
Handgun Grips
Herrett's Stocks, Inc.
Hogue Grips (Monogrip)
Jones Munitions Systems, Paul
Linebaugh Custom Sixguns, John
Logan Security Products Co. ("Streetloader" for K&L frame S&Ws)
Maloni, Russ
Monogrip
Monte Kristo Pistol Grip Co.
Mustang Custom Pistol Grips
Newell, Robert H. (custom stocks)
Nygord Precision Products
Olympic Arms, Inc.
Pachmayr Ltd.
Radical Grips
Renner Co., R.J.
Rosenberg & Sons, A. Jack
Royal Ordnance Works Ltd.
Russwood Custom Pistol Grips (custom exotic woods)
Sile Distributors
Sonderman, Robert B.
Spegel, Craig
Taurus S.A., Forjas
Tyler Mfg.-Dist., Melvin
Volquartsen Custom Ltd.
Wallace, R.D. (custom only)
Wayland Prec. Wood Prods. ("Classic" & "Double Diamond" grips)
Wilson's Gun Shop

HEARING PROTECTORS

AO Safety Prods. (ear valves, muffs)
Bausch & Lomb, Inc.
Bilsom Interntl., Inc. (ear plugs, muffs)
Clark Co., Inc., David
E-A-R, Inc.
Flents Products Co., Inc.
Marble Arms Corp.
North Consumer Prods. Div. (Lee Sonic ear valves)
Safesport Manufacturing Co.
Safety Direct (Silencio)
Smith & Wesson
Willson Safety Prods. Div. (Ray-O-Vac)

HOLSTERS AND LEATHER GOODS

A.A. Arms, Inc.
Aker Leather Products
Alessi Holsters, Inc.
Allen Co., Bob
American Sales & Mfg. Co.
Arratoonian, Andy
Bachman, Rick M.
Baker's Leather Goods, Roy
Bandcor Industries
Bang-Bang Boutique (for women)
Barami Corp.
Beeman Precision Arms, Inc. (airguns only)
Behlert Precision
Bianchi International, Inc.
Blocker's Custom Holsters, Ted
Border Guns & Leather (Old West custom)
Boyt Co., Div. of Welsh Sporting Goods
Brauer Bros. Mfg. Co.
Browning (Gen. Off.)
Bucheimer Co., J.M.
Carvajal Fabricating Co.
Cathey Enterprises, Inc.
Chace Leather Prods.
Cherokee Gun Accessories
Clements, Chas
Cobra Gunskin
Cobra Sport
Davis Leather Co., G. Wm.
DeSantis Holster & Leather Co.
El Paso Saddlery
Epps (Orillia) Northern Ltd., Ellwood (custom made)
Eutaw Company, Inc.
Faust, Inc., T.G.
Fobus International Ltd.
Galati International
GALCO International, Ltd.
Glock, Inc. (holsters)
GML Products, Inc.
Gould & Goodrich
Gunfitters, The (custom holsters)
Gun Leather Limited
Gun Parts Corp.
Hafner Enterprises, Inc.
Hebard Guns, Gil
Henigson & Associates, Steve
High North Products (1-oz. Mongoose gun sling)
Hill Speed Leather, Ernie
Holster Outpost
Horsehoe Leather Prods.
Hoyt Holster Co., Inc.
Hume, Don
Hunter Co., Inc.
John's Custom Leather
Jumbo Sports Prods.
Kane Products, Inc. (GunChaps)
Kirkpatrick Leather Co.
Kolpin Mfg., Inc.
L.A.R. Manufactring, Inc.
Lawrence Leather Co.
Lone Star Gunleather
Magnolia Sports, Inc.
Marple & Associates, Dick
Michael's of Oregon, Co. (Uncle Mike's)
Nelson Combat Leather, Bruce
Noble Co., Jim (Supreme quick-draw shoulder holster, etc.)
No-Sho Mfg. Co.
Nowlin Custom Guns/Manufacturing
Null Holsters Ltd., K.L.
Ojala Holsters, Arvo
Oklahoma Leather Products, Inc.
Old West Reproductions
Pathfinder Sports Leather
Phelps Mfg. Co.
Pony Express Sport Shop, Inc.
Proline Handgun Leather, Greg Kramer (concealment and duty rigs)
Red Head, Inc.
Renegade
Ringler Custom Leather Co.
Roy's Custom Leather Goods
Rybka Custom Leather Equipment, Thad
Safariland Ltd., Inc.
Safety Speed Holster
Schulz Industries
Shoemaker & Sons, Tex
Shootin' Accessories Ltd.
Shurkatch Corp.
Sile Distr.
Silhouette Leathers (custom holsters)
Smith Saddlery, Jesse W.
Southwind Sanctions
Sparks, Milt
Stalker, Inc.
Strong Holster Co.
Tabler Marketing (cincher)
Taylor's & Co., Inc.
Torel, Inc. (gun slings)
Triple-K Mfg. Co.
Tyler Mfg.-Dist., Melvin
Uncle Mike's
Venus Industries
Viking Leathercraft, Inc.
Whinnery, Walt
Wild Bill Cleaver (antique holstermaker)

HUNTING AND CAMP GEAR, CLOTHING, ETC.

A&B Industries, Inc.
Ace Sportswear, Inc.
Adventure 16, Inc. (camping, hunting, climbing accessories)
API Outdoors, Inc.
All Weather Outerwear
Allen Co., Bob
Atsko/Sno-Seal, Inc.
Barbour, Inc.
Bauer, Eddie
Bean, L.L.
Bear Archery (Himalayan backpack)
Big Beam (lamp)
Boss Manufacturing Company (hunting gloves and mitts)
Browning (Gen. Off.)
Brunton USA (compasses)
Cabela's (mail order)
Camp-Cap Products
Chimere, Inc.
Chippewa Shoe Co. (boots)
Clarkfield Enterprises, Inc. (camo clothing)
Coghlan's Ltd.
Crawford Co., R.M. (clothing)
Coleman Co., Inc.
Danner Shoe Mfg. Co. (boots)
Deer-Me Prod. Co. (tree steps)
Dr. O's Products, Ltd.
Dunham Co. (boots)
Duofold, Inc. (clothing)
Durango Boot
Duxbak, Inc.
Eutaw Company, Inc.
Feather Flex Decoys
Finerty, Raymond F. (Medalist apparel)
Fish-N-Hunt, Inc.
Frankonia Jagd, Hofmann & Co.
Game-Winner, Inc. (camouflage suits; orange vests)
Gander Mountain, Inc.
Glacier Glove (neoprene gloves for hunting)
Gun Club Sportswear
Hinman Outfitters, Bob
Hunter's Specialties, Inc.
Kamik Outdoor Footwear
LaCrosse Footwear, Inc.
Langenberg Hat Co.
Liberty Trouser Co.
MAG Instrument, Inc.
Marathon Rubber Prods. Co., Inc. (rain gear)
Marble Arms Corp.
Melton Shirt Co., Inc.
Molin Ind./Tru-Nord Division
Mountain View Sports, Inc.
Nelson/Weather-rite
Newbern Glove (hunting/shooting gloves)
Northlake Boot Co. (Durango)
Original Mink Oil, Inc.
Orvis Co., The (fishing gear; clothing)
Partridge Sales Ltd., John
P.A.S.T. Corp. (shooting shirts)
Pendleton Woolen Mills (OutdoorsMan cloth)
Porta Blind, Inc. (ground blind)
Precise International
Pro-Mark (shooting/hunting gloves)
Pyromid, Inc. (portable camp stove)
Ranger Mfg. Co., Inc. (camouflage suits)
Rattlers Brand (clothing)
Red Ball (boots)

Red Head, Inc.
Refrigiwear, Inc.
Re-Heater, Inc. (re-usable portable heat pack)
Remington Footwear Co.
Safari Gun Co.
Safesport Manufacturing Co.
Saf-T-Bak, Inc.
Scansport, Inc. (wool hunting packs)
Servus Rubber Co. (footwear)
Streamlight, Inc.
Swanndra New Zealand (pure wool hunting clothing)
Teledyne Co.
10-X Mfg. Products Group
Thompson, Norm
Tink's Safariland Hunting Corp. (camouflage rain gear)
Traq, Inc.
Waffen-Frankonia
Wakina
Walker Shoe Co. (boots)
Walls Industries
Warner, Glenn, Endicott Johnson (boots)
Wolverine Boots & Shoes Div. (footwear)
Woolrich Woolen Mills
Wyoming Knife Co. (saw)

KNIVES AND KNIFEMAKER'S SUPPLIES—FACTORY AND MAIL ORDER

Adventure 16, Inc.
Aitor - Cuchilleria Del Norte, S.A.
Alcas Cutlery Corp. (Cutco)
Atlanta Cutlery (mail order, supplies)
B&D Trading Co., Inc.
Baker's Leather Goods, Roy
Barteaux Machete
Bean, L.L. (mail order)
Benchmark Knives
Blackjack Knives
Blue Ridge Knives
Boker USA, Inc.
Bowen Knife Co.
Browning (Gen. Off.)
Brunton USA
Buck Knives, Inc.
Camillus Cutlery Co. (Sword Brand)
Case & Sons Cutlery Co., W.R.
Catoctin Cutlery
Chicago Cutlery Co.
Christopher Firearms Co., Inc., E. (supplies)
Clements, Chas (exotic sheaths)
Coast Cutlery Co.
Cold Steel, Inc.
Coleman Co., Inc.
Collins Brothers Div. (belt-buckle knife)
Colonial Knife Co. (Master Brand)
Compass Industries, Inc.
Creative Craftsman, Inc., The (cutlery sharpening equipment)
Crosman Blades
Custom Knifemaker's Supply
Damascus-U.S.A.
Delhi Gun House (Damascus knife blades)
Dixie Gun Works, Inc. (supplies)
Ek Commando Knife Co.
Empire Cutlery Corp.
Eze-Lap Diamond Prods. (knife sharpeners)
Fibron Products, Inc.
Fiskars
Frank, H.H.
Frost Cutlery Co.
Gerber Legendary Blades
G96 Designtech, Inc.
Green Head Corp.
Gutmann Cutlery Co., Inc.
H&B Forge Co. (throwing knives, tomahawks)
Harrington Cutlery, Inc., Russell (Dexter, Green River Works)
Henckels Zwillingswerk, Inc., J.A.
Hubertus Schneidwarenfabrik
Ibberson (Sheffield) Ltd., George
Indian Ridge Traders
Iron Mountain Knife Co.
J.A. Blades, Inc. (supplies)
Jantz Supply
Jewel Ent., Art
Joy Enterprises (Fury sporting knives)
KA-BAR Cutlery
KA-BAR Knives
Ken's Finn Knives
Kershaw Knives/Kai Cutlery USA Ltd.
Knife Importers, Inc.
Koval Knives/IRT (supplies)
Lamson & Goodnow Mfg. Co.
Lansky Sharpeners (sharpening devices)
Linder Solingen Knives
Mar Knives, Inc., Al
Matthews Cutlery (mail order)
Molin Ind./Tru-Nord Division
Murphy Co., Inc., R. (StaySharp)
Normark Corp.
Outdoor Edge Cutlery Corp.
Parker-Case
Phoenix Arms Co. Ltd., Hy-Score Works
Plaza Cutlery, Inc. (mail order)
Precise International
Queen Cutlery Co.
Randall-Made Knives
R&C Knives and Such (mail order)
Russell Co., A.G.
Sanders Custom Gun Service (mail order)
Scansport, Inc.
Schiffman, Mike (mail order)
Schrade Cutlery Corp.
Sheffield Knifemakers Supply
Smith & Wesson
Smith Saddlery, Jesse W. (sheathmakers)
Swiss Army Brands Ltd.
Tekna
Thompson/Center Arms
United Cutlery Corporation
Utica Cutlery Co. (Kutmaster)
Valor Corp.
Venus Industries
Washita Mountain Whetstone Co.
Weber Jr., Rudolf
Wenoka/Seastyle
Western Cutlery, Inc.
Whinnery, Walt (sheathmaker)
Wostenholm
Wyoming Knife Co.

LABELS, BOXES, CARTRIDGE HOLDERS

A&B Industries, Inc.
Accuracy Products (plastic ammo boxes)
Barbour, Inc.
Cabinet Mtn. Outfitter (cartridge holders)
Corbin Mfg. & Supply, Inc.
Del Rey Products
Flambeau Prods. Corp.
Gould & Goodrich
Hunter Co., Inc.
KLP, Inc.
Lakewood Products, Inc.
Marple & Associates, Dick
Peterson Instant Targets Co. (cartridge box labels; Targ-Dots)
Scharch Mfg., Inc.
Shootin' Accessories Ltd.

LOAD TESTING AND PRODUCT TESTING, (CHRONOGRAPHING, BALLISTIC STUDIES)

Ballistic Products, Inc. (manuals - loading info)
Ballistic Research (ballistic studies, pressure and velocity)
Blackwell, W.W. (internal ball. computer program for rifle cartridges)
Corbin Applied Technology
D&D Gunsmiths Ltd.
D&H Precision Tooling (pressure testing equipment)
Harrison-Hurtz Enterprises, Inc.
H-S Precision, Inc.
Hutton Rifle Ranch (ballistic studies)
Lachaussee S.A.
Lighthouse Mfg. Co., Inc.
Lomont Precision Bullets (handguns, handgun ammunition)
Maionchi - L.M.I.
Plum City Ballistics Range
Professional Hunter Supplies
Quartz-Lok
Rupert's Gun Shop
Russell's Rifle Shop (load testing and chronographing to 300 yds.)
Shooting Chrony, Inc.
SSK Industries
Sierra Bullets (chronographing, ballistic studies)
Thunderbird Cartridge Co., Inc.
Vancini, Carl A.
White Laboratory, Inc., H.P.

MISCELLANEOUS

Action, left-hand (Gentry Custom Gunmaker, David)
Action, Mauser-style only (Crandall Tool & Machine Co.)
Action, single shot (Miller Arms, Inc.)
Actions, rifle, stainless steel (Hall Manufacturing)
Activator (B.M.F. Activator, Inc.)
Adapter cartridges (Alex, Inc.)
Adapters for subcalibers
Airgun accessories, Beeman Pell seat, Pell Size, etc. (Beeman Precision Arms, Inc.)
All Rite Products, Inc.
Ammo pouches (Concorde Arms, Inc.)
Ammunition loading machines (Lachaussee S.A.)
Anodizing, black (Ivanoff, Thomas G.)
Archery (Bear Archery)
Archery target sights (ACCRA 300)
Archery sight (Hawkeye West)
Arms restoration (Mazur Restoration, Pete)
Assault rifle accessories (Cherokee Gun Accessories)
Assault rifle accessories (Feather Industries, Inc.)
Assault rifle accessories, folding stock (Ram-Line, Inc.)
Automatic firearm magazines (MEC-GAR S.R.L.)
Bedding kit, Tru-Set (Fenwal, Inc.)
Belt buckles, laser engr. hardwood (Herrett's Stocks, Inc.)
Belt buckles (Just Brass, Inc.)
Belt buckles (Pilgrim Pewter, Inc.)
Benchrest accessories (Davidson Products for Shooters)
Benchrest & accuracy shooters equipment (Bob Pease Accuracy)
Benchrest rifles & accessories (Hart & Son, Inc., Robert W.)
Body armor (Faust, Inc., T.G.)
Bore collimator, Sweany Site-A-Line optical collimator (Alley Supply Co.)
Bore illuminator, gun cleaning aid (Flashette Co.)
Bore lights (MDS, Inc.)
Brass catcher, free standing for all auto pistols and/or semi-auto rifles (M.A.M. Products, Inc.)
Brass sorters (Ben's Gun Shop)
Bumper boot jack, car (S.F. Legacy, Ltd.)
Camouflage accessories (Camofare Company)
Camouflage accessories (Camp-Cap Products)
Cannons (South Bend Replicas, Inc.)
Cartridge adapters (Sport Specialties)
Case gauge (Plum City Ballistics Range)
Case hardening compounds (Kasenit Co., Inc.)
Cased, high-grade English tools, ebony, horn, ivory handles (Huey Gun Cases, Marvin)
Caswell International Corporation
Compasses, hand warmers (The American Import Co.)
Compasses (Brunton USA)
Convert-A-Pell (Jett & Co., Inc.)
Crossbows (Barnett International)
Damascus cutlery steel (Damascus-USA)
Deer Drag (D&H Prods. Co., Inc.)
Dehumidifiers (Golden Rod Dehumidifier Co., Inc.)
Dehumidifiers (Golden Rod)
Dehumidifiers, silica gel dehumidifier (Hydrosorbent Products)
Dryer, thermo-electric (Golden Rod Dehumidifier Co., Inc.)
Dryer, thermo-electric (Golden Rod Enterprises)
Dummy rounds (Duds Ammo & Supply Co.)
E-Z Loader, for 22-cal. rifles (Del Rey Products)
Ear-valve, Lee-Sonic (North Consumer Prods. Div.)
Electric boot dryers (Baekgaard Ltd.)
Electronic practice system - handguns (Nu-Teck Ltd.)
Farrsight, sighting aids for handgunners—clip on aperture (Farr Studio)
Firearms restoration (Steve Moeller)
Firearms training (Ballistics Software Intl.)
Firearms training (Scott/McDougall Custom Gunsmiths)
Flares (Aztec International Ltd.)
Flashlights (Dynalite Products, Inc.)
Flashlights (MAG Instrument, Inc.)
Flashlights (Tekna)
Flashlights & lanterns (Streamlight, Inc.)
Game drag device (Easy Pull/Outlaw Products)
Game scent (Buck Stop Lure Co., Inc.)
Game scent, CMO scents and lures (Cabinet Mtn. Outfitter)
Game scent, scents and lures (Dr. O's Products Ltd.)
Game scent, Indian Buck lure (Rickard, Inc., Pete)
Game Scent, buck lure (Tink's Safariland Hunting Corp.)
Gas pistol (Penguin Industries, Inc.)
Grip caps (Classic Arms Corp.)
Gun bedding kit (Fenwal, Inc., Resins System Div.)
Gun, bow racks (All Rite Products, Inc.)
Gun decorating (Baron Technology, Inc.)
Gun jewelry (Pilgrim Pewter, Inc.)
Gun locks (Brown Manufacturing)
Gun photographer (Bilal, Mustafa)
Gun photographer (Hanusin, John)
Gun photographer (Macbean, Stan)
Gun photographer (Semmer, Charles)
Gun photographer (Smith, Michael L.)
Gun photographer (Weyer International)
Gun safes (Abel Safe & File Co.)
Gun safety, Gun Alert covers (Master Products, Inc.)
Gun slings (Boonie Packer Products/JFS, Inc.)
Gun slings (Torel, Inc.)
Gun vise (Pflumm Gun Mfg. Co.)
Hand exerciser (Action Products, Inc.)
Hearing protector (Clark Co., Inc., David)
Hide-A-Gun, cartridge belts, shell carriers (Ansen Enterprises)
Horsepac (Yellowstone Wilderness Supply)
Hooks for pegboards (Hugger Hooks Co.)
Hunting videos (Kulis Freeze Dry Taxidermy)
Hypodermic rifles and pistols, slaughtering pistols (Bergeron)
Indoor range (Guncraft Sports, Inc.)
Insect repellent (Armor, Div. of Buck Stop, Inc.)
Insert barrels and cartridge adapters (Sport Specialties)
Insert barrels (Gremmel Enterprises)
IR detection systems (GTS Enterprises, Inc.)

KDF, Inc.
Knife sharpeners (Lansky Sharpeners)
Knife sharpeners (Edgecraft Corp.)
Laser aim (Laser Aim, Inc.)
Laser aim (Laser Devices, Inc.)
Leather care products (EKOL Leather Care)
Leather waterproofing (Atsco/Sno-Seal, Inc.)
Lettering (Bill Adair)
Lubricants/Dry film (Dykstra, Doug)
Locks, gun (Master Lock Co.)
Lubricant/Gun Coat (Flouramics, Inc.)
Lubricants, lead removal (Muscle Products Corp./Firepower Lubricants)
Lugheads, floorplate overlays (Bell Originals, Inc., Sid)
Magazines, plastic cartridge—high impact (Defense Moulding Enterprises)
Magazines (Dibble, Derek A.)
Magazines, stainless steel (Mitchell Arms, Inc.)
Magazines (Ram-Line, Inc.)
Marsh, Mike
Max Multipurpose Ax (Forrest Tool Company)
Miniature cannons, replicas; Gatling guns (Furr Arms)
Monte Carlo pad (Hoppe's Division, Penguin Ind., Inc.)
Old Gun Industry Art (Hansen Cartridge Company)
Powderhorns (Frontier)
Powderhorns (Tennessee Valley Mfg.)
Practice wax bullets (Brazos Arms Co.)
Ransom handgun rests (Ransom Intl. Corp.)
Record books, for dealers and collectors (PFRB Company)
Reload-A-Stand, portable (Engineered Accessories)
Rifle magazines, 30-rd. Mini-14 (Butler Creek Corp.)
Rifle magazines, 25-rd. 22-cal. (Condor Mfg.)
Rifle magazines, 30-cal. M1 15 & 30-round (Miller, S.A.)
Rifle sighting device (Sure Shot of L.A., Inc.)
Rifle slings (Bianchi International, Inc.)
Rifle slings (Butler Creek Corp.)
Rifle slings (Chace Leather Prods.)
Rifle slings, 1-oz. Mongoose gun sling (High North Products)
Rifle slings (John's Custom Leather)
Rifle slings (Kirkpatrick Leather Co.)
Rifle slings (Kolpin Mfg., Inc.)
Rifle slings (Outdoor Connection, Inc.)
Rifle slings (Pathfinder Sports Leather)
Rifle slings (Schulz Industries)
RIG, NRA scoring plug (RIG Products)
Rotary flexible shaft power tools (Foredom Electric Co.)
Rubber bullets (CIDCO)
Rubber cheekpiece (Lodewick, W.H.)
Rust prevention (Rusteprufe Laboratories)
Saddle rings, studs (Goodwin, Fred)
Safaris (Africa) (Professional Hunter Specialties)
Safeties, for Rem. 870P (Harper, William E.)
Safeties, side lever for rifle (Taylor & Robbins)
Safeties (Williams Gun Sight Co.)
Safety devices (P&M Sales and Service)
Safety slug (Glaser Safety Slug)
Sav-Bore (Saunders Sptg. Gds.)
Scents (Wildlife Research Center, Inc.)
Scrimshaw (Bonham, Henry "Hank")
Scrimshaw (Boone's Custom Ivory Grips, Inc.)
Scrimshaw (Marek, George)
Scrimshaw (Sherwood, George)
Scrimshaw, handgun grips—ivory or Micarta (Taylor, Twyla)
Self defense sprays (Bushwacker Backpack & Supply Co., Inc.)
Sharpening stones, Arkansas oilstones (Russell Co., A.G.)
Shell catcher (Condor Mfg.)
Shell catchers (T&S Industries, Inc.)
Shellholders (Kolpin Mfg., Inc.)
Shooting bench (Sportsman Supply Co.)
Shooting coats (10-X Products Group)
Shooting glasses (American Optical Corp.)
Shooting glasses, Ray Ban (Bausch & Lomb, Inc.)
Shooting glasses (Bilsom Interntl, Inc.)
Shooting glasses (Willson Safety Prods. Division)
Shooting gloves, singles only, right or left (Churchill Glove Co., James)
Shooting range equipment (Caswell Internatl. Corp.)
Shooting stools (Houtz & Barwick)
Shotgun accessories, lasersights, folding stocks (Adventurer's Outpost)
Shotgun ribs (Poly Choke Div., Marble Arms Corp.)
Shotgun sight, binocular (Trius Products, Inc.)
Shotgun specialist, ventilated, free-floating ribs (Moneymaker Guncraft)
Shotgun speedloader (Armstec, Inc.)
Shotshell adapter, Plummer 410 converter (PC Co.)
Shotshell adapter, 12 ga./410 converter (Ramos, Jesse)
Sight-vise (Stuart Products, Inc.)
Slings (DTM International, Inc.)
Snap caps (Armsport, Inc.)
Snap caps (Edwards Recoil Reducer)
Sportsmen's jewelry (Bell Originals, Inc., Sid)
Springs (Wolff Co., W.C.)
Supersound, safety device (Edmund Scientific Co.)
Swivels (Boonie Packer Products/JFS, Inc.)
Swivels (Michaels of Oregon)
Swivels (Sile Distributors)
Swivels (Williams Gun Sight Co.)
Tomahawks (H&B Forge Co.)
Tree seats, treestands (A&J Products)
Treestand, climbing (API Outdoors, Inc.)
Treestands (Amacker International, Inc.)
Treestands (East Enterprises, Inc.)
Treestands (Summit Specialties, Inc.)
Treestands (Trax America, Inc.)
Treestands (Treemaster)
Tree steps (Centaur Archery, Inc.)
Tree steps (Deer Me Products Co.)
Trophies (Blackinton & Co., V.H.)
Trophies, trap & skeet shooters (Jacqueline Favre)
Video tape (Foothills Video Productions)
World hunting information (J/B Adventures & Safaris, Inc.)
Xythos-Miniature Revolver (Andres & Dworsky)

MUZZLE-LOADING GUNS, BARRELS OR EQUIPMENT

Adkins, Luther (breech plugs)
Anderson Mfg. Co. (Accra-Shot)
Antique Gun Parts, Inc. (parts)
Armi San Paolo
Armoury, Inc., The
Armsport, Inc.
Beaver Lodge (custom ML)
Bentley, John
Blackhawk East (blackpowder)
Blackhawk Mtn. (blackpowder)
Blackhawk West (blackpowder)
Blue and Gray Prods., Inc. (equipment)
Brazos Arms Co.
B-Square Co.
Buckskin Machine Works
Buffalo Bullet Co., Inc. (bullets, balls and sabots)
Burgess & Son, Robert W.
Butler Creek Corp. (poly & maxi patch)
Cache La Poudre Rifleworks (custom muzzleloaders)
Champlin, R. MacDonald (custom muzzleloaders)
Chopie Mfg., Inc. (nipple wrenches)
Connecticut Valley Arms Co. (muzzleloaders, kits)
Cumberland Knife & Gun Works
Cureton, Earl T. (powder horns)
Dangler, Homer L.
Day & Sons, Inc., Leonard
deHaas Barrels
Denver Arms, Ltd.
Desert Industries, Inc.
Dixie Gun Works, Inc.
Dixon Muzzleloading Shop, Inc.
Dyson & Son Ltd., Peter (accoutrements for ML shooter replicas)
EMF Co., Inc.
Euroarms of America, Inc.
Eutaw Company, Inc.
Fautheree, Andy (custom ML guns)
Fellowes, Ted (custom ML)
Fish, Marshall F. (antique ML repairs)
Flintlock Muzzle Loading Gun Shop, The
Forster Products, Inc.
Frontier (powderhorns)
Getz Barrel Co. (barrels)
GOEX, Inc. (blackpowder)
Gonic Arms, Inc.
Goode, A.R. (ML rifle barrels)
Green Mountain Rifle Barrel Co., Inc.
Guncraft, Inc.
Gun Parts Corp.
Gun Works, The (supplies)
Hatfield International, Inc. (squirrel rifle)
Hege Jagd-u. Sporthandels GmbH
House of Muskets, Inc., The (ML barrels and supplies)
Hughes, Steven Dodd (custom guns)
Hunkeler, A. (muzzle-loading guns)
K.B.I., Inc.
K&M Industries, Inc.
Kwik-Site Co.
Large Gun & Mach. Shop, Wm.
Lever Arms Serv. Ltd.
Lighthouse Mfg. Co., Inc.
Log Cabin Sport Shop
Lyman Products Corp.
MacDonald, R. Champlin
McCann's Muzzle-Gun Works
Modern Muzzleloading, Inc.
Montana Armory, Inc.
Mountain State Muzzleloading Supplies
Muzzleload Magnum Products (MMP)
Muzzleloaders Etc., Inc.
Navy Arms Co.
Neumann GmbH
Newman Gunshop (custom ML rifles)
October Country
Oklahoma Leather Rod., Inc.
Ox-Yoke Originals, Inc. (dry lube patches)
Peterson Gun Shop, A.W.
Phyl-Mac
Rooster Laboratories (patch and ball bullet lubricants)
R.V.I. (high grade BP accoutrements)
Scott, Inc., Tyler (Shooter's Choice black solvent; patch lube)
Sharon Gun Specialties, Inc.
Sharps Arms Co., Inc., C.
Shaw, Inc., E.R. (barrels)
Sile Distributors
Siler Locks, C.E. (flintlocks)
Single Shot, Inc.
Slipshot MTS Group
South Bend Replicas, Inc. (artillery)
Southern Bloomer Mfg. Company (cotton gun cleaning patches)
Swampfire Shop, The
Taylor's & Co., Inc.
TDP Industries, Inc.
Tennessee Valley Mfg. (powderhorns)
Ten-Ring Precision, Inc.
Thompson Bullet Lube
Track of the Wolf, Inc.
Traditions, Inc. (guns, kits, accessories)
Trail Guns Armory
Uberti USA, Inc.
Ultra Light Arms, Inc.
Upper Missouri Trading Co.
Vibra-Tek Co.
Warren Muzzle Loading Co., Inc. (blackpowder accessories)
Wells, Fred
Wescombe (parts)
Williamson-Pate Gunsmith Serv.
Winchester Sutler, Inc. (haversacks)
Winter & Associates (Olde Pennsylvania ML accessories)
Young Country Arms (paste lube for blackpowder BP fouling)

PISTOLSMITHS

Accuracy Gun Shop
Accuracy Unlimited
Accurate Plating & Weaponry, Inc.
Adair, Bill
Ahlman's, Inc.
Ahrends, Kim (custom combat conversion packages)
Aldis, Richard L.
Alpha Precision, Inc.
American Pistolsmiths Guild
Armament Gunsmithing Co., Inc.
Baer Custom Guns (accurizing 45 autos and Comp II Syst.; custom XP100s, PPC revolver)
Bain and Davis, Inc.
Baity's Custom Gunworks
Banks Pistolsmith, Ed
Bar-Sto Precision Machine (single-shot barrels for 45 ACP)
Barta's Gunsmithing
Beal, R.S., Jr. (conversions)
Behlert Precision (short actions)
Bell's Custom Shop
Bill's Gun Repair
Border Guns & Leather
Bowen Classic Arms Corp.
Brian, C.T.
Briley
Brown Products, Ed
Bustani, Leo
Campbell, Dick (PPC guns; custom)
Cannon's Guns
Caraville Manufacturing
Cellini, Vito
Chesire & Perez Dist.
Chuck's Gun Shop
Clark Custom Guns, Inc.
Combat Shop, The
Competitive Pistol Shop, The
Corkys Gun Clinic
Costa, David
Curtis Custom Shop
Custom Gun Guild
Cylinder & Slide, Inc.
Darlington Gun Works, Inc.
Davis Service Center, Bill
Day & Sons, Inc., Leonard
D&D Gunsmiths, Ltd.
Dilliot Gunsmithing, Inc.
DiStefano, Dominic (accurizing)
D&L Sports
DMG Technologies, Inc.
Duncan's Gunworks, Inc.
Dwyer, Dan
Dyson & Son Ltd., Peter
E.M.F. Company, Inc.
First Distributors, Inc., Jack
Fisher Custom Firearms
Fountain Products
Francesca Stabilizer's, Inc.
Freilich Police Equipment
Garthwaite, Jim
Genecco Gun Works, K.
Gilman-Mayfield
Giron, Robert E.
Greider Precision Products
Gunsite Gunsmithy
Gunsmithing Ltd.
Gutridge, Inc.
Hamilton, Keith
Hammond, Guy
Hanson's Gun Center
Hardison, Charles
Hebard Guns, Gil

Heinie, Richard
High Bridge Arms, Inc.
Hindman, Ace
Hoag, James W.
Irwin, Campbell H.
Ivanoff, Thomas G.
Jaeger, Inc., Paul
Jarvis Gunsmithing, Inc.
Jones, J.D.
Jungkind, Reeves C.
Jurras, L.E.
Ken's Gun Specialties
Kilham, Benjamin
Kimball, Gary
King's Gun Works, Inc.
Kontos, Michael J.
Kopec Ent., John A. (SA Colts only)
Kopp, Terry K. (rebarreling, conversions)
La Clinique du .45
LaFrance Specialties
Largent, Nelson H.
Laughridge, William R.
Lawson, John G.
Lee's Red Ramps
Linebaugh Custom Sixguns, John
Lomont Precision Bullets (Auto Mag only)
Long, George F.
Mac's .45 Shop
Mag-na-port International, Inc.
Mahony, Phillip Bruce
Marent, Rudolf (Hammerli)
Martin, Elwyn H.
Martz, John V. (custom German Lugers & P-38s)
Marvel, Alan
McMurdo, Lynn
Miller Custom
Mitchell's Accuracy Shop
Moran, Jerry
Mountain Bear Rifle Works, Inc.
Mullis Guncraft
Mustra's Custom Guns, Inc., Carl
Nastoff's 45 Shop (1911 conversions)
Neighbor, William
Novak, Wayne
Nowlin Custom Guns/Manufacturing
Nu-Line Guns
Nygord Precision Products
Oglesby & Oglesby Gunmakers, Inc.
Pachmayr Ltd.
Pacific Pistolcraft
Paris, Frank J.
Paterson Gunsmithing
Performance Specialists
Phillips & Bailey, Inc.
Pierce Pistols
Plaxco, J. Michael
Power Custom, Inc.
Practical Tools, Inc.
Precision Specialties
Ries, Chuck
Robar Co's, Inc., The
Roberts Custom Guns
Rogers Gunsmithing, Bob (custom)
Scott/McDougall Custom Gunsmiths
Seecamp Co., Inc., L.W.
Shockley, Harold H.
Shooter Shop, The
Shows, Hank
Silhouette Arms Custom 45 Shop, Inc.
Sipes Gun Shop
Spokhandguns, Inc.
Sports Shack
Sportsmen's Equipmt. Co. (specialty limiting trigger motion in autos)
SSK Industries
Steger, James R.
Strawbridge, Victor W.
Stroup, Earl R.
Swenson's 45 Shop, A.D.
300 Gunsmith Service, Inc.
Ten-Ring Precision, Inc.
Thompson, Randall
Timney Mfg., Inc.
Trapper Gun, Inc.
T.S.W. Conversions, Inc.
Ulrich, Dennis A.
Unick's Gunsmithing
Vic's Gun Refinishing
Volquartsen Custom Ltd.
Wallace, R.D.
Walters Industries
Wessinger Custom Gun & Engraving
Western Design
Williamson-Pate Gunsmith Service
Wilson's Gun Shop
Woods Pistolsmithing
Wisner's Gun Shop, Inc.

REBORING AND RERIFLING

Ackley, P.O.
Barnes Custom Shop
Bellm Contenders (rifle only)
DKT, Inc.
Francotte Et Cie S.A., Auguste
Goode, A.R.
H&S Liner Service
Irwin Gunsmith, Campbell H.
Ivanoff, Thomas G.
K-D, Inc.
Kopp, Terry K. (Inyis-A-Line bbl.; relining)
LaBounty Precision Reboring
Large Gun & Mach. Shop, Wm.
Matco, Inc.
Nu-Line Guns
Pence Precision Barrels
Redman's Reboring & Rerifling
Ridgetop Sporting Goods
Sharon Gun Specialties, Inc.
Silver Shields, Inc.
Snapp's Gunshop
Van Patten, J.W.
West, Robt. G. (barrel relining)

RELOADING TOOLS AND ACCESSORIES

ACTIV Industries, Inc. (plastic hulls, wads)
Advanced Car Mover Co., Inc. (bottom pour lead casting ladles)
Alpine's Precision Gunsmithing
American Products Co. (12-ga. shot wad)
Ammo Load, Inc.
AMT
ASI (Autoscale)
Balaance Co. (Adjustable bar for Lee Auto-Disk measure)
Ballisti-Cast, Inc.
Ballistic Products, Inc. (for shotguns)
Bartlett, J.
BE, Inc.
Belding & Mull, Inc.
Ben's Gun Shop
Berdon Machine Co. (metallic press)
Blackwell, W.W. (Load from a Disk)
Blount Sporting Equipment Division
B-Square Co.
Bullet Swaging Supply, Inc.
CCI
C&D Special Products (Clabuster Wads)
Camdex, Inc.
Carbide Die & Mfg. Co., Inc.
Carter Gun Works
Chevron Case Master
Clift Mfg., L.R. (reloading bench)
Coats, Mrs. Lester (lead wire core cutter)
Colorado Shooter's Supply (Hoch custom bullet moulds)
Colorado Sutlers Arsenal
Continental Kite & Key Co. (CONKKO) (primer pocket cleaner)
Cooper-Woodward (Perfect Lube)
Corbin Mfg. & Supply, Inc.
Custom Products (decapping tool, dies)
Denver Instrument Company
Destination North Software
Dewey Mfg. Co., J.
Dillon Precision Products, Inc.
Efemes Enterprises (Berdan decapper)
Engineered Accessories (Reload-A-Stand, portable)
Fitz Pistol Grip Co. (Fitz Flipper)
Flambeau Prods. Corp.
Forster Products, Inc.
4-D Die Co.
Fremont Tool Works
Fullmer, Geo. M. (seating die)
Green, Arthur S. (metals, fluxes, ladles for bullet casting)
Hanned Precision (22-SGB tool)
Hart & Son, Inc., Robert W.
Hensley & Gibbs (bullet moulds)
Hindman, Ace (Reloader's Logbook)
Hi-West Sales
Hollywood Loading Tools
Hornady Mfg. Co.
Huntington Die Specialties (Compact Press)
Iosso Marine Products
Javelina Products (Alox beeswax)
Jones Munitions Systems, Paul
Jones Custom Products, Neil A. (decapping tool, dies)
King & Co.
K&M Services
Lage Uniwad, Inc. (Universal shotshell wad)
Lee Precision, Inc.
Littleton, J.F.
Ljutic Industries, Inc. (plastic wads)
Lock's Phila. Gun Exch.
Lortone, Inc. (tumblers, metal polishing media)
Lyman Products Corp.
Magma Eng. Co.
Marquart Precision Co. (precision case-neck turning tool)
Mayville Eng. Co. (shotshell loader; steel shot kits)
McKillen & Heyer, Inc. (case gauge)
MCS, Inc.
MEC, Inc.
Metallic Casting & Copper Corp. (MCC)
Midway Arms, Inc. (cartridge boxes)
Millenium Safety Products, Inc. (face mask)
M&M Engineering
MMP (Tri-Cut trimmer; power powder trickler)
Mo's Competitor Supplies (neck turning tool)
Mountain South
MTM Molded Products
Multi-Scale Charge Ltd.
Muzzleload Magnum Products (MMP)
Necromancer Industries, Inc. (Compucaster automated bullet casting machine)
NEI (bullet mould)
Northeast Industrial, Inc.
Ohaus Scale
Old Western Scrounger, Inc. (press for 50-cal. B.M.G round)
Omark
Pattern Control (shotshell wads)
Pease Accuracy, Bob
Pend Oreille Sport Shop
Pflumm Gun Mfg. Co. (Drawer Vise)
Pitzer Gun Tool Co. (bullet lube/sizer)
Plum City Ballistics Range
Ponsness-Warren
P&P Tool Co. (12-ga. shot wad)
Precision Castings & Equipment, Inc. (commercial casting machine; case roller; lube/sizer)
Precision Reloading, Inc.
Quinetics Corp. (kinetic bullet puller)
Ransom Intl. Corp. (Grandmaster program loader)
Rapine Bullet Mould Mfg. Co.
RCBS
R.D.P. Tool Co., Inc. (progressive loader)
Redding, Inc.
Reloaders Specialty Mfg.
Rhino Replacement Parts (shotgun flechette rounds)
Roberts Products (Pak-Tool)
Rochester Lead Works (lead wire)
Rooster Laboratories (Universal Heater for lubricator-sizers)
Rorschach Precision Products (carboloy bullet dies)
SAECO
Sandia Die & Cartridge Co.
Scharch Mfg., Inc.
Shooters Accessory Supply (SAS)
Shootin' Accessories Ltd.
Simmons, Jerry (Pope de- and recapper)
Sport Flite Mfg., Inc. (swaging dies)
Sportsman Supply Co.
Speer
SSK Industries
Stalwart Corp. (wooden loading blocks)
Star Machine Works
Sunora Gun Shop
Taracorp Industries
Thompson Bullet Lube
Trammco, Inc. (Electra-Jacket bullet plater)
Tru-Square Metal Products (Thumbler's tumbler case polishers; Ultra Vibe 18)
T&S Industries, Inc.
Vibra Shine, Inc.
Vibra-Tek Co. (brass polisher; Brite Rouge)
Weatherby, Inc.
Webster Scale Mfg. Co.
Western Design
Whitetail Design & Engineering Ltd. (Match Prep primer pocket tool)
Widener's Reloading & Shooting Supply
Williams' Gun Shop, Ben (brass sorters, sizing machines)
Wilson, Inc., L.E.

RESTS—BENCH, PORTABLE, ETC.

Armor Metal Products (port. shoot. bench)
B-Square Co. (handgun)
Butler Creek Corp.
Clifton Arms, Inc.
Cravener's Gun Shop
Decker Shooting Products (rifle rests)
Desert Mountain Mfg. (Benchmaster rifle rest)
Hall's Shooting Products, Inc., Joe (adjustable portable)
Harris Engineering, Inc. (bipods)
Hart & Son, Inc., Robert W.
Hidalgo, Tony (adjustable shooting seat)
Holden Co., J.B.
Hoppe's Div., Penguin Industries, Inc. (benchrests and bags)
Pease Accuracy, Bob
Protektor Model Co. (sandbags)
Ransom Intl. Corp. (handgun rest)
San Angelo Sports Products, Inc.
Sinclair International, Inc.
Sportsman Supply Co. (portable bench rest)
Sports Support Systems, Inc.
Sure Shot of L.A., Inc.
Ultra Light Arms, Inc.
Wichita Engineering & Supply, Inc.
World of Targets (shooting bench—Porta Bench)

RIFLE BARREL MAKERS (See also Muzzle-Loading Guns, Barrels or Equipment)

Ackley, P.O.
Answer Products Co.
Apex Barrel Co.
Baiar, Jim
Bellm Contenders (new rifle barrels, including special and obsolete)
Borovnik KG, Ludwig
Bustani, Leo (Win.92 take-down; Trapper 357-44 magnum barrels)
Canons Delcour
Carter, Ralph L. (octagon)
Cation
Chuck's Gun Shop
Clerke Co., J.A.
Competition Limited
Desert Industries, Inc.
DKT, Inc.
Donnelly Siskiyou Gun Works, P.
Douglas Barrels, Inc.
Federal Ordnance, Inc.
Gentry Custom Gunmaker, David
Getz Barrel Co.

Goode, A.R.
Green Mountain Rifle Barrel Co., Inc.
H-S Precision, Inc.
Half Moon Rifle Shop
Hart Rifle Barrels, Inc.
Hart & Son, Inc., Robert W.
Hastings (shotguns only)
Jackalope Gun Shop
Jarvis Gunsmithing, Inc.
K-D, Inc.
KOGOT Octagon Barrels
Kopp, Terry K. (22-cal. blanks)
Krieger Barrels, Inc.
Lilja Precision Rifle Barrels, Inc.
Manufacture D'Armes Des Pyrenees Francaises - Unique
Marquart Precision Co.
Matco, Inc.
McGowen Rifle Barrels
McMillan Rifle Barrels U.S. International
Mid-America Recreation, Inc. (Pope style rifled Schuetzen rifle barrels)
Nowlin Custom Guns/Manufacturing
Nu-Line Guns
Oakland Custom Arms, Inc.
Obermeyer Rifled Barrels
Olympic Arms, Inc.
Oregon Arms, Inc.
Pell, John T. (custom octagon)
Pence Precision Barrels
Redman's Rifling & Reboring
Rocky Mountain Rifle Works, Ltd.
Sanders Custom Gun Service (importer)
Schneider Rifle Barrels, Inc., Gary
Sharon Gun Specialties, Inc.
Shaw, Inc., E.R. (also shotgun barrels)
Shilen Rifles, Inc.
Shiloh Rifle Mfg. Co., Inc.
Siskiyou Gun Works
Societa Armi Bresciane Srl
Strutz Rifle Barrels, Inc., W.C.
Verney-Carron
Wells, Fred
Wilson Arms Co.

SCOPES, MOUNTS, ACCESSORIES, OPTICAL EQUIPMENT

Action Arms Ltd.
Adco Sales, Inc. (Inter-Aims Mark V sight)
Aimpoint U.S.A. (electronic sight)
Aimtech Mount Systems
Alley Supply Co.
American Import Co., The
Anderson Mfg. Co. (lens caps: Storm King, Storm Queen)
Apel GmbH, Ernst
A.R.M.S., Inc. (mounts)
Armsport, Inc.
aus Jena
Bausch & Lomb, Inc.
Beaver Park Products, Inc.
Beeman Precision Arms, Inc. (airguns only)
B-Square Co.
Buehler Scope Mounts
Burris Co., Inc.
Bushnell
Butler Creek Corp. (lens caps)
Cape Outfitters (mount)
Celestron International (spotting scope)
Clear View Mfg. Co., Inc. (See-Thru mounts)
Compass Industries, Inc.
Conetrol Scope Mounts
Cooper Arms
Del-Sports, Inc. (EAW mounts)
D&H Prods. Co., Inc. (lens covers)
Dickson
Dynamit Nobel-RWS, Inc. (Laser sight & mounts)
Ednar, Inc.
Emerging Technologies, Inc. (Laser sight & mounts)
Europtik, Ltd.
Flaig's
Ford Ltd., J. and J.
Freeland's Scope Stands, Inc.
Fujinon, Inc. (binoculars)
GSI, Inc. (Bock mounts)
Griffin & Howe, Inc.
G.U., Inc. (Nichols Sports Optics)
Gun Parts Corp.
Gun South, Inc. (KSM mounts)
Hakko Co., Ltd.
Heckler & Koch, Inc.
Hermann Leather Co., H.J. (lens caps)
Hertel & Reuss
Holden Co., J.B. (mounts)
Imatronic, Inc. (Laser Sights)
Jaeger, Inc., Paul (Schmidt & Bender; EAW mounts, Noble)
Jason Empire, Inc.
K.B.I., Inc.
KenPatable Ent., Inc.
Kilham, Benjamin (Hutson handgun scopes)
Kmount
Kowa Optimed, Inc.
Kris Mounts
Kwik Mount Corp.
Kwik-Site
L&S Technologies, Inc.
L.A.R. Manufacturing, Inc.
Laser Devices, Inc. (Laser Sight)
Leica USA (binoculars)
Leitz
Leupold & Stevens, Inc.
Lodewick, W.H. (scope safeties)
Marble Arms Corp.
Marlin Firearms Co.
Michaels of Oregon (QD scope covers)
Military Armament Corp. (Leatherwood)
Millett Industries (mounts)
Mirador Optical Corp.
Muzzle-Nuzzle Co.
Nichols Sports Optics
Night Vision Equipment Co., Inc. (Night vision optics)
Nikon, Inc.
North American Specialties
Olympic Arms, Inc.
OMR Feinmechanik, Jagd-u. Sportwaffen GmbH
Optolyth-USA
Orchard Park Enterprise (Saddleproof mounts only)
Pachmayr Ltd.
PECAR Herbert Schwarz GmbH
Pentax Corp. (riflescopes)
Pilkington Gun Co. (QD mount)
Pioneer Marketing & Research, Inc. (German Steiner binoculars; scopes)
Precision Sport Optics
Premier Reticles (Dot reticles in Leupold)
Ram-Line, Inc. (see-thru mount for Mini-14)
Ranging, Inc.
Redfield, Inc.
Sanders Cust. Gun Serv. (MSW)
Schmidt & Bender
Seattle Binocular & Scope Repair Co.
Selsi Company, Inc. (spotting scopes, binoculars)
Shepherd Scope Ltd.
Sherwood Intl. Export Corp. (mounts)
Shooters Supply (mount for M14/M1A rifles)
Simmons Enterprises, Ernie (Nichols Sports Optics)
Simmons Outdoor Corp.
S&K Mfg. Co. (Insta-Mount)
Societa Armi Bresciane SRL
Sports Support Systems, Inc.
Springfield Armory, Inc.
SSK Industries (bases, rings)
Steiner Binoculars
Stoeger Industries
Supreme Lens Covers (lens caps)
Swarovski Optik
Swift Instruments, Inc.
Tasco Sales, Inc.
Tele-Optics (optical equipment repair services only)
Tele-Optics, Inc. (spotting scopes)
Thompson/Center Arms
Traq, Inc. (optics)
Trijicon, Inc. (rifle scopes)
Unertl Optical Co., John
United Binocular Co.
Vic's Gun Refinishing (custom claw mounts)
Wasp Shooting Systems (mounting system for Ruger Mini-14 only)
Weatherby, Inc.
Weaver, Div. of Blount Sporting Eqip.
Weaver Scope Repair Service
White Rock Tool & Die (custom mounts)
Wide View Scope Mount Corp.
Williams Gun Sight Co.
Williams, Inc., Boyd (BR)
Williams Optics, U.S.A.
York M-1 Conversions
Zeiss Optical, Inc., Carl

SHOOTING/TRAINING SCHOOLS

American Pistol Institute
American Small Arms Academy
Auto Arms
Bang Bang Boutique (women)
Bob's Tactical Indoor Shooting Range
Bilsom International, Inc.
Chapman Academy
Chelsea Gun Club of New York City, Inc.
CQB Training
Defense Training International, Inc.
Firearm Training Center, The
Firearms Academy of Seattle
Francesca Stabilizer's, Inc.
G.H. Enterprises Ltd.
Guardian Group International
Guncraft Sports, Inc. (Knoxville)
Gunfitters (certified instructors on staff)
Insights Training Center, Inc.
International Shootists, Inc.
Lethal Force Institute
Mendez, John A.
National Guild of Shotgun Shooting Instructors
Northeast Training Institute, Inc.
Nygord Precision Products
Pacific Pistolcraft
Quigley's Personal Protection Strategies, Paxton
Robar Co's, Inc., The
Rossi S.A. Metalurgica E Municoes, Amadeo
Security Awareness & Firearms Education (civilian & police firearms instruction)
Shooter's World
Shooting Arts Ltd.
Southwest Institute of Firearms Training
Starlight Training Center, Inc.
Tactical Training Center
Threat Management Institute
Unick's Gunsmithing
Yavapai Firearms Academy, Ltd.

SIGHTS, METALLIC

Alley Supply Co.
All's, The Jim J. Tembelis Co., Inc. (shotgun Accura-Sites)
Beeman Precision Arms, Inc.
Behlert Precision
Bo-Mar Tool & Mfg. Co.
Bradley Gunsight Co. (shotgun sight)
British Arms Co. Ltd.
Burris Co., Inc.
California Sight (for ML)
Cherokee Gun Accessories (Tritium Tacsight)
Clerke Co., J.A.
Daigmont Industries, Inc. (shotgun)
Farr Studio (sighting aids—clip-on aperture; the Farr Sight; the Concentrator)
Fautheree, Andy ("Calif. Sight" for ML)
Francesca Stabilizer's, Inc.
Freeland's Scope Stands, Inc.
Guardian Group Intl.
Gun Parts Corp.
Heinie, Richard
Hesco, Inc. (Meprolight sights)
Innovision Enterprises (Slug Sights)
Jaeger, Inc., Paul
Kiss Sights
Kopp, Terry K.
Lee's Red Ramps
Lofland, James W. (single shot replica)
Lyman Products Corp.
Marble Arms Corp.
Meier Works (Express sights)
Meprolight
Merit Corp.
Millett Industries
Miniature Machine Co. (MMC)
MMC Co., Inc.
Novak's .45 Shop
Omega Sales, Inc.
OMR Feinmechanik, Jagd-u. Sportwaffen GmbH
Pachmayr Ltd.
Poly Choke Div.
Slug Site Co.
Storey, Dale A./DGS, Inc.
Tradewinds, Inc.
Trijicon, Inc.
Wichita Engineering & Supply
Williams Gun Sight Co.

STOCKS (Commercial and Custom)

Ahlman's, Inc.
Air Rifle Center (refinishing, airguns only)
Angelo & Little Custom Gun Stock Blanks (blanks only)
Apel, Dietrich
Arms Ingenuity
Bain & Davis, Inc. (custom)
Balickie, Joe J.
Bartas Gunsmithing
Bartlett, Donald
Beeman Precision Arms, Inc. (airguns only)
Beitzinger Ltd., George (custom)
Belding's Custom Gun Shop
Bell & Carlson, Inc. (commercial)
Bellm Contenders
Benchmark Guns
Biesen, Al
Biesen, Roger
Billeb, Stephen L.
Billings Gunsmiths, Inc.
Bishop & Son, Inc., E.C.
Boltin, John M.
Bone, Ralph P.
Borovnik KG, Ludwig
Bowerly, Kent (custom)
Boyd's Gunstock Industries, Inc. (commercial)
Brace, Larry D.
Brgoch, Frank
Briganti Custom Gunsmith
Brown Precision, Inc.
Burkhart Gunsmithing, Don
Burres, Jack (English, Claro, Bastogne Paradox walnut blanks only)
Butler Creek
Calico Hardwoods, Inc. (blanks)
Camilli, Lou
Campbell, Dick (custom)
Cape Outfitters
Champlin Firearms, Inc.
Churchill, Winston
Clerke Co., J.A.
Clifton Arms, Inc.
Clinton River Gun Serv., Inc.
Cloward's Gun Shop (custom)
Coffin, Charles H.
Coffin, Jim
Conrad, C.A. (custom)
Costa, David (custom)
Crane Sales Co., George S. (extensions)
Cubriel, Reggie (custom stockmaker)
Custom Checkering Service
Custom Gun Guild
Custom Gun Products
Custom Gun Stocks

Dahl's Custom Stocks (custom stocks & stock blanks (hand made) custom hand checkering)
Dakota Arms, Inc.
Dangler, Homer L.
D&D Gunsmiths, Ltd. (custom)
Dever, Jack
Devereaux, R.H. "Dick"
Dixon, William
Dowtin Gunworks (DGW) (custom; blanks)
Dressel, Paul G., Jr. (custom)
Dutchmans Firearms, Inc.
Duncan's Gunworks, Inc. (custom)
Echols, D'Arcy A. (custom)
Eggleston, Jere (custom)
Emmons, Bob (custom)
Erhardt, Dennis
Eversull & Co., Inc., K.
Eyster Heritage Gunsmiths, Inc., Ken (custom)
Fajen, Inc., Reinhart
Farmer-Dressel, Sharon (custom)
Fellowes, Ted, Beaver Lodge (custom ML)
Fiberpro, Inc. (blanks; fiberglass; Kevlar)
Fisher, Jerry A.
Flaig's
Flynn's Custom Guns
Folks, Donald E. (custom trap, Skeet, livebird stocks)
Forster, Larry L.
Fountain Products (custom)
Francotte Et Cie S.A., Auguste
Frank Custom Guns, Ron
Freeland's Scope Stands, Inc.
Game Haven Gunstocks (Kevlar rifle stocks)
Garrett Accur-Lt. D.F.S. Co. (fiberglass)
Genecco Gun Works, K.
Gene's Custom Guns
Goens, Dale W.
Goodling's Gunsmithing (custom)
Goudy, Gary (custom)
Grace, Charles E.
Green, Roger M. (custom)
Greene's Machine Carving (gunstock duplicating & machining serv.; custom)
Griffin & Howe
Guncraft, Inc.
Gun Parts Corp. (commercial)
Gunsmithing Ltd.
Hanson's Gun Center
Harper's Custom Stocks
Hart & Son, Inc., Robert W. (custom)
Hecht, Hubert J., Waffen-Hecht (custom)
Heilmann, Stephen (custom)
Hensley, Darwin (custom)
Heppler, Keith M. (custom rifle)
Heydenberk, Warren
Hillmer Custom Gunstocks, Paul D.
Hi-West Sales
Hiptmayer, Klaus
Hoenig & Rodman (stock duplicating machine)
Hollis Gun Shop
H-S Precision, Inc. (Fiberglass)
Huebner, Corey O. (custom)
Hughes, Steven Dodd (custom)
Intermountain Arms (custom)
Ivanoff, Thomas G.
Jaeger, Inc., Paul
Jamison, Robert L., Jr.
Jarrett Rifles, Inc. (custom)
Jim's Gun Shop (custom)
Johnson Wood Products (blanks only)
Johnson, Neal G.
Johnson, Peter S. (custom)
Kartak Gun Works (custom)
Ken's Rifle Blanks
Kilham & Co.
Klein, Don
Klingler, Kenneth J. (custom carving only)
Knippel, Richard (custom)
Kopp, Terry K.
Kros Walnut, Inc. (Circassian walnut blanks)
Lawson Co., Harry
LeFever & Sons, Inc., Frank
Lind, Al (custom)
Logan Security Products Co., Harry M. (custom)
Makinson, Nicholas J.
Mandarino, Monte
Manley Shooting Supplies, Lowell
Matthews, Larry
Mazur Restoration, Peter (custom)
McCament, Jay
McDonald, Dennis (custom)
McFarland, Stan
McGowen Rifle Barrels
McGuire, Bill (custom)
McMillan Fiberglass Stocks, Inc.
Meadow Industries
Mercer, R.M. (custom)
Mid-America Recreation, Inc.
Miller Arms, Inc.
Miller, S.A., (gun wood)
Milliron Custom Guns & Stocks, Earl
Mitchell Arms, Inc.
Mitch's Stock Shop, Inc. (Fibercomb stocks)
Monell Custom Guns (custom)
Morrison Custom Rifles, J.W.
Morrow, Bud
MPI Stocks (fiberglass)
Mulholland, Gordon (custom)
Muzzelite Corp. (bullpup)
Nelson, Stephen E. (custom)
New England Arms Co.
New England Custom Gun Service
Newman Gun Shop (custom)
Nickels, Paul R.
Nicklas, Ted (custom)
Norman, Jim, Custom Gunstocks
Old World Gunsmithing
Olson, Vic (custom)
Or-Ün A.S. (walnut gunstock blanks)
Ottmar, Maurice
Pachmayr Ltd. (blanks and custom jobs)
Pasadena Gun Center
Paulsen Gunstocks (blanks)
Perazzi USA, Inc.
P&S Gun Service
Ranch Products
Reiswig, Wallace E. (Calif. walnut blanks)
Richards Micro-Fit Stocks (thumbhole)
R&J Gunshop (custom)
Robinson, Don (blanks only)
Robinson Firearms Mfg. Ltd.
Rogers Gunsmithing, Bob
Royal Arms
Ryan, Chad (custom)
Samco Global Arms, Inc.
Sanders Custom Gun Serv. (blanks)
Schaefer, Roy V. (commercial blanks)
Schiffman, Curt (custom)
Schiffman, Norman H. (custom)
Schwartz, David W.
Shaw's (custom only)
Sheridan Gunshop
Sherk, Dan A. (custom)
Shooting Gallery, The
Shows, Hank
Sile Distributors
Sinclair International, Inc.
Six Enterprises (fiberglass)
Snider Stocks
Speiser, Fred D.
Sportsmen's Equipment Co. (carbine conversions)
Swan, D.J. (custom)
Szweda, Robert
Talmage, William G.
Taylor's & Co., Inc.
Tecnolegno S.p.A.
Tennessee Valley Mfg. (custom, ML only)
Thurston Sports Center
Tiger-Hunt (curly maple stock blanks)
Tirelli
Trevallion Gunstocks
Tucker, James C. (custom)
Unick's Gunsmithing
Van Epps, Milton
Van Horn, Gil
Vest, John (classic rifles)
Vic's Gun Refinishing
Von Atzigen, Ed (custom)
Wallace, R.D. (custom)
Weatherby, Inc.
Weber Chris/Waffen-Weber
Weems, Cecil
Wells, Fred
Werth, Terry (custom)
West, Robert G.
Western Gunstock Mfg. Co.
Westminster Arms Ltd. (Bull-Pup kits)
Wiebe, Duane
Williams, Bob
Williamson-Pate Gunsmith Service
Windish, Jim (walnut blanks)
Winter, Robert M.
Wisner's Gun Shop, Inc.
Wright's Hardwood Sawmill (blanks only)
Yee, Mike
York M-1 Conversions
Zeeryp, Russell R.
Zollinger, Dean A.

TARGETS, BULLET AND CLAYBIRD TRAPS

Action Target, Inc.
American Whitetail Target Systems
Aztec International Ltd. (Exploding Bullseye targets)
Beeman Precision Arms, Inc. (airguns)
Birchwood-Casey
Caswell International Corp., Inc. (target carriers; commercial shooting ranges)
Champion Target Company (clay targets)
Clay Target Enterprises (clay target launching equipment)
Dapkus Co., J.G. (live bullseye targets)
Datumtech Corp. (electronic target systems)
Detroit-Armor Corp. (Shooting Ranges)
Dutchman's Firearms, Inc., The
Epps (Orillia) Northern Ltd., Ellwood (hand traps)
Feather Flex Decoys
Freeman's Animal Targets
G.H. Enterprises Ltd.
Hunterjohn
Jaro Manuf. (paper targets)
Kleen-Bore, Inc.
Maki Industries (X-Spand Target System)
MTM Molded Prods. Co.
Outers Laboratories (claybird traps)
Peterson Instant Targets, Inc. (paste-ons; Targ-Dots)
Red Star Target Co.
Remington Arms Co. (claybird traps)
Rockwood Corp.
Rocky Mountain Target Co. (Data-Targ)
Shooting Arts Ltd.
Sifre Salvador Enguix (targets)
Sight Right Co.
Su-Press-On, Inc.
Thompson Target Technology (firearms and archery targets)
Trius Products, Inc. (claybird, can thrower)
Winchester, Div. Olin Corp. (claybird traps)
White Flyer Targets
World of Targets (targets)

TAXIDERMY

Jonas, Jack H.
Kulis Freeze-Dry Taxidermy
Parker, Mark D.
Piedmont Community College

TRAP AND SKEET SHOOTERS EQUIP.

The American Import Co. (targetthrower; claybird traps)
Briley Mfg. Co. (choke tubes)
Caswell International Corp.
C&H Research (Mercury recoil suppressor)
Clymer Mfg. Co., Inc. (snap shell)
D&H Prods. Co., Inc. (snap shell)
Euroarms of America, Inc.
Eyster Heritage Gunsmiths, Inc., Ken (shotgun competition choking)
Ganton Manufacturing Ltd. (clothing)
G.H. Enterprises Ltd.
Great 870 Company, The
Griggs Products (recoil redirector)
Hall Plastics, Inc., John
Harper, William E.
Hastings
Hoppe's Division (Monte Carlo pad)
Hunter Co., Inc.
Krieghoff International, Inc.
Ljutic Industries, Inc.
Magnum Research, Inc.
Maionchi - L.M.I.
Maki Industries
Meadow Industries (stock pad, variable; muzzle rest)
Moneymaker Guncraft (free-floating, ventilated ribs)
MTM Molded Products Co. (claybird thrower)
Noble Co., Jim
Outers Laboratories (trap, claybird)
Perazzi USA, Inc.
Pro-Port, Ltd.
Protektor Model Co.
Remington Arms Co. (trap, claybird)
Shootin' Accesories Ltd.
Shurkatch Corp., Longhorn Div.
Titus Shooting Specialties, Daniel (hullbag)
Trius Products, Inc. (can thrower; trap, claybird)
Universal Clay Pigeon Traps
White Flyer Targets
Widener's Reloading & Shooting Supply
Winchester Div., Olin Corp. (trap, claybird)

TRIGGERS, RELATED EQUIPMENT

Bell Design Corp. (rifle triggers)
B.M.F. Activator, Inc.
Brownells, Inc.
Canjar Co., M.H. (triggers)
Central Specialties Co. (trigger locks only)
Cycle Dynamics, Inc.
Davis Service Center, Bill
Dayton-Traister Co. (triggers)
Electronic Trigger Systems
Flaig's (trigger shoes)
Gun Parts Corp.
Hastings
Hi-West Sales
Holmes Firearms Corp. (trigger release)
Jones, Neil A.
Meier Works (shotgun trigger guard)
Miller Single Trigger Mfg. Co.
Nettestad, Bruce A. (trigger guards)
Pachmayr Ltd. (trigger shoe)
Pacific Tool Co. (trigger shoe)
Pease Accuracy, Bob
Penrod Precision (triggers for Ruger #1,3)
Perazzi USA, Inc.
Taurus S.A., Forjas
Timney Mfg., Inc. (triggers)
Tyler Mfg.-Dist., Melvin (trigger shoe)
Williams Gun Sight Co. (trigger shoe)

MANUFACTURERS' DIRECTORY

A

A.A. Arms, Inc., 8325 Fairview Rd., Mint Hill, NC 28227/704-545-5565
A&B Industries, Inc., 7920-28 Hamilton Ave., Cincinnati, OH 45231/513-522-2992
Abel Safe & File Co., 105 North Fourth St., Fairbury, IL 61739/815-346-9280
Accu-Tek, 4525 Carter Ct., Chino, CA 91710/714-627-2404
Acculube II, Inc., 22025 70th Ave. S., Kent, WA 98032/206-395-7171
Accupro Gun Care, Div. of RTI Research Ltd., 15512-109 Ave., Surrey, BC U3R 7E8, Canada/604-583-7807
Accuracy Gun Shop, Lance Martini, 3651 University Ave., San Diego, CA 92104/619-282-8500
Accuracy Products, S.A., 14 Rue de Lawsanne, Brussels, Belgium, B-1060/32-2-539-34-42
Accuracy Unlimited, 7479 S. Dewpew St., Littleton, CO 80123
Accuracy Unlimited, Frank Glenn, 16036 N. 49th Ave., Glendale, AZ 85306/602-978-9089
Accurate Arms Co., Inc. (Propellents Div.), Rt. 1, P.O. Box 167, McEwen, TN, 37101/615-729-4207/4208
Accurate Plating & Weaponry, Inc., 1937 Calumet St., Clearwater, FL 34625/813-449-9112
Ace Sportswear, Inc., 700 Quality Rd., Fayetteville, NC 28306/919-323-1223
Ackley, P.O. (See Bellm Contenders)
Acme Custom Bullets, 2414 Clara Lane, San Antonio, TX 78213/512-680-4828
Action Ammo Ltd., P.O. Box 19630, Philadelphia, PA 19124/215-744-0100
Action Arms Ltd., P.O. Box 9573, Philadelphia, PA 19124/215-744-0100
Action Products, Inc., 22 N. Mulberry St., Hagerstown, MD 21740/301-797-1414
Action Target, Inc., P.O. Box 636, 1281 W. 220 North, Provo, UT 84603/801-377-8033
ACTIV Industries, Inc., P.O. Box F, 1000 Zigor Rd., Kearneysville, WV 25430/304-725-0451
Ad Hominem, RR 3, Orillia, ON L3V 6H3, Canada/705-689-5303
Adair, Bill, The Classic Gun, 2886 Westridge, Carrollton, TX 75006/214-418-0950
Adams, John J., P.O. Box 167, Corinth, VT 05039/802-439-5904
ADC, Inc., P.O. Box 8, Columbia City, OR 97018/800-528-0559
Adco Sales, Inc., 1 Wyman St., Woburn, MA 01801/617-935-1799
Adkins, Luther, P.O. Box 281, Shelbyville, IN 46176/317-392-3795
Advance Car Mover Co., Inc., Rowell Div., P.O. Box 1181, 112 N. Outagamie St., Appleton, WI 54912/414-734-1878
Adventure 16, Inc., 4620 Alvarado Canyon Rd., San Diego, CA 92120/619-283-6314
Adventure Game Calls, R.D. #1, Leonard Rd., Spencer, NY 14883/607-589-4611
Adventurer's Outpost, P.O. Box 70, 211 Jennifer Lane, Cottonwood, AZ 86326/800-762-7471
AFSCO Ammunition, 731 W. Third St., Owen, WI 54460/715-229-2516
Ahlman's, Inc., RR 1, P.O. Box 20, Morristown, MN 55052/507-685-4244
Ahrends, Kim, Custom Firearms, P.O. Box 203, 420 2nd Ave. NE, Clarion, IA 50525/515-532-3449
Aimpoint U.S.A., 580 Herndon Parkway, Suite 500, Herndon, VA 22070/703-471-6828
Aimtech Mount Systems, P.O. Box 223, 101 Inwood Acres, Thomasville, GA 31792/912-226-4313
Air Rifle Center, 1804 E. Sprague St., Winston Salem, NC 27107/919-784-0676
Air Rifle Specialists, 311 East Water St., Elmira, NY 14901/607-734-7340
Airmold/W.R. Grace & Co.-Conn., P.O. Box 610, Roanoke Rapids, NC 27870/919-536-2171
Aitor-Cuchilleria Del Norte, S.A., Izelaieta, 17, Ermua (Vizcaya), Spain 48260/43-17-08-50
A&J Products, 3560 Karen Ct., Hart, MI 49420/616-873-5839
Ajax Custom Grips, Inc., Div. of A. Jack Rosenberg & Sons, 11311 Stemmons, Suite #5, Dallas, TX 75229/214-241-6302
Aker Leather Products, 2248 Main St., Suite 6, Chula Vista, CA 91911/619-423-5182
Alcas Cutlery Corp., 1116 E. State St., Olean, NY 14760/716-372-3111
Alco Carrying Cases, 601 W. 26th St., New York, NY 10001/212-675-5820
Aldis, Riichard L., 3020 Hozoni Rd., Prescott, AZ 86301/602-445-6723
Alessi Holsters, Inc., 2465 Niagara Falls Blvd., Tonawanda, NY 14150/716-691-5615
Alex, Inc., P.O. Box 3034, 3420 Cameron Bridge W., Bozeman, MT 59772/406-282-7396
Alfano, Sam, 36180 Henry Gaines Rd., Pearl River, LA 70452/504-863-3364
All Rite Products, Inc., 1001 W. Cedar Knolls South, Cedar City, UT 84720/801-586-7100
All Weather Outerwear, 1270 Broadway, Rm 1005, New York, NY 10001/212-244-2690
All's, The Jim J. Tembelis Co., Inc., 280 E. Fernau Ave., Oshkosh, WI 54901/414-426-1080
Allard, Gary, Creek Side Metal & Woodcrafters, Fishers Hill, VA 22626/703-465-3903
Allen Co., Inc., 525 Burbank St., Broomfield, CO 80020/303-469-1857
Allen Co.,Bob, 214 SW Jackson, Des Moines, IA 50315/515-283-2191/800-247-8048
Alley Supply Co., P.O. Box 848, Gardnerville, NV 89410/702-782-3800
Allred Bullet Co., 932 Evergreen Dr., Logan, UT 84321/801-752-6983
Alpha Precision, Inc., 2765 Preston Rd., Good Hope, GA 30641/404-267-6163
Alpine's Precision Gunsmithing, 2401 Government Way, Coeur D'Alene, ID 83814/208-765-3559
Alsa Corp., The, 1245 McClellan, Suite 204, Los Angeles, CA 90025/213-207-4005
Altamont Mfg. Co., 510 N. Commercial St., P.O. Box 309, Thomasboro, IL 61878/217-643-3125
A&M Waterfowl, Inc., 301 Burke Drive, Ripley, TN 38063/901-635-4003
AMAC (American Military Arms Corp.), 2202 Redmond Rd., Jacksonville, AR 72076/501-982-1633
Amacker Treestands, Inc., 1212 Main St., Amacker Park, Delhi, LA 71232/318-878-9061
American Arms, Inc., 715 E. Armour Rd., N. Kansas City, MO 64116/816-474-3161
American Ballistics Company, Inc., P.O. Box 1410, Marietta, GA 30061/404-426-5311
American Bullets, 2190 C Coffee Rd., Lithonia, GA 30058
American Custom Gunmakers Guild, c/o Jan Billeb, Exec. Director, P.O. Box 812, Burlington, IA 52601-0812/319-752-6114
American Derringer Corp., P.O. Box 8983, Waco, TX 76714/817-799-9111
American Gas & Chem[illegible] Co., Ltd., 220 Pegasus Ave., Northvale, NJ 07647/201-767-730[illegible]
American Gripcraft, 323[illegible] S. Dodge #2, Tucson, AZ 85713/602-790-1222
Americ[illegible] Import Co., The, 1453 Mission St., San Francisco, CA 94103/415-863-1506
American Optical Corp., 14 Mechanic St., Southbridge, MA 01550/508-765-9711
American Pistol Institute, P.O. Box 401, Paulden, AZ 86334/602-636-4565
American Pistolsmiths Guild, 3922 Madonna Rd., Jarrettsville, MD 21084/301-557-6545
American Products Co., 14729 Spring Valley Rd., Morrison, IL 61270/815-772-3336
American Sales & Mfg. Co., P.O. Box 677, Laredo, TX 78042/512-723-6893
American Security Products Co., 11925 Pacific Ave., Fontana, CA 92335/714-685-9680, 800-421-6142
American Small Arms Academy, 1713 Far View Dr., Prescott, AZ 86301/602-778-5623
American Whitetail Target Systems, P.O. Box 41, 106 S. Church St., Tennyson, IN 47637/812-567-4527
Americase, P.O. Box 271, Waxahachie, TX 75165/800-972-2737
Amherst Arms, P.O. Box 658, Mt. Airy, MD 21771/301-829-9544
Ammo Load, Inc., 1560 E. Edinger, Suite G, Santa Ana, CA 92705/714-558-8858
Ammunition Consulting Serv., Inc., Richard Geer, 55 White Oak Circle, St. Charles, IL 60174/708-377-4625
Amrine's Gun Shop, 937 Luna Ave., Ojai, CA 93023/805-646-2376
AMT (Arcadia Machine & Tool, Inc.), 6226 Santos Diaz St., Irwindale, CA 91702/818-334-6629
Anderson Mfg. Co., 2460, Oak Harbor, WA 98277-2640/206-675-7300
Andres & Dworsky, Bergstrasse 18, A-3822 Karlstein/Thaya, Austria, Europe/0 28 44-285
Angelo & Little Custom Gun Stock Blanks, Chaffin Creek Rd., Darby, MT 59829/406-821-4530
Anschutz (See Precision Sales Intl., Inc.)
Ansen Enterprises, 1506 228th St., Torrance, CA 90501-1506/213-534-1837
Answer Products Co., 1519 Westbury Dr., Davison, MI 48423/313-653-2911
Anthony and George Ltd., Rt. 1, P.O. Box 45, Evington, VA 24550/804-821-8117
Antique Arms Co., David F. Saunders, 1110 Cleveland, Monett, MO 65708/417-235-6501
AO Safety Prods., Div. of American Optical Corp., 14 Mechanic St., Southbridge, MA 01550/508-765-9711
Apel, Dietrich, RR 2 Box 122W, Brook Rd., W. Lebanon, NH 03784/603-469-3565
Apel, GmbH, Ernst, Am Kirschberg 3, W-8708 Gerbrunn, Germany/(0)931-70 71 91
Apex Barrel Co., 808 2nd St. NW, Valley City, ND 58072/701-845-5155
API Outdoors, Inc., P.O. Box 1432, Tallulah, LA 71284/318-574-4903
Aplan, James O., HC 80 P.O. Box 793-25, Piedmont, SD 57769/605-347-5016
Arizona Custom Case, 1015 S. 23rd St., Pheonix, AZ 85034/602-273-0220
Arkansas Mallard Duck Calls, Rt. Box 182, England, AR 72046/501-842-3597
Arkfeld Mfg. & Dist. Co., Inc., Hwy 81 & Monroe Ave., P.O. Box 54, Norfolk, NE 68702-0054/402-371-9430
Armament Gunsmithing Co., Inc., 525 Route 22, Hillside, NJ 07205/908-686-0960
Armes de Chasse, P.O. Box 827, Chadds Ford, PA 19317/215-388-1146
Armfield Custom Bullets, 4775 Caroline Dr., San Diego, CA 92115/619-582-7188
Armi San Paolo, via Europa 172-A, I-25062 Concesio, Italy 030-2751725
Armite Labs., 1845 Randolph St., Los Angeles, CA 90001/213-587-7747
Armoloy Co. of Ft. Worth, 204 E. Daggett St., Fort Worth, TX 76104/817-332-5604
Armor Metal Products, 2500 Phoenix Ave., Helena, MT 59604/406-442-5560
Armor, Div. of Buck Stop, Inc., 3015 Grow Rd., Stanton, MI 48888
Armory Publications, P.O. Box 4206, Oceanside, CA 92052/619-757-3930
Armoury, Inc., The, Route 202, New Preston, CT 06777/203-868-0001
A.R.M.S., Inc. (Atlantic Research Marketing Systems), 375 West St., West Bridgewater, MA 02379/508-584-7816
Arms & Armour Press, Ltd., Villiers House, 41/47 Strand, London WC2N 5JE England
Arms Corp. of America, Inc., 4424 John Ave., Baltimore, MD 21227/301-247-6200
Arms Corp. of the Philippines (See Armscor Precision)
Arms Craft Gunsmithing, 1106 Linda Dr., Arroyo Grande, CA 93420/805-481-2830
Arms Ingenuity Co., P.O. Box 1, 51 Canal St., Weatogue, CT 06089/203-658-5624
Arms, Peripheral Data Systems, 7165 SW Fir Loop, Tigard, OR 97223/503-620-6420
Armscor Precision, 225 Lindbergh St., San Mateo, CA 94403/415-347-9556
Armsport, Inc., 3950 NW 49th St., Miami, FL 33142/305-635-7850
Armstec, Inc., 339 East Ave., Rochester, NY 14604/800-262-2832
Armurier Hiptmayer, P.O. Box 136, Eastman, Que. JOE 1P0, Canada/514-297-2492
Arratoonian, Andy, Horseshoe Leather Prods., The Cottage, Sharow, Ripon HG4 5BP, England (0765)-5858
Arrieta, S.L., Barrio Urasandi, s/n, E-20870, Elgoibar, Spain/34-43-743150
Art Jewel Enterprises Ltd., Eagle Business Ctr., 460 Randy Rd., Carol Stream, IL 60188/708-260-0400
Ashby, Isaac, P.O. Box 65, Houston, MO 65483/417-967-3787
ASI, 6226 Santos Diaz St., Irwindale, CA 91702/818-334-6629
A-Square Co., Inc., One Industrial Park, Bedford, KY 40006/502-255-7456
Atlanta Cutlery, 2143 Geesmill Rd., Conyers, GA 30208/404-922-3700
Atlanta Discount Ammo, P.O. Box 258, Clarkesville, GA 30523/404-754-9000
Atlantic Mills, Inc., 1325 Washington Ave., Asbury Park, NJ 07712/201-774-4882
Atsko/Sno-Seal, Inc., 2530 Russell SE, Orangeburg, SC 29115/803-531-1820
Atzigen, Ed von, The Custom Shop, 890 Cochrane Crescent, Peterborough, Ont., K9H 5N3 Canada/705-742-6693
Auto Arms, 738 Clearview, San Antonio, TX 78228/512-434-5450
Auto-Ordnance Corp., Williams Lane, West Hurley, NY 12491/914-679-7225
Automatic Weaponry, P.O. Box 24517, Nashville, TN 37202/615-254-1441
Autumn Sales, Inc., 1320 Lake St., Fort Worth, TX 76102/817-335-1634
A&W Repair, 2930 Schneider Dr., Arnold, MO 63010/314-287-3725
Aztec International Ltd., P.O. Box 1384, Clarkesville, GA 30523/404-754-8282

B

Bachman, Rick M. (See Old West Reproductions)
Badger Shooter's Supply, 106 S. Harding, Owen, WI 54460/715-229-2101
Baekgaard Ltd., 1855 Janke Dr., Northbrook, IL 60062/708-498-3040
Baer Custom Guns, 29601 34th Ave. N, Hillsdale, IL 61257-9755
Baiar, Jim, 490 Halfmoon Rd., Columbia Falls, MT 59912/406-892-4409
Bain & Davis, Inc., 307 E. Valley Blvd., San Gabriel, CA 91776/213-283-7449

Baity's Custom Gunworks, 414 2nd St., N. Wilkesboro, NC 28659/919-667-8785
Baker's Leather Goods, Roy, P.O. Box 893, 3161 Hwy. 344, Magnolia, AR 71753/501-234-1599,501-234-3226
Baker, Stan, 10000 Lake City Way, Seattle, WA 98125/206-522-4575
Balaance Co., 340-39 Ave. SE, P.O. Box 505, Calgary, AB T2G 1X6, Canada/403-279-0334
Balickie Custom Stocks, Joe J., 408 Trelawney Lane, Apex, NC 27502/919-362-5185
Ballard Built Cutom Bullets, P.O. Box 1443, Kingsville, TX 78364-1443/512-592-0853
Ballisti-Cast, Inc., P.O. Box 383, Pershall, ND 58770/701-862-3324
Ballistic Products, Inc., P.O. Box 408, 2105 Daniels St., Long Lake, MN 55356/612-473-1550
Ballistic Research Industries (BRI), 953 Tower Place #A, Santa Cruz, CA 95062/408-476-7981
Ballistic Research, Tom Armbrust, 1108 W. May Ave., McHenry, IL 60050/815-385-0037
Ballistica Maximus North, 107 College Park Plaza, Johnstown, PA 15904/814-266-8380
Ballistica Maximus South, 3242 Mary St., Suite S-318, Miami, FL 33133/305-446-5549
Ballistics Program Co., Inc., The, 2417 N. Patterson St., Thomasville, GA 31792/912-228-1961
Bandcor Industries, Div. of Man-Sew Corp., 6108 Sherwin Dr., Port Richey, FL 34668/813-848-0432
Bang-Bang Boutique, 720 N. Flagler Dr., Fort Lauderdale, FL 33304/305-463-7910
Banks Pistolsmith, Ed, 2762 Hwy. 41 N., Ft. Valley, GA 31030/912-987-4665
Bar-Sto Precision Machine, Irving O. Stone, Jr., 73377 Sullivan Rd., P.O. Box 1838, Twentynine Palms, CA 92277/619-367-2747
Barami Corp., 6250 East 7 Mile Rd., Detroit, MI 48234/313-891-2536
Barbour, Inc., Meadowbrook Rd., Milford, NH 03055/603-673-1313
Barnes Bullets, Inc., P.O. Box 215, American Fork, UT 84003/801-756-4222
Barnes Custom Shop (See Barnes Bullets, Inc.)
Barnett International, P.O. Box 934, 1967 Gunn Highway, Odessa, FL 33556/813-920-2241
Baron Technology, 62 Spring Hill Rd., Trumbull, CT 06611/203-452-0515
Barrett Firearms Mfg., Inc., P.O. Box 1077, Murfreesboro, TN 37133/615-896-2938
Barta's Gunsmithing, 10231 US Hwy. #10, Cato, WI 54206/414-732-4472
Barteaux Machete, P.O. Box 66464, Portland, OR 97266/503-665-2577
Bartlett, Donald, 207 So. 317th Pl., Federal Way, WA 98003/206-839-3167
Bartlett, J., 458 Corte Blanco, Upland, CA 91786
Bates, Billy R., 2905 Lynnwood Circle SW, Decatur, AL 35603/205-355-3690
Bauer, Eddie, 15010 NE 36th St., Redmond, WA 98052
Bausch & Lomb, Inc., 42 East Ave., Rochester, NY 14603/800-828-5423
B&D Trading Co., Inc., 3935 Fair Hill Rd., Fair Oaks, CA 95628/916-967-9366
BE, Inc. (See Mountain South)
Bean, L.L., 386 Main St., Freeport, ME 04032/207-865-3111
Bear Archery, RR 4, 4600 Southwest 41st Blvd., Gainesville, FL 32601/904-376-2327
Bear Hug Grips, Inc., 17230 County Rd. 338, Buena Vista, CO 81211/800-232-7710
Beaver Lodge, 9245 16th Ave. SW, Seattle, WA 98106/206-763-1698
Beaver Park Products, Inc., 840 J St., Penrose, CO 81240/719-372-6744
Beeman Precision Arms, Inc., 3440-GD Airway Dr., Santa Rosa, CA 95403/707-578-7900
Behlert Precison, Route 611 P.O. Box 63, Pipersville, PA 18947/215-766-8681
Beitzinger, George, 116-20 Atlantic Ave., Richmond Hill, NY 11419/718-847-7661
Belding & Mull, Inc., P.O. Box 428, 100 N. 4th St., Phillipsburg, PA 16866/814-342-0607
Belding's Custom Gun Shop, 10691 Sayers Rd., Munith, MI 49259/517-596-2388
B.E.L.L. (See Eldorado Custom Shop)
Bell & Carlson, Inc. (B&C), 509 N. 5th St., Atwood, KS 67730/913-626-3204
Bell Design Corp., 718 S. 2nd/P.O. Box 64, Atwood, KS 67730/913-626-3279
Bell Design Gun Services, 718 South 2nd, Atwood, KS 67730/913-626-3279
Bell Originals, Sid, Inc., R.D. 2, P.O. Box 219, Tully, NY 13159/607-842-6431
Bell's Custom Shop, 3315 Mannheim Rd., Franklin Park, IL 60131/708-678-1900
Bellm Contenders, 665 South 300 West, Price, UT 84501/801-637-9062 (price list $3)
Belltown, Ltd., 11 Camps Rd., Kent, CT 06757/203-354-5750
Ben's Gun Shop, 1151 S. Cedar Ridge, Duncanville, TX 75137/214-780-1807
Benchmark Guns, 1265 5th Ave., Yuma, AZ 85364/602-783-5161
Benchmark Knives (See Gerber Legendary Blades)
Benelli Armi, S.p.A. (See Sile Distributors—handguns; Heckler & Koch—shotguns)
Benjamin Air Rifle Co., 2600 Chicory Rd., Racine, WI 53403/414-554-7900
Bentley, John, 128-D Watson Dr., Turtle Creek, PA 15145
Berdon Machine Co., 2011 W. Washington Ave., Yakima, WA 98902/509-453-0374
Beretta U.S.A., 17601 Beretta Drive, Accokeek, MD 20607/301-283-2191
Beretta, Dr. Franco, via Rossa, 4, Concesio, Italy I-25062/030-2751955
Berger Bullets, 4234 N. 63rd Ave., Phoenix, AZ 85033/602-846-5791
Bergeron, La Bertrandiere, 42580 L'Etrat, France/77 74 01 30
Bergmann & Williams, 2450 Losee Rd., Suite F, N. Las Vegas, NV 89030/702-642-1091
Bertram Bullet Co. (See Huntington Die Specialties)
Bess, Gordon, 708 River St., Canon City, CO 81212/303-275-1073
Betz, Harold A., 817 N. Highway 90, #1109, Sierra Vista, AZ 85635/602-452-0702
BF Arms, 1123 S. Locust, Grand Island, NE 68801/308-382-1121
Bianchi International, Inc., 100 Calle Cortez, Temecula, CA 92390/714-676-5621
Biesen, Al, 5021 Rosewood, Spokane, WA 99208/509-328-9340
Biesen, Roger, 5021 W. Rosewood, Spokane, WA 99208/509-328-9340
Big 45 Frontier Gun Shop, P.O. Box 70, 515 Cliff Ave., Valley Springs, SD 57068/605-757-6248
Big Beam (See Teledyne Co.)
Big Sky Racks, Inc., P.O. Box 729, Bozeman, MT 59771/406-586-9393
Big Spring Enterprise "Bore Stores," P.O. Box 1115, Yellville, AR 72687/501-449-5297
Bilal, Mustafa, 5429 Russell Ave. NW, Suite 202, Seattle, WA 98107/206-782-4164
Bill's Gun Repair, 1007 Burlington St., Mendota, IL 61342/815-539-5786
Billeb, Stephen L., 620 N. 7th St., Burlington, IA 52601/319-753-2110
Billings Gunsmiths, Inc., Stan Wright, 1940 Grand Ave., Billings, MT 59102/406-652-3140
Billingsley & Brownell, Ross, P.O. Box 25, 620 Broadway, Dayton, WY 82836/307-655-9344 (brochure $2)
Bilsom Interntl., Inc., 109 Carpenter Dr., Sterling, VA 22170/703-834-1070
Birchwood-Casey, 7900 Fuller Rd., Eden Prairie, MN 55344/612-937-7933
Bishop & Son, Inc., E.C., 119 Main St., P.O. Box 7, Warsaw, MO 65355/816-438-5121
Bitterroot Bullet Co., P.O. Box 412, 2009 Cedar Ave., Lewiston, ID 83501/208-743-5635 (brochure: USA, Can. & Mexico $1 plus legal size env., intl. $2; lit. pkg.: USA, Can. & Mexico $7.75, Intl. $10.75)
Black Hills Ammunition, 3401 S. Hwy. 79, Rapid City, SD 57701/605-348-5150
Black Mountain Bullets, Rt. 3, P.O. Box 297, Warrenton, VA 22186/703-347-1199
Black Sheep Brand, 3220 W. Gentry Parkway, Tyler, TX 75702/214-592-3853
Blackhawk East, P.O. Box 2274, Loves Park, IL 61131
Blackhawk Mtn., P.O. Box 210, Conifer, CO 80433
Blackhawk West, P.O. Box 285, Hiawatha, KS 66434
Blackinton & Co., V.H., P.O. Box 1300, 221 John L. Dietsch Blvd., Attleboro Falls, MA 02763/508-699-4436
Blackjack Knives, 7210 Jordan Ave., #D72, Canoga Park, CA 91303/818-902-9853
Blacksmith Corp., 830 North Road 1 East, P.O. Box 1752, Chino Valley, AZ 86323/800-531-2665
Blacktail Mountain Books, 42 First Ave. West, Kalispell, MT 59901/406-257-5573
Blackwell, W.W., 9826 Sagedale, Houston, TX 77089/713-484-0935
Blakemore Game Calls, Jim, P.O. Box 10, Rt. 1, McClure, IL 62957-0010/618-661-1624
Bledsoe, Weldon, 6812 Park Place Dr., Fort Worth, TX 76118/817-589-1704
Bleile, C. Roger, 5040 Ralph Ave., Cincinnati, OH 45238/513-251-0249
Blocker's Custom Holsters, Ted, 5360 NE 112th, Portland, OR 97220/503-254-9950
Blount Sporting Equipment Division, P.O. Box 856, Lewiston, ID 83501/208-746-2351
Blue and Gray Prods., Inc., 34 West Main St., Milo, ME 04463/800-637-5579
Blue Moutain Bullets, 3420 Foothill Rd., Medford, OR 97504
Blue Ridge Knives, Rt. 6, P.O. Box 185, Marion, VA 24354-9351/703-783-6143
Blue Ridge Machinery and Tools, Inc., P.O. Box 536-GD, 2806 Putnam Ave., Hurricane, WV25526/304-562-3538/800-872-6500
B.M.F. Activator, Inc., P.O. Box 262364, Houston, TX 77207/713-477-8442
Bo-Mar Tool & Mfg. Co., Rt. 12, P.O. Box 405, Longview, TX 75605/903-759-4784
Bob's Gun Shop, P.O. Box 200, Royal, AR 71968/501-767-1970
Bob's Mexican Market, 1714-B W. Main, P.O. Box 329, Port Lavaca, TX 77979/512-987-2825
Bob's Tactical Indoor Shooting Range & Gun Shop, 122 Lafayette Rd., Salisbury, MA 01952/508-465-5561
Boessler, Erich, Gun Engraving Intl., Am Vogeltal 3, 8732 Munnerstadt, W. Germany/9733-9443
Boggs, Wm., 1816 Riverside Dr. #C, Columbus, OH 43212/614-486-6965
Boker USA, Inc., 14818 West 6th Ave., Suite #17A, Golden, CO 80401/303-279-5997
Bolden, Duane, 1295 Lassen Dr., Hanford, CA 93230/209-582-6937
Boltin, John M., 157 Park Ave., P.O. Box 644, Estill, SC 29918/803-625-2185
Bonanza (See Forster Products, Inc.)
Bondini Paolo, Via Sorrento, 345, San Carlo di Cesena, Italy I-47020/0547-663 240
Bone, Ralph P., 718 N. Atlanta, Owasso, OK 74055/918-272-9745
Bonham, Henry "Hank", P.O. Box 242, Brownsville, ME 04414/207-965-2891
Boone's Custom Ivory Grips, Inc., 562 Coyote Rd., Brinnon, WA 98320/206-796-4330
Boonie Packer Products/JFS, Inc., P.O. Box 12204, Salem, OR 97309/800-477-3244
Bor-Clear Bullets, John Bentley, 128 D Watson Dr., Turtle Creek, PA 15145/412-823-4017
Border Guns & Leather, P.O. Box 1423, 210 E. Poplar, Deming, NM 88031/505-546-2151
Borovnik KG, Ludwig, 9170 Ferlach, Bahnhofstrasse 7, Austria
Boss Manufacturing Company, 221 W. First St., Kewanee, IL 61443/309-852-2131
Bostick Wildlife Calls, Inc., P.O. Box 728, Estill, SC 29918/803-625-2210, 803-625-4512
Bourne Co., Inc., Richard A., P.O. Box 141, Hyannis Port, MA 02647/508-775-0797
Bowen Classic Arms Corp., P.O. Box 67, Louisville, TN 37777/615-984-3583
Bowen Knife Co., P.O. Box 590, Blackshear, GA 31516/912-449-4794
Bowerly, Kent, Metolious Meadows Dr., H.C.R. P.O. Box 1903, Camp Sherman, OR 97730/503-595-6028
Boyd's Gunstock Industries, Inc., 3rd & Main, P.O. Box 305, Geddes, SD 57342/605-337-2125
Boyt Co., Div. of Welsh Sporting Goods, 509 Hamilton, P.O. Drawer 668, Iowa Falls, IA 50126/515-648-4826
Brace, Larry D., 771 Blackfoot Ave., Eugene, OR 97404/503-688-1278
Bradley Gunsight Co., P.O. Box 140, Plymouth, VT 05056/203-589-0531
Brass Eagle, Inc., 7050A Bramalea Rd., Unit 19, Mississauga, Ont. L4Z 1C7, Canada/416-848-4844
Bratcher, Dan, 311 Belle Air Pl., Carthage, MO 64836/417-358-1518
Brauer Bros. Mfg. Co., 2020 Delmar Blvd., St. Louis, MO 63103/314-231-2864
Braun, M., 32, rue Notre-Dame, 2440 Luxembourg, Luxembourg
Brazos Arms Co., 17423 Autumn Trails, Houston, TX 77084/713-463-0598
Break-Free, P.O. Box 25020, Santa Ana, CA 92799/714-953-1900
Brenneke KG, Wilhelm, Ilmenauweg 2, P.O. Box 16 46, D-3012 Langenhagen, Germany/511-772288
Bretton, 19 rue Victor Grignard, Z.I. Montreynaud, 42-St. Etienne, France
Brgoch, Frank, 1580 S. 1500 East, Bountiful, UT 84010/801-295-1885
BRI (See Ballistic Research Industries)
Brian, C.T., 1101 Indiana Ct., Decatur, IL 62521/217-429-2290
Briganti Custom Gunsmith, 475 Route 32, Highland Mills, NY 10930/914-928-9573
Briley Mfg. Co., 1085-B Gessner, Houston, TX 77055/713-932-6995
British Arms Co. Ltd., P.O. Box 7, Latham, NY 12110/518-783-0773
BRNO (See T.D. Arms)
Brobst, Jim, 299 Poplar St., Hamburg, PA 19526/215-562-2103
Brooker, Dennis B., Rt. 1, P.O. Box 12A, Derby, IA 50068/515-533-2103
Brown Manufacturing, P.O. Box 9219, Akron, OH 44305/800-837-GUNS
Brown Precision, Inc., 7786 Molinos Ave., Los Molinos, CA 96055/916-384-2506
Brown Products, Ed, Rt. 2, P.O. Box 2922, Perry, MO 63462/314-565-3261
Brownell Checkering Tools, W.E., 3356 Moraga Place, San Diego, CA 92117/619-276-6146
Brownells, Inc., 222 W. Liberty, Montezuma, IA 50171/515-623-5401
Browning (Gen. Offices), Rt. 1, Morgan, UT 84050/801-876-2711
Browning (Parts & Service), Rt. 4, P.O. Box 624-B, Arnold, MO 63010/314-287-6800
Bruno Bullets/Shooters Supply, 106 N. Wyoming St., Hazelton, PA 18201/717-455-2211
Brunton USA, 620 East Monroe Ave., Riverton, WY 82501/307-856-6559
Bryco Arms (Distributed by Jennings Firearms, Inc.)
B-Square Co., P.O. Box 11281, Ft. Worth, TX 76110/817-923-0964
Bucheimer, Co., J.M., P.O. Box 280, Airport Rd., Frederick, MD 21701/301-662-5101
Buck Knives, Inc., P.O. Box 1267, 1900 Weld Blvd., El Cajon, CA 92022/619-449-1100/800-854-2557
Buck Stop Lure Co., Inc., 3600 Grow Rd., P.O. Box 636, Stanton, MI 48888/517-762-5091
Buckskin Machine Works, 3235 S. 358th St., Auburn, WA 98001/206-927-5412
Budin, Dave, Main St., Margaretville, NY 12455/914-568-4103
Buehler Scope Mounts, 17 Orinda Way, Orinda, CA 94563/415-254-3201
Buenger Ent., Box 5286, Oxnard, CA 93031/805-985-0541
Buffalo Bullet Co., Inc., 12637 Los Nietos Rd. Unit A, Santa Fe Springs, CA 90670/213-944-0322
Buffalo Rock Shooters Supply, R. Rt. 1, Ottawa, IL 61350/815-433-2471

Bull-X, Inc., 520 N. Main St., Farmer City, IL 61842/309-928-2574
Bullet Swaging Supply, Inc., P.O. Box 1056, 303 McMillan Rd., West Monroe, LA 71291/318-387-7257
Burgess & Son, Robert W., P.O. Box 3364, Warner Robins, GA 31093/912-328-7487
Burgess, Byron, 710 Bella Vista Dr., Morro Bay, CA 93442/805-772-3974
Burkhart, Don, Gunsmithing, 654 Munson Courst, Berthoud, CO 80513/303-532-0318
Burnham Bros., P.O. Box 669, 912 Hi-way 1431 West, Marble Falls, TX 78654/512-693-3112
Burres, Jack, 10333 San Fernando Road, Pacoima, CA 91331/818-899-8000
Burris Co., Inc., 331 E. 8th St., P.O. Box 1747, Greeley, CO 80632/303-356-1670
Burt, Robert B., 106 Powder Mill Rd., P.O. Box 924, Canton, CT 06019/203-693-1117
Bush Master, 451 Alliance Ave., Toronto, Ontario, M6N 2J1 Canada/416-763-4040
Bushmaster Firearms Co., 999 Roosevelt Trail, Bldg. #3, Windham, ME 04062
Bushnell, 300 N. Lone Hill Ave., San Dimas, CA 91773/714-592-8000/800-423-3537
Bushwacker Backpack & Supply Co., Inc., P.O. Box 4721, 300 Catlin #2, Missoula, MT 59806/406-728-6241
Bustani, Leo, 8195 No. Military Tr., W. Palm Beach, FL 33407/305-622-2710 (SASE f. reply)
Butler Creek Corp., 290 Arden Dr., Belgrade, MT 59714/406-388-1356
Butterfield & Butterfield, 220 San Bruno Ave., San Francisco, CA 94103/415-861-7500

C

Cabela's, 812-13th Ave., Sidney, NE 69160/308-254-5505
Cabinet Mtn. Outfitter, P.O. Box 766, Plains, MT 59859/406-826-3970
Cache La Poudre Rifleworks, 140 N. College, Ft. Collins, CO 80524/303-482-6913
Cadre Supply, P.O. Box 22074, Memphis, TN 38122/901-526-4986
Calhoon Mfg., James, 6035 Penworth Rd. SE, Calgary, AB T2A 4E9 Canada/403-235-2959
Calico Hardwoods, Inc., 1648 Airport Blvd., Windsor, CA 95492/707-546-4045
Calico Light Weapon Systems, 405 E. 19th St., Bakersfield, CA 93305/805-323-1327
California Sight, P.O. Box 4607, Pagosa Springs, CO 81157/303-731-5003
Cam Enterprises, 5090 Iron Springs Rd., P.O. Box 2, Prescott, AZ 86301
Camdex, Inc., 2330 Alger, Troy, MI 48083/313-528-2300
Cameron's, 16690 W. 11th Ave., Golden, CO 80401/303-279-7365
Camilli, Lou, 4700 Oahu Dr. NE, Albuquerque, NM 87111/505-293-5259
Camillus Cutlery Co., 54 Main St., Camillus, NY 13031/315-672-8111/800-344-0456
Camofare Company, 712 Main St. 2800, Houston, TX 77002/713-229-9253
Camp-Cap Products, P.O. Box 173, Chesterfield, MO 63006/314-532-4340
Campbell, Dick, 20000 Silver Ranch Rd., Conifer, CO 80433/303-697-0150
Can Am Enterprises, 350 Jones Rd., Fruitland, Ont. LOR ILO, Canada/416-643-4357 (catolog $2)
Canjar Co., M.H., 500 E. 45th Ave., Denver, CO 80216/303-295-2638
Cannavaro, Brian V., 600 Farm Rd., Kalispell, MT 59901/406-756-8851
Cannon Safe, Inc., 9358 Stephens St., Pico Rivera, CA 90660/213-692-0636, 800-242-1055, 800-222-1055 (CA)
Cannon's Guns, P.O. Box 357, 2387 Meridian, Victor, MT 59875/406-642-3644
Canons Delcour, 287 Rue Roosevelt, Fraipont, B-4870 Belgium/32 87 26 85 81
Cape Outfitters, Rt. 2 P.O. Box 437C, Cape Girardeau, MO 63701/314-335-4103
Caraville Manufacturing, P.O. Box 4545, Thousand Oaks, CA 91359/805-499-1234
Carbide Die & Mfg. Co., Inc., 15615 E. Arrow Hwy., Covina, CA 91706/818-337-2518
Carry-Lite, Inc., 5203 W. Clinton Ave., Milwaukee, WI 53223/414-355-3520
Carter's Wildlife Calls, Inc., Garth, P.O. Box 821, Cedar City, UT 84720/801-586-7639
Carter, Ralph L., Carter's Gun Shop, 225 G St., Penrose, CO 81240/719-372-6240
Cartridges Unlimited, 190 Bull's Bridge Rd., South Kent, CT 06785/203-927-3053
Carvajal Fabricating Co., 422 Chestnut, Unit #4, San Antonio, TX 78202/512-222-8262
Cascade Fabrication, 1090 Bailey Hill Rd. Unit A, Eugene, OR 97402/503-485-3433
Case & Sons Cutlery Co., W.R., P.O. Box 4000, Owens Way, Bradford, PA 16701/814-368-4123
Caspian Arms, 14 North Main St., Hardwick, VT 05843/802-472-6454
Caswell International Corp., 1221 Marshall St. NE, Minneapolis, MN 55413/612-379-2000
Cathey Enterprises, Inc., 3423 Milam Dr., P.O. Box 2202, Brownwood, TX 76804/915-643-2553
Cation, 32360 Edward, Madison Heights, MI 48071/313-588-0160
Catoctin Cutlery, 17 S. Main St., P.O. Box 188, Smithburg, MD 21783/301-824-7416
CCI, Div. of Blount, Inc., P.O. 856, Lewiston, ID 83501/208-746-2351
C&D Special Products, 309 Sequoya Dr., Hopkinsville, KY 42240/800-922-6287, 800-284-1746
Cedar Hill Game Call Co., Rt. 2 P.O. Box 236, Downsville, LA 71234/318-982-5632
Celestron International, P.O. Box 3587, Torrance, CA 90503
Cellini, Vito, Francesca, Inc., 3115 Old Ranch Rd., San Antonio, TX 78217/512-826-2584
Centaur Archery, Inc., 45 Hollinger Cres., Unit #1, Kitchener, Ontario, N2K 2Z1 Canada/519-743-6890
Centaur Systems, Inc., 6849 Hwy. 89 NW, Bemidji, MN 56601/218-751-8609
Central Specialties Co., 200 Lexington Dr., Buffalo Grove, IL 60089/708-537-3300
Century Gun Dist., Inc., 1467 Jason Rd., Greenfield, IN 46140/317-462-4524
Century Intl. Arms, Inc., 48 Lower Newton St., St. Albans, VT 05478/802-527-1252
CFVentures, 509 Harvey Dr., Bloomington, IN 47403
C&H Research, 155 Sunnyside Dr., Lewis, KS 67552/316-324-5445
C-H Tool & Die Corp. (See 4-D Die)
Chace Leather Prods., 507 Alden St., Fall River, MA 02722/508-678-7556
Chadick's Ltd., P.O. Box 100, Terrell, TX 75160/214-563-7577
Champion Target Company, 232 Industrial Parkway, Richmond, IN 47374/800-441-4971
Champion's Choice, Inc., 223 Space Park South, Nashville, TN 37211/615-834-6666
Champlin Firearms, Inc., P.O. Box 3191, Woodring Airport, Enid, OK 73701/405-237-7388
Champlin, R. MacDonald, P.O. Box 693, Manchester, NH 03105/603-483-8557
Chapman Academy, Rt.1, P.O. Box 60, Hallsville, MO 65255/314-696-5544
Chapman Mfg. Co., P.O. Box 250, 471 New Haven Rd., Durham, CT 06422/203-349-9228
Chapuis Armes, 21 La Gravoux, BP15, 42380 St. Bonnet-le-Chateau, France/(33)77.50.06.96
Checkmate Guns Custom Refinishing, 8232 Shaw Rd., Brooksville, FL 34602/904-799-5774
Cheddite France, S.A., 99 Route de Lyon, B.P. 112, F-26500 Bourg Les Valence, France/75 56 45 45
Chelsea Gun Club of New York City, Inc., 237 Ovington Ave., Apt. D53, Brooklyn, NY 11209/718-836-9422, 718-833-2704
Cherokee Gun Accessories, 4127 Bay St. Suite 226, Fremont, CA 94538/415-471-5770
Chesapeake Importing & Distributing Company, CIDCO, 21480 Pacific Blvd., Sterling, VA 22170/703-444-5353
Chesire & Perez Dist., 136 E. Walnut Ave., Monrovia, CA 91016/213-359-5345
CheVron Bullets, RR 1, Ottawa, IL 61350/815-433-2471
Chevron Case Master, RR 1, Ottawa, IL 61350
Chicago Cutlery Co., 5420 N. County Rd. 18, Minneapolis, MN 55428/612-533-0472
Chimere, Inc., 4406 Exchange Ave., Naples, FL 33942/813-643-4222
ChinaSports, Inc., 2010 S. Lynx Place, Ontario, CA 91761/714-923-1411
Chipmunk (See Oregon Arms, Inc.)
Chippewa Shoe Co., P.O. Box 2521, Ft. Worth, TX 76113/817-332-4385
Choate Machine & Tool Company, Inc., P.O. Box 218, Bald Knob, AR 72010/501-724-6193
Chopie Mfg., Inc., 700 Copeland Ave., LaCrosse, WI 54603/608-784-0926
Christie's East, 219 E. 67th St., New York, NY 10021/212-606-0400
Christopher Firearms Co., Inc., E., Route 128 & Ferry St., Miamitown, OH 45041/513-353-1321
Chuck's Gun Shop, P.O. Box 597, Waldo, FL 32694/904-468-2264
Churchill Glove Co., James, P.O. Box 298, Centralia, WA 98531
Churchill, Winston, Twenty Mile Stream Rd., RFD P.O. Box 29B, Proctorsville, VT 05153/802-226-7772
Cimarron Arms, 1106 Wisterwood #G, Houston, TX 77043/713-468-2007
Claridge Hi-Tec, Inc., P.O. Box 7309, Northridge, CA 91327-7309/818-700-9093
Clark Co., Inc., David, 360 Franklin St., P.O. Box 15054, Worcester, MA 01615/508-756-6216
Clark Custom Guns, Inc., James E. Clark, Rt. 2, P.O. Box 22A, Keithville, LA 71047/318-915-0836
Clark Firearms Engraving, P.O. Box 80746, San Marino, CA 91118/818-287-1652
Clark, Frank, 3714-27th St., Lubbock, TX 79410/806-799-1187
Clarkfield Enterprises, Inc., 1032 10th Ave., Clarkfield, MN 56223/612-669-7140
Classic Arms Corp., P.O. Box 8, Dunsmuir, CA 96025/916-235-2000
Clay Target Enterprises, 300 Railway Ave., Campbell, CA 95008/408-379-4829
Clearview Mfg. Co., Inc., 413 South Oakley St., Fordyce, AR 71742/501-352-8557
Clements, Chas, Handicrafts Unltd., 1741 Dallas St., Aurora, CO 80010/303-364-0403
Clenzoil Corp., P.O. Box 80226, Canton, OH 44708/216-833-9758
Clerke Co., J.A., P.O. Box 627, Pearblossom, CA 93553/805-945-0713
Clift Mfg., L.R., 3821 Hammonton Rd., Marysville, CA 95901
Clifton Arms, Inc., P.O. Box 531258, Grand Prairie, TX 75053/214-647-2500
Clinton River Gun Serv., Inc., 30016 S. River Rd., Mt. Clemens, MI 48045/313-468-1090
Cloward's Gun Shop, 4023 Aurora Ave. N, Seattle, WA 98103/206-632-2072
Clymer Mfg. Co., Inc., 1645 W. Hamlin Rd., Rochester Hills, MI 48309-3368/313-853-5555
Coast Cutlery Co. 609 SE Ankeny, Portland, OR 97214/503-234-4545
Coats, Mrs. Lester, 300 Luman Rd., Space 125, Phoenix, OR 97535/503-535-1611
Cobra Gunskin, 133-30 32nd Ave., Flushing, NY 11354/718-762-8181
Cobra Sport, s.n.c. Di Leto A&C, Via Caduti Del Lager 1, S. Romano (PISA) Italy/0039-571-450490
Cody Trading Post, Inc., 380 33rd St., P.O. Box 907, Cody, WY 82414/307-587-9502
Coffey, Barbara, Rt. 1, P.O. Box 208, Amherst, VA 24521/804-435-2259, 804-922-7249
Coffin, Charles H., 3719 Scarlet Ave., Odessa, TX 79762/915-366-4729
Coffin, Jim, 250 Country Club Lane, Albany, OR 97321/503-928-4391
Coghlan's Ltd., 121 Irene St., Winnipeg, Man., Canada R3T 4C7/204-284-9550
Cold Steel, Inc., 2128 Knoll Dr., Unit D, Ventura, CA 93003/800-255-4716, 800-624-2363
Cole-Grip, 16135 Cohasset St., Van Nuys, CA 91406/818-782-4424
Coleman Co., Inc., 250 N. St. Francis, Wichita, KS 67201
Collins Brothers Div. (See Bowen Knife Co.)
Colonial Arms, Inc., P.O. Box 636, Selma, AL 36702-0636/205-872-9455
Colonial Knife Co., P.O. Box 3327, 287 Agnes, Providence, RI 02909/401-421-1600
Colonial Repair, P.O. Box 372, Hyde Park, MA 02136/617-469-2991
Colorado School of Trades, 1575 Hoyt St., Lakewood, CO 80215/800-234-4594
Colorado Shooter's Supply, 138 So. Plum, P.O. Box 132, Fruita, CO 80446/303-887-2813
Colorado Sutlers Arsenal, P.O. Box 991, Granby, CO 80446/303-887-2813
Colt Firearms, P.O. Box 1868, Hartford, CT 06101/203-236-6311
Combat Shop, The, Rt. 1, P.O. Box 112-C, Surry, VA 23883/804-357-0881
Command Post, Inc., The, P.O. Box 1500, Crestview, FL 32536/904-682-2492
Companhia Brasileira de Cartuchos/CBC, Avenida Industrial, 3330, Santo Andre-SP-Brazil 09080/11-449-5600
Compass Industries, Inc., 104 East 25th St., New York, NY 10010/212-473-2614
Competition Bullets, Inc., 9996-29 Ave., Edmonton, Alb. T6N 1A2, Canada/403-463-2817
Competition Electronics, Inc., 3460 Precision Dr., Rockford, IL 61109/815-874-8001
Competition Limited, 1664 S. Research Loop Rd., Tucson, AZ 85710/602-722-6455
Competitive Pistol Shop, The, John Henderson, 5233 Palmer Dr., Ft. Worth, TX 76117/817-834-8479
Competitor Corporation, Inc., P.O. Box 244, West Groten, MA 01472/508-448-3521
Component Concepts, Inc., 20955 SW Regal Court, Aloha, OR 97006/503-642-3967
Concorde Arms, Inc., 27820 Fremont Ct. #3, Valencia, CA 91355/805-257-1955
Condon, Inc., David, P.O. Box 312, 14502-G Lee Rd., Chatilly, VA 22021/703-631-7748 or 109 E. Washington St., Middleburg, VA 22117/703-687-5642
Condor Mfg. Co., 418 W. Magnolia Ave., Glendale, CA 91204/818-240-3173
Conetrol Scope Mounts, Hwy. 123 South, Seguin, TX 78155
Connecticut Valley Arms Co.(CVA), 5988 Peachtree Corners East, Norcross, GA 30071/404-449-4687
Conrad, C.A., 3964 Ebert St., Winston-Salem, NC 27127/919-788-5469
Continental Kite & Key Co. (CONKKO), P.O. Box 40, Broomall, PA 19008/215-356-0711
Coonan Arms, Inc., 830 Hampden Ave., St. Paul, MN 55114/612-646-6672
Cooper Arms, P.O. Box 114, Stevensville, MT 59870/800-732-GUNS
Cooper-Woodward, 8073 Canyon Ferry Rd., Helena, MT 59601/406-375-3321
Cor-Bon Bullet & Ammo Co., 4828 Michigan Ave., Detroit, MI 48210/313-894-2373
Corbin Applied Technology, P.O. Box 2171, White City, OR 97503/503-826-5211
Corbin Mfg. & Supply, Inc., 600 Industrial Circle, P.O. Box 2659, White City, OR 97503/503-826-5211
Corkys Gun Clinic, 111 North 11th Ave., Greeley, CO 80631/303-330-0516
Corry, John, 861 Princeton Ct., Neshanic Station, NJ 08853/308-369-8019
Cosmi Americo & F., s.n.c., Via Flaminia 307, Ancona, Italy I-60020/071-88208
Costa, David, 94 Orient Ave., Arlington, MA 02174/617-643-9571
Country Armourer, The, P.O. Box 308, Ashby, MA 01431/508-386-7789
Cox, C. Ed, RD 2, Box 192, Prosperity, PA 15329/412-228-4984
CQB Training, P.O. Box 1739, Manchester, MO 63011
Craftguard, 3624 Logan Ave., Waterloo, IA 50703/319-232-2959
Crandall Tool & Machine Co., 1545 N. Mitchell St., Cadillac, MI 49601/616-775-5562

Crane & Crane Ltd., 11325 Sunrise Gold Circle, Unit F, Rancho Cordova, CA 05742/916-638-2221
Crane Sales Co., George S., P.O. Box 385, Van Nuys, CA 91409/818-505-8337
Cravener's Gun Shop, 1627-5th Ave., Ford City, PA 16226/412-763-8312
Crawford Co., R.M., P.O. Box 277, Everett, PA 15537/814-652-5701
Creative Cartridge Co., 56 Morgan Rd., Canton, CT 06019/203-693-2529
Creative Craftsman, Inc., The, 95 Highway 29 North, P.O. Box 331, Lawrenceville, GA 30246/404-963-2112
Creekside Gun Shop, Inc., Main St., Holcomb, NY 14469/716-657-6131
Crosman Airguns (a Coleman Co.), Routes 5 and 20, E. Bloomfield, NY 14443/716-657-6161
Crosman Blades, The Coleman Co., 250 N. St. Francis, Wichita, KS 67201
Crosman Products of Canada Ltd., 1173 N. Service Rd. West, Oakville, Ontario, LCM2V9 Canada/416-827-1822
Crouse's Country Cover, P.O. Box 160, Storrs, CT 06268/203-429-3720
Cubriel, Reggie, 15610 Purple Sage, San Antonio, TX 78255/512-695-3364
Cullity Restoration, Daniel, 209 Old County Rd., East Sandwich, MA 02537/508-888-1147
Cumberland Arms, Rt. 1, P.O. Box 1150, Shafer Rd., Blantons Chapel, Manchester, TN 37355
Cumberland Knife & Gun Works, 5661 Bragg Blvd., Fayetteville, NC 28303/919-867-0009
Cureton, Earl T., Rt. 2, P.O. Box 388, Willoughby Rd., Bulls Gap, TN 37711/615-235-2854
Curtis Custom Shop, 26 Novak Dr., Stafford, VA 22554/703-659-4265
Custom Checkering Service, 2124 SE Yamhill St., Portland, OR 97214/503-236-5874
Custom Chronograph, Inc., 5305 Reese Hill Rd., Sumas, WA 98295/206-988-7801
Custom Gun Guild, Frank Wood, 2646 Church Dr., Doraville, GA 30340/404-455-0346
Custom Gun Products, 5021 W. Rosewood, Spokane, WA 99208/509-328-9340
Custom Gun Stocks, Rt. 6, P.O. Box 177, McMinnville, TN 37110/615-668-3912
Custom Hunting Ammo & Arms, 2900 Fisk Rd., Howell, MI 48843/517-546-9498
Custom Knifemaker's Supply (Bob Schrimsher), P.O. Box 308, Emory, TX 75440/214-473-3330
Custom Products, Neil A. Jones, RD #1, P.O. Box 483A, Saegertown, PA 16433/814-763-2769
Custom Swaged Bullets (See Northern Precision)
Custom Tackle & Ammo, P.O. Box 1886, Farmington, NM 87499/505-632-3539
CVA (See Connecticut Valley Arms Co.)
C.W. Cartridge Co., 242 Highland Ave., Kearny, NJ 07032/201-998-1030
Cycle Dynamics, Inc., 74 Garden St., Feeding Hills, MA 01030/413-786-0141
Cylinder & Slide, Inc., 245 E. 4th St., Fremont, NE 68025/402-721-4277

D

Dade Screw Machine Products, 2319 NW 7th Ave., Miami, FL 33127/305-573-5050
Dahl's Custom Stocks, Rt. 4, P.O. Box 558, Lake Geneva, WI 53147/414-248-2464
Daigmont Industries, Inc., 422 E. Main St., Suite 207, Nacogdoches, TX 75961/409-560-4367
Daisy Mfg. Co., P.O. Box 220, Rogers, AR 72756/501-636-1200
Dakota Arms, Inc., HC 55, P.O. Box 326, Sturgis, SD 57785/605-347-4686
Daly, Charles (See Outdoor Sports HQ)
Damascus-U.S.A., Rt. 3, Box 39A Wildcat Road, Edenton, NC 27932/919-482-4992
Dangler, Homer L., P.O. Box 254, Addison, MI 49220/517-547-6745 (brochure $3)
Danner Shoe Mfg. Co., P.O. Box 30148, 12722 NE Airport Way, Portland, OR 97230/503-251-1100
Dapkus Co., J.G., P.O. Box 180, Cromwell, CT 06416/203-632-2308
Dara-Nes, Inc. (See Nesci Enterprises, Inc.)
Darlington Gun Works, Inc., P.O. Box 698, 516 S. 52 Bypass, Darlington, SC 29532/803-393-3931
Datumtech Corporation, 8575 Roll Rd., Clarence Center, NY 14032/716-741-4405
Davidson Products For Shooters, 2020 Huntington Dr., Las Cruces, NM 88001/505-522-5612
Davidson's, P.O. Box 5387, Greensboro, NC 27403/800-367-4867
Davidson, Jere, Rt. 1, P.O. Box 132, Rustburg, VA 24588/804-821-3637
Davis Industries, 15150 Sierra Bonita Lane, Chino, CA 91710/714-597-4726
Davis Leather Co., G. Wm. Davis, 3990 Valley Blvd., Unit D, Walnut, CA 91789/714-598-5620
Davis Service Center, Bill, 10173 Croydon Way #9, Sacramento, CA 95827/916-369-6789
Day & Sons, Inc., Leonard, P.O. Box 122, Flagg Hill Rd., Heath, MA 01346/413-337-8369
Dayton Traister Co., 4778 N. Monkey Hill Rd., Oak Harbor, WA 98277/206-675-3421
DBASE Consultants, 4851 Southwest Madrona St., Lake Oswego, OR 97035/503-697-0533
DBI Books, Inc., 4092 Commercial Ave., Northbrook, IL 60062/708-272-6310
D-Boone Ent., Inc., 5900 Colwyn Dr., Harrisburg, PA 17109
D&D Gunsmiths, Ltd., 363 E. Elmwood, Troy, MI 48083/313-583-1512
De Haas, Mark, RR #3, P.O. Box 77, Ridgeway, MO 64481/816-872-6308
Decker Shooting Products, 1729 Laguna Ave., Schofield, WI 54476/715-359-5873
Deepeeka Exports Pvt. Ltd., D-78, Saket, Meerut, India 250-006/0121-74483
Deer Me Products Co., P.O. Box 34, 1208 Park St., Anoka, MN 55303/612-421-8971
Defense Moulding Enterprises, 16781 Daisey Ave., Fountain Valley, CA 92708/714-842-5062
Defense Training International, Inc., 6565 Gunpark Dr., Suite 150-4, Boulder, CO 80301/303-530-7106
Del Rey Products, P.O. Box 91561, Los Angeles, CA 90009/213-823-0494
Del-Sports, Inc., Main St., Margaretville, NY 12455/914-586-4103
Delhi Gun House, 1374 Kashmere Gate, Delhi, India 110006/9111-237375, 2917344
Delorge, Ed, 2231 Hwy. 308, Thibodaux, LA 70301/504-447-1633
Delta Arms Ltd., 2316 Baynard Blvd., Wilmington, DE 19802/302-429-9298
Delta Vectors, Inc., 7119 W. 79th St., Overland Park, KS 66204/913-642-0307
Dem-Bart Checkering Tools, Inc., 6807 Bickford Ave., Snohomish, WA 98290/206-568-7356
Denver Arms, Ltd., P.O. Box 4640, Pagosa Springs, CO 81157/303-731-2295 (SASE)
Denver Bullets, Inc., 1811 W. 13th Ave., Denver, CO 80204/303-893-3146
Denver Instrument Company, 6542 Fig St., Arvada, CO 80004/800-321-1135
DeSantis Holster & Leather Co., 140 Denton Ave., P.O. Box 2039, New Hyde Park, NY 11040/516-354-8000
Desert Industries, Inc., 3261 Patrick Ln., Suite H, Las Vegas, NV 89120/702-597-10MM
Desert Mountain Mfg., P.O. Box 184, Coram, MT 59913/406-387-5381
Destination North Software, 804 Surry Rd., Wenatchee, WA 98801/509-662-6602
Detonics (See New Detonics Mfg. Corp.)
DeTreville (See Treville)
Detroit-Armor Corp., Detroit Bullet Trap Div., 2233 N. Palmer Dr., Schaumburg, IL 60103/708-397-4070
Dever, Jack, 8520 NW 90th, Oklahoma City, OK 73132/405-721-6393
Devereaux, R.H. "Dick", D.D. Custom Rifles, 5240 Mule Deer Dr., Colorado Springs, CO 80919/719-548-8468
Dewey Mfg. Co., J., P.O. Box 2014, Southbury, CT 06488/1035 Long Meadow Rd., Middlebury, CT 06762/203-598-7912
D&H Precision Tooling, 7522 Barnard Mill Rd., Ringwood, IL 60072/815-653-4011
D&H Prods. Co., Inc., 465 Denny Rd., Valencia, PA 16059/412-898-2840
Dibble, Derek A., 555 John Downey Dr., New Britain, CT 06051/203-224-2630
Dickson (See The American Import Co.)
Dilliott Gunsmithing, Inc., 657 Scarlett Rd., Dandridge, TN 37725/615-397-9204
Dillon Precision Prods., Inc., 7442 E. Butherus Dr., Scottsdale, AZ 85260/602-948-8009
DiStefano, Dominic, 4303 Friar Lane, Colorado Springs, CO 80907/303-599-3366
Dixie Gun Works, Inc., P.O. Box 130, Union City, TN 38261/901-885-0700
Dixon Muzzleloading Shop, Inc., RD 1 P.O. Box 175, Kempton, PA 19529/215-756-6271
Dixon, William, Buckhorn Gun Works, Rt. 6 P.O. Box 2230, Rapid City, SD 57702/605-787-6289
DKT, Inc., 14623 Vera Dr., Union, MI 49130/616-641-7120
D Max Industries, 1701 W. Valley Hwy. N., P.O. Box 2324, Auburn, WA 98071/206-939-5137
D&L Sports, P.O. Box 651, Gillette, WY 82717/307-686-4008
DMG Technologies, Inc., 931 Cumberland St., Lakeland, FL 33801/813-646-8888
D.O.C. Specialists (Doc & Bud Ulrich), 2209 S. Central Ave., Cicero, IL 60650/708-652-3606
Donnelly-Siskiyou Gun Works, C.P., 405 Kubli Rd., Grants Pass, OR 97527/503-846-6604
Doskocil Mfg. Co., Inc., P.O. Box 1246, Arlington, TX 76004/817-467-5116
Douglas Barrels, Inc., 5504 Big Tyler Rd., Charleston, WV 25313/304-776-1341
Dowtin Gunworks (DGW), Rt. 4 P.O. Box 930A, Flagstaff, AZ 86001/602-779-1898
Dr. O's Products Ltd., P.O. Box 111, Niverville, NY 12130/518-784-3333
Drain, Mark, SE 3211 Kamilche Point Rd., Shelton, WA 98584/206-426-5452
Dremel Mfg. Co., 4915-21st St., Racine, WI 53406
Dressel, Paul G., Jr., 209 N. 92nd Ave., Yakima, WA 98908/509-966-9233
Dri-Slide, Inc., 411 N. Darling, Fremont, MI 49412/616-924-3950
DTM International, Inc., 40 Joslyn Rd., P.O. Box 5, Lake Orion, MI 48035/313-693-6670
Du-Lite Corp., 171 River Rd., Middletown, CT 06457/203-347-2505
Dubber, Michael W., P.O. Box 312, Evansville, IN 47702/812-963-6156
Duck Call Specialists, P.O. Box 124, Jerseyville, IL 62052/618-498-4692
Duds Ammo & Supply Co., P.O. Box 393, Barton, VT 05822/802-525-3835
Duffy, Charles E., Williams Lane, West Hurley, NY 12491/914-679-2997
Duncan's Gunworks, Inc., 1619 Grand Ave., San Marcos, CA 92069/619-727-0515
Dunham Co., P.O. Box 813, Brattleboro, VT 05301/802-254-2316
Dunn, Tom M., 1342 South Poplar, Casper, WY 82601/307-237-3207
Duofold, Inc., 120 W. 45th St., 15th Floor, New York, NY 10036
DuPont (See IMR Powder Co.)
Durango Boot (See Northlake Boot Co.)
Dutchman's Firearms, Inc., The, 4143 Taylor Blvd., Louisville, KY 40215/502-366-0555
Duxbak, Inc., 903 Woods Rd., Cambridge, MD 21613/301-228-2990, 800-334-1845
Dwyer, Dan, 915 W. Washington St., San Diego, CA 92103/619-296-1501
Dykstra, Doug, 411 N. Darling, Fremont, MI 49412/616-924-3950
Dynalite Products, Inc., 215 S. Washington St., Greenfield, OH 45123/513-981-2124
Dynamit Nobel-RWS, Inc., 105 Stonehurst Court, Northvale, NJ 07647/201-767-1995
Dyson & Son Ltd., Peter, 29-31 Church St., Honley, Huddersfield, W. Yorksh. HD7 2AH, England/011-44-484-661062

E

Eagle Arms, Inc., 131 E. 22nd Ave., P.O. Box 457, Coal Valley, IL 61240/309-799-5619
Eagle Imports, Inc., 1907 Highway #35, Ocean, NJ 07712/908-531-8375
Eagle International, Inc., 5195 W. 58th Ave., Suite 300, Arvada, CO 80002/303-426-8100
E-A-R Inc., (Insta-Mold Div.), P.O. Box 2146, Boulder CO 80306/303-447-2619
East Enterprises, Inc., 2208 Mallory Place, Monroe, LA 71201/318-325-1761
Easy Pull/Outlaw Products, 316 1st St. East, Polson, MT 59860/406-883-6822
Echols, D'Arcy A., 164 W. 580 S., Providence, UT 84332/801-753-2367
Edgecraft Corp., P.O. Box 3000, Avondale, PA 19311-3000/800-342-3255
Ed's Gun House, Ed Kukowski, Route 1, P.O. Box 62, Minnesota City, MN 55952/507-689-2925
Edmund Scientific Co., 101 E. Gloucester Pike, Barrington, NJ 08033/609-543-6250
Ednar, Inc., 2-4-8 Kayabacho, Nihonbashi, Chuo-ku, Tokyo, Japan/81(Japan)-3-3667-1651
Edwards Recoil Reducer, 1104 Milton Rd., Alton, IL 62002/618-462-3257
Eezox, Inc., P.O. Box 772, Waterford, CT 06385/203-447-8282
Efemes Enterprises, P.O. Box 691, Colchester, VT 05446
Eggleston, Jere, P.O. Box 50238, Columbia, SC 29250/803-799-3402
Ek Commando Knife Co., 601 N. Lombardy St., Richmond, VA 23220/804-257-7272
Ekol Leather Care, P.O. Box 2652, 2150 Klondike Rd., West Lafayette, IN 47906/317-463-2250
E&L Mfg., Inc., 39042 N. School House, Cave Creek, AZ 85331/602-488-2598
El Paso Saddlery Co., P.O. Box 27194, El Paso, TX 79926/915-544-2233
Eldorado Cartridge Corp., P.O. Box 308, Boulder City, NV 89005/702-294-0025
Eldorado Custom Shop, P.O. Box 308, Boulder City, NV 89005/702-294-0025
Electronic Trigger Systems, 4124 Thrushwood Lane, Minnetonka, MN 55345/612-935-7829
Eley Ltd., P.O. Box 705, Wilton, Birmingham, B6 7UT, England/021-356-8899
Elite Ammunition, P.O. Box 3251, Oakbrook, IL 60522/708-366-9006
Elk River, Inc., 1225 Paonia St., Colorado Springs, CO 80915/719-574-4407
Elko Arms, Dr. L. Kortz, 28 rue Ecole Moderne, B-7400 Soignies, H.T., Belgium/32-67.33.29.34
Ellett Bros., 267 Columbia Ave., Chapin, SC 29036/803-345-3751
Ellis Sport Shop, E.W., RD 1, Route 9N, P.O. Box 315, Corinth, NY 12822/518-654-6444
Emerging Technologies, Inc., P.O. Box 3548, Little Rock, AR 72203/501-375-2227
EMF, Co., Inc., 1900 East Warner Ave. 1-D, Santa Ana, CA 92705/714-261-6611
Emmons, Bob, 11748 Robson Rd., Grafton, OH 44044/216-458-5890
Empire Cutlery Corporation, 12 Kruger Ct., Clifton, NJ 07013/201-472-5155
Engineered Accessories, 1804 S. Elm Grove Rd., New Berlin, WI 53151/414-797-0901

English Sales Co., A.G., 708 S. 12th St., Broken Arrow, OK 74012/800-222-7233
Englishtown Sporting Goods Co., Inc., David J. Maxham, 38 Main St., Englishtown, NJ 07726/201-446-7717
Enhanced Presentations, Inc., 5929 Market St., Wilmington, NC 28405/919-799-1622
Epps (Orillia) Northern Ltd., Ellwood, RR 3, Hwy. 11 North, Orillia, Ont. L3V 6H3, Canada/705-689-5333
Erhardt, Dennis, 3280 Green Meadow Dr., Helena, MT 59601/406-368-2298
Essex Arms, P.O. Box 345, Island Pond, VT 05846/802-723-4313
Estate Cartridge, Inc., P.O. Box 3702, Conroe, TX 77305/409-856-7277
Euroarms of America, Inc., 208 Piccadilly St., 1501 Lenoir Dr., P.O. Box 3277, Winchester, VA 22601/703-662-1863
European American Armory Corp., P.O. Box 3498, Hialeah, FL 33013/305-688-5656
Europtik, Ltd., P.O. Box 319, Dunmore, PA 18512/717-347-6049
Eutaw Company, Inc., P.O. Box 608, U.S. Hwy. 176 West, Holly Hill, SC 29059/803-496-3341
Evans, Robert, 332 Vine St., Oregon City, OR 97045/503-656-5693
Eversull & Co., Inc., K., Tracemont Farm, 4800 Hwy. 121, Boyce, LA 71409/318-793-8728
Excaliber Wax, Inc., 14344 County Rd. 140, Kenton, OH 43326/419-673-0512
Eyster Heritage Gunsmiths, Inc., Ken, 6441 Bishop Rd., Centerburg, OH 43011/614-625-6131
Eze-Lap Diamond Prods., P.O. Box 2229, 15164 Weststate St., Westminster, CA 92683/714-847-1555

F

Fabian Bros. Sporting Goods, Inc., 1510 Morena Blvd., Suite "G," San Diego, CA 92110/619-275-0816
Fabrique Nationale Nouvelle Herstal, S.A., Voie de Liege, 33-B-4040 Herstal, Belgium, 4040/(0)41-40 81 11
Fagan & Co., William, 22952 E. 15 Mile Rd., Mt. Clemens, MI 48043/313-465-4637
Fair Game International, P.O. Box 77234-34053, Houston, TX 77234/713-941-6269
Fajen, Inc., Reinhart, 1000 Red Bud Dr., P.O. Box 338, Warsaw, MO 65355/816-438-5111
Falling Block Works, P.O. Box 3087, Fairfax, VA 22038/703-476-0043
Fanzoj, John, P.O. Box 25, Ferlach, Austria 9170
Farm Form, Inc., 7730 Chantilly, Galveston, TX 77551/409-744-0762
Farmer-Dressel, Sharon, 209 N. 92nd Ave., Yakima, WA 98908/509-966-9233
Farr Studio, 1231 Robinhood Rd., Greenville, TN 37743/615-638-8825
Faulk's Game Call Co., Inc., 616 18th St., Lake Charles, LA 70601/318-436-9726
Faust, Inc., T.G., 544 Minor St., Reading, PA 19602/215-375-8549
Fautheree, Andy, P.O. Box 4607, Pagosa Springs, CO 81157/303-731-5003 (must send SASE)
Favre, Jacqueline, 3111 S. Valley View Blvd., Suite B-214, Las Vegas, NV 89102/702-876-6278
Feather Flex Decoys, 1655 Swan Lake Rd., Bossier City, LA 71111/318-746-8596
Feather Industries, Inc., 2500 Central Ave.#K, Boulder, CO 80301/303-442-7021
Federal Cartridge Co., 900 Ehlen Dr., Anoka, MN 55303/612-422-2840
Federal Eng. Corp., 2335 S. Michigan Ave., Chicago, IL 60616/312-842-1063
Federal Ordnance, Inc., 1443 Potrero Ave., S. El Monte, CA 91733/818-350-4161
Feinwerkbau Westinger & Altenburger GmbH & Co. KG, Neckarstrasse 43, D-7238 Oberndorf/Neckar, Germany D-7238/07423-814-0
Fellowes, Ted, Beaver Lodge, 9245 16th Ave. SW, Seattle, WA 98106/206-763-1698
Feminine Protection, Inc., 10514 Shady Trail, Dallas, TX 75220/214-351-4500
Fenwal, Inc., Resins Systems Div., 50 Main St., Ashland, MA 01721/508-881-2000 Ext. 2372
FERLIB, Armi di Ferraglio Libero, 46 Via Costa, 25063 Gardone V.T. (Brescia), Italy/030-83.75.86
Ferris Firearms, Gregg Ferris, 1827 W. Hildebrand, San Antonio, TX 78201/512-734-0304
Fiberpro, Inc., 3636 California St., San Diego, CA 92101/619-295-7703
Fibron Products, Inc., 170 Florida St., Buffalo, NY 14208/716-886-2378
Finerty, Raymond F., 803 N. Downing St., P.O. Box 914, Piqua, OH 45356/800-543-8952
Fiocchi of America, Inc., Rt. 2, P.O. Box 90-8, Ozark, MO 65721/417-725-4118
Firearm Training Center, The, 9555 Blandville Rd., West Paducah, KY 42086/502-554-5886
Firearms Academy of Seattle, P.O. Box 6691, Lynnwood, WA 98036/206-827-0533
Firearms Engravers Guild of America, Robert Evans, Secy., 332 Vine St., Oregon City, OR 97045/503-656-5693
First Distributors, Inc., Jack, 44633 Sierra Highway, Lancaster, CA 93534/805-945-6981
Fish, Marshall F., Rt. 22 N., P.O. Box 2439, Westport, NY 12993/518-962-4897
Fish-N-Hunt, Inc., 5651 Beechnut St., Houston, TX 77096/713-777-3285
Fisher Custom Firearms, 2199 S. Kittredge Way, Aurora, CO 80013/303-755-3710
Fisher, Jerry A., P.O. Box 652, 38 Buffalo Buttes, Dubois, WY 82513/307-455-2722
Fishpaw, Roy C., 101 Primrose Lane, Lynchburg, VA 24501/804-385-6667 ($2 for brochure)
Fiskars (See Gerber Legendary Blades)
Fitz Pistol Grip Co., P.O. Box 171, Douglas City, CA 96024/916-778-3136
Flaig's, 2200 Evergreen Rd., Millvale, PA 15209/412-821-1717
Flambeau Prods. Corp., 15981 Valplast Rd., Middlefield, OH 44062/216-632-1631
Flannery Engraving Co., Jeff W., 11034 Riddles Run Rd., Union, KY 41091/606-384-3127 (color catalog $5)
Flashette Co., 4725 S. Kolin Ave., Chicago, IL 60632/312-927-1302
Flayderman & Co., N., P.O. Box 2446, Ft. Lauderdale, FL 33303/305-761-8855
Flents Products Co., Inc., P.O. Box 2109, Norwalk, CT 06852/203-866-2581
Flex Gun Rods Co., Inc., P.O. Box 202, Dearborn, MI 48121/313-271-2595
Flint Creek Arms Co., David Demasi, P.O. Box 205, 136 Spring St., Phillipsburg, MT 59858
Flintlock Muzzle Loading Gun Shop, The, 1238 "G" S. Beach Blvd., Anaheim, CA 92804/714-821-6655
Floatstone Mfg. Co., 106 Powder Mill Rd., P.O. Box 765, Canton, CT 06019/203 -693-1977
Flores Publications, J., P.O. Box 163001, Miami, FL 33116
Flouramics, Inc., 103 Pleasant Ave., Upper Saddle River, NJ 07458/201-825-8110
Flow-Rite of Tennessee, Inc., P.O. Box 196, Bruceton, TN 38317/901-586-2271
Flynn's Cust. Guns, P.O. Box 7461, Alexandria, LA 71301/318-455-7130
Fobus International, Ltd., Kfar Hess, Israel 40692
Fogle, James W., RR 2, P.O. Box 258, Herrin, IL 62948/618-988-1795
Folks, Donald E., 205 W. Lincoln St., Pontiac, IL 61764/815-844-7901
Foothills Video Productions, Inc., P.O. Box 651, Spartanburg, SC 29304/803-573-7023,800-782-5358
Force 10, Inc., 3029 Fairfield Ave., Suite 223, Bridgeport, CT 06605/203-334-8282
Ford Ltd., J. and J./Sportsmatch Ltd., 16 Summer St., Leighton Buzzard, Bedfordshire, LU7 8HT England/0525-381 638
Foredom Electric Co., Rt. 6, 16 Stony Hill Rd., Bethel, CT 06801/203-792-8622
Forgett, Valmore J., Jr., 689 Bergen Blvd., Ridgefield, NJ 07657/201-945-2500
Forrest Tool Company, P.O. Box 768, 44380 Gordon Lane, Mendocino, CA 95460
Forster Products, Inc., 82 E. Lanark Ave., Lanark, IL 61046/815-493-6360
Forster, Larry L., P.O. Box 212, 220 First St. NE, Gwinner, ND 58040/701-678-2475
Fort Knox Security Products, 1051 N. Industrial Park Rd., Orem, UT 84057/801-224-7233
Forthofer's Gunsmithing, Pete, 711 Spokane Ave., Whitefish, MT 59937/406-862-2674
Fortress Publications, Inc., P.O. Box 9241, Stoney Creek, Ont. L8G 3X9, Canada/416-662-3505
Forty-Five Ranch Enterprises, 217 F St. SW, P.O. Box 1080, Miami, OK 74355/918-542-5875
Forty-Niner Trading Co., P.O. Box 792, Manteca, CA 95336/209-823-7263
Fountain Products, 492 Prospect Ave., West Springfield, MA 01089/413-781-4651
4-D Die Co., 711 N. Sandusky St., Mount Vernon, OH 43050
Fowler Bullets, 4003 Linwood Rd., Gastonia, NC 28052/704-867-3259
Francesca Stabilizer's, Inc., 3115 Old Ranch Rd., San Antonio, TX 78217/512-826-2584
Francolini, Leonard, 106 Powder Mill Rd., P.O. Box 765, Canton, CT 06019/203-693-1977
Francotte, Auguste & Cie, S.A., rue du Trois Juin 109, 4400 Herstal-Liege, Belgium/41-48.13.18
Frank Custom Guns, Ron, 7131 Richland Rd., Ft. Worth, TX 76118/817-284-4426
Frank, Henry, P.O. Box 984, 331 Karrow Ave., Whitefish, MT 59937/406-862-2681
Frankonia Jagd, Hofmann & Co., Postfach 6780, D-8700 Wurzburg 1, West Germany
Frazier Brothers Sporting Goods, 1118 N. Main St., Franklin, IN 46131/317-736-4000
Fredrick Gun Shop, 10 Elson Drive, Riverside, RI 02915/401-433-2805
Freedom Arms, Inc., P.O. Box 1776, Freedom, WY 83120/307-883-2468
Freeland's Scope Stands, Inc., 3737 14th Ave., Rock Island, IL 61201/309-788-7449
Freeman's Animal Targets, 8237 Indy Lane, Indianapolis, IN 46214/317-271-5314
Fremont Tool Works, 1214 Prairie, Ford, KS 67842/316-369-2338
Frielich Police Equipment, Frielich, R.S., 211 East 21st St., New York, NY 10010/212-254-3045
Frontier Arms Co., 2760 Tucson Hwy., Nogales, AZ 85621/602-281-0322
Frontier Cartridge Division-Hornady Mfg. Co., P.O. Box 1848, Grand Island, NE 68801/308-382-1390
Frontier, 2910 San Bernardino, Laredo, TX 78040/512-723-5409
Frost Cutlery Co., P.O. Box 21353, Chattanooga, TN 37421/800-251-7768
FTI, 1812 Margaret Ave., Annapolis, MD 21401/301-268-6451
FTL Marketing/Auto Nine Corp., 12521 Oxnard St., North Hollywood, CA 91606/818-985-2946
Fujinon, Inc., 10 High Point Dr., Wayne, NJ 07470/201-633-5600
Fullmer, Geo. M., 2499 Mavis St., Oakland, CA 94601/415-533-4193
Fulmer Antique Firearms, Chet, P.O. Box 792, (Rt. 2, Buffalo Lake), Detroit Lakes, MN 56502/218-847-7712
Furr Arms, Karl J. Furr, 91 N. 970 W., Orem, UT 84057/801-226-3877

G

G96 Designtech, Inc., 707 Commercial Ave., Carlstadt, NJ 07022/201-507-5002
Galati International, P.O. Box 326, Catawissa, MO 63015/314-257-4837
Galaxy Imports, Ltd., Inc., P.O. Box 3361, Victoria, TX 77903/512-573-4867
GALCO International, Ltd., 2019 West Quail Ave., Phoenix, AZ 85027/602-233-0956
Gamba, Renato, S.p.A., P.O. Box 48, Via Artigiani n.89, I-25063 Gardone V.T. (Brescia), Italy
Game Haven Gunstocks, 13750 Shire Rd., Wolverine, MI 49799/616-525-8257
Game-Winner, Inc., 2625 Cumberland Parkway, Suite 220, Atlanta, GA 30339/404-434-9210
Gammog, Gregory B.Gally, 16009 Kenny Rd., Laurel, MD 20707/301-725-3838
Gander Mountain, Inc., P.O. Box 128, Hwy. "W," Wilmot, WI 53192/414-862-2331, Ext. 6425
Ganton Manufacturing Ltd., Depot Lane, Seamer Rd., Scarborough, North Yorkshire, Y012 4EB England/0723 371910
Garbi, Armas Urki, #12-14, 20.600 Eibar (Guipuzcoa) Spain/43-11 38 73
Garcia National Gun Traders, Inc., 225 SW 22nd Ave., Miami, FL 33135/305-642-2355
Garrett Accur-Lt. D.F.S. Co., P.O. Box 8675, 1413B East Olive Ct., Ft. Collins, CO 80524/303-224-3067
Garthwaite, Jim, Rt. 2, P.O. Box 310, Watsontown, PA 17777/717-538-1566
Gator Guns & Repair, 6255 Spur Hwy., Kenai, AK 99611/907-283-7947
Gene's Custom Guns, P.O. Box 10534, White Bear Lake, MN 55110/612-429-5105
Genecco Gun Works, K., 10512 Lower Sacramento Rd., Stockton, CA 95210/209-951-0706
Gentry Custom Gunmaker, David, 314 N. Hoffman, Belgrade, MT 59714/406-388-4867
George, Tim and Christy, Rt. 1, P.O. Box 45, Evington, VA 24550/804-821-8117
Gerber Legendary Blades, 14200 SW 72nd Ave., Portland, OR 97223/503-639-6161
Getz Barrel Co., P.O. Box 88, Beavertown, PA 17813/717-658-7263
GFR Corp., P.O. Box 430, Andover, NH 03216/603-735-5300
G&H Decoys, Inc., P.O. Box 1208, Hwy. 75 North, Henryetta, OK 74437/918-652-3314
G.H. Enterprises Ltd., Bag 10, Okotoks, Alberta T0L 1T0 Canada/403-938-6070
Gilbert Equipment Co., Inc., 960 Downtowner Rd., Mobile, AL 36609/205-344-3322
Gillman, Edwin, 33 Valley View Dr., Hanover, PA 17331/717-632-1662
Gilman-Mayfield, 1552 N. 1st, Fresno, CA 93703/209-237-2500
Giron, Robert E., 1328 Pocono St., Pittsburg, PA 15218/412-731-6041
Glacier Glove, 4890 Aircenter Circle #206, Reno, NV 89502/702-825-8225
Glaser Safety Slug, Inc., P.O. Box 8223, Foster City, CA 94404/415-345-7677
Glass, Herb, P.O. Box 25, Bullville, NY 10915/914-361-3021
Glimm, Jerome C., 19 S. Maryland, Conrad, MT 59425/406-278-3574
Glock, Inc., 6000 Highlands Parkway, Smyrna, GA 30082/404-432-1202
GML Products, Inc., 1634-A Montgomery Hwy., Suite 196, Birmingham, AL 35216/205-979-4867
Goens, Dale W., P.O. Box 224, Cedar Crest, NM 87008/505-281-5419
Goergen, James, Rt. 2, P.O. Box 182BB, Austin, MN 55912/507-433-9280
GOEX, Inc., 1002 Springbrook Ave., Moosic, PA 18507/717-457-6724
Golden Powder International Sales, Inc., 8300 Douglas Ave., Suite 729, Dallas, TX 75225/214-373-3350
Golden Rod Dehumidifier Co., Inc., 3600 S. Harbor Blvd., Oxnard, CA 93035/800-451-6797
Gonic Arms, Inc., 134 Flagg Rd., Gonic, NH 03839/603-332-8456
Gonzalez, Ramon B., P.O. Box 370, Monticello, NY 12701/914-794-4515

Goode, A.R., 4125 NE 28th Terr., Ocala, FL 32670/904-622-9575
Goodling's Gunsmithing, R.D. #1, P.O. Box 1007, Spring Grove, PA 17632/717-225-3350
Goodwin, Fred, Silver Ridge Gun Shop, Sherman Mills, ME 04776/207-365-4451
Gordie's Gun Shop (See Gordon C. Mulholland)
Goudy, Gary, 263 Hedge Rd., Menlo Park, CA 94025/415-322-1338
Gould & Goodrich, 709 E. McNeil St., P.O. Box 1479, Lillington, NC 27546/919-893-2071
Gournet, Geoffroy G., 820 Paxinosa Ave., Easton, PA 18042/215-559-0710
Grace Metal Products, Inc., 115 Ames St., P.O. Box 67, Elk Rapids, MI 49629/616-264-8133
Grace, Charles E., 10144 Elk Lake Rd., Williamsburg, MI 49690/616-264-9483
Granger, Georges, 66 cours Fauriel, 42100 Saint Etienne, France/77-25.14.73
Grant, Howard V., Hiawatha 153, Woodruff, WI 54568/715-356-7146
Graybill, Gene, 1035 Ironville Pike, Columbia, PA 17512/717-684-6220
Great 870 Company, The, P.O. Box 6309, El Monte, CA 91734
Great Lakes Airguns, 6175 S. Park Ave., Hamburg, NY 14075/716-648-6666
Green Bay Bullets, P.O. Box 10446, 1860 Burns Ave. (54303), Green Bay, WI 54307/414-497-2949
Green Head Corp., RR 1 P.O. Box 33, Lacon, IL 61540/309-246-2155
Green Mountain Rifle Barrel Co., Inc., RFD #2, P.O. Box 8, Center Conway, NH 03813/603-356-2047
Green, Arthur S., 485 S. Robertson Blvd., Suite 5, Beverly Hills, CA 90211/213-274-1283
Green, Roger M., P.O. Box 984, 435 East Birch, Glenrock, WY 82637/307-436-9804
Greene's Machine Carving, 17200 W. 57th Ave., Golden, CO 80403/303-279-2383
Greenwald, Leon E. "Bud", 2553 S. Quitman St., Denver, CO 80219/303-935-3850
Greg Gunsmithing Repair, 3732 26th Ave. North, Robbinsdale, MN 55422/612-529-8103
Greider Precision Products, 431 Santa Marina Ct., Escondido, CA 92029/619-480-8892
Gremmel Enterprises, 271 Sterling Dr., Eugene, OR 97404/503-688-3319
Grendel, Inc., P.O. Box 908, Rockledge, FL 32955/407-636-1211
Griffin & Howe, 36 W. 44th St., Suite 1011, New York, NY 10036/212-921-0980
Griffin & Howe, Inc., 33 Claremont Rd., Bernardsville, NJ 07924/201-766-2287
Griffin's Guns & Antiques, RR 4, Peterboro, Ont., Canada K9J 6X5/705-745-7022
Griggs Products, P.O. Box 789, 270 S. Main St., Suite 103, Bountiful, UT 84010/801-295-9696
Grizzly Bullets, Joe Abrams, 2137 Hwy. 200, Trout Creek, MT 59874/406-847-2627
GRS Corp., (Glendo), P.O. Box 1153, 900 Overlander St., Emporia, KS 66801/316-343-1084
GSI, Inc., 108 Morrow Ave., P.O. Box 129, Trussville, AL 35173/205-655-8299
GTS Enterprises, Inc. (Dynaray Marketing Div.), 50 W. Hillcrest Dr., Suite 215, Thousand Oaks, CA 91360/805-373-0921
G.U., Inc., 4325 S. 120th St., Omaha, NE 68137/402-339-3530
Guardian Group International, 21 Warren St., Suite 3E, New York, NY 10007/212-619-3838
Guardsman Products, 411 N. Darling, Fremont, MI 49412/616-924-3950
Gun City, 212 West Main Ave., Bismarck, ND 58501/701-223-2304
Gun Club Sportswear, P.O. Box 477, Des Moines, IA 50302
Gun Doctor, The, 435 East Maple, Roselle, IL 60172/708-894-0668
Gun Hunter Books, Div. of Gun Hunter Trading Co., 5075 Heisig St., Beaumont, TX 77705/409-835-3006
Gun Leather Limited, 116 Lipscomb, Ft. Worth, TX 76104/817-334-0225, 800-247-0609
Gun Parts Corp., P.O. Box 2, West Hurley, NY 12491/914-679-2417
Gun Room Press, The, 127 Raritan Ave., Highland Park, NJ 08904/201-545-4344
Gun Shop, The, 5550 S. 900 East, Salt Lake City, UT 84117/801-263-3633
Gun South, Inc. (See GSI, Inc.)
Gun Works, The, 236 Main St., Springfield, OR 97477/503-741-4118
Gun-Ho Sports Cases, 110 E. 10th St., St. Paul, MN 55101/612-224-9491
Gun-Tec, P.O. Box 8125, W. Palm Beach, FL 33407 (SASE for reply)
Guncraft Books, Div. of Guncraft Sports, Inc., 125 E. Tyrone Rd., Oak Ridge, TN 378301/615-483-4024
Guncraft Sports, Inc., 125 E. Tyrone Rd., Oak Ridge, TN 37830/615-483-4024
Guncraft Sports, Inc., 10737 Dutchtown Rd., Knoxville, TN 37932/615-966-4545
Guncraft, Inc., 117 W. Pipeline, Hurst, TX 76053/817-282-1464
Gunfitters, The, P.O. 426, Cambridge, WI 53523-0426/608-764-8128
Gunline Tools, 2970 Saturn St., Brea, CA 92621/714-528-5252
Gunnerman Books, P.O. Box 214292, Auburn Hills, MI 48321/313-879-2779
Guns, 81 E. Streetsboro St., Hudson, OH 44236/216-650-4563
Gunsite Gunsmithy, P.O. Box 451, Paulden, AZ 86334/602-636-4104
Gunsmithing Ltd., 57 Unquowa Rd., Fairfield, CT 06430/203-254-0436
Gurney Engraving Method, Box 13, Sooke, BC V0S 1N0 Canada/604-642-5282
Gusdorf Corp., 11440 Lackland Rd., St. Louis, MO 63146/314-567-5249
Gutmann Cutlery Co., Inc., 120 S. Columbus Ave., Mt. Vernon, NY 10553/914-699-4044
Gutridge, Inc., 2143 Gettler St., Dyer, IN 46311/219-865-8617
Gwinnell, Bryson J., P.O. Box 248C, Maple Hill Rd., Rochester, VT 05767/802-767-3664
"Gramps" Antique Cartridges, Ellwood Epps, P.O. Box 341, Washago, Ont. L0K 2B0 Canada/705-689-5348

H

Hafner Enterprises, Inc., Rt. 1, P.O. Box 248A, Lake City, FL 32055/904-755-6481
Hagn Rifles & Actions, Martin Hagn, P.O. Box 444, Cranbrook, B.C. VIC 4H9, Canada/604-489-4861
Hakko Co Ltd., 5F Daini-Tsunemi Bldg., 1-13-12, Narimasu, Itabashiku Tokyo 175/(03)5997-7870-2
Hale, Peter, 800 E. Canyon Rd., Spanish Fork, UT 84660/801-798-8215
Half Moon Rifle Shop, 490 Halfmoon Rd., Columbia Falls, MT 59912/406-892-4409
Hall Manufacturing, 1801 Yellow Leaf Rd., Clanton, AL 35045/205-755-4094
Hall Plastics, Inc., John, P.O. Box 1526, Alvin, TX 77512/713-489-9709
Hall's Shooting Products, Inc., Joe, 443 Wells Rd., Doylestown, PA 18901/215-345-6354
Hallowell & Co., 340 West Putnam Ave., Greenwich, CT 06830/203-869-2190
Hamilton, Keith, P.O. Box 871, Gridley, CA 95948/916-846-2316
Hammans, Charles E., P.O. Box 788, 2022 McCracken, Stuttgart, AR 72106/501-673-1388
Hammerli USA, 19296 Oak Grove Circle, Groveland, CA 95321/209-962-5311
Hammond, Custom Guns Ltd., Guy, 619 S. Pandora, Gilbert, AZ 85234/602-892-3437
Hand Engravers Supply Co., 601 Springfield Dr., Albany, GA 31707/912-432-9683
Handgun Press, P.O. Box 406, Glenview, IL 60025/708-657-6500
Hanned Precision, P.O. Box 2888, Sacramento, CA 95812
Hansen & Co., 244-246 Old Post Rd., Southport, CT 06490/203-789-7337
Hansen Cartridge Co., 244 Old Post Rd., Southport, CT 06490/203-259-6222
Hanson's Gun Center, Dick Hanson, 521 S. Circle Dr., Colorado Springs, CO 80910/719-634-4220
Hanus, Bill, P.O. Box 80, Pinos Altos, NM 88053/505-536-9383
Hanusin, John, 3306 Commercial, Northbrook, IL 60062/708-564-2706
Hardin Specialty Distr., P.O. Box 338, Radcliff, KY 40159-0338/502-351-6649
Hardison, Charles, P.O. Box 356, 200 W. Baseline Rd., Lafayette, CO 80026-0356/303-666-5171
Harper's Custom Stocks, 928 Lombrano St., San Antonio, TX 78207/512-732-5780
Harper, William E., The Great 870 Co., P.O. Box 6309, El Monte, CA 91734/213-579-3077
Harrington Cutlery, Inc., Russell, Subs. of Hyde Mfg. Co., 44 River St., Southbridge, MA 01550/617-765-0201
Harris Engineering, Inc., Barlow, KY 42024/502-334-3633
Harris Enterprises, P.O. Box 105, Bly, OR 97622/503-353-2625
Harris Hand Engraving, Paul A., 10630 Janet Lee, San Antonio, TX 78230/512-391-5121
Harrison Bullet Works, 6437 E. Hobart, Mesa, AZ 85205/602-985-7844
Harrison-Hurtz Enterprises, Inc., P.O. Box 268, U.S. Hwy. 77 & Hwy. 8, Wymore, NE 68466/402-645-3378
Hart & Son, Inc., Robert W., 401 Montgomery St., Nescopeck, PA 18635/717-752-3655
Hart Rifle Barrels, Inc., RD 2, Apulia Rd., P.O. Box 182, Lafayette, NY 13084/315-677-9841
Hartmann & Weiss GmbH, Rahistedter Bahnhofstr. 47, 2000 Hamburg 73, W. Germany/040-677.55.85
Harwood, Jack O., 1191 S. Pendlebury Lane, Blackfoot, ID 83221/208-785-5368
Hastings Barrels, P.O. Box 224, Clay Center, KS 67432/913-632-2184
Hatfield International, Inc.,224 N. 4th St., St. Joseph, MO 64484/816-279-8688
Hawk Laboratories, Inc., P.O. Box 112, Station 27, Lakewood, CO 80215/303-238-1405
Hawkeye West, 3442 E. Kleindale Rd., Tucson, AZ 85716/602-326-7951
Haydel's Game Calls, Inc., 5018 Hazel Jones Rd., Bossier City, LA 71111/318-746-3586
H&B Forge Co., Rt. 2 Geisinger Rd., Shiloh, OH 44878/419-895-1856
Heatbath Corp., P.O. Box 2978, Springfield, MA 01101/413-543-3381
Hebard Guns, Gil, 125-129 Public Square, Knoxville, IL 61448
Hecht, Hubert J., Waffen-Hecht, P.O. Box 2635, Fair Oaks, CA 95628/916-966-1020
Heckler & Koch, Inc., 21480 Pacific Blvd., Sterling, VA 22170/703-450-1900
Hege Jagd-u. Sporthandels, GmbH, P.O. Box 101461, W-7770 Ueberling a. Bodensee, Germany
Heilmann, Stephen, P.O. Box 657, Grass Valley, CA 95945/916-272-8758
Heinie, Richard, 323 W. Franklin, Havana, IL 62644/309-543-4535
Henckels Zwillingswerk, Inc., J.A., 9 Skyline Dr., Hawthorne, NY 10532/914-592-7370
Hendricks, Frank E., Master Engravers, Inc., HC03, P.O. Box 334, Dripping Springs, TX 78620/512-858-7828
Henigson & Associates, Steve, 2049 Kerwood Ave., Los Angeles, CA 90025/213-305-8288
Henriksen Tool Co., Inc., 8515 Wagner Creek Rd., Talent, OR 97540/503-535-2309
Hensley & Gibbs, P.O. Box 10, Murphy, OR 97533/503-862-2341
Hensley, Darwin, P.O. Box 179, Brightwood, OR 97011/503-622-5411
Heppler's Machining, 2238 Calle Del Mundo, Santa Clara, CA 95054/408-748-9166
Heppler, Keith M., 540 Banyan Circle, Walnut Creek, CA 94598/415-934-3509
Hercules, Inc., Hercules Plaza, Wilmington, DE 19894/302-594-5000
Hermann Leather Co., H.J., Rt. 1, P.O. Box 525, Skiatook, OK 74070/918-396-1226
Herrett's Stocks, Inc., P.O. Box 741, Twin Falls, ID 83303/208-733-1498
Hertel & Reuss, Werk für Optik und Feinmechanik, GmbH, Quellhofstrasse 67, 3500 Kassell, Fed. Rep. of Germany/0561-83006
Hesco, Inc., 2821 Greenville Rd., LaGrange, GA 30240/404-884-7967
Heydenberk, Warren R.O., 1059 W. Sawmill Rd., Quakertown, PA 18951/215-538-2682
Heym, Friedrich Wilh. (See Heckler & Koch, Inc.)
Hi-West Sales, P.O. Box 2016, Cut Bank, MT 59427/406-873-5634
Hidalgo, Tony, 12701 SW 9th Pl., Davie, FL 33325/305-476-7645
High Bridge Arms, Inc., 3185 Mission St., San Francisco, CA 94110/415-282-8358
High North Products, P.O. Box 2, Antigo, WI 54409/715-623-5117
Highsmith, M.V., 2896 Walnut Grove Rd., Memphis, TN 38111/901-327-7381
Hill Speed Leather, Ernie, 4507 N. 195th Ave., Litchfield Park, AZ 85340/602-853-9222
Hillmer Custom Gunstocks, Paul D., 7251 Hudson Heights, Hudson, IA 50643/319-988-3941
Hindman, Ace, 1880 1/2 Upper Turtle Creek Rd., Kerrville, TX 78028/512-257-4290
Hinman Outfitters, Bob, 1217 W. Glen, Peoria, IL 61614/309-691-8132
Hiptmayer, Heidemarie, RR 112, #750, P.O. Box 136, Eastman, Que. J0E 1PO, Canada/514-297-2492
Hiptmayer, Klaus, P.O. Box 136, RR 112 #750, Eastman, Que. J0E 1P0, Canada/514-297-2492
Hirtenberger Patronen-, Zundhutchen- & Metallwarenfabrik, A.G., Leobersdorfer Str. 33, A2552 Hirtenberg, Austria
H.K.S. Products, 7841 Foundation Dr., Florence, KY 41042/606-342-7841
Hoag, James W., 8523 Canoga Ave., Suite C, Canoga Park, CA 91304/818-998-1510
Hobaugh, Wm. H., The Rifle Shop, P.O. Box M, Philipsburg, MT 59858/406-859-3515
Hobbie Gunsmithing, Duane A., 2412 Pattie Ave., Wichita, KS 67216/316-264-8266
Hodgdon Powder Co., Inc., 6231 Robinson, Shawnee Mission, KS 66202/913-362-9455
Hodgson, Richard, 9081 Tahoe Lane, Boulder, CO 80301
Hoenig & Rodman, 6521 Morton Dr., Boise, ID 83705/208-375-1116
Hofer, Peter, F. Lang-Str. 13, A9170 Ferlach, Austria/0-42-27-3683
Hogue Grips, P.O. Box 2038, Atascadero, CA 93423/805-466-6266
Holden Co., J.B., P.O. Box 320, Plymouth, MI 48170/313-455-4850
Holland, Dick, 422 NE 6th St., Newport, OR 97365/503-265-7556
Hollis Gun Shop, 917 Rex St., Carlsbad, NM 88220/505-835-3782
Hollywood Loading Tools (See M&M Engineering)
Holster Outpost, 950 Harry St., El Cajon, CA 92020/619-588-1222
HomeCraft Software, P.O. Box 974, Tualatin, OR 97062/503-692-3732
Hoppe's Div., Penguin Industries, Inc., Airport Industrial Mall, Coatesville, PA 19320/251-384-6000
Horizons Unlimited, 8351 Roswell Rd., Suite 168, Atlanta, GA 30350/404-683-1269
Hornady Mfg. Co., P.O. Box 1848, Grand Island, NE 68802/308-382-1390
Horsehoe Leather Prods. (See Arratoonian, Andy)
Horst, Alan K., 3221 2nd Ave., N., Great Falls, MT 59401/406-545-1831
Horton Dist. Co. Inc., Lew, 15 Walkup Drive, Westboro, MA 01581/508-366-7400
House of Muskets, Inc., The, P.O. Box 4640, Pagosa Springs, CO 81157/303-731-2295 (catalog $3)
Houtz & Barwick, P.O. Box 435, W. Church St., Elizabeth City, NC 27909/919-335-4191
Hoyt Holster Co., Inc., P.O. Box 69, 476 W. State Highway 20, Coupeville, WA 98239/206-678-6640
H&R 1871, Inc., Industrial Rowe, Gardner, MA 01440

H&S Liner Service, 515 E. 8th, Odessa, TX 79761/915-332-1021
H-S Precision, Inc., P.O. Box 2074, 1301 Turbine Dr., Rapid City, SD 57701/605-341-3006
Hubertus Schneidwarenfabrik, P.O. Box 180 106, Wuppertaler Str. 147, Solingen, Germany, D-W-5650/01149-212-59 19 94
Huebner, Corey O., 3604 S. 3rd W., Missoula, MT 59804/406-721-9647
Huey Gun Cases, Marvin, P.O. Box 22456, Kansas City, MO 64113/816-444-1637
Hugger Hooks Co., 3900 Easley Way, Golden, CO 80403/303-279-0600
Hughes, Steven Dodd, P.O. Box 11455, Eugene, OR 97440/503-485-8869 (catalog $3)
Hull, Lynn E., 14702 Old National Pike, Clear Spring, MD 21722/301-582-0204
Hume, Don, P.O. Box 351, Miami, OK 74355/918-542-6604
Hunkeler, A., Buckskin Machine Works, 3235 S. 358th St., Auburn, WA 98001/206-927-5412
Hunter Co., Inc., 3300 W. 71st Ave., Westminster, CO 80030/303-427-4626
Hunter's Specialties, Inc., 5285 Rockwell Dr. NE, Cedar Rapids, IA 52402/319-395-0321
Hunterjohn, P.O. Box 477, St. Louis, MO 63166/314-531-7250
Hunting Classics Ltd., 936 N. Marietta St., Gastonia, NC 28054/704-867-1307
Huntington Die Specialties, 601 Oro Dam Blvd., Oroville, CA 95965/916-534-1210
Hutton Rifle Ranch, P.O. Box 45236, Boise, ID 83711/208-345-8781
Hydrosorbent Products, P.O. Box 437, Ashley Falls, MA 01222/413-229-2967
Hyper-Single, Inc., 520 E. Beaver, Jenks, OK 74037/918-299-2391

I

IAI (Irwindale Arms, Inc.), 6226 Santos Diaz St., Irwindale, CA 91702/818-334-1200
Ibberson (Sheffield) Ltd., George, 25-31 Allen St., Sheffield, S3 7AW England/0742-766123
ICI-America, P.O. Box 751, Wilmington, DE 19897/302-575-3000
Idaho Ammunition Service, 2816 Mayfair Dr., Lewiston, ID 83501/208-743-0270
Imatronic, Inc., 1275 Paramount Pkwy., P.O. Box 520, Batavia, IL 60510/708-406-1920
Impact Case Company, P.O. Box 9912, Spokane, WA 99209-0912/509-467-3303
IMR Powder Co., RR 5 2 X-Plo Complex, Plattsburgh, NY 12901/518-561-9530/7810
I.N.C., Inc., P.O. Box 12767, Wichita, KS 67277/316-721-9570
Incor, Inc., P.O. Box 132, Addison, TX 75001/214-931-3500
Indian Ridge Traders (See Koval Knives/IRT)
Industria de la Escopeta S.A.L. (Indesal), P.O. Box 233, Eibar, Spain 20600/43-751800
Ingle, Ralph W., Master Engraver, #4 Missing Link, Rossville, GA 30741/404-866-5589 (color brochure $5)
Innovision Enterprises, 728 Skinner Dr., Kalamazoo, MI 49001/616-382-1681
Insights Training Center, Inc., 240 NW Gilman Blvd., Issaquah, WA 98027/206-391-4834
Interarmco (See Interarms/Walther)
Interarms, 10 Prince St., Alexandria, VA 22313/703-548-1400
Intermountain Arms, 105 E. Idaho Ave., Meridian, ID 83649/208-888-4911
International Shootists, Inc., P.O. Box 5354, Mission Hills, CA 91345/818-891-1723
Intratec, 12405 SW 130th St., Miami, FL 33186/FAX: 305-253-7207
Iosso Marine Products, 1485 Lively Blvd., Elk Grove, IL 60007/708-437-8400
Iron Mountain Knife Co., P.O. Box 2146, 850 Glen Martin Dr., Sparks, NV 89431/702-356-3632
Iron Sight Gunworks, Inc., 458 Corte Blanco, Upland, CA 91786
Ironside International Publishers, Inc., P.O. Box 55, 800 Slaters Lane, Alexandria, VA 22314/703-684-6111, ext. 224
Irwin, Campbell H., 140 Hartland Blvd., East Hartland, CT 06027/203-653-3901
Irwindale Arms, Inc. (See IAI)
Israel Military Industries Ltd. (IMI), P.O. Box 1044, Ramat Hasharon 47100, Israel/972-3-5485222
I.S.S. International Shooters Service, P.O. Box 185234, Ft. Worth, TX 76181/817-595-2090
Ithaca Gun, 891 Route 34B, King Ferry, NY 13081/315-364-7171
Ivanoff, Thomas G. (Tom's Gun Repair), 76-6 Rt. Southfork Rd., Cody, WY 82414/307-587-6949

J

J.A. Blades, Inc. (See Christopher Firearms Co., Inc., E.)
Jackalope Gun Shop, 1048 S. 5th St., Douglas, WY 82633/307-358-3441
Jaeger, Inc., Paul, P.O. Box 449, 1 Madison Ave., Grand Junction, TN 38039/901-764-6909
Jamison, R.L., Jr., 4527 Rd. 6.5 N.E., Moses Lake, WA 98837/509-762-2659
Jantz Supply, Ken, 222 E. Main, Davis, OK 73030/405-369-2316
Jaro Manuf., P.O. Box 6125, 206 E. Shaw, Pasadena, TX 77506/713-472-0417
Jarrett Rifles, Inc., 383 Brown Rd., Jackson, SC 29831/803-471-3616
Jarvis Gunsmithing, Inc., P.O. Box 173, 1123 Cherry Orchard Lane, Hamilton, MT 59840/406-961-4392
Jason Empire, Inc., 9200 Cody, P.O. Box 14930, Overland Park, KS 66214/913-888-0220
Javelina Products, P.O. Box 337, San Bernardino, CA 92402/714-882-5847
J-B Bore Cleaner, 299 Poplar St., Hamburg, PA 19526/215-562-2103
J/B Adventures & Safaris, Inc., P.O. Box 3397, Englewood, CO 80155/303-771-0977
Jenkins Recoil Pads, Inc., RR #2, P.O. Box 471, Olney, IL 62450/618-395-3416
Jennings Firearms, Inc., 3680 Research Way #1, Carson City, NV 89706/702-882-4007
Jensen Bullets, 86 N., 400 W., Blackfoot, ID 83221/208-785-5590
Jensen's Custom Ammunition, 5146 E. Pima, Tucson, AZ 85712/602-325-3346
Jett & Co., Inc., RR #3 P.O. Box 167-B, Litchfield, IL 62056/217-324-3779
JGS Precision Tool Mfg., 1141 S. Sumner Rd., Coos Bay, OR 97420/503-267-4331
Jim's Gun Shop, James R. Spradlin, 113 Arthur, Pueblo, CO 81004/719-543-9462
John's Custom Leather, 525 S. Liberty St., Blairsville, PA 15717/412-459-6802
Johns, Bill, 1412 Lisa Rae, Round Rock, TX 78664/512-255-8246
Johnson Wood Products, I.D. Johnson & Sons, Rt. #1, Strawberry Point, IA 52076/319-933-4930
Johnson, Iver, 2202 Redmond Rd., Jacksonville, AR 72706/501-982-1633
Johnson, Neal G., Gunsmithing, Inc., 111 Marvin Dr., Hampton, VA 23666/804-838-8091
Johnson, Peter S., c/o Orvis Co., 10 River Rd., Manchester, VT 05254/802-362-3622, Ext. 283
Johnston Brothers, 1889 Rte 9, Unit 22, Toms River, NJ 08756/201-240-6873
Jonad Corporation, 2091 Lakeland Ave., Lakewood, OH 44107/216-226-3161
Jonas, Jack H., 1625 So. Birch #708, Denver, CO 80222/303-757-7347
Jones Munitions Systems, Paul (See Fitz Pistol Grip Co.)
Jones, J.D., 721 Woodvue Lane, Wintersville, OH 43952/614-264-0176
Jones, Neil A. (See Custom Products)
Joy Enterprises, 801 Broad Ave., Ridgefield, NJ 07657/201-943-5920
Juenke, Vern, 25 Bitterbush Rd., Reno, NV 89523/702-345-0225
Jumbo Sports Prods., P.O. Box 280, Airport Rd., Frederick, MD 21701
Jungkind, Reeves C., 5805 N. Lamar Blvd., Austin, TX 78752/512-442-1094
Jurras, L.E., P.O. Box 680, Washington, IN 47501/812-254-7698
Just Brass, Inc., 121 Henry St., P.O. Box 112, Freeport, NY 11520/516-378-8588

K

KA-BAR Cutlery, Div. of American Consumer Prods., Inc., 31100 Solon Rd., Solon, OH 44139/216-248-7000
KA-BAR Knives, Collectors Division, P.O. Box 406, 807 W. State St., Olean, NY 14760/716-372-5611
Kalispel Metal Prods. (KMP), P.O. Box 267, Cusick, WA 99119/509-445-1121
Kamik Outdoor Footwear, 554 Montee de Liesse, Montreal, Quebec, H4T 1P1 Canada/514-341-3950
Kamyk, Steven, 9 Grandview Dr., Westfield, MA 01085/413-568-0457
Kane Products, Inc., 5572 Brecksville Rd., Cleveland, OH 44131/216-524-9962
Kartak Gun Works, 7525 S. Coast Hwy., South Beach, OR 97366/503-867-4951
Kasenit Co., Inc., P.O. Box 726, 3 King St., Mahwah, NJ 07430/201-529-3663
Kayusoft Intl., Star Route, Spray, OR 97874/503-462-3934
K.B.I., Inc., P.O. Box 6346, Harrisburg, PA 17112/717-540-8518
K-D, Inc., 665 S. 300 West, Price, UT 84501/801-637-9062
KDF, Inc., 2485 Hwy. 46 N., Seguin, TX 78155/512-379-8141
Keeler, R.H., 817 "N" St., Port Angeles, WA 98362/206-457-4702
Kehr, Roger, 7810 B Samurai Dr. SE, Olympia, WA 98503/206-456-0831
Keller Co., The, 4215 McEwen Rd., Dallas, TX 75244/214-788-4254
Kelley's, Harold Kelley, P.O. Box 125, Woburn, MA 01801/617-935-3389
Kellog's Professional Prods., Inc., 325 Pearl St., Sandusky, OH 44870/419-625-6551
Kelly, Lance, 1723 Willow Oak Dr., Edgewater, FL 32132/904-423-4933
Ken's Finn Knives, Rt. 1, P.O. Box 338, Republic, MI 49879/906-376-2132
Ken's Gun Specialties, Rt. 1 P.O. Box 147, Lakeview, AR 72642/501-431-5606
Ken's Rifle Blanks, Ken McCullough, Rt. 2 P.O. Box 85B, Weston, OR 97886/503-566-3879
Keng's Firearms Specialty, Inc., P.O. Box 44405, 875 Wharton Dr., Atlanta, GA 30336-1405/404-691-7611
KenPatable Ent., Inc., P.O. Box 19422, Louisville, KY 40219/502-239-5447
Kent Cartridge Manufacturing Co. Ltd., The, Unit 16, Branbridges Industrial Estate, East Peckham, Tonbridge, Kent, TN12 5HF England/0622-872255
Keowee Game Calls, 608 Hwy. 25 North, Travelers Rest, SC 29690/803-834-7204
Kershaw Knives/Kai Cutlery USA Ltd., Stafford Bus. Pk., 25300 SW Parkway, Wilsonville, OR 97070/503-636-0111
Kesselring Gun Shop, 400 Hwy. 99 North, Burlington, WA 98233/206-724-3113
Kilham & Co., Benjamin Kilham, Main St., P.O. Box 37, Lyme, NH 03768/603-795-4112
Kimball, Gary, 1526 N. Circle Dr., Colorado Springs, CO 80909/719-634-1274
Kimel Industries, P.O. Box 335, 3800 Old Monroe Rd., Matthews, NC 28105/704-821-7663
King & Co., Edw. R. King, P.O. Box 1242 3800 Old Monroe Rd., Bloomington, IL 61701
King's Gun Works, 1837 W. Glenoaks Blvd., Glendale, CA 91201/818-956-6010
Kingyon, Paul L., 607 N. 5th St., Burlington, IA 52601/319-752-4465
Kintrek, Inc., P.O. Box 72, Owensboro, KY 42302/502-688-8137
Kirkpatrick Leather Co., P.O. Box 3150, Laredo, TX 78044/512-723-6631
Kiss Sights, 355 N. Lantana Ave., Suite 505, Camarillo, CA 93010/805-492-4007
K&K Ammo Wrist Band, R.D. #1, P.O. Box 448-CA18, Lewistown, PA 17044/717-242-2329
Kleen-Bore, Inc., 20 Ladd Ave., Northhampton, MA 01060/413-586-7240
Klein, Don, 433 Murray Park Dr., Ripon, WI 54971/414-748-2931
Kleinendorst, K.W., RR #1, P.O. Box 1500, Hop Bottom, PA 18824/717-289-4687
Klingler, Kenneth J., P.O. Box 141, Thistle Hill, Cabot, VT 05647/802-426-3811
KLP Mfg., 215 Charles Dr., Holland, MI 49424/616-396-2575
K&M Industries, Inc., P.O. Box 66, 510 S. Main, Troy, ID 83871/208-835-2281
K&M Services, P.O. Box 363, Emigsville, PA 17318/717-764-1461
Kmount, P.O. Box 19422, Louisville, KY 40259/502-239-5447
Kneiper, Jim, P.O. Box 103, Jay, NY 12941/518-946-7944
Knife Importers, Inc., P.O. Box 1000, Manchaca, TX 78652/512-282-6860
Knight & Hale Game Calls, P.O. Box 468, Cadiz, KY 42211/502-522-3651
Knippel, Richard, 5924 Carnwood, Riverbank, CA 95367/209-869-1469
Knock on Wood Antiques, 355 Post Rd., Darien, CT 06820/203-655-9031
Kodiak Custom Bullets, 8261 Henry Circle, Anchorage, AK 99507/907-349-2282
Koevenig Engraving Service, E.J., P.O. Box 55, Rabbit Gulch, Hill City, SD 57745/605-574-2239
KOGOT Octagon Barrels, John Pell, 410 College Ave., Trinidad, CO 81082/719-846-9406
Kolpin Mfg., Inc., P.O. Box 107, 205 Depot St., Fox Lake, WI 53933/414-928-3118
Kontos, Michael J., 417 N. Huber Ct., E. Wenatchee, WA 98802/509-884-7683
Kopec Ent., John A., P.O. Box 157, S. Cow Creek Rd., Whitmore, CA 96096/916-472-3438
Kopp Publishing Co., Div. of Koppco Industries, 1301 Franklin, Lexington, MO 64067/816-259-2636
Kopp, Terry K., 1301 Franklin, Lexington, MO 64067/816-259-2636
Korth, GmbH, Robert-Bosch Str. 4, Ratzeburg, W-2418 Germany/04541-4033
Korzinek, J., R.D. #2, P.O. Box 73, Canton, PA 17724/717-673-8512 (catalog $3)
Koval Knives/IRT, 460 Schrock Rd. #D, Columbus, OH 43229/614-888-6486
Kowa Optimed, Inc., 20001 S. Vermont Ave., Torrance, CA 90502/213-327-1913
Krieger Barrels, Inc., N114 W18697 Clinton Dr., Germantown, WI 53022/414-255-9593
Kriegeskorte, A., GmbH, Jagd-und Sportwaffenfabrik, Kronacher Str. 63, P.O. Box 1930, Fürth-Stadeln, D-8510 Germany/0911-796092
Krieghoff International, Inc., P.O. Box 549, Ottsville, PA 18942/215-847-5173
Kris Mounts, 108 Lehigh St., Johnstown, PA 15905/814-539-9751
Kros Walnut, Inc., 6304 Rabbit Ears Circle, Colorado Springs, CO 80919/719-598-4929
Kudlas, John, 622-14th St. SE, Rochester, MN 55904/507-288-5579
Kulis Freeze-Dry Taxidermy, 725 Broadway Ave., Bedford, OH 44146
Kwik Mount Corp., P.O. Box 19422, Louisville, KY 40259/502-239-5447
Kwik-Site, 5555 Treadwell, Wayne, MI 48184/313-326-1500

L

LaBounty Precision Reboring, P.O. Box 186, 7968 Silver Lk. Rd., Maple Falls, WA 98266/206-599-2047
Lachaussee, S.A., 29 Rue Kerstenne, Ans, B-4430 Belgium/041-63 88 77
La Clinique du .45, 1432 Rougemont, Chambly, Quebec, J3L 2L8 Canada/514-658-1144

LaCrosse Footwear, Inc., P.O. Box 1328, La Crosse, WI 54602/608-782-3020
LaFrance Specialties, P.O. Box 178211, San Diego, CA 92117/619-293-3373
Lage Uniwad, Inc., P.O. Box 446, Victor, IA 52327/319-647-3232
Lair, Sam, 520 E. Beaver, Jenks, OK 74037/918-299-2391
Lakefield Arms Ltd., P.O. Box 129, Lakefield, Ont. K0L 2H0, Canada/705-652-8000
Lakewood Products, Inc., P.O. Box 1527, 1445 Eagle St., Rhinelander, WI 54501/715-369-3445
Lampert, Ron L., Rt. 1, P.O. Box 177, Guthrie, MN 56461/218-854-7345
Lamson & Goodnow Mfg. Co., 45 Conway St., Shelburne Falls, MA 03170/413-625-6331
Lane Bullets, Larry Clay, 1011 S. 10th St., Kansas City, KS 66105/913-621-6113
Langenberg Hat Co., P.O. Box 1860, Washington, MO 63090/314-239-1860
Lansky Sharpeners, P.O. Box 800, Buffalo, NY 14221/716-634-6333
Lapua Ltd., P.O. Box 5, Lapua, Finland SF-62101/64-310111
La Prade, Rt. 5, P.O. Box 240A, Tazewell, TN 37879
L.A.R. Manufacturing, Inc., 4133 W. Farm Rd., West Jordan, UT 84088/801-255-7106
Large Gun & Mach. Shop, Wm., James W. McKenzie, RR1, P.O. Box 188, Ironton, OH 45638/614-532-5298
Largent, Nelson H., Silver Shield's, Inc., 4464-D Chinden Blvd., Boise, ID 83714/208-323-8991
Laser Aim, Inc., 100 S. Main St., P.O. Box 581, Little Rock, AR 72203
Laser Devices, Inc., 2 Harris Ct., A4, Monterey, CA 93940/408-373-0701
Lassen Community College, P.O. Box 3000, Hiway 139, Susanville, CA 96130/916-257-6181
Laughridge, William R., Cylinder & Slide, Inc., P.O. Box 937, Fremont, NE 68025/402-721-4277
Laurona Shotguns (See Galaxy Imports Ltd., Inc.)
Lawrence Leather Co., E. McNeil St., P.O. Drawer 1479, Lillington, NC 27546/919-893-2627
Lawson Co., Harry, 3328 N. Richey Blvd., Tucson, AZ 85716/602-326-1117
Lawson, John G. (The Sight Shop), 1802 E. Columbia Ave., Tacoma, WA 98404/206-474-5465
Lea Mfg. Co., 237 E. Aurora St., Waterbury, CT 06720/203-753-5116
Lebeau-Courally, S.A., Rue Saint Gilles, 386, 4000 Liege, Belgium/32-41-52 48 43, 32-41-52 02 11
LeClear Industries, 1126 Donald Ave., P.O. Box 484, Royal Oak, MI 48068/313-588-1025
Lee Precision, Inc., 4275 Hwy. U, Hartford, WI 53027/414-673-3075
Lee's Red Ramps, P.O. Box 1249, 13223 Sheep Creek Rd., Phelan, CA 92371/619-868-5731
Lee, Mark, Mark Lee Supplies, 9901 France Court, Lakeville, MN 55044/612-461-2114
LeFever & Sons, Inc., Frank, RD #2, P.O. Box 31, Lee Center, NY 13363/315-337-6722
Legacy, Ltd., S.F., P.O. Box 1589, Bridgeport, MI 48722-1589/517-777-5200
Leibowitz, Leonard, 1205 Murrayhill Ave., Pittsburgh, PA 15217/412-361-5455
Leica USA, 156 Ludlow Ave., Northvale, NJ 07647/201-767-7500
Leitz (See Leica USA)
LEM Gun Specialties, P.O. Box 87031, College Park, GA 30337
Lethal Force Institute, P.O. Box 122, Concord, NH 03301/603-224-6814
Letschnig, Franz, Master-Engraver, R.R. 1, Martintown, Ont. K0C ISO, Canada/613-528-4843
Leupold & Stevens, Inc., P.O. Box 688, Beaverton, OR 97075/503-646-9171
Lever Arms Service Ltd., 2131 Burrard St., Vancouver, B.C., V6J 3H7 Canada/604-736-2711
Liberty Antique Gunworks, 19 Key St., P.O. Box 183, Eastport, ME 04631/207-853-2327 (catalog $5)
Liberty Trouser Co., 2301 First Ave. North, Birmingham, AL 35203/205-251-9143
Lighthouse Mfg. Co, Inc., P.O. Box 948, West Palm Beach, FL 33402/407-626-9122
Lilja Precision Rifle Barrels, Inc., 245 Compass Creek Rd., P.O. Box 372, Plains, MT 59859/406-826-3084
Lind, Al, 7821 76th Ave. SW, Tacoma, WA 98498/206-584-6361
Linder Solingen Knives, 4401 Sentry Dr., Tucker, GA 30084/404-939-6915
Lindsay, Steve, RR 2 Cedar Hills, Kearney, NE 68847/308-236-7885
Lindsley Arms Cartridge Co., Inc., P.O. Box 757, 20 Crescent St., Henniker, NH 03242/603-428-3127 (for inquiries send SASE, brochure $1)
Linebaugh Custom Sixguns, P.O. Box 1263, 930 Road 1 AB, Cody, WY 82414/307-645-3162
Lithi Bee Bullet Lube, 2161 Henry, Muskegon, MI 49441/616-755-4707
Littleton, J.F., 22 Service St., Oroville, CA 95966/916-533-6084
Ljutic Industries, Inc., P.O. Box 2117, 732 N. 16th Ave., Yakima, WA 98907/509-248-0476
Llama (See Stoeger Industries)
Lock's Phila. Gun Exch., 6700 Rowland, Philadelphia, PA 19149/215-332-6225
Loch Leven, Ind., P.O. Box 2751, Santa Rosa, CA 95405/707-573-8735
Lodewick, Walter H., 2816 NE Halsey, Portland, OR 97232/503-284-2554
Lofland, James W., 2275 Larkin Rd., Boothwyn, PA 19061/215-485-0391
Log Cabin Sport Shop, 8010 Lafayette Rd., Lodi, OH 44254/216-948-1082 (catalog $3)
Logan Security Products Co., P.O. Box 16206, Columbus, OH 43216/616-265-7386
Logan, Harry M., Box 745, Honokaa, HI 96727/808-776-1644
Lohman Mfg. Co., P.O. Box 220, Neosho, MO 64850/417-451-4438
Lomont Precision Bullets, Kent Lomont, 4236 West 700 South, Poneto, IN 46781/219-694-6792
London Guns Ltd., P.O. Box 3750, Santa Barbara, CA 93130/805-683-4141
Lone Pine Trading Post, Jct. Highways 61 and 248, Minnesota City, MN 55959/507-689-2925
Lone Star Gunleather, 1301 Brushy Bend Dr., Round Rock, TX 78681/512-255-1805
Long Island Gunsmith, Ltd., 573 Sunrise Hwy., West Babylon, NY 11704/516-321-0924
Long, George F., 1500 Rogue River Hwy., Ste. F, Grants Pass, OR 97527/503-476-7552
Lorcin Engineering Co., Inc., 6471 Mission Blvd., Riverside, CA 92509/714-682-7374
Lortone, Inc., 2856 NW Market St., Seattle, WA 98107/206-789-3100
LPS Chemical Prods., Holt Lloyd Corp., 4647 Hugh Howell Rd., P.O. Box 3050, Tucker, GA 30084/404-934-7800
L&S Technologies, Inc. (See Aimtech Mount Systems)
LT Industries, Inc., 31812 Bainbridge Rd., Solon, OH 44139/216-248-7550
Lucas, Edw. E., 32 Garfield Ave., East Brunswick, NJ 08816/201-251-5526
Lyman Products Corp., 147 West St., Middlefield, CT 06455/203-349-3421
Lynn's Specialty Gunsmithing (See McMurdo, Lynn)
Lynx-Line (See Williams Shootin' Iron Service)
"Little John's" Antique Arms, 1740 W. Laveta, Orange, CA 92668

M

Macbean, Stan, 754 North 1200 West, Orem, UT 84057/801-224-6446
Mac's .45 Shop, P.O. Box 2028, Seal Beach, CA 90740/213-438-5046
Mac-1 Airgun Distributors, 13972 Van Ness Ave., Gardena, CA 90249/213-327-3582
Mack's Sport Shop, P.O. Box 1155, Kodiak, AK 99615/907-486-4276
Madis, David, 2453 West Five Mile Pkwy., Dallas, TX 75233/214-330-7169
MAG Instrument, Inc., 1635 S. Sacramento Ave., Ontario, CA 91761/714-947-1006
Mag-Na-Port International, Inc., 41302 Executive Dr., Mr. Clemens, MI 48045/313-469-6727
Mag-Pack, P.O. Box 846, Chesterland, OH 44026
Magma Engineering Co., P.O. Box 161, Queen Creek, AZ 85242/602-987-9008
Magnolia Sports, Inc., 211 West Main, Magnolia, AR 71753/501-234-8117/800-530-7816
Magnum Research, Inc., 7110 University Ave. NE, Minneapolis, MN 55432/612-574-1868
Magnus Bullet Co., Inc., P.O. Box 2225, Birmingham, AL 35201/205-785-3357
MagSafe Ammo Co., 2725 Friendly Grove Rd. NE, Olympia, WA 98506/206-357-6383
MAGTECH Recreational Products, Inc., 5030 Paradise Rd., Suite C-211, Las Vegas, NV 89119/702-795-7191
Mahony, Phillip Bruce, 67 White Hollow Rd., Lime Rock, CT 06039/203-435-9341
Mains, Wm. H., 3111 S. Valley View Blvd., Suite B-120, Las Vegas, NV 89102/702-876-6278
Maionchi-L.M.I., Via Di Coselli--Zona Industriale Di Guamo, Lucca, Italy 55060/011 39-583 94291
Maki Industries, 26-10th St. SE, Medicine Hat, AB T1A 1P7 Canada/403-526-7997
Maki, Robert E., Hand Engravers Emporium, P.O. Box 947, Northbrook, IL 60065/708-724-8238
Makinson, Nicholas J., RR #3, Komoka, Ont. N0L 1R0 Canada/519-471-5462
Mallardtone Game Calls, 2901 16th St., Moline, IL 61265/309-762-8089
Maloni, Russ (See Russwood Custom Pistol Grips)
M.A.M. Products, Inc., 153 B Cross Slope Court, Englishtown, NJ 07726/908-536-7268
Mandall Shooting Supplies, 3616 N. Scottsdale Rd., Scottsdale, AZ 85252/602-945-2553
Mandarino, Monte, 205 Fifth Ave. East, Kalispell, MT 59901/406-257-6208
Manley Shooting Supplies, Lowell, 3684 Pine St., Deckerville, MI 48427/313-376-3665
Mannlicher (See Gun South, Inc.)
Manufacture D'Armes Des Pyrenees Francaises--Unique (M.A.P.F.), 10, Les Allees, 64700 Hendaye, France 64700/33-59 20 71 93
Mar Knives, Inc., Al, 5755 SW Jean Rd., Suite 101, Lake Oswego, OR 97035/503-635-9229
Marathon Rubber Prods. Co., Inc., 510 Sherman St., Wausau, WI 54401/715-845-6255
Marble Arms Corp., 420 Industrial Park, P.O. Box 111, Gladstone, MI 49837/906-428-3710
Marek, George, 55 Arnold St., Westfield, MA 01085/413-562-5673
Marent, Rudolf, 9711 Tiltree, Houston, TX 77075/713-946-7028
Markell, Inc., 422 Larkfield Center #235, Santa Rosa, CA 95403/707-573-0792
Marksman Products, 5622 Engineer Dr., Huntington Beach, CA 92649/714-898-7535
Marlin Firearms Co., 100 Kenna Drive, New Haven, CT 06473
Marple & Associates, Dick, 21 Dartmouth St., Hooksett, NH 03106/603-627-1837
Marquart Precision Co., P.O. Box 1740, Prescott, AZ 86302/602-445-5646
Marsh, Johnny, 1007 Drummond Dr., Nashville, TN 37211/615-834-2103
Marsh, Mike, The Croft Cottage, Main St., Nr. Matlock, Elton, Derbyshire DE4 2BY, England/062-988-669
Martin, Elwyn H., Martin's Gun Shop, 937 S. Sheridan Blvd., Lakewood, CO 80226/303-922-2184
Martz, John V., 8060 Lakeview Lane, Lincoln, CA 95648/916-645-2250
Marvel, Alan, 3922 Madonna Rd., Jarretsville, MD 21084/301-557-6545
Masen Co., John, P.O. Box 5050, Suite 165, Lewisville, TX 75028/817-430-8732
Masker Custom Rifles, Seely, 54 Woodshire S., Getzville, NY 14068/716-689-8894
Master Lock Co., 2600 N. 32nd St., Milwaukee, WI 53245/414-444-2800
Master Products, Inc., P.O. Box 8474, Van Nuys, CA 91409/818-365-0864
Matco, Inc., 1003-2nd St., N. Manchester, IN 46962/219-982-8282
Mathews & Son, Inc., Geo. E., 10224 S. Paramount Blvd., Downey, CA 90241
Matthews Cutlery, 4401 Sentry Dr., Tucker, GA 30084/404-939-6915
Matthews, Inc., Bill, P.O. Box 26727, Lakewood, CO 80226/303-922-0055
Matthews, Larry, 7525 S. Coast Hwy., South Beach, OR 97366/503-867-4951
Mauser-Werke Oberndorf, P.O. Box 1349, 7238 Oberndorf/Neckar, West Germany
Maverick Arms, Inc., Idustrial Blvd., P.O. Box 586, Eagle Pass, TX 78853/512-773-9007
Mayville Engineering Co., 715 South St., Mayville, WI 53050/414-387-4500
Mazur Restoration, Pete, 13083 Drummer Way, Grass Valley, CA 95949/916-268-2412
McCament, Jay, 1730-134th St. Ct. S., Tacoma, WA 98444/206-531-8832
McCann's Muzzle-Gun Works, 200 Federal City Rd., Pennington, NJ 08534/609-737-1707
McConnellstown Reloading & Cast Bullets, Inc., R.D. 3, P.O. Box 40, Huntingdon, PA 16652/814-627-5402
McCormick's Custom Gun Bluing, 609 NE 104th Ave., Vancouver, WA 98664/206-896-4232
McDonald, Dennis, 8359 Brady St., Peosta, IA 52068/319-556-7940
McFarland, Stan, 2221 Idella Ct., Grand Junction, CO 81505/303-243-4704
McGowen Rifle Barrels, Rt. 3., St. Anne, IL 60964/815-937-9816
McGuire, Bill, 1600 N. Eastmont Ave., East Wenatchee, WA 98802/509-884-6021
McKee Publications, 121 Eatons Neck Rd., Northport, NY 11768/516-575-5334
McKee, Arthur, 121 Eatons Neck Rd., Northport, NY 11768/516-757-8850
McKenzie, Lynton S.M., 6940 N. Alvernon Way, Tucson, AZ 85718/602-299-5090
McKillen & Heyer, Inc., 37603 Arlington Dr., P.O. Box 627, Willoughby, OH 44094/216-942-2491
McMillan Fiberglass Stocks, Inc., 21421 N. 14th Ave., Pheonix, AZ 85027/602-582-9635
McMillan Gunworks, Inc., 21438 N. 7th Ave., Suite E, Pheonix, AZ 85027/602-582-9627
McMillan Rifle Barrels, U.S. International, P.O. Box 3427, Bryan, TX 77805/409-846-3990
McMurdo, Lynn, P.O. Box 404, Afton, WY 83110/307-886-5535
McMurray & Son (See Mac-1 Airgun Distributors)
MCS, Inc. (See Mo's Competitor Supplies)
M&D Munitions Ltd., 127 Verdi St., Farmingdale, NY 11735/516-752-1038
MDS, Inc., 1640 Central Ave., St. Petersburg, FL 33712/813-894-3512
Meadow Industries, P.O. Box 450, Marlton, NJ 08053/609-953-0922
MEC, Inc. (See Mayville Engineering Co.)
MEC-Gar S.R.L., Via Madonnina, 64, Gardone V.T. (BS), Italy 25063/39-30-837687-8911719
Meier Works, Steve Hines, P.O. Box 328, 2102-2nd Ave., Canyon, TX 79015/806-655-7806

Mele, Frank, Rt. 1 P.O. Box 349, Springfork Rd., Granville, TN 38564/615-653-4414
Melton Shirt Co., Inc., 56 Harvester Ave., Batavia, NY 14020/716-343-8750
Men--Metallwerk Elisenhuette, GmbH, P.O. Box 1263, W-5408 Nassau, Germany/2604-7819
Mendez, John A., P.O. Box 1534, Radio City Station, New York, NY 10019/212-315-2580
Meprolight, 2821 Greenville Rd., LaGrange, GA 30240/404-884-7967
Mercer, R. M., 216 S. Whitewater Ave., Jefferson, WI 53549/414-674-3839
Merit Corp., Dept. GD, P.O. Box 9044, Schenectady, NY 12309/518-346-1420
Merkuria, FTC, Argentinska 38, 17005 Prague 7, Czechoslovakia
Merrill Pistol (See RPM)
Metalife Industries, P.O. Box 53, Mong Ave., Reno, PA 16343/814-436-7747
Metallic Casting & Copper Corp. (MCC), 214 E. Third St., Mt. Vernon, NY 10550/914-664-1311
Michael's Antiques, P.O. Box 591, Waldoboro, ME 04572
Michaels of Oregon Co., P.O. Box 13010, Portland, OR 97213/503-255-6890
Micro Sight Co., 242 Harbor Blvd., Belmont, CA 94002/415-591-0769
Micro-Lube, Rt. 2, P.O. Box 201, Deming, NM 88030/505-546-9116
Mid-America Recreation, Inc., 1328 5th Ave., Moline, IL 61265/309-764-5089
Midway Arms, Inc., P.O. Box 1483, Columbia, MO 65205/314-445-2400
Midwest Gun Sport, 1108 Herbert Dr., Zebulon, NC 27597/919-269-5570
Military Armament Corp., P.O. Box 120, Mt. Zion Rd., Lingleville, TX 76461/817-965-3253
Millenium Safety Products, Inc., P.O. Box 9802-916, Austin, TX 78766-0802/512-346-3876
Miller Arms, Inc., D.E. Miller, P.O. Box 260, St. Onge, SD 57779/605-578-1790
Miller Co., David, 3131 E. Greenlee Rd., Tucson, AZ 85716/602-326-3117
Miller Custom, 210 E. Julia, Clinton, IL 61727/217-935-9362
Miller Single Trigger Mfg. Co., R.D. 1, P.O. Box 99, Millersburg, PA 17061/717-692-3704
Miller, S.A., Point Roberts Sports Ltd., P.O. Box 1053, 1440 Peltier Dr., Point Roberts, WA 98281/206-945-7014
Miller, Tom, c/o Huntington's Sportsman's Store, 601 Oro Dam Blvd., Oroville, CA 95965/916-534-1210
Millett Industries, 16131 Gothard St., Huntington Beach, CA 92647/714-842-5575
Milliron Custom Guns & Stocks, Earl, 1249 NE 166th Ave., Portland, OR 97230/503-252-3725
Mills, Hugh B., Jr., 3615 Canterbury Rd., New Bern, NC 28560/919-637-4631
Miniature Machine Co. (MMC), 210 E. Poplar St., Deming, NM 88030/505-546-2151
Mirador Optical Corp., 4051 Glencoe Ave., Marina Del Rey, CA 90292/213-821-5587
Mitch's Stock Shop, Inc., 808 2nd St. NW, Valley City, ND 58072/701-845-5155
Mitchell Arms, Inc., 3400 W. MacArthur Blvd., Suite I, Santa Ana, CA 92704/714-957-5711
Mitchell's Accuracy Shop, 68 Greenridge Dr., Stafford, VA 22554/703-659-0165
Mittermeier, Frank, 3577 E. Tremont Ave., New York, NY 10465/212-828-3843
MK Arms, Inc., P.O. Box 16411, Irvine, CA 92713/714-261-2767
M&M Engineering, 10642 Arminta St., Sun Valley, CA 91352/818-842-8376
MMC Co., Inc. (See Miniature Machine Co.)
MMP, RR 6 P.O. Box 384, Harrison, AR 72601/501-741-5019
M&N Bullet Lube, P.O. Box 495, 151 NE Jefferson St., Madras, OR 97741/503-255-3750
M.O.A. Corp., 175 Carr Dr., Brookville, OH 45309/513-833-5559
Mo's Competitor Supplies, 34 Delmar Dr., Brookfield, CT 06804/203-775-1013
Modern Gun Repair School, 2538 N. 8th St., P.O. Box 5338, Phoenix, AZ 85010/602-990-8346
Modern Muzzleloading, Inc., RR 1, P.O. Box 234A, Centerville, IA 52544/515-856-2623
Moeller, Steve, 1213 4th St., Fulton, IL 61252/815-589-2300
Molin Industries/Tru-Nord Division, P.O. Box 365, 204 North 9th St., Brainerd, MN 56401/218-829-2870
MoLoc Bullets, P.O. Box 2810, Turlock, CA 95381/209-634-3642
Monell Custom Guns, Red Mill Road, RD #2, P.O. Box 96, Pine Bush, NY 12566/914-744-3021
Moneymaker Guncraft, 1420 Military Ave., Omaha, NE 68131/402-556-0226
Monogrip (See Hogue Grips)
Montana Armory, Inc., 100 Centennial Dr., Big Timber, MT 59011/406-932-4353
Monte Kristo Pistol Grip Co., P.O. Box 610, Douglas City, CA 96024/916-778-3136
Montgomery Technical College, P.O. Box 787, Troy, NC 27371/919-572-3691
Moore & Co., Wm. Larkin, 31360 Via Colinas, Suite 109, Westlake Village, CA 91360/818-889-4160
Moran, Jerry, P.O. Box 357, Mt. Morris, MI 45458-0357
Moreton/Fordyce Enterprises, P.O. Box 940, Saylorsburg, PA 18353/717-992-5742
Morrison Custom Rifles, J.W., 4015 W. Sharon, Phoenix, AZ 85029/602-978-3754
Morrow, Bud, 11 Hillside Lane, Sheridan, WY 82801/307-674-8360
Moschetti, Mitch, P.O. Box 27065, Denver, CO 80227/303-733-9593
Moss Double Tone, Inc., P.O. Box 1112, 2101 S. Kentucky, Sedalia, MO 65301/816-827-0827
Mossberg & Sons, Inc., O.F., 7 Grasso St., N. Haven, CT 06473
Mountain Arms, Rt. 3, P.O. Box 297, Warrenton, VA 22186/703-347-1199
Mountain Bear Rifle Works, Inc., Wm. Scott Bickett, 100-B Ruritan Rd., Sterling, VA 22170/703-430-0420
Mountain Hollow Game Calls, P.O. Box 121, Rt. 550 Military Rd., Cascade, MD 21719/301-241-4101
Mountain South, P.O. Box 381, Airport Industrial Park, Barnwell, SC 29812/803-259-2893
Mountain State Muzzleloading Supplies, Inc., P.O. Box 154-1, Rt. #2, Williamstown, WV 26187/304-375-7842
Mountain View Sports, Inc., P.O. Box 188, Troy, NH 03465/800-446-8782
MPI Stocks, 5655 NW St. Helens Rd., Portland, OR 97210/503-226-1215
Mrock, Larry, R.F.D. 3, P.O. Box 207, Woodhill-Hooksett Rd., Bow, NH 03301/603-224-4096 (brochure $3)
MTM Molded Products Co., P.O. Box 14117, Dayton, OH 45414/513-890-7461
Mulholland, Gordon (Gordie's Gun Shop), 1401 Fulton St., Streator, IL 61364/815-672-7202
Mullis Guncraft, 3518 Lawyers Road East, Monroe, NC 28110/704-283-8789
Multi-Scale Charge Ltd., 2446 Cawthra Rd., Bldg. 1, Unit 10, Mississauga, Ont. L5A 3K6 Canada/416-566-1255
Munger, Robert D. (See Rusteprufe Laboratories)
Munsch Gunsmithing, Tommy, Rt. 2, P.O. Box 248, Little Falls, MN 56345/612-632-6695 (list $2; other inq. SASE)
Murphy Co., Inc., R., 13 Groton-Harvard Rd., P.O. Box 376, Ayer, MA 01432/617-772-3481
Murray State College, Gunsmithing Program, 1100 S. Murray, Tishomingo, OK 73460/405-371-2371
Muscle Products Corp./Firepower Lubricants, 188 Freeport Rd., Butler, PA 16001/412-283-0567
Museum of Historical Arms, Inc., 1038 Alton Rd., Miami Beach, FL 33139/305-672-7480 (catalog $5)
Mushroom Express Bullet Co., 3147 W. U.S. 40, Greenfield, IN 46140/317-462-9390
Mustang Custom Pistol Grips (See Renner Co., R.J.)
Mustra's Custom Guns, Inc., Carl, 1002 Pennsylvania Ave., Palm Harbor, FL 34683/813-785-1403
Muzzel-Nuzzle Co., 609 N. Virginia Ave., Roswell, NM 88201/505-624-1260
Muzzlelite Corp., P.O. Box 100, Junction City, WI 54443/715-457-2431
Muzzleload Magnum Products (See MMP)
Muzzleloaders Etc., Inc., Jim Westberg, 9901 Lyndale Ave. S., Bloomington, MN 55420/612-884-1161

N

NAI/Ballistek, 1260 Oro Grande #8, Lake Havasu City, AZ 86403
Nastoff's 45 Shop, Steve Nastoff, 1057 Laverne Ave., Youngtown, OH 44511/216-799-8870
National Guild of Shotgun Shooting Instructors, 4017 Emerald St. 1, Torrance, CA 90503/213-371-1128
National Security Safe Company, Inc., P.O. Box 39, 620 S. 380 E., American Fork, UT 84003/801-756-7706
National Survival Game, Inc. (See GFR Corp.)
Nationwide Airgun Repairs, 3230 Garden Meadows, Lawrenceburg, IN 47025/812-637-1463
Navy Arms Co., 689 Bergen Blvd., Ridgefield, NJ 07657/201-945-2500
Necromancer Industries, Inc., 14 Communications Way, West Newton, PA 15089/412-872-8722
NEI, 9330 NE Halsey, Portland, OR 97220/503-255-3750
Neighbor, William (See Bill's Gun Repair)
Nelson Combat Leather, Bruce, P.O. Box 8691 CRB, Tucson, AZ 85738/602-825-9042 (catalog $3)
Nelson, Gary K., 975 Terrace Dr., Oakdale, CA 95361/209-847-4590
Nelson, Stephen E., 7365 NW Spring Creek Dr., Corvallis, OR 97330/503-745-5232
Nelson/Weather-Rite, 14760 Santa Fe Trail Dr., Lenexa, KS 66215/913-492-3200
Nesci Enterprises, Inc., P.O. Box 119, Summit St., East Hampton, CT 06424/203-267-2588
Nettestad, Bruce A., RR 1, P.O. Box 140, Pelican Rapids, MN 56572/218-863-4301
Neumann, GmbH, Untere Ringstr. 17, 8506 Langenzenn, Germany/09101-8258
New Advantage Arms Corp. (See TMI Products)
New Detonics Mfg. Corp., 21438 N. 7th Ave. #F, Phoenix, AZ 85027/602-582-4867
New England Ammunition Company, 1771 Post Rd. East, Suite 223, Westport, CT 06880/203-254-8048
New England Arms Co., P.O. Box 278, Lawrence Lane, Kittery Point, ME 03905/207-439-0593
New England Custom Gun Service (See Apel, Dietrich)
New England Firearms Co., Inc., (See H&R 1871, Inc.)
New Orleans Arms Co., 5001 Treasure St., New Orleans, LA 70186/504-944-3371
New Orleans Jewelers Supply, 206 Chartres St., New Orleans, LA 70130/504-523-3839
Newbern Glove, 301 Jefferson St., Newbern, TN 38059/901-627-2557
Newell, Robert H., 55 Coyote, Los Alamos, NM 87544/505-662-7135 (brochure $2)
Newman Gunshop, 119 Miller Rd., Agency, IA 52530/515-937-5775
NgraveR Co., 879 Raymond Hill Rd., Oakdale, CT 06370/203-848-8031
Nichols Sports Optics, P.O. Box 37669, Omaha, NE 68137/402-339-3530
Nickels, Paul R., P.O. Box 71043, Las Vegas, NV 89170/702-435-5318
Nicklas, Ted, 5504 Hegel Rd., Goodrich, MI 48438/313-797-4493
Night Vision Equipment Co., Inc., P.O. Box 266, Emmaus, PA 18049/215-391-9101
Nikon, Inc., 1300 Walt Whitman Rd., Melville, NY 11747/516-547-4200
Nitex, Inc., Ed House, P.O. Box 1706, Uvalde, TX 78801/512-278-8843
N&J Sales Co., Lime Kiln Rd., Northford, CT 06472/203-484-0247
No-Sho Mfg. Co., 10727 Glenfield Ct., Houston, TX 77096/713-723-5332
Noble Co., Jim, 1305 Columbia St., Vancouver, WA 98660/206-695-1309
Noreen, Peter H., Rt.2 P.O. Box 49, Herman, MN 56248/612-677-2682
Norinco (See Chinasports, Inc.)
NORMA (See Dynamit Nobel/RWS)
Norman, Jim, Custom Gunstocks, 14281 Cane Rd., Valley Center, CA 92082/619-749-6252
Normark Corp., 1710 E. 78th St., Minneapolis, MN 55423/612-869-3291
North American Arms, 1800 North 300 West, Spanish Fork, UT 84660/800-821-5783
North American Correspondence Schools, The Gun Pro School, Oak & Pawnee St., Scranton, PA 18515/717-342-7701
North American Specialties, 25422 Trabuco Rd. #105-328, El Toro, CA 92630/714-979-4867
North Consumer Prods. Div., 2664-B Saturn St., Brea, CA 92621/714-524-1665
North Fork Custom Gunsmithing, 428 Del Rio Rd., Roseburg, OR 97470/503-673-4467
North Wind Decoys Co., P.O. Box 1001, Fergus Falls, MN 56538/218-736-4378
Northeast Industrial, Inc. (See NEI)
Northeast Training Institute, Inc., 1142 Rockland St., Suite 380, Reading, PA 19604/215-373-1940
Northern Precision Custom Swaged Bullets, 337 S. James St., Carthage, NY 13619/315-493-3456
Northlake Boot Co., 1810 Columbia Ave., Franklin, TN 37064/615-794-1556
Nosler Bullets, Inc., 107 SW Columbia, Bend, OR 97709/503-382-3921
Novak's .45 Shop, Wayne Novak, 1206 1/2 30th St., P.O. Box 4045, Parkersburg, WV 26101/304-485-9295
Nowlin Custom Guns/Manufacturing, Rt. 1, P.O. Box 308, Claremore, OK 74017/918-342-0689
N.S.G., Inc. (See National Survival Game, Inc.)
Nu-Line Guns, 1053 Caulks Hill Rd., Harvester, MO 63303/314-441-4500 or 441-4501
Numerich Arms (See Gun Parts Corp.)
Nu-Teck Ltd., 30 Industrial Park Rd., Centerbrook, CT 06409/203-767-3573
Null Holsters Ltd., Kenneth L., Hill City Station, Resaca, GA 30735/404-625-5643
Nygord Precision Products, P.O. Box 8394, La Crescenta, CA 91214/818-352-3027

O

Oakland Custom Arms, Inc., 9191 Pine Knob Rd., Clarkston, MI 48016/313-625-1150
Oakman Turkey Calls, RD 1 P.O. Box 825, Harrisonville, PA 17228/717-485-4620
Obermeyer Rifled Barrels, 23122 60th St., Bristol, WI 53104/414-843-3537

O'Connor Rifle Products Co., Ltd., 2008 Maybank Hwy., Charleston, SC 29412/803-795-8590
October Country, P.O. Box 969, 9751 N. Government Way, Hayden Lake, ID 83835/208-772-2068
Oehler Research, Inc., P.O. Box 9135, Austin, TX 78766/512-327-6900
Oglesby & Oglesby Gunmakers, Inc., RR #5, Springfield, IL 62707/217-487-7100
Ojala Holsters, Arvo, P.O. Box 98, N. Hollywood, CA 91603/503-669-1404
Oker's Engraving, 365 Bell Rd., Bellford Mtn. Hts., P.O. Box 126, Shawnee, CO 80475/303-838-6062
Oklahoma Leather Products, Inc., 402 Newman Rd., Miami, OK 74354/918-542-6651
Old Dominion Engravers, 100 Progress Drive, Lynchburg, VA 24502/804-237-4450
Old West Reproductions, R.M. Bachman, 446 Florence South Loop, Florence, MT 59833/406-273-2615 (catalog $3)
Old Western Scrounger, Inc., 12924 Hwy. A-12, Montague, CA 96064/916-459-5445 (write for list; $2)
Old World Gunsmithing, 2901 SE 122nd, Portland, OR 97236-3205/503-760-7681
Old World Oil Products, 3827 Queen Ave. N., Minneapolis, MN 55412/612-522-5037
Olson, Vic, 5002 Countryside Dr., Imperial, MO 63052/314-296-8086
Olt Co., Phil S., P.O. Box 550, Pekin, IL 61554/309-348-3633
Olympic Arms, Inc., 624 Old Pacific Hwy. SE, Olympia, WA 98503206-456-7940
Omark Industries (See Blount Sporting Equipment Division)
Omega Sales, Inc., P.O. Box 1066, Mt. Clemens, MI 48046
OMR Feinmechanik, Jagd-und Sportwaffen, GmbH, Postfach 1231, Schutzenstr. 20, D-5400 Koblenz, Germany/0261-31865-15351
Optolyth-USA, 18805 NE Melvista Lane, Hillsboro, OR 97123/503-628-0246
Or-Un A.S., Karlitepe Mahallesi, Refah Sokak No:21-Kartal, Istanbul, Turkey 81420/901-353-1725
Orchard Park Enterprise, P.O. Box 563, Orchard Park, NY 14127/716-662-0356
Oregon Arms, Inc., 164 Schulz Rd., Central Point, OR 97502/503-664-5586
Original Mink Oil, Inc., P.O. Box 20191, 11021 NE Beach St., Portland, OR 97220/503-255-2814
Orion Bullets, P.O. Box 264, Franklin, ID 83237/208-646-2373
Orvis Co., Inc., The, 10 River Rd., Manchester, VT 05254/802-362-3622
Ottmar, Maurice, P.O. Box 657, 113 E. Fir, Coulee City, WA 99115/509-632-5717
Otto, Tim, 7 Windsor Dr., Charleston, SC 29407/803-556-0772
Outdoor Connection, Inc., The, 201 Douglas, P.O. Box 7751, Waco, TX 76712-7751/800-533-6076/817-772-5575
Outdoor Edge Cutlery Corp., 2888 Bluff St., Suite 130, Boulder, CO 80301/303-444-0937
Outdoor Sports Headquarters, Inc., 967 Watertower Lane, Dayton, OH 45449/513-865-5855
Outdoorsman's Bookstore, The, Llangorse, Brecon, County Powys LD3 7UE,(England) U.K./44-87484-660
Outers Laboratories, Div. of Blount, Route 2, Onalaska, WI 54650/608-781-5800
Owen, Harry (See Sport Specialties)
Ox-Yoke Originals, Inc., 34 Main St., Milo, ME 04463/207-943-2171

P

Pachmayr Ltd., 1875 S. Mountain Ave., Monrovia, CA 91016/818-357-7771
Pacific Pistolcraft, 1810 E. Columbia Ave., Tacoma, WA 98404/206-474-5465
P.A.C.T., Inc., P.O. Box 531525, Grand Prairie, TX 75053/214-641-0049
Pagel Gun Works, Jay A. Pagel, 1407 4th St. NW, Grand Rapids, MN 55744/218-326-3003
Paladin Press, P.O. Box 1307, Boulder, CO 80306/303-443-7250
Palcher Ammunition, Techstar Engineering, Inc., 2239 S. Huron Ave., Santa Ana, CA 92704/714-556-7384
Palmer Metal Products, 2930 N. Campbell Ave., Chicago, IL 60618/312-267-0200
Palmgren Steel Prods., Chicago Tool & Engineering Co., 8383 South Chicago Ave., Chicago, IL 60617/312-721-9675
Panavise Prods., Inc., 1485 Southern Way, Sparks, NV 90431/702-353-2900
Para-Ordnance Mfg.,Inc., 3411 McNicoll Ave., Unit #14, Scarborough, Ont. M1V 2V6, Canada/416-297-7855
Paragon Sales, Inc., P.O. Box 2022, Joliet, IL 60434/815-725-9212
Paris, Frank J., 13945 Minock Dr., Redford, MI 48239/313-255-0888
Parke-Bernet (See Sotheby's)
Parker Reproductions, 124 River Rd., Middlesex, NJ 08846/201-469-0100
Parker, Mark D., 1240 Florida Ave. #7, Longmont, CO 80501/303-772-0214
Parker-Case, P.O. Box 4000, Owens Way, Bradford, PA 16701/814-368-4123
Parker-Hale (See Navy Arms—firearms)
Parker-Hale (Precision Sports—Cleaning Supplies)
Partridge Sales Ltd., John, Trent Meadows, Rugeley, Staffordshire, WS15 2HS England/0889-584438
Pasadena Gun Center, 206 E. Shaw, Pasadena, TX 77506/713-472-0417
P.A.S.T. Corp., 210 Park Ave., Columbia, MO 65205/314-449-7278
Paterson Gunsmithing, 438 Main St., Paterson, NJ 07502/201-345-4100
Pathfinder Sports Leather, 2920 E. Chambers St., Phoenix, AZ 85040/602-276-0016
Patriot Mfg. & Sales, 2163 Oak Beach Blvd., P.O. Box 2041, Sebring, FL 33871/813-655-1798
Pattern Control, 114 N. 3rd St., Garland, TX 75040/214-494-3551
Paulsen Gunstocks, Rt. 71, P.O. Box 11, Chinook, MT 59523/406-357-3403
PC Co., 5942 Secor Rd., Toledo, OH 43623/419-472-6222
Pease Accuracy, Bob, P.O. Box 310787, Zipp Rd., New Braunfels, TX 78131/512-625-1342
PECAR Herbert Schwarz, GmbH, Kreuzbergstrasse 6, Berlin 61, 1000 Germany/030-785 73 83
Pedersen & Son, C.R., 2717 S. Pere Marquette, Ludington, MI 49431/616-843-2061
Pejsa Ballistics, 2120 Kenwood Pkwy., Minneapolis, MN 55405/612-374-3337
Pell, John T., 410 College, Trinidad, CO 81082/719-846-9406
Pence Precision Barrels, RR #2 , S. Whitley, IN 46787/219-839-4745
Pend Oreille Sport Shop, 3100 Hwy. 200 East, Sandpoint, ID 83864/208-263-2412
Pendleton Royal, P.O. Box 172, B'Ham B4 6HE, England/021-212 1385
Pendleton Woolen Mills, P.O. Box 3030, 220 N.W. Broadway, Portland, OR 97208/503-226-4801
Penguin Industries, Inc., Airport Industrial Mall, Coatesville, PA 19320/215-384-6000
Penn's Woods Products, Inc., 19 W. Pittsburgh St., Delmont, PA 15626/412-468-8311
Pennsylvania Gunsmith School, 812 Ohio River Blvd., Avalon, Pittsburgh, PA 15202/412-766-1812
Penrod Precision, 312 College Ave., P.O. Box 307, N. Manchester, IN 46962/219-981-8385
Pentax Corp., 35 Inverness Dr. E., Englewood, CO 80112/303-799-8000
Pentheny de Pentheny, 2352 Baggett Ct., Santa Rosa, CA 95401/707-573-1390
Perazzi U.S.A., Inc., 1207 S. Shamrock Ave., Monrovia, CA 91016/818-303-0068
Peregrine Industries, Inc., P.O. Box 1310, Huntington Beach, CA 92647-1310/714-847-4700
Performance Specialists, 308 Eanes School Rd., Austin, TX 78746/512-327-0119
Personal Protection Systems Ltd., Aberbeen Rd., RD #5 P.O. Box 5027-A, Moscow, PA 18444/717-842-1766
Perugini Visini & Co. s.r.l., Via Camprelle, 126, 25080 Nuvolera (Bs.), Italy
Peters, E. Larry, c/o Kimber, 9039 SE Janssen Rd., Clackamas, OR 97015/503-656-6016
Petersen Publishing Co., 8490 Sunset Blvd., Los Angeles, CA 99069
Peterson Gun Shop, A.W., 1693 Old Hwy. 441 N., Mt. Dora, FL 32757
Peterson Instant Targets, Inc. (See Lyman Products Corp.)
Pettinger Arms Books, Gerald, Route 2, Russell, IA 50238/515-535-2239
Pflumm Gun Mfg. Co., 6139 Melrose Lane, Shawnee, KS 66203/913-268-3105
PFRB Company, P.O. Box 1242, Bloomington, IL 61701/309-473-3964
Phelps Mfg. Co., P.O. Box 2266, Evansville, IN 47714/812-476-8791
Phillips & Bailey, Inc., 815A Yorkshire St., Houston, TX 77022/713-699-4288
Phoenix Arms Co. Ltd., Hy-Score Works, 40 Stonar Industrial Estate, Sandwich, Kent CT13 9LN, England/0304-61.12.21
Phyl-Mac, 609 NE 104th Ave., Vancouver, WA 98664/206-256-0579
Piedmont Community College, P.O. Box 1197, Roxboro, NC 27573/919-599-1181
Pierce Pistols, 2326 E. Hwy. 34, Newnan, GA 30263/404-253-8192
Pilgrim Pewter, Inc., RD 2, P.O. Box 219, Tully, NY 13159/607-842-6431
Pilkington Gun Co., P.O. Box 1296, Muskogee, OK 74402/918-683-9418
Pilkington, Scott, Jr., Little Trees Ramble, Monteagle, TN 37356/615-924-3475
Pine Technical College, 1100 Fourth St., Pine City, MN 55063/612-629-6764
Pioneer Guns, 5228 Montgomery Rd., Norwood, OH 45212/513-631-4871
Pioneer Marketing & Research, Inc., 216 Haddon Ave., Westmont, NJ 08108/609-854-2424
Piquette, Paul R., 80 Bradford Dr., Feeding Hills, MA 01030/413-781-8300, Ext. 682
Pitzer Gun Tool Co., RR #1, P.O. Box 200, Earlham, IA 50272/515-462-3547
Plante, Eugene T., Gene's Custom Guns, 3890 Hill Ave., P.O. Box 10534, White Bear Lake, MN 55110/612-429-5105
Plaxco, J. Michael, Rt. 1, P.O. Box 203, Roland, AR 72135/501-868-9787
Plaza Cutlery, Inc., 3333 Bristol, #161, South Coast Plaza, Costa Mesa, CA 92626/714-549-3932
Plum City Ballistics Range, Norman E. Johnson, Rt. 1, P.O. Box 29A, Plum City, WI 54761/715-647-2539
P&M Sales and Service, 5724 Gainsborough Pl., Oak Forest, IL 60452/708-687-7149
PMC-Eldorado Cartridge Co., P.O. Box 308, 12801 U.S. Hwy. 95 S., Boulder City, NV 89005/702-294-0025
PMI (See Pursuit Marketing, Inc.)
Poly Choke Div. (See Marble Arms Corp.)
Poly Technologies, Inc. (See PTK International, Inc.)
Polywad, Inc., P.O. Box 7916, Macon, GA 31209/912-477-0669
Pomeroy, Robert, RR 1 P.O. Box 50, Morison Ave., East Corinth, ME 04427/207-285-7721
Ponsness-Warren, P.O. Box 8, Rathdrum, ID 83858/208-687-2231
Pony Express Reloaders, 608 E. Co. Rd. D, Suite #3, St. Paul, MN 55117/612-483-9406
Pony Express Sport Shop, Inc., 16606 Schoenborn St., Sepulveda, CA 91343/818-895-1231
Porta Blind, Inc., 2700 Speedway, Wichita Falls, TX 76308/800-842-5545
Potts, Wayne E., 912 Poplar St., Denver, CO 80220/303-355-5462
Powell & Son (Gunmakers) Ltd., William, 35-37 Carrs Lane, Birmingham B4 7SX/21-643-0689
Power Custom, Inc., RR 2 P.O. Box 756AB, Gravois Mills, MO 65037/314-372-5684
P&P Tool Co., 125 W. Market St., Morrison, IL 61270/815-772-7618
Practical Tools, Inc., P.O. Box 63, Rd #2, Rt. 611, Pipersville, PA 18947/215-766-8681
Pragotrade, 307 Humberline Dr., Rexdale, Ontario, Canada M9W 5V1/416-675-1322
Pranger, Ed, 1414-7th St., Anacortes, WA 98221/206-293-3488
Pre-64 Winchester Parts Co., P.O. Box 8125, West Palm Beach, FL 33407 (SASE w/ request list)
Precise Chambering Co., 2499 Mavis St., Oakland, CA 94601/415-533-4193
Precise International, 15 Corporate Drive, Orangeburg, NY 10962/914-365-3500
Precise Metalsmithing Enterprises, James L. Wisner, 146 Curtis Hill Rd., Chehalis, WA 98532/206-748-3743
Precision Castings & Equipment, Inc., P.O. Box 135, Jasper, IN 47547/812-634-9167
Precision Components & Guns, Rt. 55, P.O. Box 337, Pawling, NY 12564/914-855-3040
Precision Imports, Inc., 5040 Space Center Dr., San Antonio, TX 78218/512-666-3033
Precision Munitions, Inc., P.O. Box 326, Jasper, IN 47547
Precision Prods. of Wash., Inc., N. 311 Walnut Rd., Spokane, WA 99206/509-928-0604
Precision Reloading, Inc., P.O. Box 122, Stafford Springs, CT 06076/800-223-0900
Precision Sales Intl., Inc., P.O. Box 1776, Westfield, MA 01086/413-562-5055
Precision Small Parts, Inc., 155 Carlton Rd., Charlottesville, VA 22901/804-293-6124
Precision Specialties Ltd., 131 Hendom Dr., Feeding Hills, MA 01030/413-786-3365
Precision Sport Optics, 15571 Producer Lane, Unit G, Huntington Beach, CA 92649/714-891-1309
Precision Sports, (Div. Cortland Line Co., Inc.), 3736 Kellogg Rd., P.O. Box 5588, Cortland, NY 13045-5588/607-756-2851/800-847-6787
Premier Reticles, Rt. 3, P.O. Box 369, Wardensville, WV 26851/304-874-3917
Preston Pittman Game Calls, Inc., P.O. Box 568, Lucedale, MS 39465/601-947-4417
Primos Wild Game Calls, Inc., 4436 N. State St., A-7, P.O. Box 12785, Jackson, MS 39206/601-366-1288
Pro Load Ammunition, Inc., 1120 S. Varney St., Burbank, CA 91502/818-842-6978
Pro-Mark (Div. of Wells Lamont), 6640 W. Touhy, Chicago, IL 60648/312-647-8200
Pro-Port Ltd., 41302 Executive Dr., Mt. Clemens, MI 48045/313-469-7323
Professional Gunsmiths of America, 1301 Franklin, P.O. Box 224E, Lexington, MO 64067/816-259-2636
Professional Hunter Supplies, P.O. Box 608, 468 Main St., Ferndale, CA 95536/707-786-4040
Proline Handgun Leather, Greg Kramer, 809 S. Geiger St., Tacoma, WA 98465/206-564-6652
Protecto Plastics, Div. of Penguin Ind., Airport Industrial Mall, Coatesville, PA 19320/215-384-6000
Protektor Model Co., 7 Ash St., Galeton, PA 16922/814-435-2442

PSI (See Precision Sales Intl., Inc.)
PTK International, Inc., 6030 Hwy. 85, Suite 614, Riverdale, GA 30274/404-997-5811
Puccinelli, Leonard, 5580 La Jolla Blvd., Suite 323, La Jolla, CA 92037/619-551-2629
Pursuit Marketing, Inc. (PMI), 1935 Techny Rd. Unit 16, Northbrook, IL 60062/708-272-4765
Pyrodex (See Hodgdon Powder Co., Inc.)
Pyromid, Inc., 3292 S. Highway 97, Redmond, OR 97786

Q

Quack Decoy Corp., 4 Mill St., Cumberland, RI 02864/401-723-8202
Quaker Boy, Inc., 5455 Webster Rd., Orchard Parks, NY 14127/716-662-3979
Quality Arms, Inc., P.O. Box 19477, Houston, TX 77224/713-870-8377
Quality Firearms, Inc., 4541 NW 133rd St., Miami, FL 33054/305-685-5966
Quality Parts Co., 999 Roosevelt Trail, Bldg. 3, Windham, ME 04062/800-556-SWAT
Quartz-Lok, 13137 N. 21st Lane, Phoenix, AZ 85029/602-863-2729
Queen Cutlery Co., 507 Chestnut St., Titusville, PA 16354/800-222-5233
Quigley's Personal Protection Strategies, Paxton, 9903 Santa Monica Blvd., #300, Beverly Hills, CA 90212/213-281-1762
Quinetics Corp., P.O. Box 29007, San Antonio, TX 78229/516-684-8561

R

Rabeno, Martin, Spook Hollow Trading Co., P.O. Box 37F, RD #1, Ellenville, NY 12428/914-647-4567
Radical Grips, 8774 Sepulveda Blvd., Suite 1, Sepulveda, CA 91343/818-892-8008
Rahn Gun Works, Inc., 3700 Anders Rd., P.O. Box 2, Hastings, MI 49058/616-945-9894
Raida Intertraders S.A., Raida House, 1-G Ave. de la Couronne, B1050 Brussels, Belgium
Ram-Line, Inc., 10601 W. 48th Ave., Wheat Ridge, CO 80033/303-467-0300
Ramos, Jesse, P.O. Box 7105, La Puente, CA 91744/818-369-6384
Ranch Products, P.O. Box 145, Malinta, OH 43535/313-277-3118
Randall-Made Knives, P.O. Box 1988, Orlando, FL 32802/407-855-8075 (catalog $1)
Ranger Mfg. Co., Inc., 1536 Crescent Dr., Augusta, GA 30919/404-738-3469
Ranging, Inc., Routes 5 & 20, East Bloomfield, NY 14443/716-657-6161
Ransom Intl. Corp., P.O. Box 3845, 1040 Sandretto Dr., Suite A, Prescott, AZ 86302/602-778-7899
Rapine Bullet Mould Mfg. Co., P.O. Box 1119, East Greenville, PA 18041/215-679-5413
Rattlers Brand, P.O. Box 311, 115 E. Main St., Thomaston, GA 30286/404-647-7131
Raven Arms, 1300 Bixby Dr., City of Industry, CA 91745/818-961-2511
R&C Knives and Such, P.O. Box 1047, Manteca, CA 95336/209-239-3722 (catalog $2)
RCBS, Div. of Blount, Inc., 605 Oro Dam Blvd, Oroville, CA 95965/800-533-5000
R.D.P. Tool Co., Inc., 49162 McCoy Ave., East Liverpool, OH 43920/216-385-5129
Re-Heater, Inc., 15828 S. Broadway, #C, Gardena, CA 90248
Reardon Products, P.O. Box 126, Morrison, IL 61270/815-772-3155
Red Ball, 100 Factory St., Nashua, NH 03060/603-881-4420
Red Head, Inc., P.O. Box 7100, Springfield, MO 65801/417-864-5430
Red Star Target Co., 4519 Brisebois Dr. NW, Calgary, AB T2L 2G3, Canada/403-289-7939
Redding-Hunter, Inc., 1089 Starr Rd., Cortland, NY 13045/607-753-3331
Redfield, Inc., 5800 E. Jewell Ave., Denver, CO 80224/303-757-6411
Redman's Rifling & Reboring, Rt. 3, P.O. Box 330A, Omak, WA 98841/509-826-5512
Reed Choke (See Clinton River Gun Serv., Inc.)
Refrigiwear, Inc., 71 Inip Dr., Inwood, Long Island, NY 11696
Reiswig, Wallace E., Claro Walnut Gunstock Co., 1235 Stanley Ave., Chico, CA 95928/916-342-5188
Reloaders Speciality Mfg., 7602 Carlton Rd., Coopersburg, PA 18036/215-838-9507
Remington Arms Co., 1007 Market St., Wilmington, DE 19898/302-773-5291
Remington Footwear Co., 1810 Columbia Ave., Franklin, TN 37604/800-332-2688
Renegade, P.O. Box 31546, Phoenix, AZ 85046/602-482-6777
Renner Co., R.J., P.O. Box 3543, Glendale, CA 91221-0543/818-892-8008
Reno, Wayne and Karen, 2808 Stage Stop Rd., Jefferson, CO 80456/719-836-3452
Retting, Inc., Martin B., 11029 Washington, Culver City, CA 90232/213-837-2412
Rhino Replacement Parts, P.O. Box 669, Seneca, SC 29679/803-882-0788
Rice Protective Gun Coatings, 235-30th St., West Palm Beach, FL 33407/407-848-7771
Richards Classic Oil Finish, Rt. 2, P.O. Box 325, Bedford, KY 40006/502-255-7222
Richards Micro-Fit Gun Stocks, P.O. Box 1066, Sun Valley, CA 91352/818-767-6097
Richards, John, Rt. 2, P.O. Box 325, Bedford, KY 40006/502-255-7222
Rickard, Inc., Pete, RD 1, Cobleskill, NY 12043/800-282-5663
Ridgetop Sporting Goods, P.O. Box 306, 42907 Hilligoss Ln. East, Eatonville, WA 98328/206-832-6422
Ries, Chuck, 415 Ridgecrest Dr., Grants Pass, OR 97527/503-476-5623
Rifle Shop, P.O. Box M, Philipsburg, MT 59858
RIG Products, 87 Coney Island Dr., Sparks, NV 89431/703-331-5666
Riggs, Jim, 206 Azalea, Boerne, TX 78006/512-249-8567
Riling Arms Books Co., Ray, 6844 Gorsten St., P.O. Box 18925, Philadelphia, PA 19119/215-438-2456
Ringler Custom Leather Co., P.O. Box 206, 2502 Mountain View Dr., Cody, WY 82414/307-587-6093
R.I.S. Co., Inc., 718 Timberlake Circle, Richardson, TX 75080/214-235-0933
Rizzini Battista, Via 2 Giugno 7/7Bis-25060 Marcheno (Brescia), Italy
R&J Gunshop, Bob Kerr, 133 W. Main St., John Day, OR 97845/503-575-2130
Robar Co.'s, Inc., The, 21438 N. 7th Ave., Pheonix, AZ 85027/602-581-2648
Roberts Custom Guns (See Dayton Traister Co.)
Roberts Products, 25238 SE 32nd, Issaquah, WA 98027/206-392-8172
Roberts, J.J., 166 Manassas Dr., Manassas Park, VA 22111/703-330-0448
Roberts, Wm. A., Jr., Rt. 14, P.O. Box 75, Athens, AL 35611/205-232-7027
Robinson Firearms Mfg. Ltd., 1689 Powick Rd., Kelowna, B.C., V1X 4L1 Canada/604-762-3725
Robinson, Don, Pennsylvania Hse., 36 Fairfax Crescent, Southowram, Halifax, W. Yorkshire HX3 9SW, England
Rochester Lead Works, 76 Anderson Ave., Rochester, NY 14607/716-442-8500
Rockwood Corp., 136 Lincoln Blvd., Middlesex, NJ 08846/908-560-7171
Rocky Fork Enterprises, P.O. Box 427, 878 Battle/Kidd Rd., Nolensville, TN 37135/615-941-1307
Rocky Mountain Rifle Works Ltd., 1707 14th St., Boulder, CO 80302/303-443-9189
Rocky Mountain Target Co., P.O. Box 700, Black Hawk, SD 57718/605-787-5946
Rogers Gunsmithing, Bob, P.O. Box 305, 344 S. Walnut St., Franklin Grove, IL 61031/815-456-2685
Rohner, John R. and Hans, 710 Sunshine Canyon, Boulder, CO 80302/303-444-3841
Rolston, Fred, Jr., 210 East Cummins, Tecumseh, MI 49286/517-423-6002
Rooster Laboratories, P.O. Box 412514, Kansas City, MO 64141/816-474-1622
Rorschach Precision Products, P.O. Box 151613, Irving, TX 75015/214-790-3487
Rosenberg & Sons, Jack A., 12229 Cox Lane, Dallas, TX 75234/214-241-6302
Rosser, Bob, 142 Ramsey Dr., Albertville, AL 35950/205-878-5388
Rossi S.A. Metalurgica E Municoes, Amadeo, Rua Amadeo Rossi, 143, Sao Leopoldo, RS, Brazil 93 030/0512-92-5566
Roto/Carve, 6509 Indian Hills Rd., Minneapolis, MN 55435/612-944-5150
Roy's Custom Leather Goods, (See Baker's, Roy)
Royal Arms, 1934 John Towers Ave. #A, El Cajon, CA 92020/619-448-5466
Royal Ordnance Works Ltd., P.O. Box 3245, Wilson, NC 27893/919-237-0515
RPM (R&R Sporting Arms, Inc.), 15481 N. Twin Lakes Dr., Tucson, AZ 85337/602-825-1233
R&S Industries Corp., 1312 Washington Ave., St. Louis, MO 63103/314-241-8464
Rubright Bullets, 1008 S. Quince Rd., Walnutport, PA 18088/215-767-1339
Ruger (See Sturm, Ruger & Co.)
Rundell, Joe, 6198 Frances Rd., Clio, MI 48420/313-687-0559
Runge, Robert P., 94 Grove St., Ilion, NY 13357/315-894-3036
Rupert's Gun Shop, 2202 Dick Rd., Suite B, Fenwick, MI 48834/517-248-3252
Russell Co., A.G., 1705 Hwy. 71 North, Springdale, AR 72764/501-751-7341
Russell's Rifle Shop, Rt. 5, P.O. Box 92, Georgetown, TX 78626/512-778-5338
Russwood Custom Pistol Grips, 455 Olean Rd., P.O. Box 460, East Aurora, NY 14052/716-652-7131
Rust Guardit (See Kleen-Bore, Inc.)
Rusteprufe Laboratories, 1319 Jefferson Ave., Sparta, WI 54656/608-269-4144
Rusty Duck Premium Gun Care Products, 7785 Foundation Dr., Florence, KY 41042/606-342-5553
Rutgers Book Center, Mark Aziz, 127 Raritan Ave., Highland Park, NJ 08904/201-545-4344
Rutgers Gun & Boat Center, 127 Raritan Ave., Highland Park, NJ 08904/201-545-4344
R.V.I., P.O. Box 1439 Stn. A, Vancouver, B.C. V6C 1AO, Canada/604-524-3214; U.S.: P.O. Box Q-1, 925 Boblett St., Blaine, WA 98230/206-332-6525
RWS (See Dynamit Nobel-RWS, Inc.)
Ryan, Chad, RR 3 Box 72, Cresco, IA 52136/319-547-4384
Rybka Custom Leather Equipment, Thad, 32 Havilah Hill, Odenville, AL 35120

S

SAECO (See Redding, Inc.)
Saf-T-Bak, Inc., 201 Cayuga Ave., Altoona, PA 16602
Safari Arms/SGW, 624 Old Pacific Highway SE, Olympia, WA 98503/206-456-3472
Safari Gun Co., 6410 Brandon Ave., Springfield, VA 22150/703-569-1097
Safari Outfitters Ltd., 71 Ethan Allan Hwy., Ridgefield, CT 06877/203-544-9505
Safariland Ltd., Inc., 3120 E. Mission Blvd., Ontario, CA 91761/714-923-7300
Safesport Manufacturing Co., 1100 45th Ave., Denver, CO 80211/303-433-6506
Safety Direct, 56 Coney Island Dr., Sparks, NV 89431/702-354-4451
Safety Speed Holster, 910 S. Vail Ave., Montebello, CA 90640/213-723-4140
Sailer, Anthony F. (See AFSCO Ammunition)
Salter Calls, Inc., Eddie, P.O. Box 872; Hwy. 31 South-Brewton Industrial Park, Brewton, AL 36427/205-867-2584
SAM, Inc. (See Special Service Arms Mfg., Inc.)
Samco Global Arms, Inc., 6995 NW 43rd St., Miami, FL 33166/305-593-9782
Sampson, Roger, 430 N. Grove, Mora, MN 55051/612-679-4868
San Angelo Sports Products, Inc., 909 West 14th St., San Angelo, TX 76904/915-655-7126
San Francisco Gun Exch., 124 Second St., San Francisco, CA 94105/415-982-6097
Sanders Custom Gun Serv., Bob Sanders, 2358 Tyler Lane, Louisville, KY 40205/502-454-3338
Sandia Die & Cartridge Co., 37 Atancacio Rd. NE, Albuquerque, NM 87123/505-298-5729
Sandy's Custom Gunshop, Rt. #1, P.O. Box 4, Rockport, IL 62370/217-437-4241
Sarco, Inc., 323 Union St., Stirling, NJ 07980/201-647-3800
Sardius Industries Ltd., 72 Rokach St., Ramat Gan, Israel 52542/972-3-7521353
SAS (See Corbin Mfg. & Supply, Inc.)
Sauer (See Sigarms, Inc.)
Savage Arms, Inc., Springdale Rd., Westfield, MA 01085/413-568-7001
Scansport, Inc., P.O. Box 700, Enfield, NH 03748/603-632-7654
Sceery Company, E.J., 1949 Osage Lane, Sante Fe, NM 87501/505-983-2125
Schaefer, Roy V., 101 Irving Rd., Eugene, OR 97404/503-688-4333
Scharch Mfg., Inc., 645 E. Hwy 50, Salida, CO 81201/719-539-7242
Schiffman, Curt, 12237 Powhatan Trail, Conifer, CO 80433/303-838-7128
Schiffman, Mike, 8233 S. Crystal Springs, McCammon, ID 83250/208-254-9114
Schiffman, Norman H., 12237 Powhatan Trail, Conifer, CO 80433/303-838-7128
Schmidt & Bender (See Jaeger, Inc., Paul)
Schneider Rifle Barrels, Inc., Gary, 12202 N. 62nd Pl., Scottsdale, AZ 85254/602-948-2525
Schrade Cutlery Corp., Rt. 209 North, Ellenville, NY 12428/914-647-7600
Schuck, Clay, 3645 N. 71 Ave. #25, Pheonix, AZ 85033/602-848-6685
Schulz Industries, 16247 Minnesota Ave., Paramount, CA 90723/213-439-5903
Schumakers Gun Shop, 512 Prouty Corner Lp., #A, Colville, WA 99114/509-684-4848
Schwartz Custom Guns, David W., 2505 Waller St., Eau Claire, WI 54703/715-832-1735
Schwartz Custom Guns, Wayne E., 970 E. Britton Rd., Morrice, MI 48857/517-625-4079
Scobey Duck & Goose Calls, Glynn, Rt. 3, Box 37, Newbern, TN 38059/901-643-6241
Scot Powder Co., P.O. Box 9737, Wilmington, DE 19809/302-764-9779
Scotch Hunting Products Co., Inc., 6619 Oak Orchard Rd., Elba, NY 14058/716-757-9958
Scott (Gunmakers) Ltd., W&C, Premier Works, Tame Rd., Witton, Birmingham, B6 7HS England/021-328-4107
Scott Fine Guns, Inc., Thad, P.O. Box 412, Indianola, MS 38751/601-887-5929
Scott, Inc., Tyler, 313 Rugby Ave., Suite 162, Terrace Park, OH 45174/513-831-7603
Scott/McDougall Custom Gunsmiths, 880 Piner Rd., Suite 50, Santa Rosa, CA 95403/707-546-2264
Scruggs' Game Calls, Stanley, Rt. 1, Hwy. 661, Cullen, VA 23934/804-542-4241, 800-323-4828
Seacliff International, Inc., 2210 Santa Anita, S. El Monte, CA 91733/818-350-0515
Seattle Binocular & Scope Repair Co., P.O. Box 46094, Seattle, WA 98146/206-932-3733
Security Awareness & Firearms Education, P.O. Box 864, E. 103 9th Ave., Post Falls, ID 83854/208-773-3624
Security Gun Chest (See Tread Corp.)
Seecamp Co., Inc., L.W., P.O. Box 255, New Haven, CT 06502/203-877-3429

Selsi Company, Inc., 40 Veterans Blvd., Carlstadt, NJ 07072-0497/201-935-5851
Semmer, Charles, 7885 Cyd Dr., Denver, CO 80221/303-429-6947
Seneca Run Iron Works, Inc., dba "Swagease," P.O. Box 3032, Greeley, CO 80633/303-352-1425
Servus Rubber Co., 1136 2nd St., Rock Island, IL 61201/309-786-7741
S.F. Legacy, Ltd., P.O. Box 1589, Bridgeport, MI 48722-1689/517-777-5200
S.G.S. Sporting Guns Srl., F1 Milanofiori, Assago, 20090 Italy/02-8241144, 02-8241145
Shane's Gunsmithing, P.O. Box 321, Hwy. 51 S., Minocqua, WI 54548/715-356-5414
Shappy Bullets, 76 Milldale Ave., Plantsville, CT 06479/203-621-3704
Sharon Gun Specialties, Inc., P.O. Box 336, Standward, CA 95373
Sharps Arms Co., Inc., C., (See Montana Armory)
Shaw's, Finest in Guns, 1201 La Mirada Ave., Escondido, CA 92026/619-746-2474
Shaw, Inc., E.R., Small Arms Mfg. Co., Thoms Run Rd. & Prestley, Bridgeville, PA 15017/412-221-4343
Sheffield Knifemakers Supply, P.O. Box 141, Deland, FL 32721/904-775-6453
Shell Shack, 113 E. Main, Laurel, MT 59044/406-628-8986
Shenandoah School of Gunsmithing, P.O. Box 300, Bentonville, VA 22610/703-743-1759
Shepherd Scope Ltd., P.O. Box 189, Waterloo, NE 68069/402-779-2424
Sheridan Products, Inc., 2600 Chicory Rd., Racine, WI 53403/414-554-7900
Sherk, Dan A., 9701-17th St., Dawson Creek, B.C. V1G 4H7, Canada/604-782-5630
Sherwood Intl. Export Corp., 18714 Parthenia St., Northridge, CA 91324/818-349-7600
Sherwood, George, 46 N. River Dr., Roseburg, OR 97470/503-672-3159
Shilen Rifles, Inc., P.O. Box 1300, 205 Metro Park Blvd., Ennis, TX 75119/214-875-5318
Shiloh Rifle Mfg. Co., Inc., P.O. Box 279, Big Timber, MT 59011/406-932-4454
Shirley & Co. Riflemakers, J.A., 33 Malmers Well Rd., High Wycombe, Bucks. HP13 6PD, England/0494-44.68.83
Shockley, Harold H., 204 E. Farmington Rd., Hanna City, IL 61536/309-565-4524
Shoemaker & Sons, Tex, 714 W. Cienega Ave., San Dimas, CA 91773/714-592-2071
Shooter Shop, The, 514 N. Main, Butte, MT 59701/406-723-3842
Shooter's Choice (See Venco Industries, Inc.)
Shooter's World, 3828 N. 28th Ave., Pheonix, AZ 85017/602-266-0170
Shooters Accessory Supply (SAS) (See Corbin Mfg. & Supply, Inc.)
Shooters Supply, 1120 Tieton Dr., Yakima, WA 98902/509-452-1181
Shootin' Accessories Ltd., P.O. Box 6810, Auburn, CA 95604/916-889-2220
Shootin' Shack, 1065 Silverbeach Rd. #1, Riviera Beach, FL 33403/407-842-0990
Shooting Arts Ltd., P.O. Box 621399, Littleton, CO 80162/303-933-2539
Shooting Chrony, Inc., 2480 Cawthra Rd., Unit 22, Mississauga, Ont. L5A 2X2, Canada/416-276-6292
Shooting Gallery, The, 8070 Southern Blvd., Boardman, OH 44512/216-726-7788
Shootist Supply, John Cook, 1531 Mill St., Belle Fourche, SD 57717
Shostle, Ben, The Gun Room, 1121 Burlington Dr., Muncie, IN 47302/317-282-9073
Shotguns Unlimited, 2307 Fon Du Lac Rd., Richmond, VA 23229/804-752-7115
Shows, Hank, dba The Best, 50 West 100 South, Monroe, UT 84754/801-527-4456
Shurkatch Corp., Longhorn Div., P.O. Box 858, 50 S. Elm St., Richfield Springs, NY 13439/315-858-1470
Sierra Bullets, 1400 W. Henry St., Sedalia, MO 65301/816-827-6300
Sifre, Salvador Enguix, Alpujarras 58, Apartado Correos 18, Alcira Valencia, Spain 46600/96-2414395
Sigarms, Inc., Industrial Drive, Exeter, NH 03833/603-772-2302
Sight Right Co., 249-B Maple Ave., Victor, NY 14564/716-924-5360
Sile Distributors, 7 Centre Market Pl., New York, NY 10013/212-925-4389
Siler Locks, C.E., 7 Acton Woods Rd., Candler, NC 28715/704-667-9991
Silhouette Arms Custom 45 Shop, Inc., P.O. Box 3431, N. Fort Myers, FL 33918-3431/813-656-2639
Silhouette Leathers, H.R. Brown, P.O. Box 280202, Memphis, TN 38124/901-372-5731
Silver Shield, Inc., 4464-D Chinden Blvd., Boise, ID 83714/208-323-8991
Simmons Enterprises, Ernie, 709 East Elizabethtown Rd., Manheim, PA 17545/717-664-4040
Simmons Outdoor Corp., 14530 SW 119 Ave., Miami, FL 33186/305-252-0477
Simmons, Jerry, 715 Middlebury St., Goshen, IN 46526/219-533-8546
Sinclair International, Inc., 718 Broadway, New Haven, IN 46774/219-493-1858
Sinclair, W.P., P.O. Box 1209, Warminster, Wiltshire BA12 9XJ, England/44-985-218-544
Single Shot, Inc. (See Montana Armory)
Sipes Gun Shop, 919 High St., Little Rock, AR 72202/501-376-8940
Siskiyou Gun Works, C.P. Donnelly, 405 Kubli Rd., Grants Pass, OR 97527/503-846-6604
Six Enterprises, 320-D Turtle Creek Ct., San Jose, CA 95125/408-999-0201
S&K Mfg. Co., P.O. Box 247, Pittsfield, PA 16340/814-563-7808
Skaggs, Ron E., P.O. Box 34, 114 Miles Ct., Princeton, IL 61356/815-875-8207
SKB (See Simmons Enterprises, Ernie)
Skinner, John R. (See Orvis Co., The)
Sklany, Steve, 566 Birch Grove Dr., Kalispell, MT 59901/406-755-4257
Slezak, Jerome F., 1290 Marlowe, Lakewood (Cleveland), OH 44107/216-221-1668
Slipshot MTS Group, P.O. Box 5 Postal Sta. D, Etobicoke, Ont., Canada M9A 4X1/416-762-5680
Slug Site Co., Ozark Wilds, Rt. 2 P.O. Box 158, Versailles, MO 65084/314-378-6430
Smires, Clifford L., RD 1 P.O. Box 100, Columbus, NJ 08022/609-298-3158
Smith & Wesson, 2100 Roosevelt Ave., Springfield, MA 01102/413-781-8300
Smith Saddlery, Jesse W., N. 1325 Division, Spokane, WA 99202/509-325-0622
Smith, Art, 4124 Thrushwood Lane, Minnetonka, MN 55345/612-935-7829
Smith, John, 912 Lincoln, Carpentersville, IL 60110
Smith, Mark A., P.O. Box 182, 200 N. 9th, Sinclair, WY 82334/307-324-7929
Smith, Michael, 620 Nye Circle, Chattanooga, TN 37405/615-267-8341
Smith, Ron, 5869 Straley, Ft. Worth, TX 76114/817-732-6768
Snapp's Gunshop, 6911 E. Washington Rd., Clare, MI 48617/517-386-9226
Snider Stocks, Walter S. Snider, Rt. 2 P.O. Box 147, Denton, NC 27239
Societa Armi Bresciane Srl., Via Artigiani 93, Gardone Val Trompia, Italy 25063/30-8911640, 30-8911648
Sodia Jagdgewehrfabrik, Franz, Schulhausgasse 14, 9170 Ferlach, (Karnten) Austria
Sokolovsky Corp., P.O. Box 70113, Sunnyvale, CA 94086/408-245-9268
Sonderman, Robert, 735 W. Kenton, Charleston, IL 61920/217-345-5429
Sotheby's, 1334 York Ave. at 72nd St., New York, NY 10021
South Bend Replicas, Inc., 61650 Oak Rd., South Bend, IN 46614/219-289-4500 (catalog $7)
Southeastern Community College—North Campus, 1015 Gear Ave., P.O. Drawer F, West Burlington, IA 52655/319-752-2731
Southern Ammunition Co., Inc., Rt. 1, P.O. Box 6B, Latta, SC 29565/803-752-7751
Southern Armory, P.O. Box 879, Hillsville, VA 24343/703-236-7835
Southern Bloomer Mfg. Company, P.O. Box 1621, Bristol, TN 37620/615-878-6660
Southwest Institute of Firearms Training (S.W.I.F.T.), 4610 Blue Diamond Rd., Las Vegas, NV 89118/702-897-1100
Southwind Sanctions, P.O. Box 445, Aledo, TX 76008/817-441-8917
Sparks, Milt, P.O. Box 187, Idaho City, ID 83631/208-392-6695 (brochure $2)
Special Service Arms Mfg., Inc., P.O. Box 500, Aiken, SC 29802/803-642-2224
Specialized Weapons, Inc. (The Spectre Five), P.O. Box 546, Smyrna, GA 30081/800-359-6195
Speer Products, Div. of Blount, Inc., P.O. Box 856, Lewiston, ID 83501/208-746-2351
Spegel, Craig, P.O. Box 108, Bay City, OR 97107/503-377-2697
Speiser, Fred D., 2229 Dearborn, Missoula, MT 59801/406-549-8133
Spence, George W., 115 Locust St., Steele, MO 63877/314-695-4926
Spencer Reblue Service, 1820 Tupelo Trail, Holt, MI 48842/517-694-7474
Spokhandguns, Inc., Vern D. Ewer, P.O. Box 370, 1206 Fig St., Benton City, WA 99320/509-588-5255
Sport Flite Mfg., Inc., P.O. Box 1082, Bloomfield Hills, MI 48303/313-647-3747
Sport Specialties, Harry Owen, P.O. Box 5337, Hacienda Hts., CA 91745/213-968-5806 (catalog $3)
Sportarms of Florida, 5555 NW 36 Ave., Miami, FL 33142/305-635-2411
Sporting Arms, Mfg., 311 E. 8th St., Littlefield, TX 79339/806-385-5665
Sports Innovations, Inc., P.O. Box 5181, 8505 Jacksboro Hwy., Wichita Falls, TX 76307/817-723-6015
Sports Shack, 114 S. 13th St., Nampa, ID 83687/208-466-1631
Sports Support Systems, Inc., 27281 Las Ramblas, Suite 200, Mission Viejo, CA 92691/714-367-0343
Sportsman Supply Co., 714 E. Eastwood, P.O. Box 650, Marshall, MO 65340
Sportsmen's Equipment Co., 915 W. Washington, San Diego, CA 92103/619-296-1501
Sportsmen's Exchange & Western Gun Traders, Inc., 560 S. "C" St., Oxnard, CA 93030/805-483-1917
Springfield Armory, Inc., 420 W. Main St., Geneseo, IL 61254/309-944-5631
Springfield Sporters, Inc., RD 1, Penn Run, PA 15765/412-254-2626
S&S Firearms, 74-11 Myrtle Ave., Glendale, NY 11385/718-497-1100
SSK Co., 220 N. Belvidere Ave., York, PA 17404/717-854-2897
SSK Industries, 721 Woodvue Lane, Wintersville, OH 43952/614-264-0176
Stackpole Books, Cameron & Kelker Sts., Telegraph Press Bldg., Harrisburg, PA 17105/717-234-5041
Stalker, Inc., P.O. Box 21, Fishermans Wharf Rd., Malakoff, TX 75148/903-489-1010
Stalwart Corp., P.O. Box 357, Pocatello, ID 83204/208-232-7899
Star Bonifacio Echeverria S.A., Torrekva 3, Eibar, Spain 20600/43-117340
Star Machine Works, 418 10th Ave., San Diego, CA 92101/619-232-3216
Star Reloading Co., Inc., 5520 Rock Hampton Ct., Indianapolis, IN 46268/317-872-5840
Starlight Training Center, Inc., Rt. 1, P.O. Box 88, Bronaugh, MO 64728/417-843-3555
Starnes, Ken, 1733 W. Peralta Ave., Mesa, AZ 85202/602-730-0980
Starrett Co., L.S., 121 Crescent St., Athol, MA 01331/617-249-3551
State Arms Gun Co., 815 S. Division St., Waunakee, WI 53597/608-849-5800
Steelman's Gun Shop, 10465 Beers Rd., Swartz Creek, MI 48473/313-735-4884
Steffens, Ron, 18396 Mariposa Creek Rd., Willits, CA 95490/707-485-0873
Steger, James R., 1131 Dorsey Pl., Plainfield, NJ 07062
Steiner Binoculars (See Pioneer Marketing & Research)
Steves House of Guns, Rt. 1, Minnesota City, MN 55959/507-689-2573
Stevi Machine, Inc., 4004 Highway 93 North, Stevensville, MT 59870/406-777-5401
Stewart Game Calls, Inc., Johnny, P.O. Box 7954, 5100 Fort Ave., Waco, TX 76714/817-772-3261
Steyr-Daimler-Puch (See GSI, Inc.)
Stoeger Industries, 55 Ruta Ct., S. Hackensack, NJ 07606/201-440-2700
Stoeger Publishing Co. (See Stoeger Industries)
Stone Enterprises Ltd., Rt. 609, P.O. Box 335, Wicomico Church, VA 22579/804-580-5114
Storey, Dale A., DGS, Inc., 305 N. Jefferson, Casper, WY 82601/307-237-2414
Stott's Creek Armory, Inc., RR1 P.O. Box 70, Morgantown, IN 46160/317-878-5489
Strawbridge, Victor W., 6 Pineview Dr., Dover Point, Dover, NH 03820/603-742-0013
Streamlight, Inc., 1030 W. Germantown Pike, Norristown, PA 19403/215-631-0600
Strong Holster Co., 105 Maplewood Ave., Gloucester, MA 01930/508-281-3300
Stroup, Earl R., 30506 Flossmoor Way, Hayward, CA 94544/415-471-1549
Strutz, W.C., Rifle Barrels, Inc., P.O. Box 611, Eagle River, WI 54521/715-479-4766
Stuart Products, Inc., P.O. Box 1587, Easley, SC 29641/803-859-9360
Sturm, Ruger & Co., Inc., Lacey Place, Southport, CT 06490/203-259-7843
Su-Press-On, Inc., P.O. Box 09161, Detroit, MI 48209/313-842-4222
Summit Specialties, Inc., P.O. Box 786, Decatur, AL 35602/205-353-0634
Sundance Industries, Inc., 25163 W. Avenue Stanford, Valencia, CA 91355/805-257-4807
Sunora Gun Shop, 22935 Watkins St., Buckeye, AZ 85326/602-386-3193
Super Six Limited, 13105 W. Blue Mound, Brookfield, WI 53005/414-785-9325
Supreme Lens Covers (See Butler Creek Corp.)
Sure Shot of LA., Inc., 103 Coachman Dr., Houma, LA 70360/504-876-6709
Swampfire Shop, The, 1693 Old Hwy. 441 N., Mt. Dora, FL 32757/904-383-0595
Swann, D.J., 5 Orsova Close, Eltham North, Vic. 3095, Australia/03-431-0323
Swanndri New Zealand, 152 Elm Ave., Burlingame, CA 94010/415-347-6158
Swarovski Optik, One Wholesale Way, Cranston, RI 02920/401-942-3380
Sweet Home, Inc., Subs. of Will-Burt., P.O. Box 250, Sweet Home, OR 97386/503-367-5185
Swenson's 45 Shop, A.D., P.O. Box 606, Fallbrook, CA 92028
Swift Bullet Co., 201 Main St., P.O. Box 27, Quinter, KS 67752/913-754-3959
Swift Instruments, Inc., 952 Dorchester Ave., Boston, MA 02125
Swift River Gun Works, 450 State St., Belchertown, MA 01007/413-323-4052
Swiss Army Knives, Inc., 151 Long Hill Crossroads, 37 Canal St., Shelton, CT 06484/800-243-4032
Szweda, Robert, 4120 N. Bitterwell, Prescott Valley, AZ 86314/602-662-7626

T

Tabler Marketing, 2554 Lincoln Blvd. #555, Marina Del Rey, CA 90291-5082/818-366-7485
Tactical Training Center, 574 Miami Bluff Ct., Loveland, OH 45140/513-677-8229
Talley, Dave, P.O. Box 821, Glenrock, WY 82637/307-436-8724
Talmage, William G., 451 Phantom Creek Lane, P.O. Box 512, Meadview, AZ 86444/602-564-2380
Tamarack Prods., Inc., P.O. Box 625, Wauconda, IL 60084/708-526-9333
Tank's Rifle Shop, 1324 Ohio St., Fremont, NE 68025/402-727-1317
Taracorp Industries, 16th & Cleveland Blvd., Granite City, IL 62040/618-451-4400

Tasco Sales, Inc., 7600 NW 26th St., Miami, FL 33122/305-591-3670
Taurus International, Inc., 16175 NW 49th Ave., Miami, FL 33014/305-624-1115
Taurus, S.A., Forjas, Avenida Do Forte 511, Porto Alegre, Brazil 91360/55 512-40 22 44
Taylor & Robbins, P.O. Box 164, Rixford, PA 16745/814-966-3233
Taylor's & Co., Inc., 1180 Broad Ave., Winchester, VA 22601/703-722-2017
Taylor, Twyla, P.O. Box 252, #2 Engress Rd., Oracle, AZ 85623/602-896-2860
T.D. Arms, 32464 #2 23 Mile Rd., New Baltimore, MI 48047/313-949-1890
TDP Industries, Inc., 603 Airport Blvd., Doylestown, PA 18901/215-345-8687
Tecnolegno S.p.A., Via A. Locatelli, 6/10, 24019 Zogno, Italy/0345-91114
Tekna, 101 Twin Dolphin Dr., Redwood City, CA 94065/800-225-2075
Tele-Optics, 5514 W. Lawrence Ave., Chicago, IL 60630/312-283-7757
Tele-Optics, Inc., P.O. Box 176, 219 E. Higgins Rd., Gilberts, IL 60136/708-426-7444
Teledyne Co., Big Beam, 290 E. Prairie St., Crystal Lake, IL 60014
Ten-Ring Precision, Inc., 1449 Blue Crest Lane, San Antonio, TX 78232/512-494-3063
10-X Products Group, 2915 Lyndon B. Johnson Freeway, Suite 133, Dallas, TX 75234/214-243-4016
Tennessee Valley Mfg., P.O. Box 1175, Corinth, MS 38834/601-286-5014
Tepeco, P.O. Box 342, Friendswood, TX 77546/713-482-2702
Tertin, James A. (See Jaeger, Inc., Paul)
Texas Longhorn Arms, Inc., P.O. Box 703, Richmond, TX 77469/713-341-0775
Texas Platers Supply Co., 2453 W. Five Mile Parkway, Dallas, TX 75233/214-330-7168
T.F.C. Spa, Via G. Marconi 118/B, Brescia I-25069, Italy
Theis, Terry, P.O. Box 535, Fredericksburg, TX 78624/512-997-6778
Thiewes, George W., 1846 Allen Lane, St. Charles, IL 60174/708-584-1383
Thirion, Denise, P.O. Box 408, Graton, CA 95444/707-829-1876
Thompson Bullet Lube, P.O. Box 472343, Garland, TX 75047-2343/214-271-8063
Thompson Precision, 110 Mary St., P.O. Box 251, Warren, IL 61087/815-745-3625
Thompson Target Technology, 618 Roslyn Ave., SW, Canton, OH 44710/216-453-7707
Thompson, Larry R., Larry's Gun Shop, 521 E. Lake Ave., Watsonville, CA 95076/408-724-5328
Thompson, Norm, 18905 NW Thurman St., Portland, OR 97209
Thompson, Randall, Highline Machine Co., 654 Lela Pl., Grand Junction, CO 81504/303-434-4971
Thompson/Center Arms, Farmington Rd., P.O. Box 5002, Rochester, NH 03867/603-332-2394
Threat Management Institute, 1 St. Francis Place #2801, San Francisco, CA 94107/415-777-0303
3-D Ammunition & Bullets, 112 Plum St., Doniphan, NE 68832/402-845-2285
3-Ten Corp., P.O. Box 269, Feeding Hills, MA 01030/413-789-2086
300 Gunsmith Service, Inc., 6850 S. Yosemite Ct., Englewood, CO 80112/303-773-0300
Thunderbird Cartridge Co., Inc., P.O. Box 302, Phoenix, AZ 85001/602-237-3823
Thurston Sports Center, RD #3, Turnpike Rd., Auburn, NY 13021/315-252-5357
Tiger-Hunt, Michael D. Barton, P.O. Box 379, Beaverdale, PA 15921/814-487-7956
Tillinghast, James C., P.O. Box 405GD, Hancock, NH 03449/603-525-6615 (list $2)
Timney Mfg., Inc., 3065 W. Fairmount Ave., Phoenix, AZ 85017/602-274-2999
Tink's Safariland Hunting Corp., P.O. Box 244, Madison, GA 30650/404-342-4915
Tippman Pneumatics, Inc., 3518 Adams Center Rd., Fort Wayne, IN 46825/219-749-6619
Tirelli, SNC Di Tirelli Primo & C., Via Matteotti No. 359, Gardone VT (BS), Italy 25063/030-837819
Titus, Daniel, Shooting Specialties, 872 Penn St., Bryn Mawr, PA 19010/215-525-8829
TMI Products, 930 S. Plumer Ave., Tucson, AZ 85719/602-792-1075
Tom's Gunshop, Tom Gillman, 4201 Central Ave., Hot Springs, AR 71913/501-624-3856
Torel, Inc., 1053 N. South St., P.O. Box 592, Yoakum, TX 77995/512-293-2341
Totally Dependable Products (See TDP Industries, Inc.)
Track of the Wolf, Inc., P.O. Box 653, Osseo, MN 55369-0653/612-424-2500
Tradewinds, Inc., P.O. Box 1191, Tacoma, WA 98401/206-272-4887
Traditions, Inc., 500 Main St., P.O. Box 235, Deep River, CT 06417/203-526-9555
Trafalgar Square, P.O. Box 257, N. Pomfret, VT 05053/802-457-1911
Trail Guns Armory, 1422 E. Main St., League City, TX 77573/713-332-5833
Trammco, Inc., P.O. Box 1258, Bellflower, CA 90706/213-428-5250
Trapper Gun, Inc., 18717 East 14 Mile Rd., Fraser, MI 48026/313-792-0134
Traq, Inc., Q-Products, 1444 Kansas Ave., Kansas City, KS 66105/913-371-9630
Trax America, Inc., P.O. Box 898, 1150 Eldridge, Forrest City, AR 72335/800-232-2327
Tread Corp., 1764 Granby St. NE, Roanoke, VA 24012/703-982-6881
Treemaster, P.O. Box 247, Guntersville, AL 35976/205-878-3597
Treso, Inc., P.O. Box 4640, Pagosa Springs, CO 81157/303-731-2295
Trevallion Gunstocks, David Trevallion, 9 Old Mountain Rd., Cape Neddick, ME 03902/207-361-1130
Treville, Stan de, 4129 Normal St., San Diego, CA 92103/619-298-3393
Trident Ltd., 564 Kantz Rd., Springdale, AZ 72764/501-361-2803
Trijicon, Inc., P.O. Box 2130, Farmington Hills, MI 48333/313-553-4960
Trinidad State Junior College, 600 Prospect, Trinidad, CO 81082/719-846-5631
Triple-K Mfg. Co., 2222 Commercial St., San Diego, CA 92113/619-232-2066
Trius Products, Inc., P.O. Box 25, Cleves, OH 45002/513-941-5682
Trophy Bonded Bullets, Inc., P.O. Box 262348, Houston, TX 77207/713-645-4499
Trotman Ltd., Ken, 135 Ditton Walk, Unit 11, Cambridge CB5 8QD, England
Tru-Square Metal Products, 640 First St. SW, P.O. Box 585, Auburn, WA 98001/206-833-2310
True Flight Bullet Co., 57 North Mountain Blvd., Mountaintop, PA 18707/717-474-9904
T&S Industries, Inc., 1027 Skyview Dr., West Carrollton, OH 45449/513-859-8414
T.S.W. Conversions, Inc., E. 115 Crain Rd., Paramus, NJ 07652-4017/201-265-1618
Tucker, James C., P.O. Box 38790, Sacramento, CA 95838/916-662-0503
Twin Pine Armory, P.O. Box 58, Hwy. 6, Adna, WA 98522/206-748-4590
Tyler Mfg.-Dist., Melvin, 1326 W. Britton Rd., Oklahoma City, OK 73114/405-842-8044

U

Uberti USA, Inc., 362 Limerock Rd., P.O. Box 469, Lakeville, CT 06039/203-435-8068
Ugartechea, Ignacio, Apartado 21, Eibar, Spain
Ulrich, Dennis A., "Doc" & Bud D.O.C. Specialists, 2209 S. Central Ave., Cicero, IL 60650/708-652-3606
Ultra Light Arms, Inc., P.O. Box 1270, 214 Price St., Granville, WV 26534/304-599-5687
Uncle Mike's (See Michaels of Oregon Co.)
Unertl Optical Co., John, 1224 Freedom Rd., Mars, PA 16046/412-776-9700
Unick's Gunsmithing, 5005 Center Rd., Lowellville, OH 44436/216-536-8015
United Binocular Co., 9043 S. Western Ave., Chicago, IL 60620
United Cutlery Corporation, 1425 United Blvd., Sevierville, TN 37862/615-428-2532
United States Ammunition Co. (USAC), Inc., 4500-15th St. East, Tacoma, WA 98424/206-922-7589
United States Products Co., 518 Melwood Ave., Pittsburgh, PA 15213/412-621-2130
Universal Clay Pigeon Traps, Unit 5, Dalacre Industrial Estate, Wilbarston, England LE16 8QL/01144536-771625
Upper Missouri Trading Co., 304 Harold St., Crofton, NE 68730/402-388-4844
USAC (See United States Ammunition Co.)
U.S. Arms Corp., 444 Brickell Ave., Suite P-26, Miami, FL 33131/305-371-7211
U.S. Repeating Arms Co., P.O. Box 30-300, New Haven, CT 06511/203-789-5000
Utica Cutlery Co., 820 Noyes St., Utica, NY 13503/315-733-4663

V

Vais Arms, George Vais, 4120 Willowbend, Houston, TX 77025
Valade, Robert B., 931-3rd. Ave., Seaside, OR 97138/503-738-7672
Valmet (See Stoeger Industries)
Valor Corp., 5555 NW 36th Ave., Miami, FL 33142/305-633-0127
Van Epps, Milton, Rt. 69-A, Parish, NY 13131/315-625-7251
Van Gorden, C.S., 1815 Main St., Bloomer, WI 54724/715-568-2612
Van Horn, Gil, P.O. Box 207, Llano, CA 93544
Van Patten, J.W., P.O. Box 145, Foster Hill, Milford, PA 18337/717-296-7069
Vancini, Carl A., P.O. Box 4354, Stamford, CT 06907
Venco Industries, Inc., 16770 Hilltop Park Pl., Chagrin Falls, OH 44022/216-543-8808
Venus Industries, P.O. Box 246, Sialkot-1, Pakistan
Verney-Carron, B.P. 72, 54 Boulevard Thiers, 42002 St.-Etienne Cedex 1, France/33-77.79.15.00
Vest, John, P.O. Box 1552, Susanville, CA 96130/916-257-7228
Vibra-Tek Co., 1844 Arroya Rd., Colorado Springs, CO 80906/719-634-8611
VibraShine, Inc., Rt. 1, P.O. Box 64, Mt. Olive, MS 39119/601-733-5614
Vic's Gun Refinishing, 6 Pineview Dr., Dover, NH 03820/603-742-0013
Vihtavuori Oy, 41330 Vihtavouri, Finland/358-41-779211
Viking Leathercraft, Inc., 1579A Jayken Way, Chula Vista, CA 92011/619-429-8050
Vintage Arms, Inc., Saddlehorse Place, Fairfax, VA 22030/703-968-0779
Viramontez, Ray, 601 Springfield Dr., Albany, GA 31707/912-432-9683
Vitt/Boos, 2178 Nichols Ave., Stratford, CT 06497/203-375-6859
Voere, P.O. Box 416, A-6333 Kufstein/Tirol, Austria/05372-5752
Volquartsen Custom Ltd., RR 1, Box 33A, P.O. Box 271, Carroll, IA 51401/712-792-4238
Von Atzigen, Ed, The Custom Shop, 890 Cochrane Cres., Peterborough, Ont. K9H 5N3, Canada/705-742-6693
Vorhes, David, 3042 Beecham St., Napa, CA 94558/707-226-9116

W

Waffen-Frankonia (See Frankonia Jagd, Hofmann & Co.)
Wagoner, Vernon G., 2325 E. Encanto, Mesa, AZ 85213/602-835-1307
Wahl Corp., Paul, P.O. Box 500, Bogota, NJ 07603-0500/201-261-9245
Wakina, 28150 Avenue Crocker #226, Newhall, CA 91355/805-295-8194
Waldron, Herman, P.O. Box 475, 80 N. 17th St., Pomeroy, WA 99347/509-843-1404
Walker Arms Co., Inc., Rt. 2, P.O. Box 73, Highway 80 West, Selma, AL 36701/205-872-6231
Walker Shoe Co., P.O. Box 1167, Asheboro, NC 27203-1167/919-625-1380
Wallace, R.D., Star, Rt.1 P.O. Box 76, Grandin, MO 63943/314-593-4773
Wallace, Terry, 385 San Marino, Vallejo, CA 94589/707-642-7041
Waller & Son, Inc., W., 142 New Canaan Ave., Norwalk, CT 06850/203-838-4083
Walls Industries, P.O. Box 98, 1905 N. Main St., Clebure, TX 76031/817-645-4366
Walters Industries, 6226 Park Lane, Dallas, TX 75225/214-691-6973
WAMCO, Inc., Mingo Loop, P.O. Box 337, Oquossoc, ME 04964-0337/207-864-3344
Ward & Van Valkenburg, 114-32nd Ave. N., Fargo, ND 58102/701-232-2351
Wardell Precision Handguns Ltd., Box 4132 New River Stage 1, New River, AZ 85029/602-465-7258
Wardrop, R.A., P.O. Box 245, 409 E. Marble St., Mechanicsburg, PA 17055/717-766-9663
Warenski, Julie, 590 E. 500 North, Richfield, UT 84701/801-896-5319
Warner, Glenn, Endicott Johnson, 1100 E. Main St., Endicott, NY 13760/607-770-7426
Warren Muzzleloading Co., Inc., Hwy. 21 North, Ozone, AR 72854/501-292-3268
Warren, Kenneth W., Mountain States Engraving, P.O. Box 2842, Wenatchee, WA 98802/509-663-6123
Washita Mountain Whetstone Co., P.O. Box 378, Lake Hamilton, AR 71951/501-525-3914
Wasp Shooting Systems, P.O. Box 241, Lakeview, AR 72642/501-431-5606
Waterfield Sports, Inc., P.O. Box 1155, 13611 Country Lane, Burnsville, MN 55337/612-435-8339
Watson Trophy Match Bullets, Ed, 2404 Wade Hampton Blvd., Greenville, SC 29615/803-244-7948
Wayland Prec. Wood Prods., P.O. Box 1142, Mill Valley, CA 94942/415-381-3543
Wayne, James, 2608 N. Laurent, Victoria, TX 77901/512-578-1258
WD-40 Co., P.O. Box 80607, San Diego, CA 92138-9021/619-275-1400
Weather Shield Sports Equipment, Inc., Rt. #3, Petoskey Rd., Charlevoix, MI 49720
Weatherby, Inc., 2781 Firestone Blvd., South Gate, CA 90280/213-569-7186
Weaver Products, Div. of Blount, Inc., P.O. Box 39, Onalaska, WI 54650/800-635-7656
Weaver Arms Corp., P.O. Box 8, Dexter, MO 63841/314-568-3800
Weaver Scope Repair Service, 1121 Larry Mahan Dr., Suite B, El Paso, TX 79925/915-593-1005
Weaver's Gun Shop, P.O. Box 8, Dexter, MO 63841/314-568-3101
Weber Jr., Rudolf, P.O. Box 160106, D-5650 Solingen, Germany/0212-592136
Weber, Chris/Waffen-Weber, #4-1691 Powick Rd., Kelowna, BC V1X 4L1, Canada/604-762-7575
Webster Scale Mfg. Co., P.O. Box 188, Sebring, FL 33870/813-385-6362
Weems, Cecil, P.O. Box 657, Mineral Wells, TX 76067/817-325-1462
Weihrauch KG, Hermann, Industriestr. 11, P.O. Box 20, 8744 Mellrichstadt, Germany/09776-497-499
Weisz Antique Gun Parts, P.O. Box 311, Arlington, VA 22210/703-243-9161
Welch, Sam, CVSR, P.O. Box 2110, Moab, UT 84532/801-259-8131
Wells Ltd., R.A., 3452 N. 1st Ave., Racine, WI 53402/414-639-5223
Wells, Fred, Wells Sport Store, 110 N. Summit St., Prescott, AZ 86301/602-445-3655
Wells, Rachel, 110 N. Summit St., Prescott, AZ 86301/602-445-3655
Wenoka/Seastyle, P.O. Box 8238, West Palm Beach, FL 33407/407-845-6155
Werth, Terry, 1203 Woodlawn Rd., Lincoln, IL 62656/217-732-9314
Wescombe, P.O. Box 488, Glencoe, CA 95232/209-293-7010